A TREATISE OF HUMAN NATURE

AND

CRITIQUE OF PURE REASON

David Hume
Immanuel Kant

CLASSY
PUBLISHING

A TREATISE OF HUMAN NATURE AND CRITIQUE OF PURE REASON
by David Hume & Immanuel Kant

Published by Classy Publishing, 2024

www.classypublishing.com
info@classypublishing.com

ISBN: 978-93-5522-946-5

Cover Design by Classy Publishing

CONTENTS

A TREATISE OF HUMAN NATURE

BOOK II. OF THE PASSIONS

BOOK III. OF MORALS

CRITIQUE OF PURE REASON

A TREATISE OF HUMAN NATURE

David Hume

ADVERTISEMENT

My design in the present work is sufficiently explained in the Introduction. The reader must only observe, that all the subjects I have there planned out to myself, are not treated of in these two volumes. The subjects of the Understanding and Passions make a compleat chain of reasoning by themselves; and I was willing to take advantage of this natural division, in order to try the taste of the public. If I have the good fortune to meet with success, I shall proceed to the examination of Morals, Politics, and Criticism; which will compleat this Treatise of Human Nature. The approbation of the public I consider as the greatest reward of my labours; but am determined to regard its judgment, whatever it be, as my best instruction.

INTRODUCTION

Nothing is more usual and more natural for those, who pretend to discover anything new to the world in philosophy and the sciences, than to insinuate the praises of their own systems, by decrying all those, which have been advanced before them. And indeed were they content with lamenting that ignorance, which we still lie under in the most important questions, that can come before the tribunal of human reason, there are few, who have an acquaintance with the sciences, that would not readily agree with them. It is easy for one of judgment and learning, to perceive the weak foundation even of those systems, which have obtained the greatest credit, and have carried their pretensions highest to accurate and profound reasoning. Principles taken upon trust, consequences lamely deduced from them, want of coherence in the parts, and of evidence in the whole, these are every where to be met with in the systems of the most eminent philosophers, and seem to have drawn disgrace upon philosophy itself.

Nor is there required such profound knowledge to discover the present imperfect condition of the sciences, but even the rabble without doors may, judge from the noise and clamour, which they hear, that all goes not well within. There is nothing which is not the subject of debate, and in which men of learning are not of contrary opinions. The most trivial question escapes not our controversy, and in the most momentous we are not able to give any certain decision. Disputes are multiplied, as if every thing was uncertain; and these disputes are managed with the greatest warmth, as if every thing was certain. Amidst all this bustle it is not reason, which carries the prize, but eloquence; and no man needs ever despair of gaining proselytes to the most extravagant hypothesis, who has art enough to represent it in any favourable colours. The victory is not gained by the men at arms, who manage the pike and the sword; but by the trumpeters, drummers, and musicians of the army.

From hence in my opinion arises that common prejudice against metaphysical reasonings of all kinds, even amongst those, who profess themselves scholars, and have a just value for every other part of literature. By metaphysical reasonings, they do not understand those on any particular branch of science, but every kind of argument, which is any way abstruse, and requires some attention to be comprehended. We have so often lost our labour in such researches, that we commonly reject them without hesitation, and resolve, if we must for ever be a prey to errors and delusions, that they shall at least be natural and entertaining. And indeed nothing but the most determined scepticism, along with a great degree of indolence, can justify this aversion to metaphysics. For if truth be at all within the reach of human capacity, it is certain it must lie very deep and abstruse: and to hope we shall arrive at it without pains, while the greatest geniuses have failed with the utmost pains, must certainly be esteemed sufficiently vain and presumptuous. I pretend to no such advantage in the philosophy I am going to unfold, and would esteem it a strong presumption against it, were it so very easy and obvious.

It is evident, that all the sciences have a relation, greater or less, to human nature: and that however wide any of them may seem to run from it, they still return back by one passage or another. Even. Mathematics, Natural Philosophy, and Natural Religion, are in some measure dependent on the science of MAN; since they lie under the cognizance of men, and are judged of by their powers and faculties. It is impossible to tell what changes and improvements we might make in these sciences were we thoroughly acquainted with the extent and force of human understanding, and could explain the nature of the ideas we employ, and of the operations we perform in our reasonings. And these improvements are the more to be hoped for in natural religion, as it is not content with instructing us in the nature of superior powers, but carries its views farther, to their disposition towards us, and our duties towards them; and consequently we ourselves are not only the beings, that reason, but also one of the objects, concerning which we reason.

If therefore the sciences of Mathematics, Natural Philosophy, and Natural Religion, have such a dependence on the knowledge of man, what may be expected in the other sciences, whose connexion with human nature is more close and intimate? The sole end of logic is to explain the principles and operations of our reasoning faculty, and the nature of our ideas: morals and criticism regard our tastes and sentiments: and politics consider men as united in society, and dependent on each other. In these four sciences of Logic, Morals, Criticism, and Politics, is comprehended almost everything, which it can any way import us to be acquainted with, or which can tend either to the improvement or ornament of the human mind.

Here then is the only expedient, from which we can hope for success in our philosophical researches, to leave the tedious lingering method, which we have hitherto followed, and instead of taking now and then a castle or village on the frontier, to march up directly to the capital or center of these sciences, to human nature itself; which being once masters of, we may every where else hope for an easy victory. From this station we may extend our conquests over all those sciences, which more intimately concern human life, and may afterwards proceed at leisure to discover more fully those, which are the objects of pore curiosity. There is no question of importance, whose decision is not comprised in the science of man; and there is none, which can be decided with any certainty, before we become acquainted with that science. In pretending, therefore, to explain the principles of human nature, we in effect propose a compleat system of the sciences, built on a foundation almost entirely new, and the only one upon which they can stand with any security.

And as the science of man is the-only solid foundation for the other sciences, so the only solid foundation we can give to this science itself must be laid on experience and observation. It is no astonishing reflection to consider, that the application of experimental philosophy to moral subjects should come after that to natural at the distance of above a whole century; since we find in fact, that there was about the same interval betwixt the origins of these sciences; and that reckoning from THALES to SOCRATES, the space of time is nearly equal to that betwixt, my Lord Bacon and some late philosophers in England,[1] who have begun to put the science of man on a new footing, and have engaged the attention, and excited the curiosity of the public. So true it is, that however other nations may rival us in poetry, and excel us in some other agreeable arts, the improvements in reason and philosophy can only be owing to a land of toleration and of liberty.

Nor ought we to think, that this latter improvement in the science of man will do less honour to our native country than the former in natural philosophy, but ought rather to esteem it a greater glory, upon account of the greater importance of that science, as well as the necessity it lay under of such a reformation. For to me it seems evident, that the essence of the mind being equally unknown to us with that of external bodies, it must be equally impossible to form any notion of its powers and qualities otherwise than from careful and exact experiments, and the observation of those particular effects, which result from its different circumstances and situations. And though we must endeavour to render all our principles as universal as possible, by tracing up our experiments to the utmost, and explaining all effects from the simplest and fewest causes, it is still certain we cannot go beyond experience; and any hypothesis, that pretends to discover the ultimate original qualities of human nature, ought at first to be rejected as presumptuous and chimerical.

I do not think a philosopher, who would apply himself so earnestly to the explaining the ultimate principles of the soul, would show himself a great master in that very science of human nature, which he pretends to explain, or very knowing in what is naturally satisfactory to the mind of man. For nothing is more certain, than that despair has almost the same effect upon us with enjoyment, and that we are no sooner acquainted with the impossibility of satisfying any desire, than the desire itself vanishes. When we see, that we have arrived at the utmost extent of human reason, we sit down contented, though we be perfectly satisfied in the main of our ignorance, and perceive that we can give no reason for our most general and most refined principles, beside our experience of their reality; which is the reason of the mere vulgar, and what it required no study at first to have discovered for the most particular and most extraordinary phænomenon. And as this impossibility of making any farther progress is enough to satisfy the reader, so the writer may derive a more delicate satisfaction from the free confession of his ignorance, and from his prudence in avoiding that error, into which so many have fallen, of imposing their conjectures and hypotheses on the world for the most certain principles. When

[1] Mr. *Locke*, my Lord *Shaftesbury*, Dr. *Mandeville*, Mr. *Hutchinson*, Dr. *Butler*, etc.

this mutual contentment and satisfaction can be obtained betwixt the master and scholar, I know not what more we can require of our philosophy.

But if this impossibility of explaining ultimate principles should be esteemed a defect in the science of man, I will venture to affirm, that it is a defect common to it with all the sciences, and all the arts, in which we can employ ourselves, whether they be such as are cultivated in the schools of the philosophers, or practised in the shops of the meanest artizans. None of them can go beyond experience, or establish any principles which are not founded on that authority. Moral philosophy has, indeed, this peculiar disadvantage, which is not found in natural, that in collecting its experiments, it cannot make them purposely, with premeditation, and after such a manner as to satisfy itself concerning every particular difficulty which may be. When I am at a loss to know the effects of one body upon another in any situation, I need only put them in that situation, and observe what results from it. But should I endeavour to clear up after the same manner any doubt in moral philosophy, by placing myself in the same case with that which I consider, it is evident this reflection and premeditation would so disturb the operation of my natural principles, as must render it impossible to form any just conclusion from the phenomenon. We must therefore glean up our experiments in this science from a cautious observation of human life, and take them as they appear in the common course of the world, by men's behaviour in company, in affairs, and in their pleasures. Where experiments of this kind are judiciously collected and compared, we may hope to establish on them a science which will not be inferior in certainty, and will be much superior in utility to any other of human comprehension.

BOOK I

OF THE UNDERSTANDING

PART I

Of Ideas, their Origin, Composition, Connexion, Abstraction, etc.

SECTION I

Of the Origin of our Ideas

All the perceptions of the human mind resolve themselves into two distinct kinds, which I shall call IMPRESSIONS and IDEAS. The difference betwixt these consists in the degrees of force and liveliness, with which they strike upon the mind, and make their way into our thought or consciousness. Those perceptions, which enter with most force and violence, we may name impressions: and under this name I comprehend all our sensations, passions and emotions, as they make their first appearance in the soul. By ideas I mean the faint images of these in thinking and reasoning; such as, for instance, are all the perceptions excited by the present discourse, excepting only those which arise from the sight and touch, and excepting the immediate pleasure or uneasiness it may occasion. I believe it will not be very necessary to employ many words in explaining this distinction. Every one of himself will readily perceive the difference betwixt feeling and thinking. The common degrees of these are easily distinguished; though it is not impossible but in particular instances they may very nearly approach to each other. Thus in sleep, in a fever, in madness, or in any very violent emotions of soul, our ideas may approach to our impressions, As on the other hand it sometimes happens, that our impressions are so faint and low, that we cannot distinguish them from our ideas. But notwithstanding this near resemblance in a few instances, they are in general so very different, that no-one can make a scruple to rank them under distinct heads, and assign to each a peculiar name to mark the difference.[2]

There is another division of our perceptions, which it will be convenient to observe, and which extends itself both to our impressions and ideas. This division is into SIMPLE and COMPLEX. Simple perceptions or impressions and ideas are such as admit of no distinction nor separation. The complex are the contrary to these, and may be distinguished into parts. Though a particular colour, taste, and

[2] I here make use of these terms, *impression and idea*, in a sense different from what is usual, and I hope this liberty will be allowed me. Perhaps I rather restore the word, idea, to its original sense, from which Mr Locke had perverted it, in making it stand for all our perceptions. By the terms of impression I would not be understood to express the manner, in which our lively perceptions are produced in the soul, but merely the perceptions themselves; for which there is no particular name either in the *English* or any other language, that I know of.

smell, are qualities all united together in this apple, it is easy to perceive they are not the same, but are at least distinguishable from each other.

Having by these divisions given an order and arrangement to our objects, we may now apply ourselves to consider with the more accuracy their qualities and relations. The first circumstance, that strikes my eye, is the great resemblance betwixt our impressions and ideas in every other particular, except their degree of force and vivacity. The one seem to be in a manner the reflexion of the other; so that all the perceptions of the mind are double, and appear both as impressions and ideas. When I shut my eyes and think of my chamber, the ideas I form are exact representations of the impressions I felt; nor is there any circumstance of the one, which is not to be found in the other. In running over my other perceptions, I find still the same resemblance and representation. Ideas and impressions appear always to correspond to each other. This circumstance seems to me remarkable, and engages my attention for a moment.

Upon a more accurate survey I find I have been carried away too far by the first appearance, and that I must make use of the distinction of perceptions into simple and complex, to limit this general decision, that all our ideas and impressions are resembling. I observe, that many of our complex ideas never had impressions, that corresponded to them, and that many of our complex impressions never are exactly copied in ideas. I can imagine to myself such a city as the New Jerusalem, whose pavement is gold and walls are rubies, though I never saw any such. I have seen Paris; but shall I affirm I can form such an idea of that city, as will perfectly represent all its streets and houses in their real and just proportions?

I perceive, therefore, that though there is in general a great, resemblance betwixt our complex impressions and ideas, yet the rule is not universally true, that they are exact copies of each other. We may next consider how the case stands with our simple, perceptions. After the most accurate examination, of which I am capable, I venture to affirm, that the rule here holds without any exception, and that every simple idea has a simple impression, which resembles it, and every simple impression a correspondent idea. That idea of red, which we form in the dark, and that impression which strikes our eyes in sun-shine, differ only in degree, not in nature. That the case is the same with all our simple impressions and ideas, it is impossible to prove by a particular enumeration of them. Every one may satisfy himself in this point by running over as many as he pleases. But if any one should deny this universal resemblance, I know no way of convincing him, but by desiring him to shew a simple impression, that has not a correspondent idea, or a simple idea, that has not a correspondent impression. If he does not answer this challenge, as it is certain he cannot, we may from his silence and our own observation establish our conclusion.

Thus we find, that all simple ideas and impressions resemble each other; and as the complex are formed from them, we may affirm in general, that these two species of perception are exactly correspondent. Having discovered this relation, which requires no farther examination, I am curious to find some other of their qualities. Let us consider how they stand with regard to their existence, and which of the impressions and ideas are causes, and which effects.

The full examination of this question is the subject of the present treatise; and therefore we shall here content ourselves with establishing one general proposition, THAT ALL OUR SIMPLE IDEAS IN THEIR FIRST APPEARANCE ARE DERIVED FROM SIMPLE IMPRESSIONS, WHICH ARE CORRESPONDENT TO THEM, AND WHICH THEY EXACTLY REPRESENT.

In seeking for phenomena to prove this proposition, I find only those of two kinds; but in each kind the phenomena are obvious, numerous, and conclusive. I first make myself certain, by a new, review, of what I have already asserted, that every simple impression is attended with a correspondent idea, and every simple idea with a correspondent impression. From this constant conjunction of resembling perceptions I immediately conclude, that there is a great connexion betwixt our correspondent impressions and ideas, and that the existence of the one has a considerable influence upon that of the other. Such a constant conjunction, in such an infinite number of instances, can never arise from chance; but clearly proves a dependence of the impressions on the ideas, or of the ideas on the impressions. That I may know on which side this dependence lies, I consider the order of their first appearance; and find by constant experience, that the simple impressions always take the precedence of their correspondent ideas, but never appear in the contrary order. To give a child an idea of scarlet or orange, of sweet or bitter, I present the objects, or in other words, convey to him these impressions; but proceed not so absurdly, as to endeavour to produce the impressions by exciting the ideas. Our ideas upon their appearance produce not their correspondent impressions, nor do we perceive any colour, or feel any sensation merely upon thinking of them. On the other hand we find, that any impression either of the mind or body is constantly followed by an idea, which resembles it, and is only different in the degrees of force and liveliness. The constant conjunction of our resembling perceptions, is a convincing proof, that the one are the causes of the other; and this priority of the impressions is an equal proof, that our impressions are the causes of our ideas, not our ideas of our impressions.

To confirm this I consider Another plain and convincing phænomenon; which is, that, where-ever by any accident the faculties, which give rise to any impressions, are obstructed in their operations, as when one is born blind or deaf; not only the impressions are lost, but also their correspondent ideas; so that there never appear in the mind the least traces of either of them. Nor is this only true, where the organs of sensation are entirely destroyed, but likewise where they have never been put in action to produce a particular impression. We cannot form to ourselves a just idea of the taste of a pine apple, without having actually tasted it.

There is however one contradictory phænomenon, which may prove, that it is not absolutely impossible for ideas to go before their correspondent impressions. I believe it will readily be allowed that the several distinct ideas of colours, which enter by the eyes, or those of sounds, which are conveyed by the hearing, are really different from each other, though at the same time resembling. Now if this be true of different colours, it must be no less so of the different shades of the same colour, that each of them produces a distinct idea, independent of the rest. For if this should be denied, it is possible, by the continual gradation of shades, to run a colour insensibly into what is most remote from it; and if you will not allow any of the means to be different, you cannot without absurdity deny the extremes to be the same. Suppose therefore a person to have enjoyed his sight for thirty years, and to have become perfectly well acquainted with colours of all kinds, excepting one particular shade of blue, for instance, which it never has been his fortune to meet with. Let all the different shades of that colour, except that single one, be placed before him, descending gradually from the deepest to the lightest; it is plain, that he will perceive a blank, where that shade is wanting, said will be sensible, that there is a greater distance in that place betwixt the contiguous colours, than in any other. Now I ask, whether it is possible for him, from his own imagination, to supply this deficiency, and raise up to himself the idea of that particular shade, though it had never been conveyed to him by his senses? I believe there are few but will be of opinion that he can; and this may serve as a proof, that the simple ideas are not always derived from the correspondent impressions; though the instance is so particular and singular, that it is scarce worth our observing, and does not merit that for it alone we should alter our general maxim.

But besides this exception, it may not be amiss to remark on this head, that the principle of the priority of impressions to ideas must be understood with another limitation, viz., that as our ideas are images of our impressions, so we can form secondary ideas, which are images of the primary; as appears from this very reasoning concerning them. This is not, properly speaking, an exception to the rule so much as an explanation of it. Ideas produce the images of themselves in new ideas; but as the first ideas are supposed to be derived from impressions, it still remains true, that all our simple ideas proceed either mediately or immediately, from their correspondent impressions.

This then is the first principle I establish in the science of human nature; nor ought we to despise it because of the simplicity of its appearance. For it is remarkable, that the present question concerning the precedency of our impressions or ideas, is the same with what has made so much noise in other terms, when it has been disputed whether there be any INNATE IDEAS, or whether all ideas be derived from sensation and reflexion. We may observe, that in order to prove the ideas of extension and colour not to be innate, philosophers do nothing but shew that they are conveyed by our senses. To prove the ideas of passion and desire not to be innate, they observe that we have a preceding experience of these emotions in ourselves. Now if we carefully examine these arguments, we shall find that they prove nothing but that ideas are preceded by other more lively perceptions, from which the are derived, and which they represent. I hope this clear stating of the question will remove all disputes concerning it, and win render this principle of more use in our reasonings, than it seems hitherto to have been.

SECTION II

Division of the Subject

Since it appears, that our simple impressions are prior to their correspondent ideas, and that the exceptions are very rare, method seems to require we should examine our impressions, before we consider our ideas. Impressions may be divided into two kinds, those Of SENSATION and those of REFLEXION. The first kind arises in the soul originally, from unknown causes. The second is derived in a great measure from our ideas, and that in the following order. An impression first strikes upon the senses, and makes us perceive heat or cold, thirst or hunger, pleasure or pain of some kind or other. Of this impression there is a copy taken by the mind, which remains after the impression ceases; and this we call an idea. This idea of pleasure or pain, when it returns upon the soul, produces the new impressions of desire and aversion, hope and fear, which may properly be called impressions of reflexion, because derived from it. These again are copied by the memory and imagination, and become ideas; which perhaps in their turn give rise to other impressions and ideas. So that the impressions of reflexion are only antecedent to their correspondent ideas; but posterior to those of sensation, and derived from them. The examination of our sensations belongs more to anatomists and natural philosophers than to moral; and therefore shall not at present be entered upon. And as the impressions of reflexion, viz. passions, desires, and emotions, which principally deserve our attention, arise mostly from ideas, it will be necessary to reverse that method, which at first sight seems most natural; and in order to explain the nature and principles of the human mind, give a particular account of ideas, before we proceed to impressions. For this reason I have here chosen to begin with ideas.

SECTION III

Of the Ideas of the Memory and Imagination

We find by experience, that when any impression has been present with the mind, it again makes its appearance there as an idea; and this it may do after two different ways: either when in its new appearance it retains a considerable degree of its first vivacity, and is somewhat intermediate betwixt an impression and an idea: or when it entirely loses that vivacity, and is a perfect idea. The faculty, by which we repeat our impressions in the first manner, is called the MEMORY, and the other the IMAGINATION. It is evident at first sight, that the ideas of the memory are much more lively and strong than those of the imagination, and that the former faculty paints its objects in more distinct colours, than any which are employed by the latter. When we remember any past event, the idea of it flows in upon the mind in a forcible manner; whereas in the imagination the perception is faint and languid, and cannot without difficulty be preserved by the mind steddy and uniform for any considerable time. Here then is a sensible difference betwixt one species of ideas and another. But of this more fully hereafter.[3]

There is another difference betwixt these two kinds of ideas, which is no less evident, namely that though neither the ideas, of the memory nor imagination, neither the lively nor faint ideas can make their appearance in the mind, unless their correspondent impressions have gone before to prepare the way for them, yet the imagination is not restrained to the same order and form with the original impressions; while the memory is in a manner tied down in that respect, without any power of variation.

It is evident, that the memory preserves the original form, in which its objects were presented, and that where-ever we depart from it in recollecting any thing, it proceeds from some defect or imperfection in that faculty. An historian may, perhaps, for the more convenient Carrying on of his narration, relate an event before another, to which it was in fact posterior; but then he takes notice of this disorder, if he be exact; and by that means replaces the idea in its due position. It is the same case in our recollection of those places and persons, with which we were formerly acquainted. The chief exercise of the memory is not to preserve the simple ideas, but their order and position. In short, this principle is supported by such a number of common and vulgar phaenomena, that we may spare ourselves the trouble of insisting on it any farther.

The same evidence follows us in our second principle, OF THE LIBERTY OF THE IMAGINATION TO TRANSPOSE AND CHANGE ITS IDEAS. The fables we meet with in poems and romances put this entirely out of the question. Nature there is totally confounded, and nothing mentioned but winged horses, fiery dragons, and monstrous giants. Nor will this liberty of the fancy appear strange, when we consider, that all our ideas are copyed from our impressions, and that there are not any two impressions which are perfectly inseparable. Not to mention, that this is an evident consequence of the division of ideas into simple and complex. Where-ever the imagination perceives a difference among ideas, it can easily produce a separation.

SECTION IV

Of the Connexion or Association of Ideas

As all simple ideas may be separated by the imagination, and may be united again in what form it pleases, nothing would be more unaccountable than the operations of that faculty, were it not guided by some universal principles, which render it, in some measure, uniform with itself in all times and places. Were ideas entirely

[3] Part III, Sect. 5.

loose and unconnected, chance alone would join them; and it is impossible the same simple ideas should fall regularly into complex ones (as they Commonly do) without some bond of union among them, some associating quality, by which one idea naturally introduces another. This uniting principle among ideas is not to be considered as an inseparable connexion; for that has been already excluded from the imagination: Nor yet are we to conclude, that without it the mind cannot join two ideas; for nothing is more free than that faculty: but we are only to regard it as a gentle force, which commonly prevails, and is the cause why, among other things, languages so nearly correspond to each other; nature in a manner pointing out to every one those simple ideas, which are most proper to be united in a complex one. The qualities, from which this association arises, and by which the mind is after this manner conveyed from one idea to another, are three, viz. RESEMBLANCE, CONTIGUITY in time or place, and CAUSE and EFFECT.

I believe it will not be very necessary to prove, that these qualities produce an association among ideas, and upon the appearance of one idea naturally introduce another. It is plain, that in the course of our thinking, and in the constant revolution of our ideas, our imagination runs easily from one idea to any other that resembles it, and that this quality alone is to the fancy a sufficient bond and association. It is likewise evident that as the senses, in changing their objects, are necessitated to change them regularly, and take them as they lie CONTIGUOUS to each other, the imagination must by long custom acquire the same method of thinking, and run along the parts of space and time in conceiving its objects. As to the connexion, that is made by the relation of cause and effect, we shall have occasion afterwards to examine it to the bottom, and therefore shall not at present insist upon it. It is sufficient to observe, that there is no relation, which produces a stronger connexion in the fancy, and makes one idea more readily recall another, than the relation of cause and effect betwixt their objects.

That we may understand the full extent of these relations, we must consider, that two objects are connected together in the imagination, not only when the one is immediately resembling, contiguous to, or the cause of the other, but also when there is interposed betwixt them a third object, which bears to both of them any of these relations. This may be carried on to a great length; though at the same time we may observe, that each remove considerably weakens the relation. Cousins in the fourth degree are connected by causation, if I may be allowed to use that term; but not so closely as brothers, much less as child and parent. In general we may observe, that all the relations of blood depend upon cause and effect, and are esteemed near or remote, according to the number of connecting causes interposed betwixt the persons.

Of the three relations above-mentioned this of causation is the most extensive. Two objects may be considered as placed in this relation, as well when one is the cause of any of the actions or motions of the other, as when the former is the cause of the existence of the latter. For as that action or motion is nothing but the object itself, considered in a certain light, and as the object continues the same in all its different situations, it is easy to imagine how such an influence of objects upon one another may connect them in the imagination.

We may carry this farther, and remark, not only that two objects are connected by the relation of cause and effect, when the one produces a motion or any action in the other, but also when it has a power of producing it. And this we may observe to be the source of all the relation, of interest and duty, by which men influence each other in society, and are placed in the ties of government and subordination. A master is such-a-one as by his situation, arising either from force or agreement, has a power of directing in certain particulars the actions of another, whom we call servant. A judge is one, who in all disputed cases can fix by his opinion the possession or property of any thing betwixt any members of the society. When a person is possessed of any power, there is no more required to convert it into action, but the exertion of the will; and that in every case is considered as possible, and in many as probable; especially in the case of authority, where the obedience of the subject is a pleasure and advantage to the superior.

These are therefore the principles of union or cohesion among our simple ideas, and in the imagination supply the place of that inseparable connexion, by which they are united in our memory. Here is a kind of ATTRACTION, which in the mental world will be found to have as extraordinary effects as in the natural, and to shew itself in as many and as various forms. Its effects are every where conspicuous; but as to its causes, they are mostly unknown, and must be resolved into original qualities of human nature, which I pretend not to explain. Nothing is more requisite for a true philosopher, than to restrain the intemperate desire of searching into causes, and having established any doctrine upon a sufficient number of experiments, rest contented with that, when he sees a farther examination would lead him into obscure and uncertain speculations. In that case his enquiry would be much better employed in examining the effects than the causes of his principle.

Amongst the effects of this union or association of ideas, there are none more remarkable, than those complex ideas, which are the common subjects of our thoughts and reasoning, and generally arise from some principle of union among our simple ideas. These complex ideas may be divided into Relations, Modes, and Substances. We shall briefly examine each of these in order, and shall subjoin some considerations concerning our general and particular ideas, before we leave the present subject, which may be considered as the elements of this philosophy.

SECTION V

Of Relations

The word RELATION is commonly used in two senses considerably different from each other. Either for that quality, by which two ideas are connected together in the imagination, and the one naturally introduces the other, after the manner above-explained: or for that particular circumstance, in which, even upon the arbitrary union of two ideas in the fancy, we may think proper to compare them. In common language the former is always the sense, in which we use the word, relation; and it is only in philosophy, that we extend it to mean any particular subject of comparison, without a connecting principle. Thus distance will be allowed by philosophers to be a true relation, because we acquire an idea of it by the comparing of objects: But in a common way we say, THAT NOTHING CAN BE MORE DISTANT THAN SUCH OR SUCH THINGS FROM EACH OTHER, NOTHING CAN HAVE LESS RELATION: as if distance and relation were incompatible.

It may perhaps be esteemed an endless task to enumerate all those qualities, which make objects admit of comparison, and by which the ideas of philosophical relation are produced. But if we diligently consider them, we shall find that without difficulty they may be comprised under seven general heads, which may be considered as the sources of all philosophical relation.

(1) The first is RESEMBLANCE: And this is a relation, without which no philosophical relation can exist; since no objects will admit of comparison, but what have some degree of resemblance. But though resemblance be necessary to all philosophical relation, it does not follow, that it always produces a connexion or association of ideas. When a quality becomes very general, and is common to a great many individuals, it leads not the mind directly to any one of them; but by presenting at once too great a choice, does thereby prevent the imagination from fixing on any single object.

(2) IDENTITY may be esteemed a second species of relation. This relation I here consider as applied in its strictest sense to constant and unchangeable objects; without examining the nature and foundation of personal identity, which shall find its place afterwards. Of all relations the most universal is that of identity, being common to every being whose existence has any duration.

(3) After identity the most universal and comprehensive relations are those of SPACE and TIME, which are the sources of an infinite number of comparisons, such as distant, contiguous, above, below, before, after, etc.

(4) All those objects, which admit of QUANTITY, or NUMBER, may be compared in that particular; which is another very fertile source of relation.

(5) When any two objects possess the same QUALITY in common, the DEGREES, in which they possess it, form a fifth species of relation. Thus of two objects, which are both heavy, the one may be either of greater, or less weight than the other. Two colours, that are of the same kind, may yet be of different shades, and in that respect admit of comparison.

(6) The relation of CONTRARIETY may at first sight be regarded as an exception to the rule, THAT NO RELATION OF ANY KIND CAN SUBSIST WITHOUT SOME DEGREE OF RESEMBLANCE. But let us consider, that no two ideas are in themselves contrary, except those of existence and non-existence, which are plainly resembling, as implying both of them an idea of the object; though the latter excludes the object from all times and places, in which it is supposed not to exist.

(7) All other objects, such as fire and water, heat and cold, are only found to be contrary from experience, and from the contrariety of their causes or effects; which relation of cause and effect is a seventh philosophical relation, as well as a natural one. The resemblance implied in this relation, shall be explained afterwards.

It might naturally be expected, that I should join DIFFERENCE to the other relations. But that I consider rather as a negation of relation, than as anything real or positive. Difference is of two kinds as opposed either to identity or resemblance. The first is called a difference of number; the other of KIND.

SECTION VI

Of Modes and Substances

I would fain ask those philosophers, who found so much of their reasonings on the distinction of substance and accident, and imagine we have clear ideas of each, whether the idea of substance be derived from the impressions of sensation or of reflection? If it be conveyed to us by our senses, I ask, which of them; and after what manner? If it be perceived by the eyes, it must be a colour; if by the ears, a sound; if by the palate, a taste; and so of the other senses. But I believe none will assert, that substance is either a colour, or sound, or a taste. The idea, of substance must therefore be derived from an impression of reflection, if it really exist. But the impressions of reflection resolve themselves into our passions and emotions: none of which can possibly represent a substance. We have therefore no idea of substance, distinct from that of a collection of particular qualities, nor have we any other meaning when we either talk or reason concerning it.

The idea of a substance as well as that of a mode, is nothing but a collection of Simple ideas, that are united by the imagination, and have a particular name assigned them, by which we are able to recall, either to ourselves or others, that collection. But the difference betwixt these ideas consists in this, that the particular qualities, which form a substance, are commonly referred to an unknown something, in which they are supposed to inhere; or granting this fiction should not take place, are at least supposed to be closely and inseparably connected by the relations of contiguity and causation. The effect of this is, that whatever new simple quality we discover to have the same connexion with the rest, we immediately comprehend it among them, even though it did not enter into the first conception of the substance. Thus our idea of gold may at first be a yellow colour, weight, malleableness, fusibility; but upon the discovery of its dissolubility in aqua regia, we join that to the other qualities, and suppose it to belong to the substance as much as if its idea had from the beginning made a part of the compound one. The principal of union being regarded as the chief part of the complex idea, gives entrance to whatever quality afterwards occurs, and is equally comprehended by it, as are the others, which first presented themselves.

That this cannot take place in modes, is evident from considering their nature. The simple ideas of which modes are formed, either represent qualities, which are not united by contiguity and causation, but are dispersed in different subjects; or if they be all united together, the uniting principle is not regarded as the foundation of the complex idea. The idea of a dance is an instance of the first kind of modes; that of beauty of the second. The reason is obvious, why such complex ideas cannot receive any new idea, without changing the name, which distinguishes the mode.

SECTION VII

Of Abstract Ideas

A very material question has been started concerning ABSTRACT or GENERAL ideas, WHETHER THEY BE GENERAL OR PARTICULAR IN THE MIND'S CONCEPTION OF THEM. A great philosopher[4] has disputed the received opinion in this particular, and has asserted, that all general ideas are nothing but particular ones, annexed to a certain term, which gives them a more extensive signification, and makes them recall upon occasion other individuals, which are similar to them. As I look upon this to be one of the greatest and most valuable discoveries that has been made of late years in the republic of letters, I shall here endeavour to confirm it by some arguments, which I hope will put it beyond all doubt and controversy.

It is evident, that in forming most of our general ideas, if not all of them, we abstract from every particular degree of quantity and quality, and that an object ceases not to be of any particular species on account of every small alteration in its extension, duration and other properties. It may therefore be thought, that here is a plain dilemma, that decides concerning the nature of those abstract ideas, which have afforded so much speculation to philosophers. The abstract idea of a man represents men of all sizes and all qualities; which it is concluded it cannot do, but either by representing at once all possible sizes and all possible qualities, or by, representing no particular one at all. Now it having been esteemed absurd to defend the former proposition, as implying an infinite capacity in the mind, it has been commonly inferred in favour of the latter: and our abstract ideas have been supposed to represent no particular degree either of quantity or quality. But that this inference is erroneous, I shall endeavour to make appear, first, by proving, that it is utterly impossible to conceive any quantity or quality, without forming a precise notion of its degrees: And secondly by showing, that though the capacity of the mind be not infinite, yet we can at once form a notion of all possible degrees of quantity and quality, in such a manner at least, as, however imperfect, may serve all the purposes of reflection and conversation.

[4] Dr. Berkeley. [Introd.: to 'Principles of Human Knowledge,' secs. 18 &c. Cf. also Introd. to this volume paragraphs 183 and ff.—Ed.]

To begin with the first proposition, THAT THE MIND CANNOT FORM ANY NOTION OF QUANTITY OR QUALITY WITHOUT FORMING A PRECISE NOTION OF DEGREES OF EACH; we may prove this by the three following arguments. First, We have observed, that whatever objects are different are distinguishable, and that whatever objects are distinguishable are separable by the thought and imagination. And we may here add, that these propositions are equally true in the inverse, and that whatever objects are separable are also distinguishable, and that whatever objects are distinguishable, are also different. For how is it possible we can separate what is not distinguishable, or distinguish what is not different? In order therefore to know, whether abstraction implies a separation, we need only consider it in this view, and examine, whether all the circumstances, which we abstract from in our general ideas, be such as are distinguishable and different from those, which we retain as essential parts of them. But it is evident at first sight, that the precise length of a line is not different nor distinguishable from the line itself nor the precise degree of any quality from the quality. These ideas, therefore, admit no more of separation than they do of distinction and difference. They are consequently conjoined with each other in the conception; and the general idea of a line, notwithstanding all our abstractions and refinements, has in its appearance in the mind a precise degree of quantity and quality; however it may be made to represent others, which have different degrees of both.

Secondly, it is contest, that no object can appear to the senses; or in other words, that no impression can become present to the mind, without being determined in its degrees both of quantity and quality. The confusion, in which impressions are sometimes involved, proceeds only from their faintness and unsteadiness, not from any capacity in the mind to receive any impression, which in its real existence has no particular degree nor proportion. That is a contradiction in terms; and even implies the flattest of all contradictions, viz. that it is possible for the same thing both to be and not to be.

Now since all ideas are derived from impressions, and are nothing but copies and representations of them, whatever is true of the one must be acknowledged concerning the other. Impressions and ideas differ only in their strength and vivacity. The foregoing conclusion is not founded on any particular degree of vivacity. It cannot therefore be affected by any variation in that particular. An idea is a weaker impression; and as a strong impression must necessarily have a determinate quantity and quality, the case must be the same with its copy or representative.

Thirdly, it is a principle generally received in philosophy that everything in nature is individual, and that it is utterly absurd to suppose a triangle really existent, which has no precise proportion of sides and angles. If this therefore be absurd in fact and reality, it must also be absurd in idea; since nothing of which we can form a clear and distinct idea is absurd and impossible. But to form the idea of an object, and to form an idea simply, is the same thing; the reference of the idea to an object being an extraneous denomination, of which in itself it bears no mark or character. Now as it is impossible to form an idea of an object, that is possest of quantity and quality, and yet is possest of no precise degree of either; it follows that there is an equal impossibility of forming an idea, that is not limited and confined in both these particulars. Abstract ideas are therefore in themselves individual, however they may become general in their representation. The image in the mind is only that of a particular object, though the application of it in our reasoning be the same, as if it were universal.

This application of ideas beyond their nature proceeds from our collecting all their possible degrees of quantity and quality in such an imperfect manner as may serve the purposes of life, which is the second proposition I proposed to explain. When we have found a resemblance[5] among several objects, that often occur to us, we apply the same name to all of them, whatever differences we may observe in the degrees of their quantity and quality, and whatever other differences may appear among them. After we have acquired a custom of this kind, the hearing of that name revives the idea of one of these objects, and makes the imagination conceive it with all its particular circumstances and proportions. But as the same word is supposed to have been frequently applied to other individuals, that are different in many respects from that idea, which is immediately present to the mind; the word not being able to revive the idea of all these individuals, but only touches the soul, if I may be allowed so to speak, and revives that custom, which we have acquired by surveying them. They are not really and in fact present to the mind, but only in power; nor do we draw them all out distinctly in the imagination, but keep ourselves in a readiness to survey any of them, as we may be prompted by a present design or necessity. The word raises up an individual idea, along with a certain custom; and that custom produces any other individual one, for which we may have occasion. But as the production of all the ideas, to which the name may be applied, is in most eases impossible, we abridge that work by a more partial consideration, and find but few inconveniences to arise in our reasoning from that abridgment.

For this is one of the most extraordinary circumstances in the present affair, that after the mind has produced an individual idea, upon which we reason, the

---

[5] It is evident, that even different simple ideas may have a similarity or resemblance to each other; nor is it necessary, that the point or circumstance of resemblance shoud be distinct or separable from that in which they differ. BLUE and GREEN are different simple ideas, but are more resembling than BLUE and SCARLET; tho their perfect simplicity excludes all possibility of separation or distinction. It is the same case with particular sounds, and tastes and smells. These admit of infinite resemblances upon the general appearance and comparison, without having any common circumstance the same. And of this we may be certain, even from the very abstract terms SIMPLE IDEA. They comprehend all simple ideas under them. These resemble each other in their simplicity. And yet from their very nature, which excludes all composition, this circumstance, In which they resemble, Is not distinguishable nor separable from the rest. It is the same case with all the degrees In any quality. They are all resembling and yet the quality, In any individual, Is not distinct from the degree.

attendant custom, revived by the general or abstract term, readily suggests any other individual, if by chance we form any reasoning, that agrees not with it. Thus should we mention the word triangle, and form the idea of a particular equilateral one to correspond to it, and should we afterwards assert, that the three angles of a triangle are equal to each other, the other individuals of a scalenum and isosceles, which we overlooked at first, immediately crowd in upon us, and make us perceive the falshood of this proposition, though it be true with relation to that idea, which we had formed. If the mind suggests not always these ideas upon occasion, it proceeds from some imperfection in its faculties; and such a one as is often the source of false reasoning and sophistry. But this is principally the case with those ideas which are abstruse and compounded. On other occasions the custom is more entire, and it is seldom we run into such errors.

Nay so entire is the custom, that the very same idea may be annext to several different words, and may be employed in different reasonings, without any danger of mistake. Thus the idea of an equilateral triangle of an inch perpendicular may serve us in talking of a figure, of a rectilinear figure, of a regular figure, of a triangle, and of an equilateral triangle. All these terms, therefore, are in this case attended with the same idea; but as they are wont to be applied in a greater or lesser compass, they excite their particular habits, and thereby keep the mind in a readiness to observe, that no conclusion be formed contrary to any ideas, which are usually comprized under them.

Before those habits have become entirely perfect, perhaps the mind may not be content with forming the idea of only one individual, but may run over several, in order to make itself comprehend its own meaning, and the compass of that collection, which it intends to express by the general term. That we may fix the meaning of the word, figure, we may revolve in our mind the ideas of circles, squares, parallelograms, triangles of different sizes and proportions, and may not rest on one image or idea. However this may be, it is certain that we form the idea of individuals, whenever we use any general term; that we seldom or never can exhaust these individuals; and that those, which remain, are only represented by means of that habit, by which we recall them, whenever any present occasion requires it. This then is the nature of our abstract ideas and general terms; and it is after this manner we account for the foregoing paradox, THAT SOME IDEAS ARE PARTICULAR IN THEIR NATURE, BUT GENERAL IN THEIR REPRESENTATION. A particular idea becomes general by being annexed to a general term; that is, to a term, which from a customary conjunction has a relation to many other particular ideas, and readily recalls them in the imagination.

The only difficulty, that can remain on this subject, must be with regard to that custom, which so readily recalls every particular idea, for which we may have occasion, and is excited by any word or sound, to which we commonly annex it. The most proper method, in my opinion, of giving a satisfactory explication of this act of the mind, is by producing other instances, which are analogous to it, and other principles, which facilitate its operation. To explain the ultimate causes of our mental actions is impossible. It is sufficient, if we can give any satisfactory account of them from experience and analogy.

First then I observe, that when we mention any great number, such as a thousand, the mind has generally no adequate idea of it, but only a power of producing such an idea, by its adequate idea of the decimals, under which the number is comprehended. This imperfection, however, in our ideas, is never felt in our reasonings; which seems to be an instance parallel to the present one of universal ideas.

Secondly, we have several instances of habits, which may be revived by one single word; as when a person, who has by rote any periods of a discourse, or any number of verses, will be put in remembrance of the whole, which he is at a loss to recollect, by that single word or expression, with which they begin.

Thirdly, I believe every one, who examines the situation of his mind in reasoning will agree with me, that we do not annex distinct and compleat ideas to every term we make use of, and that in talking of government, church, negotiation, conquest, we seldom spread out in our minds all the simple ideas, of which these complex ones are composed. It is however observable, that notwithstanding this imperfection we may avoid talking nonsense on these subjects, and may perceive any repugnance among the ideas, as well as if we had a fall comprehension of them. Thus if instead of saying, that in war the weaker have always recourse to negotiation, we should say, that they have always recourse to conquest, the custom, which we have acquired of attributing certain relations to ideas, still follows the words, and makes us immediately perceive the absurdity of that proposition; in the same manner as one particular idea may serve us in reasoning concerning other ideas, however different from it in several circumstances.

Fourthly, As the individuals are collected together, said placed under a general term with a view to that resemblance, which they bear to each other, this relation must facilitate their entrance in the imagination, and make them be suggested more readily upon occasion. And indeed if we consider the common progress of the thought, either in reflection or conversation, we shall find great reason to be satisfyed in this particular. Nothing is more admirable, than the readiness, with which the imagination suggests its ideas, and presents them at the very instant, in which they become necessary or useful. The fancy runs from one end of the universe to the other in collecting those ideas, which belong to any subject. One would think the whole intellectual world of ideas was at once subjected to our view, and that we did nothing but pick out such as were most proper for our purpose. There may not, however, be any present, beside those very ideas, that are thus collected by a kind of magical faculty in the soul, which, though it be always most perfect in the greatest geniuses, and is properly what we call a genius, is however inexplicable by the utmost efforts of human understanding.

Perhaps these four reflections may help to remove an difficulties to the hypothesis I have proposed concerning abstract ideas, so contrary to that, which has hitherto prevailed in philosophy, But, to tell the truth I place my chief confidence in what I have already proved concerning the impossibility of general ideas, according to the common method of explaining them. We must certainly seek some new system on this head, and there plainly is none beside what I have proposed. If ideas be particular in their nature, and at the same time finite in their number, it is only by custom they can become general in their representation, and contain an infinite number of other ideas under them.

Before I leave this subject I shall employ the same principles to explain that distinction of reason, which is so much talked of, and is so little understood, in the schools. Of this kind is the distinction betwixt figure and the body figured; motion and the body moved. The difficulty of explaining this distinction arises from the principle above explained, that all ideas, which are different, are separable. For it follows from thence, that if the figure be different from the body, their ideas must be separable as well as distinguishable: if they be not different, their ideas can neither be separable nor distinguishable. What then is meant by a distinction of reason, since it implies neither a difference nor separation.

To remove this difficulty we must have recourse to the foregoing explication of abstract ideas. It is certain that the mind would never have dreamed of distinguishing a figure from the body figured, as being in reality neither distinguishable, nor different, nor separable; did it not observe, that even in this simplicity there might be contained many different resemblances and relations. Thus when a globe of white marble is presented, we receive only the impression of a white colour disposed in a certain form, nor are we able to separate and distinguish the colour from the form. But observing afterwards a globe of black marble and a cube of white, and comparing them with our former object, we find two separate resemblances, in what formerly seemed, and really is, perfectly inseparable. After a little more practice of this kind, we begin to distinguish the figure from the colour by a distinction of reason; that is, we consider the figure and colour together, since they are in effect the same and undistinguishable; but still view them in different aspects, according to the resemblances, of which they are susceptible. When we would consider only the figure of the globe of white marble, we form in reality an idea both of the figure and colour, but tacitly carry our eye to its resemblance with the globe of black marble: And in the same manner, when we would consider its colour only, we turn our view to its resemblance with the cube of white marble. By this means we accompany our ideas with a kind of reflection, of which custom renders us, in a great measure, insensible. A person, who desires us to consider the figure of a globe of white marble without thinking on its colour, desires an impossibility but his meaning is, that we should consider the figure and colour together, but still keep in our eye the resemblance to the globe of black marble, or that to any other globe of whatever colour or substance.

PART II

Of the Ideas of Space and Time

SECTION I

Of the Infinite Divisibility of our Ideas of Space and Time

Whatever has the air of a paradox, and is contrary to the first and most unprejudiced notions of mankind, is often greedily embraced by philosophers, as shewing the superiority of their science, which could discover opinions so remote from vulgar conception. On the other hand, anything proposed to us, which causes surprize and admiration, gives such a satisfaction to the mind, that it indulges itself in those agreeable emotions, and will never be persuaded that its pleasure is entirely without foundation. From these dispositions in philosophers and their disciples arises that mutual complaisance betwixt them; while the former furnish such plenty of strange and unaccountable opinions, and the latter so readily believe them. Of this mutual complaisance I cannot give a more evident instance than in the doctrine of infinite divisibility, with the examination of which I shall begin this subject of the ideas of space and time.

It is universally allowed, that the capacity of the mind is limited, and can never attain a full and adequate conception of infinity: And though it were not allowed, it would be sufficiently evident from the plainest observation and experience. It is also obvious, that whatever is capable of being divided in infinitum, must consist of an infinite number of parts, and that it is impossible to set any bounds to the number of parts, without setting bounds at the same time to the division. It requires scarce any, induction to conclude from hence, that the idea, which we form of any finite quality, is not infinitely divisible, but that by proper distinctions and separations we may run up this idea to inferior ones, which will be perfectly simple and indivisible. In rejecting the infinite capacity of the mind, we suppose it may arrive at an end in the division of its ideas; nor are there any possible means of evading the evidence of this conclusion.

It is therefore certain, that the imagination reaches a minimum, and may raise up to itself an idea, of which it cannot conceive any sub-division, and which cannot be diminished without a total annihilation. When you tell me of the thousandth and ten thousandth part of a grain of sand, I have a distinct idea of these numbers and of their different proportions; but the images, which I form in my mind to represent the things themselves, are nothing different from each other, nor inferior to that image, by which I represent the grain of sand itself, which is supposed so vastly to exceed them. What consists of parts is distinguishable into them, and what is distinguishable is separable. But whatever we may imagine of the thing, the idea of a grain of sand is not distinguishable, nor separable into twenty, much less into a thousand, ten thousand, or an infinite number of different ideas.

It is the same case with the impressions of the senses as with the ideas of the imagination. Put a spot of ink upon paper, fix your eye upon that spot, and retire to such a distance, that, at last you lose sight of it; it is plain, that the moment before it vanished the image or impression was perfectly indivisible. It is not for want of rays of light striking on our eyes, that the minute parts of distant bodies convey not any sensible impression; but because they are removed beyond that distance, at which their impressions were reduced to a minimum, and were incapable of any farther diminution. A microscope or telescope, which renders them visible, produces not any new rays of light, but only spreads those, which always flowed from them; and by that means both gives parts to impressions, which to the naked eye appear simple and uncompounded, and advances to a minimum, what was formerly imperceptible.

We may hence discover the error of the common opinion, that the capacity of the mind is limited on both sides, and that it is impossible for the imagination to form an adequate idea, of what goes beyond a certain degree of minuteness as well as of greatness. Nothing can be more minute, than some ideas, which we form in the fancy; and images, which appear to the senses; since there are ideas and images perfectly simple and indivisible. The only defect of our senses is, that they give us disproportioned images of things, and represent as minute and uncompounded what is really great and composed of a vast number of parts. This mistake we are not sensible of: but taking the impressions of those minute objects, which appear to the senses, to be equal or nearly equal to the objects, and finding by reason, that there are other objects vastly more minute, we too hastily conclude, that these are inferior to any idea of our imagination or impression of our senses. This however is certain, that we can form ideas, which shall be no greater than the smallest atom of the animal spirits of an insect a thousand times less than a mite: And we ought rather to conclude, that the difficulty lies in enlarging our conceptions so much as to form a just notion of a mite, or even of an insect a thousand times less than a mite. For in order to form a just notion of these animals, we must have a distinct idea representing every part of them, which, according to the system of infinite divisibility, is utterly impossible, and, recording to that of indivisible parts or atoms, is extremely difficult, by reason of the vast number and multiplicity of these parts.

SECTION II

Of the Infinite Divisibility of Space and Time

Wherever ideas are adequate representations of objects, the relations, contradictions and agreements of the ideas are all applicable to the objects; and this we may in general observe to be the foundation of all human knowledge. But our ideas are adequate representations of the most minute parts of extension; and through whatever divisions and subdivisions we may suppose these parts to be arrived at, they can never become inferior to some ideas, which we form. The plain consequence is, that whatever appears impossible and contradictory upon the comparison of these ideas, must be really impossible and contradictory, without any farther excuse or evasion.

Every thing capable of being infinitely divided contains an infinite number of parts; otherwise the division would be stopt short by the indivisible parts, which we should immediately arrive at. If therefore any finite extension be infinitely divisible, it can be no contradiction to suppose, that a finite extension contains an infinite number of parts: And vice versa, if it be a contradiction to suppose, that a finite extension contains an infinite number of parts, no finite extension can be infinitely divisible. But that this latter supposition is absurd, I easily convince myself by the consideration of my clear ideas. I first take the least idea I can form of a part of extension, and being certain that there is nothing more minute than this idea, I conclude, that whatever I discover by its means must be a real quality of extension. I then repeat this idea once, twice, thrice, &c., and find the compound idea of extension, arising from its repetition, always to augment, and become double, triple, quadruple, &c., till at last it swells up to a considerable bulk, greater or smaller, in proportion as I repeat more or less the same idea. When I stop in the addition of parts, the idea of extension ceases to augment; and were I to carry on the addition in infinitum, I clearly perceive, that the idea of extension must also become infinite. Upon the whole, I conclude, that the idea of all infinite number of parts is individually the same idea with that of an infinite extension; that no finite extension is capable of containing an infinite number of parts; and consequently that no finite extension is infinitely divisible.[6]

I may subjoin another argument proposed by a noted author,[7] which seems to me very strong and beautiful. It is evident, that existence in itself belongs only to unity, and is never applicable to number, but on account of the unites, of which the number is composed. Twenty men may be said to exist; but it is only because one, two, three, four, &c. are existent, and if you deny the existence of the latter, that of the former falls of course. It is therefore utterly absurd to suppose any number to exist, and yet deny the existence of unites; and as extension is always a number, according to the common sentiment of metaphysicians, and never resolves itself into any unite or indivisible quantity, it follows, that extension can never at all exist. It is in vain to reply, that any determinate quantity of extension is an unite; but such-a-one as admits of an infinite number of fractions, and is inexhaustible

[6] It has been objected to me, that infinite divisibility supposes only an infinite number of PROPORTIONAL not of ALIQIOT parts, and that an infinite number of proportional parts does not form an infinite extension. But this distinction is entirely frivolous. Whether these parts be calld ALIQUOT or PROPORTIONAL, they cannot be inferior to those minute parts we conceive; and therefore cannot form a less extension by their conjunction.

[7] Mons. MALEZIEU

in its sub-divisions. For by the same rule these twenty men may be considered as a unit. The whole globe of the earth, nay the whole universe, may be considered as a unit. That term of unity is merely a fictitious denomination, which the mind may apply to any quantity of objects it collects together; nor can such an unity any more exist alone than number can, as being in reality a true number. But the unity, which can exist alone, and whose existence is necessary to that of all number, is of another kind, and must be perfectly indivisible, and incapable of being resolved into any lesser unity.

All this reasoning takes place with regard to time; along with an additional argument, which it may be proper to take notice of. It is a property inseparable from time, and which in a manner constitutes its essence, that each of its parts succeeds another, and that none of them, however contiguous, can ever be co-existent. For the same reason, that the year 1737 cannot concur with the present year 1738 every moment must be distinct from, and posterior or antecedent to another. It is certain then, that time, as it exists, must be composed of indivisible moments. For if in time we could never arrive at an end of division, and if each moment, as it succeeds another, were not perfectly single and indivisible, there would be an infinite number of co-existent moments, or parts of time; which I believe will be allowed to be an arrant contradiction.

The infinite divisibility of space implies that of time, as is evident from the nature of motion. If the latter, therefore, be impossible, the former must be equally so.

I doubt not but, it will readily be allowed by the most obstinate defender of the doctrine of infinite divisibility, that these arguments are difficulties, and that it is impossible to give any answer to them which will be perfectly clear and satisfactory. But here we may observe, that nothing can be more absurd, than this custom of calling a difficulty what pretends to be a demonstration, and endeavouring by that means to elude its force and evidence. It is not in demonstrations as in probabilities, that difficulties can take place, and one argument counter-ballance another, and diminish its authority. A demonstration, if just, admits of no opposite difficulty; and if not just, it is a mere sophism, and consequently can never be a difficulty. It is either irresistible, or has no manner of force. To talk therefore of objections and replies, and ballancing of arguments in such a question as this, is to confess, either that human reason is nothing but a play of words, or that the person himself, who talks so, has not a Capacity equal to such subjects. Demonstrations may be difficult to be comprehended, because of abstractedness of the subject; but can never have such difficulties as will weaken their authority, when once they are comprehended.

It is true, mathematicians are wont to say, that there are here equally strong arguments on the other side of the question, and that the doctrine of indivisible points is also liable to unanswerable objections. Before I examine these arguments and objections in detail, I will here take them in a body, and endeavour by a short and decisive reason to prove at once, that it is utterly impossible they can have any just foundation.

It is an established maxim in metaphysics, That whatever the mind clearly conceives, includes the idea of possible existence, or in other words, that nothing we imagine is absolutely impossible. We can form the idea of a golden mountain, and from thence conclude that such a mountain may actually exist. We can form no idea of a mountain without a valley, and therefore regard it as impossible.

Now it is certain we have an idea of extension; for otherwise why do we talk and reason concerning it? It is likewise certain that this idea, as conceived by the imagination, though divisible into parts or inferior ideas, is not infinitely divisible, nor consists of an infinite number of parts: For that exceeds the comprehension of our limited capacities. Here then is an idea of extension, which consists of parts or inferior ideas, that are perfectly, indivisible: consequently this idea implies no contradiction: consequently it is possible for extension really to exist conformable to it: and consequently all the arguments employed against the possibility of mathematical points are mere scholastick quibbles, and unworthy of our attention.

These consequences we may carry one step farther, and conclude that all the pretended demonstrations for the infinite divisibility of extension are equally sophistical; since it is certain these demonstrations cannot be just without proving the impossibility of mathematical points; which it is an evident absurdity to pretend to.

SECTION III

Of the other Qualities of our Idea of Space and Time

No discovery could have been made more happily for deciding all controversies concerning ideas, than that abovementioned, that impressions always take the precedency of them, and that every idea, with which the imagination is furnished, first makes its appearance in a correspondent impression. These latter perceptions are all so clear and evident, that they admit of no controversy; though many of our ideas are so obscure, that it is almost impossible even for the mind, which forms them, to tell exactly their nature and composition. Let us apply this principle, in order to discover farther the nature of our ideas of space and time.

Upon opening my eyes, and turning them to the surrounding objects, I perceive many visible bodies; and upon shutting them again, and considering the distance betwixt these bodies, I acquire the idea of extension. As every idea is derived from some impression, which is exactly similar to it, the impressions similar to this idea of extension, must either be some sensations derived from the sight, or some internal impressions arising from these sensations.

Our internal impressions are our passions, emotions, desires and aversions; none of which, I believe, will ever be asserted to be the model, from which the idea of space is derived. There remains therefore nothing but the senses, which can convey to us this original impression. Now what impression do oar senses here convey to us? This is the principal question, and decides without appeal concerning the nature of the idea.

The table before me is alone sufficient by its view to give me the idea of extension. This idea, then, is borrowed from, and represents some impression, which this moment appears to the senses. But my senses convey to me only the impressions of coloured points, disposed in a certain manner. If the eye is sensible of any thing farther, I desire it may be pointed out to me. But if it be impossible to shew any thing farther, we may conclude with certainty, that the idea of extension is nothing but a copy of these coloured points, and of the manner of their appearance.

Suppose that in the extended object, or composition of coloured points, from which we first received the idea of extension, the points were of a purple colour; it follows, that in every repetition of that idea we would not only place the points in the same order with respect to each other, but also bestow on them that precise colour, with which alone we are acquainted. But afterwards having experience of the other colours of violet, green, red, white, black, and of all the different compositions of these, and finding a resemblance in the disposition of coloured points, of which they are composed, we omit the peculiarities of colour, as far as possible, and found an abstract idea merely on that disposition of points, or manner of appearance, in which they agree. Nay even when the resemblance is carryed beyond the objects of one sense, and the impressions of touch are found to be Similar to those of sight in the disposition of their parts; this does not hinder the abstract idea from representing both, upon account of their resemblance. All abstract ideas are really nothing but particular ones, considered in a certain light; but being annexed to general terms, they are able to represent a vast variety, and to comprehend objects, which, as they are alike in some particulars, are in others vastly wide of each other.

The idea of time, being derived from the succession of our perceptions of every kind, ideas as well as impressions, and impressions of reflection as well as of sensations will afford us an instance of an abstract idea, which comprehends a still greater variety than that of space, and yet is represented in the fancy by some particular individual idea of a determinate quantity and quality.

As it is from the disposition of visible and tangible objects we receive the idea of space, so from the succession of ideas and impressions we form the idea of time, nor is it possible for time alone ever to make its appearance, or be taken notice of by the mind. A man in a sound sleep, or strongly occupyed with one thought, is insensible of time; and according as his perceptions succeed each other with greater or less rapidity, the same duration appears longer or shorter to his imagination. It has been remarked by a great philosopher, that our perceptions have certain bounds in this particular, which are fixed by the original nature and constitution of the mind, and beyond which no influence of external objects on the senses is ever able to hasten or retard our thought. If you wheel about a burning coal with rapidity, it will present to the senses an image of a circle of fire; nor will there seem to be any interval of time betwixt its revolutions; meerly because it is impossible for our perceptions to succeed each other with the same rapidity, that motion may be communicated to external objects. Wherever we have no successive perceptions, we have no notion of time, even though there be a real succession in the objects. From these phenomena, as well as from many others, we may conclude, that time cannot make its appearance to the mind, either alone, or attended with a steady unchangeable object, but is always discovered some PERCEIVABLE succession of changeable objects.

To confirm this we may add the following argument, which to me seems perfectly decisive and convincing. It is evident, that time or duration consists of different parts: For otherwise we could not conceive a longer or shorter duration. It is also evident, that these parts are not co-existent: For that quality of the co-existence of parts belongs to extension, and is what distinguishes it from duration. Now as time is composed of parts, that are not coexistent: an unchangeable object, since it produces none but coexistent impressions, produces none that can give us the idea of time; and consequently that idea must be derived from a succession of changeable objects, and time in its first appearance can never be severed from such a succession.

Having therefore found, that time in its first appearance to the mind is always conjoined with a succession of changeable objects, and that otherwise it can never fall under our notice, we must now examine whether it can be conceived without our conceiving any succession of objects, and whether it can alone form a distinct idea in the imagination.

In order to know whether any objects, which are joined in impression, be inseparable in idea, we need only consider, if they be different from each other; in which case, it is plain they may be conceived apart. Every thing, that is different is distinguishable: and everything, that is distinguishable, may be separated, according to the maxims above-explained. If on the contrary they be not different, they are not distinguishable: and if they be not distinguishable, they cannot be separated. But this is precisely the case with respect to time, compared with our successive perceptions. The idea of time is not derived from a particular impression mixed up with others, and plainly distinguishable from them; but arises altogether from the manner, in which impressions appear to the mind, without making one of the number. Five notes played on a flute give us the impression and idea of time; though time be not a sixth impression, which presents itself to the hearing or any other of the senses. Nor is it a sixth impression, which the mind by reflection finds in itself. These five sounds making their appearance in this particular manner, excite no emotion in the mind, nor produce an affection of any kind, which being observed by it can give rise to a new idea. For that is necessary to produce a new idea of reflection, nor can the mind, by revolving over a thousand times all its ideas of sensation, ever extract from them any new original idea, unless nature has so framed its faculties, that it feels some new original impression arise from such a contemplation. But here it only takes notice of the manner, in which the different sounds make their appearance; and that it may afterwards consider without considering these particular sounds, but may conjoin it with any other objects. The ideas of some objects it certainly must have, nor is it possible for it without these ideas ever to arrive at any conception of time; which since it, appears not as any primary distinct impression, can plainly be nothing but different ideas, or impressions, or objects disposed in a certain manner, that is, succeeding each other.

I know there are some who pretend, that the idea of duration is applicable in a proper sense to objects, which are perfectly unchangeable; and this I take to be the common opinion of philosophers as well as of the vulgar. But to be convinced of its falsehood we need but reflect on the foregoing conclusion, that the idea of duration is always derived from a succession of changeable objects, and can never be conveyed to the mind by any thing stedfast and unchangeable. For it inevitably follows from thence, that since the idea of duration cannot be derived from such an object, it can never-in any propriety or exactness be applied to it, nor can any thing unchangeable be ever said to have duration. Ideas always represent the Objects or impressions, from which they are derived, and can never without a fiction represent or be applied to any other. By what fiction we apply the idea of time, even to what is unchangeable, and suppose, as is common, that duration is a measure of rest as well as of motion, we shall consider afterwards.[8]

There is another very decisive argument, which establishes the present doctrine concerning our ideas of space and time, and is founded only on that simple principle, that our ideas of them are compounded of parts, which are indivisible. This argument may be worth the examining.

Every idea, that is distinguishable, being also separable, let us take one of those simple indivisible ideas, of which the compound one of extension is formed, and separating it from all others, and considering it apart, let us form a judgment of its nature and qualities.

It is plain it is not the idea of extension. For the idea of extension consists of parts; and this idea, according to the supposition, is perfectly simple and indivisible. Is it therefore nothing? That is absolutely impossible. For as the compound idea of extension, which is real, is composed of such ideas; were these so many non-entities, there would be a real existence composed of non-entities; which is absurd. Here therefore I must ask, What is our idea of a simple and indivisible point? No wonder if my answer appear somewhat new, since the question itself has scarce ever yet been thought of. We are wont to dispute concerning the nature of mathematical points, but seldom concerning the nature of their ideas.

The idea of space is conveyed to the mind by two senses, the sight and touch; nor does anything ever appear extended, that is not either visible or tangible. That compound impression, which represents extension, consists of several lesser impressions, that are indivisible to the eye or feeling, and may be called impressions of atoms or corpuscles endowed with colour and solidity. But this is not all. It is

[8] Sect 5.

not only requisite, that these atoms should be coloured or tangible, in order to discover themselves to our senses; it is also necessary we should preserve the idea of their colour or tangibility in order to comprehend them by our imagination. There is nothing but the idea of their colour or tangibility, which can render them conceivable by the mind. Upon the removal of the ideas of these sensible qualities, they are utterly annihilated to the thought or imagination.

Now such as the parts are, such is the whole. If a point be not considered as coloured or tangible, it can convey to us no idea; and consequently the idea of extension, which is composed of the ideas of these points, can never possibly exist. But if the idea of extension really can exist, as we are conscious it does, its parts must also exist; and in order to that, must be considered as coloured or tangible. We have therefore no idea of space or extension, but when we regard it as an object either of our sight or feeling.

The same reasoning will prove, that the indivisible moments of time must be filled with some real object or existence, whose succession forms the duration, and makes it be conceivable by the mind.

SECTION IV

Objections Answered

Our system concerning space and time consists of two parts, which are intimately connected together. The first depends on this chain of reasoning. The capacity of the mind is not infinite; consequently no idea of extension or duration consists of an infinite number of parts or inferior ideas, but of a finite number, and these simple and indivisible: It is therefore possible for space and time to exist conformable to this idea: And if it be possible, it is certain they actually do exist conformable to it; since their infinite divisibility is utterly impossible and contradictory.

The other part of our system is a consequence of this. The parts, into which the ideas of space and time resolve themselves, become at last indivisible; and these indivisible parts, being nothing in themselves, are inconceivable when not filled with something real and existent. The ideas of space and time are therefore no separate or distinct ideas, but merely those of the manner or order, in which objects exist: Or in other words, it is impossible to conceive either a vacuum and extension without matter, or a time, when there was no succession or change in any real existence. The intimate connexion betwixt these parts of our system is the reason why we shall examine together the objections, which have been urged against both of them, beginning with those against the finite divisibility of extension.

I. The first of these objections, which I shall take notice of, is more proper to prove this connexion and dependence of the one part upon the other, than to destroy either of them. It has often been maintained in the schools, that extension must be divisible, in infinitum, because the system of mathematical points is absurd; and that system is absurd, because a mathematical point is a non-entity, and consequently can never by its conjunction with others form a real existence. This would be perfectly decisive, were there no medium betwixt the infinite divisibility of matter, and the non-entity of mathematical points. But there is evidently a medium, viz. the bestowing a colour or solidity on these points; and the absurdity of both the extremes is a demonstration of the truth and reality of this medium. The system of physical points, which is another medium, is too absurd to need a refutation. A real extension, such as a physical point is supposed to be, can never exist without parts, different from each other; and wherever objects are different, they are distinguishable and separable by the imagination.

II. The second objection is derived from the necessity there would be of PENETRATION, if extension consisted of mathematical points. A simple and indivisible atom, that touches another, must necessarily penetrate it; for it is impossible it can touch it by its external parts, from the very supposition of its perfect simplicity, which excludes all parts. It must therefore touch it intimately, and in its whole essence, SECUNDUM SE, TOTA, ET TOTALITER; which is the very definition of penetration. But penetration is impossible: Mathematical points are of consequence equally impossible.

I answer this objection by substituting a juster idea of penetration. Suppose two bodies containing no void within their circumference, to approach each other, and to unite in such a manner that the body, which results from their union, is no more extended than either of them; it is this we must mean when we talk of penetration. But it is evident this penetration is nothing but the annihilation of one of these bodies, and the preservation of the other, without our being able to distinguish particularly which is preserved and which annihilated. Before the approach we have the idea of two bodies. After it we have the idea only of one. It is impossible for the mind to preserve any notion of difference betwixt two bodies of the same nature existing in the same place at the same time.

Taking then penetration in this sense, for the annihilation of one body upon its approach to another, I ask any one, if he sees a necessity, that a coloured or tangible point should be annihilated upon the approach of another coloured or tangible point? On the contrary, does he not evidently perceive, that from the union of these points there results an object, which is compounded and divisible, and may be distinguished into two parts, of which each preserves its existence distinct and separate, notwithstanding its contiguity to the other? Let him aid his fancy by conceiving these points to be of different colours, the better to prevent their coalition and confusion. A blue and a red point may surely lie contiguous without any penetration or annihilation. For if they cannot, what possibly can become of them? Whether shall the red or the blue be annihilated? Or if these colours unite into one, what new colour will they produce by their union?

What chiefly gives rise to these objections, and at the same time renders it so difficult to give a satisfactory answer to them, is the natural infirmity and unsteadiness both of our imagination and senses, when employed on such minute objects. Put a spot of ink upon paper, and retire to such a distance, that the spot becomes altogether invisible; you will find, that upon your return and nearer approach the spot first becomes visible by short intervals; and afterwards becomes always visible; and afterwards acquires only a new force in its colouring without augmenting its bulk; and afterwards, when it has encreased to such a degree as to be really extended, it is still difficult for the imagination to break it into its component parts, because of the uneasiness it finds in the conception of such a minute object as a single point. This infirmity affects most of our reasonings on the present subject, and makes it almost impossible to answer in an intelligible manner, and in proper expressions, many questions which may arise concerning it.

III. There have been many objections drawn from the mathematics against the indivisibility of the parts of extension: though at first sight that science seems rather favourable to the present doctrine; and if it be contrary in its DEMONSTRATIONS, it is perfectly conformable in its definitions. My present business then must be to defend the definitions, and refute the demonstrations.

A surface is DEFINed to be length and breadth without depth: A line to be length without breadth or depth: A point to be what has neither length, breadth nor depth. It is evident that all this is perfectly unintelligible upon any other supposition than that of the composition of extension by indivisible points or atoms. How else could any thing exist without length, without breadth, or without depth?

Two different answers, I find, have been made to this argument; neither of which is in my opinion satisfactory. The first is, that the objects of geometry, those surfaces, lines and points, whose proportions and positions it examines, are mere ideas in the mind; and not only never did, but never can exist in nature. They never did exist; for no one will pretend to draw a line or make a surface entirely conformable to the definition: They never can exist; for we may produce demonstrations from these very ideas to prove, that they are impossible.

But can anything be imagined more absurd and contradictory than this reasoning? Whatever can be conceived by a clear and distinct idea necessarily implies the possibility of existence; and he who pretends to prove the impossibility of its existence by any argument derived from the clear idea, in reality asserts, that we have no clear idea of it, because we have a clear idea. It is in vain to search for a contradiction in any thing that is distinctly conceived by the mind. Did it imply any contradiction, it is impossible it could ever be conceived.

There is therefore no medium betwixt allowing at least the possibility of indivisible points, and denying their idea; and it is on this latter principle, that the second answer to the foregoing argument is founded. It has been[9] pretended, that though it be impossible to conceive a length without any breadth, yet by an abstraction without a separation, we can consider the one without regarding the other; in the same manner as we may think of the length of the way betwixt two

[9] L'Art de penser.

towns, and overlook its breadth. The length is inseparable from the breadth both in nature and in our minds; but this excludes not a partial consideration, and a distinction of reason, after the manner above explained.

In refuting this answer I shall not insist on the argument, which I have already sufficiently explained, that if it be impossible for the mind to arrive at a minimum in its ideas, its capacity must be infinite, in order to comprehend the infinite number of parts, of which its idea of any extension would be composed. I shall here endeavour to find some new absurdities in this reasoning.

A surface terminates a solid; a line terminates a surface; a point terminates a line; but I assert, that if the ideas of a point, line or surface were not indivisible, it is impossible we should ever conceive these terminations: For let these ideas be supposed infinitely divisible; and then let the fancy endeavour to fix itself on the idea of the last surface, line or point; it immediately finds this idea to break into parts; and upon its seizing the last of these parts, it loses its hold by a new division, and so on in infinitum, without any possibility of its arriving at a concluding idea. The number of fractions bring it no nearer the last division, than the first idea it formed. Every particle eludes the grasp by a new fraction; like quicksilver, when we endeavour to seize it. But as in fact there must be something, which terminates the idea of every finite quantity; and as this terminating idea cannot itself consist of parts or inferior ideas; otherwise it would be the last of its parts, which finished the idea, and so on; this is a clear proof, that the ideas of surfaces, lines and points admit not of any division; those of surfaces in depth; of lines in breadth and depth; and of points in any dimension.

The school were so sensible of the force of this argument, that some of them maintained, that nature has mixed among those particles of matter, which are divisible in infinitum, a number of mathematical points, in order to give a termination to bodies; and others eluded the force of this reasoning by a heap of unintelligible cavils and distinctions. Both these adversaries equally yield the victory. A man who hides himself, confesses as evidently the superiority of his enemy, as another, who fairly delivers his arms.

Thus it appears, that the definitions of mathematics destroy the pretended demonstrations; and that if we have the idea of indivisible points, lines and surfaces conformable to the definition, their existence is certainly possible: but if we have no such idea, it is impossible we can ever conceive the termination of any figure; without which conception there can be no geometrical demonstration.

But I go farther, and maintain, that none of these demonstrations can have sufficient weight to establish such a principle, as this of infinite divisibility; and that because with regard to such minute objects, they are not properly demonstrations, being built on ideas, which are not exact, and maxims, which are not precisely true. When geometry decides anything concerning the proportions of quantity, we ought not to look for the utmost precision and exactness. None of its proofs extend so far. It takes the dimensions and proportions of figures justly; but roughly, and with some liberty. Its errors are never considerable; nor would it err at all, did it not aspire to such an absolute perfection.

I first ask mathematicians, what they mean when they say one line or surface is EQUAL to, or GREATER or LESS than another? Let any of them give an answer, to whatever sect he belongs, and whether he maintains the composition of extension by indivisible points, or by quantities divisible in infinitum. This question will embarrass both of them.

There are few or no mathematicians, who defend the hypothesis of indivisible points; and yet these have the readiest and justest answer to the present question. They need only reply, that lines or surfaces are equal, when the numbers of points in each are equal; and that as the proportion of the numbers varies, the proportion of the lines and surfaces is also varyed. But though this answer be just, as well as obvious; yet I may affirm, that this standard of equality is entirely useless, and that it never is from such a comparison we determine objects to be equal or unequal with respect to each other. For as the points, which enter into the composition of any line or surface, whether perceived by the sight or touch, are so minute and so confounded with each other, that it is utterly impossible for the mind to compute their number, such a computation will Never afford us a standard by which we may judge of proportions. No one will ever be able to determine by an exact numeration, that an inch has fewer points than a foot, or a foot fewer than an ell or any greater measure: for which reason we seldom or never consider this as the standard of equality or inequality.

As to those, who imagine, that extension is divisible in infinitum, it is impossible they can make use of this answer, or fix the equality of any line or surface by a numeration of its component parts. For since, according to their hypothesis, the least as well as greatest figures contain an infinite number of parts; and since infinite numbers, properly speaking, can neither be equal nor unequal with respect to each other; the equality or inequality of any portions of space can never depend on any proportion in the number of their parts. It is true, it may be said, that the inequality of an ell and a yard consists in the different numbers of the feet, of which they are composed; and that of a foot and a yard in the number of the inches. But as that quantity we call an inch in the one is supposed equal to what we call an inch in the other, and as it is impossible for the mind to find this equality by proceeding in infinitum with these references to inferior quantities: it is evident, that at last we must fix some standard of equality different from an enumeration of the parts.

There are some[10], who pretend, that equality is best defined by congruity, and that any two figures are equal, when upon the placing of one upon the other, all their parts correspond to and touch each other. In order to judge of this definition let us consider, that since equality is a relation, it is not, strictly speaking, a property in the figures themselves, but arises merely from the comparison, which the mind

---

[10] See Dr. Barrow's mathematical lectures.

makes betwixt them. If it consists, therefore, in this imaginary application and mutual contact of parts, we must at least have a distinct notion of these parts, and must conceive their contact. Now it is plain, that in this conception we would run up these parts to the greatest minuteness, which can possibly be conceived; since the contact of large parts would never render the figures equal. But the minutest parts we can conceive are mathematical points; and consequently this standard of equality is the same with that derived from the equality of the number of points; which we have already determined to be a just but an useless standard. We must therefore look to some other quarter for a solution of the present difficulty.

There are many philosophers, who refuse to assign any standard of equality, but assert, that it is sufficient to present two objects, that are equal, in order to give us a just notion of this proportion. All definitions, say they, are fruitless, without the perception of such objects; and where we perceive such objects, we no longer stand in need of any definition. To this reasoning, I entirely agree; and assert, that the only useful notion of equality, or inequality, is derived from the whole united appearance and the comparison of particular objects.

It is evident, that the eye, or rather the mind is often able at one view to determine the proportions of bodies, and pronounce them equal to, or greater or less than each other, without examining or comparing the number of their minute parts. Such judgments are not only common, but in many cases certain and infallible. When the measure of a yard and that of a foot are presented, the mind can no more question, that the first is longer than the second, than it can doubt of those principles, which are the most clear and self-evident.

There are therefore three proportions, which the mind distinguishes in the general appearance of its objects, and calls by the names of greater, less and equal. But though its decisions concerning these proportions be sometimes infallible, they are not always so; nor are our judgments of this kind more exempt from doubt and error than those on any other subject. We frequently correct our first opinion by a review and reflection; and pronounce those objects to be equal, which at first we esteemed unequal; and regard an object as less, though before it appeared greater than another. Nor is this the only correction, which these judgments of our senses undergo; but we often discover our error by a juxtaposition of the objects; or where that is impracticable, by the use of some common and invariable measure, which being successively applied to each, informs us of their different proportions. And even this correction is susceptible of a new correction, and of different degrees of exactness, according to the nature of the instrument, by which we measure the bodies, and the care which we employ in the comparison.

When therefore the mind is accustomed to these judgments and their corrections, and finds that the same proportion which makes two figures have in the eye that appearance, which we call equality, makes them also correspond to each other, and to any common measure, with which they are compared, we form a mixed notion of equality derived both from the looser and stricter methods of comparison. But we are not content with this. For as sound reason convinces us that there are bodies vastly more minute than those, which appear to the senses; and as a false reason would perswade us, that there are bodies infinitely more minute; we clearly perceive, that we are not possessed of any instrument or art of measuring, which can secure us from ill error and uncertainty. We are sensible, that the addition or removal of one of these minute parts, is not discernible either in the appearance or measuring; and as we imagine, that two figures, which were equal before, cannot be equal after this removal or addition, we therefore suppose some imaginary standard of equality, by which the appearances and measuring are exactly corrected, and the figures reduced entirely to that proportion. This standard is plainly imaginary. For as the very idea of equality is that of such a particular appearance corrected by juxtaposition or a common measure. The notion of any correction beyond what we have instruments and art to make, is a mere fiction of the mind, and useless as well as incomprehensible. But though this standard be only imaginary, the fiction however is very natural; nor is anything more usual, than for the mind to proceed after this manner with any action, even after the reason has ceased, which first determined it to begin. This appears very conspicuously with regard to time; where though it is evident we have no exact method of determining the proportions of parts, not even so exact as in extension, yet the various corrections of our measures, and their different degrees of exactness, have given as an obscure and implicit notion of a perfect and entire equality. The case is the same in many other subjects. A musician finding his ear becoming every day more delicate, and correcting himself by reflection and attention, proceeds with the same act of the mind, even when the subject fails him, and entertains a notion of a compleat TIERCE or OCTAVE, without being able to tell whence he derives his standard. A painter forms the same fiction with regard to colours. A mechanic with regard to motion. To the one light and shade; to the other swift and slow are imagined to be capable of an exact comparison and equality beyond the judgments of the senses.

We may apply the same reasoning to CURVE and RIGHT lines. Nothing is more apparent to the senses, than the distinction betwixt a curve and a right line; nor are there any ideas we more easily form than the ideas of these objects. But however easily we may form these ideas, it is impossible to produce any definition of them, which will fix the precise boundaries betwixt them. When we draw lines upon paper, or any continued surface, there is a certain order, by which the lines run along from one point to another, that they may produce the entire impression of a curve or right line; but this order is perfectly unknown, and nothing is observed but the united appearance. Thus even upon the system of indivisible points, we can only form a distant notion of some unknown standard to these objects. Upon that of infinite divisibility we cannot go even this length; but are reduced meerly to the general appearance, as the rule by which we determine lines to be either curve or right ones. But though we can give no perfect definition of these lines, nor produce any very exact method of distinguishing the one from the other; yet this hinders us not from correcting the first appearance by a more accurate consideration, and by a comparison with some rule, of whose rectitude from repeated trials we have a greater assurance. And it is from these corrections, and by carrying on the same action of the mind, even when its reason fails us, that we form the loose idea of a perfect standard to these figures, without being able to explain or comprehend it.

It is true, mathematicians pretend they give an exact definition of a right line, when they say, it is the shortest way betwixt two points. But in the first place I observe, that this is more properly the discovery of one of the properties of a right line, than a just deflation of it. For I ask any one, if upon mention of a right line he thinks not immediately on such a particular appearance, and if it is not by accident only that he considers this property? A right line can be comprehended alone; but this definition is unintelligible without a comparison with other lines, which we conceive to be more extended. In common life it is established as a maxim, that the straightest way is always the shortest; which would be as absurd as to say, the shortest way is always the shortest, if our idea of a right line was not different from that of the shortest way betwixt two points.

Secondly, I repeat what I have already established, that we have no precise idea of equality and inequality, shorter and longer, more than of a right line or a curve; and consequently that the one can never afford us a perfect standard for the other. An exact idea can never be built on such as are loose and undetermined.

The idea of a plain surface is as little susceptible of a precise standard as that of a right line; nor have we any other means of distinguishing such a surface, than its general appearance. It is in vain, that mathematicians represent a plain surface as produced by the flowing of a right line. It will immediately be objected, that our idea of a surface is as independent of this method of forming a surface, as our idea of an ellipse is of that of a cone; that the idea of a right line is no more precise than that of a plain surface; that a right line may flow irregularly, and by that means form a figure quite different from a plane; and that therefore we must suppose it to flow along two right lines, parallel to each other, and on the same plane; which is a description, that explains a thing by itself, and returns in a circle.

It appears, then, that the ideas which are most essential to geometry, viz. those of equality and inequality, of a right line and a plain surface, are far from being exact and determinate, according to our common method of conceiving them. Not only we are incapable of telling, if the case be in any degree doubtful, when such particular figures are equal; when such a line is a right one, and such a surface a plain one; but we can form no idea of that proportion, or of these figures, which is firm and invariable. Our appeal is still to the weak and fallible judgment, which we make from the appearance of the objects, and correct by a compass or common measure; and if we join the supposition of any farther correction, it is of such-a-one as is either useless or imaginary. In vain should we have recourse to the common topic, and employ the supposition of a deity, whose omnipotence may enable him to form a perfect geometrical figure, and describe a right line without any curve or inflexion. As the ultimate standard of these figures is derived from nothing but the senses and imagination, it is absurd to talk of any perfection beyond what these faculties can judge of; since the true perfection of any thing consists in its conformity to its standard.

Now since these ideas are so loose and uncertain, I would fain ask any mathematician what infallible assurance he has, not only of the more intricate, and obscure propositions of his science, but of the most vulgar and obvious principles? How can he prove to me, for instance, that two right lines cannot have one common segment? Or that it is impossible to draw more than one right line betwixt any two points? should he tell me, that these opinions are obviously absurd, and repugnant to our clear ideas; I would answer, that I do not deny, where two right lines incline upon each other with a sensible angle, but it is absurd to imagine them to have a common segment. But supposing these two lines to approach at the rate of an inch in twenty leagues, I perceive no absurdity in asserting, that upon their contact they become one. For, I beseech you, by what rule or standard do you judge, when you assert, that the line, in which I have supposed them to concur, cannot make the same right line with those two, that form so small an angle betwixt them? You must surely have some idea of a right line, to which this line does not agree. Do you therefore mean that it takes not the points in the same order and by the same rule, as is peculiar and essential to a right line? If so, I must inform you, that besides that in judging after this manner you allow, that extension is composed of indivisible points (which, perhaps, is more than you intend) besides this, I say, I must inform you, that neither is this the standard from which we form the idea of a right line; nor, if it were, is there any such firmness in our senses or imagination, as to determine when such an order is violated or preserved. The original standard of a right line is in reality nothing but a certain general appearance; and it is evident right lines may be made to concur with each other, and yet correspond to this standard, though corrected by all the means either practicable or imaginable.

To whatever side mathematicians turn, this dilemma still meets them. If they judge of equality, or any other proportion, by the accurate and exact standard, viz. the enumeration of the minute indivisible parts, they both employ a standard, which is useless in practice, and actually establish the indivisibility of extension, which they endeavour to explode. Or if they employ, as is usual, the inaccurate standard, derived from a comparison of objects, upon their general appearance, corrected by measuring and juxtaposition; their first principles, though certain and infallible, are too coarse to afford any such subtile inferences as they commonly draw from them. The first principles are founded on the imagination and senses: The conclusion, therefore, can never go beyond, much less contradict these faculties.

This may open our eyes a little, and let us see, that no geometrical demonstration for the infinite divisibility of extension can have so much force as what we naturally attribute to every argument, which is supported by such magnificent pretensions. At the same time we may learn the reason, why geometry falls of evidence in this single point, while all its other reasonings command our fullest assent and approbation. And indeed it seems more requisite to give the reason of this exception, than to shew, that we really must make such an exception, and regard all the mathematical arguments for infinite divisibility as utterly sophistical. For it is evident, that as no idea of quantity is infinitely divisible, there cannot be imagined a more glaring absurdity, than to endeavour to prove, that quantity itself admits of such a division; and to prove this by means of ideas, which are directly opposite in that particular. And as this absurdity is very glaring in itself, so there is no argument founded on it which is not attended with a new absurdity, and involves not an evident contradiction.

I might give as instances those arguments for infinite divisibility, which are derived from the point of contact. I know there is no mathematician, who will not refuse to be judged by the diagrams he describes upon paper, these being loose draughts, as he will tell us, and serving only to convey with greater facility certain ideas, which are the true foundation of all our reasoning. This I am satisfyed with, and am willing to rest the controversy merely upon these ideas. I desire therefore our mathematician to form, as accurately as possible, the ideas of a circle and a right line; and I then ask, if upon the conception of their contact he can conceive them as touching in a mathematical point, or if he must necessarily imagine them to concur for some space. Whichever side he chuses, he runs himself into equal difficulties. If he affirms, that in tracing these figures in his imagination, he can imagine them to touch only in a point, he allows the possibility of that idea, and consequently of the thing. If he says, that in his conception of the contact of those lines he must make them concur, he thereby acknowledges the fallacy of geometrical demonstrations, when carryed beyond a certain degree of minuteness; since it is certain he has such demonstrations against the concurrence of a circle and a right line; that is, in other words, he can prove an idea, viz. that of concurrence, to be INCOMPATIBLE with two other ideas, those of a circle and right line; though at the same time he acknowledges these ideas to be inseparable.

SECTION V

The Same Subject Continued

If the second part of my system be true, that the idea of space or extension is nothing but the idea of visible or tangible points distributed in a certain order; it follows, that we can form no idea of a vacuum, or space, where there is nothing visible or tangible. This gives rise to three objections, which I shall examine together, because the answer I shall give to one is a consequence of that which I shall make use of for the others.

First, It may be said, that men have disputed for many ages concerning a vacuum and a plenum, without being able to bring the affair to a final decision;

and philosophers, even at this day, think themselves at liberty to take part on either side, as their fancy leads them. But whatever foundation there may be for a controversy concerning the things themselves, it may be pretended, that the very dispute is decisive concerning the idea, and that it is impossible men could so long reason about a vacuum, and either refute or defend it, without having a notion of what they refuted or defended.

Secondly, If this argument should be contested, the reality or at least the possibility of the idea of a vacuum may be proved by the following reasoning. Every idea is possible, which is a necessary and infallible consequence of such as are possible. Now though we allow the world to be at present a plenum, we may easily conceive it to be deprived of motion; and this idea will certainly be allowed possible. It must also be allowed possible, to conceive the annihilation of any part of matter by the omnipotence of the deity, while the other parts remain at rest. For as every idea, that is distinguishable, is separable by the imagination; and as every idea, that is separable by the imagination, may be conceived to be separately existent; it is evident, that the existence of one particle of matter, no more implies the existence of another, than a square figure in one body implies a square figure in every one. This being granted, I now demand what results from the concurrence of these two possible ideas of rest and annihilation, and what must we conceive to follow upon the annihilation of all the air and subtile matter in the chamber, supposing the walls to remain the same, without any motion or alteration? There are some metaphysicians, who answer, that since matter and extension are the same, the annihilation of one necessarily implies that of the other; and there being now no distance betwixt the walls of the chamber, they touch each other; in the same manner as my hand touches the paper, which is immediately before me. But though this answer be very common, I defy these metaphysicians to conceive the matter according to their hypothesis, or imagine the floor and roof, with all the opposite sides of the chamber, to touch each other, while they continue in rest, and preserve the same position. For how can the two walls, that run from south to north, touch each other, while they touch the opposite ends of two walls, that run from east to west? And how can the floor and roof ever meet, while they are separated by the four walls, that lie in a contrary position? If you change their position, you suppose a motion. If you conceive any thing betwixt them, you suppose a new creation. But keeping strictly to the two ideas of rest and annihilation, it is evident, that the idea, which results from them, is not that of a contact of parts, but something else; which is concluded to be the idea of a vacuum.

The third objection carries the matter still farther, and not only asserts, that the idea of a vacuum is real and possible, but also necessary and unavoidable. This assertion is founded on the motion we observe in bodies, which, it is maintained, would be impossible and inconceivable without a vacuum, into which one body must move in order to make way for another.. I shall not enlarge upon this objection, because it principally belongs to natural philosophy, which lies without our present sphere.

In order to answer these objections, we must take the matter pretty deep, and consider the nature and origin of several ideas, lest we dispute without understanding perfectly the subject of the controversy. It is evident the idea of darkness is no positive idea, but merely the negation of light, or more properly speaking, of coloured and visible objects. A man, who enjoys his sight, receives no other perception from turning his eyes on every side, when entirely deprived of light, than what is common to him with one born blind; and it is certain such-a-one has no idea either of light or darkness. The consequence of this is, that it is not from the mere removal of visible objects we receive the impression of extension without matter; and that the idea of utter darkness can never be the same with that of vacuum.

Suppose again a man to be supported in the air, and to be softly conveyed along by some invisible power; it is evident he is sensible of nothing, and never receives the idea of extension, nor indeed any idea, from this invariable motion. Even supposing he moves his limbs to and fro, this cannot convey to him that idea. He feels in that case a certain sensation or impression, the parts of which are successive to each other, and may give him the idea of time: But certainly are not disposed in such a manner, as is necessary to convey the idea of space or the idea of space or extension.

Since then it appears, that darkness and motion, with the utter removal of every thing visible and tangible, can never give us the idea of extension without matter, or of a vacuum; the next question is, whether they can convey this idea, when mixed with something visible and tangible?

It is commonly allowed by philosophers, that all bodies, which discover themselves to the eye, appear as if painted on a plain surface, and that their different degrees of remoteness from ourselves are discovered more by reason than by the senses. When I hold up my hand before me, and spread my fingers, they are separated as perfectly by the blue colour of the firmament, as they could be by any visible object, which I could place betwixt them. In order, therefore, to know whether the sight can convey the impression and idea of a vacuum, we must suppose, that amidst an entire darkness, there are luminous bodies presented to us, whose light discovers only these bodies themselves, without giving us any impression of the surrounding objects.

We must form a parallel supposition concerning the objects of our feeling. It is not proper to suppose a perfect removal of all tangible objects: we must allow something to be perceived by the feeling; and after an interval and motion of the hand or other organ of sensation, another object of the touch to be met with; and upon leaving that, another; and so on, as often as we please. The question is, whether these intervals do not afford us the idea of extension without body?

To begin with the first case; it is evident, that when only two luminous bodies appear to the eye, we can perceive, whether they be conjoined or separate: whether they be separated by a great or small distance; and if this distance varies, we can perceive its increase or diminution, with the motion of the bodies. But as the distance is not in this case any thing coloured or visible, it may be thought that there is here a vacuum or pure extension, not only intelligible to the mind, but obvious to the very senses.

This is our natural and most familiar way of thinking; but which we shall learn to correct by a little reflection. We may observe, that when two bodies present themselves, where there was formerly an entire darkness, the only change, that is discoverable, is in the appearance of these two objects, and that all the rest continues to be as before, a perfect negation of light, and of every coloured or visible object. This is not only true of what may be said to be remote from these bodies, but also of the very distance; which is interposed betwixt them; that being nothing but darkness, or the negation of light; without parts, without composition, invariable and indivisible. Now since this distance causes no perception different from what a blind man receives from his eyes, or what is conveyed to us in the darkest night, it must partake of the same properties: And as blindness and darkness afford us no ideas of extension, it is impossible that the dark and undistinguishable distance betwixt two bodies can ever produce that idea.

The sole difference betwixt an absolute darkness and the appearance of two or more visible luminous objects consists, as I said, in the objects themselves, and in the manner they affect our senses. The angles, which the rays of light flowing from them, form with each other; the motion that is required in the eye, in its passage from one to the other; and the different parts of the organs, which are affected by them; these produce the only perceptions, from which we can judge of the distance. But as these perceptions are each of them simple and indivisible, they can never give us the idea of extension.

We may illustrate this by considering the sense of feeling, and the imaginary distance or interval interposed betwixt tangible or solid objects. I suppose two cases, viz. that of a man supported in the air, and moving his limbs to and fro, without meeting any thing tangible; and that of a man, who feeling something tangible, leaves it, and after a motion, of which he is sensible, perceives another tangible object; and I then ask, wherein consists the difference betwixt these two cases? No one will make any scruple to affirm, that it consists meerly in the perceiving those objects, and that the sensation, which arises from the motion, is in both cases the same: And as that sensation is not capable of conveying to us an idea of extension, when unaccompanyed with some other perception, it can no more give us that idea, when mixed with the impressions of tangible objects; since that mixture produces no alteration upon it.

But though motion and darkness, either alone, or attended with tangible and visible objects, convey no idea of a vacuum or extension without matter, yet they are the causes why we falsly imagine we can form such an idea. For there is a close relation betwixt that motion and darkness, and a real extension, or composition of visible and tangible objects.

First, We may observe, that two visible objects appearing in the midst of utter darkness, affect the senses in the same manner, and form the same angle by the rays, which flow from them, and meet in the eye, as if the distance betwixt them were find with visible objects, that give us a true idea of extension. The sensation of motion is likewise the same, when there is nothing tangible interposed betwixt two bodies, as when we feel a compounded body, whose different parts are placed beyond each other.

Secondly, We find by experience, that two bodies, which are so placed as to affect the senses in the same manner with two others, that have a certain extent of visible objects interposed betwixt them, are capable of receiving the same extent, without any sensible impulse or penetration, and without any change on that angle, under which they appear to the senses. In like manner, where there is one object, which we cannot feel after another without an interval, and the perceiving of that sensation we call motion in our hand or organ of sensation; experience shews us, that it is possible the same object may be felt with the same sensation of motion, along with the interposed impression of solid and tangible objects, attending the sensation. That is, in other words, an invisible and intangible distance may be converted into a visible and tangible one, without any change on the distant objects.

Thirdly, We may observe, as another relation betwixt these two kinds of distance, that they have nearly the same effects on every natural phænomenon. For as all qualities, such as heat, cold, light, attraction, &c. diminish in proportion to the distance; there is but little difference observed, whether this distance be marled out by compounded and sensible objects, or be known only by the manner, in which the distant objects affect the senses.

Here then are three relations betwixt that distance, which conveys the idea of extension, and that other, which is not filled with any coloured or solid object. The distant objects affect the senses in the same manner, whether separated by the one distance or the other; the second species of distance is found capable of receiving the first; and they both equally diminish the force of every quality.

These relations betwixt the two kinds of distance will afford us an easy reason, why the one has so often been taken for the other, and why we imagine we have an idea of extension without the idea of any object either of the sight or feeling. For we may establish it as a general maxim in this science of human nature, that wherever there is a close relation betwixt two ideas, the mind is very apt to mistake them, and in all its discourses and reasonings to use the one for the other. This phænomenon occurs on so many occasions, and is of such consequence, that I cannot forbear stopping a moment to examine its causes. I shall only premise, that we must distinguish exactly betwixt the phænomenon itself, and the causes, which I shall assign for it; and must not imagine from any uncertainty in the latter, that the former is also uncertain. The phænomenon may be real, though my explication be chimerical. The falshood of the one is no consequence of that of the other; though at the same time we may observe, that it is very natural for us to draw such a consequence; which is an evident instance of that very principle, which I endeavour to explain.

When I received the relations of resemblance, contiguity and causation, as principles of union among ideas, without examining into their causes, it was more in prosecution of my first maxim, that we must in the end rest contented with experience, than for want of something specious and plausible, which I might have displayed on that subject. It would have been easy to have made an imaginary dissection of the brain, and have shewn, why upon our conception of any idea, the animal spirits run into all the contiguous traces, and rouze up the other ideas, that are related to it. But though I have neglected any advantage, which I might have drawn from this topic in explaining the relations of ideas, I am afraid I must here have recourse to it, in order to account for the mistakes that arise from these relations. I shall therefore observe, that as the mind is endowed with a power of exciting any idea it pleases; whenever it dispatches the spirits into that region of the brain, in which the idea is placed; these spirits always excite the idea, when they run precisely into the proper traces, and rummage that cell, which belongs to the idea. But as their motion is seldom direct, and naturally turns a little to the one side or the other; for this reason the animal spirits, falling into the contiguous traces, present other related ideas in lieu of that, which the mind desired at first to survey. This change we are not always sensible of; but continuing still the same train of thought, make use of the related idea, which is presented to us, and employ it in our reasoning, as if it were the same with what we demanded. This is the cause of many mistakes and sophisms in philosophy; as will naturally be imagined, and as it would be easy to show, if there was occasion.

Of the three relations above-mentioned that of resemblance is the most fertile source of error; and indeed there are few mistakes in reasoning, which do not borrow largely from that origin. Resembling ideas are not only related together, but the actions of the mind, which we employ in considering them, are so little different, that we are not able to distinguish them. This last circumstance is of great consequence, and we may in general observe, that wherever the actions of the mind in forming any two ideas are the same or resembling, we are very apt to confound these ideas, and take the one for the other. Of this we shall see many instances in the progress of this treatise. But though resemblance be the relation, which most readily produces a mistake in ideas, yet the others of causation and contiguity may also concur in the same influence. We might produce the figures of poets and orators, as sufficient proofs of this, were it as usual, as it is reasonable, in metaphysical subjects to draw our arguments from that quarter. But lest metaphysicians should esteem this below their dignity, I shall borrow a proof from an observation, which may be made on most of their own discourses, viz. that it is usual for men to use words for ideas, and to talk instead of thinking in their reasonings. We use words for ideas, because they are commonly so closely connected that the mind easily mistakes them. And this likewise is the reason, why we substitute the idea of a distance, which is not considered either as visible or tangible, in the room of extension, which is nothing but a composition of visible or tangible points disposed in a certain order. In causing this mistake there concur both the relations of causation and resemblance. As the first species of distance is found to be convertible into the second, it is in this respect a kind of cause; and the similarity of their manner of affecting the senses, and diminishing every quality, forms the relation of resemblance.

After this chain of reasoning and explication of my principles, I am now prepared to answer all the objections that have been offered, whether derived from metaphysics or mechanics. The frequent disputes concerning a vacuum, or extension without matter prove not the reality of the idea, upon which the dispute turns; there being nothing more common, than to see men deceive themselves in this particular; especially when by means of any close relation, there is another idea presented, which may be the occasion of their mistake.

We may make almost the same answer to the second objection, derived from the conjunction of the ideas of rest and annihilation. When every thing is annihilated in the chamber, and the walls continue immoveable, the chamber must be conceived much in the same manner as at present, when the air that fills it, is not an object of the senses. This annihilation leaves to the eye, that fictitious distance, which is discovered by the different parts of the organ, that are affected, and by the degrees of light and shade;—and to the feeling, that which consists in a sensation of motion in the hand, or other member of the body. In vain should we. search any farther. On whichever side we turn this subject, we shall find that these are the only impressions such an object can produce after the supposed annihilation; and it has already been remarked, that impressions can give rise to no ideas, but to such as resemble them.

Since a body interposed betwixt two others may be supposed to be annihilated, without producing any change upon such as lie on each hand of it, it is easily conceived, how it may be created anew, and yet produce as little alteration. Now the motion of a body has much the same effect as its creation. The distant bodies are no more affected in the one case, than in the other. This suffices to satisfy the imagination, and proves there is no repugnance in such a motion. Afterwards experience comes in play to persuade us that two bodies, situated in the manner above-described, have really such a capacity of receiving body betwixt them, and that there is no obstacle to the conversion of the invisible and intangible distance into one that is visible and tangible. However natural that conversion may seem, we cannot be sure it is practicable, before we have had experience of it.

Thus I seem to have answered the three objections above-mentioned; though at the same time I am sensible, that few will be satisfyed with these answers, but will immediately propose new objections and difficulties. It will probably be said, that my reasoning makes nothing to the matter in hands and that I explain only the manner in which objects affect the senses, without endeavouring to account for their real nature and operations. Though there be nothing visible or tangible interposed betwixt two bodies, yet we find BY EXPERIENCE, that the bodies may be placed in the same manner, with regard to the eye, and require the same motion of the hand in passing from one to the other, as if divided by something visible and tangible. This invisible and intangible distance is also found by experience to contain a capacity of receiving body, or of becoming visible and tangible. Here is the whole of my system; and in no part of it have I endeavoured to explain the cause, which separates bodies after this manner, and gives them a capacity of receiving others betwixt them, without any impulse or penetration.

I answer this objection, by pleading guilty, and by confessing that my intention never was to penetrate into the nature of bodies, or explain the secret causes of their operations. For besides that this belongs not to my present purpose, I am afraid, that such an enterprise is beyond the reach of human understanding, and that we can never pretend to know body otherwise than by those external properties, which discover themselves to the senses. As to those who attempt any thing farther, I cannot approve of their ambition, till I see, in some one instance at least, that they have met with success. But at present I content myself with knowing perfectly the manner in which objects affect my senses, and their connections with each other, as far as experience informs me of them. This suffices for the conduct of life; and this also suffices for my philosophy, which pretends only to explain the nature and causes of our perceptions, or impressions and ideas.[11]

I shall conclude this subject of extension with a paradox, which will easily be explained from the foregoing reasoning. This paradox is, that if you are pleased to

---

[11] As long as we confine our speculations to the appearances of objects to our senses, without entering into disquisitions concerning their real nature and operations, we are safe from all difficulties, and can never be embarrassed by any question. Thus, if it be asked, if the invisible and intangible distance, interposed betwixt two objects, be something or nothing: It is easy to answer, that it is SOMETHING, VIZ. a property of the objects, which affect the SENSES after such a particular manner. If it be asked whether two objects, having such a distance betwixt them, touch or not: it may be answered, that this depends upon the definition of the word, TOUCH. If objects be said to touch, when there is nothing SENSIBLE interposed betwixt them, these objects touch: it objects be said to touch, when their IMAGES strike contiguous parts of the eye, and when the hand FEELS both objects successively, without any interposed motion, these objects do not touch. The appearances of objects to our senses are all consistent; and no difficulties can ever arise, but from the obscurity of the terms we make use of.

If we carry our enquiry beyond the appearances of objects to the senses, I am afraid, that most of our conclusions will be full of scepticism and uncertainty. Thus if it be asked, whether or not the invisible and intangible distance be always full of body, or of something that by an improvement of our organs might become visible or tangible, I must acknowledge, that I find no very decisive arguments on either side; though I am inclined to the contrary opinion, as being more suitable to vulgar and popular notions. If THE NEWTONIAN philosophy be rightly understood, it will be found to mean no more. A vacuum is asserted: That is, bodies are said to be placed after such a manner, is to receive bodies betwixt them, without impulsion or penetration. The real nature of this position of bodies is unknown. We are only acquainted with its effects on the senses, and its power of receiving body. Nothing is more suitable to that philosophy, than a modest scepticism to a certain degree, and a fair confession of ignorance in subjects, that exceed all human capacity.

give to the in-visible and intangible distance, or in other words, to the capacity of becoming a visible and tangible distance, the name of a vacuum, extension and matter are the same, and yet there is a vacuum. If you will not give it that name, motion is possible in a plenum, without any impulse in infinitum, without returning in a circle, and without penetration. But however we may express ourselves, we must always confess, that we have no idea of any real extension without filling it with sensible objects, and conceiving its parts as visible or tangible.

As to the doctrine, that time is nothing but the manner, in which some real objects exist; we may observe, that it is liable to the same objections as the similar doctrine with regard to extension. If it be a sufficient proof, that we have the idea of a vacuum, because we dispute and reason concerning it; we must for the same reason have the idea of time without any changeable existence; since there is no subject of dispute more frequent and common. But that we really have no such idea, is certain. For whence should it be derived? Does it arise from an impression of sensation or of reflection? Point it out distinctly to us, that we may know its nature and qualities. But if you cannot point out any such impression, you may be certain you are mistaken, when you imagine you have any such idea.

But though it be impossible to shew the impression, from which the idea of time without a changeable existence is derived; yet we can easily point out those appearances, which make us fancy we have that idea. For we may observe, that there is a continual succession of perceptions in our mind; so that the idea of time being for ever present with us; when we consider a stedfast object at five-a-clock, and regard the same at six; we are apt to apply to it that idea in the same manner as if every moment were distinguished by a different position, or an alteration of the object. The first and second appearances of the object, being compared with the succession of our perceptions, seem equally removed as if the object had really changed. To which we may add, what experience shews us, that the object was susceptible of such a number of changes betwixt these appearances; as also that the unchangeable or rather fictitious duration has the same effect upon every quality, by encreasing or diminishing it, as that succession, which is obvious to the senses. From these three relations we are apt to confound our ideas, and imagine we can form the idea of a time and duration, without any change or succession.

SECTION VI

Of the Idea of Existence, and of External Existence

It may not be amiss, before we leave this subject, to explain the ideas of existence and of external existence; which have their difficulties, as well as the ideas of space and time. By this means we shall be the better prepared for the examination of knowledge and probability, when we understand perfectly all those particular ideas, which may enter into our reasoning.

There is no impression nor idea of any kind, of which we have any consciousness or memory, that is not conceived as existent; and it is evident, that from this consciousness the most perfect idea and assurance of being is derived. From hence we may form a dilemma, the most clear and conclusive that can be imagined, viz. that since we never remember any idea or impression without attributing existence to it, the idea of existence must either be derived from a distinct impression, conjoined with every perception or object of our thought, or must be the very same with the idea of the perception or object.

As this dilemma is an evident consequence of the principle, that every idea arises from a similar impression, so our decision betwixt the propositions of the dilemma is no more doubtful. So far from there being any distinct impression, attending every impression and every idea, that I do not think there are any two distinct impressions, which are inseparably conjoined. Though certain sensations may at one time be united, we quickly find they admit of a separation, and may be presented apart. And thus, though every impression and idea we remember be considered as existent, the idea of existence is not derived from any particular impression.

The idea of existence, then, is the very same with the idea of what we conceive to be existent. To reflect on any thing simply, and to reflect on it as existent, are nothing different from each other. That idea, when conjoined with the idea of any object, makes no addition to it. Whatever we conceive, we conceive to be existent. Any idea we please to form is the idea of a being; and the idea of a being is any idea we please to form.

Whoever opposes this, must necessarily point out that distinct impression, from which the idea of entity is derived, and must prove, that this impression is inseparable from every perception we believe to be existent. This we may without hesitation conclude to be impossible.

Our foregoing reasoning[12] concerning the distinction of ideas without any real difference will not here serve us in any stead. That kind of distinction is founded on the different resemblances, which the same simple idea may have to several different ideas. But no object can be presented resembling some object with respect to its existence, and different from others in the same particular; since every object, that is presented, must necessarily be existent.

A like reasoning will account for the idea of external existence. We may observe, that it is universally allowed by philosophers, and is besides pretty obvious of itself, that nothing is ever really present with the mind but its perceptions or impressions and ideas, and that external objects become known to us only by those perceptions they occasion. To hate, to love, to think, to feel, to see; all this is nothing but to perceive.

Now since nothing is ever present to the mind but perceptions, and since all ideas are derived from something antecedently present to the mind; it follows,

[12] Part I. Sect. 7.

that it is impossible for us so much as to conceive or form an idea of any thing specifically different from ideas and impressions. Let us fix our attention out of ourselves as much as possible: Let us chase our imagination to the heavens, or to the utmost limits of the universe; we never really advance a step beyond ourselves, nor can conceive any kind of existence, but those perceptions, which have appeared in that narrow compass. This is the universe of the imagination, nor have we any idea but what is there produced.

The farthest we can go towards a conception of external objects, when supposed SPECIFICALLY different from our perceptions, is to form a relative idea of them, without pretending to comprehend the related objects. Generally speaking we do not suppose them specifically different; but only attribute to them different relations, connections and durations. But of this more fully hereafter.[13]

[13] Part IV, Sect. 2.

PART III

Of Knowledge and Probability

SECTION I

Of Knowledge

There are seven[14] different kinds of philosophical relation, viz. RESEMBLANCE, IDENTITY, RELATIONS OF TIME AND PLACE, PROPORTION IN QUANTITY OR NUMBER, DEGREES IN ANY QUALITY, CONTRARIETY and CAUSATION. These relations may be divided into two classes; into such as depend entirely on the ideas, which we compare together, and such as may be changed without any change in the ideas. It is from the idea of a triangle, that we discover the relation of equality, which its three angles bear to two right ones; and this relation is invariable, as long as our idea remains the same. On the contrary, the relations of contiguity and distance betwixt two objects may be changed merely by an alteration of their place, without any change on the objects themselves or on their ideas; and the place depends on a hundred different accidents, which cannot be foreseen by the mind. It is the same case with identity and causation. Two objects, though perfectly resembling each other, and even appearing in the same place at different times, may be numerically different: And as the power, by which one object produces another, is never discoverable merely from their idea, it is evident cause and effect are relations, of which we receive information from experience, and not from any abstract reasoning or reflection. There is no single phænomenon, even the most simple, which can be accounted for from the qualities of the objects, as they appear to us; or which we could foresee without the help of our memory and experience.

It appears, therefore, that of these seven philosophical relations, there remain only four, which depending solely upon ideas, can be the objects of knowledge and certainty. These four are RESEMBLANCE, CONTRARIETY, DEGREES IN QUALITY, and PROPORTIONS IN QUANTITY OR NUMBER. Three of these relations are discoverable at first sight, and fall more properly under the province of intuition than demonstration. When any objects resemble each other, the resemblance will at first strike the eye, or rather the mind; and seldom requires a second examination. The case is the same with contrariety, and with the degrees of any quality. No one can once doubt but existence and non-existence destroy each other, and are perfectly incompatible and contrary. And though it be impossible to judge exactly of the degrees of any quality, such as colour, taste, heat, cold, when the difference betwixt them is very small: yet it is easy to decide, that any of them

[14] Part I. Sect. 5.

is superior or inferior to another, when their difference is considerable. And this decision we always pronounce at first sight, without any enquiry or reasoning.

We might proceed, after the same manner, in fixing the proportions of quantity or number, and might at one view observe a superiority or inferiority betwixt any numbers, or figures; especially where the difference is very great and remarkable. As to equality or any exact proportion, we can only guess at it from a single consideration; except in very short numbers, or very limited portions of extension; which are comprehended in an instant, and where we perceive an impossibility of falling into any considerable error. In all other cases we must settle the proportions with some liberty, or proceed in a more artificial manner.

I have already observed, that geometry, or the art, by which we fix the proportions of figures; though it much excels both in universality and exactness, the loose judgments of the senses and imagination; yet never attains a perfect precision and exactness. It's first principles are still drawn from the general appearance of the objects; and that appearance can never afford us any security, when we examine, the prodigious minuteness of which nature is susceptible. Our ideas seem to give a perfect assurance, that no two right lines can have a common segment; but if we consider these ideas, we shall find, that they always suppose a sensible inclination of the two lines, and that where the angle they form is extremely small, we have no standard of a I @ right line so precise as to assure us of the truth of this proposition. It is the same case with most of the primary decisions of the mathematics.

There remain, therefore, algebra and arithmetic as the only sciences, in which we can carry on a chain of reasoning to any degree of intricacy, and yet preserve a perfect exactness and certainty. We are possest of a precise standard, by which we can judge of the equality and proportion of numbers; and according as they correspond or not to that standard, we determine their relations, without any possibility of error. When two numbers are so combined, as that the one has always an unite answering to every unite of the other, we pronounce them equal; and it is for want of such a standard of equality in extension, that geometry can scarce be esteemed a perfect and infallible science.

But here it may not be amiss to obviate a difficulty, which may arise from my asserting, that though geometry falls short of that perfect precision and certainty, which are peculiar to arithmetic and algebra, yet it excels the imperfect judgments of our senses and imagination. The reason why I impute any defect to geometry, is, because its original and fundamental principles are derived merely from appearances; and it may perhaps be imagined, that this defect must always attend it, and keep it from ever reaching a greater exactness in the comparison of objects or ideas, than what our eye or imagination alone is able to attain. I own that this defect so far attends it, as to keep it from ever aspiring to a full certainty: But since these fundamental principles depend on the easiest and least deceitful appearances, they bestow on their consequences a degree of exactness, of which these consequences are singly incapable. It is impossible for the eye to determine the angles of a chiliagon to be equal to 1996 right angles, or make any conjecture, that approaches this proportion; but when it determines, that right lines cannot concur; that we cannot draw more than one right line between two given points; it's mistakes can never be of any consequence. And this is the nature and use of geometry, to run us up to such appearances, as, by reason of their simplicity, cannot lead us into any considerable error.

I shall here take occasion to propose a second observation concerning our demonstrative reasonings, which is suggested by the same subject of the mathematics. It is usual with mathematicians, to pretend, that those ideas, which are their objects, are of so refined and spiritual a nature, that they fall not under the conception of the fancy, but must be comprehended by a pure and intellectual view, of which the superior faculties of the soul are alone capable. The same notion runs through most parts of philosophy, and is principally made use of to explain oar abstract ideas, and to shew how we can form an idea of a triangle, for instance, which shall neither be an isoceles nor scalenum, nor be confined to any particular length and proportion of sides. It is easy to see, why philosophers are so fond of this notion of some spiritual and refined perceptions; since by that means they cover many of their absurdities, and may refuse to submit to the decisions of clear ideas, by appealing to such as are obscure and uncertain. But to destroy this artifice, we need but reflect on that principle so oft insisted on, that all our ideas are copyed from our impressions. For from thence we may immediately conclude, that since all impressions are clear and precise, the ideas, which are copyed from them, must be of the same nature, and can never, but from our fault, contain any thing so dark and intricate. An idea is by its very nature weaker and fainter than an impression; but being in every other respect the same, cannot imply any very great mystery. If its weakness render it obscure, it is our business to remedy that defect, as much as possible, by keeping the idea steady and precise; and till we have done so, it is in vain to pretend to reasoning and philosophy.

SECTION II

Of Probability, and of the Idea of Cause and Effect

This is all I think necessary to observe concerning those four relations, which are the foundation of science; but as to the other three, which depend not upon the idea, and may be absent or present even while that remains the same, it will be proper to explain them more particularly. These three relations are identity, the situations in time and place, and causation.

All kinds of reasoning consist in nothing but a comparison, and a discovery of those relations, either constant or inconstant, which two or more objects bear to each other. This comparison we may make, either when both the objects are present to the senses, or when neither of them is present, or when only one. When both the objects are present to the senses along with the relation, we call this perception rather than reasoning; nor is there in this case any exercise of the thought, or any action, properly speaking, but a mere passive admission of the impressions through the organs of sensation. According to this way of thinking, we ought not to receive as reasoning any of the observations we may make concerning identity, and the relations of time and place; since in none of them the mind can go beyond what is immediately present to the senses, either to discover the real existence or the relations of objects. It is only causation, which produces such a connexion, as to give us assurance from the existence or action of one object, that it was followed or preceded by any other existence or action; nor can the other two relations be ever made use of in reasoning, except so far as they either affect or are affected by it. There is nothing in any objects to perswade us, that they are either always remote or always contiguous; and when from experience and observation we discover, that their relation in this particular is invariable, we, always conclude there is some secret cause, which separates or unites them. The same reasoning extends to identity. We readily suppose an object may continue individually the same, though several times absent from and present to the senses; and ascribe to it an identity, notwithstanding the interruption of the perception, whenever we conclude, that if we had kept our eye or hand constantly upon it, it would have conveyed an invariable and uninterrupted perception. But this conclusion beyond the impressions of our senses can be founded only on the connexion of cause and effect; nor can we otherwise have any security, that the object is not changed upon us, however much the new object may resemble that which was formerly present to the senses. Whenever we discover such a perfect resemblance, we consider, whether it be common in that species of objects; whether possibly or probably any cause could operate in producing the change and resemblance; and according as we determine concerning these causes and effects, we form our judgment concerning the identity of the object.

Here then it appears, that of those three relations, which depend not upon the mere ideas, the only one, that can be traced beyond our senses and informs us of existences and objects, which we do not see or feel, is causation. This relation, therefore, we shall endeavour to explain fully before we leave the subject of the understanding.

To begin regularly, we must consider the idea of causation, and see from what origin it is derived. It is impossible to reason justly, without understanding perfectly the idea concerning which we reason; and it is impossible perfectly to understand any idea, without tracing it up to its origin, and examining that primary impression, from which it arises. The examination of the impression bestows a clearness on the idea; and the examination of the idea bestows a like clearness on all our reasoning.

Let us therefore cast our eye on any two objects, which we call cause and effect, and turn them on all sides, in order to find that impression, which produces an idea, of such prodigious consequence. At first sight I perceive, that I must not search for it in any of the particular qualities of the objects; since which-ever of these qualities I pitch on, I find some object, that is not possessed of it, and yet falls under the denomination of cause or effect. And indeed there is nothing existent, either externally or internally, which is not to be considered either as a cause or an effect; though it is plain there is no one quality, which universally belongs to all beings, and gives them a title to that denomination.

The idea, then, of causation must be derived from some relation among objects; and that relation we must now endeavour to discover. I find in the first place, that whatever objects are considered as causes or effects, are contiguous; and that nothing can operate in a time or place, which is ever so little removed from those of its existence. Though distant objects may sometimes seem productive of each other, they are commonly found upon examination to be linked by a chain of causes, which are contiguous among themselves, and to the distant objects; and when in any particular instance we cannot discover this connexion, we still presume it to exist. We may therefore consider the relation of CONTIGUITY as essential to that of causation; at least may suppose it such, according to the general opinion, till we can find a more[15] proper occasion to clear up this matter, by examining what objects are or are not susceptible of juxtaposition and conjunction.

The second relation I shall observe as essential to causes and effects, is not so universally acknowledged, but is liable to some controversy. It is that of PRIORITY Of time in the cause before the effect. Some pretend that it is not absolutely necessary a cause should precede its effect; but that any object or action, in the very first moment of its existence, may exert its productive quality, and give rise to another object or action, perfectly co-temporary with itself. But beside that experience in most instances seems to contradict this opinion, we may establish the relation of priority by a kind of inference or reasoning. It is an established maxim both in natural and moral philosophy, that an object, which exists for any time in its full perfection without producing another, is not its sole cause; but is assisted by some other principle, which pushes it from its state of inactivity, and makes it exert that energy, of which it was secretly possest. Now if any cause may be perfectly co-temporary with its effect, it is certain, according to this maxim, that they must all of them be so; since any one of them, which retards its operation for a single moment, exerts not itself at that very individual time, in which it might have operated; and therefore is no proper cause. The consequence of this would be no less than the destruction of that succession of causes, which we observe in the world; and indeed, the utter annihilation of time. For if one cause were co-temporary with its effect, and this effect with its effect, and so on, it is plain there would be no such thing as succession, and all objects must be co-existent.

If this argument appear satisfactory, it is well. If not, I beg the reader to allow me the same liberty, which I have used in the preceding case, of supposing it such. For he shall find, that the affair is of no great importance.

---

[15] Part IV. Sect. 5.

Having thus discovered or supposed the two relations of contiguity and succession to be essential to causes and effects, I find I am stopt short, and can proceed no farther in considering any single instance of cause and effect. Motion in one body is regarded upon impulse as the cause of motion in another. When we consider these objects with utmost attention, we find only that the one body approaches the other; and that the motion of it precedes that of the other, but without any, sensible interval. It is in vain to rack ourselves with farther thought and reflection upon this subject. We can go no farther in considering this particular instance.

Should any one leave this instance, and pretend to define a cause, by saying it is something productive of another, it is evident he would say nothing. For what does he mean by production? Can he give any definition of it, that will not be the same with that of causation? If he can; I desire it may be produced. If he cannot; he here runs in a circle, and gives a synonimous term instead of a definition.

Shall we then rest contented with these two relations of contiguity and succession, as affording a complete idea of causation? By, no means. An object may be contiguous and prior to another, without being considered as its cause. There is a NECESSARY CONNEXION to be taken into consideration; and that relation is of much greater importance, than any of the other two above-mentioned.

Here again I turn the object on all sides, in order to discover the nature of this necessary connexion, and find the impression, or impressions, from which its idea may be derived. When I cast my eye on the known Qualities of objects, I immediately discover that the relation of cause and effect depends not in the least on them. When I consider their relations, I can find none but those of contiguity and succession; which I have already regarded as imperfect and unsatisfactory. Shall the despair of success make me assert, that I am here possest of an idea, which is not preceded by any similar impression? This would be too strong a proof of levity and inconstancy; since the contrary principle has been already so firmly established, as to admit of no farther doubt; at least, till we have more fully examined the present difficulty.

We must, therefore, proceed like those, who being in search of any thing, that lies concealed from them, and not finding it in the place they expected, beat about all the neighbouring fields, without any certain view or design, in hopes their good fortune will at last guide them to what they search for. It is necessary for us to leave the direct survey of this question concerning the nature of that necessary connexion, which enters into our idea of cause and effect; and endeavour to find some other questions, the examination of which will perhaps afford a hint, that may serve to clear up the present difficulty. Of these questions there occur two, which I shall proceed to examine, viz.

First, For what reason we pronounce it necessary, that every thing whose existence has a beginning, should also have a cause.

Secondly, Why we conclude, that such particular causes must necessarily have such particular effects; and what is the nature of that inference we draw from the one to the other, and of the belief we repose in it?

I shall only observe before I proceed any farther, that though the ideas of cause and effect be derived from the impressions of reflection as well as from those of sensation, yet for brevity's sake, I commonly mention only the latter as the origin of these ideas; though I desire that whatever I say of them may also extend to the former. Passions are connected with their objects and with one another; no less than external bodies are connected together. The same relation, then, of cause and effect, which belongs to one, must be common to all of them.

SECTION III

Why A Cause Is Always Necessary

To begin with the first question concerning the necessity of a cause: It is a general maxim in philosophy, that whatever begins to exist, must have a cause of existence. This is commonly taken for granted in all reasonings, without any proof given or demanded. It is supposed to be founded on intuition, and to be one of those maxims, which though they may be denyed with the lips, it is impossible for men in their hearts really to doubt of. But if we examine this maxim by the idea of knowledge above-explained, we shall discover in it no mark of any such intuitive certainty; but on the contrary shall find, that it is of a nature quite foreign to that species of conviction.

All certainty arises from the comparison of ideas, and from the discovery of such relations as are unalterable, so long as the ideas continue the same. These relations are RESEMBLANCE, PROPORTIONS IN QUANTITY AND NUMBER, DEGREES OF ANY QUALITY, and CONTRARIETY; none of which are implyed in this proposition, Whatever has a beginning has also a cause of existence. That proposition therefore is not intuitively certain. At least any one, who would assert it to be intuitively certain, must deny these to be the only infallible relations, and must find some other relation of that kind to be implyed in it; which it will then be time enough to examine.

But here is an argument, which proves at once, that the foregoing proposition is neither intuitively nor demonstrably certain. We can never demonstrate the necessity of a cause to every new existence, or new modification of existence, without shewing at the same time the impossibility there is, that any thing can ever begin to exist without some productive principle; and where the latter proposition cannot be proved, we must despair of ever being able to prove the former. Now that the latter proposition is utterly incapable of a demonstrative proof, we may satisfy ourselves by considering that as all distinct ideas are separable from each other, and as the ideas of cause and effect are evidently distinct, it will be easy for us to conceive any object to be non-existent this moment, and existent the next, without conjoining to it the distinct idea of a cause or productive principle. The separation, therefore, of the idea of a cause from that of a beginning of existence, is plainly possible for the imagination; and consequently the actual separation of these objects is so far possible, that it implies no contradiction nor absurdity; and is therefore incapable of being refuted by any reasoning from mere ideas; without which it is impossible to demonstrate the necessity of a cause.

Accordingly we shall find upon examination, that every demonstration, which has been produced for the necessity of a cause, is fallacious and sophistical. All the points of time and place, say some philosophers,[16] in which we can suppose any object to begin to exist, are in themselves equal; and unless there be some cause, which is peculiar to one time and to one place, and which by that means determines and fixes the existence, it must remain in eternal suspence; and the object can never begin to be, for want of something to fix its beginning. But I ask; Is there any more difficulty in supposing the time and place to be fixed without a cause, than to suppose the existence to be determined in that manner? The first question that occurs on this subject is always, whether the object shall exist or not: The next, when and where it shall begin to exist. If the removal of a cause be intuitively absurd in the one case, it must be so in the other: And if that absurdity be not clear without a proof in the one case, it will equally require one in the other. The absurdity, then, of the one supposition can never be a proof of that of the other; since they are both upon the same footing, and must stand or fall by the same reasoning.

The second argument,[17] which I find used on this head, labours under an equal difficulty. Every thing, it is said, must have a cause; for if any thing wanted a cause, it would produce ITSELF; that is, exist before it existed; which is impossible. But this reasoning is plainly unconclusive; because it supposes, that in our denial of a cause we still grant what we expressly deny, viz. that there must be a cause; which therefore is taken to be the object itself; and that, no doubt, is an evident contradiction. But to say that any thing is produced, or to express myself more properly, comes into existence, without a cause, is not to affirm, that it is itself its own cause; but on the contrary in excluding all external causes, excludes a fortiori the thing itself, which is created. An object, that exists absolutely without any cause, certainly is not its own cause; and when you assert, that the one follows from the other, you suppose the very point in questions and take it for granted, that it is utterly impossible any thing can ever begin to exist without a cause, but that, upon the exclusion of one productive principle, we must still have recourse to another.

It is exactly the same case with the third argument,[18] which has been employed to demonstrate the necessity of a cause. Whatever is produced without any cause, is

[16] Mr. Hobbes.

[17] Dr. Clarke and others.

[18] Mr. Locke.

produced by nothing; or in other words, has nothing for its cause. But nothing can never be a cause, no more than it can be something, or equal to two right angles. By the same intuition, that we perceive nothing not to be equal to two right angles, or not to be something, we perceive, that it can never be a cause; and consequently must perceive, that every object has a real cause of its existence.

I believe it will not be necessary to employ many words in shewing the weakness of this argument, after what I have said of the foregoing. They are all of them founded on the same fallacy, and are derived from the same turn of thought. It is sufficient only to observe, that when we exclude all causes we really do exclude them, and neither suppose nothing nor the object itself to be the causes of the existence; and consequently can draw no argument from the absurdity of these suppositions to prove the absurdity of that exclusion. If every thing must have a cause, it follows, that upon the exclusion of other causes we must accept of the object itself or of nothing as causes. But it is the very point in question, whether every thing must have a cause or not; and therefore, according to all just reasoning, it ought never to be taken for granted.

They are still more frivolous, who say, that every effect must have a cause, because it is implyed in the very idea of effect. Every effect necessarily pre-supposes a cause; effect being a relative term, of which cause is the correlative. But this does not prove, that every being must be preceded by a cause; no more than it follows, because every husband must have a wife, that therefore every man must be marryed. The true state of the question is, whether every object, which begins to exist, must owe its existence to a cause: and this I assert neither to be intuitively nor demonstratively certain, and hope to have proved it sufficiently by the foregoing arguments.

Since it is not from knowledge or any scientific reasoning, that we derive the opinion of the necessity of a cause to every new production, that opinion must necessarily arise from observation and experience. The next question, then, should naturally be, how experience gives rise to such a principle? But as I find it will be more convenient to sink this question in the following, Why we conclude, that such particular causes must necessarily have such particular erects, and why we form an inference from one to another? we shall make that the subject of our future enquiry. It will, perhaps, be found in the end, that the same answer will serve for both questions.

SECTION IV

Of the Component Parts of our Reasonings Concerning Cause and Effect

Though the mind in its reasonings from causes or effects carries its view beyond those objects, which it sees or remembers, it must never lose sight of them entirely, nor reason merely upon its own ideas, without some mixture of impressions, or at least of ideas of the memory, which are equivalent to impressions. When we infer effects from causes, we must establish the existence of these causes; which we have only two ways of doing, either by an immediate perception of our memory or senses, or by an inference from other causes; which causes again we must ascertain in the same manner, either by a present impression, or by an inference from their causes, and so on, till we arrive at some object, which we see or remember. It is impossible for us to carry on our inferences IN INFINITUM; and the only thing, that can stop them, is an impression of the memory or senses, beyond which there is no room for doubt or enquiry.

To give an instance of this, we may chuse any point of history, and consider for what reason we either believe or reject it. Thus we believe that Caesar was killed in the senate-house on the ides of March; and that because this fact is established on the unanimous testimony of historians, who agree to assign this precise time and place to that event. Here are certain characters and letters present either to our memory or senses; which characters we likewise remember to have been used as the signs of certain ideas; and these ideas were either in the minds of such as were immediately present at that action, and received the ideas directly from its existence; or they were derived from the testimony of others, and that again from another testimony, by a visible gradation, it will we arrive at those who were eyewitnesses and spectators of the event. It is obvious all this chain of argument or connexion of causes and effects, is at first founded on those characters or letters, which are seen or remembered, and that without the authority either of the memory or senses our whole reasoning would be chimerical and without foundation. Every link of the chain would in that case hang upon another; but there would not be any thing fixed to one end of it, capable of sustaining the whole; and consequently there would be no belief nor evidence. And this actually is the case with all hypothetical arguments, or reasonings upon a supposition; there being in them, neither any present impression, nor belief of a real existence.

I need not observe, that it is no just objection to the present doctrine, that we can reason upon our past conclusions or principles, without having recourse to those impressions, from which they first arose. For even supposing these impressions should be entirely effaced from the memory, the conviction they produced may still remain; and it is equally true, that all reasonings concerning causes and effects are originally derived from some impression; in the same manner, as the assurance of a demonstration proceeds always from a comparison of ideas, though it may continue after the comparison is forgot.

SECTION V

Of the Impressions of the Senses and Memory

In this kind of reasoning, then, from causation, we employ materials, which are of a mixed and heterogeneous nature, and which, however connected, are yet essentially different from each other. All our arguments concerning causes and effects consist both of an impression of the memory or, senses, and of the idea of that existence, which produces the object of the impression, or is produced by it. Here therefore we have three things to explain, viz. First, The original impression. Secondly, The transition to the idea of the connected cause or effect. Thirdly, The nature and qualities of that idea.

As to those impressions, which arise from the senses, their ultimate cause is, in my opinion, perfectly inexplicable by human reason, and it will always be impossible to decide with certainty, whether they arise immediately from the object, or are produced by the creative power of the mind, or are derived from the author of our being. Nor is such a question any way material to our present purpose. We may draw inferences from the coherence of our perceptions, whether they be true or false; whether they represent nature justly, or be mere illusions of the senses.

When we search for the characteristic, which distinguishes the memory from the imagination, we must immediately perceive, that it cannot lie in the simple ideas it presents to us; since both these faculties borrow their simple ideas from the impressions, and can never go beyond these original perceptions. These faculties are as little distinguished from each other by the arrangement of their complex ideas. For though it be a peculiar property of the memory to preserve the original order and position of its ideas, while the imagination transposes and changes them, as it pleases; yet this difference is not sufficient to distinguish them in their operation, or make us know the one from the other; it being impossible to recal the past impressions, in order to compare them with our present ideas, and see whether their arrangement be exactly similar. Since therefore the memory, is known, neither by the order of its complex ideas, nor the nature of its simple ones; it follows, that the difference betwixt it and the imagination lies in its superior force and vivacity. A man may indulge his fancy in feigning any past scene of adventures; nor would there be any possibility of distinguishing this from a remembrance of a like kind, were not the ideas of the imagination fainter and more obscure.

It frequently happens, that when two men have been engaged in any scene of action, the one shall remember it much better than the other, and shall have all the difficulty in the world to make his companion recollect it. He runs over several circumstances in vain; mentions the time, the place, the company, what was said, what was done on all sides; till at last he hits on some lucky circumstance, that revives the whole, and gives his friend a perfect memory of every thing. Here the person that forgets receives at first all the ideas from the discourse of the other, with the same circumstances of time and place; though he considers them as mere fictions of the imagination. But as soon as the circumstance is mentioned, that touches the memory, the very same ideas now appear in a new light, and have, in a manner, a different feeling from what they had before. Without any other alteration, beside that of the feeling, they become immediately ideas of the memory, and are assented to.

Since, therefore, the imagination can represent all the same objects that the memory can offer to us, and since those faculties are only distinguished by the different feeling of the ideas they present, it may be proper to consider what is the nature of that feeling. And here I believe every one will readily agree with me, that the ideas of the memory are more strong and lively than those of the fancy.

A painter, who intended to represent a passion or emotion of any kind, would endeavour to get a sight of a person actuated by a like emotion, in order to enliven his ideas, and give them a force and vivacity superior to what is found in those, which are mere fictions of the imagination. The more recent this memory is, the clearer is the idea; and when after a long interval he would return to the contemplation of his object, he always finds its idea to be much decayed, if not wholly obliterated. We are frequently in doubt concerning the ideas of the memory, as they become very weak and feeble; and are at a loss to determine whether any image proceeds from the fancy or the memory, when it is not drawn in such lively colours as distinguish that latter faculty. I think, I remember such an event, says one; but am not sure. A long tract of time has almost worn it out of my memory, and leaves me uncertain whether or not it be the pure offspring of my fancy.

And as an idea of the memory, by losing its force and vivacity, may degenerate to such a degree, as to be taken for an idea of the imagination; so on the other hand an idea of the imagination may acquire such a force and vivacity, as to pass for an idea of the memory, and counterfeit its effects on the belief and judgment. This is noted in the case of liars; who by the frequent repetition of their lies, come at last to believe and remember them, as realities; custom and habit having in this case, as in many others, the same influence on the mind as nature, and infixing the idea with equal force and vigour.

Thus it appears, that the belief or assent, which always attends the memory and senses, is nothing but the vivacity of those perceptions they present; and that this alone distinguishes them from the imagination. To believe is in this case to feel an immediate impression of the senses, or a repetition of that impression in the memory. It is merely the force and liveliness of the perception, which constitutes the first act of the judgment, and lays the foundation of that reasoning, which we build upon it, when we trace the relation of cause and effect.

SECTION VI

Of the Inference from the Impression to the Idea

It is easy to observe, that in tracing this relation, the inference we draw from cause to effect, is not derived merely from a survey of these particular objects, and from such a penetration into their essences as may discover the dependance of the one upon the other. There is no object, which implies the existence of any other if we consider these objects in themselves, and never look beyond the ideas which we form of them. Such an inference would amount to knowledge, and would imply the absolute contradiction and impossibility of conceiving any thing different. But as all distinct ideas are separable, it is evident there can be no impossibility of that kind. When we pass from a present impression to the idea of any object, we might possibly have separated the idea from the impression, and have substituted any other idea in its room.

It is therefore by EXPERIENCE only, that we can infer the existence of one object from that of another. The nature of experience is this. We remember to have had frequent instances of the existence of one species of objects; and also remember, that the individuals of another species of objects have always attended them, and have existed in a regular order of contiguity and succession with regard to them. Thus we remember, to have seen that species of object we call flame, and to have felt that species of sensation we call heat. We likewise call to mind their constant conjunction in all past instances. Without any farther ceremony, we call the one cause and the other effect, and infer the existence of the one from that of the other. In all those instances, from which we learn the conjunction of particular causes and effects, both the causes and effects have been perceived by the senses, and are remembered. But in all cases, wherein we reason concerning them, there is only one perceived or remembered, and the other is supplyed in conformity to our past experience.

Thus in advancing we have insensibly discovered a new relation betwixt cause and effect, when we least expected it, and were entirely employed upon another subject. This relation is their CONSTANT CONJUNCTION. Contiguity and succession are not sufficient to make us pronounce any two objects to be cause and effect, unless we perceive, that these two relations are preserved in several instances. We may now see the advantage of quitting the direct survey of this relation, in order to discover the nature of that necessary connexion, which makes so essential a part of it. There are hopes, that by this means we may at last arrive at our proposed end; though to tell the truth, this new-discovered relation of a constant conjunction seems to advance us but very little in our way. For it implies no more than this, that like objects have always been placed in like relations of contiguity and succession; and it seems evident, at least at first sight, that by this means we can never discover any new idea, and can only multiply, but not enlarge the objects of our mind. It may be thought, that what we learn not from one object, we can never learn from a hundred, which are all of the same kind, and are perfectly resembling in every circumstance. As our senses shew us in one instance two bodies, or motions, or qualities in certain relations of success and contiguity; so our memory presents us only with a multitude of instances, wherein we always find like bodies, motions, or qualities in like relations. From the mere repetition of any past impression, even to infinity, there never will arise any new original idea, such as that of a necessary connexion; and the number of impressions has in this case no more effect than if we confined ourselves to one only. But though this reasoning seems just and obvious; yet as it would be folly to despair too soon, we shall continue the thread of our discourse; and having found, that after the discovery of the constant conjunction of any objects, we always draw an inference from one object to another, we shall now examine the nature of that inference, and of the transition from the impression to the idea. Perhaps it will appear in the end, that the necessary connexion depends on the inference, instead of the inference's depending on the necessary connexion.

Since it appears, that the transition from an impression present to the memory or senses to the idea of an object, which we call cause or effect, is founded on past experience, and on our remembrance of their constant conjunction, the next question is, Whether experience produces the idea by means of the understanding or imagination; whether we are determined by reason to make the transition, or by a certain association and relation of perceptions. If reason determined us, it would proceed upon that principle, that instances, of which we have had no experience, must resemble those, of which we have had experience, and that the course of nature continues always uniformly the same. In order therefore to clear up this matter, let us consider all the arguments, upon which such a proposition may be supposed to be founded; and as these must be derived either from knowledge or probability, let us cast our eye on each of these degrees of evidence, and see whether they afford any just conclusion of this nature.

Our foregoing method of reasoning will easily convince us, that there can be no demonstrative arguments to prove, that those instances, of which we have, had no experience, resemble those, of which we have had experience. We can at least conceive a change in the course of nature; which sufficiently proves, that such a change is not absolutely impossible. To form a clear idea of any thing, is an undeniable argument for its possibility, and is alone a refutation of any pretended demonstration against it.

Probability, as it discovers not the relations of ideas, considered as such, but only those of objects, must in some respects be founded on the impressions of our memory and senses, and in some respects on our ideas. Were there no mixture of any impression in our probable reasonings, the conclusion would be entirely chimerical: And were there no mixture of ideas, the action of the mind, in observing the relation, would, properly speaking, be sensation, not reasoning. It is therefore necessary, that in all probable reasonings there be something present to the mind, either seen or remembered; and that from this we infer something connected with it, which is not seen nor remembered.

The only connexion or relation of objects, which can lead us beyond the immediate impressions of our memory and senses, is that of cause and effect; and that because it is the only one, on which we can found a just inference from one object to another. The idea of cause and effect is derived from experience, which informs us, that such particular objects, in all past instances, have been constantly conjoined with each other: And as an object similar to one of these is supposed to be immediately present in its impression, we thence presume on the existence of one similar to its usual attendant. According to this account of things, which is, I think, in every point unquestionable, probability is founded on the presumption of a resemblance betwixt those objects, of which we have had experience, and those, of which we have had none; and therefore it is impossible this presumption can arise from probability. The same principle cannot be both the cause and effect of another; and this is, perhaps, the only proposition concerning that relation, which is either intuitively or demonstratively certain.

Should any one think to elude this argument; and without determining whether our reasoning on this subject be derived from demonstration or probability, pretend that all conclusions from causes and effects are built on solid reasoning: I can only desire, that this reasoning may be produced, in order to be exposed to our examination. It may, perhaps, be said, that after experience of the constant conjunction of certain objects, we reason in the following manner. Such an object is always found to produce another. It is impossible it could have this effect, if it was not endowed with a power of production. The power necessarily implies the effect; and therefore there is a just foundation for drawing a conclusion from the existence of one object to that of its usual attendant. The past production implies a power: The power implies a new production: And the new production is what we infer from the power and the past production.

It were easy for me to shew the weakness of this reasoning, were I willing to make use of those observations, I have already made, that the idea of production is the same with that of causation, and that no existence certainly and demonstratively implies a power in any other object; or were it proper to anticipate what I shall have occasion to remark afterwards concerning the idea we form of power and efficacy. But as such a method of proceeding may seem either to weaken my system, by resting one part of it on another, or to breed a confusion in my reasoning, I shall endeavour to maintain my present assertion without any such assistance.

It shall therefore be allowed for a moment, that the production of one object by another in any one instance implies a power; and that this power is connected with its effect. But it having been already proved, that the power lies not in the sensible qualities of the cause; and there being nothing but the sensible qualities present to us; I ask, why in other instances you presume that the same power still exists, merely upon the appearance of these qualities? Your appeal to past experience decides nothing in the present case; and at the utmost can only prove, that that very object, which produced any other, was at that very instant endowed with such a power; but can never prove, that the same power must continue in the same object or collection of sensible qualities; much less, that a like power is always conjoined with like sensible qualities, should it be said, that we have experience, that the same power continues united with the same object, and that like objects are endowed with like powers, I would renew my question, why from this experience we form any conclusion beyond those past instances, of which we have had experience. If you answer this question in, the same manner as the preceding, your answer gives still occasion to a new question of the same kind, even in infinitum; which clearly proves, that the foregoing reasoning had no just foundation.

Thus not only our reason fails us in the discovery of the ultimate connexion of causes and effects, but even after experience has informed us of their constant conjunction, it is impossible for us to satisfy ourselves by our reason, why we should extend that experience beyond those particular instances, which have fallen under our observation. We suppose, but are never able to prove, that there must be a resemblance betwixt those objects, of which we have had experience, and those which lie beyond the reach of our discovery.

We have already taken notice of certain relations, which make us pass from one object to another, even though there be no reason to determine us to that transition; and this we may establish for a general rule, that wherever the mind constantly and uniformly makes a transition without any reason, it is influenced by these relations. Now this is exactly the present case. Reason can never shew us the connexion of one object with another, though aided by experience, and the observation of their constant conjunction in all past instances. When the mind, therefore, passes from the idea or impression of one object to the idea or belief of another, it is not determined by reason, but by certain principles, which associate together the ideas of these objects, and unite them in the imagination. Had ideas no more union in the fancy than objects seem to have to the understanding, we could never draw any inference from causes to effects, nor repose belief in any matter of fact. The inference, therefore, depends solely on the union of ideas.

The principles of union among ideas, I have reduced to three general ones, and have asserted, that the idea or impression of any object naturally introduces the idea of any other object, that is resembling, contiguous to, or connected with it. These principles I allow to be neither the infallible nor the sole causes of an union among ideas. They are not the infallible causes. For one may fix his attention during Sometime on any one object without looking farther. They are not the sole causes. For the thought has evidently a very irregular motion in running along its objects, and may leap from the heavens to the earth, from one end of the creation to the other, without any certain method or order. But though I allow this weakness in these three relations, and this irregularity in the imagination; yet I assert that the only general principles, which associate ideas, are resemblance, contiguity and causation.

There is indeed a principle of union among ideas, which at first sight may be esteemed different from any of these, but will be found at the bottom to depend on the same origin. When every individual of any species of objects is found by experience to be constantly united with an individual of another species, the appearance of any new individual of either species naturally conveys the thought to its usual attendant. Thus because such a particular idea is commonly annexed to such a particular word, nothing is required but the hearing of that word to produce the correspondent idea; and it will scarce be possible for the mind, by its utmost efforts, to prevent that transition. In this case it is not absolutely necessary, that upon hearing such a particular sound we should reflect on any past experience, and consider what idea has been usually connected with the sound. The imagination of itself supplies the place of this reflection, and is so accustomed to pass from the word to the idea, that it interposes not a moment's delay betwixt the hearing of the one, and the conception of the other.

But though I acknowledge this to be a true principle of association among ideas, I assert it to be the very same with that betwixt the ideas of cause and effects and to be an essential part in all our reasonings from that relation. We have no other notion of cause and effect, but that of certain objects, which have been always conjoined together, and which in all past instances have been found inseparable. We cannot penetrate into the reason of the conjunction. We only observe the thing itself, and always find that from the constant conjunction the objects acquire an union in the imagination. When the impression of one becomes present to us, we immediately form an idea of its usual attendant; and consequently we may establish this as one part of the definition of an opinion or belief, that it is an idea related to or associated with a present impression.

Thus though causation be a philosophical relation, as implying contiguity, succession, and constant conjunction, yet it is only so far as it is a natural relation, and produces an union among our ideas, that we are able to reason upon it, or draw any inference from it.

SECTION VII

Of the Nature of the Idea or Belief

The idea of an object is an essential part of the belief of it, but not the whole. We conceive many things, which we do not believe. In order then to discover more fully the nature of belief, or the qualities of those ideas we assent to, let us weigh the following considerations.

It is evident, that all reasonings from causes or effects terminate in conclusions, concerning matter of fact; that is, concerning the existence of objects or of their qualities. It is also evident, that the idea, of existence is nothing different from the idea of any object, and that when after the simple conception of any thing we would conceive it as existent, we in reality make no addition to or alteration on our first idea. Thus when we affirm, that God is existent, we simply form the idea of such a being, as he is represented to us; nor is the existence, which we attribute to him, conceived by a particular idea, which we join to the idea of his other qualities, and can again separate and distinguish from them. But I go farther; and not content with asserting, that the conception of the existence of any object is no addition to the simple conception of it, I likewise maintain, that the belief of the existence joins no new ideas to those which compose the idea of the object. When I think of God, when I think of him as existent, and when I believe him to be existent, my idea of him neither encreases nor diminishes. But as it is certain there is a great difference betwixt the simple conception of the existence of an object, and the belief of it, and as this difference lies not in the parts or composition of the idea, which we conceive; it follows, that it must lie in the manner, in which we conceive it.

Suppose a person present with me, who advances propositions, to which I do not assent, that Caesar dyed in his bed, that silver is more fusible, than lead, or mercury heavier than gold; it is evident, that notwithstanding my incredulity, I clearly understand his meaning, and form all the same ideas, which he forms. My imagination is endowed with the same powers as his; nor is it possible for him to conceive any idea, which I cannot conceive; nor conjoin any, which I cannot conjoin. I therefore ask, Wherein consists the difference betwixt believing and disbelieving any proposition? The answer is easy with regard to propositions, that are proved by intuition or demonstration. In that case, the person, who assents, not only conceives the ideas according to the proposition, but is necessarily determined to conceive them in that particular manner, either immediately or by the interposition of other ideas. Whatever is absurd is unintelligible; nor is it possible for the imagination to conceive any thing contrary to a demonstration. But as in reasonings from causation, and concerning matters of fact, this absolute necessity cannot take place, and the imagination is free to conceive both sides of the question, I still ask, Wherein consists the deference betwixt incredulity and belief? since in both cases the conception of the idea is equally possible and requisite.

It will not be a satisfactory answer to say, that a person, who does not assent to a proposition you advance; after having conceived the object in the same manner with you; immediately conceives it in a different manner, and has different ideas of it. This answer is unsatisfactory; not because it contains any falshood, but because it discovers not all the truth. It is contest, that in all cases, wherein we dissent from any person, we conceive both sides of the question; but as we can believe only one, it evidently follows, that the belief must make some difference betwixt that conception to which we assent, and that from which we dissent. We may mingle, and unite, and separate, and confound, and vary our ideas in a hundred different ways; but until there appears some principle, which fixes one of these different situations, we have in reality no opinion: And this principle, as it plainly makes no addition to our precedent ideas, can only change the manner of our conceiving them.

All the perceptions of the mind are of two kinds, viz. impressions and ideas, which differ from each other only in their different degrees of force and vivacity. Our ideas are copyed from our impressions, and represent them in all their parts. When you would any way vary the idea of a particular object, you can only encrease or diminish its force and vivacity. If you make any other change on it, it represents a different object or impression. The case is the same as in colours. A particular shade of any colour may acquire a new degree of liveliness or brightness without any other variation. But when you produce any other variation, it is no longer the same shade or colour. So that as belief does nothing but vary the manner, in which we conceive any object, it can only bestow on our ideas an additional force and vivacity. An opinion, therefore, or belief may be most accurately defined, a lively idea related to or associated with a present impression.[19]

Here are the heads of those arguments, which lead us to this conclusion. When we infer the existence of an object from that of others, some object must always be present either to the memory or senses, in order to be the foundation of our reasoning; since the mind cannot run up with its inferences IN INFINITUM. Reason can never satisfy us that the existence of any one object does ever imply that of another; so that when we pass from the impression of one to the idea or belief of another, we are not determined by reason, but by custom or a principle of association. But belief is somewhat more than a simple idea. It is a particular manner of forming an idea: And as the same idea can only be varyed by a variation of its degrees of force and vivacity; it follows upon the whole, that belief is a lively idea produced by a relation to a present impression, according to the foregoing definition.

This operation of the mind, which forms the belief of any matter of fact, seems hitherto to have been one of the greatest mysteries of philosophy; though no one has so much as suspected, that there was any difficulty in explaining it. For my part I must own, that I find a considerable difficulty in the case; and that even when I think I understand the subject perfectly, I am at a loss for terms

---

[19] We may here take occasion to observe a very remarkable error, which being frequently inculcated in the schools, has become a kind of establishd maxim, and is universally received by all logicians. This error consists in the vulgar division of the acts of the understanding, into CONCEPTION, JUDGMENT and REASONING, and in the definitions we give of them. Conception is defind to be the simple survey of one or more ideas: Judgment to be the separating or uniting of different ideas: Reasoning to be the separating or uniting of different ideas by the interposition of others, which show the relation they bear to each other. But these distinctions and definitions are faulty in very considerable articles. For FIRST, it is far from being true, that in every judgment, which we form, we unite two different ideas; since in that proposition, GOD IS, or indeed any other, which regards existence, the idea of existence is no distinct idea, which we unite with that of the object, and which is capable of forming a compound idea by the union. SECONDLY, As we can thus form a proposition, which contains only one idea, so we may exert our reason without employing more than two ideas, and without having recourse to a third to serve as a medium betwixt them. We infer a cause immediately from its effect; and this inference is not only a true species of reasoning, but the strongest of all others, and more convincing than when we interpose another idea to connect the two extremes. What we may in general affirm concerning these three acts of the understanding is, that taking them in a proper light, they all resolve themselves into the first, and are nothing but particular ways of conceiving our objects. Whether we consider a single object, or several; whether we dwell on these objects, or run from them to others; and in whatever form or order we survey them, the act of the mind exceeds not a simple conception; and the only remarkable difference, which occurs on this occasion, is, when we join belief to the conception, and are persuaded of the truth of what we conceive. This act of the mind has never yet been explain'd by any philosopher; and therefore I am at liberty to propose my hypothesis concerning it; which is, that it is only a strong and steady conception of any idea, and such as approaches in some measure to an immediate impression.

to express my meaning. I conclude, by an induction which seems to me very evident, that an opinion or belief is nothing but an idea, that is different from a fiction, not in the nature or the order of its parts, but in the manner of its being conceived. But when I would explain this manner, I scarce find any word that fully answers the case, but am obliged to have recourse to every one's feeling, in order to give him a perfect notion of this operation of the mind. An idea assented to FEELS different from a fictitious idea, that the fancy alone presents to us: And this different feeling I endeavour to explain by calling it a superior force, or vivacity, or solidity, or FIRMNESS, or steadiness. This variety of terms, which may seem so unphilosophical, is intended only to express that act of the mind, which renders realities more present to us than fictions, causes them to weigh more in the thought, and gives them a superior influence on the passions and imagination. Provided we agree about the thing, it is needless to dispute about the terms. The imagination has the command over all its ideas, and can join, and mix, and vary them in all the ways possible. It may conceive objects with all the circumstances of place and time. It may set them, in a manner, before our eyes in their true colours, just as they might have existed. But as it is impossible, that that faculty can ever, of itself, reach belief, it is evident, that belief consists not in the nature and order of our ideas, but in the manner of their conception, and in their feeling to the mind. To confess, that it is impossible to explain perfectly this feeling or manner of conception. We may make use of words, that express something near it. But its true and proper name is belief, which is a term that every one sufficiently understands in common life. And in philosophy we can go no farther, than assert, that it is something felt by the mind, which distinguishes the ideas of the judgment from the fictions of the imagination. It gives them more force and influence; makes them appear of greater importance; infixes them in the mind; and renders them the governing principles of all our actions.

This definition will also be found to be entirely conformable to every one's feeling and experience. Nothing is more evident, than that those ideas, to which we assent, are more strong, firm and vivid, than the loose reveries of a castle-builder. If one person sits down to read a book as a romance, and another as a true history, they plainly receive the same ideas, and in the same order; nor does the incredulity of the one, and the belief of the other hinder them from putting the very same sense upon their author. His words produce the same ideas in both; though his testimony has not the same influence on them. The latter has a more lively conception of all the incidents. He enters deeper into the concerns of the persons: represents to himself their actions, and characters, and friendships, and enmities: He even goes so far as to form a notion of their features, and air, and person. While the former, who gives no credit to the testimony of the author, has a more faint and languid conception of all these particulars; and except on account of the style and ingenuity of the composition, can receive little entertainment from it.

SECTION VIII

Of the Causes of Belief

Having thus explained the nature of belief, and shewn that it consists in a lively idea related to a present impression; let us now proceed to examine from what principles it is derived, and what bestows the vivacity on the idea.

I would willingly establish it as a general maxim in the science of human nature, that when any impression becomes present to us, it not only transports the mind to such ideas as are related to it, but likewise communicates to them a share of its force and vivacity. All the operations of the mind depend in a great measure on its disposition, when it performs them; and according as the spirits are more or less elevated, and the attention more or less fixed, the action will always have more or less vigour and vivacity. When therefore any object is presented, which elevates and enlivens the thought, every action, to which the mind applies itself, will be more strong and vivid, as Tong as that disposition continues, Now it is evident the continuance of the disposition depends entirely on the objects, about which the mind is employed; and that any new object naturally gives a new direction to the spirits, and changes the disposition; as on the contrary, when the mind fixes constantly on the same object, or passes easily and insensibly along related objects, the disposition has a much longer duration. Hence it happens, that when the mind is once inlivened by a present impression, it proceeds to form a more lively idea of the related objects, by a natural transition of the disposition from the one to the other. The change of the objects is so easy, that the mind is scarce sensible of it, but applies itself to the conception of the related idea with all the force and vivacity it acquired from the present impression.

If in considering the nature of relation, and that facility of transition, which is essential to it, we can satisfy ourselves concerning the reality of this phænomenon, it is well: But I must confess I place my chief confidence in experience to prove so material a principle. We may, therefore, observe, as the first experiment to our present purpose, that upon the appearance of the picture of an absent friend, our idea of him is evidently inlivened by the resemblance, and that every passion, which that idea occasions, whether of joy or sorrow, acquires new force and vigour. In producing this effect there concur both a relation and a present impression. Where the picture bears him no resemblance, or at least was not intended for him, it never so much as conveys our thought to him: And where it is absent, as well as the person; though the mind may pass from the thought of the one to that of the other; it feels its idea to be rather weekend than inlivened by that transition. We take a pleasure in viewing the picture of a friend, when it is set before us; but when it is removed, rather choose to consider him directly, than by reflexion in an image, which is equally distinct and obscure.

The ceremonies of the Roman Catholic religion may be considered as experiments of the same nature. The devotees of that strange superstition usually plead in excuse of the mummeries, with which they are upbraided, that they feel the good effect of those external motions, and postures, and actions, in enlivening their devotion, and quickening their fervour, which otherwise would decay away, if directed entirely to distant and immaterial objects. We shadow out the objects of our faith, say they, in sensible types and images, and render them more present to us by the immediate presence of these types, than it is possible for us to do, merely by an intellectual view and contemplation. Sensible objects have always a greater influence on the fancy than any other; and this influence they readily convey to those ideas, to which they are related, and which they Resemble. I shall only infer from these practices, and this reasoning, that the effect of resemblance in inlivening the idea is very common; and as in every case a resemblance and a present impression must concur, we are abundantly supplyed with experiments to prove the reality of the foregoing principle.

We may add force to these experiments by others of a different kind, in considering the effects of contiguity, as well as of resemblance. It is certain, that distance diminishes the force of every idea, and that upon our approach to any object; though it does not discover itself to our senses; it operates upon the mind with an influence that imitates an immediate impression. The thinking on any object readily transports the mind to what is contiguous; but it is only the actual presence of an object, that transports it with a superior vivacity. When I am a few miles from home, whatever relates to it touches me more nearly than when I am two hundred leagues distant; though even at that distance the reflecting on any thing in the neighbourhood of my friends and family naturally produces an idea of them. But as in this latter case, both the objects of the mind are ideas; notwithstanding there is an easy transition betwixt them; that transition alone is not able to give a superior vivacity to any of the ideas, for want of some immediate impression.[20]

---

[20] NATURANE NOBIS, IN QUIT, DATUM DICAM, AN ERRORE QUODAM, UT, CUM EA LOCA VIDEAMUS, IN QUIBUS MEMORIA DIGNOS VIROS ACCEPERIMUS MULTURN ESSE VERSATOS, MAGIS MOVEAMUR, QUAM SIQUANDO EORUM IPSORUM AUT JACTA AUDIAMUS, AUT SCRIPTUM ALIQUOD LEGAMUS? VELUT EGO NUNC MOVEOR. VENIT ENIM MIHI PLATONIS IN MENTEM: QUEM ACCIPIMUS PRIMURN HIC DISPUTARE SOLITUM: CUJUS ETIAM ILLI HORTULI PROPINQUI NON MEMORIAM SOLUM MIHI AFFERUNT, SED IPSUM VIDENTUR IN CONSPECTU MEO HIC PONERE. HIC SPEUSIPPUS, HIC XENOCRATES, HIC EJUS AUDITOR POLEMO; CUJUS IPSA ILLA SESSIO FUIT, QUAM VIDEAMUS. EQUIDEM ETIAM CURIAM NOSTRAM, HOSTILIAM DICO, NON HANC NOVAM, QUAE MIHI MINOR ESSE VIDETUR POST QUAM EST MAJOR, SOLE BARN INTUENS SCIPIONEM, CATONEM, LACLIUM, NOSTRUM VERO IN PRIMIS AVUM COGITARE. TANTA VIS ADMONITIONIS INEST IN LOCIS; UT NON SINE CAUSA EX HIS MEMORIAE DUCTA SIT DISCIPLINA. Cicero de Finibus, lib. 5.

["Should I, he said, "attribute to instinct or to some kind of illusion the fact that when we see those places in which we are told notable men spent much of their time, we are more powerfully affected than when we hear of the exploits of the men themselves or read something written? This is just what is happening to me now; for I am reminded of Plato who, we are told, was the first to make a practice of holding discussions here. Those gardens of his near by do not merely put me in mind of him; they seem to set the man himself before my very eyes. Speusippus was here; so was Xenocrates; so was his pupil, Polemo, and that very seat which we may view was his.

No one can doubt but causation has the same influence as the other two relations; of resemblance and contiguity. Superstitious people are fond of the relicks of saints and holy men, for the same reason that they seek after types and images, in order to enliven their devotion, and give them a more intimate and strong conception of those exemplary lives, which they desire to imitate. Now it is evident, one of the best relicks a devotee could procure, would be the handywork of a saint; and if his cloaths and furniture are ever to be considered in this light, it is because they were once at his disposal, and were moved and affected by him; in which respect they are to be considered as imperfect effects, and as connected with him by a shorter chain of consequences than any of those, from which we learn the reality of his existence. This phænomenon clearly proves, that a present impression with a relation of causation may, inliven any idea, and consequently produce belief or assent, according to the precedent definition of it.

But why need we seek for other arguments to prove, that a present impression with a relation or transition of the fancy may inliven any idea, when this very instance of our reasonings from cause and effect will alone suffice to that purpose? It is certain we must have an idea of every matter of fact, which we believe. It is certain, that this idea arises only from a relation to a present impression. It is certain, that the belief super-adds nothing to the idea, but only changes our manner of conceiving it, and renders it more strong and lively. The present conclusion concerning the influence of relation is the immediate consequence of all these steps; and every step appears to me sure end infallible. There enters nothing into this operation of the mind but a present impression, a lively idea, and a relation or association in the fancy betwixt the impression and idea; so that there can be no suspicion of mistake.

In order to put this whole affair in a fuller light, let us consider it as a question in natural philosophy, which we must determine by experience and observation. I suppose there is an object presented, from which I draw a certain conclusion, and form to myself ideas, which I am said to believe or assent to. Here it is evident, that however that object, which is present to my senses, and that other, whose existence I infer by reasoning, may be thought to influence each other by their particular powers or qualities; yet as the phenomenon of belief, which we at present examine, is merely internal, these powers and qualities, being entirely unknown, can have no hand in producing it. It is the present impression, which is to be considered as the true and real cause of the idea, and of the belief which attends it. We must therefore endeavour to discover by experiments the particular qualities, by which it is enabled to produce so extraordinary an effect.

"Then again, when I looked at our Senate-house (I mean the old building of Hostilius, not this new one; when it was enlarged, it diminished in my estimation), I used to think of Scipio, Cato, Laelius and in particular of my own grandfather.

"Such is the power of places to evoke associations; so it is with good reason that they are used as a basis for memory training."]

First then I observe, that the present impression has not this effect by its own proper power and efficacy, and when considered alone, as a single perception, limited to the present moment. I find, that an impression, from which, on its first appearance, I can draw no conclusion, may afterwards become the foundation of belief, when I have had experience of its usual consequences. We must in every case have observed the same impression in past instances, and have found it to be constantly conjoined with some other impression. This is confirmed by such a multitude of experiments, that it admits not of the smallest doubt.

From a second observation I conclude, that the belief, which attends the present impression, and is produced by a number of past impressions and conjunctions; that this belief, I say, arises immediately, without any new operation of the reason or imagination. Of this I can be certain, because I never am conscious of any such operation, and find nothing in the subject, on which it can be founded. Now as we call every thing CUSTOM, which proceeds from a past repetition, without any new reasoning or conclusion, we-may establish it as a certain truth, that all the belief, which follows upon any present impression, is derived solely from that origin. When we are accustomed to see two impressions conjoined together, the appearance or idea of the one immediately carries us to the idea of the other.

Being fully satisfyed on this head, I make a third set of experiments, in order to know, whether any thing be requisite, beside the customary transition, towards the production of this phænomenon of belief. I therefore change the first impression into an idea; and observe, that though the customary transition to the correlative idea still remains, yet there is in reality no belief nor perswasion. A present impression, then, is absolutely requisite to this whole operation; and when after this I compare an impression with an idea, and find that their only difference consists in their different degrees of force and vivacity, I conclude upon the whole, that belief is a more vivid and intense conception of an idea, proceeding from its relation to a present impression.

Thus all probable reasoning is nothing but a species of sensation. It is not solely in poetry and music, we must follow our taste and sentiment, but likewise in philosophy. When I am convinced of any principle, it is only an idea, which strikes more strongly upon me. When I give the preference to one set of arguments above another, I do nothing but decide from my feeling concerning the superiority of their influence. Objects have no discoverable connexion together; nor is it from any other principle but custom operating upon the imagination, that we can draw any inference from the appearance of one to the existence of another.

It will here be worth our observation, that the past experience, on which all our judgments concerning cause and effect depend, may operate on our mind in such an insensible manner as never to be taken notice of, and may even in some measure be unknown to us. A person, who stops short in his journey upon meeting a river in his way, foresees the consequences of his proceeding forward; and his knowledge of these consequences is conveyed to him by past experience, which informs him of such certain conjunctions of causes and effects. But can we think, that on this occasion he reflects on any past experience, and calls to remembrance instances, that he has seen or heard of, in order to discover the effects of water on animal bodies? No surely; this is not the method, in which he proceeds in his reasoning. The idea of sinking is so closely connected with that of water, and the idea of suffocating with that of sinking, that the mind makes the transition without the assistance of the memory. The custom operates before we have time for reflection. The objects seem so inseparable, that we interpose not a moment's delay in passing from the one to the other. But as this transition proceeds from experience, and not from any primary connexion betwixt the ideas, we must necessarily acknowledge, that experience may produce a belief and a judgment of causes and effects by a secret operation, and without being once thought of. This removes all pretext, if there yet remains any, for asserting that the mind is convinced by reasoning of that principle, that instances of which we have no experience, must necessarily resemble those, of which we have. For we here find, that the understanding or imagination can draw inferences from past experience, without reflecting on it; much more without forming any principle concerning it, or reasoning upon that principle.

In general we may observe, that in all the most established and uniform conjunctions of causes and effects, such as those of gravity, impulse, solidity, &c. the mind never carries its view expressly to consider any past experience: Though in other associations of objects, which are more rare and unusual, it may assist the custom and transition of ideas by this reflection. Nay we find in some cases, that the reflection produces the belief without the custom; or more properly speaking, that the reflection produces the custom in an oblique and artificial manner. I explain myself. It is certain, that not only in philosophy, but even in common life, we may attain the knowledge of a particular cause merely by one experiment, provided it be made with judgment, and after a careful removal of all foreign and superfluous circumstances. Now as after one experiment of this kind, the mind, upon the appearance either of the cause or the effect, can draw an inference concerning the existence of its correlative; and as a habit can never be acquired merely by one instance; it may be thought, that belief cannot in this case be esteemed the effect of custom. But this difficulty will vanish, if we consider, that though we are here supposed to have had only one experiment of a particular effect, yet we have many millions to convince us of this principle; that like objects placed in like circumstances, will always produce like effects; and as this principle has established itself by a sufficient custom, it bestows an evidence and firmness on any opinion, to which it can be applied. The connexion of the ideas is not habitual after one experiment: but this connexion is comprehended under another principle, that is habitual; which brings us back to our hypothesis. In all cases we transfer our experience to instances, of which we have no experience, either expressly or tacitly, either directly or indirectly.

I must not conclude this subject without observing, that it is very difficult to talk of the operations of the mind with perfect propriety and exactness; because common language has seldom made any very nice distinctions among them, but has generally called by the same term all such as nearly resemble each other. And as this is a source almost inevitable of obscurity and confusion in the author; so it may frequently give rise to doubts and objections in the reader, which otherwise he would never have dreamed of. Thus my general position, that an opinion or belief is nothing but a strong and lively idea derived from a present impression related to it, maybe liable to the following objection, by reason of a little ambiguity in those words strong and lively. It may be said, that not only an impression may give rise to reasoning, but that an idea may also have the same influence; especially upon my principle, that all our ideas are derived from correspondent impressions. For suppose I form at present an idea, of which I have forgot the correspondent impression, I am able to conclude from this idea, that such an impression did once exist; and as this conclusion is attended with belief, it may be asked, from whence are the qualities of force and vivacity derived, which constitute this belief? And to this I answer very readily, from the present idea. For as this idea is not here considered, as the representation of any absent object, but as a real perception in the mind, of which we are intimately conscious, it must be able to bestow on whatever is related to it the same quality, call it firmness, or solidity, or force, or vivacity, with which the mind reflects upon it, and is assured of its present existence. The idea here supplies the place of an impression, and is entirely the same, so far as regards our present purpose.

Upon the same principles we need not be surprized to hear of the remembrance of an idea: that is, of the idea of an idea, and of its force and vivacity superior to the loose conceptions of the imagination. In thinking of our past thoughts we not only delineate out the objects, of which we were thinking, but also conceive the action of the mind in the meditation, that certain JE-NE-SÇAI-QUOI, of which it is impossible to give any definition or description, but which every one sufficiently understands. When the memory offers an idea of this, and represents it as past, it is easily conceived how that idea may have more vigour and firmness, than when we think of a past thought, of which we have no remembrance.

After this any one will understand how we may form the idea of an impression and of an idea, and how we way believe the existence of an impression and of an idea.

SECTION IX

Of the Effects of other Relations and other Habits

However convincing the foregoing arguments may appear, we must not rest contented with them, but must turn the subject on every side, in order to find some new points of view, from which we may illustrate and confirm such extraordinary, and such fundamental principles. A scrupulous hesitation to receive any new hypothesis is so laudable a disposition in philosophers, and so necessary to the examination of truth, that it deserves to be complyed with, and requires that every argument be produced, which may tend to their satisfaction, and every objection removed, which may stop them in their reasoning.

I have often observed, that, beside cause and effect, the two relations of resemblance and contiguity, are to be considered as associating principles of thought, and as capable of conveying the imagination from one idea to another. I have also observed, that when of two objects connected to-ether by any of these relations, one is immediately present to the memory or senses, not only the mind is conveyed to its co-relative by means of the associating principle; but likewise conceives it with an additional force and vigour, by the united operation of that principle, and of the present impression. All this I have observed, in order to confirm by analogy, my explication of our judgments concerning cause and effect. But this very argument may, perhaps, be turned against me, and instead of a confirmation of my hypothesis, may become an objection to it. For it may be said, that if all the parts of that hypothesis be true, viz. that these three species of relation are derived from the same principles; that their effects in informing and enlivening our ideas are the same; and that belief is nothing but a more forcible and vivid conception of an idea; it should follow, that that action of the mind may not only be derived from the relation of cause and effect, but also from those of contiguity and resemblance. But as we find by experience, that belief arises only from causation, and that we can draw no inference from one object to another, except they be connected by this relation, we may conclude, that there is some error in that reasoning, which leads us into such difficulties.

This is the objection; let us now consider its solution. It is evident, that whatever is present to the memory, striking upon the mind with a vivacity, which resembles an immediate impression, must become of considerable moment in all the operations of the mind, and must easily distinguish itself above the mere fictions of the imagination. Of these impressions or ideas of the memory we form a kind of system, comprehending whatever we remember to have been present, either to our internal perception or senses; and every particular of that system, joined to the present impressions, we are pleased to call a reality. But the mind stops not here. For finding, that with this system of perceptions, there is another connected by custom, or if you will, by the relation of cause or effect, it proceeds to the consideration of their ideas; and as it feels that it is in a manner necessarily determined to view these particular ideas, and that the custom or relation, by which it is determined, admits not of the least change, it forms them into a new system, which it likewise dignifies with the title of realities. The first of these systems is the object of the memory and senses; the second of the judgment.

It is this latter principle, which peoples the world, and brings us acquainted with such existences, as by their removal in time and place, lie beyond the reach of the senses and memory. By means of it I paint the universe in my imagination, and fix my attention on any part of it I please. I form an idea of ROME, which I neither see nor remember; but which is connected with such impressions as I remember to have received from the conversation and books of travellers and historians. This idea of Rome I place in a certain situation on the idea of an object, which I call the globe. I join to it the conception of a particular government, and religion, and manners. I look backward and consider its first foundation; its several revolutions, successes, and misfortunes. All this, and everything else, which I believe, are nothing but ideas; though by their force and settled order, arising from custom and the relation of cause and effect, they distinguish themselves from the other ideas, which are merely the offspring of the imagination.

As to the influence of contiguity and resemblance, we may observe, that if the contiguous and resembling object be comprehended in this system of realities, there is no doubt but these two relations will assist that of cause and effect, and infix the related idea with more force in the imagination. This I shall enlarge upon presently. Mean while I shall carry my observation a step farther, and assert, that even where the related object is but feigned, the relation will serve to enliven the idea, and encrease its influence. A poet, no doubt, will be the better able to form a strong description of the Elysian fields, that he prompts his imagination by the view of a beautiful meadow or garden; as at another time he may by his fancy place himself in the midst of these fabulous regions, that by the feigned contiguity he may enliven his imagination.

But though I cannot altogether exclude the relations of resemblance and contiguity from operating on the fancy in this manner, it is observable that, when single, their influence is very feeble and uncertain. As the relation of cause and effect is requisite to persuade us of any real existence, so is this persuasion requisite to give force to these other relations. For where upon the appearance of an impression we not only feign another object, but likewise arbitrarily, and of our mere good-will and pleasure give it a particular relation to the impression, this can have but a small effect upon the mind; nor is there any reason, why, upon the return of the same impression, we should be determined to place the same object in the same relation to it. There is no manner of necessity for the mind to feign any resembling and contiguous objects; and if it feigns such, there is as little necessity for it always to confine itself to the same, without any difference or variation. And indeed such a fiction is founded on so little reason, that nothing but pure caprice can determine the mind to form it; and that principle being fluctuating and uncertain, it is impossible it can ever operate with any considerable degree of force and constancy. The mind forsees and anticipates the change; and even from the very first instant feels the looseness of its actions, and the weak hold it has of its objects. And as this imperfection is very sensible in every single instance, it still encreases by experience and observation, when we compare the several instances we may remember, and form a general rule against the reposing any assurance in those momentary glimpses of light, which arise in the imagination from a feigned resemblance and contiguity.

The relation of cause and effect has all the opposite advantages. The objects it presents are fixt and unalterable. The impressions of the memory never change in any considerable degree; and each impression draws along with it a precise idea, which takes its place in the imagination as something solid and real, certain and invariable. The thought is always determined to pass from the impression to the idea, and from that particular impression to that particular idea, without any choice or hesitation.

But not content with removing this objection, I shall endeavour to extract from it a proof of the present doctrine. Contiguity and resemblance have an effect much inferior to causation; but still have some effect, and augment the conviction of any opinion, and the vivacity of any conception. If this can be proved in several new instances, beside what we have already observed, it will be allowed no inconsiderable argument, that belief is nothing but a lively idea related to a present impression.

To begin with contiguity; it has been remarked among the Mahometans as well as Christians, that those pilgrims, who have seen MECCA or the HOLY LAND, are ever after more faithful and zealous believers, than those who have not had that advantage. A man, whose memory presents him with a lively image of the Red-Sea, and the Desert, and Jerusalem, and Galilee, can never doubt of any miraculous events, which are related either by Moses or the Evangelists. The lively idea of the places passes by an easy transition to the facts, which are supposed to have been related to them by contiguity, and encreases the belief by encreasing the vivacity of the conception. The remembrance of these fields and rivers has the same influence on the vulgar as a new argument; and from the same causes.

We may form a like observation concerning resemblance. We have remarked, that the conclusion, which we draw from a present object to its absent cause or effect, is never founded on any qualities, which we observe in that object, considered in itself, or, in other words, that it is impossible to determine, otherwise than by experience, what will result from any phenomenon, or what has preceded it. But though this be so evident in itself, that it seemed not to require any, proof; yet some philosophers have imagined that there is an apparent cause for the communication of motion, and that a reasonable man might immediately infer the motion of one body from the impulse of another, without having recourse to any past observation. That this opinion is false will admit of an easy proof. For if such an inference may be drawn merely from the ideas of body, of motion, and of impulse, it must amount to a demonstration, and must imply the absolute impossibility of any contrary supposition. Every effect, then, beside the communication of motion, implies a formal contradiction; and it is impossible not only that it can exist, but also that it can be conceived. But we may soon satisfy ourselves of the contrary, by forming a clear and consistent idea of one body's moving upon another, and of its rest immediately upon the contact, or of its returning back in the same line in which it came; or of its annihilation; or circular or elliptical motion: and in short, of an infinite number of other changes, which we may suppose it to undergo. These suppositions are all consistent and natural; and the reason, Why we imagine the communication of motion to be more consistent and natural not only than those suppositions, but also than any other natural effect, is founded on the relation of resemblance betwixt the cause and effect, which is here united to experience, and binds the objects in the closest and most intimate manner to each other, so as to make us imagine them to be absolutely inseparable. Resemblance, then, has the same or a parallel influence with experience; and as the only immediate effect of experience is to associate our ideas together, it follows, that all belief arises from the association of ideas, according to my hypothesis.

It is universally allowed by the writers on optics, that the eye at all times sees an equal number of physical points, and that a man on the top of a mountain has no larger an image presented to his senses, than when he is cooped up in the narrowest court or chamber. It is only by experience that he infers the greatness of the object from some peculiar qualities of the image; and this inference of the judgment he confounds with sensation, as is common on other occasions. Now it is evident, that the inference of the judgment is here much more lively than what is usual in our common reasonings, and that a man has a more vivid conception of the vast extent of the ocean from the image he receives by the eye, when he stands on the top of the high promontory, than merely from hearing the roaring of the waters. He feels a more sensible pleasure from its magnificence; which is a proof of a more lively idea: And he confounds his judgment with sensation, which is another proof of it. But as the inference is equally certain and immediate in both cases, this superior vivacity of our conception in one case can proceed from nothing but this, that in drawing an inference from the sight, beside the customary conjunction, there is also a resemblance betwixt the image and the object we infer; which strengthens the relation, and conveys the vivacity of the impression to the related idea with an easier and more natural movement.

No weakness of human nature is more universal and conspicuous than what we commonly call CREDULITY, or a too easy faith in the testimony of others; and this weakness is also very naturally accounted for from the influence of resemblance. When we receive any matter of fact upon human testimony, our faith arises from the very same origin as our inferences from causes to effects, and from effects to causes; nor is there anything but our experience of the governing principles of human nature, which can give us any assurance of the veracity of men. But though experience be the true standard of this, as well as of all other judgments, we seldom regulate ourselves entirely by it; but have a remarkable propensity to believe whatever is reported, even concerning apparitions, enchantments, and prodigies, however contrary to daily experience and observation. The words or discourses of others have an intimate connexion with certain ideas in their mind; and these ideas have also a connexion with the facts or objects, which they represent. This latter connexion is generally much over-rated, and commands our assent beyond what experience will justify; which can proceed from nothing beside the resemblance betwixt the ideas and the facts. Other effects only point out their causes in an oblique manner; but the testimony of men does it directly, and is to be considered as an image as well as an effect. No wonder, therefore, we are so rash in drawing our inferences from it, and are less guided by experience in our judgments concerning it, than in those upon any other subject.

As resemblance, when conjoined with causation, fortifies our reasonings; so the want of it in any very great degree is able almost entirely to destroy them. Of this there is a remarkable instance in the universal carelessness and stupidity of men with regard to a future state, where they show as obstinate an incredulity, as they do a blind credulity on other occasions. There is not indeed a more ample matter of wonder to the studious, and of regret to the pious man, than to observe the negligence of the bulk of mankind concerning their approaching condition; and it is with reason, that many eminent theologians have not scrupled to affirm, that though the vulgar have no formal principles of infidelity, yet they are really infidels in their hearts, and have nothing like what we can call a belief of the eternal duration of their souls. For let us consider on the one hand what divines have displayed with such eloquence concerning the importance of eternity; and at the same time reflect, that though in matters of rhetoric we ought to lay our account with some exaggeration, we must in this case allow, that the strongest figures are infinitely inferior to the subject: And after this let us view on the other hand, the prodigious security of men in this particular: I ask, if these people really believe what is inculcated on them, and what they pretend to affirm; and the answer is obviously in the negative. As belief is an act of the mind arising from custom, it is not strange the want of resemblance should overthrow what custom has established, and diminish the force of the idea, as much as that latter principle encreases it. A future state is so far removed from our comprehension, and we have so obscure an idea of the manner, in which we shall exist after the dissolution of the body, that all the reasons we can invent, however strong in themselves, and however much assisted by education, are never able with slow imaginations to surmount this difficulty, or bestow a sufficient authority and force on the idea. I rather choose to ascribe this incredulity to the faint idea we form of our future condition, derived from its want of resemblance to the present life, than to that derived from its remoteness. For I observe, that men are everywhere concerned about what may happen after their death, provided it regard this world; and that there are few to whom their name, their family, their friends, and their country are in any period of time entirely indifferent.

And indeed the want of resemblance in this case so entirely destroys belief, that except those few, who upon cool reflection on the importance of the subject, have taken care by repeated meditation to imprint in their minds the arguments for a future state, there scarce are any, who believe the immortality of the soul with a true and established judgment; such as is derived from the testimony of travellers and historians. This appears very conspicuously wherever men have occasion to compare the pleasures and pains, the rewards and punishments of this life with those of a future; even though the case does not concern themselves, and there is no violent passion to disturb their judgment. The Roman Catholicks are certainly the most zealous of any sect in the Christian world; and yet you'll find few among the more sensible people of that communion who do not blame the Gunpowder-treason, and the massacre of St. Bartholomew, as cruel and barbarous, though projected or executed against those very people, whom without any scruple they condemn to eternal and infinite punishments. All we can say in excuse for this inconsistency is, that they really do not believe what they affirm concerning a future state; nor is there any better proof of it than the very inconsistency.

We may add to this a remark; that in matters of religion men take a pleasure in being terrifyed, and that no preachers are so popular, as those who excite the most dismal and gloomy passions. In the common affairs of life, where we feel and are penetrated with the solidity of the subject, nothing can be more disagreeable than fear and terror; and it is only in dramatic performances and in religious discourses, that they ever give pleasure. In these latter cases the imagination reposes itself indolently on the idea; and the passion, being softened by the want of belief in the subject, has no more than the agreeable effect of enlivening the mind, and fixing the attention.

The present hypothesis will receive additional confirmation, if we examine the effects of other kinds of custom, as well as of other relations. To understand this we must consider, that custom, to which I attribute all belief and reasoning, may operate upon the mind in invigorating an idea after two several ways. For supposing that in all past experience we have found two objects to have been always conjoined together, it is evident, that upon the appearance of one of these objects in an impression, we must from custom make an easy transition to the idea of that object, which usually attends it; and by means of the present impression and easy transition must conceive that idea in a stronger and more lively manner, than we do any loose floating image of the fancy. But let us next suppose, that a mere idea alone, without any of this curious and almost artificial preparation, should frequently make its appearance in the mind, this idea must by degrees acquire a facility and force; and both by its firm hold and easy introduction distinguish itself from any new and unusual idea. This is the only particular, in which these two kinds of custom agree; and if it appear, that their effects on the judgment, are similar and proportionable, we may certainly conclude, that the foregoing explication of that faculty is satisfactory. But can we doubt of this agreement in their influence on the judgment, when we consider the nature and effects Of EDUCATION?

All those opinions and notions of things, to which we have been accustomed from our infancy, take such deep root, that it is impossible for us, by all the powers of reason and experience, to eradicate them; and this habit not only approaches in its influence, but even on many occasions prevails over that which a-rises from the constant and inseparable union of causes and effects. Here we most not be contented with saying, that the vividness of the idea produces the belief: We must maintain that they are individually the same. The frequent repetition of any idea infixes it in the imagination; but could never possibly of itself produce belief, if that act of the mind was, by the original constitution of our natures, annexed only to a reasoning and comparison of ideas. Custom may lead us into some false comparison of ideas. This is the utmost effect we can conceive of it. But it is certain it could never supply the place of that comparison, nor produce any act of the mind, which naturally belonged to that principle.

A person, that has lost a leg or an arm by amputation, endeavours for a long time afterwards to serve himself with them. After the death of any one, it is a common remark of the whole family, but especially of the servants, that they can scarce believe him to be dead, but still imagine him to be in his chamber or in any other place, where they were accustomed to find him. I have often heard in conversation, after talking of a person, that is any way celebrated, that one, who has no acquaintance with him, will say, I have never seen such-a-one, but almost fancy I have; so often have I heard talk of him. All these are parallel instances.

If we consider this argument from EDUCATION in a proper light, it will appear very convincing; and the more so, that it is founded on one of the most common phaenomena, that is any where to be met with. I am persuaded, that upon examination we shall find more than one half of those opinions, that prevail among mankind, to be owing to education, and that the principles, which are thus implicitely embraced, overballance those, which are owing either to abstract reasoning or experience. As liars, by the frequent repetition of their lies, come at last to remember them; so the judgment, or rather the imagination, by the like means, may have ideas so strongly imprinted on it, and conceive them in so full a light, that they may operate upon the mind in the same manner with those, which the senses, memory or reason present to us. But as education is an artificial and not a natural cause, and as its maxims are frequently contrary to reason, and even to themselves in different times and places, it is never upon that account recognized by philosophers; though in reality it be built almost on the same foundation of custom and repetition as our reasonings from causes and effects.[21]

---

[21] In general we may observe, that as our assent to all probable reasonings is founded on the vivacity of ideas, It resembles many of those whimsies and prejudices, which are rejected under the opprobrious character of being the offspring of the imagination. By this expression it appears that the word, imagination, is commonly usd in two different senses; and tho nothing be more contrary to true philosophy, than this inaccuracy, yet in the following reasonings I have often been obligd to fall into it. When I oppose the Imagination to the memory, I mean the faculty, by which we form our fainter ideas. When I oppose it to reason, I mean the same faculty, excluding only our demonstrative and probable reasonings. When I oppose it to neither, it is indifferent whether it be taken in the larger or more limited sense, or at least the context will sufficiently explain the meaning.

SECTION X

Of the Influence of Belief

But though education be disclaimed by philosophy, as a fallacious ground of assent to any opinion, it prevails nevertheless in the world, and is the cause why all systems are apt to be rejected at first as new and unusual. This perhaps will be the fate of what I have here advanced concerning belief, and though the proofs I have produced appear to me perfectly conclusive, I expect not to make many proselytes to my opinion. Men will scarce ever be persuaded, that effects of such consequence can flow from principles, which are seemingly so inconsiderable, and that the far greatest part of our reasonings with all our actions and passions, can be derived from nothing but custom and habit. To obviate this objection, I shall here anticipate a little what would more properly fall under our consideration afterwards, when we come to treat of the passions and the sense of beauty.

There is implanted in the human mind a perception of pain and pleasure, as the chief spring and moving principle of all its actions. But pain and pleasure have two ways of making their appearance in the mind; of which the one has effects very different from the other. They may either appear in impression to the actual feeling, or only in idea, as at present when I mention them. It is evident the influence of these upon our actions is far from being equal. Impressions always actuate the soul, and that in the highest degree; but it is not every idea which has the same effect. Nature has proceeded with caution in this came, and seems to have carefully avoided the inconveniences of two extremes. Did impressions alone influence the will, we should every moment of our lives be subject to the greatest calamities; because, though we foresaw their approach, we should not be provided by nature with any principle of action, which might impel us to avoid them. On the other hand, did every idea influence our actions, our condition would not be much mended. For such is the unsteadiness and activity of thought, that the images of every thing, especially of goods and evils, are always wandering in the mind; and were it moved by every idle conception of this kind, it would never enjoy a moment's peace and tranquillity.

Nature has, therefore, chosen a medium, and has neither bestowed on every idea of good and evil the power of actuating the will, nor yet has entirely excluded them from this influence. Though an idle fiction has no efficacy, yet we find by experience, that the ideas of those objects, which we believe either are or will be existent, produce in a lesser degree the same effect with those impressions, which are immediately present to the senses and perception. The effect, then, of belief is to raise up a simple idea to an equality with our impressions, and bestow on it a like influence on the passions. This effect it can only have by making an idea approach an impression in force and vivacity. For as the different degrees of force make all the original difference betwixt an impression and an idea, they must of consequence be the source of all the differences in the effects of these perceptions, and their removal, in whole or in part, the cause of every new resemblance they acquire. Wherever we can make an idea approach the impressions in force and vivacity, it will likewise imitate them in its influence on the mind; and vice versa, where it imitates them in that influence, as in the present case, this must proceed from its approaching them in force and vivacity. Belief, therefore, since it causes an idea to imitate the effects of the impressions, must make it resemble them in these qualities, and is nothing but A MORE VIVID AND INTENSE CONCEPTION OF ANY IDEA. This, then, may both serve as an additional argument for the present system, and may give us a notion after what manner our reasonings from causation are able to operate on the will and passions.

As belief is almost absolutely requisite to the exciting our passions, so the passions in their turn are very favourable to belief; and not only such facts as convey agreeable emotions, but very often such as give pain, do upon that account become more readily the objects of faith and opinion. A coward, whose fears are easily awakened, readily assents to every account of danger he meets with; as a person of a sorrowful and melancholy disposition is very credulous of every thing, that nourishes his prevailing passion. When any affecting object is presented, it gives the alarm, and excites immediately a degree of its proper passion; especially in persons who are naturally inclined to that passion. This emotion passes by an easy transition to the imagination; and diffusing itself over our idea of the affecting object, makes us form that idea with greater force and vivacity, and consequently assent to it, according to the precedent system. Admiration and surprize have the same effect as the other passions; and accordingly we may observe, that among the vulgar, quacks and projectors meet with a more easy faith upon account of their magnificent pretensions, than if they kept themselves within the bounds of moderation. The first astonishment, which naturally attends their miraculous relations, spreads itself over the whole soul, and so vivifies and enlivens the idea, that it resembles the inferences we draw from experience. This is a mystery, with which we may be already a little acquainted, and which we shall have farther occasion to be let into in the progress of this treatise.

After this account of the influence of belief on the passions, we shall find less difficulty in explaining its effects on the imagination, however extraordinary they may appear. It is certain we cannot take pleasure in any discourse, where our judgment gives no assent to those images which are presented to our fancy. The conversation of those who have acquired a habit of lying, though in affairs of no moment, never gives any satisfaction; and that because those ideas they present to us, not being attended with belief, make no impression upon the mind. Poets themselves, though liars by profession, always endeavour to give an air of truth to their fictions; and where that is totally neglected, their performances, however ingenious, will never be able to afford much pleasure. In short, we may observe, that even when ideas have no manner of influence on the will and passions, truth and reality are still requisite, in order to make them entertaining to the imagination.

But if we compare together all the phenomena that occur on this head, we shall find, that truth, however necessary it may seem in all works of genius, has no other effect than to procure an easy reception for the ideas, and to make the mind acquiesce in them with satisfaction, or at least without reluctance. But as this is an effect, which may easily be supposed to flow from that solidity and force, which, according to my system, attend those ideas that are established by reasonings from causation; it follows, that all the influence of belief upon the fancy may be explained from that system. Accordingly we may observe, that wherever that influence arises from any other principles beside truth or reality, they supply its place, and give an equal entertainment to the imagination. Poets have formed what they call a poetical system of things, which though it be believed neither by themselves nor readers, is commonly esteemed a sufficient foundation for any fiction. We have been so much accustomed to the names of MARS, JUPITER, VENUS, that in the same manner as education infixes any opinion, the constant repetition of these ideas makes them enter into the mind with facility, and prevail upon the fancy, without influencing the judgment. In like manner tragedians always borrow their fable, or at least the names of their principal actors, from some known passage in history; and that not in order to deceive the spectators; for they will frankly confess, that truth is not in any circumstance inviolably observed: but in order to procure a more easy reception into the imagination for those extraordinary events, which they represent. But this is a precaution, which is not required of comic poets, whose personages and incidents, being of a more familiar kind, enter easily into the conception, and are received without any such formality, even though at first night they be known to be fictitious, and the pure offspring of the fancy.

This mixture of truth and falshood in the fables of tragic poets not only serves our present purpose, by shewing, that the imagination can be satisfyed without any absolute belief or assurance; but may in another view be regarded as a very strong confirmation of this system. It is evident, that poets make use of this artifice of borrowing the names of their persons, and the chief events of their poems, from history, in order to procure a more easy reception for the whole, and cause it to make a deeper impression on the fancy and affections. The several incidents of the piece acquire a kind of relation by being united into one poem or representation; and if any of these incidents be an object of belief, it bestows a force and vivacity on the others, which are related to it. The vividness of the first conception diffuses itself along the relations, and is conveyed, as by so many pipes or canals, to every idea that has any communication with the primary one. This, indeed, can never amount to a perfect assurance; and that because the union among the ideas is, in a manner, accidental: But still it approaches so near, in its influence, as may convince us, that they are derived from the same origin. Belief must please the imagination by means of the force and vivacity which attends it; since every idea, which has force and vivacity, is found to be agreeable to that faculty.

To confirm this we may observe, that the assistance is mutual betwixt the judgment and fancy, as well as betwixt the judgment and passion; and that belief not only gives vigour to the imagination, but that a vigorous and strong imagination is of all talents the most proper to procure belief and authority. It is difficult for us to withhold our assent from what is painted out to us in all the colours of eloquence; and the vivacity produced by the fancy is in many cases greater than that which arises from custom and experience. We are hurried away by the lively imagination of our author or companion; and even he himself is often a victim to his own fire and genius.

Nor will it be amiss to remark, that as a lively imagination very often degenerates into madness or folly, and bears it a great resemblance in its operations; so they influence the judgment after the same manner, and produce belief from the very same principles. When the imagination, from any extraordinary ferment of the blood and spirits, acquires such a vivacity as disorders all its powers and faculties, there is no means of distinguishing betwixt truth and falshood; but every loose fiction or idea, having the same influence as the impressions of the memory, or the conclusions of the judgment, is received on the same footing, and operates with equal force on the passions. A present impression and a customary transition are now no longer necessary to enliven our ideas. Every chimera of the brain is as vivid and intense as any of those inferences, which we formerly dignifyed with the name of conclusions concerning matters of fact, and sometimes as the present impressions of the senses.

We may observe the same effect of poetry in a lesser degree; and this is common both to poetry and madness, that the vivacity they bestow on the ideas is not derived from the particular situations or connexions of the objects of these ideas, but from the present temper and disposition of the person. But how great soever the pitch may be, to which this vivacity rises, it is evident, that in poetry it never has the same feeling with that which arises in the mind, when we reason, though even upon the lowest species of probability. The mind can easily distinguish betwixt the one and the other; and whatever emotion the poetical enthusiasm may give to the spirits, it is still the mere phantom of belief or persuasion. The case is the same with the idea, as with the passion it occasions. There is no passion of the human mind but what may arise from poetry; though at the same time the feelings of the passions are very different when excited by poetical fictions, from what they are when they are from belief and reality. A passion, which is disagreeable in real life, may afford the highest entertainment in a tragedy, or epic poem. In the latter case, it lies not with that weight upon us: It feels less firm and solid: And has no other than the agreeable effect of exciting the spirits, and rouzing the attention. The difference in the passions is a clear proof of a like difference in those ideas, from which the passions are derived. Where the vivacity arises from a customary conjunction with a present impression; though the imagination may not, in appearance, be so much moved; yet there is always something more forcible and real in its actions, than in the fervors of poetry and eloquence. The force of our mental actions in this case, no more than in any other, is not to be measured by the apparent agitation of the mind. A poetical description may have a more sensible effect on the fancy, than an historical narration. It may collect more of those circumstances, that form a compleat image or picture. It may seem to set the object before us in more lively colours. But still the ideas it presents are different to the feeling from those, which arise from the memory and the judgment. There is something weak and imperfect amidst all that seeming vehemence of thought and sentiment, which attends the fictions of poetry.

We shall afterwards have occasion to remark both the resemblance and differences betwixt a poetical enthusiasm, and a serious conviction. In the mean time I cannot forbear observing, that the great difference in their feeling proceeds in some measure from reflection and GENERAL RULES. We observe, that the vigour of conception, which fictions receive from poetry and eloquence, is a circumstance merely accidental, of which every idea is equally susceptible; and that such fictions are connected with nothing that is real. This observation makes us only lend ourselves, so to speak, to the fiction: But causes the idea to feel very different from the eternal established persuasions founded on memory and custom. They are somewhat of the same kind: But the one is much inferior to the other, both in its causes and effects.

A like reflection on general rules keeps us from augmenting our belief upon every encrease of the force and vivacity of our ideas. Where an opinion admits of no doubt, or opposite probability, we attribute to it a full conviction: though the want of resemblance, or contiguity, may render its force inferior to that of other opinions. It is thus the understanding corrects the appearances of the senses, and makes us imagine, that an object at twenty foot distance seems even to the eye as large as one of the same dimensions at ten.

We may observe the same effect of poetry in a lesser degree; only with this difference, that the least reflection dissipates the illusions of poetry, and Places the objects in their proper light. It is however certain, that in the warmth of a poetical enthusiasm, a poet has a counterfeit belief, and even a kind of vision of his objects: And if there be any shadow of argument to support this belief, nothing contributes more to his full conviction than a blaze of poetical figures and images, which have their effect upon the poet himself, as well as upon his readers.

SECTION XI

Of the Probability of Chances

But in order to bestow on this system its full force and evidence, we must carry our eye from it a moment to consider its consequences, and explain from the same principles some other species of reasoning, which are derived from the same origin.

Those philosophers, who have divided human reason into knowledge and probability, and have defined the first to be that evidence, which arises from the comparison of ideas, are obliged to comprehend all our arguments from causes or effects under the general term of probability. But though every one be free to use his terms in what sense he pleases; and accordingly in the precedent part of this discourse, I have followed this method of expression; it is however certain, that in common discourse we readily affirm, that many arguments from causation exceed probability, and may be received as a superior kind of evidence. One would appear ridiculous, who would say, that it is only probable the sun will rise to-morrow, or that all men must dye; though it is plain we have no further assurance of these facts, than what experience affords us. For this reason, it would perhaps be more convenient, in order at once to preserve the common signification of words, and mark the several degrees of evidence, to distinguish human reason into three kinds, viz. THAT FROM KNOWLEDGE, FROM PROOFS, AND FROM PROBABILITIES. By knowledge, I mean the assurance arising from the comparison of ideas. By proofs, those arguments, which are derived from the relation of cause and effect, and which are entirely free from doubt and uncertainty. By probability, that evidence, which is still attended with uncertainty. It is this last species of reasoning, I proceed to examine.

Probability or reasoning from conjecture may be divided into two kinds, viz. that which is founded on chance, and that which arises from causes. We shall consider each of these in order.

The idea of cause and effect is derived from experience, which presenting us with certain objects constantly conjoined with each other, produces such a habit of surveying them in that relation, that we cannot without a sensible violence survey them iii any other. On the other hand, as chance is nothing real in itself, and, properly speaking, is merely the negation of a cause, its influence on the mind is contrary to that of causation; and it is essential to it, to leave the imagination perfectly indifferent, either to consider the existence or non-existence of that object, which is regarded as contingent. A cause traces the way to our thought, and in a manner forces us to survey such certain objects, in such certain relations. Chance can only destroy this determination of the thought, and leave the mind in its native situation of indifference; in which, upon the absence of a cause, it is instantly re-instated.

Since therefore an entire indifference is essential to chance, no one chance can possibly be superior to another, otherwise than as it is composed of a superior number of equal chances. For if we affirm that one chance can, after any other manner, be superior to another, we must at the same time affirm, that there is something, which gives it the superiority, and determines the event rather to that side than the other: That is, in other words, we must allow of a cause, and destroy the supposition of chance; which we had before established. A perfect and total indifference is essential to chance, and one total indifference can never in itself be either superior or inferior to another. This truth is not peculiar to my system, but is acknowledged by every one, that forms calculations concerning chances.

And here it is remarkable, that though chance and causation be directly contrary, yet it is impossible for us to conceive this combination of chances, which is requisite to render one hazard superior to another, without supposing a mixture of causes among the chances, and a conjunction of necessity in some particulars, with a total indifference in others. Where nothing limits the chances, every notion, that the most extravagant fancy can form, is upon a footing of equality; nor can there be any circumstance to give one the advantage above another. Thus unless we allow, that there are some causes to make the dice fall, and preserve their form in their fall, and lie upon some one of their sides, we can form no calculation concerning the laws of hazard. But supposing these causes to operate, and supposing likewise all the rest to be indifferent and to be determined by chance, it is easy to arrive at a notion of a superior combination of chances. A dye that has four sides marked with a certain number of spots, and only two with another, affords us an obvious and easy instance of this superiority. The mind is here limited by the causes to such a precise number and quality of the events; and at the same time is undetermined in its choice of any particular event.

Proceeding then in that reasoning, wherein we have advanced three steps; that chance is merely the negation of a cause, and produces a total indifference in the mind; that one negation of a cause and one total indifference can never be superior or inferior to another; and that there must always be a mixture of causes among the chances, in order to be the foundation of any reasoning: We are next to consider what effect a superior combination of chances can have upon the mind, and after what manner it influences our judgment and opinion. Here we may repeat all the same arguments we employed in examining that belief, which arises from causes; and may prove, after the same manner, that a superior number of chances produces our assent neither by demonstration nor probability. It is indeed evident that we can never by the comparison of mere ideas make any discovery, which can be of consequence in this affairs and that it is impossible to prove with certainty, that any event must fall on that side where there is a superior number of chances. To, suppose in this case any certainty, were to overthrow what we have established concerning the opposition of chances, and their perfect equality and indifference.

Should it be said, that though in an opposition of chances it is impossible to determine with certainty, on which side the event will fall, yet we can pronounce with certainty, that it is more likely and probable, it will be on that side where there is a superior number of chances, than where there is an inferior: should this be said, I would ask, what is here meant by likelihood and probability? The likelihood and probability of chances is a superior number of equal chances; and consequently when we say it is likely the event win fall on the side, which is superior, rather than on the inferior, we do no more than affirm, that where there is a superior number of chances there is actually a superior, and where there is an inferior there is an inferior; which are identical propositions, and of no consequence. The question is, by what means a superior number of equal chances operates upon the mind, and produces belief or assent; since it appears, that it is neither by arguments derived from demonstration, nor from probability.

In order to clear up this difficulty, we shall suppose a person to take a dye, formed after such a manner as that four of its sides are marked with one figure, or one number of spots, and two with another; and to put this dye into the box with an intention of throwing it: It is plain, he must conclude the one figure to be more probable than the other, and give the preference to that which is inscribed on the greatest number of sides. He in a manner believes, that this will lie uppermost; though still with hesitation and doubt, in proportion to the number of chances, which are contrary: And according as these contrary chances diminish, and the superiority encreases on the other side, his belief acquires new degrees of stability and assurance. This belief arises from an operation of the mind upon the simple and limited object before us; and therefore its nature will be the more easily discovered and explained. We have nothing but one single dye to contemplate, in order to comprehend one of the most curious operations of the understanding.

This dye, formed as above, contains three circumstances worthy of our attention. First, Certain causes, such as gravity, solidity, a cubical figure, &c. which determine it to fall, to preserve its form in its fall, and to turn up one of its sides. Secondly, A certain number of sides, which are supposed indifferent. Thirdly, A certain figure inscribed on each side. These three particulars form the whole nature of the dye, so far as relates to our present purpose; and consequently are the only circumstances regarded by the mind in its forming a judgment concerning the result of such a throw. Let us, therefore, consider gradually and carefully what must be the influence of these circumstances on the thought and imagination.

First, We have already observed, that the mind is determined by custom to pass from any cause to its effect, and that upon the appearance of the one, it is almost impossible for it not to form an idea of the other. Their constant conjunction in past instances has produced such a habit in the mind, that it always conjoins them in its thought, and infers the existence of the one from that of its usual attendant. When it considers the dye as no longer supported by the box, it can not without violence regard it as suspended in the air; but naturally places it on the table, and views it as turning up one of its sides. This is the effect of the intermingled causes, which are requisite to our forming any calculation concerning chances.

Secondly, It is supposed, that though the dye be necessarily determined to fall, and turn up one of its sides, yet there is nothing to fix the particular side, but that this is determined entirely by chance. The very nature and essence of chance is a negation of causes, and the leaving the mind in a perfect indifference among those events, which are supposed contingent. When therefore the thought is determined by the causes to consider the dye as falling and turning up one of its sides, the chances present all these sides as equal, and make us consider every one of them, one after another, as alike probable and possible. The imagination passes from the cause, viz. the throwing of the dye, to the effect, viz. the turning up one of the six sides; and feels a kind of impossibility both of stopping short in the way, and of forming any other idea. But as all these six sides are incompatible, and the dye cannot turn up above one at once, this principle directs us not to consider all of them at once as lying uppermost; which we look upon as impossible: Neither does it direct us with its entire force to any particular side; for in that case this side would be considered as certain and inevitable; but it directs us to the whole six sides after such a manner as to divide its force equally among them. We conclude in general, that some one of them must result from the throw: We run all of them over in our minds: The determination of the thought is common to all; but no more of its force falls to the share of any one, than what is suitable to its proportion with the rest. It is after this manner the original impulse, and consequently the vivacity of thought, arising from the causes, is divided and split in pieces by the intermingled chances.

We have already seen the influence of the two first qualities of the dye, viz. the causes, and the number and indifference of the sides, and have learned how they give an impulse to the thought, and divide that impulse into as many parts as there are unites in the number of sides. We must now consider the effects of the third particular, viz. the figures inscribed on each side. It is evident that where several sides have the same figure inscribe on them, they must concur in their influence on the mind, and must unite upon one image or idea of a figure all those divided impulses, that were dispersed over the several sides, upon which that figure is inscribed. Were the question only what side will be turned up, these are all perfectly equal, and no one could ever have any advantage above another. But as the question is concerning the figure, and as the same figure is presented by more than one side: it is evident, that the impulses belonging to all these sides must re-unite in that one figure, and become stronger and more forcible by the union. Four sides are supposed in the present case to have the same figure inscribed on them, and two to have another figure. The impulses of the former are, therefore, superior to those of the latter. But as the events are contrary, and it is impossible both these figures can be turned up; the impulses likewise become contrary, and the inferior destroys the superior, as far as its strength goes. The vivacity of the idea is always proportionable to the degrees of the impulse or tendency to the transition; and belief is the same with the vivacity of the idea, according to the precedent doctrine.

SECTION XII

Of the Probability of Causes

What I have said concerning the probability of chances can serve to no other purpose, than to assist us in explaining the probability of causes; since it is commonly allowed by philosophers, that what the vulgar call chance is nothing but a secret and concealed cause. That species of probability, therefore, is what we must chiefly examine.

The probabilities of causes are of several kinds; but are all derived from the same origin, viz. THE ASSOCIATION OF IDEAS TO A PRESENT IMPRESSION. As the habit, which produces the association, arises from the frequent conjunction of objects, it must arrive at its perfection by degrees, and must acquire new force from each instance, that falls under our observation. The first instance has little or no force: The second makes some addition to it: The third becomes still more sensible; and it is by these slow steps, that our judgment arrives at a full assurance. But before it attains this pitch of perfection, it passes through several inferior degrees, and in all of them is only to be esteemed a presumption or probability. The gradation, therefore, from probabilities to proofs is in many cases insensible; and the difference betwixt these kinds of evidence is more easily perceived in the remote degrees, than in the near and contiguous.

It is worthy of remark on this occasion, that though the species of probability here explained be the first in order, and naturally takes place before any entire proof can exist, yet no one, who is arrived at the age of maturity, can any longer be acquainted with it. It is true, nothing is more common than for people of the most advanced knowledge to have attained only an imperfect experience of many particular events; which naturally produces only an imperfect habit and transition: But then we must consider, that the mind, having formed another observation concerning the connexion of causes and effects, gives new force to its reasoning from that observation; and by means of it can build an argument on one single experiment, when duly prepared and examined. What we have found once to follow from any object, we conclude will for ever follow from it; and if this maxim be not always built upon as certain, it is not for want of a sufficient number of experiments, but because we frequently meet with instances to the contrary; which leads us to the second species of probability, where there is a contrariety in our experience and observation.

It would be very happy for men in the conduct of their lives and actions, were the same objects always conjoined together, and, we had nothing to fear but the mistakes of our own judgment, without having any reason to apprehend the uncertainty of nature. But as it is frequently found, that one observation is contrary to another, and that causes and effects follow not in the same order, of which we have I had experience, we are obliged to vary our reasoning on, account of this uncertainty, and take into consideration the contrariety of events. The first question, that occurs on this head, is concerning the nature and causes of the contrariety.

The vulgar, who take things according to their first appearance, attribute the uncertainty of events to such an uncertainty in the causes, as makes them often fail of their usual influence, though they meet with no obstacle nor impediment in their operation. But philosophers observing, that almost in every part of nature there is contained a vast variety of springs and principles, which are hid, by reason of their minuteness or remoteness, find that it is at least possible the contrariety of events may not proceed from any contingency in the cause, but from the secret operation of contrary causes. This possibility is converted into certainty by farther observation, when they remark, that upon an exact scrutiny, a contrariety of effects always betrays a contrariety of causes, and proceeds from their mutual hindrance and opposition. A peasant can give no better reason for the stopping of any clock or watch than to say, that commonly it does not go right: But an artizan easily perceives, that the same force in the spring or pendulum has always the same influence on the wheels; but fails of its usual effect, perhaps by reason of a grain of dust, which puts a stop to the whole movement. From the observation of several parallel instances, philosophers form a maxim, that the connexion betwixt all causes and effects is equally necessary, and that its seeming uncertainty in some instances proceeds from the secret opposition of contrary causes.

But however philosophers and the vulgar may differ in their explication of the contrariety of events, their inferences from it are always of the same kind, and founded on the same principles. A contrariety of events in the past may give us a kind of hesitating belief for the future after two several ways. First, By producing an imperfect habit and transition from the present impression to the related idea. When the conjunction of any two objects is frequent, without being entirely constant, the mind is determined to pass from one object to the other; but not with so entire a habit, as when the union is uninterrupted, and all the instances we have ever met with are uniform and of a piece-.. We find from common experience, in our actions as well as reasonings, that a constant perseverance in any course of life produces a strong inclination and tendency to continue for the future; though there are habits of inferior degrees of force, proportioned to the inferior degrees of steadiness and uniformity in our conduct.

There is no doubt but this principle sometimes takes place, and produces those inferences we draw from contrary phaenomena: though I am perswaded, that upon examination we shall not find it to be the principle, that most commonly influences the mind in this species of reasoning. When we follow only the habitual determination of the mind, we make the transition without any reflection, and interpose not a moment's delay betwixt the view of one object and the belief of that, which is often found to attend it. As the custom depends not upon any deliberation, it operates immediately, without allowing any time for reflection. But this method of proceeding we have but few instances of in our probable reasonings; and even fewer than in those, which are derived from the uninterrupted conjunction of objects. In the former species of reasoning we commonly take knowingly into consideration the contrariety of past events; we compare the different sides of the contrariety, and carefully weigh the experiments, which we have on each side: Whence we may conclude, that our reasonings of this kind arise not directly from the habit, but in an oblique manner; which we must now endeavour to explain.

It is evident, that when an object is attended with contrary effects, we judge of them only by our past experience, and always consider those as possible, which we have observed to follow from it. And as past experience regulates our judgment concerning the possibility of these effects, so it does that concerning their probability; and that effect, which has been the most common, we always esteem the most likely. Here then are two things to be considered, viz. the reasons which determine us to make the past a standard for the future, and the manner how we extract a single judgment from a contrariety of past events.

First we may observe, that the supposition, that the future resembles the past, is not founded on arguments of any kind, but is derived entirely from habit, by which we are determined to expect for the future the same train of objects, to which we have been accustomed. This habit or determination to transfer the past to the future is full and perfect; and consequently the first impulse of the imagination in this species of reasoning is endowed with the same qualities.

But, secondly, when in considering past experiments we find them of a contrary nature, this determination, though full and perfect in itself, presents us with no steady object, but offers us a number of disagreeing images in a certain order and proportion. The first impulse, therefore, is here broke into pieces, and diffuses itself over all those images, of which each partakes an equal share of that force and vivacity, that is derived from the impulse. Any of these past events may again happen; and we judge, that when they do happen, they will be mixed in the same proportion as in the past.

If our intention, therefore, be to consider the proportions of contrary events in a great number of instances, the images presented by our past experience must remain in their FIRST FORM, and preserve their first proportions. Suppose, for instance, I have found by long observation, that of twenty ships, which go to sea, only nineteen return. Suppose I see at present twenty ships that leave the port: I transfer my past experience to the future, and represent to myself nineteen of these ships as returning in safety, and one as perishing. Concerning this there can be no difficulty. But as we frequently run over those several ideas of past events, in order to form a judgment concerning one single event, which appears uncertain; this consideration must change the FIRST FORM of our ideas, and draw together the divided images presented by experience; since it is to it we refer the determination of that particular event, upon which we reason. Many of these images are supposed to concur, and a superior number to concur on one side. These agreeing images unite together, and render the idea more strong and lively, not only than a mere fiction of the imagination, but also than any idea, which is supported by a lesser number of experiments. Each new experiment is as a new stroke of the pencil, which bestows an additional vivacity on the colours without either multiplying or enlarging the figure. This operation of the mind has been so fully explained in treating of the probability of chance, that I need not here endeavour to render it more intelligible. Every past experiment may be considered as a kind of chance; I it being uncertain to us, whether the object will exist conformable to one experiment or another. And for this reason every thing that has been said on the one subject is applicable to both.

Thus upon the whole, contrary experiments produce an imperfect belief, either by weakening the habit, or by dividing and afterwards joining in different parts, that perfect habit, which makes us conclude in general, that instances, of which we have no experience, must necessarily resemble those of which we have.

To justify still farther this account of the second species of probability, where we reason with knowledge and reflection from a contrariety of past experiments, I shall propose the following considerations, without fearing to give offence by that air of subtilty, which attends them. Just reasoning ought still, perhaps, to retain its force, however subtile; in the same manner as matter preserves its solidity in the air, and fire, and animal spirits, as well as in the grosser and more sensible forms.

First, We may observe, that there is no probability so great as not to allow of a contrary possibility; because otherwise it would cease to be a probability, and would become a certainty. That probability of causes, which is most extensive, and which we at present examine, depends on a contrariety of experiments: and it is evident an experiment in the past proves at least a possibility for the future.

Secondly, The component parts of this possibility and probability are of the same nature, and differ in number only, but not in kind. It has been observed, that all single chances are entirely equal, and that the only circumstance, which can give any event, that is contingent, a superiority over another is a superior number of chances. In like manner, as the uncertainty of causes is discovery by experience, which presents us with a view of contrary events, it is plain, that when we transfer the past to the future, the known to the unknown, every past experiment has the same weight, and that it is only a superior number of them, which can throw the ballance on any side. The possibility, therefore, which enters into every reasoning of this kind, is composed of parts, which are of the same nature both among themselves, and with those, that compose the opposite probability.

Thirdly, We may establish it as a certain maxim, that in all moral as well as natural phaenomena, wherever any cause consists of a number of parts, and the effect encreases or diminishes, according to the variation of that number, the effects properly speaking, is a compounded one, and arises from the union of the several effects, that proceed from each part of the cause. Thus, because the gravity of a body encreases or diminishes by the encrease or diminution of its parts, we conclude that each part contains this quality and contributes to the gravity of the whole. The absence or presence of a part of the cause is attended with that of a proportionable part of the effect. This connexion or constant conjunction sufficiently proves the one part to be the cause of the other. As the belief which we have of any event, encreases or diminishes according to the number of chances or past experiments, it is to be considered as a compounded effect, of which each part arises from a proportionable number of chances or experiments.

Let us now join these three observations, and see what conclusion we can draw from them. To every probability there is an opposite possibility. This possibility is composed of parts, that are entirely of the same nature with those of the probability;

and consequently have the same influence on the mind and understanding. The belief, which attends the probability, is a compounded effect, and is formed by the concurrence of the several effects, which proceed from each part of the probability. Since therefore each part of the probability contributes to the production of the belief, each part of the possibility must have the same influence on the opposite side; the nature of these parts being entirely the same. The contrary belief, attending the possibility, implies a view of a certain object, as well as the probability does an opposite view. In this particular both these degrees of belief are alike. The only manner then, in which the superior number of similar component parts in the one can exert its influence, and prevail above the inferior in the other, is by producing a stronger and more lively view of its object. Each part presents a particular view; and all these views uniting together produce one general view, which is fuller and more distinct by the greater number of causes or principles, from which it is derived.

The component parts of the probability and possibility, being alike in their nature, must produce like effects; and the likeness of their effects consists in this, that each of them presents a view of a particular object. But though these parts be alike in their nature, they are very different in their quantity and number; and this difference must appear in the effect as well as the similarity. Now as the view they present is in both cases full and entire, and comprehends the object in all its parts, it is impossible that in this particular there can be any difference; nor is there any thing but a superior vivacity in the probability, arising from the concurrence of a superior number of views, which can distinguish these effects.

Here is almost the same argument in a different light. All our reasonings concerning the probability of causes are founded on the transferring of past to future. The transferring of any past experiment to the future is sufficient to give us a view of the object; whether that experiment be single or combined with others of the same kind; whether it be entire, or opposed by others of a contrary kind. Suppose, then, it acquires both these qualities of combination and opposition, it loses not upon that account its former power of presenting a view of the object, but only concurs with and opposes other experiments, that have a like influence. A question, therefore, may arise concerning the manner both of the concurrence and opposition. As to the concurrence, there is only the choice left betwixt these two hypotheses. First, That the view of the object, occasioned by the transference of each past experiment, preserves itself entire, and only multiplies the number of views. Or, SECONDLY, That it runs into the other similar and correspondent views, and gives them a superior degree of force and vivacity. But that the first hypothesis is erroneous, is evident from experience, which informs us, that the belief, attending any reasoning, consists in one conclusion, not in a multitude of similar ones, which would only distract the mind, and in many cases would be too numerous to be comprehended distinctly by any finite capacity. It remains, therefore, as the only reasonable opinion, that these similar views run into each other, and unite their forces; so as to produce a stronger and clearer view, than what arises from any one alone. This is the manner, in which past experiments concur, when they are transfered to any future event. As to the manner of their opposition, it is evident, that as the contrary views are incompatible with each other, and it is impossible the object can at once exist conformable to both of them, their influence becomes mutually destructive, and the mind is determined to the superior only with that force, which remains, after subtracting the inferior.

I am sensible how abstruse all this reasoning must appear to the generality of readers, who not being accustomed to such profound reflections on the intellectual faculties of the mind, will be apt to reject as chimerical whatever strikes not in with the common received notions, and with the easiest and most obvious principles of philosophy. And no doubt there are some pains required to enter into these arguments; though perhaps very little are necessary to perceive the imperfection of every vulgar hypothesis on this subject, and the little light, which philosophy can yet afford us in such sublime and such curious speculations. Let men be once fully perswaded of these two principles, THAT THERE, IS NOTHING IN ANY OBJECT, CONSIDERED IN ITSELF, WHICH CAN AFFORD US A REASON FOR DRAWING A CONCLUSION BEYOND it; and, THAT EVEN AFTER THE OBSERVATION OF THE FREQUENT OR CONSTANT CONJUNCTION OF OBJECTS, WE HAVE NO REASON TO DRAW ANY INFERENCE CONCERNING ANY OBJECT BEYOND THOSE OF WHICH WE HAVE HAD EXPERIENCE; I say, let men be once fully convinced of these two principles, and this will throw them so loose from all common systems, that they will make no difficulty of receiving any, which may appear the most extraordinary. These principles we have found to be sufficiently convincing, even with regard to our most certain reasonings from causation: But I shall venture to affirm, that with regard to these conjectural or probable reasonings they still acquire a new degree of evidence.

First, It is obvious, that in reasonings of this kind, it is not the object presented to us, which, considered in itself, affords us any reason to draw a conclusion concerning any other object or event. For as this latter object is supposed uncertain, and as the uncertainty is derived from a concealed contrariety of causes in the former, were any of the causes placed in the known qualities of that object, they would no longer be concealed, nor would our conclusion be uncertain.

But, secondly, it is equally obvious in this species of reasoning, that if the transference of the past to the future were founded merely on a conclusion of the understanding, it could never occasion any belief or assurance. When we transfer contrary experiments to the future, we can only repeat these contrary experiments with their particular proportions; which could not produce assurance in any single event, upon which we reason, unless the fancy melted together all those images that concur, and extracted from them one single idea or image, which is intense and lively in proportion to the number of experiments from which it is derived, and their superiority above their antagonists. Our past experience presents no determinate object; and as our belief, however faint, fixes itself on a determinate object, it is evident that the belief arises not merely from the transference of past to future, but from some operation of the fancy conjoined with it. This may lead us to conceive the manner, in which that faculty enters into all our reasonings.

I shall conclude this subject with two reflections, which may deserve our attention. The FIRST may be explained after this manner. When the mind forms a reasoning concerning any matter of fact, which is only probable, it casts its eye backward upon past experience, and transferring it to the future, is presented with so many contrary views of its object, of which those that are of the same kind uniting together, and running into one act of the mind, serve to fortify and inliven it. But suppose that this multitude of views or glimpses of an object proceeds not from experience, but from a voluntary act of the imagination; this effect does not follow, or at least, follows not in the same degree. For though custom and education produce belief by such a repetition, as is not derived from experience, yet this requires a long tract of time, along with a very frequent and undesigned repetition. In general we may pronounce, that a person who would voluntarily repeat any idea in his mind, though supported by one past experience, would be no more inclined to believe the existence of its object, than if he had contented himself with one survey of it. Beside the effect of design; each act of the mind, being separate and independent, has a separate influence, and joins not its force with that of its fellows. Not being united by any common object, producing them, they have no relation to each other; and consequently make no transition or union of forces. This phænomenon we shall understand better afterwards.

My second reflection is founded on those large probabilities, which the mind can judge of, and the minute differences it can observe betwixt them. When the chances or experiments on one side amount to ten thousand, and on the other to ten thousand and one, the judgment gives the preference to the latter, upon account of that superiority; though it is plainly impossible for the mind to run over every particular view, and distinguish the superior vivacity of the image arising from the superior number, where the difference is so inconsiderable. We have a parallel instance in the affections. It is evident, according to the principles above-mentioned, that when an object produces any passion in us, which varies according to the different quantity of the object; I say, it is evident, that the passion, properly speaking, is not a simple emotion, but a compounded one, of a great number of weaker passions, derived from a view of each part of the object. For otherwise it were impossible the passion should encrease by the encrease of these parts. Thus a man, who desires a thousand pound, has in reality a thousand or more desires which uniting together, seem to make only one passion; though the composition evidently betrays itself upon every alteration of the object, by the preference he gives to the larger number, if superior only by an unite. Yet nothing can be more certain, than that so small a difference would not be discernible in the passions, nor could render them distinguishable from each other. The difference, therefore, of our conduct in preferring the greater number depends not upon our passions, but upon custom, and general rules. We have found in a multitude of instances, that the augmenting the numbers of any sum augments the passion, where the numbers are precise and the difference sensible. The mind can perceive from its immediate feeling, that three guineas produce a greater passion than two; and this it transfers to larger numbers, because of the resemblance; and by a general rule assigns to a thousand guineas, a stronger passion than to nine hundred and ninety nine. These general rules we shall explain presently.

But beside these two species of probability, which are derived from an imperfect experience and from contrary causes, there is a third arising from ANALOGY, which differs from them in some material circumstances. According to the hypothesis above explained all kinds of reasoning from causes or effects are founded on two particulars, viz., the constant conjunction of any two objects in all past experience, and the resemblance of a present object to any one of them. The effect of these two particulars is, that the present object invigorates and inlivens the imagination; and the resemblance, along with the constant union, conveys this force and vivacity to the related idea; which we are therefore said to believe, or assent to. If you weaken either the union or resemblance, you weaken the principle of transition, and of consequence that belief, which arises from it. The vivacity of the first impression cannot be fully conveyed to the related idea, either where the conjunction of their objects is not constant, or where the present impression does not perfectly resemble any of those, whose union we are accustomed to observe. In those probabilities of chance and causes above-explained, it is the constancy of the union, which is diminished; and in the probability derived from analogy, it is the resemblance only, which is affected. Without some degree of resemblance, as well as union, it is impossible there can be any reasoning: but as this resemblance admits of many different degrees, the reasoning becomes proportionably more or less firm and certain. An experiment loses of its force, when transferred to instances, which are not exactly resembling; though it is evident it may still retain as much as may be the foundation of probability, as long as there is any resemblance remaining.

SECTION XIII

Of Unphilosophical Probability

All these kinds of probability are received by philosophers, and allowed to be reasonable foundations of belief and opinion. But there are others, that are derived from the same principles, though they have not had the good fortune to obtain the same sanction. The first probability of this kind may be accounted for thus. The diminution of the union, and of the resemblance, as above explained, diminishes the facility of the transition, and by that means weakens the evidence; and we may farther observe, that the same diminution of the evidence will follow from a diminution of the impression, and from the shading of those colours, under which it appears to the memory or senses. The argument, which we found on any matter of fact we remember, is more or less convincing according as the fact is recent or remote; and though the difference in these degrees of evidence be not received by philosophy as solid and legitimate; because in that case an argument must have a different force to day, from what it shall have a month hence; yet notwithstanding the opposition of philosophy, it is certain, this circumstance has a considerable influence on the understanding, and secretly changes the authority of the same argument, according to the different times, in which it is proposed to us. A greater force and vivacity in the impression naturally conveys a greater to the related idea; and it is on the degrees of force and vivacity, that the belief depends, according to the foregoing system.

There is a second difference, which we may frequently observe in our degrees of belief and assurance, and which never fails to take place, though disclaimed by philosophers. An experiment, that is recent and fresh in the memory, affects us more than one that is in some measure obliterated; and has a superior influence on the judgment, as well as on the passions. A lively impression produces more assurance than a faint one; because it has more original force to communicate to the related idea, which thereby acquires a greater force and vivacity. A recent observation has a like effect; because the custom and transition is there more entire, and preserves better the original force in the communication. Thus a drunkard, who has seen his companion die of a debauch, is struck with that instance for some time, and dreads a like accident for himself: But as the memory of it decays away by degrees, his former security returns, and the danger seems less certain and real.

I add, as a third instance of this kind, that though our reasonings from proofs and from probabilities be considerably different from each other, yet the former species of reasoning often degenerates insensibly into the latter, by nothing but the multitude of connected arguments. It is certain, that when an inference is drawn immediately from an object, without any intermediate cause or effect, the conviction is much stronger, and the persuasion more lively, than when the imagination is carryed through a long chain of connected arguments, however infallible the connexion of each link may be esteemed. It is from the original impression, that the vivacity of all the ideas is derived, by means of the customary transition of the imagination; and it is evident this vivacity must gradually decay in proportion to the distance, and must lose somewhat in each transition. Sometimes this distance has a greater influence than even contrary experiments would have; and a man may receive a more lively conviction from a probable reasoning, which is close and immediate, than from a long chain of consequences, though just and conclusive in each part. Nay it is seldom such reasonings produce any conviction; and one must have a very strong and firm imagination to preserve the evidence to the end, where it passes through so many, stages.

But here it may not be amiss to remark a very curious phænomenon, which the present subject suggests to us. It is evident there is no point of ancient history, of which we can have any assurance, but by passing through many millions of causes and effects, and through a chain of arguments of almost an immeasurable length. Before the knowledge of the fact could come to the first historian, it must be conveyed through many mouths; and after it is committed to writing, each new copy is a new object, of which the connexion with the foregoing is known only by experience and observation. Perhaps, therefore, it may be concluded from the precedent reasoning, that the evidence of all ancient history must now be lost; or at least, will be lost in time, as the chain of causes encreases, and runs on to a greater length. But as it seems contrary to common sense to think, that if the republic of letters, and the art of printing continue on the same footing as at present, our posterity, even after a thousand ages, can ever doubt if there has been such a man as JULIUS CAESAR; this may be considered as an objection to the present system. If belief consisted only in a certain vivacity, conveyed from an original impression, it would decay by the length of the transition, and must at last be utterly extinguished: And vice versa, if belief on some occasions be not capable of such an extinction; it must be something different from that vivacity.

Before I answer this objection I shall observe, that from this topic there has been borrowed a very celebrated argument against the Christian Religion; but with this difference, that the connexion betwixt each link of the chain in human testimony has been there supposed not to go beyond probability, and to be liable to a degree of doubt and uncertainty. And indeed it must be confest, that in this manner of considering the subject, (which however is not a true one) there is no history or tradition, but what must in the end lose all its force and evidence. Every new probability diminishes the original conviction; and however great that conviction may be supposed, it is impossible it can subsist under such re-iterated diminutions. This is true in general; though we shall find afterwards,[22] that there is one very memorable exception, which is of vast consequence in the present subject of the understanding.

Mean while to give a solution of the preceding objection upon the supposition, that historical evidence amounts at first to an entire proof; let us consider, that though the links are innumerable, that connect any original fact with the present impression, which is the foundation of belief; yet they are all of the same kind, and depend on the fidelity of Printers and Copyists. One edition passes into another, and that into a third, and so on, till we come to that volume we peruse at present. There is no variation in the steps. After we know one we know all of them; and after we have made one, we can have no scruple as to the rest. This circumstance alone preserves the evidence of history, and will perpetuate the memory of the present age to the latest posterity. If all the long chain of causes and effects, which connect any past event with any volume of history, were composed of parts different from each other, and which it were necessary for the mind distinctly to conceive, it is

[22] Part IV. Sect. 1.

impossible we should preserve to the end any belief or evidence. But as most of these proofs are perfectly resembling, the mind runs easily along them, jumps from one part to another with facility, and forms but a confused and general notion of each link. By this means a long chain of argument, has as little effect in diminishing the original vivacity, as a much shorter would have, if composed of parts, which were different from each other, and of which each required a distinct consideration.

A fourth unphilosophical species of probability is that derived from general rules, which we rashly form to ourselves, and which are the source of what we properly call PREJUDICE. An IRISHMAN cannot have wit, and a Frenchman cannot have solidity; for which reason, though the conversation of the former in any instance be visibly very agreeable, and of the latter very judicious, we have entertained such a prejudice against them, that they must be dunces or fops in spite of sense and reason. Human nature is very subject to errors of this kind; and perhaps this nation as much as any other.

Should it be demanded why men form general rules, and allow them to influence their judgment, even contrary to present observation and experience, I should reply, that in my opinion it proceeds from those very principles, on which all judgments concerning causes and effects depend. Our judgments concerning cause and effect are derived from habit and experience; and when we have been accustomed to see one object united to another, our imagination passes from the first to the second, by a natural transition, which precedes reflection, and which cannot be prevented by it. Now it is the nature of custom not only to operate with its full force, when objects are presented, that are exactly the same with those to which we have been accustomed; but also to operate in an inferior degree, when we discover such as are similar; and though the habit loses somewhat of its force by every difference, yet it is seldom entirely destroyed, where any considerable circumstances remain the same. A man, who has contracted a custom of eating fruit by the use of pears or peaches, will satisfy himself with melons, where he cannot find his favourite fruit; as one, who has become a drunkard by the use of red wines, will be carried almost with the same violence to white, if presented to him. From this principle I have accounted for that species of probability, derived from analogy, where we transfer our experience in past instances to objects which are resembling, but are not exactly the same with those concerning which we have had experience. In proportion as the resemblance decays, the probability diminishes; but still has some force as long as there remain any traces of the resemblance.

This observation we may carry farther; and may remark, that though custom be the foundation of all our judgments, yet sometimes it has an effect on the imagination in opposition to the judgment, and produces a contrariety in our sentiments concerning the same object. I explain myself. In almost all kinds of causes there is a complication of circumstances, of which some are essential, and others superfluous; some are absolutely requisite to the production of the effect, and others are only conjoined by accident. Now we may observe, that when these superfluous circumstances are numerous, and remarkable, and frequently conjoined with the essential, they have such an influence on the imagination, that even in the absence of the latter they carry us on to the conception of the usual effect, and give to that conception a force and vivacity, which make it superior to the mere fictions of the fancy. We may correct this propensity by a reflection on the nature of those circumstances: but it is still certain, that custom takes the start, and gives a biass to the imagination.

To illustrate this by a familiar instance, let us consider the case of a man, who, being hung out from a high tower in a cage of iron cannot forbear trembling, when he surveys the precipice below him, though he knows himself to be perfectly secure from falling, by his experience of the solidity of the iron, which supports him; and though the ideas of fall and descent, and harm and death, be derived solely from custom and experience. The same custom goes beyond the instances, from which it is derived, and to which it perfectly corresponds; and influences his ideas of such objects as are in some respect resembling, but fall not precisely under the same rule. The circumstances of depth and descent strike so strongly upon him, that their influence can-not be destroyed by the contrary circumstances of support and solidity, which ought to give him a perfect security. His imagination runs away with its object, and excites a passion proportioned to it. That passion returns back upon the imagination and inlivens the idea; which lively idea has a new influence on the passion, and in its turn augments its force and violence; and both his fancy and affections, thus mutually supporting each other, cause the whole to have a very great influence upon him.

But why need we seek for other instances, while the present subject of philosophical probabilities offers us so obvious an one, in the opposition betwixt the judgment and imagination arising from these effects of custom? According to my system, all reasonings are nothing but the effects of custom; and custom has no influence, but by inlivening the imagination, and giving us a strong conception of any object. It may, therefore, be concluded, that our judgment and imagination can never be contrary, and that custom cannot operate on the latter faculty after such a manner, as to render it opposite to the former. This difficulty we can remove after no other manner, than by supposing the influence of general rules. We shall afterwards take[23] notice of some general rules, by which we ought to regulate our judgment concerning causes and effects; and these rules are formed on the nature of our understanding, and on our experience of its operations in the judgments we form concerning objects. By them we learn to distinguish the accidental circumstances from the efficacious causes; and when we find that an effect can be produced without the concurrence of any particular circumstance, we conclude that that circumstance makes not a part of the efficacious cause, however frequently conjoined with it. But as this frequent conjunction necessity makes

[23] Sect. 15.

it have some effect on the imagination, in spite of the opposite conclusion from general rules, the opposition of these two principles produces a contrariety in our thoughts, and causes us to ascribe the one inference to our judgment, and the other to our imagination. The general rule is attributed to our judgment; as being more extensive and constant. The exception to the imagination, as being more capricious and uncertain.

Thus our general rules are in a manner set in opposition to each other. When an object appears, that resembles any cause in very considerable circumstances, the imagination naturally carries us to a lively conception of the usual effect, Though the object be different in the most material and most efficacious circumstances from that cause. Here is the first influence of general rules. But when we take a review of this act of the mind, and compare it with the more general and authentic operations of the understanding, we find it to be of an irregular nature, and destructive of all the most established principles of reasonings; which is the cause of our rejecting it. This is a second influence of general rules, and implies the condemnation of the former. Sometimes the one, sometimes the other prevails, according to the disposition and character of the person. The vulgar are commonly guided by the first, and wise men by the second. Mean while the sceptics may here have the pleasure of observing a new and signal contradiction in our reason, and of seeing all philosophy ready to be subverted by a principle of human nature, and again saved by a new direction of the very same principle. The following of general rules is a very unphilosophical species of probability; and yet it is only by following them that we can correct this, and all other unphilosophical probabilities.

Since we have instances, where general rules operate on the imagination even contrary to the judgment, we need not be surprized to see their effects encrease, when conjoined with that latter faculty, and to observe that they bestow on the ideas they present to us a force superior to what attends any other. Every one knows, there is an indirect manner of insinuating praise or blame, which is much less shocking than the open flattery or censure of any person. However he may communicate his sentiments by such secret insinuations, and make them known with equal certainty as by the open discovery of them, it is certain that their influence is not equally strong and powerful. One who lashes me with concealed strokes of satire, moves not my indignation to such a degree, as if he flatly told me I was a fool and coxcomb; though I equally understand his meaning, as if he did. This difference is to be attributed to the influence of general rules.

Whether a person openly, abuses me, or slyly intimates his contempt, in neither case do I immediately perceive his sentiment or opinion; and it is only by signs, that is, by its effects, I become sensible of it. The only difference, then, betwixt these two cases consists in this, that in the open discovery of his sentiments he makes use of signs, which are general and universal; and in the secret intimation employs such as are more singular and uncommon. The effect of this circumstance is, that the imagination, in running from the present impression to the absent idea, makes the transition with greater facility, and consequently conceives the object with greater force, where the connexion is common and universal, than where it is more rare and particular. Accordingly we may observe, that the open declaration of our sentiments is called the taking off the mask, as the secret intimation of our opinions is said to be the veiling of them. The difference betwixt an idea produced by a general connexion, and that arising from a particular one is here compared to the difference betwixt an impression and an idea. This difference in the imagination has a suitable effect on the passions; and this effect is augmented by another circumstance. A secret intimation of anger or contempt shews that we still have some consideration for the person, and avoid the directly abusing him. This makes a concealed satire less disagreeable; but still this depends on the same principle. For if an idea were not more feeble, when only intimated, it would never be esteemed a mark of greater respect to proceed in this method than in the other.

Sometimes scurrility is less displeasing than delicate satire, because it revenges us in a manner for the injury at the very time it is committed, by affording us a just reason to blame and contemn the person, who injures us. But this phænomenon likewise depends upon the same principle. For why do we blame all gross and injurious language, unless it be, because we esteem it contrary to good breeding and humanity? And why is it contrary, unless it be more shocking than any delicate satire? The rules of good breeding condemn whatever is openly disobliging, and gives a sensible pain and confusion to those, with whom we converse. After this is once established, abusive language is universally blamed, and gives less pain upon account of its coarseness and incivility, which render the person despicable, that employs it. It becomes less disagreeable, merely because originally it is more so; and it is more disagreeable, because it affords an inference by general and common rules, that are palpable and undeniable.

To this explication of the different influence of open and concealed flattery or satire, I shall add the consideration of another phenomenon, which is analogous to it. There are many particulars in the point of honour both of men and women, whose violations, when open and avowed, the world never excuses, but which it is more apt to overlook, when the appearances are saved, and the transgression is secret and concealed. Even those, who know with equal certainty, that the fault is committed, pardon it more easily, when the proofs seem in some measure oblique and equivocal, than when they are direct and undeniable. The same idea is presented in both cases, and, properly speaking, is equally assented to by the judgment; and yet its influence is different, because of the different manner, in which it is presented.

Now if we compare these two cases, of the open and concealed violations of the laws of honour, we shall find, that the difference betwixt them consists in this, that in the first ease the sign, from which we infer the blameable action, is single, and suffices alone to be the foundation of our reasoning and judgment; whereas in the latter the signs are numerous, and decide little or nothing when alone and unaccompanyed with many minute circumstances, which are almost imperceptible. But it is certainly true, that any reasoning is always the more convincing, the more single and united it is to the eye, and the less exercise it gives to the imagination to collect all its parts, and run from them to the correlative idea, which forms the conclusion. The labour of the thought disturbs the regular progress of the sentiments, as we shall observe presently.[24] The idea strikes not on us with ouch vivacity; and consequently has no such influence on the passion and imagination.

From the same principles we may account for those observations of the CARDINAL DE RETZ, that there are many things, in which the world wishes to be deceived; and that it more easily excuses a person in acting than in talking contrary to the decorum of his profession and character. A fault in words is commonly more open and distinct than one in actions, which admit of many palliating excuses, and decide not so clearly concerning the intention and views of the actor.

Thus it appears upon the whole, that every kind of opinion or judgment, which amounts not to knowledge, is derived entirely from the force and vivacity of the perception, and that these qualities constitute in the mind, what we call the BELIEF Of the existence of any object. This force and this vivacity are most conspicuous in the memory; and therefore our confidence in the veracity of that faculty is the greatest imaginable, and equals in many respects the assurance of a demonstration. The next degree of these qualities is that derived from the relation of cause and effect; and this too is very great, especially when the conjunction is found by experience to be perfectly constant, and when the object, which is present to us, exactly resembles those, of which we have had experience. But below this degree of evidence there are many others, which have an influence on the passions and imagination, proportioned to that degree of force and vivacity, which they communicate to the ideas. It is by habit we make the transition from cause to effect; and it is from some present impression we borrow that vivacity, which we diffuse over the correlative idea. But when we have not observed a sufficient number of instances, to produce a strong habit; or when these instances are contrary to each other; or when the resemblance is not exact; or the present impression is faint and obscure; or the experience in some measure obliterated from the memory; or the connexion dependent on a long chain of objects; or the inference derived from general rules, and yet not conformable to them: In all these cases the evidence diminishes by the diminution of the force and intenseness of the idea. This therefore is the nature of the judgment and probability.

What principally gives authority to this system is, beside the undoubted arguments, upon which each part is founded, the agreement of these parts, and the necessity of one to explain another. The belief, which attends our memory, is of the same nature with that, which is derived from our judgments: Nor is there any difference betwixt that judgment, which is derived from a constant

[24] Part IV. Sect. 1.

and uniform connexion of causes and effects, and that which depends upon an interrupted and uncertain. It is indeed evident, that in all determinations, where the mind decides from contrary experiments, it is first divided within itself, and has an inclination to either side in proportion to the number of experiments we have seen and remember. This contest is at last determined to the advantage of that side, where we observe a superior number of these experiments; but still with a diminution of force in the evidence correspondent to the number of the opposite experiments. Each possibility, of which the probability is composed, operates separately upon the imagination; and it is the larger collection of possibilities, which at last prevails, and that with a force proportionable to its superiority. All these phenomena lead directly to the precedent system; nor will it ever be possible upon any other principles to give a satisfactory and consistent explication of them. Without considering these judgments as the effects of custom on the imagination, we shall lose ourselves in perpetual contradiction and absurdity.

SECTION XIV

Of the Idea of Necessary Connexion

Having thus explained the manner, in which we reason beyond our immediate impressions, and conclude that such particular causes must have such particular effects; we must now return upon our footsteps to examine that question, which[25] first occured to us, and which we dropt in our way, viz. What is our idea of necessity, when we say that two objects are necessarily connected together. Upon this head I repeat what I have often had occasion to observe, that as we have no idea, that is not derived from an impression, we must find some impression, that gives rise to this idea of necessity, if we assert we have really such an idea. In order to this I consider, in what objects necessity is commonly supposed to lie; and finding that it is always ascribed to causes and effects, I turn my eye to two objects supposed to be placed in that relation; and examine them in all the situations, of which they are susceptible. I immediately perceive, that they are contiguous in time and place, and that the object we call cause precedes the other we call effect. In no one instance can I go any farther, nor is it possible for me to discover any third relation betwixt these objects. I therefore enlarge my view to comprehend several instances; where I find like objects always existing in like relations of contiguity and succession. At first sight this seems to serve but little to my purpose. The reflection on several instances only repeats the same objects; and therefore can never give rise to a new idea. But upon farther enquiry I find, that the repetition is not in every particular the same, but produces a new impression, and by that means the idea, which I at present examine. For after a frequent repetition, I find, that upon the appearance of one of the objects, the mind is determined by custom to consider its usual

[25] Sect. 2.

attendant, and to consider it in a stronger light upon account of its relation to the first object. It is this impression, then, or determination, which affords me the idea of necessity.

I doubt not but these consequences will at first sight be received without difficulty, as being evident deductions from principles, which we have already established, and which we have often employed in our reasonings. This evidence both in the first principles, and in the deductions, may seduce us unwarily into the conclusion, and make us imagine it contains nothing extraordinary, nor worthy of our curiosity. But though such an inadvertence may facilitate the reception of this reasoning, it will make it be the more easily forgot; for which reason I think it proper to give warning, that I have just now examined one of the most sublime questions in philosophy, viz. that concerning the power and efficacy of causes; where all the sciences seem so much interested. Such a warning will naturally rouze up the attention of the reader, and make him desire a more full account of my doctrine, as well as of the arguments, on which it is founded. This request is so reasonable, that I cannot refuse complying with it; especially as I am hopeful that these principles, the more they are examined, will acquire the more force and evidence.

There is no question, which on account of its importance, as well as difficulty, has caused more disputes both among antient and modern philosophers, than this concerning the efficacy of causes, or that quality which makes them be followed by their effects. But before they entered upon these disputes, methinks it would not have been improper to have examined what idea we have of that efficacy, which is the subject of the controversy. This is what I find principally wanting in their reasonings, and what I shall here endeavour to supply.

I begin with observing that the terms of EFFICACY, AGENCY, POWER, FORCE, ENERGY, NECESSITY, CONNEXION, and PRODUCTIVE QUALITY, are all nearly synonymous; and therefore it is an absurdity to employ any of them in defining the rest. By this observation we reject at once all the vulgar definitions, which philosophers have given of power and efficacy; and instead of searching for the idea in these definitions, must look for it in the impressions, from which it is originally derived. If it be a compound idea, it must arise from compound impressions. If simple, from simple impressions.

I believe the most general and most popular explication of this matter, is to say,[26] that finding from experience, that there are several new productions in matter, such as the motions and variations of body, and concluding that there must somewhere be a power capable of producing them, we arrive at last by this reasoning at the idea of power and efficacy. But to be convinced that this explication is more popular than philosophical, we need but reflect on two very obvious principles. First, that reason alone can never give rise to any original idea, and secondly, that reason, as distinguished from experience, can never make us conclude, that a cause or

[26] See Mr. Locke, chapter of power.

productive quality is absolutely requisite to every beginning of existence. Both these considerations have been sufficiently explained: and therefore shall not at present be any farther insisted on.

I shall only infer from them, that since reason can never give rise to the idea of efficacy, that idea must be derived from experience, and from some particular instances of this efficacy, which make their passage into the mind by the common channels of sensation or reflection. Ideas always represent their objects or impressions; and vice versa, there are some objects necessary to give rise to every idea. If we pretend, therefore, to have any just idea of this efficacy, we must produce some instance, wherein the efficacy is plainly discoverable to the mind, and its operations obvious to our consciousness or sensation. By the refusal of this, we acknowledge, that the idea is impossible and imaginary, since the principle of innate ideas, which alone can save us from this dilemma, has been already refuted, and is now almost universally rejected in the learned world. Our present business, then, must be to find some natural production, where the operation and efficacy of a cause can be clearly conceived and comprehended by the mind, without any danger of obscurity or mistake.

In this research we meet with very little encouragement from that prodigious diversity, which is found in the opinions of those philosophers, who have pretended to explain the secret force and energy of causes.[27] There are some, who maintain, that bodies operate by their substantial form; others, by their accidents or qualities; several, by their matter and form; some, by their form and accidents; others, by certain virtues and faculties distinct from all this. All these sentiments again are mixed and varyed in a thousand different ways; and form a strong presumption, that none of them have any solidity or evidence, and that the supposition of an efficacy in any of the known qualities of matter is entirely without foundation. This presumption must encrease upon us, when we consider, that these principles of substantial forms, and accidents, and faculties, are not in reality any of the known properties of bodies, but are perfectly unintelligible and inexplicable. For it is evident philosophers would never have had recourse to such obscure and uncertain principles, had they met with any satisfaction in such as are clear and intelligible; especially in such an affair as this, which must be an object of the simplest understanding, if not of the senses. Upon the whole, we may conclude, that it is impossible in any one instance to shew the principle, in which the force and agency of a cause is placed; and that the most refined and most vulgar understandings are equally at a loss in this particular. If any one think proper to refute this assertion, he need not put himself to the trouble of inventing any long reasonings: but may at once shew us an instance of a cause, where we discover the power or operating principle. This defiance we are obliged frequently to make use of, as being almost the only means of proving a negative in philosophy.

[27] See Father Malbranche, Book vi. Part 2, chap. 3. And the illustrations upon it.

The small success, which has been met with in all the attempts to fix this power, has at last obliged philosophers to conclude, that the ultimate force and efficacy of nature is perfectly unknown to us, and that it is in vain we search for it in all the known qualities of matter. In this opinion they are almost unanimous; and it is only in the inference they draw from it, that they discover any difference in their sentiments. For some of them, as the CARTESIANS in particular, having established it as a principle, that we are perfectly acquainted with the essence of matter, have very naturally inferred, that it is endowed with no efficacy, and that it is impossible for it of itself to communicate motion, or produce any of those effects, which we ascribe to it. As the essence of matter consists in extension, and as extension implies not actual motion, but only mobility; they conclude, that the energy, which produces the motion, cannot lie in the extension.

This conclusion leads them into another, which they regard as perfectly unavoidable. Matter, say they, is in itself entirely unactive, and deprived of any power, by which it may produce, or continue, or communicate motion: But since these effects are evident to our senses, and since the power, that produces them, must be placed somewhere, it must lie in the DEITY, or that divine being, who contains in his nature all excellency and perfection. It is the deity, therefore, who is the prime mover of the universe, and who not only first created matter, and gave it it's original impulse, but likewise by a continued exertion of omnipotence, supports its existence, and successively bestows on it all those motions, and configurations, and qualities, with which it is endowed.

This opinion is certainly very curious, and well worth our attention; but it will appear superfluous to examine it in this place, if we reflect a moment on our present purpose in taking notice of it. We have established it as a principle, that as all ideas are derived from impressions, or some precedent perceptions, it is impossible we can have any idea of power and efficacy, unless some instances can be produced, wherein this power is perceived to exert itself. Now, as these instances can never be discovered in body, the Cartesians, proceeding upon their principle of innate ideas, have had recourse to a supreme spirit or deity, whom they consider as the only active being in the universe, and as the immediate cause of every alteration in matter. But the principle of innate ideas being allowed to be false, it follows, that the supposition of a deity can serve us in no stead, in accounting for that idea of agency, which we search for in vain in all the objects, which are presented to our senses, or which we are internally conscious of in our own minds. For if every idea be derived from an impression, the idea of a deity proceeds from the same origin; and if no impression, either of sensation or reflection, implies any force or efficacy, it is equally impossible to discover or even imagine any such active principle in the deity. Since these philosophers, therefore, have concluded, that matter cannot be endowed with any efficacious principle, because it is impossible to discover in it such a principle; the same course of reasoning should determine them to exclude it from the supreme being. Or if they esteem that opinion absurd and impious, as it really is, I shall tell them how they may avoid it; and that is, by concluding from the very first, that they have no adequate idea of power or efficacy in any object; since neither in body nor spirit, neither in superior nor inferior natures, are they able to discover one single instance of it.

The same conclusion is unavoidable upon the hypothesis of those, who maintain the efficacy of second causes, and attribute a derivative, but a real power and energy to matter. For as they confess, that this energy lies not in any of the known qualities of matter, the difficulty still remains concerning the origin of its idea. If we have really an idea of power, we may attribute power to an unknown quality: But as it is impossible, that that idea can be derived from such a quality, and as there is nothing in known qualities, which can produce it; it follows that we deceive ourselves, when we imagine we are possest of any idea of this kind, after the manner we commonly understand it. All ideas are derived from, and represent impressions. We never have any impression, that contains any power or efficacy. We never therefore have any idea of power.

Some have asserted, that we feel an energy, or power, in our own mind; and that having in this manner acquired the idea of power, we transfer that quality to matter, where we are not able immediately to discover it. The motions of our body, and the thoughts and sentiments of our mind, (say they) obey the will; nor do we seek any farther to acquire a just notion of force or power. But to convince us how fallacious this reasoning is, we need only consider, that the will being here considered as a cause, has no more a discoverable connexion with its effects, than any material cause has with its proper effect. So far from perceiving the connexion betwixt an act of volition, and a motion of the body; it is allowed that no effect is more inexplicable from the powers and essence of thought and matter. Nor is the empire of the will over our mind more intelligible. The effect is there distinguishable and separable from the cause, and could not be foreseen without the experience of their constant conjunction. We have command over our mind to a certain degree, but beyond that, lose all empire over it: And it is evidently impossible to fix any precise bounds to our authority, where we consult not experience. In short, the actions of the mind are, in this respect, the same with those of matter. We perceive only their constant conjunction; nor can we ever reason beyond it. No internal impression has an apparent energy, more than external objects have. Since, therefore, matter is confessed by philosophers to operate by an unknown force, we should in vain hope to attain an idea of force by consulting our own minds.[28]

It has been established as a certain principle, that general or abstract ideas are nothing but individual ones taken in a certain light, and that, in reflecting on any

[28] The same imperfection attends our ideas of the Deity; but this can have no effect either on religion or morals. The order of the universe proves an omnipotent mind; that is, a mind whose will is CONSTANTLY ATTENDED with the obedience of every creature and being. Nothing more is requisite to give a foundation to all the articles of religion, nor is It necessary we shoud form a distinct idea of the force and energy of the supreme Being.

object, it is as impossible to exclude from our thought all particular degrees of quantity and quality as from the real nature of things. If we be possest, therefore, of any idea of power in general, we must also be able to conceive some particular species of it; and as power cannot subsist alone, but is always regarded as an attribute of some being or existence, we must be able to place this power in some particular being, and conceive that being as endowed with a real force and energy, by which such a particular effect necessarily results from its operation. We must distinctly and particularly conceive the connexion betwixt the cause and effect, and be able to pronounce, from a simple view of the one, that it must be followed or preceded by the other. This is the true manner of conceiving a particular power in a particular body: and a general idea being impossible without an individual; where the latter is impossible, it is certain the former can never exist. Now nothing is more evident, than that the human mind cannot form such an idea of two objects, as to conceive any connexion betwixt them, or comprehend distinctly that power or efficacy, by which they are united. Such a connexion would amount to a demonstration, and would imply the absolute impossibility for the one object not to follow, or to be conceived not to follow upon the other: Which kind of connexion has already been rejected in all cases. If any one is of a contrary opinion, and thinks he has attained a notion of power in any particular object, I desire he may point out to me that object. But till I meet with such-a-one, which I despair of, I cannot forbear concluding, that since we can never distinctly conceive how any particular power can possibly reside in any particular object, we deceive ourselves in imagining we can form any such general idea.

Thus upon the whole we may infer, that when we talk of any being, whether of a superior or inferior nature, as endowed with a power or force, proportioned to any effect; when we speak of a necessary connexion betwixt objects, and suppose, that this connexion depends upon an efficacy or energy, with which any of these objects are endowed; in all these expressions, so applied, we have really no distinct meaning, and make use only of common words, without any clear and determinate ideas. But as it is more probable, that these expressions do here lose their true meaning by being wrong applied, than that they never have any meaning; it will be proper to bestow another consideration on this subject, to see if possibly we can discover the nature and origin of those ideas, we annex to them.

Suppose two objects to be presented to us, of which the one is the cause and the other the effect; it is plain, that from the simple consideration of one, or both these objects we never shall perceive the tie by which they are united, or be able certainly to pronounce, that there is a connexion betwixt them. It is not, therefore, from any one instance, that we arrive at the idea of cause and effect, of a necessary connexion of power, of force, of energy, and of efficacy. Did we never see any but particular conjunctions of objects, entirely different from each other, we should never be able to form any such ideas.

But again; suppose we observe several instances, in which the same objects are always conjoined together, we immediately conceive a connexion betwixt them, and begin to draw an inference from one to another. This multiplicity of resembling instances, therefore, constitutes the very essence of power or connexion, and is the source from which the idea of it arises. In order, then, to understand the idea of power, we must consider that multiplicity; nor do I ask more to give a solution of that difficulty, which has so long perplexed us. For thus I reason. The repetition of perfectly similar instances can never alone give rise to an original idea, different from what is to be found in any particular instance, as has been observed, and as evidently follows from our fundamental principle, that all ideas are copyed from impressions. Since therefore the idea of power is a new original idea, not to be found in any one instance, and which yet arises from the repetition of several instances, it follows, that the repetition alone has not that effect, but must either discover or produce something new, which is the source of that idea. Did the repetition neither discover nor produce anything new, our ideas might be multiplyed by it, but would not be enlarged above what they are upon the observation of one single instance. Every enlargement, therefore, (such as the idea of power or connexion) which arises from the multiplicity of similar instances, is copyed from some effects of the multiplicity, and will be perfectly understood by understanding these effects. Wherever we find anything new to be discovered or produced by the repetition, there we must place the power, and must never look for it in any other object.

But it is evident, in the first place, that the repetition of like objects in like relations of succession and contiguity discovers nothing new in any one of them: since we can draw no inference from it, nor make it a subject either of our demonstrative or probable reasonings;[29] as has been already proved. Nay suppose we could draw an inference, it would be of no consequence in the present case; since no kind of reasoning can give rise to a new idea, such as this of power is; but wherever we reason, we must antecedently be possest of clear ideas, which may be the objects of our reasoning. The conception always precedes the understanding; and where the one is obscure, the other is uncertain; where the one fails, the other must fail also.

Secondly, It is certain that this repetition of similar objects in similar situations produces nothing new either in these objects, or in any external body. For it will readily be allowed, that the several instances we have of the conjunction of resembling causes and effects are in themselves entirely independent, and that the communication of motion, which I see result at present from the shock of two billiard-balls, is totally distinct from that which I saw result from such an impulse a twelve-month ago. These impulses have no influence on each other. They are entirely divided by time and place; and the one might have existed and communicated motion, though the other never had been in being.

There is, then, nothing new either discovered or produced in any objects by their constant conjunction, and by the uninterrupted resemblance of their relations

[29] Sect. 6.

of succession and contiguity. But it is from this resemblance, that the ideas of necessity, of power, and of efficacy, are derived. These ideas, therefore, represent not anything, that does or can belong to the objects, which are constantly conjoined. This is an argument, which, in every view we can examine it, will be found perfectly unanswerable. Similar instances are still the first source of our idea of power or necessity; at the same time that they have no influence by their similarity either on each other, or on any external object. We must, therefore, turn ourselves to some other quarter to seek the origin of that idea.

Though the several resembling instances, which give rise to the idea of power, have no influence on each other, and can never produce any new quality in the object, which can be the model of that idea, yet the observation of this resemblance produces a new impression in the mind, which is its real model. For after we have observed the resemblance in a sufficient number of instances, we immediately feel a determination of the mind to pass from one object to its usual attendant, and to conceive it in a stronger light upon account of that relation. This determination is the only effect of the resemblance; and therefore must be the same with power or efficacy, whose idea is derived from the resemblance. The several instances of resembling conjunctions lead us into the notion of power and necessity. These instances are in themselves totally distinct from each other, and have no union but in the mind, which observes them, and collects their ideas. Necessity, then, is the effect of this observation, and is nothing but an internal impression of the mind, or a determination to carry our thoughts from one object to another. Without considering it in this view, we can never arrive at the most distant notion of it, or be able to attribute it either to external or internal objects, to spirit or body, to causes or effects.

The necessary connexion betwixt causes and effects is the foundation of our inference from one to the other. The foundation of our inference is the transition arising from the accustomed union. These are, therefore, the same.

The idea of necessity arises from some impression. There is no impression conveyed by our senses, which can give rise to that idea. It must, therefore, be derived from some internal impression, or impression of reflection. There is no internal impression, which has any relation to the present business, but that propensity, which custom produces, to pass from an object to the idea of its usual attendant. This therefore is the essence of necessity. Upon the whole, necessity is something, that exists in the mind, not in objects; nor is it possible for us ever to form the most distant idea of it, considered as a quality in bodies. Either we have no idea of necessity, or necessity is nothing but that determination of the thought to pass from causes to effects, and from effects to causes, according to their experienced union.

Thus as the necessity, which makes two times two equal to four, or three angles of a triangle equal to two right ones, lies only in the act of the understanding, by which we consider and compare these ideas; in like manner the necessity or power, which unites causes and effects, lies in the determination of the mind to pass from the one to the other. The efficacy or energy of causes is neither placed in the causes themselves, nor in the deity, nor in the concurrence of these two principles; but belongs entirely to the soul, which considers the union of two or more objects in all past instances. It is here that the real power of causes is placed along with their connexion and necessity.

I am sensible, that of all the paradoxes, which I, have had, or shall hereafter have occasion to advance in the course of this treatise, the present one is the most violent, and that it is merely by dint of solid proof and reasoning I can ever hope it will have admission, and overcome the inveterate prejudices of mankind. Before we are reconciled to this doctrine, how often must we repeat to ourselves, that the simple view of any two objects or actions, however related, can never give us any idea, of power, or of a connexion betwixt them: that this idea arises from the repetition of their union: that the repetition neither discovers nor causes any thing in the objects, but has an influence only on the mind, by that customary transition it produces: that this customary transition is, therefore, the same with the power and necessity; which are consequently qualities of perceptions, not of objects, and are internally felt by the soul, and not perceivd externally in bodies? There is commonly an astonishment attending every thing extraordinary; and this astonishment changes immediately into the highest degree of esteem or contempt, according as we approve or disapprove of the subject. I am much afraid, that though the foregoing reasoning appears to me the shortest and most decisive imaginable; yet with the generality of readers the biass of the mind will prevail, and give them a prejudice against the present doctrine.

This contrary biass is easily accounted for. It is a common observation, that the mind has a great propensity to spread itself on external objects, and to conjoin with them any internal impressions, which they occasion, and which always make their appearance at the same time that these objects discover themselves to the senses. Thus as certain sounds and smells are always found to attend certain visible objects, we naturally imagine a conjunction, even in place, betwixt the objects and qualities, though the qualities be of such a nature as to admit of no such conjunction, and really exist no where. But of this more fully hereafter.[30] Mean while it is sufficient to observe, that the same propensity is the reason, why we suppose necessity and power to lie in the objects we consider, not in our mind that considers them; notwithstanding it is not possible for us to form the most distant idea of that quality, when it is not taken for the determination of the mind, to pass from the idea of an object to that of its usual attendant.

But though this be the only reasonable account we can give of necessity, the contrary notion if; so riveted in the mind from the principles above-mentioned, that I doubt not but my sentiments will be treated by many as extravagant and ridiculous.

[30] Part IV, Sect. 5.

What! the efficacy of causes lie in the determination of the mind! As if causes did not operate entirely independent of the mind, and would not continue their operation, even though there was no mind existent to contemplate them, or reason concerning them. Thought may well depend on causes for its operation, but not causes on thought. This is to reverse the order of nature, and make that secondary, which is really primary, To every operation there is a power proportioned; and this power must be placed on the body, that operates. If we remove the power from one cause, we must ascribe it to another: But to remove it from all causes, and bestow it on a being, that is no ways related to the cause or effect, but by perceiving them, is a gross absurdity, and contrary to the most certain principles of human reason.

I can only reply to all these arguments, that the case is here much the same, as if a blind man should pretend to find a great many absurdities in the supposition, that the colour of scarlet is not the same with the sound of a trumpet, nor light the same with solidity. If we have really no idea of a power or efficacy in any object, or of any real connexion betwixt causes and effects, it will be to little purpose to prove, that an efficacy is necessary in all operations. We do not understand our own meaning in talking so, but ignorantly confound ideas, which are entirely distinct from each other. I am, indeed, ready to allow, that there may be several qualities both in material and immaterial objects, with which we are utterly unacquainted; and if we please to call these POWER or EFFICACY, it will be of little consequence to the world. But when, instead of meaning these unknown qualities, we make the terms of power and efficacy signify something, of which we have a clear idea, and which is incompatible with those objects, to which we apply it, obscurity and error begin then to take place, and we are led astray by a false philosophy. This is the case, when we transfer the determination of the thought to external objects, and suppose any real intelligible connexion betwixt them; that being a quality, which can only belong to the mind that considers them.

As to what may be said, that the operations of nature are independent of our thought and reasoning, I allow it; and accordingly have observed, that objects bear to each other the relations of contiguity and succession: that like objects may be observed in several instances to have like relations; and that all this is independent of, and antecedent to the operations of the understanding. But if we go any farther, and ascribe a power or necessary connexion to these objects; this is what we can never observe in them, but must draw the idea of it from what we feel internally in contemplating them. And this I carry so far, that I am ready to convert my present reasoning into an instance of it, by a subtility, which it will not be difficult to comprehend.

When any object is presented to us, it immediately conveys to the mind a lively idea of that object, which is usually found to attend it; and this determination of the mind forms the necessary connexion of these objects. But when we change the point of view, from the objects to the perceptions; in that case the impression is to be considered as the cause, and the lively idea as the effect; and their necessary connexion is that new determination, which we feel to pass from the idea of the one to that of the other. The uniting principle among our internal perceptions is as unintelligible as that among external objects, and is not known to us any other way than by experience. Now the nature and effects of experience have been already sufficiently examined and explained. It never gives us any insight into the internal structure or operating principle of objects, but only accustoms the mind to pass from one to another.

It is now time to collect all the different parts of this reasoning, and by joining them together form an exact definition of the relation of cause and effect, which makes the subject of the present enquiry. This order would not have been excusable, of first examining our inference from the relation before we had explained the relation itself, had it been possible to proceed in a different method. But as the nature of the relation depends so much on that of the inference, we have been obliged to advance in this seemingly preposterous manner, and make use of terms before we were able exactly to define them, or fix their meaning. We shall now correct this fault by giving a precise definition of cause and effect.

There may two definitions be given of this relation, which are only different, by their presenting a different view of the same object, and making us consider it either as a philosophical or as a natural relation; either as a comparison of two ideas, or as an association betwixt them. We may define a CAUSE to be An object precedent and contiguous to another, and where all the objects resembling the former are placed in like relations of precedency and contiguity to those objects that resemble the latter. I If this definition be esteemed defective, because drawn from objects foreign to the cause, we may substitute this other definition in its place, viz. A CAUSE is an object precedent and contiguous to another, and so united with it, that the idea, of the one determines the mind to form the idea of the other, and the impression of the one to form a more lively idea of the other. 2 should this definition also be rejected for the same reason, I know no other remedy, than that the persons, who express this delicacy, should substitute a juster definition in its place. But for my part I must own my incapacity for such an undertaking. When I examine with the utmost accuracy those objects, which are commonly denominated causes and effects, I find, in considering a single instance, that the one object is precedent and contiguous to the other; and in inlarging my view to consider several instances, I find only, that like objects are constantly placed in like relations of succession and contiguity. Again, when I consider the influence of this constant conjunction, I perceive, that such a relation can never be an object of reasoning, and can never operate upon the mind, but by means of custom, which determines the imagination to make a transition from the idea of one object to that of its usual attendant, and from the impression of one to a more lively idea of the other. However extraordinary these sentiments may appear, I think it fruitless to trouble myself with any farther enquiry or reasoning upon the subject, but shall repose myself on them as on established maxims.

It will only be proper, before we leave this subject, to draw some corrollaries from it, by which we may remove several prejudices and popular errors, that have very much prevailed in philosophy. First, We may learn from the foregoing, doctrine, that all causes are of the same kind, and that in particular there is no foundation for that distinction, which we sometimes make betwixt efficient causes and causes sine qua non; or betwixt efficient causes, and formal, and material, and exemplary, and final causes. For as our idea of efficiency is derived from the constant conjunction of two objects, wherever this is observed, the cause is efficient; and where it is not, there can never be a cause of any kind. For the same reason we must reject the distinction betwixt cause and occasion, when supposed to signify any thing essentially different from each other. If constant conjunction be implyed in what we call occasion, it is a real cause. If not, it is no relation at all, and cannot give rise to any argument or reasoning.

Secondly, The same course of reasoning will make us conclude, that there is but one kind of necessity, as there is but one kind of cause, and that the common distinction betwixt moral and physical necessity is without any foundation in nature. This clearly appears from the precedent explication of necessity. It is the constant conjunction of objects, along with the determination of the mind, which constitutes a physical necessity: And the removal of these is the same thing with chance. As objects must either be conjoined or not, and as the mind must either be determined or not to pass from one object to another, it is impossible to admit of any medium betwixt chance and an absolute necessity. In weakening this conjunction and determination you do not change the nature of the necessity; since even in the operation of bodies, these have different degrees of constancy and force, without producing a different species of that relation.

The distinction, which we often make betwixt POWER and the EXERCISE of it, is equally without foundation.

Thirdly, We may now be able fully to overcome all that repugnance, which it is so natural for us to entertain against the foregoing reasoning, by which we endeavoured to prove, that the necessity of a cause to every beginning of existence is not founded on any arguments either demonstrative or intuitive. Such an opinion will not appear strange after the foregoing definitions. If we define a cause to be an object precedent and contiguous to another, and where all the objects resembling the farmer are placed in a like relation of priority and contiguity to those objects, that resemble the latter; we may easily conceive, that there is no absolute nor metaphysical necessity, that every beginning of existence should be attended with such an object. If we define a cause to be, AN OBJECT PRECEDENT AND CONTIGUOUS TO ANOTHER, AND SO UNITED WITH IT IN THE IMAGINATION, THAT THE IDEA OF THE ONE DETERMINES THE MIND TO FORM THE IDEA OF THE OTHER, AND THE IMPRESSION OF THE ONE TO FORM A MORE LIVELY IDEA OF THE OTHER; we shall make still less difficulty of assenting to this opinion. Such an influence on the mind is in itself perfectly extraordinary and incomprehensible; nor can we be certain of its reality, but from experience and observation.

I shall add as a fourth corrollary that we can never have reason to believe that any object exists, of which we cannot form an idea. For as all our reasonings concerning existence are derived from causation, and as all our reasonings concerning causation are derived from the experienced conjunction of objects, not from any reasoning or reflection, the same experience must give us a notion of these objects, and must remove all mystery from our conclusions. This is so evident, that it would scarce have merited our attention, were it not to obviate certain objections of this kind, which might arise against the following reasonings concerning matter and substance. I need not observe, that a full knowledge of the object is not requisite, but only of those qualities of it, which we believe to exist.

SECTION XV

Rules by which to Judge of Causes and Effects

According to the precedent doctrine, there are no objects which by the mere survey, without consulting experience, we can determine to be the causes of any other; and no objects, which we can certainly determine in the same manner not to be the causes. Any thing may produce any thing. Creation, annihilation, motion, reason, volition; all these may arise from one another, or from any other object we can imagine. Nor will this appear strange, if we compare two principles explained above, THAT THE CONSTANT CONJUNCTION OF OBJECTS DETERMINES THEIR CAUSATION, AND[31] THAT, PROPERTY SPEAKING, NO OBJECTS ARE CONTRARY TO EACH OTHER BUT EXISTENCE AND NON-EXISTENCE. Where objects are not contrary, nothing hinders them from having that constant conjunction, on which the relation of cause and effect totally depends.

Since therefore it is possible for all objects to become causes or effects to each other, it may be proper to fix some general rules, by which we may know when they really are so.

(1) The cause and effect must be contiguous in space and time.

(2) The cause must be prior to the effect.

(3) There must be a constant union betwixt the cause and effect. It is chiefly this quality, that constitutes the relation.

(4) The same cause always produces the same effect, and the same effect never arises but from the same cause. This principle we derive from experience, and is the source of most of our philosophical reasonings. For when by any clear experiment we have discovered the causes or effects of any phænomenon, we immediately extend our observation to every phenomenon of the same kind, without waiting for that constant repetition, from which the first idea of this relation is derived.

---

[31] Part I. Sect. 5.

(5) There is another principle, which hangs upon this, viz. that where several different objects produce the same effect, it must be by means of some quality, which we discover to be common amongst them. For as like effects imply like causes, we must always ascribe the causation to the circumstance, wherein we discover the resemblance.

(6) The following principle is founded on the same reason. The difference in the effects of two resembling objects must proceed from that particular, in which they differ. For as like causes always produce like effects, when in any instance we find our expectation to be disappointed, we must conclude that this irregularity proceeds from some difference in the causes.

(7) When any object encreases or diminishes with the encrease or diminution of its cause, it is to be regarded as a compounded effect, derived from the union of the several different effects, which arise from the several different parts of the cause. The absence or presence of one part of the cause is here supposed to be always attended with the absence or presence of a proportionable part of the effect. This constant conjunction sufficiently proves, that the one part is the cause of the other. We must, however, beware not to draw such a conclusion from a few experiments. A certain degree of heat gives pleasure; if you diminish that heat, the pleasure diminishes; but it does not follow, that if you augment it beyond a certain degree, the pleasure will likewise augment; for we find that it degenerates into pain.

(8) The eighth and last rule I shall take notice of is, that an object, which exists for any time in its full perfection without any effect, is not the sole cause of that effect, but requires to be assisted by some other principle, which may forward its influence and operation. For as like effects necessarily follow from like causes, and in a contiguous time and place, their separation for a moment shews, that these causes are not compleat ones.

Here is all the LOGIC I think proper to employ in my reasoning; and perhaps even this was not very necessary, but might have been supplyd by the natural principles of our understanding. Our scholastic head-pieces and logicians shew no such superiority above the mere vulgar in their reason and ability, as to give us any inclination to imitate them in delivering a long system of rules and precepts to direct our judgment, in philosophy. All the rules of this nature are very easy in their invention, but extremely difficult in their application; and even experimental philosophy, which seems the most natural and simple of any, requires the utmost stretch of human judgment. There is no phænomenon in nature, but what is compounded and modifyd by so many different circumstances, that in order to arrive at the decisive point, we must carefully separate whatever is superfluous, and enquire by new experiments, if every particular circumstance of the first experiment was essential to it. These new experiments are liable to a discussion of the same kind; so that the utmost constancy is requird to make us persevere in our enquiry, and the utmost sagacity to choose the right way among so many that present themselves. If this be the case even in natural philosophy, how much more in moral, where there is a much greater complication of circumstances, and where those views and sentiments, which are essential to any action of the mind, are so implicit and obscure, that they often escape our strictest attention, and are not only unaccountable in their causes, but even unknown in their existence? I am much afraid lest the small success I meet with in my enquiries will make this observation bear the air of an apology rather than of boasting.

If any thing can give me security in this particular, it will be the enlarging of the sphere of my experiments as much as possible; for which reason it may be proper in this place to examine the reasoning faculty of brutes, as well as that of human creatures.

SECTION XVI

Of the Reason of Animals

Next to the ridicule of denying an evident truth, is that of taking much pains to defend it; and no truth appears to me more evident, than that beasts are endowd with thought and reason as well as men. The arguments are in this case so obvious, that they never escape the most stupid and ignorant.

We are conscious, that we ourselves, in adapting means to ends, are guided by reason and design, and that it is not ignorantly nor casually we perform those actions, which tend to self-preservation, to the obtaining pleasure, and avoiding pain. When therefore we see other creatures, in millions of instances, perform like actions, and direct them to the ends, all our principles of reason and probability carry us with an invincible force to believe the existence of a like cause. It is needless in my opinion to illustrate this argument by the enumeration of particulars. The smallest attention will supply us with more than are requisite. The resemblance betwixt the actions of animals and those of men is so entire in this respect, that the very first action of the first animal we shall please to pitch on, will afford us an incontestable argument for the present doctrine.

This doctrine is as useful as it is obvious, and furnishes us with a kind of touchstone, by which we may try every system in this species of philosophy. It is from the resemblance of the external actions of animals to those we ourselves perform, that we judge their internal likewise to resemble ours; and the same principle of reasoning, carryd one step farther, will make us conclude that since our internal actions resemble each other, the causes, from which they are derivd, must also be resembling. When any hypothesis, therefore, is advancd to explain a mental operation, which is common to men and beasts, we must apply the same hypothesis to both; and as every true hypothesis will abide this trial, so I may venture to affirm, that no false one will ever be able to endure it. The common defect of those systems, which philosophers have employd to account for the actions of the mind, is, that they suppose such a subtility and refinement of thought, as not only exceeds the capacity of mere animals, but even of children and the common people in our own species; who are notwithstanding susceptible of the same emotions and affections as persons of the most accomplishd genius and understanding. Such a subtility is a dear proof of the falshood, as the contrary simplicity of the truth, of any system.

Let us therefore put our present system concerning the nature of the understanding to this decisive trial, and see whether it will equally account for the reasonings of beasts as for these of the human species.

Here we must make a distinction betwixt those actions of animals, which are of a vulgar nature, and seem to be on a level with their common capacities, and those more extraordinary instances of sagacity, which they sometimes discover for their own preservation, and the propagation of their species. A dog, that avoids fire and precipices, that shuns strangers, and caresses his master, affords us an instance of the first kind. A bird, that chooses with such care and nicety the place and materials of her nest, and sits upon her eggs for a due time, and in suitable season, with all the precaution that a chymist is capable of in the most delicate projection, furnishes us with a lively instance of the second.

As to the former actions, I assert they proceed from a reasoning, that is not in itself different, nor founded on different principles, from that which appears in human nature. It is necessary in the first place, that there be some impression immediately present to their memory or senses, in order to be the foundation of their judgment. From the tone of voice the dog infers his masters anger, and foresees his own punishment. From a certain sensation affecting his smell, he judges his game not to be far distant from him.

Secondly, The inference he draws from the present impression is built on experience, and on his observation of the conjunction of objects in past instances. As you vary this experience, he varies his reasoning. Make a beating follow upon one sign or motion for some time, and afterwards upon another; and he will successively draw different conclusions, according to his most recent experience.

Now let any philosopher make a trial, and endeavour to explain that act of the mind, which we call BELIEF, and give an account of the principles, from which it is derivd, independent of the influence of custom on the imagination, and let his hypothesis be equally applicable to beasts as to the human species; and after he has done this, I promise to embrace his opinion. But at the same time I demand as an equitable condition, that if my system be the only one, which can answer to all these terms, it may be receivd as entirely satisfactory and convincing. And that it is the only one, is evident almost without any reasoning. Beasts certainly never perceive any real connexion among objects. It is therefore by experience they infer one from another. They can never by any arguments form a general conclusion, that those objects, of which they have had no experience, resemble those of which they have. It is therefore by means of custom alone, that experience operates upon them. All this was sufficiently evident with respect to man. But with respect to beasts there cannot be the least suspicion of mistake; which must be ownd to be a strong confirmation, or rather an invincible proof of my system.

Nothing shews more the force of habit in reconciling us to any phaenomenoun, than this, that men are not astonished at the operations of their own reason, at the same time, that they admire the instinct of animals, and find a difficulty in explaining it, merely because it cannot be reduced to the very same principles. To consider the matter aright, reason is nothing but a wonderful and unintelligible instinct in our souls, which carries us along a certain train of ideas, and endows them with particular qualities, according to their particular situations and relations. This instinct, it is true, arises from past observation and experience; but can any one give the ultimate reason, why past experience and observation produces such an effect, any more than why nature alone shoud produce it? Nature may certainly produce whatever can arise from habit: Nay, habit is nothing but one of the principles of nature, and derives all its force from that origin.

PART IV

Of the Sceptical and other Systems of Philosophy

SECTION I

Of Scepticism with regard to Reason

In all demonstrative sciences the rules are certain and infallible; but when we apply them, our fallible said uncertain faculties are very apt to depart from them, and fall into error. We must, therefore, in every reasoning form a new judgment, as a check or controul on our first judgment or belief; and must enlarge our view to comprehend a kind of history of all the instances, wherein our understanding has deceived us, compared with those, wherein its testimony was just and true. Our reason must be considered as a kind of cause, of which truth is the natural effect; but such-a-one as by the irruption of other causes, and by the inconstancy of our mental powers, may frequently be prevented. By this means all knowledge degenerates into probability; and this probability is greater or less, according to our experience of the veracity or deceitfulness of our understanding, and according to the simplicity or intricacy of the question.

There is no Algebraist nor Mathematician so expert in his science, as to place entire confidence in any truth immediately upon his discovery of it, or regard it as any thing, but a mere probability. Every time he runs over his proofs, his confidence encreases; but still more by the approbation of his friends; and is raised to its utmost perfection by the universal assent and applauses of the learned world. Now it is evident, that this gradual encrease of assurance is nothing but the addition of new probabilities, and is derived from the constant union of causes and effects, according to past experience and observation.

In accompts of any length or importance, Merchants seldom trust to the infallible certainty of numbers for their security; but by the artificial structure of the accompts, produce a probability beyond what is derived from the skill and experience of the accomptant. For that is plainly of itself some degree of probability; though uncertain and variable, according to the degrees of his experience and length of the accompt. Now as none will maintain, that our assurance in a long numeration exceeds probability, I may safely affirm, that there scarce is any proposition concerning numbers, of which we can have a fuller security. For it is easily possible, by gradually diminishing the numbers, to reduce the longest series of addition to the most simple question, which can be formed, to an addition of two single numbers; and upon this supposition we shall find it impracticable to shew the precise limits of knowledge and of probability, or discover that particular number, at which the one ends and the other begins. But knowledge and probability are of such contrary and disagreeing natures, that they cannot well run insensibly into each other, and that because they will not divide, but must be either entirely present, or entirely absent. Besides, if any single addition were certain, every one would be so, and consequently the whole or total sum; unless the whole can be different from all its parts. I had almost said, that this was certain; but I reflect that it must reduce itself, as well as every other reasoning, and from knowledge degenerate into probability.

Since therefore all knowledge resolves itself into probability, and becomes at last of the same nature with that evidence, which we employ in common life, we must now examine this latter species of reasoning, and see on what foundation it stands.

In every judgment, which we can form concerning probability, as well as concerning knowledge, we ought always to correct the first judgment, derived from the nature of the object, by another judgment, derived from the nature of the understanding. It is certain a man of solid sense and long experience ought to have, and usually has, a greater assurance in his opinions, than one that is foolish and ignorant, and that our sentiments have different degrees of authority, even with ourselves, in proportion to the degrees of our reason and experience. In the man of the best sense and longest experience, this authority is never entire; since even such-a-one must be conscious of many errors in the past, and must still dread the like for the future. Here then arises a new species of probability to correct and regulate the first, and fix its just standard and proportion. As demonstration is subject to the controul of probability, so is probability liable to a new correction by a reflex act of the mind, wherein the nature of our understanding, and our reasoning from the first probability become our objects.

Having thus found in every probability, beside the original uncertainty inherent in the subject, a new uncertainty derived from the weakness of that faculty, which judges, and having adjusted these two together, we are obliged by our reason to add a new doubt derived from the possibility of error in the estimation we make of the truth and fidelity of our faculties. This is a doubt, which immediately occurs to us, and of which, if we would closely pursue our reason, we cannot avoid giving a decision. But this decision, though it should be favourable to our preceding judgment, being founded only on probability, must weaken still further our first evidence, and must itself be weakened by a fourth doubt of the same kind, and so on in infinitum: till at last there remain nothing of the original probability, however great we may suppose it to have been, and however small the diminution by every new uncertainty. No finite object can subsist under a decrease repeated IN INFINITUM; and even the vastest quantity, which can enter into human imagination, must in this manner be reduced to nothing. Let our first belief be never so strong, it must infallibly perish by passing through so many new examinations, of which each diminishes somewhat of its force and vigour. When I reflect on the natural fallibility of my judgment, I have less confidence in my opinions, than when I only consider the objects concerning which I reason; and when I proceed still farther, to turn the scrutiny against every successive estimation I make of my faculties, all the rules of logic require a continual diminution, and at last a total extinction of belief and evidence.

Should it here be asked me, whether I sincerely assent to this argument, which I seem to take such pains to inculcate, and whether I be really one of those sceptics, who hold that all is uncertain, and that our judgment is not in any thing possest of any measures of truth and falshood; I should reply, that this question is entirely superfluous, and that neither I, nor any other person was ever sincerely and constantly of that opinion. Nature, by an absolute and uncontroulable necessity has determined us to judge as well as to breathe and feel; nor can we any more forbear viewing certain objects in a stronger and fuller light, upon account of their customary connexion with a present impression, than we can hinder ourselves from thinking as long, as we are awake, or seeing the surrounding bodies, when we turn our eyes towards them in broad sunshine. Whoever has taken the pains to refute the cavils of this total scepticism, has really disputed without an antagonist, and endeavoured by arguments to establish a faculty, which nature has antecedently implanted in the mind, and rendered unavoidable.

My intention then in displaying so carefully the arguments of that fantastic sect, is only to make the reader sensible of the truth of my hypothesis, that all our reasonings concerning causes and effects are derived from nothing but custom; and that belief is more properly an act of the sensitive, than of the cogitative part of our natures. I have here proved, that the very same principles, which make us form a decision upon any subject, and correct that decision by the consideration of our genius and capacity, and of the situation of our mind, when we examined that subject; I say, I have proved, that these same principles, when carryed farther, and applied to every new reflex judgment, must, by continually diminishing the original evidence, at last reduce it to nothing, and utterly subvert all belief and opinion. If belief, therefore, were a simple act of the thought, without any peculiar manner of conception, or the addition of a force and vivacity, it must infallibly destroy itself, and in every case terminate in a total suspense of judgment. But as experience will sufficiently convince any one, who thinks it worth while to try, that though he can find no error in the foregoing arguments, yet he still continues to believe, and think, and reason as usual, he may safely conclude, that his reasoning and belief is some sensation or peculiar manner of conception, which it is impossible for mere ideas and reflections to destroy.

But here, perhaps, it may be demanded, how it happens, even upon my hypothesis, that these arguments above-explained produce not a total suspense of judgment, and after what manner the mind ever retains a degree of assurance in any subject? For as these new probabilities, which by their repetition perpetually diminish the original evidence, are founded on the very same principles, whether of thought or sensation, as the primary judgment, it may seem unavoidable, that in either case they must equally subvert it, and by the opposition, either of contrary thoughts or sensations, reduce the mind to a total uncertainty. I suppose, there is some question proposed to me, and that after revolving over the impressions of my memory and senses, and carrying my thoughts from them to such objects, as are commonly conjoined with them, I feel a stronger and more forcible conception on the one side, than on the other. This strong conception forms my first decision. I suppose, that afterwards I examine my judgment itself, and observing from experience, that it is sometimes just and sometimes erroneous, I consider it as regulated by contrary principles or causes, of which some lead to truth, and some to error; and in ballancing these contrary causes, I diminish by a new probability the assurance of my first decision. This new probability is liable to the same diminution as the foregoing, and so on, IN INFINITUM. It is therefore demanded, how it happens, that even after all we retain a degree of belief, which is sufficient for our purpose, either in philosophy or common life.

I answer, that after the first and second decision; as the action of the mind becomes forced and unnatural, and the ideas faint and obscure; though the principles of judgment, and the ballancing of opposite causes be the same as at the very beginning; yet their influence on the imagination, and the vigour they add to, or diminish from the thought, is by no means equal. Where the mind reaches not its objects with easiness and facility, the same principles have not the same effect as in a more natural conception of the ideas; nor does the imagination feel a sensation, which holds any proportion with that which arises from its common judgments and opinions. The attention is on the stretch: The posture of the mind is uneasy; and the spirits being diverted from their natural course, are not governed in their movements by the same laws, at least not to the same degree, as when they flow in their usual channel.

If we desire similar instances, it will not be very difficult to find them. The present subject of metaphysics will supply us abundantly. The same argument, which would have been esteemed convincing in a reasoning concerning history or politics, has little or no influence in these abstruser subjects, even though it be perfectly comprehended; and that because there is required a study and an effort of thought, in order to its being comprehended: And this effort of thought disturbs the operation of our sentiments, on which the belief depends. The case is the same in other subjects. The straining of the imagination always hinders the regular flowing of the passions and sentiments. A tragic poet, that would represent his heroes as very ingenious and witty in their misfortunes, would never touch the passions. As the emotions of the soul prevent any subtile reasoning and reflection, so these latter actions of the mind are equally prejudicial to the former. The mind, as well as the body, seems to be endowed with a certain precise degree of force and activity, which it never employs in one action, but at the expense of all the rest. This is more evidently true, where the actions are of quite different natures; since in that case the force of the mind is not only diverted, but even the disposition changed, so as to render us incapable of a sudden transition from one action to the other, and still more of performing both at once. No wonder, then, the conviction, which arises from a subtile reasoning, diminishes in proportion to the efforts, which the imagination makes to enter into the reasoning, and to conceive it in all its parts. Belief, being a lively conception, can never be entire, where it is not founded on something natural and easy.

This I take to be the true state of the question, and cannot approve of that expeditious way, which some take with the sceptics, to reject at once all their arguments without enquiry or examination. If the sceptical reasonings be strong, say they, it is a proof, that reason may have some force and authority: if weak, they can never be sufficient to invalidate all the conclusions of our understanding. This argument is not just; because the sceptical reasonings, were it possible for them to exist, and were they not destroyed by their subtility, would be successively both strong and weak, according to the successive dispositions of the mind. Reason first appears in possession of the throne, prescribing laws, and imposing maxims, with an absolute sway and authority. Her enemy, therefore, is obliged to take shelter under her protection, and by making use of rational arguments to prove the fallaciousness and imbecility of reason, produces, in a manner, a patent under her and and seal. This patent has at first an authority, proportioned to the present and immediate authority of reason, from which it is derived. But as it is supposed to be contradictory to reason, it gradually diminishes the force of that governing power and its own at the same time; till at last they both vanish away into nothing, by a regulax and just diminution. The sceptical and dogmatical reasons are of the same kind, though contrary in their operation and tendency; so that where the latter is strong, it has an enemy of equal force in the former to encounter; and as their forces were at first equal, they still continue so, as long as either of them subsists; nor does one of them lose any force in the contest, without taking as much from its antagonist. It is happy, therefore, that nature breaks the force of all sceptical arguments in time, and keeps them from having any considerable influence on the understanding. Were we to trust entirely to their self-destruction, that can never take place, until they have first subverted all conviction, and have totally destroyed human reason.

SECTION II

Of Scepticism with regard to the Senses

Thus the sceptic still continues to reason and believe, even though he asserts, that he cannot defend his reason by reason; and by the same rule he must assent to the principle concerning the existence of body, though he cannot pretend by any arguments of philosophy to maintain its veracity. Nature has not left this to his choice, and has doubtless, esteemed it an affair of too great importance to be trusted to our uncertain reasonings and speculations. We may well ask, What causes induce us to believe in the existence of body? but it is in vain to ask, Whether there be body or not? That is a point, which we must take for granted in all our reasonings.

The subject, then, of our present enquiry is concerning the causes which induce us to believe in the existence of body: And my reasonings on this head I shall begin with a distinction, which at first sight may seem superfluous, but which will contribute very much to the perfect understanding of what follows. We ought to examine apart those two questions, which are commonly confounded together, viz. Why we attribute a continued existence to objects, even when they are not present to the senses; and why we suppose them to have an existence DISTINCT from the mind and perception. Under this last head I comprehend their situation as well as relations, their external position as well as the independence of their existence and operation. These two questions concerning the continued and distinct existence of body are intimately connected together. For if the objects of our senses continue to exist, even when they are not perceived, their existence is of course independent of and distinct from the perception: and vice versa, if their existence be independent of the perception and distinct from it, they must continue to exist, even though they be not perceived. But though the decision of the one question decides the other; yet that we may the more easily discover the principles of human nature, from whence the decision arises, we shall carry along with us this distinction, and shall consider, whether it be the senses, reason, or the imagination, that produces the opinion of a continued or of a distinct existence. These are the only questions, that are intelligible on the present subject. For as to the notion of external existence, when taken for something specially different from our perceptions,[32] we have already shewn its absurdity.

To begin with the SENSES, it is evident these faculties are incapable of giving rise to the notion of the continued existence of their objects, after they no longer appear to the senses. For that is a contradiction in terms, and suppose that the senses continue to operate, even after they have ceased all manner of operation. These faculties, therefore, if they have any influence in the present case, must produce the opinion of a distinct, not of a continued existence; and in order to that, must present their impressions either as images and representations, or as these very distinct and external existences.

That our senses offer not their impressions as the images of something distinct, or independent, and external, is evident; because they convey to us nothing but a single perception, and never give us the least intimation of any thing beyond. A single perception can never produce the idea of a double existence, but by some inference either of the reason or imagination. When the mind looks farther than what immediately appears to it, its conclusions can never be put to the account of the senses; and it certainly looks farther, when from a single perception it infers a double existence, and supposes the relations of resemblance and causation betwixt them.

[32] Part. II. Sect. 6.

If our senses, therefore, suggest any idea of distinct existences, they must convey the impressions as those very existences, by a kind of fallacy and illusion. Upon this bead we may observe, that all sensations are felt by the mind, such as they really are, and that when we doubt, whether they present themselves as distinct objects, or as mere impressions, the difficulty is not concerning their nature, but concerning their relations and situation. Now if the senses presented our impressions as external to, and independent of ourselves, both the objects and ourselves must be obvious to our senses, otherwise they could not be compared by these faculties. The difficulty, then, is how fax we are ourselves the objects of our senses.

It is certain there is no question in philosophy more abstruse than that concerning identity, and the nature of the uniting principle, which constitutes a person. So far from being able by our senses merely to determine this question, we must have recourse to the most profound metaphysics to give a satisfactory answer to it; and in common life it is evident these ideas of self and person are never very fixed nor determinate. It is absurd, therefore, to imagine the senses can ever distinguish betwixt ourselves and external objects.

Add to this, that every impression, external and internal, passions, affections, sensations, pains and pleasures, are originally on the same footing; and that whatever other differences we may observe among them, they appear, all of them, in their true colours, as impressions or perceptions. And indeed, if we consider the matter aright, it is scarce possible it should be otherwise, nor is it conceivable that our senses should be more capable of deceiving us in the situation and relations, than in the nature of our impressions. For since all actions and sensations of the mind are known to us by consciousness, they must necessarily appear in every particular what they are, and be what they appear. Every thing that enters the mind, being in reality a perception, it is impossible any thing should to feeling appear different. This were to suppose, that even where we are most intimately conscious, we might be mistaken.

But not to lose time in examining, whether it is possible for our senses to deceive us, and represent our perceptions as distinct from ourselves, that is as external to and independent of us; let us consider whether they really do so, and whether this error proceeds from an immediate sensation, or from some other causes.

To begin with the question concerning EXTERNAL existence, it may perhaps be said, that setting aside the metaphysical question of the identity of a thinking substance, our own body evidently belongs to us; and as several impressions appear exterior to the body, we suppose them also exterior to ourselves. The paper, on which I write at present, is beyond my hand. The table is beyond the paper. The walls of the chamber beyond the table. And in casting my eye towards the window, I perceive a great extent of fields and buildings beyond my chamber. From all this it may be infered, that no other faculty is required, beside the senses, to convince us of the external existence of body. But to prevent this inference, we need only weigh the three following considerations. First, That, properly speaking, it is not our body we perceive, when we regard our limbs and members, but certain impressions, which enter by the senses; so that the ascribing a real and corporeal existence to these impressions, or to their objects, is an act of the mind as difficult to explain, as that which we examine at present. Secondly, Sounds, and tastes, and smelts, though commonly regarded by the mind as continued independent qualities, appear not to have any existence in extension, and consequently cannot appear to the senses as situated externally to the body. The reason, why we ascribe a place to them, shall be: considered afterwards. Thirdly, Even our sight informs us not of distance or outness (so to speak) immediately and without a certain reasoning and experience, as is acknowledged by the most rational philosophers.

As to the independency of our perceptions on ourselves, this can never be an object of the senses; but any opinion we form concerning it, must be derived from experience and observation: And we shall see afterwards, that our conclusions from experience are far from being favourable to the doctrine of the independency of our perceptions. Mean while we may observe that when we talk of real distinct existences, we have commonly more in our eye their independency than external situation in place, and think an object has a sufficient reality, when its Being is uninterrupted, and independent of the incessant revolutions, which we are conscious of in ourselves.

Thus to resume what I have said concerning the senses; they give us no notion of continued existence, because they cannot operate beyond the extent, in which they really operate. They as little produce the opinion of a distinct existence, because they neither can offer it to the mind as represented, nor as original. To offer it as represented, they must present both an object and an image. To make it appear as original, they must convey a falshood; and this falshood must lie in the relations and situation: In order to which they must be able to compare the object with ourselves; and even in that case they do not, nor is it possible they should, deceive us. We may, therefore, conclude with certainty, that the opinion of a continued and of a distinct existence never arises from the senses.

To confirm this we may observe, that there are three different kinds of impressions conveyed by the senses. The first are those of the figure, bulk, motion and solidity of bodies. The second those of colours, tastes, smells, sounds, heat and cold. The third are the pains and pleasures, that arise from the application of objects to our bodies, as by the cutting of our flesh with steel, and such like. Both philosophers and the vulgar suppose the first of these to have a distinct continued existence. The vulgar only regard the second as on the same footing. Both philosophers and the vulgar, again, esteem the third to be merely perceptions and consequently interrupted and dependent beings.

Now it is evident, that, whatever may be our philosophical opinion, colours, Sounds, heat and cold, as far as appears to the senses, exist after the same manner with motion and solidity, and that the difference we make betwixt them in this respect, arises not from the mere perception. So strong the prejudice for the distinct continued existence Of the former qualities, that when the contrary opinion is advanced by modern philosophers, people imagine they can almost refute it from their feeling and experience, and that their very senses contradict this philosophy. It is also evident, that colours, sounds, &c. are originally on the same footing with the pain that arises from steel, and pleasure that proceeds from a fire; and that the difference betwixt them is founded neither on perception nor reason, but on the imagination. For as they are confest to be, both of them, nothing but perceptions arising from the particular configurations and motions of the parts of body, wherein possibly can their difference consist? Upon the whole, then, we may conclude, that as far as the senses are judges, all perceptions are the same in the manner of their existence.

We may also observe in this instance of sounds and colours, that we can attribute a distinct continued existence to objects without ever consulting REASON, or weighing our opinions by any philosophical principles. And indeed, whatever convincing arguments philosophers may fancy they can produce to establish the belief of objects independent of the mind, it is obvious these arguments are known but to very few, and that it is not by them, that children, peasants, and the greatest part of mankind are induced to attribute objects to some impressions, and deny them to others. Accordingly we find, that all the conclusions, which the vulgar form on this head, are directly contrary to those, which are confirmed by philosophy. For philosophy informs us, that every thing, which appears to the mind, is nothing but a perception, and is interrupted, and dependent on the mind: whereas the vulgar confound perceptions and objects, and attribute a distinct continued existence to the very things they feel or see. This sentiment, then, as it is entirely unreasonable, must proceed from some other faculty than the understanding. To which we may add, that as long as we take our perceptions and objects to be the same, we can never infer the existence of the one from that of the other, nor form any argument from the relation of cause and effect; which is the only one that earl assure us of matter of fact. Even after we distinguish our perceptions from our objects, it will appear presently, that we are still incapable of reasoning from the existence of one to that of the other: So that upon the whole our reason neither does, nor is it possible it ever should, upon any supposition, give us an assurance of the continued and distinct existence of body. That opinion must be entirely owing to the IMAGINATION: which must now be the subject of our enquiry.

Since all impressions are internal and perishing existences, and appear as such, the notion of their distinct and continued existence must arise from a concurrence of some of their qualities with the qualities of the imagination, and since this notion does not extend to all of them, it must arise from certain qualities peculiar to some impressions. It will therefore be easy for us to discover these qualities by a comparison of the impressions, to which we attribute a distinct and continued existence, with those, which we regard as internal and perishing.

We may observe, then, that it is neither upon account of the involuntariness of certain impressions, as is commonly supposed, nor of their superior force and violence, that we attribute to them a reality, and continued existence, which we refuse to others, that are voluntary or feeble. For it is evident our pains and pleasures, our passions and affections, which we never suppose to have any existence beyond our perception, operate with greater violence, and are equally involuntary, as the impressions of figure and extension, colour and sound, which we suppose to be permanent beings. The heat of a fire, when moderate, is supposed to exist in the fire; but the pain, which it causes upon a near approach, is not taken to have any being, except in the perception.

These vulgar opinions, then, being rejected, we must search for some other hypothesis, by which we may discover those peculiar qualities in our impressions, which makes us attribute to them a distinct and continued existence.

After a little examination, we shall find, that all those objects, to which we attribute a continued existence, have a peculiar constancy, which distinguishes them from the impressions, whose existence depends upon our perception. Those mountains, and houses, and trees, which lie at present under my eye, have always appeared to me in the same order; and when I lose sight of them by shutting my eyes or turning my head, I soon after find them return upon me without the least alteration. My bed and table, my books and papers, present themselves in the same uniform manner, and change not upon account of any interruption in my seeing or perceivilng them. This is the case with all the impressions, whose objects are supposed to have an external existence; and is the case with no other impressions, whether gentle or violent, voluntary or involuntary.

This constancy, however, is not so perfect as not to admit of very considerable exceptions. Bodies often change their position and qualities, and after a little absence or interruption may become hardly knowable. But here it is observable, that even in these changes they preserve a coherence, and have a regular dependence on each other; which is the foundation of a kind of reasoning from causation, and produces the opinion of their continued existence. When I return to my chamber after an hour's absence, I find not my fire in the same situation, in which I left it: But then I am accustomed in other instances to see a like alteration produced in a like time, whether I am present or absent, near or remote. This coherence, therefore, in their changes is one of the characteristics of external objects, as well as their constancy.

Having found that the opinion of the continued existence of body depends on the COHERENCE, and CONSTANCY of certain impressions, I now proceed to examine after what manner these qualities give rise to so extraordinary an opinion. To begin with the coherence; we may observe, that though those internal impressions, which we regard as fleeting and perishing, have also a certain coherence or regularity in their appearances, yet it is of somewhat a different nature, from that which we discover in bodies. Our passions are found by experience to have a mutual connexion with and dependence on each other; but on no occasion is it necessary to suppose, that they have existed and operated, when they were not perceived, in order to preserve the same dependence and connexion, of which we have had experience. The case is not the same with relation to external objects. Those require a continued existence, or otherwise lose, in a great measure, the regularity of their operation. I am here seated in my chamber with my face to the fire; and all the objects, that strike my senses, are contained in a few yards around me. My memory, indeed, informs me of the existence of many objects; but then this information extends not beyond their past existence, nor do either my senses or memory give any testimony to the continuance of their being. When therefore I am thus seated, and revolve over these thoughts, I hear on a sudden a noise as of a door turning upon its hinges; and a little after see a porter, who advances towards me. This gives occasion to many new reflections and reasonings. First, I never have observed, that this noise could proceed from any thing but the motion of a door; and therefore conclude, that the present phænomenon is a contradiction to all past experience, unless the door, which I remember on the other side the chamber, be still in being. Again, I have always found, that a human body was possest of a quality, which I call gravity, and which hinders it from mounting in the air, as this porter must have done to arrive at my chamber, unless the stairs I remember be not annihilated by my absence. But this is not all. I receive a letter, which upon, opening it I perceive by the hand-writing and subscription to have come from a friend, who says he is two hundred leagues distant. It is evident I can never account for this phenomenon, conformable to my experience in other instances, without spreading out in my mind the whole sea and continent between us, and supposing the effects and continued existence of posts and ferries, according to my Memory and observation. To consider these phaenomena of the porter and letter in a certain light, they are contradictions to common experience, and may be regarded as objections to those maxims, which we form concerning the connexions of causes and effects. I am accustomed to hear such a sound, and see such an object in motion at the same time. I have not received in this particular instance both these perceptions. These observations are contrary, unless I suppose that the door still remains, and that it was opened without my perceiving it: And this supposition, which was at first entirely arbitrary and hypothetical, acquires a force and evidence by its being the only one, upon which I can reconcile these contradictions. There is scarce a moment of my life, wherein there is not a similar instance presented to me, and I have not occasion to suppose the continued existence of objects, in order to connect their past and present appearances, and give them such an union with each other, as I have found by experience to be suitable to their particular natures and circumstances. Here then I am naturally led to regard the world, as something real and durable, and as preserving its existence, even when it is no longer present to my perception.

But though this conclusion from the coherence of appearances may seem to be of the same nature with our reasonings concerning causes and effects; as being derived from custom, and regulated by past experience; we shall find upon examination, that they are at the bottom considerably different from each other, and that this inference arises from the understanding, and from custom in an indirect and oblique manner. For it will readily be allowed, that since nothing is ever really present to the mind, besides its own perceptions, it is not only impossible, that any habit should ever be acquired otherwise than by the regular succession of these perceptions, but also that any habit should ever exceed that degree of regularity. Any degree, therefore, of regularity in our perceptions, can never be a foundation for us to infer a greater degree of regularity in some objects, which are not perceived; since this supposes a contradiction, viz. a habit acquired by what was never present to the mind. But it is evident, that whenever we infer the continued existence of the objects of sense from their coherence, and the frequency of their union, it is in order to bestow on the objects a greater regularity than what is observed in our mere perceptions. We remark a connexion betwixt two kinds of objects in their past appearance to the senses, but are not able to observe this connexion to be perfectly constant, since the turning about of our head or the shutting of our eyes is able to break it. What then do we suppose in this case, but that these objects still continue their usual connexion, notwithstanding their apparent interruption, and that the irregular appearances are joined by something, of which we are insensible? But as all reasoning concerning matters of fact arises only from custom, and custom can only be the effect of repeated perceptions, the extending of custom and reasoning beyond the perceptions can never be the direct and natural effect of the constant repetition and connexion, but must arise from the co-operation of some other principles.

I have already observed,[33] in examining the foundation of mathematics, that the imagination, when set into any train of thinking, is apt to continue, even when its object fails it, and like a galley put in motion by the oars, carries on its course without any new impulse. This I have assigned for the reason, why, after considering several loose standards of equality, and correcting them by each other, we proceed to imagine so correct and exact a standard of that relation, as is not liable to the least error or variation. The same principle makes us easily entertain this opinion of the continued existence of body. Objects have a certain coherence even as they appear to our senses; but this coherence is much greater and more uniform, if we suppose the object.% to have a continued existence; and as the mind is once in the train of observing an uniformity among objects, it naturally continues, till it renders the uniformity as compleat as possible. The simple supposition of their continued existence suffices for this purpose, and gives us a notion of a much greater regularity among objects, than what they have when we look no farther than our senses.

But whatever force we may ascribe to this principle, I am afraid it is too weak to support alone so vast an edifice, as is that of the continued existence of all external

[33] Part II, Sect. 4.

bodies; and that we must join the constancy of their appearance to the coherence, in order to give a satisfactory account of that opinion. As the explication of this will lead me into a considerable compass of very profound reasoning; I think it proper, in order to avoid confusion, to give a short sketch or abridgment of my system, and afterwards draw out all its parts in their full compass. This inference from the constancy of our perceptions, like the precedent from their coherence, gives rise to the opinion of the continued existence of body, which is prior to that of its distinct existence, and produces that latter principle.

When we have been accustomed to observe a constancy in certain impressions, and have found, that the perception of the sun or ocean, for instance, returns upon us after an absence or annihilation with like parts and in a like order, as at its first appearance, we are not apt to regard these interrupted perceptions as different, (which they really are) but on the contrary consider them as individually the same, upon account of their resemblance. But as this interruption of their existence is contrary to their perfect identity, and makes us regard the first impression as annihilated, and the second as newly created, we find ourselves somewhat at a loss, and are involved in a kind of contradiction. In order to free ourselves from this difficulty, we disguise, as much as possible, the interruption, or rather remove it entirely, by supposing that these interrupted perceptions are connected by a real existence, of which we are insensible. This supposition, or idea of continued existence, acquires a force and vivacity from the memory of these broken impressions, and from that propensity, which they give us, to suppose them the same; and according to the precedent reasoning, the very essence of belief consists in the force and vivacity of the conception.

In order to justify this system, there are four things requisite. First, To explain the PRINCIPIUM INDIVIDUATIONIS, or principle of identity. Secondly, Give a reason, why the resemblance of our broken and interrupted perceptions induces us to attribute an identity to them. Thirdly, Account for that propensity, which this illusion gives, to unite these broken appearances by a continued existence. Fourthly and lastly, Explain that force and vivacity of conception, which arises from the propensity.

First, As to the principle of individuation; we may observe, that the view of any one object is not sufficient to convey the idea of identity. For in that proposition, an object is the same with itself, if the idea expressed by the word, object, were no ways distinguished from that meant by itself; we really should mean nothing, nor would the proposition contain a predicate and a subject, which however are implyed in this affirmation. One single object conveys the idea of unity, not that of identity.

On the other hand, a multiplicity of objects can never convey this idea, however resembling they may be supposed. The mind always pronounces the one not to be the other, and considers them as forming two, three, or any determinate number of objects, whose existences are entirely distinct and independent.

Since then both number and unity are incompatible with the relation of identity, it must lie in something that is neither of them. But to tell the truth, at first sight this seems utterly impossible. Betwixt unity and number there can be no medium; no more than betwixt existence and nonexistence. After one object is supposed to exist, we must either suppose another also to exist; in which case we have the idea of number: Or we must suppose it not to exist; in which case the first object remains at unity.

To remove this difficulty, let us have recourse to the idea of time or duration. I have already observ'd,[34] that time, in a strict sense, implies succession, and that when we apply its idea to any unchangeable object, it is only by a fiction of the imagination, by which the unchangeable object is supposd to participate of the changes of the co-existent objects, and in particular of that of our perceptions. This fiction of the imagination almost universally takes place; and it is by means of it, that a single object, placd before us, and surveyd for any time without our discovering in it any interruption or variation, is able to give us a notion of identity. For when we consider any two points of this time, we may place them in different lights: We may either survey them at the very same instant; in which case they give us the idea of number, both by themselves and by the object; which must be multiplyd, in order to be conceivd at once, as existent in these two different points of time: Or on the other hand, we may trace the succession of time by a like succession of ideas, and conceiving first one moment, along with the object then existent, imagine afterwards a change in the time without any VARIATION or INTERRUPTION in the object; in which case it gives us the idea of unity. Here then is an idea, which is a medium betwixt unity and number; or more properly speaking, is either of them, according to the view, in which we take it: And this idea we call that of identity. We cannot, in any propriety of speech, say, that an object is the same with itself, unless we mean, that the object existent at one time is the same with itself existent at another. By this means we make a difference, betwixt the idea meant by the word, OBJECT, and that meant by ITSELF, without going the length of number, and at the same time without restraining ourselves to a strict and absolute unity.

Thus the principle of individuation is nothing but the INVARIABLENESS and UNINTERRUPTEDNESS of any object, thro a supposd variation of time, by which the mind can trace it in the different periods of its existence, without any break of the view, and without being obligd to form the idea of multiplicity or number.

I now proceed to explain the SECOND part of my system, and shew why the constancy of our perceptions makes us ascribe to them a perfect numerical identity, tho there be very long intervals betwixt their appearance, and they have only one of the essential qualities of identity, VIZ, INVARIABLENESS. That I may avoid all ambiguity and confusion on this head, I shall observe, that I here account for the

[34] Part II, Sect. 5.

opinions and belief of the vulgar with regard to the existence of body; and therefore must entirely conform myself to their manner of thinking and of expressing themselves. Now we have already observ'd, that however philosophers may distinguish betwixt the objects and perceptions of the senses; which they suppose co-existent and resembling; yet this is a distinction, which is not comprehended by the generality of mankind, who as they perceive only one being, can never assent to the opinion of a double existence and representation. Those very sensations, which enter by the eye or ear, are with them the true objects, nor can they readily conceive that this pen or paper, which is immediately perceivd, represents another, which is different from, but resembling it. In order, therefore, to accommodate myself to their notions, I shall at first suppose; that there is only a single existence, which I shall call indifferently OBJECT or PERCEPTION, according as it shall seem best to suit my purpose, understanding by both of them what any common man means by a hat, or shoe, or stone, or any other impression, conveyd to him by his senses. I shall be sure to give warning, when I return to a more philosophical way of speaking and thinking.

To enter, therefore, upon the question concerning the source of the error and deception with regard to identity, when we attribute it to our resembling perceptions, notwithstanding their interruption; I must here recal an observation, which I have already provd and explain'd.[35] Nothing is more apt to make us mistake one idea for another, than any relation betwixt them, which associates them together in the imagination, and makes it pass with facility from one to the other. Of all relations, that of resemblance is in this respect the most efficacious; and that because it not only causes an association of ideas, but also of dispositions, and makes us conceive the one idea by an act or operation of the mind, similar to that by which we conceive the other. This circumstance I have observ'd to be of great moment; and we may establish it for a general rule, that whatever ideas place the mind in the same disposition or in similar ones, are very apt to be confounded. The mind readily passes from one to the other, and perceives not the change without a strict attention, of which, generally speaking, it is wholly incapable.

In order to apply this general maxim, we must first examine the disposition of the mind in viewing any object which preserves a perfect identity, and then find some other object, that is confounded with it, by causing a similar disposition. When we fix our thought on any object, and suppose it to continue the same for some time; it is evident we suppose the change to lie only in the time, and never exert ourselves to produce any new image or idea of the object. The faculties of the mind repose themselves in a manner, and take no more exercise, than what is necessary to continue that idea, of which we were formerly possest, and which subsists without variation or interruption. The passage from one moment to another is scarce felt, and distinguishes not itself by a different perception or idea, which may require a different direction of the spirits, in order to its conception.

[35] Part II. Sect. 5.

Now what other objects, beside identical ones, are capable of placing the mind in the same disposition, when it considers them, and of causing the same uninterrupted passage of the imagination from one idea to another? This question is of the last importance. For if we can find any such objects, we may certainly conclude, from the foregoing principle, that they are very naturally confounded with identical ones, and are taken for them in most of our reasonings. But though this question be very important, it is not very difficult nor doubtful. For I immediately reply, that a succession of related objects places the mind in this disposition, and is considered with the same smooth and uninterrupted progress of the imagination, as attends the view of the same invariable object. The very nature and essence of relation is to connect our ideas with each other, and upon the appearance of one, to facilitate the transition to its correlative. The passage betwixt related ideas is, therefore, so smooth and easy, that it produces little alteration on the mind, and seems like the continuation of the same action; and as the continuation of the same action is an effect of the continued view of the same object, it is for this reason we attribute sameness to every succession of related objects. The thought slides along the succession with equal facility, as if it considered only one object; and therefore confounds the succession with the identity.

We shall afterwards see many instances of this tendency of relation to make us ascribe an identity to different objects; but shall here confine ourselves to the present subject. We find by experience, that there is such a constancy in almost all the impressions of the senses, that their interruption produces no alteration on them, and hinders them not from returning the same in appearance and in situation as at their first existence. I survey the furniture of my chamber; I shut my eyes, and afterwards open them; and find the new perceptions to resemble perfectly those, which formerly struck my senses. This resemblance is observed in a thousand instances, and naturally connects together our ideas of these interrupted perceptions by the strongest relation, and conveys the mind with an easy transition from one to another. An easy transition or passage of the imagination, along the ideas of these different and interrupted perceptions, is almost the same disposition of mind with that in which we consider one constant and uninterrupted perception. It is therefore very natural for us to mistake the one for the other.[36]

The persons, who entertain this opinion concerning the identity of our resembling perceptions, are in general an the unthinking and unphilosophical

---

[36] This reasoning, it must be confest, is somewhat abstruse, and difficult to be comprehended; but it is remarkable, that this very difficulty may be converted into a proof of the reasoning. We may observe, that there are two relations, and both of them resemblances, which contribute to our mistaking the succession of our interrupted perceptions for an identical object. The first is, the resemblance of the perceptions: The second is the resemblance, which the act of the mind in surveying a succession of resembling objects bears to that in surveying an identical object. Now these resemblances we are apt to confound with each other; and it is natural we shoud, according to this very reasoning. But let us keep them distinct, and we shall find no difficulty in conceiving the precedent argument.

part of mankind, (that is, all of us, at one time or other) and consequently such as suppose their perceptions to be their only objects, and never think of a double existence internal and external, representing and represented. The very image, which is present to the senses, is with us the real body; and it is to these interrupted images we ascribe a perfect identity. But as the interruption of the appearance seems contrary to the identity, and naturally leads us to regard these resembling perceptions as different from each other, we here find ourselves at a loss how to reconcile such opposite opinions. The smooth passage of the imagination along the ideas of the resembling perceptions makes us ascribe to them a perfect identity. The interrupted manner of their appearance makes us consider them as so many resembling, but still distinct beings, which appear after certain intervals. The perplexity arising from this contradiction produces a propension to unite these broken appearances by the fiction of a continued existence, which is the third part of that hypothesis I proposed to explain.

Nothing is more certain from experience, than that any contradiction either to the sentiments or passions gives a sensible uneasiness, whether it proceeds from without or from within; from the opposition of external objects, or from the combat of internal principles. On the contrary, whatever strikes in with the natural propensities, and either externally forwards their satisfaction, or internally concurs with their movements, is sure to give a sensible pleasure. Now there being here an opposition betwixt the notion of the identity of resembling perceptions, and the interruption of their appearance, the mind must be uneasy in that situation, and will naturally seek relief from the uneasiness. Since the uneasiness arises from the opposition of two contrary principles, it must look for relief by sacrificing the one to the other. But as the smooth passage of our thought along our resembling perceptions makes us ascribe to them an identity, we can never without reluctance yield up that opinion. We must, therefore, turn to the other side, and suppose that our perceptions are no longer interrupted, but preserve a continued as well as an invariable existence, and are by that means entirely the same. But here the interruptions in the appearance of these perceptions are so long and frequent, that it is impossible to overlook them; and as the appearance of a perception in the mind and its existence seem at first sight entirely the same, it may be doubted, whether we can ever assent to so palpable a contradiction, and suppose a perception to exist without being present to the mind. In order to clear up this matter, and learn how the interruption in the appearance of a perception implies not necessarily an interruption in its existence, it will be proper to touch upon some principles, which we shall have occasion to explain more fully afterwards.[37]

We may begin with observing, that the difficulty in the present case is not concerning the matter of fact, or whether the mind forms such a conclusion concerning the continued existence of its perceptions, but only concerning the

[37] Sect. 6.

manner in which the conclusion is formed, and principles from which it is derived. It is certain, that almost all mankind, and even philosophers themselves, for the greatest part of their lives, take their perceptions to be their only objects, and suppose, that the very being, which is intimately present to the mind, is the real body or material existence. It is also certain, that this very perception or object is supposed to have a continued uninterrupted being, and neither to be annihilated by our absence, nor to be brought into existence by our presence. When we are absent from it, we say it still exists, but that we do not feel, we do not see it. When we are present, we say we feel, or see it. Here then may arise two questions; First, How we can satisfy ourselves in supposing a perception to be absent from the mind without being annihilated. Secondly, After what manner we conceive an object to become present to the mind, without some new creation of a perception or image; and what we mean by this seeing, and feeling, and perceiving.

As to the first question; we may observe, that what we call a mind, is nothing but a heap or collection of different perceptions, united together by certain relations, and supposed, though falsely, to be endowed with a perfect simplicity and identity. Now as every perception is distinguishable from another, and may be considered as separately existent; it evidently follows, that there is no absurdity in separating any particular perception from the mind; that is, in breaking off all its relations, with that connected mass of perceptions, which constitute a thinking being.

The same reasoning affords us an answer to the second question. If the name of perception renders not this separation from a mind absurd and contradictory, the name of object, standing for the very same thing, can never render their conjunction impossible. External objects are seen, and felt, and become present to the mind; that is, they acquire such a relation to a connected heap of perceptions, as to influence them very considerably in augmenting their number by present reflections and passions, and in storing the memory with ideas. The same continued and uninterrupted Being may, therefore, be sometimes present to the mind, and sometimes absent from it, without any real or essential change in the Being itself. An interrupted appearance to the senses implies not necessarily an interruption in the existence. The supposition of the continued existence of sensible objects or perceptions involves no contradiction. We may easily indulge our inclination to that supposition. When the exact resemblance of our perceptions makes us ascribe to them an identity, we may remove the seeming interruption by feigning a continued being, which may fill those intervals, and preserve a perfect and entire identity to our perceptions.

But as we here not only feign but believe this continued existence, the question is, from whence arises such a belief; and this question leads us to the fourth member of this system. It has been proved already, that belief in general consists in nothing, but the vivacity of an idea; and that an idea may acquire this vivacity by its relation to some present impression. Impressions are naturally the most vivid perceptions of the mind; and this quality is in part conveyed by the relation to every connected idea. The relation causes a smooth passage from the impression to the idea, and even gives a propensity to that passage. The mind falls so easily from the one perception to the other, that it scarce perceives the change, but retains in the second a considerable share of the vivacity of the first. It is excited by the lively impression; and this vivacity is conveyed to the related idea, without any great diminution in the passage, by reason of the smooth transition and the propensity of the imagination.

But suppose, that this propensity arises from some other principle, besides that of relation; it is evident it must still have the same effect, and convey the vivacity from the impression to the idea. Now this is exactly the present case. Our memory presents us with a vast number of instances of perceptions perfectly resembling each other, that return at different distances of time, and after considerable interruptions. This resemblance gives us a propension to consider these interrupted perceptions as the same; and also a propension to connect them by a continued existence, in order to justify this identity, and avoid the contradiction, in which the interrupted appearance of these perceptions seems necessarily to involve us. Here then we have a propensity to feign the continued existence of all sensible objects; and as this propensity arises from some lively impressions of the memory, it bestows a vivacity on that fiction: or in other words, makes us believe the continued existence of body. If sometimes we ascribe a continued existence to objects, which are perfectly new to us, and of whose constancy and coherence we have no experience, it is because the manner, in which they present themselves to our senses, resembles that of constant and coherent objects; and this resemblance is a source of reasoning and analogy, and leads us to attribute the same qualities to similar objects.

I believe an intelligent reader will find less difficulty to assent to this system, than to comprehend it fully and distinctly, and will allow, after a little reflection, that every part carries its own proof along with it. It is indeed evident, that as the vulgar suppose their perceptions to be their only objects, and at the same time believe the continued existence of matter, we must account for the origin of the belief upon that supposition. Now upon that supposition, it is a false opinion that any of our objects, or perceptions, are identically the same after an interruption; and consequently the opinion of their identity can never arise from reason, but must arise from the imagination. The imagination is seduced into such an opinion only by means of the resemblance of certain perceptions; since we find they are only our resembling perceptions, which we have a propension to suppose the same. This propension to bestow an identity on our resembling perceptions, produces the fiction of a continued existence; since that fiction, as well as the identity, is really false, as is acknowledged by all philosophers, and has no other effect than to remedy the interruption of our perceptions, which is the only circumstance that is contrary to their identity. In the last place this propension causes belief by means of the present impressions of the memory; since without the remembrance of former sensations, it is plain we never should have any belief of the continued existence of body. Thus in examining all these parts, we find that each of them is supported by the strongest proofs: and that all of them together form a consistent system, which is perfectly convincing. A strong propensity or inclination alone, without any present impression, will sometimes cause a belief or opinion. How much more when aided by that circumstance?

But though we are led after this manner, by the natural propensity of the imagination, to ascribe a continued existence to those sensible objects or perceptions, which we find to resemble each other in their interrupted appearance; yet a very little reflection and philosophy is sufficient to make us perceive the fallacy of that opinion. I have already observed, that there is an intimate connexion betwixt those two principles, of a continued and of a distinct or independent existence, and that we no sooner establish the one than the other follows, as a necessary consequence. It is the opinion of a continued existence, which first takes place, and without much study or reflection draws the other along with it, wherever the mind follows its first and most natural tendency. But when we compare experiments, and reason a little upon them, we quickly perceive, that the doctrine of the independent existence of our sensible perceptions is contrary to the plainest experience. This leads us backward upon our footsteps to perceive our error in attributing a continued existence to our perceptions, and is the origin of many very curious opinions, which we shall here endeavour to account for.

It will first be proper to observe a few of those experiments, which convince us, that our perceptions are not possest of any independent existence. When we press one eye with a finger, we immediately perceive all the objects to become double, and one half of them to be removed from their common and natural position. But as we do not attribute to continued existence to both these perceptions, and as they are both of the same nature, we clearly perceive, that all our perceptions are dependent on our organs, and the disposition of our nerves and animal spirits. This opinion is confirmed by the seeming encrease and diminution of objects, according to their distance; by the apparent alterations in their figure; by the changes in their colour and other qualities from our sickness and distempers: and by an infinite number of other experiments of the same kind; from all which we learn, that our sensible perceptions are not possest of any distinct or independent existence.

The natural consequence of this reasoning should be, that our perceptions have no more a continued than an independent existence; and indeed philosophers have so far run into this opinion, that they change their system, and distinguish, (as we shall do for the future) betwixt perceptions and objects, of which the former are supposed to be interrupted, and perishing, and different at every different return; the latter to be uninterrupted, and to preserve a continued existence and identity. But however philosophical this new system may be esteemed, I assert that it is only a palliative remedy, and that it contains all the difficulties of the vulgar system, with some others, that are peculiar to itself. There are no principles either of the understanding or fancy, which lead us directly to embrace this opinion of the double existence of perceptions and objects, nor can we arrive at it but by passing through the common hypothesis of the identity and continuance of our interrupted perceptions. Were we not first perswaded, that our perceptions are our only objects, and continue to exist even when they no longer make their appearance to the senses, we should never be led to think, that our perceptions and objects are different, and that our objects alone preserve a continued existence. The latter hypothesis has no primary recommendation either to reason or the imagination, but acquires all its influence on the imagination from the former. This proposition contains two parts, which we shall endeavour to prove as distinctly and clearly, as such abstruse subjects will permit.

As to the first part of the proposition, that this philosophical hypothesis has no primary recommendation, either to reason, or the imagination, we may soon satisfy ourselves with regard to reason by the following reflections. The only existences, of which we are certain, are perceptions, which being immediately present to us by consciousness, command our strongest assent, and are the first foundation of all our conclusions. The only conclusion we can draw from the existence of one thing to that of another, is by means of the relation of cause and effect, which shews, that there is a connexion betwixt them, and that the existence of one is dependent on that of the other. The idea of this relation is derived from past experience, by which we find, that two beings are constantly conjoined together, and are always present at once to the mind. But as no beings are ever present to the mind but perceptions; it follows that we may observe a conjunction or a relation of cause and effect between different perceptions, but can never observe it between perceptions and objects. It is impossible, therefore, that from the existence or any of the qualities of the former, we can ever form any conclusion concerning the existence of the latter, or ever satisfy our reason in this particular.

It is no less certain, that this philosophical system has no primary recommendation to the imagination, and that that faculty would never, of itself, and by its original tendency, have fallen upon such a principle. I confess it will be somewhat difficult to prove this to the fall satisfaction of the reader; because it implies a negative, which in many cases will not admit of any positive proof. If any one would take the pains to examine this question, and would invent a system, to account for the direct origin of this opinion from the imagination, we should be able, by the examination of that system, to pronounce a certain judgment in the present subject. Let it be taken for granted, that our perceptions are broken, and interrupted, and however like, are still different from each other; and let any one upon this supposition shew why the fancy, directly and immediately, proceeds to the belief of another existence, resembling these perceptions in their nature, but yet continued, and uninterrupted, and identical; and after he has done this to my satisfaction, I promise to renounce my present opinion. Mean while I cannot forbear concluding, from the very abstractedness and difficulty of the first supposition, that it is an improper subject for the fancy to work upon. Whoever would explain the origin of the common opinion concerning the continued and distinct existence of body, must take the mind in its common situation, and must proceed upon the supposition, that our perceptions are our only objects, and continue to exist even when they are not perceived. Though this opinion be false, it is the most natural of any, and has alone any primary recommendation to the fancy.

As to the second part of the proposition, that the philosophical system acquires all its influence on the imagination from the vulgar one; we may observe, that this is a natural and unavoidable consequence of the foregoing conclusion, that it has no primary recommendation to reason or the imagination. For as the philosophical system is found by experience to take hold of many minds, and in particular of all those, who reflect ever so little on this subject, it must derive all its authority from the vulgar system; since it has no original authority of its own. The manner, in which these two systems, though directly contrary, are connected together, may be explains, as follows.

The imagination naturally runs on in this train of thinking. Our perceptions are our only objects: Resembling perceptions are the same, however broken or uninterrupted in their appearance: This appealing interruption is contrary to the identity: The interruption consequently extends not beyond the appearance, and the perception or object really continues to exist, even when absent from us: Our sensible perceptions have, therefore, a continued and uninterrupted existence. But as a little reflection destroys this conclusion, that our perceptions have a continued existence, by shewing that they have a dependent one, it would naturally be expected, that we must altogether reject the opinion, that there is such a thing in nature as a continued existence, which is preserved even when it no longer appears to the senses. The case, however, is otherwise. Philosophers are so far from rejecting the opinion of a continued existence upon rejecting that of the independence and continuance of our sensible perceptions, that though all sects agree in the latter sentiment, the former, which is, in a manner, its necessary consequence, has been peculiar to a few extravagant sceptics; who after all maintained that opinion in words only, and were never able to bring themselves sincerely to believe it.

There is a great difference betwixt such opinions as we form after a calm and profound reflection, and such as we embrace by a kind of instinct or natural impulse, on account of their suitableness and conformity to the mind. If these opinions become contrary, it is not difficult to foresee which of them will have the advantage. As long as our attention is bent upon the subject, the philosophical and studyed principle may prevail; but the moment we relax our thoughts, nature will display herself, and draw us back to our former opinion. Nay she has sometimes such an influence, that she can stop our progress, even in the midst of our most profound reflections, and keep us from running on with all the consequences of any philosophical opinion. Thus though we clearly perceive the dependence and interruption of our perceptions, we stop short in our career, and never upon that account reject the notion of an independent and continued existence. That opinion has taken such deep root in the imagination, that it is impossible ever to eradicate it, nor will any strained metaphysical conviction of the dependence of our perceptions be sufficient for that purpose.

But though our natural and obvious principles here prevail above our studied reflections, it is certain there must be sonic struggle and opposition in the case: at least so long as these rejections retain any force or vivacity. In order to set ourselves at ease in this particular, we contrive a new hypothesis, which seems to comprehend both these principles of reason and imagination. This hypothesis is the philosophical, one of the double existence of perceptions and objects; which pleases our reason, in allowing, that our dependent perceptions are interrupted and different; and at the same time is agreeable to the imagination, in attributing a continued existence to something else, which we call objects. This philosophical system, therefore, is the monstrous offspring of two principles, which are contrary to each other, which are both at once embraced by the mind, and which are unable mutually to destroy each other. The imagination tells us, that our resembling perceptions have a continued and uninterrupted existence, and are not annihilated by their absence. Reflection tells us, that even our resembling perceptions are interrupted in their existence, and different from each other. The contradiction betwixt these opinions we elude by a new fiction, which is conformable to the hypotheses both of reflection and fancy, by ascribing these contrary qualities to different existences; the interruption to perceptions, and the continuance to objects. Nature is obstinate, and will not quit the field, however strongly attacked by reason; and at the same time reason is so clear in the point, that there is no possibility of disguising her. Not being able to reconcile these two enemies, we endeavour to set ourselves at ease as much as possible, by successively granting to each whatever it demands, and by feigning a double existence, where each may find something, that has all the conditions it desires. Were we fully convinced, that our resembling perceptions are continued, and identical, and independent, we should never run into this opinion of a double existence, since we should find satisfaction in our first supposition, and would not look beyond. Again, were we fully convinced, that our perceptions are dependent, and interrupted, and different, we should be as little inclined to embrace the opinion of a double existence; since in that case we should clearly perceive the error of our first supposition of a continued existence, and would never regard it any farther. It is therefore from the intermediate situation of the mind, that this opinion arises, and from such an adherence to these two contrary principles, as makes us seek some pretext to justify our receiving both; which happily at last is found in the system of a double existence.

Another advantage of this philosophical system is its similarity to the vulgar one; by which means we can humour our reason for a moment, when it becomes troublesome and sollicitous; and yet upon its least negligence or inattention, can easily return to our vulgar and natural notions. Accordingly we find, that philosophers neglect not this advantage; but immediately upon leaving their closets, mingle with the rest of mankind in those exploded opinions, that our perceptions are our only objects, and continue identically and uninterruptedly the same in all their interrupted appearances.

There are other particulars of this system, wherein we may remark its dependence on the fancy, in a very conspicuous manner. Of these, I shall observe the two following. First, We suppose external objects to resemble internal perceptions. I have already shewn, that the relation of cause and effect can never afford us any just conclusion from the existence or qualities of our perceptions to the existence of external continued objects: And I shall farther add, that even though they could afford such a conclusion, we should never have any reason to infer, that our objects resemble our perceptions. That opinion, therefore, is derived from nothing but the quality of the fancy above-explained, (that it borrows all its ideas from some precedent perception). We never can conceive any thing but perceptions, and therefore must make every thing resemble them.

Secondly, As we suppose our objects in general to resemble our perceptions, so we take it for granted, that every particular object resembles that perception, which it causes. The relation of cause and effect determines us to join the other of resemblance; and the ideas of these existences being already united together in the fancy by the former relation, we naturally add the latter to compleat the union. We have a strong propensity to compleat every union by joining new relations to those which we have before observed betwixt any ideas, as we shall have occasion to observe presently.[38]

Having thus given an account of all the systems both popular and philosophical, with regard to external existences, I cannot forbear giving vent to a certain sentiment, which arises upon reviewing those systems. I begun this subject with premising, that we ought to have an implicit faith in our senses, and that this would be the conclusion, I should draw from the whole of my reasoning. But to be ingenuous, I feel myself at present of a quite contrary sentiment, and am more inclined to repose no faith at all in my senses, or rather imagination, than to place in it such an implicit confidence. I cannot conceive how such trivial qualities of the fancy, conducted by such false suppositions, can ever lead to any solid and rational system. They are the coherence and constancy of our perceptions, which produce the opinion of their continued existence; though these qualities of perceptions have no perceivable connexion with such an existence. The constancy of our perceptions has the most considerable effect, and yet is attended with the greatest difficulties. It is a gross illusion to suppose, that our resembling perceptions are numerically the same; and it is this illusion, which leads us into the opinion, that these perceptions are uninterrupted, and are still existent, even when they are not present to the senses. This is the case with our popular system. And as to our philosophical one, it is liable to the same difficulties; and is over-and-above loaded with this absurdity,

[38] Sect. 5.

that it at once denies and establishes the vulgar supposition. Philosophers deny our resembling perceptions to be identically the same, and uninterrupted; and yet have so great a propensity to believe them such, that they arbitrarily invent a new set of perceptions, to which they attribute these qualities. I say, a new set of perceptions: For we may well suppose in general, but it is impossible for us distinctly to conceive, objects to be in their nature any thing but exactly the same with perceptions. What then can we look for from this confusion of groundless and extraordinary opinions but error and falshood? And how can we justify to ourselves any belief we repose in them?

This sceptical doubt, both with respect to reason and the senses, is a malady, which can never be radically cured, but must return upon us every moment, however we may chace it away, and sometimes may seem entirely free from it. It is impossible upon any system to defend either our understanding or senses; and we but expose them farther when we endeavour to justify them in that manner. As the sceptical doubt arises naturally from a profound and intense reflection on those subjects, it always encreases, the farther we carry our reflections, whether in opposition or conformity to it. Carelessness and in-attention alone can afford us any remedy. For this reason I rely entirely upon them; and take it for granted, whatever may be the reader's opinion at this present moment, that an hour hence he will be persuaded there is both an external and internal world; and going upon that supposition, I intend to examine some general systems both ancient and modern, which have been proposed of both, before I proceed to a more particular enquiry concerning our impressions. This will not, perhaps, in the end be found foreign to our present purpose.

SECTION III

Of the Antient Philosophy

Several moralists have recommended it as an excellent method of becoming acquainted with our own hearts, and knowing our progress in virtue, to recollect our dreams in a morning, and examine them with the same rigour, that we would our most serious and most deliberate actions. Our character is the same throughout, say they, and appears best where artifice, fear, and policy have no place, and men can neither be hypocrites with themselves nor others. The generosity, or baseness of our temper, our meekness or cruelty, our courage or pusilanimity, influence the fictions of the imagination with the most unbounded liberty, and discover themselves in the most glaring colours. In like manner, I am persuaded, there might be several useful discoveries made from a criticism of the fictions of the antient philosophy, concerning substances, and substantial form, and accidents, and occult qualities; which, however unreasonable and capricious, have a very intimate connexion with the principles of human nature.

It is confest by the most judicious philosophers, that our ideas of bodies are nothing but collections formed by the mind of the ideas of the several distinct sensible qualities, of which objects are composed, and which we find to have a constant union with each other. But however these qualities may in themselves be entirely distinct, it is certain we commonly regard the compound, which they form, as ONE thing, and as continuing the SAME under very considerable alterations. The acknowledged composition is evidently contrary to this supposed simplicity, and the variation to the identity. It may, therefore, be worth while to consider the causes, which make us almost universally fall into such evident contradictions, as well as the means by which we endeavour to conceal them.

It is evident, that as the ideas of the several distinct, successive qualities of objects are united together by a very close relation, the mind, in looking along the succession, must be carryed from one part of it to another by an easy transition, and will no more perceive the change, than if it contemplated the same unchangeable object. This easy transition is the effect, or rather essence of relation; I and as the imagination readily takes one idea for another, where their influence on the mind is similar; hence it proceeds, that any such succession of related qualities is readily considered as one continued object, existing without any variation. The smooth and uninterrupted progress of the thought, being alike in both cases, readily deceives the mind, and makes us ascribe an identity to the changeable succession of connected qualities.

But when we alter our method of considering the succession, and instead of traceing it gradually through the successive points of time, survey at once Any two distinct periods of its duration, and compare the different conditions of the successive qualities; in that case the variations, which were insensible when they arose gradually, do now appear of consequence, and seem entirely to destroy the identity. By this means there arises a kind of contrariety in our method of thinking, from the different points of view, in which we survey the object, and from the nearness or remoteness of those instants of time, which we compare together. When we gradually follow an object in its successive changes, the smooth progress of the thought makes us ascribe an identity to the succession; because it is by a similar act of the mind we consider an unchangeable object. When we compare its situation after a considerable change the progress of the thought is broke; and consequently we are presented with the idea of diversity: In order to reconcile which contradictions the imagination is apt to feign something unknown and invisible, which it supposes to continue the same under all these variations; and this unintelligible something it calls a substance, or original and first matter.

We entertain a like notion with regard to the simplicity of substances, and from like causes. Suppose an object perfectly simple and indivisible to be presented, along with another object, whose co-existent parts are connected together by a strong relation, it is evident the actions of the mind, in considering these two objects, are not very different. The imagination conceives the simple object at once, with facility, by a single effort of thought, without change or variation. The connexion of parts in the compound object has almost the same effect, and so unites the object within itself, that the fancy feels not the transition in passing from one part to another. Hence the colour, taste, figure, solidity, and other qualities, combined in a peach or melon, are conceived to form one thing; and that on account of their close relation, which makes them affect the thought in the same manner, as if perfectly uncompounded. But the mind rests not here. Whenever it views the object in another light, it finds that all these qualities are different, and distinguishable, and separable from each other; which view of things being destructive of its primary and more natural notions, obliges the imagination to feign an unknown something, or original substance and matter, as a principle of union or cohesion among these qualities, and as what may give the compound object a title to be called one thing, notwithstanding its diversity and composition.

The peripatetic philosophy asserts the original matter to be perfectly homogeneous in all bodies, and considers fire, water, earth, and air, as of the very same substance; on account of their gradual revolutions and changes into each other. At the same time it assigns to each of these species of objects a distinct substantial form, which it supposes to be the source of all those different qualities they possess, and to be a new foundation of simplicity and identity to each particular species. All depends on our manner of viewing the objects. When we look along the insensible changes of bodies, we suppose all of them to be of the same substance or essence. When we consider their sensible differences, we attribute to each of them a substantial and essential difference. And in order to indulge ourselves in both these ways of considering our objects, we suppose all bodies to have at once a substance and a substantial form.

The notion of accidents is an unavoidable consequence of this method of thinking with regard to substances and substantial forms; nor can we forbear looking upon colours, sounds, tastes, figures, and other properties of bodies, as existences, which cannot subsist apart, but require a subject of inhesion to sustain and support them. For having never discovered any of these sensible qualities, where, for the reasons above-mentioned, we did not likewise fancy a substance to exist; the same habit, which makes us infer a connexion betwixt cause and effect, makes us here infer a dependence of every quality on the unknown substance. The custom of imagining a dependence has the same effect as the custom of observing it would have. This conceit, however, is no more reasonable than any of the foregoing. Every quality being a distinct thing from another, may be conceived to exist apart, and may exist apart, not only from every other quality, but from that unintelligible chimera of a substance.

But these philosophers carry their fictions still farther in their sentiments concerning occult qualities, and both suppose a substance supporting, which they do not understand, and an accident supported, of which they have as imperfect an idea. The whole system, therefore, is entirely incomprehensible, and yet is derived from principles as natural as any of these above-explained.

In considering this subject we may observe a gradation of three opinions, that rise above each other, according as the persons, who form them, acquire new degrees of reason and knowledge. These opinions are that of the vulgar, that of a false philosophy, and that of the true; where we shall find upon enquiry, that the true philosophy approaches nearer to the sentiments of the vulgar, than to those of a mistaken knowledge. It is natural for men, in their common and care, less way of thinking, to imagine they perceive a connexion betwixt such objects as they have constantly found united together; and because custom has rendered it difficult to separate the ideas, they are apt to fancy such a separation to be in itself impossible and absurd. But philosophers, who abstract from the effects of custom, and compare the ideas of objects, immediately perceive the falshood of these vulgar sentiments, and discover that there is no known connexion among objects. Every different object appears to them entirely distinct and separate; and they perceive, that it is not from a view of the nature and qualities of objects we infer one from another, but only when in several instances we observe them to have been constantly conjoined. But these philosophers, instead of drawing a just inference from this observation, and concluding, that we have no idea of power or agency, separate from the mind, and belonging to causes; I say, instead of drawing this conclusion, they frequently search for the qualities, in which this agency consists, and are displeased with every system, which their reason suggests to them, in order to explain it. They have sufficient force of genius to free them from the vulgar error, that there is a natural and perceivable connexion betwixt the several sensible qualities and actions of matter; but not sufficient to keep them from ever seeking for this connexion in matter, or causes. Had they fallen upon the just conclusion, they would have returned back to the situation of the vulgar, and would have regarded all these disquisitions with indolence and indifference. At present they seem to be in a very lamentable condition, and such as the poets have given us but a faint notion of in their descriptions of the punishment of Sisyphus and Tantalus. For what can be imagined more tormenting, than to seek with eagerness, what for ever flies us; and seek for it in a place, where it is impossible it can ever exist?

But as nature seems to have observed a kind of justice and compensation in every thing, she has not neglected philosophers more than the rest of the creation; but has reserved them a consolation amid all their disappointments and afflictions. This consolation principally consists in their invention of the words: faculty and occult quality. For it being usual, after the frequent use of terms, which are really significant and intelligible, to omit the idea, which we would express by them, and to preserve only the custom, by which we recal the idea at pleasure; so it naturally happens, that after the frequent use of terms, which are wholly insignificant and unintelligible, we fancy them to be on the same footing with the precedent, and to have a secret meaning, which we might discover by reflection. The resemblance of their appearance deceives the mind, as is usual, and makes us imagine a thorough resemblance and conformity. By this means these philosophers set themselves at ease, and arrive at last, by an illusion, at the same indifference, which the people attain by their stupidity, and true philosophers by their moderate scepticism. They need only say, that any phenomenon, which puzzles them, arises from a faculty or an occult quality, and there is an end of all dispute and enquiry upon the matter.

But among all the instances, wherein the Peripatetics have shewn they were guided by every trivial propensity of the imagination, no one is more-remarkable than their sympathies, antipathies, and horrors of a vacuum. There is a very remarkable inclination in human nature, to bestow on external objects the same emotions, which it observes in itself; and to find every where those ideas, which are most present to it. This inclination, it is true, is suppressed by a little reflection, and only takes place in children, poets, and the antient philosophers. It appears in children, by their desire of beating the stones, which hurt them: In poets, by their readiness to personify every thing: And in the antient philosophers, by these fictions of sympathy and antipathy. We must pardon children, because of their age; poets, because they profess to follow implicitly the suggestions of their fancy: But what excuse shall we find to justify our philosophers in so signal a weakness?

SECTION IV

Of the Modern Philosophy

But here it may be objected, that the imagination, according to my own confession, being the ultimate judge of all systems of philosophy, I am unjust in blaming the antient philosophers for making use of that faculty, and allowing themselves to be entirely guided by it in their reasonings. In order to justify myself, I must distinguish in the imagination betwixt the principles which are permanent, irresistible, and universal; such as the customary transition from causes to effects, and from effects to causes: And the principles, which are changeable, weak, and irregular; such as those I have just now taken notice of. The former are the foundation of all our thoughts and actions, so that upon their removal human nature must immediately perish and go to ruin. The latter are neither unavoidable to mankind, nor necessary, or so much as useful in the conduct of life; but on the contrary are observed only to take place in weak minds, and being opposite to the other principles of custom and reasoning, may easily be subverted by a due contrast and opposition. For this reason the former are received by philosophy, and the latter rejected. One who concludes somebody to be near him, when he hears an articulate voice in the dark, reasons justly and naturally; though that conclusion be derived from nothing but custom, which infixes and inlivens the idea of a human creature, on account of his usual conjunction with the present impression. But one, who is tormented he knows not why, with the apprehension of spectres in the dark, may, perhaps, be said to reason, and to reason naturally too: But then it must be in the same sense, that a malady is said to be natural; as arising from natural causes, though it be contrary to health, the most agreeable and most natural situation of man.

The opinions of the antient philosophers, their fictions of substance and accident, and their reasonings concerning substantial forms and occult qualities, are like the spectres in the dark, and are derived from principles, which, however common, are neither universal nor unavoidable in human nature. The modern philosophy pretends to be entirely free from this defect, and to arise only from the solid, permanent, and consistent principles of the imagination. Upon what grounds this pretension is founded must now be the subject of our enquiry.

The fundamental principle of that philosophy is the opinion concerning colours, sounds, tastes, smells, heat and cold; which it asserts to be nothing but impressions in the mind, derived from the operation of external objects, and without any resemblance to the qualities of the objects. Upon examination, I find only one of the reasons commonly produced for this opinion to be satisfactory, viz. that derived from the variations of those impressions, even while the external object, to all appearance, continues the same. These variations depend upon several circumstances. Upon the different situations of our health: A man in a malady feels a disagreeable taste in meats, which before pleased him the most. Upon the different complexions and constitutions of men That seems bitter to one, which is sweet to another. Upon the difference of their external situation and position: Colours reflected from the clouds change according to the distance of the clouds, and according to the angle they make with the eye and luminous body. Fire also communicates the sensation of pleasure at one distance, and that of pain at another. Instances of this kind are very numerous and frequent.

The conclusion drawn from them, is likewise as satisfactory as can possibly be imagined. It is certain, that when different impressions of the same sense arise from any object, every one of these impressions has not a resembling quality existent in the object. For as the same object cannot, at the same time, be endowed with different qualities of the same sense, and as the same quality cannot resemble impressions entirely different; it evidently follows, that many of our impressions have no external model or archetype. Now from like effects we presume like causes. Many of the impressions of colour, sound, &c. are confest to be nothing but internal existences, and to arise from causes, which no ways resemble them. These impressions are in appearance nothing different from the other impressions of colour, sound, &c. We conclude, therefore, that they are, all of them, derived from a like origin.

This principle being once admitted, all the other doctrines of that philosophy seem to follow by an easy consequence. For upon the removal of sounds, colours, beat, cold, and other sensible qualities, from the rank of continued independent existences, we are reduced merely to what are called primary qualities, as the only real ones, of which we have any adequate notion. These primary qualities are extension and solidity, with their different mixtures and modifications; figure, motion, gravity, and cohesion. The generation, encrease, decay, and corruption of animals and vegetables, are nothing but changes of figure and motion; as also the operations of all bodies on each other; of fire, of light, water, air, earth, and of all the elements and powers of nature. One figure and motion produces another figure and motion; nor does there remain in the material universe any other principle, either active or passive, of which we can form the most distant idea.

I believe many objections might be made to this system But at present I shall confine myself to one, which is in my opinion very decisive. I assert, that instead of explaining the operations of external objects by its means, we utterly annihilate all these objects, and reduce ourselves to the opinions of the most extravagant scepticism concerning them. If colours, sounds, tastes, and smells be merely perceptions, nothing we can conceive is possest of a real, continued, and independent existence; not even motion, extension and solidity, which are the primary qualities chiefly insisted on.

To begin with the examination of motion; it is evident this is a quality altogether inconceivable alone, and without a reference to some other object. The idea of motion necessarily supposes that of a body moving. Now what is our idea of the moving body, without which motion is incomprehensible? It must resolve itself into the idea of extension or of solidity; and consequently the reality of motion depends upon that of these other qualities.

This opinion, which is universally acknowledged concerning motion, I have proved to be true with regard to extension; and have shewn that it is impossible to conceive extension, but as composed of parts, endowed with colour or solidity. The idea of extension is a compound idea; but as it is not compounded of an infinite number of parts or inferior ideas, it must at last resolve itself into such as are perfectly simple and indivisible. These simple and indivisible parts, not being ideas of extension, must be non entities, unless conceived as coloured or solid. Colour is excluded from any real existence. The reality, therefore, of our idea of extension depends upon the reality of that of solidity, nor can the former be just while the latter is chimerical. Let us, then, lend our attention to the examination of the idea of solidity.

The idea of solidity is that of two objects, which being impelled by the utmost force, cannot penetrate each other; but still maintain a separate and distinct existence. Solidity, therefore, is perfectly incomprehensible alone, and without the conception of some bodies, which are solid, and maintain this separate and distinct existence. Now what idea have we of these bodies? The ideas of colours, sounds, and other secondary qualities are excluded. The idea of motion depends on that of extension, and the idea of extension on that of solidity. It is impossible, therefore, that the idea of solidity can depend on either of them. For that would be to run in a circle, and make one idea depend on another, while at the same time the latter depends on the former. Our modern philosophy, therefore, leaves us no just nor satisfactory idea of solidity; nor consequently of matter.

This argument will appear entirely conclusive to every one that comprehends it; but because it may seem abstruse and intricate to the generality of readers, I hope to be excused, if I endeavour to render it more obvious by some variation of the expression. In order to form an idea of solidity, we must conceive two bodies pressing on each other without any penetration; and it is impossible to arrive at this idea, when we confine ourselves to one object, much more without conceiving any. Two non-entities cannot exclude each other from their places; because they never possess any place, nor can be endowed with any quality. Now I ask, what idea do we form of these bodies or objects, to which we suppose solidity to belong? To say, that we conceive them merely as solid, is to run on in infinitum. To affirm, that we paint them out to ourselves as extended, either resolves all into a false idea, or returns in a circle. Extension must necessarily be considered either as coloured, which is a false idea; I or as solid, which brings us back to the first question. We may make the same observation concerning mobility and figure; and upon the whole must conclude, that after the exclusion of colours, sounds, heat and cold from the rank of external existences, there remains nothing, which can afford us a just and constituent idea of body.

Add to this, that, properly speaking, solidity or impenetrability is nothing, but an impossibility of annihilation, as[39] has been already observed: For which reason it is the more necessary for us to form some distinct idea of that object, whose annihilation we suppose impossible. An impossibility of being annihilated cannot exist, and can never be conceived to exist, by itself: but necessarily requires some object or real existence, to which it may belong. Now the difficulty still remains, how to form an idea of this object or existence, without having recourse to the secondary and sensible qualities.

Nor must we omit on this occasion our accustomed method of examining ideas by considering those impressions, from which they are derived. The impressions, which enter by the sight and hearing, the smell and taste, are affirmed by modern philosophy to be without any resembling objects; and consequently the idea of solidity, which is supposed to be real, can never be derived from any of these senses. There remains, therefore, the feeling as the only sense, that can convey the impression, which is original to the idea of solidity; and indeed we naturally imagine, that we feel the solidity of bodies, and need but touch any object in order to perceive this quality. But this method of thinking is more popular than philosophical; as will appear from the following reflections.

First, It is easy to observe, that though bodies are felt by means of their solidity, yet the feeling is a quite different thing from the solidity; and that they have not the least resemblance to each other. A man, who has the palsey in one hand, has as perfect an idea of impenetrability, when he observes that hand to be supported by the table, as when he feels the same table with the other hand. An object, that presses upon any of our members, meets with resistance; and that resistance, by the motion it gives to the nerves and animal spirits, conveys a certain sensation to the mind; but it does not follow, that the sensation, motion, and resistance are any ways resembling.

---

[39] Part II. Sect. 4.

Secondly, The impressions of touch are simple impressions, except when considered with regard to their extension; which makes nothing to the present purpose: And from this simplicity I infer, that they neither represent solidity, nor any real object. For let us put two cases, viz. that of a man, who presses a stone, or any solid body, with his hand, and that of two stones, which press each other; it will readily be allowed, that these two cases are not in every respect alike, but that in the former there is conjoined with the solidity, a feeling or sensation, of which there is no appearance in the latter. In order, therefore, to make these two cases alike, it is necessary to remove some part of the impression, which the man feels by his hand, or organ of sensation; and that being impossible in a simple impression, obliges us to remove the whole, and proves that this whole impression has no archetype or model in external objects. To which we may add, that solidity necessarily supposes two bodies, along with contiguity and impulse; which being a compound object, can never be represented by a simple impression. Not to mention, that though solidity continues always invariably the same, the impressions of touch change every moment upon us; which is a clear proof that the latter are not representations of the former.

Thus there is a direct and total opposition betwixt our reason and our senses; or more properly speaking, betwixt those conclusions we form from cause and effect, and those that persuade us of the continued and independent existence of body. When we reason from cause and effect, we conclude, that neither colour, sound, taste, nor smell have a continued and independent existence. When we exclude these sensible qualities there remains nothing in the universe, which has such an existence.

SECTION V

Of the Immateriality of the Soul

Having found such contradictions and difficulties in every system concerning external objects, and in the idea of matter, which we fancy so clear and determinate, We shall naturally expect still greater difficulties and contradictions in every hypothesis concerning our internal perceptions, and the nature of the mind, which we are apt to imagine so much more obscure, and uncertain. But in this we should deceive ourselves. The intellectual world, though involved in infinite obscurities, is not perplexed with any such contradictions, as those we have discovered in the natural. What is known concerning it, agrees with itself; and what is unknown, we must be contented to leave so.

It is true, would we hearken to certain philosophers, they promise to diminish our ignorance; but I am afraid it is at the hazard of running us into contradictions, from which the subject is of itself exempted. These philosophers are the curious reasoners concerning the material or immaterial substances, in which they suppose our perceptions to inhere. In order to put a stop to these endless cavils on both sides, I know no better method, than to ask these philosophers in a few words, What they mean by substance and inhesion? And after they have answered this question, it will then be reasonable, and not till then, to enter seriously into the dispute.

This question we have found impossible to be answered with regard to matter and body: But besides that in the case of the mind, it labours under all the same difficulties, it is burthened with some additional ones, which are peculiar to that subject. As every idea is derived from a precedent impression, had we any idea of the substance of our minds, we must also have an impression of it; which is very difficult, if not impossible, to be conceived. For how can an impression represent a substance, otherwise than by resembling it? And how can an impression resemble a substance, since, according to this philosophy, it is not a substance, and has none of the peculiar qualities or characteristics of a substance?

But leaving the question of what may or may not be, for that other what actually is, I desire those philosophers, who pretend that we have an idea of the substance of our minds, to point out the impression that produces it, and tell distinctly after what manner that impression operates, and from what object it is derived. Is it an impression of sensation or of reflection? Is it pleasant, or painful, or indifferent? Does it attend us at all times, or does it only return at intervals? If at intervals, at what times principally does it return, and by what causes is it produced?

If instead of answering these questions, any one should evade the difficulty, by saying, that the definition of a substance is something which may exist by itself; and that this definition ought to satisfy us: should this be said, I should observe, that this definition agrees to every thing, that can possibly be conceived; and never will serve to distinguish substance from accident, or the soul from its perceptions. For thus I reason. Whatever is clearly conceived may exist; and whatever is clearly conceived, after any manner, may exist after the same manner. This is one principle, which has been already acknowledged. Again, every thing, which is different, is distinguishable, and every thing which is distinguishable, is separable by the imagination. This is another principle. My conclusion from both is, that since all our perceptions are different from each other, and from every thing else in the universe, they are also distinct and separable, and may be considered as separately existent, and may exist separately, and have no need of any thing else to support their existence. They are, therefore, substances, as far as this definition explains a substance.

Thus neither by considering the first origin of ideas, nor by means of a definition are we able to arrive at any satisfactory notion of substance; which seems to me a sufficient reason for abandoning utterly that dispute concerning the materiality and immateriality of the soul, and makes me absolutely condemn even the question itself. We have no perfect idea of any thing but of a perception. A substance is entirely different from a perception. We have, therefore, no idea of a substance. Inhesion in something is supposed to be requisite to support the existence of our perceptions. Nothing appears requisite to support the existence of a perception. We have, therefore, no idea of inhesion. What possibility then of answering that question, Whether perceptions inhere in a material or immaterial substance, when we do not so much as understand the meaning of the question?

There is one argument commonly employed for the immateriality of the soul, which seems to me remarkable. Whatever is extended consists of parts; and whatever consists of parts is divisible, if not in reality, at least in the imagination. But it is impossible anything divisible can be conjoined to a thought or perception, which is a being altogether inseparable and indivisible. For supposing such a conjunction, would the indivisible thought exist on the left or on the right hand of this extended divisible body? On the surface or in the middle? On the back or fore side of it? If it be conjoined with the extension, it must exist somewhere within its dimensions. If it exist within its dimensions, it must either exist in one particular part; and then that particular part is indivisible, and the perception is conjoined only with it, not with the extension: Or if the thought exists in every part, it must also be extended, and separable, and divisible, as well as the body; which is utterly absurd and contradictory. For can any one conceive a passion of a yard in length, a foot in breadth, and an inch in thickness? Thought, therefore, and extension are qualities wholly incompatible, and never can incorporate together into one subject.

This argument affects not the question concerning the substance of the soul, but only that concerning its local conjunction with matter; and therefore it may not be improper to consider in general what objects are, or are not susceptible of a local conjunction. This is a curious question, and may lead us to some discoveries of considerable moment.

The first notion of space and extension is derived solely from the senses of sight and feeling; nor is there any thing, but what is coloured or tangible, that has parts disposed after such a manner, as to convey that idea. When we diminish or encrease a relish, it is not after the same manner that we diminish or encrease any visible object; and when several sounds strike our hearing at once, custom and reflection alone make us form an idea of the degrees of the distance and contiguity of those bodies, from which they are derived. Whatever marks the place of its existence either must be extended, or must be a mathematical point, without parts or composition. What is extended must have a particular figure, as square, round, triangular; none of which will agree to a desire, or indeed to any impression or idea, except to these two senses above-mentioned. Neither ought a desire, though indivisible, to be considered as a mathematical point. For in that case it would be possible, by the addition of others, to make two, three, four desires, and these disposed and situated in such a manner, as to have a determinate length, breadth and thickness; which is evidently absurd.

It will not be surprising after this, if I deliver a maxim, which is condemned by several metaphysicians, and is esteemed contrary to the most certain principles of hum reason. This maxim is that an object may exist, and yet be no where: and I assert, that this is not only possible, but that the greatest part of beings do and must exist after this manner. An object may be said to be no where, when its parts are not so situated with respect to each other, as to form any figure or quantity; nor the whole with respect to other bodies so as to answer to our notions of contiguity or distance. Now this is evidently the case with all our perceptions and objects, except those of the sight and feeling. A moral reflection cannot be placed on the right or on the left hand of a passion, nor can a smell or sound be either of a circular or a square figure. These objects and perceptions, so far from requiring any particular place, are absolutely incompatible with it, and even the imagination cannot attribute it to them. And as to the absurdity of supposing them to be no where, we may consider, that if the passions and sentiments appear to the perception to have any particular place, the idea of extension might be derived from them, as well as from the sight and touch; contrary to what we have already established. If they APPEAR not to have any particular place, they may possibly exist in the same manner; since whatever we conceive is possible.

It will not now be necessary to prove, that those perceptions, which are simple, and exist no where, are incapable of any conjunction in place with matter or body, which is extended and divisible; since it is impossible to found a relation but on some common quality. It may be better worth our while to remark, that this question of the local conjunction of objects does not only occur in metaphysical disputes concerning the nature of the soul, but that even in common life we have every moment occasion to examine it. Thus supposing we consider a fig at one end of the table, and an olive at the other, it is evident, that in forming the complex ideas of these substances, one of the most obvious is that of their different relishes; and it is as evident, that we incorporate and conjoin these qualities with such as are coloured and tangible. The bitter taste of the one, and sweet of the other are supposed to lie in the very visible body, and to be separated from each other by the whole length of the table. This is so notable and so natural an illusion, that it may be proper to consider the principles, from which it is derived.

Though an extended object be incapable of a conjunction in place with another, that exists without any place or extension, yet are they susceptible of many other relations. Thus the taste and smell of any fruit are inseparable from its other qualities of colour and tangibility; and whichever of them be the cause or effect, it is certain they are always co-existent. Nor are they only co-existent in general, but also co-temporary in their appearance in the mind; and it is upon the application of the extended body to our senses we perceive its particular taste and smell. These relations, then, of causation, and contiguity in the time of their appearance, betwixt the extended object and the quality, which exists without any particular place, must have such an effect on the mind, that upon the appearance of one it will immediately turn its thought to the conception of the other. Nor is this all. We not only turn our thought from one to the other upon account of their relation, but likewise endeavour to give them a new relation, viz. that of a CONJUNCTION IN

PLACE, that we may render the transition more easy and natural. For it is a quality, which I shall often have occasion to remark in human nature, and shall explain more fully in its proper place, that when objects are united by any relation, we have a strong propensity to add some new relation to them, in order to compleat the union. In our arrangement of bodies we never fail to place such as are resembling, in contiguity to each other, or at least in correspondent points of view: Why? but because we feel a satisfaction in joining the relation of contiguity to that of resemblance, or the resemblance of situation to that of qualities. The effects this propensity have been[40] already observed in that resemblance, which we so readily suppose betwixt particular impressions and their external causes. But we shall not find a more evident effect of it, than in the present instance, where from the relations of causation and contiguity in time betwixt two objects, we feign likewise that of a conjunction in place, in order to strengthen the connexion.

But whatever confused notions we may form of an union in place betwixt an extended body, as a fig, and its particular taste, it is certain that upon reflection we must observe this union something altogether unintelligible and contradictory. For should we ask ourselves one obvious question, viz. if the taste, which we conceive to be contained in the circumference of the body, is in every part of it or in one only, we must quickly find ourselves at a loss, and perceive the impossibility of ever giving a satisfactory answer. We cannot rely, that it is only in one part: For experience convinces us, that every part has the same relish. We can as little reply, that it exists in every part: For then we must suppose it figured and extended; which is absurd and incomprehensible. Here then we are influenced by two principles directly contrary to each other, viz. that inclination of our fancy by which we are determined to incorporate the taste with the extended object, and our reason, which shows us the impossibility of such an union. Being divided betwixt these opposite principles, we renounce neither one nor the other, but involve the subject in such confusion and obscurity, that we no longer perceive the opposition. We suppose, that the taste exists within the circumference of the body, but in such a manner, that it fills the whole without extension, and exists entire in every part without separation. In short, we use in our most familiar way of thinking, that scholastic principle, which, when crudely proposed, appears so shocking, of TOTUM IN TOTO & TOLUM IN QUALIBET PARTE: Which is much the same, as if we should say, that a thing is in a certain place, and yet is not there.

All this absurdity proceeds from our endeavouring to bestow a place on what is utterly incapable of it; and that endeavour again arises from our inclination to compleat an union, which is founded on causation, and a contiguity of time, by attributing to the objects a conjunction in place. But if ever reason be of sufficient force to overcome prejudice, it is certain, that in the present case it must prevail. For we have only this choice left, either to suppose that some beings exist without

[40] Sect. 2, towards the end.

any place; or that they are figured and extended; or that when they are incorporated with extended objects, the whole is in the whole, and the whole in every part. The absurdity of the two last suppositions proves sufficiently the veracity of the first. Nor is there any fourth opinion. For as to the supposition of their existence in the manner of mathematical points, it resolves itself into the second opinion, and supposes, that several passions may be placed in a circular figure, and that a certain number of smells, conjoined with a certain number of sounds, may make a body of twelve cubic inches; which appears ridiculous upon the bare mentioning of it.

But though in this view of things we cannot refuse to condemn the materialists, who conjoin all thought with extension; yet a little reflection will show us equal reason for blaming their antagonists, who conjoin all thought with a simple and indivisible substance. The most vulgar philosophy informs us, that no external object can make itself known to the mind immediately, and without the interposition of an image or perception. That table, which just now appears to me, is only a perception, and all its qualities are qualities of a perception. Now the most obvious of all its qualities is extension. The perception consists of parts. These parts are so situated, as to afford us the notion of distance and contiguity; of length, breadth, and thickness. The termination of these three dimensions is what we call figure. This figure is moveable, separable, and divisible. Mobility, and separability are the distinguishing properties of extended objects. And to cut short all disputes, the very idea of extension is copyed from nothing but an impression, and consequently must perfectly agree to it. To say the idea of extension agrees to any thing, is to say it is extended.

The free-thinker may now triumph in his turn; and having found there are impressions and ideas really extended, may ask his antagonists, how they can incorporate a simple and indivisible subject with an extended perception? All the arguments of Theologians may here be retorted upon them. Is the indivisible subject, or immaterial substance, if you will, on the left or on the right hand of the perception? Is it in this particular part, or in that other? Is it in every part without being extended? Or is it entire in any one part without deserting the rest? It is impossible to give any answer to these questions, but what will both be absurd in itself, and will account for the union of our indivisible perceptions with an extended substance.

This gives me an occasion to take a-new into consideration the question concerning the substance of the soul; and though I have condemned that question as utterly unintelligible, yet I cannot forbear proposing some farther reflections concerning it. I assert, that the doctrine of the immateriality, simplicity, and indivisibility of a thinking substance is a true atheism, and will serve to justify all those sentiments, for which Spinoza is so universally infamous. From this topic, I hope at least to reap one advantage, that my adversaries will not have any pretext to render the present doctrine odious by their declamations, when they see that they can be so easily retorted on them.

The fundamental principle of the atheism of Spinoza is the doctrine of the simplicity of the universe, and the unity of that substance, in which he supposes both thought and matter to inhere. There is only one substance, says he, in the world; and that substance is perfectly simple and indivisible, and exists every where, without any local presence. Whatever we discover externally by sensation; whatever we feel internally by reflection; all these are nothing but modifications of that one, simple, and necessarily existent being, and are not possest of any separate or distinct existence. Every passion of the soul; every configuration of matter, however different and various, inhere in the same substance, and preserve in themselves their characters of distinction, without communicating them to that subject, in which they inhere. The same substratum, if I may so speak, supports the most different modifications, without any difference in itself; and varies them, without any variation. Neither time, nor place, nor all the diversity of nature are able to produce any composition or change in its perfect simplicity and identity.

I believe this brief exposition of the principles of that famous atheist will be sufficient for the present purpose, and that without entering farther into these gloomy and obscure regions, I shall be able to shew, that this hideous hypothesis is almost the same with that of the immateriality of the soul, which has become so popular. To make this evident, let us[41] remember, that as every idea is derived from a preceding perception, it is impossible our idea of a perception, and that of an object or external existence can ever represent what are specifically different from each other. Whatever difference we may suppose betwixt them, it is still incomprehensible to us; and we are obliged either to conceive an external object merely as a relation without a relative, or to make it the very same with a perception or impression.

The consequence I shall draw from this may, at first sight, appear a mere sophism; but upon the least examination will be found solid and satisfactory. I say then, that since we may suppose, but never can conceive a specific deference betwixt an object and impression; any conclusion we form concerning the connexion and repugnance of impressions, will not be known certainly to be applicable to objects; but that on the other hand, whatever conclusions of this kind we form concerning objects, will most certainly be applicable to impressions. The reason is not difficult. As an object is supposed to be different from an impression, we cannot be sure, that the circumstance, upon which we found our reasoning, is common to both, supposing we form the reasoning upon the impression. It is still possible, that the object may differ from it in that particular. But when we first form our reasoning concerning the object, it is beyond doubt, that the same reasoning must extend to the impression: And that because the quality of the object, upon which the argument is founded, must at least be conceived by the mind; and could not be conceived, unless it were common to an impression; since we have no idea but

[41] Part II, Sect. 6.

what is derived from that origin. Thus we may establish it as a certain maxim, that we can never, by any principle, but by an irregular kind[42] of reasoning from experience, discover a connexion or repugnance betwixt objects, which extends not to impressions; though the inverse proposition may not be equally true, that all the discoverable relations of impressions are common to objects.

To apply this to the present case; there are two different systems of being presented, to which I suppose myself under necessity of assigning some substance, or ground of inhesion. I observe first the universe of objects or of body: The sun, moon and stars; the earth, seas, plants, animals, men, ships, houses, and other productions either of art or nature. Here Spinoza appears, and tells me, that these are only modifications; and that the subject, in which they inhere, is simple, incompounded, and indivisible. After this I consider the other system of beings, viz. the universe of thought, or my impressions and ideas. There I observe another sun, moon and stars; an earth, and seas, covered and inhabited by plants and animals; towns, houses, mountains, rivers; and in short every thing I can discover or conceive in the first system. Upon my enquiring concerning these, Theologians present themselves, and tell me, that these also are modifications, and modifications of one simple, uncompounded, and indivisible substance. Immediately upon which I am deafened with the noise of a hundred voices, that treat the first hypothesis with detestation and scorn, and the second with applause and veneration. I turn my attention to these hypotheses to see what may be the reason of so great a partiality; and find that they have the same fault of being unintelligible, and that as far as we can understand them, they are so much alike, that it is impossible to discover any absurdity in one, which is not common to both of them. We have no idea of any quality in an object, which does not agree to, and may not represent a quality in an impression; and that because all our ideas are derived from our impressions. We can never, therefore, find any repugnance betwixt an extended object as a modification, and a simple uncompounded essence, as its substance, unless that repugnance takes place equally betwixt the perception or impression of that extended object, and the same uncompounded essence. Every idea of a quality in an object passes through an impression; and therefore every perceivable relation, whether of connexion or repugnance, must be common both to objects and impressions.

But though this argument, considered in general, seems evident beyond all doubt and contradiction, yet to make it more clear and sensible, let us survey it in detail; and see whether all the absurdities, which have been found in the system of Spinoza, may not likewise be discovered in that of Theologians.[43]

First, It has been said against Spinoza, according to the scholastic way of talking, rather than thinking, that a mode, not being any distinct or separate

[42] Such as that of Sect. 2, form the coherence of our perceptions.

[43] See *Bayle's* dictionary, article of *Spinoza*.

existence, must be the very same with its substance, and consequently the extension of the universe, must be in a manner identifyed with that, simple, uncompounded essence, in which the universe is supposed to inhere. But this, it may be pretended, is utterly impossible and inconceivable unless the indivisible substance expand itself, so as to correspond to the extension, or the extension contract itself, so as to answer to the indivisible substance. This argument seems just, as far as we can understand it; and it is plain nothing is required, but a change in the terms, to apply the same argument to our extended perceptions, and the simple essence of the soul; the ideas of objects and perceptions being in every respect the same, only attended with the supposition of a difference, that is unknown and incomprehensible.

Secondly, It has been said, that we have no idea of substance, which is not applicable to matter; nor any idea of a distinct substance, which is not applicable to every distinct portion of matter. Matter, therefore, is not a mode but a substance, and each part of matter is not a distinct mode, but a distinct substance. I have already proved, that we have no perfect idea of substance; but that taking it for something, that can exist by itself, it is evident every perception is a substance, and every distinct part of a perception a distinct substance: And consequently the one hypothesis labours under the same difficulties in this respect with the other.

Thirdly, It has been objected to the system of one simple substance in the universe, that this substance being the support or substratum of every thing, must at the very same instant be modifyed into forms, which are contrary and incompatible. The round and square figures are incompatible in the same substance at the same time. How then is it possible, that the same substance can at once be modifyed into that square table, and into this round one? I ask the same question concerning the impressions of these tables; and find that the answer is no more satisfactory in one case than in the other.

It appears, then, that to whatever side we turn, the same difficulties follow us, and that we cannot advance one step towards the establishing the simplicity and immateriality o the soul, without preparing the way for a dangerous and irrecoverable atheism. It is the same case, if instead o calling thought a modification of the soul, we should give it the more antient, and yet more modish name of an action. By an action we mean much the same thing, as what is commonly called an abstract mode; that is, something, which, properly speaking, is neither distinguishable, nor separable from its substance, and is only conceived by a distinction of reason, or an abstraction. But nothing is gained by this change of the term of modification, for that of action; nor do we free ourselves from one single difficulty by its means; as will appear from the two following reflexions.

First, I observe, that the word, action, according to this explication of it, can never justly be applied to any perception, as derived from a mind or thinking substance. Our perceptions are all really different, and separable, and distinguishable from each other, and from everything else, which we can imagine:

and therefore it is impossible to conceive, how they can be the action or abstract mode of any substance. The instance of motion, which is commonly made use of to shew after what manner perception depends, as an action, upon its substance, rather confounds than instructs us. Motion to all appearance induces no real nor essential change on the body, but only varies its relation to other objects. But betwixt a person in the morning walking a garden with company, agreeable to him; and a person in the afternoon inclosed in a dungeon, and full of terror, despair, and resentment, there seems to be a radical difference, and of quite another kind, than what is produced on a body by the change of its situation. As we conclude from the distinction and separability of their ideas, that external objects have a separate existence from each other; so when we make these ideas themselves our objects, we must draw the same conclusion concerning them, according to the precedent reasoning. At least it must be confest, that having idea of the substance of the soul, it is impossible for us to tell how it can admit of such differences, and even contrarieties of perception without any fundamental change; and consequently can never tell in what sense perceptions are actions of that substance. The use, therefore, of the word, action, unaccompanyed with any meaning, instead of that of modification, makes no addition to our knowledge, nor is of any advantage to the doctrine of the immateriality of the soul.

I add in the second place, that if it brings any advantage to that cause, it must bring an equal to the cause of atheism. For do our Theologians pretend to make a monopoly of the word, action, and may not the atheists likewise take possession of it, and affirm that plants, animals, men, &c. are nothing but particular actions of one simple universal substance, which exerts itself from a blind and absolute necessity? This you'll say is utterly absurd. I own it is unintelligible; but at the same time assert, according to the principles above-explained, that it is impossible to discover any absurdity in the supposition, that all the various objects in nature are actions of one simple substance, which absurdity will not be applicable to a like supposition concerning impressions and ideas.

From these hypotheses concerning the substance and local conjunction of our perceptions, we may pass to another, which is more intelligible than the former, and more important than the latter, viz. concerning the cause of our perceptions. Matter and motion, it is commonly said in the schools, however varyed, are still matter and motion, and produce only a difference in the position and situation of objects. Divide a body as often as you please, it is still body. Place it in any figure, nothing ever results but figure, or the relation of parts. Move it in any manner, you still find motion or a change of relation. It is absurd to imagine, that motion in a circle, for instance, should be nothing but merely motion in a circle; while motion in another direction, as in an ellipse, should also be a passion or moral reflection: That the shocking of two globular particles should become a sensation of pain, and that the meeting of two triangular ones should afford a pleasure. Now as these different shocks, and variations, and mixtures are the only changes, of which matter is susceptible, and as these never afford us any idea of thought or perception, it is concluded to be impossible, that thought can ever be caused by matter.

Few have been able to withstand the seeming evidence of this argument; and yet nothing in the world is more easy than to refute it. We need only reflect on what has been proved at large, that we are never sensible of any connexion betwixt causes and effects, and that it is only by our experience of their constant conjunction, we can arrive at any knowledge of this relation. Now as all objects, which are not contrary, are susceptible of a constant conjunction, and as no real objects are contrary;[44] I have inferred from these principles, that to consider the matter A PRIORI, any thing may produce any thing, and that we shall never discover a reason, why any object may or may not be the cause of any other, however great, or however little the resemblance may be betwixt them. This evidently destroys the precedent reasoning concerning the cause of thought or perception. For though there appear no manner of connexion betwixt motion or thought, the case is the same with all other causes and effects. Place one body of a pound weight on one end of a lever, and another body of the same weight on another end; you will never find in these bodies any principle of motion dependent on their distances from the center, more than of thought and perception. If you pretend, therefore, to prove a priori, that such a position of bodies can never cause thought; because turn it which way you will, it is nothing but a position of bodies; you must by the same course of reasoning conclude, that it can never produce motion; since there is no more apparent connexion in the one case than in the other. But as this latter conclusion is contrary to evident experience, and as it is possible we may have a like experience in the operations of the mind, and may perceive a constant conjunction of thought and motion; you reason too hastily, when from the mere consideration of the ideas, you conclude that it is impossible motion can ever produce thought, or a different position of parts give rise to a different passion or reflection. Nay it is not only possible we may have such an experience, but it is certain we have it; since every one may perceive, that the different dispositions of his body change his thoughts and sentiments. And should it be said, that this depends on the union of soul and body; I would answer, that we must separate the question concerning the substance of the mind from that concerning the cause of its thought; and that confining ourselves to the latter question we find by the comparing their ideas, that thought and motion are different from each other, and by experience, that they are constantly united; which being all the circumstances, that enter into the idea of cause and effect, when applied to the operations of matter, we may certainly conclude, that motion may be, and actually is, the cause of thought and perception.

There seems only this dilemma left us in the present case; either to assert, that nothing can be the cause of another, but where the mind can perceive the connexion in its idea of the objects: Or to maintain, that all objects, which we find constantly

[44] Part III. Sect. 15.

conjoined, are upon that account to be regarded as causes and effects. If we choose the first part of the dilemma, these are the consequences. First, We in reality affirm, that there is no such thing in the universe as a cause or productive principle, not even the deity himself; since our idea of that supreme Being is derived from particular impressions, none of which contain any efficacy, nor seem to have any connexion with any other existence. As to what may be said, that the connexion betwixt the idea of an infinitely powerful being, and that of any effect, which he wills, is necessary and unavoidable; I answer, that we have no idea of a being endowed with any power, much less of one endowed with infinite power. But if we will change expressions, we can only define power by connexion; and then in saying, that the idea, of an infinitely powerful being is connected with that of every effect, which he wills, we really do no more than assert, that a being, whose volition is connected with every effect, is connected with every effect: which is an identical proposition, and gives us no insight into the nature of this power or connexion. But, secondly, supposing, that the deity were the great and efficacious principle, which supplies the deficiency of all causes, this leads us into the grossest impieties and absurdities. For upon the same account, that we have recourse to him in natural operations, and assert that matter cannot of itself communicate motion, or produce thought, viz. because there is no apparent connexion betwixt these objects; I say, upon the very same account, we must acknowledge that the deity is the author of all our volitions and perceptions; since they have no more apparent connexion either with one another, or with the supposed but unknown substance of the soul. This agency of the supreme Being we know to have been asserted by[45] several philosophers with relation to all the actions of the mind, except volition, or rather an inconsiderable part of volition; though it is easy to perceive, that this exception is a mere pretext, to avoid the dangerous consequences of that doctrine. If nothing be active but what has an apparent power, thought is in no case any more active than matter; and if this inactivity must make us have recourse to a deity, the supreme being is the real cause of all our actions, bad as well as good, vicious as well as virtuous.

Thus we are necessarily reduced to the other side of the dilemma, viz.. that all objects, which are found to be constantly conjoined, are upon that account only to be regarded as causes and effects. Now as all objects, which are not contrary, are susceptible of a constant conjunction, and as no real objects are contrary: it follows, that for ought we can determine by the mere ideas, any thing may be the cause or effect of any thing; which evidently gives the advantage to the materialists above their antagonists.

To pronounce, then, the final decision upon the whole; the question concerning the substance of the soul is absolutely unintelligible: All our perceptions are not susceptible of a local union, either with what is extended or unextended: there being some of them of the one kind, and some of the other: And as the constant

[45] As father *Malebranche* and other *Cartesians*.

conjunction of objects constitutes the very essence of cause and effect, matter and motion may often be regarded as the causes of thought, as far as we have any notion of that relation.

It is certainly a kind of indignity to philosophy, whose sovereign authority ought every where to be acknowledged, to oblige her on every occasion to make apologies for her conclusions, and justify herself to every particular art and science, which may be offended at her. This puts one in mind of a king arrainged for high-treason against his subjects. There is only one occasion, when philosophy will think it necessary and even honourable to justify herself, and that is, when religion may seem to be in the least offended; whose rights are as dear to her as her own, and are indeed the same. If any one, therefore, should imagine that the foregoing arguments are any ways dangerous to religion, I hope the following apology will remove his apprehensions.

There is no foundation for any conclusion a priori, either concerning the operations or duration of any object, of which it is possible for the human mind to form a conception. Any object may be imagined to become entirely inactive, or to be annihilated in a moment; and it is an evident principle, that whatever we can imagine, is possible. Now this is no more true of matter, than of spirit; of an extended compounded substance, than of a simple and unextended. In both cases the metaphysical arguments for the immortality of the soul are equally inconclusive: and in both cases the moral arguments and those derived from the analogy of nature are equally strong and convincing. If my philosophy, therefore, makes no addition to the arguments for religion, I have at least the satisfaction to think it takes nothing from them, but that every thing remains precisely as before.

SECTION VI

Of Personal Identity

There are some philosophers who imagine we are every moment intimately conscious of what we call our SELF; that we feel its existence and its continuance in existence; and are certain, beyond the evidence of a demonstration, both o its perfect identity and simplicity. The strongest sensation, the most violent passion, say they, instead of distracting us from this view, only fix it the more intensely, and make us consider their influence on self either by their pain or pleasure. To attempt a farther proof of this were to weaken its evidence; since no proof can be derived from any fact, of which we are so intimately conscious; nor is there any thing, of which we can be certain, if we doubt of this.

Unluckily all these positive assertions are contrary to that very experience, which is pleaded for them, nor have we any idea of self, after the manner it is here explained. For from what impression could this idea be derived? This question it is impossible to answer without a manifest contradiction and absurdity; and yet it is a question, which must necessarily be answered, if we would have the idea of self pass for clear and intelligible, It must be some one impression, that gives rise to every real idea. But self or person is not any one impression, but that to which our several impressions and ideas are supposed to have a reference. If any impression gives rise to the idea of self, that impression must continue invariably the same, through the whole course of our lives; since self is supposed to exist after that manner. But there is no impression constant and invariable. Pain and pleasure, grief and joy, passions and sensations succeed each other, and never all exist at the same time. It cannot, therefore, be from any of these impressions, or from any other, that the idea of self is derived; and consequently there is no such idea.

But farther, what must become of all our particular perceptions upon this hypothesis? All these are different, and distinguishable, and separable from each other, and may be separately considered, and may exist separately, and have no Deed of tiny thing to support their existence. After what manner, therefore, do they belong to self; and how are they connected with it? For my part, when I enter most intimately into what I call myself, I always stumble on some particular perception or other, of heat or cold, light or shade, love or hatred, pain or pleasure. I never can catch myself at any time without a perception, and never can observe any thing but the perception. When my perceptions are removed for any time, as by sound sleep; so long am I insensible of myself, and may truly be said not to exist. And were all my perceptions removed by death, and could I neither think, nor feel, nor see, nor love, nor hate after the dissolution of my body, I should be entirely annihilated, nor do I conceive what is farther requisite to make me a perfect non-entity. If any one, upon serious and unprejudiced reflection thinks he has a different notion of himself, I must confess I call reason no longer with him. All I can allow him is, that he may be in the right as well as I, and that we are essentially different in this particular. He may, perhaps, perceive something simple and continued, which he calls himself; though I am certain there is no such principle in me.

But setting aside some metaphysicians of this kind, I may venture to affirm of the rest of mankind, that they are nothing but a bundle or collection of different perceptions, which succeed each other with an inconceivable rapidity, and are in a perpetual flux and movement. Our eyes cannot turn in their sockets without varying our perceptions. Our thought is still more variable than our sight; and all our other senses and faculties contribute to this change; nor is there any single power of the soul, which remains unalterably the same, perhaps for one moment. The mind is a kind of theatre, where several perceptions successively make their appearance; pass, re-pass, glide away, and mingle in an infinite variety of postures and situations. There is properly no simplicity in it at one time, nor identity in different; whatever natural propension we may have to imagine that simplicity and identity. The comparison of the theatre must not mislead us. They are the successive perceptions only, that constitute the mind; nor have we the most distant notion of the place, where these scenes are represented, or of the materials, of which it is composed.

What then gives us so great a propension to ascribe an identity to these successive perceptions, and to suppose ourselves possest of an invariable and uninterrupted existence through the whole course of our lives? In order to answer this question, we must distinguish betwixt personal identity, as it regards our thought or imagination, and as it regards our passions or the concern we take in ourselves. The first is our present subject; and to explain it perfectly we must take the matter pretty deep, and account for that identity, which we attribute to plants and animals; there being a great analogy betwixt it, and the identity of a self or person.

We have a distinct idea of an object, that remains invariable and uninterrupted through a supposed variation of time; and this idea we call that of identity or sameness. We have also a distinct idea of several different objects existing in succession, and connected together by a close relation; and this to an accurate view affords as perfect a notion of diversity, as if there was no manner of relation among the objects. But though these two ideas of identity, and a succession of related objects be in themselves perfectly distinct, and even contrary, yet it is certain, that in our common way of thinking they are generally confounded with each other. That action of the imagination, by which we consider the uninterrupted and invariable object, and that by which we reflect on the succession of related objects, are almost the same to the feeling, nor is there much more effort of thought required in the latter case than in the former. The relation facilitates the transition of the mind from one object to another, and renders its passage as smooth as if it contemplated one continued object. This resemblance is the cause of the confusion and mistake, and makes us substitute the notion of identity, instead of that of related objects. However at one instant we may consider the related succession as variable or interrupted, we are sure the next to ascribe to it a perfect identity, and regard it as enviable and uninterrupted. Our propensity to this mistake is so great from the resemblance above-mentioned, that we fall into it before we are aware; and though we incessantly correct ourselves by reflection, and return to a more accurate method of thinking, yet we cannot long sustain our philosophy, or take off this biass from the imagination. Our last resource is to yield to it, and boldly assert that these different related objects are in effect the same, however interrupted and variable. In order to justify to ourselves this absurdity, we often feign some new and unintelligible principle, that connects the objects together, and prevents their interruption or variation. Thus we feign the continued existence of the perceptions of our senses, to remove the interruption: and run into the notion of a soul, and self, and substance, to disguise the variation. But we may farther observe, that where we do not give rise to such a fiction, our propension to confound identity with relation is so great, that we are apt to imagine[46] something unknown and

[46] If the reader is desirous to see how a great genius may be influencd by these seemingly trivial principles of the imagination, as well as the mere vulgar, let him read my Lord SHAFTSBURY'S reasonings concerning the uniting principle of the universe, and the identity of plants and animals. See his MORALISTS: or, PHILOSOPHICAL RHAPSODY.

mysterious, connecting the parts, beside their relation; and this I take to be the case with regard to the identity we ascribe to plants and vegetables. And even when this does not take place, we still feel a propensity to confound these ideas, though we are not able fully to satisfy ourselves in that particular, nor find any thing invariable and uninterrupted to justify our notion of identity.

Thus the controversy concerning identity is not merely a dispute of words. For when we attribute identity, in an improper sense, to variable or interrupted objects, our mistake is not confined to the expression, but is commonly attended with a fiction, either of something invariable and uninterrupted, or of something mysterious and inexplicable, or at least with a propensity to such fictions. What will suffice to prove this hypothesis to the satisfaction of every fair enquirer, is to shew from daily experience and observation, that the objects, which are variable or interrupted, and yet are supposed to continue the same, are such only as consist of a succession of parts, connected together by resemblance, contiguity, or causation. For as such a succession answers evidently to our notion of diversity, it can only be by mistake we ascribe to it an identity; and as the relation of parts, which leads us into this mistake, is really nothing but a quality, which produces an association of ideas, and an easy transition of the imagination from one to another, it can only be from the resemblance, which this act of the mind bears to that, by which we contemplate one continued object, that the error arises. Our chief business, then, must be to prove, that all objects, to which we ascribe identity, without observing their invariableness and uninterruptedness, are such as consist of a succession of related objects.

In order to this, suppose any mass of matter, of which the parts are contiguous and connected, to be placed before us; it is plain we must attribute a perfect identity to this mass, provided all the parts continue uninterruptedly and invariably the same, whatever motion or change of place we may observe either in the whole or in any of the parts. But supposing some very small or inconsiderable part to be added to the mass, or subtracted from it; though this absolutely destroys the identity of the whole, strictly speaking; yet as we seldom think so accurately, we scruple not to pronounce a mass of matter the same, where we find so trivial an alteration. The passage of the thought from the object before the change to the object after it, is so smooth and easy, that we scarce perceive the transition, and are apt to imagine, that it is nothing but a continued survey of the same object.

There is a very remarkable circumstance, that attends this experiment; which is, that though the change of any considerable part in a mass of matter destroys the identity of the whole, let we must measure the greatness of the part, not absolutely, but by its proportion to the whole. The addition or diminution of a mountain would not be sufficient to produce a diversity in a planet: though the change of a very few inches would be able to destroy the identity of some bodies. It will be impossible to account for this, but by reflecting that objects operate upon the mind, and break or interrupt the continuity of its actions not according to their real greatness, but according to their proportion to each other: And therefore, since this interruption makes an object cease to appear the same, it must be the uninterrupted progress o the thought, which constitutes the imperfect identity.

This may be confirmed by another phenomenon. A change in any considerable part of a body destroys its identity; but it is remarkable, that where the change is produced gradually and insensibly we are less apt to ascribe to it the same effect. The reason can plainly be no other, than that the mind, in following the successive changes of the body, feels an easy passage from the surveying its condition in one moment to the viewing of it in another, and at no particular time perceives any interruption in its actions. From which continued perception, it ascribes a continued existence and identity to the object.

But whatever precaution we may use in introducing the changes gradually, and making them proportionable to the whole, it is certain, that where the changes are at last observed to become considerable, we make a scruple of ascribing identity to such different objects. There is, however, another artifice, by which we may induce the imagination to advance a step farther; and that is, by producing a reference of the parts to each other, and a combination to some common end or purpose. A ship, of which a considerable part has been changed by frequent reparations, is still considered as the same; nor does the difference of the materials hinder us from ascribing an identity to it. The common end, in which the parts conspire, is the same under all their variations, and affords an easy transition of the imagination from one situation of the body to another.

But this is still more remarkable, when we add a sympathy of parts to their common end, and suppose that they bear to each other, the reciprocal relation of cause and effect in all their actions and operations. This is the case with all animals and vegetables; where not only the several parts have a reference to some general purpose, but also a mutual dependence on, and connexion with each other. The effect of so strong a relation is, that though every one must allow, that in a very few years both vegetables and animals endure a total change, yet we still attribute identity to them, while their form, size, and substance are entirely altered. An oak, that grows from a small plant to a large tree, is still the same oak; though there be not one particle of matter, or figure of its parts the same. An infant becomes a man-, and is sometimes fat, sometimes lean, without any change in his identity.

We may also consider the two following phaenomena, which are remarkable in their kind. The first is, that though we commonly be able to distinguish pretty exactly betwixt numerical and specific identity, yet it sometimes happens, that we confound them, and in our thinking and reasoning employ the one for the other. Thus a man, who bears a noise, that is frequently interrupted and renewed, says, it is still the same noise; though it is evident the sounds have only a specific identity or resemblance, and there is nothing numerically the same, but the cause, which produced them. In like manner it may be said without breach of the propriety of language, that such a church, which was formerly of brick, fell to ruin, and that the parish rebuilt the same church of free-stone, and according to modern architecture. Here neither the form nor materials are the same, nor is there any thing common to the two objects, but their relation to the inhabitants of the parish; and yet this alone is sufficient to make us denominate them the same. But we must observe, that in these cases the first object is in a manner annihilated before the second comes into existence; by which means, we are never presented in any one point of time with the idea of difference and multiplicity: and for that reason are less scrupulous in calling them the same.

Secondly, We may remark, that though in a succession of related objects, it be in a manner requisite, that the change of parts be not sudden nor entire, in order to preserve the identity, yet where the objects are in their nature changeable and inconstant, we admit of a more sudden transition, than would otherwise be consistent with that relation. Thus as the nature of a river consists in the motion and change of parts; though in less than four and twenty hours these be totally altered; this hinders not the river from continuing the same during several ages. What is natural and essential to any thing is, in a manner, expected; and what is expected makes less impression, and appears of less moment, than what is unusual and extraordinary. A considerable change of the former kind seems really less to the imagination, than the most trivial alteration of the latter; and by breaking less the continuity of the thought, has less influence in destroying the identity.

We now proceed to explain the nature of personal identity, which has become so great a question ill philosophy, especially of late years in England, where all the abstruser sciences are studyed with a peculiar ardour and application. And here it is evident, the same method of reasoning must be continued which has so successfully explained the identity of plants, and animals, and ships, and houses, and of all the compounded and changeable productions either of art or nature. The identity, which we ascribe to the mind of man, is only a fictitious one, and of a like kind with that which we ascribe to vegetables and animal bodies. It cannot, therefore, have a different origin, but must proceed from a like operation of the imagination upon like objects.

But lest this argument should not convince the reader; though in my opinion perfectly decisive; let him weigh the following reasoning, which is still closer and more immediate. It is evident, that the identity, which we attribute to the human mind, however perfect we may imagine it to be, is not able to run the several different perceptions into one, and make them lose their characters of distinction and difference, which are essential to them. It is still true, that every distinct perception, which enters into the composition of the mind, is a distinct existence, and is different, and distinguishable, and separable from every other perception, either contemporary or successive. But, as, notwithstanding this distinction and separability, we suppose the whole train of perceptions to be united by identity, a question naturally arises concerning this relation of identity; whether it be something that really binds our several perceptions together, or only associates their ideas in the imagination. That is, in other words, whether in pronouncing concerning the identity of a person, we observe some real bond among his perceptions, or only feel one among the ideas we form of them. This question we might easily decide, if we would recollect what has been already proud at large, that the understanding never observes any real connexion among objects, and that even the union of cause and effect, when strictly examined, resolves itself into a customary association of ideas. For from thence it evidently follows, that identity is nothing really belonging to these different perceptions, and uniting them together; but is merely a quality, which we attribute to them, because of the union of their ideas in the imagination, when we reflect upon them. Now the only qualities, which can give ideas an union in the imagination, are these three relations above-mentioned. There are the uniting principles in the ideal world, and without them every distinct object is separable by the mind, and may be separately considered, and appears not to have any more connexion with any other object, than if disjoined by the greatest difference and remoteness. It is, therefore, on some of these three relations of resemblance, contiguity and causation, that identity depends; and as the very essence of these relations consists in their producing an easy transition of ideas; it follows, that our notions of personal identity, proceed entirely from the smooth and uninterrupted progress of the thought along a train of connected ideas, according to the principles above-explained.

The only question, therefore, which remains, is, by what relations this uninterrupted progress of our thought is produced, when we consider the successive existence of a mind or thinking person. And here it is evident we must confine ourselves to resemblance and causation, and must drop contiguity, which has little or no influence in the present case.

To begin with resemblance; suppose we could see clearly into the breast of another, and observe that succession of perceptions, which constitutes his mind or thinking principle, and suppose that he always preserves the memory of a considerable part of past perceptions; it is evident that nothing could more contribute to the bestowing a relation on this succession amidst all its variations. For what is the memory but a faculty, by which we raise up the images of past perceptions? And as an image necessarily resembles its object, must not. The frequent placing of these resembling perceptions in the chain of thought, convey the imagination more easily from one link to another, and make the whole seem like the continuance of one object? In this particular, then, the memory not only discovers the identity, but also contributes to its production, by producing the relation of resemblance among the perceptions. The case is the same whether we consider ourselves or others.

As to causation; we may observe, that the true idea of the human mind, is to consider it as a system of different perceptions or different existences, which are linked together by the relation of cause and effect, and mutually produce, destroy, influence, and modify each other. Our impressions give rise to their correspondent ideas; said these ideas in their turn produce other impressions. One thought chaces another, and draws after it a third, by which it is expelled in its turn. In this respect, I cannot compare the soul more properly to any thing than to a republic or commonwealth, in which the several members are united by the reciprocal ties of government and subordination, and give rise to other persons, who propagate the same republic in the incessant changes of its parts. And as the same individual republic may not only change its members, but also its laws and constitutions; in like manner the same person may vary his character and disposition, as well as his impressions and ideas, without losing his identity. Whatever changes he endures, his several parts are still connected by the relation of causation. And in this view our identity with regard to the passions serves to corroborate that with regard to the imagination, by the making our distant perceptions influence each other, and by giving us a present concern for our past or future pains or pleasures.

As a memory alone acquaints us with the continuance and extent of this succession of perceptions, it is to be considered, upon that account chiefly, as the source of personal identity. Had we no memory, we never should have any notion of causation, nor consequently of that chain of causes and effects, which constitute our self or person. But having once acquired this notion of causation from the memory, we can extend the same chain of causes, and consequently the identity of car persons beyond our memory, and can comprehend times, and circumstances, and actions, which we have entirely forgot, but suppose in general to have existed. For how few of our past actions are there, of which we have any memory? Who can tell me, for instance, what were his thoughts and actions on the 1st of January 1715, the 11th of March 1719, and the 3rd of August 1733? Or will he affirm, because he has entirely forgot the incidents of these days, that the present self is not the same person with the self of that time; and by that means overturn all the most established notions of personal identity? In this view, therefore, memory does not so much produce as discover personal identity, by shewing us the relation of cause and effect among our different perceptions. It will be incumbent on those, who affirm that memory produces entirely our personal identity, to give a reason why we can thus extend our identity beyond our memory.

The whole of this doctrine leads us to a conclusion, which is of great importance in the present affair, viz. that all the nice and subtile questions concerning personal identity can never possibly be decided, and are to be regarded rather as gramatical than as philosophical difficulties. Identity depends on the relations of ideas; and these relations produce identity, by means of that easy transition they occasion. But as the relations, and the easiness of the transition may diminish by insensible degrees, we have no just standard, by which we can decide any dispute concerning the time, when they acquire or lose a title to the name of identity. All the disputes concerning the identity of connected objects are merely verbal, except so fax as the relation of parts gives rise to some fiction or imaginary principle of union, as we have already observed.

What I have said concerning the first origin and uncertainty of our notion of identity, as applied to the human mind, may be extended with little or no variation to that of simplicity. An object, whose different co-existent parts are bound together by a close relation, operates upon the imagination after much the same manner as one perfectly simple and indivisible and requires not a much greater stretch of thought in order to its conception. From this similarity of operation we attribute a simplicity to it, and feign a principle of union as the support of this simplicity, and the center of all the different parts and qualities of the object.

Thus we have finished our examination of the several systems of philosophy, both of the intellectual and natural world; and in our miscellaneous way of reasoning have been led into several topics; which will either illustrate and confirm some preceding part of this discourse, or prepare the way for our following opinions. It is now time to return to a more close examination of our subject, and to proceed in the accurate anatomy of human nature, having fully explained the nature of our judgment and understandings.

SECTION VII

Conclusion of this Book

But before I launch out into those immense depths of philosophy, which lie before me, I find myself inclined to stop a moment in my present station, and to ponder that voyage, which I have undertaken, and which undoubtedly requires the utmost art and industry to be brought to a happy conclusion. Methinks I am like a man, who having struck on many shoals, and having narrowly escaped shipwreck in passing a small frith, has yet the temerity to put out to sea in the same leaky weather-beaten vessel, and even carries his ambition so far as to think of compassing the globe under these disadvantageous circumstances. My memory of past errors and perplexities, makes me diffident for the future. The wretched condition, weakness, and disorder of the faculties, I must employ in my enquiries, encrease my apprehensions. And the impossibility of amending or correcting these faculties, reduces me almost to despair, and makes me resolve to perish on the barren rock, on which I am at present, rather than venture myself upon that boundless ocean, which runs out into immensity. This sudden view of my danger strikes me with melancholy; and as it is usual for that passion, above all others, to indulge itself; I cannot forbear feeding my despair, with all those desponding reflections, which the present subject furnishes me with in such abundance.

I am first affrighted and confounded with that forelorn solitude, in which I am placed in my philosophy, and fancy myself some strange uncouth monster, who not being able to mingle and unite in society, has been expelled all human commerce, and left utterly abandoned and disconsolate. Fain would I run into the crowd for shelter and warmth; but cannot prevail with myself to mix with such deformity. I call upon others to join me, in order to make a company apart; but no one will hearken to me. Every one keeps at a distance, and dreads that storm, which beats upon me from every side. I have exposed myself to the enmity of all metaphysicians, logicians, mathematicians, and even theologians; and can I wonder at the insults I must suffer? I have declared my disapprobation of their systems; and can I be surprized, if they should express a hatred of mine and of my person? When I look abroad, I foresee on every side, dispute, contradiction, anger, calumny and detraction. When I turn my eye inward, I find nothing but doubt and ignorance. All the world conspires to oppose and contradict me; though such is my weakness, that I feel all my opinions loosen and fall of themselves, when unsupported by the approbation of others. Every step I take is with hesitation, and every new reflection makes me dread an error and absurdity in my reasoning.

For with what confidence can I venture upon such bold enterprises, when beside those numberless infirmities peculiar to myself, I find so many which are common to human nature? Can I be sure, that in leaving all established opinions I am following truth; and by what criterion shall I distinguish her, even if fortune should at last guide me on her foot-steps? After the most accurate and exact of my reasonings, I can give no reason why I should assent to it; and feel nothing but a strong propensity to consider objects strongly in that view, under which they appear to me. Experience is a principle, which instructs me in the several conjunctions of objects for the past. Habit is another principle, which determines me to expect the same for the future; and both of them conspiring to operate upon the imagination, make me form certain ideas in a more intense and lively manner, than others, which are not attended with the same advantages. Without this quality, by which the mind enlivens some ideas beyond others (which seemingly is so trivial, and so little founded on reason) we could never assent to any argument, nor carry our view beyond those few objects, which are present to our senses. Nay, even to these objects we could never attribute any existence, but what was dependent on the senses; and must comprehend them entirely in that succession of perceptions, which constitutes our self or person. Nay farther, even with relation to that succession, we could only admit of those perceptions, which are immediately present to our consciousness, nor could those lively images, with which the memory presents us, be ever received as true pictures of past perceptions. The memory, senses, and understanding are, therefore, all of them founded on the imagination, or the vivacity of our ideas.

No wonder a principle so inconstant and fallacious should lead us into errors, when implicitly followed (as it must be) in all its variations. It is this principle, which makes us reason from causes and effects; and it is the same principle, which convinces us of the continued existence of external objects, when absent from the senses. But though these two operations be equally natural and necessary in the human mind, yet in some circumstances they are[47] directly contrary, nor is it possible for us to reason justly and regularly from causes and effects, and at the same time believe the continued existence of matter. How then shall we adjust those principles together? Which of them shall we prefer? Or in case we prefer neither of them, but successively assent to both, as is usual among philosophers, with what confidence can we afterwards usurp that glorious title, when we thus knowingly embrace a manifest contradiction?

[47] Sect. 4.

This contradiction[48] would be more excusable, were it compensated by any degree of solidity and satisfaction in the other parts of our reasoning. But the case is quite contrary. When we trace up the human understanding to its first principles, we find it to lead us into such sentiments, as seem to turn into ridicule all our past pains and industry, and to discourage us from future enquiries. Nothing is more curiously enquired after by the mind of man, than the causes of every phenomenon; nor are we content with knowing the immediate causes, but push on our enquiries, till we arrive at the original and ultimate principle. We would not willingly stop before we are acquainted with that energy in the cause, by which it operates on its effect; that tie, which connects them together; and that efficacious quality, on which the tie depends. This is our aim in all our studies and reflections: And how must we be disappointed, when we learn, that this connexion, tie, or energy lies merely in ourselves, and is nothing but that determination of the mind, which is acquired by custom, and causes us to make a transition from an object to its usual attendant, and from the impression of one to the lively idea of the other? Such a discovery not only cuts off all hope of ever attaining satisfaction, but even prevents our very wishes; since it appears, that when we say we desire to know the ultimate and operating principle, as something, which resides in the external object, we either contradict ourselves, or talk without a meaning.

This deficiency in our ideas is not, indeed, perceived in common life, nor are we sensible, that in the most usual conjunctions of cause and effect we are as ignorant of the ultimate principle, which binds them together, as in the most unusual and extraordinary. But this proceeds merely from an illusion of the imagination; and the question is, how far we ought to yield to these illusions. This question is very difficult, and reduces us to a very dangerous dilemma, whichever way we answer it. For if we assent to every trivial suggestion of the fancy; beside that these suggestions are often contrary to each other; they lead us into such errors, absurdities, and obscurities, that we must at last become ashamed of our credulity. Nothing is more dangerous to reason than the flights of the imagination, and nothing has been the occasion of more mistakes among philosophers. Men of bright fancies may in this respect be compared to those angels, whom the scripture represents as covering their eyes with their wings. This has already appeared in so many instances, that we may spare ourselves the trouble of enlarging upon it any farther.

But on the other hand, if the consideration of these instances makes us take a resolution to reject all the trivial suggestions of the fancy, and adhere to the understanding, that is, to the general and more established properties of the imagination; even this resolution, if steadily executed, would be dangerous, and attended with the most fatal consequences. For I have already shewn,[49] that the understanding, when it acts alone, and according to its most general principles,

[48] Part III. Sect. 14.

[49] Sect. 1.

entirely subverts itself, and leaves not the lowest degree of evidence in any proposition, either in philosophy or common life. We save ourselves from this total scepticism only by means of that singular and seemingly trivial property of the fancy, by which we enter with difficulty into remote views of things, and are not able to accompany them with so sensible an impression, as we do those, which are more easy and natural. Shall we, then, establish it for a general maxim, that no refined or elaborate reasoning is ever to be received? Consider well the consequences of such a principle. By this means you cut off entirely all science and philosophy: You proceed upon one singular quality of the imagination, and by a parity of reason must embrace all of them: And you expressly contradict yourself; since this maxim must be built on the preceding reasoning, which will be allowed to be sufficiently refined and metaphysical. What party, then, shall we choose among these difficulties? If we embrace this principle, and condemn all refined reasoning, we run into the most manifest absurdities. If we reject it in favour of these reasonings, we subvert entirely the human understanding. We have, therefore, no choice left but betwixt a false reason and none at all. For my part, know not what ought to be done in the present case. I can only observe what is commonly done; which is, that this difficulty is seldom or never thought of; and even where it has once been present to the mind, is quickly forgot, and leaves but a small impression behind it. Very refined reflections have little or no influence upon us; and yet we do not, and cannot establish it for a rule, that they ought not to have any influence; which implies a manifest contradiction.

But what have I here said, that reflections very refined and metaphysical have little or no influence upon us? This opinion I can scarce forbear retracting, and condemning from my present feeling and experience. The intense view of these manifold contradictions and imperfections in human reason has so wrought upon me, and heated my brain, that I am ready to reject all belief and reasoning, and can look upon no opinion even as more probable or likely than another. Where am I, or what? From what causes do I derive my existence, and to what condition shall I return? Whose favour shall I court, and whose anger must I dread? What beings surround me? and on whom have, I any influence, or who have any influence on me? I am confounded with all these questions, and begin to fancy myself in the most deplorable condition imaginable, invironed with the deepest darkness, and utterly deprived of the use of every member and faculty.

Most fortunately it happens, that since reason is incapable of dispelling these clouds, nature herself suffices to that purpose, and cures me of this philosophical melancholy and delirium, either by relaxing this bent of mind, or by some avocation, and lively impression of my senses, which obliterate all these chimeras. I dine, I play a game of backgammon, I converse, and am merry with my friends; and when after three or four hours' amusement, I would return to these speculations, they appear so cold, and strained, and ridiculous, that I cannot find in my heart to enter into them any farther.

Here then I find myself absolutely and necessarily determined to live, and talk, and act like other people in the common affairs of life. But notwithstanding that my natural propensity, and the course of my animal spirits and passions reduce me to this indolent belief in the general maxims of the world, I still feel such remains of my former disposition, that I am ready to throw all my books and papers into the fire, and resolve never more to renounce the pleasures of life for the sake of reasoning and philosophy. For those are my sentiments in that splenetic humour, which governs me at present. I may, nay I must yield to the current of nature, in submitting to my senses and understanding; and in this blind submission I shew most perfectly my sceptical disposition and principles. But does it follow, that I must strive against the current of nature, which leads me to indolence and pleasure; that I must seclude myself, in some measure, from the commerce and society of men, which is so agreeable; and that I must torture my brains with subtilities and sophistries, at the very time that I cannot satisfy myself concerning the reasonableness of so painful an application, nor have any tolerable prospect of arriving by its means at truth and certainty. Under what obligation do I lie of making such an abuse of time? And to what end can it serve either for the service of mankind, or for my own private interest? No: If I must be a fool, as all those who reason or believe any thing certainly are, my follies shall at least be natural and agreeable. Where I strive against my inclination, I shall have a good reason for my resistance; and will no more be led a wandering into such dreary solitudes, and rough passages, as I have hitherto met with.

These are the sentiments of my spleen and indolence; and indeed I must confess, that philosophy has nothing to oppose to them, and expects a victory more from the returns of a serious good-humoured disposition, than from the force of reason and conviction. In all the incidents of life we ought still to preserve our scepticism. If we believe, that fire warms, or water refreshes, it is only because it costs us too much pains to think otherwise. Nay if we are philosophers, it ought only to be upon sceptical principles, and from an inclination, which we feel to the employing ourselves after that manner. Where reason is lively, and mixes itself with some propensity, it ought to be assented to. Where it does not, it never can have any title to operate upon us.

At the time, therefore, that I am tired with amusement and company, and have indulged a reverie in my chamber, or in a solitary walk by a river-side, I feel my mind all collected within itself, and am naturally inclined to carry my view into all those subjects, about which I have met with so many disputes in the course of my reading and conversation. I cannot forbear having a curiosity to be acquainted with the principles of moral good and evil, the nature and foundation of government, and the cause of those several passions and inclinations, which actuate and govern me. I am uneasy to think I approve of one object, and disapprove of another; call one thing beautiful, and another deformed; decide concerning truth and falshood, reason and folly, without knowing upon what principles I proceed. I am concerned for the condition of the learned world, which lies under such a deplorable ignorance in all these particulars. I feel an ambition to arise in me of contributing to the instruction of mankind, and of acquiring a name by my inventions and discoveries. These sentiments spring up naturally in my present disposition; and should I endeavour to banish them, by attaching myself to any other business or diversion, I feel I should be a loser in point of pleasure; and this is the origin of my philosophy.

But even suppose this curiosity and ambition should not transport me into speculations without the sphere of common life, it would necessarily happen, that from my very weakness I must be led into such enquiries. It is certain, that superstition is much more bold in its systems and hypotheses than philosophy; and while the latter contents itself with assigning new causes and principles to the phaenomena, which appear in the visible world, the former opens a world of its own, and presents us with scenes, and beings, and objects, which are altogether new. Since therefore it is almost impossible for the mind of man to rest, like those of beasts, in that narrow circle of objects, which are the subject of daily conversation and action, we ought only to deliberate concerning the choice of our guide, and ought to prefer that which is safest and most agreeable. And in this respect I make bold to recommend philosophy, and shall not scruple to give it the preference to superstition of every kind or denomination. For as superstition arises naturally and easily from the popular opinions of mankind, it seizes more strongly on the mind, and is often able to disturb us in the conduct of our lives and actions. Philosophy on the contrary, if just, can present us only with mild and moderate sentiments; and if false and extravagant, its opinions are merely the objects of a cold and general speculation, and seldom go so far as to interrupt the course of our natural propensities. The CYNICS are an extraordinary instance of philosophers, who from reasonings purely philosophical ran into as great extravagancies of conduct as any Monk or Dervise that ever was in the world. Generally speaking, the errors in religion are dangerous; those in philosophy only ridiculous.

I am sensible, that these two cases of the strength and weakness of the mind will not comprehend all mankind, and that there are in England, in particular, many honest gentlemen, who being always employed in their domestic affairs, or amusing themselves in common recreations, have carried their thoughts very little beyond those objects, which are every day exposed to their senses. And indeed, of such as these I pretend not to make philosophers, nor do I expect them either to be associates in these researches or auditors of these discoveries. They do well to keep themselves in their present situation; and instead of refining them into philosophers, I wish we could communicate to our founders of systems, a share of this gross earthy mixture, as an ingredient, which they commonly stand much in need of, and which would serve to temper those fiery particles, of which they are composed. While a warm imagination is allowed to enter into philosophy, and hypotheses embraced merely for being specious and agreeable, we can never have any steady principles, nor any sentiments, which will suit with common practice and experience. But were these hypotheses once removed, we might hope to establish a system or set of opinions, which if not true (for that, perhaps, is too much to be hoped for) might at least be satisfactory to the human mind, and might stand the test of the most critical examination. Nor should we despair of attaining this end, because of the many chimerical systems, which have successively arisen and decayed away among men, would we consider the shortness of that period, wherein these questions have been the subjects of enquiry and reasoning. Two thousand years with such long interruptions, and under such mighty discouragements are a small space of time to give any tolerable perfection to the sciences; and perhaps we are still in too early an age of the world to discover any principles, which will bear the examination of the latest posterity. For my part, my only hope is, that I may contribute a little to the advancement of knowledge, by giving in some particulars a different turn to the speculations of philosophers, and pointing out to them more distinctly those subjects, where alone they can expect assurance and conviction. Human Nature is the only science of man; and yet has been hitherto the most neglected. It will be sufficient for me, if I can bring it a little more into fashion; and the hope of this serves to compose my temper from that spleen, and invigorate it from that indolence, which sometimes prevail upon me. If the reader finds himself in the same easy disposition, let him follow me in my future speculations. If not, let him follow his inclination, and wait the returns of application and good humour. The conduct of a man, who studies philosophy in this careless manner, is more truly sceptical than that of one, who feeling in himself an inclination to it, is yet so overwhelmed with doubts and scruples, as totally to reject it. A true sceptic will be diffident of his philosophical doubts, as well as of his philosophical conviction; and will never refuse any innocent satisfaction, which offers itself, upon account of either of them.

Nor is it only proper we should in general indulge our inclination in the most elaborate philosophical researches, notwithstanding our sceptical principles, but also that we should yield to that propensity, which inclines us to be positive and certain in particular points, according to the light, in which we survey them in any particular instant. It is easier to forbear all examination and enquiry, than to check ourselves in so natural a propensity, and guard against that assurance, which always arises from an exact and full survey of an object. On such an occasion we are apt not only to forget our scepticism, but even our modesty too; and make use of such terms as these, it is evident, it is certain, it is undeniable; which a due deference to the public ought, perhaps, to prevent. I may have fallen into this fault after the example of others; but I here enter a caveat against any Objections, which may be offered on that head; and declare that such expressions were extorted from me by the present view of the object, and imply no dogmatical spirit, nor conceited idea of my own judgment, which are sentiments that I am sensible can become no body, and a sceptic still less than any other.

BOOK II

OF THE PASSIONS

PART I

Of Pride and Humility

SECTION I

Division of the Subject

As all the perceptions of the mind may be divided into impressions and ideas, so the impressions admit of another division into original and secondary. This division of the impressions is the same with that which[50] I formerly made use of when I distinguished them into impressions of sensation and reflection. Original impressions or impressions of sensation are such as without any antecedent perception arise in the soul, from the constitution of the body, from the animal spirits, or from the application of objects to the external organs. Secondary, or reflective impressions are such as proceed from some of these original ones, either immediately or by the interposition of its idea. Of the first kind are all the impressions of the senses, and all bodily pains and pleasures: Of the second are the passions, and other emotions resembling them.

It is certain, that the mind, in its perceptions, must begin somewhere; and that since the impressions precede their correspondent ideas, there must be some impressions, which without any introduction make their appearance in the soul. As these depend upon natural and physical causes, the examination of them would lead me too far from my present subject, into the sciences of anatomy and natural philosophy. For this reason I shall here confine myself to those other impressions, which I have called secondary and reflective, as arising either from the original impressions, or from their ideas. Bodily pains and pleasures are the source of many passions, both when felt and considered by the mind; but arise originally in the soul, or in the body, whichever you please to call it, without any preceding thought or perception. A fit of the gout produces a long train of passions, as grief, hope, fear; but is not derived immediately from any affection or idea. The reflective impressions may be divided into two kinds, viz. the calm and the VIOLENT. Of the first kind is the sense of beauty and deformity in action, composition, and external objects. Of the second are the passions of love and hatred, grief and joy, pride and humility. This division is far from being exact. The raptures of poetry and music frequently rise to the greatest height; while those other impressions, properly called PASSIONS, may decay into so soft an emotion, as to become, in a manner, imperceptible. But as in general the passions are more violent than the emotions arising from beauty and deformity, these impressions have been commonly distinguished from each other.

---

[50] Book I. Part I. Sect. 2.

The subject of the human mind being so copious and various, I shall here take advantage of this vulgar and spacious division, that I may proceed with the greater order; and having said all I thought necessary concerning our ideas, shall now explain those violent emotions or passions, their nature, origin, causes, and effects.

When we take a survey of the passions, there occurs a division of them into DIRECT and INDIRECT. By direct passions I understand such as arise immediately from good or evil, from pain or pleasure. By indirect such as proceed from the same principles, but by the conjunction of other qualities. This distinction I cannot at present justify or explain any farther. I can only observe in general, that under the indirect passions I comprehend pride, humility, ambition, vanity, love, hatred, envy, pity, malice, generosity, with their dependants. And under the direct passions, desire, aversion, grief, joy, hope, fear, despair and security. I shall begin with the former.

SECTION II

Of Pride and Humility, their Objects and Causes

The passions of PRIDE and HUMILITY being simple and uniform impressions, it is impossible we can ever, by a multitude of words, give a just definition of them, or indeed of any of the passions. The utmost we can pretend to is a description of them, by an enumeration of such circumstances, as attend them: But as these words, PRIDE and humility, are of general use, and the impressions they represent the most common of any, every one, of himself, will be able to form a just idea of them, without any danger of mistake. For which reason, not to lose time upon preliminaries, I shall immediately enter upon the examination of these passions.

It is evident, that pride and humility, though directly contrary, have yet the same OBJECT. This object is self, or that succession of related ideas and impressions, of which we have an intimate memory and consciousness. Here the view always fixes when we are actuated by either of these passions. According as our idea of ourself is more or less advantageous, we feel either of those opposite affections, and are elated by pride, or dejected with humility. Whatever other objects may be comprehended by the mind, they are always considered with a view to ourselves; otherwise they would never be able either to excite these passions, or produce the smallest encrease or diminution of them. When self enters not into the consideration, there is no room either for pride or humility.

But though that connected succession of perceptions, which we call SELF, be always the object of these two passions, it is impossible it can be their CAUSE, or be sufficient alone to excite them. For as these passions are directly contrary, and have the same object in common; were their object also their cause; it could never produce any degree of the one passion, but at the same time it must excite an equal degree of the other; which opposition and contrariety must destroy both. It is impossible a man can at the same time be both proud and humble; and where he has different reasons for these passions, as frequently happens, the passions either take place alternately; or if they encounter, the one annihilates the other, as far as its strength goes, and the remainder only of that, which is superior, continues to operate upon the mind. But in the present case neither of the passions could ever become superior; because supposing it to be the view only of ourself, which excited them, that being perfectly indifferent to either, must produce both in the very same proportion; or in other words, can produce neither. To excite any passion, and at the same time raise an equal share of its antagonist, is immediately to undo what was done, and must leave the mind at last perfectly calm and indifferent.

We must therefore, make a distinction betwixt the cause and the object of these passions; betwixt that idea, which excites them, and that to which they direct their view, when excited. Pride and humility, being once raised, immediately turn our attention to ourself, and regard that as their ultimate and final object; but there is something farther requisite in order to raise them: Something, which is peculiar to one of the passions, and produces not both in the very same degree. The first idea, that is presented to the mind, is that of the cause or productive principle. This excites the passion, connected with it; and that passion, when excited, turns our view to another idea, which is that of self. Here then is a passion placed betwixt two ideas, of which the one produces it, and the other is produced by it. The first idea, therefore, represents the cause, the second the object of the passion.

To begin with the causes of pride and humility; we may observe, that their most obvious and remarkable property is the vast variety of subjects, on which they may be placed. Every valuable quality of the mind, whether of the imagination, judgment, memory or disposition; wit, good-sense, learning, courage, justice, integrity; all these are the cause of pride; and their opposites of humility. Nor are these passions confined to the mind but extend their view to the body likewise. A man may be proud of his beauty, strength, agility, good mein, address in dancing, riding, and of his dexterity in any manual business or manufacture. But this is not all. The passions looking farther, comprehend whatever objects are in the least allyed or related to us. Our country, family, children, relations, riches, houses, gardens, horses, dogs, cloaths; any of these may become a cause either of pride or of humility.

From the consideration of these causes, it appears necessary we shoud make a new distinction in the causes of the passion, betwixt that QUALITY, which operates, and the subject, on which it is placed. A man, for instance, is vain of a beautiful house, which belongs to him, or which he has himself built and contrived. Here the object of the passion is himself, and the cause is the beautiful house: Which cause again is sub-divided into two parts, viz. the quality, which operates upon the passion, and the subject in which the quality inheres. The quality is the beauty, and the subject is the house, considered as his property or contrivance. Both these parts are essential, nor is the distinction vain and chimerical. Beauty, considered merely as such, unless placed upon something related to us, never produces any pride or vanity; and the strongest relation alone, without beauty, or something else in its place, has as little influence on that passion. Since, therefore, these two particulars are easily separated and there is a necessity for their conjunction, in order to produce the passion, we ought to consider them as component parts of the cause; and infix in our minds an exact idea of this distinction.

SECTION III

Whence these Objects and Causes are Derived

Being so far advanced as to observe a difference betwixt the object of the passions and their cause, and to distinguish in the cause the quality, which operates on the passions, from the subject, in which it inheres; we now proceed to examine what determines each of them to be what it is, and assigns such a particular object, and quality, and subject to these affections. By this means we shall fully understand the origin of pride and humility.

It is evident in the first place, that these passions are determined to have self for their object, not only by a natural but also by an original property. No one can doubt but this property is natural from the constancy and steadiness of its operations. It is always self, which is the object of pride and humility; and whenever the passions look beyond, it is still with a view to ourselves, nor can any person or object otherwise have any influence upon us.

That this proceeds from an original quality or primary impulse, will likewise appear evident, if we consider that it is the distinguishing characteristic of these passions Unless nature had given some original qualities to the mind, it could never have any secondary ones; because in that case it would have no foundation for action, nor could ever begin to exert itself. Now these qualities, which we must consider as original, are such as are most inseparable from the soul, and can be resolved into no other: And such is the quality, which determines the object of pride and humility. We may, perhaps, make it a greater question, whether the causes, that produce the passion, be as natural as the object, to which it is directed, and whether all that vast variety proceeds from caprice or from the constitution of the mind. This doubt we shall soon remove, if we cast our eye upon human nature, and consider that in all nations and ages, the same objects still give rise to pride and humility; and that upon the view even of a stranger, we can know pretty nearly, what will either encrease or diminish his passions of this kind. If there be any variation in this particular, it proceeds from nothing but a difference in the tempers and complexions of men; and is besides very inconsiderable. Can we imagine it possible, that while human nature remains the same, men will ever become entirely indifferent to their power, riches, beauty or personal merit, and that their pride and vanity will not be affected by these advantages?

But though the causes of pride and humility be plainly natural, we shall find upon examination, that they are not original, and that it is utterly impossible they should each of them be adapted to these passions by a particular provision, and primary constitution of nature, Beside their prodigious number, many of them are the effects of art, and arise partly from the industry, partly from the caprice, and partly from the good fortune of men, Industry produces houses, furniture, cloaths. Caprice determines their particular kinds and qualities. And good fortune frequently contributes to all this, by discovering the effects that result from the different mixtures and combinations of bodies. It is absurd, therefore, to imagine, that each of these was foreseen and provided for by nature, and that every new production of art, which causes pride or humility; instead of adapting itself to the passion by partaking of some general quality, that naturally operates on the mind; is itself the object of an original principle, which till then lay concealed in the soul, and is only by accident at last brought to light. Thus the first mechanic, that invented a fine scritoire, produced pride in him, who became possest of it, by principles different from those, which made him proud of handsome chairs and tables. As this appears evidently ridiculous, we must conclude, that each cause of pride and humility is not adapted to the passions by a distinct original quality; but that there are some one or more circumstances common to all of them, on which their efficacy depends.

Besides, we find in the course of nature, that though the effects be many, the principles, from which they arise, are commonly but few and simple, and that it is the sign of an unskilful naturalist to have recourse to a different quality, in order to explain every different operation. How much more must this be true with regard to the human mind, which being so confined a subject may justly be thought incapable of containing such a monstrous heap of principles, as would be necessary to excite the passions of pride and humility, were each distinct cause adapted to the passion by a distinct set of principles?

Here, therefore, moral philosophy is in the same condition as natural, with regard to astronomy before the time of COPERNICUS. The antients, though sensible of that maxim, THAT NATURE DOES NOTHING IN VAIN, contrived such intricate systems of the heavens, as seemed inconsistent with true philosophy, and gave place at last to something more simple and natural. To invent without scruple a new principle to every new phænomenon, instead of adapting it to the old; to overload our hypotheses with a variety of this kind; are certain proofs, that none of these principles is the just one, and that we only desire, by a number of falsehoods, to cover our ignorance of the truth.

SECTION IV

Of the Relations of Impressions and Ideas

Thus we have established two truths without any obstacle or difficulty, that IT IS FROM NATURAL PRINCIPLES THIS VARIETY OF CAUSES EXCITES PRIDE AND HUMILITY, and that IT IS NOT BY A DIFFERENT PRINCIPLE EACH DIFFERENT CAUSE IS ADAPTED TO ITS PASSION. We shall now proceed to enquire how we may reduce these principles to a lesser number, and find among the causes something common, on which their influence depends.

In order to this we must reflect on certain properties of human nature, which though they have a mighty influence on every operation both of the understanding and passions, are not commonly much insisted on by philosophers. The first of these is the association of ideas, which I have so often observed and explained. It is impossible for the mind to fix itself steadily upon one idea for any considerable time; nor can it by its utmost efforts ever arrive at such a constancy. But however changeable our thoughts may be, they are not entirely without rule and method in their changes. The rule, by which they proceed, is to pass from one object to what is resembling, contiguous to, or produced by it. When one idea is present to the imagination, any other, united by these relations, naturally follows it, and enters with more facility by means of that introduction.

The second property I shall observe in the human mind is a like association of impressions. All resembling impressions are connected together, and no sooner one arises than the rest immediately follow. Grief and disappointment give rise to anger, anger to envy, envy to malice, and malice to grief again, till the whole circle be compleated. In like manner our temper, when elevated with joy, naturally throws itself into love, generosity, pity, courage, pride, and the other resembling affections. It is difficult for the mind, when actuated by any passion, to confine itself to that passion alone, without any change or variation. Human nature is too inconstant to admit of any such regularity. Changeableness is essential to it. And to what can it so naturally change as to affections or emotions, which are suitable to the temper, and agree with that set of passions, which then prevail? It is evident, then, there is an attraction or association among impressions, as well as among ideas; though with this remarkable difference, that ideas are associated by resemblance, contiguity, and causation; and impressions only by resemblance.

In the THIRD place, it is observable of these two kinds of association, that they very much assist and forward each other, and that the transition is more easily made where they both concur in the same object. Thus a man, who, by any injury from another, is very much discomposed and ruffled in his temper, is apt to find a hundred subjects of discontent, impatience, fear, and other uneasy passions; especially if he can discover these subjects in or near the person, who was the cause of his first passion. Those principles, which forward the transition of ideas, here concur with those, which operate on the passions; and both uniting in one action, bestow on the mind a double impulse. The new passion, therefore, must arise with so much greater violence, and the transition to it must be rendered so much more easy and natural.

Upon this occasion I may cite the authority of an elegant writer, who expresses himself in the following manner.

"As the fancy delights in every thing that is great, strange, or beautiful, and is still more pleased the more it finds of these perfections in the same object, so it is capable of receiving a new satisfaction by the assistance of another sense. Thus any continued sound, as the music of birds, or a fall of waters, awakens every moment the mind of the beholder, and makes him more attentive to the several beauties of the place, that lie before him. Thus if there arises a fragrancy of smells or perfumes, they heighten the pleasure of the imagination, and make even the colours and verdure of the landschape appear more agreeable; for the ideas of both senses recommend each other, and are pleasanter together than when they enter the mind separately: As the different colours of a picture, when they are well disposed, set off one another, and receive an additional beauty from the advantage of the situation."[51] In this phænomenon we may remark the association both of impressions and ideas, as well as the mutual assistance they lend each other.

SECTION V

Of the Influence of these Relations on Pride and Humility

These principles being established on unquestionable experience, I begin to consider how we shall apply them, by revolving over all the causes of pride and humility, whether these causes be regarded, as the qualities, that operate, or as the subjects, on which the qualities are placed. In examining these qualities I immediately find many of them to concur in producing the sensation of pain and pleasure, independent of those affections, which I here endeavour to explain. Thus the beauty of our person, of itself, and by its very appearance, gives pleasure, as well as pride; and its deformity, pain as well as humility. A magnificent feast delights us, and a sordid one displeases. What I discover to be true in some instances, I suppose to be so in all; and take it for granted at present, without any farther proof, that every cause of pride, by its peculiar qualities, produces a separate pleasure, and of humility a separate uneasiness.

Again, in considering the subjects, to which these qualities adhere, I make a new supposition, which also appears probable from many obvious instances, viz, that these subjects are either parts of ourselves, or something nearly related to us. Thus the good and bad qualities of our actions and manners constitute virtue and vice, and determine our personal character, than which nothing operates more strongly on these passions. In like manner, it is the beauty or deformity of our person, houses, equipage, or furniture, by which we are rendered either vain or humble. The same qualities, when transfered to subjects, which bear us no relation, influence not in the smallest degree either of these affections.

Having thus in a manner supposed two properties of the causes of these affections, viz, that the qualities produce a separate pain or pleasure, and that the subjects, on which the qualities are placed, are related to self; I proceed to examine

[51] Addison, SPECTATOR 412, final paragraph.

the passions themselves, in order to find something in them, correspondent to the supposed properties of their causes. First, I find, that the peculiar object of pride and humility is determined by an original and natural instinct, and that it is absolutely impossible, from the primary constitution of the mind, that these passions should ever look beyond self, or that individual person. of whose actions and sentiments each of us is intimately conscious. Here at last the view always rests, when we are actuated by either of these passions; nor can we, in that situation of mind, ever lose sight of this object. For this I pretend not to give any reason; but consider such a peculiar direction of the thought as an original quality.

The SECOND quality, which I discover in these passions, and which I likewise consider an an original quality, is their sensations, or the peculiar emotions they excite in the soul, and which constitute their very being and essence. Thus pride is a pleasant sensation, and humility a painful; and upon the removal of the pleasure and pain, there is in reality no pride nor humility. Of this our very feeling convinces us; and beyond our feeling, it is here in vain to reason or dispute.

If I compare, therefore, these two established properties of the passions, viz, their object, which is self, and their sensation, which is either pleasant or painful, to the two supposed properties of the causes, viz, their relation to self, and their tendency to produce a pain or pleasure, independent of the passion; I immediately find, that taking these suppositions to be just, the true system breaks in upon me with an irresistible evidence. That cause, which excites the passion, is related to the object, which nature has attributed to the passion; the sensation, which the cause separately produces, is related to the sensation of the passion: From this double relation of ideas and impressions, the passion is derived. The one idea is easily converted into its correlative; and the one impression into that, which resembles and corresponds to it: With how much greater facility must this transition be made, where these movements mutually assist each other, and the mind receives a double impulse from the relations both of its impressions and ideas?

That we may comprehend this the better, we must suppose, that nature has given to the organs of the human mind, a certain disposition fitted to produce a peculiar impression or emotion, which we call pride: To this emotion she has assigned a certain idea, viz, that of self, which it never fails to produce. This contrivance of nature is easily conceived. We have many instances of such a situation of affairs. The nerves of the nose and palate are so disposed, as in certain circumstances to convey such peculiar sensations to the mind: The sensations of lust and hunger always produce in us the idea of those peculiar objects, which are suitable to each appetite. These two circumstances are united in pride. The organs are so disposed as to produce the passion; and the passion, after its production, naturally produces a certain idea. All this needs no proof. It is evident we never should be possest of that passion, were there not a disposition of mind proper for it; and it is as evident, that the passion always turns our view to ourselves, and makes us think of our own qualities and circumstances.

This being fully comprehended, it may now be asked, WHETHER NATURE PRODUCES THE PASSION IMMEDIATELY, OF HERSELF; OR WHETHER SHE MUST BE ASSISTED BY THE CO-OPERATION OF OTHER CAUSES? For it is observable, that in this particular her conduct is different in the different passions and sensations. The palate must be excited by an external object, in order to produce any relish: But hunger arises internally, without the concurrence of any external object. But however the case may stand with other passions and impressions, it is certain, that pride requires the assistance of some foreign object, and that the organs, which produce it, exert not themselves like the heart and arteries, by an original internal movement. For first, daily experience convinces us, that pride requires certain causes to excite it, and languishes when unsupported by some excellency in the character, in bodily accomplishments, in cloaths, equipage or fortune. SECONDLY, it is evident pride would be perpetual, if it arose immediately from nature; since the object is always the same, and there is no disposition of body peculiar to pride, as there is to thirst and hunger. Thirdly, Humility is in the very same situation with pride; and therefore, either must, upon this supposition, be perpetual likewise, or must destroy the contrary passion from, the very first moment; so that none of them could ever make its appearance. Upon the whole, we may rest satisfyed with the foregoing conclusion, that pride must have a cause, as well as an object, and that the one has no influence without the other.

The difficulty, then, is only to discover this cause, and find what it is that gives the first motion to pride, and sets those organs in action, which are naturally fitted to produce that emotion. Upon my consulting experience, in order to resolve this difficulty, I immediately find a hundred different causes, that produce pride; and upon examining these causes, I suppose, what at first I perceive to be probable, that all of them concur in two circumstances; which are, that of themselves they produce an impression, allyed to the passion, and are placed on a subject, allyed to the object of the passion. When I consider after this the nature of relation, and its effects both on the passions and ideas, I can no longer doubt, upon these suppositions, that it is the very principle, which gives rise to pride, and bestows motion on those organs, which being naturally disposed to produce that affection, require only a first impulse or beginning to their action. Any thing, that gives a pleasant sensation, and is related to self, excites the passion of pride, which is also agreeable, and has self for its object.

What I have said of pride is equally true of humility. The sensation of humility is uneasy, as that of pride is agreeable; for which reason the separate sensation, arising from the causes, must be reversed, while the relation to self continues the same. Though pride and humility are directly contrary in their effects, and in their sensations, they have notwithstanding the same object; so that it is requisite only to change the relation of impressions, without making any change upon that of ideas. Accordingly we find, that a beautiful house, belonging to ourselves, produces pride; and that the same house, still belonging to ourselves, produces humility, when by any accident its beauty is changed into deformity, and thereby the sensation of pleasure, which corresponded to pride, is transformed into pain, which is related to humility. The double relation between the ideas and impressions subsists in both cases, and produces an easy transition from the one emotion to the other.

In a word, nature has bestowed a kind of attraction on certain impressions and ideas, by which one of them, upon its appearance, naturally introduces its correlative. If these two attractions or associations of impressions and ideas concur on the same object, they mutually assist each other, and the transition of the affections and of the imagination is made with the greatest ease and facility. When an idea produces an impression, related to an impression, which is connected with an idea, related to the first idea, these two impressions must be in a manner inseparable, nor will the one in any case be unattended with the other. It is after this manner, that the particular causes of pride and humility are determined. The quality, which operates on the passion, produces separately an impression resembling it; the subject, to which the quality adheres, is related to self, the object of the passion: No wonder the whole cause, consisting of a quality and of a subject, does so unavoidably give rise to the pass on.

To illustrate this hypothesis we may compare it to that, by which I have already explained the belief attending the judgments, which we form from causation. I have observed, that in all judgments of this kind, there is always a present impression and a related idea; and that the present impression gives a vivacity to the fancy, and the relation conveys this vivacity, by an easy transition, to the related idea. Without the present impression, the attention is not fixed, nor the spirits excited. Without the relation, this attention rests on its first object, and has no farther consequence. There is evidently a great analogy betwixt that hypothesis and our present one of an impression and idea, that transfuse themselves into another impression and idea by means of their double relation: Which analogy must be allowed to be no despicable proof of both hypotheses.

SECTION VI

Limitations of this System

But before we proceed farther in this subject, and examine particularly all the causes of pride and humility, it will be proper to make some limitations to the general system, THAT ALL AGREEABLE OBJECTS, RELATED TO OURSELVES, BY AN ASSOCIATION OF IDEAS AND OF IMPRESSIONS, PRODUCE PRIDE, AND DISAGREEABLE ONES, HUMILITY: And these limitations are derived from the very nature of the subject.

I. Suppose an agreeable object to acquire a relation to self, the first passion, that appears on this occasion, is joy; and this passion discovers itself upon a slighter relation than pride and vain-glory. We may feel joy upon being present at a feast, where our senses are regard with delicacies of every kind: But it is only the master of the feast, who, beside the same joy, has the additional passion of self-applause and vanity. It is true, men sometimes boast of a great entertainment, at which they have only been present; and by so small a relation convert their pleasure into pride: But however, this must in general be owned, that joy arises from a more inconsiderable relation than vanity, and that many things, which are too foreign to produce pride, are yet able to give us a delight and pleasure, The reason of the difference may be explained thus. A relation is requisite to joy, in order to approach the object to us, and make it give us any satisfaction. But beside this, which is common to both passions, it is requisite to pride, in order to produce a transition from one passion to another, and convert the falsification into vanity. As it has a double task to perform, it must be endowed with double force and energy. To which we may add, that where agreeable objects bear not a very close relation to ourselves, they commonly do to some other person; and this latter relation not only excels, but even diminishes, and sometimes destroys the former, as we shall see afterwards.[52]

Here then is the first limitation, we must make to our general position, that every thing related to us, which produces pleasure or pain, produces likewise pride or humility. There is not only a relation required, but a close one, and a closer than is required to joy.

II. The second limitation is, that the agreeable or disagreeable object be not only closely related, but also peculiar to ourselves, or at least common to us with a few persons. It is a quality observable in human nature, and which we shall endeavour to explain afterwards, that every thing, which is often presented and to which we have been long accustomed, loses its value in our eyes, and is in a little time despised and neglected. We likewise judge of objects more from comparison than from their real and intrinsic merit; and where we cannot by some contrast enhance their value, we are apt to overlook even what is essentially good in them. These qualities of the mind have an effect upon joy as well as pride; and it is remarkable, that goods which are common to all mankind, and have become familiar to us by custom, give us little satisfaction; though perhaps of a more excellent kind, than those on which, for their singularity, we set a much higher value. But though this circumstance operates on both these passions, it has a much greater influence on vanity. We are rejoiced for many goods, which, on account of their frequency, give us no pride. Health, when it returns after a long absence, affords us a very sensible satisfaction; but is seldom regarded as a subject of vanity, because it is shared with such vast numbers.

The reason, why pride is so much more delicate in this particular than joy, I take to be, as follows. In order to excite pride, there are always two objects we must contemplate, viz. the cause or that object which produces pleasure; and self, which is the real object of the passion. But joy has only one object necessary to its production, viz. that which gives pleasure; and though it be requisite, that this

[52] Part II. Sec. 4.

bear some relation to self, yet that is only requisite in order to render it agreeable; nor is self, properly speaking, the object of this passion. Since, therefore, pride has in a manner two objects, to which it directs our view; it follows, that where neither of them have any singularity, the passion must be more weakened upon that account, than a passion, which has only one object. Upon comparing ourselves with others, as we are every moment apt to do, we find we are not in the least distinguished; and upon comparing the object we possess, we discover still the same unlucky circumstance. By two comparisons so disadvantageous the passion must be entirely destroyed.

III The third limitation is, that the pleasant or painful object be very discernible and obvious, and that not only to ourselves, but to others also. This circumstance, like the two foregoing, has an effect upon joy, as well as pride. We fancy Ourselves more happy, as well as more virtuous or beautiful, when we appear so to others; but are still more ostentatious of our virtues than of our pleasures. This proceeds from causes, which I shall endeavour to explain afterwards.

IV. The fourth limitation is derived from the inconstancy of the cause of these passions, and from the short duration of its connexion with ourselves. What is casual and inconstant gives but little joy, and less pride. We are not much satisfyed with the thing itself; and are still less apt to feel any new degrees of self-satisfaction upon its account. We foresee and anticipate its change by the imagination; which makes us little satisfyed with the thing: We compare it to ourselves, whose existence is more durable; by which means its inconstancy appears still greater. It seems ridiculous to infer an excellency in ourselves from an object, which is of so much shorter duration, and attends us during so small a part of our existence. It will be easy to comprehend the reason, why this cause operates not with the same force in joy as in pride; since the idea of self is not so essential to the former passion as to the latter.

V. I may add as a fifth limitation, or rather enlargement of this system, that general rules have a great influence upon pride and humility, as well as on all the other passions. Hence we form a notion of different ranks of men, suitable to the power of riches they are possest of; and this notion we change not upon account of any peculiarities of the health or temper of the persons, which may deprive them of all enjoyment in their possessions. This may be accounted for from the same principles, that explained the influence of general rules on the understanding. Custom readily carries us beyond the just bounds in our passions, as well as in our reasonings.

It may not be amiss to observe on this occasion, that the influence of general rules and maxims on the passions very much contributes to facilitate the effects of all the principles, which we shall explain in the progress of this treatise. For it is evident, that if a person full-grown, and of the same nature with ourselves, were on a sudden-transported into our world, he would be very much embarrased with every object, and would not readily find what degree of love or hatred, pride or humility, or any other passion he ought to attribute to it. The passions are often varyed by very inconsiderable principles; and these do not always play with a perfect regularity, especially on the first trial. But as custom and practice have brought to light all these principles, and have settled the just value of every thing; this must certainly contribute to the easy production of the passions, and guide us, by means of general established maxims, in the proportions we ought to observe in preferring one object to another. This remark may, perhaps, serve to obviate difficulties, that mayarise concerning some causes, which I shall hereafter ascribe to particular passions, and which may be esteemed too refined to operate so universally and certainly, as they are found to do.

I shall close this subject with a reflection derived from these five limitations. This reflection is, that the persons, who are proudest, and who in the eye of the world have most reason for their pride, are not always the happiest; nor the most humble always the most miserable, as may at first sight be imagined from this system. An evil may be real. though its cause has no relation to us: It may be real, without being peculiar: It may be real, without shewing itself to others: It may be real, without being constant: And it may be real, without falling under the general rules. Such evils as these will not fail to render us miserable, though they have little tendency to diminish pride: And perhaps the most real and the most solid evils of life will be found of this nature.

SECTION VII

Of Vice and Virtue

Taking these limitations along with us, let us proceed to examine the causes of pride and humility; and see, whether in every case we can discover the double relations, by which they operate on the passions. If we find that all these causes are related to self, and produce a pleasure or uneasiness separate from the passion, there will remain no farther scruple with regard to the present system. We shall principally endeavour to prove the latter point; the former being in a manner self-evident.

To begin, with vice and virtue; which are the most obvious causes of these passions; it would be entirely foreign to my present purpose to enter upon the controversy, which of late years has so much excited the curiosity of the publick. WHETHER THESE MORAL DISTINCTIONS BE FOUNDED ON NATURAL AND ORIGINAL PRINCIPLES, OR ARISE FROM INTEREST AND EDUCATION. The examination of this I reserve for the following book; and in the mean time I shall endeavour to show, that my system maintains its ground upon either of these hypotheses; which will be a strong proof of its solidity.

For granting that morality had no foundation in nature, it must still be allowed, that vice and virtue, either from self-interest or the prejudices of education, produce in us a real pain and pleasure; and this we may observe to be strenuously asserted by the defenders of that hypothesis. Every passion, habit, or turn of character (say they) which has a tendency to our advantage or prejudice, gives a delight or uneasiness; and it is from thence the approbation or disapprobation arises. We easily gain from the liberality of others, but are always in danger of losing by their avarice: Courage defends us, but cowardice lays us open to every attack: Justice is the support of society, but injustice, unless checked would quickly prove its ruin: Humility exalts; but pride mortifies us. For these reasons the former qualities are esteemed virtues, and the latter regarded as vices. Now since it is granted there is a delight or uneasiness still attending merit or demerit of every kind, this is all that is requisite for my purpose.

But I go farther, and observe, that this moral hypothesis and my present system not only agree together, but also that, allowing the former to be just, it is an absolute and invincible proof of the latter. For if all morality be founded on the pain or pleasure, which arises from the prospect of any loss or advantage, that may result from our own characters, or from those of others, all the effects of morality must-be derived from the same pain or pleasure, and among the rest, the passions of pride and humility. The very essence of virtue, according to this hypothesis, is to produce pleasure and that of vice to give pain. The virtue and vice must be part of our character in order to excite pride or humility. What farther proof can we desire for the double relation of impressions and ideas?

The same unquestionable argument may be derived from the opinion of those, who maintain that morality is something real, essential, and founded on nature. The most probable hypothesis, which has been advanced to explain the distinction betwixt vice and virtue, and the origin of moral rights and obligations, is, that from a primary constitution of nature certain characters and passions, by the very view and contemplation, produce a pain, and others in like manner excite a pleasure. The uneasiness and satisfaction are not only inseparable from vice and virtue, but constitute their very nature and essence. To approve of a character is to feel an original delight upon its appearance. To disapprove of it is to be sensible of an uneasiness. The pain and pleasure, therefore, being the primary causes of vice and virtue, must also be the causes of all their effects, and consequently of pride and humility, which are the unavoidable attendants of that distinction.

But supposing this hypothesis of moral philosophy should be allowed to be false, it is still evident, that pain and pleasure, if not the causes of vice and virtue, are at least inseparable from them. A generous and noble character affords a satisfaction even in the survey; and when presented to us, though only in a poem or fable, never fails to charm and delight us. On the other hand cruelty and treachery displease from their very nature; nor is it possible ever to reconcile us to these qualities, either in ourselves or others. Thus one hypothesis of morality is an undeniable proof of the foregoing system, and the other at worst agrees with it. But pride and humility arise not from these qualities alone of the mind, which, according to the vulgar systems of ethicks, have been comprehended as parts of moral duty, but from any other that has a connexion with pleasure and uneasiness. Nothing flatters our vanity more than the talent of pleasing by our wit, good humour, or any other accomplishment; and nothing gives us a more sensible mortification than a disappointment in any attempt of that nature. No one has ever been able to tell what wit is, and to-shew why such a system of thought must be received under that denomination, and such another rejected. It is only by taste we can decide concerning it, nor are we possest of any other standard, upon which we can form a judgment of this kind. Now what is this taste, from which true and false wit in a manner receive their being, and without which no thought can have a title to either of these denominations? It is plainly nothing but a sensation of pleasure from true wit, and of uneasiness from false, without oar being able to tell the reasons of that pleasure or uneasiness. The power of bestowing these opposite sensations is, therefore, the very essence of true and false wit; and consequently the cause of that pride or humility, which arises from them.

There may, perhaps, be some, who being accustomed to the style of the schools and pulpit, and having never considered human nature in any other light, than that in which they place it, may here be surprized to hear me talk of virtue as exciting pride, which they look upon as a vice; and of vice as producing humility, which they have been taught to consider as a virtue. But not to dispute about words, I observe, that by pride I understand that agreeable impression, which arises in the mind, when the view either of our virtue, beauty, riches or power makes us satisfyed with ourselves: and that by humility I mean the opposite impression. It is evident the former impression is not always vicious, nor the latter virtuous. The most rigid morality allows us to receive a pleasure from reflecting on a generous action; and it is by none esteemed a virtue to feel any fruitless remorses upon the thoughts of past villainy and baseness. Let us, therefore, examine these impressions, considered in themselves; and enquire into their causes, whether placed on the mind or body, without troubling ourselves at present with that merit or blame, which may attend them.

SECTION VIII

Of Beauty and Deformity

Whether we consider the body as a part of ourselves, or assent to those philosophers, who regard it as something external, it must still be allowed to be near enough connected with us to form one of these double relations, which I have asserted to be necessary to the causes of pride and humility. Wherever, therefore, we can find the other relation of impressions to join to this of ideas, we may expect with assurance either of these passions, according as the impression is pleasant or uneasy. But beauty of all kinds gives us a peculiar delight and satisfaction; as deformity produces pain, upon whatever subject it may be placed, and whether surveyed in an animate or inanimate object. If the beauty or deformity, therefore, be placed upon our own bodies, this pleasure or uneasiness must be converted into pride or humility, as having in this case all the circumstances requisite to produce a perfect transition of impressions and ideas. These opposite sensations are related to the opposite passions. The beauty or deformity is closely related to self, the object of both these passions. No wonder, then our own beauty becomes an object of pride, and deformity of humility.

But this effect of personal and bodily qualities is not only a proof of the present system, by shewing that the passions arise not in this case without all the circumstances I have required, but may be employed as a stronger and more convincing argument. If we consider all the hypotheses, which have been formed either by philosophy or common reason, to explain the difference betwixt beauty and deformity, we shall find that all of them resolve into this, that beauty is such an order and construction of parts, as either by the primary constitution of our nature, by custom, or by caprice, is fitted to give a pleasure and satisfaction to the soul. This is the distinguishing character of beauty, and forms all the difference betwixt it and deformity, whose natural tendency is to produce uneasiness. Pleasure and pain, therefore, are not only necessary attendants of beauty and deformity, but constitute their very essence. And indeed, if we consider, that a great part of the beauty, which we admire either in animals or in other objects, is derived from the idea of convenience and utility, we shall make no scruple to assent to this opinion. That shape, which produces strength, is beautiful in one animal; and that which is a sign of agility in another. The order and convenience of a palace are no less essential to its beauty, than its mere figure and appearance. In like manner the rules of architecture require, that the top of a pillar should be more slender than its base, and that because such a figure conveys to us the idea of security, which is pleasant; whereas the contrary form gives us the apprehension of danger, which is uneasy. From innumerable instances of this kind, as well as from considering that beauty like wit, cannot be defined, but is discerned only by a taste or sensation, we may conclude, that beauty is nothing but a form, which produces pleasure, as deformity is a structure of parts, which conveys pain; and since the power of producing pain and pleasure make in this manner the essence of beauty and deformity, all the effects of these qualities must be derived from the sensation; and among the rest pride and humility, which of all their effects are the most common and remarkable.

This argument I esteem just and decisive; but in order to give greater authority to the present reasoning, let us suppose it false for a moment, and see what will follow. It is certain, then, that if the power of producing pleasure and pain forms not the essence of beauty and deformity, the sensations are at least inseparable from the qualities, and it is even difficult to consider them apart. Now there is nothing common to natural and moral beauty, (both of which are the causes of pride) but this power of producing pleasure; and as a common effect supposes always a common cause, it is plain the pleasure must in both cases be the real and influencing cause of the passion. Again; there is nothing originally different betwixt the beauty of our bodies and the beauty of external and foreign objects, but that the one has a near relation to ourselves, which is wanting in the other. This original difference, therefore, must be the cause of all their other differences, and among the rest, of their different influence upon the passion of pride, which is excited by the beauty of our person, but is not affected in the least by that of foreign and external objects. Placing, then, these two conclusions together, we find they compose the preceding system betwixt them, viz, that pleasure, as a related or resembling impression, when placed on a related object by a natural transition, produces pride; and its contrary, humility. This system, then, seems already sufficiently confirmed by experience; that we have not yet exhausted all our arguments.

It is not the beauty of the body alone that produces pride, but also its strength and force. Strength is a kind of power; and therefore the desire to excel in strength is to be considered as an inferior species of ambition. For this reason the present phænomenon will be sufficiently accounted for, in explaining that passion.

Concerning all other bodily accomplishments we may observe in general, that whatever in ourselves is either useful, beautiful, or surprising, is an object of pride; and it's contrary, of humility. Now it is obvious, that every thing useful, beautiful or surprising, agrees in producing a separate pleasure and agrees in nothing else. The pleasure, therefore, with the relation to self must be the cause of the passion.

Though it should be questioned, whether beauty be not something real, and different from the power of producing pleasure, it can never be disputed, that as surprize is nothing but a pleasure arising from novelty, it is not, properly speaking, a quality in any object, but merely a passion or impression in the soul. It must, therefore, be from that impression, that pride by a natural transition arises. And it arises so naturally, that there is nothing in us or belonging to us, which produces surprize, that does not at the same time excite that other passion. Thus we are vain of the surprising adventures we have met with, the escapes we have made, and dangers we have been exposed to. Hence the origin of vulgar lying; where men without any interest, and merely out of vanity, heap up a number of extraordinary events, which are either the fictions of their brain, or if true, have at least no connexion with themselves. Their fruitful invention supplies them with a variety of adventures; and where that talent is wanting, they appropriate such as belong to others, in order to satisfy their vanity.

In this phænomenon are contained two curious experiments, which if we compare them together, according to the known rules, by which we judge of cause and effect in anatomy, natural philosophy, and other sciences, will be an undeniable argument for that influence of the double relations above-mentioned. By one of these experiments we find, that an object produces pride merely by the interposition of pleasure; and that because the quality, by which it produces pride, is in reality nothing but the power of producing pleasure. By the other experiment we find, that the pleasure produces the pride by a transition along related ideas; because when we cut off that relation the passion is immediately destroyed.. A surprising adventure, in which we have been ourselves engaged, is related to us, and by that means produces pride: But the adventures of others, though they may cause pleasure, yet for want of this relation of ideas, never excite that passion. What farther proof can be desired for the present system?

There is only one objection to this system with regard to our body: which is, that though nothing be more agreeable than health, and more painful than sickness, yet commonly men are neither proud of the one, nor mortifyed with the other. This will easily be accounted for, if we consider the second and fourth limitations, proposed to our general system. It was observed, that no object ever produces pride or humility, if it has not something peculiar to ourself; as also, that every cause of that passion must be in some measure constant, and hold some proportion to the duration of our self, which, is its object. Now as health and sickness vary incessantly to all men, and there is none, who is solely or certainly fixed in either, these accidental blessings and calamities are in a manner separated from us, and are never considered as connected with our being and existence. And that this account is just appears hence, that wherever a malady of any kind is so rooted in our constitution, that we no longer entertain any hopes of recovery, from that moment it becomes an object of humility; as is evident in old men, whom nothing mortifies more than the consideration of their age and infirmities. They endeavour, as long as possible, to conceal their blindness and deafness, their rheums and gouts; nor do they ever confess them without reluctance and uneasiness. And though young men are not ashamed of every head-ach or cold they fall into, yet no topic is so proper to mortify human pride, and make us entertain a mean opinion of our nature, than this, that we are every moment of our lives subject to such infirmities. This sufficiently proves that bodily pain and sickness are in themselves proper causes of humility; though the custom of estimating every thing by comparison more than by its intrinsic worth and value, makes us overlook these calamities, which we find to be incident to every one, and causes us to form an idea of our merit and character independent of them.

We are ashamed of such maladies as affect others, and are either dangerous or disagreeable to them. Of the epilepsy; because it gives a horror to every one present: Of the itch; because it is infectious: Of the king's-evil; because it commonly goes to posterity. Men always consider the sentiments of others in their judgment of themselves. This has evidently appeared in some of the foregoing reasonings; and will appear still more evidently, and be more fully explained afterwards.

SECTION IX

Of External Advantages and Disadvantages

But though pride and humility have the qualities of our mind and body that is self, for their natural and more immediate causes, we find by experience, that there are many other objects, which produce these affections, and that the primary one is, in some measure, obscured and lost by the multiplicity of foreign and extrinsic. We found a vanity upon houses, gardens, equipages, as well as upon personal merit and accomplishments; and though these external advantages be in themselves widely distant from thought or a person, yet they considerably influence even a passion, which is directed to that as its ultimate object. This happens when external objects acquire any particular relation to ourselves, and are associated or connected with us. A beautiful fish in the ocean, an animal in a desert, and indeed any thing that neither belongs, nor is related to us, has no manner of influence on our vanity, whatever extraordinary qualities it may be endowed with, and whatever degree of surprize and admiration it may naturally occasion. It must be some way associated with us in order to touch our pride. Its idea must hang in a manner, upon that of ourselves and the transition from the one to the other must be easy and natural.

But here it is remarkable, that though the relation of resemblance operates upon the mind in the same manner as contiguity and causation, in conveying us from one idea to another, yet it is seldom a foundation either of pride or of humility. If we resemble a person in any of the valuable parts of his character, we must, in some degree, possess the quality, in which we resemble him; and this quality we always chuse to survey directly in ourselves rather than by reflexion in another person, when we would found upon it any degree of vanity. So that though a likeness may occasionally produce that passion by suggesting a more advantageous idea of ourselves, it is there the view fixes at last, and the passion finds its ultimate and final cause.

There are instances, indeed, wherein men shew a vanity in resembling a great man in his countenance, shape, air, or other minute circumstances, that contribute not in any degree to his reputation; but it must be confessed that this extends not very far, nor is of any considerable moment in these affections. For this I assign the following reason. We can never have a vanity of resembling in trifles any person, unless he be possessed of very shining qualities, which give us a respect and veneration for him. These qualities, then, are, properly speaking, the causes of our vanity, by means of their relation to ourselves. Now after what manner are they related to ourselves? They are parts of the person we value, and consequently connected with these trifles; which are also supposed to be parts of him. These trifles are connected with the resembling qualities in us; and these qualities in us, being parts, are connected with the whole; and by that means form a chain of several links of the person we resemble. But besides that this multitude of relations must weaken the connexion; it is evident the mind, in passing from the shining qualities to the trivial ones, must by that contrast the better perceive the minuteness of the latter, and be in some measure ashamed of the comparison and resemblance.

The relation, therefore, of contiguity, or that of causation, betwixt the cause and object of pride and humility, is alone requisite to give rise to these passions; and these relations are nothing else but qualities, by which the imagination is conveyed from one idea to another. Now let us consider what effect these can possibly have upon the mind, and by what means they become so requisite to the production of the passions. It is evident, that the association of ideas operates in so silent and imperceptible a manner, that we are scarce sensible of it, and discover it more by its effects than by any immediate feeling or perception. It produces no emotion, and gives rise to no new impression of any kind, but only modifies those ideas, of which the mind was formerly possessed, and which it could recal upon occasion. From this reasoning, as well as from undoubted experience, we may conclude, that an association of ideas, however necessary, is not alone sufficient to give rise to any passion.

It is evident, then, that when the mind feels the passion either of pride or humility upon the appearance of related object, there is, beside the relation or transition of thought, an emotion or original impression produced by some other principle. The question is, whether the emotion first produced be the passion itself, or some other impression related to it. This question we cannot be long in deciding, For besides all the other arguments, with which this subject abounds, it must evidently appear, that the relation of ideas, which experience shews to be so requisite a circumstance to the production of the passion, would be entirely superfluous, were it not to second a relation of affections, and facilitate the transition from one impression to another. If nature produced immediately the passion of pride or humility, it would be compleated in itself, and would require no farther addition or encrease from any other affection. But supposing the first emotion to be only related to pride or humility, it is easily conceived to what purpose the relation of objects may serve, and how the two different associations, of impressions and ideas, by uniting their forces, may assist each other's operation. This is not only easily conceived, but I will venture to affirm it is the only manner, in which we can conceive this subject. An easy transition of ideas, which, of itself, causes no emotion, can never be necessary, or even useful to the passions, but by forwarding the transition betwixt some related impressions. Not to mention, that the same object causes a greater or smaller degree of pride, not only in proportion to the encrease or decrease of its qualities, but also to the distance or nearness of the relation; which is a clear argument for the transition of affections along the relation of ideas; since every change in the relation produces a proportionable change in the passion. Thus one part of the preceding system, concerning the relations of ideas is a sufficient proof of the other, concerning that of impressions; and is itself so evidently founded on experience, that it would be lost time to endeavour farther to prove it.

This will appear still more evidently in particular instances. Men are vain of the beauty of their country, of their county, of their parish. Here the idea of beauty plainly produces a pleasure. This pleasure is related to pride. The object or cause of this pleasure is, by the supposition, related to self, or the object of pride. By this double relation of impressions and ideas, a transition is made from the one impression to the other.

Men are also vain of the temperature of the climate, in which they were born; of the fertility of their native soil; of the goodness of the wines, fruits or victuals, produced by it; of the softness or force of their language; with other particulars of that kind. These objects have plainly a reference to the pleasures of the senses, and are originally considered as agreeable to the feeling, taste or hearing. How is it possible they could ever become objects of pride, except by means of that transition above-explained?

There are some, that discover a vanity of an opposite kind, and affect to depreciate their own country, in comparison of those, to which they have travelled. These persons find, when they are at home, and surrounded with their countrymen, that the strong relation betwixt them and their own nation is shared with so many, that it is in a manner lost to them; whereas their distant relation to a foreign country, which is formed by their having seen it and lived in it, is augmented by their considering how few there are who have done the same. For this reason they always admire the beauty, utility and rarity of what is abroad, above what is at home.

Since we can be vain of a country, climate or any inanimate object, which bears a relation to us, it is no wonder we are vain of the qualities of those, who are connected with us by blood or friendship. Accordingly we find, that the very same qualities, which in ourselves produce pride, produce also in a lesser degree the same affection, when discovered in persons related to us. The beauty, address, merit, credit and honours of their kindred are carefully displayed by the proud, as some of their most considerable sources of their vanity.

As we are proud of riches in ourselves, so to satisfy our vanity we desire that every one, who has any connexion with us, should likewise be possest of them, and are ashamed of any one, that is mean or poor, among our friends and relations. For this reason we remove the poor as far from us as possible; and as we cannot prevent poverty in some distant collaterals, and our forefathers are taken to be our nearest relations; upon this account every one affects to be of a good family, and to be descended from a long succession of rich and honourable ancestors.

I have frequently observed, that those, who boast of the antiquity of their families, are glad when they can join this circumstance, that their ancestors for many generations have been uninterrupted proprietors of the same portion of land, and that their family has never changed its possessions, or been transplanted into any other county or province. I have also observed, that it is an additional subject of vanity, when they can boast, that these possessions have been transmitted through a descent composed entirely of males, and that the honour, and fortune have never past through any female. Let us endeavour to explain these phaenomena by the foregoing system.

It is evident, that when any one boasts of the antiquity of his family, the subjects of his vanity are not merely the extent of time and number of ancestors, but also their riches and credit, which are supposed to reflect a lustre on himself on account of his relation to them. He first considers these objects; is affected by them in an agreeable manner; and then returning back to himself, through the relation of parent and child, is elevated with the passion of pride, by means of the double relation, of impressions and ideas. Since therefore the passion depends on these relations, whatever strengthens any of the relations must also encrease the passion, and whatever weakens the relations must diminish the passion. Now it is certain the identity of the possesion strengthens the relation of ideas arising from blood and kindred, and conveys the fancy with greater facility from one generation to another, from the remote ancestors to their posterity, who are both their heirs and their descendants. By this facility the impression is transmitted more entire, and excites a greater degree of pride and vanity.

The case is the same with the transmission of the honours and fortune through a succession of males without their passing through any female. It is a quality of human nature, which we shall consider[53] afterwards, that the imagination naturally turns to whatever is important and considerable; and where two objects are presented to it, a small and a great one, usually leaves the former, and dwells entirely upon the latter. As in the society of marriage, the male sex has the advantage above the female, the husband first engages our attention; and whether we consider him directly, or reach him by passing through related objects, the thought both rests upon him with greater satisfaction, and arrives at him with greater facility than his consort. It is easy to see, that this property must strengthen the child's relation to the father, and weaken that to the mother. For as all relations are nothing but a propensity to pass from one idea to another, whatever strengthens the propensity strengthens the relation; and as we have a stronger propensity to pass from the idea of the children to that of the father, than from the same idea to that of the mother, we ought to regard the former relation as the closer and more considerable. This is the reason why children commonly bear their father's name, and are esteemed to be of nobler or baser birth, according to his family. And though the mother should be possest of a superior spirit and genius to the father, as often happens, the general rule prevails, notwithstanding the exception, according to the doctrine above-explained. Nay even when a superiority of any kind is so great, or when any other reasons have such an effect, as to make the children rather represent: the mother's family than the father's, the general rule still retains such an efficacy that it weakens the relation, and makes a kind of break in the line of ancestors. The imagination runs not along them with facility, nor is able to transfer the honour and credit of the ancestors to their posterity of the same name and family so readily, as when the transition is conformable to the general rules, and passes from father to son, or from brother to brother.

SECTION X

Of Property and Riches

But the relation, which is esteemed the closest, and which of all others produces most commonly the passion of pride, is that of property. This relation it will be

[53] Part II. Sect, 2.

impossible for me fully to explain before I come to treat of justice and the other moral virtues. It is sufficient to observe on this occasion, that property may be defined, such a relation betwixt a person and an object as permits him, but forbids any other, the free use and possession of it, without violating the laws of justice and moral equity. If justice, therefore, be a virtue, which has a natural and original influence on the human mind, property may be looked upon as a particular species of causation; whether we consider the liberty it gives the proprietor to operate as he please upon the object or the advantages, which he reaps from it. It is the same case, if justice, according to the system of certain philosophers, should be esteemed an artificial and not a natural virtue. For then honour, and custom, and civil laws supply the place of natural conscience, and produce, in some degree, the same effects. This in the mean time is certain, that the mention of the property naturally carries our thought to the proprietor, and of the proprietor to the property; which being a proof of a perfect relation of ideas is all that is requisite to our present purpose. A relation of ideas, joined to that of impressions, always produces a transition of affections; and therefore, whenever any pleasure or pain arises from an object, connected with us by property. we may be certain, that either pride or humility must arise from this conjunction of relations; if the foregoing system be solid and satisfactory. And whether it be so or not, we may soon satisfy ourselves by the most cursory view of human life.

Every thing belonging to a vain man is the best that is anywhere to be found. His houses, equipage, furniture, doaths, horses, hounds, excel all others in his conceit; and it is easy to observe, that from the least advantage in any of these, he draws a new subject of pride and vanity. His wine, if you'll believe him, has a finer flavour than any other; his cookery is more exquisite; his table more orderly; his servants more expert; the air, in which he lives, more healthful; the soil he cultivates more fertile; his fruits ripen earlier and to greater perfection: Such a thing is remarkable for its novelty; such another for its antiquity: This is the workmanship of a famous artist; that belonged once to such a prince or great man: All objects, in a word, that are useful, beautiful or surprising, or are related to such, may, by means of property, give rise to this passion. These agree in giving pleasure, and agree in nothing else. This alone is common to them; and therefore must be the quality that produces the passion, which is their common effect. As every new instance is a new argument, and as the instances are here without number, I may venture to affirm, that scarce any system was ever so fully proved by experience, as that which I have here advanced.

If the property of any thing, that gives pleasure either by its utility, beauty or novelty, produces also pride by a double relation of impressions and ideas; we need not be surprized, that the power of acquiring this property, should have the same effect. Now riches are to be considered as the power of acquiring the property of what pleases; and it is only in this view they have any influence on the passions. Paper will, on many occasions, be considered as riches, and that because it may convey the power of acquiring money: And money is not riches, as it is a metal endowed with certain qualities of solidity, weight and fusibility; but only as it has a relation to the pleasures and conveniences of life. Taking then this for granted, which is in itself so evident, we may draw from it one of the strongest arguments I have yet employed to prove the influence of the double relations on pride and humility.

It has been observed in treating of the understanding, that the distinction, which we sometimes make betwixt a power and the exercise of it, is entirely frivolous, and that neither man nor any other being ought ever to be thought possest of any ability, unless it be exerted and put in action. But though this be strictly true in a just and philosophical way of thinking, it is certain it is not the philosophy of our passions; but that many things operate upon them by means of the idea and supposition of power, independent of its actual exercise. We are pleased when we acquire an ability of procuring pleasure, and are displeased when another acquires a power of giving pain. This is evident from experience; but in order to give a just explication of the matter, and account for this satisfaction and uneasiness, we must weigh the following reflections.

It is evident the error of distinguishing power from its exercise proceeds not entirely from the scholastic doctrine of free-will, which, indeed, enters very little into common life, and has but small influence on our vulgar and popular ways of thinking. According to that doctrine, motives deprive us not of free-will, nor take away our power of performing or forbearing any action. But according to common notions a man has no power, where very considerable motives lie betwixt him and the satisfaction of his desires, and determine him to forbear what he wishes to perform. I do not think I have fallen into my enemy's power, when I see him pass me in the streets with a sword by his side, while I am unprovided of any weapon. I know that the fear of the civil magistrate is as strong a restraint as any of iron, and that I am in as perfect safety as if he were chained or imprisoned. But when a person acquires such an authority over me, that not only there is no external obstacle to his actions; but also that he may punish or reward me as he pleases, without any dread of punishment in his turn, I then attribute a full power to him, and consider myself as his subject or vassal.

Now if we compare these two cases, that of a person, who has very strong motives of interest or safety to forbear any action, and that of another, who lies under no such obligation, we shall find, according to the philosophy explained in the foregoing book, that the only known difference betwixt them lies in this, that in the former case we conclude from past experience, that the person never will perform that action, and in the latter, that he possibly or probably will perform it. Nothing is more fluctuating and inconstant on many occasions, than the will of man; nor is there any thing but strong motives, which can give us an absolute certainty in pronouncing concerning any of his future actions. When we see a person free from these motives, we suppose a possibility either of his acting or forbearing; and though in general we may conclude him to be determined by motives and causes, yet this removes not the uncertainty of our judgment concerning these causes, nor the influence of that uncertainty on the passions. Since therefore we ascribe a power of performing an action to every one, who has no very powerful motive to forbear it, and refuse it to such as have; it may justly be concluded, that power has always a reference to its exercise, either actual or probable, and that we consider a person as endowed with any ability when we find from past experience, that it is probable, or at least possible he may exert it. And indeed, as our passions always regard the real existence of objects, and we always judge of this reality from past instances; nothing can be more likely of itself, without any farther reasoning, than that power consists in the possibility or probability of any action, as discovered by experience and the practice of the world.

Now it is evident, that wherever a person is in such a situation with regard to me, that there is no very powerful motive to deter him from injuring me, and consequently it is uncertain whether he will injure me or not, I must be uneasy in such a situation, and cannot consider the possibility or probability of that injury without a sensible concern. The passions are not only affected by such events as are certain and infallible, but also in an inferior degree by such as are possible and contingent. And though perhaps I never really feel any harm, and discover by the event, that, philosophically speaking, the person never had any power of harming me; since he did not exert any; this prevents not my uneasiness from the preceding uncertainty. The agreeable passions may here operate as well as the uneasy, and convey a pleasure when I perceive a good to become either possible or probable by the possibility or probability of another's bestowing it on me, upon the removal of any strong motives, which might formerly have hindered him.

But we may farther observe, that this satisfaction encreases, when any good approaches in such a manner that it is in one's own power to take or leave it, and there neither is any physical impediment, nor any very strong motive to hinder our enjoyment. As all men desire pleasure, nothing can be more probable, than its existence when there is no external obstacle to the producing it, and men perceive no danger in following their inclinations. In that case their imagination easily anticipates the satisfaction, and conveys the same joy, as if they were persuaded of its real and actual existence.

But this accounts not sufficiently for the satisfaction, which attends riches. A miser receives delight from his money; that is, from the power it affords him of procuring all the pleasures and conveniences of life, though he knows he has enjoyed his riches for forty years without ever employing them; and consequently cannot conclude by any species of reasoning, that the real existence of these pleasures is nearer, than if he were entirely deprived of all his possessions. But though he cannot form any such conclusion in a way of reasoning concerning the nearer approach of the pleasure, it is certain he imagines it to approach nearer, whenever all external obstacles are removed, along with the more powerful motives of interest and danger, which oppose it. For farther satisfaction on this head I must refer to my account of the will, where I shall[54] explain that false sensation of liberty, which makes us imagine we can perform any thing, that is not very dangerous or destructive. Whenever any other person is under no strong obligations of interest to forbear any pleasure, we judge from experience, that the pleasure will exist, and that he will probably obtain it. But when ourselves are in that situation, we judge from an illusion of the fancy, that the pleasure is still closer and more immediate. The will seems to move easily every way, and casts a shadow or image of itself, even to that side, on which it did not settle. By means of this image the enjoyment seems to approach nearer to us, and gives us the same lively satisfaction, as if it were perfectly certain and unavoidable.

It will now be easy to draw this whole reasoning to a point, and to prove, that when riches produce any pride or vanity in their possessors, as they never fail to do, it is only by means of a double relation of impressions and ideas. The very essence of riches consists in the power of procuring the pleasures and conveniences of life. The very essence of this consists in the probability of its exercise, and in its causing us to anticipate, by a true or false reasoning, the real existence of the pleasure. This anticipation of pleasure is, in itself, a very considerable pleasure; and as its cause is some possession or property, which we enjoy, and which is thereby related to us, we here dearly see all the parts of the foregoing system most exactly and distinctly drawn out before us. For the same reason, that riches cause pleasure and pride, and poverty excites uneasiness and humility, power must produce the former emotions, and slavery the latter. Power or an authority over others makes us capable of satisfying all our desires; as slavery, by subjecting us to the will of others, exposes us to a thousand wants, and mortifications.

It is here worth observing, that the vanity of power, or shame of slavery, are much augmented by the consideration of the persons, over whom we exercise our authority, or who exercise it over us. For supposing it possible to frame statues of such an admirable mechanism, that they could move and act in obedience to the will; it is evident the possession of them would give pleasure and pride, but not to such a degree, as the same authority, when exerted over sensible and rational creatures, whose condition, being compared to our own, makes it seem more agreeable and honourable. Comparison is in every case a sure method of augmenting our esteem of any thing. A rich man feels the felicity of his condition better by opposing it to that of a beggar. But there is a peculiar advantage in power, by the contrast, which is, in a manner, presented to us, betwixt ourselves and the person we command. The comparison is obvious and natural: The imagination finds it in the very subject: The passage of the thought to its conception is smooth and easy. And that this circumstance has a considerable effect in augmenting its influence, will appear afterwards in examining the nature of malice and envy.

---

[54] Part III. Sect. 2.

SECTION XI

Of the Love of Fame

But beside these original causes of pride and humility, there is a secondary one in the opinions of others, which has an equal influence on the affections. Our reputation, our character, our name are considerations of vast weight and importance; and even the other causes of pride; virtue, beauty and riches; have little influence, when not seconded by the opinions and sentiments of others. In order to account for this phænomenon it will be necessary to take some compass, and first explain the nature of sympathy.

No quality of human nature is more remarkable, both in itself and in its consequences, than that propensity we have to sympathize with others, and to receive by communication their inclinations and sentiments, however different from, or even contrary to our own. This is not only conspicuous in children, who implicitly embrace every opinion proposed to them; but also in men of the greatest judgment and understanding, who find it very difficult to follow their own reason or inclination, in opposition to that of their friends and daily companions. To this principle we ought to ascribe the great uniformity we may observe in the humours and turn of thinking of those of the same nation; and it is much more probable, that this resemblance arises from sympathy, than from any influence of the soil and climate, which, though they continue invariably the same, are not able to preserve the character of a nation the same for a century together. A good-natured man finds himself in an instant of the same humour with his company; and even the proudest and most surly take a tincture from their countrymen and acquaintance. A chearful countenance infuses a sensible complacency and serenity into my mind; as an angry or sorrowful one throws a sudden dump upon me. Hatred, resentment, esteem, love, courage, mirth and melancholy; all these passions I feel more from communication than from my own natural temper and disposition. So remarkable a phænomenon merits our attention, and must be traced up to its first principles.

When any affection is infused by sympathy, it is at first known only by its effects, and by those external signs in the countenance and conversation, which convey an idea of it. This idea is presently converted into an impression, and acquires such a degree of force and vivacity, as to become the very passion itself, and produce an equal emotion, as any original affection. However instantaneous this change of the idea into an impression may be, it proceeds from certain views and reflections, which will not escape the strict scrutiny of a philosopher, though they may the person himself, who makes them.

It is evident, that the idea, or rather impression of ourselves is always intimately present with us, and that our consciousness gives us so lively a conception of our own person, that it is not possible to imagine, that any thing can in this particular go beyond it. Whatever object, therefore, is related to ourselves must be conceived with a little vivacity of conception, according to the foregoing principles; and though this relation should not be so strong as that of causation, it must still have a considerable influence. Resemblance and contiguity are relations not to be neglected; especially when by an inference from cause and effect, and by the observation of external signs, we are informed of the real existence of the object, which is resembling or contiguous.

Now it is obvious, that nature has preserved a great resemblance among all human creatures, and that we never remark any passion or principle in others, of which, in some degree or other, we may not find a parallel in ourselves. The case is the same with the fabric of the mind, as with that of the body. However the parts may differ in shape or size, their structure and composition are in general the same. There is a very remarkable resemblance, which preserves itself amidst all their variety; and this resemblance must very much contribute to make us enter into the sentiments of others; and embrace them with facility and pleasure. Accordingly we find, that where, beside the general resemblance of our natures, there is any peculiar similarity in our manners, or character, or country, or language, it facilitates the sympathy. The stronger the relation is betwixt ourselves and any object, the more easily does the imagination make the transition, and convey to the related idea the vivacity of conception, with which we always form the idea of our own person.

Nor is resemblance the only relation, which has this effect, but receives new force from other relations, that may accompany it. The sentiments of others have little influence, when far removed from us, and require the relation of contiguity, to make them communicate themselves entirely. The relations of blood, being a species of causation, may sometimes contribute to the same effect; as also acquaintance, which operates in the same manner with education and custom; as we shall see more fully[55] afterwards. All these relations, when united together, convey the impression or consciousness of our own person to the idea of the sentiments or passions of others, and makes us conceive them in the strongest and most lively manner.

It has been remarked in the beginning of this treatise, that all ideas are borrowed from impressions, and that these two kinds of perceptions differ only in the degrees of force and vivacity, with which they strike upon the soul. The component part of ideas and impressions are precisely alike. The manner and order of their appearance may be the same. The different degrees of their force and vivacity are, therefore, the only particulars, that distinguish them: And as this difference may be removed, in some measure, by a relation betwixt the impressions and ideas, it is no wonder an idea of a sentiment or passion, may by this means be inlivened as to become the very sentiment or passion. The lively idea of any object always approaches is impression; and it is certain we may feel sickness and pain from the mere force of imagination, and make a malady real by often thinking of it. But this is most remarkable in the opinions and affections; and it is there principally that

[55] Part II. Sect. 4.

a lively idea is converted into an impression. Our affections depend more upon ourselves, and the internal operations of the mind, than any other impressions; for which reason they arise more naturally from the imagination, and from every lively idea we form of them. This is the nature and cause of sympathy; and it is after this manner we enter so deep into the opinions and affections of others, whenever we discover them.

What is principally remarkable in this whole affair is the strong confirmation these phaenomena give to the foregoing system concerning the understanding, and consequently to the present one concerning the passions; since these are analogous to each other. It is indeed evident, that when we sympathize with the passions and sentiments of others, these movements appear at first in our mind as mere ideas, and are conceived to belong to another person, as we conceive any other matter of fact. It is also evident, that the ideas of the affections of others are converted into the very impressions they represent, and that the passions arise in conformity to the images we form of them. All this is an object of the plainest experience, and depends not on any hypothesis of philosophy. That science can only be admitted to explain the phaenomena; though at the same time it must be confest, they are so clear of themselves, that there is but little occasion to employ it. For besides the relation of cause and effect, by which we are convinced of the reality of the passion, with which we sympathize; besides this, I say, we must be assisted by the relations of resemblance and contiguity, in order to feel the sympathy in its full perfection. And since these relations can entirely convert an idea into an impression, and convey the vivacity of the latter into the former, so perfectly as to lose nothing of it in the transition, we may easily conceive how the relation of cause and effect alone, may serve to strengthen and inliven an idea. In sympathy there is an evident conversion of an idea into an impression. This conversion arises from the relation of objects to ourself. Ourself is always intimately present to us. Let us compare all these circumstances, and we shall find, that sympathy is exactly correspondent to the operations of our understanding; and even contains something more surprizing and extraordinary.

It is now time to turn our view from the general consideration of sympathy, to its influence on pride and humility, when these passions arise from praise and blame, from reputation and infamy. We may observe, that no person is ever praised by another for any quality, which would not, if real, produce, of itself, a pride in the person possest of it. The elogiums either turn upon his power, or riches, or family, or virtue; all of which are subjects of vanity, that we have already explained and accounted for. It is certain, then, that if a person considered himself in the same light, in which he appears to his admirer, he would first receive a separate pleasure, and afterwards a pride or self-satisfaction, according to the hypothesis above explained. Now nothing is more natural than for us to embrace the opinions of others in this particular; both from sympathy, which renders all their sentiments intimately present to us; and from reasoning, which makes us regard their judgment, as a kind of argument for what they affirm. These two principles of authority and sympathy influence almost all our opinions; but must have a peculiar influence, when we judge of our own worth and character. Such judgments are always attended with passion;[56] and nothing tends more to disturb our understanding, and precipitate us into any opinions, however unreasonable, than their connexion with passion; which diffuses itself over the imagination, and gives an additional force to every related idea. To which we may add, that being conscious of great partiality in our own favour, we are peculiarly pleased with any thing, that confirms the good opinion we have of ourselves, and are easily shocked with whatever opposes it.

All this appears very probable in theory; but in order to bestow a full certainty on this reasoning, we must examine the phaenonena of the passions, and see if they agree with it.

Among these phaenomena we may esteem it a very favourable one to our present purposes that though fame in general be agreeable, yet we receive a much greater satisfaction from the approbation of those, whom we ourselves esteem and approve of, than of those, whom we hate and despise. In like measure we are principally mortifyed with the contempt of persons, upon whose judgment we set some value, and are, in a peat measure, indifferent about the opinions of the rest of mankind. But if the mind received from any original instinct a desire of fame and aversion to infamy, fame and infamy would influence us without distinction; and every opinion, according as it were favourable or unfavourable, would equally excite that desire or aversion. The judgment of a fool is the judgment of another person, as well as that of a wise man, and is only inferior in its influence on our own judgment.

We are not only better pleased with the approbation of a wise man than with that of a fool, but receive an additional satisfaction from the former, when it is obtained after a long and intimate acquaintance. This is accounted for after the same manner.

The praises of others never give us much pleasure, unless they concur with our own opinion, and extol us for those qualities, in which we chiefly excel. A mere soldier little values the character of eloquence: A gownman of courage: A bishop of humour: Or a merchant of learning. Whatever esteem a man may have for any quality, abstractedly considered; when he is conscious he is not possest of it; the opinions of the whole world will give him little pleasure in that particular, and that because they never will be able to draw his own opinion after them.

Nothing is more usual than for men of good families, but narrow circumstances, to leave their friends and country, and rather seek their livelihood by mean and mechanical employments among strangers, than among those, who are acquainted with their birth and education. We shall be unknown, say they, where we go. No body will suspect from what family we are sprung. We shall be removed from all

[56] Book I, Part III. Sect. 10.

our friends and acquaintance, and our poverty and meanness will by that means sit more easy upon us. In examining these sentiments, I find they afford many very convincing arguments for my present purpose.

First, We may infer from them, that the uneasiness of being contemned depends on sympathy, and that sympathy depends on the relation of objects to ourselves; since we are most uneasy under the contempt of persons, who are both related to us by blood, and contiguous in place. Hence we seek to diminish this sympathy and uneasiness by separating these relations, and placing ourselves in a contiguity to strangers, and at a distance from relations.

Secondly, We may conclude, that relations are requisite to sympathy, not absolutely considered as relations, but by their influence in converting our ideas of the sentiments of others into the very sentiments, by means of the association betwixt the idea of their persons, and that of our own. For here the relations of kindred and contiguity both subsist; but not being united in the same persons, they contribute in a less degree to the sympathy.

Thirdly, This very circumstance of the diminution of sympathy by the separation of relations is worthy of our attention. Suppose I am placed in a poor condition among strangers, and consequently am but lightly treated; I yet find myself easier in that situation, than when I was every day exposed to the contempt of my kindred and countrymen. Here I feel a double contempt; from my relations, but they are absent; from those about me, but they are strangers. This double contempt is likewise strengthened by the two relations of kindred and contiguity. But as the persons are not the same, who are connected with me by those two relations, this difference of ideas separates the impressions arising from the contempt, and keeps them from running into each other. The contempt of my neighbours has a certain influence; as has also that of my kindred: But these influences are distinct, and never unite; as when the contempt proceeds from persons who are at once both my neighbours and kindred. This phænomenon is analogous to the system of pride and humility above-explained, which may seem so extraordinary to vulgar apprehensions.

Fourthly, A person in these circumstances naturally conceals his birth from those among whom he lives, and is very uneasy, if any one suspects him to be of a family, much superior to his present fortune and way of living. Every thing in this world is judged of by comparison. What is an immense fortune for a private gentleman is beggary for a prince. A peasant would think himself happy in what cannot afford necessaries for a gentleman. When a man has either been accustomed to a more splendid way of living, or thinks himself intitled to it by his birth and quality, every thing below is disagreeable and even shameful; and it is with the greatest industry he conceals his pretensions to a better fortune. Here he himself knows his misfortunes; but as those, with whom he lives. are ignorant of them, he has the disagreeable reflection and comparison suggested only by his own thoughts, and never receives it by a sympathy with others; which must contribute very much to his ease and satisfaction.

If there be any objections to this hypothesis, THAT THE PLEASURE, WHICH WE RECEIVE FROM PRAISE, ARISES FROM A COMMUNICATION OF SENTIMENTS, we shall find, upon examination, that these objections, when taken in a proper light, will serve to confirm it. Popular fame may be agreeable even to a man, who despises the vulgar; but it is because their multitude gives them additional weight and authority. Plagiaries are delighted with praises, which they are conscious they do not deserve; but this is a kind of castle-building, where the imagination amuses itself with its own fictions, and strives to render them firm and stable by a sympathy with the sentiments of others. Proud men are most shocked with contempt, should they do not most readily assent to it; but it is because of the opposition betwixt the passion, which is natural to them, and that received by sympathy. A violent lover in like manner is very much displeased when you blame and condemn his love; though it is evident your opposition can have no influence, but by the hold it takes of himself, and by his sympathy with you. If he despises you, or perceives you are in jest, whatever you say has no effect upon him.

SECTION XII

Of the Pride and Humility of Animals

Thus in whatever light we consider this subject, we may still observe, that die causes of pride and humility correspond exactly to our hypothesis, and that nothing can excite either of these passions, unless it be both related to ourselves, and produces a pleasure or pain independent of the passion. We have not only proved, that a tendency to produce pleasure or pain is common to all the causes of pride or humility, but also that it is the only thing, which is common; and consequently is the quality, by which they operate. We have farther proved, that the most considerable causes of these passions are really nothing but the power of producing either agreeable or uneasy sensations; and therefore that all their effects, and amongst the rest, pride and humility, are derived solely from that origin. Such simple and natural principles, founded on such solid proofs, cannot fail to be received by philosophers, unless opposed by some objections, that have escaped me.

It is usual with anatomists to join their observations and experiments on human bodies to those on beasts, and from the agreement of these experiments to derive an additional argument for any particular hypothesis. It is indeed certain, that where the structure of parts in brutes is the same as in men, and the operation of these parts also the same, the causes of that operation cannot be different, and that whatever we discover to be true of the one species, may be concluded without hesitation to be certain of the other. Thus though the mixture of humours and the composition of minute parts may justly be presumed so be somewhat different in men from what it is in mere animals; and therefore any experiment we make upon the one concerning the effects of medicines will not always apply to the other; yet as the structure of the veins and muscles, the fabric and situation of the heart, of the lungs, the stomach, the liver and other parts, are the same or nearly the same in all animals, the very same hypothesis, which in one species explains muscular motion, the progress of the chyle, the circulation of the blood, must be applicable to every one; and according as it agrees or disagrees with the experiments we may make in any species of creatures, we may draw a proof of its truth or falshood on the whole. Let us, therefore, apply this method of enquiry, which is found so just and useful in reasonings concerning the body, to our present anatomy of the mind, and see what discoveries we can make by it.

In order to this we must first shew the correspondence of passions in men and animals, and afterwards compare the causes, which produce these passions.

It is plain, that almost in every species of creatures, but especially of the nobler kind, there are many evident marks of pride and humility. The very port and gait of a swan, or turkey, or peacock show the high idea he has entertained of himself, and his contempt of all others. This is the more remarkable, that in the two last species of animals, the pride always attends the beauty, and is discovered in the male only. The vanity and emulation of nightingales in singing have been commonly remarked; as likewise that of horses in swiftness, of hounds in sagacity and smell, of the bull and cock in strength, and of every other animal in his particular excellency. Add to this, that every species of creatures, which approach so often to man, as to familiarize themselves with him, show an evident pride in his approbation, and are pleased with his praises and caresses, independent of every other consideration. Nor are they the caresses of every one without distinction, which give them this vanity, but those principally of the persons they know and love; in the same manner as that passion is excited in mankind. All these are evident proofs, that pride and humility are not merely human passions, but extend themselves over the whole animal creation.

The CAUSES of these passions are likewise much the same in beasts as in us, making a just allowance for our superior knowledge and understanding. Thus animals have little or no sense of virtue or vice; they quickly lose sight of the relations of blood; and are incapable of that of right and property: For which reason the causes of their pride and humility must lie solely in the body, and can never be placed either in the mind or external objects. But so far as regards the body, the same qualities cause pride in the animal as in the human kind; and it is on beauty, strength, swiftness or some other useful or agreeable quality that this passion is always founded.

The next question is, whether, since those passions are the same, and arise from the same causes through the whole creation, the manner, in which the causes operate, be also the same. According to all rules of analogy, this is justly to be expected; and if we find upon trial, that the explication of these phaenomena, which we make use of in one species, will not apply to the rest, we may presume that that explication, however specious, is in reality without foundation.

In order to decide this question, let us consider, that there is evidently the same relation of ideas, and derived from the same causes, in the minds of animals as in those of men. A dog, that has hid a bone, often forgets the place; but when brought to it, his thought passes easily to what he formerly concealed, by means of the contiguity, which produces a relation among his ideas. In like manner, when he has been heartily beat in any place, he will tremble on his approach to it, even though he discover no signs of any present danger. The effects of resemblance are not so remarkable; but as that relation makes a considerable ingredient in causation, of which all animals shew so evident a judgment, we may conclude that the three relations of resemblance, contiguity and causation operate in the same manner upon beasts as upon human creatures.

There are also instances of the relation of impressions, sufficient to convince us, that there is an union of certain affections with each other in the inferior species of creatures as well as in the superior, and that their minds are frequently conveyed through a series of connected emotions. A dog, when elevated with joy, runs naturally into love and kindness, whether of his master or of the sex. In like manner, when full of pain and sorrow, he becomes quarrelsome and ill-natured; and that passion; which at first was grief, is by the smallest occasion converted into anger.

Thus all the internal principles, that are necessary in us to produce either pride or humility, are common to all creatures; and since the causes, which excite these passions, are likewise the same, we may justly conclude, that these causes operate after the same manner through the whole animal creation. My hypothesis Is so simple, and supposes so little reflection and judgment, that it is applicable to every sensible creature; which must not only be allowed to be a convincing proof of its veracity, but, I am confident, will be found an objection to every other system.

PART II

Of Love and Hatred

SECTION I

Of the Object and Causes of Love and Hatred

It is altogether impossible to give any definition of the passions of love and hatred; and that because they produce merely a simple impression, without any mixture or composition. Twould be as unnecessary to attempt any description of them, drawn from their nature, origin, causes and objects; and that both because these are the subjects of our present enquiry, and because these passions of themselves are sufficiently known from our common feeling and experience. This we have already observed concerning pride and humility, and here repeat it concerning love and hatred; and indeed there is so great a resemblance betwixt these two sets of passions, that we shall be obliged to begin with a kind of abridgment of our reasonings concerning the former, in order to explain the latter.

As the immediate object of pride and humility is self or that identical person, of whose thoughts, actions, and sensations we are intimately conscious; so the object of love and hatred is some other person, of whose thoughts, actions, and sensations we are not conscious. This is sufficiently evident from experience. Our love and hatred are always directed to some sensible being external to us; and when we talk of self-love, it is not in a proper sense, nor has the sensation it produces any thing in common with that tender emotion which is excited by a friend or mistress. It is the same case with hatred. We may be mortified by our own faults and follies; but never feel any anger or hatred except from the injuries of others.

But though the object of love and hatred be always some other person, it is plain that the object is not, properly speaking, the cause of these passions, or alone sufficient to excite them. For since love and hatred are directly contrary in their sensation, and have the same object in common, if that object were also their cause, it would produce these opposite passions in an equal degree; and as they must, from the very first moment, destroy each other, none of them would ever be able to make its appearance. There must, therefore, be some cause different from the object.

If we consider the causes of love and hatred, we shall find they are very much diversifyed, and have not many things in common. The virtue, knowledge, wit, good sense, good humour of any person, produce love and esteem; as the opposite qualities, hatred and contempt. The same passions arise from bodily accomplishments, such as beauty, force, swiftness, dexterity; and from their contraries; as likewise from the external advantages and disadvantages of family, possession, cloaths, nation and climate. There is not one of these objects, but what by its different qualities may produce love and esteem, or hatred and contempt.

From the view of these causes we may derive a new distinction betwixt the quality that operates, and the subject on which it is placed. A prince, that is possessed of a stately palace, commands the esteem of the people upon that account; and that first, by the beauty of the palace, and secondly, by the relation of property, which connects it with him. The removal of either of these destroys the passion; which evidently proves that the cause Is a compounded one.

Twould be tedious to trace the passions of love and hatred, through all the observations which we have formed concerning pride and humility, and which are equally applicable to both sets of passions. Twill be sufficient to remark in general, that the object of love and hatred is evidently some thinking person; and that the sensation of the former passion is always agreeable, and of the latter uneasy. We may also suppose with some shew of probability, THAT THE CAUSE OF BOTH THESE PASSIONS IS ALWAYS RELATED TO A THINKING BEING, AND THAT THE CAUSE OF THE FORMER PRODUCE A SEPARATE PLEASURE, AND OF THE LATTER A SEPARATE UNEASINESS.

One of these suppositions, viz, that the cause of love and hatred must be related to a person or thinking being, in order to produce these passions, is not only probable, but too evident to be contested. Virtue and vice, when considered in the abstract; beauty and deformity, when placed on inanimate objects; poverty and riches when belonging to a third person, excite no degree of love or hatred, esteem or contempt towards those, who have no relation to them. A person looking out at a window, sees me in the street, and beyond me a beautiful palace, with which I have no concern: I believe none will pretend, that this person will pay me the same respect, as if I were owner of the palace.

It is not so evident at first sight, that a relation of impressions is requisite to these passions, and that because in the transition the one impression is so much confounded with the other, that they become in a manner undistinguishable. But as in pride and humility, we have easily been able to make the separation, and to prove, that every cause of these passions, produces a separate pain or pleasure, I might here observe the same method with the same success, in examining particularly the several causes of love and hatred. But as I hasten a full and decisive proof of these systems, I delay this examination for a moment: And in the mean time shall endeavour to convert to my present purpose all my reasonings concerning pride and humility, by an argument that is founded on unquestionable examination.

There are few persons, that are satisfyed with their own character, or genius, or fortune, who are nor desirous of shewing themselves to the world, and of acquiring the love and approbation of mankind. Now it is evident, that the very same qualities and circumstances, which are the causes of pride or self-esteem, are also the causes of vanity or the desire of reputation; and that we always put to view those particulars with which in ourselves we are best satisfyed. But if love and esteem were not produced by the same qualities as pride, according as these qualities are related to ourselves or others, this method of proceeding would be very absurd, nor could men expect a correspondence in the sentiments of every other person, with those themselves have entertained. It is true, few can form exact systems of the passions, or make reflections on their general nature and resemblances. But without such a progress in philosophy, we are not subject to many mistakes in this particular, but are sufficiently guided by common experience, as well as by a kind of presentation; which tells us what will operate on others, by what we feel immediately in ourselves. Since then the same qualities that produce pride or humility, cause love or hatred; all the arguments that have been employed to prove, that the causes of the former passions excite a pain or pleasure independent of the passion, will be applicable with equal evidence to the causes of the latter.

SECTION II

Experiments to confirm this System

Upon duly weighing these arguments, no one will make any scruple to assent to that conclusion I draw from them, concerning the transition along related impressions and ideas, especially as it is a principle, in itself, so easy and natural. But that we may place this system beyond doubt both with regard to love and hatred, pride and humility, it will be proper to make some new experiments upon all these passions, as well as to recall a few of these observations, which I have formerly touched upon.

In order to make these experiments, let us suppose I am in company with a person, whom I formerly regarded without any sentiments either of friendship or enmity. Here I have the natural and ultimate object of all these four passions placed before me. Myself am the proper object of pride or humility; the other person of love or hatred.

Regard now with attention the nature of these passions, and their situation with respect to each other. It is evident here are four affections, placed, as it were, in a square or regular connexion with, and distance from each other. The passions of pride and humility, as well as those of love and hatred, are connected together by the identity of their object, which to the first set of passions is self, to the second some other person. These two lines of communication or connexion form two opposite sides of the square. Again, pride and love are agreeable passions; hatred and humility uneasy. This similitude of sensation betwixt pride and love, and that betwixt humility and hatred form a new connexion, and may be considered as the other two sides of the square. Upon the whole, pride is connected with humility, love with hatred, by their objects or ideas: Pride with love, humility with hatred, by their sensations or impressions.

I say then, that nothing can produce any of these passions without bearing it a double relation, viz, of ideas to the object of the passion, and of sensation to the passion itself. This we must prove by our experiments. First Experiment. To proceed with the greater order in these experiments, let us first suppose, that being placed in the situation above-mentioned, viz, in company with some other person, there is an object presented, that has no relation either of impressions or ideas to any of these passions. Thus suppose we regard together an ordinary stone, or other common object, belonging to neither of us, and causing of itself no emotion, or independent pain and pleasure: It is evident such an object will produce none of these four passions. Let us try it upon each of them successively. Let us apply it to love, to hatred, to humility, to pride; none of them ever arises in the smallest degree imaginable. Let us change the object, as oft as we please; provided still we choose one, that has neither of these two relations. Let us repeat the experiment in all the dispositions, of which the mind is susceptible. No object, in the vast variety of nature, will, in any disposition, produce any passion without these relations.

Second Experiment. Since an object, that wants both these relations can never produce any passion, let us bestow on it only one of these relations; and see what will follow. Thus suppose, I regard a stone or any common object, that belongs either to me or my companion, and by that means acquires a relation of ideas to the object of the passions: It is plain, that to consider the matter a priori, no emotion of any kind can reasonably be expected. For besides, that a relation of ideas operates secretly and calmly on the mind, it bestows an equal impulse towards the opposite passions of pride and humility, love and hatred, according as the object belongs to ourselves or others; which opposition of the passions must destroy both, and leave the mind perfectly free from any affection or emotion. This reasoning a priori is confirmed by experience. No trivial or vulgar object, that causes not a pain or pleasure, independent of the passion, will ever, by its property or other relations either to ourselves or others, be able to produce the affections of pride or humility, love or hatred.

Third Experiment. It is evident, therefore, that a relation of ideas is not able alone to give rise to these affections. Let us now remove this relation, and in its stead place a relation of impressions, by presenting an object, which is agreeable or disagreeable, but has no relation either to ourself or companion; and let us observe the consequences. To consider the matter first a priori, as in the preceding experiment; we may conclude, that the object will have a small, but an uncertain connexion with these passions. For besides, that this relation is not a cold and imperceptible one, it has not the inconvenience of the relation of ideas, nor directs us with equal force to two contrary passions, which by their opposition destroy each other. But if we consider, on the other hand, that this transition from the sensation to the affection is not forwarded by any principle, that produces a transition of ideas; but, on the contrary, that though the one impression be easily transfused into the other, yet the change of objects is supposed contrary to all the principles, that cause a transition of that kind; we may from thence infer, that nothing will ever be a steady or durable cause of any passion, that is connected with the passion merely by a relation of impressions. What our reason would conclude from analogy, after balancing these arguments, would be, that an object, which produces pleasure or uneasiness, but has no manner of connexion either with ourselves or others, may give such a turn to the disposition, as that may naturally fall into pride or love, humility or hatred, and search for other objects, upon which by a double relation, it can found these affections; but that an object, which has only one of these relations, though the most advantageous one, can never give rise to any constant and established passion.

Most fortunately all this reasoning is found to be exactly conformable to experience, and the phaenomena of the passions. Suppose I were travelling with a companion through a country, to which we are both utter strangers; it is evident, that if the prospects be beautiful, the roads agreeable, and the inns commodious, this may put me into good humour both with myself and fellow-traveller. But as we suppose, that this country has no relation either to myself or friend it can never be the immediate cause of pride or love; and therefore if I found not the passion on some other object, that bears either of us a closer relation, my emotions are rather to be considerd as the overflowings of an elevate or humane disposition, than as an established passion. The case is the same where the object produces uneasiness.

Fourth Experiment. Having found, that neither an object without any relation of ideas or impressions, nor an object, that has only one relation, can ever cause pride or humility, love or hatred; reason alone may convince us, without any farther experiment, that whatever has a double relation must necessarily excite these passions; since it is evident they must have some cause. But to leave as little room for doubt as possible, let us renew our experiments, and see whether the event in this case answers our expectation. I choose an object, such as virtue, that causes a separate satisfaction: On this object I bestow a relation to self; and find, that from this disposition of affairs, there immediately arises a passion. But what passion? That very one of pride, to which this object bears a double relation. Its idea is related to that of self, the object of the passion: The sensation it causes resembles the sensation of the passion. That I may be sure I am not mistaken in this experiment, I remove first one relation; then another; and find, that each removal destroys the passion, and leaves the object perfectly indifferent. But I am not content with this. I make a still farther trial; and instead of removing the relation, I only change it for one of a different kind. I suppose the virtue to belong to my companion, not to myself; and observe what follows from this alteration. I immediately perceive the affections wheel to about, and leaving pride, where there is only one relation, viz, of impressions, fall to the side of love, where they are attracted by a double relation of impressions and ideas. By repeating the same experiment, in changing anew the relation of ideas, I bring the affections back to pride; and by a new repetition I again place them at love or kindness. Being fully convinced of the influence of this relation, I try the effects of the other; and by changing virtue for vice, convert the pleasant impression, which arises from the former, into the disagreeable one, which proceeds from the latter. The effect still answers expectation. Vice, when placed on another, excites, by means of its double relations, the passion of hatred, instead of love, which for the same reason arises from virtue. To continue the experiment, I change anew the relation of ideas, and suppose the vice to belong to myself. What follows? What is usual. A subsequent change of the passion from hatred to humility. This humility I convert into pride by a new change of the impression; and find after all that I have compleated the round, and have by these changes brought back the passion to that very situation, in which I first found it.

But to make the matter still more certain, I alter the object; and instead of vice and virtue, make the trial upon beauty and deformity, riches and poverty, power and servitude. Each of these objects runs the circle of the passions in the same manner, by a change of their relations: And in whatever order we proceed, whether through pride, love, hatred, humility, or through humility, hatred, love, pride, the experiment is not in the least diversifyed. Esteem and contempt, indeed, arise on some occasions instead of love and hatred; but these are at the bottom the same passions, only diversifyed by some causes, which we shall explain afterwards.

Fifth Experiment. To give greater authority to these experiments, let us change the situation of affairs as much as possible, and place the passions and objects in all the different positions, of which they are susceptible. Let us suppose, beside the relations above-mentioned, that the person, along with whom I make all these experiments, is closely connected with me either by blood or friendship. He is, we shall suppose, my son or brother, or is united to me by a long and familiar acquaintance. Let us next suppose, that the cause of the passion acquires a double relation of impressions and ideas to this person; and let us see what the effects are of all these complicated attractions and relations.

Before we consider what they are in fact, let us determine what they ought to be, conformable to my hypothesis. It is plain, that, according as the impression is either pleasant or uneasy, the passion of love or hatred must arise towards the person, who is thus connected to the cause of the impression by these double relations, which I have all along required. The virtue of a brother must make me love him; as his vice or infamy must excite the contrary passion. But to judge only from the situation of affairs, I should not expect, that the affections would rest there, and never transfuse themselves into any other impression. As there is here a person, who by means of a double relation is the object of my passion, the very same reasoning leads me to think the passion will be carryed farther. The person has a relation of ideas to myself, according to the supposition; the passion, of which he is the object, by being either agreeable or uneasy, has a relation of impressions to pride or humility. It is evident, then, that one of these passions must arise from the love or hatred.

This is the reasoning I form in conformity to my hypothesis; and am pleased to find upon trial that every thing answers exactly to my expectation. The virtue or vice of a son or brother not only excites love or hatred, but by a new transition, from similar causes, gives rise to pride or humility. Nothing causes greater vanity than any shining quality in our relations; as nothing mortifies us more than their vice or infamy. This exact conformity of experience to our reasoning is a convincing proof of the solidity of that hypothesis, upon which we reason.

Sixth Experiment. This evidence will be still augmented, if we reverse the experiment, and preserving still the same relations, begin only with a different passion. Suppose, that instead of the virtue or vice of a son or brother, which causes first love or hatred, and afterwards pride or humility, we place these good or bad qualities on ourselves, without any immediate connexion with the person, who is related to us: Experience shews us, that by this change of situation the whole chain is broke, and that the mind is not conveyed from one passion to another, as in the preceding instance. We never love or hate a son or brother for the virtue or vice we discern in ourselves; though it is evident the same qualities in him give us a very sensible pride or humility. The transition from pride or humility to love or hatred is not so natural as from love or hatred to pride or humility. This may at first sight be esteemed contrary to my hypothesis; since the relations of impressions and ideas are in both cases precisely the same. Pride and humility are impressions related to love and hatred. Myself am related to the person. It should, therefore, be expected, that like causes must produce like effects, and a perfect transition arise from the double relation, as in all other cases. This difficulty we may easily solve by the following reflections.

It is evident, that as we are at all times intimately conscious of ourselves, our sentiments and passions, their ideas must strike upon us with greater vivacity than the ideas of the sentiments and passions of any other person. But every thing, that strikes upon us with vivacity, and appears in a full and strong light, forces itself, in a manner, into our consideration, and becomes present to the mind on the smallest hint and most trivial relation. For the same reason, when it is once present, it engages the attention, and keeps it from wandering to other objects, however strong may be their relation to our first object. The imagination passes easily from obscure to lively ideas, but with difficulty from lively to obscure. In the one case the relation is aided by another principle: In the other case, it is opposed by it.

Now I have observed, that those two faculties of the mind, the imagination and passions, assist each other in their operations when their propensities are similar, and when they act upon the same object. The mind has always a propensity to pass from a passion to any other related to it; and this propensity is forwarded when the object of the one passion is related to that of the other. The two impulses concur with each other, and render the whole transition more smooth and easy. But if it should happen, that while the relation of ideas, strictly speaking, continues the same, its influence, in causing a transition of the imagination, should no longer take place, it is evident its influence on the passions must also cease, as being dependent entirely on that transition. This is the reason why pride or humility is not transfused into love or hatred with the same ease, that the latter passions are changed into the former. If a person be my brother I am his likewise: but though the relations be reciprocal they have very different effects on the imagination. The passage is smooth and open from the consideration of any person related to us to that of ourself, of whom we are every moment conscious. But when the affections are once directed to ourself, the fancy passes not with the same facility from that object to any other person, how closely so ever connected with us. This easy or difficult transition of the imagination operates upon the passions, and facilitates or retards their transition, which is a clear proof, that these two faculties of the passions and imagination are connected together, and that the relations of ideas have an influence upon the affections. Besides innumerable experiments that prove this, we here find, that even when the relation remains; if by any particular circumstance its usual effect upon the fancy in producing an association or transition of ideas, is prevented; its usual effect upon the passions, in conveying us from one to another, is in like manner prevented.

Some may, perhaps, find a contradiction betwixt this phænomenon and that of sympathy, where the mind passes easily from the idea of ourselves to that of any other object related to us. But this difficulty will vanish, if we consider that in sympathy our own person is not the object of any passion, nor is there any thing, that fixes our attention on ourselves; as in the present case, where we are supposed to be actuated with pride or humility. Ourself, independent of the perception of every other object, is in reality nothing: For which reason we must turn our view to external objects; and it is natural for us to consider with most attention such as lie contiguous to us, or resemble us. But when self is the object of a passion, it is not natural to quit the consideration of it, till the passion be exhausted: in which case the double relations of impressions and ideas can no longer operate.

Seventh Experiment. To put this whole reasoning to a farther trial, let us make a new experiment; and as we have already seen the effects of related passions and ideas, let us here suppose an identity of passions along with a relation of ideas; and let us consider the effects of this new situation. It is evident a transition of the passions from the one object to the other is here in all reason to be expected; since the relation of ideas is supposed still to continue, and identity of impressions must produce a stronger connexion, than the most perfect resemblance, that can be imagined. If a double relation, therefore, of impressions and ideas is able to produce a transition from one to the other, much more an identity of impressions with a relation of ideas. Accordingly we find, that when we either love or hate any person, the passions seldom continue within their first bounds; but extend themselves towards all the contiguous objects, and comprehend the friends and relations of him we love or hate. Nothing is more natural than to bear a kindness to one brother on account of our friendship for another, without any farther examination of his character. A quarrel with one person gives us a hatred for the whole family, though entirely innocent of that, which displeases us. Instances of this kind are everywhere to be met with.

There is only one difficulty in this experiment, which it will be necessary to account for, before we proceed any farther. It is evident, that though all passions pass easily from one object to another related to it, yet this transition is made with greater facility, where the more considerable object is first presented, and the lesser follows it, than where this order is reversed, and the lesser takes the precedence. Thus it is more natural for us to love the son upon account of the father, than the father upon account of the son; the servant for the master, than the master for the servant; the subject for the prince, than the prince for the subject. In like manner we more readily contract a hatred against a whole family, where our first quarrel is with the head of it, than where we are displeased with a son, or servant, or some inferior member. In short, our passions, like other objects, descend with greater facility than they ascend.

That we may comprehend, wherein consists the difficulty of explaining this phænomenon, we must consider, that the very same reason, which determines the imagination to pass from remote to contiguous objects, with more facility than from contiguous to remote, causes it likewise to change with more ease, the less for the greater, than the greater for the less. Whatever has the greatest influence is most taken notice of; and whatever is most taken notice of, presents itself most readily to the imagination. We are more apt to over-look in any subject, what is trivial, than what appears of considerable moment; but especially if the latter takes the precedence, and first engages our attention. Thus if any accident makes us consider the Satellites of JUPITER, our fancy is naturally determined to form the idea of that planet; but if we first reflect on the principal planet, it is more natural for us to overlook its attendants. The mention of the provinces of any empire conveys our thought to the seat of the empire; but the fancy returns not with the same facility to the consideration of the provinces. The idea of the servant makes us think of the master; that of the subject carries our view to the prince. But the same relation has not an equal influence in conveying us back again. And on this is founded that reproach of Cornelia to her sons, that they ought to be ashamed she should be more known by the title of the daughter of Scipio than by that of the mother of the Gracchi. This was, in other words, exhorting them to render themselves as illustrious and famous as their grandfather, otherwise the imagination of the people, passing from her who was intermediate, and placed in an equal relation to both, would always leave them, and denominate her by what was more considerable and of greater moment. On the same principle is founded that common custom of making wives bear the name of their husbands, rather than husbands that of their wives; as also the ceremony of giving the precedency to those, whom we honour and respect. We might find many other instances to confirm this principle, were it not already sufficiently evident.

Now since the fancy finds the same facility in passing from the lesser to the greater, as from remote to contiguous, why does not this easy transition of ideas assist the transition of passions in the former case, as well as in the latter? The virtues of a friend or brother produce first love, and then pride; because in that case the imagination passes from remote to contiguous, according to its propensity.

Our own virtues produce not first pride, and then love to a friend or brother; because the passage in that case would be from contiguous to remote, contrary to its propensity. But the love or hatred of an inferior causes not readily any passion to the superior, though that be the natural propensity of the imagination: While the love or hatred of a superior, causes a passion to the inferior, contrary to its propensity. In short, the same facility of transition operates not in the same manner upon superior and inferior as upon contiguous and remote. These two phaenomena appear contradictory, and require some attention to be reconciled.

As the transition of ideas is here made contrary to the natural propensity of the imagination, that faculty must be overpowered by some stronger principle of another kind; and as there is nothing ever present to the mind but impressions and ideas, this principle must necessarily lie in the impressions. Now it has been observed, that impressions or passions are connected only by their resemblance, and that where any two passions place the mind in the same or in similar dispositions, it very naturally passes from the one to the other: As on the contrary, a repugnance in the dispositions produces a difficulty in the transition of the passions. But it is observable, that this repugnance may arise from a difference of degree as well as of kind; nor do we experience a greater difficulty in passing suddenly from a small degree of love to a small degree of hatred, than from a small to a great degree of either of these affections. A man, when calm or only moderately agitated, is so different, in every respect, from himself, when disturbed with a violent passion, that no two persons can be more unlike; nor is it easy to pass from the one extreme to the other, without a considerable interval betwixt them.

The difficulty is not less, if it be not rather greater, in passing from the strong passion to the weak, than in passing from the weak to the strong, provided the one passion upon its appearance destroys the other, and they do not both of them exist at once. But the case is entirely altered, when the passions unite together, and actuate the mind at the same time. A weak passion, when added to a strong, makes not so considerable a change in the disposition, as a strong when added to a weak; for which reason there is a closer connexion betwixt the great degree and the small, than betwixt the small degree and the great.

The degree of any passion depends upon the nature of its object; and an affection directed to a person, who is considerable in our eyes, fills and possesses the mind much more than one, which has for its object a person we esteem of less consequence. Here then the contradiction betwixt the propensities of the imagination and passion displays itself. When we turn our thought to a great and a small object, the imagination finds more facility in passing from the small to the great, than from the great to the small; but the affections find a greater difficulty: And as the affections are a more powerful principle than the imagination, no wonder they prevail over it, and draw the mind to their side. In spite of the difficulty of passing from the idea of great to that of little, a passion directed to the former, produces always a similar passion towards the latter; when the great and little are related together. The idea of the servant conveys our thought most readily to the master; but the hatred or love of the master produces with greater facility anger or good-will to the servant. The strongest passion in this case takes the precedence; and the addition of the weaker making no considerable change on the disposition, the passage is by that means rendered more easy and natural betwixt them.

As in the foregoing experiment we found, that a relation of ideas, which, by any particular circumstance, ceases to produce its usual effect of facilitating the transition of ideas, ceases likewise to operate on the passions; so in the present experiment we find the same property of the impressions. Two different degrees of the same passion are surely related together; but if the smaller be first present, it has little or no tendency to introduce the greater; and that because the addition of the great to the little, produces a more sensible alteration on the temper, than the addition of the little to the great. These phaenomena, when duly weighed, will be found convincing proofs of this hypothesis.

And these proofs will be confirmed, if we consider the manner in which the mind here reconciles the contradiction, I have observed betwixt the passions and the imagination. The fancy passes with more facility from the less to the greater, than from the greater to the less: But on the contrary a violent passion produces more easily a feeble, than that does a violent. In this opposition the passion in the end prevails over the imagination; but it is commonly by complying with it, and by seeking another quality, which may counter-ballance that principle, from whence the opposition arises. When we love the father or master of a family, we little think of his children or servants. But when these are present with us, or when it lies any ways in our power to serve them, the nearness and contiguity in this case encreases their magnitude, or at least removes that opposition, which the fancy makes to the transition of the affections. If the imagination finds a difficulty in passing from greater to less, it finds an equal facility in passing from remote to contiguous, which brings the matter to an equality, and leaves the way open from the one passion to the other.

Eighth Experiment. I have observed that the transition from love or hatred to pride or humility, is more easy than from pride or humility to love or hatred; and that the difficulty, which the imagination finds in passing from contiguous to remote, is the cause why we scarce have any instance of the latter transition of the affections. I must, however, make one exception, viz, when the very cause of the pride and humility is placed in some other person. For in that case the imagination is necessitated to consider the person, nor can it possibly confine its view to ourselves. Thus nothing more readily produces kindness and affection to any person, than his approbation of our conduct and character: As on the other hand, nothing inspires us with a stronger hatred, than his blame or contempt. Here it is evident, that the original passion is pride or humility, whose object is self; and that this passion is transfused into love or hatred, whose object is some other person, notwithstanding the rule I have already established, THAT THE

IMAGINATION PASSES WITH DIFFICULTY FROM CONTIGUOUS TO REMOTE. But the transition in this case is not made merely on account of the relation betwixt ourselves and the person; but because that very person is the real cause of our first passion, and of consequence is intimately connected with it. It is his approbation that produces pride; and disapprobation, humility. No wonder, then, the imagination returns back again attended with the related passions of love and hatred. This is not a contradiction, but an exception to the rule; and an exception that arises from the same reason with the rule itself.

Such an exception as this is, therefore, rather a confirmation of the rule. And indeed, if we consider all the eight experiments I have explained, we shall find that the same principle appears in all of them, and that it is by means of a transition arising from a double relation of impressions and ideas, pride and humility, love and hatred are produced. An object without[57] a relation, or[58] with but one, never produces either of these passions; and it is[59] found that the passion always varies in conformity to the relation. Nay we may observe, that where the relation, by any particular circumstance, has not its usual effect of producing a transition either of[60] ideas or of impressions, it ceases to operate upon the passions, and gives rise neither to pride nor love, humility nor hatred. This rule we find still to hold good,[61] even under the appearance of its contrary; and as relation is frequently experienced to have no effect; which upon examination is found to proceed from some particular circumstance, that prevents the transition; so even in instances, where that circumstance, though present, prevents not the transition, it is found to arise from some other circumstance, which counter-balances it. Thus not only the variations resolve themselves into the general principle, but even the variations of these variations.

SECTION III

Difficulties Solved

After so many and such undeniable proofs drawn from daily experience and observation, it may seem superfluous to enter into a particular examination of all the causes of love and hatred. I shall, therefore, employ the sequel of this part, First, In removing some difficulties, concerning particular causes of these passions. Secondly, In examining the compound affections, which arise from the mixture of love and hatred with other emotions.

---

[57] First Experiment.

[58] Second and Third Experiments.

[59] Fourth Experiment.

[60] Sixth Experiment.

[61] Seventh and Eighth Experiments.

Nothing is more evident, than that any person acquires our kindness, or is exposed to our ill-will, in proportion to the pleasure or uneasiness we receive from him, and that the passions keep pace exactly with the sensations in all their changes and variations. Whoever can find the means either by his services, his beauty, or his flattery, to render himself useful or agreeable to us, is sure of our affections: As on the other hand, whoever harms or displeases us never fails to excite our anger or hatred. When our own nation is at war with any other, we detest them under the character of cruel, perfidious, unjust and violent: But always esteem ourselves and allies equitable, moderate, and merciful. If the general of our enemies be successful, it is with difficulty we allow him the figure and character of a man. He is a sorcerer: He has a communication with daemons; as is reported of OLIVER CROMWELL, and the DUKE OF LUXEMBOURG: He is bloody-minded, and takes a pleasure in death and destruction. But if the success be on our side, our commander has all the opposite good qualities, and is a pattern of virtue, as well as of courage and conduct. His treachery we call policy: His cruelty is an evil inseparable from war. In short, every one of his faults we either endeavour to extenuate, or dignify it with the name of that virtue, which approaches it. It is evident the same method of thinking runs through common life.

There are some, who add another condition, and require not only that the pain and pleasure arise from the person, but likewise that it arise knowingly, and with a particular design and intention. A man, who wounds and harms us by accident, becomes not our enemy upon that account, nor do we think ourselves bound by any ties of gratitude to one, who does us any service after the same manner. By the intention we judge of the actions, and according as that is good or bad, they become causes of love or hatred.

But here we must make a distinction. If that quality in another, which pleases or displeases, be constant and inherent in his person and character, it will cause love or hatred independent of the intention: But otherwise a knowledge and design is requisite, in order to give rise to these passions. One that is disagreeable by his deformity or folly is the object of our aversion, though nothing be more certain, than that he has not the least intention of displeasing us by these qualities. But if the uneasiness proceed not from a quality, but an action, which is produced and annihilated in a moment, it is necessary, in order to produce some relation, and connect this action sufficiently with the person, that it be derived from a particular fore-thought and design. It is not enough, that the action arise from the person, and have him for its immediate cause and author. This relation alone is too feeble and inconstant to be a foundation for these passions. It reaches not the sensible and thinking part, and neither proceeds from any thing durable in him, nor leaves any thing behind it; but passes in a moment, and is as if it had never been. On the other hand, an intention shews certain qualities, which remaining after the action is performed, connect it with the person, and facilitate the transition of ideas from one to the other. We can never think of him without reflecting on these qualities;

unless repentance and a change of life have produced an alteration in that respect: In which case the passion is likewise altered. This therefore is one reason, why an intention is requisite to excite either love or hatred.

But we must farther consider, that an intention, besides its strengthening the relation of ideas, is often necessary to produce a relation of impressions, and give rise to pleasure and uneasiness. For it is observable, that the principal part of an injury is the contempt and hatred, which it shews in the person, that injures us; and without that, the mere harm gives us a less sensible uneasiness. In like manner, a good office is agreeable, chiefly because it flatters our vanity, and is a proof of the kindness and esteem of the person, who performs it. The removal of the intention, removes the mortification in the one case, and vanity in the other, and must of course cause a remarkable diminution in the passions of love and hatred.

I grant, that these effects of the removal of design, in diminishing the relations of impressions and ideas, are not entire, nor able to remove every degree of these relations. But then I ask, if the removal of design be able entirely to remove the passion of love and hatred? Experience, I am sure, informs us of the contrary, nor is there any thing more certain, than that men often fall into a violent anger for injuries, which they themselves must own to be entirely involuntary and accidental. This emotion, indeed, cannot be of long continuance; but still is sufficient to shew, that there is a natural connexion betwixt uneasiness and anger, and that the relation of impressions will operate upon a very small relation of ideas. But when the violence of the impression is once a little abated, the defect of the relation begins to be better felt; and as the character of a person is no wise interested in such injuries as are casual and involuntary, it seldom happens that on their account, we entertain a lasting enmity.

To illustrate this doctrine by a parallel instance, we may observe, that not only the uneasiness, which proceeds from another by accident, has but little force to excite our passion, but also that which arises from an acknowledged necessity and duty. One that has a real design of harming us, proceeding not from hatred and ill-will, but from justice and equity, draws not upon him our anger, if we be in any degree reasonable; notwithstanding he is both the cause, and the knowing cause of our sufferings. Let us examine a little this phænomenon.

It is evident in the first place, that this circumstance is not decisive; and though it may be able to diminish the passions, it is seldom it can entirely remove them. How few criminals are there, who have no ill-will to the person, that accuses them, or to the judge, that condemns them, even though they be conscious of their own deserts? In like manner our antagonist in a law-suit, and our competitor for any office, are commonly regarded as our enemies; though we must acknowledge, if we would but reflect a moment, that their motive is entirely as justifiable as our own.

Besides we may consider, that when we receive harm from any person, we are apt to imagine him criminal, and it is with extreme difficulty we allow of his justice and innocence. This is a clear proof, that, independent of the opinion of iniquity, any harm or uneasiness has a natural tendency to excite our hatred, and that afterwards we seek for reasons upon which we may justify and establish the passion. Here the idea of injury produces not the passion, but arises from it.

Nor is it any wonder that passion should produce the opinion of injury; since otherwise it must suffer a considerable diminution, which all the passions avoid as much as possible. The removal of injury may remove the anger, without proving that the anger arises only from the injury. The harm and the justice are two contrary objects, of which the one has a tendency to produce hatred, and the other love; and it is according to their different degrees, and our particular turn of thinking, that either of the objects prevails, and excites its proper passion.

SECTION IV

Of the Love of Relations

Having given a reason, why several actions, that cause a real pleasure or uneasiness, excite not any degree, or but a small one, of the passion of love or hatred towards the actors; it will be necessary to shew, wherein consists the pleasure or uneasiness of many objects, which we find by experience to produce these passions.

According to the preceding system there is always required a double relation of impressions and ideas betwixt the cause and effect, in order to produce either love or hatred. But though this be universally true, it is remarkable that the passion of love may be excited by only one relation of a different kind, viz, betwixt ourselves and the object; or more properly speaking, that this relation is always attended with both the others. Whoever is united to us by any connexion is always sure of a share of our love, proportioned to the connexion, without enquiring into his other qualities. Thus the relation of blood produces the strongest tie the mind is capable of in the love of parents to their children, and a lesser degree of the same affection, as the relation lessens. Nor has consanguinity alone this effect, but any other relation without exception. We love our country-men, our neighbours, those of the same trade, profession, and even name with ourselves. Every one of these relations is esteemed some tie, and gives a title to a share of our affection.

There is another phænomenon, which is parallel to this, viz, that acquaintance, without any kind of relation, gives rise to love and kindness. When we have contracted a habitude and intimacy with any person; though in frequenting his company we have not been able to discover any very valuable quality, of which he is possessed; yet we cannot forebear preferring him to strangers, of whose superior merit we are fully convinced. These two phaenomena of the effects of relation and acquaintance will give mutual light to each other, and may be both explained from the same principle.

Those, who take a pleasure in declaiming against human nature, have observed, that man is altogether insufficient to support himself; and that when you loosen all the holds, which he has of external objects, he immediately drops down into the deepest melancholy and despair. From this, say they, proceeds that continual search after amusement in gaming, in hunting, in business; by which we endeavour to forget ourselves, and excite our spirits from the languid state, into which they fall, when not sustained by some brisk and lively emotion. To this method of thinking I so far agree, that I own the mind to be insufficient, of itself, to its own entertainment, and that it naturally seeks after foreign objects, which may produce a lively sensation, and agitate the spirits. On the appearance of such an object it awakes, as it were, from a dream: The blood flows with a new tide: The heart is elevated: And the whole man acquires a vigour, which he cannot command in his solitary and calm moments. Hence company is naturally so rejoicing, as presenting the liveliest of all objects, viz, a rational and thinking Being like ourselves, who communicates to us all the actions of his mind; makes us privy to his inmost sentiments and affections; and lets us see, in the very instant of their production, all the emotions, which are caused by any object. Every lively idea is agreeable, but especially that of a passion, because such an idea becomes a kind of passion, and gives a more sensible agitation to the mind, than any other image or conception.

This being once admitted, all the rest is easy. For as the company of strangers is agreeable to us for a short time, by inlivening our thought; so the company of our relations and acquaintance must be peculiarly agreeable, because it has this effect in a greater degree, and is of more durable influence. Whatever is related to us is conceived in a lively manner by the easy transition from ourselves to the related object. Custom also, or acquaintance facilitates the entrance, and strengthens the conception of any object. The first case is parallel to our reasonings from cause and effect; the second to education. And as reasoning and education concur only in producing a lively and strong idea of any object; so is this the only particular, which is common to relation and acquaintance. This must, therefore, be the influencing quality, by which they produce all their common effects; and love or kindness being one of these effects, it must be from the force and liveliness of conception, that the passion is derived. Such a conception is peculiarly agreeable, and makes us have an affectionate regard for every thing, that produces it, when the proper object of kindness and goodwill.

It is obvious, that people associate together according to their particular tempers and dispositions, and that men of gay tempers naturally love the gay; as the serious bear an affection to the serious. This not only happens, where they remark this resemblance betwixt themselves and others, but also by the natural course of the disposition, and by a certain sympathy, which always arises betwixt similar characters. Where they remark the resemblance, it operates after the manner of a relation, by producing a connexion of ideas. Where they do not remark it, it operates by some other principle; and if this latter principle be similar to the former, it must be received as a confirmation of the foregoing reasoning.

The idea of ourselves is always intimately present to us, and conveys a sensible degree of vivacity to the idea of any other object, to which we are related. This lively idea changes by degrees into a real impression; these two kinds of perception being in a great measure the same, and differing only in their degrees of force and vivacity. But this change must be produced with the greater ease, that our natural temper gives us a propensity to the same impression, which we observe in others, and makes it arise upon any slight occasion. In that case resemblance converts the idea into an impression, not only by means of the relation, and by transfusing the original vivacity into the related idea; but also by presenting such materials as take fire from the least spark. And as in both cases a love or affection arises from the resemblance, we may learn that a sympathy with others is agreeable only by giving an emotion to the spirits, since an easy sympathy and correspondent emotions are alone common to RELATION, ACQUAINTANCE, and RESEMBLANCE.

The great propensity men have to pride may be considered as another similar phænomenon. It often happens, that after we have lived a considerable time in any city; however at first it might be disagreeable to us; yet as we become familiar with the objects, and contact an acquaintance, though merely with the streets and buildings, the aversion diminishes by degrees, and at last changes into the opposite passion. The mind finds a satisfaction and ease in the view of objects, to which it is accustomed, and naturally prefers them to others, which, though, perhaps, in themselves more valuable, are less known to it. By the same quality of the mind we are seduced into a good opinion of ourselves, and of all objects, that belong to us. They appear in a stronger light; are more agreeable; and consequently fitter subjects of pride and vanity, than any other.

It may not be amiss, in treating of the affection we bear our acquaintance and relations, to observe some pretty curious phaenomena, which attend it. It is easy to remark in common life, that children esteem their relation to their mother to be weakened, in a great measure, by her second marriage, and no longer regard her with the same eye, as if she had continued in her state of widow-hood. Nor does this happen only, when they have felt any inconveniences from her second marriage, or when her husband is much her inferior; but even without any of these considerations, and merely because she has become part of another family. This also takes place with regard to the second marriage of a father; but in a much less degree: And it is certain the ties of blood are not so much loosened in the latter case as by the marriage of a mother. These two phaenomena are remarkable in themselves, but much more so when compared.

In order to produce a perfect relation betwixt two objects, it is requisite, not only that the imagination be conveyed from one to the other by resemblance, contiguity or causation, but also that it return back from the second to the first with the same ease and facility. At first sight this may seem a necessary and unavoidable consequence. If one object resemble another, the latter object must necessarily resemble the former. If one object be the cause of another, the second object is effect to its cause. It is the same case with contiguity: And therefore the relation being always reciprocal, it may be thought, that the return of the imagination from the second to the first must also, in every case, be equally natural as its passage from the first to the second. But upon farther examination we shall easily discover our mistake. For supposing the second object, beside its reciprocal relation to the first, to have also a strong relation to a third object; in that case the thought, passing from the first object to the second, returns not back with the same facility, though the relation continues the same; but is readily carryed on to the third object, by means of the new relation, which presents itself, and gives a new impulse to the imagination. This new relation, therefore, weakens the tie betwixt the first and second objects. The fancy is by its very nature wavering and inconstant; and considers always two objects as more strongly related together, where it finds the passage equally easy both in going and returning, than where the transition is easy only in one of these motions. The double motion is a kind of a double tie, and binds the objects together in the closest and most intimate manner.

The second marriage of a mother breaks not the relation of child and parent; and that relation suffices to convey my imagination from myself to her with the greatest ease and facility. But after the imagination is arrived at this point of view, it finds its object to be surrounded with so many other relations, which challenge its regard, that it knows not which to prefer, and is at a loss what new object to pitch upon. The ties of interest and duty bind her to another family, and prevent that return of the fancy from her to myself, which is necessary to support the union. The thought has no longer the vibration, requisite to set it perfectly at ease, and indulge its inclination to change. It goes with facility, but returns with difficulty; and by that interruption finds the relation much weakened from what it would be were the passage open and easy on both sides.

Now to give a reason, why this effect follows not in the same degree upon the second marriage of a father: we may reflect on what has been proved already, that though the imagination goes easily from the view of a lesser object to that of a greater, yet it returns not with the same facility from the greater to the less. When my imagination goes from myself to my father, it passes not so readily from him to his second wife, nor considers him as entering into a different family, but as continuing the head of that family, of which I am myself a part. His superiority prevents the easy transition of the thought from him to his spouse, but keeps the passage still open for a return to myself along the same relation of child and parent. He is not sunk in the new relation he acquires; so that the double motion or vibration of thought is still easy and natural. By this indulgence of the fancy in its inconstancy, the tie of child and parent still preserves its full force and influence. A mother thinks not her tie to a son weakened, because it is shared with her husband: Nor a son his with a parent, because it is shared with a brother. The third object is here related to the first, as well as to the second; so that the imagination goes and comes along all of them with the greatest facility.

SECTION V

Of our Esteem for the Rich and Powerful

Nothing has a greater tendency to give us an esteem for any person, than his power and riches; or a contempt, than his poverty and meanness: And as esteem and contempt are to be considered as species of love and hatred, it will be proper in this place to explain these phaenomena.

Here it happens most fortunately, that the greatest difficulty is not to discover a principle capable of producing such an effect, but to choose the chief and predominant among several, that present themselves. The satisfaction we take in the riches of others, and the esteem we have for the possessors may be ascribed to three different causes. FIRST, To the objects they possess; such as houses, gardens, equipages; which, being agreeable in themselves, necessarily produce a sentiment of pleasure in every one; that either considers or surveys them. SECONDLY, To the expectation of advantage from the rich and powerful by our sharing their possessions. THIRDLY, To sympathy, which makes us partake of the satisfaction of every one, that approaches us. All these principles may concur in producing the present phænomenon. The question is, to which of them we ought principally to ascribe it.

It is certain, that the first principle, viz, the reflection on agreeable objects, has a greater influence, than what, at first sight, we may be apt to imagine. We seldom reflect on what is beautiful or ugly, agreeable or disagreeable, without an emotion of pleasure or uneasiness; and though these sensations appear not much in our common indolent way of thinking, it is easy, either in reading or conversation, to discover them. Men of wit always turn the discourse on subjects that are entertaining to the imagination; and poets never present any objects but such as are of the same nature. Mr Philips has chosen CYDER for the subject of an excellent poem. Beer would not have been so proper, as being neither so agreeable to the taste nor eye. But he would certainly have preferred wine to either of them, could his native country have afforded him so agreeable a liquor. We may learn from thence, that every thing, which is agreeable to the senses, is also in some measure agreeable to the fancy, and conveys to the thought an image of that satisfaction, which it gives by its real application to the bodily organs.

But though these reasons may induce us to comprehend this delicacy of the imagination among the causes of the respect, which we pay the rich and powerful, there are many other reasons, that may keep us from regarding it as the sole or principal. For as the ideas of pleasure can have an influence only by means of their vivacity, which makes them approach impressions, it is most natural those ideas should have that influence, which are favoured by most circumstances, and have a natural tendency to become strong and lively; such as our ideas of the passions and sensations of any human creature. Every human creature resembles ourselves, and by that means has an advantage above any other object, in operating on the imagination.

Besides, if we consider the nature of that faculty, and the great influence which all relations have upon it, we shall easily be persuaded, that however the ideas of the pleasant wines, music, or gardens, which the rich man enjoys, may become lively and agreeable, the fancy will not confine itself to them, but will carry its view to the related objects; and in particular, to the person, who possesses them. And this is the more natural, that the pleasant idea or image produces here a passion towards the person, by means of his relation to the object; so that it is unavoidable but he must enter into the original conception, since he makes the object of the derivative passion: But if he enters into the original conception, and is considered as enjoying these agreeable objects, it is sympathy, which is properly the cause of the affection; and the third principle is more powerful and universal than the first.

Add to this, that riches and power alone, even though unemployed, naturally cause esteem and respect: And consequently these passions arise not from the idea of any beautiful or agreeable objects. It is true; money implies a kind of representation of such objects, by the power it affords of obtaining them; and for that reason may still be esteemed proper to convey those agreeable images, which may give rise to the passion. But as this prospect is very distant, it is more natural for us to take a contiguous object, viz, the satisfaction, which this power affords the person, who is possest of it. And of this we shall be farther satisfyed, if we consider, that riches represent the goods of life, only by means of the will; which employs them; and therefore imply in their very nature an idea of the person, and cannot be considered without a kind of sympathy with his sensations and enjoyments.

This we may confirm by a reflection, which to some will, perhaps, appear too subtile and refined. I have already observed, that power, as distinguished from its exercise, has either no meaning at all, or is nothing but a possibility or probability of existence; by which any object approaches to reality, and has a sensible influence on the mind. I have also observed, that this approach, by an illusion of the fancy, appears much greater, when we ourselves are possest of the power, than when it is enjoyed by another; and that in the former case the objects seem to touch upon the very verge of reality, and convey almost an equal satisfaction, as if actually in our possession. Now I assert, that where we esteem a person upon account of his riches, we must enter into this sentiment of the proprietor, and that without such a sympathy the idea of the agreeable objects, which they give him the power to produce, would have but a feeble influence upon us. An avaricious man is respected for his money, though he scarce is possest of a power; that is, there scarce is a probability or even possibility of his employing it in the acquisition of the pleasures and conveniences of life. To himself alone this power seems perfect and entire; and therefore we must receive his sentiments by sympathy, before we can have a strong intense idea of these enjoyments, or esteem him upon account of them.

Thus we have found, that the first principle, viz, the agreeable idea of those objects, which riches afford the enjoyment of; resolves itself in a great measure into the third, and becomes a sympathy with the person we esteem or love. Let us now examine the second principle, viz, the agreeable expectation of advantage, and see what force we may justly attribute to it.

It is obvious, that though riches and authority undoubtedly give their owner a power of doing us service, yet this power is not to be considered as on the same footing with that, which they afford him, of pleasing himself, and satisfying his own appetites. Self-love approaches the power and exercise very near each other in the latter case; but in order to produce a similar effect in the former, we must suppose a friendship and good-will to be conjoined with the riches. Without that circumstance it is difficult to conceive on what we can found our hope of advantage from the riches of others, though there is nothing more certain, than that we naturally esteem and respect the rich, even before we discover in them any such favourable disposition towards us.

But I carry this farther, and observe, not only that we respect the rich and powerful, where they shew no inclination to serve us, but also when we lie so much out of the sphere of their activity, that they cannot even be supposed to be endowed with that power. Prisoners of war are always treated with a respect suitable to their condition; and it is certain riches go very far towards fixing the condition of any person. If birth and quality enter for a share, this still affords us an argument of the same kind. For what is it we call a man of birth, but one who is descended from a long succession of rich and powerful ancestors, and who acquires our esteem by his relation to persons whom we esteem? His ancestors, therefore, though dead, are respected, in some measure, on account of their riches, and consequently without any kind of expectation.

But not to go so far as prisoners of war and the dead to find instances of this disinterested esteem for riches, let us observe with a little attention those phaenomena that occur to us in common life and conversation. A man, who is himself of a competent fortune, upon coming into a company of strangers, naturally treats them with different degrees of respect and deference, as he is informed of their different fortunes and conditions; though it is impossible he can ever propose, and perhaps would not accept of any advantage from them. A traveller is always admitted into company, and meets with civility, in proportion as his train and equipage speak him a man of great or moderate fortune. In short, the different ranks of men are, in a great measure, regulated by riches, and that with regard to superiors as well as inferiors, strangers as well as acquaintance.

There is, indeed, an answer to these arguments, drawn from the influence of general rules. It may be pretended, that being accustomed to expect succour and protection from the rich and powerful, and to esteem them upon that account, we extend the same sentiments to those, who resemble them in their fortune, but from whom we can never hope for any advantage. The general rule still prevails, and by giving a bent to the imagination draws along the passion, in the same manner as if its proper object were real and existent.

But that this principle does not here take place, will easily appear, if we consider, that in order to establish a general rule, and extend it beyond its proper bounds, there is required a certain uniformity in our experience, and a great superiority of those instances, which are conformable to the rule, above the contrary. But here the case is quite otherwise. Of a hundred men of credit and fortune I meet with, there is not, perhaps, one from whom I can expect advantage; so that it is impossible any custom can ever prevail in the present case.

Upon the whole, there remains nothing, which can give us an esteem for power and riches, and a contempt for meanness and poverty, except the principle of sympathy, by which we enter into the sentiments of the rich and poor, and partake of their pleasure and uneasiness. Riches give satisfaction to their possessor; and this satisfaction is conveyed to the beholder by the imagination, which produces an idea resembling the original impression in force and vivacity. This agreeable idea or impression is connected with love, which is an agreeable passion. It proceeds from a thinking conscious being, which is the very object of love. From this relation of impressions, and identity of ideas, the passion arises, according to my hypothesis.

The best method of reconciling us to this opinion is to take a general survey of the universe, and observe the force of sympathy through the whole animal creation, and the easy communication of sentiments from one thinking being to another. In all creatures, that prey not upon others, and are not agitated with violent passions, there appears a remarkable desire of company, which associates them together, without any advantages they can ever propose to reap from their union. This is still more conspicuous in man, as being the creature of the universe, who has the most ardent desire of society, and is fitted for it by the most advantages. We can form no wish, which has not a reference to society. A perfect solitude is, perhaps, the greatest punishment we can suffer. Every pleasure languishes when enjoyed a-part from company, and every pain becomes more cruel and intolerable. Whatever other passions we may be actuated by; pride, ambition, avarice, curiosity, revenge or lust; the soul or animating principle of them all is sympathy; nor would they have any force, were we to abstract entirely from the thoughts and sentiments of others. Let all the powers and elements of nature conspire to serve and obey one man: Let the sun rise and set at his command: The sea and rivers roll as he pleases, and the earth furnish spontaneously whatever may be useful or agreeable to him: He will still be miserable, till you give him some one person at least, with whom he may share his happiness, and whose esteem and friendship he may enjoy.

This conclusion from a general view of human nature, we may confirm by particular instances, wherein the force of sympathy is very remarkable. Most kinds of beauty are derived from this origin; and though our first object be some senseless inanimate piece of matter, it is seldom we rest there, and carry not our view to its influence on sensible and rational creatures. A man, who shews us any house or building, takes particular care among other things to point out the convenience of the apartments, the advantages of their situation, and the little room lost in the stairs, antichambers and passages; and indeed it is evident, the chief part of the beauty consists in these particulars. The observation of convenience gives pleasure, since convenience is a beauty. But after what manner does it give pleasure? It is certain our own interest is not in the least concerned; and as this is a beauty of interest, not of form, so to speak, it must delight us merely by communication, and by our sympathizing with the proprietor of the lodging. We enter into his interest by the force of imagination, and feel the same satisfaction, that the objects naturally occasion in him.

This observation extends to tables, chairs, scritoires, chimneys, coaches, sadles, ploughs, and indeed to every work of art; it being an universal rule, that their beauty is chiefly derived from their utility, and from their fitness for that purpose, to which they are destined. But this is an advantage, that concerns only the owner, nor is there any thing but sympathy, which can interest the spectator.

It is evident, that nothing renders a field more agreeable than its fertility, and that scarce any advantages of ornament or situation will be able to equal this beauty. It is the same case with particular trees and plants, as with the field on which they grow. I know not but a plain, overgrown with furze and broom, may be, in itself, as beautiful as a hill covered with vines or olive-trees; though it will never appear so to one, who is acquainted with the value of each. But this is a beauty merely of imagination, and has no foundation in what appears to the senses. Fertility and value have a plain reference to use; and that to riches, joy, and plenty; in which though we have no hope of partaking, yet we enter into them by the vivacity of the fancy, and share them, in some measure, with the proprietor.

There is no rule in painting more reasonable than that of ballancing the figures, and placing them with the greatest exactness on their proper centers of gravity. A figure, which is not justly ballanced, is disagreeable; and that because it conveys the ideas of its fall, of harm, and of pain: Which ideas are painful, when by sympathy they acquire any degree of force and vivacity.

Add to this, that the principal part of personal beauty is an air of health and vigour, and such a construction of members as promises strength and activity. This idea of beauty cannot be accounted for but by sympathy.

In general we may remark, that the minds of men are mirrors to one another, not only because they reflect each others emotions, but also because those rays of passions, sentiments and opinions may be often reverberated, and may decay away by insensible degrees. Thus the pleasure, which a rich man receives from his possessions, being thrown upon the beholder, causes a pleasure and esteem; which sentiments again, being perceived and sympathized with, encrease the pleasure of the possessor; and being once more reflected, become a new foundation for pleasure and esteem in the beholder. There is certainly an original satisfaction in riches derived from that power, which they bestow, of enjoying all the pleasures of life; and as this is their very nature and essence, it must be the first source of all the passions, which arise from them. One of the most considerable of these passions is that of love or esteem in others, which therefore proceeds from a sympathy with the pleasure of the possessor. But the possessor has also a secondary satisfaction in riches arising from the love and esteem he acquires by them, and this satisfaction is nothing but a second reflexion of that original pleasure, which proceeded from himself. This secondary satisfaction or vanity becomes one of the principal recommendations of riches, and is the chief reason, why we either desire them for ourselves, or esteem them in others. Here then is a third rebound of the original pleasure; after which it is difficult to distinguish the images and reflexions, by reason of their faintness and confusion.

SECTION VI

Of Benevolence and Anger

Ideas may be compared to the extension and solidity of matter, and impressions, especially reflective ones, to colours, tastes, smells and other sensible qualities. Ideas never admit of a total union, but are endowed with a kind of impenetrability, by which they exclude each other, and are capable of forming a compound by their conjunction, not by their mixture. On the other hand, impressions and passions are susceptible of an entire union; and like colours, may be blended so perfectly together, that each of them may lose itself, and contribute only to vary that uniform impression, which arises from the whole. Some of the most curious phaenomena of the human mind are derived from this property of the passions.

In examining those ingredients, which are capable of uniting with love and hatred, I begin to be sensible, in some measure, of a misfortune, that has attended every system of philosophy, with which the world has been yet acquainted. It is commonly found, that in accounting for the operations of nature by any particular hypothesis; among a number of experiments, that quadrate exactly with the principles we would endeavour to establish; there is always some phænomenon, which is more stubborn, and will not so easily bend to our purpose. We need not be surprized, that this should happen in natural philosophy. The essence and composition of external bodies are so obscure, that we must necessarily, in our reasonings, or rather conjectures concerning them, involve ourselves in contradictions and absurdities. But as the perceptions of the mind are perfectly known, and I have used all imaginable caution in forming conclusions concerning them, I have always hoped to keep clear of those contradictions, which have attended every other system. Accordingly the difficulty, which I have at present in my eye, is nowise contrary to my system; but only departs a little from that simplicity, which has been hitherto its principal force and beauty.

The passions of love and hatred are always followed by, or rather conjoined with benevolence and anger. It is this conjunction, which chiefly distinguishes these affections from pride and humility. For pride and humility are pure emotions in the soul, unattended with any desire, and not immediately exciting us to action. But love and hatred are not compleated within themselves, nor rest in that emotion, which they produce, but carry the mind to something farther. Love is always followed by a desire of the happiness of the person beloved, and an aversion to his misery: As hatred produces a desire of the misery and an aversion to the happiness of the person hated. So remarkable a difference betwixt these two sets of passions of pride and humility, love and hatred, which in so many other particulars correspond to each other, merits our attention.

The conjunction of this desire and aversion with love and hatred may be accounted for by two different hypotheses. The first is, that love and hatred have not only a cause, which excites them, viz, pleasure and pain; and an object, to which they are directed, viz, a person or thinking being; but likewise an end, which they endeavour to attain, viz, the happiness or misery of the person beloved or hated; all which views, mixing together, make only one passion. According to this system, love is nothing but the desire of happiness to another person, and hatred that of misery. The desire and aversion constitute the very nature of love and hatred. They are not only inseparable but the same.

But this is evidently contrary to experience. For though it is certain we never love any person without desiring his happiness, nor hate any without wishing his misery, yet these desires arise only upon the ideas of the happiness or misery of our friend or enemy being presented by the imagination, and are not absolutely essential to love and hatred. They are the most obvious and natural sentiments of these affections, but not the only ones. The passions may express themselves in a hundred ways, and may subsist a considerable time, without our reflecting on the happiness or misery of their objects; which clearly proves, that these desires are not the same with love and hatred, nor make any essential part of them.

We may, therefore, infer, that benevolence and anger are passions different from love and hatred, and only conjoined with them, by the original constitution of the mind. As nature has given to the body certain appetites and inclinations, which she encreases, diminishes, or changes according to the situation of the fluids or solids; she has proceeded in the same manner with the mind. According as we are possessed with love or hatred, the correspondent desire of the happiness or misery of the person, who is the object of these passions, arises in the mind, and varies with each variation of these opposite passions. This order of things, abstractedly considered, is not necessary. Love and hatred might have been unattended with any such desires, or their particular connexion might have been entirely reversed. If nature had so pleased, love might have had the same effect as hatred, and hatred as love. I see no contradiction in supposing a desire of producing misery annexed to love, and of happiness to hatred. If the sensation of the passion and desire be opposite, nature could have altered the sensation without altering the tendency of the desire, and by that means made them compatible with each other.

SECTION VII

Of Compassion

But though the desire of the happiness or misery of others, according to the love or hatred we bear them, be an arbitrary and original instinct implanted in our nature, we find it may be counterfeited on many occasions, and may arise from secondary principles. Pity is a concern for, and malice a joy in the misery of others, without any friendship or enmity to occasion this concern or joy. We pity even strangers, and such as are perfectly indifferent to us: And if our ill-will to another proceed from any harm or injury, it is not, properly speaking, malice, but revenge. But if we examine these affections of pity and malice we shall find them to be secondary ones, arising from original affections, which are varied by some particular turn of thought and imagination.

It will be easy to explain the passion of pity, from the precedent reasoning concerning sympathy. We have a lively idea of every thing related to us. All human creatures are related to us by resemblance. Their persons, therefore, their interests, their passions, their pains and pleasures must strike upon us in a lively manner, and produce an emotion similar to the original one; since a lively idea is easily converted into an impression. If this be true in general, it must be more so of affliction and sorrow. These have always a stronger and more lasting influence than any pleasure or enjoyment.

A spectator of a tragedy passes through a long train of grief, terror, indignation, and other affections, which the poet represents in the persons he introduces. As many tragedies end happily, and no excellent one can be composed without some reverses of fortune, the spectator must sympathize with all these changes, and receive the fictitious joy as well as every other passion. Unless, therefore, it be asserted, that every distinct passion is communicated by a distinct original quality, and is not derived from the general principle of sympathy above-explained, it must be allowed, that all of them arise from that principle. To except any one in particular must appear highly unreasonable. As they are all first present in the mind of one person, and afterwards appear in the mind of another; and as the manner of their appearance, first as an idea, then as an impression, is in every case the same, the transition must arise from the same principle. I am at least sure, that this method of reasoning would be considered as certain, either in natural philosophy or common life.

Add to this, that pity depends, in a great measure, on the contiguity, and even sight of the object; which is a proof, that it is derived from the imagination. Not to mention that women and children are most subject to pity, as being most guided by that faculty. The same infirmity, which makes them faint at the sight of a naked sword, though in the hands of their best friend, makes them pity extremely those, whom they find in any grief or affliction. Those philosophers, who derive this passion from I know not what subtile reflections on the instability of fortune, and our being liable to the same miseries we behold, will find this observation contrary to them among a great many others, which it were easy to produce.

There remains only to take notice of a pretty remarkable phænomenon of this passion; which is, that the communicated passion of sympathy sometimes acquires strength from the weakness of its original, and even arises by a transition from affections, which have no existence. Thus when a person obtains any honourable office, or inherits a great fortune, we are always the more rejoiced for his prosperity, the less sense he seems to have of it, and the greater equanimity and indifference he shews in its enjoyment. In like manner a man, who is not dejected by misfortunes, is the more lamented on account of his patience; and if that virtue extends so far as utterly to remove all sense of uneasiness, it still farther encreases our compassion. When a person of merit falls into what is vulgarly esteemed a great misfortune, we form a notion of his condition; and carrying our fancy from the cause to the usual effect, first conceive a lively idea of his sorrow, and then feel an impression of it, entirely over-looking that greatness of mind, which elevates him above such emotions, or only considering it so far as to encrease our admiration, love and tenderness for him. We find from experience, that such a degree of passion is usually connected with such a misfortune; and though there be an exception in the present case, yet the imagination is affected by the general rule, and makes us conceive a lively idea of the passion, or rather feel the passion itself, in the same manner, as if the person were really actuated by it. From the same principles we blush for the conduct of those, who behave themselves foolishly before us; and that though they shew no sense of shame, nor seem in the least conscious of their folly. All this proceeds from sympathy; but it is of a partial kind, and views its objects only on one side, without considering the other, which has a contrary effect, and would entirely destroy that emotion, which arises from the first appearance.

We have also instances, wherein an indifference and insensibility under misfortune encreases our concern for the misfortunate, even though the indifference proceed not from any virtue and magnanimity. It is an aggravation of a murder, that it was committed upon persons asleep and in perfect security; as historians readily observe of any infant prince, who is captive in the hands of his enemies, that he is the more worthy of compassion the less sensible he is of his miserable condition. As we ourselves are here acquainted with the wretched situation of the person, it gives us a lively idea and sensation of sorrow, which is the passion that generally attends it; and this idea becomes still more lively, and the sensation more violent by a contrast with that security and indifference, which we observe in the person himself. A contrast of any kind never fails to affect the imagination, especially when presented by the subject; and it is on the imagination that pity entirely depends.[62]

[62] To prevent all ambiguity, I must observe, that where I oppose the imagination to the memory, I mean in general the faculty that presents our fainter ideas. In all other places, and particularly when it is opposed to the understanding, I understand the same faculty, excluding only our demonstrative and probable reasonings.

SECTION VIII

Of Malice and Envy

We must now proceed to account for the passion of malice, which imitates the effects of hatred, as pity does those of love; and gives us a joy in the sufferings and miseries of others, without any offence or injury on their part.

So little are men governed by reason in their sentiments and opinions, that they always judge more of objects by comparison than from their intrinsic worth and value. When the mind considers, or is accustomed to, any degree of perfection, whatever falls short of it, though really esteemable, has notwithstanding the same effect upon the passions; as what is defective and ill. This is an original quality of the soul, and similar to what we have every day experience of in our bodies. Let a man heat one hand and cool the other; the same water will, at the same time, seem both hot and cold, according to the disposition of the different organs. A small degree of any quality, succeeding a greater, produces the same sensation, as if less than it really is, and even sometimes as the opposite quality. Any gentle pain, that follows a violent one, seems as nothing, or rather becomes a pleasure; as on the other hand a violent pain, succeeding a gentle one, is doubly grievous and uneasy.

This no one can doubt of with regard to our passions and sensations. But there may arise some difficulty with regard to our ideas and objects. When an object augments or diminishes to the eye or imagination from a comparison with others, the image and idea of the object are still the same, and are equally extended in the retina, and in the brain or organ of perception. The eyes refract the rays of light, and the optic nerves convey the images to the brain in the very same manner, whether a great or small object has preceded; nor does even the imagination alter the dimensions of its object on account of a comparison with others. The question then is, how from the same impression and the same idea we can form such different judgments concerning the same object, and at one time admire its bulk, and at another despise its littleness. This variation in our judgments must certainly proceed from a variation in some perception; but as the variation lies not in the immediate impression or idea of the object, it must lie in some other impression, that accompanies it.

In order to explain this matter, I shall just touch upon two principles, one of which shall be more fully explained in the progress of this treatise; the other has been already accounted for. I believe it may safely be established for a general maxim, that no object is presented to the senses, nor image formed in the fancy, but what is accompanyed with some emotion or movement of spirits proportioned to it; and however custom may make us insensible of this sensation and cause us to confound it with the object or idea, it will be easy, by careful and exact experiments, to separate and distinguish them. For to instance only in the cases of extension and number; it is evident, that any very bulky object, such as the ocean, an extended plain, a vast chain of mountains, a wide forest: or any very numerous collection of objects, such as an army, a fleet, a crowd, excite in the mind a sensible emotion; and that the admiration, which arises on the appearance of such objects, is one of the most lively pleasures, which human nature is capable of enjoying. Now as this admiration encreases or diminishes by the encrease or diminution of the objects, we may conclude, according to our foregoing[63] principles, that it is a compound effect, proceeding from the conjunction of the several effects, which arise from each part of the cause. Every part, then, of extension, and every unite of number has a separate emotion attending it; and though that emotion be not always agreeable, yet by its conjunction with others, and by its agitating the spirits to a just pitch, it contributes to the production of admiration, which is always agreeable. If this be allowed with respect to extension and number, we can make no difficulty with respect to virtue and vice, wit and folly, riches and poverty, happiness and misery, and other objects of that kind, which are always attended with an evident emotion.

The second principle I shall take notice of is that of our adherence to general rules; which has such a mighty influence on the actions and understanding, and is able to impose on the very senses. When an object is found by experience to be always accompanyed with another; whenever the first object appears, though changed in very material circumstances; we naturally fly to the conception of the second, and form an idea of it in as lively and strong a manner, as if we had infered its existence by the justest and most authentic conclusion of our understanding. Nothing can undeceive us, not even our senses, which, instead of correcting this false judgment, are often perverted by it, and seem to authorize its errors.

The conclusion I draw from these two principles, joined to the influence of comparison above-mentioned, is very short and decisive. Every object is attended with some emotion proportioned to it; a great object with a great emotion, a small object with a small emotion. A great object, therefore, succeeding a small one makes a great emotion succeed a small one. Now a great emotion succeeding a small one becomes still greater, and rises beyond its ordinary proportion. But as there is a certain degree of an emotion, which commonly attends every magnitude of an object; when the emotion encreases, we naturally imagine that the object has likewise encreased. The effect conveys our view to its usual cause, a certain degree of emotion to a certain magnitude of the object; nor do we consider, that comparison may change the emotion without changing anything in the object. Those who are acquainted with the metaphysical part of optics and know how we transfer the judgments and conclusions of the understanding to the senses, will easily conceive this whole operation.

But leaving this new discovery of an impression, that secretly attends every idea; we must at least allow of that principle, from whence the discovery arose, that objects appear greater or less by a comparison with others. We have so many

[63] Book I. Part III. Sect. 15.

instances of this, that it is impossible we can dispute its veracity; and it is from this principle I derive the passions of malice and envy.

It is evident we must receive a greater or less satisfaction or uneasiness from reflecting on our own condition and circumstances, in proportion as they appear more or less fortunate or unhappy, in proportion to the degrees of riches, and power, and merit, and reputation, which we think ourselves possest of. Now as we seldom judge of objects from their intrinsic value, but form our notions of them from a comparison with other objects; it follows, that according as we observe a greater or less share of happiness or misery in others, we must make an estimate of our own, and feel a consequent pain or pleasure. The misery of another gives us a more lively idea of our happiness, and his happiness of our misery. The former, therefore, produces delight; and the latter uneasiness.

Here then is a kind of pity reverst, or contrary sensations arising in the beholder, from those which are felt by the person, whom he considers. In general we may observe, that in all kinds of comparison an object makes us always receive from another, to which it is compared, a sensation contrary to what arises from itself in its direct and immediate survey. A small object makes a great one appear still greater. A great object makes a little one appear less. Deformity of itself produces uneasiness; but makes us receive new pleasure by its contrast with a beautiful object, whose beauty is augmented by it; as on the other hand, beauty, which of itself produces pleasure, makes us receive a new pain by the contrast with any thing ugly, whose deformity it augments. The case, therefore, must be the same with happiness and misery. The direct survey of another's pleasure naturally gives us pleasure, and therefore produces pain when compared with our own. His pain, considered in itself, is painful to us, but augments the idea of our own happiness, and gives us pleasure.

Nor will it appear strange, that we may feel a reverst sensation from the happiness and misery of others; since we find the same comparison may give us a kind of malice against ourselves, and make us rejoice for our pains, and grieve for our pleasures. Thus the prospect of past pain is agreeable, when we are satisfyed with our present condition; as on the other hand our past pleasures give us uneasiness, when we enjoy nothing at present equal to them. The comparison being the same, as when we reflect on the sentiments of others, must be attended with the same effects.

Nay a person may extend this malice against himself, even to his present fortune, and carry it so far as designedly to seek affliction, and encrease his pains and sorrows. This may happen upon two occasions. First, Upon the distress and misfortune of a friend, or person dear to him. Secondly, Upon the feeling any remorses for a crime, of which he has been guilty. It is from the principle of comparison that both these irregular appetites for evil arise. A person, who indulges himself in any pleasure, while his friend lies under affliction, feels the reflected uneasiness from his friend more sensibly by a comparison with the original pleasure, which he himself enjoys.

This contrast, indeed, ought also to inliven the present pleasure. But as grief is here supposed to be the predominant passion, every addition falls to that side, and is swallowed up in it, without operating in the least upon the contrary affection. It is the same case with those penances, which men inflict on themselves for their past sins and failings. When a criminal reflects on the punishment he deserves, the idea of it is magnifyed by a comparison with his present ease and satisfaction; which forces him, in a manner, to seek uneasiness, in order to avoid so disagreeable a contrast.

This reasoning will account for the origin of envy as well as of malice. The only difference betwixt these passions lies in this, that envy is excited by some present enjoyment of another, which by comparison diminishes our idea of our own: Whereas malice is the unprovoked desire of producing evil to another, in order to reap a pleasure from the comparison. The enjoyment, which is the object of envy, is commonly superior to our own. A superiority naturally seems to overshade us, and presents a disagreeable comparison. But even in the case of an inferiority, we still desire a greater distance, in order to augment, still more the idea of ourself. When this distance diminishes, the comparison is less to our advantage; and consequently gives us less pleasure, and is even disagreeable. Hence arises that species of envy, which men feel, when they perceive their inferiors approaching or overtaking them in the pursuits of glory or happiness. In this envy we may see the effects of comparison twice repeated. A man, who compares himself to his inferior, receives a pleasure from the comparison: And when the inferiority decreases by the elevation of the inferior, what should only have been a decrease of pleasure, becomes a real pain, by a new comparison with its preceding condition.

It is worthy of observation concerning that envy, which arises from a superiority in others, that it is not the great disproportion betwixt ourself and another, which produces it; but on the contrary, our proximity. A common soldier bears no such envy to his general as to his sergeant or corporal; nor does an eminent writer meet with so great jealousy in common hackney scribblers, as in authors, that more nearly approach him. It may, indeed, be thought, that the greater the disproportion is, the greater must be the uneasiness from the comparison. But we may consider on the other hand, that the great disproportion cuts off the relation, and either keeps us from comparing ourselves with what is remote from us, or diminishes the effects of the comparison. Resemblance and proximity always produce a relation of ideas; and where you destroy these ties, however other accidents may bring two ideas together; as they have no bond or connecting quality to join them in the imagination; it is impossible they can remain long united, or have any considerable influence on each other.

I have observed in considering the nature of ambition, that the great feel a double pleasure in authority from the comparison of their own condition with that of their slaves; and that this comparison has a double influence, because it is natural, and presented by the subject. When the fancy, in the comparison of objects, passes not easily from the one object to the other, the action of the mind is, in a great measure, broke, and the fancy, in considering the second object, begins, as it were, upon a new footing. The impression, which attends every object, seems not greater in that case by succeeding a less of the same kind; but these two impressions are distinct, and produce their distinct effects, without any communication together. The want of relation in the ideas breaks the relation of the impressions, and by such a separation prevents their mutual operation and influence.

To confirm this we may observe, that the proximity in the degree of merit is not alone sufficient to give rise to envy, but must be assisted by other relations. A poet is not apt to envy a philosopher, or a poet of a different kind, of a different nation, or of a different age. All these differences prevent or weaken the comparison, and consequently the passion.

This too is the reason, why all objects appear great or little, merely by a comparison with those of the same species. A mountain neither magnifies nor diminishes a horse in our eyes; but when a Flemish and a Welsh horse are seen together, the one appears greater and the other less, than when viewed apart.

From the same principle we may account for that remark of historians, that any party in a civil war always choose to call in a foreign enemy at any hazard rather than submit to their fellow-citizens. Guicciardin applies this remark to the wars in Italy, where the relations betwixt the different states are, properly speaking, nothing but of name, language, and contiguity. Yet even these relations, when joined with superiority, by making the comparison more natural, make it likewise more grievous, and cause men to search for some other superiority, which may be attended with no relation, and by that means may have a less sensible influence on the imagination. The mind quickly perceives its several advantages and disadvantages; and finding its situation to be most uneasy, where superiority is conjoined with other relations, seeks its repose as much as possible, by their separation, and by breaking that association of ideas, which renders the comparison so much more natural and efficacious. When it cannot break the association, it feels a stronger desire to remove the superiority; and this is the reason why travellers are commonly so lavish of their praises to the Chinese and Persians, at the same time, that they depreciate those neighbouring nations, which may stand upon a foot of rivalship with their native country.

These examples from history and common experience are rich and curious; but we may find parallel ones in the arts, which are no less remarkable. should an author compose a treatise, of which one part was serious and profound, another light and humorous, every one would condemn so strange a mixture, and would accuse him of the neglect of all rules of art and criticism. These rules of art are founded on the qualities of human nature; and the quality of human nature, which requires a consistency in every performance is that which renders the mind incapable of passing in a moment from one passion and disposition to a quite different one. Yet this makes us not blame Mr Prior for joining his Alma and his Solomon in the same volume; though that admirable poet has succeeded perfectly well in the gaiety of the one, as well as in the melancholy of the other. Even supposing the reader should peruse these two compositions without any interval, he would feel little or no difficulty in the change of passions: Why, but because he considers these performances as entirely different, and by this break in the ideas, breaks the progress of the affections, and hinders the one from influencing or contradicting the other?

An heroic and burlesque design, united in one picture, would be monstrous; though we place two pictures of so opposite a character in the same chamber, and even close by each other, without any scruple or difficulty.

In a word, no ideas can affect each other, either by comparison, or by the passions they separately produce, unless they be united together by some relation, which may cause an easy transition of the ideas, and consequently of the emotions or impressions, attending the ideas; and may preserve the one impression in the passage of the imagination to the object of the other. This principle is very remarkable, because it is analogous to what we have observed both concerning the understanding and the passions. Suppose two objects to be presented to me, which are not connected by any kind of relation. Suppose that each of these objects separately produces a passion; and that these two passions are in themselves contrary: We find from experience, that the want of relation in the objects or ideas hinders the natural contrariety of the passions, and that the break in the transition of the thought removes the affections from each other, and prevents their opposition. It is the same case with comparison; and from both these phaenomena we may safely conclude, that the relation of ideas must forward the transition of impressions; since its absence alone is able to prevent it, and to separate what naturally should have operated upon each other. When the absence of an object or quality removes any usual or natural effect, we may certainly conclude that its presence contributes to the production of the effect.

SECTION IX

Of the Mixture of Benevolence and Anger with Compassion and Malice

Thus we have endeavoured to account for pity and malice. Both these affections arise from the imagination, according to the light, in which it places its object. When our fancy considers directly the sentiments of others, and enters deep into them, it makes us sensible of all the passions it surveys, but in a particular manner of grief or sorrow. On the contrary, when we compare the sentiments of others to our own, we feel a sensation directly opposite to the original one, viz. a joy from the grief of others, and a grief from their joy. But these are only the first foundations of the affections of pity and malice. Other passions are afterwards confounded with them. There is always a mixture of love or tenderness with pity, and of hatred or anger with malice. But it must be confessed, that this mixture seems at first sight to be contradictory to my system. For as pity is an uneasiness, and malice a joy, arising from the misery of others, pity should naturally, as in all other cases, produce hatred; and malice, love. This contradiction I endeavour to reconcile, after the following manner.

In order to cause a transition of passions, there is required a double relation of impressions and ideas, nor is one relation sufficient to produce this effect. But that we may understand the full force of this double relation, we must consider, that it is not the present sensation alone or momentary pain or pleasure, which determines the character of any passion, but the whole bent or tendency of it from the beginning to the end. One impression may be related to another, not only when their sensations are resembling, as we have all along supposed in the preceding cases; but also when their impulses or directions are similar and correspondent. This cannot take place with regard to pride and humility; because these are only pure sensations, without any direction or tendency to action. We are, therefore, to look for instances of this peculiar relation of impressions only in such affections, as are attended with a certain appetite or desire; such as those of love and hatred.

Benevolence or the appetite, which attends love, is a desire of the happiness of the person beloved, and an aversion to his misery; as anger or the appetite, which attends hatred, is a desire of the misery of the person hated, and an aversion to his happiness. A desire, therefore, of the happiness of another, and aversion to his misery, are similar to benevolence; and a desire of his misery and aversion to his happiness are correspondent to anger. Now pity is a desire of happiness to another, and aversion to his misery; as malice is the contrary appetite. Pity, then, is related to benevolence; and malice to anger: And as benevolence has been already found to be connected with love, by a natural and original quality, and anger with hatred; it is by this chain the passions of pity and malice are connected with love and hatred.

This hypothesis is founded on sufficient experience. A man, who from any motives has entertained a resolution of performing an action, naturally runs into every other view or motive, which may fortify that resolution, and give it authority and influence on the mind. To confirm us in any design, we search for motives drawn from interest, from honour, from duty. What wonder, then, that pity and benevolence, malice, and anger, being the same desires arising from different principles, should so totally mix together as to be undistinguishable? As to the connexion betwixt benevolence and love, anger and hatred, being original and primary, it admits of no difficulty.

We may add to this another experiment, viz, that benevolence and anger, and consequently love and hatred, arise when our happiness or misery have any dependance on the happiness or misery of another person, without any farther relation. I doubt not but this experiment will appear so singular as to excuse us for stopping a moment to consider it.

Suppose, that two persons of the same trade should seek employment in a town, that is not able to maintain both, it is plain the success of one is perfectly incompatible with that of the other, and that whatever is for the interest of either is contrary to that of his rival, and so vice versa. Suppose again, that two merchants, though living in different parts of the world, should enter into co-partnership together, the advantage or loss of one becomes immediately the advantage or loss of his partner, and the same fortune necessarily attends both. Now it is evident, that in the first case, hatred always follows upon the contrariety of interests; as in the second, love arises from their union. Let us consider to what principle we can ascribe these passions.

It is plain they arise not from the double relations of impressions and ideas, if we regard only the present sensation. For takeing the first case of rivalship; though the pleasure and advantage of an antagonist necessarily causes my pain and loss, yet to counter-ballance this, his pain and loss causes my pleasure and advantage; and supposing him to be unsuccessful, I may by this means receive from him a superior degree of satisfaction. In the same manner the success of a partner rejoices me, but then his misfortunes afflict me in an equal proportion; and it is easy to imagine, that the latter sentiment may in many cases preponderate. But whether the fortune of a rival or partner be good or bad, I always hate the former and love the latter.

This love of a partner cannot proceed from the relation or connexion betwixt us; in the same manner as I love a brother or countryman. A rival has almost as close a relation to me as a partner. For as the pleasure of the latter causes my pleasure, and his pain my pain; so the pleasure of the former causes my pain, and his pain my pleasure. The connexion, then, of cause and effect is the same in both cases; and if in the one case, the cause and effect have a farther relation of resemblance, they have that of contrariety in the other; which, being also a species of resemblance, leaves the matter pretty equal.

The only explication, then, we can give of this phænomenon is derived from that principle of a parallel direction above-mentioned. Our concern for our own interest gives us a pleasure in the pleasure, and a pain in the pain of a partner, after the same manner as by sympathy we feel a sensation correspondent to those, which appear in any person, who is present with us. On the other hand, the same concern for our interest makes us feel a pain in the pleasure, and a pleasure in the pain of a rival; and in short the same contrariety of sentiments as arises from comparison and malice. Since, therefore, a parallel direction of the affections, proceeding from interest, can give rise to benevolence or anger, no wonder the same parallel direction, derived from sympathy and from comparison, should have the same effect.

In general we may observe, that it is impossible to do good to others, from whatever motive, without feeling some touches of kindness and good-will towards them; as the injuries we do, not only cause hatred in the person, who suffers them, but even in ourselves. These phaenomena, indeed, may in part be accounted for from other principles.

But here there occurs a considerable objection, which it will be necessary to examine before we proceed any farther. I have endeavoured to prove, that power and riches, or poverty and meanness; which give rise to love or hatred, without producing any original pleasure or uneasiness; operate upon us by means of a secondary sensation derived from a sympathy with that pain or satisfaction, which they produce in the person, who possesses them. From a sympathy with his pleasure there arises love; from that with his uneasiness, hatred. But it is a maxim, which I have just now established, and which is absolutely necessary to the explication of the phaenomena of pity and malice, that it is not the present sensation or momentary pain or pleasure, which determines the character of any passion, but the general bent or tendency of it from the beginning to the end. For this reason, pity or a sympathy with pain produces love, and that because it interests us in the fortunes of others, good or bad, and gives us a secondary sensation correspondent to the primary; in which it has the same influence with love and benevolence. Since then this rule holds good in one case, why does it not prevail throughout, and why does sympathy in uneasiness ever produce any passion beside good-will and kindness? Is it becoming a philosopher to alter his method of reasoning, and run from one principle to its contrary, according to the particular phænomenon, which he would explain?

I have mentioned two different causes, from which a transition of passion may arise, viz, a double relation of ideas and impressions, and what is similar to it, a conformity in the tendency and direction of any two desires, which arise from different principles. Now I assert, that when a sympathy with uneasiness is weak, it produces hatred or contempt by the former cause; when strong, it produces love or tenderness by the latter. This is the solution of the foregoing difficulty, which seems so urgent; and this is a principle founded on such evident arguments, that we ought to have established it, even though it were not necessary to the explication of any phænomenon.

It is certain, that sympathy is not always limited to the present moment, but that we often feel by communication the pains and pleasures of others, which are not in being, and which we only anticipate by the force of imagination. For supposing I saw a person perfectly unknown to me, who, while asleep in the fields, was in danger of being trod under foot by horses, I should immediately run to his assistance; and in this I should be actuated by the same principle of sympathy, which makes me concerned for the present sorrows of a stranger. The bare mention of this is sufficient. Sympathy being nothing but a lively idea converted into an impression, it is evident, that, in considering the future possible or probable condition of any person, we may enter into it with so vivid a conception as to make it our own concern; and by that means be sensible of pains and pleasures, which neither belong to ourselves, nor at the present instant have any real existence.

But however we may look forward to the future in sympathizing with any person, the extending of our sympathy depends in a great measure upon our sense of his present condition. It is a great effort of imagination, to form such lively ideas even of the present sentiments of others as to feel these very sentiments; but it is impossible we could extend this sympathy to the future, without being aided by some circumstance in the present, which strikes upon us in a lively manner. When the present misery of another has any strong influence upon me, the vivacity of the conception is not confined merely to its immediate object, but diffuses its influence over all the related ideas, and gives me a lively notion of all the circumstances of that person, whether past, present, or future; possible, probable or certain. By means of this lively notion I am interested in them; take part with them; and feel a sympathetic motion in my breast, conformable to whatever I imagine in his. If I diminish the vivacity of the first conception, I diminish that of the related ideas; as pipes can convey no more water than what arises at the fountain. By this diminution I destroy the future prospect, which is necessary to interest me perfectly in the fortune of another. I may feel the present impression, but carry my sympathy no farther, and never transfuse the force of the first conception into my ideas of the related objects. If it be another's misery, which is presented in this feeble manner, I receive it by communication, and am affected with all the passions related to it: But as I am not so much interested as to concern myself in his good fortune, as well as his bad, I never feel the extensive sympathy, nor the passions related to it.

Now in order to know what passions are related to these different kinds of sympathy, we must consider, that benevolence is an original pleasure arising from the pleasure of the person beloved, and a pain proceeding from his pain: From which correspondence of impressions there arises a subsequent desire of his pleasure, and aversion to his pain. In order, then, to make a passion run parallel with benevolence, it is requisite we should feel these double impressions, correspondent to those of the person, whom we consider; nor is any one of them alone sufficient for that purpose. When we sympathize only with one impression, and that a painful one, this sympathy is related to anger and to hatred, upon account of the uneasiness it conveys to us. But as the extensive or limited sympathy depends upon the force of the first sympathy; it follows, that the passion of love or hatred depends upon the same principle. A strong impression, when communicated, gives a double tendency of the passions; which is related to benevolence and love by a similarity of direction; however painful the first impression might have been. A weak impression, that is painful, is related to anger and hatred by the resemblance of sensations. Benevolence, therefore, arises from a great degree of misery, or any degree strongly sympathized with: Hatred or contempt from a small degree, or one weakly sympathized with; which is the principle I intended to prove and explain.

Nor have we only our reason to trust to for this principle, but also experience. A certain degree of poverty produces contempt; but a degree beyond causes compassion and good-will. We may under-value a peasant or servant; but when the misery of a beggar appears very great, or is painted in very lively colours, we sympathize with him in his afflictions; and feel in our heart evident touches of pity and benevolence. The same object causes contrary passions according to its different degrees. The passions, therefore, must depend upon principles, that operate in such certain degrees, according to my hypothesis. The encrease of the sympathy has evidently the same effect as the encrease of the misery.

A barren or desolate country always seems ugly and disagreeable, and commonly inspires us with contempt for the inhabitants. This deformity, however, proceeds in a great measure from a sympathy with the inhabitants, as has been already observed; but it is only a weak one, and reaches no farther than the immediate sensation, which is disagreeable. The view of a city in ashes conveys benevolent sentiments; because we there enter so deep into the interests of the miserable inhabitants, as to wish for their prosperity, as well as feel their adversity.

But though the force of the impression generally produces pity and benevolence, it is certain, that by being carryed too far it ceases to have that effect. This, perhaps, may be worth our notice. When the uneasiness is either small in itself, or remote from us, it engages not the imagination, nor is able to convey an equal concern for the future and contingent good, as for the present and real evil Upon its acquiring greater force, we become so interested in the concerns of the person, as to be sensible both of his good and had fortune; and from that compleat sympathy there arises pity and benevolence. But it will easily be imagined, that where the present evil strikes with more than ordinary force, it may entirely engage our attention, and prevent that double sympathy, above-mentioned. Thus we find, that though every one, but especially women, are apt to contract a kindness for criminals, who go to the scaffold, and readily imagine them to be uncommonly handsome and wellshaped; yet one, who is present at the cruel execution of the rack, feels no such tender emotions; but is in a manner overcome with horror, and has no leisure to temper this uneasy sensation by any opposite sympathy.

But the instance, which makes the most clearly for my hypothesis, is that wherein by a change of the objects we separate the double sympathy even from a midling degree of the passion; in which case we find, that pity, instead of producing love and tenderness as usual, always gives rise to the contrary affection. When we observe a person in misfortunes, we are affected with pity and love; but the author of that misfortune becomes the object of our strongest hatred, and is the more detested in proportion to the degree of our compassion. Now for what reason should the same passion of pity produce love to the person, who suffers the misfortune, and hatred to the person, who causes it; unless it be because in the latter case the author bears a relation only to the misfortune; whereas in considering the sufferer we carry our view on every side, and wish for his prosperity, as well as are sensible of his affliction?

I. shall just observe, before I leave the present subject, that this phænomenon of the double sympathy, and its tendency to cause love, may contribute to the production of the kindness, which we naturally bear our relations and acquaintance. Custom and relation make us enter deeply into the sentiments of others; and whatever fortune we suppose to attend them, is rendered present to us by the imagination, and operates as if originally our own. We rejoice in their pleasures, and grieve for their sorrows, merely from the force of sympathy. Nothing that concerns them is indifferent to us; and as this correspondence of sentiments is the natural attendant of love, it readily produces that affection.

SECTION X

Of Respect and Contempt

There now remains only to explain the passion of respect and contempt, along with the amorous affection, in order to understand all the passions which have any mixture of love or hatred. Let us begin with respect and contempt.

In considering the qualities and circumstances of others, we may either regard them as they really are in themselves; or may make a comparison betwixt them and our own qualities and circumstances; or may join these two methods of consideration. The good qualities of others, from the first point of view, produce love; from the second, humility; and from the third, respect; which is a mixture of these two passions. Their bad qualities, after the same manner, cause either hatred, or pride, or contempt, according to the light in which we survey them.

That there is a mixture of pride in contempt, and of humility in respect, is, I think, too evident, from their very feeling or appearance, to require any particular proof. That this mixture arises from a tacit comparison of the person contemned or respected with ourselves is no less evident. The same man may cause either respect, love, or contempt by his condition and talents, according as the person, who considers him, from his inferior becomes his equal or superior. In changing the point of view, though the object may remain the same, its proportion to ourselves entirely alters; which is the cause of an alteration in the passions. These passions, therefore, arise from our observing the proportion; that is, from a comparison.

I have already observed, that the mind has a much stronger propensity to pride than to humility, and have endeavoured, from the principles of human nature, to assign a cause for this phænomenon. Whether my reasoning be received or not, the phænomenon is undisputed, and appears in many instances. Among the rest, it is the reason why there is a much greater mixture of pride in contempt, than of humility in respect, and why we are more elevated with the view of one below us, than mortifyed with the presence of one above us. Contempt or scorn has so strong a tincture of pride, that there scarce is any other passion discernable: Whereas in esteem or respect, love makes a more considerable ingredient than humility. The passion of vanity is so prompt, that it rouzes at the least call; while humility requires a stronger impulse to make it exert itself.

But here it may reasonably be asked, why this mixture takes place only in some cases, and appears not on every occasion. All those objects, which cause love, when placed on another person, are the causes of pride, when transfered to ourselves;

and consequently ought to be causes of humility, as well as love, while they belong to others, and are only compared to those, which we ourselves possess. In like manner every quality, which, by being directly considered, produces hatred, ought always to give rise to pride by comparison, and by a mixture of these passions of hatred and pride ought to excite contempt or scorn. The difficulty then is, why any objects ever cause pure love or hatred, and produce not always the mixt passions of respect and contempt.

I have supposed all along, that the passions of love and pride, and those of humility and hatred are similar in their sensations, and that the two former are always agreeable, and the two latter painful. But though this be universally true, it is observable, that the two agreeable, as well as the two painful passions, have some difference, and even contrarieties, which distinguish them. Nothing invigorates and exalts the mind equally with pride and vanity; though at the same time love or tenderness is rather found to weaken and infeeble it. The same difference is observable betwixt the uneasy passions. Anger and hatred bestow a new force on all our thoughts and actions; while humility and shame deject and discourage us. Of these qualities of the passions, it will be necessary to form a distinct idea. Let us remember, that pride and hatred invigorate the soul; and love and humility infeeble it.

From this it follows, that though the conformity betwixt love and hatred in the agreeableness of their sensation makes them always be excited by the same objects, yet this other contrariety is the reason, why they are excited in very different degrees. Genius and learning are pleasant and magnificent objects, and by both these circumstances are adapted to pride and vanity; but have a relation to love by their pleasure only. Ignorance and simplicity are disagreeable and mean, which in the same manner gives them a double connexion with humility, and a single one with hatred. We may, therefore, consider it as certain, that though the same object always produces love and pride, humility and hatred, according to its different situations, yet it seldom produces either the two former or the two latter passions, in the same proportion.

It is here we must seek for a solution of the difficulty above-mentioned, why any object ever excites pure love or hatred, and does not always produce respect or contempt, by a mixture of humility or pride. No quality in another gives rise to humility by comparison, unless it would have produced pride by being placed in ourselves; and vice versa no object excites pride by comparison, unless it would have produced humility by the direct survey. This is evident, objects always produce by comparison a sensation directly contrary to their original one. Suppose, therefore, an object to be presented, which is peculiarly fitted to produce love, but imperfectly to excite pride; this object, belonging to another, gives rise directly to a great degree of love, but to a small one of humility by comparison; and consequently that latter passion is scarce felt in the compound, nor is able to convert the love into respect. This is the case with good nature, good humour, facility, generosity, beauty, and many other qualities. These have a peculiar aptitude to produce love in others; but not so great a tendency to excite pride in ourselves: For which reason the view of them, as belonging to another person, produces pure love, with but a small mixture of humility and respect. It is easy to extend the same reasoning to the opposite passions.

Before we leave this subject, it may not be amiss to account for a pretty curious phænomenon, viz, why we commonly keep at a distance such as we contemn, and allow not our inferiors to approach too near even in place and situation. It has already been observed, that almost every kind of idea is attended with some emotion, even the ideas of number and extension, much more those of such objects as are esteemed of consequence in life, and fix our attention. It is not with entire indifference we can survey either a rich man or a poor one, but must feel some faint touches at least, of respect in the former case, and of contempt in the latter. These two passions are contrary to each other; but in order to make this contrariety be felt, the objects must be someway related; otherwise the affections are totally separate and distinct, and never encounter. The relation takes place wherever the persons become contiguous; which is a general reason why we are uneasy at seeing such disproportioned objects, as a rich man and a poor one, a nobleman and a porter, in that situation.

This uneasiness, which is common to every spectator, must be more sensible to the superior; and that because the near approach of the inferior is regarded as a piece of ill-breeding, and shews that he is not sensible of the disproportion, and is no way affected by it. A sense of superiority in another breeds in all men an inclination to keep themselves at a distance from him, and determines them to redouble the marks of respect and reverence, when they are obliged to approach him; and where they do not observe that conduct, it is a proof they are not sensible of his superiority. From hence too it proceeds, that any great difference in the degrees of any quality is called a distance by a common metaphor, which, however trivial it may appear, is founded on natural principles of the imagination. A great difference inclines us to produce a distance. The ideas of distance and difference are, therefore, connected together. Connected ideas are readily taken for each other; and this is in general the source of the metaphor, as we shall have occasion to observe afterwards.

SECTION XI

Of the Amorous Passion, or Love Betwixt the Sexes

Of all the compound passions, which proceed from a mixture of love and hatred with other affections, no one better deserves our attention, than that love, which arises betwixt the sexes, as well on account of its force and violence, as those curious principles of philosophy, for which it affords us an uncontestable argument. It is plain, that this affection, in its most natural state, is derived from the conjunction of three different impressions or passions, viz. The pleasing sensation arising from beauty; the bodily appetite for generation; and a generous kindness or good-will.

The origin of kindness from beauty may be explained from the foregoing reasoning. The question is how the bodily appetite is excited by it.

The appetite of generation, when confined to a certain degree, is evidently of the pleasant kind, and has a strong connexion with, all the agreeable emotions. Joy, mirth, vanity, and kindness are all incentives to this desire; as well as music, dancing, wine, and good cheer. On the other hand, sorrow, melancholy, poverty, humility are destructive of it. From this quality it is easily conceived why it should be connected with the sense of beauty.

But there is another principle that contributes to the same effect. I have observed that the parallel direction of the desires is a real relation, and no less than a resemblance in their sensation, produces a connexion among them. That we may fully comprehend the extent of this relation, we must consider, that any principal desire may be attended with subordinate ones, which are connected with it, and to which if other desires are parallel, they are by that means related to the principal one. Thus hunger may oft be considered as the primary inclination of the soul, and the desire of approaching the meat as the secondary one; since it is absolutely necessary to the satisfying that appetite. If an object, therefore, by any separate qualities, inclines us to approach the meat, it naturally encreases our appetite; as on the contrary, whatever inclines us to set our victuals at a distance, is contradictory to hunger, and diminishes our inclination to them. Now it is plain that beauty has the first effect, and deformity the second: Which is the reason why the former gives us a keener appetite for our victuals, and the latter is sufficient to disgust us at the most savoury dish that cookery has invented. All this is easily applicable to the appetite for generation.

From these two relations, viz, resemblance and a parallel desire, there arises such a connexion betwixt the sense of beauty, the bodily appetite, and benevolence, that they become in a manner inseparable: And we find from experience that it is indifferent which of them advances first; since any of them is almost sure to be attended with the related affections. One, who is inflamed with lust, feels at least a momentary kindness towards the object of it, and at the same time fancies her more beautiful than ordinary; as there are many, who begin with kindness and esteem for the wit and merit of the person, and advance from that to the other passions. But the most common species of love is that which first arises from beauty, and afterwards diffuses itself into kindness and into the bodily appetite. Kindness or esteem, and the appetite to generation, are too remote to unite easily together. The one is, perhaps, the most refined passion of the soul; the other the most gross and vulgar. The love of beauty is placed in a just medium betwixt them, and partakes of both their natures: From whence it proceeds, that it is so singularly fitted to produce both.

This account of love is not peculiar to my system, but is unavoidable on any hypothesis. The three affections, which compose this passion, are evidently distinct, and has each of them its distinct object. It is certain, therefore, that it is only by their relation they produce each other. But the relation of passions is not alone sufficient. It is likewise necessary, there should be a relation of ideas. The beauty of one person never inspires us with love for another. This then is a sensible proof of the double relation of impressions and ideas. From one instance so evident as this we may form a judgment of the rest.

This may also serve in another view to illustrate what I have insisted on concerning the origin of pride and humility, love and hatred. I have observed, that though self be the object of the first set of passions, and some other person of the second, yet these objects cannot alone be the causes of the passions; as having each of them a relation to two contrary affections, which must from the very first moment destroy each other. Here then is the situation of the mind, as I have already described it. It has certain organs naturally fitted to produce a passion; that passion, when produced, naturally turns the view to a certain object. But this not being sufficient to produce the passion, there is required some other emotion, which by a double relation of impressions and ideas may set these principles in action, and bestow on them their first impulse. This situation is still more remarkable with regard to the appetite of generation. Sex is not only the object, but also the cause of the appetite. We not only turn our view to it, when actuated by that appetite; but the reflecting on it suffices to excite the appetite. But as this cause loses its force by too great frequency, it is necessary it should be quickened by some new impulse; and that impulse we find to arise from the beauty of the person; that is, from a double relation of impressions and ideas. Since this double relation is necessary where an affection has both a distinct cause, and object, how much more so, where it has only a distinct object, without any determinate cause?

SECTION XII

Of the Love and Hatred of Animals

But to pass from the passions of love and hatred, and from their mixtures and compositions, as they appear in man, to the same affections, as they display themselves in brutes; we may observe, not only that love and hatred are common to the whole sensitive creation, but likewise that their causes, as above-explained, are of so simple a nature, that they may easily be supposed to operate on mere animals. There is no force of reflection or penetration required. Every thing is conducted by springs and principles, which are not peculiar to man, or any one species of animals. The conclusion from this is obvious in favour of the foregoing system.

Love in animals, has not for its only object animals of the same species, but extends itself farther, and comprehends almost every sensible and thinking being. A dog naturally loves a man above his own species, and very commonly meets with a return of affection.

As animals are but little susceptible either of the pleasures or pains of the imagination, they can judge of objects only by the sensible good or evil, which they produce, and from that must regulate their affections towards them. Accordingly we find, that by benefits or injuries we produce their love or hatred; and that by feeding and cherishing any animal, we quickly acquire his affections; as by beating and abusing him we never fail to draw on us his enmity and ill-will.

Love in beasts is not caused so much by relation, as in our species; and that because their thoughts are not so active as to trace relations, except in very obvious instances. Yet it is easy to remark, that on some occasions it has a considerable influence upon them. Thus acquaintance, which has the same effect as relation, always produces love in animals either to men or to each other. For the same reason any likeness among them is the source of affection. An ox confined to a park with horses, will naturally join their company, if I may so speak, but always leaves it to enjoy that of his own species, where he has the choice of both.

The affection of parents to their young proceeds from a peculiar instinct in animals, as well as in our species.

It is evident, that sympathy, or the communication of passions, takes place among animals, no less than among men. Fear, anger, courage, and other affections are frequently communicated from one animal to another, without their knowledge of that cause, which produced the original passion. Grief likewise is received by sympathy; and produces almost all the same consequences, and excites the same emotions as in our species. The howlings and lamentations of a dog produce a sensible concern in his fellows. And it is remarkable, that though almost all animals use in play the same member, and nearly the same action as in fighting; a lion, a tyger, a cat their paws; an ox his horns; a dog his teeth; a horse his heels: Yet they most carefully avoid harming their companion, even though they have nothing to fear from his resentment; which is an evident proof of the sense brutes have of each other's pain and pleasure.

Every one has observed how much more dogs are animated when they hunt in a pack, than when they pursue their game apart; and it is evident this can proceed from nothing but from sympathy. It is also well known to hunters, that this effect follows in a greater degree, and even in too great a degree, where two packs, that are strangers to each other, are joined together. We might, perhaps, be at a loss to explain this phænomenon, if we had not experience of a similar in ourselves.

Envy and malice are passions very remarkable in animals. They are perhaps more common than pity; as requiring less effort of thought and imagination.

PART III

Of the Will and Direct Passions

SECTION I

Of Liberty and Necessity

We come now to explain the direct passions, or the impressions, which arise immediately from good or evil, from pain or pleasure. Of this kind are, desire and aversion, grief and joy, hope and fear.

Of all the immediate effects of pain and pleasure, there is none more remarkable than the WILL; and though properly speaking, it be not comprehended among the passions, yet as the full understanding of its nature and properties, is necessary to the explanation of them, we shall here make it the subject of our enquiry. I desire it may be observed, that by the will, I mean nothing but the internal impression we feel and are conscious of, when we knowingly give rise to any new motion of our body, or new perception of our mind. This impression, like the preceding ones of pride and humility, love and hatred, it is impossible to define, and needless to describe any farther; for which reason we shall cut off all those definitions and distinctions, with which philosophers are wont to perplex rather than dear up this question; and entering at first upon the subject, shall examine that long disputed question concerning liberty and necessity; which occurs so naturally in treating of the will.

It is universally acknowledged, that the operations of external bodies are necessary, and that in the communication of their motion, in their attraction, and mutual cohesion, there are nor the least traces of indifference or liberty. Every object is determined by an absolute fate to a certain degree and direction of its motion, and can no more depart from that precise line, in which it moves, than it can convert itself into an angel, or spirit, or any superior substance. The actions, therefore, of matter are to be regarded as instances of necessary actions; and whatever is in this respect on the same footing with matter, must be acknowledged to be necessary. That we may know whether this be the case with the actions of the mind, we shall begin with examining matter, and considering on what the idea of a necessity in its operations are founded, and why we conclude one body or action to be the infallible cause of another.

It has been observed already, that in no single instance the ultimate connexion of any objects is discoverable, either by our senses or reason, and that we can never penetrate so far into the essence and construction of bodies, as to perceive the principle, on which their mutual influence depends. It is their constant union alone, with which we are acquainted; and it is from the constant union the necessity arises. If objects had nor an uniform and regular conjunction with each other, we should never arrive at any idea of cause and effect; and even after all, the necessity, which enters into that idea, is nothing but a determination of the mind to pass from one object to its usual attendant, and infer the existence of one from that of the other. Here then are two particulars, which we are to consider as essential to necessity, viz, the constant union and the inference of the mind; and wherever we discover these we must acknowledge a necessity. As the actions of matter have no necessity, but what is derived from these circumstances, and it is not by any insight into the essence of bodies we discover their connexion, the absence of this insight, while the union and inference remain, will never, in any case, remove the necessity. It is the observation of the union, which produces the inference; for which reason it might be thought sufficient, if we prove a constant union in the actions of the mind, in order to establish the inference, along with the necessity of these actions. But that I may bestow a greater force on my reasoning, I shall examine these particulars apart, and shall first prove from experience that our actions have a constant union with our motives, tempers, and circumstances, before I consider the inferences we draw from it.

To this end a very slight and general view of the common course of human affairs will be sufficient. There is no light, in which we can take them, that does nor confirm this principle. Whether we consider mankind according to the difference of sexes, ages, governments, conditions, or methods of education; the same uniformity and regular operation of natural principles are discernible. Like causes still produce like effects; in the same manner as in the mutual action of the elements and powers of nature.

There are different trees, which regularly produce fruit, whose relish is different from each other; and this regularity will be admitted as an instance of necessity and causes in external bodies. But are the products of Guienne and of Champagne more regularly different than the sentiments, actions, and passions of the two sexes, of which the one are distinguished by their force and maturity, the other by their delicacy and softness?

Are the changes of our body from infancy to old age more regular and certain than those of our mind and conduct? And would a man be more ridiculous, who would expect that an infant of four years old will raise a weight of three hundred pound, than one, who from a person of the same age would look for a philosophical reasoning, or a prudent and well-concerted action?

We must certainly allow, that the cohesion of the parts of matter arises from natural and necessary principles, whatever difficulty we may find in explaining them: And for a reason we must allow, that human society is founded on like principles; and our reason in the latter case, is better than even that in the former; because we not only observe, that men always seek society, but can also explain the principles, on which this universal propensity is founded. For is it more certain, that two flat pieces of marble will unite together, than that two young savages of different sexes will copulate? Do the children arise from this copulation more uniformly, than does the parents care for their safety and preservation? And after they have arrived at years of discretion by the care of their parents, are the inconveniencies attending their separation more certain than their foresight of these inconveniencies and their care of avoiding them by a close union and confederacy?

The skin, pores, muscles, and nerves of a day-labourer are different from those of a man of quality: So are his sentiments, actions and manners. The different stations of life influence the whole fabric, external and internal; and different stations arise necessarily, because uniformly, from the necessary and uniform principles of human nature. Men cannot live without society, and cannot be associated without government. Government makes a distinction of property, and establishes the different ranks of men. This produces industry, traffic, manufactures, law-suits, war, leagues, alliances, voyages, travels, cities, fleets, ports, and all those other actions and objects, which cause such a diversity, and at the same time maintain such an uniformity in human life.

Should a traveller, returning from a far country, tell us, that he had seen a climate in the fiftieth degree of northern latitude, where all the fruits ripen and come to perfection in the winter, and decay in the summer, after the same manner as in England they are produced and decay in the contrary seasons, he would find few so credulous as to believe him. I am apt to think a travellar would meet with as little credit, who should inform us of people exactly of the same character with those in Plato's republic on the one hand, or those in Hobbes's Leviathan on the other. There is a general course of nature in human actions, as well as in the operations of the sun and the climate. There are also characters peculiar to different nations and particular persons, as well as common to mankind. The knowledge of these characters is founded on the observation of an uniformity in the actions, that flow from them; and this uniformity forms the very essence of necessity.

I can imagine only one way of eluding this argument, which is by denying that uniformity of human actions, on which it is founded. As long as actions have a constant union and connexion with the situation and temper of the agent, however we may in words refuse to acknowledge the necessity, we really allow the thing. Now some may, perhaps, find a pretext to deny this regular union and connexion. For what is more capricious than human actions? What more inconstant than the desires of man? And what creature departs more widely, not only from right reason, but from his own character and disposition? An hour, a moment is sufficient to make him change from one extreme to another, and overturn what cost the greatest pain and labour to establish. Necessity is regular and certain. Human conduct is irregular and uncertain. The one, therefore, proceeds not from the other.

To this I reply, that in judging of the actions of men we must proceed upon the same maxims, as when we reason concerning external objects. When any phaenomena are constantly and invariably conjoined together, they acquire such a connexion in the imagination, that it passes from one to the other, without any doubt or hesitation. But below this there are many inferior degrees of evidence and probability, nor does one single contrariety of experiment entirely destroy all our reasoning. The mind ballances the contrary experiments, and deducting the inferior from the superior, proceeds with that degree of assurance or evidence, which remains. Even when these contrary experiments are entirely equal, we remove not the notion of causes and necessity; but supposing that the usual contrariety proceeds from the operation of contrary and concealed causes, we conclude, that the chance or indifference lies only in our judgment on account of our imperfect knowledge, not in the things themselves, which are in every case equally necessary, though to appearance not equally constant or certain. No union can be more constant and certain, than that of some actions with some motives and characters; and if in other cases the union is uncertain, it is no more than what happens in the operations of body, nor can we conclude any thing from the one irregularity, which will not follow equally from the other.

It is commonly allowed that mad-men have no liberty. But were we to judge by their actions, these have less regularity and constancy than the actions of wise-men, and consequently are farther removed from necessity. Our way of thinking in this particular is, therefore, absolutely inconsistent; but is a natural consequence of these confused ideas and undefined terms, which we so commonly make use of in our reasonings, especially on the present subject.

We must now shew, that as the union betwixt motives and actions has the same constancy, as that in any natural operations, so its influence on the understanding is also the same, in determining us to infer the existence of one from that of another. If this shall appear, there is no known circumstance, that enters into the connexion and production of the actions of matter, that is not to be found in all the operations of the mind; and consequently we cannot, without a manifest absurdity, attribute necessity to the one, and refuse into the other.

There is no philosopher, whose judgment is so riveted to this fantastical system of liberty, as not to acknowledge the force of moral evidence, and both in speculation and practice proceed upon it, as upon a reasonable foundation. Now moral evidence is nothing but a conclusion concerning the actions of men, derived from the consideration of their motives, temper and situation. Thus when we see certain characters or figures described upon paper, we infer that the person, who produced them, would affirm such facts, the death of Caesar, the success of Augustus, the cruelty of Nero; and remembering many other concurrent testimonies we conclude, that those facts were once really existant, and that so many men, without any interest, would never conspire to deceive us; especially since they must, in the attempt, expose themselves to the derision of all their contemporaries, when these facts were asserted to be recent and universally known. The same kind of reasoning runs through politics, war, commerce, economy, and indeed mixes itself so entirely in human life, that it is impossible to act or subsist a moment without having recourse to it. A prince, who imposes a tax upon his subjects, expects their compliance. A general, who conducts an army, makes account of a certain degree of courage. A merchant looks for fidelity and skill in his factor or super-cargo. A man, who gives orders for his dinner, doubts not of the obedience of his servants. In short, as nothing more nearly interests us than our own actions and those of others, the greatest part of our reasonings is employed in judgments concerning them. Now I assert, that whoever reasons after this manner, does ipso facto believe the actions of the will to arise from necessity, and that he knows not what he means, when he denies it.

All those objects, of which we call the one cause and the other effect, considered in themselves, are as distinct and separate from each other, as any two things in nature, nor can we ever, by the most accurate survey of them, infer the existence of the one from that of the other. It is only from experience and the observation of their constant union, that we are able to form this inference; and even after all, the inference is nothing but the effects of custom on the imagination. We must not here be content with saying, that the idea of cause and effect arises from objects constantly united; but must affirm, that it is the very same with the idea of those objects, and that the necessary connexion is not discovered by a conclusion of the understanding, but is merely a perception of the mind. Wherever, therefore, we observe the same union, and wherever the union operates in the same manner upon the belief and opinion, we have the idea of causes and necessity, though perhaps we may avoid those expressions. Motion in one body in all past instances, that have fallen under our observation, is followed upon impulse by motion in another. It is impossible for the mind to penetrate farther. From this constant union it forms the idea of cause and effect, and by its influence feels the necessity. As there is the same constancy, and the same influence in what we call moral evidence, I ask no more. What remains can only be a dispute of words.

And indeed, when we consider how aptly natural and moral evidence cement together, and form only one chain of argument betwixt them, we shall make no scruple to allow, that they are of the same nature, and derived from the same principles. A prisoner, who has neither money nor interest, discovers the impossibility of his escape, as well from the obstinacy of the goaler, as from the walls and bars with which he is surrounded; and in all attempts for his freedom chuses rather to work upon the stone and iron of the one, than upon the inflexible nature of the other. The same prisoner, when conducted to the scaffold, foresees his death as certainly from the constancy and fidelity of his guards as from the operation of the ax or wheel. His mind runs along a certain train of ideas: The refusal of the soldiers to consent to his escape, the action of the executioner; the separation of the head and body; bleeding, convulsive motions, and death. Here is a connected chain of natural causes and voluntary actions; but the mind feels no difference betwixt them in passing from one link to another; nor is less certain of the future event than if it were connected with the present impressions of the memory and senses by a train of causes cemented together by what we are pleased to call a physical necessity. The same experienced union has the same effect on the mind, whether the united objects be motives, volitions and actions; or figure and motion. We may change the names of things; but their nature and their operation on the understanding never change.

I dare be positive no one will ever endeavour to refute these reasonings otherwise than by altering my definitions, and assigning a different meaning to the terms of cause, and effect, and necessity, and liberty, and chance. According to my definitions, necessity makes an essential part of causation; and consequently liberty, by removing necessity, removes also causes, and is the very same thing with chance. As chance is commonly thought to imply a contradiction, and is at least directly contrary to experience, there are always the same arguments against liberty or free-will. If any one alters the definitions, I cannot pretend to argue with him, until I know the meaning he assigns to these terms.

SECTION II

The Same Subject Continued

I believe we may assign the three following reasons for the prevalance of the doctrine of liberty, however absurd it may be in one sense, and unintelligible in any other. First, After we have performed any action; though we confess we were influenced by particular views and motives; it is difficult for us to persuade ourselves we were governed by necessity, and that it was utterly impossible for us to have acted otherwise; the idea of necessity seeming to imply something of force, and violence, and constraint, of which we are not sensible. Few are capable of distinguishing betwixt the liberty of spontaniety, as it is called in the schools, and the liberty of indifference; betwixt that which is opposed to violence, and that which means a negation of necessity and causes. The first is even the most common sense of the word; and as it is only that species of liberty, which it concerns us to preserve, our thoughts have been principally turned towards it, and have almost universally confounded it with the other.

Secondly, There is a false sensation or experience even of the liberty of indifference; which is regarded as an argument for its real existence. The necessity of any action, whether of matter or of the mind, is not properly a quality in the agent, but in any thinking or intelligent being, who may consider the action, and consists in the determination of his thought to infer its existence from some preceding objects: As liberty or chance, on the other hand, is nothing but the want of that determination, and a certain looseness, which we feel in passing or not passing from the idea of one to that of the other. Now we may observe, that though in reflecting on human actions we seldom feel such a looseness or indifference, yet it very commonly happens, that in performing the actions themselves we are sensible of something like it: And as all related or resembling objects are readily taken for each other, this has been employed as a demonstrative or even an intuitive proof of human liberty. We feel that our actions are subject to our will on most occasions, and imagine we feel that the will itself is subject to nothing; because when by a denial of it we are provoked to try, we feel that it moves easily every way, and produces an image of itself even on that side, on which it did not settle. This image or faint motion, we persuade ourselves, could have been compleated into the thing itself; because, should that be denyed, we find, upon a second trial, that it can. But these efforts are all in vain; and whatever capricious and irregular actions we may perform; as the desire of showing our liberty is the sole motive of our actions; we can never free ourselves from the bonds of necessity. We may imagine we feel a liberty within ourselves; but a spectator can commonly infer our actions from our motives and character; and even where he cannot, he concludes in general, that he might, were he perfectly acquainted with every circumstance of our situation and temper, and the most secret springs of our complexion and disposition. Now this is the very essence of necessity, according to the foregoing doctrine.

A third reason why the doctrine of liberty has generally been better received in the world, than its antagonist, proceeds from religion, which has been very unnecessarily interested in this question. There is no method of reasoning more common, and yet none more blameable, than in philosophical debates to endeavour to refute any hypothesis by a pretext of its dangerous consequences to religion and morality. When any opinion leads us into absurdities, it is certainly false; but it is not certain an opinion is false, because it is of dangerous consequence. Such topics, therefore, ought entirely to be foreborn, as serving nothing to the discovery of truth, but only to make the person of an antagonist odious. This I observe in general, without pretending to draw any advantage from it. I submit myself frankly to an examination of this kind, and dare venture to affirm, that the doctrine of necessity, according to my explication of it, is not only innocent, but even advantageous to religion and morality.

I define necessity two ways, conformable to the two definitions of cause, of which it makes an essential part. I place it either in the constant union and conjunction of like objects, or in the inference of the mind from the one to the other. Now necessity, in both these senses, has universally, though tacitly, in the schools, in the pulpit, and in common life, been allowed to belong to the will of man, and no one has ever pretended to deny, that we can draw inferences concerning human actions, and that those inferences are founded on the experienced union of like actions with like motives and circumstances. The only particular in which any one can differ from me, is either, that perhaps he will refuse to call this necessity. But as long as the meaning is understood, I hope the word can do no harm. Or that he will maintain there is something else in the operations of matter. Now whether it be so or not is of no consequence to religion, whatever it may be to natural philosophy. I may be mistaken in asserting, that we have no idea of any other connexion in the actions of body, and shall be glad to be farther instructed on that head: But sure I am, I ascribe nothing to the actions of the mind, but what must readily be allowed of. Let no one, therefore, put an invidious construction on my words, by saying simply, that I assert the necessity of human actions, and place them on the same footing with the operations of senseless matter. I do not ascribe to the will that unintelligible necessity, which is supposed to lie in matter. But I ascribe to matter, that intelligible quality, call it necessity or not, which the most rigorous orthodoxy does or must allow to belong to the will. I change, therefore, nothing in the received systems, with regard to the will, but only with regard to material objects.

Nay I shall go farther, and assert, that this kind of necessity is so essential to religion and morality, that without it there must ensue an absolute subversion of both, and that every other supposition is entirely destructive to all laws both divine and human. It is indeed certain, that as all human laws are founded on rewards and punishments, it is supposed as a fundamental principle, that these motives have an influence on the mind, and both produce the good and prevent the evil actions. We may give to this influence what name we please; but as it is usually conjoined with the action, common sense requires it should be esteemed a cause, and be booked upon as an instance of that necessity, which I would establish.

This reasoning is equally solid, when applied to divine laws, so far as the deity is considered as a legislator, and is supposed to inflict punishment and bestow rewards with a design to produce obedience. But I also maintain, that even where he acts not in his magisterial capacity, but is regarded as the avenger of crimes merely on account of their odiousness and deformity, not only it is impossible, without the necessary connexion of cause and effect in human actions, that punishments could be inflicted compatible with justice and moral equity; but also that it could ever enter into the thoughts of any reasonable being to inflict them. The constant and universal object of hatred or anger is a person or creature endowed with thought and consciousness; and when any criminal or injurious actions excite that passion, it is only by their relation to the person or connexion with him. But according to the doctrine of liberty or chance, this connexion is reduced to nothing, nor are men more accountable for those actions, which are designed and premeditated, than for such as are the most casual and accidental. Actions are by their very nature temporary and perishing; and where they proceed not from some cause in the characters and disposition of the person, who performed them, they infix not themselves upon him, and can neither redound to his honour, if good, nor infamy, if evil. The action itself may be blameable; it may be contrary to all the rules of morality and religion: But the person is not responsible for it; and as it proceeded from nothing in him, that is durable or constant, and leaves nothing of that nature behind it, it is impossible he can, upon its account, become the object of punishment or vengeance. According to the hypothesis of liberty, therefore, a man is as pure and untainted, after having committed the most horrid crimes, as at the first moment of his birth, nor is his character any way concerned in his actions; since they are not derived from it, and the wickedness of the one can never be used as a proof of the depravity of the other. It is only upon the principles of necessity, that a person acquires any merit or demerit from his actions, however the common opinion may incline to the contrary.

But so inconsistent are men with themselves, that though they often assert, that necessity utterly destroys all merit and demerit either towards mankind or superior powers, yet they continue still to reason upon these very principles of necessity in all their judgments concerning this matter. Men are not blamed for such evil actions as they perform ignorantly and casually, whatever may be their consequences. Why? but because the causes of these actions are only momentary, and terminate in them alone. Men are less blamed for such evil actions, as they perform hastily and unpremeditately, than for such as proceed from thought and deliberation. For what reason? but because a hasty temper, though a constant cause in the mind, operates only by intervals, and infects not the whole character. Again, repentance wipes off every crime, especially if attended with an evident reformation of life and manners. How is this to be accounted for? But by asserting that actions render a person criminal, merely as they are proofs of criminal passions or principles in the mind; and when by any alteration of these principles they cease to be just proofs, they likewise cease to be criminal. But according to the doctrine of liberty or chance they never were just proofs, and consequently never were criminal.

Here then I turn to my adversary, and desire him to free his own system from these odious consequences before he charge them upon others. Or if he rather chuses, that this question should be decided by fair arguments before philosophers, than by declamations before the people, let him return to what I have advanced to prove that liberty and chance are synonimous; and concerning the nature of moral evidence and the regularity of human actions. Upon a review of these reasonings, I cannot doubt of an entire victory; and therefore having proved, that all actions of the will have particular causes, I proceed to explain what these causes are, and how they operate.

SECTION III

Of the Influencing Motives of the Will

Nothing is more usual in philosophy, and even in common life, than to talk of the combat of passion and reason, to give the preference to reason, and assert that men are only so far virtuous as they conform themselves to its dictates. Every rational creature, it is said, is obliged to regulate his actions by reason; and if any other motive or principle challenge the direction of his conduct, he ought to oppose it, till it be entirely subdued, or at least brought to a conformity with that superior principle. On this method of thinking the greatest part of moral philosophy, antient and modern, seems to be founded; nor is there an ampler field, as well for metaphysical arguments, as popular declamations, than this supposed pre-eminence of reason above passion. The eternity, invariableness, and divine origin of the former have been displayed to the best advantage: The blindness, unconstancy, and deceitfulness of the latter have been as strongly insisted on. In order to shew the fallacy of all this philosophy, I shall endeavour to prove first, that reason alone can never be a motive to any action of the will; and secondly, that it can never oppose passion in the direction of the will.

The understanding exerts itself after two different ways, as it judges from demonstration or probability; as it regards the abstract relations of our ideas, or those relations of objects, of which experience only gives us information. I believe it scarce will be asserted, that the first species of reasoning alone is ever the cause of any action. As its proper province is the world of ideas, and as the will always places us in that of realities, demonstration and volition seem, upon that account, to be totally removed, from each other. Mathematics, indeed, are useful in all mechanical operations, and arithmetic in almost every art and profession: But it is not of themselves they have any influence: Mechanics are the art of regulating the motions of bodies to some designed end or purpose; and the reason why we employ arithmetic in fixing the proportions of numbers, is only that we may discover the proportions of their influence and operation. A merchant is desirous of knowing the sum total of his accounts with any person: Why? but that he may learn what sum will have the same effects in paying his debt, and going to market, as all the particular articles taken together. Abstract or demonstrative reasoning, therefore, never influences any of our actions, but only as it directs our judgment concerning causes and effects; which leads us to the second operation of the understanding.

It is obvious, that when we have the prospect of pain or pleasure from any object, we feel a consequent emotion of aversion or propensity, and are carryed to avoid or embrace what will give us this uneasines or satisfaction. It is also obvious, that this emotion rests not here, but making us cast our view on every side, comprehends whatever objects are connected with its original one by the relation of cause and effect. Here then reasoning takes place to discover this relation; and according as our reasoning varies, our actions receive a subsequent variation. But it is evident in this case that the impulse arises not from reason, but is only directed by it. It is from the prospect of pain or pleasure that the aversion or propensity arises towards any object: And these emotions extend themselves to the causes and effects of that object, as they are pointed out to us by reason and experience. It can never in the least concern us to know, that such objects are causes, and such others effects, if both the causes and effects be indifferent to us. Where the objects themselves do not affect us, their connexion can never give them any influence; and it is plain, that as reason is nothing but the discovery of this connexion, it cannot be by its means that the objects are able to affect us.

Since reason alone can never produce any action, or give rise to volition, I infer, that the same faculty is as incapable of preventing volition, or of disputing the preference with any passion or emotion. This consequence is necessary. It is impossible reason could have the latter effect of preventing volition, but by giving an impulse in a contrary direction to our passion; and that impulse, had it operated alone, would have been able to produce volition. Nothing can oppose or retard the impulse of passion, but a contrary impulse; and if this contrary impulse ever arises from reason, that latter faculty must have an original influence on the will, and must be able to cause, as well as hinder any act of volition. But if reason has no original influence, it is impossible it can withstand any principle, which has such an efficacy, or ever keep the mind in suspence a moment. Thus it appears, that the principle, which opposes our passion, cannot be the same with reason, and is only called so in an improper sense. We speak not strictly and philosophically when we talk of the combat of passion and of reason. Reason is, and ought only to be the slave of the passions, and can never pretend to any other office than to serve and obey them. As this opinion may appear somewhat extraordinary, it may not be improper to confirm it by some other considerations.

A passion is an original existence, or, if you will, modification of existence, and contains not any representative quality, which renders it a copy of any other existence or modification. When I am angry, I am actually possest with the passion, and in that emotion have no more a reference to any other object, than when I am thirsty, or sick, or more than five foot high. It is impossible, therefore, that this passion can be opposed by, or be contradictory to truth and reason; since this contradiction consists in the disagreement of ideas, considered as copies, with those objects, which they represent.

What may at first occur on this head, is, that as nothing can be contrary to truth or reason, except what has a reference to it, and as the judgments of our understanding only have this reference, it must follow, that passions can be contrary to reason only so far as they are accompanyed with some judgment or opinion. According to this principle, which is so obvious and natural, it is only in two senses, that any affection can be called unreasonable. First, When a passion, such as hope or fear, grief or joy, despair or security, is founded on the supposition or the existence of objects, which really do not exist. Secondly, When in exerting any passion in action, we chuse means insufficient for the designed end, and deceive ourselves in our judgment of causes and effects. Where a passion is neither founded on false suppositions, nor chuses means insufficient for the end, the understanding can neither justify nor condemn it. It is not contrary to reason to prefer the destruction of the whole world to the scratching of my finger. It is not contrary to reason for me to chuse my total ruin, to prevent the least uneasiness of an Indian or person wholly unknown to me. It is as little contrary to reason to prefer even my own acknowledgeed lesser good to my greater, and have a more ardent affection for the former than the latter. A trivial good may, from certain circumstances, produce a desire superior to what arises from the greatest and most valuable enjoyment; nor is there any thing more extraordinary in this, than in mechanics to see one pound weight raise up a hundred by the advantage of its situation. In short, a passion must be accompanyed with some false judgment in order to its being unreasonable; and even then it is not the passion, properly speaking, which is unreasonable, but the judgment.

The consequences are evident. Since a passion can never, in any sense, be called unreasonable, but when founded on a false supposition or when it chuses means insufficient for the designed end, it is impossible, that reason and passion can ever oppose each other, or dispute for the government of the will and actions. The moment we perceive the falshood of any supposition, or the insufficiency of any means our passions yield to our reason without any opposition. I may desire any fruit as of an excellent relish; but whenever you convince me of my mistake, my longing ceases. I may will the performance of certain actions as means of obtaining any desired good; but as my willing of these actions is only secondary, and founded on the supposition, that they are causes of the proposed effect; as soon as I discover the falshood of that supposition, they must become indifferent to me.

It is natural for one, that does not examine objects with a strict philosophic eye, to imagine, that those actions of the mind are entirely the same, which produce not a different sensation, and are not immediately distinguishable to the feeling and perception. Reason, for instance, exerts itself without producing any sensible emotion; and except in the more sublime disquisitions of philosophy, or in the frivolous subtilties of the school, scarce ever conveys any pleasure or uneasiness. Hence it proceeds, that every action of the mind, which operates with the same calmness and tranquillity, is confounded with reason by all those, who judge of things from the first view and appearance. Now it is certain, there are certain calm desires and tendencies, which, though they be real passions, produce little emotion in the mind, and are more known by their effects than by the immediate feeling or sensation. These desires are of two kinds; either certain instincts originally implanted in our natures, such as benevolence and resentment, the love of life, and kindness to children; or the general appetite to good, and aversion to evil, considered merely as such. When any of these passions are calm, and cause no disorder in the soul, they are very readily taken for the determinations of reason, and are supposed to proceed from the same faculty, with that, which judges of truth and falshood. Their nature and principles have been supposed the same, because their sensations are not evidently different.

Beside these calm passions, which often determine the will, there are certain violent emotions of the same kind, which have likewise a great influence on that faculty. When I receive any injury from another, I often feel a violent passion of resentment, which makes me desire his evil and punishment, independent of all considerations of pleasure and advantage to myself. When I am immediately threatened with any grievous ill, my fears, apprehensions, and aversions rise to a great height, and produce a sensible emotion.

The common error of metaphysicians has lain in ascribing the direction of the will entirely to one of these principles, and supposing the other to have no influence. Men often act knowingly against their interest: For which reason the view of the greatest possible good does not always influence them. Men often counter-act a violent passion in prosecution of their interests and designs: It is not therefore the present uneasiness alone, which determines them. In general we may observe, that both these principles operate on the will; and where they are contrary, that either of them prevails, according to the general character or present disposition of the person. What we call strength of mind, implies the prevalence of the calm passions above the violent; though we may easily observe, there is no man so constantly possessed of this virtue, as never on any occasion to yield to the sollicitations of passion and desire. From these variations of temper proceeds the great difficulty of deciding concerning the actions and resolutions of men, where there is any contrariety of motives and passions.

SECTION IV

Of the Causes of the Violent Passions

There is not in philosophy a subject of more nice speculation than this of the different causes and effects of the calm and violent passions. It is evident passions influence not the will in proportion to their violence, or the disorder they occasion in the temper; but on the contrary, that when a passion has once become a settled principle of action, and is the predominant inclination of the soul, it commonly produces no longer any sensible agitation. As repeated custom and its own force have made every thing yield to it, it directs the actions and conduct without that opposition and emotion, which so naturally attend every momentary gust of passion. We must, therefore, distinguish betwixt a calm and a weak passion; betwixt a violent and a strong one. But notwithstanding this, it is certain, that when we would govern a man, and push him to any action, it will commonly be better policy to work upon the violent than the calm passions, and rather take him by his inclination, than what is vulgarly called his reason. We ought to place the object in such particular situations as are proper to encrease the violence of the passion. For we may observe, that all depends upon the situation of the object, and that a variation in this particular will be able to change the calm and the violent passions into each other. Both these kinds of passions pursue good, and avoid evil; and both of them are encreased or diminished by the encrease or diminution of the good or evil. But herein lies the difference betwixt them: The same good, when near, will cause a violent passion, which, when remote, produces only a calm one. As this subject belongs very properly to the present question concerning the will, we shall here examine it to the bottom, and shall consider some of those circumstances and situations of objects, which render a passion either calm or violent.

It is a remarkable property of human nature, that any emotion, which attends a passion, is easily converted into it, though in their natures they be originally different from, and even contrary to each other. It is true; in order to make a perfect union among passions, there is always required a double relation of impressions and ideas; nor is one relation sufficient for that purpose. But though this be confirmed by undoubted experience, we must understand it with its proper limitations, and must regard the double relation, as requisite only to make one passion produce another. When two passions are already produced by their separate causes, and are both present in the mind, they readily mingle and unite, though they have but one relation, and sometimes without any. The predominant passion swallows up the inferior, and converts it into itself. The spirits, when once excited, easily receive a change in their direction; and it is natural to imagine this change will come from the prevailing affection. The connexion is in many respects closer betwixt any two passions, than betwixt any passion and indifference.

When a person is once heartily in love, the little faults and caprices of his mistress, the jealousies and quarrels, to which that commerce is so subject; however unpleasant and related to anger and hatred; are yet found to give additional force to the prevailing passion. It is a common artifice of politicians, when they would affect any person very much by a matter of fact, of which they intend to inform him, first to excite his curiosity; delay as long as possible the satisfying it; and by that means raise his anxiety and impatience to the utmost, before they give him a full insight into the business. They know that his curiosity will precipitate him into the passion they design to raise, and assist the object in its influence on the mind. A soldier advancing to the battle, is naturally inspired with courage and confidence, when he thinks on his friends and fellow-soldiers; and is struck with fear and terror, when he reflects on the enemy. Whatever new emotion, therefore, proceeds from the former naturally encreases the courage; as the same emotion, proceeding from the latter, augments the fear; by the relation of ideas, and the conversion of the inferior emotion into the predominant. Hence it is that in martial discipline, the uniformity and lustre of our habit, the regularity of our figures and motions, with all the pomp and majesty of war, encourage ourselves and allies; while the same objects in the enemy strike terror into us, though agreeable and beautiful in themselves.

Since passions, however independent, are naturally transfused into each other, if they are both present at the same time; it follows, that when good or evil is placed in such a situation, as to cause any particular emotion, beside its direct passion of desire or aversion, that latter passion must acquire new force and violence.

This happens, among other cases, whenever any object excites contrary passions. For it is observable that an opposition of passions commonly causes a new emotion in the spirits, and produces more disorder, than the concurrence of any two affections of equal force. This new emotion is easily converted into the predominant passion, and encreases its violence, beyond the pitch it would have arrived at had it met with no opposition. Hence we naturally desire what is forbid, and take a pleasure in performing actions, merely because they are unlawful. The notion of duty, when opposite to the passions, is seldom able to overcome them; and when it fails of that effect, is apt rather to encrease them, by producing an opposition in our motives and principles. The same effect follows whether the opposition arises from internal motives or external obstacles. The passion commonly acquires new force and violence in both cases.

The efforts, which the mind makes to surmount the obstacle, excite the spirits and inliven the passion.

Uncertainty has the same influence as opposition. The agitation of the thought; the quick turns it makes from one view to another; the variety of passions, which succeed each other, according to the different views; All these produce an agitation in the mind, and transfuse themselves into the predominant passion.

There is not in my opinion any other natural cause, why security diminishes the passions, than because it removes that uncertainty, which encreases them. The mind, when left to itself, immediately languishes; and in order to preserve its ardour, must be every moment supported by a new flow of passion. For the same reason, despair, though contrary to security, has a like influence.

It is certain nothing more powerfully animates any affection, than to conceal some part of its object by throwing it into a kind of shade, which at the same time that it chews enough to pre-possess us in favour of the object, leaves still some work for the imagination. Besides that obscurity is always attended with a kind of uncertainty; the effort, which the fancy makes to compleat the idea, rouzes the spirits, and gives an additional force to the passion.

As despair and security, though contrary to each other, produce the same effects; so absence is observed to have contrary effects, and in different circumstances either encreases or diminishes our affections. The Duc de La Rochefoucault has very well observed, that absence destroys weak passions, but encreases strong; as the wind extinguishes a candle, but blows up a fire. Long absence naturally weakens our idea, and diminishes the passion: But where the idea is so strong and lively as to support itself, the uneasiness, arising from absence, encreases the passion and gives it new force and violence.

SECTION V

Of the Effects of Custom

But nothing has a greater effect both to encrease and diminish our passions, to convert pleasure into pain, and pain into pleasure, than custom and repetition. Custom has two original effects upon the mind, in bestowing a facility in the performance of any action or the conception of any object; and afterwards a tendency or inclination towards it; and from these we may account for all its other effects, however extraordinary.

When the soul applies itself to the performance of any action, or the conception of any object, to which it is not accustomed, there is a certain unpliableness in the faculties, and a difficulty of the spirit's moving in their new direction. As this difficulty excites the spirits, it is the source of wonder, surprize, and of all the emotions, which arise from novelty; and is in itself very agreeable, like every thing, which inlivens the mind to a moderate degree. But though surprize be agreeable in itself, yet as it puts the spirits in agitation, it not only augments our agreeable affections, but also our painful, according to the foregoing principle, that every emotion, which precedes or attends a passion, is easily converted into it. Hence every thing, that is new, is most affecting, and gives us either more pleasure or pain, than what, strictly speaking, naturally belongs to it. When it often returns upon us, the novelty wears off; the passions subside; the hurry of the spirits is over; and we survey the objects with greater tranquillity.

By degrees the repetition produces a facility of the human mind, and an infallible source of pleasure, where the facility goes not beyond a certain degree. And here it is remarkable that the pleasure, which arises from a moderate facility, has not the same tendency with that which arises from novelty, to augment the painful, as well as the agreeable affections. The pleasure of facility does not so much consist in any ferment of the spirits, as in their orderly motion; which will sometimes be so powerful as even to convert pain into pleasure, and give us a relish in time what at first was most harsh and disagreeable.

But again, as facility converts pain into pleasure, so it often converts pleasure into pain, when it is too great, and renders the actions of the mind so faint and languid, that they are no longer able to interest and support it. And indeed, scarce any other objects become disagreeable through custom; but such as are naturally attended with some emotion or affection, which is destroyed by the too frequent repetition. One can consider the clouds, and heavens, and trees, and stones, however frequently repeated, without ever feeling any aversion. But when the fair sex, or music, or good cheer, or any thing, that naturally ought to be agreeable, becomes indifferent, it easily produces the opposite affection.

But custom not only gives a facility to perform any action, but likewise an inclination and tendency towards it, where it is not entirely disagreeable, and can never be the object of inclination. And this is the reason why custom encreases all active habits, but diminishes passive, according to the observation of a late eminent philosopher. The facility takes off from the force of the passive habits by rendering the motion of the spirits faint and languid. But as in the active, the spirits are sufficiently supported of themselves, the tendency of the mind gives them new force, and bends them more strongly to the action.

SECTION VI

Of the Influence of the Imagination on the Passions

It is remarkable, that the imagination and affections have close union together, and that nothing, which affects the former, can be entirely indifferent to the latter. Wherever our ideas of good or evil acquire a new vivacity, the passions become more violent; and keep pace with the imagination in all its variations. Whether this proceeds from the principle above-mentioned, that any attendant emotion is easily converted into the predominant, I shall not determine. It is sufficient for my present purpose, that we have many instances to confirm this influence of the imagination upon the passions.

Any pleasure, with which we are acquainted, affects us more than any other, which we own to be superior, but of whose nature we are wholly ignorant. Of the one we can form a particular and determinate idea: The other we conceive under the general notion of pleasure; and it is certain, that the more general and universal any of our ideas are, the less influence they have upon the imagination. A general idea, though it be nothing but a particular one considered in a certain view, is commonly more obscure; and that because no particular idea, by which we represent a general one, is ever fixed or determinate, but may easily be changed for other particular ones, which will serve equally in the representation.

There is a noted passage in the history of Greece, which may serve for our present purpose. Themistocles told the Athenians, that he had formed a design, which would be highly useful to the public, but which it was impossible for him to communicate to them without ruining the execution, since its success depended entirely on the secrecy with which it should be conducted. The Athenians, instead of granting him full power to act as he thought fitting, ordered him to communicate his design to Aristides, in whose prudence they had an entire confidence, and whose opinion they were resolved blindly to submit to. The design of Themistocles was secretly to set fire to the fleet of all the Grecian commonwealths, which was assembled in a neighbouring port, and which being once destroyed would give the Athenians the empire of the sea without any rival Aristides returned to the assembly, and told them, that nothing could be more advantageous than the design of Themistocles but at the same time that nothing could be more unjust: Upon which the people unanimously rejected the project.

A late celebrated historian[64] admires this passage of antient history, as one of the most singular that is any where to be met.

"Here," says he, "they are not philosophers, to whom it is easy in their schools to establish the finest maxims and most sublime rules of morality, who decide that interest ought never to prevail above justice. It is a whole people interested in the proposal which is made to them, who consider it as of importance to the public good, and who notwithstanding reject it unanimously, and without hesitation, merely because it is contrary to justice."

For my part I see nothing so extraordinary in this proceeding of the Athenians. The same reasons, which render it so easy for philosophers to establish these sublime maxims, tend, in part, to diminish the merit of such a conduct in that people. Philosophers never ballance betwixt profit and honesty, because their decisions are general, and neither their passions nor imaginations are interested in the objects. And though in the present case the advantage was immediate to the Athenians, yet as it was known only under the general notion of advantage, without being

[64] Mons. Rollin [Charles Rollin, HISTOIRE ANCIENNE.(Paris 1730-38)].

conceived by any particular idea, it must have had a less considerable influence on their imaginations, and have been a less violent temptation, than if they had been acquainted with all its circumstances: Otherwise it is difficult to conceive, that a whole people, unjust and violent as men commonly are, should so unanimously have adhered to justice, and rejected any considerable advantage.

Any satisfaction, which we lately enjoyed, and of which the memory is fresh and recent, operates on the will with more violence, than another of which the traces are decayed, and almost obliterated. From whence does this proceed, but that the memory in the first case assists the fancy and gives an additional force and vigour to its conceptions? The image of the past pleasure being strong and violent, bestows these qualities on the idea of the future pleasure, which is connected with it by the relation of resemblance.

A pleasure, which is suitable to the way of life, in which we are engaged, excites more our desires and appetites than another, which is foreign to it. This phænomenon may be explained from the same principle.

Nothing is more capable of infusing any passion into the mind, than eloquence, by which objects are represented in their strongest and most lively colours. We may of ourselves acknowledge, that such an object is valuable, and such another odious; but until an orator excites the imagination, and gives force to these ideas, they may have but a feeble influence either on the will or the affections.

But eloquence is not always necessary. The bare opinion of another, especially when inforced with passion, will cause an idea of good or evil to have an influence upon us, which would otherwise have been entirely neglected. This proceeds from the principle of sympathy or communication; and sympathy, as I have already observed, is nothing but the conversion of an idea into an impression by the force of imagination.

It is remarkable, that lively passions commonly attend a lively imagination. In this respect, as well as others, the force of the passion depends as much on the temper of the person, as the nature or situation of the object.

I have already observed, that belief is nothing but a lively idea related to a present impression. This vivacity is a requisite circumstance to the exciting all our passions, the calm as well as the violent; nor has a mere fiction of the imagination any considerable influence upon either of them. It is too weak to take hold of the mind, or be attended with emotion.

SECTION VII

Of Contiguity and Distance in Space and Time

There is an easy reason, why every thing contiguous to us, either in space or time, should be conceived with a peculiar force and vivacity, and excel every other object, in its influence on the imagination. Ourself is intimately present to us, and whatever is related to self must partake of that quality. But where an object is so far removed as to have lost the advantage of this relation, why, as it is farther removed, its idea becomes still fainter and more obscure, would, perhaps, require a more particular examination.

It is obvious, that the imagination can never totally forget the points of space and time, in which we are existent; but receives such frequent advertisements of them from the passions and senses, that however it may turn its attention to foreign and remote objects, it is necessitated every moment to reflect on the present. It is also remarkable, that in the conception of those objects, which we regard as real and existent, we take them in their proper order and situation, and never leap from one object to another, which is distant from it, without running over, at least in a cursory manner, all those objects, which are interposed betwixt them. When we reflect, therefore, on any object distant from ourselves, we are obliged not only to reach it at first by passing through all the intermediate space betwixt ourselves and the object, but also to renew our progress every moment; being every moment recalled to the consideration of ourselves and our present situation. It is easily conceived, that this interruption must weaken the idea by breaking the action of the mind, and hindering the conception from being so intense and continued, as when we reflect on a nearer object. The fewer steps we make to arrive at the object, and the smoother the road is, this diminution of vivacity is less sensibly felt, but still may be observed more or less in proportion to the degrees of distance and difficulty.

Here then we are to consider two kinds of objects, the contiguous and remote; of which the former, by means of their relation to ourselves, approach an impression in force and vivacity; the latter by reason of the interruption in our manner of conceiving them, appear in a weaker and more imperfect light. This is their effect on the imagination. If my reasoning be just, they must have a proportionable effect on the will and passions. Contiguous objects must have an influence much superior to the distant and remote. Accordingly we find in common life, that men are principally concerned about those objects, which are not much removed either in space or time, enjoying the present, and leaving what is afar off to the care of chance and fortune. Talk to a man of his condition thirty years hence, and he will not regard you. Speak of what is to happen tomorrow, and he will lend you attention. The breaking of a mirror gives us more concern when at home, than the burning of a house, when abroad, and some hundred leagues distant.

But farther; though distance both in space and time has a considerable effect on the imagination, and by that means on the will and passions, yet the consequence of a removal in space are much inferior to those of a removal in time. Twenty years are certainly but a small distance of time in comparison of what history and even the memory of some may inform them of, and yet I doubt if a thousand leagues, or even the greatest distance of place this globe can admit of, will so remarkably weaken our ideas, and diminish our passions. A West-Indian merchant will tell you, that he is not without concern about what passes in Jamaica; though few extend their views so far into futurity, as to dread very remote accidents.

The cause of this phænomenon must evidently lie in the different properties of space and time. Without having recourse to metaphysics, any one may easily observe, that space or extension consists of a number of co-existent parts disposed in a certain order, and capable of being at once present to the sight or feeling. On the contrary, time or succession, though it consists likewise of parts, never presents to us more than one at once; nor is it possible for any two of them ever to be co-existent. These qualities of the objects have a suitable effect on the imagination. The parts of extension being susceptible of an union to the senses, acquire an union in the fancy; and as the appearance of one part excludes not another, the transition or passage of the thought through the contiguous parts is by that means rendered more smooth and easy. On the other hand, the incompatibility of the parts of time in their real existence separates them in the imagination, and makes it more difficult for that faculty to trace any long succession or series of events. Every part must appear single and alone, nor can regularly have entrance into the fancy without banishing what is supposed to have been immediately precedent. By this means any distance in time causes a greater interruption in the thought than an equal distance in space, and consequently weakens more considerably the idea, and consequently the passions; which depend in a great measure, on the imagination, according to my system.

There is another phænomenon of a like nature with the foregoing, viz, the superior effects of the same distance in futurity above that in the past. This difference with respect to the will is easily accounted for. As none of our actions can alter the past, it is not strange it should never determine the will. But with respect to the passions the question is yet entire, and well worth the examining.

Besides the propensity to a gradual progression through the points of space and time, we have another peculiarity in our method of thinking, which concurs in producing this phænomenon. We always follow the succession of time in placing our ideas, and from the consideration of any object pass more easily to that, which follows immediately after it, than to that which went before it. We may learn this, among other instances, from the order, which is always observed in historical narrations. Nothing but an absolute necessity can oblige an historian to break the order of time, and in his narration give the precedence to an event, which was in reality posterior to another.

This will easily be applied to the question in hand, if we reflect on what I have before observed, that the present situation of the person is always that of the imagination, and that it is from thence we proceed to the conception of any distant object. When the object is past, the progression of the thought in passing to it from the present is contrary to nature, as proceeding from one point of time to that which is preceding, and from that to another preceding, in opposition to the natural course of the succession. On the other hand, when we turn our thought to a future object, our fancy flows along the stream of time, and arrives at the object by an order, which seems most natural, passing always from one point of time to that which is immediately posterior to it. This easy progression of ideas favours the imagination, and makes it conceive its object in a stronger and fuller light, than when we are continually opposed in our passage, and are obliged to overcome the difficulties arising from the natural propensity of the fancy. A small degree of distance in the past has, therefore, a greater effect, in interupting and weakening the conception, than a much greater in the future. From this effect of it on the imagination is derived its influence on the will and passions.

There is another cause, which both contributes to the same effect, and proceeds from the same quality of the fancy, by which we are determined to trace the succession of time by a similar succession of ideas. When from the present instant we consider two points of time equally distant in the future and in the past, it is evident, that, abstractedly considered, their relation to the present is almost equal. For as the future will sometime be present, so the past was once present. If we could, therefore, remove this quality of the imagination, an equal distance in the past and in the future, would have a similar influence. Nor is this only true, when the fancy remains fixed, and from the present instant surveys the future and the past; but also when it changes its situation, and places us in different periods of time. For as on the one hand, in supposing ourselves existent in a point of time interposed betwixt the present instant and the future object, we find the future object approach to us, and the past retire, and become more distant: so on the other hand, in supposing ourselves existent in a point of time interposed betwixt the present and the past, the past approaches to us, and the future becomes more distant. But from the property of the fancy above-mentioned we rather chuse to fix our thought on the point of time interposed betwixt the present and the future, than on that betwixt the present and the past. We advance, rather than retard our existence; and following what seems the natural succession of time, proceed from past to present, and from present to future. By which means we conceive the future as flowing every moment nearer us, and the past as retiring. An equal distance, therefore, in the past and in the future, has not the same effect on the imagination; and that because we consider the one as continually encreasing, and the other as continually diminishing. The fancy anticipates the course of things, and surveys the object in that condition, to which it tends, as well as in that, which is regarded as the present.

SECTION VIII

The Same Subject Continued

Thus we have accounted for three phaenomena, which seem pretty remarkable. Why distance weakens the conception and passion: Why distance in time has a greater effect than that in space: And why distance in past time has still a greater effect than that in future. We must now consider three phaenomena, which seem to be, in a manner, the reverse of these: Why a very great distance encreases our esteem and admiration for an object; Why such a distance in time encreases it more than that in space: And a distance in past time more than that in future. The curiousness of the subject will, I hope, excuse my dwelling on it for some time.

To begin with the first phænomenon, why a great distance encreases our esteem and admiration for an object; it is evident that the mere view and contemplation of any greatness, whether successive or extended, enlarges the soul, and give it a sensible delight and pleasure. A wide plain, the ocean, eternity, a succession of several ages; all these are entertaining objects, and excel every thing, however beautiful, which accompanies not its beauty with a suitable greatness. Now when any very distant object is presented to the imagination, we naturally reflect on the interposed distance, and by that means, conceiving something great and magnificent, receive the usual satisfaction. But as the fancy passes easily from one idea to another related to it, and transports to the second all the passions excited by the first, the admiration, which is directed to the distance, naturally diffuses itself over the distant object. Accordingly we find, that it is not necessary the object should be actually distant from us, in order to cause our admiration; but that it is sufficient, if, by the natural association of ideas, it conveys our view to any considerable distance. A great traveller, though in the same chamber, will pass for a very extraordinary person; as a Greek medal, even in our cabinet, is always esteemed a valuable curiosity. Here the object, by a natural transition, conveys our views to the distance; and the admiration, which arises from that distance, by another natural transition, returns back to the object.

But though every great distance produces an admiration for the distant object, a distance in time has a more considerable effect than that in space. Antient busts and inscriptions are more valued than Japan tables: And not to mention the Greeks and Romans, it is certain we regard with more veneration the old Chaldeans and Egyptians, than the modern Chinese and Persians, and bestow more fruitless pains to dear up the history and chronology of the former, than it would cost us to make a voyage, and be certainly informed of the character, learning and government of the latter. I shall be obliged to make a digression in order to explain this phænomenon.

It is a quality very observable in human nature, that any opposition, which does not entirely discourage and intimidate us, has rather a contrary effect, and inspires us with a more than ordinary grandeur and magnanimity. In collecting our force to overcome the opposition, we invigorate the soul, and give it an elevation with which otherwise it would never have been acquainted. Compliance, by rendering our strength useless, makes us insensible of it: but opposition awakens and employs it.

This is also true in the universe. Opposition not only enlarges the soul; but the soul, when full of courage and magnanimity, in a manner seeks opposition.

Spumantemque dari pecora inter inertia votis
Optat aprum, aut fulvum descendere monte leonem.

[And, among the tamer beasts, [he] longs to be granted, in answer to his prayers,
a slavering boar, or to have a tawny lion come down from the mountain.]

Whatever supports and fills the passions is agreeable to us; as on the contrary, what weakens and infeebles them is uneasy. As opposition has the first effect, and facility the second, no wonder the mind, in certain dispositions, desires the former, and is averse to the latter.

These principles have an effect on the imagination as well as on the passions. To be convinced of this we need only consider the influence of heights and depths on that faculty. Any great elevation of place communicates a kind of pride or sublimity of imagination, and gives a fancyed superiority over those that lie below; and, vice versa, a sublime and strong imagination conveys the idea of ascent and elevation. Hence it proceeds, that we associate, in a manner, the idea of whatever is good with that of height, and evil with lowness. Heaven is supposed to be above, and hell below. A noble genius is called an elevate and sublime one. ATQUE UDAM SPERNIT HUMUM FUGIENTE PENNA. [Spurns the dank soil in winged flight.] On the contrary, a vulgar and trivial conception is stiled indifferently low or mean. Prosperity is denominated ascent, and adversity descent. Kings and princes are supposed to be placed at the top of human affairs; as peasants and day-labourers are said to be in the lowest stations. These methods of thinking, and of expressing ourselves, are not of so little consequence as they may appear at first sight.

It is evident to common sense, as well as philosophy, that there is no natural nor essential difference betwixt high and low, and that this distinction arises only from the gravitation of matter, which produces a motion from the one to the other. The very same direction, which in this part of the globe is called ascent, is denominated descent in our antipodes; which can proceed from nothing but the contrary tendency of bodies. Now it is certain, that the tendency of bodies, continually operating upon our senses, must produce, from custom, a like tendency in the fancy, and that when we consider any object situated in an ascent, the idea of its weight gives us a propensity to transport it from the place, in which it is situated, to the place immediately below it, and so on, until we come to the ground, which equally stops the body and our imagination. For a like reason we feel a difficulty in mounting, and pass not without a kind of reluctance from the inferior to that which is situated above it; as if our ideas acquired a kind of gravity from their objects. As a proof of this, do we not find, that the facility, which is so much studyed in music and poetry, is called the fail or cadency of the harmony or period; the idea of facility communicating to us that of descent, in the same manner as descent produces a facility?

Since the imagination, therefore, in running from low to high, finds an opposition in its internal qualities and principles, and since the soul, when elevated with joy and courage, in a manner seeks opposition, and throws itself with alacrity into any scene of thought or action, where its courage meets with matter to nourish and employ it; it follows, that everything, which invigorates and inlivens the soul, whether by touching the passions or imagination naturally conveys to the fancy this inclination for ascent, and determines it to run against the natural stream of its thoughts and conceptions. This aspiring progress of the imagination suits the present disposition of the mind; and the difficulty, instead of extinguishing its vigour and alacrity, has the contrary affect, of sustaining and encreasing it. Virtue, genius, power, and riches are for this reason associated with height and sublimity; as poverty, slavery, and folly are conjoined with descent and lowness. Were the case the same with us as Milton represents it to be with the angels, to whom descent is adverse, and who cannot sink without labour and compulsion, this order of things would be entirely inverted; as appears hence, that the very nature of ascent and descent is derived from the difficulty and propensity, and consequently every one of their effects proceeds from that origin.

All this is easily applied to the present question, why a considerable distance in time produces a greater veneration for the distant objects than a like removal in space. The imagination moves with more difficulty in passing from one portion of time to another, than in a transition through the parts of space; and that because space or extension appears united to our senses, while time or succession is always broken and divided. This difficulty, when joined with a small distance, interrupts and weakens the fancy: But has a contrary effect in a great removal. The mind, elevated by the vastness of its object, is still farther elevated by the difficulty of the conception; and being obliged every moment to renew its efforts in the transition from one part of time to another, feels a more vigorous and sublime disposition, than in a transition through the parts of space, where the ideas flow along with easiness and facility. In this disposition, the imagination, passing, as is usual, from the consideration of the distance to the view of the distant objects, gives us a proportionable veneration for it; and this is the reason why all the relicts of antiquity are so precious in our eyes, and appear more valuable than what is brought even from the remotest parts of the world.

The third phænomenon I have remarked will be a full confirmation of this. It is not every removal in time, which has the effect of producing veneration and esteem. We are not apt to imagine our posterity will excel us, or equal our ancestors. This phænomenon is the more remarkable, because any distance in futurity weakens not our ideas so much as an equal removal in the past. Though a removal in the past, when very great, encreases our passions beyond a like removal in the future, yet a small removal has a greater influence in diminishing them.

In our common way of thinking we are placed in a kind of middle station betwixt the past and future; and as our imagination finds a kind of difficulty in running along the former, and a facility in following the course of the latter, the difficulty conveys the notion of ascent, and the facility of the contrary. Hence we imagine our ancestors to be, in a manner, mounted above us, and our posterity to lie below us. Our fancy arrives not at the one without effort, but easily reaches the other: Which effort weakens the conception, where the distance is small; but enlarges and elevates the imagination, when attended with a suitable object. As on the other hand, the facility assists the fancy in a small removal, but takes off from its force when it contemplates any considerable distance.

It may not be improper, before we leave this subject of the will, to resume, in a few words, all that has been said concerning it, in order to set the whole more distinctly before the eyes of the reader. What we commonly understand by passion is a violent and sensible emotion of mind, when any good or evil is presented, or any object, which, by the original formation of our faculties, is fitted to excite an appetite. By reason we mean affections of the very same kind with the former; but such as operate more calmly, and cause no disorder in the temper: Which tranquillity leads us into a mistake concerning them, and causes us to regard them as conclusions only of our intellectual faculties. Both the causes and effects of these violent and calm passions are pretty variable, and depend, in a great measure, on the peculiar temper and disposition of every individual. Generally speaking, the violent passions have a more powerful influence on the will; though it is often found, that the calm ones, when corroborated by reflection, and seconded by resolution, are able to controul them in their most furious movements. What makes this whole affair more uncertain, is, that a calm passion may easily be changed into a violent one, either by a change of temper, or of the circumstances and situation of the object, as by the borrowing of force from any attendant passion, by custom, or by exciting the imagination. Upon the whole, this struggle of passion and of reason, as it is called, diversifies human life, and makes men so different not only from each other, but also from themselves in different times. Philosophy can only account for a few of the greater and more sensible events of this war; but must leave all the smaller and more delicate revolutions, as dependent on principles too fine and minute for her comprehension.

SECTION IX

Of the Direct Passions

It is easy to observe, that the passions, both direct and indirect, are founded on pain and pleasure, and that in order to produce an affection of any kind, it is only requisite to present some good or evil. Upon the removal of pain and pleasure there immediately follows a removal of love and hatred, pride and humility, desire and aversion, and of most of our reflective or secondary impressions.

The impressions, which arise from good and evil most naturally, and with the least preparation are the direct passions of desire and aversion, grief and joy, hope and fear, along with volition. The mind by an original instinct tends to unite itself with the good, and to avoid the evil, though they be conceived merely in idea, and be considered as to exist in any future period of time.

But supposing that there is an immediate impression of pain or pleasure, and that arising from an object related to ourselves or others, this does not prevent the propensity or aversion, with the consequent emotions, but by concurring with certain dormant principles of the human mind, excites the new impressions of pride or humility, love or hatred. That propensity, which unites us to the object, or separates us from it, still continues to operate, but in conjunction with the indirect passions, which arise from a double relation of impressions and ideas.

These indirect passions, being always agreeable or uneasy, give in their turn additional force to the direct passions, and encrease our desire and aversion to the object. Thus a suit of fine cloaths produces pleasure from their beauty; and this pleasure produces the direct passions, or the impressions of volition and desire. Again, when these cloaths are considered as belonging to ourself, the double relation conveys to us the sentiment of pride, which is an indirect passion; and the pleasure, which attends that passion, returns back to the direct affections, and gives new force to our desire or volition, joy or hope.

When good is certain or probable, it produces joy. When evil is in the same situation there arises GRIEF or SORROW.

When either good or evil is uncertain, it gives rise to FEAR or HOPE, according to the degrees of uncertainty on the one side or the other.

DESIRE arises from good considered simply, and AVERSION is derived from evil. The WILL exerts itself, when either the good or the absence of the evil may be attained by any action of the mind or body.

Beside good and evil, or in other words, pain and pleasure, the direct passions frequently arise from a natural impulse or instinct, which is perfectly unaccountable. Of this kind is the desire of punishment to our enemies, and of happiness to our friends; hunger, lust, and a few other bodily appetites. These passions, properly speaking, produce good and evil, and proceed not from them, like the other affections.

None of the direct affections seem to merit our particular attention, except hope and fear, which we shall here endeavour to account for. It is evident that the very same event, which by its certainty would produce grief or joy, gives always rise to fear or hope, when only probable and uncertain. In order, therefore, to understand the reason why this circumstance makes such a considerable difference, we must reflect on what I have already advanced in the preceding book concerning the nature of probability.

Probability arises from an opposition of contrary chances or causes, by which the mind is not allowed to fix on either side, but is incessantly tost from one to another, and at one moment is determined to consider an object as existent, and at another moment as the contrary. The imagination or understanding, call it which you please, fluctuates betwixt the opposite views; and though perhaps it may be oftener turned to the one side than the other, it is impossible for it, by reason of the opposition of causes or chances, to rest on either. The pro and con of the question alternately prevail; and the mind, surveying the object in its opposite principles, finds such a contrariety as utterly destroys all certainty and established opinion.

Suppose, then, that the object, concerning whose reality we are doubtful, is an object either of desire or aversion, it is evident, that, according as the mind turns itself either to the one side or the other, it must feel a momentary impression of joy or sorrow. An object, whose existence we desire, gives satisfaction, when we reflect on those causes, which produce it; and for the same reason excites grief or uneasiness from the opposite consideration: So that as the understanding, in all probable questions, is divided betwixt the contrary points of view, the affections must in the same manner be divided betwixt opposite emotions.

Now if we consider the human mind, we shall find, that with regard to the passions, it is not the nature of a wind-instrument of music, which in running over all the notes immediately loses the sound after the breath ceases; but rather resembles a string-instrument, where after each stroke the vibrations still retain some sound, which gradually and insensibly decays. The imagination is extreme quick and agile; but the passions are slow and restive: For which reason, when any object is presented, that affords a variety of views to the one, and emotions to the other; though the fancy may change its views with great celerity; each stroke will not produce a clear and distinct note of passion, but the one passion will always be mixt and confounded with the other. According as the probability inclines to good or evil, the passion of joy or sorrow predominates in the composition: Because the nature of probability is to cast a superior number of views or chances on one side; or, which is the same thing, a superior number of returns of one passion; or since the dispersed passions are collected into one, a superior degree of that passion. That is, in other words, the grief and joy being intermingled with each other, by means of the contrary views of the imagination, produce by their union the passions of hope and fear.

Upon this head there may be started a very curious question concerning that contrariety of passions, which is our present subject. It is observable, that where the objects of contrary passions are presented at once, beside the encrease of the predominant passion (which has been already explained, and commonly arises at their first shock or rencounter) it sometimes happens, that both the passions exist successively, and by short intervals; sometimes, that they destroy each other, and neither of them takes place; and sometimes that both of them remain united in the mind. It may, therefore, be asked, by what theory we can explain these variations, and to what general principle we can reduce them.

When the contrary passions arise from objects entirely different, they take place alternately, the want of relation in the ideas separating the impressions from each other, and preventing their opposition. Thus when a man is afflicted for the loss of a law-suit, and joyful for the birth of a son, the mind running from the agreeable to the calamitous object, with whatever celerity it may perform this motion, can scarcely temper the one affection with the other, and remain betwixt them in a state of indifference.

It more easily attains that calm situation, when the same event is of a mixt nature, and contains something adverse and something prosperous in its different circumstances. For in that case, both the passions, mingling with each other by means of the relation, become mutually destructive, and leave the mind in perfect tranquility.

But suppose, in the third place, that the object is not a compound of good or evil, but is considered as probable or improbable in any degree; in that case I assert, that the contrary passions will both of them be present at once in the soul, and instead of destroying and tempering each other, will subsist together, and produce a third impression or affection by their union. Contrary passions are not capable of destroying each other, except when their contrary movements exactly rencounter, and are opposite in their direction, as well as in the sensation they produce. This exact rencounter depends upon the relations of those ideas, from which they are derived, and is more or less perfect, according to the degrees of the relation. In the case of probability the contrary chances are so far related, that they determine concerning the existence or non-existence of the same object. But this relation is far from being perfect; since some of the chances lie on the side of existence, and others on that of non-existence; which are objects altogether incompatible. It is impossible by one steady view to survey the opposite chances, and the events dependent on them; but it is necessary, that the imagination should run alternately from the one to the other. Each view of the imagination produces its peculiar passion, which decays away by degrees, and is followed by a sensible vibration after the stroke. The incompatibility of the views keeps the passions from shocking in a direct line, if that expression may be allowed; and yet their relation is sufficient to mingle their fainter emotions. It is after this manner that hope and fear arise from the different mixture of these opposite passions of grief and joy, and from their imperfect union and conjunction.

Upon the whole, contrary passions succeed each other alternately, when they arise from different objects: They mutually destroy each other, when they proceed from different parts of the same: And they subsist both of them and mingle together, when they are derived from the contrary and incompatible chances or possibilities, on which any one object depends. The influence of the relations of ideas is plainly seen in this whole affair. If the objects of the contrary passions be totally different, the passions are like two opposite liquors in different bottles, which have no influence on each other. If the objects be intimately connected, the passions are like an alcali and an acid, which, being mingled, destroy each other. If the relation be more imperfect, and consists in the contradictory views of the same object, the passions are like oil and vinegar, which, however mingled, never perfectly unite and incorporate.

As the hypothesis concerning hope and fear carries its own evidence along with it, we shall be the more concise in our proofs. A few strong arguments are better than many weak ones.

The passions of fear and hope may arise when the chances are equal on both sides, and no superiority can be discovered in the one above the other. Nay, in this situation the passions are rather the strongest, as the mind has then the least foundation to rest upon, and is tossed with the greatest uncertainty. Throw in a superior degree of probability to the side of grief, you immediately see that passion diffuse itself over the composition, and tincture it into fear. Encrease the probability, and by that means the grief, the fear prevails still more and more, till at last it runs insensibly, as the joy continually diminishes, into pure grief. After you have brought it to this situation, diminish the grief, after the same manner that you encreased it; by diminishing the probability on that side, and you'll see the passion clear every moment, until it changes insensibly into hope; which again runs, after the same manner, by slow degrees, into joy, as you encrease that part of the composition by the encrease of the probability. Are not these as plain proofs, that the passions of fear and hope are mixtures of grief and joy, as in optics it is a proof, that a coloured ray of the sun passing through a prism, is a composition of two others, when, as you diminish or encrease the quantity of either, you find it prevail proportionably more or less in the composition? I am sure neither natural nor moral philosophy admits of stronger proofs.

Probability is of two kinds, either when the object is really in itself uncertain, and to be determined by chance; or when, though the object be already certain, yet it is uncertain to our judgment, which finds a number of proofs on each side of the question. Both these kinds of probabilities cause fear and hope; which can only proceed from that property, in which they agree, viz, the uncertainty and fluctuation they bestow on the imagination by that contrariety of views, which is common to both.

It is a probable good or evil, that commonly produces hope or fear; because probability, being a wavering and unconstant method of surveying an object, causes naturally a like mixture and uncertainty of passion. But we may observe, that wherever from other causes this mixture can be produced, the passions of fear and hope will arise, even though there be no probability; which must be allowed to be a convincing proof of the present hypothesis. We find that an evil, barely conceived as possible, does sometimes produce fear; especially if the evil be very great. A man cannot think of excessive pains and tortures without trembling, if he be in the least danger of suffering them. The smallness of the probability is compensated by the greatness of the evil; and the sensation is equally lively, as if the evil were more probable. One view or glimpse of the former, has the same effect as several of the latter.

But they are not only possible evils, that cause fear, but even some allowed to be impossible; as when we tremble on the brink of a precipice, though we know ourselves to be in perfect security, and have it in our choice whether we will advance a step farther. This proceeds from the immediate presence of the evil, which influences the imagination in the same manner as the certainty of it would do; but being encountered by the reflection on our security, is immediately retracted, and causes the same kind of passion, as when from a contrariety of chances contrary passions are produced.

Evils, that are certain, have sometimes the same effect in producing fear, as the possible or impossible. Thus a man in a strong prison well-guarded, without the least means of escape, trembles at the thought of the rack, to which he is sentenced.

This happens only when the certain evil is terrible and confounding; in which case the mind continually rejects it with horror, while it continually presses in upon the thought. The evil is there fixed and established, but the mind cannot endure to fix upon it; from which fluctuation and uncertainty there arises a passion of much the same appearance with fear.

But it is not only where good or evil is uncertain, as to its existence, but also as to its kind, that fear or hope arises. Let one be told by a person, whose veracity he cannot doubt of, that one of his sons is suddenly killed, it is evident the passion this event would occasion, would not settle into pure grief, till he got certain information, which of his sons he had lost. Here there is an evil certain, but the kind of it uncertain. Consequently the fear we feel on this occasion is without the least mixture of joy, and arises merely from the fluctuation of the fancy betwixt its objects. And though each side of the question produces here the same passion, yet that passion cannot settle, but receives from the imagination a tremulous and unsteady motion, resembling in its cause, as well as in its sensation, the mixture and contention of grief and joy.

From these principles we may account for a phænomenon in the passions, which at first sight seems very extraordinary, viz, that surprize is apt to change into fear, and every thing that is unexpected affrights us. The most obvious conclusion from this is, that human nature is in general pusillanimous; since upon the sudden appearance of any object. we immediately conclude it to be an evil, and without waiting till we can examine its nature, whether it be good or bad, are at first affected with fear. This I say is the most obvious conclusion; but upon farther examination we shall find that the phænomenon is otherwise to be accounted for. The suddenness and strangeness of an appearance naturally excite a commotion in the mind, like every thing for which we are not prepared, and to which we are not accustomed. This commotion, again, naturally produces a curiosity or inquisitiveness, which being very violent, from the strong and sudden impulse of the object, becomes uneasy, and resembles in its fluctuation and uncertainty, the sensation of fear or the mixed passions of grief and joy. This image of fear naturally converts into the thing itself, and gives us a real apprehension of evil, as the mind always forms its judgments more from its present disposition than from the nature of its objects.

Thus all kinds of uncertainty have a strong connexion with fear, even though they do not cause any opposition of passions by the opposite views and considerations they present to us. A person, who has left his friend in any malady, will feel more anxiety upon his account, than if he were present, though perhaps he is not only incapable of giving him assistance, but likewise of judging of the event of his sickness. In this case, though the principal object of the passion, viz, the life or death of his friend, be to him equally uncertain when present as when absent; yet there are a thousand little circumstances of his friend's situation and condition, the knowledge of which fixes the idea, and prevents that fluctuation and uncertainty so near allyed to fear. Uncertainty is, indeed, in one respect as near allyed to hope as to fear, since it makes an essential part in the composition of the former passion; but the reason, why it inclines not to that side, is, that uncertainty alone is uneasy, and has a relation of impressions to the uneasy passions.

It is thus our uncertainty concerning any minute circumstance relating to a person encreases our apprehensions of his death or misfortune. Horace has remarked this phænomenon.

Ut assidens implumibus pullis avis
Serpentium allapsus timet,
Magis relictis; non, ut adsit, auxilî
Latura plus præsentibus.

[As a bird, watching over her fledgelings, is more afraid of their being attacked by snakes if she were to leave them even though, were she to stay, she would not be any more capable of helping them, when they were with her.]

But this principle of the connexion of fear with uncertainty I carry farther, and observe that any doubt produces that passion, even though it presents nothing to us on any side but what is good and desireable. A virgin, on her bridalnight goes to bed full of fears and apprehensions, though she expects nothing but pleasure of the highest kind, and what she has long wished for. The newness and greatness of the event, the confusion of wishes and joys so embarrass the mind, that it knows not on what passion to fix itself; from whence arises a fluttering or unsettledness of the spirits which being, in some degree, uneasy, very naturally degenerates into fear.

Thus we still find, that whatever causes any fluctuation or mixture of passions, with any degree of uneasiness, always produces fear, or at least a passion so like it, that they are scarcely to be distinguished.

I have here confined myself to the examination of hope and fear in their most simple and natural situation, without considering all the variations they may receive from the mixture of different views and reflections. Terror, consternation, astonishment, anxiety, and other passions of that kind, are nothing but different species and degrees of fear. It is easy to imagine how a different situation of the object, or a different turn of thought, may change even the sensation of a passion; and this may in general account for all the particular sub-divisions of the other affections, as well as of fear. Love may shew itself in the shape of tenderness, friendship, intimacy, esteem, good-will, and in many other appearances; which at the bottom are the same affections; and arise from the same causes, though with a small variation, which it is not necessary to give any particular account of. It is for this reason I have all along confined myself to the principal passion.

The same care of avoiding prolixity is the reason why I wave the examination of the will and direct passions, as they appear in animals; since nothing is more evident, than that they are of the same nature, and excited by the same causes as in human creatures. I leave this to the reader's own observation; desiring him at the same time to consider the additional force this bestows on the present system.

SECTION X

Of Curiosity, or the Love of Truth

But methinks we have been not a little inattentive to run over so many different parts of the human mind, and examine so many passions, without taking once into the consideration that love of truth, which was the first source of all our enquiries. Twill therefore be proper, before we leave this subject, to bestow a few reflections on that passion, and shew its origin in human nature. It is an affection of so peculiar a kind, that it would have been impossible to have treated of it under any of those heads, which we have examined, without danger of obscurity and confusion.

Truth is of two kinds, consisting either in the discovery of the proportions of ideas, considered as such, or in the conformity of our ideas of objects to their real existence. It is certain, that the former species of truth, is not desired merely as truth, and that it is not the justness of our conclusions, which alone gives the pleasure. For these conclusions are equally just, when we discover the equality of two bodies by a pair of compasses, as when we learn it by a mathematical demonstration; and though in the one case the proofs be demonstrative, and in the other only sensible, yet generally speaking, the mind acquiesces with equal assurance in the one as in the other. And in an arithmetical operation, where both the truth and the assurance are of the same nature, as in the most profound algebraical problem, the pleasure is very inconsiderable, if rather it does not degenerate into pain: Which is an evident proof, that the satisfaction, which we sometimes receive from the discovery of truth, proceeds not from it, merely as such, but only as endowed with certain qualities.

The first and most considerable circumstance requisite to render truth agreeable, is the genius and capacity, which is employed in its invention and discovery. What is easy and obvious is never valued; and even what is in itself difficult, if we come to the knowledge of it without difficulty, and without any stretch of thought or judgment, is but little regarded. We love to trace the demonstrations of mathematicians; but should receive small entertainment from a person, who should barely inform us of the proportions of lines and angles, though we reposed the utmost confidence both in his judgment and veracity. In this case it is sufficient to have ears to learn the truth. We never are obliged to fix our attention or exert our genius; which of all other exercises of the mind is the most pleasant and agreeable.

But though the exercise of genius be the principal source of that satisfaction we receive from the sciences, yet I doubt, if it be alone sufficient to give us any considerable enjoyment. The truth we discover must also be of some importance. It is easy to multiply algebraical problems to infinity, nor is there any end in the discovery of the proportions of conic sections; though few mathematicians take any pleasure in these researches, but turn their thoughts to what is more useful and important. Now the question is, after what manner this utility and importance operate upon us? The difficulty on this head arises from hence, that many philosophers have consumed their time, have destroyed their health, and neglected their fortune, in the search of such truths, as they esteemed important and useful to the world, though it appeared from their whole conduct and behaviour, that they were not endowed with any share of public spirit, nor had any concern for the interests of mankind. Were they convinced, that their discoveries were of no consequence, they would entirely lose all relish for their studies, and that though the consequences be entirely indifferent to them; which seems to be a contradiction.

To remove this contradiction, we must consider, that there are certain desires and inclinations, which go no farther than the imagination, and are rather the faint shadows and images of passions, than any real affections. Thus, suppose a man, who takes a survey of the fortifications of any city; considers their strength and advantages, natural or acquired; observes the disposition and contrivance of the bastions, ramparts, mines, and other military works; it is plain, that in proportion as all these are fitted to attain their ends he will receive a suitable pleasure and satisfaction. This pleasure, as it arises from the utility, not the form of the objects, can be no other than a sympathy with the inhabitants, for whose security all this art is employed; though it is possible, that this person, as a stranger or an enemy, may in his heart have no kindness for them, or may even entertain a hatred against them.

It may indeed be objected, that such a remote sympathy is a very slight foundation for a passion, and that so much industry and application, as we frequently observe in philosophers, can never be derived from so inconsiderable an original. But here I return to what I have already remarked, that the pleasure of study conflicts chiefly in the action of the mind, and the exercise of the genius and understanding in the discovery or comprehension of any truth. If the importance of the truth be requisite to compleat the pleasure, it is not on account of any considerable addition, which of itself it brings to our enjoyment, but only because it is, in some measure, requisite to fix our attention. When we are careless and inattentive, the same action of the understanding has no effect upon us, nor is able to convey any of that satisfaction, which arises from it, when we are in another disposition.

But beside the action of the mind, which is the principal foundation of the pleasure, there is likewise required a degree of success in the attainment of the end, or the discovery of that truth we examine. Upon this head I shall make a general remark, which may be useful on many occasions, viz, that where the mind pursues any end with passion; though that passion be not derived originally from the end, but merely from the action and pursuit; yet by the natural course of the affections, we acquire a concern for the end itself, and are uneasy under any disappointment we meet with in the pursuit of it. This proceeds from the relation and parallel direction of the passions above-mentioned.

To illustrate all this by a similar instance, I shall observe, that there cannot be two passions more nearly resembling each other, than those of hunting and philosophy, whatever disproportion may at first sight appear betwixt them. It is evident, that the pleasure of hunting conflicts in the action of the mind and body; the motion, the attention, the difficulty, and the uncertainty. It is evident likewise, that these actions must be attended with an idea of utility, in order to their having any effect upon us. A man of the greatest fortune, and the farthest removed from avarice, though he takes a pleasure in hunting after patridges and pheasants, feels no satisfaction in shooting crows and magpies; and that because he considers the first as fit for the table, and the other as entirely useless. Here it is certain, that the utility or importance of itself causes no real passion, but is only requisite to support the imagination; and the same person, who over-looks a ten times greater profit in any other subject, is pleased to bring home half a dozen woodcocks or plovers, after having employed several hours in hunting after them. To make the parallel betwixt hunting and philosophy more compleat, we may observe, that though in both cases the end of our action may in itself be despised, yet in the heat of the action we acquire such an attention to this end, that we are very uneasy under any disappointments, and are sorry when we either miss our game, or fall into any error in our reasoning.

If we want another parallel to these affections, we may consider the passion of gaming, which affords a pleasure from the same principles as hunting and philosophy. It has been remarked, that the pleasure of gaming arises not from interest alone; since many leave a sure gain for this entertainment: Neither is it derived from the game alone; since the same persons have no satisfaction, when they play for nothing: But proceeds from both these causes united, though separately they have no effect. It is here, as in certain chymical preparations, where the mixture of two clear and transparent liquids produces a third, which is opaque and coloured..

The interest, which we have in any game, engages our attention, without which we can have no enjoyment, either in that or in any other action. Our attention being once engaged, the difficulty, variety, and sudden reverses of fortune, still farther interest us; and it is from that concern our satisfaction arises. Human life is so tiresome a scene, and men generally are of such indolent dispositions, that whatever amuses them, though by a passion mixt with pain, does in the main give them a sensible pleasure. And this pleasure is here encreased by the nature of the objects, which being sensible, and of a narrow compass, are entered into with facility, and are agreeable to the imagination.

The same theory, that accounts for the love of truth in mathematics and algebra may be extended to morals, politics, natural philosophy, and other studies, where we consider not the other abstract relations of ideas, but their real connexions and existence. But beside the love of knowledge, which displays itself in the sciences, there is a certain curiosity implanted in human nature, which is a passion derived from a quite different principle. Some people have an insatiable desire of knowing the actions and circumstances of their neighbours, though their interest be no way concerned in them, and they must entirely depend on others for their information;

in which case there is no room for study or application. Let us search for the reason of this phænomenon.

It has been proved at large, that the influence of belief is at once to inliven and infix any idea in the imagination, and prevent all kind of hesitation and uncertainty about it. Both these circumstances are advantageous. By the vivacity of the idea we interest the fancy, and produce, though in a lesser degree, the same pleasure, which arises from a moderate passion. As the vivacity of the idea gives pleasure, so its certainty prevents uneasiness, by fixing one particular idea in the mind, and keeping it from wavering in the choice of its objects. It is a quality of human nature, which is conspicuous on many occasions, and is common both to the mind and body, that too sudden and violent a change is unpleasant to us, and that however any objects may in themselves be indifferent, yet their alteration gives uneasiness. As it is the nature of doubt to cause a variation in the thought, and transport us suddenly from one idea to another, it must of consequence be the occasion of pain. This pain chiefly takes place, where interest, relation, or the greatness and novelty of any event interests us in it. It is not every matter of fact, of which we have a curiosity to be informed; neither are they such only as we have an interest to know. It is sufficient if the idea strikes on us with such force, and concerns us so nearly, as to give us an uneasiness in its instability and inconstancy. A stranger, when he arrives first at any town, may be entirely indifferent about knowing the history and adventures of the inhabitants; but as he becomes farther acquainted with them, and has lived any considerable time among them, he acquires the same curiosity as the natives. When we are reading the history of a nation, we may have an ardent desire of clearing up any doubt or difficulty, that occurs in it; but become careless in such researches, when the ideas of these events are, in a great measure, obliterated.

BOOK III

OF MORALS

PART I

Of Virtue and Vice in General

SECTION I

Moral Distinctions not Derived from Reason

There is an inconvenience which attends all abstruse reasoning that it may silence, without convincing an antagonist, and requires the same intense study to make us sensible of its force, that was at first requisite for its invention. When we leave our closet, and engage in the common affairs of life, its conclusions seem to vanish, like the phantoms of the night on the appearance of the morning; and it is difficult for us to retain even that conviction, which we had attained with difficulty. This is still more conspicuous in a long chain of reasoning, where we must preserve to the end the evidence of the first propositions, and where we often lose sight of all the most received maxims, either of philosophy or common life. I am not, however, without hopes, that the present system of philosophy will acquire new force as it advances; and that our reasonings concerning morals will corroborate whatever has been said concerning the UNDERSTANDING and the PASSIONS. Morality is a subject that interests us above all others: We fancy the peace of society to be at stake in every decision concerning it; and it is evident, that this concern must make our speculations appear more real and solid, than where the subject is, in a great measure, indifferent to us. What affects us, we conclude can never be a chimera; and as our passion is engaged on the one side or the other, we naturally think that the question lies within human comprehension; which, in other cases of this nature, we are apt to entertain some doubt of. Without this advantage I never should have ventured upon a third volume of such abstruse philosophy, in an age, wherein the greatest part of men seem agreed to convert reading into an amusement, and to reject every thing that requires any considerable degree of attention to be comprehended.

It has been observed, that nothing is ever present to the mind but its perceptions; and that all the actions of seeing, hearing, judging, loving, hating, and thinking, fall under this denomination. The mind can never exert itself in any action, which we may not comprehend under the term of perception; and consequently that term is no less applicable to those judgments, by which we distinguish moral good and evil, than to every other operation of the mind. To approve of one character, to condemn another, are only so many different perceptions.

Now as perceptions resolve themselves into two kinds, viz. impressions and ideas, this distinction gives rise to a question, with which we shall open up our present enquiry concerning morals. WHETHER IT IS BY MEANS OF OUR

IDEAS OR IMPRESSIONS WE DISTINGUISH BETWIXT VICE AND VIRTUE, AND PRONOUNCE AN ACTION BLAMEABLE OR PRAISEWORTHY? This will immediately cut off all loose discourses and declamations, and reduce us to something precise and exact on the present subject.

Those who affirm that virtue is nothing but a conformity to reason; that there are eternal fitnesses and unfitnesses of things, which are the same to every rational being that considers them; that the immutable measures of right and wrong impose an obligation, not only on human creatures, but also on the Deity himself: All these systems concur in the opinion, that morality, like truth, is discerned merely by ideas, and by their juxta-position and comparison. In order, therefore, to judge of these systems, we need only consider, whether it be possible, from reason alone, to distinguish betwixt moral good and evil, or whether there must concur some other principles to enable us to make that distinction.

If morality had naturally no influence on human passions and actions, it were in vain to take such pains to inculcate it; and nothing would be more fruitless than that multitude of rules and precepts, with which all moralists abound. Philosophy is commonly divided into speculative and practical; and as morality is always comprehended under the latter division, it is supposed to influence our passions and actions, and to go beyond the calm and indolent judgments of the understanding. And this is confirmed by common experience, which informs us, that men are often governed by their duties, and are detered from some actions by the opinion of injustice, and impelled to others by that of obligation.

Since morals, therefore, have an influence on the actions and affections, it follows, that they cannot be derived from reason; and that because reason alone, as we have already proved, can never have any such influence. Morals excite passions, and produce or prevent actions. Reason of itself is utterly impotent in this particular. The rules of morality therefore, are not conclusions of our reason.

No one, I believe, will deny the justness of this inference; nor is there any other means of evading it, than by denying that principle, on which it is founded. As long as it is allowed, that reason has no influence on our passions and action, it is in vain to pretend, that morality is discovered only by a deduction of reason. An active principle can never be founded on an inactive; and if reason be inactive in itself, it must remain so in all its shapes and appearances, whether it exerts itself in natural or moral subjects, whether it considers the powers of external bodies, or the actions of rational beings.

It would be tedious to repeat all the arguments, by which I have proved,[65] that reason is perfectly inert, and can never either prevent or produce any action or affection, it will be easy to recollect what has been said upon that subject. I shall only recall on this occasion one of these arguments, which I shall endeavour to render still more conclusive, and more applicable to the present subject.

---

[65] Book II. Part III. Sect 3.

Reason is the discovery of truth or falshood. Truth or falshood consists in an agreement or disagreement either to the real relations of ideas, or to real existence and matter of fact. Whatever, therefore, is not susceptible of this agreement or disagreement, is incapable of being true or false, and can never be an object of our reason. Now it is evident our passions, volitions, and actions, are not susceptible of any such agreement or disagreement; being original facts and realities, compleat in themselves, and implying no reference to other passions, volitions, and actions. It is impossible, therefore, they can be pronounced either true or false, and be either contrary or conformable to reason.

This argument is of double advantage to our present purpose. For it proves DIRECTLY, that actions do not derive their merit from a conformity to reason, nor their blame from a contrariety to it; and it proves the same truth more INDIRECTLY, by shewing us, that as reason can never immediately prevent or produce any action by contradicting or approving of it, it cannot be the source of moral good and evil, which are found to have that influence. Actions may be laudable or blameable; but they cannot be reasonable: Laudable or blameable, therefore, are not the same with reasonable or unreasonable. The merit and demerit of actions frequently contradict, and sometimes controul our natural propensities. But reason has no such influence. Moral distinctions, therefore, are not the offspring of reason. Reason is wholly inactive, and can never be the source of so active a principle as conscience, or a sense of morals.

But perhaps it may be said, that though no will or action can be immediately contradictory to reason, yet we may find such a contradiction in some of the attendants of the action, that is, in its causes or effects. The action may cause a judgment, or may be obliquely caused by one, when the judgment concurs with a passion; and by an abusive way of speaking, which philosophy will scarce allow of, the same contrariety may, upon that account, be ascribed to the action. How far this truth or falsehood may be the source of morals, it will now be proper to consider.

It has been observed, that reason, in a strict and philosophical sense, can have influence on our conduct only after two ways: Either when it excites a passion by informing us of the existence of something which is a proper object of it; or when it discovers the connexion of causes and effects, so as to afford us means of exerting any passion. These are the only kinds of judgment, which can accompany our actions, or can be said to produce them in any manner; and it must be allowed, that these judgments may often be false and erroneous. A person may be affected with passion, by supposing a pain or pleasure to lie in an object, which has no tendency to produce either of these sensations, or which produces the contrary to what is imagined. A person may also take false measures for the attaining his end, and may retard, by his foolish conduct, instead of forwarding the execution of any project. These false judgments may be thought to affect the passions and actions, which are connected with them, and may be said to render them unreasonable, in a figurative and improper way of speaking. But though this be acknowledged, it is easy to observe, that these errors are so far from being the source of all immorality, that they are commonly very innocent, and draw no manner of guilt upon the person who is so unfortunate as to fail into them. They extend not beyond a mistake of fact, which moralists have not generally supposed criminal, as being perfectly involuntary. I am more to be lamented than blamed, if I am mistaken with regard to the influence of objects in producing pain or pleasure, or if I know not the proper means of satisfying my desires. No one can ever regard such errors as a defect in my moral character. A fruit, for instance, that is really disagreeable, appears to me at a distance, and through mistake I fancy it to be pleasant and delicious. Here is one error. I choose certain means of reaching this fruit, which are not proper for my end. Here is a second error; nor is there any third one, which can ever possibly enter into our reasonings concerning actions. I ask, therefore, if a man, in this situation, and guilty of these two errors, is to be regarded as vicious and criminal, however unavoidable they might have been? Or if it be possible to imagine, that such errors are the sources of all immorality?

And here it may be proper to observe, that if moral distinctions be derived from the truth or falshood of those judgments, they must take place wherever we form the judgments; nor will there be any difference, whether the question be concerning an apple or a kingdom, or whether the error be avoidable or unavoidable. For as the very essence of morality is supposed to consist in an agreement or disagreement to reason, the other circumstances are entirely arbitrary, and can never either bestow on any action the character of virtuous or vicious, or deprive it of that character. To which we may add, that this agreement or disagreement, not admitting of degrees, all virtues and vices would of course be equal.

Should it be pretended, that though a mistake of fact be not criminal, yet a mistake of right often is; and that this may be the source of immorality: I would answer, that it is impossible such a mistake can ever be the original source of immorality, since it supposes a real right and wrong; that is, a real distinction in morals, independent of these judgments. A mistake, therefore, of right may become a species of immorality; but it is only a secondary one, and is founded on some other, antecedent to it.

As to those judgments which are the effects of our actions, and which, when false, give occasion to pronounce the actions contrary to truth and reason; we may observe, that our actions never cause any judgment, either true or false, in ourselves, and that it is only on others they have such an influence. It is certain, that an action, on many occasions, may give rise to false conclusions in others; and that a person, who through a window sees any lewd behaviour of mine with my neighbour's wife, may be so simple as to imagine she is certainly my own. In this respect my action resembles somewhat a lye or falshood; only with this difference, which is material, that I perform not the action with any intention of giving rise to a false judgment in another, but merely to satisfy my lust and passion. It causes, however, a mistake and false judgment by accident; and the falshood of its effects may be ascribed, by some odd figurative way of speaking, to the action itself. But still I can see no pretext of reason for asserting, that the tendency to cause such an error is the first spring or original source of all immorality.[66]

---

[66] One might think it were entirely superfluous to prove this, if a late author [William Wollaston, THE RELIGION OF NATURE DELINEATED (London 1722)], who has had the good fortune to obtain some reputation, had not seriously affirmed, that such a falshood is the foundation of all guilt and moral deformity. That we may discover the fallacy of his hypothesis, we need only consider, that a false conclusion is drawn from an action, only by means of an obscurity of natural principles, which makes a cause be secretly interrupted in its operation, by contrary causes, and renders the connexion betwixt two objects uncertain and variable. Now, as a like uncertainty and variety of causes take place, even in natural objects, and produce a like error in our judgment, if that tendency to produce error were the very essence of vice and immorality, it should follow, that even inanimate objects might be vicious and immoral.

It is in vain to urge, that inanimate objects act without liberty and choice. For as liberty and choice are not necessary to make an action produce in us an erroneous conclusion, they can be, in no respect, essential to morality; and I do not readily perceive, upon this system, how they can ever come to be regarded by it. If the tendency to cause error be the origin of immorality, that tendency and immorality would in every case be inseparable.

Add to this, that if I had used the precaution of shutting the windows, while I indulged myself in those liberties with my neighbour's wife, I should have been guilty of no immorality; and that because my action, being perfectly concealed, would have had no tendency to produce any false conclusion.

For the same reason, a thief, who steals in by a ladder at a window, and takes all imaginable care to cause no disturbance, is in no respect criminal. For either he will not be perceived, or if he be, it is impossible he can produce any error, nor will any one, from these circumstances, take him to be other than what he really is.

It is well known, that those who are squint-sighted, do very readily cause mistakes in others, and that we imagine they salute or are talking to one person, while they address themselves to another. Are they therefore, upon that account, immoral?

Besides, we may easily observe, that in all those arguments there is an evident reasoning in a circle. A person who takes possession of another's goods, and uses them as his own, in a manner declares them to be his own; and this falshood is the source of the immorality of injustice. But is property, or right, or obligation, intelligible, without an antecedent morality?

A man that is ungrateful to his benefactor, in a manner affirms, that he never received any favours from him. But in what manner? Is it because it is his duty to be grateful? But this supposes, that there is some antecedent rule of duty and morals. Is it because human nature is generally grateful, and makes us conclude, that a man who does any harm never received any favour from the person he harmed? But human nature is not so generally grateful, as to justify such a conclusion. Or if it were, is an exception to a general rule in every case criminal, for no other reason than because it is an exception?

But what may suffice entirely to destroy this whimsical system is, that it leaves us under the same difficulty to give a reason why truth is virtuous and falshood vicious, as to account for the merit or turpitude of any other action. I shall allow, if you please, that all immorality is derived from this supposed falshood in action, provided you can give me any plausible reason, why such a falshood is immoral. If you consider rightly of the matter, you will find yourself in the same difficulty as at the beginning.

This last argument is very conclusive; because, if there be not an evident merit or turpitude annexed to this species of truth or falahood, It can never have any influence upon our actions. For, who ever thought of forbearing any action, because others might possibly draw false conclusions from it? Or, who ever performed any, that he might give rise to true conclusions?

Thus upon the whole, it is impossible, that the distinction betwixt moral good and evil, can be made to reason; since that distinction has an influence upon our actions, of which reason alone is incapable. Reason and judgment may, indeed, be the mediate cause of an action, by prompting, or by directing a passion: But it is not pretended, that a judgment of this kind, either in its truth or falshood, is attended with virtue or vice. And as to the judgments, which are caused by our judgments, they can still less bestow those moral qualities on the actions, which are their causes.

But to be more particular, and to shew, that those eternal immutable fitnesses and unfitnesses of things cannot be defended by sound philosophy, we may weigh the following considerations.

If the thought and understanding were alone capable of fixing the boundaries of right and wrong, the character of virtuous and vicious either must lie in some relations of objects, or must be a matter of fact, which is discovered by our reasoning. This consequence is evident. As the operations of human understanding divide themselves into two kinds, the comparing of ideas, and the inferring of matter of fact; were virtue discovered by the understanding; it must be an object of one of these operations, nor is there any third operation of the understanding. which can discover it. There has been an opinion very industriously propagated by certain philosophers, that morality is susceptible of demonstration; and though no one has ever been able to advance a single step in those demonstrations; yet it is taken for granted, that this science may be brought to an equal certainty with geometry or algebra. Upon this supposition vice and virtue must consist in some relations; since it is allowed on all hands, that no matter of fact is capable of being demonstrated. Let us, therefore, begin with examining this hypothesis, and endeavour, if possible, to fix those moral qualities, which have been so long the objects of our fruitless researches. Point out distinctly the relations, which constitute morality or obligation, that we may know wherein they consist, and after what manner we must judge of them.

If you assert, that vice and virtue consist in relations susceptible of certainty and demonstration, you must confine yourself to those four relations, which alone admit of that degree of evidence; and in that case you run into absurdities, from which you will never be able to extricate yourself. For as you make the very essence of morality to lie in the relations, and as there is no one of these relations but what is applicable, not only to an irrational, but also to an inanimate object; it follows, that even such objects must be susceptible of merit or demerit. RESEMBLANCE, CONTRARIETY, DEGREES IN QUALITY, and PROPORTIONS IN QUANTITY AND NUMBER; all these relations belong as properly to matter, as to our actions, passions, and volitions. It is unquestionable, therefore, that morality lies not in any of these relations, nor the sense of it in their discovery.[67]

[67] As a proof, how confused our way of thinking on this subject commonly is, we may observe, that those who assert, that morality is demonstrable, do not say, that morality lies in the relations, and

Should it be asserted, that the sense of morality consists in the discovery of some relation, distinct from these, and that our enumeration was not compleat, when we comprehended all demonstrable relations under four general heads: To this I know not what to reply, till some one be so good as to point out to me this new relation. It is impossible to refute a system, which has never yet been explained. In such a manner of fighting in the dark, a man loses his blows in the air, and often places them where the enemy is not present.

I must, therefore, on this occasion, rest contented with requiring the two following conditions of any one that would undertake to clear up this system. First, As moral good and evil belong only to the actions of the mind, and are derived from our situation with regard to external objects, the relations, from which these moral distinctions arise, must lie only betwixt internal actions, and external objects, and must not be applicable either to internal actions, compared among themselves, or to external objects, when placed in opposition to other external objects. For as morality is supposed to attend certain relations, if these relations could belong to internal actions considered singly, it would follow, that we might be guilty of crimes in ourselves, and independent of our situation, with respect to the universe: And in like manner, if these moral relations could be applied to external objects, it would follow, that even inanimate beings would be susceptible of moral beauty and deformity. Now it seems difficult to imagine, that any relation can be discovered betwixt our passions, volitions and actions, compared to external objects, which relation might not belong either to these passions and volitions, or to these external objects, compared among themselves. But it will be still more difficult to fulfil the second condition, requisite to justify this system. According to the principles of those who maintain an abstract rational difference betwixt moral good and evil, and a natural fitness and unfitness of things, it is not only supposed, that these relations, being eternal and immutable, are the same, when considered by every rational creature, but their effects are also supposed to be necessarily the same; and it is concluded they have no less, or rather a greater, influence in directing the will of the deity, than in governing the rational and virtuous of our own species. These two particulars are evidently distinct. It is one thing to know virtue, and another to conform the will to it. In order, therefore, to prove, that the measures of right and wrong are eternal laws, obligatory on every rational mind, it is not sufficient

---

that the relations are distinguishable by reason. They only say, that reason can discover such an action, in such relations, to be virtuous, and such another vicious. It seems they thought it sufficient, if they could bring the word, Relation, into the proposition, without troubling themselves whether it was to the purpose or not. But here, I think, is plain argument. Demonstrative reason discovers only relations. But that reason, according to this hypothesis, discovers also vice and virtue. These moral qualities, therefore, must be relations. When we blame any action, in any situation, the whole complicated object, of action and situation, must form certain relations, wherein the essence of vice consists. This hypothesis is not otherwise intelligible. For what does reason discover, when it pronounces any action vicious? Does it discover a relation or a matter of fact? These questions are decisive, and must not be eluded.

to shew the relations upon which they are founded: We must also point out the connexion betwixt the relation and the will; and must prove that this connexion is so necessary, that in every well-disposed mind, it must take place and have its influence; though the difference betwixt these minds be in other respects immense and infinite. Now besides what I have already proved, that even in human nature no relation can ever alone produce any action: besides this, I say, it has been shewn, in treating of the understanding, that there is no connexion of cause and effect, such as this is supposed to be, which is discoverable otherwise than by experience, and of which we can pretend to have any security by the simple consideration of the objects. All beings in the universe, considered in themselves, appear entirely loose and independent of each other. It is only by experience we learn their influence and connexion; and this influence we ought never to extend beyond experience.

Thus it will be impossible to fulfil the first condition required to the system of eternal measures of right and wrong; because it is impossible to shew those relations, upon which such a distinction may be founded: And it is as impossible to fulfil the second condition; because we cannot prove A PRIORI, that these relations, if they really existed and were perceived, would be universally forcible and obligatory.

But to make these general reflections more clear and convincing, we may illustrate them by some particular instances, wherein this character of moral good or evil is the most universally acknowledged. Of all crimes that human creatures are capable of committing, the most horrid and unnatural is ingratitude, especially when it is committed against parents, and appears in the more flagrant instances of wounds and death. This is acknowledged by all mankind, philosophers as well as the people; the question only arises among philosophers, whether the guilt or moral deformity of this action be discovered by demonstrative reasoning, or be felt by an internal sense, and by means of some sentiment, which the reflecting on such an action naturally occasions. This question will soon be decided against the former opinion, if we can shew the same relations in other objects, without the notion of any guilt or iniquity attending them. Reason or science is nothing but the comparing of ideas, and the discovery of their relations; and if the same relations have different characters, it must evidently follow, that those characters are not discovered merely by reason. To put the affair, therefore, to this trial, let us chuse any inanimate object, such as an oak or elm; and let us suppose, that by the dropping of its seed, it produces a sapling below it, which springing up by degrees, at last overtops and destroys the parent tree: I ask, if in this instance there be wanting any relation, which is discoverable in parricide or ingratitude? Is not the one tree the cause of the other's existence; and the latter the cause of the destruction of the former, in the same manner as when a child murders his parent? It is not sufficient to reply, that a choice or will is wanting. For in the case of parricide, a will does not give rise to any DIFFERENT relations, but is only the cause from which the action is derived; and consequently produces the same relations, that in the oak or elm arise from some other principles. It is a will or choice, that determines a man to kill his parent; and they are the laws of matter and motion, that determine a sapling to destroy the oak, from which it sprung. Here then the same relations have different causes; but still the relations are the same: And as their discovery is not in both cases attended with a notion of immorality, it follows, that that notion does not arise from such a discovery.

But to chuse an instance, still more resembling; I would fain ask any one, why incest in the human species is criminal, and why the very same action, and the same relations in animals have not the smallest moral turpitude and deformity? If it be answered, that this action is innocent in animals, because they have not reason sufficient to discover its turpitude; but that man, being endowed with that faculty which ought to restrain him to his duty, the same action instantly becomes criminal to him; should this be said, I would reply, that this is evidently arguing in a circle. For before reason can perceive this turpitude, the turpitude must exist; and consequently is independent of the decisions of our reason, and is their object more properly than their effect. According to this system, then, every animal, that has sense, and appetite, and will; that is, every animal must be susceptible of all the same virtues and vices, for which we ascribe praise and blame to human creatures. All the difference is, that our superior reason may serve to discover the vice or virtue, and by that means may augment the blame or praise: But still this discovery supposes a separate being in these moral distinctions, and a being, which depends only on the will and appetite, and which, both in thought and reality, may be distinguished from the reason. Animals are susceptible of the same relations, with respect to each other, as the human species, and therefore would also be susceptible of the same morality, if the essence of morality consisted in these relations. Their want of a sufficient degree of reason may hinder them from perceiving the duties and obligations of morality, but can never hinder these duties from existing; since they must antecedently exist, in order to their being perceived. Reason must find them, and can never produce them. This argument deserves to be weighed, as being, in my opinion, entirely decisive.

Nor does this reasoning only prove, that morality consists not in any relations, that are the objects of science; but if examined, will prove with equal certainty, that it consists not in any matter of fact, which can be discovered by the understanding. This is the second part of our argument; and if it can be made evident, we may conclude, that morality is not an object of reason. But can there be any difficulty in proving, that vice and virtue are not matters of fact, whose existence we can infer by reason? Take any action allowed to be vicious: Wilful murder, for instance. Examine it in all lights, and see if you can find that matter of fact, or real existence, which you call vice. In which-ever way you take it, you find only certain passions, motives, volitions and thoughts. There is no other matter of fact in the case. The vice entirely escapes you, as long as you consider the object. You never can find it, till you turn your reflection into your own breast, and find a sentiment of disapprobation, which arises in you, towards this action. Here is a matter of fact; but it is the object of feeling, not of reason. It lies in yourself, not in the object. So that when you pronounce any action or character to be vicious, you mean nothing, but that from the constitution of your nature you have a feeling or sentiment of blame from the contemplation of it. Vice and virtue, therefore, may be compared to sounds, colours, heat and cold, which, according to modern philosophy, are not qualities in objects, but perceptions in the mind: And this discovery in morals, like that other in physics, is to be regarded as a considerable advancement of the speculative sciences; though, like that too, it has little or no influence on practice. Nothing can be more real, or concern us more, than our own sentiments of pleasure and uneasiness; and if these be favourable to virtue, and unfavourable to vice, no more can be requisite to the regulation of our conduct and behaviour.

I cannot forbear adding to these reasonings an observation, which may, perhaps, be found of some importance. In every system of morality, which I have hitherto met with, I have always remarked, that the author proceeds for some time in the ordinary way of reasoning, and establishes the being of a God, or makes observations concerning human affairs; when of a sudden I am surprized to find, that instead of the usual copulations of propositions, is, and is not, I meet with no proposition that is not connected with an ought, or an ought not. This change is imperceptible; but is, however, of the last consequence. For as this ought, or ought not, expresses some new relation or affirmation, it is necessary that it should be observed and explained; and at the same time that a reason should be given, for what seems altogether inconceivable, how this new relation can be a deduction from others, which are entirely different from it. But as authors do not commonly use this precaution, I shall presume to recommend it to the readers; and am persuaded, that this small attention would subvert all the vulgar systems of morality, and let us see, that the distinction of vice and virtue is not founded merely on the relations of objects, nor is perceived by reason.

SECTION II

Moral Distinctions Derived from a Moral Sense

Thus the course of the argument leads us to conclude, that since vice and virtue are not discoverable merely by reason, or the comparison of ideas, it must be by means of some impression or sentiment they occasion, that we are able to mark the difference betwixt them. Our decisions concerning moral rectitude and depravity are evidently perceptions; and as all perceptions are either impressions or ideas, the exclusion of the one is a convincing argument for the other. Morality, therefore, is more properly felt than judged of; though this feeling or sentiment is commonly so soft and gentle, that we are apt to confound it with an idea, according to our common custom of taking all things for the same, which have any near resemblance to each other.

The next question is, of what nature are these impressions, and after what manner do they operate upon us? Here we cannot remain long in suspense, but must pronounce the impression arising from virtue, to be agreeable, and that proceding from vice to be uneasy. Every moments experience must convince us of this. There is no spectacle so fair and beautiful as a noble and generous action; nor any which gives us more abhorrence than one that is cruel and treacherous. No enjoyment equals the satisfaction we receive from the company of those we love and esteem; as the greatest of all punishments is to be obliged to pass our lives with those we hate or contemn. A very play or romance may afford us instances of this pleasure, which virtue conveys to us; and pain, which arises from vice.

Now since the distinguishing impressions, by which moral good or evil is known, are nothing but particular pains or pleasures; it follows, that in all enquiries concerning these moral distinctions, it will be sufficient to shew the principles, which make us feel a satisfaction or uneasiness from the survey of any character, in order to satisfy us why the character is laudable or blameable. An action, or sentiment, or character is virtuous or vicious; why? because its view causes a pleasure or uneasiness of a particular kind. In giving a reason, therefore, for the pleasure or uneasiness, we sufficiently explain the vice or virtue. To have the sense of virtue, is nothing but to feel a satisfaction of a particular kind from the contemplation of a character. The very feeling constitutes our praise or admiration. We go no farther; nor do we enquire into the cause of the satisfaction. We do not infer a character to be virtuous, because it pleases: But in feeling that it pleases after such a particular manner, we in effect feel that it is virtuous. The case is the same as in our judgments concerning all kinds of beauty, and tastes, and sensations. Our approbation is implyed in the immediate pleasure they convey to us.

I have objected to the system, which establishes eternal rational measures of right and wrong, that it is impossible to shew, in the actions of reasonable creatures, any relations, which are not found in external objects; and therefore, if morality always attended these relations, it were possible for inanimate matter to become virtuous or vicious. Now it may, in like manner, be objected to the present system, that if virtue and vice be determined by pleasure and pain, these qualities must, in every case, arise from the sensations; and consequently any object, whether animate or inanimate, rational or irrational, might become morally good or evil, provided it can excite a satisfaction or uneasiness. But though this objection seems to be the very same, it has by no means the same force, in the one case as in the other. For, first, tis evident, that under the term pleasure, we comprehend sensations, which are very different from each other, and which have only such a distant resemblance, as is requisite to make them be expressed by the same abstract term. A good composition of music and a bottle of good wine equally produce pleasure; and what is more, their goodness is determined merely by the pleasure. But shall we say upon that account, that the wine is harmonious, or the music of a good flavour? In like manner an inanimate object, and the character or sentiments of any person may, both of them, give satisfaction; but as the satisfaction is different, this keeps our sentiments concerning them from being confounded, and makes us ascribe virtue to the one, and not to the other. Nor is every sentiment of pleasure or pain, which arises from characters and actions, of that peculiar kind, which makes us praise or condemn. The good qualities of an enemy are hurtful to us; but may still command our esteem and respect. It is only when a character is considered in general, without reference to our particular interest, that it causes such a feeling or sentiment, as denominates it morally good or evil. It is true, those sentiments, from interest and morals, are apt to be confounded, and naturally run into one another. It seldom happens, that we do not think an enemy vicious, and can distinguish betwixt his opposition to our interest and real villainy or baseness. But this hinders not, but that the sentiments are, in themselves, distinct; and a man of temper and judgment may preserve himself from these illusions. In like manner, though it is certain a musical voice is nothing but one that naturally gives a particular kind of pleasure; yet it is difficult for a man to be sensible, that the voice of an enemy is agreeable, or to allow it to be musical. But a person of a fine ear, who has the command of himself, can separate these feelings, and give praise to what deserves it.

SECONDLY, We may call to remembrance the preceding system of the passions, in order to remark a still more considerable difference among our pains and pleasures. Pride and humility, love and hatred are excited, when there is any thing presented to us, that both bears a relation to the object of the passion, and produces a separate sensation related to the sensation of the passion. Now virtue and vice are attended with these circumstances. They must necessarily be placed either in ourselves or others, and excite either pleasure or uneasiness; and therefore must give rise to one of these four passions; which clearly distinguishes them from the pleasure and pain arising from inanimate objects, that often bear no relation to us: And this is, perhaps, the most considerable effect that virtue and vice have upon the human mind.

It may now be asked in general, concerning this pain or pleasure, that distinguishes moral good and evil, FROM WHAT PRINCIPLES IS IT DERIVED, AND WHENCE DOES IT ARISE IN THE HUMAN MIND? To this I reply, first, that it is absurd to imagine, that in every particular instance, these sentiments are produced by an original quality and primary constitution. For as the number of our duties is, in a manner, infinite, it is impossible that our original instincts should extend to each of them, and from our very first infancy impress on the human mind all that multitude of precepts, which are contained in the compleatest system of ethics. Such a method of proceeding is not conformable to the usual maxims, by which nature is conducted, where a few principles produce all that variety we observe in the universe, and every thing is carryed on in the easiest and most simple manner. It is necessary, therefore, to abridge these primary impulses, and find some more general principles, upon which all our notions of morals are founded.

But in the second place, should it be asked, Whether we ought to search for these principles in nature, or whether we must look for them in some other origin? I would reply, that our answer to this question depends upon the definition of the word, Nature, than which there is none more ambiguous and equivocal. If nature be opposed to miracles, not only the distinction betwixt vice and virtue is natural, but also every event, which has ever happened in the world, EXCEPTING THOSE MIRACLES, ON WHICH OUR RELIGION IS FOUNDED. In saying, then, that the sentiments of vice and virtue are natural in this sense, we make no very extraordinary discovery.

But nature may also be opposed to rare and unusual; and in this sense of the word, which is the common one, there may often arise disputes concerning what is natural or unnatural; and one may in general affirm, that we are not possessed of any very precise standard, by which these disputes can be decided. Frequent and rare depend upon the number of examples we have observed; and as this number may gradually encrease or diminish, it will be impossible to fix any exact boundaries betwixt them. We may only affirm on this head, that if ever there was any thing, which could be called natural in this sense, the sentiments of morality certainly may; since there never was any nation of the world, nor any single person in any nation, who was utterly deprived of them, and who never, in any instance, shewed the least approbation or dislike of manners. These sentiments are so rooted in our constitution and temper, that without entirely confounding the human mind by disease or madness, it is impossible to extirpate and destroy them.

But nature may also be opposed to artifice, as well as to what is rare and unusual; and in this sense it may be disputed, whether the notions of virtue be natural or not. We readily forget, that the designs, and projects, and views of men are principles as necessary in their operation as heat and cold, moist and dry: But taking them to be free and entirely our own, it is usual for us to set them in opposition to the other principles of nature should it, therefore, be demanded, whether the sense of virtue be natural or artificial, I am of opinion, that it is impossible for me at present to give any precise answer to this question. Perhaps it will appear afterwards, that our sense of some virtues is artificial, and that of others natural. The discussion of this question will be more proper, when we enter upon an exact detail of each particular vice and virtue.[68]

Meanwhile it may not be amiss to observe from these definitions of natural and unnatural, that nothing can be more unphilosophical than those systems, which assert, that virtue is the same with what is natural, and vice with what is unnatural. For in the first sense of the word, Nature, as opposed to miracles, both vice and virtue are equally natural; and in the second sense, as opposed to what is unusual, perhaps virtue will be found to be the most unnatural. At least it must be owned,

[68] In the following discourse natural is also opposed sometimes to civil, sometimes to moral. The opposition will always discover the sense, in which it is taken.

that heroic virtue, being as unusual, is as little natural as the most brutal barbarity. As to the third sense of the word, it is certain, that both vice and virtue are equally artificial, and out of nature. For however it may be disputed, whether the notion of a merit or demerit in certain actions be natural or artificial, it is evident, that the actions themselves are artificial, and are performed with a certain design and intention; otherwise they could never be ranked under any of these denominations. It is impossible, therefore, that the character of natural and unnatural can ever, in any sense, mark the boundaries of vice and virtue.

Thus we are still brought back to our first position, that virtue is distinguished by the pleasure, and vice by the pain, that any action, sentiment or character gives us by the mere view and contemplation. This decision is very commodious; because it reduces us to this simple question, Why any action or sentiment upon the general view or survey, gives a certain satisfaction or uneasiness, in order to shew the origin of its moral rectitude or depravity, without looking for any incomprehensible relations and qualities, which never did exist in nature, nor even in our imagination, by any clear and distinct conception. I flatter myself I have executed a great part of my present design by a state of the question, which appears to me so free from ambiguity and obscurity.

PART II

Of Justice and Injustice

SECTION I

Justice, whether A Natural or Artificial Virtue?

I have already hinted, that our sense of every kind of virtue is not natural; but that there are some virtues, that produce pleasure and approbation by means of an artifice or contrivance, which arises from the circumstances and necessity of mankind. Of this kind I assert justice to be; and shall endeavour to defend this opinion by a short, and, I hope, convincing argument, before I examine the nature of the artifice, from which the sense of that virtue is derived.

It is evident, that when we praise any actions, we regard only the motives that produced them, and consider the actions as signs or indications of certain principles in the mind and temper. The external performance has no merit. We must look within to find the moral quality. This we cannot do directly; and therefore fix our attention on actions, as on external signs. But these actions are still considered as signs; and the ultimate object of our praise and approbation is the motive, that produced them.

After the same manner, when we require any action, or blame a person for not performing it, we always suppose, that one in that situation should be influenced by the proper motive of that action, and we esteem it vicious in him to be regardless of it. If we find, upon enquiry, that the virtuous motive was still powerful over his breast, though checked in its operation by some circumstances unknown to us, we retract our blame, and have the same esteem for him, as if he had actually performed the action, which we require of him.

It appears, therefore, that all virtuous actions derive their merit only from virtuous motives, and are considered merely as signs of those motives. From this principle I conclude, that the first virtuous motive, which bestows a merit on any action, can never be a regard to the virtue of that action, but must be some other natural motive or principle. To suppose, that the mere regard to the virtue of the action may be the first motive, which produced the action, and rendered it virtuous, is to reason in a circle. Before we can have such a regard, the action must be really virtuous; and this virtue must be derived from some virtuous motive: And consequently the virtuous motive must be different from the regard to the virtue of the action. A virtuous motive is requisite to render an action virtuous. An action must be virtuous, before we can have a regard to its virtue. Some virtuous motive, therefore, must be antecedent to that regard.

Nor is this merely a metaphysical subtilty; but enters into all our reasonings in common life, though perhaps we may not be able to place it in such distinct philosophical terms. We blame a father for neglecting his child. Why? because it shews a want of natural affection, which is the duty of every parent. Were not natural affection a duty, the care of children could not be a duty; and it were impossible we could have the duty in our eye in the attention we give to our offspring. In this case, therefore, all men suppose a motive to the action distinct from a sense of duty.

Here is a man, that does many benevolent actions; relieves the distressed, comforts the afflicted, and extends his bounty even to the greatest strangers. No character can be more amiable and virtuous. We regard these actions as proofs of the greatest humanity. This humanity bestows a merit on the actions. A regard to this merit is, therefore, a secondary consideration, and derived from the antecedent principle of humanity, which is meritorious and laudable.

In short, it may be established as an undoubted maxim, THAT NO ACTION CAN BE VIRTUOUS, OR MORALLY GOOD, UNLESS THERE BE IN HUMAN NATURE SOME MOTIVE TO PRODUCE IT, DISTINCT FROM THE SENSE OF ITS MORALITY.

But may not the sense of morality or duty produce an action, without any other motive? I answer, It may: But this is no objection to the present doctrine. When any virtuous motive or principle is common in human nature, a person, who feels his heart devoid of that motive, may hate himself upon that account, and may perform the action without the motive, from a certain sense of duty, in order to acquire by practice, that virtuous principle, or at least, to disguise to himself, as much as possible, his want of it. A man that really feels no gratitude in his temper, is still pleased to perform grateful actions, and thinks he has, by that means, fulfilled his duty. Actions are at first only considered as signs of motives: But it is usual, in this case, as in all others, to fix our attention on the signs, and neglect, in some measure, the thing signifyed. But though, on some occasions, a person may perform an action merely out of regard to its moral obligation, yet still this supposes in human nature some distinct principles, which are capable of producing the action, and whose moral beauty renders the action meritorious.

Now to apply all this to the present case; I suppose a person to have lent me a sum of money, on condition that it be restored in a few days; and also suppose, that after the expiration of the term agreed on, he demands the sum: I ask, What reason or motive have I to restore the money? It will, perhaps, be said, that my regard to justice, and abhorrence of villainy and knavery, are sufficient reasons for me, if I have the least grain of honesty, or sense of duty and obligation. And this answer, no doubt, is just and satisfactory to man in his civilized state, and when trained up according to a certain discipline and education. But in his rude and more natural condition, if you are pleased to call such a condition natural, this answer would be rejected as perfectly unintelligible and sophistical. For one in that situation would immediately ask you, WHEREIN CONSISTS THIS HONESTY AND JUSTICE, WHICH YOU FIND IN RESTORING A LOAN, AND ABSTAINING FROM THE PROPERTY OF OTHERS? It does not surely lie in the external action. It must, therefore be placed in the motive, from which the external action is derived. This motive can never be a regard to the honesty of the action. For it is a plain fallacy to say, that a virtuous motive is requisite to render an action honest, and at the same time that a regard to the honesty is the motive of the action. We can never have a regard to the virtue of an action, unless the action be antecedently virtuous. No action can be virtuous, but so far as it proceeds from a virtuous motive. A virtuous motive, therefore, must precede the regard to the virtue, and it is impossible, that the virtuous motive and the regard to the virtue can be the same.

It is requisite, then, to find some motive to acts of justice and honesty, distinct from our regard to the honesty; and in this lies the great difficulty. For should we say, that a concern for our private interest or reputation is the legitimate motive to all honest actions; it would follow, that wherever that concern ceases, honesty can no longer have place. But it is certain, that self-love, when it acts at its liberty, instead of engaging us to honest actions, is the source of all injustice and violence; nor can a man ever correct those vices, without correcting and restraining the natural movements of that appetite.

But should it be affirmed, that the reason or motive of such actions is the regard to publick interest, to which nothing is more contrary than examples of injustice and dishonesty; should this be said, I would propose the three following considerations, as worthy of our attention. First, public interest is not naturally attached to the observation of the rules of justice; but is only connected with it, after an artificial convention for the establishment of these rules, as shall be shewn more at large hereafter. Secondly, if we suppose, that the loan was secret, and that it is necessary for the interest of the person, that the money be restored in the same manner (as when the lender would conceal his riches) in that case the example ceases, and the public is no longer interested in the actions of the borrower; though I suppose there is no moralist, who will affirm, that the duty and obligation ceases. Thirdly, experience sufficiently proves, that men, in the ordinary conduct of life, look not so far as the public interest, when they pay their creditors, perform their promises, and abstain from theft, and robbery, and injustice of every kind. That is a motive too remote and too sublime to affect the generality of mankind, and operate with any force in actions so contrary to private interest as are frequently those of justice and common honesty.

In general, it may be affirmed, that there is no such passion in human minds, as the love of mankind, merely as such, independent of personal qualities, of services, or of relation to ourself. It is true, there is no human, and indeed no sensible, creature, whose happiness or misery does not, in some measure, affect us when brought near to us, and represented in lively colours: But this proceeds merely from sympathy, and is no proof of such an universal affection to mankind, since this concern extends itself beyond our own species. An affection betwixt the sexes is a passion evidently implanted in human nature; and this passion not only appears in its peculiar symptoms, but also in inflaming every other principle of affection, and raising a stronger love from beauty, wit, kindness, than what would otherwise flow from them. Were there an universal love among all human creatures, it would appear after the same manner. Any degree of a good quality would cause a stronger affection than the same degree of a bad quality would cause hatred; contrary to what we find by experience. Men's tempers are different, and some have a propensity to the tender, and others to the rougher, affections: But in the main, we may affirm, that man in general, or human nature, is nothing but the object both of love and hatred, and requires some other cause, which by a double relation of impressions and ideas, may excite these passions. In vain would we endeavour to elude this hypothesis. There are no phaenomena that point out any such kind affection to men, independent of their merit, and every other circumstance. We love company in general; but it is as we love any other amusement. An Englishman in Italy is a friend: A Euro paean in China; and perhaps a man would be beloved as such, were we to meet him in the moon. But this proceeds only from the relation to ourselves; which in these cases gathers force by being confined to a few persons.

If public benevolence, therefore, or a regard to the interests of mankind, cannot be the original motive to justice, much less can private benevolence, or a regard to the interests of the party concerned, be this motive. For what if he be my enemy, and has given me just cause to hate him? What if he be a vicious man, and deserves the hatred of all mankind? What if he be a miser, and can make no use of what I would deprive him of? What if he be a profligate debauchee, and would rather receive harm than benefit from large possessions? What if I be in necessity, and have urgent motives to acquire something to my family? In all these cases, the original motive to justice would fail; and consequently the justice itself, and along with it all property, tight, and obligation.

A rich man lies under a moral obligation to communicate to those in necessity a share of his superfluities. Were private benevolence the original motive to justice, a man would not be obliged to leave others in the possession of more than he is obliged to give them. At least the difference would be very inconsiderable. Men generally fix their affections more on what they are possessed of, than on what they never enjoyed: For this reason, it would be greater cruelty to dispossess a man of any thing, than not to give it him. But who will assert, that this is the only foundation of justice?

Besides, we must consider, that the chief reason, why men attach themselves so much to their possessions is, that they consider them as their property, and as secured to them inviolably by the laws of society. But this is a secondary consideration, and dependent on the preceding notions of justice and property.

A man's property is supposed to be fenced against every mortal, in every possible case. But private benevolence is, and ought to be, weaker in some persons, than in others: And in many, or indeed in most persons, must absolutely fail. Private benevolence, therefore, is not the original motive of justice.

From all this it follows, that we have no real or universal motive for observing the laws of equity, but the very equity and merit of that observance; and as no action can be equitable or meritorious, where it cannot arise from some separate motive, there is here an evident sophistry and reasoning in a circle. Unless, therefore, we will allow, that nature has established a sophistry, and rendered it necessary and unavoidable, we must allow, that the sense of justice and injustice is not derived from nature, but arises artificially, though necessarily from education, and human conventions.

I shall add, as a corollary to this reasoning, that since no action can be laudable or blameable, without some motives or impelling passions, distinct from the sense of morals, these distinct passions must have a great influence on that sense. It is according to their general force in human nature, that we blame or praise. In judging of the beauty of animal bodies, we always carry in our eye the economy of a certain species; and where the limbs and features observe that proportion, which is common to the species, we pronounce them handsome and beautiful. In like manner we always consider the natural and usual force of the passions, when we determine concerning vice and virtue; and if the passions depart very much from the common measures on either side, they are always disapproved as vicious. A man naturally loves his children better than his nephews, his nephews better than his cousins, his cousins better than strangers, where every thing else is equal. Hence arise our common measures of duty, in preferring the one to the other. Our sense of duty always follows the common and natural course of our passions.

To avoid giving offence, I must here observe, that when I deny justice to be a natural virtue, I make use of the word, natural, only as opposed to artificial. In another sense of the word; as no principle of the human mind is more natural than a sense of virtue; so no virtue is more natural than justice. Mankind is an inventive species; and where an invention is obvious and absolutely necessary, it may as properly be said to be natural as any thing that proceeds immediately from original principles, without the intervention of thought or reflection. Though the rules of justice be artificial, they are not arbitrary. Nor is the expression improper to call them Laws of Nature; if by natural we understand what is common to any species, or even if we confine it to mean what is inseparable from the species.

SECTION II

Of the Origin of Justice and Property

We now proceed to examine two questions, viz, CONCERNING THE MANNER, IN WHICH THE RULES OF JUSTICE ARE ESTABLISHED BY THE ARTIFICE OF MEN; and CONCERNING THE REASONS, WHICH DETERMINE US TO ATTRIBUTE TO THE OBSERVANCE OR NEGLECT OF THESE RULES A MORAL BEAUTY AND DEFORMITY. These questions will appear afterwards to be distinct. We shall begin with the former.

Of all the animals, with which this globe is peopled, there is none towards whom nature seems, at first sight, to have exercised more cruelty than towards man, in the numberless wants and necessities, with which she has loaded him, and in the slender means, which she affords to the relieving these necessities. In other creatures these two particulars generally compensate each other. If we consider the lion as a voracious and carnivorous animal, we shall easily discover him to be very necessitous; but if we turn our eye to his make and temper, his agility, his courage, his arms, and his force, we shall find, that his advantages hold proportion with his wants. The sheep and ox are deprived of all these advantages; but their appetites are moderate, and their food is of easy purchase. In man alone, this unnatural conjunction of infirmity, and of necessity, may be observed in its greatest perfection. Not only the food, which is required for his sustenance, flies his search and approach, or at least requires his labour to be produced, but he must be possessed of cloaths and lodging, to defend him against the injuries of the weather; though to consider him only in himself, he is provided neither with arms, nor force, nor other natural abilities, which are in any degree answerable to so many necessities.

It is by society alone he is able to supply his defects, and raise himself up to an equality with his fellow-creatures, and even acquire a superiority above them. By society all his infirmities are compensated; and though in that situation his wants multiply every moment upon him, yet his abilities are still more augmented, and leave him in every respect more satisfied and happy, than it is possible for him, in his savage and solitary condition, ever to become. When every individual person labours apart, and only for himself, his force is too small to execute any considerable work; his labour being employed in supplying all his different necessities, he never attains a perfection in any particular art; and as his force and success are not at all times equal, the least failure in either of these particulars must be attended with inevitable ruin and misery. Society provides a remedy for these three inconveniences. By the conjunction of forces, our power is augmented: By the partition of employments, our ability encreases: And by mutual succour we are less exposed to fortune and accidents. It is by this additional force, ability, and security, that society becomes advantageous.

But in order to form society, it is requisite not only that it be advantageous, but also that men be sensible of these advantages; and it is impossible, in their wild uncultivated state, that by study and reflection alone, they should ever be able to attain this knowledge. Most fortunately, therefore, there is conjoined to those necessities, whose remedies are remote and obscure, another necessity, which having a present and more obvious remedy, may justly be regarded as the first and original principle of human society. This necessity is no other than that natural appetite betwixt the sexes, which unites them together, and preserves their union, till a new tye takes place in their concern for their common offspring. This new concern becomes also a principle of union betwixt the parents and offspring, and forms a more numerous society; where the parents govern by the advantage of their superior strength and wisdom, and at the same time are restrained in the exercise of their authority by that natural affection, which they bear their children. In a little time, custom and habit operating on the tender minds of the children, makes them sensible of the advantages, which they may reap from society, as well as fashions them by degrees for it, by rubbing off those rough corners and untoward affections, which prevent their coalition.

For it must be confest, that however the circumstances of human nature may render an union necessary, and however those passions of lust and natural affection may seem to render it unavoidable; yet there are other particulars in our natural temper, and in our outward circumstances, which are very incommodious, and are even contrary to the requisite conjunction. Among the former, we may justly esteem our selfishness to be the most considerable. I am sensible, that generally speaking, the representations of this quality have been carried much too far; and that the descriptions, which certain philosophers delight so much to form of mankind in this particular, are as wide of nature as any accounts of monsters, which we meet with in fables and romances. So far from thinking, that men have no affection for any thing beyond themselves, I am of opinion, that though it be rare to meet with one, who loves any single person better than himself; yet it is as rare to meet with one, in whom all the kind affections, taken together, do not overbalance all the selfish. Consult common experience: Do you not see, that though the whole expence of the family be generally under the direction of the master of it, yet there are few that do not bestow the largest part of their fortunes on the pleasures of their wives, and the education of their children, reserving the smallest portion for their own proper use and entertainment. This is what we may observe concerning such as have those endearing ties; and may presume, that the case would be the same with others, were they placed in a like situation.

But though this generosity must be acknowledged to the honour of human nature, we may at the same time remark, that so noble an affection, instead of fitting men for large societies, is almost as contrary to them, as the most narrow selfishness. For while each person loves himself better than any other single person, and in his love to others bears the greatest affection to his relations and acquaintance, this must necessarily produce an oppositon of passions, and a consequent opposition of actions; which cannot but be dangerous to the new-established union.

It is however worth while to remark, that this contrariety of passions would be attended with but small danger, did it not concur with a peculiarity in our outward circumstances, which affords it an opportunity of exerting itself. There are different species of goods, which we are possessed of; the internal satisfaction of our minds, the external advantages of our body, and the enjoyment of such possessions as we have acquired by our industry and good fortune. We are perfectly secure in the enjoyment of the first. The second may be ravished from us, but can be of no advantage to him who deprives us of them. The last only are both exposed to the violence of others, and may be transferred without suffering any loss or alteration; while at the same time, there is not a sufficient quantity of them to supply every one's desires and necessities. As the improvement, therefore, of these goods is the chief advantage of society, so the instability of their possession, along with their scarcity, is the chief impediment.

In vain should we expect to find, in uncultivated nature, a remedy to this inconvenience; or hope for any inartificial principle of the human mind, which might controul those partial affections, and make us overcome the temptations arising from our circumstances. The idea of justice can never serve to this purpose, or be taken for a natural principle, capable of inspiring men with an equitable conduct towards each other. That virtue, as it is now understood, would never have been dreamed of among rude and savage men. For the notion of injury or injustice implies an immorality or vice committed against some other person: And as every immorality is derived from some defect or unsoundness of the passions, and as this defect must be judged of, in a great measure, from the ordinary course of nature in the constitution of the mind; it will be easy to know, whether we be guilty of any immorality, with regard to others, by considering the natural, and usual force of those several affections, which are directed towards them. Now it appears, that in the original frame of our mind, our strongest attention is confined to ourselves; our next is extended to our relations and acquaintance; and it is only the weakest which reaches to strangers and indifferent persons. This partiality, then, and unequal affection, must not only have an influence on our behaviour and conduct in society, but even on our ideas of vice and virtue; so as to make us regard any remarkable transgression of such a degree of partiality, either by too great an enlargement, or contraction of the affections, as vicious and immoral. This we may observe in our common judgments concerning actions, where we blame a person, who either centers all his affections in his family, or is so regardless of them, as, in any opposition of interest, to give the preference to a stranger, or mere chance acquaintance. From all which it follows, that our natural uncultivated ideas of morality, instead of providing a remedy for the partiality of our affections, do rather conform themselves to that partiality, and give it an additional force and influence.

The remedy, then, is not derived from nature, but from artifice; or more properly speaking, nature provides a remedy in the judgment and understanding, for what is irregular and incommodious in the affections. For when men, from their early education in society, have become sensible of the infinite advantages that result from it, and have besides acquired a new affection to company and conversation; and when they have observed, that the principal disturbance in society arises from those goods, which we call external, and from their looseness and easy transition from one person to another; they must seek for a remedy by putting these goods, as far as possible, on the same footing with the fixed and constant advantages of the mind and body. This can be done after no other manner, than by a convention entered into by all the members of the society to bestow stability on the possession of those external goods, and leave every one in the peaceable enjoyment of what he may acquire by his fortune and industry. By this means, every one knows what he may safely possess; and the passions ale restrained in their partial and contradictory motions. Nor is such a restraint contrary to these passions; for if so, it could never be entered into, nor maintained; but it is only contrary to their heedless and impetuous movement. Instead of departing from our own interest, or from that of our nearest friends, by abstaining from the possessions of others, we cannot better consult both these interests, than by such a convention; because it is by that means we maintain society, which is so necessary to their well-being and subsistence, as well as to our own.

This convention is not of the nature of a promise: For even promises themselves, as we shall see afterwards, arise from human conventions. It is only a general sense of common interest; which sense all the members of the society express to one another, and which induces them to regulate their conduct by certain rules. I observe, that it will be for my interest to leave another in the possession of his goods, provided he will act in the same manner with regard to me. He is sensible of a like interest in the regulation of his conduct. When this common sense of interest is mutually expressed, and is known to both, it produces a suitable resolution and behaviour. And this may properly enough be called a convention or agreement betwixt us, though without the interposition of a promise; since the actions of each of us have a reference to those of the other, and are performed upon the supposition, that something is to be performed on the other part. Two men, who pull the oars of a boat, do it by an agreement or convention, though they have never given promises to each other. Nor is the rule concerning the stability of possession the less derived from human conventions, that it arises gradually, and acquires force by a slow progression, and by our repeated experience of the inconveniences of transgressing it. On the contrary, this experience assures us still more, that the sense of interest has become common to all our fellows, and gives us a confidence of the future regularity of their conduct: And it is only on the expectation of this, that our moderation and abstinence are founded. In like manner are languages gradually established by human conventions without any promise. In like manner do gold and silver become the common measures of exchange, and are esteemed sufficient payment for what is of a hundred times their value.

After this convention, concerning abstinence from the possessions of others, is entered into, and every one has acquired a stability in his possessions, there immediately arise the ideas of justice and injustice; as also those of property, right, and obligation. The latter are altogether unintelligible without first understanding the former. Our property is nothing but those goods, whose constant possession is established by the laws of society; that is, by the laws of justice. Those, therefore, who make use of the words property, or right, or obligation, before they have explained the origin of justice, or even make use of them in that explication, are guilty of a very gross fallacy, and can never reason upon any solid foundation. A man's property is some object related to him. This relation is not natural, but moral, and founded on justice. It is very preposterous, therefore, to imagine, that we can have any idea of property, without fully comprehending the nature of justice, and shewing its origin in the artifice and contrivance of man. The origin of justice explains that of property. The same artifice gives rise to both. As our first and most natural sentiment of morals is founded on the nature of our passions, and gives the preference to ourselves and friends, above strangers; it is impossible there can be naturally any such thing as a fixed right or property, while the opposite passions of men impel them in contrary directions, and are not restrained by any convention or agreement.

No one can doubt, that the convention for the distinction of property, and for the stability of possession, is of all circumstances the most necessary to the establishment of human society, and that after the agreement for the fixing and observing of this rule, there remains little or nothing to be done towards settling a perfect harmony and concord. All the other passions, besides this of interest, are either easily restrained, or are not of such pernicious consequence, when indulged. Vanity is rather to be esteemed a social passion, and a bond of union among men. Pity and love are to be considered in the same light. And as to envy and revenge, though pernicious, they operate only by intervals, and are directed against particular persons, whom we consider as our superiors or enemies. This avidity alone, of acquiring goods and possessions for ourselves and our nearest friends, is insatiable, perpetual, universal, and directly destructive of society. There scarce is any one, who is not actuated by it; and there is no one, who has not reason to fear from it, when it acts without any restraint, and gives way to its first and most natural movements. So that upon the whole, we are to esteem the difficulties in the establishment of society, to be greater or less, according to those we encounter in regulating and restraining this passion.

It is certain, that no affection of the human mind has both a sufficient force, and a proper direction to counterbalance the love of gain, and render men fit members of society, by making them abstain from the possessions of others. Benevolence to strangers is too weak for this purpose; and as to the other passions, they rather inflame this avidity, when we observe, that the larger our possessions are, the more ability we have of gratifying all our appetites. There is no passion, therefore, capable of controlling the interested affection, but the very affection itself, by an alteration of its direction. Now this alteration must necessarily take place upon the least reflection; since it is evident, that the passion is much better satisfyed by its restraint, than by its liberty, and that in preserving society, we make much greater advances in the acquiring possessions, than in the solitary and forlorn condition, which must follow upon violence and an universal licence. The question, therefore, concerning the wickedness or goodness of human nature, enters not in the least into that other question concerning the origin of society; nor is there any thing to be considered but the degrees of men's sagacity or folly. For whether the passion of self-interest be esteemed vicious or virtuous, it is all a case; since itself alone restrains it: So that if it be virtuous, men become social by their virtue; if vicious, their vice has the same effect.

Now as it is by establishing the rule for the stability of possession, that this passion restrains itself; if that rule be very abstruse, and of difficult invention; society must be esteemed, in a manner, accidental, and the effect of many ages. But if it be found, that nothing can be more simple and obvious than that rule; that every parent, in order to preserve peace among his children, must establish it; and that these first rudiments of justice must every day be improved, as the society enlarges: If all this appear evident, as it certainly must, we may conclude, that it is utterly impossible for men to remain any considerable time in that savage condition, which precedes society; but that his very first state and situation may justly be esteemed social. This, however, hinders not, but that philosophers may, if they please, extend their reasoning to the supposed state of nature; provided they allow it to be a mere philosophical fiction, which never had, and never could have any reality. Human nature being composed of two principal parts, which are requisite in all its actions, the affections and understanding; it is certain, that the blind motions of the former, without the direction of the latter, incapacitate men for society: And it may be allowed us to consider separately the effects, that result from the separate operations of these two component parts of the mind. The same liberty may be permitted to moral, which is allowed to natural philosophers; and it is very usual with the latter to consider any motion as compounded and consisting of two parts separate from each other, though at the same time they acknowledge it to be in itself uncompounded and inseparable.

This state of nature, therefore, is to be regarded as a mere fiction, not unlike that of the golden age, which poets have invented; only with this difference, that the former is described as full of war, violence and injustice; whereas the latter is pointed out to us, as the most charming and most peaceable condition, that can possibly be imagined. The seasons, in that first age of nature, were so temperate, if we may believe the poets, that there was no necessity for men to provide themselves with cloaths and houses as a security against the violence of heat and cold. The rivers flowed with wine and milk: The oaks yielded honey; and nature spontaneously produced her greatest delicacies. Nor were these the chief advantages of that happy age. The storms and tempests were not alone removed from nature; but those more furious tempests were unknown to human breasts, which now cause such uproar, and engender such confusion. Avarice, ambition, cruelty, selfishness, were never heard of: Cordial affection, compassion, sympathy, were the only movements, with which the human mind was yet acquainted. Even the distinction of mine and thine was banished from that happy race of mortals, and carryed with them the very notions of property and obligation, justice and injustice.

This, no doubt, is to be regarded as an idle fiction; but yet deserves our attention, because nothing can more evidently shew the origin of those virtues, which are the subjects of our present enquiry. I have already observed, that justice takes its rise from human conventions; and that these are intended as a remedy to some inconveniences, which proceed from the concurrence of certain qualities of the human mind with the situation of external objects. The qualities of the mind are selfishness and limited generosity: And the situation of external objects is their easy change, joined to their scarcity in comparison of the wants and desires of men. But however philosophers may have been bewildered in those speculations, poets have been guided more infallibly, by a certain taste or common instinct, which in most kinds of reasoning goes farther than any of that art and philosophy, with which we have been yet acquainted. They easily perceived, if every man had a tender regard for another, or if nature supplied abundantly all our wants and desires, that the jealousy of interest, which justice supposes, could no longer have place; nor would there be any occasion for those distinctions and limits of property and possession, which at present are in use among mankind. Encrease to a sufficient degree the benevolence of men, or the bounty of nature, and you render justice useless, by supplying its place with much nobler virtues, and more valuable blessings. The selfishness of men is animated by the few possessions we have, in proportion to our wants; and it is to restrain this selfishness, that men have been obliged to separate themselves from the community, and to distinguish betwixt their own goods and those of others.

Nor need we have recourse to the fictions of poets to learn this; but beside the reason of the thing, may discover the same truth by common experience and observation. It is easy to remark, that a cordial affection renders all things common among friends; and that married people in particular mutually lose their property, and are unacquainted with the mine and thine, which are so necessary, and yet cause such disturbance in human society. The same effect arises from any alteration in the circumstances of mankind; as when there is such a plenty of any thing as satisfies all the desires of men: In which case the distinction of property is entirely lost, and every thing remains in common. This we may observe with regard to air and water, though the most valuable of all external objects; and may easily conclude, that if men were supplied with every thing in the same abundance, or if every one had the same affection and tender regard for every one as for himself; justice and injustice would be equally unknown among mankind.

Here then is a proposition, which, I think, may be regarded as certain, that it is only from the selfishness and confined generosity of men, along with the scanty provision nature has made for his wants, that justice derives its origin. If we look backward we shall find, that this proposition bestows an additional force on some of those observations, which we have already made on this subject.

First, we may conclude from it, that a regard to public interest, or a strong extensive benevolence, is not our first and original motive for the observation of the rules of justice; since it is allowed, that if men were endowed with such a benevolence, these rules would never have been dreamt of.

Secondly, we may conclude from the same principle, that the sense of justice is not founded on reason, or on the discovery of certain connexions and relations of ideas, which are eternal, immutable, and universally obligatory. For since it is confest, that such an alteration as that above-mentioned, in the temper and circumstances of mankind, would entirely alter our duties and obligations, it is necessary upon the common system, that the sense of virtue is derived from reason, to shew the change which this must produce in the relations and ideas. But it is evident, that the only cause, why the extensive generosity of man, and the perfect abundance of every thing, would destroy the very idea of justice, is because they render it useless; and that, on the other hand, his confined benevolence, and his necessitous condition, give rise to that virtue, only by making it requisite to the publick interest, and to that of every individual. Twas therefore a concern for our own, and the publick interest, which made us establish the laws of justice; and nothing can be more certain, than that it is not any relation of ideas, which gives us this concern, but our impressions and sentiments, without which every thing in nature is perfectly indifferent to us, and can never in the least affect us. The sense of justice, therefore, is not founded on our ideas, but on our impressions.

Thirdly, we may farther confirm the foregoing proposition, THAT THOSE IMPRESSIONS, WHICH GIVE RISE TO THIS SENSE OF JUSTICE, ARE NOT NATURAL TO THE MIND OF MAN, BUT ARISE FROM ARTIFICE AND HUMAN CONVENTIONS. For since any considerable alteration of temper and circumstances destroys equally justice and injustice; and since such an alteration has an effect only by changing our own and the publick interest; it follows, that the first establishment of the rules of justice depends on these different interests. But if men pursued the publick interest naturally, and with a hearty affection, they would never have dreamed of restraining each other by these rules; and if they pursued their own interest, without any precaution, they would run head-long into every kind of injustice and violence. These rules, therefore, are artificial, and seek their end in an oblique and indirect manner; nor is the interest, which gives rise to them, of a kind that could be pursued by the natural and inartificial passions of men.

To make this more evident, consider, that though the rules of justice are established merely by interest, their connexion with interest is somewhat singular, and is different from what may be observed on other occasions. A single act of justice is frequently contrary to public interest; and were it to stand alone, without being followed by other acts, may, in itself, be very prejudicial to society. When a man of merit, of a beneficent disposition, restores a great fortune to a miser, or a seditious bigot, he has acted justly and laudably, but the public is a real sufferer. Nor is every single act of justice, considered apart, more conducive to private interest, than to public; and it is easily conceived how a man may impoverish himself by a signal instance of integrity, and have reason to wish, that with regard to that single act, the laws of justice were for a moment suspended in the universe. But however single acts of justice may be contrary, either to public or private interest, it is certain, that the whole plan or scheme is highly conducive, or indeed absolutely requisite, both to the support of society, and the well-being of every individual. It is impossible to separate the good from the ill. Property must be stable, and must be fixed by general rules. Though in one instance the public be a sufferer, this momentary ill is amply compensated by the steady prosecution of the rule, and by the peace and order, which it establishes in society. And even every individual person must find himself a gainer, on ballancing the account; since, without justice society must immediately dissolve, and every one must fall into that savage and solitary condition, which is infinitely worse than the worst situation that can possibly be supposed in society. When therefore men have had experience enough to observe, that whatever may be the consequence of any single act of justice, performed by a single person, yet the whole system of actions, concurred in by the whole society, is infinitely advantageous to the whole, and to every part; it is not long before justice and property take place. Every member of society is sensible of this interest: Every one expresses this sense to his fellows, along with the resolution he has taken of squaring his actions by it, on condition that others will do the same. No more is requisite to induce any one of them to perform an act of justice, who has the first opportunity. This becomes an example to others. And thus justice establishes itself by a kind of convention or agreement; that is, by a sense of interest, supposed to be common to all, and where every single act is performed in expectation that others are to perform the like. Without such a convention, no one would ever have dreamed, that there was such a virtue as justice, or have been induced to conform his actions to it. Taking any single act, my justice may be pernicious in every respect; and it is only upon the supposition that others are to imitate my example, that I can be induced to embrace that virtue; since nothing but this combination can render justice advantageous, or afford me any motives to conform my self to its rules.

We come now to the second question we proposed, viz. Why we annex the idea of virtue to justice, and of vice to injustice. This question will not detain us long after the principles, which we have already established, All we can say of it at present will be dispatched in a few words: And for farther satisfaction, the reader must wait till we come to the third part of this book. The natural obligation to justice, viz, interest, has been fully explained; but as to the moral obligation, or the sentiment of right and wrong, it will first be requisite to examine the natural virtues, before we can give a full and satisfactory account of it. After men have found by experience, that their selfishness and confined generosity, acting at their liberty, totally incapacitate them for society; and at the same time have observed, that society is necessary to the satisfaction of those very passions, they are naturally induced to lay themselves under the restraint of such rules, as may render their commerce more safe and commodious. To the imposition then, and observance of these rules, both in general, and in every particular instance, they are at first induced only by a regard to interest; and this motive, on the first formation of society, is sufficiently strong and forcible. But when society has become numerous, and has encreased to a tribe or nation, this interest is more remote; nor do men so readily perceive, that disorder and confusion follow upon every breach of these rules, as in a more narrow and contracted society. But though in our own actions we may frequently lose sight of that interest, which we have in maintaining order, and may follow a lesser and more present interest, we never fail to observe the prejudice we receive, either mediately or immediately, from the injustice of others; as not being in that case either blinded by passion, or byassed by any contrary temptation. Nay when the injustice is so distant from us, as no way to affect our interest, it still displeases us; because we consider it as prejudicial to human society, and pernicious to every one that approaches the person guilty of it. We partake of their uneasiness by sympathy; and as every thing, which gives uneasiness in human actions, upon the general survey, is called Vice, and whatever produces satisfaction, in the same manner, is denominated Virtue; this is the reason why the sense of moral good and evil follows upon justice and injustice. And though this sense, in the present case, be derived only from contemplating the actions of others, yet we fail not to extend it even to our own actions. The general rule reaches beyond those instances, from which it arose; while at the same time we naturally sympathize with others in the sentiments they entertain of us. Thus self-interest is the original motive to the establishment of justice: but a sympathy with public interest is the source of the moral approbation, which attends that virtue.

Though this progress of the sentiments be natural, and even necessary, it is certain, that it is here forwarded by the artifice of politicians, who, in order to govern men more easily, and preserve peace in human society, have endeavoured to produce an esteem for justice, and an abhorrence of injustice. This, no doubt, must have its effect; but nothing can be more evident, than that the matter has been carryed too far by certain writers on morals, who seem to have employed their utmost efforts to extirpate all sense of virtue from among mankind. Any artifice of politicians may assist nature in the producing of those sentiments, which she suggests to us, and may even on some occasions, produce alone an approbation or esteem for any particular action; but it is impossible it should be the sole cause of the distinction we make betwixt vice and virtue. For if nature did not aid us in this particular, it would be in vain for politicians to talk of honourable or dishonourable, praiseworthy or blameable. These words would be perfectly unintelligible, and would no more have any idea annexed to them, than if they were of a tongue perfectly unknown to us. The utmost politicians can perform, is, to extend the natural sentiments beyond their original bounds; but still nature must furnish the materials, and give us some notion of moral distinctions.

As publick praise and blame encrease our esteem for justice; so private education and instruction contribute to the same effect. For as parents easily observe, that a man is the more useful, both to himself and others, the greater degree of probity and honour he is endowed with; and that those principles have greater force, when custom and education assist interest and reflection: For these reasons they are induced to inculcate on their children, from their earliest infancy, the principles of probity, and teach them to regard the observance of those rules, by which society is maintained, as worthy and honourable, and their violation as base and infamous. By this means the sentiments of honour may take root in their tender minds, and acquire such firmness and solidity, that they may fall little short of those principles, which are the most essential to our natures, and the most deeply radicated in our internal constitution.

What farther contributes to encrease their solidity, is the interest of our reputation, after the opinion, that a merit or demerit attends justice or injustice, is once firmly established among mankind. There is nothing, which touches us more nearly than our reputation, and nothing on which our reputation more depends than our conduct, with relation to the property of others. For this reason, every one, who has any regard to his character, or who intends to live on good terms with mankind, must fix an inviolable law to himself, never, by any temptation, to be induced to violate those principles, which are essential to a man of probity and honour.

I shall make only one observation before I leave this subject, viz, that though I assert, that in the state of nature, or that imaginary state, which preceded society, there be neither justice nor injustice, yet I assert not, that it was allowable, in such a state, to violate the property of others. I only maintain, that there was no such thing as property; and consequently could be no such thing as justice or injustice. I shall have occasion to make a similar reflection with regard to promises, when I come to treat of them; and I hope this reflection, when duly weighed, will suffice to remove all odium from the foregoing opinions, with regard to justice and injustice.

SECTION III

Of the Rules which Determine Property

Though the establishment of the rule, concerning the stability of possession, be not only useful, but even absolutely necessary to human society, it can never serve to any purpose, while it remains in such general terms. Some method must be shewn, by which we may distinguish what particular goods are to be assigned to each particular person, while the rest of mankind are excluded from their possession and enjoyment. Our next business, then, must be to discover the reasons which modify this general rule, and fit it to the common use and practice of the world.

It is obvious, that those reasons are not derived from any utility or advantage, which either the particular person or the public may reap from his enjoyment of any particular goods, beyond what would result from the possession of them by any other person. Twere better, no doubt, that every one were possessed of what is most suitable to him, and proper for his use: But besides, that this relation of fitness may be common to several at once, it is liable to so many controversies, and men are so partial and passionate in judging of these controversies, that such a loose and uncertain rule would be absolutely incompatible with the peace of human society. The convention concerning the stability of possession is entered into, in order to cut off all occasions of discord and contention; and this end would never be attained, were we allowed to apply this rule differently in every particular case, according to every particular utility, which might be discovered in such an application. Justice, in her decisions, never regards the fitness or unfitness of objects to particular persons, but conducts herself by more extensive views. Whether a man be generous, or a miser, he is equally well received by her, and obtains with the same facility a decision in his favours, even for what is entirely useless to him.

It follows therefore, that the general rule, that possession must be stable, is not applied by particular judgments, but by other general rules, which must extend to the whole society, and be inflexible either by spite or favour. To illustrate this, I propose the following instance. I first consider men in their savage and solitary condition; and suppose, that being sensible of the misery of that state, and foreseeing the advantages that would result from society, they seek each other's company, and make an offer of mutual protection and assistance. I also suppose, that they are endowed with such sagacity as immediately to perceive, that the chief impediment to this project of society and partnership lies in the avidity and selfishness of their natural temper; to remedy which, they enter into a convention for the stability of possession, and for mutual restraint and forbearance. I am sensible, that this method of proceeding is not altogether natural; but besides that I here only suppose those reflections to be formed at once, which in fact arise insensibly and by degrees; besides this, I say, it is very possible, that several persons, being by different accidents separated from the societies, to which they formerly belonged, may be obliged to form a new society among themselves; in which case they are entirely in the situation above-mentioned.

It is evident, then, that their first difficulty, in this situation, after the general convention for the establishment of society, and for the constancy of possession, is, how to separate their possessions, and assign to each his particular portion, which he must for the future inalterably enjoy. This difficulty will not detain them long; but it must immediately occur to them, as the most natural expedient, that every one continue to enjoy what he is at present master of, and that property or constant possession be conjoined to the immediate possession. Such is the effect of custom, that it not only reconciles us to any thing we have long enjoyed, but even gives us an affection for it, and makes us prefer it to other objects, which may be more valuable, but are less known to us. What has long lain under our eye, and has often been employed to our advantage, that we are always the most unwilling to part with; but can easily live without possessions, which we never have enjoyed, and are not accustomed to. It is evident, therefore, that men would easily acquiesce in this expedient, that every one continue to enjoy what he is at present possessed of; and this is the reason, why they would so naturally agree in preferring it.[69]

But we may observe, that though the rule of the assignment of property to the present possessor be natural, and by that means useful, yet its utility extends not beyond the first formation of society; nor would any thing be more pernicious, than the constant observance of it; by which restitution would be excluded, and every injustice would be authorized and rewarded. We must, therefore, seek for some other circumstance, that may give rise to property after society is once established; and of this kind, I find four most considerable, viz. Occupation, Prescription, Accession, and Succession. We shall briefly examine each of these, beginning with Occupation.

---

[69] No questions in philosophy are more difficult, than when a number of causes present themselves for the same phænomenon, to determine which is the principal and predominant. There seldom is any very precise argument to fix our choice, and men must be contented to be guided by a kind of taste or fancy, arising from analogy, and a comparison of familiar instances. Thus, in the present case, there are, no doubt, motives of public interest for most of the rules, which determine property; but still I suspect, that these rules are principally fixed by the imagination, or the more frivolous properties of our thought and conception. I shall continue to explain these causes, leaving it to the reader's choice, whether he will prefer those derived from publick utility, or those derived from the imagination. We shall begin with the right of the present possessor.

It is a quality, which I have already observed in human nature, that when two objects appear in a close relation to each other, the mind is apt to ascribe to them any additional relation, in order to compleat the union; and this inclination is so strong, as often to make us run into errors (such as that of the conjunction of thought and matter) if we find that they can serve to that purpose. Many of our impressions are incapable of place or local position; and yet those very impressions we suppose to have a local conjunction with the impressions of sight and touch, merely because they are conjoined by causation, and are already united in the imagination. Since, therefore, we can feign a new relation, and even an absurd one, in order to compleat any union, it will easily be imagined, that if there be any relations, which depend on the mind, it will readily conjoin them to any preceding relation, and unite, by a new bond, such objects as have already an union in the fancy. Thus for instance, we never fail, in our arrangement of bodies, to place those which are resembling in contiguity to each other, or at least in correspondent points of view; because we feel a satisfaction in joining the relation of contiguity to that of resemblance, or the resemblance of situation to that of qualities. And this is easily accounted for from the known properties of human nature. When the mind is determined to join certain objects, but undetermined in its choice of the particular objects, It naturally turns its eye to such as are related together. They are already united in the mind: They present themselves at the same time to the conception; and instead of requiring any new reason for their conjunction, it would require a very powerful reason to make us over-look this natural affinity. This we shall have occasion to explain more fully afterwards, when we come to treat of beauty. In the mean time, we may content ourselves with observing, that the same love of order and uniformity, which arranges the books in a library, and the chairs in a parlour, contribute to the formation of society, and to the well-being of mankind, by modifying the general rule concerning the stability of possession. And as property forms a relation betwixt a person and an object, it is natural to found it on some preceding relation; and as property Is nothing but a constant possession, secured by the laws of society, it is natural to add it to the present possession, which is a relation that resembles it. For this also has its influence. If it be natural to conjoin all sorts of relations, it is more so, to conjoin such relations as are resembling, and are related together.

The possession of all external goods is changeable and uncertain; which is one of the most considerable impediments to the establishment of society, and is the reason why, by universal agreement, express or tacite, men restrain themselves by what we now call the rules of justice and equity. The misery of the condition, which precedes this restraint, is the cause why we submit to that remedy as quickly as possible; and this affords us an easy reason, why we annex the idea of property to the first possession, or to occupation. Men are unwilling to leave property in suspense, even for the shortest time, or open the least door to violence and disorder. To which we may add, that the first possession always engages the attention most; and did we neglect it, there would be no colour of reason for assigning property to any succeeding possession.[70]

There remains nothing, but to determine exactly, what is meant by possession; and this is not so easy as may at first sight be imagined. We are said to be in possession of any thing, not only when we immediately touch it, but also when we are so situated with respect to it, as to have it in our power to use it; and may move, alter, or destroy it, according to our present pleasure or advantage. This relation, then, is a species of cause and effect; and as property is nothing but a stable possession, derived from the rules of justice, or the conventions of men, it is to be considered as the same species of relation. But here we may observe, that as the power of using any object becomes more or less certain, according as the interruptions we may meet with are more or less probable; and as this probability may increase by insensible degrees; it is in many cases impossible to determine when possession begins or ends; nor is there any certain standard, by which we can decide such controversies. A wild boar, that falls into our snares, is deemed to be in our possession, if it be impossible for him to escape. But what do we mean by impossible? How do we separate this impossibility from an improbability? And how distinguish that exactly from a probability? Mark the precise limits of the one and the other, and shew the standard, by which we may decide all disputes that may arise, and, as we find by experience, frequently do arise upon this subject.[71]

---

[70] Some philosophers account for the right of occupation, by saying, that every one has a property in his own labour; and when he joins that labour to any thing, it gives him the property of the whole: But, 1. There are several kinds of occupation, where we cannot be said to join our labour to the object we acquire: As when we possess a meadow by grazing our cattle upon it. 2. This accounts for the matter by means of accession; which is taking a needless circuit. 3. We cannot be said to join our labour to any thing but in a figurative sense. Properly speaking, we only make an alteration on it by our labour. This forms a relation betwixt us and the object; and thence arises the property, according to the preceding principles.

[71] If we seek a solution of these difficulties in reason and public interest, we never shall find satisfaction; and if we look for it in the imagination, it is evident, that the qualities, which operate upon that faculty, run so insensibly and gradually into each other, that it is impossible to give them any precise bounds or termination. The difficulties on this head must encrease, when we consider, that our judgment alters very sensibly, according to the subject, and that the same power and proximity will be deemed possession in one case, which is not esteemed such in another. A person, who has hunted

But such disputes may not only arise concerning the real existence of property and possession, but also concerning their extent; and these disputes are often susceptible of no decision, or can be decided by no other faculty than the imagination. A person who lands on the shore of a small island, that is desart and uncultivated, is deemed its possessor from the very first moment, and acquires the property of the whole; because the object is there bounded and circumscribed in the fancy, and at the same time is proportioned to the new possessor. The same person landing on a desart island, as large as Great Britain, extends his property

---

a hare to the last degree of weariness, would look upon it as an injustice for another to rush in before him, and seize his prey. But the same person advancing to pluck an apple, that hangs within his reach, has no reason to complain, if another, more alert, passes him, and takes possession. What is the reason of this difference, but that immobility, not being natural to the hare, but the effect of industry, forms in that case a strong relation with the hunter, which is wanting in the other?

Here then it appears, that a certain and infallible power of enjoyment, without touch or some other sensible relation, often produces not property: And I farther observe, that a sensible relation, without any present power, is sometimes sufficient to give a title to any object. The sight of a thing is seldom a considerable relation, and is only regarded as such, when the object is hidden, or very obscure; in which case we find, that the view alone conveys a property; according to that maxim, THAT EVEN A WHOLE CONTINENT BELONGS TO THE NATION, WHICH FIRST DISCOVERED IT. It is however remarkable that both in the case of discovery and that of possession, the first discoverer and possessor must join to the relation an intention of rendering himself proprietor, otherwise the relation will not have its effect; and that because the connexion in our fancy betwixt the property and the relation is not so great, but that it requires to be helped by such an intention.

From all these circumstances, it is easy to see how perplexed many questions may become concerning the acquisition of property by occupation; and the least effort of thought may present us with instances, which are not susceptible of any reasonable decision. If we prefer examples, which are real, to such as are feigned, we may consider the following one, which is to be met with in almost every writer, that has treated of the laws of nature. Two Grecian colonies, leaving their native country, in search of new feats, were informed that a city near them was deserted by its inhabitants. To know the truth of this report, they dispatched at once two messengers, one from each colony; who finding on their approach, that their information was true, begun a race together with an intention to take possession of the city, each of them for his countrymen. One of these messengers, finding that he was not an equal match for the other, launched his spear at the gates of the city, and was so fortunate as to fix it there before the arrival of his companion. This produced a dispute betwixt the two colonies, which of them was the proprietor of the empty city and this dispute still subsists among philosophers. For my part I find the dispute impossible to be decided, and that because the whole question hangs upon the fancy, which in this case is not possessed of any precise or determinate standard, upon which it can give sentence. To make this evident, let us consider, that if these two persons had been simply members of the colonies, and not messengers or deputies, their actions would not have been of any consequence; since in that case their relation to the colonies would have been but feeble and imperfect. Add to this, that nothing determined them to run to the gates rather than the walls, or any other part of the city, but that the gates, being the most obvious and remarkable part, satisfy the fancy best in taking them for the whole; as we find by the poets, who frequently draw their images and metaphors from them. Besides we may consider, that the touch or contact of the one messenger is not properly possession, no more than the piercing the gates with a spear; but only forms a relation; and there is a relation, in the other case, equally obvious, tho' not, perhaps, of equal force. Which of these relations, then, conveys a right and property, or whether any of them be sufficient for that effect, I leave to the decision of such as are wiser than myself.

no farther than his immediate possession; though a numerous colony are esteemed the proprietors of the whole from the instant of their debarkment.

But it often happens, that the title of first possession becomes obscure through time; and that it is impossible to determine many controversies, which may arise concerning it. In that case long possession or prescription naturally takes place, and gives a person a sufficient property in any thing he enjoys. The nature of human society admits not of any great accuracy; nor can we always remount to the first origin of things, in order to determine their present condition. Any considerable space of time sets objects at such a distance, that they seem, in a manner, to lose their reality, and have as little influence on the mind, as if they never had been in being. A man's title, that is clear and certain at present, will seem obscure and doubtful fifty years hence, even though the facts, on which it is founded, should be proved with the greatest evidence and certainty. The same facts have not the same influence after so long an interval of time. And this may be received as a convincing argument for our preceding doctrine with regard to property and justice. Possession during a long tract of time conveys a title to any object. But as it is certain, that, however every thing be produced in time, there is nothing real that is produced by time; it follows, that property being produced by time, is not any thing real in the objects, but is the off-spring of the sentiments, on which alone time is found to have any influence.[72]

We acquire the property of objects by accession, when they are connected in an intimate manner with objects that are already our property, and at the same time are inferior to them. Thus the fruits of our garden, the offspring of our cattle, and the work of our slaves, are all of them esteemed our property, even before possession. Where objects are connected together in the imagination, they are apt to be put on the same footing, and are commonly supposed to be endowed with the same qualities. We readily pass from one to the other, and make no difference in our judgments concerning them; especially if the latter be inferior to the former.[73]

---

[72] Present possession is plainly a relation betwixt a person and an object; but is not sufficient to counter-ballance the relation of first possession, unless the former be long and uninterrupted: In which case the relation is encreased on the side of the present possession, by the extent of time, and diminished on that of first possession, by the distance, This change in the relation produces a consequent change in the property.

[73] This source of property can never be explained but from the imaginations; and one may affirm, that the causes are here unmixed. We shall proceed to explain them more particularly, and illustrate them by examples from common life and experience.

It has been observed above, that the mind has a natural propensity to join relations, especially resembling ones, and finds a hind of fitness and uniformity in such an union. From this propensity are derived these laws of nature, that upon the first formation of society, property always follows the present possession; and afterwards, that it arises from first or from long possession. Now we may easily observe, that relation is not confined merely to one degree; but that from an object, that is related to us, we acquire a relation to every other object, which is related to it, and so on, till the thought loses the chain by too long a progress, However the relation may weaken by each remove, it is not immediately destroyed; but frequently connects two objects by means of an intermediate one, which is related to both. And this principle is of such force as to give rise to the right of accession, and causes us to acquire the property not only of such objects as we are immediately possessed of; but also of such as are closely connected with them.

Suppose a German, a Frenchman, and a Spaniard to come into a room, where there are placed upon the table three bottles of wine, Rhenish, Burgundy and Port; and suppose they shoued fall a quarrelling about the division of them; a person, who was chosen for umpire would naturally, to shew his impartiality, give every one the product of his own country: And this from a principle, which, in some measure, is the source of those laws of nature, that ascribe property to occupation, prescription and accession.

In all these Cases, and particularly that of accession, there is first a natural union betwixt the idea of the person and that of the object, and afterwards a new and moral union produced by that right or property, which we ascribe to the person. But here there occurs a difficulty, which merits our attention, and may afford us an opportunity of putting to tryal that singular method of reasoning, which has been employed on the present subject. I have already observed that the imagination passes with greater facility from little to great, than from great to littie, and that the transition of ideas is always easier and smoother in the former case than in the latter. Now as the right of accession arises from the easy transition of ideas, by which related objects are connected together, it shoued naturally be imagined, that the right of accession must encrease in strength, in proportion as the transition of ideas is performed with greater facility. It may, therefore, be thought, that when we have acquired the property of any small object, we shall readily consider any great object related to it as an accession, and as belonging to the proprietor of the small one; since the transition is in that case very easy from the small object to the great one, and shoued connect them together in the closest manner. But In fact the case is always found to be otherwise, The empire of Great Britain seems to draw along with it the dominion of the Orkneys, the Hebrides, the isle of Man, and the Isle of Wight; but the authority over those lesser islands does not naturally imply any title to Great Britain. In short, a small object naturally follows a great one as its accession; but a great one Is never supposed to belong to the proprietor of a small one related to it, merely on account of that property and relation. Yet in this latter case the transition of ideas is smoother from the proprietor to the small object, which is his property, and from the small object to the great one, than in the former case from the proprietor to the great object, and from the great one to the small. It may therefore be thought, that these phaenomena are objections to the foregoing hypothesis, THAT THE ASCRIBING OF PROPERTY TO ACCESSION IS NOTHING BUT AN AFFECT OF THE RELATIONS OF IDEAS, AND OF THE SMOOTH TRANSITION OF THE IMAGINATION.

It will be easy to solve this objection, if we consider the agility and unsteadiness of the imagination, with the different views, in which it is continually placing its objects. When we attribute to a person a property in two objects, we do not always pass from the person to one object, and from that to the other related to it. The objects being here to be considered as the property of the person, we are apt to join them together, and place them in the same light. Suppose, therefore, a great and a small object to be related together; if a person be strongly related to the great object, he will likewise be strongly related to both the objects, considered together, because he Is related to the most considerable part. On the contrary, if he be only related to the small object, he will not be strongly related to both, considered together, since his relation lies only with the most trivial part, which is not apt to strike us in any great degree, when we consider the whole. And this Is the reason, why small objects become accessions to great ones, and not great to small.

It is the general opinion of philosophers and civilians, that the sea is incapable of becoming the property of any nation; and that because it is impossible to take possession of it, or form any such distinct relation with it, as may be the foundation of property. Where this reason ceases, property immediately takes place. Thus the most strenuous advocates for the liberty of the seas universally allow, that friths and hays naturally belong as an accession to the proprietors of the surrounding continent. These have properly no more bond or union with the land, than the pacific ocean would have; but having an union in the fancy, and being at the same time inferior, they are of course regarded as an accession.

The property of rivers, by the laws of most nations, and by the natural turn of our thought, Is attributed to the proprietors of their banks, excepting such vast rivers as the Rhine or the Danube, which seem too large to the imagination to follow as an accession the property of the neighbouring fields. Yet even these rivers are considered as the property of that nation, thro' whose dominions they run; the idea of a nation being of a suitable bulk to correspond with them, and bear them such a relation in the fancy.

The accessions, which are made to lands bordering upon rivers, follow the land, say the civilians, provided it be made by what they call alluvion, that is, Insensibly and Imperceptibly; which are circumstances that mightily assist the imagination in the conjunction. Where there Is any considerable portion torn at once from one bank, and joined to another, it becomes not his property, whose land it falls on, till it unite with the land, and till the trees or plants have spread their roots into both. Before that, the imagination does not sufficiently join them.

There are other cases, which somewhat resemble this of accession, but which, at the bottom, are considerably different, and merit our attention. Of this kind Is the conjunction of the properties of different persons, after such a manner as not to admit of separation. The question is, to whom the united mass must belong.

Where this conjunction is of such a nature as to admit of division, but not of separation, the decision is natural and easy. The whole mass must be supposed to be common betwixt the proprietors of the several parts, and afterwards must be divided according to the proportions of these parts. But here I cannot forbear taking notice of a remarkable subtilty of the Roman law, in distinguishing betwixt confusion and commixtion. Confusion is an union of two bodies, such as different liquors, where the parts become entirely undistinguishable. Commixtion is the blending of two bodies, such as two bushels of corn, where the parts remain separate in an obvious and visible manner. As in the latter case the imagination discovers not so entire an union as in the former, but is able to trace and preserve a distinct idea of the property of each; this is the reason, why the civil law, tho' it established an entire community in the case of confusion, and after that a proportional division, yet in the case of commixtion, supposes each of the proprietors to maintain a distinct right; however necessity may at last force them to submit to the same division.

QUOD SI FRUMENTUM TITII FRUMENTO TUO MISTUM FUERIT: SIQUIDEM EX VOLUNTATE VESTRA, COMMUNE EST: QUIA SINGULA CORPORA, ID EST, SINGULA GRANA, QUAE CUJUSQUE PRO PRIA FUERUNT, EX CONSENSU VESTRO COMMUNICATA SUNT. QUOD SI CASU ID MISTUM FUERIT, VEL TITIUS ID MISCUERIT SINE TUA VOLUNT ATE, NON VIDETUR ID COMMUNE ESSE; QUIA SINGULA CORPORA IN SUA SUBSTANTIA DURANT. SED NEC MAGIS ISTIS CASIBUS COMMUNE SIT FRUMENTUM QUAM GREX INTELLIGITUR ESSE CORN MUNIS, SI PECORA TITII TUIS PECORIBUS MISTA FUERINT. SED SI AB ALTERUTRO VESTRUM TOTUM ID FRUMENTUM RETINEATUR, IN REM QUIDEM ACTIO PRO MODO FRUMENTI CUJUSQUE CORN PETIT. ARBITRIO AUTEM JUDICIS, UT IPSE AESTIMET QUALE CUJUSQUE FRUMENTUM FUERIT. Inst. Lib. IL Tit. i. Sect 28.

(In the case that your grain was mixed with that of Titius, if it was done voluntarily on the part of both of you, it is common property, inasmuch as the individual items, i.e., the single grains, which were the peculiar property of either of you, were combined with your joint consent. If, however, the mixture was accidental, or if Titius mixed it without your consent, it does not appear that it is common property, Inasmuch as the several components retain their original identity. Rather, in circumstances of this sort the grain does not become common property, any more than a herd of cattle is regarded as common property, If Titius beasts should have become mixed up with yours.

However, if all of the aforesaid corn is kept by either of you, this gives rise to a suit to determine the ownership of property, in respect of the amount of corn belonging to each. It is in the discretion of the judge to determine which is the corn belonging to either party.)

The right of succession is a very natural one, from the presumed consent of the parent or near relation, and from the general interest of mankind, which requires, that men's possessions should pass to those, who are dearest to them, in order to render them more industrious and frugal. Perhaps these causes are seconded by the influence of relation, or the association of ideas, by which we are naturally directed to consider the son after the parent's decease, and ascribe to him a title to his father's possessions. Those goods must become the property of some body: But of whom is the question. Here it is evident the persons children naturally present themselves to the mind; and being already. connected to those possessions

---

Where the properties of two persons are united after such a manner as neither to admit of division nor separation, as when one builds a house on another's ground, in that case, the whole must belong to one of the proprietors: And here I assert, that it naturally is conceived to belong to the proprietor of the most considerable part. For however the compound object may have a relation to two different persons, and carry our view at once to both of them, yet as the most considerable part principally engages our attention, and by the strict union draws the inferior along it; for this reason, the whole bears a relation to the proprietor of that part, and is regarded as his property. The only difficulty is, what we shall be pleased to call the most considerable part, and most attractive to the imagination.

This quality depends on several different circumstances, which have little connexion with each other. One part of a compound object may become more considerable than another, either because it is more constant and durable; because it is of greater value; because it is more obvious and remarkable; because it is of greater extent; or because its existence is more separate and independent. It will be easy to conceive, that, as these circumstances may be conjoined and opposed in all the different ways, and according to all the different degrees, which can be imagined, there will result many cases, where the reasons on both sides are so equally balanced, that it is impossible for us to give any satisfactory decision. Here then is the proper business of municipal laws, to fix what the principles of human nature have left undetermined.

The superficies yields to the soil, says the civil law: The writing to the paper: The canvas to the picture. These decisions do not well agree together, and are a proof of the contrariety of those principles, from which they are derived.

But of all the questions of this kind the most curious is that, which for so many ages divided the disciples of Proculus and Sabinus. Suppose a person shoued make a cup from the metal of another, or a ship from his wood, and suppose the proprietor of the metal or wood shoued demand his goods, the question is, whether he acquires a title to the cup or ship. Sabinus maintained the affirmative, and asserted that the substance or matter is the foundation of all the qualities; that it is incorruptible and immortal, and therefore superior to the form, which is casual and dependent. On the other hand, Proculus observed, that the form is the most obvious and remarkable part, and that from it bodies are denominated of this or that particular species. To which he might have added, that the matter or substance is in most bodies so fluctuating and uncertain, that it is utterly impossible to trace it in all its changes. For my part, I know not from what principles such a controversy can be certainly determined. I shall therefore content my self with observing, that the decision of Trebonian seems to me pretty ingenious; that the cup belongs to the proprietor of the metal, because it can be brought back to its first form: But that the ship belongs to the author of its form for a contrary reason. But however ingenious this reason may seem, it plainly depends upon the fancy, which by the possibility of such a reduction, finds a closer connexion and relation betwixt a cup and the proprietor of its metal, than betwixt a ship and the proprietor of its wood, where the substance is more fixed and unalterable.

by means of their deceased parent, we are apt to connect them still farther by the relation of property. Of this there are many parallel instances.[74]

SECTION IV

Of the Transference of Property by Consent

However useful, or even necessary, the stability of possession may be to human society, it is attended with very considerable inconveniences. The relation of fitness or suitableness ought never to enter into consideration, in distributing the properties of mankind; but we must govern ourselves by rules, which are more general in their application, and more free from doubt and uncertainty. Of this kind is present possession upon the first establishment of society; and afterwards occupation, prescription, accession, and succession. As these depend very much on chance, they must frequently prove contradictory both to men's wants and desires; and persons and possessions must often be very ill adjusted. This is a grand inconvenience, which calls for a remedy. To apply one directly, and allow every man to seize by violence what he judges to be fit for him, would destroy society; and therefore the rules of justice seek some medium betwixt a rigid stability, and this changeable and uncertain adjustment. But there is no medium better than that obvious one, that possession and property should always be stable, except when the proprietor consents to bestow them on some other person. This rule can have no ill consequence, in occasioning wars and dissentions; since the proprietor's consent, who alone is concerned, is taken along in the alienation: And it may serve to many good purposes in adjusting property to persons. Different parts of the earth produce different commodities; and not only so, but different men both are by nature fitted for different employments, and attain to greater perfection in any one, when they confine themselves to it alone. All this requires a mutual exchange and commerce; for which reason the translation of property by consent is founded on a law of nature, as well as its stability without such a consent.

So far is determined by a plain utility and interest. But perhaps it is from more trivial reasons, that delivery, or a sensible transference of the object is commonly required by civil laws, and also by the laws of nature, according to most authors, as

[74] In examining the different titles to authority in government, we shall meet with many reasons to convince us, that the right of succession depends, in a great measure on the imagination. Mean while I shall rest contented with observing one example, which belongs to the present subject. Suppose that a person die without children, and that a dispute arises among his relations concerning his inheritance; it is evident, that if his riches be deriv'd partly from his father, partly from his mother, the most natural way of determining such a dispute, is, to divide his possessions, and assign each part to the family, from whence it is deriv'd. Now as the person is suppos'd to have been once the full and entire proprietor of those goods; I ask, what is it makes us find a certain equity and natural reason in this partition, except it be the imagination? His affection to these families does not depend upon his possessions; for which reason his consent can never be presum'd precisely for such a partition. And as to the public interest, it seems not to be in the least concern'd on the one side or the other.

a requisite circumstance in the translation of property. The property of an object, when taken for something real, without any reference to morality, or the sentiments of the mind, is a quality perfectly insensible, and even inconceivable; nor can we form any distinct notion, either of its stability or translation. This imperfection of our ideas is less sensibly felt with regard to its stability, as it engages less our attention, and is easily past over by the mind, without any scrupulous examination. But as the translation of property from one person to another is a more remarkable event, the defect of our ideas becomes more sensible on that occasion, and obliges us to turn ourselves on every side in search of some remedy. Now as nothing more enlivens any idea than a present impression, and a relation betwixt that impression and the idea; it is natural for us to seek some false light from this quarter. In order to aid the imagination in conceiving the transference of property, we take the sensible object, and actually transfer its possession to the person, on whom we would bestow the property. The supposed resemblance of the actions, and the presence of this sensible delivery, deceive the mind, and make it fancy, that it conceives the mysterious transition of the property. And that this explication of the matter is just, appears hence, that men have invented a symbolical delivery, to satisfy the fancy, where the real one is impracticable. Thus the giving the keys of a granary is understood to be the delivery of the corn contained in it: The giving of stone and earth represents the delivery of a manor. This is a kind of superstitious practice in civil laws, and in the laws of nature, resembling the Roman catholic superstitions in religion. As the Roman catholics represent the inconceivable mysteries of the Christian religion, and render them more present to the mind, by a taper, or habit, or grimace, which is supposed to resemble them; so lawyers and moralists have run into like inventions for the same reason, and have endeavoured by those means to satisfy themselves concerning the transference of property by consent.

SECTION V

Of the Obligation of Promises

That the rule of morality, which enjoins the performance of promises, is not natural, will sufficiently appear from these two propositions, which I proceed to prove, viz, that a promise would not be intelligible, before human conventions had established it; and that even if it were intelligible, it would not be attended with any moral obligation.

I say, first, that a promise is not intelligible naturally, nor antecedent to human conventions; and that a man, unacquainted with society, could never enter into any engagements with another, even though they could perceive each other's thoughts by intuition. If promises be natural and intelligible, there must be some act of the mind attending these words, I promise; and on this act of the mind must the obligation depend. Let us, therefore, run over all the faculties of the soul, and see which of them is exerted in our promises.

The act of the mind, exprest by a promise, is not a resolution to perform any thing: For that alone never imposes any obligation. Nor is it a desire of such a performance: For we may bind ourselves without such a desire, or even with an aversion, declared and avowed. Neither is it the willing of that action, which we promise to perform: For a promise always regards some future time, and the will has an influence only on present actions. It follows, therefore, that since the act of the mind, which enters into a promise, and produces its obligation, is neither the resolving, desiring, nor willing any particular performance, it must necessarily be the willing of that obligation, which arises from the promise. Nor is this only a conclusion of philosophy; but is entirely conformable to our common ways of thinking and of expressing ourselves, when we say that we are bound by our own consent, and that the obligation arises from our mere will and pleasure. The only question then is, whether there be not a manifest absurdity in supposing this act of the mind, and such an absurdity as no man could fall into, whose ideas are not confounded with prejudice and the fallacious use of language.

All morality depends upon our sentiments; and when any action, or quality of the mind, pleases us after a certain manner, we say it is virtuous; and when the neglect, or nonperformance of it, displeases us after a like manner, we say that we lie under an obligation to perform it. A change of the obligation supposes a change of the sentiment; and a creation of a new obligation supposes some new sentiment to arise. But it is certain we can naturally no more change our own sentiments, than the motions of the heavens; nor by a single act of our will, that is, by a promise, render any action agreeable or disagreeable, moral or immoral; which, without that act, would have produced contrary impressions, or have been endowed with different qualities. It would be absurd, therefore, to will any new obligation, that is, any new sentiment of pain or pleasure; nor is it possible, that men could naturally fall into so gross an absurdity. A promise, therefore, is naturally something altogether unintelligible, nor is there any act of the mind belonging to it.[75]

[75] Were morality discoverable by reason, and not by sentiment, it would be still more evident, that promises cou'd make no alteration upon it. Morality is suppos'd to consist in relation. Every new imposition of morality, therefore, must arise from some new relation of objects; and consequently the will could not produce immediately any change in morals, but cou'd have that effect only by producing a change upon the objects. But as the moral obligation of a promise is the pure effect of the will, without the least change in any part of the universe; it follows, that promises have no natural obligation.

Shou'd it be said, that this act of the will being in effect a new object, produces new relations and new duties; I wou'd answer, that this is a pure sophism, which may be detected by a very moderate share of accuracy and exactness. To will a new obligation, is to will a new relation of objects; and therefore, if this new relation of objects were form'd by the volition itself, we should in effect will the volition; which is plainly absurd and impossible. The will has here no object to which it cou'd tend; but must return upon itself in infinitum. The new obligation depends upon new relations. The new relations depend upon a new volition. The new volition has for object a new obligation, and consequently new relations, and consequently a new volition; which volition again has in view a new obligation, relation and volition, without any termination. It is impossible, therefore, we cou'd ever

But, secondly, if there was any act of the mind belonging to it, it could not naturally produce any obligation. This appears evidently from the foregoing reasoning. A promise creates a new obligation. A new obligation supposes new sentiments to arise. The will never creates new sentiments. There could not naturally, therefore, arise any obligation from a promise, even supposing the mind could fall into the absurdity of willing that obligation.

The same truth may be proved still more evidently by that reasoning, which proved justice in general to be an artificial virtue. No action can be required of us as our duty, unless there be implanted in human nature some actuating passion or motive, capable of producing the action. This motive cannot be the sense of duty. A sense of duty supposes an antecedent obligation: And where an action is not required by any natural passion, it cannot be required by any natural obligation; since it may be omitted without proving any defect or imperfection in the mind and temper, and consequently without any vice. Now it is evident we have no motive leading us to the performance of promises, distinct from a sense of duty. If we thought, that promises had no moral obligation, we never should feel any inclination to observe them. This is not the case with the natural virtues. Though there was no obligation to relieve the miserable, our humanity would lead us to it; and when we omit that duty, the immorality of the omission arises from its being a proof, that we want the natural sentiments of humanity. A father knows it to be his duty to take care of his children: But he has also a natural inclination to it. And if no human creature had that inclination, no one could lie under any such obligation. But as there is naturally no inclination to observe promises, distinct from a sense of their obligation; it follows, that fidelity is no natural virtue, and that promises have no force, antecedent to human conventions.

If any one dissent from this, he must give a regular proof of these two propositions, viz. THAT THERE IS A PECULIAR ACT OF THE MIND, ANNEXT TO PROMISES; AND THAT CONSEQUENT TO THIS ACT OF THE MIND, THERE ARISES AN INCLINATION TO PERFORM, DISTINCT FROM A SENSE OF DUTY. I presume, that it is impossible to prove either of these two points; and therefore I venture to conclude that promises are human inventions, founded on the necessities and interests of society.

In order to discover these necessities and interests, we must consider the same qualities of human nature, which we have already found to give rise to the preceding laws of society. Men being naturally selfish, or endowed only with a confined generosity, they are not easily induced to perform any action for the interest of strangers, except with a view to some reciprocal advantage, which they had no hope of obtaining but by such a performance. Now as it frequently happens, that these mutual performances cannot be finished at the same instant, it is necessary, that

---

will a new obligation; and consequently it is impossible the will cou'd ever accompany a promise, or produce a new obligation of morality.

one party be contented to remain in uncertainty, and depend upon the gratitude of the other for a return of kindness. But so much corruption is there among men, that, generally speaking, this becomes but a slender security; and as the benefactor is here supposed to bestow his favours with a view to self-interest, this both takes off from the obligation, and sets an example to selfishness, which is the true mother of ingratitude. Were we, therefore, to follow the natural course of our passions and inclinations, we should perform but few actions for the advantage of others, from distinterested views; because we are naturally very limited in our kindness and affection: And we should perform as few of that kind, out of a regard to interest; because we cannot depend upon their gratitude. Here then is the mutual commerce of good offices in a manner lost among mankind, and every one reduced to his own skill and industry for his well-being and subsistence. The invention of the law of nature, concerning the stability of possession, has already rendered men tolerable to each other; that of the transference of property and possession by consent has begun to render them mutually advantageous: But still these laws of nature, however strictly observed, are not sufficient to render them so serviceable to each other, as by nature they are fitted to become. Though possession be stable, men may often reap but small advantage from it, while they are possessed of a greater quantity of any species of goods than they have occasion for, and at the same time suffer by the want of others. The transference of property, which is the proper remedy for this inconvenience, cannot remedy it entirely; because it can only take place with regard to such objects as are present and individual, but not to such as are absent or general. One cannot transfer the property of a particular house, twenty leagues distant; because the consent cannot be attended with delivery, which is a requisite circumstance. Neither can one transfer the property of ten bushels of corn, or five hogsheads of wine, by the mere expression and consent; because these are only general terms, and have no direct relation to any particular heap of corn, or barrels of wine. Besides, the commerce of mankind is not confined to the barter of commodities, but may extend to services and actions, which we may exchange to our mutual interest and advantage. Your corn is ripe to-day; mine will be so tomorrow. It is profitable for us both, that I should labour with you to-day, and that you should aid me to-morrow. I have no kindness for you, and know you have as little for me. I will not, therefore, take any pains upon your account; and should I labour with you upon my own account, in expectation of a return, I know I should be disappointed, and that I should in vain depend upon your gratitude. Here then I leave you to labour alone: You treat me in the same manner. The seasons change; and both of us lose our harvests for want of mutual confidence and security.

All this is the effect of the natural and inherent principles and passions of human nature; and as these passions and principles are inalterable, it may be thought, that our conduct, which depends on them, must be so too, and that it would be in vain, either for moralists or politicians, to tamper with us, or attempt to change the usual course of our actions, with a view to public interest. And indeed, did the success of their designs depend upon their success in correcting the selfishness and ingratitude of men, they would never make any progress, unless aided by omnipotence, which is alone able to new-mould the human mind, and change its character in such fundamental articles. All they can pretend to, is, to give a new direction to those natural passions, and teach us that we can better satisfy our appetites in an oblique and artificial manner, than by their headlong and impetuous motion. Hence I learn to do a service to another, without bearing him any real kindness; because I forsee, that he will return my service, in expectation of another of the same kind, and in order to maintain the same correspondence of good offices with me or with others. And accordingly, after I have served him, and he is in possession of the advantage arising from my action, he is induced to perform his part, as foreseeing the consequences of his refusal.

But though this self-interested commerce of man begins to take place, and to predominate in society, it does not entirely abolish the more generous and noble intercourse of friendship and good offices. I may still do services to such persons as I love, and am more particularly acquainted with, without any prospect of advantage; and they may make me a return in the same manner, without any view but that of recompensing my past services. In order, therefore, to distinguish those two different sorts of commerce, the interested and the disinterested, there is a certain form of words invented for the former, by which we bind ourselves to the performance of any action. This form of words constitutes what we call a promise, which is the sanction of the interested commerce of mankind. When a man says he promises any thing, he in effect expresses a resolution of performing it; and along with that, by making use of this form of words, subjects himself to the penalty of never being trusted again in case of failure. A resolution is the natural act of the mind, which promises express: But were there no more than a resolution in the case, promises would only declare our former motives, and would not create any new motive or obligation. They are the conventions of men, which create a new motive, when experience has taught us, that human affairs would be conducted much more for mutual advantage, were there certain symbols or signs instituted, by which we might give each, other security of our conduct in any particular incident, After these signs are instituted, whoever uses them is immediately bound by his interest to execute his engagements, and must never expect to be trusted any more, if he refuse to perform what he promised.

Nor is that knowledge, which is requisite to make mankind sensible of this interest in the institution and observance of promises, to be esteemed superior to the capacity of human nature, however savage and uncultivated. There needs but a very little practice of the world, to make us perceive all these consequences and advantages. The shortest experience of society discovers them to every mortal; and when each individual perceives the same sense of interest in all his fellows, he immediately performs his part of any contract, as being assured, that they will not be wanting in theirs. All of them, by concert, enter into a scheme of actions, calculated for common benefit, and agree to be true to their word; nor is there any thing requisite to form this concert or convention, but that every one have a sense of interest in the faithful fulfilling of engagements, and express that sense to other members of the society. This immediately causes that interest to operate upon them; and interest is the first obligation to the performance of promises.

Afterwards a sentiment of morals concurs with interest, and becomes a new obligation upon mankind. This sentiment of morality, in the performance of promises, arises from the same principles as that in the abstinence from the property of others. Public interest, education, and the artifices of politicians, have the same effect in both cases. The difficulties, that occur to us, in supposing a moral obligation to attend promises, we either surmount or elude. For instance; the expression of a resolution is not commonly supposed to be obligatory; and we cannot readily conceive how the making use of a certain form of words should be able to cause any material difference. Here, therefore, we feign a new act of the mind, which we call the willing an obligation; and on this we suppose the morality to depend. But we have proved already, that there is no such act of the mind, and consequently that promises impose no natural obligation.

To confirm this, we may subjoin some other reflections concerning that will, which is supposed to enter into a promise, and to cause its obligation. It is evident, that the will alone is never supposed to cause the obligation, but must be expressed by words or signs, in order to impose a tye upon any man. The expression being once brought in as subservient to the will, soon becomes the principal part of the promise; nor will a man be less bound by his word, though he secretly give a different direction to his intention, and with-hold himself both from a resolution, and from willing an obligation. But though the expression makes on most occasions the whole of the promise, yet it does not always so; and one, who should make use of any expression, of which he knows not the meaning, and which he uses without any intention of binding himself, would not certainly be bound by it. Nay, though he knows its meaning, yet if he uses it in jest only, and with such signs as shew evidently he has no serious intention of binding himself, he would not lie under any obligation of performance; but it is necessary, that the words be a perfect expression of the will, without any contrary signs. Nay, even this we must not carry so far as to imagine, that one, whom, by our quickness of understanding, we conjecture, from certain signs, to have an intention of deceiving us, is not bound by his expression or verbal promise, if we accept of it; but must limit this conclusion to those cases, where the signs are of a different kind from those of deceit. All these contradictions are easily accounted for, if the obligation of promises be merely a human invention for the convenience of society; but will never be explained, if it be something real and natural, arising from any action of the mind or body.

I shall farther observe, that since every new promise imposes a new obligation of morality on the person who promises, and since this new obligation arises from his will; it is one of the most mysterious and incomprehensible operations that can possibly be imagined, and may even be compared to TRANSUBSTANTIATION, or HOLY ORDERS,[76] where a certain form of words, along with a certain intention, changes entirely the nature of an external object, and even of a human nature. But though these mysteries be so far alike, it is very remarkable, that they differ widely in other particulars, and that this difference may be regarded as a strong proof of the difference of their origins. As the obligation of promises is an invention for the interest of society, it is warped into as many different forms as that interest requires, and even runs into direct contradictions, rather than lose sight of its object. But as those other monstrous doctines are mere priestly inventions, and have no public interest in view, they are less disturbed in their progress by new obstacles; and it must be owned, that, after the first absurdity, they follow more directly the current of reason and good sense. Theologians clearly perceived, that the external form of words, being mere sound, require an intention to make them have any efficacy; and that this intention being once considered as a requisite circumstance, its absence must equally prevent the effect, whether avowed or concealed, whether sincere or deceitful. Accordingly they have commonly determined, that the intention of the priest makes the sacrament, and that when he secretly withdraws his intention, he is highly criminal in himself; but still destroys the baptism, or communion, or holy orders. The terrible consequences of this doctrine were not able to hinder its taking place; as the inconvenience of a similar doctrine, with regard to promises, have prevented that doctrine from establishing itself. Men are always more concerned about the present life than the future; and are apt to think the smallest evil, which regards the former, more important than the greatest, which regards the latter.

We may draw the same conclusion, concerning the origin of promises, from the force, which is supposed to invalidate all contracts, and to free us from their obligation. Such a principle is a proof, that promises have no natural obligation, and are mere artificial contrivances for the convenience and advantage of society. If we consider aright of the matter, force is not essentially different from any other motive of hope or fear, which may induce us to engage our word, and lay ourselves under any obligation. A man, dangerously wounded, who promises a competent sum to a surgeon to cure him, would certainly be bound to performance; though the case be not so much different from that of one, who promises a sum to a robber, as to produce so great a difference in our sentiments of morality, if these sentiments were not built entirely on public interest and convenience.

SECTION VI

Some Farther Reflections Concerning Justice and Injustice

We have now run over the three fundamental laws of nature, that of the stability of possession, of its transference by consent, and of the performance of promises.

---

[76] I mean so far, as holy orders are suppos'd to produce the indelible character. In other respects they are only a legal qualification.

It is on the strict observance of those three laws, that the peace and security of human society entirely depend; nor is there any possibility of establishing a good correspondence among men, where these are neglected. Society is absolutely necessary for the well-being of men; and these are as necessary to the support of society. Whatever restraint they may impose on the passions of men, they are the real offspring of those passions, and are only a more artful and more refined way of satisfying them. Nothing is more vigilant and inventive than our passions; and nothing is more obvious, than the convention for the observance of these rules. Nature has, therefore, trusted this affair entirely to the conduct of men, and has not placed in the mind any peculiar original principles, to determine us to a set of actions, into which the other principles of our frame and constitution were sufficient to lead us. And to convince us the more fully of this truth, we may here stop a moment, and from a review of the preceding reasonings may draw some new arguments, to prove that those laws, however necessary, are entirely artificial, and of human invention; and consequently that justice is an artificial, and not a natural virtue.

(1) The first argument I shall make use of is derived from the vulgar definition of justice. Justice is commonly defined to be a constant and perpetual will of giving every one his due. In this definition it is supposed, that there are such things as right and property, independent of justice, and antecedent to it; and that they would have subsisted, though men had never dreamt of practising such a virtue. I have already observed, in a cursory manner, the fallacy of this opinion, and shall here continue to open up a little more distinctly my sentiments on that subject.

I shall begin with observing, that this quality, which we shall call property, is like many of the imaginary qualities of the peripatetic philosophy, and vanishes upon a more accurate inspection into the subject, when considered a-part from our moral sentiments. It is evident property does not consist in any of the sensible qualities of the object. For these may continue invariably the same, while the property changes. Property, therefore, must consist in some relation of the object. But it is not in its relation with regard to other external and inanimate objects. For these may also continue invariably the same, while the property changes. This quality, therefore, consists in the relations of objects to intelligent and rational beings. But it is not the external and corporeal relation, which forms the essence of property. For that relation may be the same betwixt inanimate objects, or with regard to brute creatures; though in those cases it forms no property. It is, therefore, in some internal relation, that the property consists; that is, in some influence, which the external relations of the object have on the mind and actions. Thus the external relation, which we call occupation or first possession, is not of itself imagined to be the property of the object, but only to cause its property. Now it is evident, this external relation causes nothing in external objects, and has only an influence on the mind, by giving us a sense of duty in abstaining from that object, and in restoring it to the first possessor. These actions are properly what we call justice;

and consequently it is on that virtue that the nature of property depends, and not the virtue on the property.

If any one, therefore, would assert, that justice is a natural virtue, and injustice a natural vice, he must assert, that abstracting from the nations of property, and right and obligation, a certain conduct and train of actions, in certain external relations of objects, has naturally a moral beauty or deformity, and causes an original pleasure or uneasiness. Thus the restoring a man's goods to him is considered as virtuous, not because nature has annexed a certain sentiment of pleasure to such a conduct, with regard to the property of others, but because she has annexed that sentiment to such a conduct, with regard to those external objects, of which others have had the first or long possession, or which they have received by the consent of those, who have had first or long possession. If nature has given us no such sentiment, there is not, naturally, nor antecedent to human conventions, any such thing as property. Now, though it seems sufficiently evident, in this dry and accurate consideration of the present subject, that nature has annexed no pleasure or sentiment of approbation to such a conduct; yet that I may leave as little room for doubt as possible, I shall subjoin a few more arguments to confirm my opinion.

First, If nature had given us a pleasure of this kind, it would have been as evident and discernible as on every other occasion; nor should we have found any difficulty to perceive, that the consideration of such actions, in such a situation, gives a certain pleasure and sentiment of approbation. We should not have been obliged to have recourse to notions of property in the definition of justice, and at the same time make use of the notions of justice in the definition of property. This deceitful method of reasoning is a plain proof, that there are contained in the subject some obscurities and difficulties, which we are not able to surmount, and which we desire to evade by this artifice.

Secondly, Those rules, by which properties, rights, and obligations are determined, have in them no marks of a natural origin but many of artifice and contrivance. They are too numerous to have proceeded from nature: They are changeable by human laws: And have all of them a direct and evident tendency to public good, and the support, of civil society. This last circumstance is remarkable upon two accounts. First, because, though the cause of the establishment of these laws had been a regard for the public good, as much as the public good is their natural tendency, they would still have been artificial, as being purposely contrived and directed to a certain end. Secondly, because, if men had been endowed with such a strong regard for public good, they would never have restrained themselves by these rules; so that the laws of justice arise from natural principles in a manner still more oblique and artificial. It is self-love which is their real origin; and as the self-love of one person is naturally contrary to that of another, these several interested passions are obliged to adjust themselves after such a manner as to concur in some system of conduct and behaviour. This system, therefore, comprehending the interest of each individual, is of course advantageous to the public; though it be not intended for that purpose by die inventors.

(2) In the second place we may observe, that all kinds of vice and virtue run insensibly into each other, and may approach by such imperceptible degrees as will make it very difficult, if not absolutely impossible, to determine when the one ends, and the other begins; and from this observation we may derive a new argument for the foregoing principle. For whatever may be the case, with regard to all kinds of vice and virtue, it is certain, that rights, and obligations, and property, admit of no such insensible gradation, but that a man either has a full and perfect property, or none at all; and is either entirely obliged to perform any action, or lies under no manner of obligation. However civil laws may talk of a perfect dominion, and of an imperfect, it is easy to observe, that this arises from a fiction, which has no foundation in reason, and can never enter into our notions of natural justice and equity. A man that hires a horse, though but for a day, has as full a right to make use of it for that time, as he whom we call its proprietor has to make use of it any other day; and it was evident, that however the use may be bounded in time or degree, the right itself is not susceptible of any such gradation, but is absolute and entire, so far as it extends. Accordingly we may observe, that this right both arises and perishes in an instant; and that a man entirely acquires the property of any object by occupation, or the consent of the proprietor; and loses it by his own consent; without any of that insensible gradation, which is remarkable in other qualities and relations, Since, therefore, this is die case with regard to property, and rights, and obligations, I ask, how it stands with regard to justice and injustice? After whatever manner you answer this question, you run into inextricable difficulties. If you reply, that justice and injustice admit of degree, and run insensibly into each other, you expressly contradict the foregoing position, that obligation and property are not susceptible of such a gradation. These depend entirely upon justice and injustice, and follow them in all their variations. Where the justice is entire, the property is also entire: Where the justice is imperfect, the property must also be imperfect And vice versa, if the property admit of no such variations, they must also be incompatible with justice. If you assent, therefore, to this last proposition, and assert, that justice and injustice are not susceptible of degrees, you in effect assert, that they are not naturally either vicious or virtuous; since vice and virtue, moral good and evil, and indeed all natural qualities, run insensibly into each other, and are, on many occasions, undistinguishable.

And here it may be worth while to observe, that though abstract reasoning, and the general maxims of philosophy and law establish this position, that property, and right, and obligation admit not of degrees, yet in our common and negligent way of thinking, we find great difficulty to entertain that opinion, and do even secretly embrace the contrary principle. An object must either be in the possession of one person or another. An action must either be performed or not. The necessity there is of choosing one side in these dilemmas, and the impossibility there often is of finding any just medium, oblige us, when we reflect on the matter, to acknowledge, that all property and obligations are entire. But on the other hand, when we consider the origin of property and obligation, and find that they depend on public utility, and sometimes on the propensities of the imagination, which are seldom entire on any side; we are naturally inclined to imagine, that these moral relations admit of an insensible gradation. Hence it is, that in references, where the consent of the parties leave the referees entire masters of the subject, they commonly discover so much equity and justice on both sides, as induces them to strike a medium, and divide the difference betwixt the parties. Civil judges, who have not this liberty, but are obliged to give a decisive sentence on some one side, are often at a loss how to determine, and are necessitated to proceed on the most frivolous reasons in the world. Half rights and obligations, which seem so natural in common life, are perfect absurdities in their tribunal; for which reason they are often obliged to take half arguments for whole ones, in order to terminate the affair one way or other.

(3) The third argument of this kind I shall make use of may be explained thus. If we consider the ordinary course of human actions, we shall find, that the mind restrains not itself by any general and universal rules; but acts on most occasions as it is determined by its present motives and inclination. As each action is a particular individual event, it must proceed from particular principles, and from our immediate situation within ourselves, and with respect to the rest of the universe. If on some occasions we extend our motives beyond those very circumstances, which gave rise to them, and form something like general rules for our conduct, it is easy to observe, that these rules are not perfectly inflexible, but allow of many exceptions. Since, therefore, this is the ordinary course of human actions, we may conclude, that the laws of justice, being universal and perfectly inflexible, can never be derived from nature, nor be the immediate offspring of any natural motive or inclination. No action can be either morally good or evil, unless there be some natural passion or motive to impel us to it, or deter us from it; and it is evident, that die morality must be susceptible of all the same variations, which are natural to the passion. Here are two persons, who dispute for an estate; of whom one is rich, a fool, and a batchelor; the other poor, a man of sense, and has a numerous family: The first is my enemy; the second my friend. Whether I be actuated in this affair by a view to public or private interest, by friendship or enmity, I must be induced to do my utmost to procure the estate to the latter. Nor would any consideration of the right and property of the persons be able to restrain me, were I actuated only by natural motives, without any combination or convention with others. For as all property depends on morality; and as all morality depends on the ordinary course of our passions and actions; and as these again are only directed by particular motives; it is evident, such a partial conduct must be suitable to the strictest morality, and could never be

a violation of property. Were men, therefore, to take the liberty of acting with regard to the laws of society, as they do in every other affair, they would conduct themselves, on most occasions, by particular judgments, and would take into consideration the characters and circumstances of the persons, as well as the general nature of the question. But it is easy to observe, that this would produce an infinite confusion in human society, and that the avidity and partiality of men would quickly bring disorder into the world, if not restrained by some general and inflexible principles. Twas, therefore, with a view to this inconvenience, that men have established those principles, and have agreed to restrain themselves by general rules, which are unchangeable by spite and favour, and by particular views of private or public interest. These rules, then, are artificially invented for a certain purpose, and are contrary to the common principles of human nature, which accommodate themselves to circumstances, and have no stated invariable method of operation.

Nor do I perceive how I can easily be mistaken in this matter. I see evidently, that when any man imposes on himself general inflexible rules in his conduct with others, he considers certain objects as their property, which he supposes to be sacred and inviolable. But no proposition can be more evident, than that property is perfectly unintelligible without first supposing justice and injustice; and that these virtues and vices are as unintelligible, unless we have motives, independent of the morality, to impel us to just actions, and deter us from unjust ones. Let those motives, therefore, be what they will, they must accommodate themselves to circumstances, and must admit of all the variations, which human affairs, in their incessant revolutions, are susceptible of. They are consequently a very improper foundation for such rigid inflexible rules as the laws of nature; and it is evident these laws can only be derived from human conventions, when men have perceived the disorders that result from following their natural and variable principles.

Upon the whole, then, we are to consider this distinction betwixt justice and injustice, as having two different foundations, viz, that of interest, when men observe, that it is impossible to live in society without restraining themselves by certain rules; and that of morality, when this interest is once observed and men receive a pleasure from the view of such actions as tend to the peace of society, and an uneasiness from such as are contrary to it. It is the voluntary convention and artifice of men, which makes the first interest take place; and therefore those laws of justice are so far to be considered as artificial. After that interest is once established and acknowledged, the sense of morality in the observance of these rules follows naturally, and of itself; though it is certain, that it is also augmented by a new artifice, and that the public instructions of politicians, and the private education of parents, contribute to the giving us a sense of honour and duty in the strict regulation of our actions with regard to the properties of others.

SECTION VII

Of the Origin of Government

Nothing is more certain, than that men are, in a great measure, governed by interest, and that even when they extend their concern beyond themselves, it is not to any great distance; nor is it usual for them, in common life, to look farther than their nearest friends and acquaintance. It is no less certain, that it is impossible for men to consult, their interest in so effectual a manner, as by an universal and inflexible observance of the rules of justice, by which alone they can preserve society, and keep themselves from falling into that wretched and savage condition, which is commonly represented as the state of nature. And as this interest, which all men have in the upholding of society, and the observation of the rules of justice, is great, so is it palpable and evident, even to the most rude and uncultivated of human race; and it is almost impossible for any one, who has had experience of society, to be mistaken in this particular. Since, therefore, men are so sincerely attached to their interest, and their interest is so much concerned in the observance of justice, and this interest is so certain and avowed; it may be asked, how any disorder can ever arise in society, and what principle there is in human nature so powerful as to overcome so strong a passion, or so violent as to obscure so clear a knowledge?

It has been observed, in treating of the passions, that men are mightily governed by the imagination, and proportion their affections more to the light, under which any object appears to them, than to its real and intrinsic value. What strikes upon them with a strong and lively idea commonly prevails above what lies in a more obscure light; and it must be a great superiority of value, that is able to compensate this advantage. Now as every thing, that is contiguous to us, either in space or time, strikes upon us with such an idea, it has a proportional effect on the will and passions, and commonly operates with more force than any object, that lies in a more distant and obscure light. Though we may be fully convinced, that the latter object excels the former, we are not able to regulate our actions by this judgment; but yield to the sollicitations of our passions, which always plead in favour of whatever is near and contiguous.

This is the reason why men so often act in contradiction to their known interest; and in particular why they prefer any trivial advantage, that is present, to the maintenance of order in society, which so much depends on the observance of justice. The consequences of every breach of equity seem to lie very remote, and are not able to counter-ballance any immediate advantage, that may be reaped from it. They are, however, never the less real for being remote; and as all men are, in some degree, subject to the same weakness, it necessarily happens, that the violations of equity must become very frequent in society, and the commerce of men, by that means, be rendered very dangerous and uncertain. You have the same propension, that I have, in favour of what is contiguous above what is remote. You are, therefore, naturally carried to commit acts of injustice as well as me. Your example both pushes me forward in this way by imitation, and also affords me a new reason for any breach of equity, by shewing me, that I should be the cully of my integrity, if I alone should impose on myself a severe restraint amidst the licentiousness of others.

This quality, therefore, of human nature, not only is very dangerous to society, but also seems, on a cursory view, to be incapable of any remedy. The remedy can only come from the consent of men; and if men be incapable of themselves to prefer remote to contiguous, they will never consent to any thing, which would oblige them to such a choice, and contradict, in so sensible a manner, their natural principles and propensities. Whoever chuses the means, chuses also the end; and if it be impossible for us to prefer what is remote, it is equally impossible for us to submit to any necessity, which would oblige us to such a method of acting.

But here it is observable, that this infirmity of human nature becomes a remedy to itself, and that we provide against our negligence about remote objects, merely because we are naturally inclined to that negligence. When we consider any objects at a distance, all their minute distinctions vanish, and we always give the preference to whatever is in itself preferable, without considering its situation and circumstances. This gives rise to what in an improper sense we call reason, which is a principle, that is often contradictory to those propensities that display themselves upon the approach of the object. In reflecting on any action, which I am to perform a twelve-month hence, I always resolve to prefer the greater good, whether at that time it will be more contiguous or remote; nor does any difference in that particular make a difference in my present intentions and resolutions. My distance from the final determination makes all those minute differences vanish, nor am I affected by any thing, but the general and more discernible qualities of good and evil. But on my nearer approach, those circumstances, which I at first over-looked, begin to appear, and have an influence on my conduct and affections. A new inclination to the present good springs up, and makes it difficult for me to adhere inflexibly to my first purpose and resolution. This natural infirmity I may very much regret, and I may endeavour, by all possible means, to free my self from it. I may have recourse to study and reflection within myself; to the advice of friends; to frequent meditation, and repeated resolution: And having experienced how ineffectual all these are, I may embrace with pleasure any other expedient, by which I may impose a restraint upon myself, and guard against this weakness.

The only difficulty, therefore, is to find out this expedient, by which men cure their natural weakness, and lay themselves under the necessity of observing the laws of justice and equity, notwithstanding their violent propension to prefer contiguous to remote. It is evident such a remedy can never be effectual without correcting this propensity; and as it is impossible to change or correct any thing material in our nature, the utmost we can do is to change our circumstances and situation, and render the observance of the laws of justice our nearest interest, and their violation our most remote. But this being impracticable with respect to all mankind, it can only take place with respect to a few, whom we thus immediately interest in the execution of justice. There are the persons, whom we call civil magistrates, kings and their ministers, our governors and rulers, who being indifferent persons to the greatest part of the state, have no interest, or but a remote one, in any act of injustice; and being satisfied with their present condition, and with their part in society, have an immediate interest in every execution of justice, which is so necessary to the upholding of society. Here then is the origin of civil government and society. Men are not able radically to cure, either in themselves or others, that narrowness of soul, which makes them prefer the present to the remote. They cannot change their natures. All they can do is to change their situation, and render the observance of justice the immediate interest of some particular persons, and its violation their more remote. These persons, then, are not only induced to observe those rules in their own conduct, but also to constrain others to a like regularity, and inforce the dictates of equity through the whole society. And if it be necessary, they may also interest others more immediately in the execution of justice, and create a number of officers, civil and military, to assist them in their government.

But this execution of justice, though the principal, is not the only advantage of government. As violent passion hinder men from seeing distinctly the interest they have in an equitable behaviour towards others; so it hinders them from seeing that equity itself, and gives them a remarkable partiality in their own favours. This inconvenience is corrected in the same manner as that above-mentioned. The same persons, who execute the laws of justice, will also decide all controversies concerning them; and being indifferent to the greatest part of the society, will decide them more equitably than every one would in his own case.

By means of these two advantages, in the execution and decision of justice, men acquire a security against each others weakness and passion, as well as against their own, and under the shelter of their governors, begin to taste at ease the sweets of society and mutual assistance. But government extends farther its beneficial influence; and not contented to protect men in those conventions they make for their mutual interest, it often obliges them to make such conventions, and forces them to seek their own advantage, by a concurrence in some common end or purpose. There is no quality in human nature, which causes more fatal errors in our conduct, than that which leads us to prefer whatever is present to the distant and remote, and makes us desire objects more according to their situation than their intrinsic value. Two neighbours may agree to drain a meadow, which they possess in common; because it is easy for them to know each others mind; and each must perceive, that the immediate consequence of his failing in his part, is, the abandoning the whole project. But it is very difficult, and indeed impossible, that a thousand persons should agree in any such action; it being difficult for them to concert so complicated a design, and still more difficult for them to execute it; while each seeks a pretext to free himself of the trouble and expence, and would lay the whole burden on others. Political society easily remedies both these inconveniences.

Magistrates find an immediate interest in the interest of any considerable part of their subjects. They need consult no body but themselves to form any scheme for the promoting of that interest. And as the failure of any one piece in the execution is connected, though not immediately, with the failure of the whole, they prevent that failure, because they find no interest in it, either immediate or remote. Thus bridges are built; harbours opened; ramparts raised; canals formed; fleets equiped; and armies disciplined every where, by the care of government, which, though composed of men subject to all human infirmities, becomes, by one of the finest and most subtle inventions imaginable, a composition, which is, in some measure, exempted from all these infirmities.

SECTION VIII

Of the Source of Allegiance

Though government be an invention very advantageous, and even in some circumstances absolutely necessary to mankind; it is not necessary in all circumstances, nor is it impossible for men to preserve society for some time, without having recourse to such an invention. Men, it is true, are always much inclined to prefer present interest to distant and remote; nor is it easy for them to resist the temptation of any advantage, that they may immediately enjoy, in apprehension of an evil that lies at a distance from them: But still this weakness is less conspicuous where the possessions, and the pleasures of life are few, and of little value, as they always are in the infancy of society. An Indian is but little tempted to dispossess another of his hut, or to steal his bow, as being already provided of the same advantages; and as to any superior fortune, which may attend one above another in hunting and fishing, it is only casual and temporary, and will have but small tendency to disturb society. And so far am I from thinking with some philosophers, that men are utterly incapable of society without government, that I assert the first rudiments of government to arise from quarrels, not among men of the same society, but among those of different societies. A less degree of riches will suffice to this latter effect, than is requisite for the former. Men fear nothing from public war and violence but the resistance they meet with, which, because they share it in common, seems less terrible; and because it comes from strangers, seems less pernicious in its consequences, than when they are exposed singly against one whose commerce is advantageous to them, and without whose society it is impossible they can subsist. Now foreign war to a society without government necessarily produces civil war. Throw any considerable goods among men, they instantly fall a quarrelling, while each strives to get possession of what pleases him, without regard to the consequences. In a foreign war the most considerable of all goods, life and limbs, are at stake; and as every one shuns dangerous ports, seizes the best arms, seeks excuse for the slightest wounds, the laws, which may be well enough observed while men were calm, can now no longer take place, when they are in such commotion.

This we find verified in the American tribes, where men live in concord and amity among themselves without any established government and never pay submission to any of their fellows, except in time of war, when their captain enjoys a shadow of authority, which he loses after their return from the field, and the establishment of peace with the neighbouring tribes. This authority, however, instructs them in the advantages of government, and teaches them to have recourse to it, when either by the pillage of war, by commerce, or by any fortuitous inventions, their riches and possessions have become so considerable as to make them forget, on every emergence, the interest they have in the preservation of peace and justice. Hence we may give a plausible reason, among others, why all governments are at first monarchical, without any mixture and variety; and why republics arise only from the abuses of monarchy and despotic power. Camps are the true mothers of cities; and as war cannot be administered, by reason of the suddenness of every exigency, without some authority in a single person, the same kind of authority naturally takes place in that civil government, which succeeds the military. And this reason I take to be more natural, than the common one derived from patriarchal government, or the authority of a father, which is said first to take place in one family, and to accustom the members of it to the government of a single person. The state of society without government is one of the most natural states of men, and must submit with the conjunction of many families, and long after the first generation. Nothing but an encrease of riches and possessions could oblige men to quit it; and so barbarous and uninstructed are all societies on their first formation, that many years must elapse before these can encrease to such a degree, as to disturb men in the enjoyment of peace and concord. But though it be possible for men to maintain a small uncultivated society without government, it is impossible they should maintain a society of any kind without justice, and the observance of those three fundamental laws concerning the stability of possession, its translation by consent, and the performance of promises. These are, therefore, antecedent to government, and are supposed to impose an obligation before the duty of allegiance to civil magistrates has once been thought of. Nay, I shall go farther, and assert, that government, upon its first establishment, would naturally be supposed. to derive its obligation from those laws of nature, and, in particular, from that concerning the performance of promises. When men have once perceived the necessity of government to maintain peace, and execute justice, they would naturally assemble together, would chuse magistrates, determine power, and promise them obedience. As a promise is supposed to be a bond or security already in use, and attended with a moral obligation, it is to be considered as the original sanction of government, and as the source of the first obligation to obedience. This reasoning appears so natural, that it has become the foundation of our fashionable system of politics, and is in a manner the creed of a party amongst us, who pride themselves, with reason, on the soundness of their philosophy, and their liberty of thought. All men, say they, are born free and equal: Government and superiority can only be established by consent: The consent of men, in establishing government, imposes on them a new obligation, unknown to the laws of nature. Men, therefore, are bound to obey their magistrates, only because they promise it; and if they had not given their word, either expressly or tacitly, to preserve allegiance, it would never have become a part of their moral duty. This conclusion, however, when carried so far as to comprehend government in all its ages and situations, is entirely erroneous; and I maintain, that though the duty of allegiance be at first grafted on the obligation of promises, and be for some time supported by that obligation, yet it quickly takes root of itself, and has an original obligation and authority, independent of all contracts. This is a principle of moment, which we must examine with care and attention, before we proceed any farther.

It is reasonable for those philosophers, who assert justice to be a natural virtue, and antecedent to human conventions, to resolve all civil allegiance into the obligation of a promise, and assert that it is our own consent alone, which binds us to any submission to magistracy. For as all government is plainly an invention of men, and the origin of most governments is known in history, it is necessary to mount higher, in order to find the source of our political duties, if we would assert them to have any natural obligation of morality. These philosophers, therefore, quickly observe, that society is as antient as the human species, and those three fundamental laws of nature as antient as society: So that taking advantage of the antiquity, and obscure origin of these laws, they first deny them to be artificial and voluntary inventions of men, and then seek to ingraft on them those other duties, which are more plainly artificial. But being once undeceived in this particular, and having found that natural, as well as civil justice, derives its origin from human conventions, we shall quickly perceive, how fruitless it is to resolve the one into the other, and seek, in the laws of nature, a stronger foundation for our political duties than interest, and human conventions; while these laws themselves are built on the very same foundation. On which ever side we turn this subject, we shall find, that these two kinds of duty are exactly on the same footing, and have the same source both of their first invention and moral obligation. They are contrived to remedy like inconveniences, and acquire their moral sanction in the same manner, from their remedying those inconveniences. These are two points, which we shall endeavour to prove as distinctly as possible.

We have already shewn, that men invented the three fundamental laws of nature, when they observed the necessity of society to their mutual subsistance, and found, that it was impossible to maintain any correspondence together, without some restraint on their natural appetites. The same self-love, therefore, which renders men so incommodious to each other, taking a new and more convenient direction, produces the rules of justice, and is the first motive of their observance. But when men have observed, that though the rules of justice be sufficient to maintain any society, yet it is impossible for them, of themselves, to observe those rules, in large and polished societies; they establish government, as a new invention to attain their ends, and preserve the old, or procure new advantages, by a more strict execution of justice. So far, therefore, our civil duties are connected with our natural, that the former are invented chiefly for the sake of the latter; and that the principal object of government is to constrain men to observe the laws of nature. In this respect, however, that law of nature, concerning the performance of promises, is only comprized along with the rest; and its exact observance is to be considered as an effect of the institution of government, and not the obedience to government as an effect of the obligation of a promise. Though the object of our civil duties be the enforcing of our natural, yet the first[77] motive of the invention, as well as performance of both, is nothing but self-interest: and since there is a separate interest in the obedience to government, from that in the performance of promises, we must also allow of a separate obligation. To obey the civil magistrate is requisite to preserve order and concord in society. To perform promises is requisite to beget mutual trust and confidence in the common offices of life. The ends, as well as the means, are perfectly distinct; nor is the one subordinate to the other.

To make this more evident, let us consider, that men will often bind themselves by promises to the performance of what it would have been their interest to perform, independent of these promises; as when they would give others a fuller security, by super-adding a new obligation of interest to that which they formerly lay under. The interest in the performance of promises, besides its moral obligation, is general, avowed, and of the last consequence in life. Other interests may be more particular and doubtful; and we are apt to entertain a greater suspicion, that men may indulge their humour, or passion, in acting contrary to them. Here, therefore, promises come naturally in play, and are often required for fuller satisfaction and security. But supposing those other interests to be as general and avowed as the interest in the performance of a promise, they will be regarded as on the same footing, and men will begin to repose the same confidence in them. Now this is exactly the case with regard to our civil duties, or obedience to the magistrate; without which no government could subsist, nor any peace or order be maintained in large societies, where there are so many possessions on the one hand, and so many wants, real or imaginary, on the other. Our civil duties, therefore, must soon detach themselves from our promises, and acquire a separate force and influence. The interest in both is of the very same kind: It is general, avowed, and prevails in all times and places. There is, then, no pretext of reason for founding the one upon the other; while each of them has a foundation peculiar to itself. We might as well resolve the obligation to abstain from the possessions of others, into the obligation of a promise, as that of allegiance. The interests are not more distinct in the one case than the other. A regard to property is not more necessary to natural society, than obedience is to civil society or government; nor is the former society more necessary to the being of mankind, than the latter to their well-being and happiness. In short, if

[77] First in time, not in dignity or force.

the performance of promises be advantageous, so is obedience to government: If the former interest be general, so is the latter: If the one interest be obvious and avowed, so is the other. And as these two rules are founded on like obligations of interest, each of them must have a peculiar authority, independent of the other.

But it is not only the natural obligations of interest, which are distinct in promises and allegiance; but also the moral obligations of honour and conscience: Nor does the merit or demerit of the one depend in the least upon that of the other. And indeed, if we consider the close connexion there is betwixt the natural and moral obligations, we shall find this conclusion to be entirely unavoidable. Our interest is always engaged on the side of obedience to magistracy; and there is nothing but a great present advantage, that can lead us to rebellion, by making us over-look the remote interest, which we have in the preserving of peace and order in society. But though a present interest may thus blind us with regard to our own actions, it takes not place with regard to those of others; nor hinders them from appearing in their true colours, as highly prejudicial to public interest, and to our own in particular. This naturally gives us an uneasiness, in considering such seditious and disloyal actions, and makes us attach to them the idea of vice and moral deformity. It is the same principle, which causes us to disapprove of all kinds of private injustice, and in particular of the breach of promises. We blame all treachery and breach of faith; because we consider, that the freedom and extent of human commerce depend entirely on a fidelity with regard to promises. We blame all disloyalty to magistrates; because we perceive, that the execution of justice, in the stability of possession, its translation by consent, and the performance of promises, is impossible, without submission to government. As there are here two interests entirely distinct from each other, they must give rise to two moral obligations, equally separate and independent. Though there was no such thing as a promise in the world, government would still be necessary in all large and civilized societies; and if promises had only their own proper obligation, without the separate sanction of government, they would have but little efficacy in such societies. This separates the boundaries of our public and private duties, and shews that the latter are more dependant on the former, than the former on the latter. Education, and the artifice of politicians, concur to bestow a farther morality on loyalty, and to brand all rebellion with a greater degree of guilt and infamy. Nor is it a wonder, that politicians should be very industrious in inculcating such notions, where their interest is so particularly concerned.

Lest those arguments should not appear entirely conclusive (as I think they are) I shall have recourse to authority, and shall prove, from the universal consent of mankind, that the obligation of submission to government is not derived from any promise of the subjects. Nor need any one wonder, that though I have all along endeavoured to establish my system on pure reason, and have scarce ever cited the judgment even of philosophers or historians on any article, I should now appeal to popular authority, and oppose the sentiments of the rabble to any philosophical reasoning. For it must be observed, that the opinions of men, in this case, carry with them a peculiar authority, and are, in a great measure, infallible. The distinction of moral good and evil is founded on the pleasure or pain, which results from the view of any sentiment, or character; and as that pleasure or pain cannot be unknown to the person who feels it, it follows,[78] that there is just so much vice or virtue in any character, as every one places in it, and that it is impossible in this particular we can ever be mistaken. And though our judgments concerning the origin of any vice or virtue, be not so certain as those concerning their degrees; yet, since the question in this case regards not any philosophical origin of an obligation, but a plain matter of fact, it is not easily conceived how we can fall into an error. A man, who acknowledges himself to be bound to another, for a certain sum, must certainly know whether it be by his own bond, or that of his father; whether it be of his mere good-will, or for money lent him; and under what conditions, and for what purposes he has bound himself. In like manner, it being certain, that there is a moral obligation to submit to government, because every one thinks so; it must be as certain, that this obligation arises not from a promise; since no one, whose judgment has not been led astray by too strict adherence to a system of philosophy, has ever yet dreamt of ascribing it to that origin. Neither magistrates nor subjects have formed this idea of our civil duties.

We find, that magistrates are so far from deriving their authority, and the obligation to obedience in their subjects, from the foundation of a promise or original contract, that they conceal, as far as possible, from their people, especially from the vulgar, that they have their origin from thence. Were this the sanction of government, our rulers would never receive it tacitly, which is the utmost that can be pretended; since what is given tacitly and insensibly can never have such influence on mankind, as what is performed expressly and openly. A tacit promise is, where the will is signified by other more diffuse signs than those of speech; but a will there must certainly be in the case, and that can never escape the person's notice, who exerted it, however silent or tacit. But were you to ask the far greatest part of the nation, whether they had ever consented to the authority of their rulers, or promised to obey them, they would be inclined to think very strangely of you; and would certainly reply, that the affair depended not on their consent, but that they were born to such an obedience. In consequence of this opinion, we frequently see them imagine such persons to be their natural rulers, as are at that time deprived of all power and authority, and whom no man, however foolish, would voluntarily chuse; and this merely because they are in that line, which ruled before, and in that degree of it, which used to succeed; though perhaps in so distant a period, that scarce any man alive could ever have given any promise of obedience. Has a

[78] This proposition must hold strictly true, with regard to every quality, that is determin'd merely by sentiment. In what sense we can talk either of a right or a wrong taste in morals, eloquence, or beauty, shall be considerd afterwards. In the mean time, it may be observ'd, that there is such an uniformity in the GENERAL sentiments of mankind, as to render such questions of but small importance.

government, then, no authority over such as these, because they never consented to it, and would esteem the very attempt of such a free choice a piece of arrogance and impiety? We find by experience, that it punishes them very freely for what it calls treason and rebellion, which, it seems, according to this system, reduces itself to common injustice. If you say, that by dwelling in its dominions, they in effect consented to the established government; I answer, that this can only be, where they think the affair depends on their choice, which few or none, beside those philosophers, have ever yet imagined. It never was pleaded as an excuse for a rebel, that the first act he performed, after he came to years of discretion, was to levy war against the sovereign of the state; and that while he was a child he could not bind himself by his own consent, and having become a man, showed plainly, by the first act he performed, that he had no design to impose on himself any obligation to obedience. We find, on the contrary, that civil laws punish this crime at the same age as any other, which is criminal, of itself, without our consent; that is, when the person is come to the full use of reason: Whereas to this crime they ought in justice to allow some intermediate time, in which a tacit consent at least might be supposed. To which we may add, that a man living under an absolute government, would owe it no allegiance; since, by its very nature, it depends not on consent. But as that is as natural and common a government as any, it must certainly occasion some obligation; and it is plain from experience, that men, who are subjected to it, do always think so. This is a clear proof, that we do not commonly esteem our allegiance to be derived from our consent or promise; and a farther proof is, that when our promise is upon any account expressly engaged, we always distinguish exactly betwixt the two obligations, and believe the one to add more force to the other, than in a repetition of the same promise. Where no promise is given, a man looks not on his faith as broken in private matters, upon account of rebellion; but keeps those two duties of honour and allegiance perfectly distinct and separate. As the uniting of them was thought by these philosophers a very subtile invention, this is a convincing proof, that it is not a true one; since no man can either give a promise, or be restrained by its sanction and obligation unknown to himself.

SECTION IX

Of the Measures of Allegiance

Those political writers, who have had recourse to a promise, or original contract, as the source of our allegiance to government, intended to establish a principle, which is perfectly just and reasonable; though the reasoning, upon which they endeavoured to establish it, was fallacious and sophistical. They would prove, that our submission to government admits of exceptions, and that an egregious tyranny in the rulers is sufficient to free the subjects from all ties of allegiance. Since men enter into society, say they, and submit themselves to government, by their free and voluntary consent, they must have in view certain advantages, which they propose to reap from it, and for which they are contented to resign their native liberty. There is, therefore, something mutual engaged on the part of the magistrate, viz, protection and security; and it is only by the hopes he affords of these advantages, that he can ever persuade men to submit to him. But when instead of protection and security, they meet with tyranny and oppression, they are freed from their promises, (as happens in all conditional contracts) and return to that state of liberty, which preceded the institution of government. Men would never be so foolish as to enter into such engagements as should turn entirely to the advantage of others, without any view of bettering their own condition. Whoever proposes to draw any profit from our submission, must engage himself, either expressly or tacitly, to make us reap some advantage from his authority; nor ought he to expect, that without the performance of his part we will ever continue in obedience.

I repeat it: This conclusion is just, though the principles be erroneous; and I flatter myself, that I can establish the same conclusion on more reasonable principles. I shall not take such a compass, in establishing our political duties, as to assert, that men perceive the advantages of government; that they institute government with a view to those advantages; that this institution requires a promise of obedience; which imposes a moral obligation to a certain degree, but being conditional, ceases to be binding, whenever the other contracting party performs not his part of the engagement. I perceive, that a promise itself arises entirely from human conventions, and is invented with a view to a certain interest. I seek, therefore, some such interest more immediately connected with government, and which may be at once the original motive to its institution, and the source of our obedience to it. This interest I find to consist in the security and protection, which we enjoy in political society, and which we can never attain, when perfectly free and independent. As interest, therefore, is the immediate sanction of government, the one can have no longer being than the other; and whenever the civil magistrate carries his oppression so far as to render his authority perfectly intolerable, we are no longer bound to submit to it. The cause ceases; the effect must cease also.

So far the conclusion is immediate and direct, concerning the natural obligation which we have to allegiance. As to the moral obligation, we may observe, that the maxim would here be false, that when the cause ceases, the effect must cease also. For there is a principle of human nature, which we have frequently taken notice of, that men are mightily addicted to general rules, and that we often carry our maxims beyond those reasons, which first induced us to establish them. Where cases are similar in many circumstances, we are apt to put them on the same footing, without considering, that they differ in the most material circumstances, and that the resemblance is more apparent than real. It may, therefore, be thought, that in the case of allegiance our moral obligation of duty will not cease, even though the natural obligation of interest, which is its cause, has ceased; and that men may be bound by conscience to submit to a tyrannical government against their own and the public interest. And indeed, to the force of this argument I so far submit, as to acknowledge, that general rules commonly extend beyond the principles, on which they are founded; and that we seldom make any exception to them, unless that exception have the qualities of a general rule, and be founded on very numerous and common instances. Now this I assert to be entirely the present case. When men submit to the authority of others, it is to procure themselves some security against the wickedness and injustice of men, who are perpetually carried, by their unruly passions, and by their present and immediate interest, to the violation of all the laws of society. But as this imperfection is inherent in human nature, we know that it must attend men in all their states and conditions; and that these, whom we chuse for rulers, do not immediately become of a superior nature to the rest of mankind, upon account of their superior power and authority. What we expect from them depends not on a change of their nature but of their situation, when they acquire a more immediate interest in the preservation of order and the execution of justice. But besides that this interest is only more immediate in the execution of justice among their subjects; besides this, I say, we may often expect, from the irregularity of human nature, that they will neglect even this immediate interest, and be transported by their passions into all the excesses of cruelty and ambition.. Our general knowledge of human nature, our observation of the past history of mankind, our experience of present times; all these causes must induce us to open the door to exceptions, and must make us conclude, that we may resist the more violent effects of supreme power, without any crime or injustice.

Accordingly we may observe, that this is both the general practice and principle of mankind, and that no nation, that could find any remedy, ever yet suffered the cruel ravages of a tyrant, or were blamed for their resistance. Those who took up arms against Dionysius or Nero, or Philip the second, have the favour of every reader in the perusal of their history: and nothing but the most violent perversion of common sense can ever lead us to condemn them. It is certain, therefore, that in all our notions of morals we never entertain such an absurdity as that of passive obedience, but make allowances for resistance in the more flagrant instances of tyranny and oppression. The general opinion of mankind has some authority in all cases; but in this of morals it is perfectly infallible. Nor is it less infallible, because men cannot distinctly explain the principles, on which it is founded. Few persons can carry on this train of reasoning:

Government is a mere human invention for the interest of society. Where the tyranny of the governor removes this interest, it also removes the natural obligation to obedience. The moral obligation is founded on the natural, and therefore must cease where that ceases; especially where the subject is such as makes us foresee very many occasions wherein the natural obligation may cease, and causes us to form a kind of general rule for the regulation of our conduct in such occurrences.

But though this train of reasoning be too subtile for the vulgar, it is certain, that all men have an implicit notion of it, and are sensible, that they owe obedience to government merely on account of the public interest; and at the same time, that human nature is so subject to frailties and passions, as may easily pervert this institution, and change their governors into tyrants and public enemies. If the sense of common interest were not our original motive to obedience, I would fain ask, what other principle is there in human nature capable of subduing the natural ambition of men, and forcing them to such a submission? Imitation and custom are not sufficient. For the question still recurs, what motive first produces those instances of submission, which we imitate, and that train of actions, which produces the custom? There evidently is no other principle than public interest; and if interest first produces obedience to government, the obligation to obedience must cease, whenever the interest ceases, in any great degree, and in a considerable number of instances.

SECTION X

Of the Objects of Allegiance

But though, on some occasions, it may be justifiable, both in sound politics and morality, to resist supreme power, it is certain, that in the ordinary course of human affairs nothing can be more pernicious and criminal; and that besides the convulsions, which always attend revolutions, such a practice tends directly to the subversion of all government, and the causing an universal anarchy and confusion among mankind. As numerous and civilized societies cannot subsist without government, so government is entirely useless without an exact obedience. We ought always to weigh the advantages, which we reap from authority, against the disadvantages; and by this means we shall become more scrupulous of putting in practice the doctrine of resistance. The common rule requires submission; and it is only in cases of grievous tyranny and oppression, that the exception can take place.

Since then such a blind submission is commonly due to magistracy, the next question is, to whom it is due, and whom we are to regard as our lawful magistrates? In order to answer this question, let us recollect what we have already established concerning the origin of government and political society. When men have once experienced the impossibility of preserving any steady order in society, while every one is his own master, and violates or observes the laws of society, according to his present interest or pleasure, they naturally run into the invention of government, and put it out of their own power, as far as possible, to transgress the laws of society. Government, therefore, arises from the same voluntary conversation of men; and it is evident, that the same convention, which establishes government, will also determine the persons who are to govern, and will remove all doubt and ambiguity in this particular. And the voluntary consent of men must here have the greater efficacy, that the authority of the magistrate does at first stand upon the foundation of a promise of the subjects, by which they bind themselves to obedience; as in every other contract or engagement. The same promise, then, which binds them to obedience, ties them down to a particular person, and makes him the object of their allegiance.

But when government has been established on this footing for some considerable time, and the separate interest, which we have in submission, has produced a separate sentiment of morality, the case is entirely altered, and a promise is no longer able to determine the particular magistrate since it is no longer considered as the foundation of government. We naturally suppose ourselves born to submission; and imagine, that such particular persons have a right to command, as we on our part are bound to obey. These notions of right and obligation are derived from nothing but the advantage we reap from government, which gives us a repugnance to practise resistance ourselves, and makes us displeased with any instance of it in others. But here it is remarkable, that in this new state of affairs, the original sanction of government, which is interest, is not admitted to determine the persons, whom we are to obey, as the original sanction did at first, when affairs were on the footing of a promise. A promise fixes and determines the persons, without any uncertainty: But it is evident, that if men were to regulate their conduct in this particular, by the view of a peculiar interest, either public or private, they would involve themselves in endless confusion, and would render all government, in a great measure, ineffectual. The private interest of every one is different; and though the public interest in itself be always one and the same, yet it becomes the source of as great dissentions, by reason of the different opinions of particular persons concerning it. The same interest, therefore, which causes us to submit to magistracy, makes us renounce itself in the choice of our magistrates, and binds us down to a certain form of government, and to particular persons, without allowing us to aspire to the utmost perfection in either. The case is here the same as in that law of nature concerning the stability of possession. It is highly advantageous, and even absolutely necessary to society, that possession should be stable; and this leads us to the establishment of such a rule: But we find, that were we to follow the same advantage, in assigning particular possessions to particular persons, we should disappoint our end, and perpetuate the confusion, which that rule is intended to prevent. We must, therefore, proceed by general rules, and regulate ourselves by general interests, in modifying the law of nature concerning the stability of possession. Nor need we fear, that our attachment to this law will diminish upon account of the seeming frivolousness of those interests, by which it is determined. The impulse of the mind is derived from a very strong interest; and those other more minute interests serve only to direct the motion, without adding any thing to it, or diminishing from it. It is the same case with government. Nothing is more advantageous to society than such an invention; and this interest is sufficient to make us embrace it with ardour and alacrity; though we are obliged afterwards to regulate and direct our devotion to government by several considerations, which are not of the same importance, and to chuse our magistrates without having in view any particular advantage from the choice.

The first of those principles I shall take notice of, as a foundation of the right of magistracy, is that which gives authority to all the most established governments of the world without exception: I mean, long possession in any one form of government, or succession of princes. It is certain, that if we remount to the first origin of every nation, we shall find, that there scarce is any race of kings, or form of a commonwealth, that is not primarily founded on usurpation and rebellion, and whose title is not at first worse than doubtful and uncertain. Time alone gives solidity to their right; and operating gradually on the minds of men, reconciles them to any authority, and makes it seem just and reasonable. Nothing causes any sentiment to have a greater influence upon us than custom, or turns our imagination more strongly to any object. When we have been long accustomed to obey any set of men, that general instinct or tendency, which we have to suppose a moral obligation attending loyalty, takes easily this direction, and chuses that set of men for its objects. It is interest which gives the general instinct; but it is custom which gives the particular direction.

And here it is observable, that the same length of time has a different influence on our sentiments of morality, according to its different influence on the mind. We naturally judge of every thing by comparison; and since in considering the fate of kingdoms and republics, we embrace a long extent of time, a small duration has not in this case a like influence on our sentiments, as when we consider any other object. One thinks he acquires a right to a horse, or a suit of cloaths, in a very short time; but a century is scarce sufficient to establish any new government, or remove all scruples in the minds of the subjects concerning it. Add to this, that a shorter period of time will suffice to give a prince a title to any additional power he may usurp, than will serve to fix his right, where the whole is an usurpation. The kings of France have not been possessed of absolute power for above two reigns; and yet nothing will appear more extravagant to Frenchmen than to talk of their liberties. If we consider what has been said concerning accession, we shall easily account for this phænomenon.

When there is no form of government established by long possession, the present possession is sufficient to supply its place, and may be regarded as the second source of all public authority. Right to authority is nothing but the constant possession of authority, maintained by the laws of society and the interests of mankind; and nothing can be more natural than to join this constant possession to the present one, according to the principles above-mentioned. If the same principles did not take place with regard to the property of private persons, it was because these principles were counter-ballanced by very strong considerations of interest; when we observed, that all restitution would by that means be prevented, and every violence be authorized and protected. And though the same motives may seem to have force, with regard to public authority, yet they are opposed by a contrary interest; which consists in the preservation of peace, and the avoiding of all changes, which, however they may be easily produced in private affairs, are unavoidably attended with bloodshed and confusion, where the public is interested.

Any one, who finding the impossibility of accounting for the right of the present possessor, by any received system of ethics, should resolve to deny absolutely that right, and assert, that it is not authorized by morality, would be justly thought to maintain a very extravagant paradox, and to shock the common sense and judgment of mankind. No maxim is more conformable, both to prudence and morals, than to submit quietly to the government, which we find established in the country where we happen to live, without enquiring too curiously into its origin and first establishment. Few governments will bear being examined so rigorously. How many kingdoms are there at present in the world, and how many more do we find in history, whose governors have no better foundation for their authority than that of present possession? To confine ourselves to the Roman and Grecian empire; is it not evident, that the long succession of emperors, from the dissolution of the Roman liberty, to the final extinction of that empire by the Turks, could not so much as pretend to any other title to the empire? The election of the senate was a mere form, which always followed the choice of the legions; and these were almost always divided in the different provinces, and nothing but the sword was able to terminate the difference. It was by the sword, therefore, that every emperor acquired, as well as defended his right; and we must either say, that all the known world, for so many ages, had no government, and owed no allegiance to any one, or must allow, that the right of the stronger, in public affairs, is to be received as legitimate, and authorized by morality, when not opposed by any other title.

The right of conquest may be considered as a third source of the title of sovereigns. This right resembles very much that of present possession; but has rather a superior force, being seconded by the notions of glory and honour, which we ascribe to conquerors, instead of the sentiments of hatred and detestation, which attend usurpers. Men naturally favour those they love; and therefore are more apt to ascribe a right to successful violence, betwixt one sovereign and another, than to the successful rebellion of a subject against his sovereign.[79]

When neither long possession, nor present possession, nor conquest take place, as when the first sovereign, who founded any monarchy, dies; in that case, the right of succession naturally prevails in their stead, and men are commonly induced to place the son of their late monarch on the throne, and suppose him to inherit his father's authority. The presumed consent of the father, the imitation of the succession to private families, the interest, which the state has in chusing the person, who is most powerful, and has the most numerous followers; all these reasons lead men to prefer the son of their late monarch to any other person.[80]

[79] It is not here asserted, that present possession or conquest are sufficient to give a title against long possession and positive laws but only that they have some force, and will be able to call the ballance where the titles are otherwise equal, and will even be sufficient sometimes to sanctify the weaker title. What degree of force they have is difficult to determine. I believe all moderate men will allow, that they have great force in all disputes concerning the rights of princes.

[80] To prevent mistakes I must observe, that this case of succession is not the same with that of hereditary monarchies, where custom has fix'd the right of succession. These depend upon the principle of long possession above explain'd.

These reasons have some weight; but I am persuaded, that to one, who considers impartially of the matter, it will appear, that there concur some principles of the imagination, along with those views of interest. The royal authority seems to be connected with the young prince even in his father's life-time, by the natural transition of the thought; and still more after his death: So that nothing is more natural than to compleat this union by a new relation, and by putting him actually in possession of what seems so naturally to belong to him.

To confirm this we may weigh the following phaenomena, which are pretty curious in their kind. In elective monarchies the right of succession has no place by the laws and settled custom; and yet its influence is so natural, that it is impossible entirely to exclude it from the imagination, and render the subjects indifferent to the son of their deceased monarch. Hence in some governments of this kind, the choice commonly falls on one or other of the royal family; and in some governments they are all excluded. Those contrary phaenomena proceed from the same principle. Where the royal family is excluded, it is from a refinement in politics, which makes people sensible of their propensity to chuse a sovereign in that family, and gives them a jealousy of their liberty, lest their new monarch, aided by this propensity, should establish his family, and destroy the freedom of elections for the future.

The history of Artaxerxes, and the younger Cyrus, may furnish us with some reflections to the same purpose. Cyrus pretended a right to the throne above his elder brother, because he was born after his father's accession. I do not pretend, that this reason was valid. I would only infer from it, that he would never have made use of such a pretext, were it not for the qualities of the imagination above-mentioned, by which we are naturally inclined to unite by a new relation whatever objects we find already united. Artaxerxes had an advantage above his brother, as being the eldest son, and the first in succession: But Cyrus was more closely related to the royal authority, as being begot after his father was invested with it.

Should it here be pretended, that the view of convenience may be the source of all the right of succession, and that men gladly take advantage of any rule, by which they can fix the successor of their late sovereign, and prevent that anarchy and confusion, which attends all new elections? To this I would answer, that I readily allow, that this motive may contribute something to the effect; but at the same time I assert, that without another principle, it is impossible such a motive should take place. The interest of a nation requires, that the succession to the crown should be fixed one way or other; but it is the same thing to its interest in what way it be fixed: So that if the relation of blood had not an effect independent of public interest, it would never have been regarded, without a positive law; and it would have been impossible, that so many positive laws of different nations could ever have concured precisely in the same views and intentions.

This leads us to consider the fifth source of authority, viz. positive laws; when the legislature establishes a certain form of government and succession of princes. At first sight it may be thought, that this must resolve into some of the preceding titles of authority. The legislative power, whence the positive law is derived, must either be established by original contract, long possession, present possession, conquest, or succession; and consequently the positive law must derive its force from some of those principles. But here it is remarkable, that though a positive law can only derive its force from these principles, yet it acquires not all the force of the principle from whence it is derived, but loses considerably in the transition; as it is natural to imagine. For instance; a government is established for many centuries on a certain system of laws, forms, and methods of succession. The legislative power, established by this long succession, changes all on a sudden the whole system of government, and introduces a new constitution in its stead. I believe few of the subjects will think themselves bound to comply with this alteration, unless it have an evident tendency to the public good: But men think themselves still at liberty to return to the antient government. Hence the notion of fundamental laws; which are supposed to be inalterable by the will of the sovereign: And of this nature the Salic law is understood to be in France. How far these fundamental laws extend is not determined in any government; nor is it possible it ever should. There is such an indefensible gradation from the most material laws to the most trivial, and from the most ancient laws to the most modern, that it will be impossible to set bounds to the legislative power, and determine how far it may innovate in the principles of government. That is the work more of imagination and passion than of reason.

Whoever considers the history of the several nations of the world; their revolutions, conquests, increase, and diminution; the manner in which their particular governments are established, and the successive right transmitted from one person to another, will soon learn to treat very lightly all disputes concerning the rights of princes, and will be convinced, that a strict adherence to any general rules, and the rigid loyalty to particular persons and families, on which some people set so high a value, are virtues that hold less of reason, than of bigotry and superstition. In this particular, the study of history confirms the reasonings of true philosophy; which, shewing us the original qualities of human nature, teaches us to regard the controversies in politics as incapable of any decision in most cases, and as entirely subordinate to the interests of peace and liberty. Where the public good does not evidently demand a change; it is certain, that the concurrence of all those titles, original contract, long possession, present possession, succession, and positive laws, forms the strongest title to sovereignty, and is justly regarded as sacred and inviolable. But when these titles are mingled and opposed in different degrees, they often occasion perplexity; and are less capable of solution from the arguments of lawyers and philosophers, than from the swords of the soldiery. Who shall tell me, for instance, whether Germanicus, or Drufus, ought to have succeeded Tiberius, had he died while they were both alive, without naming any of them for his successor? Ought the right of adoption to be received as equivalent to that of blood in a nation, where it had the same effect in private families, and had already, in two instances, taken place in the public? Ought Germanicus to be esteemed the eldest son, because he was born before Drufus; or the younger, because he was adopted after the birth of his brother? Ought the right of the elder to be regarded in a nation, where the eldest brother had no advantage in the succession to private families? Ought the Roman empire at that time to be esteemed hereditary, because of two examples; or ought it, even so early, to be regarded as belonging to the stronger, or the present possessor, as being founded on so recent an usurpation? Upon whatever principles we may pretend to answer these and such like questions, I am afraid we shall never be able to satisfy an impartial enquirer, who adopts no party in political controversies, and will be satisfied with nothing but sound reason and philosophy.

But here an English reader will be apt to enquire concerning that famous revolution, which has had such a happy influence on our constitution, and has been attended with such mighty consequences. We have already remarked, that in the case of enormous tyranny and oppression, it is lawful to take arms even against supreme power; and that as government is a mere human invention for mutual advantage and security, it no longer imposes any obligation, either natural or moral, when once it ceases to have that tendency. But though this general principle be authorized by common sense, and the practice of all ages, it is certainly impossible for the laws, or even for philosophy, to establish any particular rules, by which we may know when resistance is lawful; and decide all controversies, which may arise on that subject. This may not only happen with regard to supreme power; but it is possible, even in some constitutions, where the legislative authority is not lodged in one person, that there may be a magistrate so eminent and powerful, as to oblige the laws to keep silence in this particular. Nor would this silence be an effect only of their respect, but also of their prudence; since it is certain, that in the vast variety of circumstances, which occur in all governments, an exercise of power, in so great a magistrate, may at one time be beneficial to the public, which at another time would be pernicious and tyrannical. But notwithstanding this silence of the laws in limited monarchies, it is certain, that the people still retain the right of resistance; since it is impossible, even in the most despotic governments, to deprive them of it. The same necessity of self-preservation, and the same motive of public good, give them the same liberty in the one case as in the other. And we may farther observe, that in such mixed governments, the cases, wherein resistance is lawful, must occur much oftener, and greater indulgence be given to the subjects to defend themselves by force of arms, than in arbitrary governments. Not only where the chief magistrate enters into measures, in themselves, extremely pernicious to the public, but even when he would encroach on the other parts of the constitution, and extend his power beyond the legal bounds, it is allowable to resist and dethrone him; though such resistance and violence may, in the general tenor of the laws, be deemed unlawful and rebellious. For besides that nothing is more essential to public interest, than the preservation of public liberty; it is evident, that if such a mixed government be once supposed to be established, every part or member of the constitution must have a right of self-defence, and of maintaining its ancient bounds against the encroachment of every other authority. As matter would have been created in vain, were it deprived of a power of resistance, without which no part of it could preserve a distinct existence, and the whole might be crowded up into a single point: So it is a gross absurdity to suppose, in any government, a right without a remedy, or allow, that the supreme power is shared with the people, without allowing, that it is lawful for them to defend their share against every invader. Those, therefore, who would seem to respect our free government, and yet deny the right of resistance, have renounced all pretensions to common sense, and do not merit a serious answer.

It does not belong to my present purpose to shew, that these general principles are applicable to the late revolution; and that all the rights and privileges, which ought to be sacred to a free nation, were at that time threatened with the utmost danger. I am better pleased to leave this controverted subject, if it really admits of controversy; and to indulge myself in some philosophical reflections, which naturally arise from that important event.

First, We may observe, that should the lords and commons in our constitution, without any reason from public interest, either depose the king in being, or after his death exclude the prince, who, by laws and settled custom, ought to succeed, no one would esteem their proceedings legal, or think themselves bound to comply with them. But should the king, by his unjust practices, or his attempts for a tyrannical and despotic power, justly forfeit his legal, it then not only becomes morally lawful and suitable to the nature of political society to dethrone him; but what is more, we are apt likewise to think, that the remaining members of the constitution acquire a right of excluding his next heir, and of chusing whom they please for his successor. This is founded on a very singular quality of our thought and imagination. When a king forfeits his authority, his heir ought naturally to remain in the same situation, as if the king were removed by death; unless by mixing himself in the tyranny, he forfeit it for himself. But though this may seem reasonable, we easily comply with the contrary opinion. The deposition of a king, in such a government as ours, is certainly an act beyond all common authority, and an illegal assuming a power for public good, which, in the ordinary course of government, can belong to no member of the constitution. When the public good is so great and so evident as to justify the action, the commendable use of this licence causes us naturally to attribute to the parliament a right of using farther licences; and the antient bounds of the laws being once transgressed with approbation, we are not apt to be so strict in confining ourselves precisely within their limits. The mind naturally runs on with any train of action, which it has begun; nor do we commonly make any scruple concerning our duty, after the first action of any kind, which we perform. Thus at the revolution, no one who thought the deposition of the father justifiable, esteemed themselves to be confined to his infant son; though had that unhappy monarch died innocent at that time, and had his son, by any accident, been conveyed beyond seas, there is no doubt but a regency would have been appointed till he should come to age, and could be restored to his dominions. As the slightest properties of the imagination have an effect on the judgments of the people, it shews the wisdom of the laws and of the parliament to take advantage of such properties, and to chuse the magistrates either in or out of a line, according as the vulgar will most naturally attribute authority and right to them.

Secondly, Though the accession of the Prince of Orange to the throne might at first give occasion to many disputes, and his title be contested, it ought not now to appear doubtful, but must have acquired a sufficient authority from those three princes, who have succeeded him upon the same title. Nothing is more usual, though nothing may, at first sight, appear more unreasonable, than this way of thinking. Princes often seem to acquire a right from their successors, as well as from their ancestors; and a king, who during his life-time might justly be deemed an usurper, will be regarded by posterity as a lawful prince, because he has had the good fortune to settle his family on the throne, and entirely change the antient form of government. Julius Caesar is regarded as the first Roman emperor; while Sylla and Marius, whose titles were really the same as his, are treated as tyrants and usurpers. Time and custom give authority to all forms of government, and all successions of princes; and that power, which at first was founded only on injustice and violence, becomes in time legal and obligatory. Nor does the mind rest there; but returning back upon its footsteps, transfers to their predecessors and ancestors that right, which it naturally ascribes to the posterity, as being related together, and united in the imagination. The present king of France makes Hugh Capet a more lawful prince than Cromwell; as the established liberty of the Dutch is no inconsiderable apology for their obstinate resistance to Philip the second.

SECTION XI

Of the Laws of Nations

When civil government has been established over the greatest part of mankind, and different societies have been formed contiguous to each other, there arises a new set of duties among the neighbouring states, suitable to the nature of that commerce, which they carry on with each other. Political writers tell us, that in every kind of intercourse, a body politic is to be considered as one person; and indeed this assertion is so far just, that different nations, as well as private persons, require mutual assistance; at the same time that their selfishness and ambition are perpetual sources of war and discord. But though nations in this particular resemble individuals, yet as they are very different in other respects, no wonder they regulate themselves by different maxims, and give rise to a new set of rules, which we call the laws of nations. Under this head we may comprize the sacredness of the persons of ambassadors, the declaration of war, the abstaining from poisoned arms, with other duties of that kind, which are evidently calculated for the commerce, that is peculiar to different societies.

But though these rules be super-added to the laws of nature, the former do not entirely abolish the latter; and one may safely affirm, that the three fundamental rules of justice, the stability of possession, its transference by consent, and the performance of promises, are duties of princes, as well as of subjects. The same interest produces the same effect in both cases. Where possession has no stability, there must be perpetual war. Where property is not transferred by consent, there can be no commerce. Where promises are not observed, there can be no leagues nor alliances. The advantages, therefore, of peace, commerce, and mutual succour, make us extend to different kingdoms the same notions of justice, which take place among individuals.

There is a maxim very current in the world, which few politicians are willing to avow, but which has been authorized by the practice of all ages, that there is a system of morals calculated for princes, much more free than that which ought to govern private persons. It is evident this is not to be understood of the lesser extent of public duties and obligations; nor will any one be so extravagant as to assert, that the most solemn treaties ought to have no force among princes. For as princes do actually form treaties among themselves, they must propose some advantage from the execution of them; and the prospect of such advantage for the future must engage them to perform their part, and must establish that law of nature. The meaning, therefore, of this political maxim is, that though the morality of princes has the same extent, yet it has not the same force as that of private persons, and may lawfully be trangressed from a more trivial motive. However shocking such a proposition may appear to certain philosophers, it will be easy to defend it upon those principles, by which we have accounted for the origin of justice and equity.

When men have found by experience, that it is impossible to subsist without society, and that it is impossible to maintain society, while they give free course to their appetites; so urgent an interest quickly restrains their actions, and imposes an obligation to observe those rules, which we call the laws of justice. This obligation of interest rests nor here; but by the necessary course of the passions and sentiments, gives rise to the moral obligation of duty; while we approve of such actions as tend to the peace of society, and disapprove of such as tend to its disturbance. The same natural obligation of interest takes place among independent kingdoms, and gives rise to the same morality; so that no one of ever so corrupt morals will approve of a prince, who voluntarily, and of his own accord, breaks his word, or violates any treaty. But here we may observe, that though the intercourse of different states be advantageous, and even sometimes necessary, yet it is nor so necessary nor advantageous as that among individuals, without which it is utterly impossible for human nature ever to subsist. Since, therefore, the natural obligation to justice, among different states, is not so strong as among individuals, the moral obligation, which arises from it, must partake of its weakness; and we must necessarily give a greater indulgence to a prince or minister, who deceives another; than to a private gentleman, who breaks his word of honour.

Should it be asked, what proportion these two species of morality bear to each other? I would answer, that this is a question, to which we can never give any precise answer; nor is it possible to reduce to numbers the proportion, which we ought to fix betwixt them. One may safely affirm, that this proportion finds itself, without any art or study of men; as we may observe on many other occasions. The practice of the world goes farther in teaching us the degrees of our duty, than the most subtile philosophy, which was ever yet invented. And this may serve as a convincing proof, that all men have an implicit notion of the foundation of those moral rules concerning natural and civil justice, and are sensible, that they arise merely from human conventions, and from the interest, which we have in the preservation of peace and order. For otherwise the diminution of the interest would never produce a relaxation of the morality, and reconcile us more easily to any transgression of justice among princes and republics, than in the private commerce of one subject with another.

SECTION XII

Of Chastity and Modesty

If any difficulty attend this system concerning the laws of nature and nations, it will be with regard to the universal approbation or blame, which follows their observance or transgression, and which some may not think sufficiently explained from the general interests of society. To remove, as far as possible, all scruples of this kind, I shall here consider another set of duties, viz, the modesty and chastity which belong to the fair sex: And I doubt not but these virtues will be found to be still more conspicuous instances of the operation of those principles, which I have insisted on.

There are some philosophers, who attack the female virtues with great vehemence, and fancy they have gone very far in detecting popular errors, when they can show, that there is no foundation in nature for all that exterior modesty, which we require in the expressions, and dress, and behaviour of the fair sex. I believe I may spare myself the trouble of insisting on so obvious a subject, and may proceed, without farther preparation, to examine after what manner such notions arise from education, from the voluntary conventions of men, and from the interest of society.

Whoever considers the length and feebleness of human infancy, with the concern which both sexes naturally have for their offspring, will easily perceive, that there must be an union of male and female for the education of the young, and that this union must be of considerable duration. But in order to induce the men to impose on themselves this restraint, and undergo chearfully all the fatigues and expences, to which it subjects them, they must believe, that the children are their own, and that their natural instinct is not directed to a wrong object, when they give a loose to love and tenderness. Now if we examine the structure of the human body, we shall find, that this security is very difficult to be attained on our part; and that since, in the copulation of the sexes, the principle of generation goes from the man to the woman, an error may easily take place on the side of the former, though it be utterly impossible with regard to the latter. From this trivial and anatomical observation is derived that vast difference betwixt the education and duties of the two sexes.

Were a philosopher to examine the matter a priori, he would reason after the following manner. Men are induced to labour for the maintenance and education of their children, by the persuasion that they are really their own; and therefore it is reasonable, and even necessary, to give them some security in this particular. This security cannot consist entirely in the imposing of severe punishments on any transgressions of conjugal fidelity on the part of the wife; since these public punishments cannot be inflicted without legal proof, which it is difficult to meet with in this subject. What restraint, therefore, shall we impose on women, in order to counter-balance so strong a temptation as they have to infidelity? There seems to be no restraint possible, but in the punishment of bad fame or reputation; a punishment, which has a mighty influence on the human mind, and at the same time is inflicted by the world upon surmizes, and conjectures, and proofs, that would never be received in any court of judicature. In order, therefore, to impose a due restraint on the female sex, we must attach a peculiar degree of shame to their infidelity, above what arises merely from its injustice, and must bestow proportionable praises on their chastity.

But though this be a very strong motive to fidelity, our philosopher would quickly discover, that it would not alone be sufficient to that purpose. All human creatures, especially of the female sex, are apt to over-look remote motives in favour of any present temptation: The temptation is here the strongest imaginable: Its approaches are insensible and seducing: And a woman easily finds, or flatters herself she shall find, certain means of securing her reputation, and preventing all the pernicious consequences of her pleasures. It is necessary, therefore, that, beside the infamy attending such licences, there should be some preceding backwardness or dread, which may prevent their first approaches, and may give the female sex a repugnance to all expressions, and postures, and liberties, that have an immediate relation to that enjoyment.

Such would be the reasonings of our speculative philosopher: But I am persuaded, that if he had not a perfect knowledge of human nature, he would be apt to regard them as mere chimerical speculations, and would consider the infamy attending infidelity, and backwardness to all its approaches, as principles that were rather to be wished than hoped for in the world. For what means, would he say, of persuading mankind, that the transgressions of conjugal duty are more infamous than any other kind of injustice, when it is evident they are more excusable, upon account of the greatness of the temptation? And what possibility of giving a backwardness to the approaches of a pleasure, to which nature has inspired so strong a propensity; and a propensity that it is absolutely necessary in the end to comply with, for the support of the species?

But speculative reasonings, which cost so much pains to philosophers, are often formed by the world naturally, and without reflection: As difficulties, which seem unsurmountable in theory, are easily got over in practice. Those, who have an interest in the fidelity of women, naturally disapprove of their infidelity, and all the approaches to it. Those, who have no interest, are carried along with the stream. Education takes possession of the ductile minds of the fair sex in their infancy. And when a general rule of this kind is once established, men are apt to extend it beyond those principles, from which it first arose. Thus batchelors, however debauched, cannot chuse but be shocked with any instance of lewdness or impudence in women. And though all these maxims have a plain reference to generation, yet women past child-bearing have no more privilege in this respect, than those who are in the flower of their youth and beauty. Men have undoubtedly an implicit notion, that all those ideas of modesty and decency have a regard to generation; since they impose not the same laws, with the same force, on the male sex, where that reason takes not place. The exception is there obvious and extensive, and founded on a remarkable difference, which produces a clear separation and disjunction of ideas. But as the case is not the same with regard to the different ages of women, for this reason, though men know, that these notions are founded on the public interest, yet the general rule carries us beyond the original principle, and makes us extend the notions of modesty over the whole sex, from their earliest infancy to their extremest old-age and infirmity.

Courage, which is the point of honour among men, derives its merit, in a great measure, from artifice, as well as the chastity of women; though it has also some foundation in nature, as we shall see afterwards.

As to the obligations which the male sex lie under, with regard to chastity, we may observe, that according to the general notions of the world, they bear nearly the same proportion to the obligations of women, as the obligations of the law of nations do to those of the law of nature. It is contrary to the interest of civil society, that men should have an entire liberty of indulging their appetites in venereal enjoyment: But as this interest is weaker than in the case of the female sex, the moral obligation, arising from it, must be proportionably weaker. And to prove this we need only appeal to the practice and sentiments of all nations and ages.

PART III

Of the other Virtues and Vices

SECTION I

Of the Origin of the Natural Virtues and Vices

We come now to the examination of such virtues and vices as are entirely natural, and have no dependance on the artifice and contrivance of men. The examination of these will conclude this system of morals.

The chief spring or actuating principle of the human mind is pleasure or pain; and when these sensations are removed, both from our thought and feeling, we are, in a great measure, incapable of passion or action, of desire or volition. The most immediate effects of pleasure and pain are the propense and averse motions of the mind; which are diversified into volition, into desire and aversion, grief and joy, hope and fear, according as the pleasure or pain changes its situation, and becomes probable or improbable, certain or uncertain, or is considered as out of our power for the present moment. But when along with this, the objects, that cause pleasure or pain, acquire a relation to ourselves or others; they still continue to excite desire and aversion, grief and joy: But cause, at the same time, the indirect passions of pride or humility, love or hatred, which in this case have a double relation of impressions and ideas to the pain or pleasure.

We have already observed, that moral distinctions depend entirely on certain peculiar sentiments of pain and pleasure, and that whatever mental quality in ourselves or others gives us a satisfaction, by the survey or reflection, is of course virtuous; as every thing of this nature, that gives uneasiness, is vicious. Now since every quality in ourselves or others, which gives pleasure, always causes pride or love; as every one, that produces uneasiness, excites humility or hatred: It follows, that these two particulars are to be considered as equivalent, with regard to our mental qualities, virtue and the power of producing love or pride, vice and the power of producing humility or hatred. In every case, therefore, we must judge of the one by the other; and may pronounce any quality of the mind virtuous, which causes love or pride; and any one vicious, which causes hatred or humility.

If any action be either virtuous or vicious, it is only as a sign of some quality or character. It must depend upon durable principles of the mind, which extend over the whole conduct, and enter into the personal character. Actions themselves, not proceeding from any constant principle, have no influence on love or hatred, pride or humility; and consequently are never considered in morality.

This reflection is self-evident, and deserves to be attended to, as being of the utmost importance in the present subject. We are never to consider any single action in our enquiries concerning the origin of morals; but only the quality or character from which the action proceeded. These alone are durable enough to affect our sentiments concerning the person. Actions are, indeed, better indications of a character than words, or even wishes and sentiments; but it is only so far as they are such indications, that they are attended with love or hatred, praise or blame.

To discover the true origin of morals, and of that love or hatred, which arises from mental qualities, we must take the matter pretty deep, and compare some principles, which have been already examined and explained.

We may begin with considering a-new the nature and force of sympathy. The minds of all men are similar in their feelings and operations; nor can any one be actuated by any affection, of which all others are not, in some degree, susceptible. As in strings equally wound up, the motion of one communicates itself to the rest; so all the affections readily pass from one person to another, and beget correspondent movements in every human creature. When I see the effects of passion in the voice and gesture of any person, my mind immediately passes from these effects to their causes, and forms such a lively idea of the passion, as is presently converted into the passion itself. In like manner, when I perceive the causes of any emotion, my mind is conveyed to the effects, and is actuated with a like emotion. Were I present at any of the more terrible operations of surgery, it is certain, that even before it begun, the preparation of the instruments, the laying of the bandages in order, the heating of the irons, with all the signs of anxiety and concern in the patient and assistants, would have a great effect upon my mind, and excite the strongest sentiments of pity and terror. No passion of another discovers itself immediately to the mind. We are only sensible of its causes or effects. From these we infer the passion: And consequently these give rise to our sympathy.

Our sense of beauty depends very much on this principle; and where any object has atendency to produce pleasure in its possessor, it is always regarded as beautiful; as every object, that has a tendency to produce pain, is disagreeable and deformed. Thus the conveniency of a house, the fertility of a field, the strength of a horse, the capacity, security, and swift-sailing of a vessel, form the principal beauty of these several objects. Here the object, which is denominated beautiful, pleases only by its tendency to produce a certain effect. That effect is the pleasure or advantage of some other person. Now the pleasure of a stranger, for whom we have no friendship, pleases us only by sympathy. To this principle, therefore, is owing the beauty, which we find in every thing that is useful. How considerable a part this is of beauty can easily appear upon reflection. Wherever an object has a tendency to produce pleasure in the possessor, or in other words, is the proper cause of pleasure, it is sure to please the spectator, by a delicate sympathy with the possessor. Most of the works of art are esteemed beautiful, in proportion to their fitness for the use of man, and even many of the productions of nature derive their beauty from that source. Handsome and beautiful, on most occasions, is nor an absolute but a relative quality, and pleases us by nothing but its tendency to produce an end that is agreeable.[81]

The same principle produces, in many instances, our sentiments of morals, as well as those of beauty. No virtue is more esteemed than justice, and no vice more detested than injustice; nor are there any qualities, which go farther to the fixing the character, either as amiable or odious. Now justice is a moral virtue, merely because it has that tendency to the good of mankind; and, indeed, is nothing but an artificial invention to that purpose. The same may be said of allegiance, of the laws of nations, of modesty, and of good-manners. All these are mere human contrivances for the interest of society. And since there is a very strong sentiment of morals, which in all nations, and all ages, has attended them, we must allow, that the reflecting on the tendency of characters and mental qualities, is sufficient to give us the sentiments of approbation and blame. Now as the means to an end can only be agreeable, where the end is agreeable; and as the good of society, where our own interest is not concerned, or that of our friends, pleases only by sympathy: It follows, that sympathy is the source of the esteem, which we pay to all the artificial virtues.

Thus it appears, that sympathy is a very powerful principle in human nature, that it has a great influence on our taste of beauty, and that it produces our sentiment of morals in all the artificial virtues. From thence we may presume, that it also gives rise to many of the other virtues; and that qualities acquire our approbation, because of their tendency to the good of mankind. This presumption must become a certainty, when we find that most of those qualities, which we naturally approve of, have actually that tendency, and render a man a proper member of society: While the qualities, which we naturally disapprove of, have a contrary tendency, and render any intercourse with the person dangerous or disagreeable. For having found, that such tendencies have force enough to produce the strongest sentiment of morals, we can never reasonably, in these cases, look for any other cause of approbation or blame; it being an inviolable maxim in philosophy, that where any particular cause is sufficient for an effect, we ought to rest satisfied with it, and ought not to multiply causes without necessity. We have happily attained experiments in the artificial virtues, where the tendency of qualities to the good of society, is the sole cause of our approbation, without any suspicion of the concurrence of another principle. From thence we learn the force of that principle. And where that principle may take place, and the quality approved of is really beneficial to society, a true philosopher will never require any other principle to account for the strongest approbation and esteem.

---

[81] Decentior equus cujus astricta sunt ilia; sed idem velocior. Pulcher aspectu sit athieta, cujus lacertos exercitatio expressit; idem certamini paratior. Nunquam vero species ab utilitate dividitur. Sed hoc quidem discernere, modici judicii est. Quinct. lib. 8. (A horse with narrow flanks looks more comely; It also moves faster. An athlete whose muscles have been developed by training presents a handsome appearance; he is also better prepared for the contest. Attractive appearance is invariably associated with efficient functioning. Yet it takes no outstanding powers of judgement to wake this distinction.)

That many of the natural virtues have this tendency to the good of society, no one can doubt of. Meekness, beneficence, charity, generosity, clemency, moderation, equity bear the greatest figure among the moral qualities, and are commonly denominated the social virtues, to mark their tendency to the good of society. This goes so far, that some philosophers have represented all moral distinctions as the effect of artifice and education, when skilful politicians endeavoured to restrain the turbulent passions of men, and make them operate to the public good, by the notions of honour and shame. This system, however, is nor consistent with experience. For, first, there are other virtues and vices beside those which have this tendency to the public advantage and loss. Secondly, had not men a natural sentiment of approbation and blame, it could never be excited by politicians; nor would the words laudable and praise-worthy, blameable and odious be any more intelligible, than if they were a language perfectly known to us, as we have already observed. But though this system be erroneous, it may teach us, that moral distinctions arise, in a great measure, from the tendency of qualities and characters to the interests of society, and that it is our concern for that interest, which makes us approve or disapprove of them. Now we have no such extensive concern for society but from sympathy; and consequently it is that principle, which takes us so far out of ourselves, as to give us the same pleasure or uneasiness in the characters of others, as if they had a tendency to our own advantage or loss.

The only difference betwixt the natural virtues and justice lies in this, that the good, which results from the former, arises from every single act, and is the object of some natural passion: Whereas a single act of justice, considered in itself, may often be contrary to the public good; and it is only the concurrence of mankind, in a general scheme or system of action, which is advantageous. When I relieve persons in distress, my natural humanity is my motive; and so far as my succour extends, so far have I promoted the happiness of my fellow-creatures. But if we examine all the questions, that come before any tribunal of justice, we shall find, that, considering each case apart, it would as often be an instance of humanity to decide contrary to the laws of justice as conformable them. Judges take from a poor man to give to a rich; they bestow on the dissolute the labour of the industrious; and put into the hands of the vicious the means of harming both themselves and others. The whole scheme, however, of law and justice is advantageous to the society; and it was with a view to this advantage, that men, by their voluntary conventions, established it. After it is once established by these conventions, it is naturally attended with a strong sentiment of morals; which can proceed from nothing but our sympathy with the interests of society. We need no other explication of that esteem, which attends such of the natural virtues, as have a tendency to the public good. I must farther add, that there are several circumstances, which render this hypothesis much more probable with regard to the natural than the artificial virtues. It is certain that the imagination is more affected by what is particular, than by what is general; and that the sentiments are always moved with difficulty, where their objects are, in any degree, loose and undetermined: Now every particular act of justice is not beneficial to society, but the whole scheme or system: And it may not, perhaps, be any individual person for whom we are concerned, who receives benefit from justice, but the whole society alike. On the contrary, every particular act of generosity, or relief of the industrious and indigent, is beneficial; and is beneficial to a particular person, who is not undeserving of it. It is more natural, therefore, to think, that the tendencies of the latter virtue will affect our sentiments, and command our approbation, than those of the former; and therefore, since we find, that the approbation of the former arises from their tendencies, we may ascribe, with better reason, the same cause to the approbation of the latter. In any number of similar effects, if a cause can be discovered for one, we ought to extend that cause to all the other effects, which can be accounted for by it: But much more, if these other effects be attended with peculiar circumstances, which facilitate the operation of that cause.

Before I proceed farther, I must observe two remarkable circumstances in this affair, which may seem objections to the present system. The first may be thus explained. When any quality, or character, has a tendency to the good of mankind, we are pleased with it, and approve of it; because it presents the lively idea of pleasure; which idea affects us by sympathy, and is itself a kind of pleasure. But as this sympathy is very variable, it may be thought that our sentiments of morals must admit of all the same variations. We sympathize more with persons contiguous to us, than with persons remote from us: With our acquaintance, than with strangers: With our countrymen, than with foreigners. But notwithstanding this variation of our sympathy, we give the same approbation to the same moral qualities in China as in England. They appear equally virtuous, and recommend themselves equally to the esteem of a judicious spectator. The sympathy varies without a variation in our esteem. Our esteem, therefore, proceeds not from sympathy.

To this I answer: The approbation of moral qualities most certainly is not derived from reason, or any comparison of ideas; but proceeds entirely from a moral taste, and from certain sentiments of pleasure or disgust, which arise upon the contemplation and view of particular qualities or characters. Now it is evident, that those sentiments, whence-ever they are derived, must vary according to the distance or contiguity of the objects; nor can I feel the same lively pleasure from the virtues of a person, who lived in Greece two thousand years ago, that I feel from the virtues of a familiar friend and acquaintance. Yet I do not say, that I esteem the one more than the other: And therefore, if the variation of the sentiment, without a variation of the esteem, be an objection, it must have equal force against every other system, as against that of sympathy. But to consider the matter a-right, it has no force at all; and it is the easiest matter in the world to account for it. Our situation, with regard both to persons and things, is in continual fluctuation; and a man, that lies at a distance from us, may, in a little time, become a familiar acquaintance. Besides, every particular man has a peculiar position with regard to others; and it is impossible we could ever converse together on any reasonable terms, were each of us to consider characters and persons, only as they appear from his peculiar point of view. In order, therefore, to prevent those continual contradictions, and arrive at a more stable judgment of things, we fix on some steady and general points of view; and always, in our thoughts, place ourselves in them, whatever may be our present situation. In like manner, external beauty is determined merely by pleasure; and it is evident, a beautiful countenance cannot give so much pleasure, when seen at the distance of twenty paces, as when it is brought nearer us. We say not, however, that it appears to us less beautiful: Because we know what effect it will have in such a position, and by that reflection we correct its momentary appearance.

In general, all sentiments of blame or praise are variable, according to our situation of nearness or remoteness, with regard to the person blamed or praised, and according to the present disposition of our mind. But these variations we regard not in our general decision, but still apply the terms expressive of our liking or dislike, in the same manner, as if we remained in one point of view. Experience soon teaches us this method of correcting our sentiments, or at least, of correcting our language, where the sentiments are more stubborn and inalterable. Our servant, if diligent and faithful, may excite stronger sentiments of love and kindness than Marcus Brutus, as represented in history; but we say not upon that account, that the former character is more laudable than the latter. We know, that were we to approach equally near to that renowned patriot, he would command a much higher degree of affection and admiration. Such corrections are common with regard to all the senses; and indeed it were impossible we could ever make use of language, or communicate our sentiments to one another, did we not correct the momentary appearances of things, and overlook our present situation.

It is therefore from the influence of characters and qualities, upon those who have an intercourse with any person, that we blame or praise him. We consider not whether the persons, affected by the qualities, be our acquaintance or strangers, countrymen or foreigners. Nay, we over-look our own interest in those general judgments; and blame not a man for opposing us in any of our pretensions, when his own interest is particularly concerned. We make allowance for a certain degree of selfishness in men; because we know it to be inseparable from human nature, and inherent in our frame and constitution. By this reflection we correct those sentiments of blame, which so naturally arise upon any opposition.

But however the general principle of our blame or praise may be corrected by those other principles, it is certain, they are not altogether efficacious, nor do our passions often correspond entirely to the present theory. It is seldom men heartily love what lies at a distance from them, and what no way redounds to their particular benefit; as it is no less rare to meet with persons, who can pardon another any opposition he makes to their interest, however justifiable that opposition may be by the general rules of morality. Here we are contented with saying, that reason requires such an Impartial conduct, but that it is seldom we can bring ourselves to it, and that our passions do not readily follow the determination of our judgment. This language will be easily understood, if we consider what we formerly said concerning that reason, which is able to oppose our passion; and which we have found to be nothing but a general calm determination of the passions, founded on some distant view or reflection. When we form our judgments of persons, merely from the tendency of their characters to our own benefit, or to that of our friends, we find so many contradictions to our sentiments in society and conversation, and such an uncertainty from the incessant changes of our situation, that we seek some other standard of merit and demerit, which may not admit of so great variation. Being thus loosened from our first station, we cannot afterwards fix ourselves so commodiously by any means as by a sympathy with those, who have any commerce with the person we consider. This is far from being as lively as when our own interest is concerned, or that of our particular friends; nor has it such an influence on our love and hatred: But being equally conformable to our calm and general principles, it is said to have an equal authority over our reason, and to command our judgment and opinion. We blame equally a bad action, which we read of in history, with one performed in our neighbourhood the other day: The meaning of which is, that we know from reflection, that the former action would excite as strong sentiments of disapprobation as the latter, were it placed in the same position.

I now proceed to the second remarkable circumstance, which I proposed to take notice of. Where a person is possessed of a character, that in its natural tendency is beneficial to society, we esteem him virtuous, and are delighted with the view of his character, even though particular accidents prevent its operation, and incapacitate him from being serviceable to his friends and country. Virtue in rags is still virtue; and the love, which it procures, attends a man into a dungeon or desart, where the virtue can no longer be exerted in action, and is lost to all the world. Now this may be esteemed an objection to the present system. Sympathy interests us in the good of mankind; and if sympathy were the source of our esteem for virtue, that sentiment of approbation could only take place, where the virtue actually attained its end, and was beneficial to mankind. Where it fails of its end, it is only an imperfect means; and therefore can never acquire any merit from that end. The goodness of an end can bestow a merit on such means alone as are compleat, and actually produce the end.

To this we may reply, that where any object, in all its parts, is fitted to attain any agreeable end, it naturally gives us pleasure, and is esteemed beautiful, even though some external circumstances be wanting to render it altogether effectual. It is sufficient if every thing be compleat in the object itself. A house, that is contrived with great judgment for all the commodities of life, pleases us upon that account; though perhaps we are sensible, that no one will ever dwell in it. A fertile soil, and a happy climate, delight us by a reflection on the happiness which they would afford the inhabitants, though at present the country be desart and uninhabited. A man, whose limbs and shape promise strength and activity, is esteemed handsome, though condemned to perpetual imprisonment. The imagination has a set of passions belonging to it, upon which our sentiments of beauty much depend. These passions are moved by degrees of liveliness and strength, which are inferior to belief, and independent of the real existence of their objects. Where a character is, in every respect, fitted to be beneficial to society, the imagination passes easily from the cause to the effect, without considering that there are some circumstances wanting to render the cause a complete one. General rules create a species of probability, which sometimes influences the judgment, and always the imagination.

It is true, when the cause is compleat, and a good disposition is attended with good fortune, which renders it really beneficial to society, it gives a stronger pleasure to the spectator, and is attended with a more lively sympathy. We are more affected by it; and yet we do not say that it is more virtuous, or that we esteem it more. We know, that an alteration of fortune may render the benevolent disposition entirely impotent; and therefore we separate, as much as possible, the fortune from the disposition. The case is the same, as when we correct the different sentiments of virtue, which proceed from its different distances from ourselves. The passions do not always follow our corrections; but these corrections serve sufficiently to regulate our abstract notions, and are alone regarded, when we pronounce in general concerning the degrees of vice and virtue.

It is observed by critics, that all words or sentences, which are difficult to the pronunciation, are disagreeable to the ear. There is no difference, whether a man hear them pronounced, or read them silently to himself. When I run over a book with my eye, I imagine I hear it all; and also, by the force of imagination, enter into the uneasiness, which the delivery of it would give the speaker. The uneasiness is not real; but as such a composition of words has a natural tendency to produce it, this is sufficient to affect the mind with a painful sentiment, and render the discourse harsh and disagreeable. It is a similar case, where any real quality is, by accidental circumstances, rendered impotent, and is deprived of its natural influence on society.

Upon these principles we may easily remove any contradiction, which may appear to be betwixt the extensive sympathy, on which our sentiments of virtue depend, and that limited generosity which I have frequently observed to be natural to men, and which justice and property suppose, according to the precedent reasoning. My sympathy with another may give me the sentiment of pain and disapprobation, when any object is presented, that has a tendency to give him uneasiness; though I may not be willing to sacrifice any thing of my own interest, or cross any of my passions, for his satisfaction. A house may displease me by being ill-contrived for the convenience of the owner; and yet I may refuse to give a shilling towards the rebuilding of it. Sentiments must touch the heart, to make them controul our passions: But they need not extend beyond the imagination, to make them influence our taste. When a building seems clumsy and tottering to the eye, it is ugly and disagreeable; though we be fully assured of the solidity of the workmanship. It is a kind of fear, which causes this sentiment of disapprobation; but the passion is not the same with that which we feel, when obliged to stand under a wall, that we really think tottering and insecure. The seeming tendencies of objects affect the mind: And the emotions they excite are of a like species with those, which proceed from the real consequences of objects, but their feeling is different. Nay, these emotions are so different in their feeling, that they may often be contrary, without destroying each other; as when the fortifications of a city belonging to an enemy are esteemed beautiful upon account of their strength, though we could wish that they were entirely destroyed. The imagination adheres to the general views of things, and distinguishes the feelings they produce, from those which arise from our particular and momentary situation.

If we examine the panegyrics that are commonly made of great men, we shall find, that most of the qualities, which are attributed to them, may be divided into two kinds, viz. such as make them perform their part in society; and such as render them serviceable to themselves, and enable them to promote their own interest. Their prudence, temperance, frugality, industry, assiduity, enterprize, dexterity, are celebrated, as well as their generosity and humanity. If we ever give an indulgence to any quality, that disables a man from making a figure in life, it is to that of indolence, which is not supposed to deprive one of his parts and capacity, but only suspends their exercise; and that without any inconvenience to the person himself, since it is, in some measure, from his own choice. Yet indolence is always allowed to be a fault, and a very great one, if extreme: Nor do a man's friends ever acknowledge him to be subject to it, but in order to save his character in more material articles. He could make a figure, say they, if he pleased to give application: His understanding is sound, his conception quick, and his memory tenacious; but he hates business, and is indifferent about his fortune. And this a man sometimes may make even a subject of vanity; though with the air of confessing a fault: Because he may think, that his incapacity for business implies much more noble qualities; such as a philosophical spirit, a fine taste, a delicate wit, or a relish for pleasure and society. But take any other case: Suppose a quality, that without being an indication of any other good qualities, incapacitates a man always for business, and is destructive to his interest; such as a blundering understanding, and a wrong judgment of every thing in life; inconstancy and irresolution; or a want of address in the management of men and business: These are all allowed to be imperfections in a character; and many men would rather acknowledge the greatest crimes, than have it suspected, that they are, in any degree, subject to them.

It is very happy, in our philosophical researches, when we find the same phænomenon diversified by a variety of circumstances; and by discovering what is common among them, can the better assure ourselves of the truth of any hypothesis we may make use of to explain it. Were nothing esteemed virtue but what were beneficial to society, I am persuaded, that the foregoing explication of the moral sense ought still to be received, and that upon sufficient evidence: But this evidence must grow upon us, when we find other kinds of virtue, which will not admit of any explication except from that hypothesis. Here is a man, who is not remarkably defective in his social qualities; but what principally recommends him is his dexterity in business, by which he has extricated himself from the greatest difficulties, and conducted the most delicate affairs with a singular address and prudence. I find an esteem for him immediately to arise in me: His company is a satisfaction to me; and before I have any farther acquaintance with him, I would rather do him a service than another, whose character is in every other respect equal, but is deficient in that particular. In this case, the qualities that please me are all considered as useful to the person, and as having a tendency to promote his interest and satisfaction. They are only regarded as means to an end, and please me in proportion to their fitness for that end. The end, therefore, must be agreeable to me. But what makes the end agreeable? The person is a stranger: I am no way interested in him, nor lie under any obligation to him: His happiness concerns not me, farther than the happiness of every human, and indeed of every sensible creature: That is, it affects me only by sympathy. From that principle, whenever I discover his happiness and good, whether in its causes or effects, I enter so deeply into it, that it gives me a sensible emotion. The appearance of qualities, that have a tendency to promote it, have an agreeable effect upon my imagination, and command my love and esteem.

This theory may serve to explain, why the same qualities, in all cases, produce both pride and love, humility and hatred; and the same man is always virtuous or vicious, accomplished or despicable to others, who is so to himself. A person, in whom we discover any passion or habit, which originally is only incommodious to himself, becomes always disagreeable to us, merely on its account; as on the other hand, one whose character is only dangerous and disagreeable to others, can never be satisfied with himself, as long as he is sensible of that disadvantage. Nor is this observable only with regard to characters and manners, but may be remarked even in the most minute circumstances. A violent cough in another gives us uneasiness; though in itself it does not in the least affect us. A man will be mortified, if you tell him he has a stinking breath; though it is evidently no annoyance to himself. Our fancy easily changes its situation; and either surveying ourselves as we appear to others, or considering others as they feel themselves, we enter, by that means, into sentiments, which no way belong to us, and in which nothing but sympathy is able to interest us. And this sympathy we sometimes carry so far, as even to be displeased with a quality commodious to us, merely because it displeases others, and makes us disagreeable in their eyes; though perhaps we never can have any interest in rendering ourselves agreeable to them.

There have been many systems of morality advanced by philosophers in all ages; but if they are strictly examined, they may be reduced to two, which alone merit our attention. Moral good and evil are certainly distinguished by our sentiments, not by reason: But these sentiments may arise either from the mere species or appearance of characters and passions, or from reflections on their tendency to the happiness of mankind, and of particular persons. My opinion is, that both these causes are intermixed in our judgments of morals; after the same manner as they are in our decisions concerning most kinds of external beauty: Though I am also of opinion, that reflections on the tendencies of actions have by far the greatest influence, and determine all the great lines of our duty. There are, however, instances, in cases of less moment, wherein this immediate taste or sentiment produces our approbation. Wit, and a certain easy and disengaged behaviour, are qualities immediately agreeable to others, and command their love and esteem. Some of these qualities produce satisfaction in others by particular original principles of human nature, which cannot be accounted for: Others may be resolved into principles, which are more general. This will best appear upon a particular enquiry.

As some qualities acquire their merit from their being immediately agreeable to others, without any tendency to public interest; so some are denominated virtuous from their being immediately agreeable to the person himself, who possesses them. Each of the passions and operations of the mind has a particular feeling, which must be either agreeable or disagreeable. The first is virtuous, the second vicious. This particular feeling constitutes the very nature of the passion; and therefore needs not be accounted for.

But however directly the distinction of vice and virtue may seem to flow from the immediate pleasure or uneasiness, which particular qualities cause to ourselves or others; it is easy to observe, that it has also a considerable dependence on the principle of sympathy so often insisted on. We approve of a person, who is possessed of qualities immediately agreeable to those, with whom he has any commerce; though perhaps we ourselves never reaped any pleasure from them. We also approve of one, who is possessed of qualities, that are immediately agreeable to himself; though they be of no service to any mortal. To account for this we must have recourse to the foregoing principles.

Thus, to take a general review of the present hypothesis: Every quality of the mind is denominated virtuous, which gives pleasure by the mere survey; as every quality, which produces pain, is called vicious. This pleasure and this pain may arise from four different sources. For we reap a pleasure from the view of a character, which is naturally fitted to be useful to others, or to the person himself, or which is agreeable to others, or to the person himself. One may, perhaps, be surprized. that amidst all these interests and pleasures, we should forget our own, which touch us so nearly on every other occasion. But we shall easily satisfy ourselves on this head, when we consider, that every particular person's pleasure and interest being different, it is impossible men could ever agree in their sentiments and judgments, unless they chose some common point of view, from which they might survey their object, and which might cause it to appear the same to all of them. Now in judging of characters, the only interest or pleasure, which appears the same to every spectator, is that of the person himself, whose character is examined; or that of persons, who have a connexion with him. And though such interests and pleasures touch us more faintly than our own, yet being more constant and universal, they counter-ballance the latter even in practice, and are alone admitted in speculation as the standard of virtue and morality. They alone produce that particular feeling or sentiment, on which moral distinctions depend.

As to the good or ill desert of virtue or vice, it is an evident consequence of the sentiments of pleasure or uneasiness. These sentiments produce love or hatred; and love or hatred, by the original constitution of human passion, is attended with benevolence or anger; that is, with a desire of making happy the person we love, and miserable the person we hate. We have treated of this more fully on another occasion.

SECTION II

Of Greatness of Mind

It may now be proper to illustrate this general system of morals, by applying it to particular instances of virtue and vice, and shewing how their merit or demerit arises from the four sources here explained. We shall begin with examining the passions of pride and humility, and shall consider the vice or virtue that lies in their excesses or just proportion. An excessive pride or overweaning conceit of ourselves is always esteemed vicious, and is universally hated; as modesty, or a just sense of our weakness, is esteemed virtuous, and procures the good-will of every-one. Of the four sources of moral distinctions, this is to be ascribed to the third; viz, the immediate agreeableness and disagreeableness of a quality to others, without any reflections on the tendency of that quality.

In order to prove this, we must have recourse to two principles, which are very conspicuous in human nature. The first of these is the sympathy, and communication of sentiments and passions above-mentioned. So close and intimate is the correspondence of human souls, that no sooner any person approaches me, than he diffuses on me all his opinions, and draws along my judgment in a greater or lesser degree. And though, on many occasions, my sympathy with him goes not so far as entirely to change my sentiments, and way of thinking; yet it seldom is so weak as not to disturb the easy course of my thought, and give an authority to that opinion, which is recommended to me by his assent and approbation. Nor is it any way material upon what subject he and I employ our thoughts. Whether we judge of an indifferent person, or of my own character, my sympathy gives equal force to his decision: And even his sentiments of his own merit make me consider him in the same light, in which he regards himself.

This principle of sympathy is of so powerful and insinuating a nature, that it enters into most of our sentiments and passions, and often takes place under the appearance of its contrary. For it is remarkable, that when a person opposes me in any thing, which I am strongly bent upon, and rouzes up my passion by contradiction, I have always a degree of sympathy with him, nor does my commotion proceed from any other origin. We may here observe an evident conflict or rencounter of opposite principles and passions. On the one side there is that passion or sentiment, which is natural to me; and it is observable, that the stronger this passion is, the greater is the commotion. There must also be some passion or sentiment on the other side; and this passion can proceed from nothing but sympathy. The sentiments of others can never affect us, but by becoming, in some measure, our own; in which case they operate upon us, by opposing and encreasing our passions, in the very same manner, as if they had been originally derived from our own temper and disposition. While they remain concealed in the minds of others, they can never have an influence upon us: And even when they are known, if they went no farther than the imagination, or conception; that faculty is so accustomed to objects of every different kind, that a mere idea, though contrary to our sentiments and inclinations, would never alone be able to affect us.

The second principle I shall take notice of is that of comparison, or the variation of our judgments concerning objects, according to the proportion they bear to those with which we compare them. We judge more, of objects by comparison, than by their intrinsic worth and value; and regard every thing as mean, when set in opposition to what is superior of the same kind. But no comparison is more obvious than that with ourselves; and hence it is that on all occasions it takes place, and mixes with most of our passions. This kind of comparison is directly contrary to sympathy in its operation, as we have observed in treating of compassion and malice.[82] IN ALL KINDS OF COMPARISON AN OBJECT MAKES US ALWAYS RECEIVE FROM ANOTHER, TO WHICH IT IS COMPARED, A SENSATION CONTRARY TO WHAT ARISES FROM ITSELF IN ITS DIRECT AND IMMEDIATE SURVEY. THE DIRECT SURVEY OF ANOTHER'S PLEASURE NATURALLY GIVES US PLEASURE; AND THEREFORE PRODUCES PAIN, WHEN COMPARED WITH OUR OWN. HIS PAIN, CONSIDERED IN ITSELF, IS PAINFUL; BUT AUGMENTS THE IDEA OF OUR OWN HAPPINESS, AND GIVES US PLEASURE.

Since then those principles of sympathy, and a comparison with ourselves, are directly contrary, it may be worth while to consider, what general rules can be formed, beside the particular temper of the person, for the prevalence of the one or the other. Suppose I am now in safety at land, and would willingly reap some pleasure from this consideration: I must think on the miserable condition of those who are at sea in a storm, and must endeavour to render this idea as strong and lively as possible, in order to make me more sensible of my own happiness. But whatever pains I may take, the comparison will never have an equal efficacy, as if

[82] Book II. Part II. Sect. VIII.

I were really on the shore,[83] and saw a ship at a distance tossed by a tempest, and in danger every moment of perishing on a rock or sand-bank. But suppose this idea to become still more lively. Suppose the ship to be driven so near me, that I can perceive distinctly the horror, painted on the countenance of the seamen and passengers, hear their lamentable cries, see the dearest friends give their last adieu, or embrace with a resolution to perish in each others arms: No man has so savage a heart as to reap any pleasure from such a spectacle, or withstand the motions of the tenderest compassion and sympathy. It is evident, therefore, there is a medium in this case; and that if the idea be too feint, it has no influence by comparison; and on the other hand, if it be too strong, it operates on us entirely by sympathy, which is the contrary to comparison. Sympathy being the conversion of an idea into an impression, demands a greater force and vivacity in the idea than is requisite to comparison.

All this is easily applied to the present subject. We sink very much in our own eyes, when in the presence of a great man, or one of a superior genius; and this humility makes a considerable ingredient in that respect, which we pay our superiors, according to our foregoing reasonings on that passion.[84] Sometimes even envy and hatred arise from the comparison; but in the greatest part of men, it rests at respect and esteem. As sympathy has such a powerful influence on the human mind, it causes pride to have, in some measure, the same effect as merit; and by making us enter into those elevated sentiments, which the proud man entertains of himself, presents that comparison, which is so mortifying and disagreeable. Our judgment does not entirely accompany him in the flattering conceit, in which he pleases himself; but still is so shaken as to receive the idea it presents, and to give it an influence above the loose conceptions of the imagination. A man, who, in an idle humour, would form a notion of a person of a merit very much superior to his own, would not be mortified by that fiction: But when a man, whom we are really persuaded to be of inferior merit, is presented to us; if we observe in him any extraordinary degree of pride and self-conceit; the firm persuasion he has of his own merit, takes hold of the imagination, and diminishes us in our own eyes, in the same manner, as if he were really possessed of all the good qualities which he so liberally attributes to himself. Our idea is here precisely in that medium, which is requisite to make it operate on us by comparison. Were it accompanied with belief, and did the person appear to have the same merit, which he assumes to himself, it would have a contrary effect, and would operate on us by sympathy. The influence

[83] Suave mari magno turbantibus aequora ventis E terra magnum alterius spectare laborem; Non quia vexari quenquam eat jucunda voluptas, Sed quibus ipse malls caress qula cernere sauv' est. LUCRET.

(There is something pleasant in watching, from dry land, the great difficulties another man is undergoing out on the high sea, with the winds lashing the waters. This is not because one derives delight from any man's distress, but because it is pleasurable to perceive from what troubles one is oneself free.)

[84] Book II. Part II. Sect. X.

of that principle would then be superior to that of comparison, contrary to what happens where the person's merit seems below his pretensions.

The necessary consequence of these principles is, that pride, or an over-weaning conceit of ourselves, must be vicious; since it causes uneasiness in all men, and presents them every moment with a disagreeable comparison. It is a trite observation in philosophy, and even in common life and conversation, that it is our own pride, which makes us so much displeased with the pride of other people; and that vanity becomes insupportable to us merely because we are vain. The gay naturally associate themselves with the gay, and the amorous with the amorous: But the proud never can endure the proud, and rather seek the company of those who are of an opposite disposition. As we are, all of us, proud in some degree, pride is universally blamed and condemned by all mankind; as having a natural tendency to cause uneasiness in others by means of comparison. And this effect must follow the more naturally, that those, who have an ill-grounded conceit of themselves, are for ever making those comparisons, nor have they any other method of supporting their vanity. A man of sense and merit is pleased with himself, independent of all foreign considerations: But a fool must always find some person, that is more foolish, in order to keep himself in good humour with his own parts and understanding.

But though an over-weaning conceit of our own merit be vicious and disagreeable, nothing can be more laudable, than to have a value for ourselves, where we really have qualities that are valuable. The utility and advantage of any quality to ourselves is a source of virtue, as well as its agreeableness to others; and it is certain, that nothing is more useful to us in the conduct of life, than a due degree of pride, which makes us sensible of our own merit, and gives us a confidence and assurance in all our projects and enterprizes. Whatever capacity any one may be endowed with, it is entirely useless to him, if he be not acquainted with it, and form not designs suitable to it. It is requisite on all occasions to know our own force; and were it allowable to err on either side, it would be more advantageous to over-rate our merit, than to form ideas of it, below its just standard. Fortune commonly favours the bold and enterprizing; and nothing inspires us with more boldness than a good opinion of ourselves.

Add to this, that though pride, or self-applause, be sometimes disagreeable to others, it is always agreeable to ourselves; as on the other hand, modesty, though it gives pleasure to every one, who observes it, produces often uneasiness in the person endowed with it. Now it has been observed, that our own sensations determine the vice and virtue of any quality, as well as those sensations, which it may excite in others.

Thus self-satisfaction and vanity may not only be allowable, but requisite in a character. It is, however, certain, that good-breeding and decency require that we should avoid all signs and expressions, which tend directly to show that passion. We have, all of us, a wonderful partiality for ourselves, and were we always to give vent to our sentiments in this particular, we should mutually cause the greatest indignation in each other, not only by the immediate presence of so disagreeable a subject of comparison, but also by the contrariety of our judgments. In like manner, therefore, as we establish the laws of nature, in order to secure property in society, and prevent the opposition of self-interest; we establish the rules of good-breeding, in order to prevent the opposition of men's pride, and render conversation agreeable and inoffensive. Nothing is more disagreeable than a man's over-weaning conceit of himself: Every one almost has a strong propensity to this vice: No one can well distinguish in himself betwixt the vice and virtue, or be certain, that his esteem of his own merit is well-founded: For these reasons, all direct expressions of this passion are condemned; nor do we make any exception to this rule in favour of men of sense and merit. They are not allowed to do themselves justice openly, in words, no more than other people; and even if they show a reserve and secret doubt in doing themselves justice in their own thoughts, they will be more applauded. That impertinent, and almost universal propensity of men, to over-value themselves, has given us such a prejudice against self-applause, that we are apt to condemn it, by a general rule, wherever we meet with it; and it is with some difficulty we give a privilege to men of sense, even in their most secret thoughts. At least, it must be owned, that some disguise in this particular is absolutely requisite; and that if we harbour pride in our breasts, we must carry a fair outside, and have the appearance of modesty and mutual deference in all our conduct and behaviour. We must, on every occasion, be ready to prefer others to ourselves; to treat them with a kind of deference, even though they be our equals; to seem always the lowest and least in the company, where we are not very much distinguished above them: And if we observe these rules in our conduct, men will have more indulgence for our secret sentiments, when we discover them in an oblique manner.

I believe no one, who has any practice of the world, and can penetrate into the inward sentiments of men, will assert, that the humility, which good-breeding and decency require of us, goes beyond the outside, or that a thorough sincerity in this particular is esteemed a real part of our duty. On the contrary, we may observe, that a genuine and hearty pride, or self-esteem, if well concealed and well founded, is essential to the character of a man of honour, and that there is no quality of the mind, which is more indispensibly requisite to procure the esteem and approbation of mankind. There are certain deferences and mutual submissions, which custom requires of the different ranks of men towards each other; and whoever exceeds in this particular, if through interest, is accused of meanness; if through ignorance, of simplicity. It is necessary, therefore, to know our rank and station in the world, whether it be fixed by our birth, fortune, employments, talents or reputation. It is necessary to feel the sentiment and passion of pride in conformity to it, and to regulate our actions accordingly. And should it be said, that prudence may suffice to regulate our actions in this particular, without any real pride, I would observe, that here the object of prudence is to conform our actions to the general usage and custom; and, that it is impossible those tacit airs of superiority should ever have been established and authorized by custom, unless men were generally proud, and unless that passion were generally approved, when well-grounded.

If we pass from common life and conversation to history, this reasoning acquires new force, when we observe, that all those great actions and sentiments, which have become the admiration of mankind, are founded on nothing but pride and self-esteem. Go, says Alexander the Great to his soldiers, when they refused to follow him to the Indies, go tell your countrymen, that you left Alexander corn pleating the conquest of the world. This passage was always particularly admired by the prince of Conde, as we learn from St Evremond.

"ALEXANDER," said that prince, "abandoned by his soldiers, among barbarians, not yet fully subdued, felt in himself such a dignity of right and of empire, that he could not believe it possible any one could refuse to obey him. Whether in Europe or in Asia, among Greeks or Persians, all was indifferent to him: Wherever he found men, he fancied he found subjects."

In general we may observe, that whatever we call heroic virtue, and admire under the character of greatness and elevation of mind, is either nothing but a steady and well-established pride and self-esteem, or partakes largely of that passion. Courage, intrepidity, ambition, love of glory, magnanimity, and all the other shining virtues of that kind, have plainly a strong mixture of self-esteem in them, and derive a great part of their merit from that origin. Accordingly we find, that many religious declaimers decry those virtues as purely pagan and natural, and represent to us the excellency of the Christian religion, which places humility in the rank of virtues, and corrects the judgment of the world, and even of philosophers, who so generally admire all the efforts of pride and ambition. Whether this virtue of humility has been rightly understood, I shall not pretend to determine. I am content with the concession, that the world naturally esteems a well-regulated pride, which secretly animates our conduct, without breaking out into such indecent expressions of vanity, as many offend the vanity of others.

The merit of pride or self-esteem is derived from two circumstances, viz, its utility and its agreeableness to ourselves; by which it capacitates us for business, and, at the same time, gives us an immediate satisfaction. When it goes beyond its just bounds, it loses the first advantage, and even becomes prejudicial; which is the reason why we condemn an extravagant pride and ambition, however regulated by the decorums of good-breeding and politeness. But as such a passion is still agreeable, and conveys an elevated and sublime sensation to the person, who is actuated by it, the sympathy with that satisfaction diminishes considerably the blame, which naturally attends its dangerous influence on his conduct and behaviour. Accordingly we may observe, that an excessive courage and magnanimity, especially when it displays itself under the frowns of fortune, contributes in a great measure, to the character of a hero, and will render a person the admiration of posterity; at the same time, that it ruins his affairs, and leads him into dangers and difficulties, with which otherwise he would never have been acquainted.

Heroism, or military glory, is much admired by the generality of mankind. They consider it as the most sublime kind of merit. Men of cool reflection are not so sanguine in their praises of it. The infinite confusions and disorder, which it has caused in the world, diminish much of its merit in their eyes. When they would oppose the popular notions on this head, they always paint out the evils, which this supposed virtue has produced in human society; the subversion of empires, the devastation of provinces, the sack of cities. As long as these are present to us, we are more inclined to hate than admire the ambition of heroes. But when we fix our view on the person himself, who is the author of all this mischief, there is something so dazzling in his character, the mere contemplation of it so elevates the mind, that we cannot refuse it our admiration. The pain, which we receive from its tendency to the prejudice of society, is over-powered by a stronger and more immediate sympathy.

Thus our explication of the merit or demerit, which attends the degrees of pride or self-esteem, may serve as a strong argument for the preceding hypothesis, by shewing the effects of those principles above explained in all the variations of our judgments concerning that passion. Nor will this reasoning be advantageous to us only by shewing, that the distinction of vice and virtue arises from the four principles of the advantage and of the pleasure of the person himself, and of others: But may also afford us a strong proof of some under-parts of that hypothesis.

No one, who duly considers of this matter, will make any scruple of allowing, that any piece of in-breeding, or any expression of pride and haughtiness, is displeasing to us, merely because it shocks our own pride, and leads us by sympathy into a comparison, which causes the disagreeable passion of humility. Now as an insolence of this kind is blamed even in a person who has always been civil to ourselves in particular; nay, in one, whose name is only known to us in history; it follows, that our disapprobation proceeds from a sympathy with others, and from the reflection, that such a character is highly displeasing and odious to every one, who converses or has any intercourse with the person possest of it. We sympathize with those people in their uneasiness; and as their uneasiness proceeds in part from a sympathy with the person who insults them, we may here observe a double rebound of the sympathy; which is a principle very similar to what we have observed.[85]

SECTION III

Of Goodness and Benevolence

Having thus explained the origin of that praise and approbation, which attends every thing we call great in human affections; we now proceed to give an account of their goodness, and shew whence its merit is derived.

[85] Book II. Part II. Sect. V.

When experience has once given us a competent knowledge of human affairs, and has taught us the proportion they bear to human passion, we perceive, that the generosity of men is very limited, and that it seldom extends beyond their friends and family, or, at most, beyond their native country. Being thus acquainted with the nature of man, we expect not any impossibilities from him; but confine our view to that narrow circle, in which any person moves, in order to form a judgment of his moral character. When the natural tendency of his passions leads him to be serviceable and useful within his sphere, we approve of his character, and love his person, by a sympathy with the sentiments of those, who have a more particular connexion with him. We are quickly obliged to forget our own interest in our judgments of this kind, by reason of the perpetual contradictions, we meet with in society and conversation, from persons that are not placed in the same situation, and have not the same interest with ourselves. The only point of view, in which our sentiments concur with those of others, is, when we consider the tendency of any passion to the advantage or harm of those, who have any immediate connexion or intercourse with the person possessed of it. And though this advantage or harm be often very remote from ourselves, yet sometimes it is very near us, and interests us strongly by sympathy. This concern we readily extend to other cases, that are resembling; and when these are very remote, our sympathy is proportionably weaker, and our praise or blame fainter and more doubtful. The case is here the same as in our judgments concerning external bodies. All objects seem to diminish by their distance: But though the appearance of objects to our senses be the original standard, by which we judge of them, yet we do not say, that they actually diminish by the distance; but correcting the appearance by reflection, arrive at a more constant and established judgment concerning them. In like manner, though sympathy be much fainter than our concern for ourselves, and a sympathy with persons remote from us much fainter than that with persons near and contiguous; yet we neglect all these differences in our calm judgments concerning the characters of men. Besides, that we ourselves often change our situation in this particular, we every day meet with persons, who are in a different situation from ourselves, and who could never converse with us on any reasonable terms, were we to remain constantly in that situation and point of view, which is peculiar to us. The intercourse of sentiments, therefore, in society and conversation, makes us form some general inalterable standard, by which we may approve or disapprove of characters and manners. And though the heart does not always take part with those general notions, or regulate its love and hatred by them, yet are they sufficient for discourse, and serve all our purposes in company, in the pulpit, on the theatre, and in the schools.

From these principles we may easily account for that merit, which is commonly ascribed to generosity, humanity, compassion, gratitude, friendship, fidelity, zeal, disinterestedness, liberality, and all those other qualities, which form the character of good and benevolent. A propensity to the tender passions makes a man agreeable and useful in all the parts of life; and gives a just direction to all his other quailties, which otherwise may become prejudicial to society. Courage and ambition, when not regulated by benevolence, are fit only to make a tyrant and public robber. It is the same case with judgment and capacity, and all the qualities of that kind. They are indifferent in themselves to the interests of society, and have a tendency to the good or ill of mankind, according as they are directed by these other passions.

As Love is immediately agreeable to the person, who is actuated by it, and hatred immediately disagreeable; this may also be a considerable reason, why we praise all the passions that partake of the former, and blame all those that have any considerable share of the latter. It is certain we are infinitely touched with a tender sentiment, as well as with a great one. The tears naturally start in our eyes at the conception of it; nor can we forbear giving a loose to the same tenderness towards the person who exerts it. All this seems to me a proof, that our approbation has, in those cases, an origin different from the prospect of utility and advantage, either to ourselves or others. To which we may add, that men naturally, without reflection, approve of that character, which is most like their own. The man of a mild disposition and tender affections, in forming a notion of the most perfect virtue, mixes in it more of benevolence and humanity, than the man of courage and enterprize, who naturally looks upon a certain elevation of mind as the most accomplished character. This must evidently proceed from an immediate sympathy, which men have with characters similar to their own. They enter with more warmth into such sentiments, and feel more sensibly the pleasure, which arises from them.

It is remarkable, that nothing touches a man of humanity more than any instance of extraordinary delicacy in love or friendship, where a person is attentive to the smallest concerns of his friend, and is willing to sacrifice to them the most considerable interest of his own. Such delicacies have little influence on society; because they make us regard the greatest trifles: But they are the more engaging, the more minute the concern is, and are a proof of the highest merit in any one, who is capable of them. The passions are so contagious, that they pass with the greatest facility from one person to another, and produce correspondent movements in all human breasts. Where friendship appears in very signal instances, my heart catches the same passion, and is warmed by those warm sentiments, that display themselves before me. Such agreeable movements must give me an affection to every one that excites them. This is the case with every thing that is agreeable in any person. The transition from pleasure to love is easy: But the transition must here be still more easy; since the agreeable sentiment, which is excited by sympathy, is love itself; and there is nothing required but to change the object.

Hence the peculiar merit of benevolence in all its shapes and appearances. Hence even its weaknesses are virtuous and amiable; and a person, whose grief upon the loss of a friend were excessive, would be esteemed upon that account. His tenderness bestows a merit, as it does a pleasure, on his melancholy.

We are not, however, to imagine, that all the angry passions are vicious, though they are disagreeable. There is a certain indulgence due to human nature in this respect. Anger and hatred are passions inherent in Our very frame and constitutions. The want of them, on some occasions, may even be a proof of weakness and imbecillity. And where they appear only in a low degree, we not only excuse them because they are natural; but even bestow our applauses on them, because they are inferior to what appears in the greatest part of mankind.

Where these angry passions rise up to cruelty, they form the most detested of all vices. All the pity and concern which we have for the miserable sufferers by this vice, turns against the person guilty of it, and produces a stronger hatred than we are sensible of on any other occasion. Even when the vice of inhumanity rises not to this extreme degree, our sentiments concerning it are very much influenced by reflections on the harm that results from it. And we may observe in general, that if we can find any quality in a person, which renders him incommodious to those, who live and converse with him, we always allow it to be a fault or blemish, without any farther examination. On the other hand, when we enumerate the good qualities of any person, we always mention those parts of his character, which render him a safe companion, an easy friend, a gentle master, an agreeable husband, or an indulgent father. We consider him with all his relations in society; and love or hate him, according as he affects those, who have any immediate intercourse with him. And it is a most certain rule, that if there be no relation of life, in which I could not wish to stand to a particular person, his character must so far be allowed to be perfect. If he be as little wanting to himself as to others, his character is entirely perfect. This is the ultimate test of merit and virtue.

SECTION IV

Of Natural Abilities

No distinction is more usual in all systems of ethics, than that betwixt natural abilities and moral virtues; where the former are placed on the same footing with bodily endowments, and are supposed to have no merit or moral worth annexed to them. Whoever considers the matter accurately, will find, that a dispute upon this head would be merely a dispute of words, and that though these qualities are not altogether of the same kind, yet they agree in the most material circumstances. They are both of them equally mental qualities: And both of them equally produce pleasure; and have of course an equal tendency to procure the love and esteem of mankind. There are few, who are not as jealous of their character, with regard to sense and knowledge, as to honour and courage; and much more than with regard to temperance and sobriety. Men are even afraid of passing for goodnatured; lest that should be taken for want of understanding: And often boast of more debauches than they have been really engaged in, to give themselves airs of fire and spirit. In short, the figure a man makes in the world, the reception he meets with in company, the esteem paid him by his acquaintance; all these advantages depend almost as much upon his good sense and judgment, as upon any other part of his character. Let a man have the best intentions in the world, and be the farthest from all injustice and violence, he will never be able to make himself be much regarded without a moderate share, at least, of parts and understanding. Since then natural abilities, though, perhaps, inferior, yet are on the same footing, both as to their causes and effects, with those qualities which we call moral virtues, why should we make any distinction betwixt them?

Though we refuse to natural abilities the title of virtues, we must allow, that they procure the love and esteem of mankind; that they give a new lustre to the other virtues; and that a man possessed of them is much more intitled to our good-will and services, than one entirely void of them. It may, indeed, be pretended that the sentiment of approbation, which those qualities produce, besides its being inferior, is also somewhat different from that, which attends the other virtues. But this, in my opinion, is not a sufficient reason for excluding them from the catalogue of virtues. Each of the virtues, even benevolence, justice, gratitude, integrity, excites a different sentiment or feeling in the spectator. The characters of Caesar and Cato, as drawn by Sallust, are both of them virtuous, in the strictest sense of the word; but in a different way: Nor are the sentiments entirely the same, which arise from them. The one produces love; the other esteem: The one is amiable; the other awful: We could wish to meet with the one character in a friend; the other character we would be ambitious of in ourselves. In like manner, the approbation which attends natural abilities, may be somewhat different to the feeling from that, which arises from the other virtues, without making them entirely of a different species. And indeed we may observe, that the natural abilities, no more than the other virtues, produce not, all of them, the same kind of approbation. Good sense and genius beget esteem: Wit and humour excite love.[86]

Those, who represent the distinction betwixt natural abilities and moral virtues as very material, may say, that the former are entirely involuntary, and have therefore no merit attending them, as having no dependance on liberty and free-will. But to this I answer, first, that many of those qualities, which all moralists, especially the antients, comprehend under the title of moral virtues, are equally involuntary and necessary, with the qualities of the judgment and imagination. Of this nature are constancy, fortitude, magnanimity; and, in short, all the qualities which form the great man. I might say the same, in some degree, of the others; it being almost impossible for the mind to change its character in any considerable article, or cure itself of a passionate or splenetic temper, when they are natural to it. The greater degree there is of these blameable qualities, the more vicious they

[86] Love and esteem are at the bottom the same passions, and arise from like causes. The qualities, that produce both, are agreeable, and give pleasure. But where this pleasure is severe and serious; or where its object is great, and makes a strong impression; or where it produces any degree of humility and awe: In all these cases, the passion, which arises from the pleasure, is more properly denominated esteem than love. Benevolence attends both: But is connected with love in a more eminent degree.

become, and yet they are the less voluntary. Secondly, I would have anyone give me a reason, why virtue and vice may not be involuntary, as well as beauty and deformity. These moral distinctions arise from the natural distinctions of pain and pleasure; and when we receive those feelings from the general consideration of any quality or character, we denominate it vicious or virtuous. Now I believe no one will assert, that a quality can never produce pleasure or pain to the person who considers it, unless it be perfectly voluntary in the person who possesses it. Thirdly, As to free-will, we have shewn that it has no place with regard to the actions, no more than the qualities of men. It is not a just consequence, that what is voluntary is free. Our actions are more voluntary than our judgments; but we have not more liberty in the one than in the other.

But though this distinction betwixt voluntary and involuntary be not sufficient to justify the distinction betwixt natural abilities and moral virtues, yet the former distinction will afford us a plausible reason, why moralists have invented the latter. Men have observed, that though natural abilities and moral qualities be in the main on the same footing, there is, however, this difference betwixt them, that the former are almost invariable by any art or industry; while the latter, or at least, the actions, that proceed from them, may be changed by the motives of rewards and punishments, praise and blame. Hence legislators, and divines, and moralists, have principally applied themselves to the regulating these voluntary actions, and have endeavoured to produce additional motives, for being virtuous in that particular. They knew, that to punish a man for folly, or exhort him to be prudent and sagacious, would have but little effect; though the same punishments and exhortations, with regard to justice and injustice, might have a considerable influence. But as men, in common life and conversation, do not carry those ends in view, but naturally praise or blame whatever pleases or displeases them, they do not seem much to regard this distinction, but consider prudence under the character of virtue as well as benevolence, and penetration as well as justice. Nay, we find, that all moralists, whose judgment is not perverted by a strict adherence to a system, enter into the same way of thinking; and that the antient moralists in particular made no scruple of placing prudence at the head of the cardinal virtues. There is a sentiment of esteem and approbation, which may be excited, in some degree, by any faculty of the mind, in its perfect state and condition; and to account for this sentiment is the business of Philosophers. It belongs to Grammarians to examine what qualities are entitled to the denomination of virtue; nor will they find, upon trial, that this is so easy a task, as at first sight they may be apt to imagine.

The principal reason why natural abilities are esteemed, is because of their tendency to be useful to the person, who is possessed of them. It is impossible to execute any design with success, where it is not conducted with prudence and discretion; nor will the goodness of our intentions alone suffice to procure us a happy issue to our enterprizes. Men are superior to beasts principally by the superiority of their reason; and they are the degrees of the same faculty, which set such an infinite difference betwixt one man and another. All the advantages of art are owing to human reason; and where fortune is not very capricious, the most considerable part of these advantages must fall to the share of the prudent and sagacious.

When it is asked, whether a quick or a slow apprehension be most valuable? whether one, that at first view penetrates into a subject, but can perform nothing upon study; or a contrary character, which must work out every thing by dint of application? whether a clear head, or a copious invention? whether a profound genius, or a sure judgment? in short, what character, or peculiar understanding, is more excellent than another? It is evident we can answer none of these questions, without considering which of those qualities capacitates a man best for the world, and carries him farthest in any of his undertakings.

There are many other qualities of the mind, whose merit is derived from the same origin, industry, perseverance, patience, activity, vigilance, application, constancy, with other virtues of that kind, which it will be easy to recollect, are esteemed valuable upon no other account, than their advantage in the conduct of life. It is the same case with temperance, frugality, economy, resolution: As on the other hand, prodigality, luxury, irresolution, uncertainty, are vicious, merely because they draw ruin upon us, and incapacitate us for business and action.

As wisdom and good-sense are valued, because they are useful to the person possessed of them; so wit and eloquence are valued, because they are immediately agreeable to others. On the other hand, good humour is loved and esteemed, because it is immediately agreeable to the person himself. It is evident, that the conversation of a man of wit is very satisfactory; as a chearful good-humoured companion diffuses a joy over the whole company, from a sympathy with his gaiety. These qualities, therefore, being agreeable, they naturally beget love and esteem, and answer to all the characters of virtue.

It is difficult to tell, on many occasions, what it is that renders one man's conversation so agreeable and entertaining, and another's so insipid and distasteful. As conversation is a transcript of the mind as well as books, the same qualities, which render the one valuable, must give us an esteem for the other. This we shall consider afterwards. In the mean time it may be affirmed in general, that all the merit a man may derive from his conversation (which, no doubt, may be very considerable) arises from nothing but the pleasure it conveys to those who are present.

In this view, cleanliness is also to be regarded as a virtue; since it naturally renders us agreeable to others, and is a very considerable source of love and affection. No one will deny, that a negligence in this particular is a fault; and as faults are nothing but smaller vices, and this fault can have no other origin than the uneasy sensation, which it excites in others, we may in this instance, seemingly so trivial, dearly discover the origin of the moral distinction of vice and virtue in other instances.

Besides all those qualities, which render a person lovely or valuable, there is also a certain JE-NE-SAIS-QUOI of agreeable and handsome, that concurs to the same effect. In this case, as well as in that of wit and eloquence, we must have recourse to a certain sense, which acts without reflection, and regards not the tendencies of qualities and characters. Some moralists account for all the sentiments of virtue by this sense. Their hypothesis is very plausible. Nothing but a particular enquiry can give the preference to any other hypothesis. When we find, that almost all the virtues have such particular tendencies; and also find, that these tendencies are sufficient alone to give a strong sentiment of approbation: We cannot doubt, after this, that qualities are approved of, in proportion to the advantage, which results from them.

The decorum or indecorum of a quality, with regard to the age, or character, or station, contributes also to its praise or blame. This decorum depends, in a great measure, upon experience. It is usual to see men lose their levity, as they advance in years. Such a degree of gravity, therefore, and such years, are connected together in our thoughts. When we observe them separated in any person's character, this imposes a kind of violence on our imagination, and is disagreeable.

That faculty of the soul, which, of all others, is of the least consequence to the character, and has the least virtue or vice in its several degrees, at the same time, that it admits of a great variety of degrees, is the memory. Unless it rise up to that stupendous height as to surprize us, or sink so low as, in some measure, to affect the judgment, we commonly take no notice of its variations, nor ever mention them to the praise or dispraise of any person. It is so far from being a virtue to have a good memory, that men generally affect to complain of a bad one; and endeavouring to persuade the world, that what they say is entirely of their own invention, sacrifice it to the praise of genius and judgment. Yet to consider the matter abstractedly, it would be difficult to give a reason, why the faculty of recalling past ideas with truth and clearness, should not have as much merit in it, as the faculty of placing our present ideas, in such an order, as to form true propositions and opinions. The reason of the difference certainly must be, that the memory is exerted without any sensation of pleasure or pain; and in all its middling degrees serves almost equally well in business and affairs. But the least variations in the judgment are sensibly felt in their consequences; while at the same time that faculty is never exerted in any eminent degree, without an extraordinary delight and satisfaction. The sympathy with this utility and pleasure bestows a merit on the understanding; and the absence of it makes us consider the memory as a faculty very indifferent to blame or praise.

Before I leave this subject of natural abilities, I must observe, that, perhaps, one source of the esteem and affection, which attends them, is derived from the importance and weight, which they bestow on the person possessed of them. He becomes of greater consequence in life. His resolutions and actions affect a greater number of his fellow-creatures. Both his friendship and enmity are of moment.

And it is easy to observe, that whoever is elevated, after this manner, above the rest of mankind, must excite in us the sentiments of esteem and approbation. Whatever is important engages our attention, fixes our thought, and is contemplated with satisfaction. The histories of kingdoms are more interesting than domestic stories: The histories of great empires more than those of small cities and principalities: And the histories of wars and revolutions more than those of peace and order. We sympathize with the persons that suffer, in all the various sentiments which belong to their fortunes. The mind is occupied by the multitude of the objects, and by the strong passions, that display themselves. And this occupation or agitation of the mind is commonly agreeable and amusing. The same theory accounts for the esteem and regard we pay to men of extraordinary parts and abilities. The good and ill of multitudes are connected with their actions. Whatever they undertake is important, and challenges our attention. Nothing is to be over-looked and despised, that regards them. And where any person can excite these sentiments, he soon acquires our esteem; unless other circumstances of his character render him odious and disagreeable.

SECTION V

Some Farther Reflections Concerning the Natural Virtues

It has been observed, in treating of the passions, that pride and humility, love and hatred, are excited by any advantages or disadvantages of the mind, body, or fortune; and that these advantages or disadvantages have that effect by producing a separate impression of pain or pleasure. The pain or pleasure, which arises from the general survey or view of any action or quality of the mind, constitutes its vice or virtue, and gives rise to our approbation or blame, which is nothing but a fainter and more imperceptible love or hatred. We have assigned four different sources of this pain and pleasure; and in order to justify more fully that hypothesis, it may here be proper to observe, that the advantages or disadvantages of the body and of fortune, produce a pain or pleasure from the very same principles. The tendency of any object to be useful to the person possessed of it, or to others; to convey pleasure to him or to others; all these circumstances convey an immediate pleasure to the person, who considers the object, and command his love and approbation.

To begin with the advantages of the body; we may observe a phænomenon, which might appear somewhat trivial and ludicrous, if any thing could be trivial, which fortified a conclusion of such importance, or ludicrous, which was employed in a philosophical reasoning. It is a general remark, that those we call good women's men, who have either signalized themselves by their amorous exploits, or whose make of body promises any extraordinary vigour of that kind, are well received by the fair sex, and naturally engage the affections even of those, whose virtue prevents any design of ever giving employment to those talents. Here it is evident, that the ability of such a person to give enjoyment, is the real source of that love and esteem he meets with among the females; at the same time that the women, who love and esteem him, have no prospect of receiving that enjoyment themselves, and can only be affected by means of their sympathy with one, that has a commerce of love with him. This instance is singular, and merits our attention.

Another source of the pleasure we receive from considering bodily advantages, is their utility to the person himself, who is possessed of them. It is certain, that a considerable part of the beauty of men, as well as of other animals, consists in such a conformation of members, as we find by experience to be attended with strength and agility, and to capacitate the creature for any action or exercise. Broad shoulders, a lank belly, firm joints, taper legs; all these are beautiful in our species because they are signs of force and vigour, which being advantages we naturally sympathize with, they convey to the beholder a share of that satisfaction they produce in the possessor.

So far as to the utility, which may attend any quality of the body. As to the immediate pleasure, it is certain, that an air of health, as well as of strength and agility, makes a considerable part of beauty; and that a sickly air in another is always disagreeable, upon account of that idea of pain and uneasiness, which it conveys to us. On the other hand, we are pleased with the regularity of our own features, though it be neither useful to ourselves nor others; and it is necessary at a distance, to make it convey to us any satisfaction. We commonly consider ourselves as we appear in the eyes of others, and sympathize with the advantageous sentiments they entertain with regard to us.

How far the advantages of fortune produce esteem and approbation from the same principles, we may satisfy ourselves by reflecting on our precedent reasoning on that subject. We have observed, that our approbation of those, who are possessed of the advantages of fortune, may be ascribed to three different causes. First, To that immediate pleasure, which a rich man gives us, by the view of the beautiful cloaths, equipage, gardens, or houses, which he possesses. Secondly, To the advantage, which we hope to reap from him by his generosity and liberality. Thirdly, To the pleasure and advantage, which he himself reaps from his possessions, and which produce an agreeable sympathy in us. Whether we ascribe our esteem of the rich and great to one or all of these causes, we may clearly see the traces of those principles, which give rise to the sense of vice and virtue. I believe most people, at first sight, will be inclined to ascribe our esteem of the rich to self-interest, and the prospect of advantage. But as it is certain, that our esteem or deference extends beyond any prospect of advantage to ourselves, it is evident, that that sentiment must proceed from a sympathy with those, who are dependent on the person we esteem and respect, and who have an immediate connexion with him. We consider him as a person capable of contributing to the happiness or enjoyment of his fellow-creatures, whose sentiments, with regard to him, we naturally embrace. And this consideration will serve to justify my hypothesis in preferring the third principle to the other two, and ascribing our esteem of the rich to a sympathy with the pleasure and advantage, which they themselves receive from their possessions. For as even the other two principles cannot operate to a due extent, or account for all the phaenomena, without having recourse to a sympathy of one kind or other; it is much more natural to chuse that sympathy, which is immediate and direct, than that which is remote and indirect. To which we may add, that where the riches or power are very great, and render the person considerable and important in the world, the esteem attending them, may, in part, be ascribed to another source, distinct from these three, viz. their interesting the mind by a prospect of the multitude, and importance of their consequences: Though, in order to account for the operation of this principle, we must also have recourse to sympathy; as we have observed in the preceding section.

It may not be amiss, on this occasion, to remark the flexibility of our sentiments, and the several changes they so readily receive from the objects, with which they are conjoined. All the sentiments of approbation, which attend any particular species of objects, have a great resemblance to each other, though derived from different sources; and, on the other hand, those sentiments, when directed to different objects, are different to the feeling, though derived from the same source. Thus the beauty of all visible objects causes a pleasure pretty much the same, though it be sometimes derived from the mere species and appearance of the objects; sometimes from sympathy, and an idea of their utility. In like manner, whenever we survey the actions and characters of men, without any particular interest in them, the pleasure, or pain, which arises from the survey (with some minute differences) is, in the main, of the same kind, though perhaps there be a great diversity in the causes, from which it is derived. On the other hand, a convenient house, and a virtuous character, cause not the same feeling of approbation; even though the source of our approbation be the same, and flow from sympathy and an idea of their utility. There is something very inexplicable in this variation of our feelings; but it is what we have experience of with regard to all our passions and sentiments.

SECTION VI

Conclusion of this Book

Thus upon the whole I am hopeful, that nothing is wanting to an accurate proof of this system of ethics. We are certain, that sympathy is a very powerful principle in human nature. We are also certain, that it has a great influence on our sense of beauty, when we regard external objects, as well as when we judge of morals. We find, that it has force sufficient to give us the strongest sentiments of approbation, when it operates alone, without the concurrence of any other principle; as in the cases of justice, allegiance, chastity, and good-manners. We may observe, that all the circumstances requisite for its operation are found in most of the virtues; which have, for the most part, a tendency to the good of society, or to that of the person possessed of them. If we compare all these circumstances, we shall not doubt, that sympathy is the chief source of moral distinctions; especially when we reflect, that no objection can be raised against this hypothesis in one case, which will not extend to all cases. Justice is certainly approved of for no other reason, than because it has a tendency to the public good: And the public good is indifferent to us, except so far as sympathy interests us in it. We may presume the like with regard to all the other virtues, which have a like tendency to the public good. They must derive all their merit from our sympathy with those, who reap any advantage from them: As the virtues, which have a tendency to the good of the person possessed of them, derive their merit from our sympathy with him.

Most people will readily allow, that the useful qualities of the mind are virtuous, because of their utility. This way of thinking is so natural, and occurs on so many occasions, that few will make any scruple of admitting it. Now this being once admitted, the force of sympathy must necessarily be acknowledged. Virtue is considered as means to an end. Means to an end are only valued so far as the end is valued. But the happiness of strangers affects us by sympathy alone. To that principle, therefore, we are to ascribe the sentiment of approbation, which arises from the survey of all those virtues, that are useful to society, or to the person possessed of them. These form the most considerable part of morality.

Were it proper in such a subject to bribe the reader's assent, or employ any thing but solid argument, we are here abundantly supplied with topics to engage the affections. All lovers of virtue (and such we all are in speculation, however we may degenerate in practice) must certainly be pleased to see moral distinctions derived from so noble a source, which gives us a just notion both of the generosity and capacity of human nature. It requires but very little knowledge of human affairs to perceive, that a sense of morals is a principle inherent in the soul, and one of the most powerful that enters into the composition. But this sense must certainly acquire new force, when reflecting on itself, it approves of those principles, from whence it is derived, and finds nothing but what is great and good in its rise and origin. Those who resolve the sense of morals into original instincts of the human mind, may defend the cause of virtue with sufficient authority; but want the advantage, which those possess, who account for that sense by an extensive sympathy with mankind. According to their system, not only virtue must be approved of, but also the sense of virtue: And not only that sense, but also the principles, from whence it is derived. So that nothing is presented on any side, but what is laudable and good.

This observation may be extended to justice, and the other virtues of that kind. Though justice be artificial, the sense of its morality is natural. It is the combination of men, in a system of conduct, which renders any act of justice beneficial to society. But when once it has that tendency, we naturally approve of it; and if we did not so, it is impossible any combination or convention could ever produce that sentiment.

Most of the inventions of men are subject to change. They depend upon humour and caprice. They have a vogue for a time, and then sink into oblivion. It may, perhaps, be apprehended, that if justice were allowed to be a human invention, it must be placed on the same footing. But the cases are widely different. The interest, on which justice is founded, is the greatest imaginable, and extends to all times and places. It cannot possibly be served by any other invention. It is obvious, and discovers itself on the very first formation of society. All these causes render the rules of justice stedfast and immutable; at least, as immutable as human nature. And if they were founded on original instincts, could they have any greater stability?

The same system may help us to form a just notion of the happiness, as well as of the dignity of virtue, and may interest every principle of our nature in the embracing and cherishing that noble quality. Who indeed does not feel an accession of alacrity in his pursuits of knowledge and ability of every kind, when he considers, that besides the advantage, which immediately result from these acquisitions, they also give him a new lustre in the eyes of mankind, and are universally attended with esteem and approbation? And who can think any advantages of fortune a sufficient compensation for the least breach of the social virtues, when he considers, that not only his character with regard to others, but also his peace and inward satisfaction entirely depend upon his strict observance of them; and that a mind will never be able to bear its own survey, that has been wanting in its part to mankind and society? But I forbear insisting on this subject. Such reflections require a work apart, very different from the genius of the present. The anatomist ought never to emulate the painter; nor in his accurate dissections and portraitures of the smaller parts of the human body, pretend to give his figures any graceful and engaging attitude or expression. There is even something hideous, or at least minute in the views of things, which he presents; and it is necessary the objects should be set more at a distance, and be more covered up from sight, to make them engaging to the eye and imagination. An anatomist, however, is admirably fitted to give advice to a painter; and it is even impracticable to excel in the latter art, without the assistance of the former. We must have an exact knowledge of the parts, their situation and connexion, before we can design with any elegance or correctness. And thus the most abstract speculations concerning human nature, however cold and unentertaining, become subservient to practical morality; and may render this latter science more correct in its precepts, and more persuasive in its exhortations.

APPENDIX

There is nothing I would more willingly lay hold of, than an opportunity of confessing my errors; and should esteem such a return to truth and reason to be more honourable than the most unerring judgment. A man, who is free from mistakes, can pretend to no praises, except from the justness of his understanding: But a man, who corrects his mistakes, shews at once the justness of his understanding, and the candour and ingenuity of his temper. I have not yet been so fortunate as to discover any very considerable mistakes in the reasonings delivered in the preceding volumes, except on one article: But I have found by experience, that some of my expressions have not been so well chosen, as to guard against all mistakes in the readers; and it is chiefly to remedy this defect, I have subjoined the following appendix.

We can never be induced to believe any matter of fact, except where its cause, or its effect, is present to us; but what the nature is of that belief, which arises from the relation of cause and effect, few have had the curiosity to ask themselves. In my opinion, this dilemma is inevitable. Either the belief is some new idea, such as that of reality or existence, which we join to the simple conception of an object, or it is merely a peculiar feeling or sentiment. That it is not a new idea, annexed to the simple conception, may be evinced from these two arguments. First, We have no abstract idea of existence, distinguishable and separable from the idea of particular objects. It is impossible, therefore, that this idea of existence can be annexed to the idea of any object, or form the difference betwixt a simple conception and belief. Secondly, The mind has the command over all its ideas, and can separate, unite, mix, and vary them, as it pleases; so that if belief consisted merely in a new idea, annexed to the conception, it would be in a man's power to believe what he pleased. We may, therefore, conclude, that belief consists merely in a certain feeling or sentiment; in something, that depends not on the will, but must arise from certain determinate causes and principles, of which we are not masters. When we are convinced of any matter of fact, we do nothing but conceive it, along with a certain feeling, different from what attends the mere reveries of the imagination. And when we express our incredulity concerning any fact, we mean, that the arguments for the fact produce not that feeling. Did not the belief consist in a sentiment different from our mere conception, whatever objects were presented by the wildest imagination, would be on an equal footing with the most established truths founded on history and experience. There is nothing but the feeling, or sentiment, to distinguish the one from the other.

This, therefore, being regarded as an undoubted truth, that belief is nothing but a peculiar feeling, different from the simple conception, the next question, that naturally occurs, is, what is the nature of this feeling, or sentiment, and whether it be analogous to any other sentiment of the human mind? This question is important. For if it be not analogous to any other sentiment, we must despair of explaining its causes, and must consider it as an original principle of the human mind. If it be analogous, we may hope to explain its causes from analogy, and trace it up to more general principles. Now that there is a greater firmness and solidity in the conceptions, which are the objects of conviction and assurance, than in the loose and indolent reveries of a castle-builder, every one will readily own. They strike upon us with more force; they are more present to us; the mind has a firmer hold of them, and is more actuated and moved by them. It acquiesces in them; and, in a manner, fixes and reposes itself on them. In short, they approach nearer to the impressions, which are immediately present to us; and are therefore analogous to many other operations of the mind.

There is not, in my opinion, any possibility of evading this conclusion, but by asserting, that belief, beside the simple conception, consists in some impression or feeling, distinguishable from the conception. It does not modify the conception, and render it more present and intense: It is only annexed to it, after the same manner that will and desire are annexed to particular conceptions of good and pleasure. But the following considerations will, I hope, be sufficient to remove this hypothesis. First, It is directly contrary to experience, and our immediate consciousness. All men have ever allowed reasoning to be merely an operation of our thoughts or ideas; and however those ideas may be varied to the feeling, there is nothing ever enters into our conclusions but ideas, or our fainter conceptions. For instance; I hear at present a person's voice, whom I am acquainted with; and this sound comes from the next room. This impression of my senses immediately conveys my thoughts to the person, along with all the surrounding objects. I paint them out to myself as existent at present, with the same qualities and relations, that I formerly knew them possessed of. These ideas take faster hold of my mind, than the ideas of an inchanted castle. They are different to the feeling; but there is no distinct or separate impression attending them. It is the same case when I recollect the several incidents of a journey, or the events of any history. Every particular fact is there the object of belief. Its idea is modified differently from the loose reveries of a castle-builder: But no distinct impression attends every distinct idea, or conception of matter of fact. This is the subject of plain experience. If ever this experience can be disputed on any occasion, it is when the mind has been agitated with doubts and difficulties; and afterwards, upon taking the object in a new point of view, or being presented with a new argument, fixes and reposes itself in one settled conclusion and belief. In this case there is a feeling distinct and separate from the conception. The passage from doubt and agitation to tranquility and repose, conveys a satisfaction and pleasure to the mind. But take any other case. Suppose I see the legs and thighs of a person in motion, while some interposed object conceals the rest of his body. Here it is certain, the imagination spreads out the whole figure. I give him a head and shoulders, and breast and neck. These members I conceive and believe him to be possessed of. Nothing can be more evident, than that this whole operation is performed by the thought or imagination alone. The transition is immediate. The ideas presently strike us. Their customary connexion with the present impression, varies them and modifies them in a certain manner, but produces no act of the mind, distinct from this peculiarity of conception. Let any one examine his own mind, and he will evidently find this to be the truth.

Secondly, Whatever may be the case, with regard to this distinct impression, it must be allowed, that the mind has a firmer hold, or more steady conception of what it takes to be matter of fact, than of fictions. Why then look any farther, or multiply suppositions without necessity?

Thirdly, We can explain the causes of the firm conception, but not those of any separate impression. And not only so, but the causes of the firm conception exhaust the whole subject, and nothing is left to produce any other effect. An inference concerning a matter of fact is nothing but the idea of an object, that is frequently conjoined, or is associated with a present impression. This is the whole of it. Every part is requisite to explain, from analogy, the more steady conception; and nothing remains capable of producing any distinct impression.

Fourthly, The effects of belief, in influencing the passions and imagination, can all be explained from the firm conception; and there is no occasion to have recourse to any other principle. These arguments, with many others, enumerated in the foregoing volumes, sufficiently prove, that belief only modifies the idea or conception; and renders it different to the feeling, without producing any distinct impression. Thus upon a general view of the subject, there appear to be two questions of importance, which we may venture to recommend to the consideration of philosophers, Whether there be any thing to distinguish belief from the simple conception beside the feeling of sentiment? And, Whether this feeling be any thing but a firmer conception, or a faster hold, that we take of the object?

If, upon impartial enquiry, the same conclusion, that I have formed, be assented to by philosophers, the next business is to examine the analogy, which there is betwixt belief, and other acts of the mind, and find the cause of the firmness and strength of conception: And this I do not esteem a difficult task. The transition from a present impression, always enlivens and strengthens any idea. When any object is presented, the idea of its usual attendant immediately strikes us, as something real and solid. It is felt, rather than conceived, and approaches the impression, from which it is derived, in its force and influence. This I have proved at large. I cannot add any new arguments.

I had entertained some hopes, that however deficient our theory of the intellectual world might be, it would be free from those contradictions, and absurdities, which seem to attend every explication, that human reason can give of the material world. But upon a more strict review of the section concerning personal identity, I find myself involved in such a labyrinth, that, I must confess, I neither know how to correct my former opinions, nor how to render them consistent. If this be not a good general reason for scepticism, it is at least a sufficient one (if I were not already abundantly supplied) for me to entertain a diffidence and modesty in all my decisions. I shall propose the arguments on both sides, beginning with those that induced me to deny the strict and proper identity and simplicity of a self or thinking being.

When we talk of self or substance, we must have an idea annexed to these terms, otherwise they are altogether unintelligible. Every idea is derived from preceding impressions; and we have no impression of self or substance, as something simple and individual. We have, therefore, no idea of them in that sense.

Whatever is distinct, is distinguishable; and whatever is distinguishable, is separable by the thought or imagination. All perceptions are distinct. They are, therefore, distinguishable, and separable, and may be conceived as separately existent, and may exist separately, without any contradiction or absurdity.

When I view this table and that chimney, nothing is present to me but particular perceptions, which are of a like nature with all the other perceptions. This is the doctrine of philosophers. But this table, which is present to me, and the chimney, may and do exist separately. This is the doctrine of the vulgar, and implies no contradiction. There is no contradiction, therefore, in extending the same doctrine to all the perceptions.

In general, the following reasoning seems satisfactory. All ideas are borrowed from preceding perceptions. Our ideas of objects, therefore, are derived from that source. Consequently no proposition can be intelligible or consistent with regard to objects, which is not so with regard to perceptions. But it is intelligible and consistent to say, that objects exist distinct and independent, without any common simple substance or subject of inhesion. This proposition, therefore, can never be absurd with regard to perceptions.

When I turn my reflection on myself, I never can perceive this self without some one or more perceptions; nor can I ever perceive any thing but the perceptions. It is the composition of these, therefore, which forms the self. We can conceive a thinking being to have either many or few perceptions. Suppose the mind to be reduced even below the life of an oyster. Suppose it to have only one perception, as of thirst or hunger. Consider it in that situation. Do you conceive any thing but merely that perception? Have you any notion of self or substance? If not, the addition of other perceptions can never give you that notion.

The annihilation, which some people suppose to follow upon death, and which entirely destroys this self, is nothing but an extinction of all particular perceptions; love and hatred, pain and pleasure, thought and sensation. These therefore must be the same with self; since the one cannot survive the other.

Is self the same with substance? If it be, how can that question have place, concerning the subsistence of self, under a change of substance? If they be distinct, what is the difference betwixt them? For my part, I have a notion of neither, when conceived distinct from particular perceptions.

Philosophers begin to be reconciled to the principle, that we have no idea of external substance, distinct from the ideas of particular qualities. This must pave the way for a like principle with regard to the mind, that we have no notion of it, distinct from the particular perceptions.

So far I seem to be attended with sufficient evidence. But having thus loosened all our particular perceptions, when I proceed to explain the principle of connexion, which binds them together, and makes us attribute to them a real simplicity and identity; I am sensible, that my account is very defective, and that nothing but the seeming evidence of the precedent reasonings could have induced me to receive it. If perceptions are distinct existences, they form a whole only by being connected together. But no connexions among distinct existences are ever discoverable by human understanding. We only feel a connexion or determination of the thought, to pass from one object to another. It follows, therefore, that the thought alone finds personal identity, when reflecting on the train of past perceptions, that compose a mind, the ideas of them are felt to be connected together, and naturally introduce each other. However extraordinary this conclusion may seem, it need not surprize us. Most philosophers seem inclined to think, that personal identity arises from consciousness; and consciousness is nothing but a reflected thought or perception. The present philosophy, therefore, has so far a promising aspect. But all my hopes vanish, when I come to explain the principles, that unite our successive perceptions in our thought or consciousness. I cannot discover any theory, which gives me satisfaction on this head.

In short there are two principles, which I cannot render consistent; nor is it in my power to renounce either of them, viz, that all our distinct perceptions are distinct existences, and that the mind never perceives any real connexion among distinct existences. Did our perceptions either inhere in something simple and individual, or did the mind perceive some real connexion among them, there would be no difficulty in the case. For my part, I must plead the privilege of a sceptic, and confess, that this difficulty is too hard for my understanding. I pretend not, however, to pronounce it absolutely insuperable. Others, perhaps, or myself, upon more mature reflections, may discover some hypothesis, that will reconcile those contradictions.

I shall also take this opportunity of confessing two other errors of less importance, which more mature reflection has discovered to me in my reasoning. The first may be found in Vol. I. page 106. where I say, that the distance betwixt two bodies is known, among other things, by the angles, which the rays of light flowing from the bodies make with each other. It is certain, that these angles are not known to the mind, and consequently can never discover the distance. The second error may be found in Vol. I. page 144 where I say, that two ideas of the same object can only be different by their different degrees of force and vivacity. I believe there are other differences among ideas, which cannot properly be comprehended under these terms. Had I said, that two ideas of the same object can only be different by their different feeling, I should have been nearer the truth.

CRITIQUE OF PURE REASON

Immanuel Kant

Translated by
J. M. D. Meiklejohn

PREFACE TO THE FIRST EDITION 1781

Human reason, in one sphere of its cognition, is called upon to consider questions, which it cannot decline, as they are presented by its own nature, but which it cannot answer, as they transcend every faculty of the mind.

It falls into this difficulty without any fault of its own. It begins with principles, which cannot be dispensed with in the field of experience, and the truth and sufficiency of which are, at the same time, insured by experience. With these principles it rises, in obedience to the laws of its own nature, to ever higher and more remote conditions. But it quickly discovers that, in this way, its labours must remain ever incomplete, because new questions never cease to present themselves; and thus it finds itself compelled to have recourse to principles which transcend the region of experience, while they are regarded by common sense without distrust. It thus falls into confusion and contradictions, from which it conjectures the presence of latent errors, which, however, it is unable to discover, because the principles it employs, transcending the limits of experience, cannot be tested by that criterion. The arena of these endless contests is called *Metaphysic.*

Time was, when she was the *queen* of all the sciences; and, if we take the will for the deed, she certainly deserves, so far as regards the high importance of her object-matter, this title of honour. Now, it is the fashion of the time to heap contempt and scorn upon her; and the matron mourns, forlorn and forsaken, like Hecuba:

> Modo maxima rerum,
> Tot generis, natisque potens...
> Nunc trahor exul, inops.
>
> —Ovid, Metamorphoses. xiii

At first, her government, under the administration of the *dogmatists*, was an absolute *despotism*. But, as the legislative continued to show traces of the ancient barbaric rule, her empire gradually broke up, and intestine wars introduced the reign of *anarchy;* while the *sceptics*, like nomadic tribes, who hate a permanent habitation and settled mode of living, attacked from time to time those who had organized themselves into civil communities. But their number was, very happily, small; and thus they could not entirely put a stop to the exertions of those who persisted in raising new edifices, although on no settled or uniform plan. In recent times the hope dawned upon us of seeing those disputes settled, and the legitimacy of her claims established by a kind of *physiology* of the human understanding—that of the celebrated Locke. But it was found that—although it was affirmed that this so-called queen could not refer her descent to any higher source than that of common experience, a circumstance which necessarily brought suspicion on her claims—as this *genealogy* was incorrect, she persisted in the advancement of her claims to sovereignty. Thus metaphysics necessarily fell back into the antiquated and rotten constitution of *dogmatism*, and again became obnoxious to the contempt from which efforts had been made to save it. At present, as all methods, according to the general persuasion, have been tried in vain, there reigns nought but weariness and complete *indifferentism*—the mother of chaos and night in the scientific world, but at the same time the source of, or at least the prelude to, the re-creation and reinstallation of a science, when it has fallen into confusion, obscurity, and disuse from ill directed effort.

For it is in reality vain to profess *indifference* in regard to such inquiries, the object of which cannot be indifferent to humanity. Besides, these pretended *indifferentists*, however much they may try to disguise themselves by the assumption of a popular style and by changes on the language of the schools, unavoidably fall into metaphysical declarations and propositions, which they profess to regard with so much contempt. At the same time, this indifference, which has arisen in the world of science, and which relates to that kind of knowledge which we should wish to see destroyed the last, is a phenomenon that well deserves our attention and reflection. It is plainly not the effect of the levity, but of the matured *judgement*[1] of the age, which refuses to be any longer entertained with illusory knowledge, It is, in fact, a call to reason, again to undertake the most laborious of all tasks—that of self-examination, and to establish a tribunal, which may secure it in its well-grounded claims, while it pronounces against all baseless assumptions and pretensions, not in an arbitrary manner, but according to its own eternal and unchangeable laws. This tribunal is nothing less than the *Critical Investigation of Pure Reason.*

I do not mean by this a criticism of books and systems, but a critical inquiry into the faculty of reason, with reference to the cognitions to which it strives to attain *without the aid of experience;* in other words, the solution of the question regarding the possibility or impossibility of metaphysics, and the determination of the origin, as well as of the extent and limits of this science. All this must be done on the basis of principles.

This path—the only one now remaining—has been entered upon by me; and I flatter myself that I have, in this way, discovered the cause of—and consequently the mode of removing—all the errors which have hitherto set reason at variance with itself, in the sphere of non-empirical thought. I have not returned an evasive answer

---

[1] We very often hear complaints of the shallowness of the present age, and of the decay of profound science. But I do not think that those which rest upon a secure foundation, such as mathematics, physical science, etc., in the least deserve this reproach, but that they rather maintain their ancient fame, and in the latter case, indeed, far surpass it. The same would be the case with the other kinds of cognition, if their principles were but firmly established. In the absence of this security, indifference, doubt, and finally, severe criticism are rather signs of a profound habit of thought. Our age is the age of criticism, to which everything must be subjected. The sacredness of religion, and the authority of legislation, are by many regarded as grounds of exemption from the examination of this tribunal. But, if they are exempted, they become the subjects of just suspicion, and cannot lay claim to sincere respect, which reason accords only to that which has stood the test of a free and public examination.

to the questions of reason, by alleging the inability and limitation of the faculties of the mind; I have, on the contrary, examined them completely in the light of principles, and, after having discovered the cause of the doubts and contradictions into which reason fell, have solved them to its perfect satisfaction. It is true, these questions have not been solved as dogmatism, in its vain fancies and desires, had expected; for it can only be satisfied by the exercise of magical arts, and of these I have no knowledge. But neither do these come within the compass of our mental powers; and it was the duty of philosophy to destroy the illusions which had their origin in misconceptions, whatever darling hopes and valued expectations may be ruined by its explanations. My chief aim in this work has been thoroughness; and I make bold to say that there is not a single metaphysical problem that does not find its solution, or at least the key to its solution, here. Pure reason is a perfect unity; and therefore, if the principle presented by it prove to be insufficient for the solution of even a single one of those questions to which the very nature of reason gives birth, we must reject it, as we could not be perfectly certain of its sufficiency in the case of the others.

While I say this, I think I see upon the countenance of the reader signs of dissatisfaction mingled with contempt, when he hears declarations which sound so boastful and extravagant; and yet they are beyond comparison more moderate than those advanced by the commonest author of the commonest philosophical programme, in which the dogmatist professes to demonstrate the simple nature of the soul, or the necessity of a primal being. Such a dogmatist promises to extend human knowledge beyond the limits of possible experience; while I humbly confess that this is completely beyond my power. Instead of any such attempt, I confine myself to the examination of reason alone and its pure thought; and I do not need to seek far for the sum-total of its cognition, because it has its seat in my own mind. Besides, common logic presents me with a complete and systematic catalogue of all the simple operations of reason; and it is my task to answer the question how far reason can go, without the material presented and the aid furnished by experience.

So much for the completeness and thoroughness necessary in the execution of the present task. The aims set before us are not arbitrarily proposed, but are imposed upon us by the nature of cognition itself.

The above remarks relate to the *matter* of our critical inquiry. As regards the *form*, there are two indispensable conditions, which any one who undertakes so difficult a task as that of a critique of pure reason, is bound to fulfil. These conditions are *certitude* and *clearness*.

As regards *certitude*, I have fully convinced myself that, in this sphere of thought, *opinion* is perfectly inadmissible, and that everything which bears the least semblance of an hypothesis must be excluded, as of no value in such discussions. For it is a necessary condition of every cognition that is to be established upon *à priori* grounds that it shall be held to be absolutely necessary; much more is this the case with an attempt to determine all pure *à priori* cognition, and to furnish the standard—and consequently an example—of all apodeictic (philosophical) certitude. Whether I have succeeded in what I professed to do, it is for the reader to determine; it is the author's business merely to adduce grounds and reasons, without determining what influence these ought to have on the mind of his judges. But, lest anything he may have said may become the innocent cause of doubt in their minds, or tend to weaken the effect which his arguments might otherwise produce—he may be allowed to point out those passages which may occasion mistrust or difficulty, although these do not concern the main purpose of the present work. He does this solely with the view of removing from the mind of the reader any doubts which might affect his judgement of the work as a whole, and in regard to its ultimate aim.

I know no investigations more necessary for a full insight into the nature of the faculty which we call *understanding*, and at the same time for the determination of the rules and limits of its use, than those undertaken in the second chapter of the "Transcendental Analytic," under the title of *Deduction of the Pure Conceptions of the Understanding;* and they have also cost me by far the greatest labour—labour which, I hope, will not remain uncompensated. The view there taken, which goes somewhat deeply into the subject, has two sides. The one relates to the objects of the pure understanding, and is intended to demonstrate and to render comprehensible the objective validity of its *à priori* conceptions; and it forms for this reason an essential part of the Critique. The other considers the pure understanding itself, its possibility and its powers of cognition—that is, from a subjective point of view; and, although this exposition is of great importance, it does not belong essentially to the main purpose of the work, because the grand question is what and how much can reason and understanding, apart from experience, cognize, and not, how is the *faculty of thought* itself possible? As the latter is an inquiry into the cause of a given effect, and has thus in it some semblance of an hypothesis (although, as I shall show on another occasion, this is really not the fact), it would seem that, in the present instance, I had allowed myself to enounce a mere *opinion*, and that the reader must therefore be at liberty to hold a different *opinion*. But I beg to remind him that, if my subjective deduction does not produce in his mind the conviction of its certitude at which I aimed, the objective deduction, with which alone the present work is properly concerned, is in every respect satisfactory.

As regards *clearness*, the reader has a right to demand, in the first place, *discursive* or logical clearness, that is, on the basis of conceptions, and, secondly, *intuitive* or æsthetic clearness, by means of intuitions, that is, by examples or other modes of illustration *in concreto*. I have done what I could for the first kind of intelligibility. This was essential to my purpose; and it thus became the accidental cause of my inability to do complete justice to the second requirement. I have been almost always at a loss, during the progress of this work, how to settle this question. Examples and illustrations always appeared to me necessary, and, in the first sketch of the Critique, naturally fell into their proper places. But I very soon became aware of the magnitude of my task, and the numerous problems with which I should be engaged; and, as I perceived that this critical investigation would, even if delivered in the driest *scholastic* manner, be far from being brief, I found it unadvisable to enlarge it still more with examples and explanations, which are necessary only from a *popular* point of view. I was induced to take this course from the consideration also that the present work is not intended for popular use, that those devoted to science do not require such helps, although they are always acceptable, and that they would have materially interfered with my present purpose. Abbé Terrasson remarks with great justice that, if we estimate the size of a work, not from the number of its pages, but from the time which we require to make ourselves master of it, it may be said of many a book—*that it would be much shorter, if it were not so short*. On the other hand, as regards the comprehensibility of a system of speculative cognition, connected under a single principle, we may say with equal justice: many a book would have been much clearer, if it had not been intended to be so very clear. For explanations and examples, and other helps to intelligibility, aid us in the comprehension of *parts*, but they distract the attention, dissipate the mental power of the reader, and stand in the way of his forming a clear conception of the *whole;* as he cannot attain soon enough to a survey of the system, and the colouring and embellishments bestowed upon it prevent his observing its articulation or organization—which is the most important consideration with him, when he comes to judge of its unity and stability.

The reader must naturally have a strong inducement to co-operate with the present author, if he has formed the intention of erecting a complete and solid edifice of metaphysical science, according to the plan now laid before him. Metaphysics, as here represented, is the only science which admits of completion—and with little labour, if it is united, in a short time; so that nothing will be left to future generations except the task of illustrating and applying it *didactically*. For this science is nothing more than the inventory of all that is given us by *pure reason*, systematically arranged. Nothing can escape our notice; for what reason produces from itself cannot lie concealed, but must be brought to the light by reason itself, so soon as we have discovered the common principle of the ideas we seek. The perfect unity of this kind of cognitions, which are based upon pure conceptions, and uninfluenced by any empirical element, or any peculiar intuition leading to determinate experience, renders this completeness not only practicable, but also necessary.

Tecum habita, et nôris quam sit tibi curta supellex.

—Persius. Satirae iv. 52.

Such a system of pure speculative reason I hope to be able to publish under the title of *Metaphysic of Nature*[2]. The content of this work (which will not be half

[2] In contradistinction to the Metaphysic of Ethics. This work was never published.

so long) will be very much richer than that of the present Critique, which has to discover the sources of this cognition and expose the conditions of its possibility, and at the same time to clear and level a fit foundation for the scientific edifice. In the present work, I look for the patient hearing and the impartiality of a *judge;* in the other, for the good-will and assistance of a *co-labourer*. For, however complete the list of *principles* for this system may be in the Critique, the correctness of the system requires that no *deduced* conceptions should be absent. These cannot be presented *à priori*, but must be gradually discovered; and, while the *synthesis* of conceptions has been fully exhausted in the Critique, it is necessary that, in the proposed work, the same should be the case with their *analysis*. But this will be rather an amusement than a labour.

PREFACE TO THE SECOND EDITION 1787

Whether the treatment of that portion of our knowledge which lies within the province of pure reason advances with that undeviating certainty which characterizes the progress of *science*, we shall be at no loss to determine. If we find those who are engaged in metaphysical pursuits, unable to come to an understanding as to the method which they ought to follow; if we find them, after the most elaborate preparations, invariably brought to a stand before the goal is reached, and compelled to retrace their steps and strike into fresh paths, we may then feel quite sure that they are far from having attained to the certainty of scientific progress and may rather be said to be merely groping about in the dark. In these circumstances we shall render an important service to reason if we succeed in simply indicating the path along which it must travel, in order to arrive at any results—even if it should be found necessary to abandon many of those aims which, without reflection, have been proposed for its attainment.

That *Logic* has advanced in this sure course, even from the earliest times, is apparent from the fact that, since Aristotle, it has been unable to advance a step and, thus, to all appearance has reached its completion. For, if some of the moderns have thought to enlarge its domain by introducing *psychological* discussions on the mental faculties, such as imagination and wit, *metaphysical*, discussions on the origin of knowledge and the different kinds of certitude, according to the difference of the objects (idealism, scepticism, and so on), or *anthropological* discussions on prejudices, their causes and remedies: this attempt, on the part of these authors, only shows their ignorance of the peculiar nature of logical science. We do not enlarge but disfigure the sciences when we lose sight of their respective limits and allow them to run into one another. Now logic is enclosed within limits which admit of perfectly clear definition; it is a science which has for its object nothing but the exposition and proof of the *formal* laws of all thought, whether it be *à priori* or empirical, whatever be its origin or its object, and whatever the difficulties—natural or accidental—which it encounters in the human mind.

The early success of logic must be attributed exclusively to the narrowness of its field, in which abstraction may, or rather must, be made of all the objects of cognition with their characteristic distinctions, and in which the understanding has only to deal with itself and with its own forms. It is, obviously, a much more difficult task for reason to strike into the sure path of science, where it has to deal not simply with itself, but with objects external to itself. Hence, logic is properly only a *propædeutic*—forms, as it were, the vestibule of the sciences; and while it is necessary to enable us to form a correct judgement with regard to the various branches of knowledge, still the acquisition of real, substantive knowledge is to be sought only in the sciences properly so called, that is, in the objective sciences.

Now these sciences, if they can be termed rational at all, must contain elements of *à priori* cognition, and this cognition may stand in a twofold relation to its object. Either it may have to *determine* the conception of the object—which must be supplied extraneously, or it may have to *establish its reality*. The former is *theoretical*, the latter *practical*, rational cognition. In both, the *pure* or *à priori* element must be treated first, and must be carefully distinguished from that which is supplied from other sources. Any other method can only lead to irremediable confusion.

Mathematics and *physics* are the two theoretical sciences which have to determine their objects *à priori*. The former is purely *à priori*, the latter is partially so, but is also dependent on other sources of cognition.

In the earliest times of which history affords us any record, *mathematics* had already entered on the sure course of science, among that wonderful nation, the Greeks. Still it is not to be supposed that it was as easy for this science to strike into, or rather to construct for itself, that royal road, as it was for logic, in which reason has only to deal with itself. On the contrary, I believe that it must have remained long—chiefly among the Egyptians—in the stage of blind groping after its true aims and destination, and that it was revolutionized by the happy idea of one man, who struck out and determined for all time the path which this science must follow, and which admits of an indefinite advancement. The history of this intellectual revolution—much more important in its results than the discovery of the passage round the celebrated Cape of Good Hope—and of its author, has not been preserved. But Diogenes Laertius, in naming the supposed discoverer of some of the simplest elements of geometrical demonstration—elements which, according to the ordinary opinion, do not even require to be proved—makes it apparent that the change introduced by the first indication of this new path, must have seemed of the utmost importance to the mathematicians of that age, and it has thus been secured against the chance of oblivion. A new light must have flashed on the mind of the first man (*Thales*, or whatever may have been his name) who demonstrated the properties of the *isosceles* triangle. For he found that it was not sufficient to meditate on the figure, as it lay before his eyes, or the conception of it, as it existed in his mind, and thus endeavour to get at the knowledge of its properties, but that it was necessary to produce these properties, as it were, by a positive *à priori construction;* and that, in order to arrive with certainty at *à priori* cognition, he must not attribute to the object any other properties than those which necessarily followed from that which he had himself, in accordance with his conception, placed in the object.

A much longer period elapsed before *Physics* entered on the highway of science. For it is only about a century and a half since the wise BACON gave a new direction to physical studies, or rather—as others were already on the right track—imparted fresh vigour to the pursuit of this new direction. Here, too, as in the case of mathematics, we find evidence of a rapid intellectual revolution. In the remarks which follow I shall confine myself to the *empirical* side of natural science.

When GALILEI experimented with balls of a definite weight on the inclined plane, when TORRICELLI caused the air to sustain a weight which he had calculated beforehand to be equal to that of a definite column of water, or when STAHL, at a later period, converted metals into lime, and reconverted lime into metal, by the addition and subtraction of certain elements;[3] a light broke upon all natural philosophers. They learned that reason only perceives that which it produces after its own design; that it must not be content to follow, as it were, in the leading-strings of nature, but must proceed in advance with principles of judgement according to unvarying laws, and compel nature to reply its questions. For accidental observations, made according to no preconceived plan, cannot be united under a necessary law. But it is this that reason seeks for and requires. It is only the principles of reason which can give to concordant phenomena the validity of laws, and it is only when experiment is directed by these rational principles that it can have any real utility. Reason must approach nature with the view, indeed, of receiving information from it, not, however, in the character of a pupil, who listens to all that his master chooses to tell him, but in that of a judge, who compels the witnesses to reply to those questions which he himself thinks fit to propose. To this single idea must the revolution be ascribed, by which, after groping in the dark for so many centuries, natural science was at length conducted into the path of certain progress.

We come now to *metaphysics*, a purely speculative science, which occupies a completely isolated position and is entirely independent of the teachings of experience. It deals with mere conceptions—not, like mathematics, with conceptions applied to intuition—and in it, reason is the pupil of itself alone. It is the oldest of the sciences, and would still survive, even if all the rest were swallowed up in the abyss of an all-destroying barbarism. But it has not yet had the good fortune to attain to the sure scientific method. This will be apparent; if we apply the tests which we proposed at the outset. We find that reason perpetually comes to a stand, when it attempts to gain *à priori* the perception even of those laws which the most common experience confirms. We find it compelled to retrace its steps in innumerable instances, and to abandon the path on which it had entered, because this does not lead to the desired result. We find, too, that those who are engaged in metaphysical pursuits are far from being able to agree among themselves, but that, on the contrary, this science appears to furnish an arena specially adapted for the display of skill or the exercise of strength in mock-contests—a field in which no combatant ever yet succeeded in gaining an inch of ground, in which, at least, no victory was ever yet crowned with permanent possession.

This leads us to inquire why it is that, in metaphysics, the sure path of science has not hitherto been found. Shall we suppose that it is impossible to discover it?

---

[3] I do not here follow with exactness the history of the experimental method, of which, indeed, the first steps are involved in some obscurity.

Why then should nature have visited our reason with restless aspirations after it, as if it were one of our weightiest concerns? Nay, more, how little cause should we have to place confidence in our reason, if it abandons us in a matter about which, most of all, we desire to know the truth—and not only so, but even allures us to the pursuit of vain phantoms, only to betray us in the end? Or, if the path has only hitherto been missed, what indications do we possess to guide us in a renewed investigation, and to enable us to hope for greater success than has fallen to the lot of our predecessors?

It appears to me that the examples of mathematics and natural philosophy, which, as we have seen, were brought into their present condition by a sudden revolution, are sufficiently remarkable to fix our attention on the essential circumstances of the change which has proved so advantageous to them, and to induce us to make the experiment of imitating them, so far as the analogy which, as rational sciences, they bear to metaphysics may permit. It has hitherto been assumed that our cognition must conform to the objects; but all attempts to ascertain anything about these objects *à priori*, by means of conceptions, and thus to extend the range of our knowledge, have been rendered abortive by this assumption. Let us then make the experiment whether we may not be more successful in metaphysics, if we assume that the objects must conform to our cognition. This appears, at all events, to accord better with the *possibility* of our gaining the end we have in view, that is to say, of arriving at the cognition of objects *à priori*, of determining something with respect to these objects, before they are given to us. We here propose to do just what COPERNICUS did in attempting to explain the celestial movements. When he found that he could make no progress by assuming that all the heavenly bodies revolved round the spectator, he reversed the process, and tried the experiment of assuming that the spectator revolved, while the stars remained at rest. We may make the same experiment with regard to the intuition of objects. If the intuition must conform to the nature of the objects, I do not see how we can know anything of them *à priori*. If, on the other hand, the object conforms to the nature of our faculty of intuition, I can then easily conceive the possibility of such an *à priori* knowledge. Now as I cannot rest in the mere intuitions, but—if they are to become cognitions—must refer them, as *representations*, to something, as *object*, and must determine the latter by means of the former, here again there are two courses open to me. *Either*, first, I may assume that the conceptions, by which I effect this determination, conform to the object—and in this case I am reduced to the same perplexity as before; *or* secondly, I may assume that the objects, or, which is the same thing, that *experience*, in which alone as given objects they are cognized, conform to my conceptions—and then I am at no loss how to proceed. For experience itself is a mode of cognition which requires understanding. Before objects, are given to me, that is, *à priori*, I must presuppose in myself laws of the understanding which are expressed in conceptions *à priori*. To these conceptions, then, all the objects of experience must necessarily conform. Now there are objects which reason *thinks*, and that necessarily, but which cannot be given in experience, or, at least, cannot be given *so* as reason thinks them. The attempt to think these objects will hereafter furnish an excellent test of the new method of thought which we have adopted, and which is based on the principle that we only cognize in things *à priori* that which we ourselves place in them.[4]

This attempt succeeds as well as we could desire, and promises to metaphysics, in its first part—that is, where it is occupied with conceptions *à priori*, of which the corresponding objects may be given in experience—the certain course of science. For by this new method we are enabled perfectly to explain the possibility of *à priori* cognition, and, what is more, to demonstrate satisfactorily the laws which lie *à priori* at the foundation of nature, as the sum of the objects of experience—neither of which was possible according to the procedure hitherto followed. But from this deduction of the faculty of *à priori* cognition in the first part of metaphysics, we derive a surprising result, and one which, to all appearance, militates against the great end of metaphysics, as treated in the second part. For we come to the conclusion that our faculty of cognition is unable to transcend the limits of possible experience; and yet this is precisely the most essential object of this science. The estimate of our rational cognition *à priori* at which we arrive is that it has only to do with phenomena, and that things in themselves, while possessing a real existence, lie beyond its sphere. Here we are enabled to put the justice of this estimate to the test. For that which of necessity impels us to transcend the limits of experience and of all phenomena is the *unconditioned*, which reason absolutely requires in things as they are in themselves, in order to complete the series of conditions. Now, if it appears that when, on the one hand, we assume that our cognition conforms to its objects as things in themselves, *the unconditioned cannot be thought without contradiction*, and that when, on the other hand, we assume that our representation of things as they are given to us, does not conform to these things as they are in themselves, but that these objects, as phenomena, conform to our mode of representation, *the contradiction disappears:* we shall then be convinced of the truth of that which we began by assuming for the sake of experiment; we may look upon it as established that the unconditioned does not lie in things as we know

[4] This method, accordingly, which we have borrowed from the natural philosopher, consists in seeking for the elements of pure reason in that *which admits of confirmation or refutation by experiment.* Now the propositions of pure reason, especially when they transcend the limits of possible experience, do not admit of our making any experiment with their *objects*, as in natural science. Hence, with regard to those *conceptions* and *principles* which we assume *à priori*, our only course will be to view them from two different sides. We must regard one and the same conception, *on the one hand*, in relation to experience as an object of the senses and of the understanding, *on the other hand*, in relation to reason, isolated and transcending the limits of experience, as an object of mere thought. Now if we find that, when we regard things from this double point of view, the result is in harmony with the principle of pure reason, but that, when we regard them from a single point of view, reason is involved in self-contradiction, then the experiment will establish the correctness of this distinction.

them, or as they are given to us, but in things as they are in themselves, beyond the range of our cognition.[5]

But, after we have thus denied the power of speculative reason to make any progress in the sphere of the supersensible, it still remains for our consideration whether data do not exist in *practical* cognition which may enable us to determine the transcendent conception of the unconditioned, to rise beyond the limits of all possible experience from a *practical* point of view, and thus to satisfy the great ends of metaphysics. Speculative reason has thus, at least, made room for such an extension of our knowledge: and, if it must leave this space vacant, still it does not rob us of the liberty to fill it up, if we can, by means of practical data—nay, it even challenges us to make the attempt.[6]

This attempt to introduce a complete revolution in the procedure of metaphysics, after the *example* of the geometricians and natural philosophers, constitutes the aim of the Critique of Pure Speculative Reason. It is a treatise on the method to be followed, not a system of the science itself. But, at the same time, it marks out and defines both the external boundaries and the internal structure of this science. For pure speculative reason has this peculiarity, that, in choosing the various objects of thought, it is able to define the limits of its own faculties, and even to give a complete enumeration of the possible modes of proposing problems to itself, and thus to sketch out the entire system of metaphysics. For, on the one hand, in cognition *à priori*, nothing must be attributed to the objects but what the thinking subject derives from itself; and, on the other hand, reason is, in regard to the principles of cognition, a perfectly distinct, independent unity, in which, as in an organized body, every member exists for the sake of the others, and all for the sake of each, so that no principle can be viewed, with safety, in one relationship, unless it is, at the same time, viewed in relation to the total use of pure reason. Hence, too, metaphysics has this singular advantage—an advantage which falls to the lot of no other science which has to do with *objects*—that, if

[5] This experiment of pure reason has a great similarity to that of the *Chemists*, which they term the experiment of *reduction*, or, more usually, the *synthetic* process. The *analysis* of the metaphysician separates pure cognition *à priori* into two heterogeneous elements, viz., the cognition of things as phenomena, and of things in themselves. *Dialectic* combines these again into harmony with the necessary rational idea of the unconditioned, and finds that this harmony never results except through the above distinction, which is, therefore, concluded to be just.

[6] So the central laws of the movements of the heavenly bodies established the truth of that which Copernicus, first, assumed only as a hypothesis, and, at the same time, brought to light that invisible force (Newtonian attraction) which holds the universe together. The latter would have remained forever undiscovered, if Copernicus had not ventured on the experiment—contrary to the senses but still just—of looking for the observed movements not in the heavenly bodies, but in the spectator. In this Preface I treat the new metaphysical method as a hypothesis with the view of rendering apparent the first attempts at such a change of method, which are always hypothetical. But in the Critique itself it will be demonstrated, not hypothetically, but apodeictically, from the nature of our representations of space and time, and from the elementary conceptions of the understanding.

once it is conducted into the sure path of science, by means of this criticism, it can then take in the whole sphere of its cognitions, and can thus complete its work, and leave it for the use of posterity, as a capital which can never receive fresh accessions. For metaphysics has to deal only with principles and with the limitations of its own employment as determined by these principles. To this perfection it is, therefore, bound, as the fundamental science, to attain, and to it the maxim may justly be applied:

> Nil actum reputans, si quid superesset agendum.

But, it will be asked, what kind of a treasure is this that we propose to bequeath to posterity? What is the real value of this system of metaphysics, purified by criticism, and thereby reduced to a permanent condition? A cursory view of the present work will lead to the supposition that its use is merely *negative*, that it only serves to warn us against venturing, with speculative reason, beyond the limits of experience. This is, in fact, its primary use. But this, at once, assumes a *positive* value, when we observe that the principles with which speculative reason endeavours to transcend its limits lead inevitably, not to the *extension*, but to the *contraction* of the use of reason, inasmuch as they threaten to extend the limits of sensibility, which is their proper sphere, over the entire realm of thought and, thus, to supplant the pure (practical) use of reason. So far, then, as this criticism is occupied in confining speculative reason within its proper bounds, it is only negative; but, inasmuch as it thereby, at the same time, removes an obstacle which impedes and even threatens to destroy the use of practical reason, it possesses a positive and very important value. In order to admit this, we have only to be convinced that there is an absolutely necessary use of pure reason—the moral use—in which it inevitably transcends the limits of sensibility, without the aid of speculation, requiring only to be insured against the effects of a speculation which would involve it in contradiction with itself. To deny the positive advantage of the service which this criticism renders us would be as absurd as to maintain that the system of police is productive of no positive benefit, since its main business is to prevent the violence which citizen has to apprehend from citizen, that so each may pursue his vocation in peace and security. That space and time are only forms of sensible intuition, and hence are only conditions of the existence of things as phenomena; that, moreover, we have no conceptions of the understanding, and, consequently, no elements for the cognition of things, except in so far as a corresponding intuition can be given to these conceptions; that, accordingly, we can have no cognition of an object, as a thing in itself, but only as an object of sensible intuition, that is, as phenomenon—all this is proved in the analytical part of the Critique; and from this the limitation of all possible speculative cognition to the mere objects of *experience*, follows as a necessary result. At the same time, it must be carefully borne in mind that, while we surrender the power of *cognizing*, we still reserve the power of *thinking* objects, as things in themselves.[7] For, otherwise, we should require to affirm the existence of an appearance, without something that appears—which would be absurd. Now let us suppose, for a moment, that we had not undertaken this criticism and, accordingly, had not drawn the necessary distinction between things as objects of experience and things as they are in themselves. The principle of causality, and, by consequence, the mechanism of nature as determined by causality, would then have absolute validity in relation to all things as efficient causes. I should then be unable to assert, with regard to one and the same being, e.g., the human soul, that its will is *free*, and yet, at the same time, subject to natural necessity, that is, *not free*, without falling into a palpable contradiction, for in both propositions I should take the soul in *the same signification*, as a thing in general, as a thing in itself—as, without previous criticism, I could not but take it. Suppose now, on the other hand, that we *have* undertaken this criticism, and have learnt that an object may be taken in *two senses*, first, as a phenomenon, secondly, as a thing in itself; and that, according to the deduction of the conceptions of the understanding, the principle of causality has reference only to things in the first sense. We then see how it does not involve any contradiction to assert, on the one hand, that the will, in the phenomenal sphere—in visible action—is necessarily obedient to the law of nature, and, in so far, *not free;* and, on the other hand, that, as belonging to a thing in itself, it is not subject to that law, and, accordingly, is *free*. Now, it is true that I cannot, by means of speculative reason, and still less by empirical observation, *cognize* my soul as a thing in itself and consequently, cannot cognize liberty as the property of a being to which I ascribe effects in the world of sense. For, to do so, I must cognize this being as existing, and yet not in time, which—since I cannot support my conception by any intuition—is impossible. At the same time, while I cannot *cognize*, I can quite well *think* freedom, that is to say, my representation of it involves at least no contradiction, if we bear in mind the critical distinction of the two modes of representation (the sensible and the intellectual) and the consequent limitation of the conceptions of the pure understanding and of the principles which flow from them. Suppose now that morality necessarily presupposed liberty, in the strictest sense, as a property of our will; suppose that reason contained certain practical, original principles *à priori*, which were absolutely impossible without this presupposition; and suppose, at the same time, that speculative reason had

[7] In order to *cognize* an object, I must be able to prove its possibility, either from its reality as attested by experience, or *à priori*, by means of reason. But I can *think* what I please, provided only I do not contradict myself; that is, provided my conception is a possible thought, though I may be unable to answer for the existence of a corresponding object in the sum of possibilities. But something more is required before I can attribute to such a conception objective validity, that is real possibility—the other possibility being merely logical. We are not, however, confined to theoretical sources of cognition for the means of satisfying this additional requirement, but may derive them from practical sources.

proved that liberty was incapable of being thought at all. It would then follow that the moral presupposition must give way to the speculative affirmation, the opposite of which involves an obvious contradiction, and that *liberty* and, with it, morality must yield to the *mechanism of nature;* for the negation of morality involves no contradiction, except on the presupposition of liberty. Now morality does not require the speculative cognition of liberty; it is enough that I can think it, that its conception involves no contradiction, that it does not interfere with the mechanism of nature. But even this requirement we could not satisfy, if we had not learnt the twofold sense in which things may be taken; and it is only in this way that the doctrine of morality and the doctrine of nature are confined within their proper limits. For this result, then, we are indebted to a criticism which warns us of our unavoidable ignorance with regard to things in themselves, and establishes the necessary limitation of our theoretical *cognition* to mere phenomena.

The positive value of the critical principles of pure reason in relation to the conception of *God* and of the *simple nature* of the *soul,* admits of a similar exemplification; but on this point I shall not dwell. I cannot even make the assumption—as the practical interests of morality require—of God, freedom, and immortality, if I do not deprive speculative reason of its pretensions to transcendent insight. For to arrive at these, it must make use of principles which, in fact, extend only to the objects of possible experience, and which cannot be applied to objects beyond this sphere without converting them into phenomena, and thus rendering the *practical extension* of pure reason impossible. I must, therefore, abolish *knowledge,* to make room for *belief.* The dogmatism of metaphysics, that is, the presumption that it is possible to advance in metaphysics without previous criticism, is the true source of the unbelief (always dogmatic) which militates against morality.

Thus, while it may be no very difficult task to bequeath a legacy to posterity, in the shape of a system of metaphysics constructed in accordance with the Critique of Pure Reason, still the value of such a bequest is not to be depreciated. It will render an important service to reason, by substituting the certainty of scientific method for that random groping after results without the guidance of principles, which has hitherto characterized the pursuit of metaphysical studies. It will render an important service to the inquiring mind of youth, by leading the student to apply his powers to the cultivation of genuine science, instead of wasting them, as at present, on speculations which can never lead to any result, or on the idle attempt to invent new ideas and opinions. But, above all, it will confer an inestimable benefit on morality and religion, by showing that all the objections urged against them may be silenced for ever by the *Socratic* method, that is to say, by proving the ignorance of the objector. For, as the world has never been, and, no doubt, never will be without a system of metaphysics of one kind or another, it is the highest and weightiest concern of philosophy to render it powerless for harm, by closing up the sources of error.

This important change in the field of the sciences, this loss of its fancied possessions, to which speculative reason must submit, does not prove in any way detrimental to the general interests of humanity. The advantages which the world has derived from the teachings of pure reason are not at all impaired. The loss falls, in its whole extent, on the *monopoly of the schools*, but does not in the slightest degree touch the *interests of mankind*. I appeal to the most obstinate dogmatist, whether the proof of the continued existence of the soul after death, derived from the simplicity of its substance; of the freedom of the will in opposition to the general mechanism of nature, drawn from the subtle but impotent distinction of subjective and objective practical necessity; or of the existence of God, deduced from the conception of an *ens realissimum*—the contingency of the changeable, and the necessity of a prime mover, has ever been able to pass beyond the limits of the schools, to penetrate the public mind, or to exercise the slightest influence on its convictions. It must be admitted that this has not been the case and that, owing to the unfitness of the common understanding for such subtle speculations, it can never be expected to take place. On the contrary, it is plain that *the hope of a future life* arises from the feeling, which exists in the breast of every man, that the temporal is inadequate to meet and satisfy the demands of his nature. In like manner, it cannot be doubted that the clear exhibition of duties in opposition to all the claims of inclination, gives rise to the consciousness of *freedom*, and that the glorious order, beauty, and providential care, everywhere displayed in nature, give rise to the belief in a wise and great Author of the Universe. Such is the genesis of these general convictions of mankind, so far as they depend on rational grounds; and this public property not only remains undisturbed, but is even raised to greater importance, by the doctrine that the schools have no right to arrogate to themselves a more profound insight into a matter of general human concernment than that to which the great mass of men, ever held by us in the highest estimation, can without difficulty attain, and that the schools should, therefore, confine themselves to the elaboration of these universally comprehensible and, from a moral point of view, amply satisfactory proofs. The change, therefore, affects only the arrogant pretensions of the schools, which would gladly retain, in their own exclusive possession, the key to the truths which they impart to the public.

Quod mecum nescit, solus vult scire videri.

At the same time it does not deprive the speculative philosopher of his just title to be the sole depositor of a science which benefits the public without its knowledge—I mean, the Critique of Pure Reason. This can never become popular and, indeed, has no occasion to be so; for finespun arguments in favour of useful truths make just as little impression on the public mind as the equally subtle objections brought against these truths. On the other hand, since both inevitably force themselves on every man who rises to the height of speculation, it becomes the manifest duty of the schools to enter upon a thorough investigation of the rights of speculative reason and, thus, to prevent the scandal which metaphysical controversies are sure, sooner or later, to cause even to the masses. It is only by criticism that metaphysicians (and, as such, theologians too) can be saved from these controversies and from the consequent perversion of their doctrines. Criticism alone can strike a blow at the root of materialism, fatalism, atheism, free-thinking, fanaticism, and superstition, which are universally injurious—as well as of idealism and scepticism, which are dangerous to the schools, but can scarcely pass over to the public. If governments think proper to interfere with the affairs of the learned, it would be more consistent with a wise regard for the interests of science, as well as for those of society, to favour a criticism of this kind, by which alone the labours of reason can be established on a firm basis, than to support the ridiculous despotism of the schools, which raise a loud cry of danger to the public over the destruction of cobwebs, of which the public has never taken any notice, and the loss of which, therefore, it can never feel.

This critical science is not opposed to the *dogmatic procedure* of reason in pure cognition; for pure cognition must always be dogmatic, that is, must rest on strict demonstration from sure principles *à priori*—but to *dogmatism*, that is, to the presumption that it is possible to make any progress with a pure cognition, derived from (philosophical) conceptions, according to the principles which reason has long been in the habit of employing—without first inquiring in what way and by what right reason has come into the possession of these principles. Dogmatism is thus the dogmatic procedure of pure reason *without previous criticism of its own powers*, and in opposing this procedure, we must not be supposed to lend any countenance to that loquacious shallowness which arrogates to itself the name of popularity, nor yet to scepticism, which makes short work with the whole science of metaphysics. On the contrary, our criticism is the necessary preparation for a thoroughly scientific system of metaphysics which must perform its task entirely *à priori*, to the complete satisfaction of speculative reason, and must, therefore, be treated, not popularly, but scholastically. In carrying out the plan which the Critique prescribes, that is, in the future system of metaphysics, we must have recourse to the strict method of the celebrated WOLF, the greatest of all dogmatic philosophers. He was the first to point out the necessity of establishing fixed principles, of clearly defining our conceptions, and of subjecting our demonstrations to the most severe scrutiny, instead of rashly jumping at conclusions. The example which he set served to awaken that spirit of profound and thorough investigation which is not yet extinct in Germany. He would have been peculiarly well fitted to give a truly scientific character to metaphysical studies, had it occurred to him to prepare the field by a criticism of the *organum*, that is, of pure reason itself. That he failed to perceive the necessity of such a procedure must be ascribed to the dogmatic mode of thought which characterized his age, and on this point the philosophers of his time, as well as of all previous times, have nothing to reproach each other with. Those who reject at once the method of Wolf, and of the Critique of Pure Reason, can have no other aim but to shake off the fetters of *science*, to change labour into sport, certainty into opinion, and philosophy into philodoxy.

In this *second edition*, I have endeavoured, as far as possible, to remove the difficulties and obscurity which, without fault of mine perhaps, have given rise to many misconceptions even among acute thinkers. In the propositions themselves, and in the demonstrations by which they are supported, as well as in the form and the entire plan of the work, I have found nothing to alter; which must be attributed partly to the long examination to which I had subjected the whole before offering it to the public and partly to the nature of the case. For pure speculative reason is an organic structure in which there is nothing isolated or independent, but every Single part is essential to all the rest; and hence, the slightest imperfection, whether defect or positive error, could not fail to betray itself in use. I venture, further, to hope, that this system will maintain the same unalterable character for the future. I am led to entertain this confidence, not by vanity, but by the evidence which the equality of the result affords, when we proceed, first, from the simplest elements up to the complete whole of pure reason and, and then, backwards from the whole to each part. We find that the attempt to make the slightest alteration, in any part, leads inevitably to contradictions, not merely in this system, but in human reason itself. At the same time, there is still much room for improvement in the *exposition* of the doctrines contained in this work. In the present edition, I have endeavoured to remove misapprehensions of the æsthetical part, especially with regard to the conception of time; to clear away the obscurity which has been found in the deduction of the conceptions of the understanding; to supply the supposed want of sufficient evidence in the demonstration of the principles of the pure understanding; and, lastly, to obviate the misunderstanding of the paralogisms which immediately precede the Rational Psychology. Beyond this point—the end of the second main division of the "Transcendental Dialectic"—I have not extended my alterations,[8]

[8] The only addition, properly so called—and that only in the method of proof—which I have made in the present edition, consists of a new refutation of psychological *Idealism*, and a strict demonstration—the only one possible, as I believe—of the objective reality of external intuition. However harmless idealism may be considered—although in reality it is not so—in regard to the essential ends of metaphysics, it must still remain a scandal to philosophy and to the general human reason to be obliged to assume, as an article of mere belief, the existence of things external to ourselves (from which, yet, we derive the whole material of cognition for the internal sense), and not to be able to oppose a satisfactory proof to any one who may call it in question. As there is some obscurity of expression in the demonstration as it stands in the text, I propose to alter the passage in question as follows: "But this permanent cannot be an intuition in me. For all the determining grounds of my existence which can be found in me are representations and, as such, do themselves require a permanent, distinct from them, which may determine my existence in relation to their changes, that is, my existence in time, wherein they change." It may, probably, be urged in opposition to this proof that, after all, I am only conscious immediately of that which is in me, that is, of my *representation* of external things, and that, consequently, it must always remain uncertain whether anything corresponding to this representation does or does not exist externally to me. But I am conscious, through internal *experience*, of my *existence in time* (consequently, also, of the determinability of the

partly from want of time, and partly because I am not aware that any portion of the remainder has given rise to misconceptions among intelligent and impartial critics, whom I do not here mention with that praise which is their due, but who will find that their suggestions have been attended to in the work itself.

In attempting to render the exposition of my views as intelligible as possible, I have been compelled to leave out or abridge various passages which were not essential to the completeness of the work, but which many readers might consider useful in other respects, and might be unwilling to miss. This trifling loss, which could not be avoided without swelling the book beyond due limits, may be supplied, at the pleasure of the reader, by a comparison with the first edition, and will, I hope, be more than compensated for by the greater clearness of the exposition as it now stands.

I have observed, with pleasure and thankfulness, in the pages of various reviews and treatises, that the spirit of profound and thorough investigation is not extinct in Germany, though it may have been overborne and silenced for a time by the

---

former in the latter), and that is more than the simple consciousness of my representation. It is, in fact, the same as the *empirical consciousness of my existence*, which can only be determined in relation to something, which, while connected with my existence, is *external to me*. This consciousness of my existence in time is, therefore, identical with the consciousness of a relation to something external to me, and it is, therefore, experience, not fiction, sense, not imagination, which inseparably connects the external with my internal sense. For the external sense is, in itself, the relation of intuition to something real, external to me; and the reality of this something, as opposed to the mere imagination of it, rests solely on its inseparable connection with internal experience as the condition of its possibility. If with the *intellectual consciousness* of my existence, in the representation: *I am*, which accompanies all my judgements, and all the operations of my understanding, I could, at the same time, connect a determination of my existence by *intellectual intuition*, then the consciousness of a relation to something external to me would not be necessary. But the internal intuition in which alone my existence can be determined, though preceded by that purely intellectual consciousness, is itself sensible and attached to the condition of time. Hence this determination of my existence, and consequently my internal experience itself, must depend on something permanent which is not in me, which can be, therefore, only in something external to me, to which I must look upon myself as being related. Thus the reality of the external sense is necessarily connected with that of the internal, in order to the possibility of experience in general; that is, I am just as certainly conscious that there are things external to me related to my sense as I am that I myself exist as determined in time. But in order to ascertain to what given intuitions objects, external me, really correspond, in other words, what intuitions belong to the external sense and not to imagination, I must have recourse, in every particular case, to those rules according to which experience in general (even internal experience) is distinguished from imagination, and which are always based on the proposition that there really is an external experience.—We may add the remark that the representation of something *permanent* in existence, is not the same thing as the *permanent representation;* for a representation may be very variable and changing—as all our representations, even that of matter, are—and yet refer to something permanent, which must, therefore, be distinct from all my representations and external to me, the existence of which is necessarily included in the determination of my own existence, and with it constitutes *one* experience—an experience which would not even be possible internally, if it were not also at the same time, in part, external. To the question *How?* we are no more able to reply, than we are, in general, to think the stationary in time, the coexistence of which with the variable, produces the conception of change.

fashionable tone of a licence in thinking, which gives itself the airs of genius, and that the difficulties which beset the paths of criticism have not prevented energetic and acute thinkers from making themselves masters of the science of pure reason to which these paths conduct—a science which is not popular, but scholastic in its character, and which alone can hope for a lasting existence or possess an abiding value. To these deserving men, who so happily combine profundity of view with a talent for lucid exposition—a talent which I myself am not conscious of possessing—I leave the task of removing any obscurity which may still adhere to the statement of my doctrines. For, in this case, the danger is not that of being refuted, but of being misunderstood. For my own part, I must henceforward abstain from controversy, although I shall carefully attend to all suggestions, whether from friends or adversaries, which may be of use in the future elaboration of the system of this Propædeutic. As, during these labours, I have advanced pretty far in years this month I reach my sixty-fourth year—it will be necessary for me to economize time, if I am to carry out my plan of elaborating the metaphysics of nature as well as of morals, in confirmation of the correctness of the principles established in this Critique of Pure Reason, both speculative and practical; and I must, therefore, leave the task of clearing up the obscurities of the present work—inevitable, perhaps, at the outset—as well as, the defence of the whole, to those deserving men, who have made my system their own. A philosophical system cannot come forward armed at all points like a mathematical treatise, and hence it may be quite possible to take objection to particular passages, while the organic structure of the system, considered as a unity, has no danger to apprehend. But few possess the ability, and still fewer the inclination, to take a comprehensive view of a new system. By confining the view to particular passages, taking these out of their connection and comparing them with one another, it is easy to pick out apparent contradictions, especially in a work written with any freedom of style. These contradictions place the work in an unfavourable light in the eyes of those who rely on the judgement of others, but are easily reconciled by those who have mastered the idea of the whole. If a theory possesses stability in itself, the action and reaction which seemed at first to threaten its existence serve only, in the course of time, to smooth down any superficial roughness or inequality, and—if men of insight, impartiality, and truly popular gifts, turn their attention to it—to secure to it, in a short time, the requisite elegance also.

KÖNIGSBERG
April 1787.

INTRODUCTION

I. Of the difference between Pure and Empirical Knowledge

That all our knowledge begins with experience there can be no doubt. For how is it possible that the faculty of cognition should be awakened into exercise otherwise than by means of objects which affect our senses, and partly of themselves produce representations, partly rouse our powers of understanding into activity, to compare to connect, or to separate these, and so to convert the raw material of our sensuous impressions into a knowledge of objects, which is called experience? In respect of time, therefore, no knowledge of ours is antecedent to experience, but begins with it.

But, though all our knowledge begins with experience, it by no means follows that all arises out of experience. For, on the contrary, it is quite possible that our empirical knowledge is a compound of that which we receive through impressions, and that which the faculty of cognition supplies from itself (sensuous impressions giving merely the occasion), an addition which we cannot distinguish from the original element given by sense, till long practice has made us attentive to, and skilful in separating it. It is, therefore, a question which requires close investigation, and not to be answered at first sight, whether there exists a knowledge altogether independent of experience, and even of all sensuous impressions? Knowledge of this kind is called à priori, in contradistinction to empirical knowledge, which has its sources à posteriori, that is, in experience.

But the expression, "à priori," is not as yet definite enough adequately to indicate the whole meaning of the question above started. For, in speaking of knowledge which has its sources in experience, we are wont to say, that this or that may be known à priori, because we do not derive this knowledge immediately from experience, but from a general rule, which, however, we have itself borrowed from experience. Thus, if a man undermined his house, we say, "he might know à priori that it would have fallen;" that is, he needed not to have waited for the experience that it did actually fall. But still, à priori, he could not know even this much. For, that bodies are heavy, and, consequently, that they fall when their supports are taken away, must have been known to him previously, by means of experience.

By the term "knowledge à priori," therefore, we shall in the sequel understand, not such as is independent of this or that kind of experience, but such as is absolutely so of all experience. Opposed to this is empirical knowledge, or that which is possible only à posteriori, that is, through experience. Knowledge à priori is either pure or impure. Pure knowledge à priori is that with which no empirical element is mixed up. For example, the proposition, "Every change has a cause," is a proposition à priori, but impure, because change is a conception which can only be derived from experience.

II. The Human Intellect, even in an Unphilosophical State, is in Possession of Certain Cognitions "à priori"

The question now is as to a criterion, by which we may securely distinguish a pure from an empirical cognition. Experience no doubt teaches us that this or that object is constituted in such and such a manner, but not that it could not possibly exist otherwise. Now, in the first place, if we have a proposition which contains the idea of necessity in its very conception, it is priori. If, moreover, it is not derived from any other proposition, unless from one equally involving the idea of necessity, it is absolutely priori. Secondly, an empirical judgement never exhibits strict and absolute, but only assumed and comparative universality (by induction); therefore, the most we can say is—so far as we have hitherto observed, there is no exception to this or that rule. If, on the other hand, a judgement carries with it strict and absolute universality, that is, admits of no possible exception, it is not derived from experience, but is valid absolutely à priori.

Empirical universality is, therefore, only an arbitrary extension of validity, from that which may be predicated of a proposition valid in most cases, to that which is asserted of a proposition which holds good in all; as, for example, in the affirmation, "All bodies are heavy." When, on the contrary, strict universality characterizes a judgement, it necessarily indicates another peculiar source of knowledge, namely, a faculty of cognition à priori. Necessity and strict universality, therefore, are infallible tests for distinguishing pure from empirical knowledge, and are inseparably connected with each other. But as in the use of these criteria the empirical limitation is sometimes more easily detected than the contingency of the judgement, or the unlimited universality which we attach to a judgement is often a more convincing proof than its necessity, it may be advisable to use the criteria separately, each being by itself infallible.

Now, that in the sphere of human cognition we have judgements which are necessary, and in the strictest sense universal, consequently pure à priori, it will be an easy matter to show. If we desire an example from the sciences, we need only take any proposition in mathematics. If we cast our eyes upon the commonest operations of the understanding, the proposition, "Every change must have a cause," will amply serve our purpose. In the latter case, indeed, the conception of a cause so plainly involves the conception of a necessity of connection with an effect, and of a strict universality of the law, that the very notion of a cause would entirely disappear, were we to derive it, like Hume, from a frequent association of what happens with that which precedes; and the habit thence originating of connecting representations—the necessity inherent in the judgement being therefore merely subjective. Besides, without seeking for such examples of principles existing à priori in cognition, we might easily show that such principles are the indispensable basis of the possibility of experience itself, and consequently prove their existence à priori. For whence could our experience itself acquire certainty, if all the rules on which it depends were themselves empirical, and consequently fortuitous? No one, therefore, can admit the validity of the use of such rules as first principles. But, for the present, we may content ourselves with having established the fact, that we do possess and exercise a faculty of pure à priori cognition; and, secondly, with having pointed out the proper tests of such cognition, namely, universality and necessity.

Not only in judgements, however, but even in conceptions, is an à priori origin manifest. For example, if we take away by degrees from our conceptions of a body all that can be referred to mere sensuous experience—colour, hardness or softness, weight, even impenetrability—the body will then vanish; but the space which it occupied still remains, and this it is utterly impossible to annihilate in thought. Again, if we take away, in like manner, from our empirical conception of any object, corporeal or incorporeal, all properties which mere experience has taught us to connect with it, still we cannot think away those through which we cogitate it as substance, or adhering to substance, although our conception of substance is more determined than that of an object. Compelled, therefore, by that necessity with which the conception of substance forces itself upon us, we must confess that it has its seat in our faculty of cognition à priori.

III. Philosophy stands in need of a Science which shall Determine the Possibility, Principles, and Extent of Human Knowledge "à priori"

Of far more importance than all that has been above said, is the consideration that certain of our cognitions rise completely above the sphere of all possible experience, and by means of conceptions, to which there exists in the whole extent of experience no corresponding object, seem to extend the range of our judgements beyond its bounds. And just in this transcendental or supersensible sphere, where experience affords us neither instruction nor guidance, lie the investigations of reason, which, on account of their importance, we consider far preferable to, and as having a far more elevated aim than, all that the understanding can achieve within the sphere of sensuous phenomena. So high a value do we set upon these investigations, that even at the risk of error, we persist in following them out, and permit neither doubt nor disregard nor indifference to restrain us from the pursuit. These unavoidable problems of mere pure reason are God, freedom (of will), and immortality. The science which, with all its preliminaries, has for its especial object the solution of these problems is named metaphysics—a science which is at the very outset dogmatical, that is, it confidently takes upon itself the execution of this task without any previous investigation of the ability or inability of reason for such an undertaking.

Now the safe ground of experience being thus abandoned, it seems nevertheless natural that we should hesitate to erect a building with the cognitions we possess, without knowing whence they come, and on the strength of principles, the origin of which is undiscovered. Instead of thus trying to build without a foundation, it is rather to be expected that we should long ago have put the question, how the understanding can arrive at these à priori cognitions, and what is the extent, validity, and worth which they may possess? We say, "This is natural enough," meaning by the word natural, that which is consistent with a just and reasonable way of thinking; but if we understand by the term, that which usually happens, nothing indeed could be more natural and more comprehensible than that this investigation should be left long unattempted. For one part of our pure knowledge, the science of mathematics, has been long firmly established, and thus leads us to form flattering expectations with regard to others, though these may be of quite a different nature. Besides, when we get beyond the bounds of experience, we are of course safe from opposition in that quarter; and the charm of widening the range of our knowledge is so great that, unless we are brought to a standstill by some evident contradiction, we hurry on undoubtingly in our course. This, however, may be avoided, if we are sufficiently cautious in the construction of our fictions, which are not the less fictions on that account.

Mathematical science affords us a brilliant example, how far, independently of all experience, we may carry our à priori knowledge. It is true that the mathematician occupies himself with objects and cognitions only in so far as they can be represented by means of intuition. But this circumstance is easily overlooked, because the said intuition can itself be given à priori, and therefore is hardly to be distinguished from a mere pure conception. Deceived by such a proof of the power of reason, we can perceive no limits to the extension of our knowledge. The light dove cleaving in free flight the thin air, whose resistance it feels, might imagine that her movements would be far more free and rapid in airless space. Just in the same way did Plato, abandoning the world of sense because of the narrow limits it sets to the understanding, venture upon the wings of ideas beyond it, into the void space of pure intellect. He did not reflect that he made no real progress by all his efforts; for he met with no resistance which might serve him for a support, as it were, whereon to rest, and on which he might apply his powers, in order to let the intellect acquire momentum for its progress. It is, indeed, the common fate of human reason in speculation, to finish the imposing edifice of thought as rapidly as possible, and then for the first time to begin to examine whether the foundation is a solid one or no. Arrived at this point, all sorts of excuses are sought after, in order to console us for its want of stability, or rather, indeed, to enable Us to dispense altogether with so late and dangerous an investigation. But what frees us during the process of building from all apprehension or suspicion, and flatters us into the belief of its solidity, is this. A great part, perhaps the greatest part, of the business of our reason consists in the analysation of the conceptions which we already possess of objects. By this means we gain a multitude of cognitions, which although really nothing more than elucidations or explanations of that which (though in a confused manner) was already thought in our conceptions, are, at least in respect of their form, prized as new introspections; whilst, so far as regards their matter or content, we have really made no addition to our conceptions, but only disinvolved them. But as this process does furnish a real priori knowledge, which has a sure progress and useful results, reason, deceived by this, slips in, without being itself aware of it, assertions of a quite different kind; in which, to given conceptions it adds others, à priori indeed, but entirely foreign to them, without our knowing how it arrives at these, and, indeed, without such a question ever suggesting itself. I shall therefore at once proceed to examine the difference between these two modes of knowledge.

IV. Of the Difference Between Analytical and Synthetical Judgements

In all judgements wherein the relation of a subject to the predicate is cogitated (I mention affirmative judgements only here; the application to negative will be very easy), this relation is possible in two different ways. Either the predicate B belongs to the subject A, as somewhat which is contained (though covertly) in the conception A; or the predicate B lies completely out of the conception A, although it stands in connection with it. In the first instance, I term the judgement analytical, in the second, synthetical. Analytical judgements (affirmative) are therefore those in which the connection of the predicate with the subject is cogitated through identity; those in which this connection is cogitated without identity, are called synthetical judgements. The former may be called explicative, the latter augmentative judgements; because the former add in the predicate nothing to the conception of the subject, but only analyse it into its constituent conceptions, which were thought already in the subject, although in a confused manner; the latter add to our conceptions of the subject a predicate which was not contained in it, and which no analysis could ever have discovered therein. For example, when I say, "All bodies are extended," this is an analytical judgement. For I need not go beyond the conception of body in order to find extension connected with it, but merely analyse the conception, that is, become conscious of the manifold properties which I think in that conception, in order to discover this predicate in it: it is therefore an analytical judgement. On the other hand, when I say, "All bodies are heavy," the predicate is something totally different from that which I think in the mere conception of a body. By the addition of such a predicate, therefore, it becomes a synthetical judgement.

Judgements of experience, as such, are always synthetical. For it would be absurd to think of grounding an analytical judgement on experience, because in forming such a judgement I need not go out of the sphere of my conceptions, and therefore recourse to the testimony of experience is quite unnecessary. That "bodies are extended" is not an empirical judgement, but a proposition which stands firm à priori. For before addressing myself to experience, I already have in my conception all the requisite conditions for the judgement, and I have only to extract the predicate from the conception, according to the principle of contradiction, and thereby at the same time become conscious of the necessity of the judgement, a necessity which I could never learn from experience. On the other hand, though at first I do not at all include the predicate of weight in my conception of body in general, that conception still indicates an object of experience, a part of the totality of experience, to which I can still add other parts; and this I do when I recognize by observation that bodies are heavy. I can cognize beforehand by analysis the conception of body through the characteristics of extension, impenetrability, shape, etc., all which are cogitated in this conception. But now I extend my knowledge, and looking back on experience from which I had derived this conception of body, I find weight at all times connected with the above characteristics, and therefore I synthetically add to my conceptions this as a predicate, and say, "All bodies are heavy." Thus it is experience upon which rests the possibility of the synthesis of the predicate of weight with the conception of body, because both conceptions, although the one is not contained in the other, still belong to one another (only contingently, however), as parts of a whole, namely, of experience, which is itself a synthesis of intuitions.

But to synthetical judgements à priori, such aid is entirely wanting. If I go out of and beyond the conception A, in order to recognize another B as connected with it, what foundation have I to rest on, whereby to render the synthesis possible? I have here no longer the advantage of looking out in the sphere of experience for what I want. Let us take, for example, the proposition, "Everything that happens has a cause." In the conception of "something that happens," I indeed think an existence which a certain time antecedes, and from this I can derive analytical judgements. But the conception of a cause lies quite out of the above conception, and indicates something entirely different from "that which happens," and is consequently not contained in that conception. How then am I able to assert concerning the general conception—"that which happens"—something entirely different from that conception, and to recognize the conception of cause although not contained in it, yet as belonging to it, and even necessarily? what is here the unknown = X, upon which the understanding rests when it believes it has found, out of the conception A a foreign predicate B, which it nevertheless considers to be connected with it? It cannot be experience, because the principle adduced annexes the two representations, cause and effect, to the representation existence, not only with universality, which experience cannot give, but also with the expression of necessity, therefore completely à priori and from pure conceptions. Upon such synthetical, that is augmentative propositions, depends the whole aim of our speculative knowledge à priori; for although analytical judgements are indeed highly important and necessary, they are so, only to arrive at that clearness of conceptions which is requisite for a sure and extended synthesis, and this alone is a real acquisition.

V. In all Theoretical Sciences of Reason, Synthetical Judgements "à priori" are contained as Principles

1. Mathematical judgements are always synthetical. Hitherto this fact, though incontestably true and very important in its consequences, seems to have escaped the analysts of the human mind, nay, to be in complete opposition to all their conjectures. For as it was found that mathematical conclusions all proceed according to the principle of contradiction (which the nature of every apodeictic certainty requires), people became persuaded that the fundamental principles of the science also were recognized and admitted in the same way. But the notion is fallacious; for although a synthetical proposition can certainly be discerned by means of the principle of contradiction, this is possible only when another synthetical proposition precedes, from which the latter is deduced, but never of itself.

Before all, be it observed, that proper mathematical propositions are always judgements à priori, and not empirical, because they carry along with them the conception of necessity, which cannot be given by experience. If this be demurred to, it matters not; I will then limit my assertion to pure mathematics, the very conception of which implies that it consists of knowledge altogether non-empirical and à priori.

We might, indeed at first suppose that the proposition 7 + 5 = 12 is a merely analytical proposition, following (according to the principle of contradiction) from the conception of a sum of seven and five. But if we regard it more narrowly, we find that our conception of the sum of seven and five contains nothing more than the uniting of both sums into one, whereby it cannot at all be cogitated what this single number is which embraces both. The conception of twelve is by no means obtained by merely cogitating the union of seven and five; and we may analyse our conception of such a possible sum as long as we will, still we shall never discover in it the notion of twelve. We must go beyond these conceptions, and have recourse to an intuition which corresponds to one of the two—our five fingers, for example, or like Segner in his Arithmetic five points, and so by degrees, add the units contained in the five given in the intuition, to the conception of seven. For I first take the number 7, and, for the conception of 5 calling in the aid of the fingers of my hand as objects of intuition, I add the units, which I before took together to make up the number 5, gradually now by means of the material image my hand, to the number 7, and by this process, I at length see the number 12 arise. That 7 should be added to 5, I have certainly cogitated in my conception of a sum = 7 + 5, but not that this sum was equal to 12. Arithmetical propositions are therefore always synthetical, of which we may become more clearly convinced by trying large numbers. For it will thus become quite evident that, turn and twist our conceptions as we may, it is impossible, without having recourse to intuition, to arrive at the sum total or product by means of the mere analysis of our conceptions. Just as little is any principle of pure geometry analytical. "A straight line between two points is the shortest," is a synthetical proposition. For my conception of straight contains no notion of quantity, but is merely qualitative. The conception of the shortest is therefore fore wholly an addition, and by no analysis can it be extracted from our conception of a straight line. Intuition must therefore here lend its aid, by means of which, and thus only, our synthesis is possible.

Some few principles preposited by geometricians are, indeed, really analytical, and depend on the principle of contradiction. They serve, however, like identical propositions, as links in the chain of method, not as principles—for example, a = a, the whole is equal to itself, or (a+b) —> a, the whole is greater than its part. And yet even these principles themselves, though they derive their validity from pure conceptions, are only admitted in mathematics because they can be presented in intuition. What causes us here commonly to believe that the predicate of such apodeictic judgements is already contained in our conception, and that the judgement is therefore analytical, is merely the equivocal nature of the expression. We must join in thought a certain predicate to a given conception, and this necessity cleaves already to the conception. But the question is, not what we must join in thought to the given conception, but what we really think therein, though only obscurely, and then it becomes manifest that the predicate pertains to these conceptions, necessarily indeed, yet not as thought in the conception itself, but by virtue of an intuition, which must be added to the conception.

2. The science of natural philosophy (physics) contains in itself synthetical judgements à priori, as principles. I shall adduce two propositions. For instance, the proposition, "In all changes of the material world, the quantity of matter remains unchanged"; or, that, "In all communication of motion, action and reaction must always be equal." In both of these, not only is the necessity, and therefore their origin à priori clear, but also that they are synthetical propositions. For in the conception of matter, I do not cogitate its permanency, but merely its presence in space, which it fills. I therefore really go out of and beyond the conception of matter, in order to think on to it something à priori, which I did not think in it. The proposition is therefore not analytical, but synthetical, and nevertheless conceived à priori; and so it is with regard to the other propositions of the pure part of natural philosophy.

3. As to metaphysics, even if we look upon it merely as an attempted science, yet, from the nature of human reason, an indispensable one, we find that it must contain synthetical propositions à priori. It is not merely the duty of metaphysics to dissect, and thereby analytically to illustrate the conceptions which we form à priori of things; but we seek to widen the range of our à priori knowledge. For this purpose, we must avail ourselves of such principles as add something to the original conception—something not identical with, nor contained in it, and by means of synthetical judgements à priori, leave far behind us the limits of experience; for example, in the proposition, "the world must have a beginning," and such like. Thus metaphysics, according to the proper aim of the science, consists merely of synthetical propositions à priori.

VI. The Universal Problem of Pure Reason

It is extremely advantageous to be able to bring a number of investigations under the formula of a single problem. For in this manner, we not only facilitate our own labour, inasmuch as we define it clearly to ourselves, but also render it more easy for others to decide whether we have done justice to our undertaking. The proper problem of pure reason, then, is contained in the question: "How are synthetical judgements à priori possible?"

That metaphysical science has hitherto remained in so vacillating a state of uncertainty and contradiction, is only to be attributed to the fact that this great problem, and perhaps even the difference between analytical and synthetical judgements, did not sooner suggest itself to philosophers. Upon the solution of this problem, or upon sufficient proof of the impossibility of synthetical knowledge à priori, depends the existence or downfall of the science of metaphysics. Among philosophers, David Hume came the nearest of all to this problem; yet it never acquired in his mind sufficient precision, nor did he regard the question in its universality. On the contrary, he stopped short at the synthetical proposition of the connection of an effect with its cause (principium causalitatis), insisting that such proposition à priori was impossible. According to his conclusions, then, all that we term metaphysical science is a mere delusion, arising from the fancied insight of reason into that which is in truth borrowed from experience, and to which habit has given the appearance of necessity. Against this assertion, destructive to all pure philosophy, he would have been guarded, had he had our problem before his eyes in its universality. For he would then have perceived that, according to his own argument, there likewise could not be any pure mathematical science, which assuredly cannot exist without synthetical propositions à priori—an absurdity from which his good understanding must have saved him.

In the solution of the above problem is at the same time comprehended the possibility of the use of pure reason in the foundation and construction of all sciences which contain theoretical knowledge à priori of objects, that is to say, the answer to the following questions:

How is pure mathematical science possible?
How is pure natural science possible?

Respecting these sciences, as they do certainly exist, it may with propriety be asked, how they are possible?—for that they must be possible is shown by the fact of their really existing.[9] But as to metaphysics, the miserable progress it has hitherto made, and the fact that of no one system yet brought forward, far as regards its true

[9] As to the existence of pure natural science, or physics, perhaps many may still express doubts. But we have only to look at the different propositions which are commonly treated of at the commencement of proper (empirical) physical science—those, for example, relating to the permanence of the same quantity of matter, the vis inertiae, the equality of action and reaction, etc.—to be soon convinced

aim, can it be said that this science really exists, leaves any one at liberty to doubt with reason the very possibility of its existence.

Yet, in a certain sense, this kind of knowledge must unquestionably be looked upon as given; in other words, metaphysics must be considered as really existing, if not as a science, nevertheless as a natural disposition of the human mind (metaphysica naturalis). For human reason, without any instigations imputable to the mere vanity of great knowledge, unceasingly progresses, urged on by its own feeling of need, towards such questions as cannot be answered by any empirical application of reason, or principles derived therefrom; and so there has ever really existed in every man some system of metaphysics. It will always exist, so soon as reason awakes to the exercise of its power of speculation. And now the question arises: "How is metaphysics, as a natural disposition, possible?" In other words, how, from the nature of universal human reason, do those questions arise which pure reason proposes to itself, and which it is impelled by its own feeling of need to answer as well as it can?

But as in all the attempts hitherto made to answer the questions which reason is prompted by its very nature to propose to itself, for example, whether the world had a beginning, or has existed from eternity, it has always met with unavoidable contradictions, we must not rest satisfied with the mere natural disposition of the mind to metaphysics, that is, with the existence of the faculty of pure reason, whence, indeed, some sort of metaphysical system always arises; but it must be possible to arrive at certainty in regard to the question whether we know or do not know the things of which metaphysics treats. We must be able to arrive at a decision on the subjects of its questions, or on the ability or inability of reason to form any judgement respecting them; and therefore either to extend with confidence the bounds of our pure reason, or to set strictly defined and safe limits to its action. This last question, which arises out of the above universal problem, would properly run thus: "How is metaphysics possible as a science?"

Thus, the critique of reason leads at last, naturally and necessarily, to science; and, on the other hand, the dogmatical use of reason without criticism leads to groundless assertions, against which others equally specious can always be set, thus ending unavoidably in scepticism.

Besides, this science cannot be of great and formidable prolixity, because it has not to do with objects of reason, the variety of which is inexhaustible, but merely with Reason herself and her problems; problems which arise out of her own bosom, and are not proposed to her by the nature of outward things, but by her own nature. And when once Reason has previously become able completely to understand her own power in regard to objects which she meets with in experience, it will be easy to determine securely the extent and limits of her attempted application to objects beyond the confines of experience.

---

that they form a science of pure physics (physica pura, or rationalis), which well deserves to be separately exposed as a special science, in its whole extent, whether that be great or confined.

We may and must, therefore, regard the attempts hitherto made to establish metaphysical science dogmatically as non-existent. For what of analysis, that is, mere dissection of conceptions, is contained in one or other, is not the aim of, but only a preparation for metaphysics proper, which has for its object the extension, by means of synthesis, of our à priori knowledge. And for this purpose, mere analysis is of course useless, because it only shows what is contained in these conceptions, but not how we arrive, à priori, at them; and this it is her duty to show, in order to be able afterwards to determine their valid use in regard to all objects of experience, to all knowledge in general. But little self-denial, indeed, is needed to give up these pretensions, seeing the undeniable, and in the dogmatic mode of procedure, inevitable contradictions of Reason with herself, have long since ruined the reputation of every system of metaphysics that has appeared up to this time. It will require more firmness to remain undeterred by difficulty from within, and opposition from without, from endeavouring, by a method quite opposed to all those hitherto followed, to further the growth and fruitfulness of a science indispensable to human reason—a science from which every branch it has borne may be cut away, but whose roots remain indestructible.

VII. Idea and Division of a Particular Science, under the Name of a Critique of Pure Reason

From all that has been said, there results the idea of a particular science, which may be called the Critique of Pure Reason. For reason is the faculty which furnishes us with the principles of knowledge à priori. Hence, pure reason is the faculty which contains the principles of cognizing anything absolutely à priori. An organon of pure reason would be a compendium of those principles according to which alone all pure cognitions à priori can be obtained. The completely extended application of such an organon would afford us a system of pure reason. As this, however, is demanding a great deal, and it is yet doubtful whether any extension of our knowledge be here possible, or, if so, in what cases; we can regard a science of the mere criticism of pure reason, its sources and limits, as the propædeutic to a system of pure reason. Such a science must not be called a doctrine, but only a critique of pure reason; and its use, in regard to speculation, would be only negative, not to enlarge the bounds of, but to purify, our reason, and to shield it against error—which alone is no little gain. I apply the term transcendental to all knowledge which is not so much occupied with objects as with the mode of our cognition of these objects, so far as this mode of cognition is possible à priori. A system of such conceptions would be called transcendental philosophy. But this, again, is still beyond the bounds of our present essay. For as such a science must contain a complete exposition not only of our synthetical à priori, but of our analytical à priori knowledge, it is of too wide a range for our present purpose, because we do not require to carry our analysis any farther than is necessary to understand, in their full extent, the principles of synthesis à priori, with which alone we have to do. This investigation, which we cannot properly call a doctrine, but only a transcendental critique, because it aims not at the enlargement, but at the correction and guidance, of our knowledge, and is to serve as a touchstone of the worth or worthlessness of all knowledge à priori, is the sole object of our present essay. Such a critique is consequently, as far as possible, a preparation for an organon; and if this new organon should be found to fail, at least for a canon of pure reason, according to which the complete system of the philosophy of pure reason, whether it extend or limit the bounds of that reason, might one day be set forth both analytically and synthetically. For that this is possible, nay, that such a system is not of so great extent as to preclude the hope of its ever being completed, is evident. For we have not here to do with the nature of outward objects, which is infinite, but solely with the mind, which judges of the nature of objects, and, again, with the mind only in respect of its cognition à priori. And the object of our investigations, as it is not to be sought without, but, altogether within, ourselves, cannot remain concealed, and in all probability is limited enough to be completely surveyed and fairly estimated, according to its worth or worthlessness. Still less let the reader here expect a critique of books and systems of pure reason; our present object is exclusively a critique of the faculty of pure reason itself. Only when we make this critique our foundation, do we possess a pure touchstone for estimating the philosophical value of ancient and modern writings on this subject; and without this criterion, the incompetent historian or judge decides upon and corrects the groundless assertions of others with his own, which have themselves just as little foundation.

Transcendental philosophy is the idea of a science, for which the Critique of Pure Reason must sketch the whole plan architectonically, that is, from principles, with a full guarantee for the validity and stability of all the parts which enter into the building. It is the system of all the principles of pure reason. If this Critique itself does not assume the title of transcendental philosophy, it is only because, to be a complete system, it ought to contain a full analysis of all human knowledge à priori. Our critique must, indeed, lay before us a complete enumeration of all the radical conceptions which constitute the said pure knowledge. But from the complete analysis of these conceptions themselves, as also from a complete investigation of those derived from them, it abstains with reason; partly because it would be deviating from the end in view to occupy itself with this analysis, since this process is not attended with the difficulty and insecurity to be found in the synthesis, to which our critique is entirely devoted, and partly because it would be inconsistent with the unity of our plan to burden this essay with the vindication of the completeness of such an analysis and deduction, with which, after all, we have at present nothing to do. This completeness of the analysis of these radical conceptions, as well as of the deduction from the conceptions à priori which may be given by the analysis, we can, however, easily attain, provided only that we are in possession of all these radical conceptions, which are to serve as principles of the synthesis, and that in respect of this main purpose nothing is wanting.

To the Critique of Pure Reason, therefore, belongs all that constitutes transcendental philosophy; and it is the complete idea of transcendental philosophy, but still not the science itself; because it only proceeds so far with the analysis as is necessary to the power of judging completely of our synthetical knowledge à priori.

The principal thing we must attend to, in the division of the parts of a science like this, is that no conceptions must enter it which contain aught empirical; in other words, that the knowledge à priori must be completely pure. Hence, although the highest principles and fundamental conceptions of morality are certainly cognitions à priori, yet they do not belong to transcendental philosophy; because, though they certainly do not lay the conceptions of pain, pleasure, desires, inclinations, etc. (which are all of empirical origin), at the foundation of its precepts, yet still into the conception of duty—as an obstacle to be overcome, or as an incitement which should not be made into a motive—these empirical conceptions must necessarily enter, in the construction of a system of pure morality. Transcendental philosophy is consequently a philosophy of the pure and merely speculative reason. For all that is practical, so far as it contains motives, relates to feelings, and these belong to empirical sources of cognition.

If we wish to divide this science from the universal point of view of a science in general, it ought to comprehend, first, a Doctrine of the Elements, and, secondly, a Doctrine of the Method of pure reason. Each of these main divisions will have its subdivisions, the separate reasons for which we cannot here particularize. Only so much seems necessary, by way of introduction of premonition, that there are two sources of human knowledge (which probably spring from a common, but to us unknown root), namely, sense and understanding. By the former, objects are given to us; by the latter, thought. So far as the faculty of sense may contain representations à priori, which form the conditions under which objects are given, in so far it belongs to transcendental philosophy. The transcendental doctrine of sense must form the first part of our science of elements, because the conditions under which alone the objects of human knowledge are given must precede those under which they are thought.

I

TRANSCENDENTAL DOCTRINE OF ELEMENTS

FIRST PART

TRANSCENDENTAL ÆSTHETIC

§ I. Introductory

In whatsoever mode, or by whatsoever means, our knowledge may relate to objects, it is at least quite clear that the only manner in which it immediately relates to them is by means of an intuition. To this as the indispensable groundwork, all thought points. But an intuition can take place only in so far as the object is given to us. This, again, is only possible, to man at least, on condition that the object affect the mind in a certain manner. The capacity for receiving representations (receptivity) through the mode in which we are affected by objects, objects, is called sensibility. By means of sensibility, therefore, objects are given to us, and it alone furnishes us with intuitions; by the understanding they are thought, and from it arise conceptions. But an thought must directly, or indirectly, by means of certain signs, relate ultimately to intuitions; consequently, with us, to sensibility, because in no other way can an object be given to us.

The effect of an object upon the faculty of representation, so far as we are affected by the said object, is sensation. That sort of intuition which relates to an object by means of sensation is called an empirical intuition. The undetermined object of an empirical intuition is called phenomenon. That which in the phenomenon corresponds to the sensation, I term its matter; but that which effects that the content of the phenomenon can be arranged under certain relations, I call its form. But that in which our sensations are merely arranged, and by which they are susceptible of assuming a certain form, cannot be itself sensation. It is, then, the matter of all phenomena that is given to us à posteriori; the form must lie ready à priori for them in the mind, and consequently can be regarded separately from all sensation.

I call all representations pure, in the transcendental meaning of the word, wherein nothing is met with that belongs to sensation. And accordingly we find existing in the mind à priori, the pure form of sensuous intuitions in general, in which all the manifold content of the phenomenal world is arranged and viewed under certain relations. This pure form of sensibility I shall call pure intuition. Thus, if I take away from our representation of a body all that the understanding thinks as belonging to it, as substance, force, divisibility, etc., and also whatever belongs to sensation, as impenetrability, hardness, colour, etc.; yet there is still something left us from this empirical intuition, namely, extension and shape. These belong to pure intuition, which exists à priori in the mind, as a mere form of sensibility, and without any real object of the senses or any sensation.

The science of all the principles of sensibility à priori, I call transcendental æsthetic.[10] There must, then, be such a science forming the first part of the transcendental doctrine of elements, in contradistinction to that part which contains the principles of pure thought, and which is called transcendental logic.

In the science of transcendental æsthetic accordingly, we shall first isolate sensibility or the sensuous faculty, by separating from it all that is annexed to its perceptions by the conceptions of understanding, so that nothing be left but empirical intuition. In the next place we shall take away from this intuition all that belongs to sensation, so that nothing may remain but pure intuition, and the mere form of phenomena, which is all that the sensibility can afford à priori. From this investigation it will be found that there are two pure forms of sensuous intuition, as principles of knowledge à priori, namely, space and time. To the consideration of these we shall now proceed.

SECTION I—Of Space

§ 2. Metaphysical Exposition of this Conception

By means of the external sense (a property of the mind), we represent to ourselves objects as without us, and these all in space. Herein alone are their shape, dimensions, and relations to each other determined or determinable. The internal sense, by means of which the mind contemplates itself or its internal state, gives, indeed, no intuition of the soul as an object; yet there is nevertheless a determinate

[10] The Germans are the only people who at present use this word to indicate what others call the critique of taste. At the foundation of this term lies the disappointed hope, which the eminent analyst, Baumgarten, conceived, of subjecting the criticism of the beautiful to principles of reason, and so of elevating its rules into a science. But his endeavours were vain. For the said rules or criteria are, in respect to their chief sources, merely empirical, consequently never can serve as determinate laws à priori, by which our judgement in matters of taste is to be directed. It is rather our judgement which forms the proper test as to the correctness of the principles. On this account it is advisable to give up the use of the term as designating the critique of taste, and to apply it solely to that doctrine, which is true science—the science of the laws of sensibility—and thus come nearer to the language and the sense of the ancients in their well-known division of the objects of cognition into aiotheta kai noeta, or to share it with speculative philosophy, and employ it partly in a transcendental, partly in a psychological signification.

form, under which alone the contemplation of our internal state is possible, so that all which relates to the inward determinations of the mind is represented in relations of time. Of time we cannot have any external intuition, any more than we can have an internal intuition of space. What then are time and space? Are they real existences? Or, are they merely relations or determinations of things, such, however, as would equally belong to these things in themselves, though they should never become objects of intuition; or, are they such as belong only to the form of intuition, and consequently to the subjective constitution of the mind, without which these predicates of time and space could not be attached to any object? In order to become informed on these points, we shall first give an exposition of the conception of space. By exposition, I mean the clear, though not detailed, representation of that which belongs to a conception; and an exposition is metaphysical when it contains that which represents the conception as given à priori.

1. Space is not a conception which has been derived from outward experiences. For, in order that certain sensations may relate to something without me (that is, to something which occupies a different part of space from that in which I am); in like manner, in order that I may represent them not merely as without, of, and near to each other, but also in separate places, the representation of space must already exist as a foundation. Consequently, the representation of space cannot be borrowed from the relations of external phenomena through experience; but, on the contrary, this external experience is itself only possible through the said antecedent representation.

2. Space then is a necessary representation à priori, which serves for the foundation of all external intuitions. We never can imagine or make a representation to ourselves of the non-existence of space, though we may easily enough think that no objects are found in it. It must, therefore, be considered as the condition of the possibility of phenomena, and by no means as a determination dependent on them, and is a representation à priori, which necessarily supplies the basis for external phenomena.

3. Space is no discursive, or as we say, general conception of the relations of things, but a pure intuition. For, in the first place, we can only represent to ourselves one space, and, when we talk of divers spaces, we mean only parts of one and the same space. Moreover, these parts cannot antecede this one all-embracing space, as the component parts from which the aggregate can be made up, but can be cogitated only as existing in it. Space is essentially one, and multiplicity in it, consequently the general notion of spaces, of this or that space, depends solely upon limitations. Hence it follows that an à priori intuition (which is not empirical) lies at the root of all our conceptions of space. Thus, moreover, the principles of geometry—for example, that "in a triangle, two sides together are greater than the third," are never deduced from general conceptions of line and triangle, but from intuition, and this à priori, with apodeictic certainty.

4. Space is represented as an infinite given quantity. Now every conception must indeed be considered as a representation which is contained in an infinite multitude of different possible representations, which, therefore, comprises these under itself; but no conception, as such, can be so conceived, as if it contained within itself an infinite multitude of representations. Nevertheless, space is so conceived of, for all parts of space are equally capable of being produced to infinity. Consequently, the original representation of space is an intuition à priori, and not a conception.

§ 3. Transcendental Exposition of the Conception of Space

By a transcendental exposition, I mean the explanation of a conception, as a principle, whence can be discerned the possibility of other synthetical à priori cognitions. For this purpose, it is requisite, firstly, that such cognitions do really flow from the given conception; and, secondly, that the said cognitions are only possible under the presupposition of a given mode of explaining this conception.

Geometry is a science which determines the properties of space synthetically, and yet à priori. What, then, must be our representation of space, in order that such a cognition of it may be possible? It must be originally intuition, for from a mere conception, no propositions can be deduced which go out beyond the conception, and yet this happens in geometry. (Introd. V.) But this intuition must be found in the mind à priori, that is, before any perception of objects, consequently must be pure, not empirical, intuition. For geometrical principles are always apodeictic, that is, united with the consciousness of their necessity, as: "Space has only three dimensions." But propositions of this kind cannot be empirical judgements, nor conclusions from them. (Introd. II.) Now, how can an external intuition anterior to objects themselves, and in which our conception of objects can be determined à priori, exist in the human mind? Obviously not otherwise than in so far as it has its seat in the subject only, as the formal capacity of the subject's being affected by objects, and thereby of obtaining immediate representation, that is, intuition; consequently, only as the form of the external sense in general.

Thus it is only by means of our explanation that the possibility of geometry, as a synthetical science à priori, becomes comprehensible. Every mode of explanation which does not show us this possibility, although in appearance it may be similar to ours, can with the utmost certainty be distinguished from it by these marks.

§ 4. Conclusions from the foregoing Conceptions

(a) Space does not represent any property of objects as things in themselves, nor does it represent them in their relations to each other; in other words, space does not represent to us any determination of objects such as attaches to the objects themselves, and would remain, even though all subjective conditions of the intuition were abstracted. For neither absolute nor relative determinations of objects can be intuited prior to the existence of the things to which they belong, and therefore not à priori.

(b) Space is nothing else than the form of all phenomena of the external sense, that is, the subjective condition of the sensibility, under which alone external intuition is possible. Now, because the receptivity or capacity of the subject to be affected by objects necessarily antecedes all intuitions of these objects, it is easily understood how the form of all phenomena can be given in the mind previous to all actual perceptions, therefore à priori, and how it, as a pure intuition, in which all objects must be determined, can contain principles of the relations of these objects prior to all experience.

It is therefore from the human point of view only that we can speak of space, extended objects, etc. If we depart from the subjective condition, under which alone we can obtain external intuition, or, in other words, by means of which we are affected by objects, the representation of space has no meaning whatsoever. This predicate is only applicable to things in so far as they appear to us, that is, are objects of sensibility. The constant form of this receptivity, which we call sensibility, is a necessary condition of all relations in which objects can be intuited as existing without us, and when abstraction of these objects is made, is a pure intuition, to which we give the name of space. It is clear that we cannot make the special conditions of sensibility into conditions of the possibility of things, but only of the possibility of their existence as far as they are phenomena. And so we may correctly say that space contains all which can appear to us externally, but not all things considered as things in themselves, be they intuited or not, or by whatsoever subject one will. As to the intuitions of other thinking beings, we cannot judge whether they are or are not bound by the same conditions which limit our own intuition, and which for us are universally valid. If we join the limitation of a judgement to the conception of the subject, then the judgement will possess unconditioned validity. For example, the proposition, "All objects are beside each other in space," is valid only under the limitation that these things are taken as objects of our sensuous intuition. But if I join the condition to the conception and say, "All things, as external phenomena, are beside each other in space," then the rule is valid universally, and without any limitation. Our expositions, consequently, teach the reality (i.e., the objective validity) of space in regard of all which can be presented to us externally as object, and at the same time also the ideality of space in regard to objects when they are considered by means of reason as things in themselves, that is, without reference to the constitution of our sensibility. We maintain, therefore, the empirical reality of space in regard to all possible external experience, although we must admit its transcendental ideality; in other words, that it is nothing, so soon as we withdraw the condition upon which the possibility of all experience depends and look upon space as something that belongs to things in themselves.

But, with the exception of space, there is no representation, subjective and referring to something external to us, which could be called objective à priori. For there are no other subjective representations from which we can deduce synthetical propositions à priori, as we can from the intuition of space. (See § 3.) Therefore, to speak accurately, no ideality whatever belongs to these, although they agree in this respect with the representation of space, that they belong merely to the subjective nature of the mode of sensuous perception; such a mode, for example, as that of sight, of hearing, and of feeling, by means of the sensations of colour, sound, and heat, but which, because they are only sensations and not intuitions, do not of themselves give us the cognition of any object, least of all, an à priori cognition. My purpose, in the above remark, is merely this: to guard any one against illustrating the asserted ideality of space by examples quite insufficient, for example, by colour, taste, etc.; for these must be contemplated not as properties of things, but only as changes in the subject, changes which may be different in different men. For, in such a case, that which is originally a mere phenomenon, a rose, for example, is taken by the empirical understanding for a thing in itself, though to every different eye, in respect of its colour, it may appear different. On the contrary, the transcendental conception of phenomena in space is a critical admonition, that, in general, nothing which is intuited in space is a thing in itself, and that space is not a form which belongs as a property to things; but that objects are quite unknown to us in themselves, and what we call outward objects, are nothing else but mere representations of our sensibility, whose form is space, but whose real correlate, the thing in itself, is not known by means of these representations, nor ever can be, but respecting which, in experience, no inquiry is ever made.

SECTION II—Of Time

§ 5. Metaphysical Exposition of this Conception

1. Time is not an empirical conception. For neither coexistence nor succession would be perceived by us, if the representation of time did not exist as a foundation à priori. Without this presupposition we could not represent to ourselves that things exist together at one and the same time, or at different times, that is, contemporaneously, or in succession.
2. Time is a necessary representation, lying at the foundation of all our intuitions. With regard to phenomena in general, we cannot think away time from them, and represent them to ourselves as out of and unconnected with time, but we can quite well represent to ourselves time void of phenomena. Time is therefore given à priori. In it alone is all reality of phenomena possible. These may all be annihilated in thought, but time itself, as the universal condition of their possibility, cannot be so annulled.

3. On this necessity à priori is also founded the possibility of apodeictic principles of the relations of time, or axioms of time in general, such as: "Time has only one dimension," "Different times are not coexistent but successive" (as different spaces are not successive but coexistent). These principles cannot be derived from experience, for it would give neither strict universality, nor apodeictic certainty. We should only be able to say, "so common experience teaches us," but not "it must be so." They are valid as rules, through which, in general, experience is possible; and they instruct us respecting experience, and not by means of it.
4. Time is not a discursive, or as it is called, general conception, but a pure form of the sensuous intuition. Different times are merely parts of one and the same time. But the representation which can only be given by a single object is an intuition. Besides, the proposition that different times cannot be coexistent could not be derived from a general conception. For this proposition is synthetical, and therefore cannot spring out of conceptions alone. It is therefore contained immediately in the intuition and representation of time.
5. The infinity of time signifies nothing more than that every determined quantity of time is possible only through limitations of one time lying at the foundation. Consequently, the original representation, time, must be given as unlimited. But as the determinate representation of the parts of time and of every quantity of an object can only be obtained by limitation, the complete representation of time must not be furnished by means of conceptions, for these contain only partial representations. Conceptions, on the contrary, must have immediate intuition for their basis.

§ 6 Transcendental Exposition of the Conception of Time

I may here refer to what is said above (§ 5, 3), where, for or sake of brevity, I have placed under the head of metaphysical exposition, that which is properly transcendental. Here I shall add that the conception of change, and with it the conception of motion, as change of place, is possible only through and in the representation of time; that if this representation were not an intuition (internal) à priori, no conception, of whatever kind, could render comprehensible the possibility of change, in other words, of a conjunction of contradictorily opposed predicates in one and the same object, for example, the presence of a thing in a place and the non-presence of the same thing in the same place. It is only in time that it is possible to meet with two contradictorily opposed determinations in one thing, that is, after each other. Thus our conception of time explains the possibility of so much synthetical knowledge à priori, as is exhibited in the general doctrine of motion, which is not a little fruitful.

§ 7. Conclusions from the above Conceptions

(a) Time is not something which subsists of itself, or which inheres in things as an objective determination, and therefore remains, when abstraction is made of the subjective conditions of the intuition of things. For in the former case, it would be something real, yet without presenting to any power of perception any real object. In the latter case, as an order or determination inherent in things themselves, it could not be antecedent to things, as their condition, nor discerned or intuited by means of synthetical propositions à priori. But all this is quite possible when we regard time as merely the subjective condition under which all our intuitions take place. For in that case, this form of the inward intuition can be represented prior to the objects, and consequently à priori.

(b) Time is nothing else than the form of the internal sense, that is, of the intuitions of self and of our internal state. For time cannot be any determination of outward phenomena. It has to do neither with shape nor position; on the contrary, it determines the relation of representations in our internal state. And precisely because this internal intuition presents to us no shape or form, we endeavour to supply this want by analogies, and represent the course of time by a line progressing to infinity, the content of which constitutes a series which is only of one dimension; and we conclude from the properties of this line as to all the properties of time, with this single exception, that the parts of the line are coexistent, whilst those of time are successive. From this it is clear also that the representation of time is itself an intuition, because all its relations can be expressed in an external intuition.

(c) Time is the formal condition à priori of all phenomena whatsoever. Space, as the pure form of external intuition, is limited as a condition à priori to external phenomena alone. On the other hand, because all representations, whether they have or have not external things for their objects, still in themselves, as determinations of the mind, belong to our internal state; and because this internal state is subject to the formal condition of the internal intuition, that is, to time—time is a condition à priori of all phenomena whatsoever—the immediate condition of all internal, and thereby the mediate condition of all external phenomena. If I can say à priori, "All outward phenomena are in space, and determined à priori according to the relations of space," I can also, from the principle of the internal sense, affirm universally, "All phenomena in general, that is, all objects of the senses, are in time and stand necessarily in relations of time."

If we abstract our internal intuition of ourselves and all external intuitions, possible only by virtue of this internal intuition and presented to us by our faculty of representation, and consequently take objects as they are in themselves, then time is nothing. It is only of objective validity in regard to phenomena, because these are things which we regard as objects of our senses. It no longer objective we, make abstraction of the sensuousness of our intuition, in other words, of that mode of representation which is peculiar to us, and speak of things in general. Time is therefore merely a subjective condition of our (human) intuition (which is always sensuous, that is, so far as we are affected by objects), and in itself, independently of the mind or subject, is nothing. Nevertheless, in respect of all phenomena, consequently of all things which come within the sphere of our experience, it is necessarily objective. We cannot say, "All things are in time," because in this conception of things in general, we abstract and make no mention of any sort of intuition of things. But this is the proper condition under which time belongs to our representation of objects. If we add the condition to the conception, and say, "All things, as phenomena, that is, objects of sensuous intuition, are in time," then the proposition has its sound objective validity and universality à priori.

What we have now set forth teaches, therefore, the empirical reality of time; that is, its objective validity in reference to all objects which can ever be presented to our senses. And as our intuition is always sensuous, no object ever can be presented to us in experience, which does not come under the conditions of time. On the other hand, we deny to time all claim to absolute reality; that is, we deny that it, without having regard to the form of our sensuous intuition, absolutely inheres in things as a condition or property. Such properties as belong to objects as things in themselves never can be presented to us through the medium of the senses. Herein consists, therefore, the transcendental ideality of time, according to which, if we abstract the subjective conditions of sensuous intuition, it is nothing, and cannot be reckoned as subsisting or inhering in objects as things in themselves, independently of its relation to our intuition. This ideality, like that of space, is not to be proved or illustrated by fallacious analogies with sensations, for this reason—that in such arguments or illustrations, we make the presupposition that the phenomenon, in which such and such predicates inhere, has objective reality, while in this case we can only find such an objective reality as is itself empirical, that is, regards the object as a mere phenomenon. In reference to this subject, see the remark in Section I (§ 4)

§ 8. Elucidation

Against this theory, which grants empirical reality to time, but denies to it absolute and transcendental reality, I have heard from intelligent men an objection so unanimously urged that I conclude that it must naturally present itself to every reader to whom these considerations are novel. It runs thus: "Changes are real" (this the continual change in our own representations demonstrates, even though the existence of all external phenomena, together with their changes, is denied). Now, changes are only possible in time, and therefore time must be something real. But there is no difficulty in answering this. I grant the whole argument. Time, no doubt, is something real, that is, it is the real form of our internal intuition. It therefore has subjective reality, in reference to our internal experience, that is, I have really the representation of time and of my determinations therein. Time, therefore, is not to be regarded as an object, but as the mode of representation of myself as an object. But if I could intuite myself, or be intuited by another being, without this condition of sensibility, then those very determinations which we now represent to ourselves as changes, would present to us a knowledge in which the representation of time, and consequently of change, would not appear. The empirical reality of time, therefore, remains, as the condition of all our experience. But absolute reality, according to what has been said above, cannot be granted it. Time is nothing but the form of our internal intuition.[11] If we take away from it the special condition of our sensibility, the conception of time also vanishes; and it inheres not in the objects themselves, but solely in the subject (or mind) which intuites them.

But the reason why this objection is so unanimously brought against our doctrine of time, and that too by disputants who cannot start any intelligible arguments against the doctrine of the ideality of space, is this—they have no hope of demonstrating apodeictically the absolute reality of space, because the doctrine of idealism is against them, according to which the reality of external objects is not capable of any strict proof. On the other hand, the reality of the object of our internal sense (that is, myself and my internal state) is clear immediately through consciousness. The former—external objects in space—might be a mere delusion, but the latter—the object of my internal perception—is undeniably real. They do not, however, reflect that both, without question of their reality as representations, belong only to the genus phenomenon, which has always two aspects, the one, the object considered as a thing in itself, without regard to the mode of intuiting it, and the nature of which remains for this very reason problematical, the other, the form of our intuition of the object, which must be sought not in the object as a thing in itself, but in the subject to which it appears—which form of intuition nevertheless belongs really and necessarily to the phenomenal object.

Time and space are, therefore, two sources of knowledge, from which, à priori, various synthetical cognitions can be drawn. Of this we find a striking example in the cognitions of space and its relations, which form the foundation of pure mathematics. They are the two pure forms of all intuitions, and thereby make synthetical propositions à priori possible. But these sources of knowledge being merely conditions of our sensibility, do therefore, and as such, strictly determine their own range and purpose, in that they do not and cannot present objects as things in themselves, but are applicable to them solely in so far as they are considered as

[11] I can indeed say "my representations follow one another, or are successive"; but this means only that we are conscious of them as in a succession, that is, according to the form of the internal sense. Time, therefore, is not a thing in itself, nor is it any objective determination pertaining to, or inherent in things.

sensuous phenomena. The sphere of phenomena is the only sphere of their validity, and if we venture out of this, no further objective use can be made of them. For the rest, this formal reality of time and space leaves the validity of our empirical knowledge unshaken; for our certainty in that respect is equally firm, whether these forms necessarily inhere in the things themselves, or only in our intuitions of them. On the other hand, those who maintain the absolute reality of time and space, whether as essentially subsisting, or only inhering, as modifications, in things, must find themselves at utter variance with the principles of experience itself. For, if they decide for the first view, and make space and time into substances, this being the side taken by mathematical natural philosophers, they must admit two self-subsisting nonentities, infinite and eternal, which exist (yet without there being anything real) for the purpose of containing in themselves everything that is real. If they adopt the second view of inherence, which is preferred by some metaphysical natural philosophers, and regard space and time as relations (contiguity in space or succession in time), abstracted from experience, though represented confusedly in this state of separation, they find themselves in that case necessitated to deny the validity of mathematical doctrines à priori in reference to real things (for example, in space)—at all events their apodeictic certainty. For such certainty cannot be found in an à posteriori proposition; and the conceptions à priori of space and time are, according to this opinion, mere creations of the imagination, having their source really in experience, inasmuch as, out of relations abstracted from experience, imagination has made up something which contains, indeed, general statements of these relations, yet of which no application can be made without the restrictions attached thereto by nature. The former of these parties gains this advantage, that they keep the sphere of phenomena free for mathematical science. On the other hand, these very conditions (space and time) embarrass them greatly, when the understanding endeavours to pass the limits of that sphere. The latter has, indeed, this advantage, that the representations of space and time do not come in their way when they wish to judge of objects, not as phenomena, but merely in their relation to the understanding. Devoid, however, of a true and objectively valid à priori intuition, they can neither furnish any basis for the possibility of mathematical cognitions à priori, nor bring the propositions of experience into necessary accordance with those of mathematics. In our theory of the true nature of these two original forms of the sensibility, both difficulties are surmounted.

In conclusion, that transcendental æsthetic cannot contain any more than these two elements—space and time, is sufficiently obvious from the fact that all other conceptions appertaining to sensibility, even that of motion, which unites in itself both elements, presuppose something empirical. Motion, for example, presupposes the perception of something movable. But space considered in itself contains nothing movable, consequently motion must be something which is found in space only through experience—in other words, an empirical datum. In like manner, transcendental æsthetic cannot number the conception of change among its data à priori; for time itself does not change, but only something which is in time. To acquire the conception of change, therefore, the perception of some existing object and of the succession of its determinations, in one word, experience, is necessary.

§ 9. General Remarks on Transcendental Æsthetic

I. In order to prevent any misunderstanding, it will be requisite, in the first place, to recapitulate, as clearly as possible, what our opinion is with respect to the fundamental nature of our sensuous cognition in general. We have intended, then, to say that all our intuition is nothing but the representation of phenomena; that the things which we intuite, are not in themselves the same as our representations of them in intuition, nor are their relations in themselves so constituted as they appear to us; and that if we take away the subject, or even only the subjective constitution of our senses in general, then not only the nature and relations of objects in space and time, but even space and time themselves disappear; and that these, as phenomena, cannot exist in themselves, but only in us. What may be the nature of objects considered as things in themselves and without reference to the receptivity of our sensibility is quite unknown to us. We know nothing more than our mode of perceiving them, which is peculiar to us, and which, though not of necessity pertaining to every animated being, is so to the whole human race. With this alone we have to do. Space and time are the pure forms thereof; sensation the matter. The former alone can we cognize à priori, that is, antecedent to all actual perception; and for this reason such cognition is called pure intuition. The latter is that in our cognition which is called cognition à posteriori, that is, empirical intuition. The former appertain absolutely and necessarily to our sensibility, of whatsoever kind our sensations may be; the latter may be of very diversified character. Supposing that we should carry our empirical intuition even to the very highest degree of clearness, we should not thereby advance one step nearer to a knowledge of the constitution of objects as things in themselves. For we could only, at best, arrive at a complete cognition of our own mode of intuition, that is of our sensibility, and this always under the conditions originally attaching to the subject, namely, the conditions of space and time; while the question: "What are objects considered as things in themselves?" remains unanswerable even after the most thorough examination of the phenomenal world.

To say, then, that all our sensibility is nothing but the confused representation of things containing exclusively that which belongs to them as things in themselves, and this under an accumulation of characteristic marks and partial representations which we cannot distinguish in consciousness, is a falsification of the conception of sensibility and phenomenization, which renders our whole doctrine thereof empty and useless. The difference between a confused and a clear representation is merely logical and has nothing to do with content. No doubt the conception of right, as employed by a sound understanding, contains all that the most subtle investigation could unfold from it, although, in the ordinary practical use of the word, we are not conscious of the manifold representations comprised in the conception. But we cannot for this reason assert that the ordinary conception is a sensuous one, containing a mere phenomenon, for right cannot appear as a phenomenon; but the conception of it lies in the understanding, and represents a property (the moral property) of actions, which belongs to them in themselves. On the other hand, the representation in intuition of a body contains nothing which could belong to an object considered as a thing in itself, but merely the phenomenon or appearance of something, and the mode in which we are affected by that appearance; and this receptivity of our faculty of cognition is called sensibility, and remains toto caelo different from the cognition of an object in itself, even though we should examine the content of the phenomenon to the very bottom.

It must be admitted that the Leibnitz-Wolfian philosophy has assigned an entirely erroneous point of view to all investigations into the nature and origin of our cognitions, inasmuch as it regards the distinction between the sensuous and the intellectual as merely logical, whereas it is plainly transcendental, and concerns not merely the clearness or obscurity, but the content and origin of both. For the faculty of sensibility not only does not present us with an indistinct and confused cognition of objects as things in themselves, but, in fact, gives us no knowledge of these at all. On the contrary, so soon as we abstract in thought our own subjective nature, the object represented, with the properties ascribed to it by sensuous intuition, entirely disappears, because it was only this subjective nature that determined the form of the object as a phenomenon.

In phenomena, we commonly, indeed, distinguish that which essentially belongs to the intuition of them, and is valid for the sensuous faculty of every human being, from that which belongs to the same intuition accidentally, as valid not for the sensuous faculty in general, but for a particular state or organization of this or that sense. Accordingly, we are accustomed to say that the former is a cognition which represents the object itself, whilst the latter presents only a particular appearance or phenomenon thereof. This distinction, however, is only empirical. If we stop here (as is usual), and do not regard the empirical intuition as itself a mere phenomenon (as we ought to do), in which nothing that can appertain to a thing in itself is to be found, our transcendental distinction is lost, and we believe that we cognize objects as things in themselves, although in the whole range of the sensuous world, investigate the nature of its objects as profoundly as we may, we have to do with nothing but phenomena. Thus, we call the rainbow a mere appearance of phenomenon in a sunny shower, and the rain, the reality or thing in itself; and this is right enough, if we understand the latter conception in a merely physical sense, that is, as that which in universal experience, and under whatever conditions of sensuous perception, is known in intuition to be so and so determined, and not otherwise. But if we consider this empirical datum generally, and inquire, without reference to its accordance with all our senses, whether there can be discovered in it aught which represents an object as a thing in itself (the raindrops of course are not such, for they are, as phenomena, empirical objects), the question of the relation of the representation to the object is transcendental; and not only are the raindrops mere phenomena, but even their circular form, nay, the space itself through which they fall, is nothing in itself, but both are mere modifications or fundamental dispositions of our sensuous intuition, whilst the transcendental object remains for us utterly unknown.

The second important concern of our æsthetic is that it does not obtain favour merely as a plausible hypothesis, but possess as undoubted a character of certainty as can be demanded of any theory which is to serve for an organon. In order fully to convince the reader of this certainty, we shall select a case which will serve to make its validity apparent, and also to illustrate what has been said in § 3.

Suppose, then, that space and time are in themselves objective, and conditions of the—possibility of objects as things in themselves. In the first place, it is evident that both present us, with very many apodeictic and synthetic propositions à priori, but especially space—and for this reason we shall prefer it for investigation at present. As the propositions of geometry are cognized synthetically à priori, and with apodeictic certainty, I inquire: Whence do you obtain propositions of this kind, and on what basis does the understanding rest, in order to arrive at such absolutely necessary and universally valid truths?

There is no other way than through intuitions or conceptions, as such; and these are given either à priori or à posteriori. The latter, namely, empirical conceptions, together with the empirical intuition on which they are founded, cannot afford any synthetical proposition, except such as is itself also empirical, that is, a proposition of experience. But an empirical proposition cannot possess the qualities of necessity and absolute universality, which, nevertheless, are the characteristics of all geometrical propositions. As to the first and only means to arrive at such cognitions, namely, through mere conceptions or intuitions à priori, it is quite clear that from mere conceptions no synthetical cognitions, but only analytical ones, can be obtained. Take, for example, the proposition: "Two straight lines cannot enclose a space, and with these alone no figure is possible," and try to deduce it from the conception of a straight line and the number two; or take the proposition: "It is possible to construct a figure with three straight lines," and endeavour, in like manner, to deduce it from the mere conception of a straight line and the number three. All your endeavours are in vain, and you find yourself forced to have recourse to intuition, as, in fact, geometry always does. You therefore give yourself an object in intuition. But of what kind is this intuition? Is it a pure à priori, or is it an empirical intuition? If the latter, then neither an universally valid, much less an apodeictic proposition can arise from it, for experience never can give us any such proposition. You must, therefore, give yourself an object à priori in intuition, and upon that ground your synthetical proposition. Now if there did not exist within you a faculty of intuition à priori; if this subjective condition were not in respect to its form also the universal condition à priori under which alone the object of this external intuition is itself possible; if the object (that is, the triangle) were something in itself, without relation to you the subject; how could you affirm that that which lies necessarily in your subjective conditions in order to construct a triangle, must also necessarily belong to the triangle in itself? For to your conceptions of three lines, you could not add anything new (that is, the figure); which, therefore, must necessarily be found in the object, because the object is given before your cognition, and not by means of it. If, therefore, space (and time also) were not a mere form of your intuition, which contains conditions à priori, under which alone things can become external objects for you, and without which subjective conditions the objects are in themselves nothing, you could not construct any synthetical proposition whatsoever regarding external objects. It is therefore not merely possible or probable, but indubitably certain, that space and time, as the necessary conditions of all our external and internal experience, are merely subjective conditions of all our intuitions, in relation to which all objects are therefore mere phenomena, and not things in themselves, presented to us in this particular manner. And for this reason, in respect to the form of phenomena, much may be said à priori, whilst of the thing in itself, which may lie at the foundation of these phenomena, it is impossible to say anything.

II. In confirmation of this theory of the ideality of the external as well as internal sense, consequently of all objects of sense, as mere phenomena, we may especially remark that all in our cognition that belongs to intuition contains nothing more than mere relations. (The feelings of pain and pleasure, and the will, which are not cognitions, are excepted.) The relations, to wit, of place in an intuition (extension), change of place (motion), and laws according to which this change is determined (moving forces). That, however, which is present in this or that place, or any operation going on, or result taking place in the things themselves, with the exception of change of place, is not given to us by intuition. Now by means of mere relations, a thing cannot be known in itself; and it may therefore be fairly concluded, that, as through the external sense nothing but mere representations of relations are given us, the said external sense in its representation can contain only the relation of the object to the subject, but not the essential nature of the object as a thing in itself.

The same is the case with the internal intuition, not only because, in the internal intuition, the representation of the external senses constitutes the material with which the mind is occupied; but because time, in which we place, and which itself antecedes the consciousness of, these representations in experience, and which, as the formal condition of the mode according to which objects are placed in the mind, lies at the foundation of them, contains relations of the successive, the coexistent, and of that which always must be coexistent with succession, the permanent. Now that which, as representation, can antecede every exercise of thought (of an object), is intuition; and when it contains nothing but relations, it is the form of the intuition, which, as it presents us with no representation, except in so far as something is placed in the mind, can be nothing else than the mode in which the mind is affected by its own activity, to wit—its presenting to itself representations, consequently the mode in which the mind is affected by itself; that is, it can be nothing but an internal sense in respect to its form. Everything that is represented through the medium of sense is so far phenomenal; consequently, we must either refuse altogether to admit an internal sense, or the subject, which is the object of that sense, could only be represented by it as phenomenon, and not as it would judge of itself, if its intuition were pure spontaneous activity, that is, were intellectual. The difficulty here lies wholly in the question: How can the subject have an internal intuition of itself? But this difficulty is common to every theory. The consciousness of self (apperception) is the simple representation of the "ego"; and if by means of that representation alone, all the manifold representations in the subject were spontaneously given, then our internal intuition would be intellectual. This consciousness in man requires an internal perception of the manifold representations which are previously given in the subject; and the manner in which these representations are given in the mind without spontaneity, must, on account of this difference (the want of spontaneity), be called sensibility. If the faculty of self-consciousness is to apprehend what lies in the mind, it must all act that and can in this way alone produce an intuition of self. But the form of this intuition, which lies in the original constitution of the mind, determines, in the representation of time, the manner in which the manifold representations are to combine themselves in the mind; since the subject intuites itself, not as it would represent itself immediately and spontaneously, but according to the manner in which the mind is internally affected, consequently, as it appears, and not as it is.

III. When we say that the intuition of external objects, and also the self-intuition of the subject, represent both, objects and subject, in space and time, as they affect our senses, that is, as they appear—this is by no means equivalent to asserting that these objects are mere illusory appearances. For when we speak of things as phenomena, the objects, nay, even the properties which we ascribe to them, are looked upon as really given; only that, in so far as this or that property depends upon the mode of intuition of the subject, in the relation of the given object to the subject, the object as phenomenon is to be distinguished from the object as a thing in itself. Thus I do not say that bodies seem or appear to be external to me, or that my soul seems merely to be given in my self-consciousness, although I maintain that the properties of space and time, in conformity to which I set both, as the condition of their existence, abide in my mode of intuition, and not in the objects in themselves. It would be my own fault, if out of that which I should reckon as phenomenon, I made mere illusory appearance.[12] But this will not happen, because of our principle of the ideality of all sensuous intuitions. On the contrary, if we ascribe objective reality to these forms of representation, it becomes impossible to avoid changing everything into mere appearance. For if we regard space and time as properties, which must be found in objects as things in themselves, as sine quibus non of the possibility of their existence, and reflect on the absurdities in which we then find ourselves involved, inasmuch as we are compelled to admit the existence of two infinite things, which are nevertheless not substances, nor anything really inhering in substances, nay, to admit that they are the necessary conditions of the existence of all things, and moreover, that they must continue to exist, although all existing things were annihilated—we cannot blame the good Berkeley for degrading bodies to mere illusory appearances. Nay, even our own existence, which would in this case depend upon the self-existent reality of such a mere nonentity as time, would necessarily be changed with it into mere appearance—an absurdity which no one has as yet been guilty of.

IV. In natural theology, where we think of an object—God—which never can be an object of intuition to us, and even to himself can never be an object of sensuous intuition, we carefully avoid attributing to his intuition the conditions of space and time—and intuition all his cognition must be, and not thought, which always includes limitation. But with what right can we do this if we make them forms of objects as things in themselves, and such, moreover, as would continue to exist as à priori conditions of the existence of things, even though the things themselves were annihilated? For as conditions of all existence in general, space and time must be conditions of the existence of the Supreme Being also. But if we do not thus make them objective forms of all things, there is no other way left than to make them subjective forms of our mode of intuition—external and internal; which is called sensuous, because it is not primitive, that is, is not such as gives in itself the existence of the object of the intuition (a mode of intuition which, so far as we can judge, can belong only to the Creator), but is dependent on the existence of the object, is possible, therefore, only on condition that the representative faculty of the subject is affected by the object.

---

[12] The predicates of the phenomenon can be affixed to the object itself in relation to our sensuous faculty; for example, the red colour or the perfume to the rose. But (illusory) appearance never can be attributed as a predicate to an object, for this very reason, that it attributes to this object in itself that which belongs to it only in relation to our sensuous faculty, or to the subject in general, e.g., the two handles which were formerly ascribed to Saturn. That which is never to be found in the object itself, but always in the relation of the object to the subject, and which moreover is inseparable from our representation of the object, we denominate phenomenon. Thus the predicates of space and time are rightly attributed to objects of the senses as such, and in this there is no illusion. On the contrary, if I ascribe redness of the rose as a thing in itself, or to Saturn his handles, or extension to all external objects, considered as things in themselves, without regarding the determinate relation of these objects to the subject, and without limiting my judgement to that relation—then, and then only, arises illusion.

It is, moreover, not necessary that we should limit the mode of intuition in space and time to the sensuous faculty of man. It may well be that all finite thinking beings must necessarily in this respect agree with man (though as to this we cannot decide), but sensibility does not on account of this universality cease to be sensibility, for this very reason, that it is a deduced (intuitus derivativus), and not an original (intuitus originarius), consequently not an intellectual intuition, and this intuition, as such, for reasons above mentioned, seems to belong solely to the Supreme Being, but never to a being dependent, quoad its existence, as well as its intuition (which its existence determines and limits relatively to given objects). This latter remark, however, must be taken only as an illustration, and not as any proof of the truth of our æsthetical theory.

§ 10. Conclusion of the Transcendental Æsthetic

We have now completely before us one part of the solution of the grand general problem of transcendental philosophy, namely, the question: "How are synthetical propositions à priori possible?" That is to say, we have shown that we are in possession of pure à priori intuitions, namely, space and time, in which we find, when in a judgement à priori we pass out beyond the given conception, something which is not discoverable in that conception, but is certainly found à priori in the intuition which corresponds to the conception, and can be united synthetically with it. But the judgements which these pure intuitions enable us to make, never reach farther than to objects of the senses, and are valid only for objects of possible experience.

SECOND PART
TRANSCENDENTAL LOGIC

INTRODUCTION
Idea of a Transcendental Logic

I. Of Logic in General

Our knowledge springs from two main sources in the mind, first of which is the faculty or power of receiving representations (receptivity for impressions); the second is the power of cognizing by means of these representations (spontaneity in the production of conceptions). Through the first an object is given to us; through the second, it is, in relation to the representation (which is a mere determination of the mind), thought. Intuition and conceptions constitute, therefore, the elements of all our knowledge, so that neither conceptions without an intuition in some way corresponding to them, nor intuition without conceptions, can afford us a cognition. Both are either pure or empirical. They are empirical, when sensation (which presupposes the actual presence of the object) is contained in them; and pure, when no sensation is mixed with the representation. Sensations we may call the matter of sensuous cognition. Pure intuition consequently contains merely the form under which something is intuited, and pure conception only the form of the thought of an object. Only pure intuitions and pure conceptions are possible à priori; the empirical only à posteriori.

We apply the term sensibility to the receptivity of the mind for impressions, in so far as it is in some way affected; and, on the other hand, we call the faculty of spontaneously producing representations, or the spontaneity of cognition, understanding. Our nature is so constituted that intuition with us never can be other than sensuous, that is, it contains only the mode in which we are affected by objects. On the other hand, the faculty of thinking the object of sensuous intuition is the understanding. Neither of these faculties has a preference over the other. Without the sensuous faculty no object would be given to us, and without the understanding no object would be thought. Thoughts without content are void; intuitions without conceptions, blind. Hence it is as necessary for the mind to make its conceptions sensuous (that is, to join to them the object in intuition), as to make its intuitions intelligible (that is, to bring them under conceptions). Neither of these faculties can exchange its proper function. Understanding cannot intuite, and the sensuous faculty cannot think. In no other way than from the united operation of both, can knowledge arise. But no one ought, on this account, to overlook the difference of the elements contributed by each; we have rather great reason carefully to separate and distinguish them. We therefore distinguish the science of the laws of sensibility, that is, æsthetic, from the science of the laws of the understanding, that is, logic.

Now, logic in its turn may be considered as twofold—namely, as logic of the general, or of the particular use of the understanding. The first contains the absolutely necessary laws of thought, without which no use whatsoever of the understanding is possible, and gives laws therefore to the understanding, without regard to the difference of objects on which it may be employed. The logic of the particular use of the understanding contains the laws of correct thinking upon a particular class of objects. The former may be called elemental logic—the latter, the organon of this or that particular science. The latter is for the most part employed in the schools, as a propædeutic to the sciences, although, indeed, according to the course of human reason, it is the last thing we arrive at, when the science has been already matured, and needs only the finishing touches towards its correction and completion; for our knowledge of the objects of our attempted science must be tolerably extensive and complete before we can indicate the laws by which a science of these objects can be established.

General logic is again either pure or applied. In the former, we abstract all the empirical conditions under which the understanding is exercised; for example, the influence of the senses, the play of the fantasy or imagination, the laws of the memory, the force of habit, of inclination, etc., consequently also, the sources of prejudice—in a word, we abstract all causes from which particular cognitions arise, because these causes regard the understanding under certain circumstances of its application, and, to the knowledge of them experience is required. Pure general logic has to do, therefore, merely with pure à priori principles, and is a canon of understanding and reason, but only in respect of the formal part of their use, be the content what it may, empirical or transcendental. General logic is called applied, when it is directed to the laws of the use of the understanding, under the subjective empirical conditions which psychology teaches us. It has therefore empirical principles, although, at the same time, it is in so far general, that it applies to the exercise of the understanding, without regard to the difference of objects. On this account, moreover, it is neither a canon of the understanding in general, nor an organon of a particular science, but merely a cathartic of the human understanding.

In general logic, therefore, that part which constitutes pure logic must be carefully distinguished from that which constitutes applied (though still general) logic. The former alone is properly science, although short and dry, as the methodical exposition of an elemental doctrine of the understanding ought to be. In this, therefore, logicians must always bear in mind two rules:

1. As general logic, it makes abstraction of all content of the cognition of the understanding, and of the difference of objects, and has to do with nothing but the mere form of thought.

2. As pure logic, it has no empirical principles, and consequently draws nothing (contrary to the common persuasion) from psychology, which therefore has no influence on the canon of the understanding. It is a demonstrated doctrine, and everything in it must be certain completely à priori.

What I called applied logic (contrary to the common acceptation of this term, according to which it should contain certain exercises for the scholar, for which pure logic gives the rules), is a representation of the understanding, and of the rules of its necessary employment in concreto, that is to say, under the accidental conditions of the subject, which may either hinder or promote this employment, and which are all given only empirically. Thus applied logic treats of attention, its impediments and consequences, of the origin of error, of the state of doubt, hesitation, conviction, etc., and to it is related pure general logic in the same way that pure morality, which contains only the necessary moral laws of a free will, is related to practical ethics, which considers these laws under all the impediments of feelings, inclinations, and passions to which men are more or less subjected, and which never can furnish us with a true and demonstrated science, because it, as well as applied logic, requires empirical and psychological principles.

II. Of Transcendental Logic

General logic, as we have seen, makes abstraction of all content of cognition, that is, of all relation of cognition to its object, and regards only the logical form in the relation of cognitions to each other, that is, the form of thought in general. But as we have both pure and empirical intuitions (as transcendental æsthetic proves), in like manner a distinction might be drawn between pure and empirical thought (of objects). In this case, there would exist a kind of logic, in which we should not make abstraction of all content of cognition; for or logic which should comprise merely the laws of pure thought (of an object), would of course exclude all those cognitions which were of empirical content. This kind of logic would also examine the origin of our cognitions of objects, so far as that origin cannot be ascribed to the objects themselves; while, on the contrary, general logic has nothing to do with the origin of our cognitions, but contemplates our representations, be they given primitively à priori in ourselves, or be they only of empirical origin, solely according to the laws which the understanding observes in employing them in the process of thought, in relation to each other. Consequently, general logic treats of the form of the understanding only, which can be applied to representations, from whatever source they may have arisen.

And here I shall make a remark, which the reader must bear well in mind in the course of the following considerations, to wit, that not every cognition à priori, but only those through which we cognize that and how certain representations (intuitions or conceptions) are applied or are possible only à priori; that is to say, the à priori possibility of cognition and the à priori use of it are transcendental. Therefore neither is space, nor any à priori geometrical determination of space, a transcendental Representation, but only the knowledge that such a representation is not of empirical origin, and the possibility of its relating to objects of experience, although itself à priori, can be called transcendental. So also, the application of space to objects in general would be transcendental; but if it be limited to objects of sense it is empirical. Thus, the distinction of the transcendental and empirical belongs only to the critique of cognitions, and does not concern the relation of these to their object.

Accordingly, in the expectation that there may perhaps be conceptions which relate à priori to objects, not as pure or sensuous intuitions, but merely as acts of pure thought (which are therefore conceptions, but neither of empirical nor æsthetical origin)—in this expectation, I say, we form to ourselves, by anticipation, the idea of a science of pure understanding and rational cognition, by means of which we may cogitate objects entirely à priori. A science of this kind, which should determine the origin, the extent, and the objective validity of such cognitions, must be called transcendental logic, because it has not, like general logic, to do with the laws of understanding and reason in relation to empirical as well as pure rational cognitions without distinction, but concerns itself with these only in an à priori relation to objects.

III. Of the Division of General Logic into Analytic and Dialectic

The old question with which people sought to push logicians into a corner, so that they must either have recourse to pitiful sophisms or confess their ignorance, and consequently the vanity of their whole art, is this: "What is truth?" The definition of the word truth, to wit, "the accordance of the cognition with its object," is presupposed in the question; but we desire to be told, in the answer to it, what is the universal and secure criterion of the truth of every cognition.

To know what questions we may reasonably propose is in itself a strong evidence of sagacity and intelligence. For if a question be in itself absurd and unsusceptible of a rational answer, it is attended with the danger—not to mention the shame that falls upon the person who proposes it—of seducing the unguarded listener into making absurd answers, and we are presented with the ridiculous spectacle of one (as the ancients said) "milking the he-goat, and the other holding a sieve."

If truth consists in the accordance of a cognition with its object, this object must be, ipso facto, distinguished from all others; for a cognition is false if it does not accord with the object to which it relates, although it contains something which may be affirmed of other objects. Now an universal criterion of truth would be that which is valid for all cognitions, without distinction of their objects. But it is evident that since, in the case of such a criterion, we make abstraction of all the content of a cognition (that is, of all relation to its object), and truth relates precisely to this content, it must be utterly absurd to ask for a mark of the truth of this content of cognition; and that, accordingly, a sufficient, and at the same time universal, test of truth cannot possibly be found. As we have already termed the content of a cognition its matter, we shall say: "Of the truth of our cognitions in respect of their matter, no universal test can be demanded, because such a demand is self-contradictory."

On the other hand, with regard to our cognition in respect of its mere form (excluding all content), it is equally manifest that logic, in so far as it exhibits the universal and necessary laws of the understanding, must in these very laws present us with criteria of truth. Whatever contradicts these rules is false, because thereby the understanding is made to contradict its own universal laws of thought; that is, to contradict itself. These criteria, however, apply solely to the form of truth, that is, of thought in general, and in so far they are perfectly accurate, yet not sufficient. For although a cognition may be perfectly accurate as to logical form, that is, not self-contradictory, it is notwithstanding quite possible that it may not stand in agreement with its object. Consequently, the merely logical criterion of truth, namely, the accordance of a cognition with the universal and formal laws of understanding and reason, is nothing more than the conditio sine qua non, or negative condition of all truth. Farther than this logic cannot go, and the error which depends not on the form, but on the content of the cognition, it has no test to discover.

General logic, then, resolves the whole formal business of understanding and reason into its elements, and exhibits them as principles of all logical judging of our cognitions. This part of logic may, therefore, be called analytic, and is at least the negative test of truth, because all cognitions must first of an be estimated and tried according to these laws before we proceed to investigate them in respect of their content, in order to discover whether they contain positive truth in regard to their object. Because, however, the mere form of a cognition, accurately as it may accord with logical laws, is insufficient to supply us with material (objective) truth, no one, by means of logic alone, can venture to predicate anything of or decide concerning objects, unless he has obtained, independently of logic, well-grounded information about them, in order afterwards to examine, according to logical laws, into the use and connection, in a cohering whole, of that information, or, what is still better, merely to test it by them. Notwithstanding, there lies so seductive a charm in the possession of a specious art like this—an art which gives to all our cognitions the form of the understanding, although with respect to the content thereof we may be sadly deficient—that general logic, which is merely a canon of judgement, has been employed as an organon for the actual production, or rather for the semblance of production, of objective assertions, and has thus been grossly misapplied. Now general logic, in its assumed character of organon, is called dialectic.

Different as are the significations in which the ancients used this term for a science or an art, we may safely infer, from their actual employment of it, that with them it was nothing else than a logic of illusion—a sophistical art for giving ignorance, nay, even intentional sophistries, the colouring of truth, in which the thoroughness of procedure which logic requires was imitated, and their topic employed to cloak the empty pretensions. Now it may be taken as a safe and useful warning, that general logic, considered as an organon, must always be a logic of illusion, that is, be dialectical, for, as it teaches us nothing whatever respecting the content of our cognitions, but merely the formal conditions of their accordance with the understanding, which do not relate to and are quite indifferent in respect of objects, any attempt to employ it as an instrument (organon) in order to extend and enlarge the range of our knowledge must end in mere prating; any one being able to maintain or oppose, with some appearance of truth, any single assertion whatever.

Such instruction is quite unbecoming the dignity of philosophy. For these reasons we have chosen to denominate this part of logic dialectic, in the sense of a critique of dialectical illusion, and we wish the term to be so understood in this place.

IV. Of the Division of Transcendental Logic into Transcendental Analytic and Dialectic

In transcendental logic we isolate the understanding (as in transcendental æsthetic the sensibility) and select from our cognition merely that part of thought which has its origin in the understanding alone. The exercise of this pure cognition, however, depends upon this as its condition, that objects to which it may be applied be given to us in intuition, for without intuition the whole of our cognition is without objects, and is therefore quite void. That part of transcendental logic, then, which treats of the elements of pure cognition of the understanding, and of the principles without which no object at all can be thought, is transcendental analytic, and at the same time a logic of truth. For no cognition can contradict it, without losing at the same time all content, that is, losing all reference to an object, and therefore all truth. But because we are very easily seduced into employing these pure cognitions and principles of the understanding by themselves, and that even beyond the boundaries of experience, which yet is the only source whence we can obtain matter (objects) on which those pure conceptions may be employed—understanding runs the risk of making, by means of empty sophisms, a material and objective use of the mere formal principles of the pure understanding, and of passing judgements on objects without distinction—objects which are not given to us, nay, perhaps cannot be given to us in any way. Now, as it ought properly to be only a canon for judging of the empirical use of the understanding, this kind of logic is misused when we seek to employ it as an organon of the universal and unlimited exercise of the understanding, and attempt with the pure understanding alone to judge synthetically, affirm, and determine respecting objects in general.

In this case the exercise of the pure understanding becomes dialectical. The second part of our transcendental logic must therefore be a critique of dialectical illusion, and this critique we shall term transcendental dialectic—not meaning it as an art of producing dogmatically such illusion (an art which is unfortunately too current among the practitioners of metaphysical juggling), but as a critique of understanding and reason in regard to their hyperphysical use. This critique will expose the groundless nature of the pretensions of these two faculties, and invalidate their claims to the discovery and enlargement of our cognitions merely by means of transcendental principles, and show that the proper employment of these faculties is to test the judgements made by the pure understanding, and to guard it from sophistical delusion.

FIRST DIVISION

TRANSCENDENTAL LOGIC

TRANSCENDENTAL ANALYTIC. § 1

Transcendental analytic is the dissection of the whole of our à priori knowledge into the elements of the pure cognition of the understanding. In order to effect our purpose, it is necessary: (1) That the conceptions be pure and not empirical; (2) That they belong not to intuition and sensibility, but to thought and understanding; (3) That they be elementary conceptions, and as such, quite different from deduced or compound conceptions; (4) That our table of these elementary conceptions be complete, and fill up the whole sphere of the pure understanding. Now this completeness of a science cannot be accepted with confidence on the guarantee of a mere estimate of its existence in an aggregate formed only by means of repeated experiments and attempts. The completeness which we require is possible only by means of an idea of the totality of the à priori cognition of the understanding, and through the thereby determined division of the conceptions which form the said whole; consequently, only by means of their connection in a system. Pure understanding distinguishes itself not merely from everything empirical, but also completely from all sensibility. It is a unity self-subsistent, self-sufficient, and not to be enlarged by any additions from without. Hence the sum of its cognition constitutes a system to be determined by and comprised under an idea; and the completeness and articulation of this system can at the same time serve as a test of the correctness and genuineness of all the parts of cognition that belong to it. The whole of this part of transcendental logic consists of two books, of which the one contains the conceptions, and the other the principles of pure understanding.

BOOK I

Analytic of Conceptions. § 2

By the term Analytic of Conceptions, I do not understand the analysis of these, or the usual process in philosophical investigations of dissecting the conceptions which present themselves, according to their content, and so making them clear; but I mean the hitherto little attempted dissection of the faculty of understanding itself, in order to investigate the possibility of conceptions à priori, by looking for them in the understanding alone, as their birthplace, and analysing the pure use of this faculty. For this is the proper duty of a transcendental philosophy; what remains is the logical treatment of the conceptions in philosophy in general. We shall therefore follow up the pure conceptions even to their germs and beginnings in the human understanding, in which they lie, until they are developed on occasions presented by experience, and, freed by the same understanding from the empirical conditions attaching to them, are set forth in their unalloyed purity.

Chapter I

Of the Transcendental Clue to the Discovery of all Pure Conceptions of the Understanding

Introductory § 3

When we call into play a faculty of cognition, different conceptions manifest themselves according to the different circumstances, and make known this faculty, and assemble themselves into a more or less extensive collection, according to the time or penetration that has been applied to the consideration of them. Where this process, conducted as it is mechanically, so to speak, will end, cannot be determined with certainty. Besides, the conceptions which we discover in this haphazard manner present themselves by no means in order and systematic unity, but are at last coupled together only according to resemblances to each other, and arranged in series, according to the quantity of their content, from the simpler to the more complex—series which are anything but systematic, though not altogether without a certain kind of method in their construction.

Transcendental philosophy has the advantage, and moreover the duty, of searching for its conceptions according to a principle; because these conceptions spring pure and unmixed out of the understanding as an absolute unity, and therefore must be connected with each other according to one conception or idea. A connection of this kind, however, furnishes us with a ready prepared rule, by which its proper place may be assigned to every pure conception of the understanding, and the completeness of the system of all be determined à priori—both which would otherwise have been dependent on mere choice or chance.

Section I. Of the Logical Use of the Understanding in General § 4

The understanding was defined above only negatively, as a non-sensuous faculty of cognition. Now, independently of sensibility, we cannot possibly have any intuition; consequently, the understanding is no faculty of intuition. But besides intuition there is no other mode of cognition, except through conceptions; consequently, the cognition of every, at least of every human, understanding is a cognition through conceptions—not intuitive, but discursive. All intuitions, as sensuous, depend on affections; conceptions, therefore, upon functions. By the word function I understand the unity of the act of arranging diverse representations under one common representation. Conceptions, then, are based on the spontaneity of thought, as sensuous intuitions are on the receptivity of impressions. Now, the understanding cannot make any other use of these conceptions than to judge by means of them. As no representation, except an intuition, relates immediately to its object, a conception never relates immediately to an object, but only to some other representation thereof, be that an intuition or itself a conception. A judgement, therefore, is the mediate cognition of an object, consequently the representation of a representation of it. In every judgement there is a conception which applies to, and is valid for many other conceptions, and which among these comprehends also a given representation, this last being immediately connected with an object. For example, in the judgement—"All bodies are divisible," our conception of divisible applies to various other conceptions; among these, however, it is here particularly applied to the conception of body, and this conception of body relates to certain phenomena which occur to us. These objects, therefore, are mediately represented by the conception of divisibility. All judgements, accordingly, are functions of unity in our representations, inasmuch as, instead of an immediate, a higher representation, which comprises this and various others, is used for our cognition of the object, and thereby many possible cognitions are collected into one. But we can reduce all acts of the understanding to judgements, so that understanding may be represented as the faculty of judging. For it is, according to what has been said above, a faculty of thought. Now thought is cognition by means of conceptions. But conceptions, as predicates of possible judgements, relate to some representation of a yet undetermined object. Thus the conception of body indicates something—for example, metal—which can be cognized by means of that conception. It is therefore a conception, for the reason alone that other representations are contained under it, by means of which it can relate to objects. It is therefore the predicate to a possible judgement; for example: "Every metal is a body." All the functions of the understanding therefore can be discovered, when we can completely exhibit the functions of unity in judgements. And that this may be effected very easily, the following section will show.

Section II. Of the Logical Function of the Understanding in Judgements § 5

If we abstract all the content of a judgement, and consider only the intellectual form thereof, we find that the function of thought in a judgement can be brought under four heads, of which each contains three momenta. These may be conveniently represented in the following table:

1

Quantity of judgements

Universal

Particular

Singular

2		3
Quality		*Relation*
Affirmative		Categorical
Negative		Hypothetical
Infinite		Disjunctive
	4	
	Modality	
	Problematical	
	Assertorical	
	Apodeictical	

As this division appears to differ in some, though not essential points, from the usual technique of logicians, the following observations, for the prevention of otherwise possible misunderstanding, will not be without their use.

1. Logicians say, with justice, that in the use of judgements in syllogisms, singular judgements may be treated like universal ones. For, precisely because a singular judgement has no extent at all, its predicate cannot refer to a part of that which is contained in the conception of the subject and be excluded from the rest. The predicate is valid for the whole conception just as if it were a general conception, and had extent, to the whole of which the predicate applied. On the other hand, let us compare a singular with a general judgement, merely as a cognition, in regard to quantity. The singular judgement relates to the general one, as unity to infinity, and is therefore in itself essentially different. Thus, if we estimate a singular judgement (*judicium singulare*) not merely according to its intrinsic validity as a judgement, but also as a cognition generally, according to its quantity in comparison with that of other cognitions, it is then entirely different from a general judgement (*judicium commune*), and in a complete table of the momenta of thought deserves a separate place—though, indeed, this would not be necessary in a logic limited merely to the consideration of the use of judgements in reference to each other.

2. In like manner, in transcendental logic, infinite must be distinguished from affirmative judgements, although in general logic they are rightly enough classed under affirmative. General logic abstracts all content of the predicate (though it be negative), and only considers whether the said predicate be affirmed or denied of the subject. But transcendental logic considers also the worth or content of this logical affirmation—an affirmation by means of a merely negative predicate, and inquires how much the sum total of our cognition gains by this affirmation. For example, if I say of the soul, "It is not mortal"—by this negative judgement I should at least ward off error. Now, by the proposition, "The soul is not mortal," I have, in respect of the logical form, really affirmed, inasmuch as I thereby place the soul in the unlimited sphere of immortal beings. Now, because of the whole sphere of possible existences, the mortal occupies one part, and the immortal the other, neither more nor less is affirmed by the proposition than that the soul is one among

the infinite multitude of things which remain over, when I take away the whole mortal part. But by this proceeding we accomplish only this much, that the infinite sphere of all possible existences is in so far limited that the mortal is excluded from it, and the soul is placed in the remaining part of the extent of this sphere. But this part remains, notwithstanding this exception, infinite, and more and more parts may be taken away from the whole sphere, without in the slightest degree thereby augmenting or affirmatively determining our conception of the soul. These judgements, therefore, infinite in respect of their logical extent, are, in respect of the content of their cognition, merely limitative; and are consequently entitled to a place in our transcendental table of all the momenta of thought in judgements, because the function of the understanding exercised by them may perhaps be of importance in the field of its pure à priori cognition.

3. All relations of thought in judgements are those (a) of the predicate to the subject; (b) of the principle to its consequence; (c) of the divided cognition and all the members of the division to each other. In the first of these three classes, we consider only two conceptions; in the second, two judgements; in the third, several judgements in relation to each other. The hypothetical proposition, "If perfect justice exists, the obstinately wicked are punished," contains properly the relation to each other of two propositions, namely, "Perfect justice exists," and "The obstinately wicked are punished." Whether these propositions are in themselves true is a question not here decided. Nothing is cogitated by means of this judgement except a certain consequence. Finally, the disjunctive judgement contains a relation of two or more propositions to each other—a relation not of consequence, but of logical opposition, in so far as the sphere of the one proposition excludes that of the other. But it contains at the same time a relation of community, in so far as all the propositions taken together fill up the sphere of the cognition. The disjunctive judgement contains, therefore, the relation of the parts of the whole sphere of a cognition, since the sphere of each part is a complemental part of the sphere of the other, each contributing to form the sum total of the divided cognition. Take, for example, the proposition, "The world exists either through blind chance, or through internal necessity, or through an external cause." Each of these propositions embraces a part of the sphere of our possible cognition as to the existence of a world; all of them taken together, the whole sphere. To take the cognition out of one of these spheres, is equivalent to placing it in one of the others; and, on the other hand, to place it in one sphere is equivalent to taking it out of the rest. There is, therefore, in a disjunctive judgement a certain community of cognitions, which consists in this, that they mutually exclude each other, yet thereby determine, as a whole, the true cognition, inasmuch as, taken together, they make up the complete content of a particular given cognition. And this is all that I find necessary, for the sake of what follows, to remark in this place.

4. The modality of judgements is a quite peculiar function, with this distinguishing characteristic, that it contributes nothing to the content of a

judgement (for besides quantity, quality, and relation, there is nothing more that constitutes the content of a judgement), but concerns itself only with the value of the copula in relation to thought in general. Problematical judgements are those in which the affirmation or negation is accepted as merely possible (ad libitum). In the assertorical, we regard the proposition as real (true); in the apodeictical, we look on it as necessary.[13] Thus the two judgements (antecedens et consequens), the relation of which constitutes a hypothetical judgement, likewise those (the members of the division) in whose reciprocity the disjunctive consists, are only problematical. In the example above given the proposition, "There exists perfect justice," is not stated assertorically, but as an ad libitum judgement, which someone may choose to adopt, and the consequence alone is assertorical. Hence such judgements may be obviously false, and yet, taken problematically, be conditions of our cognition of the truth. Thus the proposition, "The world exists only by blind chance," is in the disjunctive judgement of problematical import only: that is to say, one may accept it for the moment, and it helps us (like the indication of the wrong road among all the roads that one can take) to find out the true proposition. The problematical proposition is, therefore, that which expresses only logical possibility (which is not objective); that is, it expresses a free choice to admit the validity of such a proposition—a merely arbitrary reception of it into the understanding. The assertorical speaks of logical reality or truth; as, for example, in a hypothetical syllogism, the antecedens presents itself in a problematical form in the major, in an assertorical form in the minor, and it shows that the proposition is in harmony with the laws of the understanding. The apodeictical proposition cogitates the assertorical as determined by these very laws of the understanding, consequently as affirming à priori, and in this manner it expresses logical necessity. Now because all is here gradually incorporated with the understanding—inasmuch as in the first place we judge problematically; then accept assertorically our judgement as true; lastly, affirm it as inseparably united with the understanding, that is, as necessary and apodeictical—we may safely reckon these three functions of modality as so many momenta of thought.

Section III. Of the Pure Conceptions of the Understanding, or Categories § 6

General logic, as has been repeatedly said, makes abstraction of all content of cognition, and expects to receive representations from some other quarter, in order, by means of analysis, to convert them into conceptions. On the contrary, transcendental logic has lying before it the manifold content of à priori sensibility, which transcendental æsthetic presents to it in order to give matter to the pure conceptions of the understanding, without which transcendental logic would have

[13] Just as if thought were in the first instance a function of the understanding; in the second, of judgement; in the third, of reason. A remark which will be explained in the sequel.

no content, and be therefore utterly void. Now space and time contain an infinite diversity of determinations of pure à priori intuition, but are nevertheless the condition of the mind's receptivity, under which alone it can obtain representations of objects, and which, consequently, must always affect the conception of these objects. But the spontaneity of thought requires that this diversity be examined after a certain manner, received into the mind, and connected, in order afterwards to form a cognition out of it. This Process I call synthesis.

By the word synthesis, in its most general signification, I understand the process of joining different representations to each other and of comprehending their diversity in one cognition. This synthesis is pure when the diversity is not given empirically but à priori (as that in space and time). Our representations must be given previously to any analysis of them; and no conceptions can arise, quoad their content, analytically. But the synthesis of a diversity (be it given à priori or empirically) is the first requisite for the production of a cognition, which in its beginning, indeed, may be crude and confused, and therefore in need of analysis—still, synthesis is that by which alone the elements of our cognitions are collected and united into a certain content, consequently it is the first thing on which we must fix our attention, if we wish to investigate the origin of our knowledge.

Synthesis, generally speaking, is, as we shall afterwards see, the mere operation of the imagination—a blind but indispensable function of the soul, without which we should have no cognition whatever, but of the working of which we are seldom even conscious. But to reduce this synthesis to conceptions is a function of the understanding, by means of which we attain to cognition, in the proper meaning of the term.

Pure synthesis, represented generally, gives us the pure conception of the understanding. But by this pure synthesis, I mean that which rests upon a basis of à priori synthetical unity. Thus, our numeration (and this is more observable in large numbers) is a synthesis according to conceptions, because it takes place according to a common basis of unity (for example, the decade). By means of this conception, therefore, the unity in the synthesis of the manifold becomes necessary.

By means of analysis different representations are brought under one conception—an operation of which general logic treats. On the other hand, the duty of transcendental logic is to reduce to conceptions, not representations, but the pure synthesis of representations. The first thing which must be given to us for the sake of the à priori cognition of all objects, is the diversity of the pure intuition; the synthesis of this diversity by means of the imagination is the second; but this gives, as yet, no cognition. The conceptions which give unity to this pure synthesis, and which consist solely in the representation of this necessary synthetical unity, furnish the third requisite for the cognition of an object, and these conceptions are given by the understanding.

The same function which gives unity to the different representation in a judgement, gives also unity to the mere synthesis of different representations in an intuition; and this unity we call the pure conception of the understanding. Thus, the same understanding, and by the same operations, whereby in conceptions, by means of analytical unity, it produced the logical form of a judgement, introduces, by means of the synthetical unity of the manifold in intuition, a transcendental content into its representations, on which account they are called pure conceptions of the understanding, and they apply à priori to objects, a result not within the power of general logic.

In this manner, there arise exactly so many pure conceptions of the understanding, applying à priori to objects of intuition in general, as there are logical functions in all possible judgements. For there is no other function or faculty existing in the understanding besides those enumerated in that table. These conceptions we shall, with Aristotle, call categories, our purpose being originally identical with his, notwithstanding the great difference in the execution.

TABLE OF THE CATEGORIES

1
Of Quantity
Unity
Plurality
Totality

2
Of Quality
Reality
Negation
Limitation

3
Of Relation
Of Inherence and Subsistence (substantia et accidens)
Of Causality and Dependence (cause and effect)
Of Community (reciprocity between the agent and patient)

4
Of Modality
Possibility—Impossibility
Existence—Non-existence
Necessity—Contingence

This, then, is a catalogue of all the originally pure conceptions of the synthesis which the understanding contains à priori, and these conceptions alone entitle it to be called a pure understanding; inasmuch as only by them it can render the manifold of intuition conceivable, in other words, think an object of intuition. This division is made systematically from a common principle, namely the faculty of judgement (which is just the same as the power of thought), and has not arisen rhapsodically from a search at haphazard after pure conceptions, respecting the full number of which we never could be certain, inasmuch as we employ induction alone in our search, without considering that in this way we can never understand wherefore precisely these conceptions, and none others, abide in the pure understanding. It was a design worthy of an acute thinker like Aristotle, to search for these fundamental conceptions. Destitute, however, of any guiding principle, he picked them up just as they occurred to him, and at first hunted out ten, which he called categories (predicaments). Afterwards be believed that he had discovered five others, which were added under the name of post predicaments. But his catalogue still remained defective. Besides, there are to be found among them some of the modes of pure sensibility (quando, ubi, situs, also prius, simul), and likewise an empirical conception (motus)—which can by no means belong to this genealogical register of the pure understanding. Moreover, there are deduced conceptions (actio, passio) enumerated among the original conceptions, and, of the latter, some are entirely wanting.

With regard to these, it is to be remarked, that the categories, as the true primitive conceptions of the pure understanding, have also their pure deduced conceptions, which, in a complete system of transcendental philosophy, must by no means be passed over; though in a merely critical essay we must be contented with the simple mention of the fact.

Let it be allowed me to call these pure, but deduced conceptions of the understanding, the predicables of the pure understanding, in contradistinction to predicaments. If we are in possession of the original and primitive, the deduced and subsidiary conceptions can easily be added, and the genealogical tree of the understanding completely delineated. As my present aim is not to set forth a complete system, but merely the principles of one, I reserve this task for another time. It may be easily executed by any one who will refer to the ontological manuals, and subordinate to the category of causality, for example, the predicables of force, action, passion; to that of community, those of presence and resistance; to the categories of modality, those of origination, extinction, change; and so with the rest. The categories combined with the modes of pure sensibility, or with one another, afford a great number of deduced à priori conceptions; a complete enumeration of which would be a useful and not unpleasant, but in this place a perfectly dispensable, occupation.

I purposely omit the definitions of the categories in this treatise. I shall analyse these conceptions only so far as is necessary for the doctrine of method, which is to form a part of this critique. In a system of pure reason, definitions of them would be with justice demanded of me, but to give them here would only bide from our view the main aim of our investigation, at the same time raising doubts and objections, the consideration of which, without injustice to our main purpose, may be very well postponed till another opportunity. Meanwhile, it ought to be sufficiently clear, from the little we have already said on this subject, that the formation of a complete vocabulary of pure conceptions, accompanied by all the requisite explanations, is not only a possible, but an easy undertaking. The compartments already exist; it is only necessary to fill them up; and a systematic topic like the present, indicates with perfect precision the proper place to which each conception belongs, while it readily points out any that have not yet been filled up.

§ 7

Our table of the categories suggests considerations of some importance, which may perhaps have significant results in regard to the scientific form of all rational cognitions. For, that this table is useful in the theoretical part of philosophy, nay, indispensable for the sketching of the complete plan of a science, so far as that science rests upon conceptions à priori, and for dividing it mathematically, according to fixed principles, is most manifest from the fact that it contains all the elementary conceptions of the understanding, nay, even the form of a system of these in the understanding itself, and consequently indicates all the momenta, and also the internal arrangement of a projected speculative science, as I have elsewhere shown.[14] Here follow some of these observations.

I. This table, which contains four classes of conceptions of the understanding, may, in the first instance, be divided into two classes, the first of which relates to objects of intuition—pure as well as empirical; the second, to the existence of these objects, either in relation to one another, or to the understanding.

The former of these classes of categories I would entitle the mathematical, and the latter the dynamical categories. The former, as we see, has no correlates; these are only to be found in the second class. This difference must have a ground in the nature of the human understanding.

II. The number of the categories in each class is always the same, namely, three—a fact which also demands some consideration, because in all other cases division à priori through conceptions is necessarily dichotomy. It is to be added, that the third category in each triad always arises from the combination of the second with the first.

Thus totality is nothing else but plurality contemplated as unity; limitation is merely reality conjoined with negation; community is the causality of a substance, reciprocally determining, and determined by other substances; and finally, necessity is nothing but existence, which is given through the possibility itself. Let it not be supposed, however, that the third category is merely a deduced, and not a primitive conception of the pure understanding. For the conjunction of the first and second, in order to produce the third conception, requires a particular function of the understanding, which is by no means identical with those which are exercised in the first and second. Thus, the conception of a number (which belongs to the category of totality) is not always possible, where the conceptions of multitude and unity exist (for example, in the representation of the infinite). Or, if I conjoin the conception of a cause with that of a substance, it does not follow

[14] In the "Metaphysical Principles of Natural Science."

that the conception of influence, that is, how one substance can be the cause of something in another substance, will be understood from that. Thus it is evident that a particular act of the understanding is here necessary; and so in the other instances.

III. With respect to one category, namely, that of community, which is found in the third class, it is not so easy as with the others to detect its accordance with the form of the disjunctive judgement which corresponds to it in the table of the logical functions.

In order to assure ourselves of this accordance, we must observe that in every disjunctive judgement, the sphere of the judgement (that is, the complex of all that is contained in it) is represented as a whole divided into parts; and, since one part cannot be contained in the other, they are cogitated as co-ordinated with, not subordinated to each other, so that they do not determine each other unilaterally, as in a linear series, but reciprocally, as in an aggregate—(if one member of the division is posited, all the rest are excluded; and conversely).

Now a like connection is cogitated in a whole of things; for one thing is not subordinated, as effect, to another as cause of its existence, but, on the contrary, is co-ordinated contemporaneously and reciprocally, as a cause in relation to the determination of the others (for example, in a body—the parts of which mutually attract and repel each other). And this is an entirely different kind of connection from that which we find in the mere relation of the cause to the effect (the principle to the consequence), for in such a connection the consequence does not in its turn determine the principle, and therefore does not constitute, with the latter, a whole—just as the Creator does not with the world make up a whole. The process of understanding by which it represents to itself the sphere of a divided conception, is employed also when we think of a thing as divisible; and in the same manner as the members of the division in the former exclude one another, and yet are connected in one sphere, so the understanding represents to itself the parts of the latter, as having—each of them—an existence (as substances), independently of the others, and yet as united in one whole.

§ 8

In the transcendental philosophy of the ancients there exists one more leading division, which contains pure conceptions of the understanding, and which, although not numbered among the categories, ought, according to them, as conceptions à priori, to be valid of objects. But in this case they would augment the number of the categories; which cannot be. These are set forth in the proposition, so renowned among the schoolmen—'*Quodlibet ens est UNUM, VERUM, BONUM*.' Now, though the inferences from this principle were mere tautological propositions, and though it is allowed only by courtesy to retain a place in modern metaphysics, yet a thought which maintained itself for such a length of time, however empty it seems to be, deserves an investigation of its origin, and justifies the conjecture that it must be grounded in some law of the understanding, which, as is often the case, has only been erroneously interpreted. These pretended transcendental predicates are, in fact, nothing but logical requisites and criteria of all cognition of objects, and they employ, as the basis for this cognition, the categories of quantity, namely, unity, plurality, and totality. But these, which must be taken as material conditions, that is, as belonging to the possibility of things themselves, they employed merely in a formal signification, as belonging to the logical requisites of all cognition, and yet most unguardedly changed these criteria of thought into properties of objects, as things in themselves. Now, in every cognition of an object, there is unity of conception, which may be called qualitative unity, so far as by this term we understand only the unity in our connection of the manifold; for example, unity of the theme in a play, an oration, or a story. Secondly, there is truth in respect of the deductions from it. The more true deductions we have from a given conception, the more criteria of its objective reality. This we might call the qualitative plurality of characteristic marks, which belong to a conception as to a common foundation, but are not cogitated as a quantity in it. Thirdly, there is perfection—which consists in this, that the plurality falls back upon the unity of the conception, and accords completely with that conception and with no other. This we may denominate qualitative completeness. Hence it is evident that these logical criteria of the possibility of cognition are merely the three categories of quantity modified and transformed to suit an unauthorized manner of applying them. That is to say, the three categories, in which the unity in the production of the quantum must be homogeneous throughout, are transformed solely with a view to the connection of heterogeneous parts of cognition in one act of consciousness, by means of the quality of the cognition, which is the principle of that connection. Thus the criterion of the possibility of a conception (not of its object) is the definition of it, in which the unity of the conception, the truth of all that may be immediately deduced from it, and finally, the completeness of what has been thus deduced, constitute the requisites for the reproduction of the whole conception. Thus also, the criterion or test of an hypothesis is the intelligibility of the received principle of explanation, or its unity (without help from any subsidiary hypothesis)—the truth of our deductions from it (consistency with each other and with experience)—and lastly, the completeness of the principle of the explanation of these deductions, which refer to neither more nor less than what was admitted in the hypothesis, restoring analytically and à posteriori, what was cogitated synthetically and à priori. By the conceptions, therefore, of unity, truth, and perfection, we have made no addition to the transcendental table of the categories, which is complete without them. We have, on the contrary, merely employed the three categories of quantity, setting aside their application to objects of experience, as general logical laws of the consistency of cognition with itself.

Chapter II

Of the Deduction of the Pure Conceptions of the Understanding

Section I. Of the Principles of a Transcendental Deduction in general § 9

Teachers of jurisprudence, when speaking of rights and claims, distinguish in a cause the question of right (quid juris) from the question of fact (quid facti), and while they demand proof of both, they give to the proof of the former, which goes to establish right or claim in law, the name of deduction. Now we make use of a great number of empirical conceptions, without opposition from any one; and consider ourselves, even without any attempt at deduction, justified in attaching to them a sense, and a supposititious signification, because we have always experience at hand to demonstrate their objective reality. There exist also, however, usurped conceptions, such as fortune, fate, which circulate with almost universal indulgence, and yet are occasionally challenged by the question, "quid juris?" In such cases, we have great difficulty in discovering any deduction for these terms, inasmuch as we cannot produce any manifest ground of right, either from experience or from reason, on which the claim to employ them can be founded.

Among the many conceptions, which make up the very variegated web of human cognition, some are destined for pure use à priori, independent of all experience; and their title to be so employed always requires a deduction, inasmuch as, to justify such use of them, proofs from experience are not sufficient; but it is necessary to know how these conceptions can apply to objects without being derived from experience. I term, therefore, an examination of the manner in which conceptions can apply à priori to objects, the transcendental deduction of conceptions, and I distinguish it from the empirical deduction, which indicates the mode in which conception is obtained through experience and reflection thereon; consequently, does not concern itself with the right, but only with the fact of our obtaining conceptions in such and such a manner. We have already seen that we are in possession of two perfectly different kinds of conceptions, which nevertheless agree with each other in this, that they both apply to objects completely à priori. These are the conceptions of space and time as forms of sensibility, and the categories as pure conceptions of the understanding. To attempt an empirical deduction of either of these classes would be labour in vain, because the distinguishing characteristic of their nature consists in this, that they apply to their objects, without having borrowed anything from experience towards the representation of them. Consequently, if a deduction of these conceptions is necessary, it must always be transcendental.

Meanwhile, with respect to these conceptions, as with respect to all our cognition, we certainly may discover in experience, if not the principle of their possibility, yet the occasioning causes of their production. It will be found that the impressions of sense give the first occasion for bringing into action the whole faculty of cognition, and for the production of experience, which contains two very dissimilar elements, namely, a matter for cognition, given by the senses, and a certain form for the arrangement of this matter, arising out of the inner fountain of pure intuition and thought; and these, on occasion given by sensuous impressions, are called into exercise and produce conceptions. Such an investigation into the first efforts of our faculty of cognition to mount from particular perceptions to general conceptions is undoubtedly of great utility; and we have to thank the celebrated Locke for having first opened the way for this inquiry. But a deduction of the pure à priori conceptions of course never can be made in this way, seeing that, in regard to their future employment, which must be entirely independent of experience, they must have a far different certificate of birth to show from that of a descent from experience. This attempted physiological derivation, which cannot properly be called deduction, because it relates merely to a quaestio facti, I shall entitle an explanation of the possession of a pure cognition. It is therefore manifest that there can only be a transcendental deduction of these conceptions and by no means an empirical one; also, that all attempts at an empirical deduction, in regard to pure à priori conceptions, are vain, and can only be made by one who does not understand the altogether peculiar nature of these cognitions.

But although it is admitted that the only possible deduction of pure à priori cognition is a transcendental deduction, it is not, for that reason, perfectly manifest that such a deduction is absolutely necessary. We have already traced to their sources the conceptions of space and time, by means of a transcendental deduction, and we have explained and determined their objective validity à priori. Geometry, nevertheless, advances steadily and securely in the province of pure à priori cognitions, without needing to ask from philosophy any certificate as to the pure and legitimate origin of its fundamental conception of space. But the use of the conception in this science extends only to the external world of sense, the pure form of the intuition of which is space; and in this world, therefore, all geometrical cognition, because it is founded upon à priori intuition, possesses immediate evidence, and the objects of this cognition are given à priori (as regards their form) in intuition by and through the cognition itself. With the pure conceptions of understanding, on the contrary, commences the absolute necessity of seeking a transcendental deduction, not only of these conceptions themselves, but likewise of space, because, inasmuch as they make affirmations concerning objects not by means of the predicates of intuition and sensibility, but of pure thought à priori, they apply to objects without any of the conditions of sensibility. Besides, not being founded on experience, they are not presented with any object in à priori intuition upon which, antecedently to experience, they might base their synthesis. Hence results, not only doubt as to the objective validity and proper limits of their use, but that even our conception of space is rendered equivocal; inasmuch as we are very ready with the aid of the categories, to carry the use of this conception beyond the conditions of sensuous intuition—and, for this reason, we have already found a transcendental deduction of it needful. The reader, then, must be quite convinced of the absolute necessity of a transcendental deduction, before taking a single step in the field of pure reason; because otherwise he goes to work blindly, and after he has wondered about in all directions, returns to the state of utter ignorance from which he started. He ought, moreover, clearly to recognize beforehand the unavoidable difficulties in his undertaking, so that he may not afterwards complain of the obscurity in which the subject itself is deeply involved, or become too soon impatient of the obstacles in his path; because we have a choice of only two things—either at once to give up all pretensions to knowledge beyond the limits of possible experience, or to bring this critical investigation to completion.

We have been able, with very little trouble, to make it comprehensible how the conceptions of space and time, although à priori cognitions, must necessarily apply to external objects, and render a synthetical cognition of these possible, independently of all experience. For inasmuch as only by means of such pure form of sensibility an object can appear to us, that is, be an object of empirical intuition, space and time are pure intuitions, which contain à priori the condition of the possibility of objects as phenomena, and an à priori synthesis in these intuitions possesses objective validity.

On the other hand, the categories of the understanding do not represent the conditions under which objects are given to us in intuition; objects can consequently appear to us without necessarily connecting themselves with these, and consequently without any necessity binding on the understanding to contain à priori the conditions of these objects. Thus we find ourselves involved in a difficulty which did not present itself in the sphere of sensibility, that is to say, we cannot discover how the subjective conditions of thought can have objective validity, in other words, can become conditions of the possibility of all cognition of objects; for phenomena may certainly be given to us in intuition without any help from the functions of the understanding. Let us take, for example, the conception of cause, which indicates a peculiar kind of synthesis, namely, that with something, A, something entirely different, B, is connected according to a law. It is not à priori manifest why phenomena should contain anything of this kind (we are of course debarred from appealing for proof to experience, for the objective validity of this conception must be demonstrated à priori), and it hence remains doubtful à priori, whether such a conception be not quite void and without any corresponding object among phenomena. For that objects of sensuous intuition must correspond to the formal conditions of sensibility existing à priori in the mind is quite evident, from the fact that without these they could not be objects for us; but that they must also correspond to the conditions which understanding requires for the synthetical unity of thought is an assertion, the grounds for which are not so easily to be discovered. For phenomena might be so constituted as not to correspond to the conditions of the unity of thought; and all things might lie in such confusion that, for example, nothing could be met with in the sphere of phenomena to suggest a law of synthesis, and so correspond to the conception of cause and effect; so that this conception would be quite void, null, and without significance. Phenomena would nevertheless continue to present objects to our intuition; for mere intuition does not in any respect stand in need of the functions of thought.

If we thought to free ourselves from the labour of these investigations by saying: "Experience is constantly offering us examples of the relation of cause and effect in phenomena, and presents us with abundant opportunity of abstracting the conception of cause, and so at the same time of corroborating the objective validity of this conception"; we should in this case be overlooking the fact, that the conception of cause cannot arise in this way at all; that, on the contrary, it must either have an à priori basis in the understanding, or be rejected as a mere chimera. For this conception demands that something, A, should be of such a nature that something else, B, should follow from it necessarily, and according to an absolutely universal law. We may certainly collect from phenomena a law, according to which this or that usually happens, but the element of necessity is not to be found in it. Hence it is evident that to the synthesis of cause and effect belongs a dignity, which is utterly wanting in any empirical synthesis; for it is no mere mechanical synthesis, by means of addition, but a dynamical one; that is to say, the effect is not to be cogitated as merely annexed to the cause, but as posited by and through the cause, and resulting from it. The strict universality of this law never can be a characteristic of empirical laws, which obtain through induction only a comparative universality, that is, an extended range of practical application. But the pure conceptions of the understanding would entirely lose all their peculiar character, if we treated them merely as the productions of experience.

Transition to the Transcendental Deduction of the Categories § 10

There are only two possible ways in which synthetical representation and its objects can coincide with and relate necessarily to each other, and, as it were, meet together. Either the object alone makes the representation possible, or the representation alone makes the object possible. In the former case, the relation between them is only empirical, and an à priori representation is impossible. And this is the case with phenomena, as regards that in them which is referable to mere sensation. In the latter case—although representation alone (for of its causality, by means of the will, we do not here speak) does not produce the object as to its existence, it must nevertheless be à priori determinative in regard to the object, if it is only by means of the representation that we can cognize anything as an object. Now there are only two conditions of the possibility of a cognition of objects;

firstly, intuition, by means of which the object, though only as phenomenon, is given; secondly, conception, by means of which the object which corresponds to this intuition is thought. But it is evident from what has been said on æsthetic that the first condition, under which alone objects can be intuited, must in fact exist, as a formal basis for them, à priori in the mind. With this formal condition of sensibility, therefore, all phenomena necessarily correspond, because it is only through it that they can be phenomena at all; that is, can be empirically intuited and given. Now the question is whether there do not exist, à priori in the mind, conceptions of understanding also, as conditions under which alone something, if not intuited, is yet thought as object. If this question be answered in the affirmative, it follows that all empirical cognition of objects is necessarily conformable to such conceptions, since, if they are not presupposed, it is impossible that anything can be an object of experience. Now all experience contains, besides the intuition of the senses through which an object is given, a conception also of an object that is given in intuition. Accordingly, conceptions of objects in general must lie as à priori conditions at the foundation of all empirical cognition; and consequently, the objective validity of the categories, as à priori conceptions, will rest upon this, that experience (as far as regards the form of thought) is possible only by their means. For in that case they apply necessarily and à priori to objects of experience, because only through them can an object of experience be thought.

The whole aim of the transcendental deduction of all à priori conceptions is to show that these conceptions are à priori conditions of the possibility of all experience. Conceptions which afford us the objective foundation of the possibility of experience are for that very reason necessary. But the analysis of the experiences in which they are met with is not deduction, but only an illustration of them, because from experience they could never derive the attribute of necessity. Without their original applicability and relation to all possible experience, in which all objects of cognition present themselves, the relation of the categories to objects, of whatever nature, would be quite incomprehensible.

The celebrated Locke, for want of due reflection on these points, and because he met with pure conceptions of the understanding in experience, sought also to deduce them from experience, and yet proceeded so inconsequently as to attempt, with their aid, to arrive it cognitions which lie far beyond the limits of all experience. David Hume perceived that, to render this possible, it was necessary that the conceptions should have an à priori origin. But as he could not explain how it was possible that conceptions which are not connected with each other in the understanding must nevertheless be thought as necessarily connected in the object—and it never occurred to him that the understanding itself might, perhaps, by means of these conceptions, be the author of the experience in which its objects were presented to it—he was forced to drive these conceptions from experience, that is, from a subjective necessity arising from repeated association of experiences erroneously considered to be objective—in one word, from habit.

But he proceeded with perfect consequence and declared it to be impossible, with such conceptions and the principles arising from them, to overstep the limits of experience. The empirical derivation, however, which both of these philosophers attributed to these conceptions, cannot possibly be reconciled with the fact that we do possess scientific à priori cognitions, namely, those of pure mathematics and general physics.

The former of these two celebrated men opened a wide door to extravagance—(for if reason has once undoubted right on its side, it will not allow itself to be confined to set limits, by vague recommendations of moderation); the latter gave himself up entirely to scepticism—a natural consequence, after having discovered, as he thought, that the faculty of cognition was not trustworthy. We now intend to make a trial whether it be not possible safely to conduct reason between these two rocks, to assign her determinate limits, and yet leave open for her the entire sphere of her legitimate activity.

I shall merely premise an explanation of what the categories are. They are conceptions of an object in general, by means of which its intuition is contemplated as determined in relation to one of the logical functions of judgement. The following will make this plain. The function of the categorical judgement is that of the relation of subject to predicate; for example, in the proposition: "All bodies are divisible." But in regard to the merely logical use of the understanding, it still remains undetermined to which Of these two conceptions belongs the function Of subject and to which that of predicate. For we could also say: "Some divisible is a body." But the category of substance, when the conception of a body is brought under it, determines that; and its empirical intuition in experience must be contemplated always as subject and never as mere predicate. And so with all the other categories.

Section II. Transcendental Deduction of the pure Conceptions of the Understanding

Of the Possibility of a Conjunction of the manifold representations given by Sense § 11

The manifold content in our representations can be given in an intuition which is merely sensuous—in other words, is nothing but susceptibility; and the form of this intuition can exist à priori in our faculty of representation, without being anything else but the mode in which the subject is affected. But the conjunction (conjunctio) of a manifold in intuition never can be given us by the senses; it cannot therefore be contained in the pure form of sensuous intuition, for it is a spontaneous act of the faculty of representation. And as we must, to distinguish it from sensibility, entitle this faculty understanding; so all conjunction whether conscious or unconscious, be it of the manifold in intuition, sensuous or non-sensuous, or of several conceptions—is an act of the understanding. To this act we shall give the general appellation of synthesis, thereby to indicate, at the same time, that we cannot represent anything as conjoined in the object without having previously conjoined it ourselves. Of all mental notions, that of conjunction is the only one which cannot be given through objects, but can be originated only by the subject itself, because it is an act of its purely spontaneous activity. The reader will easily enough perceive that the possibility of conjunction must be grounded in the very nature of this act, and that it must be equally valid for all conjunction, and that analysis, which appears to be its contrary, must, nevertheless, always presuppose it; for where the understanding has not previously conjoined, it cannot dissect or analyse, because only as conjoined by it, must that which is to be analysed have been given to our faculty of representation.

But the conception of conjunction includes, besides the conception of the manifold and of the synthesis of it, that of the unity of it also. Conjunction is the representation of the synthetical unity of the manifold.[15] This idea of unity, therefore, cannot arise out of that of conjunction; much rather does that idea, by combining itself with the representation of the manifold, render the conception of conjunction possible. This unity, which à priori precedes all conceptions of conjunction, is not the category of unity (§ 6); for all the categories are based upon logical functions of judgement, and in these functions we already have conjunction, and consequently unity of given conceptions. It is therefore evident that the category of unity presupposes conjunction. We must therefore look still higher for this unity (as qualitative, § 8), in that, namely, which contains the ground of the unity of diverse conceptions in judgements, the ground, consequently, of the possibility of the existence of the understanding, even in regard to its logical use.

Of the Originally Synthetical Unity of Apperception § 12

The "I think" must accompany all my representations, for otherwise something would be represented in me which could not be thought; in other words, the representation would either be impossible, or at least be, in relation to me, nothing. That representation which can be given previously to all thought is called intuition. All the diversity or manifold content of intuition, has, therefore, a necessary relation to the "I think," in the subject in which this diversity is found. But this representation, "I think," is an act of spontaneity; that is to say, it cannot be regarded as belonging to mere sensibility. I call it pure apperception, in order to distinguish it from empirical; or primitive apperception, because it is self-

[15] Whether the representations are in themselves identical, and consequently whether one can be thought analytically by means of and through the other, is a question which we need not at present consider. Our Consciousness of the one, when we speak of the manifold, is always distinguishable from our consciousness of the other; and it is only respecting the synthesis of this (possible) consciousness that we here treat.

consciousness which, whilst it gives birth to the representation "I think," must necessarily be capable of accompanying all our representations. It is in all acts of consciousness one and the same, and unaccompanied by it, no representation can exist for me. The unity of this apperception I call the transcendental unity of self-consciousness, in order to indicate the possibility of à priori cognition arising from it. For the manifold representations which are given in an intuition would not all of them be my representations, if they did not all belong to one self-consciousness, that is, as my representations (even although I am not conscious of them as such), they must conform to the condition under which alone they can exist together in a common self-consciousness, because otherwise they would not all without exception belong to me. From this primitive conjunction follow many important results.

For example, this universal identity of the apperception of the manifold given in intuition contains a synthesis of representations and is possible only by means of the consciousness of this synthesis. For the empirical consciousness which accompanies different representations is in itself fragmentary and disunited, and without relation to the identity of the subject. This relation, then, does not exist because I accompany every representation with consciousness, but because I join one representation to another, and am conscious of the synthesis of them. Consequently, only because I can connect a variety of given representations in one consciousness, is it possible that I can represent to myself the identity of consciousness in these representations; in other words, the analytical unity of apperception is possible only under the presupposition of a synthetical unity.[16] The thought, "These representations given in intuition belong all of them to me," is accordingly just the same as, "I unite them in one self-consciousness, or can at least so unite them"; and although this thought is not itself the consciousness of the synthesis of representations, it presupposes the possibility of it; that is to say, for the reason alone that I can comprehend the variety of my representations in one consciousness, do I call them my representations, for otherwise I must have as many-coloured and various a self as are the representations of which I am conscious. Synthetical unity of the manifold in intuitions, as given à priori, is therefore the foundation of the identity of apperception itself, which antecedes à priori all

[16] All general conceptions—as such—depend, for their existence, on the analytical unity of consciousness. For example, when I think of red in general, I thereby think to myself a property which (as a characteristic mark) can be discovered somewhere, or can be united with other representations; consequently, it is only by means of a forethought possible synthetical unity that I can think to myself the analytical. A representation which is cogitated as common to different representations, is regarded as belonging to such as, besides this common representation, contain something different; consequently it must be previously thought in synthetical unity with other although only possible representations, before I can think in it the analytical unity of consciousness which makes it a conceptas communis. And thus the synthetical unity of apperception is the highest point with which we must connect every operation of the understanding, even the whole of logic, and after it our transcendental philosophy; indeed, this faculty is the understanding itself.

determinate thought. But the conjunction of representations into a conception is not to be found in objects themselves, nor can it be, as it were, borrowed from them and taken up into the understanding by perception, but it is on the contrary an operation of the understanding itself, which is nothing more than the faculty of conjoining à priori and of bringing the variety of given representations under the unity of apperception. This principle is the highest in all human cognition.

This fundamental principle of the necessary unity of apperception is indeed an identical, and therefore analytical, proposition; but it nevertheless explains the necessity for a synthesis of the manifold given in an intuition, without which the identity of self-consciousness would be incogitable. For the ego, as a simple representation, presents us with no manifold content; only in intuition, which is quite different from the representation ego, can it be given us, and by means of conjunction it is cogitated in one self-consciousness. An understanding, in which all the manifold should be given by means of consciousness itself, would be intuitive; our understanding can only think and must look for its intuition to sense. I am, therefore, conscious of my identical self, in relation to all the variety of representations given to me in an intuition, because I call all of them my representations. In other words, I am conscious myself of a necessary à priori synthesis of my representations, which is called the original synthetical unity of apperception, under which rank all the representations presented to me, but that only by means of a synthesis.

The Principle of the Synthetical Unity of Apperception is the highest Principle of all exercise of the Understanding § 13

The supreme principle of the possibility of all intuition in relation to sensibility was, according to our transcendental æsthetic, that all the manifold in intuition be subject to the formal conditions of space and time. The supreme principle of the possibility of it in relation to the understanding is that all the manifold in it be subject to conditions of the originally synthetical unity or apperception.[17] To the former of these two principles are subject all the various representations of intuition, in so far as they are given to us; to the latter, in so far as they must be capable of conjunction in one consciousness; for without this nothing can be thought or cognized, because the given representations would not have in common

[17] Space and time, and all portions thereof, are intuitions; consequently are, with a manifold for their content, single representations. (See the Transcendental Æsthetic.) Consequently, they are not pure conceptions, by means of which the same consciousness is found in a great number of representations; but, on the contrary, they are many representations contained in one, the consciousness of which is, so to speak, compounded. The unity of consciousness is nevertheless synthetical and, therefore, primitive. From this peculiar character of consciousness follow many important consequences. (See § 21.)

the act Of the apperception "I think" and therefore could not be connected in one self-consciousness.

Understanding is, to speak generally, the faculty Of cognitions. These consist in the determined relation of given representation to an object. But an object is that, in the conception of which the manifold in a given intuition is united. Now all union of representations requires unity of consciousness in the synthesis of them. Consequently, it is the unity of consciousness alone that constitutes the possibility of representations relating to an object, and therefore of their objective validity, and of their becoming cognitions, and consequently, the possibility of the existence of the understanding itself.

The first pure cognition of understanding, then, upon which is founded all its other exercise, and which is at the same time perfectly independent of all conditions of mere sensuous intuition, is the principle of the original synthetical unity of apperception. Thus the mere form of external sensuous intuition, namely, space, affords us, per se, no cognition; it merely contributes the manifold in à priori intuition to a possible cognition. But, in order to cognize something in space (for example, a line), I must draw it, and thus produce synthetically a determined conjunction of the given manifold, so that the unity of this act is at the same time the unity of consciousness (in the conception of a line), and by this means alone is an object (a determinate space) cognized. The synthetical unity of consciousness is, therefore, an objective condition of all cognition, which I do not merely require in order to cognize an object, but to which every intuition must necessarily be subject, in order to become an object for me; because in any other way, and without this synthesis, the manifold in intuition could not be united in one consciousness.

This proposition is, as already said, itself analytical, although it constitutes the synthetical unity, the condition of all thought; for it states nothing more than that all my representations in any given intuition must be subject to the condition which alone enables me to connect them, as my representation with the identical self, and so to unite them synthetically in one apperception, by means of the general expression, "I think."

But this principle is not to be regarded as a principle for every possible understanding, but only for the understanding by means of whose pure apperception in the thought I am, no manifold content is given. The understanding or mind which contained the manifold in intuition, in and through the act itself of its own self-consciousness, in other words, an understanding by and in the representation of which the objects of the representation should at the same time exist, would not require a special act of synthesis of the manifold as the condition of the unity of its consciousness, an act of which the human understanding, which thinks only and cannot intuite, has absolute need. But this principle is the first principle of all the operations of our understanding, so that we cannot form the least conception of any other possible understanding, either of one such as should be itself intuition, or possess a sensuous intuition, but with forms different from those of space and time.

What Objective Unity of Self-consciousness is § 14

It is by means of the transcendental unity of apperception that all the manifold, given in an intuition is united into a conception of the object. On this account it is called objective, and must be distinguished from the subjective unity of consciousness, which is a determination of the internal sense, by means of which the said manifold in intuition is given empirically to be so united. Whether I can be empirically conscious of the manifold as coexistent or as successive, depends upon circumstances, or empirical conditions. Hence the empirical unity of consciousness by means of association of representations, itself relates to a phenomenal world and is wholly contingent. On the contrary, the pure form of intuition in time, merely as an intuition, which contains a given manifold, is subject to the original unity of consciousness, and that solely by means of the necessary relation of the manifold in intuition to the "I think," consequently by means of the pure synthesis of the understanding, which lies à priori at the foundation of all empirical synthesis. The transcendental unity of apperception is alone objectively valid; the empirical which we do not consider in this essay, and which is merely a unity deduced from the former under given conditions in concreto, possesses only subjective validity. One person connects the notion conveyed in a word with one thing, another with another thing; and the unity of consciousness in that which is empirical, is, in relation to that which is given by experience, not necessarily and universally valid.

The Logical Form of all Judgements consists in the Objective Unity of Apperception of the Conceptions contained therein § 15

I could never satisfy myself with the definition which logicians give of a judgement. It is, according to them, the representation of a relation between two conceptions. I shall not dwell here on the faultiness of this definition, in that it suits only for categorical and not for hypothetical or disjunctive judgements, these latter containing a relation not of conceptions but of judgements themselves—a blunder from which many evil results have followed.[18] It is more important for our present purpose to observe, that this definition does not determine in what the said relation consists.

But if I investigate more closely the relation of given cognitions in every judgement, and distinguish it, as belonging to the understanding, from the relation which is produced according to laws of the reproductive imagination (which has

[18]The tedious doctrine of the four syllogistic figures concerns only categorical syllogisms; and although it is nothing more than an artifice by surreptitiously introducing immediate conclusions (consequentiae immediatae) among the premises of a pure syllogism, to give ism give rise to an appearance of more modes of drawing a conclusion than that in the first figure, the artifice would not have had much success, had not its authors succeeded in bringing categorical judgements into exclusive respect, as those to which all others must be referred—a doctrine, however, which, according to § 5, is utterly false.

only subjective validity), I find that judgement is nothing but the mode of bringing given cognitions under the objective unit of apperception. This is plain from our use of the term of relation is in judgements, in order to distinguish the objective unity of given representations from the subjective unity. For this term indicates the relation of these representations to the original apperception, and also their necessary unity, even although the judgement is empirical, therefore contingent, as in the judgement: "All bodies are heavy." I do not mean by this, that these representations do necessarily belong to each other in empirical intuition, but that by means of the necessary unity of appreciation they belong to each other in the synthesis of intuitions, that is to say, they belong to each other according to principles of the objective determination of all our representations, in so far as cognition can arise from them, these principles being all deduced from the main principle of the transcendental unity of apperception. In this way alone can there arise from this relation a judgement, that is, a relation which has objective validity, and is perfectly distinct from that relation of the very same representations which has only subjective validity—a relation, to wit, which is produced according to laws of association. According to these laws, I could only say: "When I hold in my hand or carry a body, I feel an impression of weight"; but I could not say: "It, the body, is heavy"; for this is tantamount to saying both these representations are conjoined in the object, that is, without distinction as to the condition of the subject, and do not merely stand together in my perception, however frequently the perceptive act may be repeated.

All Sensuous Intuitions are subject to the Categories, as Conditions under which alone the manifold Content of them can be united in one Consciousness § 16

The manifold content given in a sensuous intuition comes necessarily under the original synthetical unity of apperception, because thereby alone is the unity of intuition possible (§ 13). But that act of the understanding, by which the manifold content of given representations (whether intuitions or conceptions) is brought under one apperception, is the logical function of judgements (§ 15). All the manifold, therefore, in so far as it is given in one empirical intuition, is determined in relation to one of the logical functions of judgement, by means of which it is brought into union in one consciousness. Now the categories are nothing else than these functions of judgement so far as the manifold in a given intuition is determined in relation to them (§ 9). Consequently, the manifold in a given intuition is necessarily subject to the categories of the understanding.

Observation § 17

The manifold in an intuition, which I call mine, is represented by means of the synthesis of the understanding, as belonging to the necessary unity of self-consciousness, and this takes place by means of the category.[19] The category indicates accordingly that the empirical consciousness of a given manifold in an intuition is subject to a pure self-consciousness à priori, in the same manner as an empirical intuition is subject to a pure sensuous intuition, which is also à priori. In the above proposition, then, lies the beginning of a deduction of the pure conceptions of the understanding. Now, as the categories have their origin in the understanding alone, independently of sensibility, I must in my deduction make abstraction of the mode in which the manifold of an empirical intuition is given, in order to fix my attention exclusively on the unity which is brought by the understanding into the intuition by means of the category. In what follows (§ 22), it will be shown, from the mode in which the empirical intuition is given in the faculty of sensibility, that the unity which belongs to it is no other than that which the category (according to § 16) imposes on the manifold in a given intuition, and thus, its à priori validity in regard to all objects of sense being established, the purpose of our deduction will be fully attained.

But there is one thing in the above demonstration of which I could not make abstraction, namely, that the manifold to be intuited must be given previously to the synthesis of the understanding, and independently of it. How this takes place remains here undetermined. For if I cogitate an understanding which was itself intuitive (as, for example, a divine understanding which should not represent given objects, but by whose representation the objects themselves should be given or produced), the categories would possess no significance in relation to such a faculty of cognition. They are merely rules for an understanding, whose whole power consists in thought, that is, in the act of submitting the synthesis of the manifold which is presented to it in intuition from a very different quarter, to the unity of apperception; a faculty, therefore, which cognizes nothing per se, but only connects and arranges the material of cognition, the intuition, namely, which must be presented to it by means of the object. But to show reasons for this peculiar character of our understandings, that it produces unity of apperception à priori only by means of categories, and a certain kind and number thereof, is as impossible as to explain why we are endowed with precisely so many functions of judgement and no more, or why time and space are the only forms of our intuition.

In Cognition, its Application to Objects of Experience is the only legitimate use of the Category § 18

To think an object and to cognize an object are by no means the same thing. In cognition there are two elements: firstly, the conception, whereby an object is cogitated (the category); and, secondly, the intuition, whereby the object is given.

[19] The proof of this rests on the represented unity of intuition, by means of which an object is given, and which always includes in itself a synthesis of the manifold to be intuited, and also the relation of this latter to unity of apperception.

For supposing that to the conception a corresponding intuition could not be given, it would still be a thought as regards its form, but without any object, and no cognition of anything would be possible by means of it, inasmuch as, so far as I knew, there existed and could exist nothing to which my thought could be applied. Now all intuition possible to us is sensuous; consequently, our thought of an object by means of a pure conception of the understanding, can become cognition for us only in so far as this conception is applied to objects of the senses. Sensuous intuition is either pure intuition (space and time) or empirical intuition—of that which is immediately represented in space and time by means of sensation as real. Through the determination of pure intuition we obtain à priori cognitions of objects, as in mathematics, but only as regards their form as phenomena; whether there can exist things which must be intuited in this form is not thereby established. All mathematical conceptions, therefore, are not per se cognition, except in so far as we presuppose that there exist things which can only be represented conformably to the form of our pure sensuous intuition. But things in space and time are given only in so far as they are perceptions (representations accompanied with sensation), therefore only by empirical representation. Consequently the pure conceptions of the understanding, even when they are applied to intuitions à priori (as in mathematics), produce cognition only in so far as these (and therefore the conceptions of the understanding by means of them) can be applied to empirical intuitions. Consequently the categories do not, even by means of pure intuition afford us any cognition of things; they can only do so in so far as they can be applied to empirical intuition. That is to say, the categories serve only to render empirical cognition possible. But this is what we call experience. Consequently, in cognition, their application to objects of experience is the only legitimate use of the categories.

§ 19

The foregoing proposition is of the utmost importance, for it determines the limits of the exercise of the pure conceptions of the understanding in regard to objects, just as transcendental æsthetic determined the limits of the exercise of the pure form of our sensuous intuition. Space and time, as conditions of the possibility of the presentation of objects to us, are valid no further than for objects of sense, consequently, only for experience. Beyond these limits they represent to us nothing, for they belong only to sense, and have no reality apart from it. The pure conceptions of the understanding are free from this limitation, and extend to objects of intuition in general, be the intuition like or unlike to ours, provided only it be sensuous, and not intellectual. But this extension of conceptions beyond the range of our intuition is of no advantage; for they are then mere empty conceptions of objects, as to the possibility or impossibility of the existence of which they furnish us with no means of discovery. They are mere forms of thought, without objective reality, because we have no intuition to which the synthetical unity of apperception, which alone the categories contain, could be applied, for the purpose of determining an object. Our sensuous and empirical intuition can alone give them significance and meaning.

If, then, we suppose an object of a non-sensuous intuition to be given we can in that case represent it by all those predicates which are implied in the presupposition that nothing appertaining to sensuous intuition belongs to it; for example, that it is not extended, or in space; that its duration is not time; that in it no change (the effect of the determinations in time) is to be met with, and so on. But it is no proper knowledge if I merely indicate what the intuition of the object is not, without being able to say what is contained in it, for I have not shown the possibility of an object to which my pure conception of understanding could be applicable, because I have not been able to furnish any intuition corresponding to it, but am only able to say that our intuition is not valid for it. But the most important point is this, that to a something of this kind not one category can be found applicable. Take, for example, the conception of substance, that is, something that can exist as subject, but never as mere predicate; in regard to this conception I am quite ignorant whether there can really be anything to correspond to such a determination of thought, if empirical intuition did not afford me the occasion for its application. But of this more in the sequel.

Of the Application of the Categories to Objects of the Senses in general § 20

The pure conceptions of the understanding apply to objects of intuition in general, through the understanding alone, whether the intuition be our own or some other, provided only it be sensuous, but are, for this very reason, mere forms of thought, by means of which alone no determined object can be cognized. The synthesis or conjunction of the manifold in these conceptions relates, we have said, only to the unity of apperception, and is for this reason the ground of the possibility of à priori cognition, in so far as this cognition is dependent on the understanding. This synthesis is, therefore, not merely transcendental, but also purely intellectual. But because a certain form of sensuous intuition exists in the mind à priori which rests on the receptivity of the representative faculty (sensibility), the understanding, as a spontaneity, is able to determine the internal sense by means of the diversity of given representations, conformably to the synthetical unity of apperception, and thus to cogitate the synthetical unity of the apperception of the manifold of sensuous intuition à priori, as the condition to which must necessarily be submitted all objects of human intuition. And in this manner the categories as mere forms of thought receive objective reality, that is, application to objects which are given to us in intuition, but that only as phenomena, for it is only of phenomena that we are capable of à priori intuition.

This synthesis of the manifold of sensuous intuition, which is possible and necessary à priori, may be called figurative (synthesis speciosa), in contradistinction to that which is cogitated in the mere category in regard to the manifold of an intuition in general, and is called connection or conjunction of the understanding (synthesis intellectualis). Both are transcendental, not merely because they themselves precede à priori all experience, but also because they form the basis for the possibility of other cognition à priori.

But the figurative synthesis, when it has relation only to the originally synthetical unity of apperception, that is to the transcendental unity cogitated in the categories, must, to be distinguished from the purely intellectual conjunction, be entitled the transcendental synthesis of imagination. Imagination is the faculty of representing an object even without its presence in intuition. Now, as all our intuition is sensuous, imagination, by reason of the subjective condition under which alone it can give a corresponding intuition to the conceptions of the understanding, belongs to sensibility. But in so far as the synthesis of the imagination is an act of spontaneity, which is determinative, and not, like sense, merely determinable, and which is consequently able to determine sense à priori, according to its form, conformably to the unity of apperception, in so far is the imagination a faculty of determining sensibility à priori, and its synthesis of intuitions according to the categories must be the transcendental synthesis of the imagination. It is an operation of the understanding on sensibility, and the first application of the understanding to objects of possible intuition, and at the same time the basis for the exercise of the other functions of that faculty. As figurative, it is distinguished from the merely intellectual synthesis, which is produced by the understanding alone, without the aid of imagination. Now, in so far as imagination is spontaneity, I sometimes call it also the productive imagination, and distinguish it from the reproductive, the synthesis of which is subject entirely to empirical laws, those of association, namely, and which, therefore, contributes nothing to the explanation of the possibility of à priori cognition, and for this reason belongs not to transcendental philosophy, but to psychology.

We have now arrived at the proper place for explaining the paradox which must have struck every one in our exposition of the internal sense (§ 6), namely—how this sense represents us to our own consciousness, only as we appear to ourselves, not as we are in ourselves, because, to wit, we intuite ourselves only as we are inwardly affected. Now this appears to be contradictory, inasmuch as we thus stand in a passive relation to ourselves; and therefore in the systems of psychology, the internal sense is commonly held to be one with the faculty of apperception, while we, on the contrary, carefully distinguish them.

That which determines the internal sense is the understanding, and its original power of conjoining the manifold of intuition, that is, of bringing this under an apperception (upon which rests the possibility of the understanding itself). Now, as the human understanding is not in itself a faculty of intuition, and is unable to exercise such a power, in order to conjoin, as it were, the manifold of its own intuition, the synthesis of understanding is, considered per se, nothing but the unity of action, of which, as such, it is self-conscious, even apart from sensibility, by which, moreover, it is able to determine our internal sense in respect of the manifold which may be presented to it according to the form of sensuous intuition. Thus, under the name of a transcendental synthesis of imagination, the understanding exercises an activity upon the passive subject, whose faculty it is; and so we are right in saying that the internal sense is affected thereby. Apperception and its synthetical unity are by no means one and the same with the internal sense. The former, as the source of all our synthetical conjunction, applies, under the name of the categories, to the manifold of intuition in general, prior to all sensuous intuition of objects. The internal sense, on the contrary, contains merely the form of intuition, but without any synthetical conjunction of the manifold therein, and consequently does not contain any determined intuition, which is possible only through consciousness of the determination of the manifold by the transcendental act of the imagination (synthetical influence of the understanding on the internal sense), which I have named figurative synthesis.

This we can indeed always perceive in ourselves. We cannot cogitate a geometrical line without drawing it in thought, nor a circle without describing it, nor represent the three dimensions of space without drawing three lines from the same point perpendicular to one another. We cannot even cogitate time, unless, in drawing a straight line (which is to serve as the external figurative representation of time), we fix our attention on the act of the synthesis of the manifold, whereby we determine successively the internal sense, and thus attend also to the succession of this determination. Motion as an act of the subject (not as a determination of an object),[20] consequently the synthesis of the manifold in space, if we make abstraction of space and attend merely to the act by which we determine the internal sense according to its form, is that which produces the conception of succession. The understanding, therefore, does by no means find in the internal sense any such synthesis of the manifold, but produces it, in that it affects this sense. At the same time, how "I who think" is distinct from the "i" which intuites itself (other modes of intuition being cogitable as at least possible), and yet one and the same with this latter as the same subject; how, therefore, I am able to say: "I, as an intelligence and thinking subject, cognize myself as an object thought, so far as I am, moreover, given to myself in intuition—only, like other phenomena, not as I am in myself, and as considered by the understanding, but merely as I appear"—is a question that has in it neither more nor less difficulty than the question—

[20] Motion of an object in space does not belong to a pure science, consequently not to geometry; because, that a thing is movable cannot be known à priori, but only from experience. But motion, considered as the description of a space, is a pure act of the successive synthesis of the manifold in external intuition by means of productive imagination, and belongs not only to geometry, but even to transcendental philosophy.

"How can I be an object to myself?" or this—"How I can be an object of my own intuition and internal perceptions?" But that such must be the fact, if we admit that space is merely a pure form of the phenomena of external sense, can be clearly proved by the consideration that we cannot represent time, which is not an object of external intuition, in any other way than under the image of a line, which we draw in thought, a mode of representation without which we could not cognize the unity of its dimension, and also that we are necessitated to take our determination of periods of time, or of points of time, for all our internal perceptions from the changes which we perceive in outward things. It follows that we must arrange the determinations of the internal sense, as phenomena in time, exactly in the same manner as we arrange those of the external senses in space. And consequently, if we grant, respecting this latter, that by means of them we know objects only in so far as we are affected externally, we must also confess, with regard to the internal sense, that by means of it we intuite ourselves only as we are internally affected by ourselves; in other words, as regards internal intuition, we cognize our own subject only as phenomenon, and not as it is in itself.[21]

§ 21

On the other hand, in the transcendental synthesis of the manifold content of representations, consequently in the synthetical unity of apperception, I am conscious of myself, not as I appear to myself, nor as I am in myself, but only that "I am." This representation is a thought, not an intuition. Now, as in order to cognize ourselves, in addition to the act of thinking, which subjects the manifold of every possible intuition to the unity of apperception, there is necessary a determinate mode of intuition, whereby this manifold is given; although my own existence is certainly not mere phenomenon (much less mere illusion), the determination of my existence[22] Can only take place conformably to the form of the internal sense,

[21] I do not see why so much difficulty should be found in admitting that our internal sense is affected by ourselves. Every act of attention exemplifies it. In such an act the understanding determines the internal sense by the synthetical conjunction which it cogitates, conformably to the internal intuition which corresponds to the manifold in the synthesis of the understanding. How much the mind is usually affected thereby every one will be able to perceive in himself.

[22] The "I think" expresses the act of determining my own existence. My existence is thus already given by the act of consciousness; but the mode in which I must determine my existence, that is, the mode in which I must place the manifold belonging to my existence, is not thereby given. For this purpose intuition of self is required, and this intuition possesses a form given à priori, namely, time, which is sensuous, and belongs to our receptivity of the determinable. Now, as I do not possess another intuition of self which gives the determining in me (of the spontaneity of which I am conscious), prior to the act of determination, in the same manner as time gives the determinable, it is clear that I am unable to determine my own existence as that of a spontaneous being, but I am only able to represent to myself the spontaneity of my thought, that is, of my determination, and my existence remains ever determinable in a purely sensuous manner, that is to say, like the existence of a phenomenon. But it is because of this spontaneity that I call myself an intelligence.

according to the particular mode in which the manifold which I conjoin is given in internal intuition, and I have therefore no knowledge of myself as I am, but merely as I appear to myself. The consciousness of self is thus very far from a knowledge of self, in which I do not use the categories, whereby I cogitate an object, by means of the conjunction of the manifold in one apperception. In the same way as I require, for the sake of the cognition of an object distinct from myself, not only the thought of an object in general (in the category), but also an intuition by which to determine that general conception, in the same way do I require, in order to the cognition of myself, not only the consciousness of myself or the thought that I think myself, but in addition an intuition of the manifold in myself, by which to determine this thought. It is true that I exist as an intelligence which is conscious only of its faculty of conjunction or synthesis, but subjected in relation to the manifold which this intelligence has to conjoin to a limitative conjunction called the internal sense. My intelligence (that is, I) can render that conjunction or synthesis perceptible only according to the relations of time, which are quite beyond the proper sphere of the conceptions of the understanding and consequently cognize itself in respect to an intuition (which cannot possibly be intellectual, nor given by the understanding), only as it appears to itself, and not as it would cognize itself, if its intuition were intellectual.

Transcendental Deduction of the universally possible employment in experience of the Pure Conceptions of the Understanding. § 22

In the metaphysical deduction, the à priori origin of categories was proved by their complete accordance with the general logical of thought; in the transcendental deduction was exhibited the possibility of the categories as à priori cognitions of objects of an intuition in general (§ 16 and 17).At present we are about to explain the possibility of cognizing, à priori, by means of the categories, all objects which can possibly be presented to our senses, not, indeed, according to the form of their intuition, but according to the laws of their conjunction or synthesis, and thus, as it were, of prescribing laws to nature and even of rendering nature possible. For if the categories were inadequate to this task, it would not be evident to us why everything that is presented to our senses must be subject to those laws which have an à priori origin in the understanding itself.

I premise that by the term synthesis of apprehension I understand the combination of the manifold in an empirical intuition, whereby perception, that is, empirical consciousness of the intuition (as phenomenon), is possible.

We have à priori forms of the external and internal sensuous intuition in the representations of space and time, and to these must the synthesis of apprehension of the manifold in a phenomenon be always comformable, because the synthesis itself can only take place according to these forms. But space and time are not merely forms of sensuous intuition, but intuitions themselves (which contain a manifold), and therefore contain à priori the determination of the unity of this manifold.[23] (See the Transcendent Æsthetic.) Therefore is unity of the synthesis of the manifold without or within us, consequently also a conjunction to which all that is to be represented as determined in space or time must correspond, given à priori along with (not in) these intuitions, as the condition of the synthesis of all apprehension of them. But this synthetical unity can be no other than that of the conjunction of the manifold of a given intuition in general, in a primitive act of consciousness, according to the categories, but applied to our sensuous intuition. Consequently all synthesis, whereby alone is even perception possible, is subject to the categories. And, as experience is cognition by means of conjoined perceptions, the categories are conditions of the possibility of experience and are therefore valid à priori for all objects of experience.

When, then, for example, I make the empirical intuition of a house by apprehension of the manifold contained therein into a perception, the necessary unity of space and of my external sensuous intuition lies at the foundation of this act, and I, as it were, draw the form of the house conformably to this synthetical unity of the manifold in space. But this very synthetical unity remains, even when I abstract the form of space, and has its seat in the understanding, and is in fact the category of the synthesis of the homogeneous in an intuition; that is to say, the category of quantity, to which the aforesaid synthesis of apprehension, that is, the perception, must be completely conformable.[24]

To take another example, when I perceive the freezing of water, I apprehend two states (fluidity and solidity), which, as such, stand toward each other mutually in a relation of time. But in the time, which I place as an internal intuition, at the foundation of this phenomenon, I represent to myself synthetical unity of the manifold, without which the aforesaid relation could not be given in an intuition as determined (in regard to the succession of time). Now this synthetical unity, as the à priori condition under which I conjoin the manifold of an intuition, is, if I make abstraction of the permanent form of my internal intuition (that is to say, of

[23] Space represented as an object (as geometry really requires it to be) contains more than the mere form of the intuition; namely, a combination of the manifold given according to the form of sensibility into a representation that can be intuited; so that the form of the intuition gives us merely the manifold, but the formal intuition gives unity of representation. In the æsthetic, I regarded this unity as belonging entirely to sensibility, for the purpose of indicating that it antecedes all conceptions, although it presupposes a synthesis which does not belong to sense, through which alone, however, all our conceptions of space and time are possible. For as by means of this unity alone (the understanding determining the sensibility) space and time are given as intuitions, it follows that the unity of this intuition à priori belongs to space and time, and not to the conception of the understanding (§ 20).

[24] In this manner it is proved, that the synthesis of apprehension, which is empirical, must necessarily be conformable to the synthesis of apperception, which is intellectual, and contained à priori in the category. It is one and the same spontaneity which at one time, under the name of imagination, at another under that of understanding, produces conjunction in the manifold of intuition.

time), the category of cause, by means of which, when applied to my sensibility, I determine everything that occurs according to relations of time. Consequently apprehension in such an event, and the event itself, as far as regards the possibility of its perception, stands under the conception of the relation of cause and effect: and so in all other cases.

Categories are conceptions which prescribe laws à priori to phenomena, consequently to nature as the complex of all phenomena (natura materialiter spectata). And now the question arises—inasmuch as these categories are not derived from nature, and do not regulate themselves according to her as their model (for in that case they would be empirical)—how it is conceivable that nature must regulate herself according to them, in other words, how the categories can determine à priori the synthesis of the manifold of nature, and yet not derive their origin from her. The following is the solution of this enigma.

It is not in the least more difficult to conceive how the laws of the phenomena of nature must harmonize with the understanding and with its à priori form—that is, its faculty of conjoining the manifold—than it is to understand how the phenomena themselves must correspond with the à priori form of our sensuous intuition. For laws do not exist in the phenomena any more than the phenomena exist as things in themselves. Laws do not exist except by relation to the subject in which the phenomena inhere, in so far as it possesses understanding, just as phenomena have no existence except by relation to the same existing subject in so far as it has senses. To things as things in themselves, conformability to law must necessarily belong independently of an understanding to cognize them. But phenomena are only representations of things which are utterly unknown in respect to what they are in themselves. But as mere representations, they stand under no law of conjunction except that which the conjoining faculty prescribes. Now that which conjoins the manifold of sensuous intuition is imagination, a mental act to which understanding contributes unity of intellectual synthesis, and sensibility, manifoldness of apprehension. Now as all possible perception depends on the synthesis of apprehension, and this empirical synthesis itself on the transcendental, consequently on the categories, it is evident that all possible perceptions, and therefore everything that can attain to empirical consciousness, that is, all phenomena of nature, must, as regards their conjunction, be subject to the categories. And nature (considered merely as nature in general) is dependent on them, as the original ground of her necessary conformability to law (as natura formaliter spectata). But the pure faculty (of the understanding) of prescribing laws à priori to phenomena by means of mere categories, is not competent to enounce other or more laws than those on which a nature in general, as a conformability to law of phenomena of space and time, depends. Particular laws, inasmuch as they concern empirically determined phenomena, cannot be entirely deduced from pure laws, although they all stand under them. Experience must be superadded in order to know these particular laws; but in regard to experience in general, and everything that can be cognized as an object thereof, these à priori laws are our only rule and guide.

Result of this Deduction of the Conceptions of the Understanding. § 23

We cannot think any object except by means of the categories; we cannot cognize any thought except by means of intuitions corresponding to these conceptions. Now all our intuitions are sensuous, and our cognition, in so far as the object of it is given, is empirical. But empirical cognition is experience; consequently no à priori cognition is possible for us, except of objects of possible experience.[25]

But this cognition, which is limited to objects of experience, is not for that reason derived entirely, from, experience, but—and this is asserted of the pure intuitions and the pure conceptions of the understanding—there are, unquestionably, elements of cognition, which exist in the mind à priori. Now there are only two ways in which a necessary harmony of experience with the conceptions of its objects can be cogitated. Either experience makes these conceptions possible, or the conceptions make experience possible. The former of these statements will not hold good with respect to the categories (nor in regard to pure sensuous intuition), for they are à priori conceptions, and therefore independent of experience. The assertion of an empirical origin would attribute to them a sort of generatio aequivoca. Consequently, nothing remains but to adopt the second alternative (which presents us with a system, as it were, of the epigenesis of pure reason), namely, that on the part of the understanding the categories do contain the grounds of the possibility of all experience. But with respect to the questions how they make experience possible, and what are the principles of the possibility thereof with which they present us in their application to phenomena, the following section on the transcendental exercise of the faculty of judgement will inform the reader.

It is quite possible that someone may propose a species of preformation-system of pure reason—a middle way between the two—to wit, that the categories are neither innate and first à priori principles of cognition, nor derived from experience, but are merely subjective aptitudes for thought implanted in us contemporaneously with our existence, which were so ordered and disposed by our Creator, that their exercise perfectly harmonizes with the laws of nature which regulate experience. Now, not to mention that with such an hypothesis it is impossible to say at what

[25] Lest my readers should stumble at this assertion, and the conclusions that may be too rashly drawn from it, I must remind them that the categories in the act of thought are by no means limited by the conditions of our sensuous intuition, but have an unbounded sphere of action. It is only the cognition of the object of thought, the determining of the object, which requires intuition. In the absence of intuition, our thought of an object may still have true and useful consequences in regard to the exercise of reason by the subject. But as this exercise of reason is not always directed on the determination of the object, in other words, on cognition thereof, but also on the determination of the subject and its volition, I do not intend to treat of it in this place.

point we must stop in the employment of predetermined aptitudes, the fact that the categories would in this case entirely lose that character of necessity which is essentially involved in the very conception of them, is a conclusive objection to it. The conception of cause, for example, which expresses the necessity of an effect under a presupposed condition, would be false, if it rested only upon such an arbitrary subjective necessity of uniting certain empirical representations according to such a rule of relation. I could not then say—"The effect is connected with its cause in the object (that is, necessarily)," but only, "I am so constituted that I can think this representation as so connected, and not otherwise." Now this is just what the sceptic wants. For in this case, all our knowledge, depending on the supposed objective validity of our judgement, is nothing but mere illusion; nor would there be wanting people who would deny any such subjective necessity in respect to themselves, though they must feel it. At all events, we could not dispute with any one on that which merely depends on the manner in which his subject is organized.

Short view of the above Deduction.

The foregoing deduction is an exposition of the pure conceptions of the understanding (and with them of all theoretical à priori cognition), as principles of the possibility of experience, but of experience as the determination of all phenomena in space and time in general—of experience, finally, from the principle of the original synthetical unity of apperception, as the form of the understanding in relation to time and space as original forms of sensibility.

I consider the division by paragraphs to be necessary only up to this point, because we had to treat of the elementary conceptions. As we now proceed to the exposition of the employment of these, I shall not designate the chapters in this manner any further.

BOOK II

Analytic of Principles

General logic is constructed upon a plan which coincides exactly with the division of the higher faculties of cognition. These are, understanding, judgement, and reason. This science, accordingly, treats in its analytic of conceptions, judgements, and conclusions in exact correspondence with the functions and order of those mental powers which we include generally under the generic denomination of understanding.

As this merely formal logic makes abstraction of all content of cognition, whether pure or empirical, and occupies itself with the mere form of thought (discursive cognition), it must contain in its analytic a canon for reason. For the form of reason has its law, which, without taking into consideration the particular nature of the cognition about which it is employed, can be discovered à priori, by the simple analysis of the action of reason into its momenta.

Transcendental logic, limited as it is to a determinate content, that of pure à priori cognitions, to wit, cannot imitate general logic in this division. For it is evident that the transcendental employment of reason is not objectively valid, and therefore does not belong to the logic of truth (that is, to analytic), but as a logic of illusion, occupies a particular department in the scholastic system under the name of transcendental dialectic.

Understanding and judgement accordingly possess in transcendental logic a canon of objectively valid, and therefore true exercise, and are comprehended in the analytical department of that logic. But reason, in her endeavours to arrive by à priori means at some true statement concerning objects and to extend cognition beyond the bounds of possible experience, is altogether dialectic, and her illusory assertions cannot be constructed into a canon such as an analytic ought to contain.

Accordingly, the analytic of principles will be merely a canon for the faculty of judgement, for the instruction of this faculty in its application to phenomena of the pure conceptions of the understanding, which contain the necessary condition for the establishment of à priori laws. On this account, although the subject of the following chapters is the especial principles of understanding, I shall make use of the term Doctrine of the faculty of judgement, in order to define more particularly my present purpose.

INTRODUCTION

Of the Transcendental Faculty of judgement in General

If understanding in general be defined as the faculty of laws or rules, the faculty of judgement may be termed the faculty of subsumption under these rules; that is, of distinguishing whether this or that does or does not stand under a given rule (casus datae legis). General logic contains no directions or precepts for the faculty of judgement, nor can it contain any such. For as it makes abstraction of all content of cognition, no duty is left for it, except that of exposing analytically the mere form of cognition in conceptions, judgements, and conclusions, and of thereby establishing formal rules for all exercise of the understanding. Now if this logic wished to give some general direction how we should subsume under these rules, that is, how we should distinguish whether this or that did or did not stand under them, this again could not be done otherwise than by means of a rule. But this rule, precisely because it is a rule, requires for itself direction from the faculty of judgement. Thus, it is evident that the understanding is capable of being instructed by rules, but that the judgement is a peculiar talent, which does not, and cannot require tuition, but only exercise. This faculty is therefore the specific quality of the so-called mother wit, the want of which no scholastic discipline can compensate.

For although education may furnish, and, as it were, engraft upon a limited understanding rules borrowed from other minds, yet the power of employing these rules correctly must belong to the pupil himself; and no rule which we can prescribe to him with this purpose is, in the absence or deficiency of this gift of nature, secure from misuse.[26] A physician therefore, a judge or a statesman, may have in his head many admirable pathological, juridical, or political rules, in a degree that may enable him to be a profound teacher in his particular science, and yet in the application of these rules he may very possibly blunder—either because he is wanting in natural judgement (though not in understanding) and, whilst he can comprehend the general in abstracto, cannot distinguish whether a particular case in concreto ought to rank under the former; or because his faculty of judgement has not been sufficiently exercised by examples and real practice. Indeed, the grand and only use of examples, is to sharpen the judgement. For as regards the correctness and precision of the insight of the understanding, examples

[26] Deficiency in judgement is properly that which is called stupidity; and for such a failing we know no remedy. A dull or narrow-minded person, to whom nothing is wanting but a proper degree of understanding, may be improved by tuition, even so far as to deserve the epithet of learned. But as such persons frequently labour under a deficiency in the faculty of judgement, it is not uncommon to find men extremely learned who in the application of their science betray a lamentable degree this irremediable want.

are commonly injurious rather than otherwise, because, as casus in terminis they seldom adequately fulfil the conditions of the rule. Besides, they often weaken the power of our understanding to apprehend rules or laws in their universality, independently of particular circumstances of experience; and hence, accustom us to employ them more as formulae than as principles. Examples are thus the go-cart of the judgement, which he who is naturally deficient in that faculty cannot afford to dispense with.

But although general logic cannot give directions to the faculty of judgement, the case is very different as regards transcendental logic, insomuch that it appears to be the especial duty of the latter to secure and direct, by means of determinate rules, the faculty of judgement in the employment of the pure understanding. For, as a doctrine, that is, as an endeavour to enlarge the sphere of the understanding in regard to pure à priori cognitions, philosophy is worse than useless, since from all the attempts hitherto made, little or no ground has been gained. But, as a critique, in order to guard against the mistakes of the faculty of judgement (lapsus judicii) in the employment of the few pure conceptions of the understanding which we possess, although its use is in this case purely negative, philosophy is called upon to apply all its acuteness and penetration.

But transcendental philosophy has this peculiarity, that besides indicating the rule, or rather the general condition for rules, which is given in the pure conception of the understanding, it can, at the same time, indicate à priori the case to which the rule must be applied. The cause of the superiority which, in this respect, transcendental philosophy possesses above all other sciences except mathematics, lies in this: it treats of conceptions which must relate à priori to their objects, whose objective validity consequently cannot be demonstrated à posteriori, and is, at the same time, under the obligation of presenting in general but sufficient tests, the conditions under which objects can be given in harmony with those conceptions; otherwise they would be mere logical forms, without content, and not pure conceptions of the understanding.

Our transcendental doctrine of the faculty of judgement will contain two chapters. The first will treat of the sensuous condition under which alone pure conceptions of the understanding can be employed—that is, of the schematism of the pure understanding. The second will treat of those synthetical judgements which are derived à priori from pure conceptions of the understanding under those conditions, and which lie à priori at the foundation of all other cognitions, that is to say, it will treat of the principles of the pure understanding.

TRANSCENDENTAL DOCTRINE OF THE FACULTY OF JUDGEMENT OR, ANALYTIC OF PRINCIPLES

Chapter I

Of the Schematism at of the Pure Conceptions of the Understanding

In all subsumptions of an object under a conception, the representation of the object must be homogeneous with the conception; in other words, the conception must contain that which is represented in the object to be subsumed under it. For this is the meaning of the expression: "An object is contained under a conception." Thus the empirical conception of a plate is homogeneous with the pure geometrical conception of a circle, inasmuch as the roundness which is cogitated in the former is intuited in the latter.

But pure conceptions of the understanding, when compared with empirical intuitions, or even with sensuous intuitions in general, are quite heterogeneous, and never can be discovered in any intuition. How then is the subsumption of the latter under the former, and consequently the application of the categories to phenomena, possible?—For it is impossible to say, for example: "Causality can be intuited through the senses and is contained in the phenomenon."—This natural and important question forms the real cause of the necessity of a transcendental doctrine of the faculty of judgement, with the purpose, to wit, of showing how pure conceptions of the understanding can be applied to phenomena. In all other sciences, where the conceptions by which the object is thought in the general are not so different and heterogeneous from those which represent the object in concreto—as it is given, it is quite unnecessary to institute any special inquiries concerning the application of the former to the latter.

Now it is quite clear that there must be some third thing, which on the one side is homogeneous with the category, and with the phenomenon on the other, and so makes the application of the former to the latter possible. This mediating representation must be pure (without any empirical content), and yet must on the one side be intellectual, on the other sensuous. Such a representation is the transcendental schema.

The conception of the understanding contains pure synthetical unity of the manifold in general. Time, as the formal condition of the manifold of the internal sense, consequently of the conjunction of all representations, contains à priori a manifold in the pure intuition. Now a transcendental determination of time is so far homogeneous with the category, which constitutes the unity thereof, that it is universal and rests upon a rule à priori. On the other hand, it is so far homogeneous with the phenomenon, inasmuch as time is contained in every empirical representation of the manifold. Thus an application of the category to phenomena becomes possible, by means of the transcendental determination of time, which, as the schema of the conceptions of the understanding, mediates the subsumption of the latter under the former.

After what has been proved in our deduction of the categories, no one, it is to be hoped, can hesitate as to the proper decision of the question, whether the employment of these pure conceptions of the understanding ought to be merely empirical or also transcendental; in other words, whether the categories, as conditions of a possible experience, relate à priori solely to phenomena, or whether, as conditions of the possibility of things in general, their application can be extended to objects as things in themselves. For we have there seen that conceptions are quite impossible, and utterly without signification, unless either to them, or at least to the elements of which they consist, an object be given; and that, consequently, they cannot possibly apply to objects as things in themselves without regard to the question whether and how these may be given to us; and, further, that the only manner in which objects can be given to us is by means of the modification of our sensibility; and, finally, that pure à priori conceptions, in addition to the function of the understanding in the category, must contain à priori formal conditions of sensibility (of the internal sense, namely), which again contain the general condition under which alone the category can be applied to any object. This formal and pure condition of sensibility, to which the conception of the understanding is restricted in its employment, we shall name the schema of the conception of the understanding, and the procedure of the understanding with these schemata we shall call the schematism of the pure understanding.

The schema is, in itself, always a mere product of the imagination. But, as the synthesis of imagination has for its aim no single intuition, but merely unity in the determination of sensibility, the schema is clearly distinguishable from the image. Thus, if I place five points one after another.... this is an image of the number five. On the other hand, if I only think a number in general, which may be either five or a hundred, this thought is rather the representation of a method of representing in an image a sum (e.g., a thousand) in conformity with a conception, than the image itself, an image which I should find some little difficulty in reviewing, and comparing with the conception. Now this representation of a general procedure of the imagination to present its image to a conception, I call the schema of this conception.

In truth, it is not images of objects, but schemata, which lie at the foundation of our pure sensuous conceptions. No image could ever be adequate to our conception of a triangle in general. For the generalness of the conception it never could attain to, as this includes under itself all triangles, whether right-angled, acute-angled, etc., whilst the image would always be limited to a single part of this sphere. The schema of the triangle can exist nowhere else than in thought, and it indicates a rule of the synthesis of the imagination in regard to pure figures in space. Still less is an object of experience, or an image of the object, ever to the empirical conception. On the contrary, the conception always relates immediately to the schema of the imagination, as a rule for the determination of our intuition, in conformity with a certain general conception. The conception of a dog indicates a rule, according to which my imagination can delineate the figure of a four-footed animal in general, without being limited to any particular individual form which experience presents to me, or indeed to any possible image that I can represent to myself in concreto. This schematism of our understanding in regard to phenomena and their mere form, is an art, hidden in the depths of the human soul, whose true modes of action we shall only with difficulty discover and unveil. Thus much only can we say: "The image is a product of the empirical faculty of the productive imagination—the schema of sensuous conceptions (of figures in space, for example) is a product, and, as it were, a monogram of the pure imagination à priori, whereby and according to which images first become possible, which, however, can be connected with the conception only mediately by means of the schema which they indicate, and are in themselves never fully adequate to it." On the other hand, the schema of a pure conception of the understanding is something that cannot be reduced into any image—it is nothing else than the pure synthesis expressed by the category, conformably, to a rule of unity according to conceptions. It is a transcendental product of the imagination, a product which concerns the determination of the internal sense, according to conditions of its form (time) in respect to all representations, in so far as these representations must be conjoined à priori in one conception, conformably to the unity of apperception.

Without entering upon a dry and tedious analysis of the essential requisites of transcendental schemata of the pure conceptions of the understanding, we shall rather proceed at once to give an explanation of them according to the order of the categories, and in connection therewith.

For the external sense the pure image of all quantities (quantorum) is space; the pure image of all objects of sense in general, is time. But the pure schema of quantity (quantitatis) as a conception of the understanding, is number, a representation which comprehends the successive addition of one to one (homogeneous quantities). Thus, number is nothing else than the unity of the synthesis of the manifold in a homogeneous intuition, by means of my generating time itself in my apprehension of the intuition.

Reality, in the pure conception of the understanding, is that which corresponds to a sensation in general; that, consequently, the conception of which indicates a being (in time). Negation is that the conception of which represents a not-being (in time). The opposition of these two consists therefore in the difference of one and the same time, as a time filled or a time empty. Now as time is only the form of intuition, consequently of objects as phenomena, that which in objects corresponds to sensation is the transcendental matter of all objects as things in themselves (Sachheit, reality). Now every sensation has a degree or quantity by which it can fill time, that is to say, the internal sense in respect of the representation of an object, more or less, until it vanishes into nothing (= 0 = negatio). Thus there is a relation and connection between reality and negation, or rather a transition from the former to the latter, which makes every reality representable to us as a quantum; and the schema of a reality as the quantity of something in so far as it fills time, is exactly this continuous and uniform generation of the reality in time, as we descend in time from the sensation which has a certain degree, down to the vanishing thereof, or gradually ascend from negation to the quantity thereof.

The schema of substance is the permanence of the real in time; that is, the representation of it as a substratum of the empirical determination of time; a substratum which therefore remains, whilst all else changes. (Time passes not, but in it passes the existence of the changeable. To time, therefore, which is itself unchangeable and permanent, corresponds that which in the phenomenon is unchangeable in existence, that is, substance, and it is only by it that the succession and coexistence of phenomena can be determined in regard to time.)

The schema of cause and of the causality of a thing is the real which, when posited, is always followed by something else. It consists, therefore, in the succession of the manifold, in so far as that succession is subjected to a rule.

The schema of community (reciprocity of action and reaction), or the reciprocal causality of substances in respect of their accidents, is the coexistence of the determinations of the one with those of the other, according to a general rule.

The schema of possibility is the accordance of the synthesis of different representations with the conditions of time in general (as, for example, opposites cannot exist together at the same time in the same thing, but only after each other), and is therefore the determination of the representation of a thing at any time.

The schema of reality is existence in a determined time.

The schema of necessity is the existence of an object in all time.

It is clear, from all this, that the schema of the category of quantity contains and represents the generation (synthesis) of time itself, in the successive apprehension of an object; the schema of quality the synthesis of sensation with the representation of time, or the filling up of time; the schema of relation the relation of perceptions to each other in all time (that is, according to a rule of the determination of time): and finally, the schema of modality and its categories, time itself, as the correlative of the determination of an object—whether it does belong to time, and how. The schemata, therefore, are nothing but à priori determinations of time according to rules, and these, in regard to all possible objects, following the arrangement of the categories, relate to the series in time, the content in time, the order in time, and finally, to the complex or totality in time.

Hence it is apparent that the schematism of the understanding, by means of the transcendental synthesis of the imagination, amounts to nothing else than the unity of the manifold of intuition in the internal sense, and thus indirectly to the unity of apperception, as a function corresponding to the internal sense (a receptivity). Thus, the schemata of the pure conceptions of the understanding are the true and only conditions whereby our understanding receives an application to objects, and consequently significance. Finally, therefore, the categories are only capable of empirical use, inasmuch as they serve merely to subject phenomena to the universal rules of synthesis, by means of an à priori necessary unity (on account of the necessary union of all consciousness in one original apperception); and so to render them susceptible of a complete connection in one experience. But within this whole of possible experience lie all our cognitions, and in the universal relation to this experience consists transcendental truth, which antecedes all empirical truth, and renders the latter possible.

It is, however, evident at first sight, that although the schemata of sensibility are the sole agents in realizing the categories, they do, nevertheless, also restrict them, that is, they limit the categories by conditions which lie beyond the sphere of understanding—namely, in sensibility. Hence the schema is properly only the phenomenon, or the sensuous conception of an object in harmony with the category. (Numerus est quantitas phaenomenon—sensatio realitas phaenomenon; constans et perdurabile rerum substantia phaenomenon—aeternitas, necessitas, phaenomena, etc.) Now, if we remove a restrictive condition, we thereby amplify, it appears, the formerly limited conception. In this way, the categories in their pure signification, free from all conditions of sensibility, ought to be valid of things as they are, and not, as the schemata represent them, merely as they appear; and consequently the categories must have a significance far more extended, and wholly independent of all schemata. In truth, there does always remain to the pure conceptions of the understanding, after abstracting every sensuous condition, a value and significance, which is, however, merely logical. But in this case, no object is given them, and therefore they have no meaning sufficient to afford us a conception of an object. The notion of substance, for example, if we leave out the sensuous determination of permanence, would mean nothing more than a something which can be cogitated as subject, without the possibility of becoming a predicate to anything else. Of this representation I can make nothing, inasmuch as it does not indicate to me what determinations the thing possesses which must thus be valid as premier subject. Consequently, the categories, without schemata are merely functions of the understanding for the production of conceptions, but do not represent any object. This significance they derive from sensibility, which at the same time realizes the understanding and restricts it.

Chapter II

System of all Principles of the Pure Understanding

In the foregoing chapter we have merely considered the general conditions under which alone the transcendental faculty of judgement is justified in using the pure conceptions of the understanding for synthetical judgements. Our duty at present is to exhibit in systematic connection those judgements which the understanding really produces à priori. For this purpose, our table of the categories will certainly afford us the natural and safe guidance. For it is precisely the categories whose application to possible experience must constitute all pure à priori cognition of the understanding; and the relation of which to sensibility will, on that very account, present us with a complete and systematic catalogue of all the transcendental principles of the use of the understanding.

Principles à priori are so called, not merely because they contain in themselves the grounds of other judgements, but also because they themselves are not grounded in higher and more general cognitions. This peculiarity, however, does not raise them altogether above the need of a proof. For although there could be found no higher cognition, and therefore no objective proof, and although such a principle rather serves as the foundation for all cognition of the object, this by no means hinders us from drawing a proof from the subjective sources of the possibility of the cognition of an object. Such a proof is necessary, moreover, because without it the principle might be liable to the imputation of being a mere gratuitous assertion.

In the second place, we shall limit our investigations to those principles which relate to the categories. For as to the principles of transcendental æsthetic, according to which space and time are the conditions of the possibility of things as phenomena, as also the restriction of these principles, namely, that they cannot be applied to objects as things in themselves—these, of course, do not fall within the scope of our present inquiry. In like manner, the principles of mathematical science form no part of this system, because they are all drawn from intuition, and not from the pure conception of the understanding. The possibility of these principles, however, will necessarily be considered here, inasmuch as they are synthetical judgements à priori, not indeed for the purpose of proving their accuracy and apodeictic certainty, which is unnecessary, but merely to render conceivable and deduce the possibility of such evident à priori cognitions.

But we shall have also to speak of the principle of analytical judgements, in opposition to synthetical judgements, which is the proper subject of our inquiries, because this very opposition will free the theory of the latter from all ambiguity, and place it clearly before our eyes in its true nature.

Section I. Of the Supreme Principle of all Analytical Judgements

Whatever may be the content of our cognition, and in whatever manner our cognition may be related to its object, the universal, although only negative conditions of all our judgements is that they do not contradict themselves; otherwise these judgements are in themselves (even without respect to the object) nothing. But although there may exist no contradiction in our judgement, it may nevertheless connect conceptions in such a manner that they do not correspond to the object, or without any grounds either à priori or à posteriori for arriving at such a judgement, and thus, without being self-contradictory, a judgement may nevertheless be either false or groundless.

Now, the proposition: "No subject can have a predicate that contradicts it," is called the principle of contradiction, and is a universal but purely negative criterion of all truth. But it belongs to logic alone, because it is valid of cognitions, merely as cognitions and without respect to their content, and declares that the contradiction entirely nullifies them. We can also, however, make a positive use of this principle, that is, not merely to banish falsehood and error (in so far as it rests upon contradiction), but also for the cognition of truth. For if the judgement is analytical, be it affirmative or negative, its truth must always be recognizable by means of the principle of contradiction. For the contrary of that which lies and is cogitated as conception in the cognition of the object will be always properly negatived, but the conception itself must always be affirmed of the object, inasmuch as the contrary thereof would be in contradiction to the object.

We must therefore hold the principle of contradiction to be the universal and fully sufficient Principle of all analytical cognition. But as a sufficient criterion of truth, it has no further utility or authority. For the fact that no cognition can be at variance with this principle without nullifying itself, constitutes this principle the sine qua non, but not the determining ground of the truth of our cognition. As our business at present is properly with the synthetical part of our knowledge only, we shall always be on our guard not to transgress this inviolable principle; but at the same time not to expect from it any direct assistance in the establishment of the truth of any synthetical proposition.

There exists, however, a formula of this celebrated principle—a principle merely formal and entirely without content—which contains a synthesis that has been inadvertently and quite unnecessarily mixed up with it. It is this: "It is impossible for a thing to be and not to be at the same time." Not to mention the superfluousness of the addition of the word impossible to indicate the apodeictic certainty, which ought to be self-evident from the proposition itself, the proposition is affected by the condition of time, and as it were says: "A thing = A, which is something = B, cannot at the same time be non-B." But both, B as well as non-B, may quite well exist in succession. For example, a man who is young cannot at the same time be old; but the same man can very well be at one time young, and at another not young, that is, old. Now the principle of contradiction as a merely logical proposition must not by any means limit its application merely to relations of time, and consequently a formula like the preceding is quite foreign to its true purpose. The misunderstanding arises in this way. We first of all separate a predicate of a thing from the conception of the thing, and afterwards connect with this predicate its opposite, and hence do not establish any contradiction with the subject, but only with its predicate, which has been conjoined with the subject synthetically—a contradiction, moreover, which obtains only when the first and second predicate are affirmed in the same time. If I say: "A man who is ignorant is not learned," the condition "at the same time" must be added, for he who is at one time ignorant, may at another be learned. But if I say: "No ignorant man is a learned man," the proposition is analytical, because the characteristic ignorance is now a constituent part of the conception of the subject; and in this case the negative proposition is evident immediately from the proposition of contradiction, without the necessity of adding the condition "the same time." This is the reason why I have altered the formula of this principle—an alteration which shows very clearly the nature of an analytical proposition.

Section II. Of the Supreme Principle of all Synthetical Judgements

The explanation of the possibility of synthetical judgements is a task with which general logic has nothing to do; indeed she needs not even be acquainted with its name. But in transcendental logic it is the most important matter to be dealt with—indeed the only one, if the question is of the possibility of synthetical judgements à priori, the conditions and extent of their validity. For when this question is fully decided, it can reach its aim with perfect ease, the determination, to wit, of the extent and limits of the pure understanding.

In an analytical judgement I do not go beyond the given conception, in order to arrive at some decision respecting it. If the judgement is affirmative, I predicate of the conception only that which was already cogitated in it; if negative, I merely exclude from the conception its contrary. But in synthetical judgements, I must go beyond the given conception, in order to cogitate, in relation with it, something quite different from that which was cogitated in it, a relation which is consequently never one either of identity or contradiction, and by means of which the truth or error of the judgement cannot be discerned merely from the judgement itself.

Granted, then, that we must go out beyond a given conception, in order to compare it synthetically with another, a third thing is necessary, in which alone the synthesis of two conceptions can originate. Now what is this tertium quid that is to be the medium of all synthetical judgements? It is only a complex in which all our representations are contained, the internal sense to wit, and its form à priori, time.

The synthesis of our representations rests upon the imagination; their synthetical unity (which is requisite to a judgement), upon the unity of apperception. In this, therefore, is to be sought the possibility of synthetical judgements, and as all three contain the sources of à priori representations, the possibility of pure synthetical judgements also; nay, they are necessary upon these grounds, if we are to possess a knowledge of objects, which rests solely upon the synthesis of representations.

If a cognition is to have objective reality, that is, to relate to an object, and possess sense and meaning in respect to it, it is necessary that the object be given in some way or another. Without this, our conceptions are empty, and we may indeed have thought by means of them, but by such thinking we have not, in fact, cognized anything, we have merely played with representation. To give an object, if this expression be understood in the sense of "to present" the object, not mediately but immediately in intuition, means nothing else than to apply the representation of it to experience, be that experience real or only possible. Space and time themselves, pure as these conceptions are from all that is empirical, and certain as it is that they are represented fully à priori in the mind, would be completely without objective validity, and without sense and significance, if their necessary use in the objects of experience were not shown. Nay, the representation of them is a mere schema, that always relates to the reproductive imagination, which calls up the objects of experience, without which they have no meaning. And so it is with all conceptions without distinction.

The possibility of experience is, then, that which gives objective reality to all our à priori cognitions. Now experience depends upon the synthetical unity of phenomena, that is, upon a synthesis according to conceptions of the object of phenomena in general, a synthesis without which experience never could become knowledge, but would be merely a rhapsody of perceptions, never fitting together into any connected text, according to rules of a thoroughly united (possible) consciousness, and therefore never subjected to the transcendental and necessary unity of apperception. Experience has therefore for a foundation, à priori principles of its form, that is to say, general rules of unity in the synthesis of phenomena, the objective reality of which rules, as necessary conditions even of the possibility of experience can which rules, as necessary conditions—even of the possibility of experience—can always be shown in experience. But apart from this relation, à priori synthetical propositions are absolutely impossible, because they have no third term, that is, no pure object, in which the synthetical unity can exhibit the objective reality of its conceptions.

Although, then, respecting space, or the forms which productive imagination describes therein, we do cognize much à priori in synthetical judgements, and are really in no need of experience for this purpose, such knowledge would nevertheless amount to nothing but a busy trifling with a mere chimera, were not space to be considered as the condition of the phenomena which constitute the material of external experience. Hence those pure synthetical judgements do relate, though but mediately, to possible experience, or rather to the possibility of experience, and upon that alone is founded the objective validity of their synthesis.

While then, on the one hand, experience, as empirical synthesis, is the only possible mode of cognition which gives reality to all other synthesis; on the other hand, this latter synthesis, as cognition à priori, possesses truth, that is, accordance with its object, only in so far as it contains nothing more than what is necessary to the synthetical unity of experience.

Accordingly, the supreme principle of all synthetical judgements is: "Every object is subject to the necessary conditions of the synthetical unity of the manifold of intuition in a possible experience."

À priori synthetical judgements are possible when we apply the formal conditions of the à priori intuition, the synthesis of the imagination, and the necessary unity of that synthesis in a transcendental apperception, to a possible cognition of experience, and say: "The conditions of the possibility of experience in general are at the same time conditions of the possibility of the objects of experience, and have, for that reason, objective validity in an à priori synthetical judgement."

Section III. Systematic Representation of all Synthetical Principles of the Pure Understanding

That principles exist at all is to be ascribed solely to the pure understanding, which is not only the faculty of rules in regard to that which happens, but is even the source of principles according to which everything that can be presented to us as an object is necessarily subject to rules, because without such rules we never could attain to cognition of an object. Even the laws of nature, if they are contemplated as principles of the empirical use of the understanding, possess also a characteristic of necessity, and we may therefore at least expect them to be determined upon grounds which are valid à priori and antecedent to all experience. But all laws of nature, without distinction, are subject to higher principles of the understanding, inasmuch as the former are merely applications of the latter to particular cases of experience. These higher principles alone therefore give the conception, which contains the necessary condition, and, as it were, the exponent of a rule; experience, on the other hand, gives the case which comes under the rule.

There is no danger of our mistaking merely empirical principles for principles of the pure understanding, or conversely; for the character of necessity, according to conceptions which distinguish the latter, and the absence of this in every empirical proposition, how extensively valid soever it may be, is a perfect safeguard against confounding them. There are, however, pure principles à priori, which nevertheless I should not ascribe to the pure understanding—for this reason, that they are not derived from pure conceptions, but (although by the mediation of the understanding) from pure intuitions. But understanding is the faculty of conceptions. Such principles mathematical science possesses, but their application to experience, consequently their objective validity, nay the possibility of such à priori synthetical cognitions (the deduction thereof) rests entirely upon the pure understanding.

On this account, I shall not reckon among my principles those of mathematics; though I shall include those upon the possibility and objective validity à priori, of principles of the mathematical science, which, consequently, are to be looked upon as the principle of these, and which proceed from conceptions to intuition, and not from intuition to conceptions.

In the application of the pure conceptions of the understanding to possible experience, the employment of their synthesis is either mathematical or dynamical, for it is directed partly on the intuition alone, partly on the existence of a phenomenon. But the à priori conditions of intuition are in relation to a possible experience absolutely necessary, those of the existence of objects of a possible empirical intuition are in themselves contingent. Hence the principles of the mathematical use of the categories will possess a character of absolute necessity, that is, will be apodeictic; those, on the other hand, of the dynamical use, the character of an à priori necessity indeed, but only under the condition of empirical thought in an experience, therefore only mediately and indirectly. Consequently they will not possess that immediate evidence which is peculiar to the former, although their application to experience does not, for that reason, lose its truth and certitude. But of this point we shall be better able to judge at the conclusion of this system of principles.

The table of the categories is naturally our guide to the table of principles, because these are nothing else than rules for the objective employment of the former. Accordingly, all principles of the pure understanding are:

1
Axioms
of Intuition

2
Anticipations
of Perception

3
Analogies
of Experience

4
Postulates of
Empirical Thought
in general

These appellations I have chosen advisedly, in order that we might not lose sight of the distinctions in respect of the evidence and the employment of these principles. It will, however, soon appear that—a fact which concerns both the evidence of these principles, and the à priori determination of phenomena—according to the categories of quantity and quality (if we attend merely to the form of these), the principles of these categories are distinguishable from those of the two others, in as much as the former are possessed of an intuitive, but the latter of a merely discursive, though in both instances a complete, certitude. I shall therefore call the former mathematical, and the latter dynamical principles.[27] It must be observed, however, that by these terms I mean just as little in the one case the principles of mathematics as those of general (physical) dynamics in the other. I have here in view merely the principles of the pure understanding, in their application to the internal sense (without distinction of the representations given therein), by means of which the sciences of mathematics and dynamics become possible. Accordingly, I have named these principles rather with reference to their application than their content; and I shall now proceed to consider them in the order in which they stand in the table.

1. AXIOMS OF INTUITION.

The principle of these is: All Intuitions are Extensive Quantities.

PROOF.

All phenomena contain, as regards their form, an intuition in space and time, which lies à priori at the foundation of all without exception. Phenomena, therefore, cannot be apprehended, that is, received into empirical consciousness otherwise than through the synthesis of a manifold, through which the representations of a determinate space or time are generated; that is to say, through the composition of the homogeneous and the consciousness of the synthetical unity of this manifold (homogeneous). Now the consciousness of a homogeneous manifold in intuition, in so far as thereby the representation of an object is rendered possible, is the conception of a quantity (quanti). Consequently, even the perception of an object as phenomenon is possible only through the same synthetical unity of the manifold of the given sensuous intuition, through which the unity of the composition of the homogeneous manifold in the conception of a quantity is cogitated; that is to say, all phenomena are quantities, and extensive quantities, because as intuitions in space or time they must be represented by means of the same synthesis through which space and time themselves are determined.

---

[27] All combination (conjunctio) is either composition (compositio) or connection (nexus). The former is the synthesis of a manifold, the parts of which do not necessarily belong to each other. For example, the two triangles into which a square is divided by a diagonal, do not necessarily belong to each other, and of this kind is the synthesis of the homogeneous in everything that can be mathematically considered. This synthesis can be divided into those of aggregation and coalition, the former of which is applied to extensive, the latter to intensive quantities. The second sort of combination (nexus) is the synthesis of a manifold, in so far as its parts do belong necessarily to each other; for example, the accident to a substance, or the effect to the cause. Consequently it is a synthesis of that which though heterogeneous, is represented as connected à priori. This combination—not an arbitrary one—I entitle dynamical because it concerns the connection of the existence of the manifold. This, again, may be divided into the physical synthesis, of the phenomena divided among each other, and the metaphysical synthesis, or the connection of phenomena à priori in the faculty of cognition.

An extensive quantity I call that wherein the representation of the parts renders possible (and therefore necessarily antecedes) the representation of the whole. I cannot represent to myself any line, however small, without drawing it in thought, that is, without generating from a point all its parts one after another, and in this way alone producing this intuition. Precisely the same is the case with every, even the smallest, portion of time. I cogitate therein only the successive progress from one moment to another, and hence, by means of the different portions of time and the addition of them, a determinate quantity of time is produced. As the pure intuition in all phenomena is either time or space, so is every phenomenon in its character of intuition an extensive quantity, inasmuch as it can only be cognized in our apprehension by successive synthesis (from part to part). All phenomena are, accordingly, to be considered as aggregates, that is, as a collection of previously given parts; which is not the case with every sort of quantities, but only with those which are represented and apprehended by us as extensive.

On this successive synthesis of the productive imagination, in the generation of figures, is founded the mathematics of extension, or geometry, with its axioms, which express the conditions of sensuous intuition à priori, under which alone the schema of a pure conception of external intuition can exist; for example, "be tween two points only one straight line is possible," "two straight lines cannot enclose a space," etc. These are the axioms which properly relate only to quantities (quanta) as such.

But, as regards the quantity of a thing (quantitas), that is to say, the answer to the question: "How large is this or that object?" although, in respect to this question, we have various propositions synthetical and immediately certain (indemonstrabilia); we have, in the proper sense of the term, no axioms. For example, the propositions: "If equals be added to equals, the wholes are equal"; "If equals be taken from equals, the remainders are equal"; are analytical, because I am immediately conscious of the identity of the production of the one quantity with the production of the other; whereas axioms must be à priori synthetical propositions. On the other hand, the self-evident propositions as to the relation of numbers, are certainly synthetical but not universal, like those of geometry, and for this reason cannot be called axioms, but numerical formulae. That 7 + 5 = 12 is not an analytical proposition. For neither in the representation of seven, nor of five, nor of the composition of the two numbers, do I cogitate the number twelve. (Whether I cogitate the number in the addition of both, is not at present the question; for in the case of an analytical proposition, the only point is whether I really cogitate the predicate in the representation of the subject.) But although the proposition is synthetical, it is nevertheless only a singular proposition. In so far as regard is here had merely to the synthesis of the homogeneous (the units), it cannot take place except in one manner, although our use of these numbers is afterwards general. If I say: "A triangle can be constructed with three lines, any two of which taken together are greater than the third," I exercise merely the pure function of the productive imagination, which may draw the lines longer or shorter and construct the angles at its pleasure. On the contrary, the number seven is possible only in one manner, and so is likewise the number twelve, which results from the synthesis of seven and five. Such propositions, then, cannot be termed axioms (for in that case we should have an infinity of these), but numerical formulae.

This transcendental principle of the mathematics of phenomena greatly enlarges our à priori cognition. For it is by this principle alone that pure mathematics is rendered applicable in all its precision to objects of experience, and without it the validity of this application would not be so self-evident; on the contrary, contradictions and confusions have often arisen on this very point. Phenomena are not things in themselves. Empirical intuition is possible only through pure intuition (of space and time); consequently, what geometry affirms of the latter, is indisputably valid of the former. All evasions, such as the statement that objects of sense do not conform to the rules of construction in space (for example, to the rule of the infinite divisibility of lines or angles), must fall to the ground. For, if these objections hold good, we deny to space, and with it to all mathematics, objective validity, and no longer know wherefore, and how far, mathematics can be applied to phenomena. The synthesis of spaces and times as the essential form of all intuition, is that which renders possible the apprehension of a phenomenon, and therefore every external experience, consequently all cognition of the objects of experience; and whatever mathematics in its pure use proves of the former, must necessarily hold good of the latter. All objections are but the chicaneries of an ill-instructed reason, which erroneously thinks to liberate the objects of sense from the formal conditions of our sensibility, and represents these, although mere phenomena, as things in themselves, presented as such to our understanding. But in this case, no à priori synthetical cognition of them could be possible, consequently not through pure conceptions of space and the science which determines these conceptions, that is to say, geometry, would itself be impossible.

2. ANTICIPATIONS OF PERCEPTION.

The principle of these is: In all phenomena the Real, that which is an object of sensation, has Intensive Quantity, that is, has a Degree.

PROOF.

Perception is empirical consciousness, that is to say, a consciousness which contains an element of sensation. Phenomena as objects of perception are not pure, that is, merely formal intuitions, like space and time, for they cannot be perceived in themselves.[28] They contain, then, over and above the intuition, the materials for an object (through which is represented something existing in space or time), that is to

[28] They can be perceived only as phenomena, and some part of them must always belong to the non-ego; whereas pure intuitions are entirely the products of the mind itself, and as such are cognized *in themselves.—Tr*

say, they contain the real of sensation, as a representation merely subjective, which gives us merely the consciousness that the subject is affected, and which we refer to some external object. Now, a gradual transition from empirical consciousness to pure consciousness is possible, inasmuch as the real in this consciousness entirely vanishes, and there remains a merely formal consciousness (à priori) of the manifold in time and space; consequently there is possible a synthesis also of the production of the quantity of a sensation from its commencement, that is, from the pure intuition = 0 onwards up to a certain quantity of the sensation. Now as sensation in itself is not an objective representation, and in it is to be found neither the intuition of space nor of time, it cannot possess any extensive quantity, and yet there does belong to it a quantity (and that by means of its apprehension, in which empirical consciousness can within a certain time rise from nothing = 0 up to its given amount), consequently an intensive quantity. And thus we must ascribe intensive quantity, that is, a degree of influence on sense to all objects of perception, in so far as this perception contains sensation.

All cognition, by means of which I am enabled to cognize and determine à priori what belongs to empirical cognition, may be called an anticipation; and without doubt this is the sense in which Epicurus employed his expression prholepsis. But as there is in phenomena something which is never cognized à priori, which on this account constitutes the proper difference between pure and empirical cognition, that is to say, sensation (as the matter of perception), it follows, that sensation is just that element in cognition which cannot be at all anticipated. On the other hand, we might very well term the pure determinations in space and time, as well in regard to figure as to quantity, anticipations of phenomena, because they represent à priori that which may always be given à posteriori in experience. But suppose that in every sensation, as sensation in general, without any particular sensation being thought of, there existed something which could be cognized à priori, this would deserve to be called anticipation in a special sense—special, because it may seem surprising to forestall experience, in that which concerns the matter of experience, and which we can only derive from itself. Yet such really is the case here.

Apprehension[29], by means of sensation alone, fills only one moment, that is, if I do not take into consideration a succession of many sensations. As that in the phenomenon, the apprehension of which is not a successive synthesis advancing from parts to an entire representation, sensation has therefore no extensive quantity; the want of sensation in a moment of time would represent it as empty, consequently = 0. That which in the empirical intuition corresponds to sensation is reality (realitas phaenomenon); that which corresponds to the absence of it, negation = 0. Now every sensation is capable of a diminution, so that it can decrease, and thus gradually disappear. Therefore, between reality in a phenomenon and

[29] Apprehension is the Kantian word for preception, in the largest sense in which we employ that term. It is the genus which includes under i, as species, perception proper and sensation proper—Tr

negation, there exists a continuous concatenation of many possible intermediate sensations, the difference of which from each other is always smaller than that between the given sensation and zero, or complete negation. That is to say, the real in a phenomenon has always a quantity, which however is not discoverable in apprehension, inasmuch as apprehension take place by means of mere sensation in one instant, and not by the successive synthesis of many sensations, and therefore does not progress from parts to the whole. Consequently, it has a quantity, but not an extensive quantity.

Now that quantity which is apprehended only as unity, and in which plurality can be represented only by approximation to negation = O, I term intensive quantity. Consequently, reality in a phenomenon has intensive quantity, that is, a degree. If we consider this reality as cause (be it of sensation or of another reality in the phenomenon, for example, a change), we call the degree of reality in its character of cause a momentum, for example, the momentum of weight; and for this reason, that the degree only indicates that quantity the apprehension of which is not successive, but instantaneous. This, however, I touch upon only in passing, for with causality I have at present nothing to do.

Accordingly, every sensation, consequently every reality in phenomena, however small it may be, has a degree, that is, an intensive quantity, which may always be lessened, and between reality and negation there exists a continuous connection of possible realities, and possible smaller perceptions. Every colour—for example, red—has a degree, which, be it ever so small, is never the smallest, and so is it always with heat, the momentum of weight, etc.

This property of quantities, according to which no part of them is the smallest possible (no part simple), is called their continuity. Space and time are quanta continua, because no part of them can be given, without enclosing it within boundaries (points and moments), consequently, this given part is itself a space or a time. Space, therefore, consists only of spaces, and time of times. Points and moments are only boundaries, that is, the mere places or positions of their limitation. But places always presuppose intuitions which are to limit or determine them; and we cannot conceive either space or time composed of constituent parts which are given before space or time. Such quantities may also be called flowing, because synthesis (of the productive imagination) in the production of these quantities is a progression in time, the continuity of which we are accustomed to indicate by the expression flowing.

All phenomena, then, are continuous quantities, in respect both to intuition and mere perception (sensation, and with it reality). In the former case they are extensive quantities; in the latter, intensive. When the synthesis of the manifold of a phenomenon is interrupted, there results merely an aggregate of several phenomena, and not properly a phenomenon as a quantity, which is not produced by the mere continuation of the productive synthesis of a certain kind, but by the repetition of a synthesis always ceasing. For example, if I call thirteen dollars a sum or quantity of money, I employ the term quite correctly, inasmuch as I understand by thirteen dollars the value of a mark in standard silver, which is, to be sure, a continuous quantity, in which no part is the smallest, but every part might constitute a piece of money, which would contain material for still smaller pieces. If, however, by the words thirteen dollars I understand so many coins (be their value in silver what it may), it would be quite erroneous to use the expression a quantity of dollars; on the contrary, I must call them aggregate, that is, a number of coins. And as in every number we must have unity as the foundation, so a phenomenon taken as unity is a quantity, and as such always a continuous quantity (quantum continuum).

Now, seeing all phenomena, whether considered as extensive or intensive, are continuous quantities, the proposition: "All change (transition of a thing from one state into another) is continuous," might be proved here easily, and with mathematical evidence, were it not that the causality of a change lies, entirely beyond the bounds of a transcendental philosophy, and presupposes empirical principles. For of the possibility of a cause which changes the condition of things, that is, which determines them to the contrary to a certain given state, the understanding gives us à priori no knowledge; not merely because it has no insight into the possibility of it (for such insight is absent in several à priori cognitions), but because the notion of change concerns only certain determinations of phenomena, which experience alone can acquaint us with, while their cause lies in the unchangeable. But seeing that we have nothing which we could here employ but the pure fundamental conceptions of all possible experience, among which of course nothing empirical can be admitted, we dare not, without injuring the unity of our system, anticipate general physical science, which is built upon certain fundamental experiences.

Nevertheless, we are in no want of proofs of the great influence which the principle above developed exercises in the anticipation of perceptions, and even in supplying the want of them, so far as to shield us against the false conclusions which otherwise we might rashly draw.

If all reality in perception has a degree, between which and negation there is an endless sequence of ever smaller degrees, and if, nevertheless, every sense must have a determinate degree of receptivity for sensations; no perception, and consequently no experience is possible, which can prove, either immediately or mediately, an entire absence of all reality in a phenomenon; in other words, it is impossible ever to draw from experience a proof of the existence of empty space or of empty time. For in the first place, an entire absence of reality in a sensuous intuition cannot of course be an object of perception; secondly, such absence cannot be deduced from the contemplation of any single phenomenon, and the difference of the degrees in its reality; nor ought it ever to be admitted in explanation of any phenomenon. For if even the complete intuition of a determinate space or time is thoroughly real, that is, if no part thereof is empty, yet because every reality has its degree, which, with the extensive quantity of the phenomenon unchanged, can diminish through endless gradations down to nothing (the void), there must be infinitely graduated degrees, with which space or time is filled, and the intensive quantity in different phenomena may be smaller or greater, although the extensive quantity of the intuition remains equal and unaltered.

We shall give an example of this. Almost all natural philosophers, remarking a great difference in the quantity of the matter of different kinds in bodies with the same volume (partly on account of the momentum of gravity or weight, partly on account of the momentum of resistance to other bodies in motion), conclude unanimously that this volume (extensive quantity of the phenomenon) must be void in all bodies, although in different proportion. But who would suspect that these for the most part mathematical and mechanical inquirers into nature should ground this conclusion solely on a metaphysical hypothesis—a sort of hypothesis which they profess to disparage and avoid? Yet this they do, in assuming that the real in space (I must not here call it impenetrability or weight, because these are empirical conceptions) is always identical, and can only be distinguished according to its extensive quantity, that is, multiplicity. Now to this presupposition, for which they can have no ground in experience, and which consequently is merely metaphysical, I oppose a transcendental demonstration, which it is true will not explain the difference in the filling up of spaces, but which nevertheless completely does away with the supposed necessity of the above-mentioned presupposition that we cannot explain the said difference otherwise than by the hypothesis of empty spaces. This demonstration, moreover, has the merit of setting the understanding at liberty to conceive this distinction in a different manner, if the explanation of the fact requires any such hypothesis. For we perceive that although two equal spaces may be completely filled by matters altogether different, so that in neither of them is there left a single point wherein matter is not present, nevertheless, every reality has its degree (of resistance or of weight), which, without diminution of the extensive quantity, can become less and less ad infinitum, before it passes into nothingness and disappears. Thus an expansion which fills a space—for example, caloric, or any other reality in the phenomenal world—can decrease in its degrees to infinity, yet without leaving the smallest part of the space empty; on the contrary, filling it with those lesser degrees as completely as another phenomenon could with greater. My intention here is by no means to maintain that this is really the case with the difference of matters, in regard to their specific gravity; I wish only to prove, from a principle of the pure understanding, that the nature of our perceptions makes such a mode of explanation possible, and that it is erroneous to regard the real in a phenomenon as equal quoad its degree, and different only quoad its aggregation and extensive quantity, and this, too, on the pretended authority of an à priori principle of the understanding.

Nevertheless, this principle of the anticipation of perception must somewhat startle an inquirer whom initiation into transcendental philosophy has rendered cautious. We must naturally entertain some doubt whether or not the understanding can enounce any such synthetical proposition as that respecting the degree of all reality in phenomena, and consequently the possibility of the internal difference of sensation itself—abstraction being made of its empirical quality. Thus it is a question not unworthy of solution: "How the understanding can pronounce synthetically and à priori respecting phenomena, and thus anticipate these, even in that which is peculiarly and merely empirical, that, namely, which concerns sensation itself?"

The quality of sensation is in all cases merely empirical, and cannot be represented à priori (for example, colours, taste, etc.). But the real—that which corresponds to sensation—in opposition to negation = 0, only represents something the conception of which in itself contains a being (ein seyn), and signifies nothing but the synthesis in an empirical consciousness. That is to say, the empirical consciousness in the internal sense can be raised from 0 to every higher degree, so that the very same extensive quantity of intuition, an illuminated surface, for example, excites as great a sensation as an aggregate of many other surfaces less illuminated. We can therefore make complete abstraction of the extensive quantity of a phenomenon, and represent to ourselves in the mere sensation in a certain momentum, a synthesis of homogeneous ascension from 0 up to the given empirical consciousness, All sensations therefore as such are given only à posteriori, but this property thereof, namely, that they have a degree, can be known à priori. It is worthy of remark, that in respect to quantities in general, we can cognize à priori only a single quality, namely, continuity; but in respect to all quality (the real in phenomena), we cannot cognize à priori anything more than the intensive quantity thereof, namely, that they have a degree. All else is left to experience.

3. ANALOGIES OF EXPERIENCE.

The principle of these is: Experience is possible only through the representation of a necessary connection of Perceptions.

PROOF.

Experience is an empirical cognition; that is to say, a cognition which determines an object by means of perceptions. It is therefore a synthesis of perceptions, a synthesis which is not itself contained in perception, but which contains the synthetical unity of the manifold of perception in a consciousness; and this unity constitutes the essential of our cognition of objects of the senses, that is, of experience (not merely of intuition or sensation). Now in experience our perceptions come together contingently, so that no character of necessity in their connection appears, or can appear from the perceptions themselves, because apprehension is only a placing together of the manifold of empirical intuition, and no representation of a necessity in the connected existence of the phenomena which apprehension brings together, is to be discovered therein. But as experience is a cognition of objects by means of perceptions, it follows that the relation of the existence of the existence of the manifold must be represented in experience not as it is put together in time, but as it is objectively in time. And as time itself cannot be perceived, the determination of the existence of objects in time can only take place by means of their connection in time in general, consequently only by means of à priori connecting conceptions. Now as these conceptions always possess the character of necessity, experience is possible only by means of a representation of the necessary connection of perception.

The three modi of time are permanence, succession, and coexistence. Accordingly, there are three rules of all relations of time in phenomena, according to which the existence of every phenomenon is determined in respect of the unity of all time, and these antecede all experience and render it possible.

The general principle of all three analogies rests on the necessary unity of apperception in relation to all possible empirical consciousness (perception) at every time, consequently, as this unity lies à priori at the foundation of all mental operations, the principle rests on the synthetical unity of all phenomena according to their relation in time. For the original apperception relates to our internal sense (the complex of all representations), and indeed relates à priori to its form, that is to say, the relation of the manifold empirical consciousness in time. Now this manifold must be combined in original apperception according to relations of time—a necessity imposed by the à priori transcendental unity of apperception, to which is subjected all that can belong to my (i.e., my own) cognition, and therefore all that can become an object for me. This synthetical and à priori determined unity in relation of perceptions in time is therefore the rule: "All empirical determinations of time must be subject to rules of the general determination of time"; and the analogies of experience, of which we are now about to treat, must be rules of this nature.

These principles have this peculiarity, that they do not concern phenomena, and the synthesis of the empirical intuition thereof, but merely the existence of phenomena and their relation to each other in regard to this existence. Now the mode in which we apprehend a thing in a phenomenon can be determined à priori in such a manner that the rule of its synthesis can give, that is to say, can produce this à priori intuition in every empirical example. But the existence of phenomena cannot be known à priori, and although we could arrive by this path at a conclusion of the fact of some existence, we could not cognize that existence determinately, that is to say, we should be incapable of anticipating in what respect the empirical intuition of it would be distinguishable from that of others.

The two principles above mentioned, which I called mathematical, in consideration of the fact of their authorizing the application of mathematic phenomena, relate to these phenomena only in regard to their possibility, and instruct us how phenomena, as far as regards their intuition or the real in their perception, can be generated according to the rules of a mathematical synthesis. Consequently, numerical quantities, and with them the determination of a phenomenon as a quantity, can be employed in the one case as well as in the other.

Thus, for example, out of 200,000 illuminations by the moon, I might compose and give à priori, that is construct, the degree of our sensations of the sun-light.[30] We may therefore entitle these two principles constitutive.

The case is very different with those principles whose province it is to subject the existence of phenomena to rules à priori. For as existence does not admit of being constructed, it is clear that they must only concern the relations of existence and be merely regulative principles. In this case, therefore, neither axioms nor anticipations are to be thought of. Thus, if a perception is given us, in a certain relation of time to other (although undetermined) perceptions, we cannot then say à priori, what and how great (in quantity) the other perception necessarily connected with the former is, but only how it is connected, quoad its existence, in this given modus of time. Analogies in philosophy mean something very different from that which they represent in mathematics. In the latter they are formulae, which enounce the equality of two relations of quantity, and are always constitutive, so that if two terms of the proportion are given, the third is also given, that is, can be constructed by the aid of these formulae. But in philosophy, analogy is not the equality of two quantitative but of two qualitative relations. In this case, from three given terms, I can give à priori and cognize the relation to a fourth member, but not this fourth term itself, although I certainly possess a rule to guide me in the search for this fourth term in experience, and a mark to assist me in discovering it. An analogy of experience is therefore only a rule according to which unity of experience must arise out of perceptions in respect to objects (phenomena) not as a constitutive, but merely as a regulative principle. The same holds good also of the postulates of empirical thought in general, which relate to the synthesis of mere intuition (which concerns the form of phenomena), the synthesis of perception (which concerns the matter of phenomena), and the synthesis of experience (which concerns the relation of these perceptions). For they are only regulative principles, and clearly distinguishable from the mathematical, which are constitutive, not indeed in regard to the certainty which both possess à priori, but in the mode of evidence thereof, consequently also in the manner of demonstration.

But what has been observed of all synthetical propositions, and must be particularly remarked in this place, is this, that these analogies possess significance and validity, not as principles of the transcendental, but only as principles of the empirical use of the understanding, and their truth can therefore be proved only as such, and that consequently the phenomena must not be subjoined directly under the categories, but only under their schemata. For if the objects to which those principles must be applied were things in themselves, it would be quite

[30] Kant's meaning is: The two principles enunciated under the heads of "Axioms of Intuition," and "Anticipations of Perception," authorize the application to phenomena of determinations of size and number, that is of mathematic. For example, I may compute the light of the sun, and say that its quantity is a certain number of times greater than that of the moon. In the same way, heat is measured by the comparison of its different effects on water, &c., and on mercury in a thermometer.—Tr

impossible to cognize aught concerning them synthetically à priori. But they are nothing but phenomena; a complete knowledge of which—a knowledge to which all principles à priori must at last relate—is the only possible experience. It follows that these principles can have nothing else for their aim than the conditions of the empirical cognition in the unity of synthesis of phenomena. But this synthesis is cogitated only in the schema of the pure conception of the understanding, of whose unity, as that of a synthesis in general, the category contains the function unrestricted by any sensuous condition. These principles will therefore authorize us to connect phenomena according to an analogy, with the logical and universal unity of conceptions, and consequently to employ the categories in the principles themselves; but in the application of them to experience, we shall use only their schemata, as the key to their proper application, instead of the categories, or rather the latter as restricting conditions, under the title of "formulae" of the former.

A. FIRST ANALOGY.

Principle of the Permanence of Substance.

In all changes of phenomena, substance is permanent, and the quantum thereof in nature is neither increased nor diminished.

PROOF.

All phenomena exist in time, wherein alone as substratum, that is, as the permanent form of the internal intuition, coexistence and succession can be represented. Consequently time, in which all changes of phenomena must be cogitated, remains and changes not, because it is that in which succession and coexistence can be represented only as determinations thereof. Now, time in itself cannot be an object of perception. It follows that in objects of perception, that is, in phenomena, there must be found a substratum which represents time in general, and in which all change or coexistence can be perceived by means of the relation of phenomena to it. But the substratum of all reality, that is, of all that pertains to the existence of things, is substance; all that pertains to existence can be cogitated only as a determination of substance. Consequently, the permanent, in relation to which alone can all relations of time in phenomena be determined, is substance in the world of phenomena, that is, the real in phenomena, that which, as the substratum of all change, remains ever the same. Accordingly, as this cannot change in existence, its quantity in nature can neither be increased nor diminished.

Our apprehension of the manifold in a phenomenon is always successive, is Consequently always changing. By it alone we could, therefore, never determine whether this manifold, as an object of experience, is coexistent or successive, unless it had for a foundation something fixed and permanent, of the existence of which all succession and coexistence are nothing but so many modes (modi of time). Only in the permanent, then, are relations of time possible (for simultaneity and succession are the only relations in time); that is to say, the permanent is the substratum of our empirical representation of time itself, in which alone all determination of time is possible. Permanence is, in fact, just another expression for time, as the abiding correlate of all existence of phenomena, and of all change, and of all coexistence. For change does not affect time itself, but only the phenomena in time (just as coexistence cannot be regarded as a modus of time itself, seeing that in time no parts are coexistent, but all successive). If we were to attribute succession to time itself, we should be obliged to cogitate another time, in which this succession would be possible. It is only by means of the permanent that existence in different parts of the successive series of time receives a quantity, which we entitle duration. For in mere succession, existence is perpetually vanishing and recommencing, and therefore never has even the least quantity. Without the permanent, then, no relation in time is possible. Now, time in itself is not an object of perception; consequently the permanent in phenomena must be regarded as the substratum of all determination of time, and consequently also as the condition of the possibility of all synthetical unity of perceptions, that is, of experience; and all existence and all change in time can only be regarded as a mode in the existence of that which abides unchangeably. Therefore, in all phenomena, the permanent is the object in itself, that is, the substance (phenomenon); but all that changes or can change belongs only to the mode of the existence of this substance or substances, consequently to its determinations.

I find that in all ages not only the philosopher, but even the common understanding, has preposited this permanence as a substratum of all change in phenomena; indeed, I am compelled to believe that they will always accept this as an indubitable fact. Only the philosopher expresses himself in a more precise and definite manner, when he says: "In all changes in the world, the substance remains, and the accidents alone are changeable." But of this decidedly synthetical proposition, I nowhere meet with even an attempt at proof; nay, it very rarely has the good fortune to stand, as it deserves to do, at the head of the pure and entirely à priori laws of nature. In truth, the statement that substance is permanent, is tautological. For this very permanence is the ground on which we apply the category of substance to the phenomenon; and we should have been obliged to prove that in all phenomena there is something permanent, of the existence of which the changeable is nothing but a determination. But because a proof of this nature cannot be dogmatical, that is, cannot be drawn from conceptions, inasmuch as it concerns a synthetical proposition à priori, and as philosophers never reflected that such propositions are valid only in relation to possible experience, and therefore cannot be proved except by means of a deduction of the possibility of experience, it is no wonder that while it has served as the foundation of all experience (for we feel the need of it in empirical cognition), it has never been supported by proof.

A philosopher was asked: "What is the weight of smoke?" He answered: "Subtract from the weight of the burnt wood the weight of the remaining ashes, and you will have the weight of the smoke." Thus he presumed it to be incontrovertible that even in fire the matter (substance) does not perish, but that only the form of it undergoes a change. In like manner was the saying: "From nothing comes nothing," only another inference from the principle or permanence, or rather of the ever-abiding existence of the true subject in phenomena. For if that in the phenomenon which we call substance is to be the proper substratum of all determination of time, it follows that all existence in past as well as in future time, must be determinable by means of it alone. Hence we are entitled to apply the term substance to a phenomenon, only because we suppose its existence in all time, a notion which the word permanence does not fully express, as it seems rather to be referable to future time. However, the internal necessity perpetually to be, is inseparably connected with the necessity always to have been, and so the expression may stand as it is. "Gigni de nihilo nihil; in nihilum nil posse reverti,"[31] are two propositions which the ancients never parted, and which people nowadays sometimes mistakenly disjoin, because they imagine that the propositions apply to objects as things in themselves, and that the former might be inimical to the dependence (even in respect of its substance also) of the world upon a supreme cause. But this apprehension is entirely needless, for the question in this case is only of phenomena in the sphere of experience, the unity of which never could be possible, if we admitted the possibility that new things (in respect of their substance) should arise. For in that case, we should lose altogether that which alone can represent the unity of time, to wit, the identity of the substratum, as that through which alone all change possesses complete and thorough unity. This permanence is, however, nothing but the manner in which we represent to ourselves the existence of things in the phenomenal world.

The determinations of a substance, which are only particular modes of its existence, are called accidents. They are always real, because they concern the existence of substance (negations are only determinations, which express the non-existence of something in the substance). Now, if to this real in the substance we ascribe a particular existence (for example, to motion as an accident of matter), this existence is called inherence, in contradistinction to the existence of substance, which we call subsistence. But hence arise many misconceptions, and it would be a more accurate and just mode of expression to designate the accident only as the mode in which the existence of a substance is positively determined. Meanwhile, by reason of the conditions of the logical exercise of our understanding, it is impossible to avoid separating, as it were, that which in the existence of a substance is subject to change, whilst the substance remains, and regarding it in relation to that which is properly permanent and radical. On this account, this category of substance stands under the title of relation, rather because it is the condition thereof than because it contains in itself any relation.

Now, upon this notion of permanence rests the proper notion of the conception change. Origin and extinction are not changes of that which originates or becomes

[31] Persius, Satirae, iii.83-84.

extinct. Change is but a mode of existence, which follows on another mode of existence of the same object; hence all that changes is permanent, and only the condition thereof changes. Now since this mutation affects only determinations, which can have a beginning or an end, we may say, employing an expression which seems somewhat paradoxical: "Only the permanent (substance) is subject to change; the mutable suffers no change, but rather alternation, that is, when certain determinations cease, others begin."

Change, when, cannot be perceived by us except in substances, and origin or extinction in an absolute sense, that does not concern merely a determination of the permanent, cannot be a possible perception, for it is this very notion of the permanent which renders possible the representation of a transition from one state into another, and from non-being to being, which, consequently, can be empirically cognized only as alternating determinations of that which is permanent. Grant that a thing absolutely begins to be; we must then have a point of time in which it was not. But how and by what can we fix and determine this point of time, unless by that which already exists? For a void time—preceding—is not an object of perception; but if we connect this beginning with objects which existed previously, and which continue to exist till the object in question in question begins to be, then the latter can only be a determination of the former as the permanent. The same holds good of the notion of extinction, for this presupposes the empirical representation of a time, in which a phenomenon no longer exists.

Substances (in the world of phenomena) are the substratum of all determinations of time. The beginning of some, and the ceasing to be of other substances, would utterly do away with the only condition of the empirical unity of time; and in that case phenomena would relate to two different times, in which, side by side, existence would pass; which is absurd. For there is only one time in which all different times must be placed, not as coexistent, but as successive.

Accordingly, permanence is a necessary condition under which alone phenomena, as things or objects, are determinable in a possible experience. But as regards the empirical criterion of this necessary permanence, and with it of the substantiality of phenomena, we shall find sufficient opportunity to speak in the sequel.

B. SECOND ANALOGY.

Principle of the Succession of Time According to the Law of Causality. All changes take place according to the law of the connection of Cause and Effect.

PROOF.

(That all phenomena in the succession of time are only changes, that is, a successive being and non-being of the determinations of substance, which is permanent; consequently that a being of substance itself which follows on the non-being thereof, or a non-being of substance which follows on the being thereof, in other words, that the origin or extinction of substance itself, is impossible—all this has been fully established in treating of the foregoing principle. This principle might have been expressed as follows: "All alteration (succession) of phenomena is merely change"; for the changes of substance are not origin or extinction, because the conception of change presupposes the same subject as existing with two opposite determinations, and consequently as permanent. After this premonition, we shall proceed to the proof.)

I perceive that phenomena succeed one another, that is to say, a state of things exists at one time, the opposite of which existed in a former state. In this case, then, I really connect together two perceptions in time. Now connection is not an operation of mere sense and intuition, but is the product of a synthetical faculty of imagination, which determines the internal sense in respect of a relation of time. But imagination can connect these two states in two ways, so that either the one or the other may antecede in time; for time in itself cannot be an object of perception, and what in an object precedes and what follows cannot be empirically determined in relation to it. I am only conscious, then, that my imagination places one state before and the other after; not that the one state antecedes the other in the object. In other words, the objective relation of the successive phenomena remains quite undetermined by means of mere perception. Now in order that this relation may be cognized as determined, the relation between the two states must be so cogitated that it is thereby determined as necessary, which of them must be placed before and which after, and not conversely. But the conception which carries with it a necessity of synthetical unity, can be none other than a pure conception of the understanding which does not lie in mere perception; and in this case it is the conception of "the relation of cause and effect," the former of which determines the latter in time, as its necessary consequence, and not as something which might possibly antecede (or which might in some cases not be perceived to follow). It follows that it is only because we subject the sequence of phenomena, and consequently all change, to the law of causality, that experience itself, that is, empirical cognition of phenomena, becomes possible; and consequently, that phenomena themselves, as objects of experience, are possible only by virtue of this law.

Our apprehension of the manifold of phenomena is always successive. The representations of parts succeed one another. Whether they succeed one another in the object also, is a second point for reflection, which was not contained in the former. Now we may certainly give the name of object to everything, even to every representation, so far as we are conscious thereof; but what this word may mean in the case of phenomena, not merely in so far as they (as representations) are objects, but only in so far as they indicate an object, is a question requiring deeper consideration. In so far as they, regarded merely as representations, are at the same time objects of consciousness, they are not to be distinguished from apprehension, that is, reception into the synthesis of imagination, and we must therefore say: "The manifold of phenomena is always produced successively in the mind." If phenomena were things in themselves, no man would be able to conjecture from the succession of our representations how this manifold is connected in the object; for we have to do only with our representations. How things may be in themselves, without regard to the representations through which they affect us, is utterly beyond the sphere of our cognition. Now although phenomena are not things in themselves, and are nevertheless the only thing given to us to be cognized, it is my duty to show what sort of connection in time belongs to the manifold in phenomena themselves, while the representation of this manifold in apprehension is always successive. For example, the apprehension of the manifold in the phenomenon of a house which stands before me, is successive. Now comes the question whether the manifold of this house is in itself successive—which no one will be at all willing to grant. But, so soon as I raise my conception of an object to the transcendental signification thereof, I find that the house is not a thing in itself, but only a phenomenon, that is, a representation, the transcendental object of which remains utterly unknown. What then am I to understand by the question: "How can the manifold be connected in the phenomenon itself—not considered as a thing in itself, but merely as a phenomenon?" Here that which lies in my successive apprehension is regarded as representation, whilst the phenomenon which is given me, notwithstanding that it is nothing more than a complex of these representations, is regarded as the object thereof, with which my conception, drawn from the representations of apprehension, must harmonize. It is very soon seen that, as accordance of the cognition with its object constitutes truth, the question now before us can only relate to the formal conditions of empirical truth; and that the phenomenon, in opposition to the representations of apprehension, can only be distinguished therefrom as the object of them, if it is subject to a rule which distinguishes it from every other apprehension, and which renders necessary a mode of connection of the manifold. That in the phenomenon which contains the condition of this necessary rule of apprehension, is the object.

Let us now proceed to our task. That something happens, that is to say, that something or some state exists which before was not, cannot be empirically perceived, unless a phenomenon precedes, which does not contain in itself this state. For a reality which should follow upon a void time, in other words, a beginning, which no state of things precedes, can just as little be apprehended as the void time itself. Every apprehension of an event is therefore a perception which follows upon another perception. But as this is the case with all synthesis of apprehension, as I have shown above in the example of a house, my apprehension of an event is not yet sufficiently distinguished from other apprehensions. But I remark also that if in a phenomenon which contains an occurrence, I call the antecedent state of my perception, A, and the following state, B, the perception B can only follow A in apprehension, and the perception A cannot follow B, but only precede it. For example, I see a ship float down the stream of a river. My perception of its place lower down follows upon my perception of its place higher up the course of the river, and it is impossible that, in the apprehension of this phenomenon, the vessel should be perceived first below and afterwards higher up the stream. Here, therefore, the order in the sequence of perceptions in apprehension is determined; and by this order apprehension is regulated. In the former example, my perceptions in the apprehension of a house might begin at the roof and end at the foundation, or vice versa; or I might apprehend the manifold in this empirical intuition, by going from left to right, and from right to left. Accordingly, in the series of these perceptions, there was no determined order, which necessitated my beginning at a certain point, in order empirically to connect the manifold. But this rule is always to be met with in the perception of that which happens, and it makes the order of the successive perceptions in the apprehension of such a phenomenon necessary.

I must, therefore, in the present case, deduce the subjective sequence of apprehension from the objective sequence of phenomena, for otherwise the former is quite undetermined, and one phenomenon is not distinguishable from another. The former alone proves nothing as to the connection of the manifold in an object, for it is quite arbitrary. The latter must consist in the order of the manifold in a phenomenon, according to which order the apprehension of one thing (that which happens) follows that of another thing (which precedes), in conformity with a rule. In this way alone can I be authorized to say of the phenomenon itself, and not merely of my own apprehension, that a certain order or sequence is to be found therein. That is, in other words, I cannot arrange my apprehension otherwise than in this order.

In conformity with this rule, then, it is necessary that in that which antecedes an event there be found the condition of a rule, according to which in this event follows always and necessarily; but I cannot reverse this and go back from the event, and determine (by apprehension) that which antecedes it. For no phenomenon goes back from the succeeding point of time to the preceding point, although it does certainly relate to a preceding point of time; from a given time, on the other hand, there is always a necessary progression to the determined succeeding time. Therefore, because there certainly is something that follows, I must of necessity connect it with something else, which antecedes, and upon which it follows, in conformity with a rule, that is necessarily, so that the event, as conditioned, affords certain indication of a condition, and this condition determines the event.

Let us suppose that nothing precedes an event, upon which this event must follow in conformity with a rule. All sequence of perception would then exist only in apprehension, that is to say, would be merely subjective, and it could not thereby be objectively determined what thing ought to precede, and what ought to follow in perception. In such a case, we should have nothing but a play of representations, which would possess no application to any object. That is to say, it would not be possible through perception to distinguish one phenomenon from another, as regards relations of time; because the succession in the act of apprehension would always be of the same sort, and therefore there would be nothing in the phenomenon to determine the succession, and to render a certain sequence objectively necessary. And, in this case, I cannot say that two states in a phenomenon follow one upon the other, but only that one apprehension follows upon another. But this is merely subjective, and does not determine an object, and consequently cannot be held to be cognition of an object—not even in the phenomenal world.

Accordingly, when we know in experience that something happens, we always presuppose that something precedes, whereupon it follows in conformity with a rule. For otherwise I could not say of the object that it follows; because the mere succession in my apprehension, if it be not determined by a rule in relation to something preceding, does not authorize succession in the object. Only, therefore, in reference to a rule, according to which phenomena are determined in their sequence, that is, as they happen, by the preceding state, can I make my subjective synthesis (of apprehension) objective, and it is only under this presupposition that even the experience of an event is possible.

No doubt it appears as if this were in thorough contradiction to all the notions which people have hitherto entertained in regard to the procedure of the human understanding. According to these opinions, it is by means of the perception and comparison of similar consequences following upon certain antecedent phenomena that the understanding is led to the discovery of a rule, according to which certain events always follow certain phenomena, and it is only by this process that we attain to the conception of cause. Upon such a basis, it is clear that this conception must be merely empirical, and the rule which it furnishes us with—"Everything that happens must have a cause"—would be just as contingent as experience itself. The universality and necessity of the rule or law would be perfectly spurious attributes of it. Indeed, it could not possess universal validity, inasmuch as it would not in this case be à priori, but founded on deduction. But the same is the case with this law as with other pure à priori representations (e.g., space and time), which we can draw in perfect clearness and completeness from experience, only because we had already placed them therein, and by that means, and by that alone, had rendered experience possible. Indeed, the logical clearness of this representation of a rule, determining the series of events, is possible only when we have made use thereof in experience. Nevertheless, the recognition of this rule, as a condition of the synthetical unity of phenomena in time, was the ground of experience itself and consequently preceded it à priori.

It is now our duty to show by an example that we never, even in experience, attribute to an object the notion of succession or effect (of an event—that is, the happening of something that did not exist before), and distinguish it from the subjective succession of apprehension, unless when a rule lies at the foundation, which compels us to observe this order of perception in preference to any other, and that, indeed, it is this necessity which first renders possible the representation of a succession in the object.

We have representations within us, of which also we can be conscious. But, however widely extended, however accurate and thoroughgoing this consciousness may be, these representations are still nothing more than representations, that is, internal determinations of the mind in this or that relation of time. Now how happens it that to these representations we should set an object, or that, in addition to their subjective reality, as modifications, we should still further attribute to them a certain unknown objective reality? It is clear that objective significancy cannot consist in a relation to another representation (of that which we desire to term object), for in that case the question again arises: "How does this other representation go out of itself, and obtain objective significancy over and above the subjective, which is proper to it, as a determination of a state of mind?" If we try to discover what sort of new property the relation to an object gives to our subjective representations, and what new importance they thereby receive, we shall find that this relation has no other effect than that of rendering necessary the connection of our representations in a certain manner, and of subjecting them to a rule; and that conversely, it is only because a certain order is necessary in the relations of time of our representations, that objective significancy is ascribed to them.

In the synthesis of phenomena, the manifold of our representations is always successive. Now hereby is not represented an object, for by means of this succession, which is common to all apprehension, no one thing is distinguished from another. But so soon as I perceive or assume that in this succession there is a relation to a state antecedent, from which the representation follows in accordance with a rule, so soon do I represent something as an event, or as a thing that happens; in other words, I cognize an object to which I must assign a certain determinate position in time, which cannot be altered, because of the preceding state in the object. When, therefore, I perceive that something happens, there is contained in this representation, in the first place, the fact, that something antecedes; because, it is only in relation to this that the phenomenon obtains its proper relation of time, in other words, exists after an antecedent time, in which it did not exist. But it can receive its determined place in time only by the presupposition that something existed in the foregoing state, upon which it follows inevitably and always, that is, in conformity with a rule. From all this it is evident that, in the first place, I cannot reverse the order of succession, and make that which happens precede that upon which it follows; and that, in the second place, if the antecedent state be posited, a certain determinate event inevitably and necessarily follows. Hence it follows that there exists a certain order in our representations, whereby the present gives a sure indication of some previously existing state, as a correlate, though still undetermined, of the existing event which is given—a correlate which itself relates to the event as its consequence, conditions it, and connects it necessarily with itself in the series of time.

If then it be admitted as a necessary law of sensibility, and consequently a formal condition of all perception, that the preceding necessarily determines the succeeding time (inasmuch as I cannot arrive at the succeeding except through the preceding), it must likewise be an indispensable law of empirical representation of the series of time that the phenomena of the past determine all phenomena in the succeeding time, and that the latter, as events, cannot take place, except in so far as the former determine their existence in time, that is to say, establish it according to a rule. For it is of course only in phenomena that we can empirically cognize this continuity in the connection of times.

For all experience and for the possibility of experience, understanding is indispensable, and the first step which it takes in this sphere is not to render the representation of objects clear, but to render the representation of an object in general, possible. It does this by applying the order of time to phenomena, and their existence. In other words, it assigns to each phenomenon, as a consequence, a place in relation to preceding phenomena, determined à priori in time, without which it could not harmonize with time itself, which determines a place à priori to all its parts. This determination of place cannot be derived from the relation of phenomena to absolute time (for it is not an object of perception); but, on the contrary, phenomena must reciprocally determine the places in time of one another, and render these necessary in the order of time. In other words, whatever follows or happens, must follow in conformity with a universal rule upon that which was contained in the foregoing state. Hence arises a series of phenomena, which, by means of the understanding, produces and renders necessary exactly the same order and continuous connection in the series of our possible perceptions, as is found à priori in the form of internal intuition (time), in which all our perceptions must have place.

That something happens, then, is a perception which belongs to a possible experience, which becomes real only because I look upon the phenomenon as determined in regard to its place in time, consequently as an object, which can always be found by means of a rule in the connected series of my perceptions. But this rule of the determination of a thing according to succession in time is as follows: "In what precedes may be found the condition, under which an event always (that is, necessarily) follows." From all this it is obvious that the principle of cause and effect is the principle of possible experience, that is, of objective cognition of phenomena, in regard to their relations in the succession of time.

The proof of this fundamental proposition rests entirely on the following momenta of argument. To all empirical cognition belongs the synthesis of the manifold by the imagination, a synthesis which is always successive, that is, in which the representations therein always follow one another. But the order of succession in imagination is not determined, and the series of successive representations may be taken retrogressively as well as progressively. But if this synthesis is a synthesis of apprehension (of the manifold of a given phenomenon), then the order is determined in the object, or to speak more accurately, there is therein an order of successive synthesis which determines an object, and according to which something necessarily precedes, and when this is posited, something else necessarily follows. If, then, my perception is to contain the cognition of an event, that is, of something which really happens, it must be an empirical judgement, wherein we think that the succession is determined; that is, it presupposes another phenomenon, upon which this event follows necessarily, or in conformity with a rule. If, on the contrary, when I posited the antecedent, the event did not necessarily follow, I should be obliged to consider it merely as a subjective play of my imagination, and if in this I represented to myself anything as objective, I must look upon it as a mere dream. Thus, the relation of phenomena (as possible perceptions), according to which that which happens is, as to its existence, necessarily determined in time by something which antecedes, in conformity with a rule—in other words, the relation of cause and effect—is the condition of the objective validity of our empirical judgements in regard to the sequence of perceptions, consequently of their empirical truth, and therefore of experience. The principle of the relation of causality in the succession of phenomena is therefore valid for all objects of experience, because it is itself the ground of the possibility of experience.

Here, however, a difficulty arises, which must be resolved. The principle of the connection of causality among phenomena is limited in our formula to the succession thereof, although in practice we find that the principle applies also when the phenomena exist together in the same time, and that cause and effect may be simultaneous. For example, there is heat in a room, which does not exist in the open air. I look about for the cause, and find it to be the fire, Now the fire as the cause is simultaneous with its effect, the heat of the room. In this case, then, there is no succession as regards time, between cause and effect, but they are simultaneous; and still the law holds good. The greater part of operating causes in nature are simultaneous with their effects, and the succession in time of the latter is produced only because the cause cannot achieve the total of its effect in one moment. But at the moment when the effect first arises, it is always simultaneous with the causality of its cause, because, if the cause had but a moment before ceased to be, the effect could not have arisen. Here it must be specially remembered that we must consider the order of time and not the lapse thereof. The relation remains, even though no time has elapsed. The time between the causality of the cause and its immediate effect may entirely vanish, and the cause and effect be thus simultaneous, but the relation of the one to the other remains always determinable according to time. If, for example, I consider a leaden ball, which lies upon a cushion and makes a hollow in it, as a cause, then it is simultaneous with the effect. But I distinguish the two through the relation of time of the dynamical connection of both. For if I lay the ball upon the cushion, then the hollow follows upon the before smooth surface; but supposing the cushion has, from some cause or another, a hollow, there does not thereupon follow a leaden ball.

Thus, the law of succession of time is in all instances the only empirical criterion of effect in relation to the causality of the antecedent cause. The glass is the cause of the rising of the water above its horizontal surface, although the two phenomena are contemporaneous. For, as soon as I draw some water with the glass from a larger vessel, an effect follows thereupon, namely, the change of the horizontal state which the water had in the large vessel into a concave, which it assumes in the glass.

This conception of causality leads us to the conception of action; that of action, to the conception of force; and through it, to the conception of substance. As I do not wish this critical essay, the sole purpose of which is to treat of the sources of our synthetical cognition à priori, to be crowded with analyses which merely explain, but do not enlarge the sphere of our conceptions, I reserve the detailed explanation of the above conceptions for a future system of pure reason. Such an analysis, indeed, executed with great particularity, may already be found in well-known works on this subject. But I cannot at present refrain from making a few remarks on the empirical criterion of a substance, in so far as it seems to be more evident and more easily recognized through the conception of action than through that of the permanence of a phenomenon.

Where action (consequently activity and force) exists, substance also must exist, and in it alone must be sought the seat of that fruitful source of phenomena. Very well. But if we are called upon to explain what we mean by substance, and wish to avoid the vice of reasoning in a circle, the answer is by no means so easy. How shall we conclude immediately from the action to the permanence of that which acts, this being nevertheless an essential and peculiar criterion of substance (phenomenon)? But after what has been said above, the solution of this question becomes easy enough, although by the common mode of procedure—merely analysing our conceptions—it would be quite impossible. The conception of action indicates the relation of the subject of causality to the effect. Now because all effect consists in that which happens, therefore in the changeable, the last subject thereof is the permanent, as the substratum of all that changes, that is, substance. For according to the principle of causality, actions are always the first ground of all change in phenomena and, consequently, cannot be a property of a subject which itself changes, because if this were the case, other actions and another subject would be necessary to determine this change. From all this it results that action alone, as an empirical criterion, is a sufficient proof of the presence of substantiality, without any necessity on my part of endeavouring to discover the permanence of substance by a comparison. Besides, by this mode of induction we could not attain to the completeness which the magnitude and strict universality of the conception requires. For that the primary subject of the causality of all arising and passing away, all origin and extinction, cannot itself (in the sphere of phenomena) arise and pass away, is a sound and safe conclusion, a conclusion which leads us to the conception of empirical necessity and permanence in existence, and consequently to the conception of a substance as phenomenon.

When something happens, the mere fact of the occurrence, without regard to that which occurs, is an object requiring investigation. The transition from the non-being of a state into the existence of it, supposing that this state contains no quality which previously existed in the phenomenon, is a fact of itself demanding inquiry. Such an event, as has been shown in No. A, does not concern substance (for substance does not thus originate), but its condition or state. It is therefore only change, and not origin from nothing. If this origin be regarded as the effect of a foreign cause, it is termed creation, which cannot be admitted as an event among phenomena, because the very possibility of it would annihilate the unity of experience. If, however, I regard all things not as phenomena, but as things in themselves and objects of understanding alone, they, although substances, may be considered as dependent, in respect of their existence, on a foreign cause. But this would require a very different meaning in the words, a meaning which could not apply to phenomena as objects of possible experience.

How a thing can be changed, how it is possible that upon one state existing in one point of time, an opposite state should follow in another point of time—of this we have not the smallest conception à priori. There is requisite for this the knowledge of real powers, which can only be given empirically; for example, knowledge of moving forces, or, in other words, of certain successive phenomena (as movements) which indicate the presence of such forces. But the form of every change, the condition under which alone it can take place as the coming into existence of another state (be the content of the change, that is, the state which is changed, what it may), and consequently the succession of the states themselves can very well be considered à priori, in relation to the law of causality and the conditions of time.[32]

When a substance passes from one state, a, into another state, b, the point of time in which the latter exists is different from, and subsequent to that in which the former existed. In like manner, the second state, as reality (in the phenomenon), differs from the first, in which the reality of the second did not exist, as b from zero. That is to say, if the state, b, differs from the state, a, only in respect to quantity, the change is a coming into existence of b -a, which in the former state did not exist, and in relation to which that state is = O.

Now the question arises how a thing passes from one state = a, into another state = b. Between two moments there is always a certain time, and between two states existing in these moments there is always a difference having a certain quantity (for all parts of phenomena are in their turn quantities). Consequently, every transition from one state into another is always effected in a time contained between two moments, of which the first determines the state which leaves, and the second determines the state into the thing passes. The thing leaves, and the second determines the state into which the thing Both moments, then, are limitations of

[32] It must be remarked that I do not speak of the change of certain relations, but of the change of the state. Thus, when a body moves in a uniform manner, it does not change its state (of motion); but only when all motion increases or decreases.

the time of a change, consequently of the intermediate state between both, and as such they belong to the total of the change. Now every change has a cause, which evidences its causality in the whole time during which the charge takes place. The cause, therefore, does not produce the change all at once or in one moment, but in a time, so that, as the time gradually increases from the commencing instant, a, to its completion at b, in like manner also, the quantity of the reality (b - a) is generated through the lesser degrees which are contained between the first and last. All change is therefore possible only through a continuous action of the causality, which, in so far as it is uniform, we call a momentum. The change does not consist of these momenta, but is generated or produced by them as their effect.

Such is the law of the continuity of all change, the ground of which is that neither time itself nor any phenomenon in time consists of parts which are the smallest possible, but that, notwithstanding, the state of a thing passes in the process of a change through all these parts, as elements, to its second state. There is no smallest degree of reality in a phenomenon, just as there is no smallest degree in the quantity of time; and so the new state of reality grows up out of the former state, through all the infinite degrees thereof, the differences of which one from another, taken all together, are less than the difference between o and a.

It is not our business to inquire here into the utility of this principle in the investigation of nature. But how such a proposition, which appears so greatly to extend our knowledge of nature, is possible completely à priori, is indeed a question which deserves investigation, although the first view seems to demonstrate the truth and reality of the principle, and the question, how it is possible, may be considered superfluous. For there are so many groundless pretensions to the enlargement of our knowledge by pure reason that we must take it as a general rule to be mistrustful of all such, and without a thoroughgoing and radical deduction, to believe nothing of the sort even on the clearest dogmatical evidence.

Every addition to our empirical knowledge, and every advance made in the exercise of our perception, is nothing more than an extension of the determination of the internal sense, that is to say, a progression in time, be objects themselves what they may, phenomena, or pure intuitions. This progression in time determines everything, and is itself determined by nothing else. That is to say, the parts of the progression exist only in time, and by means of the synthesis thereof, and are not given antecedently to it. For this reason, every transition in perception to anything which follows upon another in time, is a determination of time by means of the production of this perception. And as this determination of time is, always and in all its parts, a quantity, the perception produced is to be considered as a quantity which proceeds through all its degrees—no one of which is the smallest possible—from zero up to its determined degree. From this we perceive the possibility of cognizing à priori a law of changes—a law, however, which concerns their form merely. We merely anticipate our own apprehension, the formal condition of which, inasmuch as it is itself to be found in the mind antecedently to all given phenomena, must certainly be capable of being cognized à priori.

Thus, as time contains the sensuous condition à priori of the possibility of a continuous progression of that which exists to that which follows it, the understanding, by virtue of the unity of apperception, contains the condition à priori of the possibility of a continuous determination of the position in time of all phenomena, and this by means of the series of causes and effects, the former of which necessitate the sequence of the latter, and thereby render universally and for all time, and by consequence, objectively, valid the empirical cognition of the relations of time.

C. THIRD ANALOGY.

Principle of Coexistence, According to the Law of Reciprocity or Community.

All substances, in so far as they can be perceived in space at the same time, exist in a state of complete reciprocity of action.

PROOF.

Things are coexistent, when in empirical intuition the perception of the one can follow upon the perception of the other, and vice versa—which cannot occur in the succession of phenomena, as we have shown in the explanation of the second principle. Thus I can perceive the moon and then the earth, or conversely, first the earth and then the moon; and for the reason that my perceptions of these objects can reciprocally follow each other, I say, they exist contemporaneously. Now coexistence is the existence of the manifold in the same time. But time itself is not an object of perception; and therefore we cannot conclude from the fact that things are placed in the same time, the other fact, that the perception of these things can follow each other reciprocally. The synthesis of the imagination in apprehension would only present to us each of these perceptions as present in the subject when the other is not present, and contrariwise; but would not show that the objects are coexistent, that is to say, that, if the one exists, the other also exists in the same time, and that this is necessarily so, in order that the perceptions may be capable of following each other reciprocally. It follows that a conception of the understanding or category of the reciprocal sequence of the determinations of phenomena (existing, as they do, apart from each other, and yet contemporaneously), is requisite to justify us in saying that the reciprocal succession of perceptions has its foundation in the object, and to enable us to represent coexistence as objective. But that relation of substances in which the one contains determinations the ground of which is in the other substance, is the relation of influence. And, when this influence is reciprocal, it is the relation of community or reciprocity. Consequently the coexistence of substances in space cannot be cognized in experience otherwise than under the precondition of their reciprocal action. This is therefore the condition of the possibility of things themselves as objects of experience.

Things are coexistent, in so far as they exist in one and the same time. But how can we know that they exist in one and the same time? Only by observing that the order in the synthesis of apprehension of the manifold is arbitrary and a matter of indifference, that is to say, that it can proceed from A, through B, C, D, to E, or contrariwise from E to A. For if they were successive in time (and in the order, let us suppose, which begins with A), it is quite impossible for the apprehension in perception to begin with E and go backwards to A, inasmuch as A belongs to past time and, therefore, cannot be an object of apprehension.

Let us assume that in a number of substances considered as phenomena each is completely isolated, that is, that no one acts upon another. Then I say that the coexistence of these cannot be an object of possible perception and that the existence of one cannot, by any mode of empirical synthesis, lead us to the existence of another. For we imagine them in this case to be separated by a completely void space, and thus perception, which proceeds from the one to the other in time, would indeed determine their existence by means of a following perception, but would be quite unable to distinguish whether the one phenomenon follows objectively upon the first, or is coexistent with it.

Besides the mere fact of existence, then, there must be something by means of which A determines the position of B in time and, conversely, B the position of A; because only under this condition can substances be empirically represented as existing contemporaneously. Now that alone determines the position of another thing in time which is the cause of it or of its determinations. Consequently every substance (inasmuch as it can have succession predicated of it only in respect of its determinations) must contain the causality of certain determinations in another substance, and at the same time the effects of the causality of the other in itself. That is to say, substances must stand (mediately or immediately) in dynamical community with each other, if coexistence is to be cognized in any possible experience. But, in regard to objects of experience, that is absolutely necessary without which the experience of these objects would itself be impossible. Consequently it is absolutely necessary that all substances in the world of phenomena, in so far as they are coexistent, stand in a relation of complete community of reciprocal action to each other.

The word community has in our language[33] two meanings, and contains the two notions conveyed in the Latin communio and commercium. We employ it in this place in the latter sense—that of a dynamical community, without which even the community of place (communio spatii) could not be empirically cognized. In our experiences it is easy to observe that it is only the continuous influences in all parts of space that can conduct our senses from one object to another; that the light which plays between our eyes and the heavenly bodies produces a mediating community between them and us, and thereby evidences their coexistence with us; that we cannot empirically change our position (perceive this change), unless

[33] German

the existence of matter throughout the whole of space rendered possible the perception of the positions we occupy; and that this perception can prove the contemporaneous existence of these places only through their reciprocal influence, and thereby also the coexistence of even the most remote objects—although in this case the proof is only mediate. Without community, every perception (of a phenomenon in space) is separated from every other and isolated, and the chain of empirical representations, that is, of experience, must, with the appearance of a new object, begin entirely de novo, without the least connection with preceding representations, and without standing towards these even in the relation of time. My intention here is by no means to combat the notion of empty space; for it may exist where our perceptions cannot exist, inasmuch as they cannot reach thereto, and where, therefore, no empirical perception of coexistence takes place. But in this case it is not an object of possible experience.

The following remarks may be useful in the way of explanation. In the mind, all phenomena, as contents of a possible experience, must exist in community (communio) of apperception or consciousness, and in so far as it is requisite that objects be represented as coexistent and connected, in so far must they reciprocally determine the position in time of each other and thereby constitute a whole. If this subjective community is to rest upon an objective basis, or to be applied to substances as phenomena, the perception of one substance must render possible the perception of another, and conversely. For otherwise succession, which is always found in perceptions as apprehensions, would be predicated of external objects, and their representation of their coexistence be thus impossible. But this is a reciprocal influence, that is to say, a real community (commercium) of substances, without which therefore the empirical relation of coexistence would be a notion beyond the reach of our minds. By virtue of this commercium, phenomena, in so far as they are apart from, and nevertheless in connection with each other, constitute a compositum reale. Such composita are possible in many different ways. The three dynamical relations then, from which all others spring, are those of inherence, consequence, and composition.

These, then, are the three analogies of experience. They are nothing more than principles of the determination of the existence of phenomena in time, according to the three modi of this determination; to wit, the relation to time itself as a quantity (the quantity of existence, that is, duration), the relation in time as a series or succession, finally, the relation in time as the complex of all existence (simultaneity). This unity of determination in regard to time is thoroughly dynamical; that is to say, time is not considered as that in which experience determines immediately to every existence its position; for this is impossible, inasmuch as absolute time is not an object of perception, by means of which phenomena can be connected with each other. On the contrary, the rule of the understanding, through which alone the existence of phenomena can receive synthetical unity as regards relations of time, determines for every phenomenon its position in time, and consequently à priori, and with validity for all and every time.

By nature, in the empirical sense of the word, we understand the totality of phenomena connected, in respect of their existence, according to necessary rules, that is, laws. There are therefore certain laws (which are moreover à priori) which make nature possible; and all empirical laws can exist only by means of experience, and by virtue of those primitive laws through which experience itself becomes possible. The purpose of the analogies is therefore to represent to us the unity of nature in the connection of all phenomena under certain exponents, the only business of which is to express the relation of time (in so far as it contains all existence in itself) to the unity of apperception, which can exist in synthesis only according to rules. The combined expression of all is this: "All phenomena exist in one nature, and must so exist, inasmuch as without this à priori unity, no unity of experience, and consequently no determination of objects in experience, is possible."

As regards the mode of proof which we have employed in treating of these transcendental laws of nature, and the peculiar character of we must make one remark, which will at the same time be important as a guide in every other attempt to demonstrate the truth of intellectual and likewise synthetical propositions à priori. Had we endeavoured to prove these analogies dogmatically, that is, from conceptions; that is to say, had we employed this method in attempting to show that everything which exists, exists only in that which is permanent—that every thing or event presupposes the existence of something in a preceding state, upon which it follows in conformity with a rule—lastly, that in the manifold, which is coexistent, the states coexist in connection with each other according to a rule, all our labour would have been utterly in vain. For more conceptions of things, analyse them as we may, cannot enable us to conclude from the existence of one object to the existence of another. What other course was left for us to pursue? This only, to demonstrate the possibility of experience as a cognition in which at last all objects must be capable of being presented to us, if the representation of them is to possess any objective reality. Now in this third, this mediating term, the essential form of which consists in the synthetical unity of the apperception of all phenomena, we found à priori conditions of the universal and necessary determination as to time of all existences in the world of phenomena, without which the empirical determination thereof as to time would itself be impossible, and we also discovered rules of synthetical unity à priori, by means of which we could anticipate experience. For want of this method, and from the fancy that it was possible to discover a dogmatical proof of the synthetical propositions which are requisite in the empirical employment of the understanding, has it happened that a proof of the principle of sufficient reason has been so often attempted, and always in vain. The other two analogies nobody has ever thought of, although they have always been silently employed by the mind,[34] because the guiding thread

[34] The unity of the universe, in which all phenomena to be connected, is evidently a mere consequence of the admitted principle of the community of all substances which are coexistent. For were

furnished by the categories was wanting, the guide which alone can enable us to discover every hiatus, both in the system of conceptions and of principles.

4. THE POSTULATES OF EMPIRICAL THOUGHT.

1. That which agrees with the formal conditions (intuition and conception) of experience, is possible.
2. That which coheres with the material conditions of experience (sensation), is real.
3. That whose coherence with the real is determined according to universal conditions of experience is (exists) necessary.

Explanation.

The categories of modality possess this peculiarity, that they do not in the least determine the object, or enlarge the conception to which they are annexed as predicates, but only express its relation to the faculty of cognition. Though my conception of a thing is in itself complete, I am still entitled to ask whether the object of it is merely possible, or whether it is also real, or, if the latter, whether it is also necessary. But hereby the object itself is not more definitely determined in thought, but the question is only in what relation it, including all its determinations, stands to the understanding and its employment in experience, to the empirical faculty of judgement, and to the reason of its application to experience.

For this very reason, too, the categories of modality are nothing more than explanations of the conceptions of possibility, reality, and necessity, as employed in experience, and at the same time, restrictions of all the categories to empirical use alone, not authorizing the transcendental employment of them. For if they are to have something more than a merely logical significance, and to be something more than a mere analytical expression of the form of thought, and to have a relation to things and their possibility, reality, or necessity, they must concern possible experience and its synthetical unity, in which alone objects of cognition can be given.

The postulate of the possibility of things requires also, that the conception of the things agree with the formal conditions of our experience in general. But this, that is to say, the objective form of experience, contains all the kinds of synthesis which are requisite for the cognition of objects. A conception which contains a synthesis must be regarded as empty and, without reference to an object, if its synthesis does not belong to experience—either as borrowed from it, and in this case it is called an empirical conception, or such as is the ground and à priori condition of

substances isolated, they could not as parts constitute a whole, and were their connection (reciprocal action of the manifold) not necessary from the very fact of coexistence, we could not conclude from the fact of the latter as a merely ideal relation to the former as a real one. We have, however, shown in its place that community is the proper ground of the possibility of an empirical cognition of coexistence, and that we may therefore properly reason from the latter to the former as its condition.

experience (its form), and in this case it is a pure conception, a conception which nevertheless belongs to experience, inasmuch as its object can be found in this alone. For where shall we find the criterion or character of the possibility of an object which is cogitated by means of an à priori synthetical conception, if not in the synthesis which constitutes the form of empirical cognition of objects? That in such a conception no contradiction exists is indeed a necessary logical condition, but very far from being sufficient to establish the objective reality of the conception, that is, the possibility of such an object as is thought in the conception. Thus, in the conception of a figure which is contained within two straight lines, there is no contradiction, for the conceptions of two straight lines and of their junction contain no negation of a figure. The impossibility in such a case does not rest upon the conception in itself, but upon the construction of it in space, that is to say, upon the conditions of space and its determinations. But these have themselves objective reality, that is, they apply to possible things, because they contain à priori the form of experience in general.

And now we shall proceed to point out the extensive utility and influence of this postulate of possibility. When I represent to myself a thing that is permanent, so that everything in it which changes belongs merely to its state or condition, from such a conception alone I never can cognize that such a thing is possible. Or, if I represent to myself something which is so constituted that, when it is posited, something else follows always and infallibly, my thought contains no self-contradiction; but whether such a property as causality is to be found in any possible thing, my thought alone affords no means of judging. Finally, I can represent to myself different things (substances) which are so constituted that the state or condition of one causes a change in the state of the other, and reciprocally; but whether such a relation is a property of things cannot be perceived from these conceptions, which contain a merely arbitrary synthesis. Only from the fact, therefore, that these conceptions express à priori the relations of perceptions in every experience, do we know that they possess objective reality, that is, transcendental truth; and that independent of experience, though not independent of all relation to form of an experience in general and its synthetical unity, in which alone objects can be empirically cognized.

But when we fashion to ourselves new conceptions of substances, forces, action, and reaction, from the material presented to us by perception, without following the example of experience in their connection, we create mere chimeras, of the possibility of which we cannot discover any criterion, because we have not taken experience for our instructress, though we have borrowed the conceptions from her. Such fictitious conceptions derive their character of possibility not, like the categories, à priori, as conceptions on which all experience depends, but only, à posteriori, as conceptions given by means of experience itself, and their possibility must either be cognized à posteriori and empirically, or it cannot be cognized at all. A substance which is permanently present in space, yet without filling it (like that tertium quid between matter and the thinking subject which some have tried to introduce into metaphysics), or a peculiar fundamental power of the mind of intuiting the future by anticipation (instead of merely inferring from past and present events), or, finally, a power of the mind to place itself in community of thought with other men, however distant they may be—these are conceptions the possibility of which has no ground to rest upon. For they are not based upon experience and its known laws; and, without experience, they are a merely arbitrary conjunction of thoughts, which, though containing no internal contradiction, has no claim to objective reality, neither, consequently, to the possibility of such an object as is thought in these conceptions. As far as concerns reality, it is self-evident that we cannot cogitate such a possibility in concreto without the aid of experience; because reality is concerned only with sensation, as the matter of experience, and not with the form of thought, with which we can no doubt indulge in shaping fancies.

But I pass by everything which derives its possibility from reality in experience, and I purpose treating here merely of the possibility of things by means of à priori conceptions. I maintain, then, that the possibility of things is not derived from such conceptions per se, but only when considered as formal and objective conditions of an experience in general.

It seems, indeed, as if the possibility of a triangle could be cognized from the conception of it alone (which is certainly independent of experience); for we can certainly give to the conception a corresponding object completely à priori, that is to say, we can construct it. But as a triangle is only the form of an object, it must remain a mere product of the imagination, and the possibility of the existence of an object corresponding to it must remain doubtful, unless we can discover some other ground, unless we know that the figure can be cogitated under the conditions upon which all objects of experience rest. Now, the facts that space is a formal condition à priori of external experience, that the formative synthesis, by which we construct a triangle in imagination, is the very same as that we employ in the apprehension of a phenomenon for the purpose of making an empirical conception of it, are what alone connect the notion of the possibility of such a thing, with the conception of it. In the same manner, the possibility of continuous quantities, indeed of quantities in general, for the conceptions of them are without exception synthetical, is never evident from the conceptions in themselves, but only when they are considered as the formal conditions of the determination of objects in experience. And where, indeed, should we look for objects to correspond to our conceptions, if not in experience, by which alone objects are presented to us? It is, however, true that without antecedent experience we can cognize and characterize the possibility of things, relatively to the formal conditions, under which something is determined in experience as an object, consequently, completely à priori. But still this is possible only in relation to experience and within its limits.

The postulate concerning the cognition of the reality of things requires perception, consequently conscious sensation, not indeed immediately, that is, of the object itself, whose existence is to be cognized, but still that the object have some connection with a real perception, in accordance with the analogies of experience, which exhibit all kinds of real connection in experience.

From the mere conception of a thing it is impossible to conclude its existence. For, let the conception be ever so complete, and containing a statement of all the determinations of the thing, the existence of it has nothing to do with all this, but only with thew question whether such a thing is given, so that the perception of it can in every case precede the conception. For the fact that the conception of it precedes the perception, merely indicates the possibility of its existence; it is perception which presents matter to the conception, that is the sole criterion of reality. Prior to the perception of the thing, however, and therefore comparatively à priori, we are able to cognize its existence, provided it stands in connection with some perceptions according to the principles of the empirical conjunction of these, that is, in conformity with the analogies of perception. For, in this case, the existence of the supposed thing is connected with our perception in a possible experience, and we are able, with the guidance of these analogies, to reason in the series of possible perceptions from a thing which we do really perceive to the thing we do not perceive. Thus, we cognize the existence of a magnetic matter penetrating all bodies from the perception of the attraction of the steel-filings by the magnet, although the constitution of our organs renders an immediate perception of this matter impossible for us. For, according to the laws of sensibility and the connected context of our perceptions, we should in an experience come also on an immediate empirical intuition of this matter, if our senses were more acute—but this obtuseness has no influence upon and cannot alter the form of possible experience in general. Our knowledge of the existence of things reaches as far as our perceptions, and what may be inferred from them according to empirical laws, extend. If we do not set out from experience, or do not proceed according to the laws of the empirical connection of phenomena, our pretensions to discover the existence of a thing which we do not immediately perceive are vain. Idealism, however, brings forward powerful objections to these rules for proving existence mediately. This is, therefore, the proper place for its refutation.

REFUTATION OF IDEALISM.

Idealism—I mean material idealism—is the theory which declares the existence of objects in space without us to be either () doubtful and indemonstrable, or (2) false and impossible. The first is the problematical idealism of Descartes, who admits the undoubted certainty of only one empirical assertion (assertio), to wit, "I am." The second is the dogmatical idealism of Berkeley, who maintains that space, together with all the objects of which it is the inseparable condition, is a thing which is in itself impossible, and that consequently the objects in space are mere products of the imagination. The dogmatical theory of idealism is unavoidable, if we regard space as a property of things in themselves; for in that case it is, with all to which it serves as condition, a nonentity. But the foundation for this kind of idealism we have already destroyed in the transcendental æsthetic. Problematical idealism, which makes no such assertion, but only alleges our incapacity to prove the existence of anything besides ourselves by means of immediate experience, is a theory rational and evidencing a thorough and philosophical mode of thinking, for it observes the rule not to form a decisive judgement before sufficient proof be shown. The desired proof must therefore demonstrate that we have experience of external things, and not mere fancies. For this purpose, we must prove, that our internal and, to Descartes, indubitable experience is itself possible only under the previous assumption of external experience.

THEOREM.

The simple but empirically determined consciousness of my own existence proves the existence of external objects in space.

PROOF

I am conscious of my own existence as determined in time. All determination in regard to time presupposes the existence of something permanent in perception. But this permanent something cannot be something in me, for the very reason that my existence in time is itself determined by this permanent something. It follows that the perception of this permanent existence is possible only through a thing without me and not through the mere representation of a thing without me. Consequently, the determination of my existence in time is possible only through the existence of real things external to me. Now, consciousness in time is necessarily connected with the consciousness of the possibility of this determination in time. Hence it follows that consciousness in time is necessarily connected also with the existence of things without me, inasmuch as the existence of these things is the condition of determination in time. That is to say, the consciousness of my own existence is at the same time an immediate consciousness of the existence of other things without me.

Remark I. The reader will observe, that in the foregoing proof the game which idealism plays is retorted upon itself, and with more justice. It assumed that the only immediate experience is internal and that from this we can only infer the existence of external things. But, as always happens, when we reason from given effects to determined causes, idealism has reasoned with too much haste and uncertainty, for it is quite possible that the cause of our representations may lie in ourselves, and that we ascribe it falsely to external things. But our proof shows that external experience is properly immediate,[35] that only by virtue of it—not,

[35] The immediate consciousness of the existence of external things is, in the preceding theorem, not presupposed, but proved, by the possibility of this consciousness understood by us or not. The question as to the possibility of it would stand thus: "Have we an internal sense, but no external

indeed, the consciousness of our own existence, but certainly the determination of our existence in time, that is, internal experience—is possible. It is true, that the representation "I am," which is the expression of the consciousness which can accompany all my thoughts, is that which immediately includes the existence of a subject. But in this representation we cannot find any knowledge of the subject, and therefore also no empirical knowledge, that is, experience. For experience contains, in addition to the thought of something existing, intuition, and in this case it must be internal intuition, that is, time, in relation to which the subject must be determined. But the existence of external things is absolutely requisite for this purpose, so that it follows that internal experience is itself possible only mediately and through external experience.

Remark II. Now with this view all empirical use of our faculty of cognition in the determination of time is in perfect accordance. Its truth is supported by the fact that it is possible to perceive a determination of time only by means of a change in external relations (motion) to the permanent in space (for example, we become aware of the sun's motion by observing the changes of his relation to the objects of this earth). But this is not all. We find that we possess nothing permanent that can correspond and be submitted to the conception of a substance as intuition, except matter. This idea of permanence is not itself derived from external experience, but is an à priori necessary condition of all determination of time, consequently also of the internal sense in reference to our own existence, and that through the existence of external things. In the representation "I," the consciousness of myself is not an intuition, but a merely intellectual representation produced by the spontaneous activity of a thinking subject. It follows, that this "i" has not any predicate of intuition, which, in its character of permanence, could serve as correlate to the determination of time in the internal sense—in the same way as impenetrability is the correlate of matter as an empirical intuition.

Remark III. From the fact that the existence of external things is a necessary condition of the possibility of a determined consciousness of ourselves, it does not follow that every intuitive representation of external things involves the existence of these things, for their representations may very well be the mere products of the imagination (in dreams as well as in madness); though, indeed, these are themselves created by the reproduction of previous external perceptions, which, as has been shown, are possible only through the reality of external objects. The sole aim of our remarks has, however, been to prove that internal experience in general is possible only through external experience in general. Whether this or that

sense, and is our belief in external perception a mere delusion?" But it is evident that, in order merely to fancy to ourselves anything as external, that is, to present it to the sense in intuition we must already possess an external sense, and must thereby distinguish immediately the mere receptivity of an external intuition from the spontaneity which characterizes every act of imagination. For merely to imagine also an external sense, would annihilate the faculty of intuition itself which is to be determined by the imagination.

supposed experience be purely imaginary must be discovered from its particular determinations and by comparing these with the criteria of all real experience.

Finally, as regards the third postulate, it applies to material necessity in existence, and not to merely formal and logical necessity in the connection of conceptions. Now as we cannot cognize completely à priori the existence of any object of sense, though we can do so comparatively à priori, that is, relatively to some other previously given existence—a cognition, however, which can only be of such an existence as must be contained in the complex of experience, of which the previously given perception is a part—the necessity of existence can never be cognized from conceptions, but always, on the contrary, from its connection with that which is an object of perception. But the only existence cognized, under the condition of other given phenomena, as necessary, is the existence of effects from given causes in conformity with the laws of causality. It is consequently not the necessity of the existence of things (as substances), but the necessity of the state of things that we cognize, and that not immediately, but by means of the existence of other states given in perception, according to empirical laws of causality. Hence it follows that the criterion of necessity is to be found only in the law of possible experience—that everything which happens is determined à priori in the phenomenon by its cause. Thus we cognize only the necessity of effects in nature, the causes of which are given us. Moreover, the criterion of necessity in existence possesses no application beyond the field of possible experience, and even in this it is not valid of the existence of things as substances, because these can never be considered as empirical effects, or as something that happens and has a beginning. Necessity, therefore, regards only the relations of phenomena according to the dynamical law of causality, and the possibility grounded thereon, of reasoning from some given existence (of a cause) à priori to another existence (of an effect). "Everything that happens is hypothetically necessary," is a principle which subjects the changes that take place in the world to a law, that is, to a rule of necessary existence, without which nature herself could not possibly exist. Hence the proposition, "Nothing happens by blind chance (in mundo non datur casus)," is an à priori law of nature. The case is the same with the proposition, "Necessity in nature is not blind," that is, it is conditioned, consequently intelligible necessity (non datur fatum). Both laws subject the play of change to "a nature of things (as phenomena)," or, which is the same thing, to the unity of the understanding, and through the understanding alone can changes belong to an experience, as the synthetical unity of phenomena. Both belong to the class of dynamical principles. The former is properly a consequence of the principle of causality—one of the analogies of experience. The latter belongs to the principles of modality, which to the determination of causality adds the conception of necessity, which is itself, however, subject to a rule of the understanding. The principle of continuity forbids any leap in the series of phenomena regarded as changes (in mundo non datur saltus); and likewise, in the complex of all empirical intuitions in space, any break or hiatus between two phenomena (non datur hiatus)—for we can so express the principle, that experience can admit nothing which proves the existence of a vacuum, or which even admits it as a part of an empirical synthesis. For, as regards a vacuum or void, which we may cogitate as out and beyond the field of possible experience (the world), such a question cannot come before the tribunal of mere understanding, which decides only upon questions that concern the employment of given phenomena for the construction of empirical cognition. It is rather a problem for ideal reason, which passes beyond the sphere of a possible experience and aims at forming a judgement of that which surrounds and circumscribes it, and the proper place for the consideration of it is the transcendental dialectic. These four propositions, "In mundo non datur hiatus, non datur saltus, non datur casus, non datur fatum," as well as all principles of transcendental origin, we could very easily exhibit in their proper order, that is, in conformity with the order of the categories, and assign to each its proper place. But the already practised reader will do this for himself, or discover the clue to such an arrangement. But the combined result of all is simply this, to admit into the empirical synthesis nothing which might cause a break in or be foreign to the understanding and the continuous connection of all phenomena, that is, the unity of the conceptions of the understanding. For in the understanding alone is the unity of experience, in which all perceptions must have their assigned place, possible.

Whether the field of possibility be greater than that of reality, and whether the field of the latter be itself greater than that of necessity, are interesting enough questions, and quite capable of synthetic solution, questions, however, which come under the jurisdiction of reason alone. For they are tantamount to asking whether all things as phenomena do without exception belong to the complex and connected whole of a single experience, of which every given perception is a part which therefore cannot be conjoined with any other phenomena—or, whether my perceptions can belong to more than one possible experience? The understanding gives to experience, according to the subjective and formal conditions, of sensibility as well as of apperception, the rules which alone make this experience possible. Other forms of intuition besides those of space and time, other forms of understanding besides the discursive forms of thought, or of cognition by means of conceptions, we can neither imagine nor make intelligible to ourselves; and even if we could, they would still not belong to experience, which is the only mode of cognition by which objects are presented to us. Whether other perceptions besides those which belong to the total of our possible experience, and consequently whether some other sphere of matter exists, the understanding has no power to decide, its proper occupation being with the synthesis of that which is given. Moreover, the poverty of the usual arguments which go to prove the existence of a vast sphere of possibility, of which all that is real (every object of experience) is but a small part, is very remarkable. "All real is possible"; from this follows naturally, according to the logical laws of conversion, the particular proposition: "Some possible is real." Now this seems to be equivalent to: "Much is possible that is not real." No doubt it does seem as if we ought to consider the sum of the possible to be greater than that of the real, from the fact that something must be added to the former to constitute the latter. But this notion of adding to the possible is absurd. For that which is not in the sum of the possible, and consequently requires to be added to it, is manifestly impossible. In addition to accordance with the formal conditions of experience, the understanding requires a connection with some perception; but that which is connected with this perception is real, even although it is not immediately perceived. But that another series of phenomena, in complete coherence with that which is given in perception, consequently more than one all-embracing experience is possible, is an inference which cannot be concluded from the data given us by experience, and still less without any data at all. That which is possible only under conditions which are themselves merely possible, is not possible in any respect. And yet we can find no more certain ground on which to base the discussion of the question whether the sphere of possibility is wider than that of experience.

I have merely mentioned these questions, that in treating of the conception of the understanding, there might be no omission of anything that, in the common opinion, belongs to them. In reality, however, the notion of absolute possibility (possibility which is valid in every respect) is not a mere conception of the understanding, which can be employed empirically, but belongs to reason alone, which passes the bounds of all empirical use of the understanding. We have, therefore, contented ourselves with a merely critical remark, leaving the subject to be explained in the sequel.

Before concluding this fourth section, and at the same time the system of all principles of the pure understanding, it seems proper to mention the reasons which induced me to term the principles of modality postulates. This expression I do not here use in the sense which some more recent philosophers, contrary to its meaning with mathematicians, to whom the word properly belongs, attach to it—that of a proposition, namely, immediately certain, requiring neither deduction nor proof. For if, in the case of synthetical propositions, however evident they may be, we accord to them without deduction, and merely on the strength of their own pretensions, unqualified belief, all critique of the understanding is entirely lost; and, as there is no want of bold pretensions, which the common belief (though for the philosopher this is no credential) does not reject, the understanding lies exposed to every delusion and conceit, without the power of refusing its assent to those assertions, which, though illegitimate, demand acceptance as veritable axioms. When, therefore, to the conception of a thing an à priori determination is synthetically added, such a proposition must obtain, if not a proof, at least a deduction of the legitimacy of its assertion.

The principles of modality are, however, not objectively synthetical, for the predicates of possibility, reality, and necessity do not in the least augment the conception of that of which they are affirmed, inasmuch as they contribute nothing to the representation of the object. But as they are, nevertheless, always synthetical, they are so merely subjectively. That is to say, they have a reflective power, and apply to the conception of a thing, of which, in other respects, they affirm nothing, the faculty of cognition in which the conception originates and has its seat. So that if the conception merely agree with the formal conditions of experience, its object is called possible; if it is in connection with perception, and determined thereby, the object is real; if it is determined according to conceptions by means of the connection of perceptions, the object is called necessary. The principles of modality therefore predicate of a conception nothing more than the procedure of the faculty of cognition which generated it. Now a postulate in mathematics is a practical proposition which contains nothing but the synthesis by which we present an object to ourselves, and produce the conception of it, for example—"With a given line, to describe a circle upon a plane, from a given point"; and such a proposition does not admit of proof, because the procedure, which it requires, is exactly that by which alone it is possible to generate the conception of such a figure. With the same right, accordingly, can we postulate the principles of modality, because they do not augment[36] the conception of a thing but merely indicate the manner in which it is connected with the faculty of cognition.

GENERAL REMARK ON THE SYSTEM OF PRINCIPLES.

It is very remarkable that we cannot perceive the possibility of a thing from the category alone, but must always have an intuition, by which to make evident the objective reality of the pure conception of the understanding. Take, for example, the categories of relation. How (1) a thing can exist only as a subject, and not as a mere determination of other things, that is, can be substance; or how (2), because something exists, some other thing must exist, consequently how a thing can be a cause; or how (3), when several things exist, from the fact that one of these things exists, some consequence to the others follows, and reciprocally, and in this way a community of substances can be possible—are questions whose solution cannot be obtained from mere conceptions. The very same is the case with the other categories; for example, how a thing can be of the same sort with many others, that is, can be a quantity, and so on. So long as we have not intuition we cannot know whether we do really think an object by the categories, and where an object can anywhere be found to cohere with them, and thus the truth is established, that the categories are not in themselves cognitions, but mere forms of thought for the construction of cognitions from given intuitions. For the same reason is it true

[36] When I think the reality of a thing, I do really think more than the possibility, but not in the thing; for that can never contain more in reality than was contained in its complete possibility. But while the notion of possibility is merely the notion of a position of thing in relation to the understanding (its empirical use), reality is the conjunction of the thing with perception.

that from categories alone no synthetical proposition can be made. For example: "In every existence there is substance," that is, something that can exist only as a subject and not as mere predicate; or, "Everything is a quantity"—to construct propositions such as these, we require something to enable us to go out beyond the given conception and connect another with it. For the same reason the attempt to prove a synthetical proposition by means of mere conceptions, for example: "Everything that exists contingently has a cause," has never succeeded. We could never get further than proving that, without this relation to conceptions, we could not conceive the existence of the contingent, that is, could not à priori through the understanding cognize the existence of such a thing; but it does not hence follow that this is also the condition of the possibility of the thing itself that is said to be contingent. If, accordingly; we look back to our proof of the principle of causality, we shall find that we were able to prove it as valid only of objects of possible experience, and, indeed, only as itself the principle of the possibility of experience, Consequently of the cognition of an object given in empirical intuition, and not from mere conceptions. That, however, the proposition: "Everything that is contingent must have a cause," is evident to every one merely from conceptions, is not to be denied. But in this case the conception of the contingent is cogitated as involving not the category of modality (as that the non-existence of which can be conceived) but that of relation (as that which can exist only as the consequence of something else), and so it is really an identical proposition: "That which can exist only as a consequence, has a cause." In fact, when we have to give examples of contingent existence, we always refer to changes, and not merely to the possibility of conceiving the opposite.[37] But change is an event, which, as such, is possible only through a cause, and considered per se its non-existence is therefore possible, and we become cognizant of its contingency from the fact that it can exist only as the effect of a cause. Hence, if a thing is assumed to be contingent, it is an analytical proposition to say, it has a cause.

But it is still more remarkable that, to understand the possibility of things according to the categories and thus to demonstrate the objective reality of the latter, we require not merely intuitions, but external intuitions. If, for example, we take the pure conceptions of relation, we find that (1) for the purpose of presenting to the conception of substance something permanent in intuition

---

[37] We can easily conceive the non-existence of matter; but the ancients did not thence infer its contingency. But even the alternation of the existence and non-existence of a given state in a thing, in which all change consists, by no means proves the contingency of that state—the ground of proof being the reality of its opposite. For example, a body is in a state of rest after motion, but we cannot infer the contingency of the motion from the fact that the former is the opposite of the latter. For this opposite is merely a logical and not a real opposite to the other. If we wish to demonstrate the contingency of the motion, what we ought to prove is that, instead of the motion which took place in the preceding point of time, it was possible for the body to have been then in rest, not, that it is afterwards in rest; for in this case, both opposites are perfectly consistent with each other.

corresponding thereto and thus of demonstrating the objective reality of this conception, we require an intuition (of matter) in space, because space alone is permanent and determines things as such, while time, and with it all that is in the internal sense, is in a state of continual flow; (2) in order to represent change as the intuition corresponding to the conception of causality, we require the representation of motion as change in space; in fact, it is through it alone that changes, the possibility of which no pure understanding can perceive, are capable of being intuited. Change is the connection of determinations contradictorily opposed to each other in the existence of one and the same thing. Now, how it is possible that out of a given state one quite opposite to it in the same thing should follow, reason without an example can not only not conceive, but cannot even make intelligible without intuition; and this intuition is the motion of a point in space; the existence of which in different spaces (as a consequence of opposite determinations) alone makes the intuition of change possible. For, in order to make even internal change cognitable, we require to represent time, as the form of the internal sense, figuratively by a line, and the internal change by the drawing of that line (motion), and consequently are obliged to employ external intuition to be able to represent the successive existence of ourselves in different states. The proper ground of this fact is that all change to be perceived as change presupposes something permanent in intuition, while in the internal sense no permanent intuition is to be found. Lastly, the objective possibility of the category of community cannot be conceived by mere reason, and consequently its objective reality cannot be demonstrated without an intuition, and that external in space. For how can we conceive the possibility of community, that is, when several substances exist, that some effect on the existence of the one follows from the existence of the other, and reciprocally, and therefore that, because something exists in the latter, something else must exist in the former, which could not be understood from its own existence alone? For this is the very essence of community—which is inconceivable as a property of things which are perfectly isolated. Hence, Leibnitz, in attributing to the substances of the world—as cogitated by the understanding alone—a community, required the mediating aid of a divinity; for, from their existence, such a property seemed to him with justice inconceivable. But we can very easily conceive the possibility of community (of substances as phenomena) if we represent them to ourselves as in space, consequently in external intuition. For external intuition contains in itself à priori formal external relations, as the conditions of the possibility of the real relations of action and reaction, and therefore of the possibility of community. With the same ease can it be demonstrated, that the possibility of things as quantities, and consequently the objective reality of the category of quantity, can be grounded only in external intuition, and that by its means alone is the notion of quantity appropriated by the internal sense. But I must avoid prolixity, and leave the task of illustrating this by examples to the reader's own reflection.

The above remarks are of the greatest importance, not only for the confirmation of our previous confutation of idealism, but still more when the subject of self-cognition by mere internal consciousness and the determination of our own nature without the aid of external empirical intuitions is under discussion, for the indication of the grounds of the possibility of such a cognition.

The result of the whole of this part of the analytic of principles is, therefore: "All principles of the pure understanding are nothing more than à priori principles of the possibility of experience, and to experience alone do all à priori synthetical propositions apply and relate"; indeed, their possibility itself rests entirely on this relation.

Chapter III

Of the Ground of the Division of all Objects into Phenomena and Noumena

We have now not only traversed the region of the pure understanding and carefully surveyed every part of it, but we have also measured it, and assigned to everything therein its proper place. But this land is an island, and enclosed by nature herself within unchangeable limits. It is the land of truth (an attractive word), surrounded by a wide and stormy ocean, the region of illusion, where many a fog-bank, many an iceberg, seems to the mariner, on his voyage of discovery, a new country, and, while constantly deluding him with vain hopes, engages him in dangerous adventures, from which he never can desist, and which yet he never can bring to a termination. But before venturing upon this sea, in order to explore it in its whole extent, and to arrive at a certainty whether anything is to be discovered there, it will not be without advantage if we cast our eyes upon the chart of the land that we are about to leave, and to ask ourselves, firstly, whether we cannot rest perfectly contented with what it contains, or whether we must not of necessity be contented with it, if we can find nowhere else a solid foundation to build upon; and, secondly, by what title we possess this land itself, and how we hold it secure against all hostile claims? Although, in the course of our analytic, we have already given sufficient answers to these questions, yet a summary recapitulation of these solutions may be useful in strengthening our conviction, by uniting in one point the momenta of the arguments.

We have seen that everything which the understanding draws from itself, without borrowing from experience, it nevertheless possesses only for the behoof and use of experience. The principles of the pure understanding, whether constitutive à priori (as the mathematical principles), or merely regulative (as the dynamical), contain nothing but the pure schema, as it were, of possible experience. For experience possesses its unity from the synthetical unity which the understanding, originally and from itself, imparts to the synthesis of the imagination in relation to apperception, and in à priori relation to and agreement with which phenomena, as data for a possible cognition, must stand. But although these rules of the understanding are not only à priori true, but the very source of all truth, that is, of the accordance of our cognition with objects, and on this ground, that they contain the basis of the possibility of experience, as the ensemble of all cognition, it seems to us not enough to propound what is true—we desire also to be told what we want to know. If, then, we learn nothing more by this critical examination than what we should have practised in the merely empirical use of the understanding, without any such subtle inquiry, the presumption is that the advantage we reap from it is not worth the labour bestowed upon it. It may certainly be answered that no rash curiosity is more prejudicial to the enlargement of our knowledge than that which must know beforehand the utility of this or that piece of information which we seek, before we have entered on the needful investigations, and before one could form the least conception of its utility, even though it were placed before our eyes. But there is one advantage in such transcendental inquiries which can be made comprehensible to the dullest and most reluctant learner—this, namely, that the understanding which is occupied merely with empirical exercise, and does not reflect on the sources of its own cognition, may exercise its functions very well and very successfully, but is quite unable to do one thing, and that of very great importance, to determine, namely, the bounds that limit its employment, and to know what lies within or without its own sphere. This purpose can be obtained only by such profound investigations as we have instituted. But if it cannot distinguish whether certain questions lie within its horizon or not, it can never be sure either as to its claims or possessions, but must lay its account with many humiliating corrections, when it transgresses, as it unavoidably will, the limits of its own territory, and loses itself in fanciful opinions and blinding illusions.

That the understanding, therefore, cannot make of its à priori principles, or even of its conceptions, other than an empirical use, is a proposition which leads to the most important results. A transcendental use is made of a conception in a fundamental proposition or principle, when it is referred to things in general and considered as things in themselves; an empirical use, when it is referred merely to phenomena, that is, to objects of a possible experience. That the latter use of a conception is the only admissible one is evident from the reasons following. For every conception are requisite, firstly, the logical form of a conception (of thought) general; and, secondly, the possibility of presenting to this an object to which it may apply. Failing this latter, it has no sense, and utterly void of content, although it may contain the logical function for constructing a conception from certain data. Now, object cannot be given to a conception otherwise than by intuition, and, even if a pure intuition antecedent to the object is à priori possible, this pure intuition can itself obtain objective validity only from empirical intuition, of which it is itself but the form. All conceptions, therefore, and with them all principles, however high the degree of their à priori possibility, relate to empirical intuitions, that is, to data towards a possible experience. Without this they possess no objective validity, but are mere play of imagination or of understanding with images or notions. Let us take, for example, the conceptions of mathematics, and first in its pure intuitions. "Space has three dimensions"—"Between two points there can be only one straight line," etc. Although all these principles, and the representation of the object with which this science occupies itself, are generated in the mind entirely à priori, they would nevertheless have no significance if we were not always able to exhibit their significance in and by means of phenomena (empirical objects). Hence it is requisite that an abstract conception be made sensuous, that is, that an object corresponding to it in intuition be forthcoming, otherwise the conception remains, as we say, without sense, that is, without meaning. Mathematics fulfils this requirement by the construction of the figure, which is a phenomenon evident to the senses. The same science finds support and significance in number; this in its turn finds it in the fingers, or in counters, or in lines and points. The conception itself is always produced à priori, together with the synthetical principles or formulas from such conceptions; but the proper employment of them, and their application to objects, can exist nowhere but in experience, the possibility of which, as regards its form, they contain à priori.

That this is also the case with all of the categories and the principles based upon them is evident from the fact that we cannot render intelligible the possibility of an object corresponding to them without having recourse to the conditions of sensibility, consequently, to the form of phenomena, to which, as their only proper objects, their use must therefore be confined, inasmuch as, if this condition is removed, all significance, that is, all relation to an object, disappears, and no example can be found to make it comprehensible what sort of things we ought to think under such conceptions.

The conception of quantity cannot be explained except by saying that it is the determination of a thing whereby it can be cogitated how many times one is placed in it. But this "how many times" is based upon successive repetition, consequently upon time and the synthesis of the homogeneous therein. Reality, in contradistinction to negation, can be explained only by cogitating a time which is either filled therewith or is void. If I leave out the notion of permanence (which is existence in all time), there remains in the conception of substance nothing but the logical notion of subject, a notion of which I endeavour to realize by representing to myself something that can exist only as a subject. But not only am I perfectly ignorant of any conditions under which this logical prerogative can belong to a thing, I can make nothing out of the notion, and draw no inference from it, because no object to which to apply the conception is determined, and we consequently do not know whether it has any meaning at all. In like manner, if I leave out the notion of time, in which something follows upon some other thing in conformity with a rule, I can find nothing in the pure category, except that there is a something of such a sort that from it a conclusion may be drawn as to the existence of some other thing. But in this case it would not only be impossible to distinguish between a cause and an effect, but, as this power to draw conclusions requires conditions of which I am quite ignorant, the conception is not determined as to the mode in which it ought to apply to an object. The so-called principle: "Everything that is contingent has a cause," comes with a gravity and self-assumed authority that seems to require no support from without. But, I ask, what is meant by contingent? The answer is that the non-existence of which is possible. But I should like very well to know by what means this possibility of non-existence is to be cognized, if we do not represent to ourselves a succession in the series of phenomena, and in this succession an existence which follows a non-existence, or conversely, consequently, change. For to say, that the non-existence of a thing is not self-contradictory is a lame appeal to a logical condition, which is no doubt a necessary condition of the existence of the conception, but is far from being sufficient for the real objective possibility of non-existence. I can annihilate in thought every existing substance without self-contradiction, but I cannot infer from this their objective contingency in existence, that is to say, the possibility of their non-existence in itself. As regards the category of community, it may easily be inferred that, as the pure categories of substance and causality are incapable of a definition and explanation sufficient to determine their object without the aid of intuition, the category of reciprocal causality in the relation of substances to each other (commercium) is just as little susceptible thereof. Possibility, existence, and necessity nobody has ever yet been able to explain without being guilty of manifest tautology, when the definition has been drawn entirely from the pure understanding. For the substitution of the logical possibility of the conception—the condition of which is that it be not self-contradictory, for the transcendental possibility of things—the condition of which is that there be an object corresponding to the conception, is a trick which can only deceive the inexperienced.[38]

It follows incontestably, that the pure conceptions of the understanding are incapable of transcendental, and must always be of empirical use alone, and that the principles of the pure understanding relate only to the general conditions of a possible experience, to objects of the senses, and never to things in general, apart from the mode in which we intuite them.

Transcendental analytic has accordingly this important result, to wit, that the understanding is competent effect nothing à priori, except the anticipation of the form of a possible experience in general, and that, as that which is not phenomenon cannot be an object of experience, it can never overstep the limits of sensibility, within which alone objects are presented to us. Its principles are merely principles of the exposition of phenomena, and the proud name of an ontology, which professes to present synthetical cognitions à priori of things in general in a systematic doctrine, must give place to the modest title of analytic of the pure understanding.

Thought is the act of referring a given intuition to an object. If the mode of this intuition is unknown to us, the object is merely transcendental, and the conception of the understanding is employed only transcendentally, that is, to produce unity in the thought of a manifold in general. Now a pure category, in which all conditions of sensuous intuition—as the only intuition we possess—are abstracted,

[38] In one word, to none of these conceptions belongs a corresponding object, and consequently their real possibility cannot be demonstrated, if we take away sensuous intuition—the only intuition which we possess—and there then remains nothing but the logical possibility, that is, the fact that the conception or thought is possible—which, however, is not the question; what we want to know being, whether it relates to an object and thus possesses any meaning.

does not determine an object, but merely expresses the thought of an object in general, according to different modes. Now, to employ a conception, the function of judgement is required, by which an object is subsumed under the conception, consequently the at least formal condition, under which something can be given in intuition. Failing this condition of judgement (schema), subsumption is impossible; for there is in such a case nothing given, which may be subsumed under the conception. The merely transcendental use of the categories is therefore, in fact, no use at all and has no determined, or even, as regards its form, determinable object. Hence it follows that the pure category is incompetent to establish a synthetical à priori principle, and that the principles of the pure understanding are only of empirical and never of transcendental use, and that beyond the sphere of possible experience no synthetical à priori principles are possible.

It may be advisable, therefore, to express ourselves thus. The pure categories, apart from the formal conditions of sensibility, have a merely transcendental meaning, but are nevertheless not of transcendental use, because this is in itself impossible, inasmuch as all the conditions of any employment or use of them (in judgements) are absent, to wit, the formal conditions of the subsumption of an object under these conceptions. As, therefore, in the character of pure categories, they must be employed empirically, and cannot be employed transcendentally, they are of no use at all, when separated from sensibility, that is, they cannot be applied to an object. They are merely the pure form of the employment of the understanding in respect of objects in general and of thought, without its being at the same time possible to think or to determine any object by their means. But there lurks at the foundation of this subject an illusion which it is very difficult to avoid. The categories are not based, as regards their origin, upon sensibility, like the forms of intuition, space, and time; they seem, therefore, to be capable of an application beyond the sphere of sensuous objects. But this is not the case. They are nothing but mere forms of thought, which contain only the logical faculty of uniting à priori in consciousness the manifold given in intuition. Apart, then, from the only intuition possible for us, they have still less meaning than the pure sensuous forms, space and time, for through them an object is at least given, while a mode of connection of the manifold, when the intuition which alone gives the manifold is wanting, has no meaning at all. At the same time, when we designate certain objects as phenomena or sensuous existences, thus distinguishing our mode of intuiting them from their own nature as things in themselves, it is evident that by this very distinction we as it were place the latter, considered in this their own nature, although we do not so intuite them, in opposition to the former, or, on the other hand, we do so place other possible things, which are not objects of our senses, but are cogitated by the understanding alone, and call them intelligible existences (noumena). Now the question arises whether the pure conceptions of our understanding do possess significance in respect of these latter, and may possibly be a mode of cognizing them.

But we are met at the very commencement with an ambiguity, which may easily occasion great misapprehension. The understanding, when it terms an object in a certain relation phenomenon, at the same time forms out of this relation a representation or notion of an object in itself, and hence believes that it can form also conceptions of such objects. Now as the understanding possesses no other fundamental conceptions besides the categories, it takes for granted that an object considered as a thing in itself must be capable of being thought by means of these pure conceptions, and is thereby led to hold the perfectly undetermined conception of an intelligible existence, a something out of the sphere of our sensibility, for a determinate conception of an existence which we can cognize in some way or other by means of the understanding.

If, by the term noumenon, we understand a thing so far as it is not an object of our sensuous intuition, thus making abstraction of our mode of intuiting it, this is a noumenon in the negative sense of the word. But if we understand by it an object of a non-sensuous intuition, we in this case assume a peculiar mode of intuition, an intellectual intuition, to wit, which does not, however, belong to us, of the very possibility of which we have no notion—and this is a noumenon in the positive sense.

The doctrine of sensibility is also the doctrine of noumena in the negative sense, that is, of things which the understanding is obliged to cogitate apart from any relation to our mode of intuition, consequently not as mere phenomena, but as things in themselves. But the understanding at the same time comprehends that it cannot employ its categories for the consideration of things in themselves, because these possess significance only in relation to the unity of intuitions in space and time, and that they are competent to determine this unity by means of general à priori connecting conceptions only on account of the pure ideality of space and time. Where this unity of time is not to be met with, as is the case with noumena, the whole use, indeed the whole meaning of the categories is entirely lost, for even the possibility of things to correspond to the categories is in this case incomprehensible. On this point, I need only refer the reader to what I have said at the commencement of the General Remark appended to the foregoing chapter. Now, the possibility of a thing can never be proved from the fact that the conception of it is not self-contradictory, but only by means of an intuition corresponding to the conception. If, therefore, we wish to apply the categories to objects which cannot be regarded as phenomena, we must have an intuition different from the sensuous, and in this case the objects would be a noumena in the positive sense of the word. Now, as such an intuition, that is, an intellectual intuition, is no part of our faculty of cognition, it is absolutely impossible for the categories to possess any application beyond the limits of experience. It may be true that there are intelligible existences to which our faculty of sensuous intuition has no relation, and cannot be applied, but our conceptions of the understanding, as mere forms of thought for our sensuous intuition, do not extend to these. What, therefore, we call noumenon must be understood by us as such in a negative sense.

If I take away from an empirical intuition all thought (by means of the categories), there remains no cognition of any object; for by means of mere intuition nothing is cogitated, and, from the existence of such or such an affection of sensibility in me, it does not follow that this affection or representation has any relation to an object without me. But if I take away all intuition, there still remains the form of thought, that is, the mode of determining an object for the manifold of a possible intuition. Thus the categories do in some measure really extend further than sensuous intuition, inasmuch as they think objects in general, without regard to the mode (of sensibility) in which these objects are given. But they do not for this reason apply to and determine a wider sphere of objects, because we cannot assume that such can be given, without presupposing the possibility of another than the sensuous mode of intuition, a supposition we are not justified in making.

I call a conception problematical which contains in itself no contradiction, and which is connected with other cognitions as a limitation of given conceptions, but whose objective reality cannot be cognized in any manner. The conception of a noumenon, that is, of a thing which must be cogitated not as an object of sense, but as a thing in itself (solely through the pure understanding), is not self-contradictory, for we are not entitled to maintain that sensibility is the only possible mode of intuition. Nay, further, this conception is necessary to restrain sensuous intuition within the bounds of phenomena, and thus to limit the objective validity of sensuous cognition; for things in themselves, which lie beyond its province, are called noumena for the very purpose of indicating that this cognition does not extend its application to all that the understanding thinks. But, after all, the possibility of such noumena is quite incomprehensible, and beyond the sphere of phenomena, all is for us a mere void; that is to say, we possess an understanding whose province does problematically extend beyond this sphere, but we do not possess an intuition, indeed, not even the conception of a possible intuition, by means of which objects beyond the region of sensibility could be given us, and in reference to which the understanding might be employed assertorically. The conception of a noumenon is therefore merely a limitative conception and therefore only of negative use. But it is not an arbitrary or fictitious notion, but is connected with the limitation of sensibility, without, however, being capable of presenting us with any positive datum beyond this sphere.

The division of objects into phenomena and noumena, and of the world into a mundus sensibilis and intelligibilis is therefore quite inadmissible in a positive sense, although conceptions do certainly admit of such a division; for the class of noumena have no determinate object corresponding to them, and cannot therefore possess objective validity. If we abandon the senses, how can it be made conceivable that the categories (which are the only conceptions that could serve as conceptions for noumena) have any sense or meaning at all, inasmuch as something more than the mere unity of thought, namely, a possible intuition, is requisite for their application to an object? The conception of a noumenon, considered as merely problematical, is, however, not only admissible, but, as a limitative conception of sensibility, absolutely necessary. But, in this case, a noumenon is not a particular intelligible object for our understanding; on the contrary, the kind of understanding to which it could belong is itself a problem, for we cannot form the most distant conception of the possibility of an understanding which should cognize an object, not discursively by means of categories, but intuitively in a non-sensuous intuition. Our understanding attains in this way a sort of negative extension. That is to say, it is not limited by, but rather limits, sensibility, by giving the name of noumena to things, not considered as phenomena, but as things in themselves. But it at the same time prescribes limits to itself, for it confesses itself unable to cognize these by means of the categories, and hence is compelled to cogitate them merely as an unknown something.

I find, however, in the writings of modern authors, an entirely different use of the expressions, mundus sensibilis and intelligibilis, which quite departs from the meaning of the ancients—an acceptation in which, indeed, there is to be found no difficulty, but which at the same time depends on mere verbal quibbling. According to this meaning, some have chosen to call the complex of phenomena, in so far as it is intuited, mundus sensibilis, but in so far as the connection thereof is cogitated according to general laws of thought, mundus intelligibilis. Astronomy, in so far as we mean by the word the mere observation of the starry heaven, may represent the former; a system of astronomy, such as the Copernican or Newtonian, the latter. But such twisting of words is a mere sophistical subterfuge, to avoid a difficult question, by modifying its meaning to suit our own convenience. To be sure, understanding and reason are employed in the cognition of phenomena; but the question is, whether these can be applied when the object is not a phenomenon and in this sense we regard it if it is cogitated as given to the understanding alone, and not to the senses. The question therefore is whether, over and above the empirical use of the understanding, a transcendental use is possible, which applies to the noumenon as an object. This question we have answered in the negative.

When therefore we say, the senses represent objects as they appear, the understanding as they are, the latter statement must not be understood in a transcendental, but only in an empirical signification, that is, as they must be represented in the complete connection of phenomena, and not according to what they may be, apart from their relation to possible experience, consequently not as objects of the pure understanding. For this must ever remain unknown to us. Nay, it is also quite unknown to us whether any such transcendental or extraordinary cognition is possible under any circumstances, at least, whether it is possible by means of our categories. Understanding and sensibility, with us, can determine objects only in conjunction. If we separate them, we have intuitions without conceptions, or conceptions without intuitions; in both cases, representations, which we cannot apply to any determinate object.

If, after all our inquiries and explanations, any one still hesitates to abandon the mere transcendental use of the categories, let him attempt to construct with them a synthetical proposition. It would, of course, be unnecessary for this purpose to construct an analytical proposition, for that does not extend the sphere of the understanding, but, being concerned only about what is cogitated in the conception itself, it leaves it quite undecided whether the conception has any relation to objects, or merely indicates the unity of thought—complete abstraction being made of the modi in which an object may be given: in such a proposition, it is sufficient for the understanding to know what lies in the conception—to what it applies is to it indifferent. The attempt must therefore be made with a synthetical and so-called transcendental principle, for example: "Everything that exists, exists as substance," or, "Everything that is contingent exists as an effect of some other thing, viz., of its cause." Now I ask, whence can the understanding draw these synthetical propositions, when the conceptions contained therein do not relate to possible experience but to things in themselves (noumena)? Where is to be found the third term, which is always requisite PURE site in a synthetical proposition, which may connect in the same proposition conceptions which have no logical (analytical) connection with each other? The proposition never will be demonstrated, nay, more, the possibility of any such pure assertion never can be shown, without making reference to the empirical use of the understanding, and thus, ipso facto, completely renouncing pure and non-sensuous judgement. Thus the conception of pure and merely intelligible objects is completely void of all principles of its application, because we cannot imagine any mode in which they might be given, and the problematical thought which leaves a place open for them serves only, like a void space, to limit the use of empirical principles, without containing at the same time any other object of cognition beyond their sphere.

APPENDIX

Of the Equivocal Nature or Amphiboly of the Conceptions of Reflection from the Confusion of the Transcendental with the Empirical use of the Understanding.

Reflection (reflexio) is not occupied about objects themselves, for the purpose of directly obtaining conceptions of them, but is that state of the mind in which we set ourselves to discover the subjective conditions under which we obtain conceptions. It is the consciousness of the relation of given representations to the different sources or faculties of cognition, by which alone their relation to each other can be rightly determined. The first question which occurs in considering our representations is to what faculty of cognition do they belong? To the understanding or to the senses? Many judgements are admitted to be true from mere habit or inclination; but, because reflection neither precedes nor follows, it is held to be a judgement that has its origin in the understanding. All judgements do not require examination, that is, investigation into the grounds of their truth. For, when they are immediately certain (for example: "Between two points there can be only one straight line"), no better or less mediate test of their truth can be found than that which they themselves contain and express. But all judgement, nay, all comparisons require reflection, that is, a distinction of the faculty of cognition to which the given conceptions belong. The act whereby I compare my representations with the faculty of cognition which originates them, and whereby I distinguish whether they are compared with each other as belonging to the pure understanding or to sensuous intuition, I term transcendental reflection. Now, the relations in which conceptions can stand to each other are those of identity and difference, agreement and opposition, of the internal and external, finally, of the determinable and the determining (matter and form). The proper determination of these relations rests on the question, to what faculty of cognition they subjectively belong, whether to sensibility or understanding? For, on the manner in which we solve this question depends the manner in which we must cogitate these relations.

Before constructing any objective judgement, we compare the conceptions that are to be placed in the judgement, and observe whether there exists identity (of many representations in one conception), if a general judgement is to be constructed, or difference, if a particular; whether there is agreement when affirmative; and opposition when negative judgements are to be constructed, and so on. For this reason we ought to call these conceptions, conceptions of comparison (conceptus comparationis). But as, when the question is not as to the logical form, but as to the content of conceptions, that is to say, whether the things themselves are identical or different, in agreement or opposition, and so on, the things can have a twofold relation to our faculty of cognition, to wit, a relation either to sensibility or to the understanding, and as on this relation depends their relation to each other, transcendental reflection, that is, the relation of given representations to one or the other faculty of cognition, can alone determine this latter relation. Thus we shall not be able to discover whether the things are identical or different, in agreement or opposition, etc., from the mere conception of the things by means of comparison (comparatio), but only by distinguishing the mode of cognition to which they belong, in other words, by means of transcendental reflection. We may, therefore, with justice say, that logical reflection is mere comparison, for in it no account is taken of the faculty of cognition to which the given conceptions belong, and they are consequently, as far as regards their origin, to be treated as homogeneous; while transcendental reflection (which applies to the objects themselves) contains the ground of the possibility of objective comparison of representations with each other, and is therefore very different from the former, because the faculties of cognition to which they belong are not even the same. Transcendental reflection is a duty which no one can neglect who wishes to establish an à priori judgement upon things. We shall now proceed to fulfil this duty, and thereby throw not a little light on the question as to the determination of the proper business of the understanding.

1. Identity and Difference. When an object is presented to us several times, but always with the same internal determinations (qualitas et quantitas), it, if an object of pure understanding, is always the same, not several things, but only one thing (numerica identitas); but if a phenomenon, we do not concern ourselves with comparing the conception of the thing with the conception of some other, but, although they may be in this respect perfectly the same, the difference of place at the same time is a sufficient ground for asserting the numerical difference of these objects (of sense). Thus, in the case of two drops of water, we may make complete abstraction of all internal difference (quality and quantity), and, the fact that they are intuited at the same time in different places, is sufficient to justify us in holding them to be numerically different. Leibnitz regarded phenomena as things in themselves, consequently as intelligibilia, that is, objects of pure understanding (although, on account of the confused nature of their representations, he gave them the name of phenomena), and in this case his principle of the indiscernible (principium identatis indiscernibilium) is not to be impugned. But, as phenomena are objects of sensibility, and, as the understanding, in respect of them, must be employed empirically and not purely or transcendentally, plurality and numerical difference are given by space itself as the condition of external phenomena. For one part of space, although it may be perfectly similar and equal to another part, is still without it, and for this reason alone is different from the latter, which is added to it in order to make up a greater space. It follows that this must hold good of all things that are in the different parts of space at the same time, however similar and equal one may be to another.

2. Agreement and Opposition. When reality is represented by the pure understanding (realitas noumenon), opposition between realities is incogitable—

such a relation, that is, that when these realities are connected in one subject, they annihilate the effects of each other and may be represented in the formula 3 -3 = 0. On the other hand, the real in a phenomenon (realitas phaenomenon) may very well be in mutual opposition, and, when united in the same subject, the one may completely or in part annihilate the effect or consequence of the other; as in the case of two moving forces in the same straight line drawing or impelling a point in opposite directions, or in the case of a pleasure counterbalancing a certain amount of pain.

3. The Internal and External. In an object of the pure understanding, only that is internal which has no relation (as regards its existence) to anything different from itself. On the other hand, the internal determinations of a substantia phaenomenon in space are nothing but relations, and it is itself nothing more than a complex of mere relations. Substance in space we are cognizant of only through forces operative in it, either drawing others towards itself (attraction), or preventing others from forcing into itself (repulsion and impenetrability). We know no other properties that make up the conception of substance phenomenal in space, and which we term matter. On the other hand, as an object of the pure understanding, every substance must have internal determination and forces. But what other internal attributes of such an object can I think than those which my internal sense presents to me? That, to wit, which in either itself thought, or something analogous to it. Hence Leibnitz, who looked upon things as noumena, after denying them everything like external relation, and therefore also composition or combination, declared that all substances, even the component parts of matter, were simple substances with powers of representation, in one word, monads.

4. Matter and Form. These two conceptions lie at the foundation of all other reflection, so inseparably are they connected with every mode of exercising the understanding. The former denotes the determinable in general, the second its determination, both in a transcendental sense, abstraction being made of every difference in that which is given, and of the mode in which it is determined. Logicians formerly termed the universal, matter, the specific difference of this or that part of the universal, form. In a judgement one may call the given conceptions logical matter (for the judgement), the relation of these to each other (by means of the copula), the form of the judgement. In an object, the composite parts thereof (essentialia) are the matter; the mode in which they are connected in the object, the form. In respect to things in general, unlimited reality was regarded as the matter of all possibility, the limitation thereof (negation) as the form, by which one thing is distinguished from another according to transcendental conceptions. The understanding demands that something be given (at least in the conception), in order to be able to determine it in a certain manner. Hence, in a conception of the pure understanding, the matter precedes the form, and for this reason Leibnitz first assumed the existence of things (monads) and of an internal power of representation in them, in order

to found upon this their external relation and the community their state (that is, of their representations). Hence, with him, space and time were possible—the former through the relation of substances, the latter through the connection of their determinations with each other, as causes and effects. And so would it really be, if the pure understanding were capable of an immediate application to objects, and if space and time were determinations of things in themselves. But being merely sensuous intuitions, in which we determine all objects solely as phenomena, the form of intuition (as a subjective property of sensibility) must antecede all matter (sensations), consequently space and time must antecede all phenomena and all data of experience, and rather make experience itself possible. But the intellectual philosopher could not endure that the form should precede the things themselves and determine their possibility; an objection perfectly correct, if we assume that we intuite things as they are, although with confused representation. But as sensuous intuition is a peculiar subjective condition, which is à priori at the foundation of all perception, and the form of which is primitive, the form must be given per se, and so far from matter (or the things themselves which appear) lying at the foundation of experience (as we must conclude, if we judge by mere conceptions), the very possibility of itself presupposes, on the contrary, a given formal intuition (space and time).

REMARK ON THE AMPHIBOLY OF THE CONCEPTIONS OF REFLECTION.

Let me be allowed to term the position which we assign to a conception either in the sensibility or in the pure understanding, the transcendental place. In this manner, the appointment of the position which must be taken by each conception according to the difference in its use, and the directions for determining this place to all conceptions according to rules, would be a transcendental topic, a doctrine which would thoroughly shield us from the surreptitious devices of the pure understanding and the delusions which thence arise, as it would always distinguish to what faculty of cognition each conception properly belonged. Every conception, every title, under which many cognitions rank together, may be called a logical place. Upon this is based the logical topic of Aristotle, of which teachers and rhetoricians could avail themselves, in order, under certain titles of thought, to observe what would best suit the matter they had to treat, and thus enable themselves to quibble and talk with fluency and an appearance of profundity.

Transcendental topic, on the contrary, contains nothing more than the above-mentioned four titles of all comparison and distinction, which differ from categories in this respect, that they do not represent the object according to that which constitutes its conception (quantity, reality), but set forth merely the comparison of representations, which precedes our conceptions of things. But this comparison requires a previous reflection, that is, a determination of the place to which the representations of the things which are compared belong, whether, to wit, they are cogitated by the pure understanding, or given by sensibility.

Conceptions may be logically compared without the trouble of inquiring to what faculty their objects belong, whether as noumena, to the understanding, or as phenomena, to sensibility. If, however, we wish to employ these conceptions in respect of objects, previous transcendental reflection is necessary. Without this reflection I should make a very unsafe use of these conceptions, and construct pretended synthetical propositions which critical reason cannot acknowledge and which are based solely upon a transcendental amphiboly, that is, upon a substitution of an object of pure understanding for a phenomenon.

For want of this doctrine of transcendental topic, and consequently deceived by the amphiboly of the conceptions of reflection, the celebrated Leibnitz constructed an intellectual system of the world, or rather, believed himself competent to cognize the internal nature of things, by comparing all objects merely with the understanding and the abstract formal conceptions of thought. Our table of the conceptions of reflection gives us the unexpected advantage of being able to exhibit the distinctive peculiarities of his system in all its parts, and at the same time of exposing the fundamental principle of this peculiar mode of thought, which rested upon naught but a misconception. He compared all things with each other merely by means of conceptions, and naturally found no other differences than those by which the understanding distinguishes its pure conceptions one from another. The conditions of sensuous intuition, which contain in themselves their own means of distinction, he did not look upon as primitive, because sensibility was to him but a confused mode of representation and not any particular source of representations. A phenomenon was for him the representation of the thing in itself, although distinguished from cognition by the understanding only in respect of the logical form—the former with its usual want of analysis containing, according to him, a certain mixture of collateral representations in its conception of a thing, which it is the duty of the understanding to separate and distinguish. In one word, Leibnitz intellectualized phenomena, just as Locke, in his system of noogony (if I may be allowed to make use of such expressions), sensualized the conceptions of the understanding, that is to say, declared them to be nothing more than empirical or abstract conceptions of reflection. Instead of seeking in the understanding and sensibility two different sources of representations, which, however, can present us with objective judgements of things only in conjunction, each of these great men recognized but one of these faculties, which, in their opinion, applied immediately to things in themselves, the other having no duty but that of confusing or arranging the representations of the former.

Accordingly, the objects of sense were compared by Leibnitz as things in general merely in the understanding.

1st. He compares them in regard to their identity or difference—as judged by the understanding. As, therefore, he considered merely the conceptions of objects, and not their position in intuition, in which alone objects can be given, and left quite out of sight the transcendental locale of these conceptions—

whether, that is, their object ought to be classed among phenomena, or among things in themselves, it was to be expected that he should extend the application of the principle of indiscernibles, which is valid solely of conceptions of things in general, to objects of sense (mundus phaenomenon), and that he should believe that he had thereby contributed in no small degree to extend our knowledge of nature. In truth, if I cognize in all its inner determinations a drop of water as a thing in itself, I cannot look upon one drop as different from another, if the conception of the one is completely identical with that of the other. But if it is a phenomenon in space, it has a place not merely in the understanding (among conceptions), but also in sensuous external intuition (in space), and in this case, the physical locale is a matter of indifference in regard to the internal determinations of things, and one place, B, may contain a thing which is perfectly similar and equal to another in a place, A, just as well as if the two things were in every respect different from each other. Difference of place without any other conditions, makes the plurality and distinction of objects as phenomena, not only possible in itself, but even necessary. Consequently, the above so-called law is not a law of nature. It is merely an analytical rule for the comparison of things by means of mere conceptions.

2nd. The principle: "Realities (as simple affirmations) never logically contradict each other," is a proposition perfectly true respecting the relation of conceptions, but, whether as regards nature, or things in themselves (of which we have not the slightest conception), is without any the least meaning. For real opposition, in which A -B is = 0, exists everywhere, an opposition, that is, in which one reality united with another in the same subject annihilates the effects of the other—a fact which is constantly brought before our eyes by the different antagonistic actions and operations in nature, which, nevertheless, as depending on real forces, must be called realitates phaenomena. General mechanics can even present us with the empirical condition of this opposition in an à priori rule, as it directs its attention to the opposition in the direction of forces—a condition of which the transcendental conception of reality can tell us nothing. Although M. Leibnitz did not announce this proposition with precisely the pomp of a new principle, he yet employed it for the establishment of new propositions, and his followers introduced it into their Leibnitzio-Wolfian system of philosophy. According to this principle, for example, all evils are but consequences of the limited nature of created beings, that is, negations, because these are the only opposite of reality. (In the mere conception of a thing in general this is really the case, but not in things as phenomena.) In like manner, the upholders of this system deem it not only possible, but natural also, to connect and unite all reality in one being, because they acknowledge no other sort of opposition than that of contradiction (by which the conception itself of a thing is annihilated), and find themselves unable to conceive an opposition of reciprocal destruction, so to speak, in which one real cause destroys the effect of another, and the conditions of whose representation we meet with only in sensibility.

3rd. The Leibnitzian monadology has really no better foundation than on this philosopher's mode of falsely representing the difference of the internal and external solely in relation to the understanding. Substances, in general, must have something inward, which is therefore free from external relations, consequently from that of composition also. The simple—that which can be represented by a unit—is therefore the foundation of that which is internal in things in themselves. The internal state of substances cannot therefore consist in place, shape, contact, or motion, determinations which are all external relations, and we can ascribe to them no other than that whereby we internally determine our faculty of sense itself, that is to say, the state of representation. Thus, then, were constructed the monads, which were to form the elements of the universe, the active force of which consists in representation, the effects of this force being thus entirely confined to themselves.

For the same reason, his view of the possible community of substances could not represent it but as a predetermined harmony, and by no means as a physical influence. For inasmuch as everything is occupied only internally, that is, with its own representations, the state of the representations of one substance could not stand in active and living connection with that of another, but some third cause operating on all without exception was necessary to make the different states correspond with one another. And this did not happen by means of assistance applied in each particular case (systema assistentiae), but through the unity of the idea of a cause occupied and connected with all substances, in which they necessarily receive, according to the Leibnitzian school, their existence and permanence, consequently also reciprocal correspondence, according to universal laws.

4th. This philosopher's celebrated doctrine of space and time, in which he intellectualized these forms of sensibility, originated in the same delusion of transcendental reflection. If I attempt to represent by the mere understanding, the external relations of things, I can do so only by employing the conception of their reciprocal action, and if I wish to connect one state of the same thing with another state, I must avail myself of the notion of the order of cause and effect. And thus Leibnitz regarded space as a certain order in the community of substances, and time as the dynamical sequence of their states. That which space and time possess proper to themselves and independent of things, he ascribed to a necessary confusion in our conceptions of them, whereby that which is a mere form of dynamical relations is held to be a self-existent intuition, antecedent even to things themselves. Thus space and time were the intelligible form of the connection of things (substances and their states) in themselves. But things were intelligible substances (substantiae noumena). At the same time, he made these conceptions valid of phenomena, because he did not allow to sensibility a peculiar mode of intuition, but sought all, even the empirical representation of objects, in the understanding, and left to sense naught but the despicable task of confusing and disarranging the representations of the former.

But even if we could frame any synthetical proposition concerning things in themselves by means of the pure understanding (which is impossible), it could not apply to phenomena, which do not represent things in themselves. In such a case I should be obliged in transcendental reflection to compare my conceptions only under the conditions of sensibility, and so space and time would not be determinations of things in themselves, but of phenomena. What things may be in themselves, I know not and need not know, because a thing is never presented to me otherwise than as a phenomenon.

I must adopt the same mode of procedure with the other conceptions of reflection. Matter is substantia phaenomenon. That in it which is internal I seek to discover in all parts of space which it occupies, and in all the functions and operations it performs, and which are indeed never anything but phenomena of the external sense. I cannot therefore find anything that is absolutely, but only what is comparatively internal, and which itself consists of external relations. The absolutely internal in matter, and as it should be according to the pure understanding, is a mere chimera, for matter is not an object for the pure understanding. But the transcendental object, which is the foundation of the phenomenon which we call matter, is a mere nescio quid, the nature of which we could not understand, even though someone were found able to tell us. For we can understand nothing that does not bring with it something in intuition corresponding to the expressions employed. If, by the complaint of being unable to perceive the internal nature of things, it is meant that we do not comprehend by the pure understanding what the things which appear to us may be in themselves, it is a silly and unreasonable complaint; for those who talk thus really desire that we should be able to cognize, consequently to intuite, things without senses, and therefore wish that we possessed a faculty of cognition perfectly different from the human faculty, not merely in degree, but even as regards intuition and the mode thereof, so that thus we should not be men, but belong to a class of beings, the possibility of whose existence, much less their nature and constitution, we have no means of cognizing. By observation and analysis of phenomena we penetrate into the interior of nature, and no one can say what progress this knowledge may make in time. But those transcendental questions which pass beyond the limits of nature, we could never answer, even although all nature were laid open to us, because we have not the power of observing our own mind with any other intuition than that of our internal sense. For herein lies the mystery of the origin and source of our faculty of sensibility. Its application to an object, and the transcendental ground of this unity of subjective and objective, lie too deeply concealed for us, who cognize ourselves only through the internal sense, consequently as phenomena, to be able to discover in our existence anything but phenomena, the non-sensuous cause of which we at the same time earnestly desire to penetrate to.

The great utility of this critique of conclusions arrived at by the processes of mere reflection consists in its clear demonstration of the nullity of all conclusions respecting objects which are compared with each other in the understanding alone, while it at the same time confirms what we particularly insisted on, namely, that, although phenomena are not included as things in themselves among the objects of the pure understanding, they are nevertheless the only things by which our cognition can possess objective reality, that is to say, which give us intuitions to correspond with our conceptions.

When we reflect in a purely logical manner, we do nothing more than compare conceptions in our understanding, to discover whether both have the same content, whether they are self-contradictory or not, whether anything is contained in either conception, which of the two is given, and which is merely a mode of thinking that given. But if I apply these conceptions to an object in general (in the transcendental sense), without first determining whether it is an object of sensuous or intellectual intuition, certain limitations present themselves, which forbid us to pass beyond the conceptions and render all empirical use of them impossible. And thus these limitations prove that the representation of an object as a thing in general is not only insufficient, but, without sensuous determination and independently of empirical conditions, self-contradictory; that we must therefore make abstraction of all objects, as in logic, or, admitting them, must think them under conditions of sensuous intuition; that, consequently, the intelligible requires an altogether peculiar intuition, which we do not possess, and in the absence of which it is for us nothing; while, on the other hand phenomena cannot be objects in themselves. For, when I merely think things in general, the difference in their external relations cannot constitute a difference in the things themselves; on the contrary, the former presupposes the latter, and if the conception of one of two things is not internally different from that of the other, I am merely thinking the same thing in different relations. Further, by the addition of one affirmation (reality) to the other, the positive therein is really augmented, and nothing is abstracted or withdrawn from it; hence the real in things cannot be in contradiction with or opposition to itself—and so on.

The true use of the conceptions of reflection in the employment of the understanding has, as we have shown, been so misconceived by Leibnitz, one of the most acute philosophers of either ancient or modern times, that he has been misled into the construction of a baseless system of intellectual cognition, which professes to determine its objects without the intervention of the senses. For this reason, the exposition of the cause of the amphiboly of these conceptions, as the origin of these false principles, is of great utility in determining with certainty the proper limits of the understanding.

It is right to say whatever is affirmed or denied of the whole of a conception can be affirmed or denied of any part of it (dictum de omni et nullo); but it would be absurd so to alter this logical proposition as to say whatever is not contained in a general conception is likewise not contained in the particular conceptions which rank under it; for the latter are particular conceptions, for the very reason that their content is greater than that which is cogitated in the general conception. And yet the whole intellectual system of Leibnitz is based upon this false principle, and with it must necessarily fall to the ground, together with all the ambiguous principles in reference to the employment of the understanding which have thence originated.

Leibnitz's principle of the identity of indiscernibles or indistinguishables is really based on the presupposition that, if in the conception of a thing a certain distinction is not to be found, it is also not to be met with in things themselves; that, consequently, all things are completely identical (numero eadem) which are not distinguishable from each other (as to quality or quantity) in our conceptions of them. But, as in the mere conception of anything abstraction has been made of many necessary conditions of intuition, that of which abstraction has been made is rashly held to be non-existent, and nothing is attributed to the thing but what is contained in its conception.

The conception of a cubic foot of space, however I may think it, is in itself completely identical. But two cubic feet in space are nevertheless distinct from each other from the sole fact of their being in different places (they are numero diversa); and these places are conditions of intuition, wherein the object of this conception is given, and which do not belong to the conception, but to the faculty of sensibility. In like manner, there is in the conception of a thing no contradiction when a negative is not connected with an affirmative; and merely affirmative conceptions cannot, in conjunction, produce any negation. But in sensuous intuition, wherein reality (take for example, motion) is given, we find conditions (opposite directions)—of which abstraction has been made in the conception of motion in general—which render possible a contradiction or opposition (not indeed of a logical kind)—and which from pure positives produce zero = 0. We are therefore not justified in saying that all reality is in perfect agreement and harmony, because no contradiction is discoverable among its conceptions.[39] According to mere conceptions, that which is internal is the substratum of all relations or external determinations. When, therefore, I abstract all conditions of intuition, and confine myself solely to the conception of a thing in general, I can make abstraction of all external relations, and there must nevertheless remain a conception of that which indicates no relation, but merely internal determinations. Now it seems to follow that in everything (substance) there is something which is absolutely internal and which antecedes all external determinations, inasmuch as it renders them possible; and that therefore this substratum is something which

[39] If any one wishes here to have recourse to the usual subterfuge, and to say, that at least realitates noumena cannot be in opposition to each other, it will be requisite for him to adduce an example of this pure and non-sensuous reality, that it may be understood whether the notion represents something or nothing. But an example cannot be found except in experience, which never presents to us anything more than phenomena; and thus the proposition means nothing more than that the conception which contains only affirmatives does not contain anything negative—a proposition nobody ever doubted.

does not contain any external relations and is consequently simple (for corporeal things are never anything but relations, at least of their parts external to each other); and, inasmuch as we know of no other absolutely internal determinations than those of the internal sense, this substratum is not only simple, but also, analogously with our internal sense, determined through representations, that is to say, all things are properly monads, or simple beings endowed with the power of representation. Now all this would be perfectly correct, if the conception of a thing were the only necessary condition of the presentation of objects of external intuition. It is, on the contrary, manifest that a permanent phenomenon in space (impenetrable extension) can contain mere relations, and nothing that is absolutely internal, and yet be the primary substratum of all external perception. By mere conceptions I cannot think anything external, without, at the same time, thinking something internal, for the reason that conceptions of relations presuppose given things, and without these are impossible. But, as an intuition there is something (that is, space, which, with all it contains, consists of purely formal, or, indeed, real relations) which is not found in the mere conception of a thing in general, and this presents to us the substratum which could not be cognized through conceptions alone, I cannot say: because a thing cannot be represented by mere conceptions without something absolutely internal, there is also, in the things themselves which are contained under these conceptions, and in their intuition nothing external to which something absolutely internal does not serve as the foundation. For, when we have made abstraction of all the conditions of intuition, there certainly remains in the mere conception nothing but the internal in general, through which alone the external is possible. But this necessity, which is grounded upon abstraction alone, does not obtain in the case of things themselves, in so far as they are given in intuition with such determinations as express mere relations, without having anything internal as their foundation; for they are not things of a thing of which we can neither for they are not things in themselves, but only phenomena. What we cognize in matter is nothing but relations (what we call its internal determinations are but comparatively internal). But there are some self-subsistent and permanent, through which a determined object is given. That I, when abstraction is made of these relations, have nothing more to think, does not destroy the conception of a thing as phenomenon, nor the conception of an object in abstracto, but it does away with the possibility of an object that is determinable according to mere conceptions, that is, of a noumenon. It is certainly startling to hear that a thing consists solely of relations; but this thing is simply a phenomenon, and cannot be cogitated by means of the mere categories: it does itself consist in the mere relation of something in general to the senses. In the same way, we cannot cogitate relations of things in abstracto, if we commence with conceptions alone, in any other manner than that one is the cause of determinations in the other; for that is itself the conception of the understanding or category of relation. But, as in this case we make abstraction of all intuition, we lose altogether the mode in which the manifold determines to each of its parts its place, that is, the form of sensibility (space); and yet this mode antecedes all empirical causality.

If by intelligible objects we understand things which can be thought by means of the pure categories, without the need of the schemata of sensibility, such objects are impossible. For the condition of the objective use of all our conceptions of understanding is the mode of our sensuous intuition, whereby objects are given; and, if we make abstraction of the latter, the former can have no relation to an object. And even if we should suppose a different kind of intuition from our own, still our functions of thought would have no use or signification in respect thereof. But if we understand by the term, objects of a non-sensuous intuition, in respect of which our categories are not valid, and of which we can accordingly have no knowledge (neither intuition nor conception), in this merely negative sense noumena must be admitted. For this is no more than saying that our mode of intuition is not applicable to all things, but only to objects of our senses, that consequently its objective validity is limited, and that room is therefore left for another kind of intuition, and thus also for things that may be objects of it. But in this sense the conception of a noumenon is problematical, that is to say, it is the notion of that it that it is possible, nor that it is impossible, inasmuch as we do not know of any mode of intuition besides the sensuous, or of any other sort of conceptions than the categories—a mode of intuition and a kind of conception neither of which is applicable to a non-sensuous object. We are on this account incompetent to extend the sphere of our objects of thought beyond the conditions of our sensibility, and to assume the existence of objects of pure thought, that is, of noumena, inasmuch as these have no true positive signification. For it must be confessed of the categories that they are not of themselves sufficient for the cognition of things in themselves and, without the data of sensibility, are mere subjective forms of the unity of the understanding. Thought is certainly not a product of the senses, and in so far is not limited by them, but it does not therefore follow that it may be employed purely and without the intervention of sensibility, for it would then be without reference to an object. And we cannot call a noumenon an object of pure thought; for the representation thereof is but the problematical conception of an object for a perfectly different intuition and a perfectly different understanding from ours, both of which are consequently themselves problematical. The conception of a noumenon is therefore not the conception of an object, but merely a problematical conception inseparably connected with the limitation of our sensibility. That is to say, this conception contains the answer to the question: "Are there objects quite unconnected with, and independent of, our intuition?"—a question to which only an indeterminate answer can be given. That answer is: "Inasmuch as sensuous intuition does not apply to all things without distinction, there remains room for other and different objects." The existence of these problematical objects is therefore not absolutely denied, in the absence of a determinate conception of them, but, as no category is valid in respect of them, neither must they be admitted as objects for our understanding.

Understanding accordingly limits sensibility, without at the same time enlarging its own field. While, moreover, it forbids sensibility to apply its forms and modes to things in themselves and restricts it to the sphere of phenomena, it cogitates an object in itself, only, however, as a transcendental object, which is the cause of a phenomenon (consequently not itself a phenomenon), and which cannot be thought either as a quantity or as reality, or as substance (because these conceptions always require sensuous forms in which to determine an object)—an object, therefore, of which we are quite unable to say whether it can be met with in ourselves or out of us, whether it would be annihilated together with sensibility, or, if this were taken away, would continue to exist. If we wish to call this object a noumenon, because the representation of it is non-sensuous, we are at liberty to do so. But as we can apply to it none of the conceptions of our understanding, the representation is for us quite void, and is available only for the indication of the limits of our sensuous intuition, thereby leaving at the same time an empty space, which we are competent to fill by the aid neither of possible experience, nor of the pure understanding.

The critique of the pure understanding, accordingly, does not permit us to create for ourselves a new field of objects beyond those which are presented to us as phenomena, and to stray into intelligible worlds; nay, it does not even allow us to endeavour to form so much as a conception of them. The specious error which leads to this—and which is a perfectly excusable one—lies in the fact that the employment of the understanding, contrary to its proper purpose and destination, is made transcendental, and objects, that is, possible intuitions, are made to regulate themselves according to conceptions, instead of the conceptions arranging themselves according to the intuitions, on which alone their own objective validity rests. Now the reason of this again is that apperception, and with it thought, antecedes all possible determinate arrangement of representations. Accordingly we think something in general and determine it on the one hand sensuously, but, on the other, distinguish the general and in abstracto represented object from this particular mode of intuiting it. In this case there remains a mode of determining the object by mere thought, which is really but a logical form without content, which, however, seems to us to be a mode of the existence of the object in itself (noumenon), without regard to intuition which is limited to our senses.

Before ending this transcendental analytic, we must make an addition, which, although in itself of no particular importance, seems to be necessary to the completeness of the system. The highest conception, with which a transcendental philosophy commonly begins, is the division into possible and impossible. But as all division presupposes a divided conception, a still higher one must exist, and this is the conception of an object in general—problematically understood and without its being decided whether it is something or nothing. As the categories are the only conceptions which apply to objects in general, the distinguishing of an object, whether it is something or nothing, must proceed according to the order and direction of the categories.

1. To the categories of quantity, that is, the conceptions of all, many, and one, the conception which annihilates all, that is, the conception of none, is opposed. And thus the object of a conception, to which no intuition can be found to correspond, is = nothing. That is, it is a conception without an object (ens rationis), like noumena, which cannot be considered possible in the sphere of reality, though they must not therefore be held to be impossible—or like certain new fundamental forces in matter, the existence of which is cogitable without contradiction, though, as examples from experience are not forthcoming, they must not be regarded as possible.

2. Reality is something; negation is nothing, that is, a conception of the absence of an object, as cold, a shadow (nihil privativum).

3. The mere form of intuition, without substance, is in itself no object, but the merely formal condition of an object (as phenomenon), as pure space and pure time. These are certainly something, as forms of intuition, but are not themselves objects which are intuited (ens imaginarium).

4. The object of a conception which is self-contradictory, is nothing, because the conception is nothing—is impossible, as a figure composed of two straight lines (nihil negativum).

The table of this division of the conception of nothing (the corresponding division of the conception of something does not require special description) must therefore be arranged as follows:

NOTHING
AS

1
As Empty Conception
without object,
ens rationis

2
Empty object of
a conception,
nihil privativum

3
Empty intuition
without object,
ens imaginarium

4
Empty object
without conception,
nihil negativum

We see that the ens rationis is distinguished from the nihil negativum or pure nothing by the consideration that the former must not be reckoned among possibilities, because it is a mere fiction—though not self-contradictory, while the latter is completely opposed to all possibility, inasmuch as the conception annihilates itself. Both, however, are empty conceptions. On the other hand, the nihil privativum and ens imaginarium are empty data for conceptions. If light be not given to the senses, we cannot represent to ourselves darkness, and if extended objects are not perceived, we cannot represent space. Neither the negation, nor the mere form of intuition can, without something real, be an object.

SECOND DIVISION

TRANSCENDENTAL LOGIC

TRANSCENDENTAL DIALECTIC

Introduction

I. Of Transcendental Illusory Appearance

We termed dialectic in general a logic of appearance. This does not signify a doctrine of probability; for probability is truth, only cognized upon insufficient grounds, and though the information it gives us is imperfect, it is not therefore deceitful. Hence it must not be separated from the analytical part of logic. Still less must phenomenon and appearance be held to be identical. For truth or illusory appearance does not reside in the object, in so far as it is intuited, but in the judgement upon the object, in so far as it is thought. It is, therefore, quite correct to say that the senses do not err, not because they always judge correctly, but because they do not judge at all. Hence truth and error, consequently also, illusory appearance as the cause of error, are only to be found in a judgement, that is, in the relation of an object to our understanding. In a cognition which completely harmonizes with the laws of the understanding, no error can exist. In a representation of the senses—as not containing any judgement—there is also no error. But no power of nature can of itself deviate from its own laws. Hence neither the understanding per se (without the influence of another cause), nor the senses per se, would fall into error; the former could not, because, if it acts only according to its own laws, the effect (the judgement) must necessarily accord with these laws. But in accordance with the laws of the understanding consists the formal element in all truth. In the senses there is no judgement—neither a true nor a false one. But, as we have no source of cognition besides these two, it follows that error is caused solely by the unobserved influence of the sensibility upon the understanding. And thus it happens that the subjective grounds of a judgement and are confounded with the objective, and cause them to deviate from their proper determination,[40] just as a body in motion would always of itself proceed in a straight line, but if another impetus gives to it a different direction, it will then start off into a curvilinear line of motion. To

[40] Sensibility, subjected to the understanding, as the object upon which the understanding employs its functions, is the source of real cognitions. But, in so far as it exercises an influence upon the action of the understanding and determines it to judgement, sensibility is itself the cause of error.

distinguish the peculiar action of the understanding from the power which mingles with it, it is necessary to consider an erroneous judgement as the diagonal between two forces, that determine the judgement in two different directions, which, as it were, form an angle, and to resolve this composite operation into the simple ones of the understanding and the sensibility. In pure à priori judgements this must be done by means of transcendental reflection, whereby, as has been already shown, each representation has its place appointed in the corresponding faculty of cognition, and consequently the influence of the one faculty upon the other is made apparent.

It is not at present our business to treat of empirical illusory appearance (for example, optical illusion), which occurs in the empirical application of otherwise correct rules of the understanding, and in which the judgement is misled by the influence of imagination. Our purpose is to speak of transcendental illusory appearance, which influences principles—that are not even applied to experience, for in this case we should possess a sure test of their correctness—but which leads us, in disregard of all the warnings of criticism, completely beyond the empirical employment of the categories and deludes us with the chimera of an extension of the sphere of the pure understanding. We shall term those principles the application of which is confined entirely within the limits of possible experience, immanent; those, on the other hand, which transgress these limits, we shall call transcendent principles. But by these latter I do not understand principles of the transcendental use or misuse of the categories, which is in reality a mere fault of the judgement when not under due restraint from criticism, and therefore not paying sufficient attention to the limits of the sphere in which the pure understanding is allowed to exercise its functions; but real principles which exhort us to break down all those barriers, and to lay claim to a perfectly new field of cognition, which recognizes no line of demarcation. Thus transcendental and transcendent are not identical terms. The principles of the pure understanding, which we have already propounded, ought to be of empirical and not of transcendental use, that is, they are not applicable to any object beyond the sphere of experience. A principle which removes these limits, nay, which authorizes us to overstep them, is called transcendent. If our criticism can succeed in exposing the illusion in these pretended principles, those which are limited in their employment to the sphere of experience may be called, in opposition to the others, immanent principles of the pure understanding.

Logical illusion, which consists merely in the imitation of the form of reason (the illusion in sophistical syllogisms), arises entirely from a want of due attention to logical rules. So soon as the attention is awakened to the case before us, this illusion totally disappears. Transcendental illusion, on the contrary, does not cease to exist, even after it has been exposed, and its nothingness clearly perceived by means of transcendental criticism. Take, for example, the illusion in the proposition: "The world must have a beginning in time." The cause of this is as follows. In our reason, subjectively considered as a faculty of human cognition, there exist fundamental rules and maxims of its exercise, which have completely the appearance of objective principles. Now from this cause it happens that the subjective necessity of a certain connection of our conceptions, is regarded as an objective necessity of the determination of things in themselves. This illusion it is impossible to avoid, just as we cannot avoid perceiving that the sea appears to be higher at a distance than it is near the shore, because we see the former by means of higher rays than the latter, or, which is a still stronger case, as even the astronomer cannot prevent himself from seeing the moon larger at its rising than some time afterwards, although he is not deceived by this illusion.

Transcendental dialectic will therefore content itself with exposing the illusory appearance in transcendental judgements, and guarding us against it; but to make it, as in the case of logical illusion, entirely disappear and cease to be illusion is utterly beyond its power. For we have here to do with a natural and unavoidable illusion, which rests upon subjective principles and imposes these upon us as objective, while logical dialectic, in the detection of sophisms, has to do merely with an error in the logical consequence of the propositions, or with an artificially constructed illusion, in imitation of the natural error. There is, therefore, a natural and unavoidable dialectic of pure reason—not that in which the bungler, from want of the requisite knowledge, involves himself, nor that which the sophist devises for the purpose of misleading, but that which is an inseparable adjunct of human reason, and which, even after its illusions have been exposed, does not cease to deceive, and continually to lead reason into momentary errors, which it becomes necessary continually to remove.

II. Of Pure Reason as the Seat of Transcendental Illusory Appearance

A. OF REASON IN GENERAL.

All our knowledge begins with sense, proceeds thence to understanding, and ends with reason, beyond which nothing higher can be discovered in the human mind for elaborating the matter of intuition and subjecting it to the highest unity of thought. At this stage of our inquiry it is my duty to give an explanation of this, the highest faculty of cognition, and I confess I find myself here in some difficulty. Of reason, as of the understanding, there is a merely formal, that is, logical use, in which it makes abstraction of all content of cognition; but there is also a real use, inasmuch as it contains in itself the source of certain conceptions and principles, which it does not borrow either from the senses or the understanding. The former faculty has been long defined by logicians as the faculty of mediate conclusion in contradistinction to immediate conclusions (consequentiae immediatae); but the nature of the latter, which itself generates conceptions, is not to be understood from this definition. Now as a division of reason into a logical and a transcendental faculty presents itself here, it becomes necessary to seek for a higher conception of this source of cognition which shall comprehend both conceptions. In this we may expect, according to the analogy of the conceptions of the understanding, that the logical conception will give us the key to the transcendental, and that the table of the functions of the former will present us with the clue to the conceptions of reason.

In the former part of our transcendental logic, we defined the understanding to be the faculty of rules; reason may be distinguished from understanding as the faculty of principles.

The term principle is ambiguous, and commonly signifies merely a cognition that may be employed as a principle, although it is not in itself, and as regards its proper origin, entitled to the distinction. Every general proposition, even if derived from experience by the process of induction, may serve as the major in a syllogism; but it is not for that reason a principle. Mathematical axioms (for example, there can be only one straight line between two points) are general à priori cognitions, and are therefore rightly denominated principles, relatively to the cases which can be subsumed under them. But I cannot for this reason say that I cognize this property of a straight line from principles—I cognize it only in pure intuition.

Cognition from principles, then, is that cognition in which I cognize the particular in the general by means of conceptions. Thus every syllogism is a form of the deduction of a cognition from a principle. For the major always gives a conception, through which everything that is subsumed under the condition thereof is cognized according to a principle. Now as every general cognition may serve as the major in a syllogism, and the understanding presents us with such general à priori propositions, they may be termed principles, in respect of their possible use.

But if we consider these principles of the pure understanding in relation to their origin, we shall find them to be anything rather than cognitions from conceptions. For they would not even be possible à priori, if we could not rely on the assistance of pure intuition (in mathematics), or on that of the conditions of a possible experience. That everything that happens has a cause, cannot be concluded from the general conception of that which happens; on the contrary the principle of causality instructs us as to the mode of obtaining from that which happens a determinate empirical conception.

Synthetical cognitions from conceptions the understanding cannot supply, and they alone are entitled to be called principles. At the same time, all general propositions may be termed comparative principles.

It has been a long-cherished wish—that (who knows how late), may one day, be happily accomplished—that the principles of the endless variety of civil laws should be investigated and exposed; for in this way alone can we find the secret of simplifying legislation. But in this case, laws are nothing more than limitations of our freedom upon conditions under which it subsists in perfect harmony with itself; they consequently have for their object that which is completely our own work, and of which we ourselves may be the cause by means of these conceptions. But how objects as things in themselves—how the nature of things is subordinated to principles and is to be determined, according to conceptions, is a question which it seems well nigh impossible to answer. Be this, however, as it may—for on this point our investigation is yet to be made—it is at least manifest from what we have said that cognition from principles is something very different from cognition by means of the understanding, which may indeed precede other cognitions in the form of a principle, but in itself—in so far as it is synthetical—is neither based upon mere thought, nor contains a general proposition drawn from conceptions alone.

The understanding may be a faculty for the production of unity of phenomena by virtue of rules; the reason is a faculty for the production of unity of rules (of the understanding) under principles. Reason, therefore, never applies directly to experience, or to any sensuous object; its object is, on the contrary, the understanding, to the manifold cognition of which it gives a unity à priori by means of conceptions—a unity which may be called rational unity, and which is of a nature very different from that of the unity produced by the understanding.

The above is the general conception of the faculty of reason, in so far as it has been possible to make it comprehensible in the absence of examples. These will be given in the sequel.

B. OF THE LOGICAL USE OF REASON.

A distinction is commonly made between that which is immediately cognized and that which is inferred or concluded. That in a figure which is bounded by three straight lines there are three angles, is an immediate cognition; but that these angles are together equal to two right angles, is an inference or conclusion. Now, as we are constantly employing this mode of thought and have thus become quite accustomed to it, we no longer remark the above distinction, and, as in the case of the so-called deceptions of sense, consider as immediately perceived, what has really been inferred. In every reasoning or syllogism, there is a fundamental proposition, afterwards a second drawn from it, and finally the conclusion, which connects the truth in the first with the truth in the second—and that infallibly. If the judgement concluded is so contained in the first proposition that it can be deduced from it without the meditation of a third notion, the conclusion is called immediate (consequentia immediata); I prefer the term conclusion of the understanding. But if, in addition to the fundamental cognition, a second judgement is necessary for the production of the conclusion, it is called a conclusion of the reason. In the proposition: All men are mortal, are contained the propositions: Some men are mortal, Nothing that is not mortal is a man, and these are therefore immediate conclusions from the first. On the other hand, the proposition: all the learned are mortal, is not contained in the main proposition (for the conception of a learned man does not occur in it), and it can be deduced from the main proposition only by means of a mediating judgement.

In every syllogism I first cogitate a rule (the major) by means of the understanding. In the next place I subsume a cognition under the condition of the rule (and this is the minor) by means of the judgement. And finally I determine my cognition by means of the predicate of the rule (this is the conclusio), consequently, I determine it à priori by means of the reason. The relations, therefore, which the major proposition, as the rule, represents between a cognition and its condition, constitute the different kinds of syllogisms. These are just threefold—analogously with all judgements, in so far as they differ in the mode of expressing the relation of a cognition in the understanding—namely, categorical, hypothetical, and disjunctive.

When as often happens, the conclusion is a judgement which may follow from other given judgements, through which a perfectly different object is cogitated, I endeavour to discover in the understanding whether the assertion in this conclusion does not stand under certain conditions according to a general rule. If I find such a condition, and if the object mentioned in the conclusion can be subsumed under the given condition, then this conclusion follows from a rule which is also valid for other objects of cognition. From this we see that reason endeavours to subject the great variety of the cognitions of the understanding to the smallest possible number of principles (general conditions), and thus to produce in it the highest unity.

C. OF THE PURE USE OF REASON.

Can we isolate reason, and, if so, is it in this case a peculiar source of conceptions and judgements which spring from it alone, and through which it can be applied to objects; or is it merely a subordinate faculty, whose duty it is to give a certain form to given cognitions—a form which is called logical, and through which the cognitions of the understanding are subordinated to each other, and lower rules to higher (those, to wit, whose condition comprises in its sphere the condition of the others), in so far as this can be done by comparison? This is the question which we have at present to answer. Manifold variety of rules and unity of principles is a requirement of reason, for the purpose of bringing the understanding into complete accordance with itself, just as understanding subjects the manifold content of intuition to conceptions, and thereby introduces connection into it. But this principle prescribes no law to objects, and does not contain any ground of the possibility of cognizing or of determining them as such, but is merely a subjective law for the proper arrangement of the content of the understanding. The purpose of this law is, by a comparison of the conceptions of the understanding, to reduce them to the smallest possible number, although, at the same time, it does not justify us in demanding from objects themselves such a uniformity as might contribute to the convenience and the enlargement of the sphere of the understanding, or in expecting that it will itself thus receive from them objective validity. In one word, the question is: "does reason in itself, that is, does pure reason contain à priori synthetical principles and rules, and what are those principles?"

The formal and logical procedure of reason in syllogisms gives us sufficient information in regard to the ground on which the transcendental principle of reason in its pure synthetical cognition will rest.

1. Reason, as observed in the syllogistic process, is not applicable to intuitions, for the purpose of subjecting them to rules—for this is the province of the understanding with its categories—but to conceptions and judgements. If pure reason does apply to objects and the intuition of them, it does so not immediately, but mediately—through the understanding and its judgements, which have a direct relation to the senses and their intuition, for the purpose of determining their objects. The unity of reason is therefore not the unity of a possible experience, but is essentially different from this unity, which is that of the understanding. That everything which happens has a cause, is not a principle cognized and prescribed by reason. This principle makes the unity of experience possible and borrows nothing from reason, which, without a reference to possible experience, could never have produced by means of mere conceptions any such synthetical unity.

2. Reason, in its logical use, endeavours to discover the general condition of its judgement (the conclusion), and a syllogism is itself nothing but a judgement by means of the subsumption of its condition under a general rule (the major). Now as this rule may itself be subjected to the same process of reason, and thus the condition of the condition be sought (by means of a prosyllogism) as long as the process can be continued, it is very manifest that the peculiar principle of reason in its logical use is to find for the conditioned cognition of the understanding the unconditioned whereby the unity of the former is completed.

But this logical maxim cannot be a principle of pure reason, unless we admit that, if the conditioned is given, the whole series of conditions subordinated to one another—a series which is consequently itself unconditioned—is also given, that is, contained in the object and its connection.

But this principle of pure reason is evidently synthetical; for, analytically, the conditioned certainly relates to some condition, but not to the unconditioned. From this principle also there must originate different synthetical propositions, of which the pure understanding is perfectly ignorant, for it has to do only with objects of a possible experience, the cognition and synthesis of which is always conditioned. The unconditioned, if it does really exist, must be especially considered in regard to the determinations which distinguish it from whatever is conditioned, and will thus afford us material for many à priori synthetical propositions.

The principles resulting from this highest principle of pure reason will, however, be transcendent in relation to phenomena, that is to say, it will be impossible to make any adequate empirical use of this principle. It is therefore completely different from all principles of the understanding, the use made of which is entirely immanent, their object and purpose being merely the possibility of experience. Now our duty in the transcendental dialectic is as follows. To discover whether the principle that the series of conditions (in the synthesis of phenomena, or of thought in general) extends to the unconditioned is objectively true, or not; what consequences result therefrom affecting the empirical use of the understanding, or rather whether there exists any such objectively valid proposition of reason, and whether it is not, on the contrary, a merely logical precept which directs us to ascend perpetually to still higher conditions, to approach completeness in the series of them, and thus to introduce into our cognition the highest possible unity of reason. We must ascertain, I say, whether this requirement of reason has not been regarded, by a misunderstanding, as a transcendental principle of pure reason, which postulates a thorough completeness in the series of conditions in objects themselves. We must show, moreover, the misconceptions and illusions that intrude into syllogisms, the major proposition of which pure reason has supplied—a proposition which has perhaps more of the character of a petitio than of a postulatum—and that proceed from experience upwards to its conditions. The solution of these problems is our task in transcendental dialectic, which we are about to expose even at its source, that lies deep in human reason. We shall divide it into two parts, the first of which will treat of the transcendent conceptions of pure reason, the second of transcendent and dialectical syllogisms.

TRANSCENDENTAL DIALECTIC

BOOK I

OF THE CONCEPTIONS OF PURE REASON

The conceptions of pure reason—we do not here speak of the possibility of them—are not obtained by reflection, but by inference or conclusion. The conceptions of understanding are also cogitated à priori antecedently to experience, and render it possible; but they contain nothing but the unity of reflection upon phenomena, in so far as these must necessarily belong to a possible empirical consciousness. Through them alone are cognition and the determination of an object possible. It is from them, accordingly, that we receive material for reasoning, and antecedently to them we possess no à priori conceptions of objects from which they might be deduced, On the other hand, the sole basis of their objective reality consists in the necessity imposed on them, as containing the intellectual form of all experience, of restricting their application and influence to the sphere of experience.

But the term, conception of reason, or rational conception, itself indicates that it does not confine itself within the limits of experience, because its object-matter is a cognition, of which every empirical cognition is but a part—nay, the whole of possible experience may be itself but a part of it—a cognition to which no actual experience ever fully attains, although it does always pertain to it. The aim of rational conceptions is the comprehension, as that of the conceptions of understanding is the understanding of perceptions. If they contain the unconditioned, they relate to that to which all experience is subordinate, but which is never itself an object of experience—that towards which reason tends in all its conclusions from experience, and by the standard of which it estimates the degree of their empirical use, but which is never itself an element in an empirical synthesis. If, notwithstanding, such conceptions possess objective validity, they may be called conceptus ratiocinati (conceptions legitimately concluded); in cases where they do not, they have been admitted on account of having the appearance of being correctly concluded, and may be called conceptus ratiocinantes (sophistical conceptions). But as this can only be sufficiently demonstrated in that part of our treatise which relates to the dialectical conclusions of reason, we shall omit any consideration of it in this place. As we called the pure conceptions of the understanding categories, we shall also distinguish those of pure reason by a new name and call them transcendental ideas. These terms, however, we must in the first place explain and justify.

Section I—Of Ideas in General

Despite the great wealth of words which European languages possess, the thinker finds himself often at a loss for an expression exactly suited to his conception, for want of which he is unable to make himself intelligible either to others or to himself. To coin new words is a pretension to legislation in language which is seldom successful; and, before recourse is taken to so desperate an expedient, it is advisable to examine the dead and learned languages, with the hope and the probability that we may there meet with some adequate expression of the notion we have in our minds. In this case, even if the original meaning of the word has become somewhat uncertain, from carelessness or want of caution on the part of the authors of it, it is always better to adhere to and confirm its proper meaning—even although it may be doubtful whether it was formerly used in exactly this sense—than to make our labour vain by want of sufficient care to render ourselves intelligible.

For this reason, when it happens that there exists only a single word to express a certain conception, and this word, in its usual acceptation, is thoroughly adequate to the conception, the accurate distinction of which from related conceptions is of great importance, we ought not to employ the expression improvidently, or, for the sake of variety and elegance of style, use it as a synonym for other cognate words. It is our duty, on the contrary, carefully to preserve its peculiar signification, as otherwise it easily happens that when the attention of the reader is no longer particularly attracted to the expression, and it is lost amid the multitude of other words of very different import, the thought which it conveyed, and which it alone conveyed, is lost with it.

Plato employed the expression idea in a way that plainly showed he meant by it something which is never derived from the senses, but which far transcends even the conceptions of the understanding (with which Aristotle occupied himself), inasmuch as in experience nothing perfectly corresponding to them could be found. Ideas are, according to him, archetypes of things themselves, and not merely keys to possible experiences, like the categories. In his view they flow from the highest reason, by which they have been imparted to human reason, which, however, exists no longer in its original state, but is obliged with great labour to recall by reminiscence—which is called philosophy—the old but now sadly obscured ideas. I will not here enter upon any literary investigation of the sense which this sublime philosopher attached to this expression. I shall content myself with remarking that it is nothing unusual, in common conversation as well as in written works, by comparing the thoughts which an author has delivered upon a subject, to understand him better than he understood himself inasmuch as he may not have sufficiently determined his conception, and thus have sometimes spoken, nay even thought, in opposition to his own opinions.

Plato perceived very clearly that our faculty of cognition has the feeling of a much higher vocation than that of merely spelling out phenomena according to synthetical unity, for the purpose of being able to read them as experience, and that our reason naturally raises itself to cognitions far too elevated to admit of the possibility of an object given by experience corresponding to them—cognitions which are nevertheless real, and are not mere phantoms of the brain.

This philosopher found his ideas especially in all that is practical,[41] that is, which rests upon freedom, which in its turn ranks under cognitions that are the peculiar product of reason. He who would derive from experience the conceptions of virtue, who would make (as many have really done) that, which at best can but serve as an imperfectly illustrative example, a model for or the formation of a perfectly adequate idea on the subject, would in fact transform virtue into a nonentity changeable according to time and circumstance and utterly incapable of being employed as a rule. On the contrary, every one is conscious that, when any one is held up to him as a model of virtue, he compares this so-called model with the true original which he possesses in his own mind and values him according to this standard. But this standard is the idea of virtue, in relation to which all possible objects of experience are indeed serviceable as examples—proofs of the practicability in a certain degree of that which the conception of virtue demands—but certainly not as archetypes. That the actions of man will never be in perfect accordance with all the requirements of the pure ideas of reason, does not prove the thought to be chimerical. For only through this idea are all judgements as to moral merit or demerit possible; it consequently lies at the foundation of every approach to moral perfection, however far removed from it the obstacles in human nature—indeterminable as to degree—may keep us.

The Platonic Republic has become proverbial as an example—and a striking one—of imaginary perfection, such as can exist only in the brain of the idle thinker; and Brucker ridicules the philosopher for maintaining that a prince can never govern well, unless he is participant in the ideas. But we should do better to follow up this thought and, where this admirable thinker leaves us without assistance, employ new efforts to place it in clearer light, rather than carelessly fling it aside as useless, under the very miserable and pernicious pretext of impracticability. A constitution of the greatest possible human freedom according to laws, by which the liberty of every individual can consist with the liberty of every other (not of the greatest possible happiness, for this follows necessarily from the former), is, to say the least, a necessary idea, which must be placed at the foundation not only of the first plan of the constitution of a state, but of all its laws. And, in this, it not necessary at the outset to take account of the obstacles which lie in our way—

[41] He certainly extended the application of his conception to speculative cognitions also, provided they were given pure and completely à priori, nay, even to mathematics, although this science cannot possess an object otherwhere than in Possible experience. I cannot follow him in this, and as little can I follow him in his mystical deduction of these ideas, or in his hypostatization of them; although, in truth, the elevated and exaggerated language which he employed in describing them is quite capable of an interpretation more subdued and more in accordance with fact and the nature of things.

obstacles which perhaps do not necessarily arise from the character of human nature, but rather from the previous neglect of true ideas in legislation. For there is nothing more pernicious and more unworthy of a philosopher, than the vulgar appeal to a so-called adverse experience, which indeed would not have existed, if those institutions had been established at the proper time and in accordance with ideas; while, instead of this, conceptions, crude for the very reason that they have been drawn from experience, have marred and frustrated all our better views and intentions. The more legislation and government are in harmony with this idea, the more rare do punishments become and thus it is quite reasonable to maintain, as Plato did, that in a perfect state no punishments at all would be necessary. Now although a perfect state may never exist, the idea is not on that account the less just, which holds up this maximum as the archetype or standard of a constitution, in order to bring legislative government always nearer and nearer to the greatest possible perfection. For at what precise degree human nature must stop in its progress, and how wide must be the chasm which must necessarily exist between the idea and its realization, are problems which no one can or ought to determine—and for this reason, that it is the destination of freedom to overstep all assigned limits between itself and the idea.

But not only in that wherein human reason is a real causal agent and where ideas are operative causes (of actions and their objects), that is to say, in the region of ethics, but also in regard to nature herself, Plato saw clear proofs of an origin from ideas. A plant, and animal, the regular order of nature—probably also the disposition of the whole universe—give manifest evidence that they are possible only by means of and according to ideas; that, indeed, no one creature, under the individual conditions of its existence, perfectly harmonizes with the idea of the most perfect of its kind—just as little as man with the idea of humanity, which nevertheless he bears in his soul as the archetypal standard of his actions; that, notwithstanding, these ideas are in the highest sense individually, unchangeably, and completely determined, and are the original causes of things; and that the totality of connected objects in the universe is alone fully adequate to that idea. Setting aside the exaggerations of expression in the writings of this philosopher, the mental power exhibited in this ascent from the ectypal mode of regarding the physical world to the architectonic connection thereof according to ends, that is, ideas, is an effort which deserves imitation and claims respect. But as regards the principles of ethics, of legislation, and of religion, spheres in which ideas alone render experience possible, although they never attain to full expression therein, he has vindicated for himself a position of peculiar merit, which is not appreciated only because it is judged by the very empirical rules, the validity of which as principles is destroyed by ideas. For as regards nature, experience presents us with rules and is the source of truth, but in relation to ethical laws experience is the parent of illusion, and it is in the highest degree reprehensible to limit or to deduce the laws which dictate what I ought to do, from what is done.

We must, however, omit the consideration of these important subjects, the development of which is in reality the peculiar duty and dignity of philosophy, and confine ourselves for the present to the more humble but not less useful task of preparing a firm foundation for those majestic edifices of moral science. For this foundation has been hitherto insecure from the many subterranean passages which reason in its confident but vain search for treasures has made in all directions. Our present duty is to make ourselves perfectly acquainted with the transcendental use made of pure reason, its principles and ideas, that we may be able properly to determine and value its influence and real worth. But before bringing these introductory remarks to a close, I beg those who really have philosophy at heart—and their number is but small—if they shall find themselves convinced by the considerations following as well as by those above, to exert themselves to preserve to the expression idea its original signification, and to take care that it be not lost among those other expressions by which all sorts of representations are loosely designated—that the interests of science may not thereby suffer. We are in no want of words to denominate adequately every mode of representation, without the necessity of encroaching upon terms which are proper to others. The following is a graduated list of them. The genus is representation in general (representatio). Under it stands representation with consciousness (perceptio). A perception which relates solely to the subject as a modification of its state, is a sensation (sensatio), an objective perception is a cognition (cognitio). A cognition is either an intuition or a conception (intuitus vel conceptus). The former has an immediate relation to the object and is singular and individual; the latter has but a mediate relation, by means of a characteristic mark which may be common to several things. A conception is either empirical or pure. A pure conception, in so far as it has its origin in the understanding alone, and is not the conception of a pure sensuous image, is called notio. A conception formed from notions, which transcends the possibility of experience, is an idea, or a conception of reason. To one who has accustomed himself to these distinctions, it must be quite intolerable to hear the representation of the colour red called an idea. It ought not even to be called a notion or conception of understanding.

Section II. Of Transcendental Ideas

Transcendental analytic showed us how the mere logical form of our cognition can contain the origin of pure conceptions à priori, conceptions which represent objects antecedently to all experience, or rather, indicate the synthetical unity which alone renders possible an empirical cognition of objects. The form of judgements—converted into a conception of the synthesis of intuitions—produced the categories which direct the employment of the understanding in experience. This consideration warrants us to expect that the form of syllogisms, when applied to synthetical unity of intuitions, following the rule of the categories, will contain the origin of particular à priori conceptions, which we may call pure conceptions of reason or transcendental ideas, and which will determine the use of the understanding in the totality of experience according to principles.

The function of reason in arguments consists in the universality of a cognition according to conceptions, and the syllogism itself is a judgement which is determined à priori in the whole extent of its condition. The proposition: "Caius is mortal," is one which may be obtained from experience by the aid of the understanding alone; but my wish is to find a conception which contains the condition under which the predicate of this judgement is given—in this case, the conception of man—and after subsuming under this condition, taken in its whole extent (all men are mortal), I determine according to it the cognition of the object thought, and say: "Caius is mortal."

Hence, in the conclusion of a syllogism we restrict a predicate to a certain object, after having thought it in the major in its whole extent under a certain condition. This complete quantity of the extent in relation to such a condition is called universality (universalitas). To this corresponds totality (universitas) of conditions in the synthesis of intuitions. The transcendental conception of reason is therefore nothing else than the conception of the totality of the conditions of a given conditioned. Now as the unconditioned alone renders possible totality of conditions, and, conversely, the totality of conditions is itself always unconditioned; a pure rational conception in general can be defined and explained by means of the conception of the unconditioned, in so far as it contains a basis for the synthesis of the conditioned.

To the number of modes of relation which the understanding cogitates by means of the categories, the number of pure rational conceptions will correspond. We must therefore seek for, first, an unconditioned of the categorical synthesis in a subject; secondly, of the hypothetical synthesis of the members of a series; thirdly, of the disjunctive synthesis of parts in a system.

There are exactly the same number of modes of syllogisms, each of which proceeds through prosyllogisms to the unconditioned—one to the subject which cannot be employed as predicate, another to the presupposition which supposes nothing higher than itself, and the third to an aggregate of the members of the complete division of a conception. Hence the pure rational conceptions of totality in the synthesis of conditions have a necessary foundation in the nature of human reason—at least as modes of elevating the unity of the understanding to the unconditioned. They may have no valid application, corresponding to their transcendental employment, in concreto, and be thus of no greater utility than to direct the understanding how, while extending them as widely as possible, to maintain its exercise and application in perfect consistence and harmony.

But, while speaking here of the totality of conditions and of the unconditioned as the common title of all conceptions of reason, we again light upon an expression which we find it impossible to dispense with, and which nevertheless, owing to the ambiguity attaching to it from long abuse, we cannot employ with safety. The word absolute is one of the few words which, in its original signification, was perfectly adequate to the conception it was intended to convey—a conception which no other word in the same language exactly suits, and the loss—or, which is the same thing, the incautious and loose employment—of which must be followed by the loss of the conception itself. And, as it is a conception which occupies much of the attention of reason, its loss would be greatly to the detriment of all transcendental philosophy. The word absolute is at present frequently used to denote that something can be predicated of a thing considered in itself and intrinsically. In this sense absolutely possible would signify that which is possible in itself (interne)—which is, in fact, the least that one can predicate of an object. On the other hand, it is sometimes employed to indicate that a thing is valid in all respects—for example, absolute sovereignty. Absolutely possible would in this sense signify that which is possible in all relations and in every respect; and this is the most that can be predicated of the possibility of a thing. Now these significations do in truth frequently coincide. Thus, for example, that which is intrinsically impossible, is also impossible in all relations, that is, absolutely impossible. But in most cases they differ from each other toto caelo, and I can by no means conclude that, because a thing is in itself possible, it is also possible in all relations, and therefore absolutely. Nay, more, I shall in the sequel show that absolute necessity does not by any means depend on internal necessity, and that, therefore, it must not be considered as synonymous with it. Of an opposite which is intrinsically impossible, we may affirm that it is in all respects impossible, and that, consequently, the thing itself, of which this is the opposite, is absolutely necessary; but I cannot reason conversely and say, the opposite of that which is absolutely necessary is intrinsically impossible, that is, that the absolute necessity of things is an internal necessity. For this internal necessity is in certain cases a mere empty word with which the least conception cannot be connected, while the conception of the necessity of a thing in all relations possesses very peculiar determinations. Now as the loss of a conception of great utility in speculative science cannot be a matter of indifference to the philosopher, I trust that the proper determination and careful preservation of the expression on which the conception depends will likewise be not indifferent to him.

In this enlarged signification, then, shall I employ the word absolute, in opposition to that which is valid only in some particular respect; for the latter is restricted by conditions, the former is valid without any restriction whatever.

Now the transcendental conception of reason has for its object nothing else than absolute totality in the synthesis of conditions and does not rest satisfied till it has attained to the absolutely, that is, in all respects and relations, unconditioned. For pure reason leaves to the understanding everything that immediately relates to the object of intuition or rather to their synthesis in imagination. The former restricts itself to the absolute totality in the employment of the conceptions of the understanding and aims at carrying out the synthetical unity which is cogitated in the category, even to the unconditioned. This unity may hence be called the rational unity of phenomena, as the other, which the category expresses, may be termed the unity of the understanding. Reason, therefore, has an immediate relation to the use of the understanding, not indeed in so far as the latter contains the ground of possible experience (for the conception of the absolute totality of conditions is not a conception that can be employed in experience, because no experience is unconditioned), but solely for the purpose of directing it to a certain unity, of which the understanding has no conception, and the aim of which is to collect into an absolute whole all acts of the understanding. Hence the objective employment of the pure conceptions of reason is always transcendent, while that of the pure conceptions of the understanding must, according to their nature, be always immanent, inasmuch as they are limited to possible experience.

I understand by idea a necessary conception of reason, to which no corresponding object can be discovered in the world of sense. Accordingly, the pure conceptions of reason at present under consideration are transcendental ideas. They are conceptions of pure reason, for they regard all empirical cognition as determined by means of an absolute totality of conditions. They are not mere fictions, but natural and necessary products of reason, and have hence a necessary relation to the whole sphere of the exercise of the understanding. And, finally, they are transcendent, and overstep the limits of all experiences, in which, consequently, no object can ever be presented that would be perfectly adequate to a transcendental idea. When we use the word idea, we say, as regards its object (an object of the pure understanding), a great deal, but as regards its subject (that is, in respect of its reality under conditions of experience), exceedingly little, because the idea, as the conception of a maximum, can never be completely and adequately presented in concreto. Now, as in the merely speculative employment of reason the latter is properly the sole aim, and as in this case the approximation to a conception, which is never attained in practice, is the same thing as if the conception were non-existent—it is commonly said of the conception of this kind, "it is only an idea." So we might very well say, "the absolute totality of all phenomena is only an idea," for, as we never can present an adequate representation of it, it remains for us a problem incapable of solution. On the other hand, as in the practical use of the understanding we have only to do with action and practice according to rules, an idea of pure reason can always be given really in concreto, although only partially, nay, it is the indispensable condition of all practical employment of reason. The practice or execution of the idea is always limited and defective, but nevertheless within indeterminable boundaries, consequently always under the influence of the conception of an absolute perfection. And thus the practical idea is always in the highest degree fruitful, and in relation to real actions indispensably necessary. In the idea, pure reason possesses even causality and the power of producing that which its conception contains. Hence we cannot say of wisdom, in a disparaging way, "it is only an idea." For, for the very reason that it is the idea of the necessary unity of all possible aims, it must be for all practical exertions and endeavours the primitive condition and rule—a rule which, if not constitutive, is at least limitative.

Now, although we must say of the transcendental conceptions of reason, "they are only ideas," we must not, on this account, look upon them as superfluous and nugatory. For, although no object can be determined by them, they can be of great utility, unobserved and at the basis of the edifice of the understanding, as the canon for its extended and self-consistent exercise—a canon which, indeed, does not enable it to cognize more in an object than it would cognize by the help of its own conceptions, but which guides it more securely in its cognition. Not to mention that they perhaps render possible a transition from our conceptions of nature and the non-ego to the practical conceptions, and thus produce for even ethical ideas keeping, so to speak, and connection with the speculative cognitions of reason. The explication of all this must be looked for in the sequel.

But setting aside, in conformity with our original purpose, the consideration of the practical ideas, we proceed to contemplate reason in its speculative use alone, nay, in a still more restricted sphere, to wit, in the transcendental use; and here must strike into the same path which we followed in our deduction of the categories. That is to say, we shall consider the logical form of the cognition of reason, that we may see whether reason may not be thereby a source of conceptions which enables us to regard objects in themselves as determined synthetically à priori, in relation to one or other of the functions of reason.

Reason, considered as the faculty of a certain logical form of cognition, is the faculty of conclusion, that is, of mediate judgement—by means of the subsumption of the condition of a possible judgement under the condition of a given judgement. The given judgement is the general rule (major). The subsumption of the condition of another possible judgement under the condition of the rule is the minor. The actual judgement, which enounces the assertion of the rule in the subsumed case, is the conclusion (conclusio). The rule predicates something generally under a certain condition. The condition of the rule is satisfied in some particular case. It follows that what was valid in general under that condition must also be considered as valid in the particular case which satisfies this condition. It is very plain that reason attains to a cognition, by means of acts of the understanding which constitute a series of conditions. When I arrive at the proposition, "All bodies are changeable," by beginning with the more remote cognition (in which the conception of body does not appear, but which nevertheless contains the condition of that conception), "All compound is changeable," by proceeding from this to a less remote cognition, which stands under the condition of the former, "Bodies are compound," and hence to a third, which at length connects for me the remote cognition (changeable) with the one before me, "Consequently, bodies are changeable"—I have arrived at a cognition (conclusion) through a series of conditions (premisses). Now every series, whose exponent (of the categorical or hypothetical judgement) is given, can be continued; consequently the same procedure of reason conducts us to the ratiocinatio polysyllogistica, which is a series of syllogisms, that can be continued either on the side of the conditions (per prosyllogismos) or of the conditioned (per episyllogismos) to an indefinite extent.

But we very soon perceive that the chain or series of prosyllogisms, that is, of deduced cognitions on the side of the grounds or conditions of a given cognition, in other words, the ascending series of syllogisms must have a very different relation to the faculty of reason from that of the descending series, that is, the progressive procedure of reason on the side of the conditioned by means of episyllogisms. For, as in the former case the cognition (conclusio) is given only as conditioned, reason can attain to this cognition only under the presupposition that all the members of the series on the side of the conditions are given (totality in the series of premisses), because only under this supposition is the judgement we may be considering possible à priori; while on the side of the conditioned or the inferences, only an incomplete and becoming, and not a presupposed or given series, consequently only a potential progression, is cogitated. Hence, when a cognition is contemplated as conditioned, reason is compelled to consider the series of conditions in an ascending line as completed and given in their totality. But if the very same condition is considered at the same time as the condition of other cognitions, which together constitute a series of inferences or consequences in a descending line, reason may preserve a perfect indifference, as to how far this progression may extend *a parte posteriori*, and whether the totality of this series is possible, because it stands in no need of such a series for the purpose of arriving at the conclusion before it, inasmuch as this conclusion is sufficiently guaranteed and determined on grounds a parte priori. It may be the case, that upon the side of the conditions the series of premisses has a first or highest condition, or it may not possess this, and so be a parte priori unlimited; but it must, nevertheless, contain totality of conditions, even admitting that we never could succeed in completely apprehending it; and the whole series must be unconditionally true, if the conditioned, which is considered as an inference resulting from it, is to be held as true. This is a requirement of reason, which announces its cognition as determined à priori and as necessary, either in itself—and in this case it needs no grounds to rest upon—or, if it is deduced, as a member of a series of grounds, which is itself unconditionally true.

Section III. System of Transcendental Ideas

We are not at present engaged with a logical dialectic, which makes complete abstraction of the content of cognition and aims only at unveiling the illusory appearance in the form of syllogisms. Our subject is transcendental dialectic, which must contain, completely à priori, the origin of certain cognitions drawn from pure reason, and the origin of certain deduced conceptions, the object of which cannot be given empirically and which therefore lie beyond the sphere of the faculty of understanding. We have observed, from the natural relation which the transcendental use of our cognition, in syllogisms as well as in judgements, must have to the logical, that there are three kinds of dialectical arguments, corresponding to the three modes of conclusion, by which reason attains to cognitions on principles; and that in all it is the business of reason to ascend from the conditioned synthesis, beyond which the understanding never proceeds, to the unconditioned which the understanding never can reach.

Now the most general relations which can exist in our representations are: 1st, the relation to the subject; 2nd, the relation to objects, either as phenomena, or as objects of thought in general. If we connect this subdivision with the main division, all the relations of our representations, of which we can form either a conception or an idea, are threefold: 1. The relation to the subject; 2. The relation to the manifold of the object as a phenomenon; 3. The relation to all things in general.

Now all pure conceptions have to do in general with the synthetical unity of representations; conceptions of pure reason (transcendental ideas), on the other hand, with the unconditional synthetical unity of all conditions. It follows that all transcendental ideas arrange themselves in three classes, the first of which contains the absolute (unconditioned) unity of the thinking subject, the second the absolute unity of the series of the conditions of a phenomenon, the third the absolute unity of the condition of all objects of thought in general.

The thinking subject is the object-matter of Psychology; the sum total of all phenomena (the world) is the object-matter of Cosmology; and the thing which contains the highest condition of the possibility of all that is cogitable (the being of all beings) is the object-matter of all Theology. Thus pure reason presents us with the idea of a transcendental doctrine of the soul (psychologia rationalis), of a transcendental science of the world (cosmologia rationalis), and finally of a transcendental doctrine of God (theologia transcendentalis). Understanding cannot originate even the outline of any of these sciences, even when connected with the highest logical use of reason, that is, all cogitable syllogisms—for the purpose of proceeding from one object (phenomenon) to all others, even to the utmost limits of the empirical synthesis. They are, on the contrary, pure and genuine products, or problems, of pure reason.

What modi of the pure conceptions of reason these transcendental ideas are will be fully exposed in the following chapter. They follow the guiding thread of the categories. For pure reason never relates immediately to objects, but to the conceptions of these contained in the understanding. In like manner, it will be made manifest in the detailed explanation of these ideas—how reason, merely through the synthetical use of the same function which it employs in a categorical syllogism, necessarily attains to the conception of the absolute unity of the thinking subject—how the logical procedure in hypothetical ideas necessarily produces the idea of the absolutely unconditioned in a series of given conditions, and finally—how the mere form of the disjunctive syllogism involves the highest conception of a being of all beings: a thought which at first sight seems in the highest degree paradoxical.

An objective deduction, such as we were able to present in the case of the categories, is impossible as regards these transcendental ideas. For they have, in truth, no relation to any object, in experience, for the very reason that they are only ideas. But a subjective deduction of them from the nature of our reason is possible, and has been given in the present chapter.

It is easy to perceive that the sole aim of pure reason is the absolute totality of the synthesis on the side of the conditions, and that it does not concern itself with the absolute completeness on the Part of the conditioned. For of the former alone does she stand in need, in order to preposit the whole series of conditions, and thus present them to the understanding à priori. But if we once have a completely (and unconditionally) given condition, there is no further necessity, in proceeding with the series, for a conception of reason; for the understanding takes of itself every step downward, from the condition to the conditioned. Thus the transcendental ideas are available only for ascending in the series of conditions, till we reach the unconditioned, that is, principles. As regards descending to the conditioned, on the other hand, we find that there is a widely extensive logical use which reason makes of the laws of the understanding, but that a transcendental use thereof is impossible; and that when we form an idea of the absolute totality of such a synthesis, for example, of the whole series of all future changes in the world, this idea is a mere ens rationis, an arbitrary fiction of thought, and not a necessary presupposition of reason. For the possibility of the conditioned presupposes the totality of its conditions, but not of its consequences. Consequently, this conception is not a transcendental idea—and it is with these alone that we are at present occupied.

Finally, it is obvious that there exists among the transcendental ideas a certain connection and unity, and that pure reason, by means of them, collects all its cognitions into one system. From the cognition of self to the cognition of the world, and through these to the supreme being, the progression is so natural, that it seems to resemble the logical march of reason from the premisses to the conclusion.[42] Now whether there lies unobserved at the foundation of these ideas an analogy of the same kind as exists between the logical and transcendental procedure of reason, is another of those questions, the answer to which we must not expect till we arrive

[42] The science of Metaphysics has for the proper object of its inquiries only three grand ideas: GOD, FREEDOM, and IMMORTALITY, and it aims at showing, that the second conception, conjoined with the first, must lead to the third, as a necessary conclusion. All the other subjects with which it occupies itself, are merely means for the attainment and realization of these ideas. It does not require these ideas for the construction of a science of nature, but, on the contrary, for the purpose of passing beyond the sphere of nature. A complete insight into and comprehension of them would render Theology, Ethics, and, through the conjunction of both, Religion, solely dependent on the speculative faculty of reason. In a systematic representation of these ideas the above-mentioned arrangement—the synthetical one—would be the most suitable; but in the investigation which must necessarily precede it, the analytical, which reverses this arrangement, would be better adapted to our purpose, as in it we should proceed from that which experience immediately presents to us—psychology, to cosmology, and thence to theology.

at a more advanced stage in our inquiries. In this cursory and preliminary view, we have, meanwhile, reached our aim. For we have dispelled the ambiguity which attached to the transcendental conceptions of reason, from their being commonly mixed up with other conceptions in the systems of philosophers, and not properly distinguished from the conceptions of the understanding; we have exposed their origin and, thereby, at the same time their determinate number, and presented them in a systematic connection, and have thus marked out and enclosed a definite sphere for pure reason.

TRANSCENDENTAL DIALECTIC

BOOK II

OF THE DIALECTICAL PROCEDURE OF PURE REASON

It may be said that the object of a merely transcendental idea is something of which we have no conception, although the idea may be a necessary product of reason according to its original laws. For, in fact, a conception of an object that is adequate to the idea given by reason, is impossible. For such an object must be capable of being presented and intuited in a Possible experience. But we should express our meaning better, and with less risk of being misunderstood, if we said that we can have no knowledge of an object, which perfectly corresponds to an idea, although we may possess a problematical conception thereof.

Now the transcendental (subjective) reality at least of the pure conceptions of reason rests upon the fact that we are led to such ideas by a necessary procedure of reason. There must therefore be syllogisms which contain no empirical premisses, and by means of which we conclude from something that we do know, to something of which we do not even possess a conception, to which we, nevertheless, by an unavoidable illusion, ascribe objective reality. Such arguments are, as regards their result, rather to be termed sophisms than syllogisms, although indeed, as regards their origin, they are very well entitled to the latter name, inasmuch as they are not fictions or accidental products of reason, but are necessitated by its very nature. They are sophisms, not of men, but of pure reason herself, from which the Wisest cannot free himself. After long labour he may be able to guard against the error, but he can never be thoroughly rid of the illusion which continually mocks and misleads him.

Of these dialectical arguments there are three kinds, corresponding to the number of the ideas which their conclusions present. In the argument or syllogism of the first class, I conclude, from the transcendental conception of the subject contains no manifold, the absolute unity of the subject itself, of which I cannot in this manner attain to a conception. This dialectical argument I shall call the transcendental paralogism. The second class of sophistical arguments is occupied with the transcendental conception of the absolute totality of the series of conditions for a given phenomenon, and I conclude, from the fact that I have always a self-contradictory conception of the unconditioned synthetical unity of the series upon one side, the truth of the opposite unity, of which I have nevertheless no conception. The condition of reason in these dialectical arguments, I shall term the antinomy of pure reason. Finally, according to the third kind of sophistical argument, I conclude, from the totality of the conditions of thinking objects in general, in so far as they can be given, the absolute synthetical unity of all conditions of the possibility of things in general; that is, from things which I do not know in their mere transcendental conception, I conclude a being of all beings which I know still less by means of a transcendental conception, and of whose unconditioned necessity I can form no conception whatever. This dialectical argument I shall call the ideal of pure reason.

Chapter I

Of the Paralogisms of Pure Reason

The logical paralogism consists in the falsity of an argument in respect of its form, be the content what it may. But a transcendental paralogism has a transcendental foundation, and concludes falsely, while the form is correct and unexceptionable. In this manner the paralogism has its foundation in the nature of human reason, and is the parent of an unavoidable, though not insoluble, mental illusion.

We now come to a conception which was not inserted in the general list of transcendental conceptions, and yet must be reckoned with them, but at the same time without in the least altering, or indicating a deficiency in that table. This is the conception, or, if the term is preferred, the judgement, "I think." But it is readily perceived that this thought is as it were the vehicle of all conceptions in general, and consequently of transcendental conceptions also, and that it is therefore regarded as a transcendental conception, although it can have no peculiar claim to be so ranked, inasmuch as its only use is to indicate that all thought is accompanied by consciousness. At the same time, pure as this conception is from empirical content (impressions of the senses), it enables us to distinguish two different kinds of objects. "I," as thinking, am an object of the internal sense, and am called soul. That which is an object of the external senses is called body. Thus the expression, "I," as a thinking being, designates the object-matter of psychology, which may be called "the rational doctrine of the soul," inasmuch as in this science I desire to know nothing of the soul but what, independently of all experience (which determines me in concreto), may be concluded from this conception "I," in so far as it appears in all thought.

Now, the rational doctrine of the soul is really an undertaking of this kind. For if the smallest empirical element of thought, if any particular perception of my internal state, were to be introduced among the grounds of cognition of this science, it would not be a rational, but an empirical doctrine of the soul. We have thus before us a pretended science, raised upon the single proposition, "I think," whose foundation or want of foundation we may very properly, and agreeably with the nature of a transcendental philosophy, here examine. It ought not to be objected that in this proposition, which expresses the perception of one's self, an internal experience is asserted, and that consequently the rational doctrine of the soul which is founded upon it, is not pure, but partly founded upon an empirical principle. For this internal perception is nothing more than the mere apperception, "I think," which in fact renders all transcendental conceptions possible, in which we say, "I think substance, cause, etc." For internal experience in general and its possibility, or perception in general, and its relation to other perceptions, unless some particular distinction or determination thereof is empirically given, cannot be regarded as empirical cognition, but as cognition of the empirical, and belongs to the investigation of the possibility of every experience, which is certainly transcendental. The smallest object of experience (for example, only pleasure or pain), that should be included in the general representation of self-consciousness, would immediately change the rational into an empirical psychology.

"I think" is therefore the only text of rational psychology, from which it must develop its whole system. It is manifest that this thought, when applied to an object (myself), can contain nothing but transcendental predicates thereof; because the least empirical predicate would destroy the purity of the science and its independence of all experience.

But we shall have to follow here the guidance of the categories—only, as in the present case a thing, "I," as thinking being, is at first given, we shall—not indeed change the order of the categories as it stands in the table—but begin at the category of substance, by which at the a thing in itself is represented and proceeds backwards through the series. The topic of the rational doctrine of the soul, from which everything else it may contain must be deduced, is accordingly as follows:

1
The Soul is
SUBSTANCE

2
As regards its quality
it is SIMPLE

3
As regards the different
times in which it exists,
it is numerically identical,
that is UNITY, not Plurality.

4
It is in relation to possible objects in space[43]

From these elements originate all the conceptions of pure psychology, by combination alone, without the aid of any other principle. This substance, merely as an object of the internal sense, gives the conception of Immateriality; as simple substance, that of Incorruptibility; its identity, as intellectual substance, gives the conception of Personality; all these three together, Spirituality. Its relation to objects in space gives us the conception of connection (commercium) with bodies.

[43] The reader, who may not so easily perceive the psychological sense of these expressions, taken here in their transcendental abstraction, and cannot guess why the latter attribute of the soul belongs to the category of existence, will find the expressions sufficiently explained and justified in the sequel. I have, moreover, to apologize for the Latin terms which have been employed, instead of their German synonyms, contrary to the rules of correct writing. But I judged it better to sacrifice elegance to perspicuity.

Thus it represents thinking substance as the principle of life in matter, that is, as a soul (anima), and as the ground of Animality; and this, limited and determined by the conception of spirituality, gives us that of Immortality.

Now to these conceptions relate four paralogisms of a transcendental psychology, which is falsely held to be a science of pure reason, touching the nature of our thinking being. We can, however, lay at the foundation of this science nothing but the simple and in itself perfectly contentless representation "i" which cannot even be called a conception, but merely a consciousness which accompanies all conceptions. By this "I," or "He," or "It," who or which thinks, nothing more is represented than a transcendental subject of thought = x, which is cognized only by means of the thoughts that are its predicates, and of which, apart from these, we cannot form the least conception. Hence in a perpetual circle, inasmuch as we must always employ it, in order to frame any judgement respecting it. And this inconvenience we find it impossible to rid ourselves of, because consciousness in itself is not so much a representation distinguishing a particular object, as a form of representation in general, in so far as it may be termed cognition; for in and by cognition alone do I think anything.

It must, however, appear extraordinary at first sight that the condition under which I think, and which is consequently a property of my subject, should be held to be likewise valid for every existence which thinks, and that we can presume to base upon a seemingly empirical proposition a judgement which is apodeictic and universal, to wit, that everything which thinks is constituted as the voice of my consciousness declares it to be, that is, as a self-conscious being. The cause of this belief is to be found in the fact that we necessarily attribute to things à priori all the properties which constitute conditions under which alone we can cogitate them. Now I cannot obtain the least representation of a thinking being by means of external experience, but solely through self-consciousness. Such objects are consequently nothing more than the transference of this consciousness of mine to other things which can only thus be represented as thinking beings. The proposition, "I think," is, in the present case, understood in a problematical sense, not in so far as it contains a perception of an existence (like the Cartesian "Cogito, ergo sum"), but in regard to its mere possibility—for the purpose of discovering what properties may be inferred from so simple a proposition and predicated of the subject of it.

If at the foundation of our pure rational cognition of thinking beings there lay more than the mere Cogito—if we could likewise call in aid observations on the play of our thoughts, and the thence derived natural laws of the thinking self, there would arise an empirical psychology which would be a kind of physiology of the internal sense and might possibly be capable of explaining the phenomena of that sense. But it could never be available for discovering those properties which do not belong to possible experience (such as the quality of simplicity), nor could it make any apodeictic enunciation on the nature of thinking beings: it would therefore not be a rational psychology.

Now, as the proposition "I think" (in the problematical sense) contains the form of every judgement in general and is the constant accompaniment of all the categories, it is manifest that conclusions are drawn from it only by a transcendental employment of the understanding. This use of the understanding excludes all empirical elements; and we cannot, as has been shown above, have any favourable conception beforehand of its procedure. We shall therefore follow with a critical eye this proposition through all the predicaments of pure psychology; but we shall, for brevity's sake, allow this examination to proceed in an uninterrupted connection.

Before entering on this task, however, the following general remark may help to quicken our attention to this mode of argument. It is not merely through my thinking that I cognize an object, but only through my determining a given intuition in relation to the unity of consciousness in which all thinking consists. It follows that I cognize myself, not through my being conscious of myself as thinking, but only when I am conscious of the intuition of myself as determined in relation to the function of thought. All the modi of self-consciousness in thought are hence not conceptions of objects (conceptions of the understanding—categories); they are mere logical functions, which do not present to thought an object to be cognized, and cannot therefore present my Self as an object. Not the consciousness of the determining, but only that of the determinable self, that is, of my internal intuition (in so far as the manifold contained in it can be connected conformably with the general condition of the unity of apperception in thought), is the object.

1. In all judgements I am the determining subject of that relation which constitutes a judgement. But that the I which thinks, must be considered as in thought always a subject, and as a thing which cannot be a predicate to thought, is an apodeictic and identical proposition. But this proposition does not signify that I, as an object, am, for myself, a self-subsistent being or substance. This latter statement—an ambitious one—requires to be supported by data which are not to be discovered in thought; and are perhaps (in so far as I consider the thinking self merely as such) not to be discovered in the thinking self at all.

2. That the I or Ego of apperception, and consequently in all thought, is singular or simple, and cannot be resolved into a plurality of subjects, and therefore indicates a logically simple subject—this is self-evident from the very conception of an Ego, and is consequently an analytical proposition. But this is not tantamount to declaring that the thinking Ego is a simple substance—for this would be a synthetical proposition. The conception of substance always relates to intuitions, which with me cannot be other than sensuous, and which consequently lie completely out of the sphere of the understanding and its thought: but to this sphere belongs the affirmation that the Ego is simple in thought. It would indeed be surprising, if the conception of "substance," which in other cases requires so much labour to distinguish from the other elements presented by intuition—so much

trouble, too, to discover whether it can be simple (as in the case of the parts of matter)—should be presented immediately to me, as if by revelation, in the poorest mental representation of all.

3. The proposition of the identity of my Self amidst all the manifold representations of which I am conscious, is likewise a proposition lying in the conceptions themselves, and is consequently analytical. But this identity of the subject, of which I am conscious in all its representations, does not relate to or concern the intuition of the subject, by which it is given as an object. This proposition cannot therefore enounce the identity of the person, by which is understood the consciousness of the identity of its own substance as a thinking being in all change and variation of circumstances. To prove this, we should require not a mere analysis of the proposition, but synthetical judgements based upon a given intuition.

4. I distinguish my own existence, as that of a thinking being, from that of other things external to me—among which my body also is reckoned. This is also an analytical proposition, for other things are exactly those which I think as different or distinguished from myself. But whether this consciousness of myself is possible without things external to me; and whether therefore I can exist merely as a thinking being (without being man)—cannot be known or inferred from this proposition.

Thus we have gained nothing as regards the cognition of myself as object, by the analysis of the consciousness of my Self in thought. The logical exposition of thought in general is mistaken for a metaphysical determination of the object.

Our Critique would be an investigation utterly superfluous, if there existed a possibility of proving à priori, that all thinking beings are in themselves simple substances, as such, therefore, possess the inseparable attribute of personality, and are conscious of their existence apart from and unconnected with matter. For we should thus have taken a step beyond the world of sense, and have penetrated into the sphere of noumena; and in this case the right could not be denied us of extending our knowledge in this sphere, of establishing ourselves, and, under a favouring star, appropriating to ourselves possessions in it. For the proposition: "Every thinking being, as such, is simple substance," is an à priori synthetical proposition; because in the first place it goes beyond the conception which is the subject of it, and adds to the mere notion of a thinking being the mode of its existence, and in the second place annexes a predicate (that of simplicity) to the latter conception—a predicate which it could not have discovered in the sphere of experience. It would follow that à priori synthetical propositions are possible and legitimate, not only, as we have maintained, in relation to objects of possible experience, and as principles of the possibility of this experience itself, but are applicable to things in themselves—an inference which makes an end of the whole of this Critique, and obliges us to fall back on the old mode of metaphysical procedure. But indeed the danger is not so great, if we look a little closer into the question.

There lurks in the procedure of rational Psychology a paralogism, which is represented in the following syllogism:

That which cannot be cogitated otherwise than as subject, does not exist otherwise than as subject, and is therefore substance.

A thinking being, considered merely as such, cannot be cogitated otherwise than as subject.

Therefore it exists also as such, that is, as substance.

In the major we speak of a being that can be cogitated generally and in every relation, consequently as it may be given in intuition. But in the minor we speak of the same being only in so far as it regards itself as subject, relatively to thought and the unity of consciousness, but not in relation to intuition, by which it is presented as an object to thought. Thus the conclusion is here arrived at by a Sophisma figurae dictionis.[44]

That this famous argument is a mere paralogism, will be plain to any one who will consider the general remark which precedes our exposition of the principles of the pure understanding, and the section on noumena. For it was there proved that the conception of a thing, which can exist per se—only as a subject and never as a predicate, possesses no objective reality; that is to say, we can never know whether there exists any object to correspond to the conception; consequently, the conception is nothing more than a conception, and from it we derive no proper knowledge. If this conception is to indicate by the term substance, an object that can be given, if it is to become a cognition, we must have at the foundation of the cognition a permanent intuition, as the indispensable condition of its objective reality. For through intuition alone can an object be given. But in internal intuition there is nothing permanent, for the Ego is but the consciousness of my thought. If then, we appeal merely to thought, we cannot discover the necessary condition of the application of the conception of substance—that is, of a subject existing per se—to the subject as a thinking being. And thus the conception of the simple nature of substance, which is connected with the objective reality of this conception, is shown to be also invalid, and to be, in fact, nothing more than the logical qualitative unity of self-consciousness in thought; whilst we remain perfectly ignorant whether the subject is composite or not.

Refutation of the Argument of Mendelssohn for the Substantiality or Permanence of the Soul.

---

[44] Thought is taken in the two premisses in two totally different senses. In the major it is considered as relating and applying to objects in general, consequently to objects of intuition also. In the minor, we understand it as relating merely to self-consciousness. In this sense, we do not cogitate an object, but merely the relation to the self-consciousness of the subject, as the form of thought. In the former premiss we speak of things which cannot be cogitated otherwise than as subjects. In the second, we do not speak of things, but of thought (all objects being abstracted), in which the Ego is always the subject of consciousness. Hence the conclusion cannot be, "I cannot exist otherwise than as subject"; but only "I can, in cogitating my existence, employ my Ego only as the subject of the judgement." But this is an identical proposition, and throws no light on the mode of my existence.

This acute philosopher easily perceived the insufficiency of the common argument which attempts to prove that the soul—it being granted that it is a simple being—cannot perish by dissolution or decomposition; he saw it is not impossible for it to cease to be by extinction, or disappearance. He endeavoured to prove in his Phaedo, that the soul cannot be annihilated, by showing that a simple being cannot cease to exist. Inasmuch as, he said, a simple existence cannot diminish, nor gradually lose portions of its being, and thus be by degrees reduced to nothing (for it possesses no parts, and therefore no multiplicity), between the moment in which it is, and the moment in which it is not, no time can be discovered—which is impossible. But this philosopher did not consider that, granting the soul to possess this simple nature, which contains no parts external to each other and consequently no extensive quantity, we cannot refuse to it any less than to any other being, intensive quantity, that is, a degree of reality in regard to all its faculties, nay, to all that constitutes its existence. But this degree of reality can become less and less through an infinite series of smaller degrees. It follows, therefore, that this supposed substance—this thing, the permanence of which is not assured in any other way, may, if not by decomposition, by gradual loss (remissio) of its powers (consequently by elanguescence, if I may employ this expression), be changed into nothing. For consciousness itself has always a degree, which may be lessened.[45] Consequently the faculty of being conscious may be diminished; and so with all other faculties. The permanence of the soul, therefore, as an object of the internal sense, remains undemonstrated, nay, even indemonstrable. Its permanence in life is evident, per se, inasmuch as the thinking being (as man) is to itself, at the same time, an object of the external senses. But this does not authorize the rational psychologist to affirm, from mere conceptions, its permanence beyond life.[46]

---

[45] Clearness is not, as logicians maintain, the consciousness of a representation. For a certain degree of consciousness, which may not, however, be sufficient for recollection, is to be met with in many dim representations. For without any consciousness at all, we should not be able to recognize any difference in the obscure representations we connect; as we really can do with many conceptions, such as those of right and justice, and those of the musician, who strikes at once several notes in improvising a piece of music. But a representation is clear, in which our consciousness is sufficient for the consciousness of the difference of this representation from others. If we are only conscious that there is a difference, but are not conscious of the difference—that is, what the difference is—the representation must be termed obscure. There is, consequently, an infinite series of degrees of consciousness down to its entire disappearance.

[46] There are some who think they have done enough to establish a new possibility in the mode of the existence of souls, when they have shown that there is no contradiction in their hypotheses on this subject. Such are those who affirm the possibility of thought—of which they have no other knowledge than what they derive from its use in connecting empirical intuitions presented in this our human life—after this life has ceased. But it is very easy to embarrass them by the introduction of counter-possibilities, which rest upon quite as good a foundation. Such, for example, is the possibility of the division of a simple substance into several substances; and conversely, of the coalition of several into one simple substance. For, although divisibility presupposes composition, it does not necessarily require a composition of substances, but only of the degrees (of the several

If, now, we take the above propositions—as they must be accepted as valid for all thinking beings in the system of rational psychology—in synthetical connection, and proceed, from the category of relation, with the proposition: "All thinking beings are, as such, substances," backwards through the series, till the circle is completed; we come at last to their existence, of which, in this system of rational psychology, substances are held to be conscious, independently of external things; nay, it is asserted that, in relation to the permanence which is a necessary characteristic of substance, they can of themselves determine external things. It follows that idealism—at least problematical idealism, is perfectly unavoidable in this rationalistic system. And, if the existence of outward things is not held to be requisite to the determination of the existence of a substance in time, the existence of these outward things at all, is a gratuitous assumption which remains without the possibility of a proof.

But if we proceed analytically—the "I think" as a proposition containing in itself an existence as given, consequently modality being the principle—and dissect this proposition, in order to ascertain its content, and discover whether and how this Ego determines its existence in time and space without the aid of anything external; the propositions of rationalistic psychology would not begin with the conception of a thinking being, but with a reality, and the properties of a thinking being in general would be deduced from the mode in which this reality is cogitated, after everything empirical had been abstracted; as is shown in the following table:

---

faculties) of one and the same substance. Now we can cogitate all the powers and faculties of the soul—even that of consciousness—as diminished by one half, the substance still remaining. In the same way we can represent to ourselves without contradiction, this obliterated half as preserved, not in the soul, but without it; and we can believe that, as in this case every thing that is real in the soul, and has a degree—consequently its entire existence—has been halved, a particular substance would arise out of the soul. For the multiplicity, which has been divided, formerly existed, but not as a multiplicity of substances, but of every reality as the quantum of existence in it; and the unity of substance was merely a mode of existence, which by this division alone has been transformed into a plurality of subsistence. In the same manner several simple substances might coalesce into one, without anything being lost except the plurality of subsistence, inasmuch as the one substance would contain the degree of reality of all the former substances. Perhaps, indeed, the simple substances, which appear under the form of matter, might (not indeed by a mechanical or chemical influence upon each other, but by an unknown influence, of which the former would be but the phenomenal appearance), by means of such a dynamical division of the parent-souls, as intensive quantities, produce other souls, while the former repaired the loss thus sustained with new matter of the same sort. I am far from allowing any value to such chimeras; and the principles of our analytic have clearly proved that no other than an empirical use of the categories—that of substance, for example—is possible. But if the rationalist is bold enough to construct, on the mere authority of the faculty of thought—without any intuition, whereby an object is given—a self-subsistent being, merely because the unity of apperception in thought cannot allow him to believe it a composite being, instead of declaring, as he ought to do, that he is unable to explain the possibility of a thinking nature; what ought to hinder the materialist, with as complete an independence of experience, to employ the principle of the rationalist in a directly opposite manner—still preserving the formal unity required by his opponent?

1
I think,

2
as Subject,

3
as simple Subject,

4
as identical Subject,
in every state of my thought.

Now, inasmuch as it is not determined in this second proposition, whether I can exist and be cogitated only as subject, and not also as a predicate of another being, the conception of a subject is here taken in a merely logical sense; and it remains undetermined, whether substance is to be cogitated under the conception or not. But in the third proposition, the absolute unity of apperception—the simple Ego in the representation to which all connection and separation, which constitute thought, relate, is of itself important; even although it presents us with no information about the constitution or subsistence of the subject. Apperception is something real, and the simplicity of its nature is given in the very fact of its possibility. Now in space there is nothing real that is at the same time simple; for points, which are the only simple things in space, are merely limits, but not constituent parts of space. From this follows the impossibility of a definition on the basis of materialism of the constitution of my Ego as a merely thinking subject. But, because my existence is considered in the first proposition as given, for it does not mean, "Every thinking being exists" (for this would be predicating of them absolute necessity), but only, "I exist thinking"; the proposition is quite empirical, and contains the determinability of my existence merely in relation to my representations in time. But as I require for this purpose something that is permanent, such as is not given in internal intuition; the mode of my existence, whether as substance or as accident, cannot be determined by means of this simple self-consciousness. Thus, if materialism is inadequate to explain the mode in which I exist, spiritualism is likewise as insufficient; and the conclusion is that we are utterly unable to attain to any knowledge of the constitution of the soul, in so far as relates to the possibility of its existence apart from external objects.

And, indeed, how should it be possible, merely by the aid of the unity of consciousness—which we cognize only for the reason that it is indispensable to the possibility of experience—to pass the bounds of experience (our existence in this life); and to extend our cognition to the nature of all thinking beings by means of the empirical—but in relation to every sort of intuition, perfectly undetermined—proposition, "I think"?

There does not then exist any rational psychology as a doctrine furnishing any addition to our knowledge of ourselves. It is nothing more than a discipline, which sets impassable limits to speculative reason in this region of thought, to prevent it, on the one hand, from throwing itself into the arms of a soulless materialism, and, on the other, from losing itself in the mazes of a baseless spiritualism. It teaches us to consider this refusal of our reason to give any satisfactory answer to questions which reach beyond the limits of this our human life, as a hint to abandon fruitless speculation; and to direct, to a practical use, our knowledge of ourselves—which, although applicable only to objects of experience, receives its principles from a higher source, and regulates its procedure as if our destiny reached far beyond the boundaries of experience and life.

From all this it is evident that rational psychology has its origin in a mere misunderstanding. The unity of consciousness, which lies at the basis of the categories, is considered to be an intuition of the subject as an object; and the category of substance is applied to the intuition. But this unity is nothing more than the unity in thought, by which no object is given; to which therefore the category of substance—which always presupposes a given intuition—cannot be applied. Consequently, the subject cannot be cognized. The subject of the categories cannot, therefore, for the very reason that it cogitates these, frame any conception of itself as an object of the categories; for, to cogitate these, it must lay at the foundation its own pure self-consciousness—the very thing that it wishes to explain and describe. In like manner, the subject, in which the representation of time has its basis, cannot determine, for this very reason, its own existence in time. Now, if the latter is impossible, the former, as an attempt to determine itself by means of the categories as a thinking being in general, is no less so.[47]

Thus, then, appears the vanity of the hope of establishing a cognition which is to extend its rule beyond the limits of experience—a cognition which is one of the highest interests of humanity; and thus is proved the futility of the attempt of

[47] The "I think" is, as has been already stated, an empirical proposition, and contains the proposition, "I exist." But I cannot say, "Everything, which thinks, exists"; for in this case the property of thought would constitute all beings possessing it, necessary beings. Hence my existence cannot be considered as an inference from the proposition, "I think," as Descartes maintained—because in this case the major premiss, "Everything, which thinks, exists," must precede—but the two propositions are identical. The proposition, "I think," expresses an undetermined empirical intuition, that perception (proving consequently that sensation, which must belong to sensibility, lies at the foundation of this proposition); but it precedes experience, whose province it is to determine an object of perception by means of the categories in relation to time; and existence in this proposition is not a category, as it does not apply to an undetermined given object, but only to one of which we have a conception, and about which we wish to know whether it does or does not exist, out of, and apart from this conception. An undetermined perception signifies here merely something real that has been given, only, however, to thought in general—but not as a phenomenon, nor as a thing in itself (noumenon), but only as something that really exists, and is designated as such in the proposition, "I think." For it must be remarked that, when I call the proposition, "I think," an empirical proposition, I do not thereby mean that the Ego in the proposition is an empirical representation; on the contrary, it is purely intellectual, because it belongs to thought in general. But without some empirical representation, which presents to the mind material for thought, the mental act, "I think," would not take place; and the empirical is only the condition of the application or employment of the pure intellectual faculty.

speculative philosophy in this region of thought. But, in this interest of thought, the severity of criticism has rendered to reason a not unimportant service, by the demonstration of the impossibility of making any dogmatical affirmation concerning an object of experience beyond the boundaries of experience. She has thus fortified reason against all affirmations of the contrary. Now, this can be accomplished in only two ways. Either our proposition must be proved apodeictically; or, if this is unsuccessful, the sources of this inability must be sought for, and, if these are discovered to exist in the natural and necessary limitation of our reason, our opponents must submit to the same law of renunciation and refrain from advancing claims to dogmatic assertion.

But the right, say rather the necessity to admit a future life, upon principles of the practical conjoined with the speculative use of reason, has lost nothing by this renunciation; for the merely speculative proof has never had any influence upon the common reason of men. It stands upon the point of a hair, so that even the schools have been able to preserve it from falling only by incessantly discussing it and spinning it like a top; and even in their eyes it has never been able to present any safe foundation for the erection of a theory. The proofs which have been current among men, preserve their value undiminished; nay, rather gain in clearness and unsophisticated power, by the rejection of the dogmatical assumptions of speculative reason. For reason is thus confined within her own peculiar province—the arrangement of ends or aims, which is at the same time the arrangement of nature; and, as a practical faculty, without limiting itself to the latter, it is justified in extending the former, and with it our own existence, beyond the boundaries of experience and life. If we turn our attention to the analogy of the nature of living beings in this world, in the consideration of which reason is obliged to accept as a principle that no organ, no faculty, no appetite is useless, and that nothing is superfluous, nothing disproportionate to its use, nothing unsuited to its end; but that, on the contrary, everything is perfectly conformed to its destination in life—we shall find that man, who alone is the final end and aim of this order, is still the only animal that seems to be excepted from it. For his natural gifts—not merely as regards the talents and motives that may incite him to employ them, but especially the moral law in him—stretch so far beyond all mere earthly utility and advantage, that he feels himself bound to prize the mere consciousness of probity, apart from all advantageous consequences—even the shadowy gift of posthumous fame—above everything; and he is conscious of an inward call to constitute himself, by his conduct in this world—without regard to mere sublunary interests—the citizen of a better. This mighty, irresistible proof—accompanied by an ever-increasing knowledge of the conformability to a purpose in everything we see around us, by the conviction of the boundless immensity of creation, by the consciousness of a certain illimitableness in the possible extension of our knowledge, and by a desire commensurate therewith—remains to humanity, even after the theoretical cognition of ourselves has failed to establish the necessity of an existence after death.

Conclusion of the Solution of the Psychological Paralogism

The dialectical illusion in rational psychology arises from our confounding an idea of reason (of a pure intelligence) with the conception—in every respect undetermined—of a thinking being in general. I cogitate myself in behalf of a possible experience, at the same time making abstraction of all actual experience; and infer therefrom that I can be conscious of myself apart from experience and its empirical conditions. I consequently confound the possible abstraction of my empirically determined existence with the supposed consciousness of a possible separate existence of my thinking self; and I believe that I cognize what is substantial in myself as a transcendental subject, when I have nothing more in thought than the unity of consciousness, which lies at the basis of all determination of cognition.

The task of explaining the community of the soul with the body does not properly belong to the psychology of which we are here speaking; because it proposes to prove the personality of the soul apart from this communion (after death), and is therefore transcendent in the proper sense of the word, although occupying itself with an object of experience—only in so far, however, as it ceases to be an object of experience. But a sufficient answer may be found to the question in our system. The difficulty which lies in the execution of this task consists, as is well known, in the presupposed heterogeneity of the object of the internal sense (the soul) and the objects of the external senses; inasmuch as the formal condition of the intuition of the one is time, and of that of the other space also. But if we consider that both kinds of objects do not differ internally, but only in so far as the one appears externally to the other—consequently, that what lies at the basis of phenomena, as a thing in itself, may not be heterogeneous; this difficulty disappears. There then remains no other difficulty than is to be found in the question—how a community of substances is possible; a question which lies out of the region of psychology, and which the reader, after what in our analytic has been said of primitive forces and faculties, will easily judge to be also beyond the region of human cognition.

GENERAL REMARK

On the Transition from Rational Psychology to Cosmology.

The proposition, "I think," or, "I exist thinking," is an empirical proposition. But such a proposition must be based on empirical intuition, and the object cogitated as a phenomenon; and thus our theory appears to maintain that the soul, even in thought, is merely a phenomenon; and in this way our consciousness itself, in fact, abuts upon nothing.

Thought, per se, is merely the purely spontaneous logical function which operates to connect the manifold of a possible intuition; and it does not represent the subject of consciousness as a phenomenon—for this reason alone, that it pays no attention to the question whether the mode of intuiting it is sensuous or intellectual. I therefore do not represent myself in thought either as I am, or as

I appear to myself; I merely cogitate myself as an object in general, of the mode of intuiting which I make abstraction. When I represent myself as the subject of thought, or as the ground of thought, these modes of representation are not related to the categories of substance or of cause; for these are functions of thought applicable only to our sensuous intuition. The application of these categories to the Ego would, however, be necessary, if I wished to make myself an object of knowledge. But I wish to be conscious of myself only as thinking; in what mode my Self is given in intuition, I do not consider, and it may be that I, who think, am a phenomenon—although not in so far as I am a thinking being; but in the consciousness of myself in mere thought I am a being, though this consciousness does not present to me any property of this being as material for thought.

But the proposition, "I think," in so far as it declares, "I exist thinking," is not the mere representation of a logical function. It determines the subject (which is in this case an object also) in relation to existence; and it cannot be given without the aid of the internal sense, whose intuition presents to us an object, not as a thing in itself, but always as a phenomenon. In this proposition there is therefore something more to be found than the mere spontaneity of thought; there is also the receptivity of intuition, that is, my thought of myself applied to the empirical intuition of myself. Now, in this intuition the thinking self must seek the conditions of the employment of its logical functions as categories of substance, cause, and so forth; not merely for the purpose of distinguishing itself as an object in itself by means of the representation "I," but also for the purpose of determining the mode of its existence, that is, of cognizing itself as noumenon. But this is impossible, for the internal empirical intuition is sensuous, and presents us with nothing but phenomenal data, which do not assist the object of pure consciousness in its attempt to cognize itself as a separate existence, but are useful only as contributions to experience.

But, let it be granted that we could discover, not in experience, but in certain firmly-established à priori laws of the use of pure reason—laws relating to our existence, authority to consider ourselves as legislating à priori in relation to our own existence and as determining this existence; we should, on this supposition, find ourselves possessed of a spontaneity, by which our actual existence would be determinable, without the aid of the conditions of empirical intuition. We should also become aware that in the consciousness of our existence there was an à priori content, which would serve to determine our own existence—an existence only sensuously determinable—relatively, however, to a certain internal faculty in relation to an intelligible world.

But this would not give the least help to the attempts of rational psychology. For this wonderful faculty, which the consciousness of the moral law in me reveals, would present me with a principle of the determination of my own existence which is purely intellectual—but by what predicates? By none other than those which are given in sensuous intuition. Thus I should find myself in the same position in rational psychology which I formerly occupied, that is to say, I should find myself still in need of sensuous intuitions, in order to give significance to my conceptions of substance and cause, by means of which alone I can possess a knowledge of myself: but these intuitions can never raise me above the sphere of experience. I should be justified, however, in applying these conceptions, in regard to their practical use, which is always directed to objects of experience—in conformity with their analogical significance when employed theoretically—to freedom and its subject. At the same time, I should understand by them merely the logical functions of subject and predicate, of principle and consequence, in conformity with which all actions are so determined, that they are capable of being explained along with the laws of nature, conformably to the categories of substance and cause, although they originate from a very different principle. We have made these observations for the purpose of guarding against misunderstanding, to which the doctrine of our intuition of self as a phenomenon is exposed. We shall have occasion to perceive their utility in the sequel.

Chapter II

The Antinomy of Pure Reason

We showed in the introduction to this part of our work, that all transcendental illusion of pure reason arose from dialectical arguments, the schema of which logic gives us in its three formal species of syllogisms—just as the categories find their logical schema in the four functions of all judgements. The first kind of these sophistical arguments related to the unconditioned unity of the subjective conditions of all representations in general (of the subject or soul), in correspondence with the categorical syllogisms, the major of which, as the principle, enounces the relation of a predicate to a subject. The second kind of dialectical argument will therefore be concerned, following the analogy with hypothetical syllogisms, with the unconditioned unity of the objective conditions in the phenomenon; and, in this way, the theme of the third kind to be treated of in the following chapter will be the unconditioned unity of the objective conditions of the possibility of objects in general.

But it is worthy of remark that the transcendental paralogism produced in the mind only a one-third illusion, in regard to the idea of the subject of our thought; and the conceptions of reason gave no ground to maintain the contrary proposition. The advantage is completely on the side of Pneumatism; although this theory itself passes into naught, in the crucible of pure reason.

Very different is the case when we apply reason to the objective synthesis of phenomena. Here, certainly, reason establishes, with much plausibility, its principle of unconditioned unity; but it very soon falls into such contradictions that it is compelled, in relation to cosmology, to renounce its pretensions.

For here a new phenomenon of human reason meets us—a perfectly natural antithetic, which does not require to be sought for by subtle sophistry, but into which reason of itself unavoidably falls. It is thereby preserved, to be sure, from the slumber of a fancied conviction—which a merely one-sided illusion produces; but it is at the same time compelled, either, on the one hand, to abandon itself to a despairing scepticism, or, on the other, to assume a dogmatical confidence and obstinate persistence in certain assertions, without granting a fair hearing to the other side of the question. Either is the death of a sound philosophy, although the former might perhaps deserve the title of the euthanasia of pure reason.

Before entering this region of discord and confusion, which the conflict of the laws of pure reason (antinomy) produces, we shall present the reader with some considerations, in explanation and justification of the method we intend to follow in our treatment of this subject. I term all transcendental ideas, in so far as they relate to the absolute totality in the synthesis of phenomena, cosmical conceptions;

partly on account of this unconditioned totality, on which the conception of the world-whole is based—a conception, which is itself an idea—partly because they relate solely to the synthesis of phenomena—the empirical synthesis; while, on the other hand, the absolute totality in the synthesis of the conditions of all possible things gives rise to an ideal of pure reason, which is quite distinct from the cosmical conception, although it stands in relation with it. Hence, as the paralogisms of pure reason laid the foundation for a dialectical psychology, the antinomy of pure reason will present us with the transcendental principles of a pretended pure (rational) cosmology—not, however, to declare it valid and to appropriate it, but—as the very term of a conflict of reason sufficiently indicates, to present it as an idea which cannot be reconciled with phenomena and experience.

Section I. System of Cosmological Ideas

That We may be able to enumerate with systematic precision these ideas according to a principle, we must remark, in the first place, that it is from the understanding alone that pure and transcendental conceptions take their origin; that the reason does not properly give birth to any conception, but only frees the conception of the understanding from the unavoidable limitation of a possible experience, and thus endeavours to raise it above the empirical, though it must still be in connection with it. This happens from the fact that, for a given conditioned, reason demands absolute totality on the side of the conditions (to which the understanding submits all phenomena), and thus makes of the category a transcendental idea. This it does that it may be able to give absolute completeness to the empirical synthesis, by continuing it to the unconditioned (which is not to be found in experience, but only in the idea). Reason requires this according to the principle: If the conditioned is given the whole of the conditions, and consequently the absolutely unconditioned, is also given, whereby alone the former was possible. First, then, the transcendental ideas are properly nothing but categories elevated to the unconditioned; and they may be arranged in a table according to the titles of the latter. But, secondly, all the categories are not available for this purpose, but only those in which the synthesis constitutes a series—of conditions subordinated to, not co-ordinated with, each other. Absolute totality is required of reason only in so far as concerns the ascending series of the conditions of a conditioned; not, consequently, when the question relates to the descending series of consequences, or to the aggregate of the co-ordinated conditions of these consequences. For, in relation to a given conditioned, conditions are presupposed and considered to be given along with it. On the other hand, as the consequences do not render possible their conditions, but rather presuppose them—in the consideration of the procession of consequences (or in the descent from the given condition to the conditioned), we may be quite unconcerned whether the series ceases or not; and their totality is not a necessary demand of reason.

Thus we cogitate—and necessarily—a given time completely elapsed up to a given moment, although that time is not determinable by us. But as regards time future, which is not the condition of arriving at the present, in order to conceive it; it is quite indifferent whether we consider future time as ceasing at some point, or as prolonging itself to infinity. Take, for example, the series m, n, o, in which n is given as conditioned in relation to m, but at the same time as the condition of o, and let the series proceed upwards from the conditioned n to m (l, k, i, etc.), and also downwards from the condition n to the conditioned o (p, q, r, etc.)—I must presuppose the former series, to be able to consider n as given, and n is according to reason (the totality of conditions) possible only by means of that series. But its possibility does not rest on the following series o, p, q, r, which for this reason cannot be regarded as given, but only as capable of being given (dabilis).

I shall term the synthesis of the series on the side of the conditions—from that nearest to the given phenomenon up to the more remote—regressive; that which proceeds on the side of the conditioned, from the immediate consequence to the more remote, I shall call the progressive synthesis. The former proceeds in antecedentia, the latter in consequentia. The cosmological ideas are therefore occupied with the totality of the regressive synthesis, and proceed in antecedentia, not in consequentia. When the latter takes place, it is an arbitrary and not a necessary problem of pure reason; for we require, for the complete understanding of what is given in a phenomenon, not the consequences which succeed, but the grounds or principles which precede.

In order to construct the table of ideas in correspondence with the table of categories, we take first the two primitive quanta of all our intuitions, time and space. Time is in itself a series (and the formal condition of all series), and hence, in relation to a given present, we must distinguish à priori in it the antecedentia as conditions (time past) from the consequentia (time future). Consequently, the transcendental idea of the absolute totality of the series of the conditions of a given conditioned, relates merely to all past time. According to the idea of reason, the whole past time, as the condition of the given moment, is necessarily cogitated as given. But, as regards space, there exists in it no distinction between progressus and regressus; for it is an aggregate and not a series—its parts existing together at the same time. I can consider a given point of time in relation to past time only as conditioned, because this given moment comes into existence only through the past time rather through the passing of the preceding time. But as the parts of space are not subordinated, but co-ordinated to each other, one part cannot be the condition of the possibility of the other; and space is not in itself, like time, a series. But the synthesis of the manifold parts of space—(the syntheses whereby we apprehend space)—is nevertheless successive; it takes place, therefore, in time, and contains a series. And as in this series of aggregated spaces (for example, the feet in a rood), beginning with a given portion of space, those which continue to be annexed form the condition of the limits of the former—the measurement of a space must also be regarded as a synthesis of the series of the conditions of a given conditioned. It differs, however, in this respect from that of time, that the side of the conditioned is not in itself distinguishable from the side of the condition; and, consequently, regressus and progressus in space seem to be identical. But, inasmuch as one part of space is not given, but only limited, by and through another, we must also consider every limited space as conditioned, in so far as it presupposes some other space as the condition of its limitation, and so on. As regards limitation, therefore, our procedure in space is also a regressus, and the transcendental idea of the absolute totality of the synthesis in a series of conditions applies to space also; and I am entitled to demand the absolute totality of the phenomenal synthesis in space as well as in time. Whether my demand can be satisfied is a question to be answered in the sequel.

Secondly, the real in space—that is, matter—is conditioned. Its internal conditions are its parts, and the parts of parts its remote conditions; so that in this case we find a regressive synthesis, the absolute totality of which is a demand of reason. But this cannot be obtained otherwise than by a complete division of parts, whereby the real in matter becomes either nothing or that which is not matter, that is to say, the simple. Consequently we find here also a series of conditions and a progress to the unconditioned.

Thirdly, as regards the categories of a real relation between phenomena, the category of substance and its accidents is not suitable for the formation of a transcendental idea; that is to say, reason has no ground, in regard to it, to proceed regressively with conditions. For accidents (in so far as they inhere in a substance) are co-ordinated with each other, and do not constitute a series. And, in relation to substance, they are not properly subordinated to it, but are the mode of existence of the substance itself. The conception of the substantial might nevertheless seem to be an idea of the transcendental reason. But, as this signifies nothing more than the conception of an object in general, which subsists in so far as we cogitate in it merely a transcendental subject without any predicates; and as the question here is of an unconditioned in the series of phenomena—it is clear that the substantial can form no member thereof. The same holds good of substances in community, which are mere aggregates and do not form a series. For they are not subordinated to each other as conditions of the possibility of each other; which, however, may be affirmed of spaces, the limits of which are never determined in themselves, but always by some other space. It is, therefore, only in the category of causality that we can find a series of causes to a given effect, and in which we ascend from the latter, as the conditioned, to the former as the conditions, and thus answer the question of reason.

Fourthly, the conceptions of the possible, the actual, and the necessary do not conduct us to any series—excepting only in so far as the contingent in existence must always be regarded as conditioned, and as indicating, according to a law of the understanding, a condition, under which it is necessary to rise to a higher, till in the totality of the series, reason arrives at unconditioned necessity.

There are, accordingly, only four cosmological ideas, corresponding with the four titles of the categories. For we can select only such as necessarily furnish us with a series in the synthesis of the manifold.

1
The absolute Completeness
of the
COMPOSITION
of the given totality of all phenomena.

2
The absolute Completeness
of the
DIVISION
of given totality in a phenomenon.

3
The absolute Completeness
of the
ORIGINATION
of a phenomenon.

4
The absolute Completeness
of the DEPENDENCE of the EXISTENCE
of what is changeable in a phenomenon.

We must here remark, in the first place, that the idea of absolute totality relates to nothing but the exposition of phenomena, and therefore not to the pure conception of a totality of things. Phenomena are here, therefore, regarded as given, and reason requires the absolute completeness of the conditions of their possibility, in so far as these conditions constitute a series—consequently an absolutely (that is, in every respect) complete synthesis, whereby a phenomenon can be explained according to the laws of the understanding.

Secondly, it is properly the unconditioned alone that reason seeks in this serially and regressively conducted synthesis of conditions. It wishes, to speak in another way, to attain to completeness in the series of premisses, so as to render it unnecessary to presuppose others. This unconditioned is always contained in the absolute totality of the series, when we endeavour to form a representation of it in thought. But this absolutely complete synthesis is itself but an idea; for it is impossible, at least before hand, to know whether any such synthesis is possible in the case of phenomena. When we represent all existence in thought by means of pure conceptions of the understanding, without any conditions of sensuous intuition, we may say with justice that for a given conditioned the whole series of conditions subordinated to each other is also given; for the former is only given through the latter. But we find in the case of phenomena a particular limitation of the mode in which conditions are given, that is, through the successive synthesis of the manifold of intuition, which must be complete in the regress. Now whether this completeness is sensuously possible, is a problem. But the idea of it lies in the reason—be it possible or impossible to connect with the idea adequate empirical conceptions. Therefore, as in the absolute totality of the regressive synthesis of the manifold in a phenomenon (following the guidance of the categories, which represent it as a series of conditions to a given conditioned) the unconditioned is necessarily contained—it being still left unascertained whether and how this totality exists; reason sets out from the idea of totality, although its proper and final aim is the unconditioned—of the whole series, or of a part thereof.

This unconditioned may be cogitated—either as existing only in the entire series, all the members of which therefore would be without exception conditioned and only the totality absolutely unconditioned—and in this case the regressus is called infinite; or the absolutely unconditioned is only a part of the series, to which the other members are subordinated, but which Is not itself submitted to any other condition.[48] In the former case the series is a parte priori unlimited (without beginning), that is, infinite, and nevertheless completely given. But the regress in it is never completed, and can only be called potentially infinite. In the second case there exists a first in the series. This first is called, in relation to past time, the beginning of the world; in relation to space, the limit of the world; in relation to the parts of a given limited whole, the simple; in relation to causes, absolute spontaneity (liberty); and in relation to the existence of changeable things, absolute physical necessity.

We possess two expressions, world and nature, which are generally interchanged. The first denotes the mathematical total of all phenomena and the totality of their synthesis—in its progress by means of composition, as well as by division. And the world is termed nature,[49] when it is regarded as a dynamical whole—when our attention is not directed to the aggregation in space and time, for the purpose of cogitating it as a quantity, but to the unity in the existence of phenomena. In

[48] The absolute totality of the series of conditions to a given conditioned is always unconditioned; because beyond it there exist no other conditions, on which it might depend. But the absolute totality of such a series is only an idea, or rather a problematical conception, the possibility of which must be investigated—particularly in relation to the mode in which the unconditioned, as the transcendental idea which is the real subject of inquiry, may be contained therein.

[49] Nature, understood adjective (formaliter), signifies the complex of the determinations of a thing, connected according to an internal principle of causality. On the other hand, we understand by nature, substantive (materialiter), the sum total of phenomena, in so far as they, by virtue of an internal principle of causality, are connected with each other throughout. In the former sense we speak of the nature of liquid matter, of fire, etc., and employ the word only adjective; while, if speaking of the objects of nature, we have in our minds the idea of a subsisting whole.

this case the condition of that which happens is called a cause; the unconditioned causality of the cause in a phenomenon is termed liberty; the conditioned cause is called in a more limited sense a natural cause. The conditioned in existence is termed contingent, and the unconditioned necessary. The unconditioned necessity of phenomena may be called natural necessity.

The ideas which we are at present engaged in discussing I have called cosmological ideas; partly because by the term world is understood the entire content of all phenomena, and our ideas are directed solely to the unconditioned among phenomena; partly also, because world, in the transcendental sense, signifies the absolute totality of the content of existing things, and we are directing our attention only to the completeness of the synthesis—although, properly, only in regression. In regard to the fact that these ideas are all transcendent, and, although they do not transcend phenomena as regards their mode, but are concerned solely with the world of sense (and not with noumena), nevertheless carry their synthesis to a degree far above all possible experience—it still seems to me that we can, with perfect propriety, designate them cosmical conceptions. As regards the distinction between the mathematically and the dynamically unconditioned which is the aim of the regression of the synthesis, I should call the two former, in a more limited signification, cosmical conceptions, the remaining two transcendent physical conceptions. This distinction does not at present seem to be of particular importance, but we shall afterwards find it to be of some value.

Section II. Antithetic of Pure Reason

Thetic is the term applied to every collection of dogmatical propositions. By antithetic I do not understand dogmatical assertions of the opposite, but the self-contradiction of seemingly dogmatical cognitions (thesis cum antithesis), in none of which we can discover any decided superiority. Antithetic is not, therefore, occupied with one-sided statements, but is engaged in considering the contradictory nature of the general cognitions of reason and its causes. Transcendental antithetic is an investigation into the antinomy of pure reason, its causes and result. If we employ our reason not merely in the application of the principles of the understanding to objects of experience, but venture with it beyond these boundaries, there arise certain sophistical propositions or theorems. These assertions have the following peculiarities: They can find neither confirmation nor confutation in experience; and each is in itself not only self-consistent, but possesses conditions of its necessity in the very nature of reason—only that, unluckily, there exist just as valid and necessary grounds for maintaining the contrary proposition.

The questions which naturally arise in the consideration of this dialectic of pure reason, are therefore: 1st. In what propositions is pure reason unavoidably subject to an antinomy? 2nd. What are the causes of this antinomy? 3rd. Whether and in what way can reason free itself from this self-contradiction?

A dialectical proposition or theorem of pure reason must, according to what has been said, be distinguishable from all sophistical propositions, by the fact that it is not an answer to an arbitrary question, which may be raised at the mere pleasure of any person, but to one which human reason must necessarily encounter in its progress. In the second place, a dialectical proposition, with its opposite, does not carry the appearance of a merely artificial illusion, which disappears as soon as it is investigated, but a natural and unavoidable illusion, which, even when we are no longer deceived by it, continues to mock us and, although rendered harmless, can never be completely removed.

This dialectical doctrine will not relate to the unity of understanding in empirical conceptions, but to the unity of reason in pure ideas. The conditions of this doctrine are—inasmuch as it must, as a synthesis according to rules, be conformable to the understanding, and at the same time as the absolute unity of the synthesis, to the reason—that, if it is adequate to the unity of reason, it is too great for the understanding, if according with the understanding, it is too small for the reason. Hence arises a mutual opposition, which cannot be avoided, do what we will.

These sophistical assertions of dialectic open, as it were, a battle-field, where that side obtains the victory which has been permitted to make the attack, and he is compelled to yield who has been unfortunately obliged to stand on the defensive. And hence, champions of ability, whether on the right or on the wrong side, are certain to carry away the crown of victory, if they only take care to have the right to make the last attack, and are not obliged to sustain another onset from their opponent. We can easily believe that this arena has been often trampled by the feet of combatants, that many victories have been obtained on both sides, but that the last victory, decisive of the affair between the contending parties, was won by him who fought for the right, only if his adversary was forbidden to continue the tourney. As impartial umpires, we must lay aside entirely the consideration whether the combatants are fighting for the right or for the wrong side, for the true or for the false, and allow the combat to be first decided. Perhaps, after they have wearied more than injured each other, they will discover the nothingness of their cause of quarrel and part good friends.

This method of watching, or rather of originating, a conflict of assertions, not for the purpose of finally deciding in favour of either side, but to discover whether the object of the struggle is not a mere illusion, which each strives in vain to reach, but which would be no gain even when reached—this procedure, I say, may be termed the sceptical method. It is thoroughly distinct from scepticism—the principle of a technical and scientific ignorance, which undermines the foundations of all knowledge, in order, if possible, to destroy our belief and confidence therein. For the sceptical method aims at certainty, by endeavouring to discover in a conflict of this kind, conducted honestly and intelligently on both sides, the point of misunderstanding; just as wise legislators derive, from the embarrassment of judges in lawsuits, information in regard to the defective and ill-defined parts of their statutes. The antinomy which reveals itself in the application of laws, is for our limited wisdom the best criterion of legislation. For the attention of reason, which in abstract speculation does not easily become conscious of its errors, is thus roused to the momenta in the determination of its principles.

But this sceptical method is essentially peculiar to transcendental philosophy, and can perhaps be dispensed with in every other field of investigation. In mathematics its use would be absurd; because in it no false assertions can long remain hidden, inasmuch as its demonstrations must always proceed under the guidance of pure intuition, and by means of an always evident synthesis. In experimental philosophy, doubt and delay may be very useful; but no misunderstanding is possible, which cannot be easily removed; and in experience means of solving the difficulty and putting an end to the dissension must at last be found, whether sooner or later. Moral philosophy can always exhibit its principles, with their practical consequences, in concreto—at least in possible experiences, and thus escape the mistakes and ambiguities of abstraction. But transcendental propositions, which lay claim to insight beyond the region of possible experience, cannot, on the one hand, exhibit their abstract synthesis in any à priori intuition, nor, on the other, expose a lurking error by the help of experience. Transcendental reason, therefore, presents us with no other criterion than that of an attempt to reconcile such assertions, and for this purpose to permit a free and unrestrained conflict between them. And this we now proceed to arrange.[50]

FIRST CONFLICT OF THE TRANSCENDENTAL IDEAS. THESIS.

The world has a beginning in time, and is also limited in regard to space.

PROOF.

Granted that the world has no beginning in time; up to every given moment of time, an eternity must have elapsed, and therewith passed away an infinite series of successive conditions or states of things in the world. Now the infinity of a series consists in the fact that it never can be completed by means of a successive synthesis. It follows that an infinite series already elapsed is impossible and that, consequently, a beginning of the world is a necessary condition of its existence. And this was the first thing to be proved.

As regards the second, let us take the opposite for granted. In this case, the world must be an infinite given total of coexistent things. Now we cannot cogitate the dimensions of a quantity, which is not given within certain limits of an intuition,[51] in any other way than by means of the synthesis of its parts, and the

[50] The antinomies stand in the order of the four transcendental ideas above detailed.

[51] We may consider an undetermined quantity as a whole, when it is enclosed within limits, although we cannot construct or ascertain its totality by measurement, that is, by the successive synthesis of

total of such a quantity only by means of a completed synthesis, or the repeated addition of unity to itself. Accordingly, to cogitate the world, which fills all spaces, as a whole, the successive synthesis of the parts of an infinite world must be looked upon as completed, that is to say, an infinite time must be regarded as having elapsed in the enumeration of all co-existing things; which is impossible. For this reason an infinite aggregate of actual things cannot be considered as a given whole, consequently, not as a contemporaneously given whole. The world is consequently, as regards extension in space, not infinite, but enclosed in limits. And this was the second thing to be proved.

ANTITHESIS.

The world has no beginning, and no limits in space, but is, in relation both to time and space, infinite.

PROOF.

For let it be granted that it has a beginning. A beginning is an existence which is preceded by a time in which the thing does not exist. On the above supposition, it follows that there must have been a time in which the world did not exist, that is, a void time. But in a void time the origination of a thing is impossible; because no part of any such time contains a distinctive condition of being, in preference to that of non-being (whether the supposed thing originate of itself, or by means of some other cause). Consequently, many series of things may have a beginning in the world, but the world itself cannot have a beginning, and is, therefore, in relation to past time, infinite.

As regards the second statement, let us first take the opposite for granted—that the world is finite and limited in space; it follows that it must exist in a void space, which is not limited. We should therefore meet not only with a relation of things in space, but also a relation of things to space. Now, as the world is an absolute whole, out of and beyond which no object of intuition, and consequently no correlate to which can be discovered, this relation of the world to a void space is merely a relation to no object. But such a relation, and consequently the limitation of the world by void space, is nothing. Consequently, the world, as regards space, is not limited, that is, it is infinite in regard to extension.[52]

---

its parts. For its limits of themselves determine its completeness as a whole.

[52] Space is merely the form of external intuition (formal intuition), and not a real object which can be externally perceived. Space, prior to all things which determine it (fill or limit it), or, rather, which present an empirical intuition conformable to it, is, under the title of absolute space, nothing but the mere possibility of external phenomena, in so far as they either exist in themselves, or can annex themselves to given intuitions. Empirical intuition is therefore not a composition of phenomena and space (of perception and empty intuition). The one is not the correlate of the other in a synthesis, but they are vitally connected in the same empirical intuition, as matter and form. If we wish to set one of these two apart from the other—space from phenomena—there arise all sorts of empty

OBSERVATIONS ON THE FIRST ANTINOMY. ON THE THESIS.

In bringing forward these conflicting arguments, I have not been on the search for sophisms, for the purpose of availing myself of special pleading, which takes advantage of the carelessness of the opposite party, appeals to a misunderstood statute, and erects its unrighteous claims upon an unfair interpretation. Both proofs originate fairly from the nature of the case, and the advantage presented by the mistakes of the dogmatists of both parties has been completely set aside.

The thesis might also have been unfairly demonstrated, by the introduction of an erroneous conception of the infinity of a given quantity. A quantity is infinite, if a greater than itself cannot possibly exist. The quantity is measured by the number of given units—which are taken as a standard—contained in it. Now no number can be the greatest, because one or more units can always be added. It follows that an infinite given quantity, consequently an infinite world (both as regards time and extension) is impossible. It is, therefore, limited in both respects. In this manner I might have conducted my proof; but the conception given in it does not agree with the true conception of an infinite whole. In this there is no representation of its quantity, it is not said how large it is; consequently its conception is not the conception of a maximum. We cogitate in it merely its relation to an arbitrarily assumed unit, in relation to which it is greater than any number. Now, just as the unit which is taken is greater or smaller, the infinite will be greater or smaller; but the infinity, which consists merely in the relation to this given unit, must remain always the same, although the absolute quantity of the whole is not thereby cognized.

The true (transcendental) conception of infinity is: that the successive synthesis of unity in the measurement of a given quantum can never be completed.[53] Hence it follows, without possibility of mistake, that an eternity of actual successive states up to a given (the present) moment cannot have elapsed, and that the world must therefore have a beginning.

In regard to the second part of the thesis, the difficulty as to an infinite and yet elapsed series disappears; for the manifold of a world infinite in extension is contemporaneously given. But, in order to cogitate the total of this manifold, as we cannot have the aid of limits constituting by themselves this total in intuition, we are obliged to give some account of our conception, which in this case cannot proceed from the whole to the determined quantity of the parts, but must demonstrate the possibility of a whole by means of a successive synthesis of the parts. But as this

---

determinations of external intuition, which are very far from being possible perceptions. For example, motion or rest of the world in an infinite empty space, or a determination of the mutual relation of both, cannot possibly be perceived, and is therefore merely the predicate of a notional entity.

[53] The quantum in this sense contains a congeries of given units, which is greater than any number—and this is the mathematical conception of the infinite.

synthesis must constitute a series that cannot be completed, it is impossible for us to cogitate prior to it, and consequently not by means of it, a totality. For the conception of totality itself is in the present case the representation of a completed synthesis of the parts; and this completion, and consequently its conception, is impossible.

ON THE ANTITHESIS.

The proof in favour of the infinity of the cosmical succession and the cosmical content is based upon the consideration that, in the opposite case, a void time and a void space must constitute the limits of the world. Now I am not unaware, that there are some ways of escaping this conclusion. It may, for example, be alleged, that a limit to the world, as regards both space and time, is quite possible, without at the same time holding the existence of an absolute time before the beginning of the world, or an absolute space extending beyond the actual world—which is impossible. I am quite well satisfied with the latter part of this opinion of the philosophers of the Leibnitzian school. Space is merely the form of external intuition, but not a real object which can itself be externally intuited; it is not a correlate of phenomena, it is the form of phenomena itself. Space, therefore, cannot be regarded as absolutely and in itself something determinative of the existence of things, because it is not itself an object, but only the form of possible objects. Consequently, things, as phenomena, determine space; that is to say, they render it possible that, of all the possible predicates of space (size and relation), certain may belong to reality. But we cannot affirm the converse, that space, as something self-subsistent, can determine real things in regard to size or shape, for it is in itself not a real thing. Space (filled or void)[54] may therefore be limited by phenomena, but phenomena cannot be limited by an empty space without them. This is true of time also. All this being granted, it is nevertheless indisputable, that we must assume these two nonentities, void space without and void time before the world, if we assume the existence of cosmical limits, relatively to space or time.

For, as regards the subterfuge adopted by those who endeavour to evade the consequence—that, if the world is limited as to space and time, the infinite void must determine the existence of actual things in regard to their dimensions—it arises solely from the fact that instead of a sensuous world, an intelligible world—of which nothing is known—is cogitated; instead of a real beginning (an existence, which is preceded by a period in which nothing exists), an existence which presupposes no other condition than that of time; and, instead of limits of extension, boundaries of the universe. But the question relates to the mundus phaenomenon, and its quantity; and in this case we cannot make abstraction of the conditions of

[54] It is evident that what is meant here is, that empty space, in so far as it is limited by phenomena—space, that is, within the world—does not at least contradict transcendental principles, and may therefore, as regards them, be admitted, although its possibility cannot on that account be affirmed.

sensibility, without doing away with the essential reality of this world itself. The world of sense, if it is limited, must necessarily lie in the infinite void. If this, and with it space as the à priori condition of the possibility of phenomena, is left out of view, the whole world of sense disappears. In our problem is this alone considered as given. The mundus intelligibilis is nothing but the general conception of a world, in which abstraction has been made of all conditions of intuition, and in relation to which no synthetical proposition—either affirmative or negative—is possible.

SECOND CONFLICT OF TRANSCENDENTAL IDEAS. THESIS.

Every composite substance in the world consists of simple parts; and there exists nothing that is not either itself simple, or composed of simple parts.

PROOF.

For, grant that composite substances do not consist of simple parts; in this case, if all combination or composition were annihilated in thought, no composite part, and (as, by the supposition, there do not exist simple parts) no simple part would exist. Consequently, no substance; consequently, nothing would exist. Either, then, it is impossible to annihilate composition in thought; or, after such annihilation, there must remain something that subsists without composition, that is, something that is simple. But in the former case the composite could not itself consist of substances, because with substances composition is merely a contingent relation, apart from which they must still exist as self-subsistent beings. Now, as this case contradicts the supposition, the second must contain the truth—that the substantial composite in the world consists of simple parts.

It follows, as an immediate inference, that the things in the world are all, without exception, simple beings—that composition is merely an external condition pertaining to them—and that, although we never can separate and isolate the elementary substances from the state of composition, reason must cogitate these as the primary subjects of all composition, and consequently, as prior thereto—and as simple substances.

ANTITHESIS.

No composite thing in the world consists of simple parts; and there does not exist in the world any simple substance.

PROOF.

Let it be supposed that a composite thing (as substance) consists of simple parts. Inasmuch as all external relation, consequently all composition of substances, is possible only in space; the space, occupied by that which is composite, must consist of the same number of parts as is contained in the composite. But space does not consist of simple parts, but of spaces. Therefore, every part of the composite must occupy a space. But the absolutely primary parts of what is composite are simple. It follows that what is simple occupies a space. Now, as everything real that occupies a space, contains a manifold the parts of which are external to each other, and is consequently composite—and a real composite, not of accidents (for these cannot exist external to each other apart from substance), but of substances—it follows that the simple must be a substantial composite, which is self-contradictory.

The second proposition of the antithesis—that there exists in the world nothing that is simple—is here equivalent to the following: The existence of the absolutely simple cannot be demonstrated from any experience or perception either external or internal; and the absolutely simple is a mere idea, the objective reality of which cannot be demonstrated in any possible experience; it is consequently, in the exposition of phenomena, without application and object. For, let us take for granted that an object may be found in experience for this transcendental idea; the empirical intuition of such an object must then be recognized to contain absolutely no manifold with its parts external to each other, and connected into unity. Now, as we cannot reason from the non-consciousness of such a manifold to the impossibility of its existence in the intuition of an object, and as the proof of this impossibility is necessary for the establishment and proof of absolute simplicity; it follows that this simplicity cannot be inferred from any perception whatever. As, therefore, an absolutely simple object cannot be given in any experience, and the world of sense must be considered as the sum total of all possible experiences: nothing simple exists in the world.

This second proposition in the antithesis has a more extended aim than the first. The first merely banishes the simple from the intuition of the composite; while the second drives it entirely out of nature. Hence we were unable to demonstrate it from the conception of a given object of external intuition (of the composite), but we were obliged to prove it from the relation of a given object to a possible experience in general.

OBSERVATIONS ON THE SECOND ANTINOMY. THESIS.

When I speak of a whole, which necessarily consists of simple parts, I understand thereby only a substantial whole, as the true composite; that is to say, I understand that contingent unity of the manifold which is given as perfectly isolated (at least in thought), placed in reciprocal connection, and thus constituted a unity. Space ought not to be called a compositum but a totum, for its parts are possible in the whole, and not the whole by means of the parts. It might perhaps be called a compositum ideale, but not a compositum reale. But this is of no importance. As space is not a composite of substances (and not even of real accidents), if I abstract all composition therein—nothing, not even a point, remains; for a point is possible only as the limit of a space—consequently of a composite. Space and time, therefore, do not consist of simple parts. That which belongs only to the condition or state of a substance, even although it possesses a quantity (motion or change, for example), likewise does not consist of simple parts. That is to say, a certain degree of change does not originate from the addition of many simple changes. Our inference of the simple from the composite is valid only of self-subsisting things. But the accidents of a state are not self-subsistent. The proof, then, for the necessity of the simple, as the component part of all that is substantial and composite, may prove a failure, and the whole case of this thesis be lost, if we carry the proposition too far, and wish to make it valid of everything that is composite without distinction—as indeed has really now and then happened. Besides, I am here speaking only of the simple, in so far as it is necessarily given in the composite—the latter being capable of solution into the former as its component parts. The proper signification of the word monas (as employed by Leibnitz) ought to relate to the simple, given immediately as simple substance (for example, in consciousness), and not as an element of the composite. As an clement, the term atomus would be more appropriate. And as I wish to prove the existence of simple substances, only in relation to, and as the elements of, the composite, I might term the antithesis of the second Antinomy, transcendental Atomistic. But as this word has long been employed to designate a particular theory of corporeal phenomena (moleculae), and thus presupposes a basis of empirical conceptions, I prefer calling it the dialectical principle of Monadology.

ANTITHESIS.

Against the assertion of the infinite subdivisibility of matter whose ground of proof is purely mathematical, objections have been alleged by the Monadists. These objections lay themselves open, at first sight, to suspicion, from the fact that they do not recognize the clearest mathematical proofs as propositions relating to the constitution of space, in so far as it is really the formal condition of the possibility of all matter, but regard them merely as inferences from abstract but arbitrary conceptions, which cannot have any application to real things. Just as if it were possible to imagine another mode of intuition than that given in the primitive intuition of space; and just as if its à priori determinations did not apply to everything, the existence of which is possible, from the fact alone of its filling space. If we listen to them, we shall find ourselves required to cogitate, in addition to the mathematical point, which is simple—not, however, a part, but a mere limit of space—physical points, which are indeed likewise simple, but possess the peculiar property, as parts of space, of filling it merely by their aggregation. I shall not repeat here the common and clear refutations of this absurdity, which are to be found everywhere in numbers: every one knows that it is impossible to undermine the evidence of mathematics by mere discursive conceptions; I shall only remark that, if in this case philosophy endeavours to gain an advantage over mathematics by sophistical artifices, it is because it forgets that the discussion relates solely to Phenomena and their conditions. It is not sufficient to find the conception of the simple for the pure conception of the composite, but we must discover for the intuition of the composite (matter), the intuition of the simple. Now this, according to the laws of sensibility, and consequently in the case of objects of sense, is utterly impossible. In the case of a whole composed of substances, which is cogitated solely by the pure understanding, it may be necessary to be in possession of the simple before composition is possible. But this does not hold good of the Totum substantiale phaenomenon, which, as an empirical intuition in space, possesses the necessary property of containing no simple part, for the very reason that no part of space is simple. Meanwhile, the Monadists have been subtle enough to escape from this difficulty, by presupposing intuition and the dynamical relation of substances as the condition of the possibility of space, instead of regarding space as the condition of the possibility of the objects of external intuition, that is, of bodies. Now we have a conception of bodies only as phenomena, and, as such, they necessarily presuppose space as the condition of all external phenomena. The evasion is therefore in vain; as, indeed, we have sufficiently shown in our Æsthetic. If bodies were things in themselves, the proof of the Monadists would be unexceptionable.

The second dialectical assertion possesses the peculiarity of having opposed to it a dogmatical proposition, which, among all such sophistical statements, is the only one that undertakes to prove in the case of an object of experience, that which is properly a transcendental idea—the absolute simplicity of substance. The proposition is that the object of the internal sense, the thinking Ego, is an absolute simple substance. Without at present entering upon this subject—as it has been considered at length in a former chapter—I shall merely remark that, if something is cogitated merely as an object, without the addition of any synthetical determination of its intuition—as happens in the case of the bare representation, I—it is certain that no manifold and no composition can be perceived in such a representation. As, moreover, the predicates whereby I cogitate this object are merely intuitions of the internal sense, there cannot be discovered in them anything to prove the existence of a manifold whose parts are external to each other, and, consequently, nothing to prove the existence of real composition. Consciousness, therefore, is so constituted that, inasmuch as the thinking subject is at the same time its own object, it cannot divide itself—although it can divide its inhering determinations. For every object in relation to itself is absolute unity. Nevertheless, if the subject is regarded externally, as an object of intuition, it must, in its character of phenomenon, possess the property of composition. And it must always be regarded in this manner, if we wish to know whether there is or is not contained in it a manifold whose parts are external to each other.

THIRD CONFLICT OF THE TRANSCENDENTAL IDEAS. THESIS.

Causality according to the laws of nature, is not the only causality operating to originate the phenomena of the world. A causality of freedom is also necessary to account fully for these phenomena.

PROOF.

Let it be supposed, that there is no other kind of causality than that according to the laws of nature. Consequently, everything that happens presupposes a previous condition, which it follows with absolute certainty, in conformity with a rule. But this previous condition must itself be something that has happened (that has arisen in time, as it did not exist before), for, if it has always been in existence, its consequence or effect would not thus originate for the first time, but would likewise have always existed. The causality, therefore, of a cause, whereby something happens, is itself a thing that has happened. Now this again presupposes, in conformity with the law of nature, a previous condition and its causality, and this another anterior to the former, and so on. If, then, everything happens solely in accordance with the laws of nature, there cannot be any real first beginning of things, but only a subaltern or comparative beginning. There cannot, therefore, be a completeness of series on the side of the causes which originate the one from the other. But the law of nature is that nothing can happen without a sufficient à priori determined cause. The proposition therefore—if all causality is possible only in accordance with the laws of nature—is, when stated in this unlimited and general manner, self-contradictory. It follows that this cannot be the only kind of causality.

From what has been said, it follows that a causality must be admitted, by means of which something happens, without its cause being determined according to necessary laws by some other cause preceding. That is to say, there must exist an absolute spontaneity of cause, which of itself originates a series of phenomena which proceeds according to natural laws—consequently transcendental freedom, without which even in the course of nature the succession of phenomena on the side of causes is never complete.

ANTITHESIS.

There is no such thing as freedom, but everything in the world happens solely according to the laws of nature.

PROOF.

Granted, that there does exist freedom in the transcendental sense, as a peculiar kind of causality, operating to produce events in the world—a faculty, that is to say, of originating a state, and consequently a series of consequences from that state. In this case, not only the series originated by this spontaneity, but the determination of this spontaneity itself to the production of the series, that is to say, the causality itself must have an absolute commencement, such that nothing can precede to determine this action according to unvarying laws. But every beginning of action presupposes in the acting cause a state of inaction; and a dynamically primal beginning of action presupposes a state, which has no connection—as regards causality—with the preceding state of the cause—which does not, that is, in any wise result from it. Transcendental freedom is therefore opposed to the natural law of cause and effect, and such a conjunction of successive states in effective causes is destructive of the possibility of unity in experience and for that reason not to be found in experience—is consequently a mere fiction of thought.

We have, therefore, nothing but nature to which we must look for connection and order in cosmical events. Freedom—independence of the laws of nature—is certainly a deliverance from restraint, but it is also a relinquishing of the guidance of law and rule. For it cannot be alleged that, instead of the laws of nature, laws of freedom may be introduced into the causality of the course of nature. For, if freedom were determined according to laws, it would be no longer freedom, but merely nature. Nature, therefore, and transcendental freedom are distinguishable as conformity to law and lawlessness. The former imposes upon understanding the difficulty of seeking the origin of events ever higher and higher in the series of causes, inasmuch as causality is always conditioned thereby; while it compensates this labour by the guarantee of a unity complete and in conformity with law. The latter, on the contrary, holds out to the understanding the promise of a point of rest in the chain of causes, by conducting it to an unconditioned causality, which professes to have the power of spontaneous origination, but which, in its own utter blindness, deprives it of the guidance of rules, by which alone a completely connected experience is possible.

OBSERVATIONS ON THE THIRD ANTINOMY. ON THE THESIS.

The transcendental idea of freedom is far from constituting the entire content of the psychological conception so termed, which is for the most part empirical. It merely presents us with the conception of spontaneity of action, as the proper ground for imputing freedom to the cause of a certain class of objects. It is, however, the true stumbling-stone to philosophy, which meets with unconquerable difficulties in the way of its admitting this kind of unconditioned causality. That element in the question of the freedom of the will, which has for so long a time placed speculative reason in such perplexity, is properly only transcendental, and concerns the question, whether there must be held to exist a faculty of spontaneous origination of a series of successive things or states. How such a faculty is possible is not a necessary inquiry; for in the case of natural causality itself, we are obliged to content ourselves with the à priori knowledge that such a causality must be presupposed, although we are quite incapable of comprehending how the being of one thing is possible through the being of another, but must for this information look entirely to experience. Now we have demonstrated this necessity of a free first beginning of a series of phenomena, only in so far as it is required for the comprehension of an origin of the world, all following states being regarded as a succession according to laws of nature alone. But, as there has thus been proved the existence of a faculty which can of itself originate a series in time—although we are unable to explain how it can exist—we feel ourselves authorized to admit, even in the midst of the natural course of events, a beginning, as regards causality, of different successions of phenomena, and at the same time to attribute to all substances a faculty of free action. But we ought in this case not to allow ourselves to fall into a common misunderstanding, and to suppose that, because a successive series in the world can only have a comparatively first beginning—another state or condition of things always preceding—an absolutely first beginning of a series in the course of nature is impossible. For we are not speaking here of an absolutely first beginning in relation to time, but as regards causality alone. When, for example, I, completely of my own free will, and independently of the necessarily determinative influence of natural causes, rise from my chair, there commences with this event, including its material consequences in infinitum, an absolutely new series; although, in relation to time, this event is merely the continuation of a preceding series. For this resolution and act of mine do not form part of the succession of effects in nature, and are not mere continuations of it; on the contrary, the determining causes of nature cease to operate in reference to this event, which certainly succeeds the acts of nature, but does not proceed from them. For these reasons, the action of a free agent must be termed, in regard to causality, if not in relation to time, an absolutely primal beginning of a series of phenomena.

The justification of this need of reason to rest upon a free act as the first beginning of the series of natural causes is evident from the fact, that all philosophers of antiquity (with the exception of the Epicurean school) felt themselves obliged, when constructing a theory of the motions of the universe, to accept a prime mover, that is, a freely acting cause, which spontaneously and prior to all other causes evolved this series of states. They always felt the need of going beyond mere nature, for the purpose of making a first beginning comprehensible.

ON THE ANTITHESIS.

The assertor of the all-sufficiency of nature in regard to causality (transcendental Physiocracy), in opposition to the doctrine of freedom, would defend his view of the question somewhat in the following manner. He would say, in answer to the sophistical arguments of the opposite party: If you do not accept a mathematical first, in relation to time, you have no need to seek a dynamical first, in regard to causality. Who compelled you to imagine an absolutely primal condition of the world, and therewith an absolute beginning of the gradually progressing successions of phenomena—and, as some foundation for this fancy of yours, to set bounds to unlimited nature? Inasmuch as the substances in the world have always existed—at least the unity of experience renders such a supposition quite necessary—there is no difficulty in believing also, that the changes in the conditions of these substances have always existed; and, consequently, that a first beginning, mathematical or dynamical, is by no means required. The possibility of such an infinite derivation, without any initial member from which all the others result, is certainly quite incomprehensible. But, if you are rash enough to deny the enigmatical secrets of nature for this reason, you will find yourselves obliged to deny also the existence of many fundamental properties of natural objects (such as fundamental forces), which you can just as little comprehend; and even the possibility of so simple a conception as that of change must present to you insuperable difficulties. For if experience did not teach you that it was real, you never could conceive à priori the possibility of this ceaseless sequence of being and non-being.

But if the existence of a transcendental faculty of freedom is granted—a faculty of originating changes in the world—this faculty must at least exist out of and apart from the world; although it is certainly a bold assumption, that, over and above the complete content of all possible intuitions, there still exists an object which cannot be presented in any possible perception. But, to attribute to substances in the world itself such a faculty, is quite inadmissible; for, in this case; the connection of phenomena reciprocally determining and determined according to general laws, which is termed nature, and along with it the criteria of empirical truth, which enable us to distinguish experience from mere visionary dreaming, would almost entirely disappear. In proximity with such a lawless faculty of freedom, a system of nature is hardly cogitable; for the laws of the latter would be continually subject to the intrusive influences of the former, and the course of phenomena, which would otherwise proceed regularly and uniformly, would become thereby confused and disconnected.

FOURTH CONFLICT OF THE TRANSCENDENTAL IDEAS. THESIS.

There exists either in, or in connection with the world—either as a part of it, or as the cause of it—an absolutely necessary being.

PROOF.

The world of sense, as the sum total of all phenomena, contains a series of changes. For, without such a series, the mental representation of the series of time itself, as the condition of the possibility of the sensuous world, could not be presented to us.[55] But every change stands under its condition, which precedes it in time and renders it necessary. Now the existence of a given condition presupposes a complete series of conditions up to the absolutely unconditioned, which alone is absolutely necessary. It follows that something that is absolutely necessary must exist, if change exists as its consequence. But this necessary thing itself belongs to the sensuous world. For suppose it to exist out of and apart from it, the series of cosmical changes would receive from it a beginning, and yet this necessary cause would not itself belong to the world of sense. But this is impossible. For, as the beginning of a series in time is determined only by that which precedes it in

[55] Objectively, time, as the formal condition of the possibility of change, precedes all changes; but subjectively, and in consciousness, the representation of time, like every other, is given solely by occasion of perception.

time, the supreme condition of the beginning of a series of changes must exist in the time in which this series itself did not exist; for a beginning supposes a time preceding, in which the thing that begins to be was not in existence. The causality of the necessary cause of changes, and consequently the cause itself, must for these reasons belong to time—and to phenomena, time being possible only as the form of phenomena. Consequently, it cannot be cogitated as separated from the world of sense—the sum total of all phenomena. There is, therefore, contained in the world, something that is absolutely necessary—whether it be the whole cosmical series itself, or only a part of it.

ANTITHESIS.

An absolutely necessary being does not exist, either in the world, or out of it—as its cause.

PROOF.

Grant that either the world itself is necessary, or that there is contained in it a necessary existence. Two cases are possible. First, there must either be in the series of cosmical changes a beginning, which is unconditionally necessary, and therefore uncaused—which is at variance with the dynamical law of the determination of all phenomena in time; or, secondly, the series itself is without beginning, and, although contingent and conditioned in all its parts, is nevertheless absolutely necessary and unconditioned as a whole—which is self-contradictory. For the existence of an aggregate cannot be necessary, if no single part of it possesses necessary existence.

Grant, on the other hand, that an absolutely necessary cause exists out of and apart from the world. This cause, as the highest member in the series of the causes of cosmical changes, must originate or begin[56] the existence of the latter and their series. In this case it must also begin to act, and its causality would therefore belong to time, and consequently to the sum total of phenomena, that is, to the world. It follows that the cause cannot be out of the world; which is contradictory to the hypothesis. Therefore, neither in the world, nor out of it (but in causal connection with it), does there exist any absolutely necessary being.

OBSERVATIONS ON THE FOURTH ANTINOMY. ON THE THESIS.

To demonstrate the existence of a necessary being, I cannot be permitted in this place to employ any other than the cosmological argument, which ascends from the conditioned in phenomena to the unconditioned in conception—the unconditioned being considered the necessary condition of the absolute totality of

[56] The word begin is taken in two senses. The first is active—the cause being regarded as beginning a series of conditions as its effect (infit). The second is passive—the causality in the cause itself beginning to operate (fit). I reason here from the first to the second.

the series. The proof, from the mere idea of a supreme being, belongs to another principle of reason and requires separate discussion.

The pure cosmological proof demonstrates the existence of a necessary being, but at the same time leaves it quite unsettled, whether this being is the world itself, or quite distinct from it. To establish the truth of the latter view, principles are requisite, which are not cosmological and do not proceed in the series of phenomena. We should require to introduce into our proof conceptions of contingent beings—regarded merely as objects of the understanding, and also a principle which enables us to connect these, by means of mere conceptions, with a necessary being. But the proper place for all such arguments is a transcendent philosophy, which has unhappily not yet been established.

But, if we begin our proof cosmologically, by laying at the foundation of it the series of phenomena, and the regress in it according to empirical laws of causality, we are not at liberty to break off from this mode of demonstration and to pass over to something which is not itself a member of the series. The condition must be taken in exactly the same signification as the relation of the conditioned to its condition in the series has been taken, for the series must conduct us in an unbroken regress to this supreme condition. But if this relation is sensuous, and belongs to the possible empirical employment of understanding, the supreme condition or cause must close the regressive series according to the laws of sensibility and consequently, must belong to the series of time. It follows that this necessary existence must be regarded as the highest member of the cosmical series.

Certain philosophers have, nevertheless, allowed themselves the liberty of making such a saltus (metabasis eis allo gonos). From the changes in the world they have concluded their empirical contingency, that is, their dependence on empirically-determined causes, and they thus admitted an ascending series of empirical conditions: and in this they are quite right. But as they could not find in this series any primal beginning or any highest member, they passed suddenly from the empirical conception of contingency to the pure category, which presents us with a series—not sensuous, but intellectual—whose completeness does certainly rest upon the existence of an absolutely necessary cause. Nay, more, this intellectual series is not tied to any sensuous conditions; and is therefore free from the condition of time, which requires it spontaneously to begin its causality in time. But such a procedure is perfectly inadmissible, as will be made plain from what follows.

In the pure sense of the categories, that is contingent the contradictory opposite of which is possible. Now we cannot reason from empirical contingency to intellectual. The opposite of that which is changed—the opposite of its state—is actual at another time, and is therefore possible. Consequently, it is not the contradictory opposite of the former state. To be that, it is necessary that, in the same time in which the preceding state existed, its opposite could have existed in its place; but such a cognition is not given us in the mere phenomenon of change.

A body that was in motion = A, comes into a state of rest = non-A. Now it cannot be concluded from the fact that a state opposite to the state A follows it, that the contradictory opposite of A is possible; and that A is therefore contingent. To prove this, we should require to know that the state of rest could have existed in the very same time in which the motion took place. Now we know nothing more than that the state of rest was actual in the time that followed the state of motion; consequently, that it was also possible. But motion at one time, and rest at another time, are not contradictorily opposed to each other. It follows from what has been said that the succession of opposite determinations, that is, change, does not demonstrate the fact of contingency as represented in the conceptions of the pure understanding; and that it cannot, therefore, conduct us to the fact of the existence of a necessary being. Change proves merely empirical contingency, that is to say, that the new state could not have existed without a cause, which belongs to the preceding time. This cause—even although it is regarded as absolutely necessary—must be presented to us in time, and must belong to the series of phenomena.

ON THE ANTITHESIS.

The difficulties which meet us, in our attempt to rise through the series of phenomena to the existence of an absolutely necessary supreme cause, must not originate from our inability to establish the truth of our mere conceptions of the necessary existence of a thing. That is to say, our objections not be ontological, but must be directed against the causal connection with a series of phenomena of a condition which is itself unconditioned. In one word, they must be cosmological and relate to empirical laws. We must show that the regress in the series of causes (in the world of sense) cannot conclude with an empirically unconditioned condition, and that the cosmological argument from the contingency of the cosmical state—a contingency alleged to arise from change—does not justify us in accepting a first cause, that is, a prime originator of the cosmical series.

The reader will observe in this antinomy a very remarkable contrast. The very same grounds of proof which established in the thesis the existence of a supreme being, demonstrated in the antithesis—and with equal strictness—the non-existence of such a being. We found, first, that a necessary being exists, because the whole time past contains the series of all conditions, and with it, therefore, the unconditioned (the necessary); secondly, that there does not exist any necessary being, for the same reason, that the whole time past contains the series of all conditions—which are themselves, therefore, in the aggregate, conditioned. The cause of this seeming incongruity is as follows. We attend, in the first argument, solely to the absolute totality of the series of conditions, the one of which determines the other in time, and thus arrive at a necessary unconditioned. In the second, we consider, on the contrary, the contingency of everything that is determined in the series of time—for every event is preceded by a time, in which the condition itself must be determined as conditioned—and thus everything that is unconditioned or absolutely necessary disappears. In both, the mode of proof is quite in accordance with the common procedure of human reason, which often falls into discord with itself, from considering an object from two different points of view. Herr von Mairan regarded the controversy between two celebrated astronomers, which arose from a similar difficulty as to the choice of a proper standpoint, as a phenomenon of sufficient importance to warrant a separate treatise on the subject. The one concluded: the moon revolves on its own axis, because it constantly presents the same side to the earth; the other declared that the moon does not revolve on its own axis, for the same reason. Both conclusions were perfectly correct, according to the point of view from which the motions of the moon were considered.

Section III. Of the Interest of Reason in these Self-contradictions

We have thus completely before us the dialectical procedure of the cosmological ideas. No possible experience can present us with an object adequate to them in extent. Nay, more, reason itself cannot cogitate them as according with the general laws of experience. And yet they are not arbitrary fictions of thought. On the contrary, reason, in its uninterrupted progress in the empirical synthesis, is necessarily conducted to them, when it endeavours to free from all conditions and to comprehend in its unconditioned totality that which can only be determined conditionally in accordance with the laws of experience. These dialectical propositions are so many attempts to solve four natural and unavoidable problems of reason. There are neither more, nor can there be less, than this number, because there are no other series of synthetical hypotheses, limiting à priori the empirical synthesis.

The brilliant claims of reason striving to extend its dominion beyond the limits of experience, have been represented above only in dry formulae, which contain merely the grounds of its pretensions. They have, besides, in conformity with the character of a transcendental philosophy, been freed from every empirical element; although the full splendour of the promises they hold out, and the anticipations they excite, manifests itself only when in connection with empirical cognitions. In the application of them, however, and in the advancing enlargement of the employment of reason, while struggling to rise from the region of experience and to soar to those sublime ideas, philosophy discovers a value and a dignity, which, if it could but make good its assertions, would raise it far above all other departments of human knowledge—professing, as it does, to present a sure foundation for our highest hopes and the ultimate aims of all the exertions of reason. The questions: whether the world has a beginning and a limit to its extension in space; whether there exists anywhere, or perhaps, in my own thinking Self, an indivisible and indestructible unity—or whether nothing but what is divisible and transitory exists; whether I am a free agent, or, like other beings, am bound in the chains of nature and fate; whether, finally, there is a supreme cause of the world, or all our thought and speculation must end with nature and the order of external things—are questions for the solution of which the mathematician would willingly exchange his whole science; for in it there is no satisfaction for the highest aspirations and most ardent desires of humanity. Nay, it may even be said that the true value of mathematics—that pride of human reason—consists in this: that she guides reason to the knowledge of nature—in her greater as well as in her less manifestations—in her beautiful order and regularity—guides her, moreover, to an insight into the wonderful unity of the moving forces in the operations of nature, far beyond the expectations of a philosophy building only on experience; and that she thus encourages philosophy to extend the province of reason beyond all experience, and at the same time provides it with the most excellent materials for supporting its investigations, in so far as their nature admits, by adequate and accordant intuitions.

Unfortunately for speculation—but perhaps fortunately for the practical interests of humanity—reason, in the midst of her highest anticipations, finds herself hemmed in by a press of opposite and contradictory conclusions, from which neither her honour nor her safety will permit her to draw back. Nor can she regard these conflicting trains of reasoning with indifference as mere passages at arms, still less can she command peace; for in the subject of the conflict she has a deep interest. There is no other course left open to her than to reflect with herself upon the origin of this disunion in reason—whether it may not arise from a mere misunderstanding. After such an inquiry, arrogant claims would have to be given up on both sides; but the sovereignty of reason over understanding and sense would be based upon a sure foundation.

We shall at present defer this radical inquiry and, in the meantime, consider for a little what side in the controversy we should most willingly take, if we were obliged to become partisans at all. As, in this case, we leave out of sight altogether the logical criterion of truth, and merely consult our own interest in reference to the question, these considerations, although inadequate to settle the question of right in either party, will enable us to comprehend how those who have taken part in the struggle, adopt the one view rather than the other—no special insight into the subject, however, having influenced their choice. They will, at the same time, explain to us many other things by the way—for example, the fiery zeal on the one side and the cold maintenance of their cause on the other; why the one party has met with the warmest approbations, and the other has always been repulsed by irreconcilable prejudices.

There is one thing, however, that determines the proper point of view, from which alone this preliminary inquiry can be instituted and carried on with the proper completeness—and that is the comparison of the principles from which both sides, thesis and antithesis, proceed. My readers would remark in the propositions of the antithesis a complete uniformity in the mode of thought and a perfect unity of principle. Its principle was that of pure empiricism, not only in the explication of the phenomena in the world, but also in the solution of the transcendental ideas, even of that of the universe itself. The affirmations of the thesis, on the contrary, were based, in addition to the empirical mode of explanation employed in the series of phenomena, on intellectual propositions; and its principles were in so far not simple. I shall term the thesis, in view of its essential characteristic, the dogmatism of pure reason.

On the side of Dogmatism, or of the thesis, therefore, in the determination of the cosmological ideas, we find:

1. A practical interest, which must be very dear to every right-thinking man. That the word has a beginning—that the nature of my thinking self is simple, and therefore indestructible—that I am a free agent, and raised above the compulsion of nature and her laws—and, finally, that the entire order of things, which form the world, is dependent upon a Supreme Being, from whom the whole receives unity and connection—these are so many foundation-stones of morality and religion. The antithesis deprives us of all these supports—or, at least, seems so to deprive us.

2. A speculative interest of reason manifests itself on this side. For, if we take the transcendental ideas and employ them in the manner which the thesis directs, we can exhibit completely à priori the entire chain of conditions, and understand the derivation of the conditioned—beginning from the unconditioned. This the antithesis does not do; and for this reason does not meet with so welcome a reception. For it can give no answer to our question respecting the conditions of its synthesis—except such as must be supplemented by another question, and so on to infinity. According to it, we must rise from a given beginning to one still higher; every part conducts us to a still smaller one; every event is preceded by another event which is its cause; and the conditions of existence rest always upon other and still higher conditions, and find neither end nor basis in some self-subsistent thing as the primal being.

3. This side has also the advantage of popularity; and this constitutes no small part of its claim to favour. The common understanding does not find the least difficulty in the idea of the unconditioned beginning of all synthesis—accustomed, as it is, rather to follow our consequences than to seek for a proper basis for cognition. In the conception of an absolute first, moreover—the possibility of which it does not inquire into—it is highly gratified to find a firmly-established point of departure for its attempts at theory; while in the restless and continuous ascent from the conditioned to the condition, always with one foot in the air, it can find no satisfaction.

On the side of the antithesis, or Empiricism, in the determination of the cosmological ideas:

1. We cannot discover any such practical interest arising from pure principles of reason as morality and religion present. On the contrary, pure empiricism seems to empty them of all their power and influence. If there does not exist a Supreme Being distinct from the world—if the world is without beginning, consequently

without a Creator—if our wills are not free, and the soul is divisible and subject to corruption just like matter—the ideas and principles of morality lose all validity and fall with the transcendental ideas which constituted their theoretical support.

2. But empiricism, in compensation, holds out to reason, in its speculative interests, certain important advantages, far exceeding any that the dogmatist can promise us. For, when employed by the empiricist, understanding is always upon its proper ground of investigation—the field of possible experience, the laws of which it can explore, and thus extend its cognition securely and with clear intelligence without being stopped by limits in any direction. Here can it and ought it to find and present to intuition its proper object—not only in itself, but in all its relations; or, if it employ conceptions, upon this ground it can always present the corresponding images in clear and unmistakable intuitions. It is quite unnecessary for it to renounce the guidance of nature, to attach itself to ideas, the objects of which it cannot know; because, as mere intellectual entities, they cannot be presented in any intuition. On the contrary, it is not even permitted to abandon its proper occupation, under the pretence that it has been brought to a conclusion (for it never can be), and to pass into the region of idealizing reason and transcendent conceptions, which it is not required to observe and explore the laws of nature, but merely to think and to imagine—secure from being contradicted by facts, because they have not been called as witnesses, but passed by, or perhaps subordinated to the so-called higher interests and considerations of pure reason.

Hence the empiricist will never allow himself to accept any epoch of nature for the first—the absolutely primal state; he will not believe that there can be limits to his outlook into her wide domains, nor pass from the objects of nature, which he can satisfactorily explain by means of observation and mathematical thought—which he can determine synthetically in intuition, to those which neither sense nor imagination can ever present in concreto; he will not concede the existence of a faculty in nature, operating independently of the laws of nature—a concession which would introduce uncertainty into the procedure of the understanding, which is guided by necessary laws to the observation of phenomena; nor, finally, will he permit himself to seek a cause beyond nature, inasmuch as we know nothing but it, and from it alone receive an objective basis for all our conceptions and instruction in the unvarying laws of things.

In truth, if the empirical philosopher had no other purpose in the establishment of his antithesis than to check the presumption of a reason which mistakes its true destination, which boasts of its insight and its knowledge, just where all insight and knowledge cease to exist, and regards that which is valid only in relation to a practical interest, as an advancement of the speculative interests of the mind (in order, when it is convenient for itself, to break the thread of our physical investigations, and, under pretence of extending our cognition, connect them with transcendental ideas, by means of which we really know only that we know nothing)—if, I say, the empiricist rested satisfied with this benefit, the principle advanced by him would be a maxim recommending moderation in the pretensions of reason and modesty in its affirmations, and at the same time would direct us to the right mode of extending the province of the understanding, by the help of the only true teacher, experience. In obedience to this advice, intellectual hypotheses and faith would not be called in aid of our practical interests; nor should we introduce them under the pompous titles of science and insight. For speculative cognition cannot find an objective basis any other where than in experience; and, when we overstep its limits our synthesis, which requires ever new cognitions independent of experience, has no substratum of intuition upon which to build.

But if—as often happens—empiricism, in relation to ideas, becomes itself dogmatic and boldly denies that which is above the sphere of its phenomenal cognition, it falls itself into the error of intemperance—an error which is here all the more reprehensible, as thereby the practical interest of reason receives an irreparable injury.

And this constitutes the opposition between Epicureanism[57] and Platonism.

Both Epicurus and Plato assert more in their systems than they know. The former encourages and advances science—although to the prejudice of the practical; the latter presents us with excellent principles for the investigation of the practical, but, in relation to everything regarding which we can attain to speculative cognition, permits reason to append idealistic explanations of natural phenomena, to the great injury of physical investigation.

3. In regard to the third motive for the preliminary choice of a party in this war of assertions, it seems very extraordinary that empiricism should be utterly unpopular. We should be inclined to believe that the common understanding would receive it with pleasure—promising as it does to satisfy it without passing the bounds of experience and its connected order; while transcendental dogmatism obliges it to rise to conceptions which far surpass the intelligence and ability of the most practised thinkers. But in this, in truth, is to be found its real motive. For the common understanding thus finds itself in a situation where not even the most learned can have the advantage of it. If it understands little or nothing

[57] It is, however, still a matter of doubt whether Epicurus ever propounded these principles as directions for the objective employment of the understanding. If, indeed, they were nothing more than maxims for the speculative exercise of reason, he gives evidence therein a more genuine philosophic spirit than any of the philosophers of antiquity. That, in the explanation of phenomena, we must proceed as if the field of inquiry had neither limits in space nor commencement in time; that we must be satisfied with the teaching of experience in reference to the material of which the world is posed; that we must not look for any other mode of the origination of events than that which is determined by the unalterable laws of nature; and finally, that we not employ the hypothesis of a cause distinct from the world to account for a phenomenon or for the world itself—are principles for the extension of speculative philosophy, and the discovery of the true sources of the principles of morals, which, however little conformed to in the present day, are undoubtedly correct. At the same time, any one desirous of ignoring, in mere speculation, these dogmatical propositions, need not for that reason be accused of denying them.

about these transcendental conceptions, no one can boast of understanding any more; and although it may not express itself in so scholastically correct a manner as others, it can busy itself with reasoning and arguments without end, wandering among mere ideas, about which one can always be very eloquent, because we know nothing about them; while, in the observation and investigation of nature, it would be forced to remain dumb and to confess its utter ignorance. Thus indolence and vanity form of themselves strong recommendations of these principles. Besides, although it is a hard thing for a philosopher to assume a principle, of which he can give to himself no reasonable account, and still more to employ conceptions, the objective reality of which cannot be established, nothing is more usual with the common understanding. It wants something which will allow it to go to work with confidence. The difficulty of even comprehending a supposition does not disquiet it, because—not knowing what comprehending means—it never even thinks of the supposition it may be adopting as a principle; and regards as known that with which it has become familiar from constant use. And, at last, all speculative interests disappear before the practical interests which it holds dear; and it fancies that it understands and knows what its necessities and hopes incite it to assume or to believe. Thus the empiricism of transcendentally idealizing reason is robbed of all popularity; and, however prejudicial it may be to the highest practical principles, there is no fear that it will ever pass the limits of the schools, or acquire any favour or influence in society or with the multitude.

Human reason is by nature architectonic. That is to say, it regards all cognitions as parts of a possible system, and hence accepts only such principles as at least do not incapacitate a cognition to which we may have attained from being placed along with others in a general system. But the propositions of the antithesis are of a character which renders the completion of an edifice of cognitions impossible. According to these, beyond one state or epoch of the world there is always to be found one more ancient; in every part always other parts themselves divisible; preceding every event another, the origin of which must itself be sought still higher; and everything in existence is conditioned, and still not dependent on an unconditioned and primal existence. As, therefore, the antithesis will not concede the existence of a first beginning which might be available as a foundation, a complete edifice of cognition, in the presence of such hypothesis, is utterly impossible. Thus the architectonic interest of reason, which requires a unity—not empirical, but à priori and rational—forms a natural recommendation for the assertions of the thesis in our antinomy.

But if any one could free himself entirely from all considerations of interest, and weigh without partiality the assertions of reason, attending only to their content, irrespective of the consequences which follow from them; such a person, on the supposition that he knew no other way out of the confusion than to settle the truth of one or other of the conflicting doctrines, would live in a state of continual hesitation. Today, he would feel convinced that the human will is free; to-morrow, considering the indissoluble chain of nature, he would look on freedom as a mere illusion and declare nature to be all-in-all. But, if he were called to action, the play of the merely speculative reason would disappear like the shapes of a dream, and practical interest would dictate his choice of principles. But, as it well befits a reflective and inquiring being to devote certain periods of time to the examination of its own reason—to divest itself of all partiality, and frankly to communicate its observations for the judgement and opinion of others; so no one can be blamed for, much less prevented from, placing both parties on their trial, with permission to end themselves, free from intimidation, before intimidation, before a sworn jury of equal condition with themselves—the condition of weak and fallible men.

Section IV. Of the necessity imposed upon Pure Reason of presenting a Solution of its Transcendental Problems

To avow an ability to solve all problems and to answer all questions would be a profession certain to convict any philosopher of extravagant boasting and self-conceit, and at once to destroy the confidence that might otherwise have been reposed in him. There are, however, sciences so constituted that every question arising within their sphere must necessarily be capable of receiving an answer from the knowledge already possessed, for the answer must be received from the same sources whence the question arose. In such sciences it is not allowable to excuse ourselves on the plea of necessary and unavoidable ignorance; a solution is absolutely requisite. The rule of right and wrong must help us to the knowledge of what is right or wrong in all possible cases; otherwise, the idea of obligation or duty would be utterly null, for we cannot have any obligation to that which we cannot know. On the other hand, in our investigations of the phenomena of nature, much must remain uncertain, and many questions continue insoluble; because what we know of nature is far from being sufficient to explain all the phenomena that are presented to our observation. Now the question is: Whether there is in transcendental philosophy any question, relating to an object presented to pure reason, which is unanswerable by this reason; and whether we must regard the subject of the question as quite uncertain, so far as our knowledge extends, and must give it a place among those subjects, of which we have just so much conception as is sufficient to enable us to raise a question—faculty or materials failing us, however, when we attempt an answer.

Now I maintain that, among all speculative cognition, the peculiarity of transcendental philosophy is that there is no question, relating to an object presented to pure reason, which is insoluble by this reason; and that the profession of unavoidable ignorance—the problem being alleged to be beyond the reach of our faculties—cannot free us from the obligation to present a complete and satisfactory answer. For the very conception which enables us to raise the question must give us the power of answering it; inasmuch as the object, as in the case of right and wrong, is not to be discovered out of the conception.

But, in transcendental philosophy, it is only the cosmological questions to which we can demand a satisfactory answer in relation to the constitution of their object; and the philosopher is not permitted to avail himself of the pretext of necessary ignorance and impenetrable obscurity. These questions relate solely to the cosmological ideas. For the object must be given in experience, and the question relates to the adequateness of the object to an idea. If the object is transcendental and therefore itself unknown; if the question, for example, is whether the object—the something, the phenomenon of which (internal—in ourselves) is thought—that is to say, the soul, is in itself a simple being; or whether there is a cause of all things, which is absolutely necessary—in such cases we are seeking for our idea an object, of which we may confess that it is unknown to us, though we must not on that account assert that it is impossible. [58]The cosmological ideas alone posses the peculiarity that we can presuppose the object of them and the empirical synthesis requisite for the conception of that object to be given; and the question, which arises from these ideas, relates merely to the progress of this synthesis, in so far as it must contain absolute totality—which, however, is not empirical, as it cannot be given in any experience. Now, as the question here is solely in regard to a thing as the object of a possible experience and not as a thing in itself, the answer to the transcendental cosmological question need not be sought out of the idea, for the question does not regard an object in itself. The question in relation to a possible experience is not, "What can be given in an experience in concreto" but "what is contained in the idea, to which the empirical synthesis must approximate." The question must therefore be capable of solution from the idea alone. For the idea is a creation of reason itself, which therefore cannot disclaim the obligation to answer or refer us to the unknown object.

It is not so extraordinary, as it at first sight appears, that a science should demand and expect satisfactory answers to all the questions that may arise within its own sphere (questiones domesticae), although, up to a certain time, these answers may not have been discovered. There are, in addition to transcendental philosophy, only two pure sciences of reason; the one with a speculative, the other with a practical content—pure mathematics and pure ethics. Has any one ever

[58] The question, "What is the constitution of a transcendental object?" is unanswerable—we are unable to say what it is; but we can perceive that the question itself is nothing; because it does not relate to any object that can be presented to us. For this reason, we must consider all the questions raised in transcendental psychology as answerable and as really answered; for they relate to the transcendental subject of all internal phenomena, which is not itself phenomenon and consequently not given as an object, in which, moreover, none of the categories—and it is to them that the question is properly directed—find any conditions of its application. Here, therefore, is a case where no answer is the only proper answer. For a question regarding the constitution of a something which cannot be cogitated by any determined predicate, being completely beyond the sphere of objects and experience, is perfectly null and void.

heard it alleged that, from our complete and necessary ignorance of the conditions, it is uncertain what exact relation the diameter of a circle bears to the circle in rational or irrational numbers? By the former the sum cannot be given exactly, by the latter only approximately; and therefore we decide that the impossibility of a solution of the question is evident. Lambert presented us with a demonstration of this. In the general principles of morals there can be nothing uncertain, for the propositions are either utterly without meaning, or must originate solely in our rational conceptions. On the other hand, there must be in physical science an infinite number of conjectures, which can never become certainties; because the phenomena of nature are not given as objects dependent on our conceptions. The key to the solution of such questions cannot, therefore, be found in our conceptions, or in pure thought, but must lie without us and for that reason is in many cases not to be discovered; and consequently a satisfactory explanation cannot be expected. The questions of transcendental analytic, which relate to the deduction of our pure cognition, are not to be regarded as of the same kind as those mentioned above; for we are not at present treating of the certainty of judgements in relation to the origin of our conceptions, but only of that certainty in relation to objects.

We cannot, therefore, escape the responsibility of at least a critical solution of the questions of reason, by complaints of the limited nature of our faculties, and the seemingly humble confession that it is beyond the power of our reason to decide, whether the world has existed from all eternity or had a beginning—whether it is infinitely extended, or enclosed within certain limits—whether anything in the world is simple, or whether everything must be capable of infinite divisibility—whether freedom can originate phenomena, or whether everything is absolutely dependent on the laws and order of nature—and, finally, whether there exists a being that is completely unconditioned and necessary, or whether the existence of everything is conditioned and consequently dependent on something external to itself, and therefore in its own nature contingent. For all these questions relate to an object, which can be given nowhere else than in thought. This object is the absolutely unconditioned totality of the synthesis of phenomena. If the conceptions in our minds do not assist us to some certain result in regard to these problems, we must not defend ourselves on the plea that the object itself remains hidden from and unknown to us. For no such thing or object can be given—it is not to be found out of the idea in our minds. We must seek the cause of our failure in our idea itself, which is an insoluble problem and in regard to which we obstinately assume that there exists a real object corresponding and adequate to it. A clear explanation of the dialectic which lies in our conception, will very soon enable us to come to a satisfactory decision in regard to such a question.

The pretext that we are unable to arrive at certainty in regard to these problems may be met with this question, which requires at least a plain answer: "From what source do the ideas originate, the solution of which involves you in such difficulties? Are you seeking for an explanation of certain phenomena; and do you expect these ideas to give you the principles or the rules of this explanation?" Let it be granted, that all nature was laid open before you; that nothing was hid from your senses and your consciousness. Still, you could not cognize in concreto the object of your ideas in any experience. For what is demanded is not only this full and complete intuition, but also a complete synthesis and the consciousness of its absolute totality; and this is not possible by means of any empirical cognition. It follows that your question—your idea—is by no means necessary for the explanation of any phenomenon; and the idea cannot have been in any sense given by the object itself. For such an object can never be presented to us, because it cannot be given by any possible experience. Whatever perceptions you may attain to, you are still surrounded by conditions—in space, or in time—and you cannot discover anything unconditioned; nor can you decide whether this unconditioned is to be placed in an absolute beginning of the synthesis, or in an absolute totality of the series without beginning. A whole, in the empirical signification of the term, is always merely comparative. The absolute whole of quantity (the universe), of division, of derivation, of the condition of existence, with the question—whether it is to be produced by finite or infinite synthesis, no possible experience can instruct us concerning. You will not, for example, be able to explain the phenomena of a body in the least degree better, whether you believe it to consist of simple, or of composite parts; for a simple phenomenon—and just as little an infinite series of composition—can never be presented to your perception. Phenomena require and admit of explanation, only in so far as the conditions of that explanation are given in perception; but the sum total of that which is given in phenomena, considered as an absolute whole, is itself a perception—and we cannot therefore seek for explanations of this whole beyond itself, in other perceptions. The explanation of this whole is the proper object of the transcendental problems of pure reason.

Although, therefore, the solution of these problems is unattainable through experience, we must not permit ourselves to say that it is uncertain how the object of our inquiries is constituted. For the object is in our own mind and cannot be discovered in experience; and we have only to take care that our thoughts are consistent with each other, and to avoid falling into the amphiboly of regarding our idea as a representation of an object empirically given, and therefore to be cognized according to the laws of experience. A dogmatical solution is therefore not only unsatisfactory but impossible. The critical solution, which may be a perfectly certain one, does not consider the question objectively, but proceeds by inquiring into the basis of the cognition upon which the question rests.

Section V. Sceptical Exposition of the Cosmological Problems presented in the four Transcendental Ideas

We should be quite willing to desist from the demand of a dogmatical answer to our questions, if we understood beforehand that, be the answer what it may, it would only serve to increase our ignorance, to throw us from one incomprehensibility into another, from one obscurity into another still greater, and perhaps lead us into irreconcilable contradictions. If a dogmatical affirmative or negative answer is demanded, is it at all prudent to set aside the probable grounds of a solution which lie before us and to take into consideration what advantage we shall gain, if the answer is to favour the one side or the other? If it happens that in both cases the answer is mere nonsense, we have in this an irresistible summons to institute a critical investigation of the question, for the purpose of discovering whether it is based on a groundless presupposition and relates to an idea, the falsity of which would be more easily exposed in its application and consequences than in the mere representation of its content. This is the great utility of the sceptical mode of treating the questions addressed by pure reason to itself. By this method we easily rid ourselves of the confusions of dogmatism, and establish in its place a temperate criticism, which, as a genuine cathartic, will successfully remove the presumptuous notions of philosophy and their consequence—the vain pretension to universal science.

If, then, I could understand the nature of a cosmological idea and perceive, before I entered on the discussion of the subject at all, that, whatever side of the question regarding the unconditioned of the regressive synthesis of phenomena it favoured—it must either be too great or too small for every conception of the understanding—I would be able to comprehend how the idea, which relates to an object of experience—an experience which must be adequate to and in accordance with a possible conception of the understanding—must be completely void and without significance, inasmuch as its object is inadequate, consider it as we may. And this is actually the case with all cosmological conceptions, which, for the reason above mentioned, involve reason, so long as it remains attached to them, in an unavoidable antinomy. For suppose:

First, that the world has no beginning—in this case it is too large for our conception; for this conception, which consists in a successive regress, cannot overtake the whole eternity that has elapsed. Grant that it has a beginning, it is then too small for the conception of the understanding. For, as a beginning presupposes a time preceding, it cannot be unconditioned; and the law of the empirical employment of the understanding imposes the necessity of looking for a higher condition of time; and the world is, therefore, evidently too small for this law.

The same is the case with the double answer to the question regarding the extent, in space, of the world. For, if it is infinite and unlimited, it must be too large for every possible empirical conception. If it is finite and limited, we have a right to ask: "What determines these limits?" Void space is not a self-subsistent correlate of things, and cannot be a final condition—and still less an empirical condition, forming a part of a possible experience. For how can we have any experience or perception of an absolute void? But the absolute totality of the empirical synthesis requires that the unconditioned be an empirical conception. Consequently, a finite world is too small for our conception.

Secondly, if every phenomenon (matter) in space consists of an infinite number of parts, the regress of the division is always too great for our conception; and if the division of space must cease with some member of the division (the simple), it is too small for the idea of the unconditioned. For the member at which we have discontinued our division still admits a regress to many more parts contained in the object.

Thirdly, suppose that every event in the world happens in accordance with the laws of nature; the causality of a cause must itself be an event and necessitates a regress to a still higher cause, and consequently the unceasing prolongation of the series of conditions a parte priori. Operative nature is therefore too large for every conception we can form in the synthesis of cosmical events.

If we admit the existence of spontaneously produced events, that is, of free agency, we are driven, in our search for sufficient reasons, on an unavoidable law of nature and are compelled to appeal to the empirical law of causality, and we find that any such totality of connection in our synthesis is too small for our necessary empirical conception.

Fourthly, if we assume the existence of an absolutely necessary being—whether it be the world or something in the world, or the cause of the world—we must place it in a time at an infinite distance from any given moment; for, otherwise, it must be dependent on some other and higher existence. Such an existence is, in this case, too large for our empirical conception, and unattainable by the continued regress of any synthesis.

But if we believe that everything in the world—be it condition or conditioned—is contingent; every given existence is too small for our conception. For in this case we are compelled to seek for some other existence upon which the former depends.

We have said that in all these cases the cosmological idea is either too great or too small for the empirical regress in a synthesis, and consequently for every possible conception of the understanding. Why did we not express ourselves in a manner exactly the reverse of this and, instead of accusing the cosmological idea of over stepping or of falling short of its true aim, possible experience, say that, in the first case, the empirical conception is always too small for the idea, and in the second too great, and thus attach the blame of these contradictions to the empirical regress? The reason is this. Possible experience can alone give reality to our conceptions; without it a conception is merely an idea, without truth or relation to an object. Hence a possible empirical conception must be the standard by which we are to judge whether an idea is anything more than an idea and fiction of thought, or whether it relates to an object in the world. If we say of a thing that in relation to some other thing it is too large or too small, the former is considered as existing for the sake of the latter, and requiring to be adapted to it. Among the trivial subjects of discussion in the old schools of dialectics was this question: "If a ball cannot pass through a hole, shall we say that the ball is too large or the hole too small?" In this case it is indifferent what expression we employ; for we do not know which exists for the sake of the other. On the other hand, we cannot say: "The man is too long for his coat"; but: "The coat is too short for the man."

We are thus led to the well-founded suspicion that the cosmological ideas, and all the conflicting sophistical assertions connected with them, are based upon a false and fictitious conception of the mode in which the object of these ideas is presented to us; and this suspicion will probably direct us how to expose the illusion that has so long led us astray from the truth.

Section VI. Transcendental Idealism as the Key to the Solution of Pure Cosmological Dialectic

In the transcendental æsthetic we proved that everything intuited in space and time, all objects of a possible experience, are nothing but phenomena, that is, mere representations; and that these, as presented to us—as extended bodies, or as series of changes—have no self-subsistent existence apart from human thought. This doctrine I call Transcendental Idealism.[59] The realist in the transcendental sense regards these modifications of our sensibility, these mere representations, as things subsisting in themselves.

It would be unjust to accuse us of holding the long-decried theory of empirical idealism, which, while admitting the reality of space, denies, or at least doubts, the existence of bodies extended in it, and thus leaves us without a sufficient criterion of reality and illusion. The supporters of this theory find no difficulty in admitting the reality of the phenomena of the internal sense in time; nay, they go the length of maintaining that this internal experience is of itself a sufficient proof of the real existence of its object as a thing in itself.

Transcendental idealism allows that the objects of external intuition—as intuited in space, and all changes in time—as represented by the internal sense, are real. For, as space is the form of that intuition which we call external, and, without objects in space, no empirical representation could be given us, we can and ought to regard extended bodies in it as real. The case is the same with representations in time. But time and space, with all phenomena therein, are not in themselves things. They are nothing but representations and cannot exist out of and apart from the mind. Nay, the sensuous internal intuition of the mind (as the object of consciousness), the determination of which is represented by the succession of different states in time, is not the real, proper self, as it exists in itself—not the transcendental subject—but only a phenomenon, which is presented to the sensibility of this, to us, unknown being. This internal phenomenon cannot be admitted to be a self-subsisting thing; for its condition is time, and time cannot be the condition of a thing in itself. But the empirical truth of phenomena in space and time is guaranteed beyond the

[59] I have elsewhere termed this theory formal idealism, to distinguish it from material idealism, which doubts or denies the existence of external things. To avoid ambiguity, it seems advisable in many cases to employ this term instead of that mentioned in the text.

possibility of doubt, and sufficiently distinguished from the illusion of dreams or fancy—although both have a proper and thorough connection in an experience according to empirical laws. The objects of experience then are not things in themselves, but are given only in experience, and have no existence apart from and independently of experience. That there may be inhabitants in the moon, although no one has ever observed them, must certainly be admitted; but this assertion means only, that we may in the possible progress of experience discover them at some future time. For that which stands in connection with a perception according to the laws of the progress of experience is real. They are therefore really existent, if they stand in empirical connection with my actual or real consciousness, although they are not in themselves real, that is, apart from the progress of experience.

There is nothing actually given—we can be conscious of nothing as real, except a perception and the empirical progression from it to other possible perceptions. For phenomena, as mere representations, are real only in perception; and perception is, in fact, nothing but the reality of an empirical representation, that is, a phenomenon. To call a phenomenon a real thing prior to perception means either that we must meet with this phenomenon in the progress of experience, or it means nothing at all. For I can say only of a thing in itself that it exists without relation to the senses and experience. But we are speaking here merely of phenomena in space and time, both of which are determinations of sensibility, and not of things in themselves. It follows that phenomena are not things in themselves, but are mere representations, which if not given in us—in perception—are non-existent.

The faculty of sensuous intuition is properly a receptivity—a capacity of being affected in a certain manner by representations, the relation of which to each other is a pure intuition of space and time—the pure forms of sensibility. These representations, in so far as they are connected and determinable in this relation (in space and time) according to laws of the unity of experience, are called objects. The non-sensuous cause of these representations is completely unknown to us and hence cannot be intuited as an object. For such an object could not be represented either in space or in time; and without these conditions intuition or representation is impossible. We may, at the same time, term the non-sensuous cause of phenomena the transcendental object—but merely as a mental correlate to sensibility, considered as a receptivity. To this transcendental object we may attribute the whole connection and extent of our possible perceptions, and say that it is given and exists in itself prior to all experience. But the phenomena, corresponding to it, are not given as things in themselves, but in experience alone. For they are mere representations, receiving from perceptions alone significance and relation to a real object, under the condition that this or that perception—indicating an object—is in complete connection with all others in accordance with the rules of the unity of experience. Thus we can say: "The things that really existed in past time are given in the transcendental object of experience." But these are to me real objects, only in so far as I can represent to my own mind, that a regressive series of possible perceptions—following the indications of history, or the footsteps of cause and effect—in accordance with empirical laws—that, in one word, the course of the world conducts us to an elapsed series of time as the condition of the present time. This series in past time is represented as real, not in itself, but only in connection with a possible experience. Thus, when I say that certain events occurred in past time, I merely assert the possibility of prolonging the chain of experience, from the present perception, upwards to the conditions that determine it according to time.

If I represent to myself all objects existing in all space and time, I do not thereby place these in space and time prior to all experience; on the contrary, such a representation is nothing more than the notion of a possible experience, in its absolute completeness. In experience alone are those objects, which are nothing but representations, given. But, when I say they existed prior to my experience, this means only that I must begin with the perception present to me and follow the track indicated until I discover them in some part or region of experience. The cause of the empirical condition of this progression—and consequently at what member therein I must stop, and at what point in the regress I am to find this member—is transcendental, and hence necessarily incognizable. But with this we have not to do; our concern is only with the law of progression in experience, in which objects, that is, phenomena, are given. It is a matter of indifference, whether I say, "I may in the progress of experience discover stars, at a hundred times greater distance than the most distant of those now visible," or, "Stars at this distance may be met in space, although no one has, or ever will discover them." For, if they are given as things in themselves, without any relation to possible experience, they are for me non-existent, consequently, are not objects, for they are not contained in the regressive series of experience. But, if these phenomena must be employed in the construction or support of the cosmological idea of an absolute whole, and when we are discussing a question that oversteps the limits of possible experience, the proper distinction of the different theories of the reality of sensuous objects is of great importance, in order to avoid the illusion which must necessarily arise from the misinterpretation of our empirical conceptions.

Section VII. Critical Solution of the Cosmological Problem

The antinomy of pure reason is based upon the following dialectical argument: "If that which is conditioned is given, the whole series of its conditions is also given; but sensuous objects are given as conditioned; consequently..." This syllogism, the major of which seems so natural and evident, introduces as many cosmological ideas as there are different kinds of conditions in the synthesis of phenomena, in so far as these conditions constitute a series. These ideas require absolute totality in the series, and thus place reason in inextricable embarrassment. Before proceeding to expose the fallacy in this dialectical argument, it will be necessary to have a correct understanding of certain conceptions that appear in it.

In the first place, the following proposition is evident, and indubitably certain: "If the conditioned is given, a regress in the series of all its conditions is thereby imperatively required." For the very conception of a conditioned is a conception of something related to a condition, and, if this condition is itself conditioned, to another condition—and so on through all the members of the series. This proposition is, therefore, analytical and has nothing to fear from transcendental criticism. It is a logical postulate of reason: to pursue, as far as possible, the connection of a conception with its conditions.

If, in the second place, both the conditioned and the condition are things in themselves, and if the former is given, not only is the regress to the latter requisite, but the latter is really given with the former. Now, as this is true of all the members of the series, the entire series of conditions, and with them the unconditioned, is at the same time given in the very fact of the conditioned, the existence of which is possible only in and through that series, being given. In this case, the synthesis of the conditioned with its condition, is a synthesis of the understanding merely, which represents things as they are, without regarding whether and how we can cognize them. But if I have to do with phenomena, which, in their character of mere representations, are not given, if I do not attain to a cognition of them (in other words, to themselves, for they are nothing more than empirical cognitions), I am not entitled to say: "If the conditioned is given, all its conditions (as phenomena) are also given." I cannot, therefore, from the fact of a conditioned being given, infer the absolute totality of the series of its conditions. For phenomena are nothing but an empirical synthesis in apprehension or perception, and are therefore given only in it. Now, in speaking of phenomena it does not follow that, if the conditioned is given, the synthesis which constitutes its empirical condition is also thereby given and presupposed; such a synthesis can be established only by an actual regress in the series of conditions. But we are entitled to say in this case that a regress to the conditions of a conditioned, in other words, that a continuous empirical synthesis is enjoined; that, if the conditions are not given, they are at least required; and that we are certain to discover the conditions in this regress.

We can now see that the major, in the above cosmological syllogism, takes the conditioned in the transcendental signification which it has in the pure category, while the minor speaks of it in the empirical signification which it has in the category as applied to phenomena. There is, therefore, a dialectical fallacy in the syllogism—a sophisma figurae dictionis. But this fallacy is not a consciously devised one, but a perfectly natural illusion of the common reason of man. For, when a thing is given as conditioned, we presuppose in the major its conditions and their series, unperceived, as it were, and unseen; because this is nothing more than the logical requirement of complete and satisfactory premisses for a given conclusion. In this case, time is altogether left out in the connection of the conditioned with the condition; they are supposed to be given in themselves, and contemporaneously. It is, moreover, just as natural to regard phenomena (in the minor) as things in themselves and as objects presented to the pure understanding, as in the major, in which complete abstraction was made of all conditions of intuition. But it is under these conditions alone that objects are given. Now we overlooked a remarkable distinction between the conceptions. The synthesis of the conditioned with its condition, and the complete series of the latter (in the major) are not limited by time, and do not contain the conception of succession. On the contrary, the empirical synthesis and the series of conditions in the phenomenal world—subsumed in the minor—are necessarily successive and given in time alone. It follows that I cannot presuppose in the minor, as I did in the major, the absolute totality of the synthesis and of the series therein represented; for in the major all the members of the series are given as things in themselves—without any limitations or conditions of time, while in the minor they are possible only in and through a successive regress, which cannot exist, except it be actually carried into execution in the world of phenomena.

After this proof of the viciousness of the argument commonly employed in maintaining cosmological assertions, both parties may now be justly dismissed, as advancing claims without grounds or title. But the process has not been ended by convincing them that one or both were in the wrong and had maintained an assertion which was without valid grounds of proof. Nothing seems to be clearer than that, if one maintains: "The world has a beginning," and another: "The world has no beginning," one of the two must be right. But it is likewise clear that, if the evidence on both sides is equal, it is impossible to discover on what side the truth lies; and the controversy continues, although the parties have been recommended to peace before the tribunal of reason. There remains, then, no other means of settling the question than to convince the parties, who refute each other with such conclusiveness and ability, that they are disputing about nothing, and that a transcendental illusion has been mocking them with visions of reality where there is none. The mode of adjusting a dispute which cannot be decided upon its own merits, we shall now proceed to lay before our readers.

*

Zeno of Elea, a subtle dialectician, was severely reprimanded by Plato as a sophist, who, merely from the base motive of exhibiting his skill in discussion, maintained and subverted the same proposition by arguments as powerful and convincing on the one side as on the other. He maintained, for example, that God (who was probably nothing more, in his view, than the world) is neither finite nor infinite, neither in motion nor in rest, neither similar nor dissimilar to any other thing. It seemed to those philosophers who criticized his mode of discussion that his purpose was to deny completely both of two self-contradictory propositions—which is absurd. But I cannot believe that there is any justice in this accusation. The first of these propositions I shall presently consider in a more detailed manner. With regard to the others, if by the word of God he understood merely the Universe, his meaning must have been—that it cannot be permanently present in one place—that is, at rest—nor be capable of changing its place—that is, of moving—because all places are in the universe, and the universe itself is, therefore, in no place. Again, if the universe contains in itself everything that exists, it cannot be similar or dissimilar to any other thing, because there is, in fact, no other thing with which it can be compared. If two opposite judgements presuppose a contingent impossible, or arbitrary condition, both—in spite of their opposition (which is, however, not properly or really a contradiction)—fall away; because the condition, which ensured the validity of both, has itself disappeared.

If we say: "Everybody has either a good or a bad smell," we have omitted a third possible judgement—it has no smell at all; and thus both conflicting statements may be false. If we say: "It is either good-smelling or not good-smelling (vel suaveolens vel non-suaveolens)," both judgements are contradictorily opposed; and the contradictory opposite of the former judgement—some bodies are not good-smelling—embraces also those bodies which have no smell at all. In the preceding pair of opposed judgements (per disparata), the contingent condition of the conception of body (smell) attached to both conflicting statements, instead of having been omitted in the latter, which is consequently not the contradictory opposite of the former.

If, accordingly, we say: "The world is either infinite in extension, or it is not infinite (non est infinitus)"; and if the former proposition is false, its contradictory opposite—the world is not infinite—must be true. And thus I should deny the existence of an infinite, without, however affirming the existence of a finite world. But if we construct our proposition thus: "The world is either infinite or finite (non-infinite)," both statements may be false. For, in this case, we consider the world as per se determined in regard to quantity, and while, in the one judgement, we deny its infinite and consequently, perhaps, its independent existence; in the other, we append to the world, regarded as a thing in itself, a certain determination—that of finitude; and the latter may be false as well as the former, if the world is not given as a thing in itself, and thus neither as finite nor as infinite in quantity. This kind of opposition I may be allowed to term dialectical; that of contradictories may be called analytical opposition. Thus then, of two dialectically opposed judgements both may be false, from the fact, that the one is not a mere contradictory of the other, but actually enounces more than is requisite for a full and complete contradiction.

When we regard the two propositions—"The world is infinite in quantity," and, "The world is finite in quantity," as contradictory opposites, we are assuming that the world—the complete series of phenomena—is a thing in itself. For it remains as a permanent quantity, whether I deny the infinite or the finite regress in the series of its phenomena. But if we dismiss this assumption—this transcendental illusion—and deny that it is a thing in itself, the contradictory opposition is metamorphosed into a merely dialectical one; and the world, as not existing in itself—independently of the regressive series of my representations—exists in like manner neither as a whole which is infinite nor as a whole which is finite in itself. The universe exists for me only in the empirical regress of the series of phenomena and not per se. If, then, it is always conditioned, it is never completely or as a whole; and it is, therefore, not an unconditioned whole and does not exist as such, either with an infinite, or with a finite quantity.

What we have here said of the first cosmological idea—that of the absolute totality of quantity in phenomena—applies also to the others. The series of conditions is discoverable only in the regressive synthesis itself, and not in the phenomenon considered as a thing in itself—given prior to all regress. Hence I am compelled to say: "The aggregate of parts in a given phenomenon is in itself neither finite nor infinite; and these parts are given only in the regressive synthesis of decomposition—a synthesis which is never given in absolute completeness, either as finite, or as infinite." The same is the case with the series of subordinated causes, or of the conditioned up to the unconditioned and necessary existence, which can never be regarded as in itself, and in its totality, either as finite or as infinite; because, as a series of subordinate representations, it subsists only in the dynamical regress and cannot be regarded as existing previously to this regress, or as a self-subsistent series of things.

Thus the antinomy of pure reason in its cosmological ideas disappears. For the above demonstration has established the fact that it is merely the product of a dialectical and illusory opposition, which arises from the application of the idea of absolute totality—admissible only as a condition of things in themselves—to phenomena, which exist only in our representations, and—when constituting a series—in a successive regress. This antinomy of reason may, however, be really profitable to our speculative interests, not in the way of contributing any dogmatical addition, but as presenting to us another material support in our critical investigations. For it furnishes us with an indirect proof of the transcendental ideality of phenomena, if our minds were not completely satisfied with the direct proof set forth in the Trancendental Æsthetic. The proof would proceed in the following dilemma. If the world is a whole existing in itself, it must be either finite or infinite. But it is neither finite nor infinite—as has been shown, on the one side, by the thesis, on the other, by the antithesis. Therefore the world—the content of all phenomena—is not a whole existing in itself. It follows that phenomena are nothing, apart from our representations. And this is what we mean by transcendental ideality.

This remark is of some importance. It enables us to see that the proofs of the fourfold antinomy are not mere sophistries—are not fallacious, but grounded on the nature of reason, and valid—under the supposition that phenomena are things in themselves. The opposition of the judgements which follow makes it evident that a fallacy lay in the initial supposition, and thus helps us to discover the true constitution of objects of sense. This transcendental dialectic does not favour scepticism, although it presents us with a triumphant demonstration of the advantages of the sceptical method, the great utility of which is apparent in the antinomy, where the arguments of reason were allowed to confront each other in undiminished force. And although the result of these conflicts of reason is not what we expected—although we have obtained no positive dogmatical addition to metaphysical science—we have still reaped a great advantage in the correction of our judgements on these subjects of thought.

Section VIII. Regulative Principle of Pure Reason in relation to the Cosmological Ideas

The cosmological principle of totality could not give us any certain knowledge in regard to the maximum in the series of conditions in the world of sense, considered as a thing in itself. The actual regress in the series is the only means of approaching this maximum. This principle of pure reason, therefore, may still be considered as valid—not as an axiom enabling us to cogitate totality in the object as actual, but as a problem for the understanding, which requires it to institute and to continue, in conformity with the idea of totality in the mind, the regress in the series of the conditions of a given conditioned. For in the world of sense, that is, in space and time, every condition which we discover in our investigation of phenomena is itself conditioned; because sensuous objects are not things in themselves (in which case an absolutely unconditioned might be reached in the progress of cognition), but are merely empirical representations the conditions of which must always be found in intuition. The principle of reason is therefore properly a mere rule—prescribing a regress in the series of conditions for given phenomena, and prohibiting any pause or rest on an absolutely unconditioned. It is, therefore, not a principle of the possibility of experience or of the empirical cognition of sensuous objects—consequently not a principle of the understanding; for every experience is confined within certain proper limits determined by the given intuition. Still less is it a constitutive principle of reason authorizing us to extend our conception of the sensuous world beyond all possible experience. It is merely a principle for the enlargement and extension of experience as far as is possible for human faculties. It forbids us to consider any empirical limits as absolute. It is, hence, a principle of reason, which, as a rule, dictates how we ought to proceed in our empirical regress, but is unable to anticipate or indicate prior to the empirical regress what is given in the object itself. I have termed it for this reason a regulative principle of reason; while the principle of the absolute totality of the series of conditions, as existing in itself and given in the object, is a constitutive cosmological principle. This distinction will at once demonstrate the falsehood of the constitutive principle, and prevent us from attributing (by a transcendental subreptio) objective reality to an idea, which is valid only as a rule.

In order to understand the proper meaning of this rule of pure reason, we must notice first that it cannot tell us what the object is, but only how the empirical regress is to be proceeded with in order to attain to the complete conception of the object. If it gave us any information in respect to the former statement, it would be a constitutive principle—a principle impossible from the nature of pure reason. It will not therefore enable us to establish any such conclusions as: "The series of conditions for a given conditioned is in itself finite," or, "It is infinite." For, in this case, we should be cogitating in the mere idea of absolute totality, an object which is not and cannot be given in experience; inasmuch as we should be attributing a reality objective and independent of the empirical synthesis, to a series of phenomena. This idea of reason cannot then be regarded as valid—except as a rule for the regressive synthesis in the series of conditions, according to which we must proceed from the conditioned, through all intermediate and subordinate conditions, up to the unconditioned; although this goal is unattained and unattainable. For the absolutely unconditioned cannot be discovered in the sphere of experience.

We now proceed to determine clearly our notion of a synthesis which can never be complete. There are two terms commonly employed for this purpose. These terms are regarded as expressions of different and distinguishable notions, although the ground of the distinction has never been clearly exposed. The term employed by the mathematicians is progressus in infinitum. The philosophers prefer the expression progressus in indefinitum. Without detaining the reader with an examination of the reasons for such a distinction, or with remarks on the right or wrong use of the terms, I shall endeavour clearly to determine these conceptions, so far as is necessary for the purpose in this Critique.

We may, with propriety, say of a straight line, that it may be produced to infinity. In this case the distinction between a progressus in infinitum and a progressus in indefinitum is a mere piece of subtlety. For, although when we say, "Produce a straight line," it is more correct to say in indefinitum than in infinitum; because the former means, "Produce it as far as you please," the second, "You must not cease to produce it"; the expression in infinitum is, when we are speaking of the power to do it, perfectly correct, for we can always make it longer if we please—on to infinity. And this remark holds good in all cases, when we speak of a progressus, that is, an advancement from the condition to the conditioned; this possible advancement always proceeds to infinity. We may proceed from a given pair in the descending line of generation from father to son, and cogitate a never-ending line of descendants from it. For in such a case reason does not demand absolute totality in the series, because it does not presuppose it as a condition and as given (datum), but merely as conditioned, and as capable of being given (dabile).

Very different is the case with the problem: "How far the regress, which ascends from the given conditioned to the conditions, must extend"; whether I can say: "It is a regress in infinitum," or only "in indefinitum"; and whether, for example, setting out from the human beings at present alive in the world, I may ascend in the series of their ancestors, in infinitum—or whether all that can be said is, that so far as I have proceeded, I have discovered no empirical ground for considering the series limited, so that I am justified, and indeed, compelled to search for ancestors still further back, although I am not obliged by the idea of reason to presuppose them.

My answer to this question is: "If the series is given in empirical intuition as a whole, the regress in the series of its internal conditions proceeds in infinitum; but, if only one member of the series is given, from which the regress is to proceed to absolute totality, the regress is possible only in indefinitum." For example, the division of a portion of matter given within certain limits—of a body, that is—proceeds in infinitum. For, as the condition of this whole is its part, and the condition of the part a part of the part, and so on, and as in this regress of decomposition an unconditioned indivisible member of the series of conditions is not to be found; there are no reasons or grounds in experience for stopping in the division, but, on the contrary, the more remote members of the division are actually and empirically given prior to this division. That is to say, the division proceeds to infinity. On the other hand, the series of ancestors of any given human being is not given, in its absolute totality, in any experience, and yet the regress proceeds from every genealogical member of this series to one still higher, and does not meet with any empirical limit presenting an absolutely unconditioned member of the series. But as the members of such a series are not contained in the empirical intuition of the whole, prior to the regress, this regress does not proceed to infinity, but only in indefinitum, that is, we are called upon to discover other and higher members, which are themselves always conditioned.

In neither case—the regressus in infinitum, nor the regressus in indefinitum, is the series of conditions to be considered as actually infinite in the object itself. This might be true of things in themselves, but it cannot be asserted of phenomena, which, as conditions of each other, are only given in the empirical regress itself. Hence, the question no longer is, "What is the quantity of this series of conditions in itself—is it finite or infinite?" for it is nothing in itself; but, "How is the empirical regress to be commenced, and how far ought we to proceed with it?" And here a signal distinction in the application of this rule becomes apparent. If the whole is given empirically, it is possible to recede in the series of its internal conditions to infinity. But if the whole is not given, and can only be given by and through the empirical regress, I can only say: "It is possible to infinity, to proceed to still higher conditions in the series." In the first case, I am justified in asserting that more members are empirically given in the object than I attain to in the regress (of decomposition). In the second case, I am justified only in saying, that I can always proceed further in the regress, because no member of the series is given as absolutely conditioned, and thus a higher member is possible, and an inquiry with regard to it is necessary. In the one case it is necessary to find other members of the series, in the other it is necessary to inquire for others, inasmuch as experience presents no absolute limitation of the regress. For, either you do not possess a perception which absolutely limits your empirical regress, and in this case the regress cannot be regarded as complete; or, you do possess such a limitative perception, in which case it is not a part of your series (for that which limits must be distinct from that which is limited by it), and it is incumbent you to continue your regress up to this condition, and so on.

These remarks will be placed in their proper light by their application in the following section.

Section IX. Of the Empirical Use of the Regulative Principle of Reason with regard to the Cosmological Ideas

We have shown that no transcendental use can be made either of the conceptions of reason or of understanding. We have shown, likewise, that the demand of absolute totality in the series of conditions in the world of sense arises from a transcendental employment of reason, resting on the opinion that phenomena are to be regarded as things in themselves. It follows that we are not required to answer the question respecting the absolute quantity of a series—whether it is in itself limited or unlimited. We are only called upon to determine how far we must proceed in the empirical regress from condition to condition, in order to discover, in conformity with the rule of reason, a full and correct answer to the questions proposed by reason itself.

This principle of reason is hence valid only as a rule for the extension of a possible experience—its invalidity as a principle constitutive of phenomena in themselves having been sufficiently demonstrated. And thus, too, the antinomial conflict of reason with itself is completely put an end to; inasmuch as we have not only presented a critical solution of the fallacy lurking in the opposite statements of reason, but have shown the true meaning of the ideas which gave rise to these statements. The dialectical principle of reason has, therefore, been changed into a doctrinal principle. But in fact, if this principle, in the subjective signification which we have shown to be its only true sense, may be guaranteed as a principle of the unceasing extension of the employment of our understanding, its influence and value are just as great as if it were an axiom for the à priori determination of objects. For such an axiom could not exert a stronger influence on the extension and rectification of our knowledge, otherwise than by procuring for the principles of the understanding the most widely expanded employment in the field of experience.

I. Solution of the Cosmological Idea of the Totality of the Composition of Phenomena in the Universe

Here, as well as in the case of the other cosmological problems, the ground of the regulative principle of reason is the proposition that in our empirical regress no experience of an absolute limit, and consequently no experience of a condition, which is itself absolutely unconditioned, is discoverable. And the truth of this proposition itself rests upon the consideration that such an experience must represent to us phenomena as limited by nothing or the mere void, on which our continued regress by means of perception must abut—which is impossible.

Now this proposition, which declares that every condition attained in the empirical regress must itself be considered empirically conditioned, contains the rule in terminis, which requires me, to whatever extent I may have proceeded in the ascending series, always to look for some higher member in the series—whether this member is to become known to me through experience, or not.

Nothing further is necessary, then, for the solution of the first cosmological problem, than to decide, whether, in the regress to the unconditioned quantity of the universe (as regards space and time), this never limited ascent ought to be called a regressus in infinitum or indefinitum.

The general representation which we form in our minds of the series of all past states or conditions of the world, or of all the things which at present exist in it, is itself nothing more than a possible empirical regress, which is cogitated—although in an undetermined manner—in the mind, and which gives rise to the conception of a series of conditions for a given object.[60] Now I have a conception of the universe, but not an intuition—that is, not an intuition of it as a whole. Thus I cannot infer the magnitude of the regress from the quantity or magnitude of the world, and determine the former by means of the latter; on the contrary, I must first of all form a conception of the quantity or magnitude of the world from the magnitude of the empirical regress. But of this regress I know nothing more than that I ought to proceed from every given member of the series of conditions to one still higher. But the quantity of the universe is not thereby determined, and we cannot affirm that this regress proceeds in infinitum. Such an affirmation would anticipate the members of the series which have not yet been reached, and represent the number of them as beyond the grasp of any empirical synthesis; it would consequently determine the cosmical quantity prior to the regress (although only in a negative manner)—which is impossible. For the world is not given in its totality in any intuition: consequently, its quantity cannot be given prior to the regress. It follows that we are unable to make any declaration respecting the cosmical quantity in itself—not even that the regress in it is a regress in infinitum; we must only endeavour to attain to a conception of the quantity of the universe, in conformity with the rule which determines the empirical regress in it. But this rule merely requires us never to admit an absolute limit to our series—how far

[60] The cosmical series can neither be greater nor smaller than the possible empirical regress, upon which its conception is based. And as this regress cannot be a determinate infinite regress, still less a determinate finite (absolutely limited), it is evident that we cannot regard the world as either finite or infinite, because the regress, which gives us the representation of the world, is neither finite nor infinite.

soever we may have proceeded in it, but always, on the contrary, to subordinate every phenomenon to some other as its condition, and consequently to proceed to this higher phenomenon. Such a regress is, therefore, the regressus in indefinitum, which, as not determining a quantity in the object, is clearly distinguishable from the regressus in infinitum.

It follows from what we have said that we are not justified in declaring the world to be infinite in space, or as regards past time. For this conception of an infinite given quantity is empirical; but we cannot apply the conception of an infinite quantity to the world as an object of the senses. I cannot say, "The regress from a given perception to everything limited either in space or time, proceeds in infinitum," for this presupposes an infinite cosmical quantity; neither can I say, "It is finite," for an absolute limit is likewise impossible in experience. It follows that I am not entitled to make any assertion at all respecting the whole object of experience—the world of sense; I must limit my declarations to the rule according to which experience or empirical knowledge is to be attained.

To the question, therefore, respecting the cosmical quantity, the first and negative answer is: "The world has no beginning in time, and no absolute limit in space."

For, in the contrary case, it would be limited by a void time on the one hand, and by a void space on the other. Now, since the world, as a phenomenon, cannot be thus limited in itself for a phenomenon is not a thing in itself; it must be possible for us to have a perception of this limitation by a void time and a void space. But such a perception—such an experience is impossible; because it has no content. Consequently, an absolute cosmical limit is empirically, and therefore absolutely, impossible.[61]

From this follows the affirmative answer: "The regress in the series of phenomena—as a determination of the cosmical quantity, proceeds in indefinitum." This is equivalent to saying: "The world of sense has no absolute quantity, but the empirical regress (through which alone the world of sense is presented to us on the side of its conditions) rests upon a rule, which requires it to proceed from every member of the series, as conditioned, to one still more remote (whether through personal experience, or by means of history, or the chain of cause and effect), and not to cease at any point in this extension of the possible empirical employment of the understanding." And this is the proper and only use which reason can make of its principles.

[61] The reader will remark that the proof presented above is very different from the dogmatical demonstration given in the antithesis of the first antinomy. In that demonstration, it was taken for granted that the world is a thing in itself—given in its totality prior to all regress, and a determined position in space and time was denied to it—if it was not considered as occupying all time and all space. Hence our conclusion differed from that given above; for we inferred in the antithesis the actual infinity of the world.

The above rule does not prescribe an unceasing regress in one kind of phenomena. It does not, for example, forbid us, in our ascent from an individual human being through the line of his ancestors, to expect that we shall discover at some point of the regress a primeval pair, or to admit, in the series of heavenly bodies, a sun at the farthest possible distance from some centre. All that it demands is a perpetual progress from phenomena to phenomena, even although an actual perception is not presented by them (as in the case of our perceptions being so weak as that we are unable to become conscious of them), since they, nevertheless, belong to possible experience.

Every beginning is in time, and all limits to extension are in space. But space and time are in the world of sense. Consequently phenomena in the world are conditionally limited, but the world itself is not limited, either conditionally or unconditionally.

For this reason, and because neither the world nor the cosmical series of conditions to a given conditioned can be completely given, our conception of the cosmical quantity is given only in and through the regress and not prior to it—in a collective intuition. But the regress itself is really nothing more than the determining of the cosmical quantity, and cannot therefore give us any determined conception of it—still less a conception of a quantity which is, in relation to a certain standard, infinite. The regress does not, therefore, proceed to infinity (an infinity given), but only to an indefinite extent, for or the of presenting to us a quantity—realized only in and through the regress itself.

II. Solution of the Cosmological Idea of the Totality of the Division of a Whole given in Intuition

When I divide a whole which is given in intuition, I proceed from a conditioned to its conditions. The division of the parts of the whole (subdivisio or decompositio) is a regress in the series of these conditions. The absolute totality of this series would be actually attained and given to the mind, if the regress could arrive at simple parts. But if all the parts in a continuous decomposition are themselves divisible, the division, that is to say, the regress, proceeds from the conditioned to its conditions in infinitum; because the conditions (the parts) are themselves contained in the conditioned, and, as the latter is given in a limited intuition, the former are all given along with it. This regress cannot, therefore, be called a regressus in indefinitum, as happened in the case of the preceding cosmological idea, the regress in which proceeded from the conditioned to the conditions not given contemporaneously and along with it, but discoverable only through the empirical regress. We are not, however, entitled to affirm of a whole of this kind, which is divisible in infinitum, that it consists of an infinite number of parts. For, although all the parts are contained in the intuition of the whole, the whole division is not contained therein. The division is contained only in the progressing decomposition—in the regress itself, which is the condition of the possibility and actuality of the series. Now, as this regress is infinite, all the members (parts) to which it attains must be contained in the given whole as an aggregate. But the complete series of division is not contained therein. For this series, being infinite in succession and always incomplete, cannot represent an infinite number of members, and still less a composition of these members into a whole.

To apply this remark to space. Every limited part of space presented to intuition is a whole, the parts of which are always spaces—to whatever extent subdivided. Every limited space is hence divisible to infinity.

Let us again apply the remark to an external phenomenon enclosed in limits, that is, a body. The divisibility of a body rests upon the divisibility of space, which is the condition of the possibility of the body as an extended whole. A body is consequently divisible to infinity, though it does not, for that reason, consist of an infinite number of parts.

It certainly seems that, as a body must be cogitated as substance in space, the law of divisibility would not be applicable to it as substance. For we may and ought to grant, in the case of space, that division or decomposition, to any extent, never can utterly annihilate composition (that is to say, the smallest part of space must still consist of spaces); otherwise space would entirely cease to exist—which is impossible. But, the assertion on the other hand that when all composition in matter is annihilated in thought, nothing remains, does not seem to harmonize with the conception of substance, which must be properly the subject of all composition and must remain, even after the conjunction of its attributes in space—which constituted a body—is annihilated in thought. But this is not the case with substance in the phenomenal world, which is not a thing in itself cogitated by the pure category. Phenomenal substance is not an absolute subject; it is merely a permanent sensuous image, and nothing more than an intuition, in which the unconditioned is not to be found.

But, although this rule of progress to infinity is legitimate and applicable to the subdivision of a phenomenon, as a mere occupation or filling of space, it is not applicable to a whole consisting of a number of distinct parts and constituting a quantum discretum—that is to say, an organized body. It cannot be admitted that every part in an organized whole is itself organized, and that, in analysing it to infinity, we must always meet with organized parts; although we may allow that the parts of the matter which we decompose in infinitum, may be organized. For the infinity of the division of a phenomenon in space rests altogether on the fact that the divisibility of a phenomenon is given only in and through this infinity, that is, an undetermined number of parts is given, while the parts themselves are given and determined only in and through the subdivision; in a word, the infinity of the division necessarily presupposes that the whole is not already divided in se. Hence our division determines a number of parts in the whole—a number which extends just as far as the actual regress in the division; while, on the other hand, the very notion of a body organized to infinity represents the whole as already and in itself divided. We expect, therefore, to find in it a determinate, but at the same time, infinite, number of parts—which is self-contradictory. For we should thus have a whole containing a series of members which could not be completed in any regress—which is infinite, and at the same time complete in an organized composite. Infinite divisibility is applicable only to a quantum continuum, and is based entirely on the infinite divisibility of space, But in a quantum discretum the multitude of parts or units is always determined, and hence always equal to some number. To what extent a body may be organized, experience alone can inform us; and although, so far as our experience of this or that body has extended, we may not have discovered any inorganic part, such parts must exist in possible experience. But how far the transcendental division of a phenomenon must extend, we cannot know from experience—it is a question which experience cannot answer; it is answered only by the principle of reason which forbids us to consider the empirical regress, in the analysis of extended body, as ever absolutely complete.

Concluding Remark on the Solution of the Transcendental Mathematical Ideas—and Introductory to the Solution of the Dynamical Ideas.

We presented the antinomy of pure reason in a tabular form, and we endeavoured to show the ground of this self-contradiction on the part of reason, and the only means of bringing it to a conclusion—namely, by declaring both contradictory statements to be false. We represented in these antinomies the conditions of phenomena as belonging to the conditioned according to relations of space and time—which is the usual supposition of the common understanding. In this respect, all dialectical representations of totality, in the series of conditions to a given conditioned, were perfectly homogeneous. The condition was always a member of the series along with the conditioned, and thus the homogeneity of the whole series was assured. In this case the regress could never be cogitated as complete; or, if this was the case, a member really conditioned was falsely regarded as a primal member, consequently as unconditioned. In such an antinomy, therefore, we did not consider the object, that is, the conditioned, but the series of conditions belonging to the object, and the magnitude of that series. And thus arose the difficulty—a difficulty not to be settled by any decision regarding the claims of the two parties, but simply by cutting the knot—by declaring the series proposed by reason to be either too long or too short for the understanding, which could in neither case make its conceptions adequate with the ideas.

But we have overlooked, up to this point, an essential difference existing between the conceptions of the understanding which reason endeavours to raise to the rank of ideas—two of these indicating a mathematical, and two a dynamical synthesis of phenomena. Hitherto, it was necessary to signalize this distinction; for, just as in our general representation of all transcendental ideas, we considered them under phenomenal conditions, so, in the two mathematical ideas, our discussion is concerned solely with an object in the world of phenomena. But as we are now about to proceed to the consideration of the dynamical conceptions of the understanding, and their adequateness with ideas, we must not lose sight of this distinction. We shall find that it opens up to us an entirely new view of the conflict in which reason is involved. For, while in the first two antinomies, both parties were dismissed, on the ground of having advanced statements based upon false hypothesis; in the present case the hope appears of discovering a hypothesis which may be consistent with the demands of reason, and, the judge completing the statement of the grounds of claim, which both parties had left in an unsatisfactory state, the question may be settled on its own merits, not by dismissing the claimants, but by a comparison of the arguments on both sides. If we consider merely their extension, and whether they are adequate with ideas, the series of conditions may be regarded as all homogeneous. But the conception of the understanding which lies at the basis of these ideas, contains either a synthesis of the homogeneous (presupposed in every quantity—in its composition as well as in its division) or of the heterogeneous, which is the case in the dynamical synthesis of cause and effect, as well as of the necessary and the contingent.

Thus it happens that in the mathematical series of phenomena no other than a sensuous condition is admissible—a condition which is itself a member of the series; while the dynamical series of sensuous conditions admits a heterogeneous condition, which is not a member of the series, but, as purely intelligible, lies out of and beyond it. And thus reason is satisfied, and an unconditioned placed at the head of the series of phenomena, without introducing confusion into or discontinuing it, contrary to the principles of the understanding.

Now, from the fact that the dynamical ideas admit a condition of phenomena which does not form a part of the series of phenomena, arises a result which we should not have expected from an antinomy. In former cases, the result was that both contradictory dialectical statements were declared to be false. In the present case, we find the conditioned in the dynamical series connected with an empirically unconditioned, but non-sensuous condition; and thus satisfaction is done to the understanding on the one hand and to the reason on the other.[62] While, moreover, the dialectical arguments for unconditioned totality in mere phenomena fall to the ground, both propositions of reason may be shown to be true in their proper signification. This could not happen in the case of the cosmological ideas which demanded a mathematically unconditioned unity; for no condition could be placed at the head of the series of phenomena, except one which was itself a phenomenon and consequently a member of the series.

---

[62] For the understanding cannot admit among phenomena a condition which is itself empirically unconditioned. But if it is possible to cogitate an intelligible condition—one which is not a member of the series of phenomena—for a conditioned phenomenon, without breaking the series of empirical conditions, such a condition may be admissible as empirically unconditioned, and the empirical regress continue regular, unceasing, and intact.

III. Solution of the Cosmological Idea of the Totality of the Deduction of Cosmical Events from their Causes

There are only two modes of causality cogitable—the causality of nature or of freedom. The first is the conjunction of a particular state with another preceding it in the world of sense, the former following the latter by virtue of a law. Now, as the causality of phenomena is subject to conditions of time, and the preceding state, if it had always existed, could not have produced an effect which would make its first appearance at a particular time, the causality of a cause must itself be an effect—must itself have begun to be, and therefore, according to the principle of the understanding, itself requires a cause.

We must understand, on the contrary, by the term freedom, in the cosmological sense, a faculty of the spontaneous origination of a state; the causality of which, therefore, is not subordinated to another cause determining it in time. Freedom is in this sense a pure transcendental idea, which, in the first place, contains no empirical element; the object of which, in the second place, cannot be given or determined in any experience, because it is a universal law of the very possibility of experience, that everything which happens must have a cause, that consequently the causality of a cause, being itself something that has happened, must also have a cause. In this view of the case, the whole field of experience, how far soever it may extend, contains nothing that is not subject to the laws of nature. But, as we cannot by this means attain to an absolute totality of conditions in reference to the series of causes and effects, reason creates the idea of a spontaneity, which can begin to act of itself, and without any external cause determining it to action, according to the natural law of causality.

It is especially remarkable that the practical conception of freedom is based upon the transcendental idea, and that the question of the possibility of the former is difficult only as it involves the consideration of the truth of the latter. Freedom, in the practical sense, is the independence of the will of coercion by sensuous impulses. A will is sensuous, in so far as it is pathologically affected (by sensuous impulses); it is termed animal (arbitrium brutum), when it is pathologically necessitated. The human will is certainly an arbitrium sensitivum, not brutum, but liberum; because sensuousness does not necessitate its action, a faculty existing in man of self-determination, independently of all sensuous coercion.

It is plain that, if all causality in the world of sense were natural—and natural only—every event would be determined by another according to necessary laws, and that, consequently, phenomena, in so far as they determine the will, must necessitate every action as a natural effect from themselves; and thus all practical freedom would fall to the ground with the transcendental idea. For the latter presupposes that although a certain thing has not happened, it ought to have happened, and that, consequently, its phenomenal cause was not so powerful and determinative as to exclude the causality of our will—a causality capable of producing effects independently of and even in opposition to the power of natural causes, and capable, consequently, of spontaneously originating a series of events.

Here, too, we find it to be the case, as we generally found in the self-contradictions and perplexities of a reason which strives to pass the bounds of possible experience, that the problem is properly not physiological, but transcendental. The question of the possibility of freedom does indeed concern psychology; but, as it rests upon dialectical arguments of pure reason, its solution must engage the attention of transcendental philosophy. Before attempting this solution, a task which transcendental philosophy cannot decline, it will be advisable to make a remark with regard to its procedure in the settlement of the question.

If phenomena were things in themselves, and time and space forms of the existence of things, condition and conditioned would always be members of the same series; and thus would arise in the present case the antinomy common to all transcendental ideas—that their series is either too great or too small for the understanding. The dynamical ideas, which we are about to discuss in this and the following section, possess the peculiarity of relating to an object, not considered as a quantity, but as an existence; and thus, in the discussion of the present question, we may make abstraction of the quantity of the series of conditions, and consider merely the dynamical relation of the condition to the conditioned. The question, then, suggests itself, whether freedom is possible; and, if it is, whether it can consist with the universality of the natural law of causality; and, consequently, whether we enounce a proper disjunctive proposition when we say: "Every effect must have its origin either in nature or in freedom," or whether both cannot exist together in the same event in different relations. The principle of an unbroken connection between all events in the phenomenal world, in accordance with the unchangeable laws of nature, is a well-established principle of transcendental analytic which admits of no exception. The question, therefore, is: "Whether an effect, determined according to the laws of nature, can at the same time be produced by a free agent, or whether freedom and nature mutually exclude each other?" And here, the common but fallacious hypothesis of the absolute reality of phenomena manifests its injurious influence in embarrassing the procedure of reason. For if phenomena are things in themselves, freedom is impossible. In this case, nature is the complete and all-sufficient cause of every event; and condition and conditioned, cause and effect are contained in the same series, and necessitated by the same law. If, on the contrary, phenomena are held to be, as they are in fact, nothing more than mere representations, connected with each other in accordance with empirical laws, they must have a ground which is not phenomenal. But the causality of such an intelligible cause is not determined or determinable by phenomena; although its effects, as phenomena, must be determined by other phenomenal existences. This cause and its causality exist therefore out of and apart from the series of phenomena; while its effects do exist and are discoverable in the series of empirical conditions. Such an effect may therefore be considered to be free in relation to its intelligible cause, and necessary in relation to the phenomena from which it is a necessary consequence—a distinction which, stated in this perfectly general and abstract manner, must appear in the highest degree subtle and obscure. The sequel will explain. It is sufficient, at present, to remark that, as the complete and unbroken connection of phenomena is an unalterable law of nature, freedom is impossible—on the supposition that phenomena are absolutely real. Hence those philosophers who adhere to the common opinion on this subject can never succeed in reconciling the ideas of nature and freedom.

Possibility of Freedom in Harmony with the Universal Law of Natural Necessity.

That element in a sensuous object which is not itself sensuous, I may be allowed to term intelligible. If, accordingly, an object which must be regarded as a sensuous phenomenon possesses a faculty which is not an object of sensuous intuition, but by means of which it is capable of being the cause of phenomena, the causality of an object or existence of this kind may be regarded from two different points of view. It may be considered to be intelligible, as regards its action—the action of a thing which is a thing in itself, and sensuous, as regards its effects—the effects of a phenomenon belonging to the sensuous world. We should accordingly, have to form both an empirical and an intellectual conception of the causality of such a faculty or power—both, however, having reference to the same effect. This twofold manner of cogitating a power residing in a sensuous object does not run counter to any of the conceptions which we ought to form of the world of phenomena or of a possible experience. Phenomena—not being things in themselves—must have a transcendental object as a foundation, which determines them as mere representations; and there seems to be no reason why we should not ascribe to this transcendental object, in addition to the property of self-phenomenization, a causality whose effects are to be met with in the world of phenomena, although it is not itself a phenomenon. But every effective cause must possess a character, that is to say, a law of its causality, without which it would cease to be a cause. In the above case, then, every sensuous object would possess an empirical character, which guaranteed that its actions, as phenomena, stand in complete and harmonious connection, conformably to unvarying natural laws, with all other phenomena, and can be deduced from these, as conditions, and that they do thus, in connection with these, constitute a series in the order of nature. This sensuous object must, in the second place, possess an intelligible character, which guarantees it to be the cause of those actions, as phenomena, although it is not itself a phenomenon nor subordinate to the conditions of the world of sense. The former may be termed the character of the thing as a phenomenon, the latter the character of the thing as a thing in itself.

Now this active subject would, in its character of intelligible subject, be subordinate to no conditions of time, for time is only a condition of phenomena, and not of things in themselves. No action would begin or cease to be in this subject; it would consequently be free from the law of all determination of time—the law of change, namely, that everything which happens must have a cause in the phenomena of a preceding state. In one word, the causality of the subject, in so far as it is intelligible, would not form part of the series of empirical conditions which determine and necessitate an event in the world of sense. Again, this intelligible character of a thing cannot be immediately cognized, because we can perceive nothing but phenomena, but it must be capable of being cogitated in harmony with the empirical character; for we always find ourselves compelled to place, in thought, a transcendental object at the basis of phenomena although we can never know what this object is in itself.

In virtue of its empirical character, this subject would at the same time be subordinate to all the empirical laws of causality, and, as a phenomenon and member of the sensuous world, its effects would have to be accounted for by a reference to preceding phenomena. Eternal phenomena must be capable of influencing it; and its actions, in accordance with natural laws, must explain to us how its empirical character, that is, the law of its causality, is to be cognized in and by means of experience. In a word, all requisites for a complete and necessary determination of these actions must be presented to us by experience.

In virtue of its intelligible character, on the other hand (although we possess only a general conception of this character), the subject must be regarded as free from all sensuous influences, and from all phenomenal determination. Moreover, as nothing happens in this subject—for it is a noumenon, and there does not consequently exist in it any change, demanding the dynamical determination of time, and for the same reason no connection with phenomena as causes—this active existence must in its actions be free from and independent of natural necessity, for this necessity exists only in the world of phenomena. It would be quite correct to say that it originates or begins its effects in the world of sense from itself, although the action productive of these effects does not begin in itself. We should not be in this case affirming that these sensuous effects began to exist of themselves, because they are always determined by prior empirical conditions—by virtue of the empirical character, which is the phenomenon of the intelligible character—and are possible only as constituting a continuation of the series of natural causes. And thus nature and freedom, each in the complete and absolute signification of these terms, can exist, without contradiction or disagreement, in the same action.

Exposition of the Cosmological Idea of Freedom in Harmony with the Universal Law of Natural Necessity.

I have thought it advisable to lay before the reader at first merely a sketch of the solution of this transcendental problem, in order to enable him to form with greater ease a clear conception of the course which reason must adopt in the solution. I shall now proceed to exhibit the several momenta of this solution, and to consider them in their order.

The natural law that everything which happens must have a cause, that the causality of this cause, that is, the action of the cause (which cannot always have existed, but must be itself an event, for it precedes in time some effect which it has originated), must have itself a phenomenal cause, by which it is determined and, and, consequently, all events are empirically determined in an order of nature—this law, I say, which lies at the foundation of the possibility of experience, and of a connected system of phenomena or nature is a law of the understanding, from which no departure, and to which no exception, can be admitted. For to except even a single phenomenon from its operation is to exclude it from the sphere of possible experience and thus to admit it to be a mere fiction of thought or phantom of the brain.

Thus we are obliged to acknowledge the existence of a chain of causes, in which, however, absolute totality cannot be found. But we need not detain ourselves with this question, for it has already been sufficiently answered in our discussion of the antinomies into which reason falls, when it attempts to reach the unconditioned in the series of phenomena. If we permit ourselves to be deceived by the illusion of transcendental idealism, we shall find that neither nature nor freedom exists. Now the question is: "Whether, admitting the existence of natural necessity in the world of phenomena, it is possible to consider an effect as at the same time an effect of nature and an effect of freedom—or, whether these two modes of causality are contradictory and incompatible?"

No phenomenal cause can absolutely and of itself begin a series. Every action, in so far as it is productive of an event, is itself an event or occurrence, and presupposes another preceding state, in which its cause existed. Thus everything that happens is but a continuation of a series, and an absolute beginning is impossible in the sensuous world. The actions of natural causes are, accordingly, themselves effects, and presuppose causes preceding them in time. A primal action which forms an absolute beginning, is beyond the causal power of phenomena.

Now, is it absolutely necessary that, granting that all effects are phenomena, the causality of the cause of these effects must also be a phenomenon and belong to the empirical world? Is it not rather possible that, although every effect in the phenomenal world must be connected with an empirical cause, according to the universal law of nature, this empirical causality may be itself the effect of a non-empirical and intelligible causality—its connection with natural causes remaining nevertheless intact? Such a causality would be considered, in reference to phenomena, as the primal action of a cause, which is in so far, therefore, not phenomenal, but, by reason of this faculty or power, intelligible; although it must, at the same time, as a link in the chain of nature, be regarded as belonging to the sensuous world.

A belief in the reciprocal causality of phenomena is necessary, if we are required to look for and to present the natural conditions of natural events, that is to say, their causes. This being admitted as unexceptionably valid, the requirements of the understanding, which recognizes nothing but nature in the region of phenomena, are satisfied, and our physical explanations of physical phenomena may proceed in their regular course, without hindrance and without opposition. But it is no stumbling-block in the way, even assuming the idea to be a pure fiction, to admit that there are some natural causes in the possession of a faculty which is not empirical, but intelligible, inasmuch as it is not determined to action by empirical conditions, but purely and solely upon grounds brought forward by the understanding—this action being still, when the cause is phenomenized, in perfect accordance with the laws of empirical causality. Thus the acting subject, as a causal phenomenon, would continue to preserve a complete connection with nature and natural conditions; and the phenomenon only of the subject (with all its phenomenal causality) would contain certain conditions, which, if we ascend from the empirical to the transcendental object, must necessarily be regarded as intelligible. For, if we attend, in our inquiries with regard to causes in the world of phenomena, to the directions of nature alone, we need not trouble ourselves about the relation in which the transcendental subject, which is completely unknown to us, stands to these phenomena and their connection in nature. The intelligible ground of phenomena in this subject does not concern empirical questions. It has to do only with pure thought; and, although the effects of this thought and action of the pure understanding are discoverable in phenomena, these phenomena must nevertheless be capable of a full and complete explanation, upon purely physical grounds and in accordance with natural laws. And in this case we attend solely to their empirical and omit all consideration of their intelligible character (which is the transcendental cause of the former) as completely unknown, except in so far as it is exhibited by the latter as its empirical symbol. Now let us apply this to experience. Man is a phenomenon of the sensuous world and, at the same time, therefore, a natural cause, the causality of which must be regulated by empirical laws. As such, he must possess an empirical character, like all other natural phenomena. We remark this empirical character in his actions, which reveal the presence of certain powers and faculties. If we consider inanimate or merely animal nature, we can discover no reason for ascribing to ourselves any other than a faculty which is determined in a purely sensuous manner. But man, to whom nature reveals herself only through sense, cognizes himself not only by his senses, but also through pure apperception; and this in actions and internal determinations, which he cannot regard as sensuous impressions. He is thus to himself, on the one hand, a phenomenon, but on the other hand, in respect of certain faculties, a purely intelligible object—intelligible, because its action cannot be ascribed to sensuous receptivity. These faculties are understanding and reason. The latter, especially, is in a peculiar manner distinct from all empirically-conditioned faculties, for it employs ideas alone in the consideration of its objects, and by means of these determines the understanding, which then proceeds to make an empirical use of its own conceptions, which, like the ideas of reason, are pure and non-empirical.

That reason possesses the faculty of causality, or that at least we are compelled so to represent it, is evident from the imperatives, which in the sphere of the practical we impose on many of our executive powers. The words I ought express a species of necessity, and imply a connection with grounds which nature does not and cannot present to the mind of man. Understanding knows nothing in nature but that which is, or has been, or will be. It would be absurd to say that anything in nature ought to be other than it is in the relations of time in which it stands; indeed, the ought, when we consider merely the course of nature, has neither application nor meaning. The question, "What ought to happen in the sphere of nature?" is just as absurd as the question, "What ought to be the properties of a circle?" All that we are entitled to ask is, "What takes place in nature?" or, in the latter case, "What are the properties of a circle?"

But the idea of an ought or of duty indicates a possible action, the ground of which is a pure conception; while the ground of a merely natural action is, on the contrary, always a phenomenon. This action must certainly be possible under physical conditions, if it is prescribed by the moral imperative ought; but these physical or natural conditions do not concern the determination of the will itself, they relate to its effects alone, and the consequences of the effect in the world of phenomena. Whatever number of motives nature may present to my will, whatever sensuous impulses—the moral ought it is beyond their power to produce. They may produce a volition, which, so far from being necessary, is always conditioned—a volition to which the ought enunciated by reason, sets an aim and a standard, gives permission or prohibition. Be the object what it may, purely sensuous—as pleasure, or presented by pure reason—as good, reason will not yield to grounds which have an empirical origin. Reason will not follow the order of things presented by experience, but, with perfect spontaneity, rearranges them according to ideas, with which it compels empirical conditions to agree. It declares, in the name of these ideas, certain actions to be necessary which nevertheless have not taken place and which perhaps never will take place; and yet presupposes that it possesses the faculty of causality in relation to these actions. For, in the absence of this supposition, it could not expect its ideas to produce certain effects in the world of experience.

Now, let us stop here and admit it to be at least possible that reason does stand in a really causal relation to phenomena. In this case it must—pure reason as it is—exhibit an empirical character. For every cause supposes a rule, according to which certain phenomena follow as effects from the cause, and every rule requires uniformity in these effects; and this is the proper ground of the conception of a cause—as a faculty or power. Now this conception (of a cause) may be termed the empirical character of reason; and this character is a permanent one, while the effects produced appear, in conformity with the various conditions which accompany and partly limit them, in various forms.

Thus the volition of every man has an empirical character, which is nothing more than the causality of his reason, in so far as its effects in the phenomenal world manifest the presence of a rule, according to which we are enabled to examine, in their several kinds and degrees, the actions of this causality and the rational grounds for these actions, and in this way to decide upon the subjective principles of the volition. Now we learn what this empirical character is only from phenomenal effects, and from the rule of these which is presented by experience; and for this reason all the actions of man in the world of phenomena are determined by his empirical character, and the co-operative causes of nature. If, then, we could investigate all the phenomena of human volition to their lowest foundation in the mind, there would be no action which we could not anticipate with certainty, and recognize to be absolutely necessary from its preceding conditions. So far as relates to this empirical character, therefore, there can be no freedom; and it is only in the light of this character that we can consider the human will, when we confine ourselves to simple observation and, as is the case in anthropology, institute a physiological investigation of the motive causes of human actions.

But when we consider the same actions in relation to reason—not for the purpose of explaining their origin, that is, in relation to speculative reason, but to practical reason, as the producing cause of these actions—we shall discover a rule and an order very different from those of nature and experience. For the declaration of this mental faculty may be that what has and could not but take place in the course of nature, ought not to have taken place. Sometimes, too, we discover, or believe that we discover, that the ideas of reason did actually stand in a causal relation to certain actions of man; and that these actions have taken place because they were determined, not by empirical causes, but by the act of the will upon grounds of reason.

Now, granting that reason stands in a causal relation to phenomena; can an action of reason be called free, when we know that, sensuously, in its empirical character, it is completely determined and absolutely necessary? But this empirical character is itself determined by the intelligible character. The latter we cannot cognize; we can only indicate it by means of phenomena, which enable us to have an immediate cognition only of the empirical character.[63] An action, then, in so far as it is to be ascribed to an intelligible cause, does not result from it in accordance with empirical laws. That is to say, not the conditions of pure reason, but only their effects in the internal sense, precede the act. Pure reason, as a purely intelligible faculty, is not subject to the conditions of time. The causality of reason in its intelligible character does not begin to be; it does not make its appearance at

[63] The real morality of actions—their merit or demerit, and even that of our own conduct, is completely unknown to us. Our estimates can relate only to their empirical character. How much is the result of the action of free will, how much is to be ascribed to nature and to blameless error, or to a happy constitution of temperament (merito fortunae), no one can discover, nor, for this reason, determine with perfect justice.

a certain time, for the purpose of producing an effect. If this were not the case, the causality of reason would be subservient to the natural law of phenomena, which determines them according to time, and as a series of causes and effects in time; it would consequently cease to be freedom and become a part of nature. We are therefore justified in saying: "If reason stands in a causal relation to phenomena, it is a faculty which originates the sensuous condition of an empirical series of effects." For the condition, which resides in the reason, is non-sensuous, and therefore cannot be originated, or begin to be. And thus we find—what we could not discover in any empirical series—a condition of a successive series of events itself empirically unconditioned. For, in the present case, the condition stands out of and beyond the series of phenomena—it is intelligible, and it consequently cannot be subjected to any sensuous condition, or to any time-determination by a preceding cause.

But, in another respect, the same cause belongs also to the series of phenomena. Man is himself a phenomenon. His will has an empirical character, which is the empirical cause of all his actions. There is no condition—determining man and his volition in conformity with this character—which does not itself form part of the series of effects in nature, and is subject to their law—the law according to which an empirically undetermined cause of an event in time cannot exist. For this reason no given action can have an absolute and spontaneous origination, all actions being phenomena, and belonging to the world of experience. But it cannot be said of reason, that the state in which it determines the will is always preceded by some other state determining it. For reason is not a phenomenon, and therefore not subject to sensuous conditions; and, consequently, even in relation to its causality, the sequence or conditions of time do not influence reason, nor can the dynamical law of nature, which determines the sequence of time according to certain rules, be applied to it.

Reason is consequently the permanent condition of all actions of the human will. Each of these is determined in the empirical character of the man, even before it has taken place. The intelligible character, of which the former is but the sensuous schema, knows no before or after; and every action, irrespective of the time-relation in which it stands with other phenomena, is the immediate effect of the intelligible character of pure reason, which, consequently, enjoys freedom of action, and is not dynamically determined either by internal or external preceding conditions. This freedom must not be described, in a merely negative manner, as independence of empirical conditions, for in this case the faculty of reason would cease to be a cause of phenomena; but it must be regarded, positively, as a faculty which can spontaneously originate a series of events. At the same time, it must not be supposed that any beginning can take place in reason; on the contrary, reason, as the unconditioned condition of all action of the will, admits of no time-conditions, although its effect does really begin in a series of phenomena—a beginning which is not, however, absolutely primal.

I shall illustrate this regulative principle of reason by an example, from its employment in the world of experience; proved it cannot be by any amount of experience, or by any number of facts, for such arguments cannot establish the truth of transcendental propositions. Let us take a voluntary action—for example, a falsehood—by means of which a man has introduced a certain degree of confusion into the social life of humanity, which is judged according to the motives from which it originated, and the blame of which and of the evil consequences arising from it, is imputed to the offender. We at first proceed to examine the empirical character of the offence, and for this purpose we endeavour to penetrate to the sources of that character, such as a defective education, bad company, a shameless and wicked disposition, frivolity, and want of reflection—not forgetting also the occasioning causes which prevailed at the moment of the transgression. In this the procedure is exactly the same as that pursued in the investigation of the series of causes which determine a given physical effect. Now, although we believe the action to have been determined by all these circumstances, we do not the less blame the offender. We do not blame him for his unhappy disposition, nor for the circumstances which influenced him, nay, not even for his former course of life; for we presuppose that all these considerations may be set aside, that the series of preceding conditions may be regarded as having never existed, and that the action may be considered as completely unconditioned in relation to any state preceding, just as if the agent commenced with it an entirely new series of effects. Our blame of the offender is grounded upon a law of reason, which requires us to regard this faculty as a cause, which could have and ought to have otherwise determined the behaviour of the culprit, independently of all empirical conditions. This causality of reason we do not regard as a co-operating agency, but as complete in itself. It matters not whether the sensuous impulses favoured or opposed the action of this causality, the offence is estimated according to its intelligible character—the offender is decidedly worthy of blame, the moment he utters a falsehood. It follows that we regard reason, in spite of the empirical conditions of the act, as completely free, and therefore, as in the present case, culpable.

The above judgement is complete evidence that we are accustomed to think that reason is not affected by sensuous conditions, that in it no change takes place—although its phenomena, in other words, the mode in which it appears in its effects, are subject to change—that in it no preceding state determines the following, and, consequently, that it does not form a member of the series of sensuous conditions which necessitate phenomena according to natural laws. Reason is present and the same in all human actions and at all times; but it does not itself exist in time, and therefore does not enter upon any state in which it did not formerly exist. It is, relatively to new states or conditions, determining, but not determinable. Hence we cannot ask: "Why did not reason determine itself in a different manner?" The question ought to be thus stated: "Why did not reason employ its power of causality to determine certain phenomena in a different manner?" But this is a question which admits of no answer. For a different intelligible character would have exhibited a different empirical character; and, when we say that, in spite of the course which his whole former life has taken, the offender could have refrained from uttering the falsehood, this means merely that the act was subject to the power and authority—permissive or prohibitive—of reason. Now, reason is not subject in its causality to any conditions of phenomena or of time; and a difference in time may produce a difference in the relation of phenomena to each other—for these are not things and therefore not causes in themselves—but it cannot produce any difference in the relation in which the action stands to the faculty of reason.

Thus, then, in our investigation into free actions and the causal power which produced them, we arrive at an intelligible cause, beyond which, however, we cannot go; although we can recognize that it is free, that is, independent of all sensuous conditions, and that, in this way, it may be the sensuously unconditioned condition of phenomena. But for what reason the intelligible character generates such and such phenomena and exhibits such and such an empirical character under certain circumstances, it is beyond the power of our reason to decide. The question is as much above the power and the sphere of reason as the following would be: "Why does the transcendental object of our external sensuous intuition allow of no other form than that of intuition in space?" But the problem, which we were called upon to solve, does not require us to entertain any such questions. The problem was merely this—whether freedom and natural necessity can exist without opposition in the same action. To this question we have given a sufficient answer; for we have shown that, as the former stands in a relation to a different kind of condition from those of the latter, the law of the one does not affect the law of the other and that, consequently, both can exist together in independence of and without interference with each other.

The reader must be careful to remark that my intention in the above remarks has not been to prove the actual existence of freedom, as a faculty in which resides the cause of certain sensuous phenomena. For, not to mention that such an argument would not have a transcendental character, nor have been limited to the discussion of pure conceptions—all attempts at inferring from experience what cannot be cogitated in accordance with its laws, must ever be unsuccessful. Nay, more, I have not even aimed at demonstrating the possibility of freedom; for this too would have been a vain endeavour, inasmuch as it is beyond the power of the mind to cognize the possibility of a reality or of a causal power by the aid of mere à priori conceptions. Freedom has been considered in the foregoing remarks only as a transcendental idea, by means of which reason aims at originating a series of conditions in the world of phenomena with the help of that which is sensuously unconditioned, involving itself, however, in an antinomy with the laws which itself prescribes for the conduct of the understanding. That this antinomy is based upon a mere illusion, and that nature and freedom are at least not opposed—this was the only thing in our power to prove, and the question which it was our task to solve.

IV. Solution of the Cosmological Idea of the Totality of the Dependence of Phenomenal Existences

In the preceding remarks, we considered the changes in the world of sense as constituting a dynamical series, in which each member is subordinated to another—as its cause. Our present purpose is to avail ourselves of this series of states or conditions as a guide to an existence which may be the highest condition of all changeable phenomena, that is, to a necessary being. Our endeavour to reach, not the unconditioned causality, but the unconditioned existence, of substance. The series before us is therefore a series of conceptions, and not of intuitions (in which the one intuition is the condition of the other).

But it is evident that, as all phenomena are subject to change and conditioned in their existence, the series of dependent existences cannot embrace an unconditioned member, the existence of which would be absolutely necessary. It follows that, if phenomena were things in themselves, and—as an immediate consequence from this supposition—condition and conditioned belonged to the same series of phenomena, the existence of a necessary being, as the condition of the existence of sensuous phenomena, would be perfectly impossible.

An important distinction, however, exists between the dynamical and the mathematical regress. The latter is engaged solely with the combination of parts into a whole, or with the division of a whole into its parts; and therefore are the conditions of its series parts of the series, and to be consequently regarded as homogeneous, and for this reason, as consisting, without exception, of phenomena. If the former regress, on the contrary, the aim of which is not to establish the possibility of an unconditioned whole consisting of given parts, or of an unconditioned part of a given whole, but to demonstrate the possibility of the deduction of a certain state from its cause, or of the contingent existence of substance from that which exists necessarily, it is not requisite that the condition should form part of an empirical series along with the conditioned.

In the case of the apparent antinomy with which we are at present dealing, there exists a way of escape from the difficulty; for it is not impossible that both of the contradictory statements may be true in different relations. All sensuous phenomena may be contingent, and consequently possess only an empirically conditioned existence, and yet there may also exist a non-empirical condition of the whole series, or, in other words, a necessary being. For this necessary being, as an intelligible condition, would not form a member—not even the highest member—of the series; the whole world of sense would be left in its empirically determined existence uninterfered with and uninfluenced. This would also form a ground of distinction between the modes of solution employed for the third and fourth antinomies. For, while in the consideration of freedom in the former antinomy, the thing itself—the cause (substantia phaenomenon)—was regarded as belonging to the series of conditions, and only its causality to the intelligible world—we are obliged in the present case to cogitate this necessary being as purely intelligible and as existing entirely apart from the world of sense (as an ens extramundanum); for otherwise it would be subject to the phenomenal law of contingency and dependence.

In relation to the present problem, therefore, the regulative principle of reason is that everything in the sensuous world possesses an empirically conditioned existence—that no property of the sensuous world possesses unconditioned necessity—that we are bound to expect, and, so far as is possible, to seek for the empirical condition of every member in the series of conditions—and that there is no sufficient reason to justify us in deducing any existence from a condition which lies out of and beyond the empirical series, or in regarding any existence as independent and self-subsistent; although this should not prevent us from recognizing the possibility of the whole series being based upon a being which is intelligible, and for this reason free from all empirical conditions.

But it has been far from my intention, in these remarks, to prove the existence of this unconditioned and necessary being, or even to evidence the possibility of a purely intelligible condition of the existence of all sensuous phenomena. As bounds were set to reason, to prevent it from leaving the guiding thread of empirical conditions and losing itself in transcendent theories which are incapable of concrete presentation; so it was my purpose, on the other hand, to set bounds to the law of the purely empirical understanding, and to protest against any attempts on its part at deciding on the possibility of things, or declaring the existence of the intelligible to be impossible, merely on the ground that it is not available for the explanation and exposition of phenomena. It has been shown, at the same time, that the contingency of all the phenomena of nature and their empirical conditions is quite consistent with the arbitrary hypothesis of a necessary, although purely intelligible condition, that no real contradiction exists between them and that, consequently, both may be true. The existence of such an absolutely necessary being may be impossible; but this can never be demonstrated from the universal contingency and dependence of sensuous phenomena, nor from the principle which forbids us to discontinue the series at some member of it, or to seek for its cause in some sphere of existence beyond the world of nature. Reason goes its way in the empirical world, and follows, too, its peculiar path in the sphere of the transcendental.

The sensuous world contains nothing but phenomena, which are mere representations, and always sensuously conditioned; things in themselves are not, and cannot be, objects to us. It is not to be wondered at, therefore, that we are not justified in leaping from some member of an empirical series beyond the world of sense, as if empirical representations were things in themselves, existing apart from their transcendental ground in the human mind, and the cause of whose existence may be sought out of the empirical series. This would certainly be the case with contingent things; but it cannot be with mere representations of things, the contingency of which is itself merely a phenomenon and can relate to no other regress than that which determines phenomena, that is, the empirical. But to cogitate an intelligible ground of phenomena, as free, moreover, from the contingency of the latter, conflicts neither with the unlimited nature of the empirical regress, nor with the complete contingency of phenomena. And the demonstration of this was the only thing necessary for the solution of this apparent antinomy. For if the condition of every conditioned—as regards its existence—is sensuous, and for this reason a part of the same series, it must be itself conditioned, as was shown in the antithesis of the fourth antinomy. The embarrassments into which a reason, which postulates the unconditioned, necessarily falls, must, therefore, continue to exist; or the unconditioned must be placed in the sphere of the intelligible. In this way, its necessity does not require, nor does it even permit, the presence of an empirical condition: and it is, consequently, unconditionally necessary.

The empirical employment of reason is not affected by the assumption of a purely intelligible being; it continues its operations on the principle of the contingency of all phenomena, proceeding from empirical conditions to still higher and higher conditions, themselves empirical. Just as little does this regulative principle exclude the assumption of an intelligible cause, when the question regards merely the pure employment of reason—in relation to ends or aims. For, in this case, an intelligible cause signifies merely the transcendental and to us unknown ground of the possibility of sensuous phenomena, and its existence, necessary and independent of all sensuous conditions, is not inconsistent with the contingency of phenomena, or with the unlimited possibility of regress which exists in the series of empirical conditions.

Concluding Remarks on the Antinomy of Pure Reason.

So long as the object of our rational conceptions is the totality of conditions in the world of phenomena, and the satisfaction, from this source, of the requirements of reason, so long are our ideas transcendental and cosmological. But when we set the unconditioned—which is the aim of all our inquiries—in a sphere which lies out of the world of sense and possible experience, our ideas become transcendent. They are then not merely serviceable towards the completion of the exercise of reason (which remains an idea, never executed, but always to be pursued); they detach themselves completely from experience and construct for themselves objects, the material of which has not been presented by experience, and the objective reality of which is not based upon the completion of the empirical series, but upon pure à priori conceptions. The intelligible object of these transcendent ideas may be conceded, as a transcendental object. But we cannot cogitate it as a thing determinable by certain distinct predicates relating to its internal nature, for it has no connection with empirical conceptions; nor are we justified in affirming the existence of any such object. It is, consequently, a mere product of the mind alone. Of all the cosmological ideas, however, it is that occasioning the fourth antinomy which compels us to venture upon this step. For the existence of phenomena, always conditioned and never self-subsistent, requires us to look for an object different from phenomena—an intelligible object, with which all contingency must cease. But, as we have allowed ourselves to assume the existence of a self-subsistent reality out of the field of experience, and are therefore obliged to regard phenomena as merely a contingent mode of representing intelligible objects employed by beings which are themselves intelligences—no other course remains for us than to follow analogy and employ the same mode in forming some conception of intelligible things, of which we have not the least knowledge, which nature taught us to use in the formation of empirical conceptions. Experience made us acquainted with the contingent. But we are at present engaged in the discussion of things which are not objects of experience; and must, therefore, deduce our knowledge of them from that which is necessary absolutely and in itself, that is, from pure conceptions. Hence the first step which we take out of the world of sense obliges us to begin our system of new cognition with the investigation of a necessary being, and to deduce from our conceptions of it all our conceptions of intelligible things. This we propose to attempt in the following chapter.

Chapter III

The Ideal of Pure Reason

Section I. Of the Ideal in General

We have seen that pure conceptions do not present objects to the mind, except under sensuous conditions; because the conditions of objective reality do not exist in these conceptions, which contain, in fact, nothing but the mere form of thought. They may, however, when applied to phenomena, be presented in concreto; for it is phenomena that present to them the materials for the formation of empirical conceptions, which are nothing more than concrete forms of the conceptions of the understanding. But ideas are still further removed from objective reality than categories; for no phenomenon can ever present them to the human mind in concreto. They contain a certain perfection, attainable by no possible empirical cognition; and they give to reason a systematic unity, to which the unity of experience attempts to approximate, but can never completely attain.

But still further removed than the idea from objective reality is the Ideal, by which term I understand the idea, not in concreto, but in individuo—as an individual thing, determinable or determined by the idea alone. The idea of humanity in its complete perfection supposes not only the advancement of all the powers and faculties, which constitute our conception of human nature, to a complete attainment of their final aims, but also everything which is requisite for the complete determination of the idea; for of all contradictory predicates, only one can conform with the idea of the perfect man. What I have termed an ideal was in Plato's philosophy an idea of the divine mind—an individual object present to its pure intuition, the most perfect of every kind of possible beings, and the archetype of all phenomenal existences.

Without rising to these speculative heights, we are bound to confess that human reason contains not only ideas, but ideals, which possess, not, like those of Plato, creative, but certainly practical power—as regulative principles, and form the basis of the perfectibility of certain actions. Moral conceptions are not perfectly pure conceptions of reason, because an empirical element—of pleasure or pain—lies at the foundation of them. In relation, however, to the principle, whereby reason sets bounds to a freedom which is in itself without law, and consequently when we attend merely to their form, they may be considered as pure conceptions of reason. Virtue and wisdom in their perfect purity are ideas. But the wise man of the Stoics is an ideal, that is to say, a human being existing only in thought and in complete conformity with the idea of wisdom. As the idea provides a rule, so the ideal serves as an archetype for the perfect and complete determination of the copy. Thus the conduct of this wise and divine man serves us as a standard of action, with which we may compare and judge ourselves, which may help us to reform ourselves, although the perfection it demands can never be attained by us. Although we cannot concede objective reality to these ideals, they are not to be considered as chimeras; on the contrary, they provide reason with a standard, which enables it to estimate, by comparison, the degree of incompleteness in the objects presented to it. But to aim at realizing the ideal in an example in the world of experience—to describe, for instance, the character of the perfectly wise man in a romance—is impracticable. Nay more, there is something absurd in the attempt; and the result must be little edifying, as the natural limitations, which are continually breaking in upon the perfection and completeness of the idea, destroy the illusion in the story and throw an air of suspicion even on what is good in the idea, which hence appears fictitious and unreal.

Such is the constitution of the ideal of reason, which is always based upon determinate conceptions, and serves as a rule and a model for limitation or of criticism. Very different is the nature of the ideals of the imagination. Of these it is impossible to present an intelligible conception; they are a kind of monogram, drawn according to no determinate rule, and forming rather a vague picture—the production of many diverse experiences—than a determinate image. Such are the ideals which painters and physiognomists profess to have in their minds, and which can serve neither as a model for production nor as a standard for appreciation. They may be termed, though improperly, sensuous ideals, as they are declared to be models of certain possible empirical intuitions. They cannot, however, furnish rules or standards for explanation or examination.

In its ideals, reason aims at complete and perfect determination according to à priori rules; and hence it cogitates an object, which must be completely determinable in conformity with principles, although all empirical conditions are absent, and the conception of the object is on this account transcendent.

Section II. Of the Transcendental Ideal (Prototypon Trancendentale)

Every conception is, in relation to that which is not contained in it, undetermined and subject to the principle of determinability. This principle is that, of every two contradictorily opposed predicates, only one can belong to a conception. It is a purely logical principle, itself based upon the principle of contradiction; inasmuch as it makes complete abstraction of the content and attends merely to the logical form of the cognition.

But again, everything, as regards its possibility, is also subject to the principle of complete determination, according to which one of all the possible contradictory predicates of things must belong to it. This principle is not based merely upon that of contradiction; for, in addition to the relation between two contradictory predicates, it regards everything as standing in a relation to the sum of possibilities, as the sum total of all predicates of things, and, while presupposing this sum as an à priori condition, presents to the mind everything as receiving the possibility of its individual existence from the relation it bears to, and the share it possesses in, the aforesaid sum of possibilities.[64] The principle of complete determination relates the content and not to the logical form. It is the principle of the synthesis of all the predicates which are required to constitute the complete conception of a thing, and not a mere principle analytical representation, which enounces that one of two contradictory predicates must belong to a conception. It contains, moreover, a transcendental presupposition—that, namely, of the material for all possibility, which must contain à priori the data for this or that particular possibility.

The proposition, everything which exists is completely determined, means not only that one of every pair of given contradictory attributes, but that one of all possible attributes, is always predicable of the thing; in it the predicates are not merely compared logically with each other, but the thing itself is transcendentally compared with the sum-total of all possible predicates. The proposition is equivalent to saying: "To attain to a complete knowledge of a thing, it is necessary to possess a knowledge of everything that is possible, and to determine it thereby in a positive or negative manner." The conception of complete determination is consequently a conception which cannot be presented in its totality in concreto, and is therefore based upon an idea, which has its seat in the reason—the faculty which prescribes to the understanding the laws of its harmonious and perfect exercise.

Now, although this idea of the sum-total of all possibility, in so far as it forms the condition of the complete determination of everything, is itself undetermined in relation to the predicates which may constitute this sum-total, and we cogitate in it merely the sum-total of all possible predicates—we nevertheless find, upon closer examination, that this idea, as a primitive conception of the mind, excludes a large number of predicates—those deduced and those irreconcilable with others, and that it is evolved as a conception completely determined à priori. Thus it becomes the conception of an individual object, which is completely determined by and through the mere idea, and must consequently be termed an ideal of pure reason.

When we consider all possible predicates, not merely logically, but transcendentally, that is to say, with reference to the content which may be cogitated as existing in them à priori, we shall find that some indicate a being, others merely a non-being. The logical negation expressed in the word not does not properly belong to a conception, but only to the relation of one conception to another in a judgement, and is consequently quite insufficient to present to the

[64] Thus this principle declares everything to possess a relation to a common correlate—the sum-total of possibility, which, if discovered to exist in the idea of one individual thing, would establish the affinity of all possible things, from the identity of the ground of their complete determination. The determinability of every conception is subordinate to the universality (Allgemeinheit, universalitas) of the principle of excluded middle; the determination of a thing to the totality (Allheit, universitas) of all possible predicates.

mind the content of a conception. The expression not mortal does not indicate that a non-being is cogitated in the object; it does not concern the content at all. A transcendental negation, on the contrary, indicates non-being in itself, and is opposed to transcendental affirmation, the conception of which of itself expresses a being. Hence this affirmation indicates a reality, because in and through it objects are considered to be something—to be things; while the opposite negation, on the other hand, indicates a mere want, or privation, or absence, and, where such negations alone are attached to a representation, the non-existence of anything corresponding to the representation.

Now a negation cannot be cogitated as determined, without cogitating at the same time the opposite affirmation. The man born blind has not the least notion of darkness, because he has none of light; the vagabond knows nothing of poverty, because he has never known what it is to be in comfort;[65] the ignorant man has no conception of his ignorance, because he has no conception of knowledge. All conceptions of negatives are accordingly derived or deduced conceptions; and realities contain the data, and, so to speak, the material or transcendental content of the possibility and complete determination of all things.

If, therefore, a transcendental substratum lies at the foundation of the complete determination of things—a substratum which is to form the fund from which all possible predicates of things are to be supplied, this substratum cannot be anything else than the idea of a sum-total of reality (omnitudo realitatis). In this view, negations are nothing but limitations—a term which could not, with propriety, be applied to them, if the unlimited (the all) did not form the true basis of our conception.

This conception of a sum-total of reality is the conception of a thing in itself, regarded as completely determined; and the conception of an ens realissimum is the conception of an individual being, inasmuch as it is determined by that predicate of all possible contradictory predicates, which indicates and belongs to being. It is, therefore, a transcendental ideal which forms the basis of the complete determination of everything that exists, and is the highest material condition of its possibility—a condition on which must rest the cogitation of all objects with respect to their content. Nay, more, this ideal is the only proper ideal of which the human mind is capable; because in this case alone a general conception of a thing is completely determined by and through itself, and cognized as the representation of an individuum.

The logical determination of a conception is based upon a disjunctive syllogism, the major of which contains the logical division of the extent of a general

[65] The investigations and calculations of astronomers have taught us much that is wonderful; but the most important lesson we have received from them is the discovery of the abyss of our ignorance in relation to the universe—an ignorance the magnitude of which reason, without the information thus derived, could never have conceived. This discovery of our deficiencies must produce a great change in the determination of the aims of human reason.

conception, the minor limits this extent to a certain part, while the conclusion determines the conception by this part. The general conception of a reality cannot be divided à priori, because, without the aid of experience, we cannot know any determinate kinds of reality, standing under the former as the genus. The transcendental principle of the complete determination of all things is therefore merely the representation of the sum-total of all reality; it is not a conception which is the genus of all predicates under itself, but one which comprehends them all within itself. The complete determination of a thing is consequently based upon the limitation of this total of reality, so much being predicated of the thing, while all that remains over is excluded—a procedure which is in exact agreement with that of the disjunctive syllogism and the determination of the objects in the conclusion by one of the members of the division. It follows that reason, in laying the transcendental ideal at the foundation of its determination of all possible things, takes a course in exact analogy with that which it pursues in disjunctive syllogisms—a proposition which formed the basis of the systematic division of all transcendental ideas, according to which they are produced in complete parallelism with the three modes of syllogistic reasoning employed by the human mind.

It is self-evident that reason, in cogitating the necessary complete determination of things, does not presuppose the existence of a being corresponding to its ideal, but merely the idea of the ideal—for the purpose of deducing from the unconditional totality of complete determination, The ideal is therefore the prototype of all things, which, as defective copies (ectypa), receive from it the material of their possibility, and approximate to it more or less, though it is impossible that they can ever attain to its perfection.

The possibility of things must therefore be regarded as derived—except that of the thing which contains in itself all reality, which must be considered to be primitive and original. For all negations—and they are the only predicates by means of which all other things can be distinguished from the ens realissimum—are mere limitations of a greater and a higher—nay, the highest reality; and they consequently presuppose this reality, and are, as regards their content, derived from it. The manifold nature of things is only an infinitely various mode of limiting the conception of the highest reality, which is their common substratum; just as all figures are possible only as different modes of limiting infinite space. The object of the ideal of reason—an object existing only in reason itself—is also termed the primal being (ens originarium); as having no existence superior to him, the supreme being (ens summum); and as being the condition of all other beings, which rank under it, the being of all beings (ens entium). But none of these terms indicate the objective relation of an actually existing object to other things, but merely that of an idea to conceptions; and all our investigations into this subject still leave us in perfect uncertainty with regard to the existence of this being.

A primal being cannot be said to consist of many other beings with an existence which is derivative, for the latter presuppose the former, and therefore cannot be constitutive parts of it. It follows that the ideal of the primal being must be cogitated as simple.

The deduction of the possibility of all other things from this primal being cannot, strictly speaking, be considered as a limitation, or as a kind of division of its reality; for this would be regarding the primal being as a mere aggregate—which has been shown to be impossible, although it was so represented in our first rough sketch. The highest reality must be regarded rather as the ground than as the sum-total of the possibility of all things, and the manifold nature of things be based, not upon the limitation of the primal being itself, but upon the complete series of effects which flow from it. And thus all our powers of sense, as well as all phenomenal reality, may be with propriety regarded as belonging to this series of effects, while they could not have formed parts of the idea, considered as an aggregate. Pursuing this track, and hypostatizing this idea, we shall find ourselves authorized to determine our notion of the Supreme Being by means of the mere conception of a highest reality, as one, simple, all-sufficient, eternal, and so on—in one word, to determine it in its unconditioned completeness by the aid of every possible predicate. The conception of such a being is the conception of God in its transcendental sense, and thus the ideal of pure reason is the object-matter of a transcendental theology.

But, by such an employment of the transcendental idea, we should be over stepping the limits of its validity and purpose. For reason placed it, as the conception of all reality, at the basis of the complete determination of things, without requiring that this conception be regarded as the conception of an objective existence. Such an existence would be purely fictitious, and the hypostatizing of the content of the idea into an ideal, as an individual being, is a step perfectly unauthorized. Nay, more, we are not even called upon to assume the possibility of such an hypothesis, as none of the deductions drawn from such an ideal would affect the complete determination of things in general—for the sake of which alone is the idea necessary.

It is not sufficient to circumscribe the procedure and the dialectic of reason; we must also endeavour to discover the sources of this dialectic, that we may have it in our power to give a rational explanation of this illusion, as a phenomenon of the human mind. For the ideal, of which we are at present speaking, is based, not upon an arbitrary, but upon a natural, idea. The question hence arises: How happens it that reason regards the possibility of all things as deduced from a single possibility, that, to wit, of the highest reality, and presupposes this as existing in an individual and primal being?

The answer is ready; it is at once presented by the procedure of transcendental analytic. The possibility of sensuous objects is a relation of these objects to thought, in which something (the empirical form) may be cogitated à priori; while that which constitutes the matter—the reality of the phenomenon (that element which corresponds to sensation)—must be given from without, as otherwise it could not even be cogitated by, nor could its possibility be presentable to the mind. Now, a sensuous object is completely determined, when it has been compared with all phenomenal predicates, and represented by means of these either positively or negatively. But, as that which constitutes the thing itself—the real in a phenomenon, must be given, and that, in which the real of all phenomena is given, is experience, one, sole, and all-embracing—the material of the possibility of all sensuous objects must be presupposed as given in a whole, and it is upon the limitation of this whole that the possibility of all empirical objects, their distinction from each other and their complete determination, are based. Now, no other objects are presented to us besides sensuous objects, and these can be given only in connection with a possible experience; it follows that a thing is not an object to us, unless it presupposes the whole or sum-total of empirical reality as the condition of its possibility. Now, a natural illusion leads us to consider this principle, which is valid only of sensuous objects, as valid with regard to things in general. And thus we are induced to hold the empirical principle of our conceptions of the possibility of things, as phenomena, by leaving out this limitative condition, to be a transcendental principle of the possibility of things in general.

We proceed afterwards to hypostatize this idea of the sum-total of all reality, by changing the distributive unity of the empirical exercise of the understanding into the collective unity of an empirical whole—a dialectical illusion, and by cogitating this whole or sum of experience as an individual thing, containing in itself all empirical reality. This individual thing or being is then, by means of the above-mentioned transcendental subreption, substituted for our notion of a thing which stands at the head of the possibility of all things, the real conditions of whose complete determination it presents.[66]

Section III. Of the Arguments employed by Speculative Reason in Proof of the Existence of a Supreme Being

Notwithstanding the pressing necessity which reason feels, to form some presupposition that shall serve the understanding as a proper basis for the complete determination of its conceptions, the idealistic and factitious nature of such a presupposition is too evident to allow reason for a moment to persuade itself into a belief of the objective existence of a mere creation of its own thought. But there are other considerations which compel reason to seek out some resting place in the regress from the conditioned to the unconditioned, which is not given

[66] This ideal of the ens realissimum—although merely a mental representation—is first objectivized, that is, has an objective existence attributed to it, then hypostatized, and finally, by the natural progress of reason to the completion of unity, personified, as we shall show presently. For the regulative unity of experience is not based upon phenomena themselves, but upon the connection of the variety of phenomena by the understanding in a consciousness, and thus the unity of the supreme reality and the complete determinability of all things, seem to reside in a supreme understanding, and, consequently, in a conscious intelligence.

as an actual existence from the mere conception of it, although it alone can give completeness to the series of conditions. And this is the natural course of every human reason, even of the most uneducated, although the path at first entered it does not always continue to follow. It does not begin from conceptions, but from common experience, and requires a basis in actual existence. But this basis is insecure, unless it rests upon the immovable rock of the absolutely necessary. And this foundation is itself unworthy of trust, if it leave under and above it empty space, if it do not fill all, and leave no room for a why or a wherefore, if it be not, in one word, infinite in its reality.

If we admit the existence of some one thing, whatever it may be, we must also admit that there is something which exists necessarily. For what is contingent exists only under the condition of some other thing, which is its cause; and from this we must go on to conclude the existence of a cause which is not contingent, and which consequently exists necessarily and unconditionally. Such is the argument by which reason justifies its advances towards a primal being.

Now reason looks round for the conception of a being that may be admitted, without inconsistency, to be worthy of the attribute of absolute necessity, not for the purpose of inferring à priori, from the conception of such a being, its objective existence (for if reason allowed itself to take this course, it would not require a basis in given and actual existence, but merely the support of pure conceptions), but for the purpose of discovering, among all our conceptions of possible things, that conception which possesses no element inconsistent with the idea of absolute necessity. For that there must be some absolutely necessary existence, it regards as a truth already established. Now, if it can remove every existence incapable of supporting the attribute of absolute necessity, excepting one—this must be the absolutely necessary being, whether its necessity is comprehensible by us, that is, deducible from the conception of it alone, or not.

Now that, the conception of which contains a therefore to every wherefore, which is not defective in any respect whatever, which is all-sufficient as a condition, seems to be the being of which we can justly predicate absolute necessity—for this reason, that, possessing the conditions of all that is possible, it does not and cannot itself require any condition. And thus it satisfies, in one respect at least, the requirements of the conception of absolute necessity. In this view, it is superior to all other conceptions, which, as deficient and incomplete, do not possess the characteristic of independence of all higher conditions. It is true that we cannot infer from this that what does not contain in itself the supreme and complete condition—the condition of all other things—must possess only a conditioned existence; but as little can we assert the contrary, for this supposed being does not possess the only characteristic which can enable reason to cognize by means of an à priori conception the unconditioned and necessary nature of its existence.

The conception of an ens realissimum is that which best agrees with the conception of an unconditioned and necessary being. The former conception does not satisfy all the requirements of the latter; but we have no choice, we are obliged to adhere to it, for we find that we cannot do without the existence of a necessary being; and even although we admit it, we find it out of our power to discover in the whole sphere of possibility any being that can advance well-grounded claims to such a distinction.

The following is, therefore, the natural course of human reason. It begins by persuading itself of the existence of some necessary being. In this being it recognizes the characteristics of unconditioned existence. It then seeks the conception of that which is independent of all conditions, and finds it in that which is itself the sufficient condition of all other things—in other words, in that which contains all reality. But the unlimited all is an absolute unity, and is conceived by the mind as a being one and supreme; and thus reason concludes that the Supreme Being, as the primal basis of all things, possesses an existence which is absolutely necessary.

This conception must be regarded as in some degree satisfactory, if we admit the existence of a necessary being, and consider that there exists a necessity for a definite and final answer to these questions. In such a case, we cannot make a better choice, or rather we have no choice at all, but feel ourselves obliged to declare in favour of the absolute unity of complete reality, as the highest source of the possibility of things. But if there exists no motive for coming to a definite conclusion, and we may leave the question unanswered till we have fully weighed both sides—in other words, when we are merely called upon to decide how much we happen to know about the question, and how much we merely flatter ourselves that we know—the above conclusion does not appear to be so great advantage, but, on the contrary, seems defective in the grounds upon which it is supported.

For, admitting the truth of all that has been said, that, namely, the inference from a given existence (my own, for example) to the existence of an unconditioned and necessary being is valid and unassailable; that, in the second place, we must consider a being which contains all reality, and consequently all the conditions of other things, to be absolutely unconditioned; and admitting too, that we have thus discovered the conception of a thing to which may be attributed, without inconsistency, absolute necessity—it does not follow from all this that the conception of a limited being, in which the supreme reality does not reside, is therefore incompatible with the idea of absolute necessity. For, although I do not discover the element of the unconditioned in the conception of such a being—an element which is manifestly existent in the sum-total of all conditions—I am not entitled to conclude that its existence is therefore conditioned; just as I am not entitled to affirm, in a hypothetical syllogism, that where a certain condition does not exist (in the present, completeness, as far as pure conceptions are concerned), the conditioned does not exist either. On the contrary, we are free to consider all limited beings as likewise unconditionally necessary, although we are unable to infer this from the general conception which we have of them. Thus conducted, this argument is incapable of giving us the least notion of the properties of a necessary being, and must be in every respect without result.

This argument continues, however, to possess a weight and an authority, which, in spite of its objective insufficiency, it has never been divested of. For, granting that certain responsibilities lie upon us, which, as based on the ideas of reason, deserve to be respected and submitted to, although they are incapable of a real or practical application to our nature, or, in other words, would be responsibilities without motives, except upon the supposition of a Supreme Being to give effect and influence to the practical laws: in such a case we should be bound to obey our conceptions, which, although objectively insufficient, do, according to the standard of reason, preponderate over and are superior to any claims that may be advanced from any other quarter. The equilibrium of doubt would in this case be destroyed by a practical addition; indeed, Reason would be compelled to condemn herself, if she refused to comply with the demands of the judgement, no superior to which we know—however defective her understanding of the grounds of these demands might be.

This argument, although in fact transcendental, inasmuch as it rests upon the intrinsic insufficiency of the contingent, is so simple and natural, that the commonest understanding can appreciate its value. We see things around us change, arise, and pass away; they, or their condition, must therefore have a cause. The same demand must again be made of the cause itself—as a datum of experience. Now it is natural that we should place the highest causality just where we place supreme causality, in that being, which contains the conditions of all possible effects, and the conception of which is so simple as that of an all-embracing reality. This highest cause, then, we regard as absolutely necessary, because we find it absolutely necessary to rise to it, and do not discover any reason for proceeding beyond it. Thus, among all nations, through the darkest polytheism glimmer some faint sparks of monotheism, to which these idolaters have been led, not from reflection and profound thought, but by the study and natural progress of the common understanding.

There are only three modes of proving the existence of a Deity, on the grounds of speculative reason.

All the paths conducting to this end begin either from determinate experience and the peculiar constitution of the world of sense, and rise, according to the laws of causality, from it to the highest cause existing apart from the world—or from a purely indeterminate experience, that is, some empirical existence—or abstraction is made of all experience, and the existence of a supreme cause is concluded from à priori conceptions alone. The first is the physico-theological argument, the second the cosmological, the third the ontological. More there are not, and more there cannot be.

I shall show it is as unsuccessful on the one path—the empirical—as on the other—the transcendental, and that it stretches its wings in vain, to soar beyond the world of sense by the mere might of speculative thought. As regards the order in which we must discuss those arguments, it will be exactly the reverse of that in which reason, in the progress of its development, attains to them—the order in which they are placed above. For it will be made manifest to the reader that, although experience presents the occasion and the starting-point, it is the transcendental idea of reason which guides it in its pilgrimage and is the goal of all its struggles. I shall therefore begin with an examination of the transcendental argument, and afterwards inquire what additional strength has accrued to this mode of proof from the addition of the empirical element.

Section IV. Of the Impossibility of an Ontological Proof of the Existence of God

It is evident from what has been said that the conception of an absolutely necessary being is a mere idea, the objective reality of which is far from being established by the mere fact that it is a need of reason. On the contrary, this idea serves merely to indicate a certain unattainable perfection, and rather limits the operations than, by the presentation of new objects, extends the sphere of the understanding. But a strange anomaly meets us at the very threshold; for the inference from a given existence in general to an absolutely necessary existence seems to be correct and unavoidable, while the conditions of the understanding refuse to aid us in forming any conception of such a being.

Philosophers have always talked of an absolutely necessary being, and have nevertheless declined to take the trouble of conceiving whether—and how—a being of this nature is even cogitable, not to mention that its existence is actually demonstrable. A verbal definition of the conception is certainly easy enough: it is something the non-existence of which is impossible. But does this definition throw any light upon the conditions which render it impossible to cogitate the non-existence of a thing—conditions which we wish to ascertain, that we may discover whether we think anything in the conception of such a being or not? For the mere fact that I throw away, by means of the word unconditioned, all the conditions which the understanding habitually requires in order to regard anything as necessary, is very far from making clear whether by means of the conception of the unconditionally necessary I think of something, or really of nothing at all.

Nay, more, this chance-conception, now become so current, many have endeavoured to explain by examples which seemed to render any inquiries regarding its intelligibility quite needless. Every geometrical proposition—a triangle has three angles—it was said, is absolutely necessary; and thus people talked of an object which lay out of the sphere of our understanding as if it were perfectly plain what the conception of such a being meant.

All the examples adduced have been drawn, without exception, from judgements, and not from things. But the unconditioned necessity of a judgement does not form the absolute necessity of a thing. On the contrary, the absolute necessity of a judgement is only a conditioned necessity of a thing, or of the predicate in a judgement. The proposition above-mentioned does not enounce that three angles necessarily exist, but, upon condition that a triangle exists, three angles must necessarily exist—in it. And thus this logical necessity has been the source of the greatest delusions. Having formed an à priori conception of a thing, the content of which was made to embrace existence, we believed ourselves safe in concluding that, because existence belongs necessarily to the object of the conception (that is, under the condition of my positing this thing as given), the existence of the thing is also posited necessarily, and that it is therefore absolutely necessary—merely because its existence has been cogitated in the conception.

If, in an identical judgement, I annihilate the predicate in thought, and retain the subject, a contradiction is the result; and hence I say, the former belongs necessarily to the latter. But if I suppress both subject and predicate in thought, no contradiction arises; for there is nothing at all, and therefore no means of forming a contradiction. To suppose the existence of a triangle and not that of its three angles, is self-contradictory; but to suppose the non-existence of both triangle and angles is perfectly admissible. And so is it with the conception of an absolutely necessary being. Annihilate its existence in thought, and you annihilate the thing itself with all its predicates; how then can there be any room for contradiction? Externally, there is nothing to give rise to a contradiction, for a thing cannot be necessary externally; nor internally, for, by the annihilation or suppression of the thing itself, its internal properties are also annihilated. God is omnipotent—that is a necessary judgement. His omnipotence cannot be denied, if the existence of a Deity is posited—the existence, that is, of an infinite being, the two conceptions being identical. But when you say, God does not exist, neither omnipotence nor any other predicate is affirmed; they must all disappear with the subject, and in this judgement there cannot exist the least self-contradiction.

You have thus seen that when the predicate of a judgement is annihilated in thought along with the subject, no internal contradiction can arise, be the predicate what it may. There is no possibility of evading the conclusion—you find yourselves compelled to declare: There are certain subjects which cannot be annihilated in thought. But this is nothing more than saying: There exist subjects which are absolutely necessary—the very hypothesis which you are called upon to establish. For I find myself unable to form the slightest conception of a thing which when annihilated in thought with all its predicates, leaves behind a contradiction; and contradiction is the only criterion of impossibility in the sphere of pure à priori conceptions.

Against these general considerations, the justice of which no one can dispute, one argument is adduced, which is regarded as furnishing a satisfactory demonstration from the fact. It is affirmed that there is one and only one conception, in which the non-being or annihilation of the object is self-contradictory, and this is the conception of an ens realissimum. It possesses, you say, all reality, and you feel yourselves justified in admitting the possibility of such a being. (This I am willing to grant for the present, although the existence of a conception which is not self-contradictory is far from being sufficient to prove the possibility of an object.)[67] Now the notion of all reality embraces in it that of existence; the notion of existence lies, therefore, in the conception of this possible thing. If this thing is annihilated in thought, the internal possibility of the thing is also annihilated, which is self-contradictory.

I answer: It is absurd to introduce—under whatever term disguised—into the conception of a thing, which is to be cogitated solely in reference to its possibility, the conception of its existence. If this is admitted, you will have apparently gained the day, but in reality have enounced nothing but a mere tautology. I ask, is the proposition, this or that thing (which I am admitting to be possible) exists, an analytical or a synthetical proposition? If the former, there is no addition made to the subject of your thought by the affirmation of its existence; but then the conception in your minds is identical with the thing itself, or you have supposed the existence of a thing to be possible, and then inferred its existence from its internal possibility—which is but a miserable tautology. The word reality in the conception of the thing, and the word existence in the conception of the predicate, will not help you out of the difficulty. For, supposing you were to term all positing of a thing reality, you have thereby posited the thing with all its predicates in the conception of the subject and assumed its actual existence, and this you merely repeat in the predicate. But if you confess, as every reasonable person must, that every existential proposition is synthetical, how can it be maintained that the predicate of existence cannot be denied without contradiction?—a property which is the characteristic of analytical propositions, alone.

I should have a reasonable hope of putting an end for ever to this sophistical mode of argumentation, by a strict definition of the conception of existence, did not my own experience teach me that the illusion arising from our confounding a logical with a real predicate (a predicate which aids in the determination of a thing) resists almost all the endeavours of explanation and illustration. A logical predicate may be what you please, even the subject may be predicated of itself; for logic pays no regard to the content of a judgement. But the determination of a conception is a predicate, which adds to and enlarges the conception. It must not, therefore, be contained in the conception.

Being is evidently not a real predicate, that is, a conception of something which is added to the conception of some other thing. It is merely the positing

[67] A conception is always possible, if it is not self-contradictory. This is the logical criterion of possibility, distinguishing the object of such a conception from the nihil negativum. But it may be, notwithstanding, an empty conception, unless the objective reality of this synthesis, but which it is generated, is demonstrated; and a proof of this kind must be based upon principles of possible experience, and not upon the principle of analysis or contradiction. This remark may be serviceable as a warning against concluding, from the possibility of a conception—which is logical—the possibility of a thing—which is real.

of a thing, or of certain determinations in it. Logically, it is merely the copula of a judgement. The proposition, God is omnipotent, contains two conceptions, which have a certain object or content; the word is, is no additional predicate—it merely indicates the relation of the predicate to the subject. Now, if I take the subject (God) with all its predicates (omnipotence being one), and say: God is, or, There is a God, I add no new predicate to the conception of God, I merely posit or affirm the existence of the subject with all its predicates—I posit the object in relation to my conception. The content of both is the same; and there is no addition made to the conception, which expresses merely the possibility of the object, by my cogitating the object—in the expression, it is—as absolutely given or existing. Thus the real contains no more than the possible. A hundred real dollars contain no more than a hundred possible dollars. For, as the latter indicate the conception, and the former the object, on the supposition that the content of the former was greater than that of the latter, my conception would not be an expression of the whole object, and would consequently be an inadequate conception of it. But in reckoning my wealth there may be said to be more in a hundred real dollars than in a hundred possible dollars—that is, in the mere conception of them. For the real object—the dollars—is not analytically contained in my conception, but forms a synthetical addition to my conception (which is merely a determination of my mental state), although this objective reality—this existence—apart from my conceptions, does not in the least degree increase the aforesaid hundred dollars.

By whatever and by whatever number of predicates—even to the complete determination of it—I may cogitate a thing, I do not in the least augment the object of my conception by the addition of the statement: This thing exists. Otherwise, not exactly the same, but something more than what was cogitated in my conception, would exist, and I could not affirm that the exact object of my conception had real existence. If I cogitate a thing as containing all modes of reality except one, the mode of reality which is absent is not added to the conception of the thing by the affirmation that the thing exists; on the contrary, the thing exists—if it exist at all—with the same defect as that cogitated in its conception; otherwise not that which was cogitated, but something different, exists. Now, if I cogitate a being as the highest reality, without defect or imperfection, the question still remains—whether this being exists or not? For, although no element is wanting in the possible real content of my conception, there is a defect in its relation to my mental state, that is, I am ignorant whether the cognition of the object indicated by the conception is possible à posteriori. And here the cause of the present difficulty becomes apparent. If the question regarded an object of sense merely, it would be impossible for me to confound the conception with the existence of a thing. For the conception merely enables me to cogitate an object as according with the general conditions of experience; while the existence of the object permits me to cogitate it as contained in the sphere of actual experience. At the same time, this connection with the world of experience does not in the least augment the conception, although a possible perception has been added to the experience of the mind. But if we cogitate existence by the pure category alone, it is not to be wondered at, that we should find ourselves unable to present any criterion sufficient to distinguish it from mere possibility.

Whatever be the content of our conception of an object, it is necessary to go beyond it, if we wish to predicate existence of the object. In the case of sensuous objects, this is attained by their connection according to empirical laws with some one of my perceptions; but there is no means of cognizing the existence of objects of pure thought, because it must be cognized completely à priori. But all our knowledge of existence (be it immediately by perception, or by inferences connecting some object with a perception) belongs entirely to the sphere of experience—which is in perfect unity with itself; and although an existence out of this sphere cannot be absolutely declared to be impossible, it is a hypothesis the truth of which we have no means of ascertaining.

The notion of a Supreme Being is in many respects a highly useful idea; but for the very reason that it is an idea, it is incapable of enlarging our cognition with regard to the existence of things. It is not even sufficient to instruct us as to the possibility of a being which we do not know to exist. The analytical criterion of possibility, which consists in the absence of contradiction in propositions, cannot be denied it. But the connection of real properties in a thing is a synthesis of the possibility of which an à priori judgement cannot be formed, because these realities are not presented to us specifically; and even if this were to happen, a judgement would still be impossible, because the criterion of the possibility of synthetical cognitions must be sought for in the world of experience, to which the object of an idea cannot belong. And thus the celebrated Leibnitz has utterly failed in his attempt to establish upon à priori grounds the possibility of this sublime ideal being.

The celebrated ontological or Cartesian argument for the existence of a Supreme Being is therefore insufficient; and we may as well hope to increase our stock of knowledge by the aid of mere ideas, as the merchant to augment his wealth by the addition of noughts to his cash account.

Section V. Of the Impossibility of a Cosmological Proof of the Existence of God

It was by no means a natural course of proceeding, but, on the contrary, an invention entirely due to the subtlety of the schools, to attempt to draw from a mere idea a proof of the existence of an object corresponding to it. Such a course would never have been pursued, were it not for that need of reason which requires it to suppose the existence of a necessary being as a basis for the empirical regress, and that, as this necessity must be unconditioned and à priori, reason is bound to discover a conception which shall satisfy, if possible, this requirement, and enable us to attain to the à priori cognition of such a being. This conception was thought to be found in the idea of an ens realissimum, and thus this idea was employed for the attainment of a better defined knowledge of a necessary being, of the existence of which we were convinced, or persuaded, on other grounds. Thus reason was seduced from her natural courage; and, instead of concluding with the conception of an ens realissimum, an attempt was made to begin with it, for the purpose of inferring from it that idea of a necessary existence which it was in fact called in to complete. Thus arose that unfortunate ontological argument, which neither satisfies the healthy common sense of humanity, nor sustains the scientific examination of the philosopher.

The cosmological proof, which we are about to examine, retains the connection between absolute necessity and the highest reality; but, instead of reasoning from this highest reality to a necessary existence, like the preceding argument, it concludes from the given unconditioned necessity of some being its unlimited reality. The track it pursues, whether rational or sophistical, is at least natural, and not only goes far to persuade the common understanding, but shows itself deserving of respect from the speculative intellect; while it contains, at the same time, the outlines of all the arguments employed in natural theology—arguments which always have been, and still will be, in use and authority. These, however adorned, and hid under whatever embellishments of rhetoric and sentiment, are at bottom identical with the arguments we are at present to discuss. This proof, termed by Leibnitz the argumentum a contingentia mundi, I shall now lay before the reader, and subject to a strict examination.

It is framed in the following manner: If something exists, an absolutely necessary being must likewise exist. Now I, at least, exist. Consequently, there exists an absolutely necessary being. The minor contains an experience, the major reasons from a general experience to the existence of a necessary being.[68] Thus this argument really begins at experience, and is not completely à priori, or ontological. The object of all possible experience being the world, it is called the cosmological proof. It contains no reference to any peculiar property of sensuous objects, by which this world of sense might be distinguished from other possible worlds; and in this respect it differs from the physico-theological proof, which is based upon the consideration of the peculiar constitution of our sensuous world.

The proof proceeds thus: A necessary being can be determined only in one way, that is, it can be determined by only one of all possible opposed predicates; consequently, it must be completely determined in and by its conception. But there is only a single conception of a thing possible, which completely determines the thing à priori: that is, the conception of the ens realissimum. It follows that the

[68] This inference is too well known to require more detailed discussion. It is based upon the spurious transcendental law of causality, that everything which is contingent has a cause, which, if itself contingent, must also have a cause; and so on, till the series of subordinated causes must end with an absolutely necessary cause, without which it would not possess completeness.

conception of the ens realissimum is the only conception by and in which we can cogitate a necessary being. Consequently, a Supreme Being necessarily exists.

In this cosmological argument are assembled so many sophistical propositions that speculative reason seems to have exerted in it all her dialectical skill to produce a transcendental illusion of the most extreme character. We shall postpone an investigation of this argument for the present, and confine ourselves to exposing the stratagem by which it imposes upon us an old argument in a new dress, and appeals to the agreement of two witnesses, the one with the credentials of pure reason, and the other with those of empiricism; while, in fact, it is only the former who has changed his dress and voice, for the purpose of passing himself off for an additional witness. That it may possess a secure foundation, it bases its conclusions upon experience, and thus appears to be completely distinct from the ontological argument, which places its confidence entirely in pure à priori conceptions. But this experience merely aids reason in making one step—to the existence of a necessary being. What the properties of this being are cannot be learned from experience; and therefore reason abandons it altogether, and pursues its inquiries in the sphere of pure conception, for the purpose of discovering what the properties of an absolutely necessary being ought to be, that is, what among all possible things contain the conditions (requisita) of absolute necessity. Reason believes that it has discovered these requisites in the conception of an ens realissimum—and in it alone, and hence concludes: The ens realissimum is an absolutely necessary being. But it is evident that reason has here presupposed that the conception of an ens realissimum is perfectly adequate to the conception of a being of absolute necessity, that is, that we may infer the existence of the latter from that of the former—a proposition which formed the basis of the ontological argument, and which is now employed in the support of the cosmological argument, contrary to the wish and professions of its inventors. For the existence of an absolutely necessary being is given in conceptions alone. But if I say: "The conception of the ens realissimum is a conception of this kind, and in fact the only conception which is adequate to our idea of a necessary being," I am obliged to admit, that the latter may be inferred from the former. Thus it is properly the ontological argument which figures in the cosmological, and constitutes the whole strength of the latter; while the spurious basis of experience has been of no further use than to conduct us to the conception of absolute necessity, being utterly insufficient to demonstrate the presence of this attribute in any determinate existence or thing. For when we propose to ourselves an aim of this character, we must abandon the sphere of experience, and rise to that of pure conceptions, which we examine with the purpose of discovering whether any one contains the conditions of the possibility of an absolutely necessary being. But if the possibility of such a being is thus demonstrated, its existence is also proved; for we may then assert that, of all possible beings there is one which possesses the attribute of necessity—in other words, this being possesses an absolutely necessary existence.

All illusions in an argument are more easily detected when they are presented in the formal manner employed by the schools, which we now proceed to do.

If the proposition: "Every absolutely necessary being is likewise an ens realissimum," is correct (and it is this which constitutes the nervus probandi of the cosmological argument), it must, like all affirmative judgements, be capable of conversion—the conversio per accidens, at least. It follows, then, that some entia realissima are absolutely necessary beings. But no ens realissimum is in any respect different from another, and what is valid of some is valid of all. In this present case, therefore, I may employ simple conversion, and say: "Every ens realissimum is a necessary being." But as this proposition is determined à priori by the conceptions contained in it, the mere conception of an ens realissimum must possess the additional attribute of absolute necessity. But this is exactly what was maintained in the ontological argument, and not recognized by the cosmological, although it formed the real ground of its disguised and illusory reasoning.

Thus the second mode employed by speculative reason of demonstrating the existence of a Supreme Being, is not only, like the first, illusory and inadequate, but possesses the additional blemish of an ignoratio elenchi—professing to conduct us by a new road to the desired goal, but bringing us back, after a short circuit, to the old path which we had deserted at its call.

I mentioned above that this cosmological argument contains a perfect nest of dialectical assumptions, which transcendental criticism does not find it difficult to expose and to dissipate. I shall merely enumerate these, leaving it to the reader, who must by this time be well practised in such matters, to investigate the fallacies residing therein.

The following fallacies, for example, are discoverable in this mode of proof: 1. The transcendental principle: "Everything that is contingent must have a cause"—a principle without significance, except in the sensuous world. For the purely intellectual conception of the contingent cannot produce any synthetical proposition, like that of causality, which is itself without significance or distinguishing characteristic except in the phenomenal world. But in the present case it is employed to help us beyond the limits of its sphere. 2. "From the impossibility of an infinite ascending series of causes in the world of sense a first cause is inferred"; a conclusion which the principles of the employment of reason do not justify even in the sphere of experience, and still less when an attempt is made to pass the limits of this sphere. 3. Reason allows itself to be satisfied upon insufficient grounds, with regard to the completion of this series. It removes all conditions (without which, however, no conception of Necessity can take place); and, as after this it is beyond our power to form any other conceptions, it accepts this as a completion of the conception it wishes to form of the series. 4. The logical possibility of a conception of the total of reality (the criterion of this possibility being the absence of contradiction) is confounded with the transcendental, which requires a principle of the practicability of such a synthesis—a principle which again refers us to the world of experience. And so on.

The aim of the cosmological argument is to avoid the necessity of proving the existence of a necessary being priori from mere conceptions—a proof which must be ontological, and of which we feel ourselves quite incapable. With this purpose, we reason from an actual existence—an experience in general, to an absolutely necessary condition of that existence. It is in this case unnecessary to demonstrate its possibility. For after having proved that it exists, the question regarding its possibility is superfluous. Now, when we wish to define more strictly the nature of this necessary being, we do not look out for some being the conception of which would enable us to comprehend the necessity of its being—for if we could do this, an empirical presupposition would be unnecessary; no, we try to discover merely the negative condition (conditio sine qua non), without which a being would not be absolutely necessary. Now this would be perfectly admissible in every sort of reasoning, from a consequence to its principle; but in the present case it unfortunately happens that the condition of absolute necessity can be discovered in but a single being, the conception of which must consequently contain all that is requisite for demonstrating the presence of absolute necessity, and thus entitle me to infer this absolute necessity à priori. That is, it must be possible to reason conversely, and say: The thing, to which the conception of the highest reality belongs, is absolutely necessary. But if I cannot reason thus—and I cannot, unless I believe in the sufficiency of the ontological argument—I find insurmountable obstacles in my new path, and am really no farther than the point from which I set out. The conception of a Supreme Being satisfies all questions à priori regarding the internal determinations of a thing, and is for this reason an ideal without equal or parallel, the general conception of it indicating it as at the same time an ens individuum among all possible things. But the conception does not satisfy the question regarding its existence—which was the purpose of all our inquiries; and, although the existence of a necessary being were admitted, we should find it impossible to answer the question: What of all things in the world must be regarded as such?

It is certainly allowable to admit the existence of an all-sufficient being—a cause of all possible effects—for the purpose of enabling reason to introduce unity into its mode and grounds of explanation with regard to phenomena. But to assert that such a being necessarily exists, is no longer the modest enunciation of an admissible hypothesis, but the boldest declaration of an apodeictic certainty; for the cognition of that which is absolutely necessary must itself possess that character.

The aim of the transcendental ideal formed by the mind is either to discover a conception which shall harmonize with the idea of absolute necessity, or a conception which shall contain that idea. If the one is possible, so is the other; for reason recognizes that alone as absolutely necessary which is necessary from its conception. But both attempts are equally beyond our power—we find it impossible to satisfy the understanding upon this point, and as impossible to induce it to remain at rest in relation to this incapacity.

Unconditioned necessity, which, as the ultimate support and stay of all existing things, is an indispensable requirement of the mind, is an abyss on the verge of which human reason trembles in dismay. Even the idea of eternity, terrible and sublime as it is, as depicted by Haller, does not produce upon the mental vision such a feeling of awe and terror; for, although it measures the duration of things, it does not support them. We cannot bear, nor can we rid ourselves of the thought that a being, which we regard as the greatest of all possible existences, should say to himself: I am from eternity to eternity; beside me there is nothing, except that which exists by my will; whence then am I? Here all sinks away from under us; and the greatest, as the smallest, perfection, hovers without stay or footing in presence of the speculative reason, which finds it as easy to part with the one as with the other.

Many physical powers, which evidence their existence by their effects, are perfectly inscrutable in their nature; they elude all our powers of observation. The transcendental object which forms the basis of phenomena, and, in connection with it, the reason why our sensibility possesses this rather than that particular kind of conditions, are and must ever remain hidden from our mental vision; the fact is there, the reason of the fact we cannot see. But an ideal of pure reason cannot be termed mysterious or inscrutable, because the only credential of its reality is the need of it felt by reason, for the purpose of giving completeness to the world of synthetical unity. An ideal is not even given as a cogitable object, and therefore cannot be inscrutable; on the contrary, it must, as a mere idea, be based on the constitution of reason itself, and on this account must be capable of explanation and solution. For the very essence of reason consists in its ability to give an account, of all our conceptions, opinions, and assertions—upon objective, or, when they happen to be illusory and fallacious, upon subjective grounds.

Detection and Explanation of the Dialectical Illusion in all Transcendental Arguments for the Existence of a Necessary Being.

Both of the above arguments are transcendental; in other words, they do not proceed upon empirical principles. For, although the cosmological argument professed to lay a basis of experience for its edifice of reasoning, it did not ground its procedure upon the peculiar constitution of experience, but upon pure principles of reason—in relation to an existence given by empirical consciousness; utterly abandoning its guidance, however, for the purpose of supporting its assertions entirely upon pure conceptions. Now what is the cause, in these transcendental arguments, of the dialectical, but natural, illusion, which connects the conceptions of necessity and supreme reality, and hypostatizes that which cannot be anything but an idea? What is the cause of this unavoidable step on the part of reason, of admitting that some one among all existing things must be necessary, while it falls back from the assertion of the existence of such a being as from an abyss? And how does reason proceed to explain this anomaly to itself, and from the wavering condition of a timid and reluctant approbation—always again withdrawn—arrive at a calm and settled insight into its cause?

It is something very remarkable that, on the supposition that something exists, I cannot avoid the inference that something exists necessarily. Upon this perfectly natural—but not on that account reliable—inference does the cosmological argument rest. But, let me form any conception whatever of a thing, I find that I cannot cogitate the existence of the thing as absolutely necessary, and that nothing prevents me—be the thing or being what it may—from cogitating its non-existence. I may thus be obliged to admit that all existing things have a necessary basis, while I cannot cogitate any single or individual thing as necessary. In other words, I can never complete the regress through the conditions of existence, without admitting the existence of a necessary being; but, on the other hand, I cannot make a commencement from this being.

If I must cogitate something as existing necessarily as the basis of existing things, and yet am not permitted to cogitate any individual thing as in itself necessary, the inevitable inference is that necessity and contingency are not properties of things themselves—otherwise an internal contradiction would result; that consequently neither of these principles are objective, but merely subjective principles of reason—the one requiring us to seek for a necessary ground for everything that exists, that is, to be satisfied with no other explanation than that which is complete à priori, the other forbidding us ever to hope for the attainment of this completeness, that is, to regard no member of the empirical world as unconditioned. In this mode of viewing them, both principles, in their purely heuristic and regulative character, and as concerning merely the formal interest of reason, are quite consistent with each other. The one says: "You must philosophize upon nature," as if there existed a necessary primal basis of all existing things, solely for the purpose of introducing systematic unity into your knowledge, by pursuing an idea of this character—a foundation which is arbitrarily admitted to be ultimate; while the other warns you to consider no individual determination, concerning the existence of things, as such an ultimate foundation, that is, as absolutely necessary, but to keep the way always open for further progress in the deduction, and to treat every determination as determined by some other. But if all that we perceive must be regarded as conditionally necessary, it is impossible that anything which is empirically given should be absolutely necessary.

It follows from this that you must accept the absolutely necessary as out of and beyond the world, inasmuch as it is useful only as a principle of the highest possible unity in experience, and you cannot discover any such necessary existence in the would, the second rule requiring you to regard all empirical causes of unity as themselves deduced.

The philosophers of antiquity regarded all the forms of nature as contingent; while matter was considered by them, in accordance with the judgement of the common reason of mankind, as primal and necessary. But if they had regarded matter, not relatively—as the substratum of phenomena, but absolutely and in itself—as an independent existence, this idea of absolute necessity would have immediately disappeared. For there is nothing absolutely connecting reason with such an existence; on the contrary, it can annihilate it in thought, always and without self-contradiction. But in thought alone lay the idea of absolute necessity. A regulative principle must, therefore, have been at the foundation of this opinion. In fact, extension and impenetrability—which together constitute our conception of matter—form the supreme empirical principle of the unity of phenomena, and this principle, in so far as it is empirically unconditioned, possesses the property of a regulative principle. But, as every determination of matter which constitutes what is real in it—and consequently impenetrability—is an effect, which must have a cause, and is for this reason always derived, the notion of matter cannot harmonize with the idea of a necessary being, in its character of the principle of all derived unity. For every one of its real properties, being derived, must be only conditionally necessary, and can therefore be annihilated in thought; and thus the whole existence of matter can be so annihilated or suppressed. If this were not the case, we should have found in the world of phenomena the highest ground or condition of unity—which is impossible, according to the second regulative principle. It follows that matter, and, in general, all that forms part of the world of sense, cannot be a necessary primal being, nor even a principle of empirical unity, but that this being or principle must have its place assigned without the world. And, in this way, we can proceed in perfect confidence to deduce the phenomena of the world and their existence from other phenomena, just as if there existed no necessary being; and we can at the same time, strive without ceasing towards the attainment of completeness for our deduction, just as if such a being—the supreme condition of all existences—were presupposed by the mind.

These remarks will have made it evident to the reader that the ideal of the Supreme Being, far from being an enouncement of the existence of a being in itself necessary, is nothing more than a regulative principle of reason, requiring us to regard all connection existing between phenomena as if it had its origin from an all-sufficient necessary cause, and basing upon this the rule of a systematic and necessary unity in the explanation of phenomena. We cannot, at the same time, avoid regarding, by a transcendental subreptio, this formal principle as constitutive, and hypostatizing this unity. Precisely similar is the case with our notion of space. Space is the primal condition of all forms, which are properly just so many different limitations of it; and thus, although it is merely a principle of sensibility, we cannot help regarding it as an absolutely necessary and self-subsistent thing—as an object given à priori in itself. In the same way, it is quite natural that, as the systematic unity of nature cannot be established as a principle for the empirical employment of reason, unless it is based upon the idea of an ens realissimum, as the supreme cause, we should regard this idea as a real object, and this object, in its character of supreme condition, as absolutely necessary, and that in this way a regulative should be transformed into a constitutive principle. This interchange becomes evident when I regard this supreme being, which, relatively to the world, was absolutely (unconditionally) necessary, as a thing per se. In this case, I find it impossible to represent this necessity in or by any conception, and it exists merely in my own mind, as the formal condition of thought, but not as a material and hypostatic condition of existence.

Section VI. Of the Impossibility of a Physico-Theological Proof

If, then, neither a pure conception nor the general experience of an existing being can provide a sufficient basis for the proof of the existence of the Deity, we can make the attempt by the only other mode—that of grounding our argument upon a determinate experience of the phenomena of the present world, their constitution and disposition, and discover whether we can thus attain to a sound conviction of the existence of a Supreme Being. This argument we shall term the physico-theological argument. If it is shown to be insufficient, speculative reason cannot present us with any satisfactory proof of the existence of a being corresponding to our transcendental idea.

It is evident from the remarks that have been made in the preceding sections, that an answer to this question will be far from being difficult or unconvincing. For how can any experience be adequate with an idea? The very essence of an idea consists in the fact that no experience can ever be discovered congruent or adequate with it. The transcendental idea of a necessary and all-sufficient being is so immeasurably great, so high above all that is empirical, which is always conditioned, that we hope in vain to find materials in the sphere of experience sufficiently ample for our conception, and in vain seek the unconditioned among things that are conditioned, while examples, nay, even guidance is denied us by the laws of empirical synthesis.

If the Supreme Being forms a link in the chain of empirical conditions, it must be a member of the empirical series, and, like the lower members which it precedes, have its origin in some higher member of the series. If, on the other hand, we disengage it from the chain, and cogitate it as an intelligible being, apart from the series of natural causes—how shall reason bridge the abyss that separates the latter from the former? All laws respecting the regress from effects to causes, all synthetical additions to our knowledge relate solely to possible experience and the objects of the sensuous world, and, apart from them, are without significance.

The world around us opens before our view so magnificent a spectacle of order, variety, beauty, and conformity to ends, that whether we pursue our observations into the infinity of space in the one direction, or into its illimitable divisions in the other, whether we regard the world in its greatest or its least manifestations—even after we have attained to the highest summit of knowledge which our weak minds can reach, we find that language in the presence of wonders so inconceivable has lost its force, and number its power to reckon, nay, even thought fails to conceive adequately, and our conception of the whole dissolves into an astonishment without power of expression—all the more eloquent that it is dumb. Everywhere around us we observe a chain of causes and effects, of means and ends, of death and birth; and, as nothing has entered of itself into the condition in which we find it, we are constantly referred to some other thing, which itself suggests the same inquiry regarding its cause, and thus the universe must sink into the abyss of nothingness, unless we admit that, besides this infinite chain of contingencies, there exists something that is primal and self-subsistent—something which, as the cause of this phenomenal world, secures its continuance and preservation.

This highest cause—what magnitude shall we attribute to it? Of the content of the world we are ignorant; still less can we estimate its magnitude by comparison with the sphere of the possible. But this supreme cause being a necessity of the human mind, what is there to prevent us from attributing to it such a degree of perfection as to place it above the sphere of all that is possible? This we can easily do, although only by the aid of the faint outline of an abstract conception, by representing this being to ourselves as containing in itself, as an individual substance, all possible perfection—a conception which satisfies that requirement of reason which demands parsimony in principles, which is free from self-contradiction, which even contributes to the extension of the employment of reason in experience, by means of the guidance afforded by this idea to order and system, and which in no respect conflicts with any law of experience.

This argument always deserves to be mentioned with respect. It is the oldest, the clearest, and that most in conformity with the common reason of humanity. It animates the study of nature, as it itself derives its existence and draws ever new strength from that source. It introduces aims and ends into a sphere in which our observation could not of itself have discovered them, and extends our knowledge of nature, by directing our attention to a unity, the principle of which lies beyond nature. This knowledge of nature again reacts upon this idea—its cause; and thus our belief in a divine author of the universe rises to the power of an irresistible conviction.

For these reasons it would be utterly hopeless to attempt to rob this argument of the authority it has always enjoyed. The mind, unceasingly elevated by these considerations, which, although empirical, are so remarkably powerful, and continually adding to their force, will not suffer itself to be depressed by the doubts suggested by subtle speculation; it tears itself out of this state of uncertainty, the moment it casts a look upon the wondrous forms of nature and the majesty of the universe, and rises from height to height, from condition to condition, till it has elevated itself to the supreme and unconditioned author of all.

But although we have nothing to object to the reasonableness and utility of this procedure, but have rather to commend and encourage it, we cannot approve of the claims which this argument advances to demonstrative certainty and to a reception upon its own merits, apart from favour or support by other arguments. Nor can it injure the cause of morality to endeavour to lower the tone of the arrogant sophist, and to teach him that modesty and moderation which are the properties of a belief that brings calm and content into the mind, without prescribing to it an unworthy subjection. I maintain, then, that the physico-theological argument is insufficient of itself to prove the existence of a Supreme Being, that it must entrust this to the ontological argument—to which it serves merely as an introduction, and that, consequently, this argument contains the only possible ground of proof (possessed by speculative reason) for the existence of this being.

The chief momenta in the physico-theological argument are as follow: 1. We observe in the world manifest signs of an arrangement full of purpose, executed with great wisdom, and argument in whole of a content indescribably various, and of an extent without limits. 2. This arrangement of means and ends is entirely foreign to the things existing in the world—it belongs to them merely as a contingent attribute; in other words, the nature of different things could not of itself, whatever means were employed, harmoniously tend towards certain purposes, were they not chosen and directed for these purposes by a rational and disposing principle, in accordance with certain fundamental ideas. 3. There exists, therefore, a sublime and wise cause (or several), which is not merely a blind, all-powerful nature, producing the beings and events which fill the world in unconscious fecundity, but a free and intelligent cause of the world. 4. The unity of this cause may be inferred from the unity of the reciprocal relation existing between the parts of the world, as portions of an artistic edifice—an inference which all our observation favours, and all principles of analogy support.

In the above argument, it is inferred from the analogy of certain products of nature with those of human art, when it compels Nature to bend herself to its purposes, as in the case of a house, a ship, or a watch, that the same kind of causality—namely, understanding and will—resides in nature. It is also declared that the internal possibility of this freely-acting nature (which is the source of all art, and perhaps also of human reason) is derivable from another and superhuman art—a conclusion which would perhaps be found incapable of standing the test of subtle transcendental criticism. But to neither of these opinions shall we at present object. We shall only remark that it must be confessed that, if we are to discuss the subject of cause at all, we cannot proceed more securely than with the guidance of the analogy subsisting between nature and such products of design—these being the only products whose causes and modes of organization are completely known to us. Reason would be unable to satisfy her own requirements, if she passed from a causality which she does know, to obscure and indemonstrable principles of explanation which she does not know.

According to the physico-theological argument, the connection and harmony existing in the world evidence the contingency of the form merely, but not of the matter, that is, of the substance of the world. To establish the truth of the latter opinion, it would be necessary to prove that all things would be in themselves incapable of this harmony and order, unless they were, even as regards their substance, the product of a supreme wisdom. But this would require very different grounds of proof from those presented by the analogy with human art. This proof can at most, therefore, demonstrate the existence of an architect of the world, whose efforts are limited by the capabilities of the material with which he works, but not of a creator of the world, to whom all things are subject. Thus this argument is utterly insufficient for the task before us—a demonstration of the existence of an all-sufficient being. If we wish to prove the contingency of matter, we must have recourse to a transcendental argument, which the physico-theological was constructed expressly to avoid.

We infer, from the order and design visible in the universe, as a disposition of a thoroughly contingent character, the existence of a cause proportionate thereto. The conception of this cause must contain certain determinate qualities, and it must therefore be regarded as the conception of a being which possesses all power, wisdom, and so on, in one word, all perfection—the conception, that is, of an all-sufficient being. For the predicates of very great, astonishing, or immeasurable power and excellence, give us no determinate conception of the thing, nor do they inform us what the thing may be in itself. They merely indicate the relation existing between the magnitude of the object and the observer, who compares it with himself and with his own power of comprehension, and are mere expressions of praise and reverence, by which the object is either magnified, or the observing subject depreciated in relation to the object. Where we have to do with the magnitude (of the perfection) of a thing, we can discover no determinate conception, except that which comprehends all possible perfection or completeness, and it is only the total (omnitudo) of reality which is completely determined in and through its conception alone.

Now it cannot be expected that any one will be bold enough to declare that he has a perfect insight into the relation which the magnitude of the world he contemplates bears (in its extent as well as in its content) to omnipotence, into that of the order and design in the world to the highest wisdom, and that of the unity of the world to the absolute unity of a Supreme Being. Physico-theology is therefore incapable of presenting a determinate conception of a supreme cause of the world, and is therefore insufficient as a principle of theology—a theology which is itself to be the basis of religion.

The attainment of absolute totality is completely impossible on the path of empiricism. And yet this is the path pursued in the physico-theological argument. What means shall we employ to bridge the abyss?

After elevating ourselves to admiration of the magnitude of the power, wisdom, and other attributes of the author of the world, and finding we can advance no further, we leave the argument on empirical grounds, and proceed to infer the contingency of the world from the order and conformity to aims that are observable in it. From this contingency we infer, by the help of transcendental conceptions alone, the existence of something absolutely necessary; and, still advancing, proceed from the conception of the absolute necessity of the first cause to the completely determined or determining conception thereof—the conception of an all-embracing reality. Thus the physico-theological, failing in its undertaking, recurs in its embarrassment to the cosmological argument; and, as this is merely the ontological argument in disguise, it executes its design solely by the aid of pure reason, although it at first professed to have no connection with this faculty and to base its entire procedure upon experience alone.

The physico-theologians have therefore no reason to regard with such contempt the transcendental mode of argument, and to look down upon it, with the conceit of clear-sighted observers of nature, as the brain-cobweb of obscure speculatists. For, if they reflect upon and examine their own arguments, they will find that, after following for some time the path of nature and experience, and discovering themselves no nearer their object, they suddenly leave this path and pass into the region of pure possibility, where they hope to reach upon the wings of ideas what had eluded all their empirical investigations. Gaining, as they think, a firm footing after this immense leap, they extend their determinate conception—into the possession of which they have come, they know not how—over the whole sphere of creation, and explain their ideal, which is entirely a product of pure reason, by illustrations drawn from experience—though in a degree miserably unworthy of the grandeur of the object, while they refuse to acknowledge that they have arrived at this cognition or hypothesis by a very different road from that of experience.

Thus the physico-theological is based upon the cosmological, and this upon the ontological proof of the existence of a Supreme Being; and as besides these three there is no other path open to speculative reason, the ontological proof, on the ground of pure conceptions of reason, is the only possible one, if any proof of a proposition so far transcending the empirical exercise of the understanding is possible at all.

Section VII. Critique of all Theology based upon Speculative Principles of Reason

If by the term theology I understand the cognition of a primal being, that cognition is based either upon reason alone (theologia rationalis) or upon revelation (theologia revelata). The former cogitates its object either by means of pure transcendental conceptions, as an ens originarium, realissimum, ens entium, and is termed transcendental theology; or, by means of a conception derived from the nature of our own mind, as a supreme intelligence, and must then be entitled natural theology. The person who believes in a transcendental theology alone, is termed a deist; he who acknowledges the possibility of a natural theology also, a theist. The former admits that we can cognize by pure reason alone the existence of a Supreme Being, but at the same time maintains that our conception of this being is purely transcendental, and that all we can say of it is that it possesses all reality, without being able to define it more closely. The second asserts that reason is capable of presenting us, from the analogy with nature, with a more definite conception of this being, and that its operations, as the cause of all things, are the results of intelligence and free will. The former regards the Supreme Being as the cause of the world—whether by the necessity of his nature, or as a free agent, is left undetermined; the latter considers this being as the author of the world.

Transcendental theology aims either at inferring the existence of a Supreme Being from a general experience, without any closer reference to the world to which this experience belongs, and in this case it is called cosmotheology; or it endeavours to cognize the existence of such a being, through mere conceptions, without the aid of experience, and is then termed ontotheology.

Natural theology infers the attributes and the existence of an author of the world, from the constitution of, the order and unity observable in, the world, in which two modes of causality must be admitted to exist—those of nature and freedom. Thus it rises from this world to a supreme intelligence, either as the principle of all natural, or of all moral order and perfection. In the former case it is termed physico-theology, in the latter, ethical or moral-theology.[69]

As we are wont to understand by the term God not merely an eternal nature, the operations of which are insensate and blind, but a Supreme Being, who is the free and intelligent author of all things, and as it is this latter view alone that can be of interest to humanity, we might, in strict rigour, deny to the deist any belief in God at all, and regard him merely as a maintainer of the existence of a primal being or thing—the supreme cause of all other things. But, as no one ought to be blamed, merely because he does not feel himself justified in maintaining a certain opinion, as if he altogether denied its truth and asserted the opposite, it is more correct—as it is less harsh—to say, the deist believes in a God, the theist in a living God (summa intelligentia). We shall now proceed to investigate the sources of all these attempts of reason to establish the existence of a Supreme Being.

It may be sufficient in this place to define theoretical knowledge or cognition as knowledge of that which is, and practical knowledge as knowledge of that which ought to be. In this view, the theoretical employment of reason is that by which I cognize à priori (as necessary) that something is, while the practical is that by which I cognize à priori what ought to happen. Now, if it is an indubitably certain, though at the same time an entirely conditioned truth, that something is, or ought to happen, either a certain determinate condition of this truth is absolutely

[69] Not theological ethics; for this science contains ethical laws, which presuppose the existence of a Supreme Governor of the world; while moral-theology, on the contrary, is the expression of a conviction of the existence of a Supreme Being, founded upon ethical laws.

necessary, or such a condition may be arbitrarily presupposed. In the former case the condition is postulated (per thesin), in the latter supposed (per hypothesin). There are certain practical laws—those of morality—which are absolutely necessary. Now, if these laws necessarily presuppose the existence of some being, as the condition of the possibility of their obligatory power, this being must be postulated, because the conditioned, from which we reason to this determinate condition, is itself cognized à priori as absolutely necessary. We shall at some future time show that the moral laws not merely presuppose the existence of a Supreme Being, but also, as themselves absolutely necessary in a different relation, demand or postulate it—although only from a practical point of view. The discussion of this argument we postpone for the present.

When the question relates merely to that which is, not to that which ought to be, the conditioned which is presented in experience is always cogitated as contingent. For this reason its condition cannot be regarded as absolutely necessary, but merely as relatively necessary, or rather as needful; the condition is in itself and à priori a mere arbitrary presupposition in aid of the cognition, by reason, of the conditioned. If, then, we are to possess a theoretical cognition of the absolute necessity of a thing, we cannot attain to this cognition otherwise than à priori by means of conceptions; while it is impossible in this way to cognize the existence of a cause which bears any relation to an existence given in experience.

Theoretical cognition is speculative when it relates to an object or certain conceptions of an object which is not given and cannot be discovered by means of experience. It is opposed to the cognition of nature, which concerns only those objects or predicates which can be presented in a possible experience.

The principle that everything which happens (the empirically contingent) must have a cause, is a principle of the cognition of nature, but not of speculative cognition. For, if we change it into an abstract principle, and deprive it of its reference to experience and the empirical, we shall find that it cannot with justice be regarded any longer as a synthetical proposition, and that it is impossible to discover any mode of transition from that which exists to something entirely different—termed cause. Nay, more, the conception of a cause likewise that of the contingent—loses, in this speculative mode of employing it, all significance, for its objective reality and meaning are comprehensible from experience alone.

When from the existence of the universe and the things in it the existence of a cause of the universe is inferred, reason is proceeding not in the natural, but in the speculative method. For the principle of the former enounces, not that things themselves or substances, but only that which happens or their states—as empirically contingent, have a cause: the assertion that the existence of substance itself is contingent is not justified by experience, it is the assertion of a reason employing its principles in a speculative manner. If, again, I infer from the form of the universe, from the way in which all things are connected and act and react upon each other, the existence of a cause entirely distinct from the universe—this would again be a judgement of purely speculative reason; because the object in this case—the cause—can never be an object of possible experience. In both these cases the principle of causality, which is valid only in the field of experience—useless and even meaningless beyond this region, would be diverted from its proper destination.

Now I maintain that all attempts of reason to establish a theology by the aid of speculation alone are fruitless, that the principles of reason as applied to nature do not conduct us to any theological truths, and, consequently, that a rational theology can have no existence, unless it is founded upon the laws of morality. For all synthetical principles of the understanding are valid only as immanent in experience; while the cognition of a Supreme Being necessitates their being employed transcendentally, and of this the understanding is quite incapable. If the empirical law of causality is to conduct us to a Supreme Being, this being must belong to the chain of empirical objects—in which case it would be, like all phenomena, itself conditioned. If the possibility of passing the limits of experience be admitted, by means of the dynamical law of the relation of an effect to its cause, what kind of conception shall we obtain by this procedure? Certainly not the conception of a Supreme Being, because experience never presents us with the greatest of all possible effects, and it is only an effect of this character that could witness to the existence of a corresponding cause. If, for the purpose of fully satisfying the requirements of Reason, we recognize her right to assert the existence of a perfect and absolutely necessary being, this can be admitted only from favour, and cannot be regarded as the result of irresistible demonstration. The physico-theological proof may add weight to others—if other proofs there are—by connecting speculation with experience; but in itself it rather prepares the mind for theological cognition, and gives it a right and natural direction, than establishes a sure foundation for theology.

It is now perfectly evident that transcendental questions admit only of transcendental answers—those presented à priori by pure conceptions without the least empirical admixture. But the question in the present case is evidently synthetical—it aims at the extension of our cognition beyond the bounds of experience—it requires an assurance respecting the existence of a being corresponding with the idea in our minds, to which no experience can ever be adequate. Now it has been abundantly proved that all à priori synthetical cognition is possible only as the expression of the formal conditions of a possible experience; and that the validity of all principles depends upon their immanence in the field of experience, that is, their relation to objects of empirical cognition or phenomena. Thus all transcendental procedure in reference to speculative theology is without result.

If any one prefers doubting the conclusiveness of the proofs of our analytic to losing the persuasion of the validity of these old and time honoured arguments, he at least cannot decline answering the question—how he can pass the limits of all possible experience by the help of mere ideas. If he talks of new arguments, or of improvements upon old arguments, I request him to spare me. There is certainly no great choice in this sphere of discussion, as all speculative arguments must at last look for support to the ontological, and I have, therefore, very little to fear from the argumentative fecundity of the dogmatical defenders of a non-sensuous reason. Without looking upon myself as a remarkably combative person, I shall not decline the challenge to detect the fallacy and destroy the pretensions of every attempt of speculative theology. And yet the hope of better fortune never deserts those who are accustomed to the dogmatical mode of procedure. I shall, therefore, restrict myself to the simple and equitable demand that such reasoners will demonstrate, from the nature of the human mind as well as from that of the other sources of knowledge, how we are to proceed to extend our cognition completely à priori, and to carry it to that point where experience abandons us, and no means exist of guaranteeing the objective reality of our conceptions. In whatever way the understanding may have attained to a conception, the existence of the object of the conception cannot be discovered in it by analysis, because the cognition of the existence of the object depends upon the object's being posited and given in itself apart from the conception. But it is utterly impossible to go beyond our conception, without the aid of experience—which presents to the mind nothing but phenomena, or to attain by the help of mere conceptions to a conviction of the existence of new kinds of objects or supernatural beings.

But although pure speculative reason is far from sufficient to demonstrate the existence of a Supreme Being, it is of the highest utility in correcting our conception of this being—on the supposition that we can attain to the cognition of it by some other means—in making it consistent with itself and with all other conceptions of intelligible objects, clearing it from all that is incompatible with the conception of an ens summun, and eliminating from it all limitations or admixtures of empirical elements.

Transcendental theology is still therefore, notwithstanding its objective insufficiency, of importance in a negative respect; it is useful as a test of the procedure of reason when engaged with pure ideas, no other than a transcendental standard being in this case admissible. For if, from a practical point of view, the hypothesis of a Supreme and All-sufficient Being is to maintain its validity without opposition, it must be of the highest importance to define this conception in a correct and rigorous manner—as the transcendental conception of a necessary being, to eliminate all phenomenal elements (anthropomorphism in its most extended signification), and at the same time to overflow all contradictory assertions—be they atheistic, deistic, or anthropomorphic. This is of course very easy; as the same arguments which demonstrated the inability of human reason to affirm the existence of a Supreme Being must be alike sufficient to prove the invalidity of its denial. For it is impossible to gain from the pure speculation of reason demonstration that there exists no Supreme Being, as the ground of all that exists, or that this being possesses none of those properties which we regard as analogical with the dynamical qualities of a thinking being, or that, as the anthropomorphists would have us believe, it is subject to all the limitations which sensibility imposes upon those intelligences which exist in the world of experience.

A Supreme Being is, therefore, for the speculative reason, a mere ideal, though a faultless one—a conception which perfects and crowns the system of human cognition, but the objective reality of which can neither be proved nor disproved by pure reason. If this defect is ever supplied by a moral theology, the problematic transcendental theology which has preceded, will have been at least serviceable as demonstrating the mental necessity existing for the conception, by the complete determination of it which it has furnished, and the ceaseless testing of the conclusions of a reason often deceived by sense, and not always in harmony with its own ideas. The attributes of necessity, infinitude, unity, existence apart from the world (and not as a world soul), eternity (free from conditions of time), omnipresence (free from conditions of space), omnipotence, and others, are pure transcendental predicates; and thus the accurate conception of a Supreme Being, which every theology requires, is furnished by transcendental theology alone.

APPENDIX

Of the Regulative Employment of the Ideas of Pure Reason

The result of all the dialectical attempts of pure reason not only confirms the truth of what we have already proved in our Transcendental Analytic, namely, that all inferences which would lead us beyond the limits of experience are fallacious and groundless, but it at the same time teaches us this important lesson, that human reason has a natural inclination to overstep these limits, and that transcendental ideas are as much the natural property of the reason as categories are of the understanding. There exists this difference, however, that while the categories never mislead us, outward objects being always in perfect harmony therewith, ideas are the parents of irresistible illusions, the severest and most subtle criticism being required to save us from the fallacies which they induce.

Whatever is grounded in the nature of our powers will be found to be in harmony with the final purpose and proper employment of these powers, when once we have discovered their true direction and aim. We are entitled to suppose, therefore, that there exists a mode of employing transcendental ideas which is proper and immanent; although, when we mistake their meaning, and regard them as conceptions of actual things, their mode of application is transcendent and delusive. For it is not the idea itself, but only the employment of the idea in relation to possible experience, that is transcendent or immanent. An idea is employed transcendently, when it is applied to an object falsely believed to be adequate with and to correspond to it; imminently, when it is applied solely to the employment of the understanding in the sphere of experience. Thus all errors of subreptio—of misapplication, are to be ascribed to defects of judgement, and not to understanding or reason.

Reason never has an immediate relation to an object; it relates immediately to the understanding alone. It is only through the understanding that it can be employed in the field of experience. It does not form conceptions of objects, it merely arranges them and gives to them that unity which they are capable of possessing when the sphere of their application has been extended as widely as possible. Reason avails itself of the conception of the understanding for the sole purpose of producing totality in the different series. This totality the understanding does not concern itself with; its only occupation is the connection of experiences, by which series of conditions in accordance with conceptions are established. The object of reason is, therefore, the understanding and its proper destination. As the latter brings unity into the diversity of objects by means of its conceptions, so the former brings unity into the diversity of conceptions by means of ideas; as it sets the final aim of a collective unity to the operations of the understanding, which without this occupies itself with a distributive unity alone.

I accordingly maintain that transcendental ideas can never be employed as constitutive ideas, that they cannot be conceptions of objects, and that, when thus considered, they assume a fallacious and dialectical character. But, on the other hand, they are capable of an admirable and indispensably necessary application to objects—as regulative ideas, directing the understanding to a certain aim, the guiding lines towards which all its laws follow, and in which they all meet in one point. This point—though a mere idea (focus imaginarius), that is, not a point from which the conceptions of the understanding do really proceed, for it lies beyond the sphere of possible experience—serves, notwithstanding, to give to these conceptions the greatest possible unity combined with the greatest possible extension. Hence arises the natural illusion which induces us to believe that these lines proceed from an object which lies out of the sphere of empirical cognition, just as objects reflected in a mirror appear to be behind it. But this illusion—which we may hinder from imposing upon us—is necessary and unavoidable, if we desire to see, not only those objects which lie before us, but those which are at a great distance behind us; that is to say, when, in the present case, we direct the aims of the understanding, beyond every given experience, towards an extension as great as can possibly be attained.

If we review our cognitions in their entire extent, we shall find that the peculiar business of reason is to arrange them into a system, that is to say, to give them connection according to a principle. This unity presupposes an idea—the idea of the form of a whole (of cognition), preceding the determinate cognition of the parts, and containing the conditions which determine à priori to every part its place and relation to the other parts of the whole system. This idea, accordingly, demands complete unity in the cognition of the understanding—not the unity of a contingent aggregate, but that of a system connected according to necessary laws. It cannot be affirmed with propriety that this idea is a conception of an object; it is merely a conception of the complete unity of the conceptions of objects, in so far as this unity is available to the understanding as a rule. Such conceptions of reason are not derived from nature; on the contrary, we employ them for the interrogation and investigation of nature, and regard our cognition as defective so long as it is not adequate to them. We admit that such a thing as pure earth, pure water, or pure air, is not to be discovered. And yet we require these conceptions (which have their origin in the reason, so far as regards their absolute purity and completeness) for the purpose of determining the share which each of these natural causes has in every phenomenon. Thus the different kinds of matter are all referred to earths, as mere weight; to salts and inflammable bodies, as pure force; and finally, to water and air, as the vehicula of the former, or the machines employed by them in their operations—for the purpose of explaining the chemical action and reaction of bodies in accordance with the idea of a mechanism. For, although not actually so expressed, the influence of such ideas of reason is very observable in the procedure of natural philosophers.

If reason is the faculty of deducing the particular from the general, and if the general be certain in se and given, it is only necessary that the judgement should subsume the particular under the general, the particular being thus necessarily determined. I shall term this the demonstrative or apodeictic employment of reason. If, however, the general is admitted as problematical only, and is a mere idea, the particular case is certain, but the universality of the rule which applies to this particular case remains a problem. Several particular cases, the certainty of which is beyond doubt, are then taken and examined, for the purpose of discovering whether the rule is applicable to them; and if it appears that all the particular cases which can be collected follow from the rule, its universality is inferred, and at the same time, all the causes which have not, or cannot be presented to our observation, are concluded to be of the same character with those which we have observed. This I shall term the hypothetical employment of the reason.

The hypothetical exercise of reason by the aid of ideas employed as problematical conceptions is properly not constitutive. That is to say, if we consider the subject strictly, the truth of the rule, which has been employed as an hypothesis, does not follow from the use that is made of it by reason. For how can we know all the possible cases that may arise? some of which may, however, prove exceptions to the universality of the rule. This employment of reason is merely regulative, and its sole aim is the introduction of unity into the aggregate of our particular cognitions, and thereby the approximating of the rule to universality.

The object of the hypothetical employment of reason is therefore the systematic unity of cognitions; and this unity is the criterion of the truth of a rule. On the other hand, this systematic unity—as a mere idea—is in fact merely a unity projected, not to be regarded as given, but only in the light of a problem—a problem which serves, however, as a principle for the various and particular exercise of the understanding in experience, directs it with regard to those cases which are not presented to our observation, and introduces harmony and consistency into all its operations.

All that we can be certain of from the above considerations is that this systematic unity is a logical principle, whose aim is to assist the understanding, where it cannot of itself attain to rules, by means of ideas, to bring all these various rules under one principle, and thus to ensure the most complete consistency and connection that can be attained. But the assertion that objects and the understanding by which they are cognized are so constituted as to be determined to systematic unity, that this may be postulated à priori, without any reference to the interest of reason, and that we are justified in declaring all possible cognitions—empirical and others—to possess systematic unity, and to be subject to general principles from which, notwithstanding their various character, they are all derivable such an assertion can be founded only upon a transcendental principle of reason, which would render this systematic unity not subjectively and logically—in its character of a method, but objectively necessary.

We shall illustrate this by an example. The conceptions of the understanding make us acquainted, among many other kinds of unity, with that of the causality of a substance, which is termed power. The different phenomenal manifestations of the same substance appear at first view to be so very dissimilar that we are inclined to assume the existence of just as many different powers as there are different effects—as, in the case of the human mind, we have feeling, consciousness, imagination, memory, wit, analysis, pleasure, desire and so on. Now we are required by a logical maxim to reduce these differences to as small a number as possible, by comparing them and discovering the hidden identity which exists. We must inquire, for example, whether or not imagination (connected with consciousness), memory, wit, and analysis are not merely different forms of understanding and reason. The idea of a fundamental power, the existence of which no effort of logic can assure us of, is the problem to be solved, for the systematic representation of the existing variety of powers. The logical principle of reason requires us to produce as great a unity as is possible in the system of our cognitions; and the more the phenomena of this and the other power are found to be identical, the more probable does it become, that they are nothing but different manifestations of one and the same power, which may be called, relatively speaking, a fundamental power. And so with other cases.

These relatively fundamental powers must again be compared with each other, to discover, if possible, the one radical and absolutely fundamental power of which they are but the manifestations. But this unity is purely hypothetical. It is not maintained, that this unity does really exist, but that we must, in the interest of reason, that is, for the establishment of principles for the various rules presented by experience, try to discover and introduce it, so far as is practicable, into the sphere of our cognitions.

But the transcendental employment of the understanding would lead us to believe that this idea of a fundamental power is not problematical, but that it possesses objective reality, and thus the systematic unity of the various powers or forces in a substance is demanded by the understanding and erected into an apodeictic or necessary principle. For, without having attempted to discover the unity of the various powers existing in nature, nay, even after all our attempts have failed, we notwithstanding presuppose that it does exist, and may be, sooner or later, discovered. And this reason does, not only, as in the case above adduced, with regard to the unity of substance, but where many substances, although all to a certain extent homogeneous, are discoverable, as in the case of matter in general. Here also does reason presuppose the existence of the systematic unity of various powers—inasmuch as particular laws of nature are subordinate to general laws; and parsimony in principles is not merely an economical principle of reason, but an essential law of nature.

We cannot understand, in fact, how a logical principle of unity can of right exist, unless we presuppose a transcendental principle, by which such a systematic unit—as a property of objects themselves—is regarded as necessary à priori. For with what right can reason, in its logical exercise, require us to regard the variety of forces which nature displays, as in effect a disguised unity, and to deduce them from one fundamental force or power, when she is free to admit that it is just as possible that all forces should be different in kind, and that a systematic unity is not conformable to the design of nature? In this view of the case, reason would be proceeding in direct opposition to her own destination, by setting as an aim an idea which entirely conflicts with the procedure and arrangement of nature. Neither can we assert that reason has previously inferred this unity from the contingent nature of phenomena. For the law of reason which requires us to seek for this unity is a necessary law, inasmuch as without it we should not possess a faculty of reason, nor without reason a consistent and self-accordant mode of employing the understanding, nor, in the absence of this, any proper and sufficient criterion of empirical truth. In relation to this criterion, therefore, we must suppose the idea of the systematic unity of nature to possess objective validity and necessity.

We find this transcendental presupposition lurking in different forms in the principles of philosophers, although they have neither recognized it nor confessed to themselves its presence. That the diversities of individual things do not exclude identity of species, that the various species must be considered as merely different determinations of a few genera, and these again as divisions of still higher races, and so on—that, accordingly, a certain systematic unity of all possible empirical conceptions, in so far as they can be deduced from higher and more general conceptions, must be sought for, is a scholastic maxim or logical principle, without which reason could not be employed by us. For we can infer the particular from the general, only in so far as general properties of things constitute the foundation upon which the particular rest.

That the same unity exists in nature is presupposed by philosophers in the well-known scholastic maxim, which forbids us unnecessarily to augment the number of entities or principles (entia praeter necessitatem non esse multiplicanda). This maxim asserts that nature herself assists in the establishment of this unity of reason, and that the seemingly infinite diversity of phenomena should not deter us from the expectation of discovering beneath this diversity a unity of fundamental properties, of which the aforesaid variety is but a more or less determined form. This unity, although a mere idea, thinkers have found it necessary rather to moderate the desire than to encourage it. It was considered a great step when chemists were able to reduce all salts to two main genera—acids and alkalis; and they regard this difference as itself a mere variety, or different manifestation of one and the same fundamental material. The different kinds of earths (stones and even metals) chemists have endeavoured to reduce to three, and afterwards to two; but still, not content with this advance, they cannot but think that behind these diversities there lurks but one genus—nay, that even salts and earths have a common principle. It might be conjectured that this is merely an economical plan of reason, for the purpose of sparing itself trouble, and an attempt of a purely hypothetical character, which, when successful, gives an appearance of probability to the principle of explanation employed by the reason. But a selfish purpose of this kind is easily to be distinguished from the idea, according to which every one presupposes that this unity is in accordance with the laws of nature, and that reason does not in this case request, but requires, although we are quite unable to determine the proper limits of this unity.

If the diversity existing in phenomena—a diversity not of form (for in this they may be similar) but of content—were so great that the subtlest human reason could never by comparison discover in them the least similarity (which is not impossible), in this case the logical law of genera would be without foundation, the conception of a genus, nay, all general conceptions would be impossible, and the faculty of the understanding, the exercise of which is restricted to the world of conceptions, could not exist. The logical principle of genera, accordingly, if it is to be applied to nature (by which I mean objects presented to our senses), presupposes a transcendental principle. In accordance with this principle, homogeneity is necessarily presupposed in the variety of phenomena (although we are unable to determine à priori the degree of this homogeneity), because without it no empirical conceptions, and consequently no experience, would be possible.

The logical principle of genera, which demands identity in phenomena, is balanced by another principle—that of species, which requires variety and diversity in things, notwithstanding their accordance in the same genus, and directs the understanding to attend to the one no less than to the other. This principle (of the faculty of distinction) acts as a check upon the reason and reason exhibits in this respect a double and conflicting interest—on the one hand, the interest in the extent (the interest of generality) in relation to genera; on the other, that of the content (the interest of individuality) in relation to the variety of species. In the former case, the understanding cogitates more under its conceptions, in the latter it cogitates more in them. This distinction manifests itself likewise in the habits of thought peculiar to natural philosophers, some of whom—the remarkably speculative heads—may be said to be hostile to heterogeneity in phenomena, and have their eyes always fixed on the unity of genera, while others—with a strong empirical tendency—aim unceasingly at the analysis of phenomena, and almost destroy in us the hope of ever being able to estimate the character of these according to general principles.

The latter mode of thought is evidently based upon a logical principle, the aim of which is the systematic completeness of all cognitions. This principle authorizes me, beginning at the genus, to descend to the various and diverse contained under it; and in this way extension, as in the former case unity, is assured to the system. For if we merely examine the sphere of the conception which indicates a genus, we cannot discover how far it is possible to proceed in the division of that sphere; just as it is impossible, from the consideration of the space occupied by matter, to determine how far we can proceed in the division of it. Hence every genus must contain different species, and these again different subspecies; and as each of the latter must itself contain a sphere (must be of a certain extent, as a conceptus communis), reason demands that no species or sub-species is to be considered as the lowest possible. For a species or sub-species, being always a conception, which contains only what is common to a number of different things, does not completely determine any individual thing, or relate immediately to it, and must consequently contain other conceptions, that is, other sub-species under it. This law of specification may be thus expressed: entium varietates non temere sunt minuendae.

But it is easy to see that this logical law would likewise be without sense or application, were it not based upon a transcendental law of specification, which certainly does not require that the differences existing phenomena should be infinite in number, for the logical principle, which merely maintains the indeterminateness of the logical sphere of a conception, in relation to its possible division, does not authorize this statement; while it does impose upon the understanding the duty of searching for subspecies to every species, and minor differences in every difference. For, were there no lower conceptions, neither could there be any higher. Now the understanding cognizes only by means of conceptions; consequently, how far soever it may proceed in division, never by mere intuition, but always by lower and lower conceptions. The cognition of phenomena in their complete determination (which is possible only by means of the understanding) requires an unceasingly continued specification of conceptions, and a progression to ever smaller differences, of which abstraction had been made in the conception of the species, and still more in that of the genus.

This law of specification cannot be deduced from experience; it can never present us with a principle of so universal an application. Empirical specification very soon stops in its distinction of diversities, and requires the guidance of the transcendental law, as a principle of the reason—a law which imposes on us the necessity of never ceasing in our search for differences, even although these may not present themselves to the senses. That absorbent earths are of different kinds could only be discovered by obeying the anticipatory law of reason, which imposes upon the understanding the task of discovering the differences existing between these earths, and supposes that nature is richer in substances than our senses would indicate. The faculty of the understanding belongs to us just as much under the presupposition of differences in the objects of nature, as under the condition that these objects are homogeneous, because we could not possess conceptions, nor make any use of our understanding, were not the phenomena included under these conceptions in some respects dissimilar, as well as similar, in their character.

Reason thus prepares the sphere of the understanding for the operations of this faculty: 1. By the principle of the homogeneity of the diverse in higher genera; 2. By the principle of the variety of the homogeneous in lower species; and, to complete the systematic unity, it adds, 3. A law of the affinity of all conceptions which prescribes a continuous transition from one species to every other by the gradual increase of diversity. We may term these the principles of the homogeneity, the specification, and the continuity of forms. The latter results from the union of the two former, inasmuch as we regard the systematic connection as complete in thought, in the ascent to higher genera, as well as in the descent to lower species. For all diversities must be related to each other, as they all spring from one highest genus, descending through the different gradations of a more and more extended determination.

We may illustrate the systematic unity produced by the three logical principles in the following manner. Every conception may be regarded as a point, which, as the standpoint of a spectator, has a certain horizon, which may be said to enclose a number of things that may be viewed, so to speak, from that centre. Within this horizon there must be an infinite number of other points, each of which has its own horizon, smaller and more circumscribed; in other words, every species contains sub-species, according to the principle of specification, and the logical horizon consists of smaller horizons (subspecies), but not of points (individuals), which possess no extent. But different horizons or genera, which include under them so many conceptions, may have one common horizon, from which, as from a mid-point, they may be surveyed; and we may proceed thus, till we arrive at the highest genus, or universal and true horizon, which is determined by the highest conception, and which contains under itself all differences and varieties, as genera, species, and subspecies.

To this highest standpoint I am conducted by the law of homogeneity, as to all lower and more variously-determined conceptions by the law of specification. Now as in this way there exists no void in the whole extent of all possible conceptions, and as out of the sphere of these the mind can discover nothing, there arises from the presupposition of the universal horizon above mentioned, and its complete division, the principle: Non datur vacuum formarum. This principle asserts that there are not different primitive and highest genera, which stand isolated, so to speak, from each other, but all the various genera are mere divisions and limitations of one highest and universal genus; and hence follows immediately the principle: Datur continuum formarum. This principle indicates that all differences of species limit each other, and do not admit of transition from one to another by a saltus, but only through smaller degrees of the difference between the one species and the other. In one word, there are no species or sub-species which (in the view of reason) are the nearest possible to each other; intermediate species or sub-species being always possible, the difference of which from each of the former is always smaller than the difference existing between these.

The first law, therefore, directs us to avoid the notion that there exist different primal genera, and enounces the fact of perfect homogeneity; the second imposes a check upon this tendency to unity and prescribes the distinction of sub-species, before proceeding to apply our general conceptions to individuals. The third unites both the former, by enouncing the fact of homogeneity as existing even in the most various diversity, by means of the gradual transition from one species to another. Thus it indicates a relationship between the different branches or species, in so far as they all spring from the same stem.

But this logical law of the continuum specierum (formarum logicarum) presupposes a transcendental principle (lex continui in natura), without which the understanding might be led into error, by following the guidance of the former, and thus perhaps pursuing a path contrary to that prescribed by nature. This law must, consequently, be based upon pure transcendental, and not upon empirical, considerations. For, in the latter case, it would come later than the system; whereas it is really itself the parent of all that is systematic in our cognition of nature. These principles are not mere hypotheses employed for the purpose of experimenting upon nature; although when any such connection is discovered, it forms a solid ground for regarding the hypothetical unity as valid in the sphere of nature—and thus they are in this respect not without their use. But we go farther, and maintain that it is manifest that these principles of parsimony in fundamental causes, variety in effects, and affinity in phenomena, are in accordance both with reason and nature, and that they are not mere methods or plans devised for the purpose of assisting us in our observation of the external world.

But it is plain that this continuity of forms is a mere idea, to which no adequate object can be discovered in experience. And this for two reasons. First, because the species in nature are really divided, and hence form quanta discreta; and, if the gradual progression through their affinity were continuous, the intermediate members lying between two given species must be infinite in number, which is impossible. Secondly, because we cannot make any determinate empirical use of this law, inasmuch as it does not present us with any criterion of affinity which could aid us in determining how far we ought to pursue the graduation of differences: it merely contains a general indication that it is our duty to seek for and, if possible, to discover them.

When we arrange these principles of systematic unity in the order conformable to their employment in experience, they will stand thus: Variety, Affinity, Unity, each of them, as ideas, being taken in the highest degree of their completeness. Reason presupposes the existence of cognitions of the understanding, which have a direct relation to experience, and aims at the ideal unity of these cognitions—a unity which far transcends all experience or empirical notions. The affinity of the diverse, notwithstanding the differences existing between its parts, has a relation to things, but a still closer one to the mere properties and powers of things. For example, imperfect experience may represent the orbits of the planets as circular. But we discover variations from this course, and we proceed to suppose that the planets revolve in a path which, if not a circle, is of a character very similar to it. That is to say, the movements of those planets which do not form a circle will approximate more or less to the properties of a circle, and probably form an ellipse. The paths of comets exhibit still greater variations, for, so far as our observation extends, they do not return upon their own course in a circle or ellipse. But we proceed to the conjecture that comets describe a parabola, a figure which is closely allied to the ellipse. In fact, a parabola is merely an ellipse, with its longer axis produced to an indefinite extent. Thus these principles conduct us to a unity in the genera of the forms of these orbits, and, proceeding farther, to a unity as regards the cause of the motions of the heavenly bodies—that is, gravitation. But we go on extending our conquests over nature, and endeavour to explain all seeming deviations from these rules, and even make additions to our system which no experience can ever substantiate—for example, the theory, in affinity with that of ellipses, of hyperbolic paths of comets, pursuing which, these bodies leave our solar system and, passing from sun to sun, unite the most distant parts of the infinite universe, which is held together by the same moving power.

The most remarkable circumstance connected with these principles is that they seem to be transcendental, and, although only containing ideas for the guidance of the empirical exercise of reason, and although this empirical employment stands to these ideas in an asymptotic relation alone (to use a mathematical term), that is, continually approximate, without ever being able to attain to them, they possess, notwithstanding, as à priori synthetical propositions, objective though undetermined validity, and are available as rules for possible experience. In the elaboration of our experience, they may also be employed with great advantage, as heuristic[70] principles. A transcendental deduction of them cannot be made; such a deduction being always impossible in the case of ideas, as has been already shown.

We distinguished, in the Transcendental Analytic, the dynamical principles of the understanding, which are regulative principles of intuition, from the mathematical, which are constitutive principles of intuition. These dynamical laws are, however, constitutive in relation to experience, inasmuch as they render the conceptions without which experience could not exist possible à priori. But the principles of pure reason cannot be constitutive even in regard to empirical conceptions, because no sensuous schema corresponding to them can be discovered, and they cannot therefore have an object in concreto. Now, if I grant that they cannot be employed in the sphere of experience, as constitutive principles, how shall I secure for them employment and objective validity as regulative principles, and in what way can they be so employed?

The understanding is the object of reason, as sensibility is the object of the understanding. The production of systematic unity in all the empirical operations of the understanding is the proper occupation of reason; just as it is the business of the understanding to connect the various content of phenomena by means of conceptions, and subject them to empirical laws. But the operations of the understanding are, without the schemata of sensibility, undetermined; and, in the

[70] From the Greek, eurhioko.

same manner, the unity of reason is perfectly undetermined as regards the conditions under which, and the extent to which, the understanding ought to carry the systematic connection of its conceptions. But, although it is impossible to discover in intuition a schema for the complete systematic unity of all the conceptions of the understanding, there must be some analogon of this schema. This analogon is the idea of the maximum of the division and the connection of our cognition in one principle. For we may have a determinate notion of a maximum and an absolutely perfect, all the restrictive conditions which are connected with an indeterminate and various content having been abstracted. Thus the idea of reason is analogous with a sensuous schema, with this difference, that the application of the categories to the schema of reason does not present a cognition of any object (as is the case with the application of the categories to sensuous schemata), but merely provides us with a rule or principle for the systematic unity of the exercise of the understanding. Now, as every principle which imposes upon the exercise of the understanding à priori compliance with the rule of systematic unity also relates, although only in an indirect manner, to an object of experience, the principles of pure reason will also possess objective reality and validity in relation to experience. But they will not aim at determining our knowledge in regard to any empirical object; they will merely indicate the procedure, following which the empirical and determinate exercise of the understanding may be in complete harmony and connection with itself—a result which is produced by its being brought into harmony with the principle of systematic unity, so far as that is possible, and deduced from it.

I term all subjective principles, which are not derived from observation of the constitution of an object, but from the interest which Reason has in producing a certain completeness in her cognition of that object, maxims of reason. Thus there are maxims of speculative reason, which are based solely upon its speculative interest, although they appear to be objective principles.

When principles which are really regulative are regarded as constitutive, and employed as objective principles, contradictions must arise; but if they are considered as mere maxims, there is no room for contradictions of any kind, as they then merely indicate the different interests of reason, which occasion differences in the mode of thought. In effect, Reason has only one single interest, and the seeming contradiction existing between her maxims merely indicates a difference in, and a reciprocal limitation of, the methods by which this interest is satisfied.

This reasoner has at heart the interest of diversity—in accordance with the principle of specification; another, the interest of unity—in accordance with the principle of aggregation. Each believes that his judgement rests upon a thorough insight into the subject he is examining, and yet it has been influenced solely by a greater or less degree of adherence to some one of the two principles, neither of which are objective, but originate solely from the interest of reason, and on this account to be termed maxims rather than principles. When I observe intelligent men disputing about the distinctive characteristics of men, animals, or plants, and even of minerals, those on the one side assuming the existence of certain national characteristics, certain well-defined and hereditary distinctions of family, race, and so on, while the other side maintain that nature has endowed all races of men with the same faculties and dispositions, and that all differences are but the result of external and accidental circumstances—I have only to consider for a moment the real nature of the subject of discussion, to arrive at the conclusion that it is a subject far too deep for us to judge of, and that there is little probability of either party being able to speak from a perfect insight into and understanding of the nature of the subject itself. Both have, in reality, been struggling for the twofold interest of reason; the one maintaining the one interest, the other the other. But this difference between the maxims of diversity and unity may easily be reconciled and adjusted; although, so long as they are regarded as objective principles, they must occasion not only contradictions and polemic, but place hinderances in the way of the advancement of truth, until some means is discovered of reconciling these conflicting interests, and bringing reason into union and harmony with itself.

The same is the case with the so-called law discovered by Leibnitz, and supported with remarkable ability by Bonnet—the law of the continuous gradation of created beings, which is nothing more than an inference from the principle of affinity; for observation and study of the order of nature could never present it to the mind as an objective truth. The steps of this ladder, as they appear in experience, are too far apart from each other, and the so-called petty differences between different kinds of animals are in nature commonly so wide separations that no confidence can be placed in such views (particularly when we reflect on the great variety of things, and the ease with which we can discover resemblances), and no faith in the laws which are said to express the aims and purposes of nature. On the other hand, the method of investigating the order of nature in the light of this principle, and the maxim which requires us to regard this order—it being still undetermined how far it extends—as really existing in nature, is beyond doubt a legitimate and excellent principle of reason—a principle which extends farther than any experience or observation of ours and which, without giving us any positive knowledge of anything in the region of experience, guides us to the goal of systematic unity.

Of the Ultimate End of the Natural Dialectic of Human Reason.

The ideas of pure reason cannot be, of themselves and in their own nature, dialectical; it is from their misemployment alone that fallacies and illusions arise. For they originate in the nature of reason itself, and it is impossible that this supreme tribunal for all the rights and claims of speculation should be itself undeserving of confidence and promotive of error. It is to be expected, therefore, that these ideas have a genuine and legitimate aim. It is true, the mob of sophists raise against reason the cry of inconsistency and contradiction, and affect to despise the government of that faculty, because they cannot understand its constitution, while it is to its beneficial influences alone that they owe the position and the intelligence which enable them to criticize and to blame its procedure.

We cannot employ an à priori conception with certainty, until we have made a transcendental deduction therefore. The ideas of pure reason do not admit of the same kind of deduction as the categories. But if they are to possess the least objective validity, and to represent anything but mere creations of thought (entia rationis ratiocinantis), a deduction of them must be possible. This deduction will complete the critical task imposed upon pure reason; and it is to this part Of our labours that we now proceed.

There is a great difference between a thing's being presented to the mind as an object in an absolute sense, or merely as an ideal object. In the former case I employ my conceptions to determine the object; in the latter case nothing is present to the mind but a mere schema, which does not relate directly to an object, not even in a hypothetical sense, but which is useful only for the purpose of representing other objects to the mind, in a mediate and indirect manner, by means of their relation to the idea in the intellect. Thus I say the conception of a supreme intelligence is a mere idea; that is to say, its objective reality does not consist in the fact that it has an immediate relation to an object (for in this sense we have no means of establishing its objective validity), it is merely a schema constructed according to the necessary conditions of the unity of reason—the schema of a thing in general, which is useful towards the production of the highest degree of systematic unity in the empirical exercise of reason, in which we deduce this or that object of experience from the imaginary object of this idea, as the ground or cause of the said object of experience. In this way, the idea is properly a heuristic, and not an ostensive, conception; it does not give us any information respecting the constitution of an object, it merely indicates how, under the guidance of the idea, we ought to investigate the constitution and the relations of objects in the world of experience. Now, if it can be shown that the three kinds of transcendental ideas (psychological, cosmological, and theological), although not relating directly to any object nor determining it, do nevertheless, on the supposition of the existence of an ideal object, produce systematic unity in the laws of the empirical employment of the reason, and extend our empirical cognition, without ever being inconsistent or in opposition with it—it must be a necessary maxim of reason to regulate its procedure according to these ideas. And this forms the transcendental deduction of all speculative ideas, not as constitutive principles of the extension of our cognition beyond the limits of our experience, but as regulative principles of the systematic unity of empirical cognition, which is by the aid of these ideas arranged and emended within its own proper limits, to an extent unattainable by the operation of the principles of the understanding alone.

I shall make this plainer. Guided by the principles involved in these ideas, we must, in the first place, so connect all the phenomena, actions, and feelings of the mind, as if it were a simple substance, which, endowed with personal identity, possesses a permanent existence (in this life at least), while its states, among which those of the body are to be included as external conditions, are in continual change. Secondly, in cosmology, we must investigate the conditions of all natural phenomena, internal as well as external, as if they belonged to a chain infinite and without any prime or supreme member, while we do not, on this account, deny the existence of intelligible grounds of these phenomena, although we never employ them to explain phenomena, for the simple reason that they are not objects of our cognition. Thirdly, in the sphere of theology, we must regard the whole system of possible experience as forming an absolute, but dependent and sensuously-conditioned unity, and at the same time as based upon a sole, supreme, and all-sufficient ground existing apart from the world itself—a ground which is a self-subsistent, primeval and creative reason, in relation to which we so employ our reason in the field of experience, as if all objects drew their origin from that archetype of all reason. In other words, we ought not to deduce the internal phenomena of the mind from a simple thinking substance, but deduce them from each other under the guidance of the regulative idea of a simple being; we ought not to deduce the phenomena, order, and unity of the universe from a supreme intelligence, but merely draw from this idea of a supremely wise cause the rules which must guide reason in its connection of causes and effects.

Now there is nothing to hinder us from admitting these ideas to possess an objective and hyperbolic existence, except the cosmological ideas, which lead reason into an antinomy: the psychological and theological ideas are not antinomial. They contain no contradiction; and how, then, can any one dispute their objective reality, since he who denies it knows as little about their possibility as we who affirm? And yet, when we wish to admit the existence of a thing, it is not sufficient to convince ourselves that there is no positive obstacle in the way; for it cannot be allowable to regard mere creations of thought, which transcend, though they do not contradict, all our conceptions, as real and determinate objects, solely upon the authority of a speculative reason striving to compass its own aims. They cannot, therefore, be admitted to be real in themselves; they can only possess a comparative reality—that of a schema of the regulative principle of the systematic unity of all cognition. They are to be regarded not as actual things, but as in some measure analogous to them. We abstract from the object of the idea all the conditions which limit the exercise of our understanding, but which, on the other hand, are the sole conditions of our possessing a determinate conception of any given thing. And thus we cogitate a something, of the real nature of which we have not the least conception, but which we represent to ourselves as standing in a relation to the whole system of phenomena, analogous to that in which phenomena stand to each other.

By admitting these ideal beings, we do not really extend our cognitions beyond the objects of possible experience; we extend merely the empirical unity of our experience, by the aid of systematic unity, the schema of which is furnished by the idea, which is therefore valid—not as a constitutive, but as a regulative principle.

For although we posit a thing corresponding to the idea—a something, an actual existence—we do not on that account aim at the extension of our cognition by means of transcendent conceptions. This existence is purely ideal, and not objective; it is the mere expression of the systematic unity which is to be the guide of reason in the field of experience. There are no attempts made at deciding what the ground of this unity may be, or what the real nature of this imaginary being.

Thus the transcendental and only determinate conception of God, which is presented to us by speculative reason, is in the strictest sense deistic. In other words, reason does not assure us of the objective validity of the conception; it merely gives us the idea of something, on which the supreme and necessary unity of all experience is based. This something we cannot, following the analogy of a real substance, cogitate otherwise than as the cause of all things operating in accordance with rational laws, if we regard it as an individual object; although we should rest contented with the idea alone as a regulative principle of reason, and make no attempt at completing the sum of the conditions imposed by thought. This attempt is, indeed, inconsistent with the grand aim of complete systematic unity in the sphere of cognition—a unity to which no bounds are set by reason.

Hence it happens that, admitting a divine being, I can have no conception of the internal possibility of its perfection, or of the necessity of its existence. The only advantage of this admission is that it enables me to answer all other questions relating to the contingent, and to give reason the most complete satisfaction as regards the unity which it aims at attaining in the world of experience. But I cannot satisfy reason with regard to this hypothesis itself; and this proves that it is not its intelligence and insight into the subject, but its speculative interest alone which induces it to proceed from a point lying far beyond the sphere of our cognition, for the purpose of being able to consider all objects as parts of a systematic whole.

Here a distinction presents itself, in regard to the way in which we may cogitate a presupposition—a distinction which is somewhat subtle, but of great importance in transcendental philosophy. I may have sufficient grounds to admit something, or the existence of something, in a relative point of view (suppositio relativa), without being justified in admitting it in an absolute sense (suppositio absoluta). This distinction is undoubtedly requisite, in the case of a regulative principle, the necessity of which we recognize, though we are ignorant of the source and cause of that necessity, and which we assume to be based upon some ultimate ground, for the purpose of being able to cogitate the universality of the principle in a more determinate way. For example, I cogitate the existence of a being corresponding to a pure transcendental idea. But I cannot admit that this being exists absolutely and in itself, because all of the conceptions by which I can cogitate an object in a determinate manner fall short of assuring me of its existence; nay, the conditions of the objective validity of my conceptions are excluded by the idea—by the very fact of its being an idea. The conceptions of reality, substance, causality, nay, even that of necessity in existence, have no significance out of the sphere of empirical cognition, and cannot, beyond that sphere, determine any object. They may, accordingly, be employed to explain the possibility of things in the world of sense, but they are utterly inadequate to explain the possibility of the universe itself considered as a whole; because in this case the ground of explanation must lie out of and beyond the world, and cannot, therefore, be an object of possible experience. Now, I may admit the existence of an incomprehensible being of this nature—the object of a mere idea, relatively to the world of sense; although I have no ground to admit its existence absolutely and in itself. For if an idea (that of a systematic and complete unity, of which I shall presently speak more particularly) lies at the foundation of the most extended empirical employment of reason, and if this idea cannot be adequately represented in concreto, although it is indispensably necessary for the approximation of empirical unity to the highest possible degree—I am not only authorized, but compelled, to realize this idea, that is, to posit a real object corresponding thereto. But I cannot profess to know this object; it is to me merely a something, to which, as the ground of systematic unity in cognition, I attribute such properties as are analogous to the conceptions employed by the understanding in the sphere of experience. Following the analogy of the notions of reality, substance, causality, and necessity, I cogitate a being, which possesses all these attributes in the highest degree; and, as this idea is the offspring of my reason alone, I cogitate this being as self-subsistent reason, and as the cause of the universe operating by means of ideas of the greatest possible harmony and unity. Thus I abstract all conditions that would limit my idea, solely for the purpose of rendering systematic unity possible in the world of empirical diversity, and thus securing the widest possible extension for the exercise of reason in that sphere. This I am enabled to do, by regarding all connections and relations in the world of sense, as if they were the dispositions of a supreme reason, of which our reason is but a faint image. I then proceed to cogitate this Supreme Being by conceptions which have, properly, no meaning or application, except in the world of sense. But as I am authorized to employ the transcendental hypothesis of such a being in a relative respect alone, that is, as the substratum of the greatest possible unity in experience—I may attribute to a being which I regard as distinct from the world, such properties as belong solely to the sphere of sense and experience. For I do not desire, and am not justified in desiring, to cognize this object of my idea, as it exists in itself; for I possess no conceptions sufficient for this task, those of reality, substance, causality, nay, even that of necessity in existence, losing all significance, and becoming merely the signs of conceptions, without content and without applicability, when I attempt to carry them beyond the limits of the world of sense. I cogitate merely the relation of a perfectly unknown being to the greatest possible systematic unity of experience, solely for the purpose of employing it as the schema of the regulative principle which directs reason in its empirical exercise.

It is evident, at the first view, that we cannot presuppose the reality of this transcendental object, by means of the conceptions of reality, substance, causality, and so on, because these conceptions cannot be applied to anything that is distinct from the world of sense. Thus the supposition of a Supreme Being or cause is purely relative; it is cogitated only in behalf of the systematic unity of experience; such a being is but a something, of whose existence in itself we have not the least conception. Thus, too, it becomes sufficiently manifest why we required the idea of a necessary being in relation to objects given by sense, although we can never have the least conception of this being, or of its absolute necessity.

And now we can clearly perceive the result of our transcendental dialectic, and the proper aim of the ideas of pure reason—which become dialectical solely from misunderstanding and inconsiderateness. Pure reason is, in fact, occupied with itself, and not with any object. Objects are not presented to it to be embraced in the unity of an empirical conception; it is only the cognitions of the understanding that are presented to it, for the purpose of receiving the unity of a rational conception, that is, of being connected according to a principle. The unity of reason is the unity of system; and this systematic unity is not an objective principle, extending its dominion over objects, but a subjective maxim, extending its authority over the empirical cognition of objects. The systematic connection which reason gives to the empirical employment of the understanding not only advances the extension of that employment, but ensures its correctness, and thus the principle of a systematic unity of this nature is also objective, although only in an indefinite respect (principium vagum). It is not, however, a constitutive principle, determining an object to which it directly relates; it is merely a regulative principle or maxim, advancing and strengthening the empirical exercise of reason, by the opening up of new paths of which the understanding is ignorant, while it never conflicts with the laws of its exercise in the sphere of experience.

But reason cannot cogitate this systematic unity, without at the same time cogitating an object of the idea—an object that cannot be presented in any experience, which contains no concrete example of a complete systematic unity. This being (ens rationis ratiocinatae) is therefore a mere idea and is not assumed to be a thing which is real absolutely and in itself. On the contrary, it forms merely the problematical foundation of the connection which the mind introduces among the phenomena of the sensuous world. We look upon this connection, in the light of the above-mentioned idea, as if it drew its origin from the supposed being which corresponds to the idea. And yet all we aim at is the possession of this idea as a secure foundation for the systematic unity of experience—a unity indispensable to reason, advantageous to the understanding, and promotive of the interests of empirical cognition.

We mistake the true meaning of this idea when we regard it as an enouncement, or even as a hypothetical declaration of the existence of a real thing, which we are to regard as the origin or ground of a systematic constitution of the universe. On the contrary, it is left completely undetermined what the nature or properties of this so-called ground may be. The idea is merely to be adopted as a point of view, from which this unity, so essential to reason and so beneficial to the understanding, may be regarded as radiating. In one word, this transcendental thing is merely the schema of a regulative principle, by means of which Reason, so far as in her lies, extends the dominion of systematic unity over the whole sphere of experience.

The first object of an idea of this kind is the ego, considered merely as a thinking nature or soul. If I wish to investigate the properties of a thinking being, I must interrogate experience. But I find that I can apply none of the categories to this object, the schema of these categories, which is the condition of their application, being given only in sensuous intuition. But I cannot thus attain to the cognition of a systematic unity of all the phenomena of the internal sense. Instead, therefore, of an empirical conception of what the soul really is, reason takes the conception of the empirical unity of all thought, and, by cogitating this unity as unconditioned and primitive, constructs the rational conception or idea of a simple substance which is in itself unchangeable, possessing personal identity, and in connection with other real things external to it; in one word, it constructs the idea of a simple self-subsistent intelligence. But the real aim of reason in this procedure is the attainment of principles of systematic unity for the explanation of the phenomena of the soul. That is, reason desires to be able to represent all the determinations of the internal sense as existing in one subject, all powers as deduced from one fundamental power, all changes as mere varieties in the condition of a being which is permanent and always the same, and all phenomena in space as entirely different in their nature from the procedure of thought. Essential simplicity (with the other attributes predicated of the ego) is regarded as the mere schema of this regulative principle; it is not assumed that it is the actual ground of the properties of the soul. For these properties may rest upon quite different grounds, of which we are completely ignorant; just as the above predicates could not give us any knowledge of the soul as it is in itself, even if we regarded them as valid in respect of it, inasmuch as they constitute a mere idea, which cannot be represented in concreto. Nothing but good can result from a psychological idea of this kind, if we only take proper care not to consider it as more than an idea; that is, if we regard it as valid merely in relation to the employment of reason, in the sphere of the phenomena of the soul. Under the guidance of this idea, or principle, no empirical laws of corporeal phenomena are called in to explain that which is a phenomenon of the internal sense alone; no windy hypotheses of the generation, annihilation, and palingenesis of souls are admitted. Thus the consideration of this object of the internal sense is kept pure, and unmixed with heterogeneous elements; while the investigation of reason aims at reducing all the grounds of explanation employed in this sphere of knowledge to a single principle. All this is best effected, nay, cannot be effected otherwise than by means of such a schema, which requires us to regard this ideal thing as an actual existence. The psychological idea is, therefore, meaningless and inapplicable, except as the schema of a regulative conception. For, if I ask whether the soul is not really of a spiritual nature—it is a question which has no meaning.

From such a conception has been abstracted, not merely all corporeal nature, but all nature, that is, all the predicates of a possible experience; and consequently, all the conditions which enable us to cogitate an object to this conception have disappeared. But, if these conditions are absent, it is evident that the conception is meaningless.

The second regulative idea of speculative reason is the conception of the universe. For nature is properly the only object presented to us, in regard to which reason requires regulative principles. Nature is twofold—thinking and corporeal nature. To cogitate the latter in regard to its internal possibility, that is, to determine the application of the categories to it, no idea is required—no representation which transcends experience. In this sphere, therefore, an idea is impossible, sensuous intuition being our only guide; while, in the sphere of psychology, we require the fundamental idea (I), which contains à priori a certain form of thought namely, the unity of the ego. Pure reason has, therefore, nothing left but nature in general, and the completeness of conditions in nature in accordance with some principle. The absolute totality of the series of these conditions is an idea, which can never be fully realized in the empirical exercise of reason, while it is serviceable as a rule for the procedure of reason in relation to that totality. It requires us, in the explanation of given phenomena (in the regress or ascent in the series), to proceed as if the series were infinite in itself, that is, were prolonged in indefinitum; while on the other hand, where reason is regarded as itself the determining cause (in the region of freedom), we are required to proceed as if we had not before us an object of sense, but of the pure understanding. In this latter case, the conditions do not exist in the series of phenomena, but may be placed quite out of and beyond it, and the series of conditions may be regarded as if it had an absolute beginning from an intelligible cause. All this proves that the cosmological ideas are nothing but regulative principles, and not constitutive; and that their aim is not to realize an actual totality in such series. The full discussion of this subject will be found in its proper place in the chapter on the antinomy of pure reason.

The third idea of pure reason, containing the hypothesis of a being which is valid merely as a relative hypothesis, is that of the one and all-sufficient cause of all cosmological series, in other words, the idea of God. We have not the slightest ground absolutely to admit the existence of an object corresponding to this idea; for what can empower or authorize us to affirm the existence of a being of the highest perfection—a being whose existence is absolutely necessary—merely because we possess the conception of such a being? The answer is: It is the existence of the world which renders this hypothesis necessary. But this answer makes it perfectly evident that the idea of this being, like all other speculative ideas, is essentially nothing more than a demand upon reason that it shall regulate the connection which it and its subordinate faculties introduce into the phenomena of the world by principles of systematic unity and, consequently, that it shall regard all phenomena as originating from one all-embracing being, as the supreme and all-sufficient cause. From this it is plain that the only aim of reason in this procedure is the establishment of its own formal rule for the extension of its dominion in the world of experience; that it does not aim at an extension of its cognition beyond the limits of experience; and that, consequently, this idea does not contain any constitutive principle.

The highest formal unity, which is based upon ideas alone, is the unity of all things—a unity in accordance with an aim or purpose; and the speculative interest of reason renders it necessary to regard all order in the world as if it originated from the intention and design of a supreme reason. This principle unfolds to the view of reason in the sphere of experience new and enlarged prospects, and invites it to connect the phenomena of the world according to teleological laws, and in this way to attain to the highest possible degree of systematic unity. The hypothesis of a supreme intelligence, as the sole cause of the universe—an intelligence which has for us no more than an ideal existence—is accordingly always of the greatest service to reason. Thus, if we presuppose, in relation to the figure of the earth (which is round, but somewhat flattened at the poles),[71] or that of mountains or seas, wise designs on the part of an author of the universe, we cannot fail to make, by the light of this supposition, a great number of interesting discoveries. If we keep to this hypothesis, as a principle which is purely regulative, even error cannot be very detrimental. For, in this case, error can have no more serious consequences than that, where we expected to discover a teleological connection (nexus finalis), only a mechanical or physical connection appears. In such a case, we merely fail to find the additional form of unity we expected, but we do not lose the rational unity which the mind requires in its procedure in experience. But even a miscarriage of this sort cannot affect the law in its general and teleological relations. For although we may convict an anatomist of an error, when he connects the limb of some animal with a certain purpose, it is quite impossible to prove in a single case that any arrangement of nature, be it what it may, is entirely without aim or design. And thus medical physiology, by the aid of a principle presented to it by pure reason, extends its very limited empirical knowledge of the purposes of the different parts of an organized body so far that it may be asserted with the utmost confidence, and with the approbation of all reflecting men, that every organ or bodily part of an animal has its use and answers a certain design. Now, this is a supposition which, if regarded as of a constitutive character, goes much farther than any experience

[71] The advantages which a circular form, in the case of the earth, has over every other, are well known. But few are aware that the slight flattening at the poles, which gives it the figure of a spheroid, is the only cause which prevents the elevations of continents or even of mountains, perhaps thrown up by some internal convulsion, from continually altering the position of the axis of the earth—and that to some considerable degree in a short time. The great protuberance of the earth under the Equator serves to overbalance the impetus of all other masses of earth, and thus to preserve the axis of the earth, so far as we can observe, in its present position. And yet this wise arrangement has been unthinkingly explained from the equilibrium of the formerly fluid mass.

or observation of ours can justify. Hence it is evident that it is nothing more than a regulative principle of reason, which aims at the highest degree of systematic unity, by the aid of the idea of a causality according to design in a supreme cause—a cause which it regards as the highest intelligence.

If, however, we neglect this restriction of the idea to a purely regulative influence, reason is betrayed into numerous errors. For it has then left the ground of experience, in which alone are to be found the criteria of truth, and has ventured into the region of the incomprehensible and unsearchable, on the heights of which it loses its power and collectedness, because it has completely severed its connection with experience.

The first error which arises from our employing the idea of a Supreme Being as a constitutive (in repugnance to the very nature of an idea), and not as a regulative principle, is the error of inactive reason (ignava ratio).[72] We may so term every principle which requires us to regard our investigations of nature as absolutely complete, and allows reason to cease its inquiries, as if it had fully executed its task. Thus the psychological idea of the ego, when employed as a constitutive principle for the explanation of the phenomena of the soul, and for the extension of our knowledge regarding this subject beyond the limits of experience—even to the condition of the soul after death—is convenient enough for the purposes of pure reason, but detrimental and even ruinous to its interests in the sphere of nature and experience. The dogmatizing spiritualist explains the unchanging unity of our personality through all changes of condition from the unity of a thinking substance, the interest which we take in things and events that can happen only after our death, from a consciousness of the immaterial nature of our thinking subject, and so on. Thus he dispenses with all empirical investigations into the cause of these internal phenomena, and with all possible explanations of them upon purely natural grounds; while, at the dictation of a transcendent reason, he passes by the immanent sources of cognition in experience, greatly to his own ease and convenience, but to the sacrifice of all, genuine insight and intelligence. These prejudicial consequences become still more evident, in the case of the dogmatical treatment of our idea of a Supreme Intelligence, and the theological system of nature (physico-theology) which is falsely based upon it. For, in this case, the aims which we observe in nature, and often those which we merely fancy to exist, make the investigation of causes a very easy task, by directing us to refer such and such phenomena immediately to the unsearchable will and counsel of the Supreme Wisdom, while we ought to investigate their causes in the general laws of the mechanism of matter. We are thus recommended to consider the labour

[72] This was the term applied by the old dialecticians to a sophistical argument, which ran thus: If it is your fate to die of this disease, you will die, whether you employ a physician or not. Cicero says that this mode of reasoning has received this appellation, because, if followed, it puts an end to the employment of reason in the affairs of life. For a similar reason, I have applied this designation to the sophistical argument of pure reason.

of reason as ended, when we have merely dispensed with its employment, which is guided surely and safely only by the order of nature and the series of changes in the world—which are arranged according to immanent and general laws. This error may be avoided, if we do not merely consider from the view-point of final aims certain parts of nature, such as the division and structure of a continent, the constitution and direction of certain mountain-chains, or even the organization existing in the vegetable and animal kingdoms, but look upon this systematic unity of nature in a perfectly general way, in relation to the idea of a Supreme Intelligence. If we pursue this advice, we lay as a foundation for all investigation the conformity to aims of all phenomena of nature in accordance with universal laws, for which no particular arrangement of nature is exempt, but only cognized by us with more or less difficulty; and we possess a regulative principle of the systematic unity of a teleological connection, which we do not attempt to anticipate or predetermine. All that we do, and ought to do, is to follow out the physico-mechanical connection in nature according to general laws, with the hope of discovering, sooner or later, the teleological connection also. Thus, and thus only, can the principle of final unity aid in the extension of the employment of reason in the sphere of experience, without being in any case detrimental to its interests.

The second error which arises from the misconception of the principle of systematic unity is that of perverted reason (perversa ratio, usteron roteron rationis). The idea of systematic unity is available as a regulative principle in the connection of phenomena according to general natural laws; and, how far soever we have to travel upon the path of experience to discover some fact or event, this idea requires us to believe that we have approached all the more nearly to the completion of its use in the sphere of nature, although that completion can never be attained. But this error reverses the procedure of reason. We begin by hypostatizing the principle of systematic unity, and by giving an anthropomorphic determination to the conception of a Supreme Intelligence, and then proceed forcibly to impose aims upon nature. Thus not only does teleology, which ought to aid in the completion of unity in accordance with general laws, operate to the destruction of its influence, but it hinders reason from attaining its proper aim, that is, the proof, upon natural grounds, of the existence of a supreme intelligent cause. For, if we cannot presuppose supreme finality in nature à priori, that is, as essentially belonging to nature, how can we be directed to endeavour to discover this unity and, rising gradually through its different degrees, to approach the supreme perfection of an author of all—a perfection which is absolutely necessary, and therefore cognizable à priori? The regulative principle directs us to presuppose systematic unity absolutely and, consequently, as following from the essential nature of things—but only as a unity of nature, not merely cognized empirically, but presupposed à priori, although only in an indeterminate manner. But if I insist on basing nature upon the foundation of a supreme ordaining Being, the unity of nature is in effect lost. For, in this case, it is quite foreign and unessential to the nature of things, and cannot be cognized from the general laws of nature. And thus arises a vicious circular argument, what ought to have been proved having been presupposed.

To take the regulative principle of systematic unity in nature for a constitutive principle, and to hypostatize and make a cause out of that which is properly the ideal ground of the consistent and harmonious exercise of reason, involves reason in inextricable embarrassments. The investigation of nature pursues its own path under the guidance of the chain of natural causes, in accordance with the general laws of nature, and ever follows the light of the idea of an author of the universe—not for the purpose of deducing the finality, which it constantly pursues, from this Supreme Being, but to attain to the cognition of his existence from the finality which it seeks in the existence of the phenomena of nature, and, if possible, in that of all things to cognize this being, consequently, as absolutely necessary. Whether this latter purpose succeed or not, the idea is and must always be a true one, and its employment, when merely regulative, must always be accompanied by truthful and beneficial results.

Complete unity, in conformity with aims, constitutes absolute perfection. But if we do not find this unity in the nature of the things which go to constitute the world of experience, that is, of objective cognition, consequently in the universal and necessary laws of nature, how can we infer from this unity the idea of the supreme and absolutely necessary perfection of a primal being, which is the origin of all causality? The greatest systematic unity, and consequently teleological unity, constitutes the very foundation of the possibility of the most extended employment of human reason. The idea of unity is therefore essentially and indissolubly connected with the nature of our reason. This idea is a legislative one; and hence it is very natural that we should assume the existence of a legislative reason corresponding to it, from which the systematic unity of nature—the object of the operations of reason—must be derived.

In the course of our discussion of the antinomies, we stated that it is always possible to answer all the questions which pure reason may raise; and that the plea of the limited nature of our cognition, which is unavoidable and proper in many questions regarding natural phenomena, cannot in this case be admitted, because the questions raised do not relate to the nature of things, but are necessarily originated by the nature of reason itself, and relate to its own internal constitution. We can now establish this assertion, which at first sight appeared so rash, in relation to the two questions in which reason takes the greatest interest, and thus complete our discussion of the dialectic of pure reason.

If, then, the question is asked, in relation to transcendental theology,[73] first, whether there is anything distinct from the world, which contains the ground of

[73] After what has been said of the psychological idea of the ego and its proper employment as a regulative principle of the operations of reason, I need not enter into details regarding the

cosmical order and connection according to general laws? The answer is: Certainly. For the world is a sum of phenomena; there must, therefore, be some transcendental basis of these phenomena, that is, a basis cogitable by the pure understanding alone. If, secondly, the question is asked whether this being is substance, whether it is of the greatest reality, whether it is necessary, and so forth? I answer that this question is utterly without meaning. For all the categories which aid me in forming a conception of an object cannot be employed except in the world of sense, and are without meaning when not applied to objects of actual or possible experience. Out of this sphere, they are not properly conceptions, but the mere marks or indices of conceptions, which we may admit, although they cannot, without the help of experience, help us to understand any subject or thing. If, thirdly, the question is whether we may not cogitate this being, which is distinct from the world, in analogy with the objects of experience? The answer is: Undoubtedly, but only as an ideal, and not as a real object. That is, we must cogitate it only as an unknown substratum of the systematic unity, order, and finality of the world—a unity which reason must employ as the regulative principle of its investigation of nature. Nay, more, we may admit into the idea certain anthropomorphic elements, which are promotive of the interests of this regulative principle. For it is no more than an idea, which does not relate directly to a being distinct from the world, but to the regulative principle of the systematic unity of the world, by means, however, of a schema of this unity—the schema of a Supreme Intelligence, who is the wisely-designing author of the universe. What this basis of cosmical unity may be in itself, we know not—we cannot discover from the idea; we merely know how we ought to employ the idea of this unity, in relation to the systematic operation of reason in the sphere of experience.

But, it will be asked again, can we on these grounds, admit the existence of a wise and omnipotent author of the world? Without doubt; and not only so, but we must assume the existence of such a being. But do we thus extend the limits of our knowledge beyond the field of possible experience? By no means. For we have merely presupposed a something, of which we have no conception, which we do not know as it is in itself; but, in relation to the systematic disposition of the universe, which we must presuppose in all our observation of nature, we have cogitated this unknown being in analogy with an intelligent existence (an empirical conception), that is to say, we have endowed it with those attributes, which, judging from the nature of our own reason, may contain the ground of such a systematic unity. This idea is therefore valid only relatively to the employment in experience of our reason. But if we attribute to it absolute and objective validity, we overlook the fact that it is merely an ideal being that we cogitate; and, by setting out from

---

transcendental illusion by which the systematic unity of all the various phenomena of the internal sense is hypostatized. The procedure is in this case very similar to that which has been discussed in our remarks on the theological ideal.

a basis which is not determinable by considerations drawn from experience, we place ourselves in a position which incapacitates us from applying this principle to the empirical employment of reason.

But, it will be asked further, can I make any use of this conception and hypothesis in my investigations into the world and nature? Yes, for this very purpose was the idea established by reason as a fundamental basis. But may I regard certain arrangements, which seemed to have been made in conformity with some fixed aim, as the arrangements of design, and look upon them as proceeding from the divine will, with the intervention, however, of certain other particular arrangements disposed to that end? Yes, you may do so; but at the same time you must regard it as indifferent, whether it is asserted that divine wisdom has disposed all things in conformity with his highest aims, or that the idea of supreme wisdom is a regulative principle in the investigation of nature, and at the same time a principle of the systematic unity of nature according to general laws, even in those cases where we are unable to discover that unity. In other words, it must be perfectly indifferent to you whether you say, when you have discovered this unity: God has wisely willed it so; or: Nature has wisely arranged this. For it was nothing but the systematic unity, which reason requires as a basis for the investigation of nature, that justified you in accepting the idea of a supreme intelligence as a schema for a regulative principle; and, the farther you advance in the discovery of design and finality, the more certain the validity of your idea. But, as the whole aim of this regulative principle was the discovery of a necessary and systematic unity in nature, we have, in so far as we attain this, to attribute our success to the idea of a Supreme Being; while, at the same time, we cannot, without involving ourselves in contradictions, overlook the general laws of nature, as it was in reference to them alone that this idea was employed. We cannot, I say, overlook the general laws of nature, and regard this conformity to aims observable in nature as contingent or hyperphysical in its origin; inasmuch as there is no ground which can justify us in the admission of a being with such properties distinct from and above nature. All that we are authorized to assert is that this idea may be employed as a principle, and that the properties of the being which is assumed to correspond to it may be regarded as systematically connected in analogy with the causal determination of phenomena.

For the same reasons we are justified in introducing into the idea of the supreme cause other anthropomorphic elements (for without these we could not predicate anything of it); we may regard it as allowable to cogitate this cause as a being with understanding, the feelings of pleasure and displeasure, and faculties of desire and will corresponding to these. At the same time, we may attribute to this being infinite perfection—a perfection which necessarily transcends that which our knowledge of the order and design in the world authorize us to predicate of it. For the regulative law of systematic unity requires us to study nature on the supposition that systematic and final unity in infinitum is everywhere discoverable, even in the highest diversity. For, although we may discover little of this cosmical perfection, it belongs to the legislative prerogative of reason to require us always to seek for and to expect it; while it must always be beneficial to institute all inquiries into nature in accordance with this principle. But it is evident that, by this idea of a supreme author of all, which I place as the foundation of all inquiries into nature, I do not mean to assert the existence of such a being, or that I have any knowledge of its existence; and, consequently, I do not really deduce anything from the existence of this being, but merely from its idea, that is to say, from the nature of things in this world, in accordance with this idea. A certain dim consciousness of the true use of this idea seems to have dictated to the philosophers of all times the moderate language used by them regarding the cause of the world. We find them employing the expressions wisdom and care of nature, and divine wisdom, as synonymous—nay, in purely speculative discussions, preferring the former, because it does not carry the appearance of greater pretensions than such as we are entitled to make, and at the same time directs reason to its proper field of action—nature and her phenomena.

Thus, pure reason, which at first seemed to promise us nothing less than the extension of our cognition beyond the limits of experience, is found, when thoroughly examined, to contain nothing but regulative principles, the virtue and function of which is to introduce into our cognition a higher degree of unity than the understanding could of itself. These principles, by placing the goal of all our struggles at so great a distance, realize for us the most thorough connection between the different parts of our cognition, and the highest degree of systematic unity. But, on the other hand, if misunderstood and employed as constitutive principles of transcendent cognition, they become the parents of illusions and contradictions, while pretending to introduce us to new regions of knowledge.

Thus all human cognition begins with intuitions, proceeds from thence to conceptions, and ends with ideas. Although it possesses, in relation to all three elements, à priori sources of cognition, which seemed to transcend the limits of all experience, a thoroughgoing criticism demonstrates that speculative reason can never, by the aid of these elements, pass the bounds of possible experience, and that the proper destination of this highest faculty of cognition is to employ all methods, and all the principles of these methods, for the purpose of penetrating into the innermost secrets of nature, by the aid of the principles of unity (among all kinds of which teleological unity is the highest), while it ought not to attempt to soar above the sphere of experience, beyond which there lies nought for us but the void inane. The critical examination, in our Transcendental Analytic, of all the propositions which professed to extend cognition beyond the sphere of experience, completely demonstrated that they can only conduct us to a possible experience. If we were not distrustful even of the clearest abstract theorems, if we were not allured by specious and inviting prospects to escape from the constraining power of their evidence, we might spare ourselves the laborious examination of all the dialectical arguments which a transcendent reason adduces in support of its pretensions; for we should know with the most complete certainty that, however honest such professions might be, they are null and valueless, because they relate to a kind of knowledge to which no man can by any possibility attain. But, as there is no end to discussion, if we cannot discover the true cause of the illusions by which even the wisest are deceived, and as the analysis of all our transcendent cognition into its elements is of itself of no slight value as a psychological study, while it is a duty incumbent on every philosopher—it was found necessary to investigate the dialectical procedure of reason in its primary sources. And as the inferences of which this dialectic is the parent are not only deceitful, but naturally possess a profound interest for humanity, it was advisable at the same time, to give a full account of the momenta of this dialectical procedure, and to deposit it in the archives of human reason, as a warning to all future metaphysicians to avoid these causes of speculative error.

II

TRANSCENDENTAL DOCTRINE OF METHOD

If we regard the sum of the cognition of pure speculative reason as an edifice, the idea of which, at least, exists in the human mind, it may be said that we have in the Transcendental Doctrine of Elements examined the materials and determined to what edifice these belong, and what its height and stability. We have found, indeed, that, although we had purposed to build for ourselves a tower which should reach to Heaven, the supply of materials sufficed merely for a habitation, which was spacious enough for all terrestrial purposes, and high enough to enable us to survey the level plain of experience, but that the bold undertaking designed necessarily failed for want of materials—not to mention the confusion of tongues, which gave rise to endless disputes among the labourers on the plan of the edifice, and at last scattered them over all the world, each to erect a separate building for himself, according to his own plans and his own inclinations. Our present task relates not to the materials, but to the plan of an edifice; and, as we have had sufficient warning not to venture blindly upon a design which may be found to transcend our natural powers, while, at the same time, we cannot give up the intention of erecting a secure abode for the mind, we must proportion our design to the material which is presented to us, and which is, at the same time, sufficient for all our wants.

I understand, then, by the transcendental doctrine of method, the determination of the formal conditions of a complete system of pure reason. We shall accordingly have to treat of the discipline, the canon, the architectonic, and, finally, the history of pure reason. This part of our Critique will accomplish, from the transcendental point of view, what has been usually attempted, but miserably executed, under the name of practical logic. It has been badly executed, I say, because general logic, not being limited to any particular kind of cognition (not even to the pure cognition of the understanding) nor to any particular objects, it cannot, without borrowing from other sciences, do more than present merely the titles or signs of possible methods and the technical expressions, which are employed in the systematic parts of all sciences; and thus the pupil is made acquainted with names, the meaning and application of which he is to learn only at some future time.

Chapter I

The Discipline of Pure Reason

Negative judgements—those which are so not merely as regards their logical form, but in respect of their content—are not commonly held in especial respect. They are, on the contrary, regarded as jealous enemies of our insatiable desire for knowledge; and it almost requires an apology to induce us to tolerate, much less to prize and to respect them.

All propositions, indeed, may be logically expressed in a negative form; but, in relation to the content of our cognition, the peculiar province of negative judgements is solely to prevent error. For this reason, too, negative propositions, which are framed for the purpose of correcting false cognitions where error is absolutely impossible, are undoubtedly true, but inane and senseless; that is, they are in reality purposeless and, for this reason, often very ridiculous. Such is the proposition of the schoolman that Alexander could not have subdued any countries without an army.

But where the limits of our possible cognition are very much contracted, the attraction to new fields of knowledge great, the illusions to which the mind is subject of the most deceptive character, and the evil consequences of error of no inconsiderable magnitude—the negative element in knowledge, which is useful only to guard us against error, is of far more importance than much of that positive instruction which makes additions to the sum of our knowledge. The restraint which is employed to repress, and finally to extirpate the constant inclination to depart from certain rules, is termed discipline. It is distinguished from culture, which aims at the formation of a certain degree of skill, without attempting to repress or to destroy any other mental power, already existing. In the cultivation of a talent, which has given evidence of an impulse towards self-development, discipline takes a negative,[74] culture and doctrine a positive, part.

That natural dispositions and talents (such as imagination and wit), which ask a free and unlimited development, require in many respects the corrective influence of discipline, every one will readily grant. But it may well appear strange that reason, whose proper duty it is to prescribe rules of discipline to all the other powers of the mind, should itself require this corrective. It has, in fact, hitherto

[74] I am well aware that, in the language of the schools, the term discipline is usually employed as synonymous with instruction. But there are so many cases in which it is necessary to distinguish the notion of the former, as a course of corrective training, from that of the latter, as the communication of knowledge, and the nature of things itself demands the appropriation of the most suitable expressions for this distinction, that it is my desire that the former terms should never be employed in any other than a negative signification.

escaped this humiliation, only because, in presence of its magnificent pretensions and high position, no one could readily suspect it to be capable of substituting fancies for conceptions, and words for things.

Reason, when employed in the field of experience, does not stand in need of criticism, because its principles are subjected to the continual test of empirical observations. Nor is criticism requisite in the sphere of mathematics, where the conceptions of reason must always be presented in concreto in pure intuition, and baseless or arbitrary assertions are discovered without difficulty. But where reason is not held in a plain track by the influence of empirical or of pure intuition, that is, when it is employed in the transcendental sphere of pure conceptions, it stands in great need of discipline, to restrain its propensity to overstep the limits of possible experience and to keep it from wandering into error. In fact, the utility of the philosophy of pure reason is entirely of this negative character. Particular errors may be corrected by particular animadversions, and the causes of these errors may be eradicated by criticism. But where we find, as in the case of pure reason, a complete system of illusions and fallacies, closely connected with each other and depending upon grand general principles, there seems to be required a peculiar and negative code of mental legislation, which, under the denomination of a discipline, and founded upon the nature of reason and the objects of its exercise, shall constitute a system of thorough examination and testing, which no fallacy will be able to withstand or escape from, under whatever disguise or concealment it may lurk.

But the reader must remark that, in this the second division of our transcendental Critique the discipline of pure reason is not directed to the content, but to the method of the cognition of pure reason. The former task has been completed in the doctrine of elements. But there is so much similarity in the mode of employing the faculty of reason, whatever be the object to which it is applied, while, at the same time, its employment in the transcendental sphere is so essentially different in kind from every other, that, without the warning negative influence of a discipline specially directed to that end, the errors are unavoidable which spring from the unskillful employment of the methods which are originated by reason but which are out of place in this sphere.

Section I. The Discipline of Pure Reason in the Sphere of Dogmatism

The science of mathematics presents the most brilliant example of the extension of the sphere of pure reason without the aid of experience. Examples are always contagious; and they exert an especial influence on the same faculty, which naturally flatters itself that it will have the same good fortune in other case as fell to its lot in one fortunate instance. Hence pure reason hopes to be able to extend its empire in the transcendental sphere with equal success and security, especially when it applies the same method which was attended with such brilliant results in the science of mathematics. It is, therefore, of the highest importance for us to know whether the method of arriving at demonstrative certainty, which is termed mathematical, be identical with that by which we endeavour to attain the same degree of certainty in philosophy, and which is termed in that science dogmatical.

Philosophical cognition is the cognition of reason by means of conceptions; mathematical cognition is cognition by means of the construction of conceptions. The construction of a conception is the presentation à priori of the intuition which corresponds to the conception. For this purpose a non-empirical intuition is requisite, which, as an intuition, is an individual object; while, as the construction of a conception (a general representation), it must be seen to be universally valid for all the possible intuitions which rank under that conception. Thus I construct a triangle, by the presentation of the object which corresponds to this conception, either by mere imagination, in pure intuition, or upon paper, in empirical intuition, in both cases completely à priori, without borrowing the type of that figure from any experience. The individual figure drawn upon paper is empirical; but it serves, notwithstanding, to indicate the conception, even in its universality, because in this empirical intuition we keep our eye merely on the act of the construction of the conception, and pay no attention to the various modes of determining it, for example, its size, the length of its sides, the size of its angles, these not in the least affecting the essential character of the conception.

Philosophical cognition, accordingly, regards the particular only in the general; mathematical the general in the particular, nay, in the individual. This is done, however, entirely à priori and by means of pure reason, so that, as this individual figure is determined under certain universal conditions of construction, the object of the conception, to which this individual figure corresponds as its schema, must be cogitated as universally determined.

The essential difference of these two modes of cognition consists, therefore, in this formal quality; it does not regard the difference of the matter or objects of both. Those thinkers who aim at distinguishing philosophy from mathematics by asserting that the former has to do with quality merely, and the latter with quantity, have mistaken the effect for the cause. The reason why mathematical cognition can relate only to quantity is to be found in its form alone. For it is the conception of quantities only that is capable of being constructed, that is, presented à priori in intuition; while qualities cannot be given in any other than an empirical intuition. Hence the cognition of qualities by reason is possible only through conceptions. No one can find an intuition which shall correspond to the conception of reality, except in experience; it cannot be presented to the mind à priori and antecedently to the empirical consciousness of a reality. We can form an intuition, by means of the mere conception of it, of a cone, without the aid of experience; but the colour of the cone we cannot know except from experience. I cannot present an intuition of a cause, except in an example which experience offers to me. Besides, philosophy, as well as mathematics, treats of quantities; as, for example, of totality, infinity, and so on. Mathematics, too, treats of the difference of lines and surfaces—as spaces of different quality, of the continuity of extension—as a quality thereof. But, although in such cases they have a common object, the mode in which reason considers that object is very different in philosophy from what it is in mathematics. The former confines itself to the general conceptions; the latter can do nothing with a mere conception, it hastens to intuition. In this intuition it regards the conception in concreto, not empirically, but in an à priori intuition, which it has constructed; and in which, all the results which follow from the general conditions of the construction of the conception are in all cases valid for the object of the constructed conception.

Suppose that the conception of a triangle is given to a philosopher and that he is required to discover, by the philosophical method, what relation the sum of its angles bears to a right angle. He has nothing before him but the conception of a figure enclosed within three right lines, and, consequently, with the same number of angles. He may analyse the conception of a right line, of an angle, or of the number three as long as he pleases, but he will not discover any properties not contained in these conceptions. But, if this question is proposed to a geometrician, he at once begins by constructing a triangle. He knows that two right angles are equal to the sum of all the contiguous angles which proceed from one point in a straight line; and he goes on to produce one side of his triangle, thus forming two adjacent angles which are together equal to two right angles. He then divides the exterior of these angles, by drawing a line parallel with the opposite side of the triangle, and immediately perceives that he has thus got an exterior adjacent angle which is equal to the interior. Proceeding in this way, through a chain of inferences, and always on the ground of intuition, he arrives at a clear and universally valid solution of the question.

But mathematics does not confine itself to the construction of quantities (quanta), as in the case of geometry; it occupies itself with pure quantity also (quantitas), as in the case of algebra, where complete abstraction is made of the properties of the object indicated by the conception of quantity. In algebra, a certain method of notation by signs is adopted, and these indicate the different possible constructions of quantities, the extraction of roots, and so on. After having thus denoted the general conception of quantities, according to their different relations, the different operations by which quantity or number is increased or diminished are presented in intuition in accordance with general rules. Thus, when one quantity is to be divided by another, the signs which denote both are placed in the form peculiar to the operation of division; and thus algebra, by means of a symbolical construction of quantity, just as geometry, with its ostensive or geometrical construction (a construction of the objects themselves), arrives at results which discursive cognition cannot hope to reach by the aid of mere conceptions.

Now, what is the cause of this difference in the fortune of the philosopher and the mathematician, the former of whom follows the path of conceptions, while the latter pursues that of intuitions, which he represents, à priori, in correspondence with his conceptions? The cause is evident from what has been already demonstrated in the introduction to this Critique. We do not, in the present case, want to discover analytical propositions, which may be produced merely by analysing our conceptions—for in this the philosopher would have the advantage over his rival; we aim at the discovery of synthetical propositions—such synthetical propositions, moreover, as can be cognized à priori. I must not confine myself to that which I actually cogitate in my conception of a triangle, for this is nothing more than the mere definition; I must try to go beyond that, and to arrive at properties which are not contained in, although they belong to, the conception. Now, this is impossible, unless I determine the object present to my mind according to the conditions, either of empirical, or of pure, intuition. In the former case, I should have an empirical proposition (arrived at by actual measurement of the angles of the triangle), which would possess neither universality nor necessity; but that would be of no value. In the latter, I proceed by geometrical construction, by means of which I collect, in a pure intuition, just as I would in an empirical intuition, all the various properties which belong to the schema of a triangle in general, and consequently to its conception, and thus construct synthetical propositions which possess the attribute of universality.

It would be vain to philosophize upon the triangle, that is, to reflect on it discursively; I should get no further than the definition with which I had been obliged to set out. There are certainly transcendental synthetical propositions which are framed by means of pure conceptions, and which form the peculiar distinction of philosophy; but these do not relate to any particular thing, but to a thing in general, and enounce the conditions under which the perception of it may become a part of possible experience. But the science of mathematics has nothing to do with such questions, nor with the question of existence in any fashion; it is concerned merely with the properties of objects in themselves, only in so far as these are connected with the conception of the objects.

In the above example, we merely attempted to show the great difference which exists between the discursive employment of reason in the sphere of conceptions, and its intuitive exercise by means of the construction of conceptions. The question naturally arises: What is the cause which necessitates this twofold exercise of reason, and how are we to discover whether it is the philosophical or the mathematical method which reason is pursuing in an argument?

All our knowledge relates, finally, to possible intuitions, for it is these alone that present objects to the mind. An à priori or non-empirical conception contains either a pure intuition—and in this case it can be constructed; or it contains nothing but the synthesis of possible intuitions, which are not given à priori. In this latter case, it may help us to form synthetical à priori judgements, but only in the discursive method, by conceptions, not in the intuitive, by means of the construction of conceptions.

The only à priori intuition is that of the pure form of phenomena—space and time. A conception of space and time as quanta may be presented à priori in intuition, that is, constructed, either alone with their quality (figure), or as pure quantity (the mere synthesis of the homogeneous), by means of number. But the matter of phenomena, by which things are given in space and time, can be presented only in perception, à posteriori. The only conception which represents à priori this empirical content of phenomena is the conception of a thing in general; and the à priori synthetical cognition of this conception can give us nothing more than the rule for the synthesis of that which may be contained in the corresponding à posteriori perception; it is utterly inadequate to present an à priori intuition of the real object, which must necessarily be empirical.

Synthetical propositions, which relate to things in general, an à priori intuition of which is impossible, are transcendental. For this reason transcendental propositions cannot be framed by means of the construction of conceptions; they are à priori, and based entirely on conceptions themselves. They contain merely the rule, by which we are to seek in the world of perception or experience the synthetical unity of that which cannot be intuited à priori. But they are incompetent to present any of the conceptions which appear in them in an à priori intuition; these can be given only à posteriori, in experience, which, however, is itself possible only through these synthetical principles.

If we are to form a synthetical judgement regarding a conception, we must go beyond it, to the intuition in which it is given. If we keep to what is contained in the conception, the judgement is merely analytical—it is merely an explanation of what we have cogitated in the conception. But I can pass from the conception to the pure or empirical intuition which corresponds to it. I can proceed to examine my conception in concreto, and to cognize, either à priori or a posterio, what I find in the object of the conception. The former—à priori cognition—is rational-mathematical cognition by means of the construction of the conception; the latter—à posteriori cognition—is purely empirical cognition, which does not possess the attributes of necessity and universality. Thus I may analyse the conception I have of gold; but I gain no new information from this analysis, I merely enumerate the different properties which I had connected with the notion indicated by the word. My knowledge has gained in logical clearness and arrangement, but no addition has been made to it. But if I take the matter which is indicated by this name, and submit it to the examination of my senses, I am enabled to form several synthetical—although still empirical—propositions. The mathematical conception of a triangle I should construct, that is, present à priori in intuition, and in this way attain to rational-synthetical cognition. But when the transcendental conception of reality, or substance, or power is presented to my mind, I find that it does not relate to or indicate either an empirical or pure intuition, but that it indicates merely the synthesis of empirical intuitions, which cannot of course be given à priori. The synthesis in such a conception cannot proceed à priori—without the aid of experience—to the intuition which corresponds to the conception; and, for this reason, none of these conceptions can produce a determinative synthetical proposition, they can never present more than a principle of the synthesis[75] of possible empirical intuitions. A transcendental proposition is, therefore, a synthetical cognition of reason by means of pure conceptions and the discursive method, and it renders possible all synthetical unity in empirical cognition, though it cannot present us with any intuition à priori.

There is thus a twofold exercise of reason. Both modes have the properties of universality and an à priori origin in common, but are, in their procedure, of widely different character. The reason of this is that in the world of phenomena, in which alone objects are presented to our minds, there are two main elements—the form of intuition (space and time), which can be cognized and determined completely à priori, and the matter or content—that which is presented in space and time, and which, consequently, contains a something—an existence corresponding to our powers of sensation. As regards the latter, which can never be given in a determinate mode except by experience, there are no à priori notions which relate to it, except the undetermined conceptions of the synthesis of possible sensations, in so far as these belong (in a possible experience) to the unity of consciousness. As regards the former, we can determine our conceptions à priori in intuition, inasmuch as we are ourselves the creators of the objects of the conceptions in space and time—these objects being regarded simply as quanta. In the one case, reason proceeds according to conceptions and can do nothing more than subject phenomena to these—which can only be determined empirically, that is, à posteriori—in conformity, however, with those conceptions as the rules of all empirical synthesis. In the other case, reason proceeds by the construction of conceptions; and, as these conceptions relate to an à priori intuition, they may be given and determined in pure intuition à priori, and without the aid of empirical data. The examination and consideration of everything that exists in space or time—whether it is a quantum or not, in how far the particular something (which fills space or time) is a primary substratum, or a mere determination of some other existence, whether it relates to anything else—either as cause or effect, whether its existence is isolated or in reciprocal connection with and dependence upon others, the possibility of this existence, its reality and necessity or opposites—all these form part of the cognition of reason on the ground of conceptions, and this cognition is termed philosophical. But to determine à priori an intuition in space (its figure), to divide time into periods, or merely to cognize the quantity of an intuition in space and time, and to determine

[75] In the case of the conception of cause, I do really go beyond the empirical conception of an event—but not to the intuition which presents this conception in concreto, but only to the time-conditions, which may be found in experience to correspond to the conception. My procedure is, therefore, strictly according to conceptions; I cannot in a case of this kind employ the construction of conceptions, because the conception is merely a rule for the synthesis of perceptions, which are not pure intuitions, and which, therefore, cannot be given à priori.

it by number—all this is an operation of reason by means of the construction of conceptions, and is called mathematical.

The success which attends the efforts of reason in the sphere of mathematics naturally fosters the expectation that the same good fortune will be its lot, if it applies the mathematical method in other regions of mental endeavour besides that of quantities. Its success is thus great, because it can support all its conceptions by à priori intuitions and, in this way, make itself a master, as it were, over nature; while pure philosophy, with its à priori discursive conceptions, bungles about in the world of nature, and cannot accredit or show any à priori evidence of the reality of these conceptions. Masters in the science of mathematics are confident of the success of this method; indeed, it is a common persuasion that it is capable of being applied to any subject of human thought. They have hardly ever reflected or philosophized on their favourite science—a task of great difficulty; and the specific difference between the two modes of employing the faculty of reason has never entered their thoughts. Rules current in the field of common experience, and which common sense stamps everywhere with its approval, are regarded by them as axiomatic. From what source the conceptions of space and time, with which (as the only primitive quanta) they have to deal, enter their minds, is a question which they do not trouble themselves to answer; and they think it just as unnecessary to examine into the origin of the pure conceptions of the understanding and the extent of their validity. All they have to do with them is to employ them. In all this they are perfectly right, if they do not overstep the limits of the sphere of nature. But they pass, unconsciously, from the world of sense to the insecure ground of pure transcendental conceptions (instabilis tellus, innabilis unda), where they can neither stand nor swim, and where the tracks of their footsteps are obliterated by time; while the march of mathematics is pursued on a broad and magnificent highway, which the latest posterity shall frequent without fear of danger or impediment.

As we have taken upon us the task of determining, clearly and certainly, the limits of pure reason in the sphere of transcendentalism, and as the efforts of reason in this direction are persisted in, even after the plainest and most expressive warnings, hope still beckoning us past the limits of experience into the splendours of the intellectual world—it becomes necessary to cut away the last anchor of this fallacious and fantastic hope. We shall, accordingly, show that the mathematical method is unattended in the sphere of philosophy by the least advantage—except, perhaps, that it more plainly exhibits its own inadequacy—that geometry and philosophy are two quite different things, although they go hand in hand in the field of natural science, and, consequently, that the procedure of the one can never be imitated by the other.

The evidence of mathematics rests upon definitions, axioms, and demonstrations. I shall be satisfied with showing that none of these forms can be employed or imitated in philosophy in the sense in which they are understood by mathematicians; and that the geometrician, if he employs his method in philosophy, will succeed only in building card-castles, while the employment of the philosophical method in mathematics can result in nothing but mere verbiage. The essential business of philosophy, indeed, is to mark out the limits of the science; and even the mathematician, unless his talent is naturally circumscribed and limited to this particular department of knowledge, cannot turn a deaf ear to the warnings of philosophy, or set himself above its direction.

I. Of Definitions. A definition is, as the term itself indicates, the representation, upon primary grounds, of the complete conception of a thing within its own limits.[76] Accordingly, an empirical conception cannot be defined, it can only be explained. For, as there are in such a conception only a certain number of marks or signs, which denote a certain class of sensuous objects, we can never be sure that we do not cogitate under the word which indicates the same object, at one time a greater, at another a smaller number of signs. Thus, one person may cogitate in his conception of gold, in addition to its properties of weight, colour, malleability, that of resisting rust, while another person may be ignorant of this quality. We employ certain signs only so long as we require them for the sake of distinction; new observations abstract some and add new ones, so that an empirical conception never remains within permanent limits. It is, in fact, useless to define a conception of this kind. If, for example, we are speaking of water and its properties, we do not stop at what we actually think by the word water, but proceed to observation and experiment; and the word, with the few signs attached to it, is more properly a designation than a conception of the thing. A definition in this case would evidently be nothing more than a determination of the word. In the second place, no à priori conception, such as those of substance, cause, right, fitness, and so on, can be defined. For I can never be sure, that the clear representation of a given conception (which is given in a confused state) has been fully developed, until I know that the representation is adequate with its object. But, inasmuch as the conception, as it is presented to the mind, may contain a number of obscure representations, which we do not observe in our analysis, although we employ them in our application of the conception, I can never be sure that my analysis is complete, while examples may make this probable, although they can never demonstrate the fact. Instead of the word definition, I should rather employ the term exposition—a more modest expression, which the critic may accept without surrendering his doubts as to the completeness of the analysis of any such conception. As, therefore, neither empirical nor à priori conceptions are capable of definition, we have to see whether

[76] The definition must describe the conception completely that is, omit none of the marks or signs of which it composed; within its own limits, that is, it must be precise, and enumerate no more signs than belong to the conception; and on primary grounds, that is to say, the limitations of the bounds of the conception must not be deduced from other conceptions, as in this case a proof would be necessary, and the so-called definition would be incapable of taking its place at the head of all the judgements we have to form regarding an object.

the only other kind of conceptions—arbitrary conceptions—can be subjected to this mental operation. Such a conception can always be defined; for I must know thoroughly what I wished to cogitate in it, as it was I who created it, and it was not given to my mind either by the nature of my understanding or by experience. At the same time, I cannot say that, by such a definition, I have defined a real object. If the conception is based upon empirical conditions, if, for example, I have a conception of a clock for a ship, this arbitrary conception does not assure me of the existence or even of the possibility of the object. My definition of such a conception would with more propriety be termed a declaration of a project than a definition of an object. There are no other conceptions which can bear definition, except those which contain an arbitrary synthesis, which can be constructed à priori. Consequently, the science of mathematics alone possesses definitions. For the object here thought is presented à priori in intuition; and thus it can never contain more or less than the conception, because the conception of the object has been given by the definition—and primarily, that is, without deriving the definition from any other source. Philosophical definitions are, therefore, merely expositions of given conceptions, while mathematical definitions are constructions of conceptions originally formed by the mind itself; the former are produced by analysis, the completeness of which is never demonstratively certain, the latter by a synthesis. In a mathematical definition the conception is formed, in a philosophical definition it is only explained. From this it follows:

(a) That we must not imitate, in philosophy, the mathematical usage of commencing with definitions—except by way of hypothesis or experiment. For, as all so-called philosophical definitions are merely analyses of given conceptions, these conceptions, although only in a confused form, must precede the analysis; and the incomplete exposition must precede the complete, so that we may be able to draw certain inferences from the characteristics which an incomplete analysis has enabled us to discover, before we attain to the complete exposition or definition of the conception. In one word, a full and clear definition ought, in philosophy, rather to form the conclusion than the commencement of our labours.[77] In mathematics, on the contrary, we cannot have a conception prior to the definition; it is the definition which gives us the conception, and it must for this reason form the commencement of every chain of mathematical reasoning.

[77] Philosophy abounds in faulty definitions, especially such as contain some of the elements requisite to form a complete definition. If a conception could not be employed in reasoning before it had been defined, it would fare ill with all philosophical thought. But, as incompletely defined conceptions may always be employed without detriment to truth, so far as our analysis of the elements contained in them proceeds, imperfect definitions, that is, propositions which are properly not definitions, but merely approximations thereto, may be used with great advantage. In mathematics, definition belongs ad esse, in philosophy ad melius esse. It is a difficult task to construct a proper definition. Jurists are still without a complete definition of the idea of right.

(b) Mathematical definitions cannot be erroneous. For the conception is given only in and through the definition, and thus it contains only what has been cogitated in the definition. But although a definition cannot be incorrect, as regards its content, an error may sometimes, although seldom, creep into the form. This error consists in a want of precision. Thus the common definition of a circle—that it is a curved line, every point in which is equally distant from another point called the centre—is faulty, from the fact that the determination indicated by the word curved is superfluous. For there ought to be a particular theorem, which may be easily proved from the definition, to the effect that every line, which has all its points at equal distances from another point, must be a curved line—that is, that not even the smallest part of it can be straight. Analytical definitions, on the other hand, may be erroneous in many respects, either by the introduction of signs which do not actually exist in the conception, or by wanting in that completeness which forms the essential of a definition. In the latter case, the definition is necessarily defective, because we can never be fully certain of the completeness of our analysis. For these reasons, the method of definition employed in mathematics cannot be imitated in philosophy.

2. Of Axioms. These, in so far as they are immediately certain, are à priori synthetical principles. Now, one conception cannot be connected synthetically and yet immediately with another; because, if we wish to proceed out of and beyond a conception, a third mediating cognition is necessary. And, as philosophy is a cognition of reason by the aid of conceptions alone, there is to be found in it no principle which deserves to be called an axiom. Mathematics, on the other hand, may possess axioms, because it can always connect the predicates of an object à priori, and without any mediating term, by means of the construction of conceptions in intuition. Such is the case with the proposition: Three points can always lie in a plane. On the other hand, no synthetical principle which is based upon conceptions, can ever be immediately certain (for example, the proposition: Everything that happens has a cause), because I require a mediating term to connect the two conceptions of event and cause—namely, the condition of time-determination in an experience, and I cannot cognize any such principle immediately and from conceptions alone. Discursive principles are, accordingly, very different from intuitive principles or axioms. The former always require deduction, which in the case of the latter may be altogether dispensed with. Axioms are, for this reason, always self-evident, while philosophical principles, whatever may be the degree of certainty they possess, cannot lay any claim to such a distinction. No synthetical proposition of pure transcendental reason can be so evident, as is often rashly enough declared, as the statement, twice two are four. It is true that in the Analytic I introduced into the list of principles of the pure understanding, certain axioms of intuition; but the principle there discussed was

not itself an axiom, but served merely to present the principle of the possibility of axioms in general, while it was really nothing more than a principle based upon conceptions. For it is one part of the duty of transcendental philosophy to establish the possibility of mathematics itself. Philosophy possesses, then, no axioms, and has no right to impose its à priori principles upon thought, until it has established their authority and validity by a thoroughgoing deduction.

3. Of Demonstrations. Only an apodeictic proof, based upon intuition, can be termed a demonstration. Experience teaches us what is, but it cannot convince us that it might not have been otherwise. Hence a proof upon empirical grounds cannot be apodeictic. À priori conceptions, in discursive cognition, can never produce intuitive certainty or evidence, however certain the judgement they present may be. Mathematics alone, therefore, contains demonstrations, because it does not deduce its cognition from conceptions, but from the construction of conceptions, that is, from intuition, which can be given à priori in accordance with conceptions. The method of algebra, in equations, from which the correct answer is deduced by reduction, is a kind of construction—not geometrical, but by symbols—in which all conceptions, especially those of the relations of quantities, are represented in intuition by signs; and thus the conclusions in that science are secured from errors by the fact that every proof is submitted to ocular evidence. Philosophical cognition does not possess this advantage, it being required to consider the general always in abstracto (by means of conceptions), while mathematics can always consider it in concreto (in an individual intuition), and at the same time by means of à priori representation, whereby all errors are rendered manifest to the senses. The former—discursive proofs—ought to be termed acroamatic proofs, rather than demonstrations, as only words are employed in them, while demonstrations proper, as the term itself indicates, always require a reference to the intuition of the object.

It follows from all these considerations that it is not consonant with the nature of philosophy, especially in the sphere of pure reason, to employ the dogmatical method, and to adorn itself with the titles and insignia of mathematical science. It does not belong to that order, and can only hope for a fraternal union with that science. Its attempts at mathematical evidence are vain pretensions, which can only keep it back from its true aim, which is to detect the illusory procedure of reason when transgressing its proper limits, and by fully explaining and analysing our conceptions, to conduct us from the dim regions of speculation to the clear region of modest self-knowledge. Reason must not, therefore, in its transcendental endeavours, look forward with such confidence, as if the path it is pursuing led straight to its aim, nor reckon with such security upon its premisses, as to consider it unnecessary to take a step back, or to keep a strict watch for errors, which, overlooked in the principles, may be detected in the arguments themselves—in which case it may be requisite either to determine these principles with greater strictness, or to change them entirely.

I divide all apodeictic propositions, whether demonstrable or immediately certain, into dogmata and mathemata. A direct synthetical proposition, based on conceptions, is a dogma; a proposition of the same kind, based on the construction of conceptions, is a mathema. Analytical judgements do not teach us any more about an object than what was contained in the conception we had of it; because they do not extend our cognition beyond our conception of an object, they merely elucidate the conception. They cannot therefore be with propriety termed dogmas. Of the two kinds of à priori synthetical propositions above mentioned, only those which are employed in philosophy can, according to the general mode of speech, bear this name; those of arithmetic or geometry would not be rightly so denominated. Thus the customary mode of speaking confirms the explanation given above, and the conclusion arrived at, that only those judgements which are based upon conceptions, not on the construction of conceptions, can be termed dogmatical.

Thus, pure reason, in the sphere of speculation, does not contain a single direct synthetical judgement based upon conceptions. By means of ideas, it is, as we have shown, incapable of producing synthetical judgements, which are objectively valid; by means of the conceptions of the understanding, it establishes certain indubitable principles, not, however, directly on the basis of conceptions, but only indirectly by means of the relation of these conceptions to something of a purely contingent nature, namely, possible experience. When experience is presupposed, these principles are apodeictically certain, but in themselves, and directly, they cannot even be cognized à priori. Thus the given conceptions of cause and event will not be sufficient for the demonstration of the proposition: Every event has a cause. For this reason, it is not a dogma; although from another point of view, that of experience, it is capable of being proved to demonstration. The proper term for such a proposition is principle, and not theorem (although it does require to be proved), because it possesses the remarkable peculiarity of being the condition of the possibility of its own ground of proof, that is, experience, and of forming a necessary presupposition in all empirical observation.

If then, in the speculative sphere of pure reason, no dogmata are to be found; all dogmatical methods, whether borrowed from mathematics, or invented by philosophical thinkers, are alike inappropriate and inefficient. They only serve to conceal errors and fallacies, and to deceive philosophy, whose duty it is to see that reason pursues a safe and straight path. A philosophical method may, however, be systematical. For our reason is, subjectively considered, itself a system, and, in the sphere of mere conceptions, a system of investigation according to principles of unity, the material being supplied by experience alone. But this is not the proper place for discussing the peculiar method of transcendental philosophy, as our present task is simply to examine whether our faculties are capable of erecting an edifice on the basis of pure reason, and how far they may proceed with the materials at their command.

Section II. The Discipline of Pure Reason in Polemics

Reason must be subject, in all its operations, to criticism, which must always be permitted to exercise its functions without restraint; otherwise its interests are imperilled and its influence obnoxious to suspicion. There is nothing, however useful, however sacred it may be, that can claim exemption from the searching examination of this supreme tribunal, which has no respect of persons. The very existence of reason depends upon this freedom; for the voice of reason is not that of a dictatorial and despotic power, it is rather like the vote of the citizens of a free state, every member of which must have the privilege of giving free expression to his doubts, and possess even the right of veto.

But while reason can never decline to submit itself to the tribunal of criticism, it has not always cause to dread the judgement of this court. Pure reason, however, when engaged in the sphere of dogmatism, is not so thoroughly conscious of a strict observance of its highest laws, as to appear before a higher judicial reason with perfect confidence. On the contrary, it must renounce its magnificent dogmatical pretensions in philosophy.

Very different is the case when it has to defend itself, not before a judge, but against an equal. If dogmatical assertions are advanced on the negative side, in opposition to those made by reason on the positive side, its justification kat authrhopon is complete, although the proof of its propositions is kat aletheian unsatisfactory.

By the polemic of pure reason I mean the defence of its propositions made by reason, in opposition to the dogmatical counter-propositions advanced by other parties. The question here is not whether its own statements may not also be false; it merely regards the fact that reason proves that the opposite cannot be established with demonstrative certainty, nor even asserted with a higher degree of probability. Reason does not hold her possessions upon sufferance; for, although she cannot show a perfectly satisfactory title to them, no one can prove that she is not the rightful possessor.

It is a melancholy reflection that reason, in its highest exercise, falls into an antithetic; and that the supreme tribunal for the settlement of differences should not be at union with itself. It is true that we had to discuss the question of an apparent antithetic, but we found that it was based upon a misconception. In conformity with the common prejudice, phenomena were regarded as things in themselves, and thus an absolute completeness in their synthesis was required in the one mode or in the other (it was shown to be impossible in both); a demand entirely out of place in regard to phenomena. There was, then, no real self-contradiction of reason in the propositions: The series of phenomena given in themselves has an absolutely first beginning; and: This series is absolutely and in itself without beginning. The two propositions are perfectly consistent with each other, because phenomena as phenomena are in themselves nothing, and consequently the hypothesis that they are things in themselves must lead to self-contradictory inferences.

But there are cases in which a similar misunderstanding cannot be provided against, and the dispute must remain unsettled. Take, for example, the theistic proposition: There is a Supreme Being; and on the other hand, the atheistic counter-statement: There exists no Supreme Being; or, in psychology: Everything that thinks possesses the attribute of absolute and permanent unity, which is utterly different from the transitory unity of material phenomena; and the counter-proposition: The soul is not an immaterial unity, and its nature is transitory, like that of phenomena. The objects of these questions contain no heterogeneous or contradictory elements, for they relate to things in themselves, and not to phenomena. There would arise, indeed, a real contradiction, if reason came forward with a statement on the negative side of these questions alone. As regards the criticism to which the grounds of proof on the affirmative side must be subjected, it may be freely admitted, without necessitating the surrender of the affirmative propositions, which have, at least, the interest of reason in their favour—an advantage which the opposite party cannot lay claim to.

I cannot agree with the opinion of several admirable thinkers—Sulzer among the rest—that, in spite of the weakness of the arguments hitherto in use, we may hope, one day, to see sufficient demonstrations of the two cardinal propositions of pure reason—the existence of a Supreme Being, and the immortality of the soul. I am certain, on the contrary, that this will never be the case. For on what ground can reason base such synthetical propositions, which do not relate to the objects of experience and their internal possibility? But it is also demonstratively certain that no one will ever be able to maintain the contrary with the least show of probability. For, as he can attempt such a proof solely upon the basis of pure reason, he is bound to prove that a Supreme Being, and a thinking subject in the character of a pure intelligence, are impossible. But where will he find the knowledge which can enable him to enounce synthetical judgements in regard to things which transcend the region of experience? We may, therefore, rest assured that the opposite never will be demonstrated. We need not, then, have recourse to scholastic arguments; we may always admit the truth of those propositions which are consistent with the speculative interests of reason in the sphere of experience, and form, moreover, the only means of uniting the speculative with the practical interest. Our opponent, who must not be considered here as a critic solely, we can be ready to meet with a non liquet which cannot fail to disconcert him; while we cannot deny his right to a similar retort, as we have on our side the advantage of the support of the subjective maxim of reason, and can therefore look upon all his sophistical arguments with calm indifference.

From this point of view, there is properly no antithetic of pure reason. For the only arena for such a struggle would be upon the field of pure theology and psychology; but on this ground there can appear no combatant whom we need to fear. Ridicule and boasting can be his only weapons; and these may be laughed at, as mere child's play. This consideration restores to Reason her courage; for what source of confidence could be found, if she, whose vocation it is to destroy error, were at variance with herself and without any reasonable hope of ever reaching a state of permanent repose?

Everything in nature is good for some purpose. Even poisons are serviceable; they destroy the evil effects of other poisons generated in our system, and must always find a place in every complete pharmacopoeia. The objections raised against the fallacies and sophistries of speculative reason, are objections given by the nature of this reason itself, and must therefore have a destination and purpose which can only be for the good of humanity. For what purpose has Providence raised many objects, in which we have the deepest interest, so far above us, that we vainly try to cognize them with certainty, and our powers of mental vision are rather excited than satisfied by the glimpses we may chance to seize? It is very doubtful whether it is for our benefit to advance bold affirmations regarding subjects involved in such obscurity; perhaps it would even be detrimental to our best interests. But it is undoubtedly always beneficial to leave the investigating, as well as the critical reason, in perfect freedom, and permit it to take charge of its own interests, which are advanced as much by its limitation, as by its extension of its views, and which always suffer by the interference of foreign powers forcing it, against its natural tendencies, to bend to certain preconceived designs.

Allow your opponent to say what he thinks reasonable, and combat him only with the weapons of reason. Have no anxiety for the practical interests of humanity—these are never imperilled in a purely speculative dispute. Such a dispute serves merely to disclose the antinomy of reason, which, as it has its source in the nature of reason, ought to be thoroughly investigated. Reason is benefited by the examination of a subject on both sides, and its judgements are corrected by being limited. It is not the matter that may give occasion to dispute, but the manner. For it is perfectly permissible to employ, in the presence of reason, the language of a firmly rooted faith, even after we have been obliged to renounce all pretensions to knowledge.

If we were to ask the dispassionate David Hume—a philosopher endowed, in a degree that few are, with a well-balanced judgement: What motive induced you to spend so much labour and thought in undermining the consoling and beneficial persuasion that reason is capable of assuring us of the existence, and presenting us with a determinate conception of a Supreme Being?—his answer would be: Nothing but the desire of teaching reason to know its own powers better, and, at the same time, a dislike of the procedure by which that faculty was compelled to support foregone conclusions, and prevented from confessing the internal weaknesses which it cannot but feel when it enters upon a rigid self-examination. If, on the other hand, we were to ask Priestley—a philosopher who had no taste for transcendental speculation, but was entirely devoted to the principles of empiricism—what his motives were for overturning those two main pillars of religion—the doctrines of the freedom of the will and the immortality of the soul (in his view the hope of a future life is but the expectation of the miracle of resurrection)—this philosopher, himself a zealous and pious teacher of religion, could give no other answer than this: I acted in the interest of reason, which always suffers, when certain objects are explained and judged by a reference to other supposed laws than those of material nature—the only laws which we know in a determinate manner. It would be unfair to decry the latter philosopher, who endeavoured to harmonize his paradoxical opinions with the interests of religion, and to undervalue an honest and reflecting man, because he finds himself at a loss the moment he has left the field of natural science. The same grace must be accorded to Hume, a man not less well-disposed, and quite as blameless in his moral character, and who pushed his abstract speculations to an extreme length, because, as he rightly believed, the object of them lies entirely beyond the bounds of natural science, and within the sphere of pure ideas.

What is to be done to provide against the danger which seems in the present case to menace the best interests of humanity? The course to be pursued in reference to this subject is a perfectly plain and natural one. Let each thinker pursue his own path; if he shows talent, if he gives evidence of profound thought, in one word, if he shows that he possesses the power of reasoning—reason is always the gainer. If you have recourse to other means, if you attempt to coerce reason, if you raise the cry of treason to humanity, if you excite the feelings of the crowd, which can neither understand nor sympathize with such subtle speculations—you will only make yourselves ridiculous. For the question does not concern the advantage or disadvantage which we are expected to reap from such inquiries; the question is merely how far reason can advance in the field of speculation, apart from all kinds of interest, and whether we may depend upon the exertions of speculative reason, or must renounce all reliance on it. Instead of joining the combatants, it is your part to be a tranquil spectator of the struggle—a laborious struggle for the parties engaged, but attended, in its progress as well as in its result, with the most advantageous consequences for the interests of thought and knowledge. It is absurd to expect to be enlightened by Reason, and at the same time to prescribe to her what side of the question she must adopt. Moreover, reason is sufficiently held in check by its own power, the limits imposed on it by its own nature are sufficient; it is unnecessary for you to place over it additional guards, as if its power were dangerous to the constitution of the intellectual state. In the dialectic of reason there is no victory gained which need in the least disturb your tranquility.

The strife of dialectic is a necessity of reason, and we cannot but wish that it had been conducted long ere this with that perfect freedom which ought to be its essential condition. In this case, we should have had at an earlier period a matured and profound criticism, which must have put an end to all dialectical disputes, by exposing the illusions and prejudices in which they originated.

There is in human nature an unworthy propensity—a propensity which, like everything that springs from nature, must in its final purpose be conducive to the good of humanity—to conceal our real sentiments, and to give expression only to certain received opinions, which are regarded as at once safe and promotive of the common good. It is true, this tendency, not only to conceal our real sentiments, but to profess those which may gain us favour in the eyes of society, has not only civilized, but, in a certain measure, moralized us; as no one can break through the outward covering of respectability, honour, and morality, and thus the seemingly-good examples which we see around us form an excellent school for moral improvement, so long as our belief in their genuineness remains unshaken. But this disposition to represent ourselves as better than we are, and to utter opinions which are not our own, can be nothing more than a kind of provisionary arrangement of nature to lead us from the rudeness of an uncivilized state, and to teach us how to assume at least the appearance and manner of the good we see. But when true principles have been developed, and have obtained a sure foundation in our habit of thought, this conventionalism must be attacked with earnest vigour, otherwise it corrupts the heart, and checks the growth of good dispositions with the mischievous weed of fair appearances.

I am sorry to remark the same tendency to misrepresentation and hypocrisy in the sphere of speculative discussion, where there is less temptation to restrain the free expression of thought. For what can be more prejudicial to the interests of intelligence than to falsify our real sentiments, to conceal the doubts which we feel in regard to our statements, or to maintain the validity of grounds of proof which we well know to be insufficient? So long as mere personal vanity is the source of these unworthy artifices—and this is generally the case in speculative discussions, which are mostly destitute of practical interest, and are incapable of complete demonstration—the vanity of the opposite party exaggerates as much on the other side; and thus the result is the same, although it is not brought about so soon as if the dispute had been conducted in a sincere and upright spirit. But where the mass entertains the notion that the aim of certain subtle speculators is nothing less than to shake the very foundations of public welfare and morality—it seems not only prudent, but even praise worthy, to maintain the good cause by illusory arguments, rather than to give to our supposed opponents the advantage of lowering our declarations to the moderate tone of a merely practical conviction, and of compelling us to confess our inability to attain to apodeictic certainty in speculative subjects. But we ought to reflect that there is nothing, in the world more fatal to the maintenance of a good cause than deceit, misrepresentation, and falsehood. That the strictest laws of honesty should be observed in the discussion of a purely speculative subject is the least requirement that can be made. If we could reckon with security even upon so little, the conflict of speculative reason regarding the important questions of God, immortality, and freedom, would have been either decided long ago, or would very soon be brought to a conclusion. But, in general, the uprightness of the defence stands in an inverse ratio to the goodness of the cause; and perhaps more honesty and fairness are shown by those who deny than by those who uphold these doctrines.

I shall persuade myself, then, that I have readers who do not wish to see a righteous cause defended by unfair arguments. Such will now recognize the fact that, according to the principles of this Critique, if we consider not what is, but what ought to be the case, there can be really no polemic of pure reason. For how can two persons dispute about a thing, the reality of which neither can present in actual or even in possible experience? Each adopts the plan of meditating on his idea for the purpose of drawing from the idea, if he can, what is more than the idea, that is, the reality of the object which it indicates. How shall they settle the dispute, since neither is able to make his assertions directly comprehensible and certain, but must restrict himself to attacking and confuting those of his opponent? All statements enounced by pure reason transcend the conditions of possible experience, beyond the sphere of which we can discover no criterion of truth, while they are at the same time framed in accordance with the laws of the understanding, which are applicable only to experience; and thus it is the fate of all such speculative discussions that while the one party attacks the weaker side of his opponent, he infallibly lays open his own weaknesses.

The critique of pure reason may be regarded as the highest tribunal for all speculative disputes; for it is not involved in these disputes, which have an immediate relation to certain objects and not to the laws of the mind, but is instituted for the purpose of determining the rights and limits of reason.

Without the control of criticism, reason is, as it were, in a state of nature, and can only establish its claims and assertions by war. Criticism, on the contrary, deciding all questions according to the fundamental laws of its own institution, secures to us the peace of law and order, and enables us to discuss all differences in the more tranquil manner of a legal process. In the former case, disputes are ended by victory, which both sides may claim and which is followed by a hollow armistice; in the latter, by a sentence, which, as it strikes at the root of all speculative differences, ensures to all concerned a lasting peace. The endless disputes of a dogmatizing reason compel us to look for some mode of arriving at a settled decision by a critical investigation of reason itself; just as Hobbes maintains that the state of nature is a state of injustice and violence, and that we must leave it and submit ourselves to the constraint of law, which indeed limits individual freedom, but only that it may consist with the freedom of others and with the common good of all.

This freedom will, among other things, permit of our openly stating the difficulties and doubts which we are ourselves unable to solve, without being decried on that account as turbulent and dangerous citizens. This privilege forms part of the native rights of human reason, which recognizes no other judge than the universal reason of humanity; and as this reason is the source of all progress and improvement, such a privilege is to be held sacred and inviolable. It is unwise, moreover, to denounce as dangerous any bold assertions against, or rash attacks upon, an opinion which is held by the largest and most moral class of the community; for that would be giving them an importance which they do not deserve. When I hear that the freedom of the will, the hope of a future life, and the existence of God have been overthrown by the arguments of some able writer, I feel a strong desire to read his book; for I expect that he will add to my knowledge and impart greater clearness and distinctness to my views by the argumentative power shown in his writings. But I am perfectly certain, even before I have opened the book, that he has not succeeded in a single point, not because I believe I am in possession of irrefutable demonstrations of these important propositions, but because this transcendental critique, which has disclosed to me the power and the limits of pure reason, has fully convinced me that, as it is insufficient to establish the affirmative, it is as powerless, and even more so, to assure us of the truth of the negative answer to these questions. From what source does this free-thinker derive his knowledge that there is, for example, no Supreme Being? This proposition lies out of the field of possible experience, and, therefore, beyond the limits of human cognition. But I would not read at, all the answer which the dogmatical maintainer of the good cause makes to his opponent, because I know well beforehand, that he will merely attack the fallacious grounds of his adversary, without being able to establish his own assertions. Besides, a new illusory argument, in the construction of which talent and acuteness are shown, is suggestive of new ideas and new trains of reasoning, and in this respect the old and everyday sophistries are quite useless. Again, the dogmatical opponent of religion gives employment to criticism, and enables us to test and correct its principles, while there is no occasion for anxiety in regard to the influence and results of his reasoning.

But, it will be said, must we not warn the youth entrusted to academical care against such writings, must we not preserve them from the knowledge of these dangerous assertions, until their judgement is ripened, or rather until the doctrines which we wish to inculcate are so firmly rooted in their minds as to withstand all attempts at instilling the contrary dogmas, from whatever quarter they may come?

If we are to confine ourselves to the dogmatical procedure in the sphere of pure reason, and find ourselves unable to settle such disputes otherwise than by becoming a party in them, and setting counter-assertions against the statements advanced by our opponents, there is certainly no plan more advisable for the moment, but, at the same time, none more absurd and inefficient for the future, than this retaining of the youthful mind under guardianship for a time, and thus preserving it—for so long at least—from seduction into error. But when, at a later period, either curiosity, or the prevalent fashion of thought places such writings in their hands, will the so-called convictions of their youth stand firm? The young thinker, who has in his armoury none but dogmatical weapons with which to resist the attacks of his opponent, and who cannot detect the latent dialectic which lies in his own opinions as well as in those of the opposite party, sees the advance of illusory arguments and grounds of proof which have the advantage of novelty, against as illusory grounds of proof destitute of this advantage, and which, perhaps, excite the suspicion that the natural credulity of his youth has been abused by his instructors. He thinks he can find no better means of showing that he has out grown the discipline of his minority than by despising those well-meant warnings, and, knowing no system of thought but that of dogmatism, he drinks deep draughts of the poison that is to sap the principles in which his early years were trained.

Exactly the opposite of the system here recommended ought to be pursued in academical instruction. This can only be effected, however, by a thorough training in the critical investigation of pure reason. For, in order to bring the principles of this critique into exercise as soon as possible, and to demonstrate their perfect even in the presence of the highest degree of dialectical illusion, the student ought to examine the assertions made on both sides of speculative questions step by step, and to test them by these principles. It cannot be a difficult task for him to show the fallacies inherent in these propositions, and thus he begins early to feel his own power of securing himself against the influence of such sophistical arguments, which must finally lose, for him, all their illusory power. And, although the same blows which overturn the edifice of his opponent are as fatal to his own speculative structures, if such he has wished to rear; he need not feel any sorrow in regard to this seeming misfortune, as he has now before him a fair prospect into the practical region in which he may reasonably hope to find a more secure foundation for a rational system.

There is, accordingly, no proper polemic in the sphere of pure reason. Both parties beat the air and fight with their own shadows, as they pass beyond the limits of nature, and can find no tangible point of attack—no firm footing for their dogmatical conflict. Fight as vigorously as they may, the shadows which they hew down, immediately start up again, like the heroes in Walhalla, and renew the bloodless and unceasing contest.

But neither can we admit that there is any proper sceptical employment of pure reason, such as might be based upon the principle of neutrality in all speculative disputes. To excite reason against itself, to place weapons in the hands of the party on the one side as well as in those of the other, and to remain an undisturbed and sarcastic spectator of the fierce struggle that ensues, seems, from the dogmatical point of view, to be a part fitting only a malevolent disposition. But, when the sophist evidences an invincible obstinacy and blindness, and a pride which no criticism can moderate, there is no other practicable course than to oppose to this pride and obstinacy similar feelings and pretensions on the other side, equally well or ill founded, so that reason, staggered by the reflections thus forced upon it, finds it necessary to moderate its confidence in such pretensions and to listen to the advice of criticism. But we cannot stop at these doubts, much less regard the conviction of our ignorance, not only as a cure for the conceit natural to dogmatism, but as the settlement of the disputes in which reason is involved with itself. On the contrary, scepticism is merely a means of awakening reason from its dogmatic dreams and exciting it to a more careful investigation into its own powers and pretensions. But, as scepticism appears to be the shortest road to a permanent peace in the domain of philosophy, and as it is the track pursued by the many who aim at giving a philosophical colouring to their contemptuous dislike of all inquiries of this kind, I think it necessary to present to my readers this mode of thought in its true light.

Scepticism not a Permanent State for Human Reason.

The consciousness of ignorance—unless this ignorance is recognized to be absolutely necessary ought, instead of forming the conclusion of my inquiries, to be the strongest motive to the pursuit of them. All ignorance is either ignorance of things or of the limits of knowledge. If my ignorance is accidental and not necessary, it must incite me, in the first case, to a dogmatical inquiry regarding the objects of which I am ignorant; in the second, to a critical investigation into the bounds of all possible knowledge. But that my ignorance is absolutely necessary and unavoidable, and that it consequently absolves from the duty of all further investigation, is a fact which cannot be made out upon empirical grounds—from observation—but upon critical grounds alone, that is, by a thoroughgoing investigation into the primary sources of cognition. It follows that the determination of the bounds of reason can be made only on à priori grounds; while the empirical limitation of reason, which is merely an indeterminate cognition of an ignorance that can never be completely removed, can take place only à posteriori. In other words, our empirical knowledge is limited by that which yet remains for us to know. The former cognition of our ignorance, which is possible only on a rational basis, is a science; the latter is merely a perception, and we cannot say how far the inferences drawn from it may extend. If I regard the earth, as it really appears to my senses, as a flat surface, I am ignorant how far this surface extends. But experience teaches me that, how far soever I go, I always see before me a space in which I can proceed farther; and thus I know the limits—merely visual—of my actual knowledge of the earth, although I am ignorant of the limits of the earth itself. But if I have got so far as to know that the earth is a sphere, and that its surface is spherical, I can cognize à priori and determine upon principles, from my knowledge of a small part of this surface—say to the extent of a degree—the diameter and circumference of the earth; and although I am ignorant of the objects which this surface contains, I have a perfect knowledge of its limits and extent.

The sum of all the possible objects of our cognition seems to us to be a level surface, with an apparent horizon—that which forms the limit of its extent, and which has been termed by us the idea of unconditioned totality. To reach this limit by empirical means is impossible, and all attempts to determine it à priori according to a principle, are alike in vain. But all the questions raised by pure reason relate to that which lies beyond this horizon, or, at least, in its boundary line.

The celebrated David Hume was one of those geographers of human reason who believe that they have given a sufficient answer to all such questions by declaring them to lie beyond the horizon of our knowledge—a horizon which, however, Hume was unable to determine. His attention especially was directed to the principle of causality; and he remarked with perfect justice that the truth of this principle, and even the objective validity of the conception of a cause, was not commonly based upon clear insight, that is, upon à priori cognition. Hence he concluded that this law does not derive its authority from its universality and necessity, but merely from its general applicability in the course of experience, and a kind of subjective necessity thence arising, which he termed habit. From the inability of reason to establish this principle as a necessary law for the acquisition of all experience, he inferred the nullity of all the attempts of reason to pass the region of the empirical.

This procedure of subjecting the facta of reason to examination, and, if necessary, to disapproval, may be termed the censura of reason. This censura must inevitably lead us to doubts regarding all transcendent employment of principles. But this is only the second step in our inquiry. The first step in regard to the subjects of pure reason, and which marks the infancy of that faculty, is that of dogmatism. The second, which we have just mentioned, is that of scepticism, and it gives evidence that our judgement has been improved by experience. But a third step is necessary—indicative of the maturity and manhood of the judgement, which now lays a firm foundation upon universal and necessary principles. This is the period of criticism, in which we do not examine the facta of reason, but reason itself, in the whole extent of its powers, and in regard to its capability of à priori cognition; and thus we determine not merely the empirical and ever-shifting bounds of our knowledge, but its necessary and eternal limits. We demonstrate from indubitable principles, not merely our ignorance in respect to this or that subject, but in regard to all possible questions of a certain class. Thus scepticism is a resting place for reason, in which it may reflect on its dogmatical wanderings and gain some knowledge of the region in which it happens to be, that it may pursue its way with greater certainty; but it cannot be its permanent dwelling-place. It must take up its abode only in the region of complete certitude, whether this relates to the cognition of objects themselves, or to the limits which bound all our cognition.

Reason is not to be considered as an indefinitely extended plane, of the bounds of which we have only a general knowledge; it ought rather to be compared to a sphere, the radius of which may be found from the curvature of its surface—that is, the nature of à priori synthetical propositions—and, consequently, its circumference and extent. Beyond the sphere of experience there are no objects which it can cognize; nay, even questions regarding such supposititious objects relate only to the subjective principles of a complete determination of the relations which exist between the understanding-conceptions which lie within this sphere.

We are actually in possession of à priori synthetical cognitions, as is proved by the existence of the principles of the understanding, which anticipate experience. If any one cannot comprehend the possibility of these principles, he may have some reason to doubt whether they are really à priori; but he cannot on this account declare them to be impossible, and affirm the nullity of the steps which reason may have taken under their guidance. He can only say: If we perceived their origin and their authenticity, we should be able to determine the extent and limits of reason; but, till we can do this, all propositions regarding the latter are mere random assertions. In this view, the doubt respecting all dogmatical philosophy, which proceeds without the guidance of criticism, is well grounded; but we cannot therefore deny to reason the ability to construct a sound philosophy, when the way has been prepared by a thorough critical investigation. All the conceptions produced, and all the questions raised, by pure reason, do not lie in the sphere of experience, but in that of reason itself, and hence they must be solved, and shown to be either valid or inadmissible, by that faculty. We have no right to decline the solution of such problems, on the ground that the solution can be discovered only from the nature of things, and under pretence of the limitation of human faculties, for reason is the sole creator of all these ideas, and is therefore bound either to establish their validity or to expose their illusory nature.

The polemic of scepticism is properly directed against the dogmatist, who erects a system of philosophy without having examined the fundamental objective principles on which it is based, for the purpose of evidencing the futility of his designs, and thus bringing him to a knowledge of his own powers. But, in itself, scepticism does not give us any certain information in regard to the bounds of our knowledge. All unsuccessful dogmatical attempts of reason are facia, which it is always useful to submit to the censure of the sceptic. But this cannot help us to any decision regarding the expectations which reason cherishes of better success in future endeavours; the investigations of scepticism cannot, therefore, settle the dispute regarding the rights and powers of human reason.

Hume is perhaps the ablest and most ingenious of all sceptical philosophers, and his writings have, undoubtedly, exerted the most powerful influence in awakening reason to a thorough investigation into its own powers. It will, therefore, well repay our labours to consider for a little the course of reasoning which he followed and the errors into which he strayed, although setting out on the path of truth and certitude.

Hume was probably aware, although he never clearly developed the notion, that we proceed in judgements of a certain class beyond our conception of the object. I have termed this kind of judgement synthetical. As regard the manner in which I pass beyond my conception by the aid of experience, no doubts can be entertained. Experience is itself a synthesis of perceptions; and it employs perceptions to increment the conception, which I obtain by means of another perception. But we feel persuaded that we are able to proceed beyond a conception, and to extend our cognition à priori. We attempt this in two ways—either, through the pure understanding, in relation to that which may become an object of experience, or, through pure reason, in relation to such properties of things, or of the existence of things, as can never be presented in any experience. This sceptical philosopher did not distinguish these two kinds of judgements, as he ought to have done, but regarded this augmentation of conceptions, and, if we may so express ourselves, the spontaneous generation of understanding and reason, independently of the impregnation of experience, as altogether impossible. The so-called à priori principles of these faculties he consequently held to be invalid and imaginary, and regarded them as nothing but subjective habits of thought originating in experience, and therefore purely empirical and contingent rules, to which we attribute a spurious necessity and universality. In support of this strange assertion, he referred us to the generally acknowledged principle of the relation between cause and effect. No faculty of the mind can conduct us from the conception of a thing to the existence of something else; and hence he believed he could infer that, without experience, we possess no source from which we can augment a conception, and no ground sufficient to justify us in framing a judgement that is to extend our cognition à priori. That the light of the sun, which shines upon a piece of wax, at the same time melts it, while it hardens clay, no power of the understanding could infer from the conceptions which we previously possessed of these substances; much less is there any à priori law that could conduct us to such a conclusion, which experience alone can certify. On the other hand, we have seen in our discussion of transcendental logic, that, although we can never proceed immediately beyond the content of the conception which is given us, we can always cognize completely à priori—in relation, however, to a third term, namely, possible experience—the law of its connection with other things. For example, if I observe that a piece of wax melts, I can cognize à priori that there must have been something (the sun's heat) preceding, which this law; although, without the aid of experience, I could not cognize à priori and in a determinate manner either the cause from the effect, or the effect from the cause. Hume was, therefore, wrong in inferring, from the contingency of the determination according to law, the contingency of the law itself; and the passing beyond the conception of a thing to possible experience (which is an à priori proceeding, constituting the objective reality of the conception), he confounded with our synthesis of objects in actual experience, which is always, of course, empirical. Thus, too, he regarded the principle of affinity, which has its seat in the understanding and indicates a necessary connection, as a mere rule of association, lying in the imitative faculty of imagination, which can present only contingent, and not objective connections.

The sceptical errors of this remarkably acute thinker arose principally from a defect, which was common to him with the dogmatists, namely, that he had never made a systematic review of all the different kinds of à priori synthesis performed by the understanding. Had he done so, he would have found, to take one example among many, that the principle of permanence was of this character, and that it, as well as the principle of causality, anticipates experience. In this way he might have been able to describe the determinate limits of the à priori operations of understanding and reason. But he merely declared the understanding to be limited, instead of showing what its limits were; he created a general mistrust in the power of our faculties, without giving us any determinate knowledge of the bounds of our necessary and unavoidable ignorance; he examined and condemned some of the principles of the understanding, without investigating all its powers with the completeness necessary to criticism. He denies, with truth, certain powers to the understanding, but he goes further, and declares it to be utterly inadequate to the à priori extension of knowledge, although he has not fully examined all the powers which reside in the faculty; and thus the fate which always overtakes scepticism meets him too. That is to say, his own declarations are doubted, for his objections were based upon facta, which are contingent, and not upon principles, which can alone demonstrate the necessary invalidity of all dogmatical assertions.

As Hume makes no distinction between the well-grounded claims of the understanding and the dialectical pretensions of reason, against which, however, his attacks are mainly directed, reason does not feel itself shut out from all attempts at the extension of à priori cognition, and hence it refuses, in spite of a few checks in this or that quarter, to relinquish such efforts. For one naturally arms oneself to resist an attack, and becomes more obstinate in the resolve to establish the claims he has advanced. But a complete review of the powers of reason, and the conviction thence arising that we are in possession of a limited field of action, while we must admit the vanity of higher claims, puts an end to all doubt and dispute, and induces reason to rest satisfied with the undisturbed possession of its limited domain.

To the uncritical dogmatist, who has not surveyed the sphere of his understanding, nor determined, in accordance with principles, the limits of possible cognition, who, consequently, is ignorant of his own powers, and believes he will discover them by the attempts he makes in the field of cognition, these attacks of scepticism are not only dangerous, but destructive. For if there is one proposition in his chain of reasoning which he cannot prove, or the fallacy in which he cannot evolve in accordance with a principle, suspicion falls on all his statements, however plausible they may appear.

And thus scepticism, the bane of dogmatical philosophy, conducts us to a sound investigation into the understanding and the reason. When we are thus far advanced, we need fear no further attacks; for the limits of our domain are clearly marked out, and we can make no claims nor become involved in any disputes regarding the region that lies beyond these limits. Thus the sceptical procedure in philosophy does not present any solution of the problems of reason, but it forms an excellent exercise for its powers, awakening its circumspection, and indicating the means whereby it may most fully establish its claims to its legitimate possessions.

Section III. The Discipline of Pure Reason in Hypothesis

This critique of reason has now taught us that all its efforts to extend the bounds of knowledge, by means of pure speculation, are utterly fruitless. So much the wider field, it may appear, lies open to hypothesis; as, where we cannot know with certainty, we are at liberty to make guesses and to form suppositions.

Imagination may be allowed, under the strict surveillance of reason, to invent suppositions; but, these must be based on something that is perfectly certain—and that is the possibility of the object. If we are well assured upon this point, it is allowable to have recourse to supposition in regard to the reality of the object; but this supposition must, unless it is utterly groundless, be connected, as its ground of explanation, with that which is really given and absolutely certain. Such a supposition is termed a hypothesis.

It is beyond our power to form the least conception à priori of the possibility of dynamical connection in phenomena; and the category of the pure understanding will not enable us to excogitate any such connection, but merely helps us to understand it, when we meet with it in experience. For this reason we cannot, in accordance with the categories, imagine or invent any object or any property of an object not given, or that may not be given in experience, and employ it in a hypothesis; otherwise, we should be basing our chain of reasoning upon mere chimerical fancies, and not upon conceptions of things. Thus, we have no right to assume the existence of new powers, not existing in nature—for example, an understanding with a non-sensuous intuition, a force of attraction without contact, or some new kind of substances occupying space, and yet without the property of impenetrability—and, consequently, we cannot assume that there is any other kind of community among substances than that observable in experience, any kind of presence than that in space, or any kind of duration than that in time. In one word, the conditions of possible experience are for reason the only conditions of the possibility of things; reason cannot venture to form, independently of these conditions, any conceptions of things, because such conceptions, although not self-contradictory, are without object and without application.

The conceptions of reason are, as we have already shown, mere ideas, and do not relate to any object in any kind of experience. At the same time, they do not indicate imaginary or possible objects. They are purely problematical in their nature and, as aids to the heuristic exercise of the faculties, form the basis of the regulative principles for the systematic employment of the understanding in the field of experience. If we leave this ground of experience, they become mere fictions of thought, the possibility of which is quite indemonstrable; and they cannot, consequently, be employed as hypotheses in the explanation of real phenomena. It is quite admissible to cogitate the soul as simple, for the purpose of enabling ourselves to employ the idea of a perfect and necessary unity of all the faculties of the mind as the principle of all our inquiries into its internal phenomena, although we cannot cognize this unity in concreto. But to assume that the soul is a simple substance (a transcendental conception) would be enouncing a proposition which is not only indemonstrable—as many physical hypotheses are—but a proposition which is purely arbitrary, and in the highest degree rash. The simple is never presented in experience; and, if by substance is here meant the permanent object of sensuous intuition, the possibility of a simple phenomenon is perfectly inconceivable. Reason affords no good grounds for admitting the existence of intelligible beings, or of intelligible properties of sensuous things, although—as we have no conception either of their possibility or of their impossibility—it will always be out of our power to affirm dogmatically that they do not exist. In the explanation of given phenomena, no other things and no other grounds of explanation can be employed than those which stand in connection with the given phenomena according to the known laws of experience. A transcendental hypothesis, in which a mere idea of reason is employed to explain the phenomena of nature, would not give us any better insight into a phenomenon, as we should be trying to explain what we do not sufficiently understand from known empirical principles, by what we do not understand at all. The principles of such a hypothesis might conduce to the satisfaction of reason, but it would not assist the understanding in its application to objects. Order and conformity to aims in the sphere of nature must be themselves explained upon natural grounds and according to natural laws; and the wildest hypotheses, if they are only physical, are here more admissible than a hyperphysical hypothesis, such as that of a divine author. For such a hypothesis would introduce the principle of ignava ratio, which requires us to give up the search for causes that might be discovered in the course of experience and to rest satisfied with a mere idea. As regards the absolute totality of the grounds of explanation in the series of these causes, this can be no hindrance to the understanding in the case of phenomena; because, as they are to us nothing more than phenomena, we have no right to look for anything like completeness in the synthesis of the series of their conditions.

Transcendental hypotheses are therefore inadmissible; and we cannot use the liberty of employing, in the absence of physical, hyperphysical grounds of explanation. And this for two reasons; first, because such hypothesis do not advance reason, but rather stop it in its progress; secondly, because this licence would render fruitless all its exertions in its own proper sphere, which is that of experience. For, when the explanation of natural phenomena happens to be difficult, we have constantly at hand a transcendental ground of explanation, which lifts us above the necessity of investigating nature; and our inquiries are brought to a close, not because we have obtained all the requisite knowledge, but because we abut upon a principle which is incomprehensible and which, indeed, is so far back in the track of thought as to contain the conception of the absolutely primal being.

The next requisite for the admissibility of a hypothesis is its sufficiency. That is, it must determine à priori the consequences which are given in experience and which are supposed to follow from the hypothesis itself. If we require to employ auxiliary hypotheses, the suspicion naturally arises that they are mere fictions; because the necessity for each of them requires the same justification as in the case of the original hypothesis, and thus their testimony is invalid. If we suppose the existence of an infinitely perfect cause, we possess sufficient grounds for the explanation of the conformity to aims, the order and the greatness which we observe in the universe; but we find ourselves obliged, when we observe the evil in the world and the exceptions to these laws, to employ new hypothesis in support of the original one. We employ the idea of the simple nature of the human soul as the foundation of all the theories we may form of its phenomena; but when we meet with difficulties in our way, when we observe in the soul phenomena similar to the changes which take place in matter, we require to call in new auxiliary hypotheses. These may, indeed, not be false, but we do not know them to be true, because the only witness to their certitude is the hypothesis which they themselves have been called in to explain.

We are not discussing the above-mentioned assertions regarding the immaterial unity of the soul and the existence of a Supreme Being as dogmata, which certain philosophers profess to demonstrate à priori, but purely as hypotheses. In the former case, the dogmatist must take care that his arguments possess the apodeictic certainty of a demonstration. For the assertion that the reality of such ideas is probable is as absurd as a proof of the probability of a proposition in geometry. Pure abstract reason, apart from all experience, can either cognize nothing at all; and hence the judgements it enounces are never mere opinions, they are either apodeictic certainties, or declarations that nothing can be known on the subject. Opinions and probable judgements on the nature of things can only be employed to explain given phenomena, or they may relate to the effect, in accordance with empirical laws, of an actually existing cause. In other words, we must restrict the sphere of opinion to the world of experience and nature. Beyond this region opinion is mere invention; unless we are groping about for the truth on a path not yet fully known, and have some hopes of stumbling upon it by chance.

But, although hypotheses are inadmissible in answers to the questions of pure speculative reason, they may be employed in the defence of these answers. That is to say, hypotheses are admissible in polemic, but not in the sphere of dogmatism. By the defence of statements of this character, I do not mean an attempt at discovering new grounds for their support, but merely the refutation of the arguments of opponents. All à priori synthetical propositions possess the peculiarity that, although the philosopher who maintains the reality of the ideas contained in the proposition is not in possession of sufficient knowledge to establish the certainty of his statements, his opponent is as little able to prove the truth of the opposite. This equality of fortune does not allow the one party to be superior to the other in the sphere of speculative cognition; and it is this sphere, accordingly, that is the proper arena of these endless speculative conflicts. But we shall afterwards show that, in relation to its practical exercise, Reason has the right of admitting what, in the field of pure speculation, she would not be justified in supposing, except upon perfectly sufficient grounds; because all such suppositions destroy the necessary completeness of speculation—a condition which the practical reason, however, does not consider to be requisite. In this sphere, therefore, Reason is mistress of a possession, her title to which she does not require to prove—which, in fact, she could not do. The burden of proof accordingly rests upon the opponent. But as he has just as little knowledge regarding the subject discussed, and is as little able to prove the non-existence of the object of an idea, as the philosopher on the other side is to demonstrate its reality, it is evident that there is an advantage on the side of the philosopher who maintains his proposition as a practically necessary supposition (melior est conditio possidentis). For he is at liberty to employ, in self-defence, the same weapons as his opponent makes use of in attacking him; that is, he has a right to use hypotheses not for the purpose of supporting the arguments in favour of his own propositions, but to show that his opponent knows no more than himself regarding the subject under discussion and cannot boast of any speculative advantage.

Hypotheses are, therefore, admissible in the sphere of pure reason only as weapons for self-defence, and not as supports to dogmatical assertions. But the opposing party we must always seek for in ourselves. For speculative reason is, in the sphere of transcendentalism, dialectical in its own nature. The difficulties and objections we have to fear lie in ourselves. They are like old but never superannuated claims; and we must seek them out, and settle them once and for ever, if we are to expect a permanent peace. External tranquility is hollow and unreal. The root of these contradictions, which lies in the nature of human reason, must be destroyed; and this can only be done by giving it, in the first instance, freedom to grow, nay, by nourishing it, that it may send out shoots, and thus betray its own existence. It is our duty, therefore, to try to discover new objections, to put weapons in the bands of our opponent, and to grant him the most favourable position in the arena that he can wish. We have nothing to fear from these concessions; on the contrary, we may rather hope that we shall thus make ourselves master of a possession which no one will ever venture to dispute.

The thinker requires, to be fully equipped, the hypotheses of pure reason, which, although but leaden weapons (for they have not been steeled in the armoury of experience), are as useful as any that can be employed by his opponents. If, accordingly, we have assumed, from a non-speculative point of view, the immaterial nature of the soul, and are met by the objection that experience seems to prove that the growth and decay of our mental faculties are mere modifications of the sensuous organism—we can weaken the force of this objection by the assumption that the body is nothing but the fundamental phenomenon, to which, as a necessary condition, all sensibility, and consequently all thought, relates in the present state of our existence; and that the separation of soul and body forms the conclusion of the sensuous exercise of our power of cognition and the beginning of the intellectual. The body would, in this view of the question, be regarded, not as the cause of thought, but merely as its restrictive condition, as promotive of the sensuous and animal, but as a hindrance to the pure and spiritual life; and the dependence of the animal life on the constitution of the body, would not prove that the whole life of man was also dependent on the state of the organism. We might go still farther, and discover new objections, or carry out to their extreme consequences those which have already been adduced.

Generation, in the human race as well as among the irrational animals, depends on so many accidents—of occasion, of proper sustenance, of the laws enacted by the government of a country of vice even, that it is difficult to believe in the eternal existence of a being whose life has begun under circumstances so mean and trivial, and so entirely dependent upon our own control. As regards the continuance of the existence of the whole race, we need have no difficulties, for accident in single cases is subject to general laws; but, in the case of each individual, it would seem as if we could hardly expect so wonderful an effect from causes so insignificant. But, in answer to these objections, we may adduce the transcendental hypothesis that all life is properly intelligible, and not subject to changes of time, and that it neither began in birth, nor will end in death. We may assume that this life is nothing more than a sensuous representation of pure spiritual life; that the whole world of sense is but an image, hovering before the faculty of cognition which we exercise in this sphere, and with no more objective reality than a dream; and that if we could intuite ourselves and other things as they really are, we should see ourselves in a world of spiritual natures, our connection with which did not begin at our birth and will not cease with the destruction of the body. And so on.

We cannot be said to know what has been above asserted, nor do we seriously maintain the truth of these assertions; and the notions therein indicated are not even ideas of reason, they are purely fictitious conceptions. But this hypothetical procedure is in perfect conformity with the laws of reason. Our opponent mistakes the absence of empirical conditions for a proof of the complete impossibility of all that we have asserted; and we have to show him that he has not exhausted the whole sphere of possibility and that he can as little compass that sphere by the laws of experience and nature, as we can lay a secure foundation for the operations of reason beyond the region of experience. Such hypothetical defences against the pretensions of an opponent must not be regarded as declarations of opinion. The philosopher abandons them, so soon as the opposite party renounces its dogmatical conceit. To maintain a simply negative position in relation to propositions which rest on an insecure foundation, well befits the moderation of a true philosopher; but to uphold the objections urged against an opponent as proofs of the opposite statement is a proceeding just as unwarrantable and arrogant as it is to attack the position of a philosopher who advances affirmative propositions regarding such a subject.

It is evident, therefore, that hypotheses, in the speculative sphere, are valid, not as independent propositions, but only relatively to opposite transcendent assumptions. For, to make the principles of possible experience conditions of the possibility of things in general is just as transcendent a procedure as to maintain the objective reality of ideas which can be applied to no objects except such as lie without the limits of possible experience. The judgements enounced by pure reason must be necessary, or they must not be enounced at all. Reason cannot trouble herself with opinions. But the hypotheses we have been discussing are merely problematical judgements, which can neither be confuted nor proved; while, therefore, they are not personal opinions, they are indispensable as answers to objections which are liable to be raised. But we must take care to confine them to this function, and guard against any assumption on their part of absolute validity, a proceeding which would involve reason in inextricable difficulties and contradictions.

Section IV. The Discipline of Pure Reason in Relation to Proofs

It is a peculiarity, which distinguishes the proofs of transcendental synthetical propositions from those of all other à priori synthetical cognitions, that reason, in the case of the former, does not apply its conceptions directly to an object, but is first obliged to prove, à priori, the objective validity of these conceptions and the possibility of their syntheses. This is not merely a prudential rule, it is essential to the very possibility of the proof of a transcendental proposition. If I am required to pass, à priori, beyond the conception of an object, I find that it is utterly impossible without the guidance of something which is not contained in the conception. In mathematics, it is à priori intuition that guides my synthesis; and, in this case, all our conclusions may be drawn immediately from pure intuition. In transcendental cognition, so long as we are dealing only with conceptions of the understanding, we are guided by possible experience. That is to say, a proof in the sphere of transcendental cognition does not show that the given conception (that of an event, for example) leads directly to another conception (that of a cause)—for this would be a saltus which nothing can justify; but it shows that experience itself, and consequently the object of experience, is impossible without the connection indicated by these conceptions. It follows that such a proof must demonstrate the possibility of arriving, synthetically and à priori, at a certain knowledge of things, which was not contained in our conceptions of these things. Unless we pay particular attention to this requirement, our proofs, instead of pursuing the straight path indicated by reason, follow the tortuous road of mere subjective association. The illusory conviction, which rests upon subjective causes of association, and which is considered as resulting from the perception of a real and objective natural affinity, is always open to doubt and suspicion. For this reason, all the attempts which have been made to prove the principle of sufficient reason, have, according to the universal admission of philosophers, been quite unsuccessful; and, before the appearance of transcendental criticism, it was considered better, as this principle could not be abandoned, to appeal boldly to the common sense of mankind (a proceeding which always proves that the problem, which reason ought to solve, is one in which philosophers find great difficulties), rather than attempt to discover new dogmatical proofs.

But, if the proposition to be proved is a proposition of pure reason, and if I aim at passing beyond my empirical conceptions by the aid of mere ideas, it is necessary that the proof should first show that such a step in synthesis is possible (which it is not), before it proceeds to prove the truth of the proposition itself. The so-called proof of the simple nature of the soul from the unity of apperception, is a very plausible one. But it contains no answer to the objection, that, as the notion of absolute simplicity is not a conception which is directly applicable to a perception, but is an idea which must be inferred—if at all—from observation, it is by no means evident how the mere fact of consciousness, which is contained in all thought, although in so far a simple representation, can conduct me to the consciousness and cognition of a thing which is purely a thinking substance. When I represent to my mind the power of my body as in motion, my body in this thought is so far absolute unity, and my representation of it is a simple one; and hence I can indicate this representation by the motion of a point, because I have made abstraction of the size or volume of the body. But I cannot hence infer that, given merely the moving power of a body, the body may be cogitated as simple substance, merely because the representation in my mind takes no account of its content in space, and is consequently simple. The simple, in abstraction, is very different from the objectively simple; and hence the Ego, which is simple in the first sense, may, in the second sense, as indicating the soul itself, be a very complex conception, with a very various content. Thus it is evident that in all such arguments there lurks a paralogism. We guess (for without some such surmise our suspicion would not be excited in reference to a proof of this character) at the presence of the paralogism, by keeping ever before us a criterion of the possibility of those synthetical propositions which aim at proving more than experience can teach us. This criterion is obtained from the observation that such proofs do not lead us directly from the subject of the proposition to be proved to the required predicate, but find it necessary to presuppose the possibility of extending our cognition à priori by means of ideas. We must, accordingly, always use the greatest caution; we require, before attempting any proof, to consider how it is possible to extend the sphere of cognition by the operations of pure reason, and from what source we are to derive knowledge, which is not obtained from the analysis of conceptions, nor relates, by anticipation, to possible experience. We shall thus spare ourselves much severe and fruitless labour, by not expecting from reason what is beyond its power, or rather by subjecting it to discipline, and teaching it to moderate its vehement desires for the extension of the sphere of cognition.

The first rule for our guidance is, therefore, not to attempt a transcendental proof, before we have considered from what source we are to derive the principles upon which the proof is to be based, and what right we have to expect that our conclusions from these principles will be veracious. If they are principles of the understanding, it is vain to expect that we should attain by their means to ideas of pure reason; for these principles are valid only in regard to objects of possible experience. If they are principles of pure reason, our labour is alike in vain. For the principles of reason, if employed as objective, are without exception dialectical and possess no validity or truth, except as regulative principles of the systematic employment of reason in experience. But when such delusive proof are presented to us, it is our duty to meet them with the non liquet of a matured judgement; and, although we are unable to expose the particular sophism upon which the proof is based, we have a right to demand a deduction of the principles employed in it; and, if these principles have their origin in pure reason alone, such a deduction is absolutely impossible. And thus it is unnecessary that we should trouble ourselves with the exposure and confutation of every sophistical illusion; we may, at once, bring all dialectic, which is inexhaustible in the production of fallacies, before the bar of critical reason, which tests the principles upon which all dialectical procedure is based. The second peculiarity of transcendental proof is that a transcendental proposition cannot rest upon more than a single proof. If I am drawing conclusions, not from conceptions, but from intuition corresponding to a conception, be it pure intuition, as in mathematics, or empirical, as in natural science, the intuition which forms the basis of my inferences presents me with materials for many synthetical propositions, which I can connect in various modes, while, as it is allowable to proceed from different points in the intention, I can arrive by different paths at the same proposition.

But every transcendental proposition sets out from a conception, and posits the synthetical condition of the possibility of an object according to this conception. There must, therefore, be but one ground of proof, because it is the conception alone which determines the object; and thus the proof cannot contain anything more than the determination of the object according to the conception. In our Transcendental Analytic, for example, we inferred the principle: Every event has a cause, from the only condition of the objective possibility of our conception of an event. This is that an event cannot be determined in time, and consequently cannot form a part of experience, unless it stands under this dynamical law. This is the only possible ground of proof; for our conception of an event possesses objective validity, that is, is a true conception, only because the law of causality determines an object to which it can refer. Other arguments in support of this principle have been attempted—such as that from the contingent nature of a phenomenon; but when this argument is considered, we can discover no criterion of contingency, except the fact of an event—of something happening, that is to say, the existence which is preceded by the non-existence of an object, and thus we fall back on the very thing to be proved. If the proposition: "Every thinking being is simple," is to be proved, we keep to the conception of the ego, which is simple, and to which all thought has a relation. The same is the case with the transcendental proof of the existence of a Deity, which is based solely upon the harmony and reciprocal fitness of the conceptions of an ens realissimum and a necessary being, and cannot be attempted in any other manner.

This caution serves to simplify very much the criticism of all propositions of reason. When reason employs conceptions alone, only one proof of its thesis is possible, if any. When, therefore, the dogmatist advances with ten arguments in favour of a proposition, we may be sure that not one of them is conclusive. For if he possessed one which proved the proposition he brings forward to demonstration—as must always be the case with the propositions of pure reason—what need is there for any more? His intention can only be similar to that of the advocate who had different arguments for different judges; this availing himself of the weakness of those who examine his arguments, who, without going into any profound investigation, adopt the view of the case which seems most probable at first sight and decide according to it.

The third rule for the guidance of pure reason in the conduct of a proof is that all transcendental proofs must never be apagogic or indirect, but always ostensive or direct. The direct or ostensive proof not only establishes the truth of the proposition to be proved, but exposes the grounds of its truth; the apagogic, on the other hand, may assure us of the truth of the proposition, but it cannot enable us to comprehend the grounds of its possibility. The latter is, accordingly, rather an auxiliary to an argument, than a strictly philosophical and rational mode of procedure. In one respect, however, they have an advantage over direct proofs, from the fact that the mode of arguing by contradiction, which they employ, renders our understanding of the question more clear, and approximates the proof to the certainty of an intuitional demonstration.

The true reason why indirect proofs are employed in different sciences is this. When the grounds upon which we seek to base a cognition are too various or too profound, we try whether or not we may not discover the truth of our cognition from its consequences. The modus ponens of reasoning from the truth of its inferences to the truth of a proposition would be admissible if all the inferences that can be drawn from it are known to be true; for in this case there can be only one possible ground for these inferences, and that is the true one. But this is a quite impracticable procedure, as it surpasses all our powers to discover all the possible inferences that can be drawn from a proposition. But this mode of reasoning is employed, under favour, when we wish to prove the truth of an hypothesis; in which case we admit the truth of the conclusion—which is supported by analogy—that, if all the inferences we have drawn and examined agree with the proposition assumed, all other possible inferences will also agree with it. But, in this way, an hypothesis can never be established as a demonstrated truth. The modus tollens of reasoning from known inferences to the unknown proposition, is not only a rigorous, but a very easy mode of proof. For, if it can be shown that but one inference from a proposition is false, then the proposition must itself be false. Instead, then, of examining, in an ostensive argument, the whole series of the grounds on which the truth of a proposition rests, we need only take the opposite of this proposition, and if one inference from it be false, then must the opposite be itself false; and, consequently, the proposition which we wished to prove must be true.

The apagogic method of proof is admissible only in those sciences where it is impossible to mistake a subjective representation for an objective cognition. Where this is possible, it is plain that the opposite of a given proposition may contradict merely the subjective conditions of thought, and not the objective cognition; or it may happen that both propositions contradict each other only under a subjective condition, which is incorrectly considered to be objective, and, as the condition is itself false, both propositions may be false, and it will, consequently, be impossible to conclude the truth of the one from the falseness of the other.

In mathematics such subreptions are impossible; and it is in this science, accordingly, that the indirect mode of proof has its true place. In the science of nature, where all assertion is based upon empirical intuition, such subreptions may be guarded against by the repeated comparison of observations; but this mode of proof is of little value in this sphere of knowledge. But the transcendental efforts of pure reason are all made in the sphere of the subjective, which is the real medium of all dialectical illusion; and thus reason endeavours, in its premisses, to impose upon us subjective representations for objective cognitions. In the transcendental sphere of pure reason, then, and in the case of synthetical propositions, it is inadmissible to support a statement by disproving the counter-statement. For only two cases are possible; either, the counter-statement is nothing but the enouncement of the inconsistency of the opposite opinion with the subjective conditions of reason, which does not affect the real case (for example, we cannot comprehend the unconditioned necessity of the existence of a being, and hence every speculative proof of the existence of such a being must be opposed on subjective grounds, while the possibility of this being in itself cannot with justice be denied); or, both propositions, being dialectical in their nature, are based upon an impossible conception. In this latter case the rule applies: non entis nulla sunt predicata; that is to say, what we affirm and what we deny, respecting such an object, are equally untrue, and the apagogic mode of arriving at the truth is in this case impossible. If, for example, we presuppose that the world of sense is given in itself in its totality, it is false, either that it is infinite, or that it is finite and limited in space. Both are false, because the hypothesis is false. For the notion of phenomena (as mere representations) which are given in themselves (as objects) is self-contradictory; and the infinitude of this imaginary whole would, indeed, be unconditioned, but would be inconsistent (as everything in the phenomenal world is conditioned) with the unconditioned determination and finitude of quantities which is presupposed in our conception.

The apagogic mode of proof is the true source of those illusions which have always had so strong an attraction for the admirers of dogmatical philosophy. It may be compared to a champion who maintains the honour and claims of the party he has adopted by offering battle to all who doubt the validity of these claims and the purity of that honour; while nothing can be proved in this way, except the respective strength of the combatants, and the advantage, in this respect, is always on the side of the attacking party. Spectators, observing that each party is alternately conqueror and conquered, are led to regard the subject of dispute as beyond the power of man to decide upon. But such an opinion cannot be justified; and it is sufficient to apply to these reasoners the remark:

Non defensoribus istis
Tempus eget.

Each must try to establish his assertions by a transcendental deduction of the grounds of proof employed in his argument, and thus enable us to see in what way the claims of reason may be supported. If an opponent bases his assertions upon subjective grounds, he may be refuted with ease; not, however to the advantage of the dogmatist, who likewise depends upon subjective sources of cognition and is in like manner driven into a corner by his opponent. But, if parties employ the direct method of procedure, they will soon discover the difficulty, nay, the impossibility of proving their assertions, and will be forced to appeal to prescription and precedence; or they will, by the help of criticism, discover with ease the dogmatical illusions by which they had been mocked, and compel reason to renounce its exaggerated pretensions to speculative insight and to confine itself within the limits of its proper sphere—that of practical principles.

Chapter II

The Canon of Pure Reason

It is a humiliating consideration for human reason that it is incompetent to discover truth by means of pure speculation, but, on the contrary, stands in need of discipline to check its deviations from the straight path and to expose the illusions which it originates. But, on the other hand, this consideration ought to elevate and to give it confidence, for this discipline is exercised by itself alone, and it is subject to the censure of no other power. The bounds, moreover, which it is forced to set to its speculative exercise, form likewise a check upon the fallacious pretensions of opponents; and thus what remains of its possessions, after these exaggerated claims have been disallowed, is secure from attack or usurpation. The greatest, and perhaps the only, use of all philosophy of pure reason is, accordingly, of a purely negative character. It is not an organon for the extension, but a discipline for the determination, of the limits of its exercise; and without laying claim to the discovery of new truth, it has the modest merit of guarding against error.

At the same time, there must be some source of positive cognitions which belong to the domain of pure reason and which become the causes of error only from our mistaking their true character, while they form the goal towards which reason continually strives. How else can we account for the inextinguishable desire in the human mind to find a firm footing in some region beyond the limits of the world of experience? It hopes to attain to the possession of a knowledge in which it has the deepest interest. It enters upon the path of pure speculation; but in vain. We have some reason, however, to expect that, in the only other way that lies open to it—the path of practical reason—it may meet with better success.

I understand by a canon a list of the à priori principles of the proper employment of certain faculties of cognition. Thus general logic, in its analytical department, is a formal canon for the faculties of understanding and reason. In the same way, Transcendental Analytic was seen to be a canon of the pure understanding; for it alone is competent to enounce true à priori synthetical cognitions. But, when no proper employment of a faculty of cognition is possible, no canon can exist. But the synthetical cognition of pure speculative reason is, as has been shown, completely impossible. There cannot, therefore, exist any canon for the speculative exercise of this faculty—for its speculative exercise is entirely dialectical; and, consequently, transcendental logic, in this respect, is merely a discipline, and not a canon. If, then, there is any proper mode of employing the faculty of pure reason—in which case there must be a canon for this faculty—this canon will relate, not to the speculative, but to the practical use of reason. This canon we now proceed to investigate.

Section I. Of the Ultimate End of the Pure Use of Reason

There exists in the faculty of reason a natural desire to venture beyond the field of experience, to attempt to reach the utmost bounds of all cognition by the help of ideas alone, and not to rest satisfied until it has fulfilled its course and raised the sum of its cognitions into a self-subsistent systematic whole. Is the motive for this endeavour to be found in its speculative, or in its practical interests alone?

Setting aside, at present, the results of the labours of pure reason in its speculative exercise, I shall merely inquire regarding the problems the solution of which forms its ultimate aim, whether reached or not, and in relation to which all other aims are but partial and intermediate. These highest aims must, from the nature of reason, possess complete unity; otherwise the highest interest of humanity could not be successfully promoted.

The transcendental speculation of reason relates to three things: the freedom of the will, the immortality of the soul, and the existence of God. The speculative interest which reason has in those questions is very small; and, for its sake alone, we should not undertake the labour of transcendental investigation—a labour full of toil and ceaseless struggle. We should be loth to undertake this labour, because the discoveries we might make would not be of the smallest use in the sphere of concrete or physical investigation. We may find out that the will is free, but this knowledge only relates to the intelligible cause of our volition. As regards the phenomena or expressions of this will, that is, our actions, we are bound, in obedience to an inviolable maxim, without which reason cannot be employed in the sphere of experience, to explain these in the same way as we explain all the other phenomena of nature, that is to say, according to its unchangeable laws. We may have discovered the spirituality and immortality of the soul, but we cannot employ this knowledge to explain the phenomena of this life, nor the peculiar nature of the future, because our conception of an incorporeal nature is purely negative and does not add anything to our knowledge, and the only inferences to be drawn from it are purely fictitious. If, again, we prove the existence of a supreme intelligence, we should be able from it to make the conformity to aims existing in the arrangement of the world comprehensible; but we should not be justified in deducing from it any particular arrangement or disposition, or inferring any where it is not perceived. For it is a necessary rule of the speculative use of reason that we must not overlook natural causes, or refuse to listen to the teaching of experience, for the sake of deducing what we know and perceive from something that transcends all our knowledge. In one word, these three propositions are, for the speculative reason, always transcendent, and cannot be employed as immanent principles in relation to the objects of experience; they are, consequently, of no use to us in this sphere, being but the valueless results of the severe but unprofitable efforts of reason.

If, then, the actual cognition of these three cardinal propositions is perfectly useless, while Reason uses her utmost endeavours to induce us to admit them, it is plain that their real value and importance relate to our practical, and not to our speculative interest.

I term all that is possible through free will, practical. But if the conditions of the exercise of free volition are empirical, reason can have only a regulative, and not a constitutive, influence upon it, and is serviceable merely for the introduction of unity into its empirical laws. In the moral philosophy of prudence, for example, the sole business of reason is to bring about a union of all the ends, which are aimed at by our inclinations, into one ultimate end—that of happiness—and to show the agreement which should exist among the means of attaining that end. In this sphere, accordingly, reason cannot present to us any other than pragmatical laws of free action, for our guidance towards the aims set up by the senses, and is incompetent to give us laws which are pure and determined completely à priori. On the other hand, pure practical laws, the ends of which have been given by reason entirely à priori, and which are not empirically conditioned, but are, on the contrary, absolutely imperative in their nature, would be products of pure reason. Such are the moral laws; and these alone belong to the sphere of the practical exercise of reason, and admit of a canon.

All the powers of reason, in the sphere of what may be termed pure philosophy, are, in fact, directed to the three above-mentioned problems alone. These again have a still higher end—the answer to the question, what we ought to do, if the will is free, if there is a God and a future world. Now, as this problem relates to our in reference to the highest aim of humanity, it is evident that the ultimate intention of nature, in the constitution of our reason, has been directed to the moral alone.

We must take care, however, in turning our attention to an object which is foreign[78] to the sphere of transcendental philosophy, not to injure the unity of our system by digressions, nor, on the other hand, to fail in clearness, by saying too little on the new subject of discussion. I hope to avoid both extremes, by keeping as close as possible to the transcendental, and excluding all psychological, that is, empirical, elements.

I have to remark, in the first place, that at present I treat of the conception of freedom in the practical sense only, and set aside the corresponding transcendental conception, which cannot be employed as a ground of explanation in the phenomenal world, but is itself a problem for pure reason. A will is purely animal (arbitrium brutum) when it is determined by sensuous impulses or instincts only, that is, when it is determined in a pathological manner. A will, which can

[78] All practical conceptions relate to objects of pleasure and pain, and consequently—in an indirect manner, at least—to objects of feeling. But as feeling is not a faculty of representation, but lies out of the sphere of our powers of cognition, the elements of our judgements, in so far as they relate to pleasure or pain, that is, the elements of our practical judgements, do not belong to transcendental philosophy, which has to do with pure à priori cognitions alone.

be determined independently of sensuous impulses, consequently by motives presented by reason alone, is called a free will (arbitrium liberum); and everything which is connected with this free will, either as principle or consequence, is termed practical. The existence of practical freedom can be proved from experience alone. For the human will is not determined by that alone which immediately affects the senses; on the contrary, we have the power, by calling up the notion of what is useful or hurtful in a more distant relation, of overcoming the immediate impressions on our sensuous faculty of desire. But these considerations of what is desirable in relation to our whole state, that is, is in the end good and useful, are based entirely upon reason. This faculty, accordingly, enounces laws, which are imperative or objective laws of freedom and which tell us what ought to take place, thus distinguishing themselves from the laws of nature, which relate to that which does take place. The laws of freedom or of free will are hence termed practical laws.

Whether reason is not itself, in the actual delivery of these laws, determined in its turn by other influences, and whether the action which, in relation to sensuous impulses, we call free, may not, in relation to higher and more remote operative causes, really form a part of nature—these are questions which do not here concern us. They are purely speculative questions; and all we have to do, in the practical sphere, is to inquire into the rule of conduct which reason has to present. Experience demonstrates to us the existence of practical freedom as one of the causes which exist in nature, that is, it shows the causal power of reason in the determination of the will. The idea of transcendental freedom, on the contrary, requires that reason—in relation to its causal power of commencing a series of phenomena—should be independent of all sensuous determining causes; and thus it seems to be in opposition to the law of nature and to all possible experience. It therefore remains a problem for the human mind. But this problem does not concern reason in its practical use; and we have, therefore, in a canon of pure reason, to do with only two questions, which relate to the practical interest of pure reason: Is there a God? and, Is there a future life? The question of transcendental freedom is purely speculative, and we may therefore set it entirely aside when we come to treat of practical reason. Besides, we have already discussed this subject in the antinomy of pure reason.

Section II. Of the Ideal of the Summum Bonum as a Determining Ground of the Ultimate End of Pure Reason

Reason conducted us, in its speculative use, through the field of experience and, as it can never find complete satisfaction in that sphere, from thence to speculative ideas—which, however, in the end brought us back again to experience, and thus fulfilled the purpose of reason, in a manner which, though useful, was not at all in accordance with our expectations. It now remains for us to consider whether pure reason can be employed in a practical sphere, and whether it will here conduct us to those ideas which attain the highest ends of pure reason, as we have just stated them. We shall thus ascertain whether, from the point of view of its practical interest, reason may not be able to supply us with that which, on the speculative side, it wholly denies us.

The whole interest of reason, speculative as well as practical, is centred in the three following questions:

1. WHAT CAN I KNOW?
2. WHAT OUGHT I TO DO?
3. WHAT MAY I HOPE?

The first question is purely speculative. We have, as I flatter myself, exhausted all the replies of which it is susceptible, and have at last found the reply with which reason must content itself, and with which it ought to be content, so long as it pays no regard to the practical. But from the two great ends to the attainment of which all these efforts of pure reason were in fact directed, we remain just as far removed as if we had consulted our ease and declined the task at the outset. So far, then, as knowledge is concerned, thus much, at least, is established, that, in regard to those two problems, it lies beyond our reach.

The second question is purely practical. As such it may indeed fall within the province of pure reason, but still it is not transcendental, but moral, and consequently cannot in itself form the subject of our criticism.

The third question: If I act as I ought to do, what may I then hope?—is at once practical and theoretical. The practical forms a clue to the answer of the theoretical, and—in its highest form—speculative question. For all hoping has happiness for its object and stands in precisely the same relation to the practical and the law of morality as knowing to the theoretical cognition of things and the law of nature. The former arrives finally at the conclusion that something is (which determines the ultimate end), because something ought to take place; the latter, that something is (which operates as the highest cause), because something does take place.

Happiness is the satisfaction of all our desires; extensive, in regard to their multiplicity; intensive, in regard to their degree; and protensive, in regard to their duration. The practical law based on the motive of happiness I term a pragmatical law (or prudential rule); but that law, assuming such to exist, which has no other motive than the worthiness of being happy, I term a moral or ethical law. The first tells us what we have to do, if we wish to become possessed of happiness; the second dictates how we ought to act, in order to deserve happiness. The first is based upon empirical principles; for it is only by experience that I can learn either what inclinations exist which desire satisfaction, or what are the natural means of satisfying them. The second takes no account of our desires or the means of satisfying them, and regards only the freedom of a rational being, and the necessary conditions under which alone this freedom can harmonize with the distribution of happiness according to principles. This second law may therefore rest upon mere ideas of pure reason, and may be cognized à priori.

I assume that there are pure moral laws which determine, entirely à priori (without regard to empirical motives, that is, to happiness), the conduct of a rational being, or in other words, to use which it makes of its freedom, and that these laws are absolutely imperative (not merely hypothetically, on the supposition of other empirical ends), and therefore in all respects necessary. I am warranted in assuming this, not only by the arguments of the most enlightened moralists, but by the moral judgement of every man who will make the attempt to form a distinct conception of such a law.

Pure reason, then, contains, not indeed in its speculative, but in its practical, or, more strictly, its moral use, principles of the possibility of experience, of such actions, namely, as, in accordance with ethical precepts, might be met with in the history of man. For since reason commands that such actions should take place, it must be possible for them to take place; and hence a particular kind of systematic unity—the moral—must be possible. We have found, it is true, that the systematic unity of nature could not be established according to speculative principles of reason, because, while reason possesses a causal power in relation to freedom, it has none in relation to the whole sphere of nature; and, while moral principles of reason can produce free actions, they cannot produce natural laws. It is, then, in its practical, but especially in its moral use, that the principles of pure reason possess objective reality.

I call the world a moral world, in so far as it may be in accordance with all the ethical laws—which, by virtue of the freedom of reasonable beings, it can be, and according to the necessary laws of morality it ought to be. But this world must be conceived only as an intelligible world, inasmuch as abstraction is therein made of all conditions (ends), and even of all impediments to morality (the weakness or pravity of human nature). So far, then, it is a mere idea—though still a practical idea—which may have, and ought to have, an influence on the world of sense, so as to bring it as far as possible into conformity with itself. The idea of a moral world has, therefore, objective reality, not as referring to an object of intelligible intuition—for of such an object we can form no conception whatever—but to the world of sense—conceived, however, as an object of pure reason in its practical use—and to a corpus mysticum of rational beings in it, in so far as the liberum arbitrium of the individual is placed, under and by virtue of moral laws, in complete systematic unity both with itself and with the freedom of all others.

That is the answer to the first of the two questions of pure reason which relate to its practical interest: Do that which will render thee worthy of happiness. The second question is this: If I conduct myself so as not to be unworthy of happiness, may I hope thereby to obtain happiness? In order to arrive at the solution of this question, we must inquire whether the principles of pure reason, which prescribe à priori the law, necessarily also connect this hope with it.

I say, then, that just as the moral principles are necessary according to reason in its practical use, so it is equally necessary according to reason in its theoretical use to assume that every one has ground to hope for happiness in the measure in which he has made himself worthy of it in his conduct, and that therefore the system of morality is inseparably (though only in the idea of pure reason) connected with that of happiness.

Now in an intelligible, that is, in the moral world, in the conception of which we make abstraction of all the impediments to morality (sensuous desires), such a system of happiness, connected with and proportioned to morality, may be conceived as necessary, because freedom of volition—partly incited, and partly restrained by moral laws—would be itself the cause of general happiness; and thus rational beings, under the guidance of such principles, would be themselves the authors both of their own enduring welfare and that of others. But such a system of self-rewarding morality is only an idea, the carrying out of which depends upon the condition that every one acts as he ought; in other words, that all actions of reasonable beings be such as they would be if they sprung from a Supreme Will, comprehending in, or under, itself all particular wills. But since the moral law is binding on each individual in the use of his freedom of volition, even if others should not act in conformity with this law, neither the nature of things, nor the causality of actions and their relation to morality, determine how the consequences of these actions will be related to happiness; and the necessary connection of the hope of happiness with the unceasing endeavour to become worthy of happiness, cannot be cognized by reason, if we take nature alone for our guide. This connection can be hoped for only on the assumption that the cause of nature is a supreme reason, which governs according to moral laws.

I term the idea of an intelligence in which the morally most perfect will, united with supreme blessedness, is the cause of all happiness in the world, so far as happiness stands in strict relation to morality (as the worthiness of being happy), the ideal of the supreme Good. It is only, then, in the ideal of the supreme original good, that pure reason can find the ground of the practically necessary connection of both elements of the highest derivative good, and accordingly of an intelligible, that is, moral world. Now since we are necessitated by reason to conceive ourselves as belonging to such a world, while the senses present to us nothing but a world of phenomena, we must assume the former as a consequence of our conduct in the world of sense (since the world of sense gives us no hint of it), and therefore as future in relation to us. Thus God and a future life are two hypotheses which, according to the principles of pure reason, are inseparable from the obligation which this reason imposes upon us.

Morality per se constitutes a system. But we can form no system of happiness, except in so far as it is dispensed in strict proportion to morality. But this is only possible in the intelligible world, under a wise author and ruler. Such a ruler, together with life in such a world, which we must look upon as future, reason finds itself compelled to assume; or it must regard the moral laws as idle dreams, since the necessary consequence which this same reason connects with them must, without this hypothesis, fall to the ground. Hence also the moral laws are universally regarded as commands, which they could not be did they not connect à priori adequate consequences with their dictates, and thus carry with them promises and threats. But this, again, they could not do, did they not reside in a necessary being, as the Supreme Good, which alone can render such a teleological unity possible.

Leibnitz termed the world, when viewed in relation to the rational beings which it contains, and the moral relations in which they stand to each other, under the government of the Supreme Good, the kingdom of Grace, and distinguished it from the kingdom of Nature, in which these rational beings live, under moral laws, indeed, but expect no other consequences from their actions than such as follow according to the course of nature in the world of sense. To view ourselves, therefore, as in the kingdom of grace, in which all happiness awaits us, except in so far as we ourselves limit our participation in it by actions which render us unworthy of happiness, is a practically necessary idea of reason.

Practical laws, in so far as they are subjective grounds of actions, that is, subjective principles, are termed maxims. The judgements of moral according to in its purity and ultimate results are framed according ideas; the observance of its laws, according to maxims.

The whole course of our life must be subject to moral maxims; but this is impossible, unless with the moral law, which is a mere idea, reason connects an efficient cause which ordains to all conduct which is in conformity with the moral law an issue either in this or in another life, which is in exact conformity with our highest aims. Thus, without a God and without a world, invisible to us now, but hoped for, the glorious ideas of morality are, indeed, objects of approbation and of admiration, but cannot be the springs of purpose and action. For they do not satisfy all the aims which are natural to every rational being, and which are determined à priori by pure reason itself, and necessary.

Happiness alone is, in the view of reason, far from being the complete good. Reason does not approve of it (however much inclination may desire it), except as united with desert. On the other hand, morality alone, and with it, mere desert, is likewise far from being the complete good. To make it complete, he who conducts himself in a manner not unworthy of happiness, must be able to hope for the possession of happiness. Even reason, unbiased by private ends, or interested considerations, cannot judge otherwise, if it puts itself in the place of a being whose business it is to dispense all happiness to others. For in the practical idea both points are essentially combined, though in such a way that participation in happiness is rendered possible by the moral disposition, as its condition, and not conversely, the moral disposition by the prospect of happiness. For a disposition which should require the prospect of happiness as its necessary condition would not be moral, and hence also would not be worthy of complete happiness—a happiness which, in the view of reason, recognizes no limitation but such as arises from our own immoral conduct.

Happiness, therefore, in exact proportion with the morality of rational beings (whereby they are made worthy of happiness), constitutes alone the supreme good of a world into which we absolutely must transport ourselves according to the commands of pure but practical reason. This world is, it is true, only an intelligible world; for of such a systematic unity of ends as it requires, the world of sense gives us no hint. Its reality can be based on nothing else but the hypothesis of a supreme original good. In it independent reason, equipped with all the sufficiency of a supreme cause, founds, maintains, and fulfils the universal order of things, with the most perfect teleological harmony, however much this order may be hidden from us in the world of sense.

This moral theology has the peculiar advantage, in contrast with speculative theology, of leading inevitably to the conception of a sole, perfect, and rational First Cause, whereof speculative theology does not give us any indication on objective grounds, far less any convincing evidence. For we find neither in transcendental nor in natural theology, however far reason may lead us in these, any ground to warrant us in assuming the existence of one only Being, which stands at the head of all natural causes, and on which these are entirely dependent. On the other hand, if we take our stand on moral unity as a necessary law of the universe, and from this point of view consider what is necessary to give this law adequate efficiency and, for us, obligatory force, we must come to the conclusion that there is one only supreme will, which comprehends all these laws in itself. For how, under different wills, should we find complete unity of ends? This will must be omnipotent, that all nature and its relation to morality in the world may be subject to it; omniscient, that it may have knowledge of the most secret feelings and their moral worth; omnipresent, that it may be at hand to supply every necessity to which the highest weal of the world may give rise; eternal, that this harmony of nature and liberty may never fail; and so on.

But this systematic unity of ends in this world of intelligences—which, as mere nature, is only a world of sense, but, as a system of freedom of volition, may be termed an intelligible, that is, moral world (regnum gratiae)—leads inevitably also to the teleological unity of all things which constitute this great whole, according to universal natural laws—just as the unity of the former is according to universal and necessary moral laws—and unites the practical with the speculative reason. The world must be represented as having originated from an idea, if it is to harmonize with that use of reason without which we cannot even consider ourselves as worthy of reason—namely, the moral use, which rests entirely on the idea of the supreme good. Hence the investigation of nature receives a teleological direction, and becomes, in its widest extension, physico-theology. But this, taking its rise in moral order as a unity founded on the essence of freedom, and not accidentally instituted by external commands, establishes the teleological view of nature on grounds which must be inseparably connected with the internal possibility of things. This gives rise to a transcendental theology, which takes the ideal of the highest ontological perfection as a principle of systematic unity; and this principle connects all things according to universal and necessary natural laws, because all things have their origin in the absolute necessity of the one only Primal Being.

What use can we make of our understanding, even in respect of experience, if we do not propose ends to ourselves? But the highest ends are those of morality, and it is only pure reason that can give us the knowledge of these. Though supplied with these, and putting ourselves under their guidance, we can make no teleological use of the knowledge of nature, as regards cognition, unless nature itself has established teleological unity. For without this unity we should not even possess reason, because we should have no school for reason, and no cultivation through objects which afford the materials for its conceptions. But teleological unity is a necessary unity, and founded on the essence of the individual will itself. Hence this will, which is the condition of the application of this unity in concreto, must be so likewise. In this way the transcendental enlargement of our rational cognition would be, not the cause, but merely the effect of the practical teleology which pure reason imposes upon us.

Hence, also, we find in the history of human reason that, before the moral conceptions were sufficiently purified and determined, and before men had attained to a perception of the systematic unity of ends according to these conceptions and from necessary principles, the knowledge of nature, and even a considerable amount of intellectual culture in many other sciences, could produce only rude and vague conceptions of the Deity, sometimes even admitting of an astonishing indifference with regard to this question altogether. But the more enlarged treatment of moral ideas, which was rendered necessary by the extreme pure moral law of our religion, awakened the interest, and thereby quickened the perceptions of reason in relation to this object. In this way, and without the help either of an extended acquaintance with nature, or of a reliable transcendental insight (for these have been wanting in all ages), a conception of the Divine Being was arrived at, which we now hold to be the correct one, not because speculative reason convinces us of its correctness, but because it accords with the moral principles of reason. Thus it is to pure reason, but only in its practical use, that we must ascribe the merit of having connected with our highest interest a cognition, of which mere speculation was able only to form a conjecture, but the validity of which it was unable to establish—and of having thereby rendered it, not indeed a demonstrated dogma, but a hypothesis absolutely necessary to the essential ends of reason.

But if practical reason has reached this elevation, and has attained to the conception of a sole Primal Being as the supreme good, it must not, therefore, imagine that it has transcended the empirical conditions of its application, and risen to the immediate cognition of new objects; it must not presume to start from the conception which it has gained, and to deduce from it the moral laws themselves. For it was these very laws, the internal practical necessity of which led us to the hypothesis of an independent cause, or of a wise ruler of the universe, who should give them effect. Hence we are not entitled to regard them as accidental and derived from the mere will of the ruler, especially as we have no conception of such a will, except as formed in accordance with these laws. So far, then, as practical reason has the right to conduct us, we shall not look upon actions as binding on us, because they are the commands of God, but we shall regard them as divine commands, because we are internally bound by them. We shall study freedom under the teleological unity which accords with principles of reason; we shall look upon ourselves as acting in conformity with the divine will only in so far as we hold sacred the moral law which reason teaches us from the nature of actions themselves, and we shall believe that we can obey that will only by promoting the weal of the universe in ourselves and in others. Moral theology is, therefore, only of immanent use. It teaches us to fulfil our destiny here in the world, by placing ourselves in harmony with the general system of ends, and warns us against the fanaticism, nay, the crime of depriving reason of its legislative authority in the moral conduct of life, for the purpose of directly connecting this authority with the idea of the Supreme Being. For this would be, not an immanent, but a transcendent use of moral theology, and, like the transcendent use of mere speculation, would inevitably pervert and frustrate the ultimate ends of reason.

Section III. Of Opinion, Knowledge, and Belief

The holding of a thing to be true is a phenomenon in our understanding which may rest on objective grounds, but requires, also, subjective causes in the mind of the person judging. If a judgement is valid for every rational being, then its ground is objectively sufficient, and it is termed a conviction. If, on the other hand, it has its ground in the particular character of the subject, it is termed a persuasion.

Persuasion is a mere illusion, the ground of the judgement, which lies solely in the subject, being regarded as objective. Hence a judgement of this kind has only private validity—is only valid for the individual who judges, and the holding of a thing to be true in this way cannot be communicated. But truth depends upon agreement with the object, and consequently the judgements of all understandings, if true, must be in agreement with each other (consentientia uni tertio consentiunt inter se). Conviction may, therefore, be distinguished, from an external point of view, from persuasion, by the possibility of communicating it and by showing its validity for the reason of every man; for in this case the presumption, at least, arises that the agreement of all judgements with each other, in spite of the different characters of individuals, rests upon the common ground of the agreement of each with the object, and thus the correctness of the judgement is established.

Persuasion, accordingly, cannot be subjectively distinguished from conviction, that is, so long as the subject views its judgement simply as a phenomenon of its own mind. But if we inquire whether the grounds of our judgement, which are valid for us, produce the same effect on the reason of others as on our own, we have then the means, though only subjective means, not, indeed, of producing conviction, but of detecting the merely private validity of the judgement; in other words, of discovering that there is in it the element of mere persuasion.

If we can, in addition to this, develop the subjective causes of the judgement, which we have taken for its objective grounds, and thus explain the deceptive judgement as a phenomenon in our mind, apart altogether from the objective character of the object, we can then expose the illusion and need be no longer deceived by it, although, if its subjective cause lies in our nature, we cannot hope altogether to escape its influence.

I can only maintain, that is, affirm as necessarily valid for every one, that which produces conviction. Persuasion I may keep for myself, if it is agreeable to me; but I cannot, and ought not, to attempt to impose it as binding upon others.

Holding for true, or the subjective validity of a judgement in relation to conviction (which is, at the same time, objectively valid), has the three following degrees: opinion, belief, and knowledge. Opinion is a consciously insufficient judgement, subjectively as well as objectively. Belief is subjectively sufficient, but is recognized as being objectively insufficient. Knowledge is both subjectively and objectively sufficient. Subjective sufficiency is termed conviction (for myself); objective sufficiency is termed certainty (for all). I need not dwell longer on the explanation of such simple conceptions.

I must never venture to be of opinion, without knowing something, at least, by which my judgement, in itself merely problematical, is brought into connection with the truth—which connection, although not perfect, is still something more than an arbitrary fiction. Moreover, the law of such a connection must be certain. For if, in relation to this law, I have nothing more than opinion, my judgement is but a play of the imagination, without the least relation to truth. In the judgements of pure reason, opinion has no place. For, as they do not rest on empirical grounds and as the sphere of pure reason is that of necessary truth and à priori cognition, the principle of connection in it requires universality and necessity, and consequently perfect certainty—otherwise we should have no guide to the truth at all. Hence it is absurd to have an opinion in pure mathematics; we must know, or abstain from forming a judgement altogether. The case is the same with the maxims of morality. For we must not hazard an action on the mere opinion that it is allowed, but we must know it to be so. In the transcendental sphere of reason, on the other hand, the term opinion is too weak, while the word knowledge is too strong. From the merely speculative point of view, therefore, we cannot form a judgement at all. For the subjective grounds of a judgement, such as produce belief, cannot be admitted in speculative inquiries, inasmuch as they cannot stand without empirical support and are incapable of being communicated to others in equal measure.

But it is only from the practical point of view that a theoretically insufficient judgement can be termed belief. Now the practical reference is either to skill or to morality; to the former, when the end proposed is arbitrary and accidental, to the latter, when it is absolutely necessary.

If we propose to ourselves any end whatever, the conditions of its attainment are hypothetically necessary. The necessity is subjectively, but still only comparatively, sufficient, if I am acquainted with no other conditions under which the end can be attained. On the other hand, it is sufficient, absolutely and for every one, if I know for certain that no one can be acquainted with any other conditions under which the attainment of the proposed end would be possible. In the former case my supposition—my judgement with regard to certain conditions—is a merely accidental belief; in the latter it is a necessary belief. The physician must pursue some course in the case of a patient who is in danger, but is ignorant of the nature of the disease. He observes the symptoms, and concludes, according to the best of his judgement, that it is a case of phthisis. His belief is, even in his own judgement, only contingent: another man might, perhaps come nearer the truth. Such a belief, contingent indeed, but still forming the ground of the actual use of means for the attainment of certain ends, I term Pragmatical belief.

The usual test, whether that which any one maintains is merely his persuasion, or his subjective conviction at least, that is, his firm belief, is a bet. It frequently happens that a man delivers his opinions with so much boldness and assurance, that he appears to be under no apprehension as to the possibility of his being in error. The offer of a bet startles him, and makes him pause. Sometimes it turns out that his persuasion may be valued at a ducat, but not at ten. For he does not hesitate, perhaps, to venture a ducat, but if it is proposed to stake ten, he immediately becomes aware of the possibility of his being mistaken—a possibility which has hitherto escaped his observation. If we imagine to ourselves that we have to stake the happiness of our whole life on the truth of any proposition, our judgement drops its air of triumph, we take the alarm, and discover the actual strength of our belief. Thus pragmatical belief has degrees, varying in proportion to the interests at stake.

Now, in cases where we cannot enter upon any course of action in reference to some object, and where, accordingly, our judgement is purely theoretical, we can still represent to ourselves, in thought, the possibility of a course of action, for which we suppose that we have sufficient grounds, if any means existed of ascertaining the truth of the matter. Thus we find in purely theoretical judgements an analogon of practical judgements, to which the word belief may properly be applied, and which we may term doctrinal belief. I should not hesitate to stake my all on the truth of the proposition—if there were any possibility of bringing it to the test of experience—that, at least, some one of the planets, which we see, is inhabited. Hence I say that I have not merely the opinion, but the strong belief, on the correctness of which I would stake even many of the advantages of life, that there are inhabitants in other worlds.

Now we must admit that the doctrine of the existence of God belongs to doctrinal belief. For, although in respect to the theoretical cognition of the universe I do not require to form any theory which necessarily involves this idea, as the condition of my explanation of the phenomena which the universe presents, but, on the contrary, am rather bound so to use my reason as if everything were mere nature, still teleological unity is so important a condition of the application of my reason to nature, that it is impossible for me to ignore it—especially since, in addition to these considerations, abundant examples of it are supplied by experience. But the sole condition, so far as my knowledge extends, under which this unity can be my guide in the investigation of nature, is the assumption that a supreme intelligence has ordered all things according to the wisest ends. Consequently, the hypothesis of a wise author of the universe is necessary for my guidance in the investigation of nature—is the condition under which alone I can fulfil an end which is contingent indeed, but by no means unimportant. Moreover, since the result of my attempts so frequently confirms the utility of this assumption, and since nothing decisive can be adduced against it, it follows that it would be saying far too little to term my judgement, in this case, a mere opinion, and that, even in this theoretical connection, I may assert that I firmly believe in God. Still, if we use words strictly, this must not be called a practical, but a doctrinal belief, which the theology of nature (physico-theology) must also produce in my mind. In the wisdom of a Supreme Being, and in the shortness of life, so inadequate to the development of the glorious powers of human nature, we may find equally sufficient grounds for a doctrinal belief in the future life of the human soul.

The expression of belief is, in such cases, an expression of modesty from the objective point of view, but, at the same time, of firm confidence, from the subjective. If I should venture to term this merely theoretical judgement even so much as a hypothesis which I am entitled to assume; a more complete conception, with regard to another world and to the cause of the world, might then be justly required of me than I am, in reality, able to give. For, if I assume anything, even as a mere hypothesis, I must, at least, know so much of the properties of such a being as will enable me, not to form the conception, but to imagine the existence of it. But the word belief refers only to the guidance which an idea gives me, and to its subjective influence on the conduct of my reason, which forces me to hold it fast, though I may not be in a position to give a speculative account of it.

But mere doctrinal belief is, to some extent, wanting in stability. We often quit our hold of it, in consequence of the difficulties which occur in speculation, though in the end we inevitably return to it again.

It is quite otherwise with moral belief. For in this sphere action is absolutely necessary, that is, I must act in obedience to the moral law in all points. The end is here incontrovertibly established, and there is only one condition possible, according to the best of my perception, under which this end can harmonize with all other ends, and so have practical validity—namely, the existence of a God and of a future world. I know also, to a certainty, that no one can be acquainted with any other conditions which conduct to the same unity of ends under the moral law.

But since the moral precept is, at the same time, my maxim (as reason requires that it should be), I am irresistibly constrained to believe in the existence of God and in a future life; and I am sure that nothing can make me waver in this belief, since I should thereby overthrow my moral maxims, the renunciation of which would render me hateful in my own eyes.

Thus, while all the ambitious attempts of reason to penetrate beyond the limits of experience end in disappointment, there is still enough left to satisfy us in a practical point of view. No one, it is true, will be able to boast that he knows that there is a God and a future life; for, if he knows this, he is just the man whom I have long wished to find. All knowledge, regarding an object of mere reason, can be communicated; and I should thus be enabled to hope that my own knowledge would receive this wonderful extension, through the instrumentality of his instruction. No, my conviction is not logical, but moral certainty; and since it rests on subjective grounds (of the moral sentiment), I must not even say: It is morally certain that there is a God, etc., but: I am morally certain, that is, my belief in God and in another world is so interwoven with my moral nature that I am under as little apprehension of having the former torn from me as of losing the latter.

The only point in this argument that may appear open to suspicion is that this rational belief presupposes the existence of moral sentiments. If we give up this assumption, and take a man who is entirely indifferent with regard to moral laws, the question which reason proposes, becomes then merely a problem for speculation and may, indeed, be supported by strong grounds from analogy, but not by such as will compel the most obstinate scepticism to give way.[79] But in these questions no man is free from all interest. For though the want of good sentiments may place him beyond the influence of moral interests, still even in this case enough may be left to make him fear the existence of God and a future life. For he cannot pretend to any certainty of the non-existence of God and of a future life, unless—since it could only be proved by mere reason, and therefore apodeictically—he is prepared to establish the impossibility of both, which certainly no reasonable man would undertake to do. This would be a negative belief, which could not, indeed, produce morality and good sentiments, but still could produce an analogon of these, by operating as a powerful restraint on the outbreak of evil dispositions.

But, it will be said, is this all that pure reason can effect, in opening up prospects beyond the limits of experience? Nothing more than two articles of belief? Common sense could have done as much as this, without taking the philosophers to counsel in the matter!

[79] The human mind (as, I believe, every rational being must of necessity do) takes a natural interest in morality, although this interest is not undivided, and may not be practically in preponderance. If you strengthen and increase it, you will find the reason become docile, more enlightened, and more capable of uniting the speculative interest with the practical. But if you do not take care at the outset, or at least midway, to make men good, you will never force them into an honest belief.

I shall not here eulogize philosophy for the benefits which the laborious efforts of its criticism have conferred on human reason—even granting that its merit should turn out in the end to be only negative—for on this point something more will be said in the next section. But, I ask, do you require that that knowledge which concerns all men, should transcend the common understanding, and should only be revealed to you by philosophers? The very circumstance which has called forth your censure, is the best confirmation of the correctness of our previous assertions, since it discloses, what could not have been foreseen, that Nature is not chargeable with any partial distribution of her gifts in those matters which concern all men without distinction and that, in respect to the essential ends of human nature, we cannot advance further with the help of the highest philosophy, than under the guidance which nature has vouchsafed to the meanest understanding.

Chapter III

The Architectonic of Pure Reason

By the term architectonic I mean the art of constructing a system. Without systematic unity, our knowledge cannot become science; it will be an aggregate, and not a system. Thus architectonic is the doctrine of the scientific in cognition, and therefore necessarily forms part of our methodology.

Reason cannot permit our knowledge to remain in an unconnected and rhapsodistic state, but requires that the sum of our cognitions should constitute a system. It is thus alone that they can advance the ends of reason. By a system I mean the unity of various cognitions under one idea. This idea is the conception—given by reason—of the form of a whole, in so far as the conception determines à priori not only the limits of its content, but the place which each of its parts is to occupy. The scientific idea contains, therefore, the end and the form of the whole which is in accordance with that end. The unity of the end, to which all the parts of the system relate, and through which all have a relation to each other, communicates unity to the whole system, so that the absence of any part can be immediately detected from our knowledge of the rest; and it determines à priori the limits of the system, thus excluding all contingent or arbitrary additions. The whole is thus an organism (articulatio), and not an aggregate (coacervatio); it may grow from within (per intussusceptionem), but it cannot increase by external additions (per appositionem). It is, thus, like an animal body, the growth of which does not add any limb, but, without changing their proportions, makes each in its sphere stronger and more active.

We require, for the execution of the idea of a system, a schema, that is, a content and an arrangement of parts determined à priori by the principle which the aim of the system prescribes. A schema which is not projected in accordance with an idea, that is, from the standpoint of the highest aim of reason, but merely empirically, in accordance with accidental aims and purposes (the number of which cannot be predetermined), can give us nothing more than technical unity. But the schema which is originated from an idea (in which case reason presents us with aims à priori, and does not look for them to experience), forms the basis of architectonical unity. A science, in the proper acceptation of that term, cannot be formed technically, that is, from observation of the similarity existing between different objects, and the purely contingent use we make of our knowledge in concreto with reference to all kinds of arbitrary external aims; its constitution must be framed on architectonical principles, that is, its parts must be shown to possess an essential affinity, and be capable of being deduced from one supreme and internal aim or end, which forms the condition of the possibility of the scientific whole. The schema of a science must give à priori the plan of it (monogramma), and the division of the whole into parts, in conformity with the idea of the science; and it must also distinguish this whole from all others, according to certain understood principles.

No one will attempt to construct a science, unless he have some idea to rest on as a proper basis. But, in the elaboration of the science, he finds that the schema, nay, even the definition which he at first gave of the science, rarely corresponds with his idea; for this idea lies, like a germ, in our reason, its parts undeveloped and hid even from microscopical observation. For this reason, we ought to explain and define sciences, not according to the description which the originator gives of them, but according to the idea which we find based in reason itself, and which is suggested by the natural unity of the parts of the science already accumulated. For it will of ten be found that the originator of a science and even his latest successors remain attached to an erroneous idea, which they cannot render clear to themselves, and that they thus fail in determining the true content, the articulation or systematic unity, and the limits of their science.

It is unfortunate that, only after having occupied ourselves for a long time in the collection of materials, under the guidance of an idea which lies undeveloped in the mind, but not according to any definite plan of arrangement—nay, only after we have spent much time and labour in the technical disposition of our materials, does it become possible to view the idea of a science in a clear light, and to project, according to architectonical principles, a plan of the whole, in accordance with the aims of reason. Systems seem, like certain worms, to be formed by a kind of generatio aequivoca—by the mere confluence of conceptions, and to gain completeness only with the progress of time. But the schema or germ of all lies in reason; and thus is not only every system organized according to its own idea, but all are united into one grand system of human knowledge, of which they form members. For this reason, it is possible to frame an architectonic of all human cognition, the formation of which, at the present time, considering the immense materials collected or to be found in the ruins of old systems, would not indeed be very difficult. Our purpose at present is merely to sketch the plan of the architectonic of all cognition given by pure reason; and we begin from the point where the main root of human knowledge divides into two, one of which is reason. By reason I understand here the whole higher faculty of cognition, the rational being placed in contradistinction to the empirical.

If I make complete abstraction of the content of cognition, objectively considered, all cognition is, from a subjective point of view, either historical or rational. Historical cognition is cognitio ex datis, rational, cognitio ex principiis. Whatever may be the original source of a cognition, it is, in relation to the person who possesses it, merely historical, if he knows only what has been given him from another quarter, whether that knowledge was communicated by direct experience or by instruction. Thus the Person who has learned a system of philosophy—say the Wolfian—although he has a perfect knowledge of all the principles, definitions, and arguments in that philosophy, as well as of the divisions that have been made of the system, possesses really no more than an historical knowledge of the Wolfian system; he knows only what has been told him, his judgements are only those which he has received from his teachers. Dispute the validity of a definition, and he is completely at a loss to find another. He has formed his mind on another's; but the imitative faculty is not the productive. His knowledge has not been drawn from reason; and although, objectively considered, it is rational knowledge, subjectively, it is merely historical. He has learned this or that philosophy and is merely a plaster cast of a living man. Rational cognitions which are objective, that is, which have their source in reason, can be so termed from a subjective point of view, only when they have been drawn by the individual himself from the sources of reason, that is, from principles; and it is in this way alone that criticism, or even the rejection of what has been already learned, can spring up in the mind.

All rational cognition is, again, based either on conceptions, or on the construction of conceptions. The former is termed philosophical, the latter mathematical. I have already shown the essential difference of these two methods of cognition in the first chapter. A cognition may be objectively philosophical and subjectively historical—as is the case with the majority of scholars and those who cannot look beyond the limits of their system, and who remain in a state of pupilage all their lives. But it is remarkable that mathematical knowledge, when committed to memory, is valid, from the subjective point of view, as rational knowledge also, and that the same distinction cannot be drawn here as in the case of philosophical cognition. The reason is that the only way of arriving at this knowledge is through the essential principles of reason, and thus it is always certain and indisputable; because reason is employed in concreto—but at the same time à priori—that is, in pure and, therefore, infallible intuition; and thus all causes of illusion and error are excluded. Of all the à priori sciences of reason, therefore, mathematics alone can be learned. Philosophy—unless it be in an historical manner—cannot be learned; we can at most learn to philosophize.

Philosophy is the system of all philosophical cognition. We must use this term in an objective sense, if we understand by it the archetype of all attempts at philosophizing, and the standard by which all subjective philosophies are to be judged. In this sense, philosophy is merely the idea of a possible science, which does not exist in concreto, but to which we endeavour in various ways to approximate, until we have discovered the right path to pursue—a path overgrown by the errors and illusions of sense—and the image we have hitherto tried in vain to shape has become a perfect copy of the great prototype. Until that time, we cannot learn philosophy—it does not exist; if it does, where is it, who possesses it, and how shall we know it? We can only learn to philosophize; in other words, we can only exercise our powers of reasoning in accordance with general principles, retaining at the same time, the right of investigating the sources of these principles, of testing, and even of rejecting them.

Until then, our conception of philosophy is only a scholastic conception—a conception, that is, of a system of cognition which we are trying to elaborate into a science; all that we at present know being the systematic unity of this cognition, and consequently the logical completeness of the cognition for the desired end. But there is also a cosmical conception (conceptus cosmicus) of philosophy, which has always formed the true basis of this term, especially when philosophy was personified and presented to us in the ideal of a philosopher. In this view philosophy is the science of the relation of all cognition to the ultimate and essential aims of human reason (teleologia rationis humanae), and the philosopher is not merely an artist—who occupies himself with conceptions—but a lawgiver, legislating for human reason. In this sense of the word, it would be in the highest degree arrogant to assume the title of philosopher, and to pretend that we had reached the perfection of the prototype which lies in the idea alone.

The mathematician, the natural philosopher, and the logician—how far soever the first may have advanced in rational, and the two latter in philosophical knowledge—are merely artists, engaged in the arrangement and formation of conceptions; they cannot be termed philosophers. Above them all, there is the ideal teacher, who employs them as instruments for the advancement of the essential aims of human reason. Him alone can we call philosopher; but he nowhere exists. But the idea of his legislative power resides in the mind of every man, and it alone teaches us what kind of systematic unity philosophy demands in view of the ultimate aims of reason. This idea is, therefore, a cosmical conception.[80]

In view of the complete systematic unity of reason, there can only be one ultimate end of all the operations of the mind. To this all other aims are subordinate, and nothing more than means for its attainment. This ultimate end is the destination of man, and the philosophy which relates to it is termed moral philosophy. The superior position occupied by moral philosophy, above all other spheres for the operations of reason, sufficiently indicates the reason why the ancients always included the idea—and in an especial manner—of moralist in that of philosopher. Even at the present day, we call a man who appears to have the power of self-government, even although his knowledge may be very limited, by the name of philosopher.

The legislation of human reason, or philosophy, has two objects—nature and freedom—and thus contains not only the laws of nature, but also those of ethics, at first in two separate systems, which, finally, merge into one grand philosophical system of cognition. The philosophy of nature relates to that which is, that of ethics to that which ought to be.

But all philosophy is either cognition on the basis of pure reason, or the cognition of reason on the basis of empirical principles. The former is termed pure, the latter empirical philosophy.

---

[80] By a cosmical conception, I mean one in which all men necessarily take an interest; the aim of a science must accordingly be determined according to scholastic conceptions, if it is regarded merely as a means to certain arbitrarily proposed ends.

The philosophy of pure reason is either propædeutic, that is, an inquiry into the powers of reason in regard to pure à priori cognition, and is termed critical philosophy; or it is, secondly, the system of pure reason—a science containing the systematic presentation of the whole body of philosophical knowledge, true as well as illusory, given by pure reason—and is called metaphysic. This name may, however, be also given to the whole system of pure philosophy, critical philosophy included, and may designate the investigation into the sources or possibility of à priori cognition, as well as the presentation of the à priori cognitions which form a system of pure philosophy—excluding, at the same time, all empirical and mathematical elements.

Metaphysic is divided into that of the speculative and that of the practical use of pure reason, and is, accordingly, either the metaphysic of nature, or the metaphysic of ethics. The former contains all the pure rational principles—based upon conceptions alone (and thus excluding mathematics)—of all theoretical cognition; the latter, the principles which determine and necessitate à priori all action. Now moral philosophy alone contains a code of laws—for the regulation of our actions—which are deduced from principles entirely à priori. Hence the metaphysic of ethics is the only pure moral philosophy, as it is not based upon anthropological or other empirical considerations. The metaphysic of speculative reason is what is commonly called metaphysic in the more limited sense. But as pure moral philosophy properly forms a part of this system of cognition, we must allow it to retain the name of metaphysic, although it is not requisite that we should insist on so terming it in our present discussion.

It is of the highest importance to separate those cognitions which differ from others both in kind and in origin, and to take great care that they are not confounded with those with which they are generally found connected. What the chemist does in the analysis of substances, what the mathematician in pure mathematics, is, in a still higher degree, the duty of the philosopher, that the value of each different kind of cognition, and the part it takes in the operations of the mind, may be clearly defined. Human reason has never wanted a metaphysic of some kind, since it attained the power of thought, or rather of reflection; but it has never been able to keep this sphere of thought and cognition pure from all admixture of foreign elements. The idea of a science of this kind is as old as speculation itself; and what mind does not speculate—either in the scholastic or in the popular fashion? At the same time, it must be admitted that even thinkers by profession have been unable clearly to explain the distinction between the two elements of our cognition—the one completely à priori, the other à posteriori; and hence the proper definition of a peculiar kind of cognition, and with it the just idea of a science which has so long and so deeply engaged the attention of the human mind, has never been established. When it was said: "Metaphysic is the science of the first principles of human cognition," this definition did not signalize a peculiarity in kind, but only a difference in degree; these first principles were thus declared to be more general than others, but no criterion of distinction from empirical principles was given. Of these some are more general, and therefore higher, than others; and—as we cannot distinguish what is completely à priori from that which is known to be à posteriori—where shall we draw the line which is to separate the higher and so-called first principles, from the lower and subordinate principles of cognition? What would be said if we were asked to be satisfied with a division of the epochs of the world into the earlier centuries and those following them? "Does the fifth, or the tenth century belong to the earlier centuries?" it would be asked. In the same way I ask: Does the conception of extension belong to metaphysics? You answer, "Yes." Well, that of body too? "Yes." And that of a fluid body? You stop, you are unprepared to admit this; for if you do, everything will belong to metaphysics. From this it is evident that the mere degree of subordination—of the particular to the general—cannot determine the limits of a science; and that, in the present case, we must expect to find a difference in the conceptions of metaphysics both in kind and in origin. The fundamental idea of metaphysics was obscured on another side by the fact that this kind of à priori cognition showed a certain similarity in character with the science of mathematics. Both have the property in common of possessing an à priori origin; but, in the one, our knowledge is based upon conceptions, in the other, on the construction of conceptions. Thus a decided dissimilarity between philosophical and mathematical cognition comes out—a dissimilarity which was always felt, but which could not be made distinct for want of an insight into the criteria of the difference. And thus it happened that, as philosophers themselves failed in the proper development of the idea of their science, the elaboration of the science could not proceed with a definite aim, or under trustworthy guidance. Thus, too, philosophers, ignorant of the path they ought to pursue and always disputing with each other regarding the discoveries which each asserted he had made, brought their science into disrepute with the rest of the world, and finally, even among themselves.

All pure à priori cognition forms, therefore, in view of the peculiar faculty which originates it, a peculiar and distinct unity; and metaphysic is the term applied to the philosophy which attempts to represent that cognition in this systematic unity. The speculative part of metaphysic, which has especially appropriated this appellation—that which we have called the metaphysic of nature—and which considers everything, as it is (not as it ought to be), by means of à priori conceptions, is divided in the following manner.

Metaphysic, in the more limited acceptation of the term, consists of two parts—transcendental philosophy and the physiology of pure reason. The former presents the system of all the conceptions and principles belonging to the understanding and the reason, and which relate to objects in general, but not to any particular given objects (Ontologia); the latter has nature for its subject-matter, that is, the sum of given objects—whether given to the senses, or, if we will, to some other kind of intuition—and is accordingly physiology, although only rationalis. But the use of the faculty of reason in this rational mode of regarding nature is either physical or hyperphysical, or, more properly speaking, immanent or transcendent. The former relates to nature, in so far as our knowledge regarding it may be applied in experience (in concreto); the latter to that connection of the objects of experience, which transcends all experience. Transcendent physiology has, again, an internal and an external connection with its object, both, however, transcending possible experience; the former is the physiology of nature as a whole, or transcendental cognition of the world, the latter of the connection of the whole of nature with a being above nature, or transcendental cognition of God.

Immanent physiology, on the contrary, considers nature as the sum of all sensuous objects, consequently, as it is presented to us—but still according to à priori conditions, for it is under these alone that nature can be presented to our minds at all. The objects of immanent physiology are of two kinds: 1. Those of the external senses, or corporeal nature; 2. The object of the internal sense, the soul, or, in accordance with our fundamental conceptions of it, thinking nature. The metaphysics of corporeal nature is called physics; but, as it must contain only the principles of an à priori cognition of nature, we must term it rational physics. The metaphysics of thinking nature is called psychology, and for the same reason is to be regarded as merely the rational cognition of the soul.

Thus the whole system of metaphysics consists of four principal parts: 1. Ontology; 2. Rational Physiology; 3. Rational cosmology; and 4. Rational theology. The second part—that of the rational doctrine of nature—may be subdivided into two, physica rationalis[81] and psychologia rationalis.

The fundamental idea of a philosophy of pure reason of necessity dictates this division; it is, therefore, architectonical—in accordance with the highest aims of reason, and not merely technical, or according to certain accidentally-observed similarities existing between the different parts of the whole science. For this reason, also, is the division immutable and of legislative authority. But the reader may observe in it a few points to which he ought to demur, and which may weaken his conviction of its truth and legitimacy.

In the first place, how can I desire an à priori cognition or metaphysic of objects, in so far as they are given à posteriori? and how is it possible to cognize the nature of things according to à priori principles, and to attain to a rational physiology? The answer is this. We take from experience nothing more than is requisite to present

[81] It must not be supposed that I mean by this appellation what is generally called physica general is, and which is rather mathematics than a philosophy of nature. For the metaphysic of nature is completely different from mathematics, nor is it so rich in results, although it is of great importance as a critical test of the application of pure understanding—cognition to nature. For want of its guidance, even mathematicians, adopting certain common notions—which are, in fact, metaphysical—have unconsciously crowded their theories of nature with hypotheses, the fallacy of which becomes evident upon the application of the principles of this metaphysic, without detriment, however, to the employment of mathematics in this sphere of cognition.

us with an object (in general) of the external or of the internal sense; in the former case, by the mere conception of matter (impenetrable and inanimate extension), in the latter, by the conception of a thinking being—given in the internal empirical representation, I think. As to the rest, we must not employ in our metaphysic of these objects any empirical principles (which add to the content of our conceptions by means of experience), for the purpose of forming by their help any judgements respecting these objects.

Secondly, what place shall we assign to empirical psychology, which has always been considered a part of metaphysics, and from which in our time such important philosophical results have been expected, after the hope of constructing an à priori system of knowledge had been abandoned? I answer: It must be placed by the side of empirical physics or physics proper; that is, must be regarded as forming a part of applied philosophy, the à priori principles of which are contained in pure philosophy, which is therefore connected, although it must not be confounded, with psychology. Empirical psychology must therefore be banished from the sphere of metaphysics, and is indeed excluded by the very idea of that science. In conformity, however, with scholastic usage, we must permit it to occupy a place in metaphysics—but only as an appendix to it. We adopt this course from motives of economy; as psychology is not as yet full enough to occupy our attention as an independent study, while it is, at the same time, of too great importance to be entirely excluded or placed where it has still less affinity than it has with the subject of metaphysics. It is a stranger who has been long a guest; and we make it welcome to stay, until it can take up a more suitable abode in a complete system of anthropology—the pendant to empirical physics.

The above is the general idea of metaphysics, which, as more was expected from it than could be looked for with justice, and as these pleasant expectations were unfortunately never realized, fell into general disrepute. Our Critique must have fully convinced the reader that, although metaphysics cannot form the foundation of religion, it must always be one of its most important bulwarks, and that human reason, which naturally pursues a dialectical course, cannot do without this science, which checks its tendencies towards dialectic and, by elevating reason to a scientific and clear self-knowledge, prevents the ravages which a lawless speculative reason would infallibly commit in the sphere of morals as well as in that of religion. We may be sure, therefore, whatever contempt may be thrown upon metaphysics by those who judge a science not by its own nature, but according to the accidental effects it may have produced, that it can never be completely abandoned, that we must always return to it as to a beloved one who has been for a time estranged, because the questions with which it is engaged relate to the highest aims of humanity, and reason must always labour either to attain to settled views in regard to these, or to destroy those which others have already established.

Metaphysic, therefore—that of nature, as well as that of ethics, but in an especial manner the criticism which forms the propædeutic to all the operations of reason—forms properly that department of knowledge which may be termed, in the truest sense of the word, philosophy. The path which it pursues is that of science, which, when it has once been discovered, is never lost, and never misleads. Mathematics, natural science, the common experience of men, have a high value as means, for the most part, to accidental ends—but at last also, to those which are necessary and essential to the existence of humanity. But to guide them to this high goal, they require the aid of rational cognition on the basis of pure conceptions, which, be it termed as it may, is properly nothing but metaphysics.

For the same reason, metaphysics forms likewise the completion of the culture of human reason. In this respect, it is indispensable, setting aside altogether the influence which it exerts as a science. For its subject-matter is the elements and highest maxims of reason, which form the basis of the possibility of some sciences and of the use of all. That, as a purely speculative science, it is more useful in preventing error than in the extension of knowledge, does not detract from its value; on the contrary, the supreme office of censor which it occupies assures to it the highest authority and importance. This office it administers for the purpose of securing order, harmony, and well-being to science, and of directing its noble and fruitful labours to the highest possible aim—the happiness of all mankind.

Chapter IV

The History of Pure Reason

This title is placed here merely for the purpose of designating a division of the system of pure reason of which I do not intend to treat at present. I shall content myself with casting a cursory glance, from a purely transcendental point of view—that of the nature of pure reason—on the labours of philosophers up to the present time. They have aimed at erecting an edifice of philosophy; but to my eye this edifice appears to be in a very ruinous condition.

It is very remarkable, although naturally it could not have been otherwise, that, in the infancy of philosophy, the study of the nature of God and the constitution of a future world formed the commencement, rather than the conclusion, as we should have it, of the speculative efforts of the human mind. However rude the religious conceptions generated by the remains of the old manners and customs of a less cultivated time, the intelligent classes were not thereby prevented from devoting themselves to free inquiry into the existence and nature of God; and they easily saw that there could be no surer way of pleasing the invisible ruler of the world, and of attaining to happiness in another world at least, than a good and honest course of life in this. Thus theology and morals formed the two chief motives, or rather the points of attraction in all abstract inquiries. But it was the former that especially occupied the attention of speculative reason, and which afterwards became so celebrated under the name of metaphysics.

I shall not at present indicate the periods of time at which the greatest changes in metaphysics took place, but shall merely give a hasty sketch of the different ideas which occasioned the most important revolutions in this sphere of thought. There are three different ends in relation to which these revolutions have taken place.

1. In relation to the object of the cognition of reason, philosophers may be divided into sensualists and intellectualists. Epicurus may be regarded as the head of the former, Plato of the latter. The distinction here signalized, subtle as it is, dates from the earliest times, and was long maintained. The former asserted that reality resides in sensuous objects alone, and that everything else is merely imaginary; the latter, that the senses are the parents of illusion and that truth is to be found in the understanding alone. The former did not deny to the conceptions of the understanding a certain kind of reality; but with them it was merely logical, with the others it was mystical. The former admitted intellectual conceptions, but declared that sensuous objects alone possessed real existence. The latter maintained that all real objects were intelligible, and believed that the pure understanding possessed a faculty of

intuition apart from sense, which, in their opinion, served only to confuse the ideas of the understanding.

2. In relation to the origin of the pure cognitions of reason, we find one school maintaining that they are derived entirely from experience, and another that they have their origin in reason alone. Aristotle may be regarded as the head of the empiricists, and Plato of the noologists. Locke, the follower of Aristotle in modern times, and Leibnitz of Plato (although he cannot be said to have imitated him in his mysticism), have not been able to bring this question to a settled conclusion. The procedure of Epicurus in his sensual system, in which he always restricted his conclusions to the sphere of experience, was much more consequent than that of Aristotle and Locke. The latter especially, after having derived all the conceptions and principles of the mind from experience, goes so far, in the employment of these conceptions and principles, as to maintain that we can prove the existence of God and the existence of God and the immortality of them objects lying beyond the soul—both of them of possible experience—with the same force of demonstration as any mathematical proposition.
3. In relation to method. Method is procedure according to principles. We may divide the methods at present employed in the field of inquiry into the naturalistic and the scientific. The naturalist of pure reason lays it down as his principle that common reason, without the aid of science—which he calls sound reason, or common sense—can give a more satisfactory answer to the most important questions of metaphysics than speculation is able to do. He must maintain, therefore, that we can determine the content and circumference of the moon more certainly by the naked eye, than by the aid of mathematical reasoning. But this system is mere misology reduced to principles; and, what is the most absurd thing in this doctrine, the neglect of all scientific means is paraded as a peculiar method of extending our cognition. As regards those who are naturalists because they know no better, they are certainly not to be blamed. They follow common sense, without parading their ignorance as a method which is to teach us the wonderful secret, how we are to find the truth which lies at the bottom of the well of Democritus.

> Quod sapio satis est mihi, non ego curo Esse quod
> Arcesilas aerumnosiqueSolones. PERSIUS
>
> —Satirae, iii. 78-79.

is their motto, under which they may lead a pleasant and praiseworthy life, without troubling themselves with science or troubling science with them.

As regards those who wish to pursue a scientific method, they have now the choice of following either the dogmatical or the sceptical, while they are bound never to desert the systematic mode of procedure. When I mention, in relation to the former, the celebrated Wolf, and as regards the latter, David Hume, I may leave, in accordance with my present intention, all others unnamed. The critical path alone is still open. If my reader has been kind and patient enough to accompany me on this hitherto untravelled route, he can now judge whether, if he and others will contribute their exertions towards making this narrow footpath a high road of thought, that which many centuries have failed to accomplish may not be executed before the close of the present—namely, to bring Reason to perfect contentment in regard to that which has always, but without permanent results, occupied her powers and engaged her ardent desire for knowledge.

www.ingramcontent.com/pod-product-compliance
Lightning Source LLC
LaVergne TN
LVHW020427070526
838199LV00004B/316